THE CAMBRIDGE HISTORY
OF THE BRITISH EMPIRE

VOLUME FOUR

Cambridge University Press
Fetter Lane, London

New York
Bombay, Calcutta, Madras
Toronto
Macmillan

Tokyo
Maruzen-Kabushiki-Kaisha

THE
CAMBRIDGE HISTORY
OF THE
BRITISH EMPIRE

VOLUME IV
BRITISH INDIA
1497–1858

Edited by

H. H. DODWELL, M.A.

*Professor of the History and Culture of the British Dominions
in Asia, in the University of London*

CAMBRIDGE
AT THE UNIVERSITY PRESS
1929

This volume can also be obtained
as Volume V of
The Cambridge History of India

PRINTED IN GREAT BRITAIN

PREFACE

I GREATLY regret having to record the deaths of two contributors, Mr S. M. Edwardes, and Lt.-Col. C. E. Luard, while this volume was in preparation. Dr Surendranath Sen, however, was kind enough to revise Chapters XIV and XXII, with their bibliographies.

The spelling of proper names is generally that of the *Imperial Gazetteer*; all diacritical marks have been omitted.

The reader will find that in this and the following volume the scale of treatment has had to be materially reduced. The period covered by them is much shorter, but it is also incomparably fuller, and the allocation of space has offered many difficult problems. In the circumstances it seemed to me desirable to economise as much as possible in the space given to political history in order to provide room for an outline of the development of the administrative system, a subject on which easily accessible information is scanty and inadequate. I have thus been able to make room not only for the chapters dealing with this topic in the present volume but for a longer series of chapters in the next.

H. H. D.

SCHOOL OF ORIENTAL STUDIES
LONDON

TABLE OF CONTENTS

CHAPTER I
THE PORTUGUESE IN INDIA

By Sir E. Denison Ross, C.I.E., Professor of Persian in the University of London, and Director of the School of Oriental Studies.

	PAGE
The sea-route to India	1
Alexander VI's bulls	2
Historical sources	3
Political state of South India	3
Settlement at Calicut	3
Cabral's voyage	5
da Gama's second voyage	6
d'Albuquerque's first voyage	7
Pacheco's defence of Cochin	7
Almeida's government	8
The Egyptian squadron	9
d'Albuquerque's government	10
Capture of Malacca	11
Attack on Aden	11
Portuguese suzerainty over Ormuz	12
Lopo Soares's and Diogo Lopes's expeditions to the Red Sea	13
Vasco da Gama's return and death	13
The Portuguese in Gujarat	14
First siege of Diu	15
Garcia de Noronha	15
Estavão da Gama	16
Dom João de Castro	16
Portuguese policy	17
Later governors	18
Cession of Daman	19
Siege of Goa	20
Akbar in Gujarat	22
Portuguese relations with the Moghuls	23
Union of the Spanish and Portuguese crowns	24
Portuguese in Ceylon	24

CHAPTER II
THE DUTCH IN INDIA

By P. Geyl, Litt.D., Professor of Dutch History and Institutions in the University of London.

Early voyages of the Dutch to the east	28
Linschoten and Houtman	29
The United Company	30
Early factories in the Archipelago	31
Coromandel factories	33

PAGE

Havart's description 36
Their organisation 37
Factories in Bengal 40
Early attempts on Ceylon 41
Conquest of Ceylon 42
The Ten Years' Truce 44
Renewal of war with the Portuguese 47
Capture of Colombo 47
Capture of Negapatam 49
Capture of the Malabar fortresses 49
Organisation in Malabar 51
Relations with the King of Kandi 51
Religious policy 53
Misgovernment of Vuyst and Versluys 54
Renewed war and treaty with Kandi 1766 54
Naval power of the Dutch 55
Finance and organisation 57
Peculation 58
Attempted reforms 59
Relations with the French 59
Fall of the Company 60

CHAPTER III

THE FRENCH FACTORIES IN INDIA

By HENRI FROIDEVAUX.

Early voyages to the east 61
Madagascar 62
Colbert's company 63
Preparatory measures 65
Early factories 66
La Haye's expedition 67
Trinkomali 69
St Thomé 69
Pondichery 70
Martin's work 71
Dutch capture of Pondichery 72
Decadence of the company 73
Law's company 74
Mahé 74
Lenoir and Dumas 75

CHAPTER IV

THE EAST INDIA COMPANY, 1600–1740

By SIR WILLIAM FOSTER, C.I.E., late Historiographer to the India Office.

Formation of the East India Company 76
Early voyages 77
Hawkins at Agra 77
Conflicts with the Portuguese 78
Roe's embassy 80
The capture of Ormuz 81

CONTENTS

	PAGE
The Anglo-Dutch alliance	82
The Convention of Goa	85
The first Dutch War	86
Cession of Bombay	87
Trade from Surat	87
Early factories in Eastern India	89
The Company 1635–55	89
Courteen's Association	90
The Assada scheme and the United Joint Stock	91
Trade and trading conditions	91
The question of private trade	94
Cromwell's charter	95
Attacks on the Company	96
The Scottish East India Company	97
The English Company	98
The United Company	99
Rise of Bombay	100
Maratha troubles	101
Sir Josia Child's policy	101
Sir John Child at Bombay	102
The Coromandel factories	103
Disputes between the London and English Companies' servants	105
The Bengal factories	106
The Moghul War	107
Foundation of Calcutta	108
The Company 1709–40	108
Development of trade	109
Surman's embassy	111
Troubles in Bengal	112
Madras 1700–1740	113
Bombay 1700–1740	113
The Danish East India Company	114
The Ostend Company	115
Other foreign Companies	116

CHAPTER V

THE WAR OF THE AUSTRIAN SUCCESSION

By H. H. DODWELL, M.A., Professor of the History and Culture of the
British Dominions in Asia, in the University of London.

Situation of the Carnatic	117
The Maratha raid 1740	118
Anwar-ud-din nawab	119
Neutrality proposals	119
Barnett's squadron	120
La Bourdonnais captures Madras	120
Dupleix's quarrel with La Bourdonnais	121
Attitude of the nawab	121
French military successes	122
Siege of Pondichery	123
Treaty of Aix-la-Chapelle	124

CHAPTER VI

DUPLEIX AND BUSSY

By ALFRED MARTINEAU, Professor of Colonial History at the Sorbonne, formerly Governor of the French Settlements in India.

	PAGE
English projects in Tanjore	125
Dupleix's agreement with Chanda Sahib	126
Overthrow of Anwar-ud-din	126
Overthrow of Nasir Jang	127
Struggles round Trichinopoly	128
Death of Chanda Sahib and surrender of Law	130
Action of Vikravandi	130
Clive's successes in the Carnatic	131
French alliance with Morari Rao and Nandi Raja	131
Further attempts on Trichinopoly	131
Conference of Sadras	132
Recall of Dupleix	132
Bussy's expedition	134
Ghazi-ud-din's attempt and death	135
Grant of the Sarkars	136
Bussy's position	137
Intrigues against Bussy	138
Bussy's success	139
His recall	140

CHAPTER VII

CLIVE IN BENGAL, 1756–60

By H. H. DODWELL.

Accession of Siraj-ud-daula	141
His attitude towards the English	141
Capture of Calcutta	143
Expedition of recovery	144
Neutrality discussions with the French	145
Capture of Chandernagore	146
Discontent in Bengal	147
The conspiracy	148
Campaign of Plassey	149
Omichand's affair	151
Clive and the Hindu officials	151
Rotation government project	153
The shahzada in Bihar	153
The Dutch project	153
Clive's achievement	155

CHAPTER VIII

THE SEVEN YEARS' WAR

By H. H. DODWELL.

Military situation in 1756	157
Influence of Clive's success in Bengal	157
French reinforcements	158
Lally's expedition	158

PAGE

Capture of Fort St David 159
The Tanjore expedition 159
The naval action 3 August, 1758 160
The siege of Madras 160
Forde's campaign 162
d'Aché's final defeat 163
Battle of Wandiwash 163
Hyder 'Ali and the French 163
Siege of Pondichery 164
The causes of the French failure 164

CHAPTER IX

BENGAL, 1760–72

By H. H. DODWELL.

Situation on Clive's departure 166
Caillaud's campaign 1760 166
Holwell's views on English policy 167
Mir Ja'far replaced by Mir Kasim 168
Affairs of Shah 'Alam 169
Ramnarayan's abandonment 170
The internal trade question 170
The quarrel with Mir Kasim 171
Vansittart's policy 172
Expulsion of Mir Kasim and the war with Oudh 173
The Bengal mutinies 174
Restoration of Mir Ja'far 174
Najm-ud-daula's accession 174
Clive's reappointment as governor 175
His settlement in Oudh 175
Arrangements with Shah 'Alam and the diwanni 176
The question of presents 177
The salt company 178
The batta question 178
The officers' mutiny 179
Clive's Military Fund 180
Clive's character 180
Verelst and Cartier 180

CHAPTER X

THE EAST INDIA COMPANY AND THE STATE, 1772–86

By P. E. ROBERTS, M.A., Fellow of Worcester College, Oxford.

East Indian affairs in parliament 181
Position of the East India Company 182
Parliamentary measures of 1767 184
Debates of March, 1772 184
Select and secret committees appointed 186
Attacks on the Company 187
The Regulating Act 188
The acts of 1779 and 1780 191
The select and secret committees of 1781 192
Attempt to recall Hastings 193

PAGE

Dundas's India bi 194
Fox's India bills 195
Supported by Burke 196
Fox's commissioners 199
Pitt's India Act 200
The Board of Control 200
Hastings's views 203
Supplementary acts of 1786 203

CHAPTER XI

THE EARLY REFORMS OF WARREN HASTINGS IN BENGAL

By P. E. ROBERTS.

Warren Hastings's early service 205
Appointed governor of Bengal 205
Position in 1772 206
The dual government 206
Despatch of the supervisors 207
Hastings entrusted with their duties 207
Commercial reforms 208
Abolition of the dual government 209
Trial of Muhammad Reza Khan 209
Efficacy of the reforms 211
Abuse of patronage 212
Salaries and allowances 213

CHAPTER XII

EXTERNAL RELATIONS AND THE ROHILLA WAR

By P. E. ROBERTS.

Shah 'Alam withdraws from the Company's protection . . 215
Transfer of Kora and Allahabad to Oudh 216
Rohilkhand and the Marathas 217
The Rohilla treaty with Oudh 217
The conference at Benares 218
Decision to attack the Rohillas 219
Question of the Rohilla War 220
The Rohilla atrocities 222
Condemned by the Company 223

CHAPTER XIII

HASTINGS AND HIS COLLEAGUES

By P. E. ROBERTS.

The majority in council 225
Richard Barwell 226
Hastings's position 227
His conditional resignation 228
The compact with Francis 229

PAGE

Later councillors 230
Hastings's love of power 231
The majority attack on Hastings 232
Nandakumar's accusations 233
Nandakumar's trial 235
Misconduct of the majority and of Hastings . . . 239
Position of the Supreme Court 240
Character of Impey 241
Projected amalgamation of the Courts 242
Disputes with the Supreme Court 243
Impey and the Sadr Court 244
Impey's impeachment 246
The Supreme Court amended 247

CHAPTER XIV

THE FIRST CONFLICT OF THE COMPANY WITH THE MARATHAS, 1761–82

By the late LT.-COL. C. E. LUARD, C.I.E.

The accession of Madhu Rao 249
Raghunath Rao's regency 249
Struggle between Raghunath Rao and Madhu Rao . . 250
Position of the English 251
Maratha war with Hyder 'Ali 252
Death of Madhu Rao 253
Raghunath Rao's recovery of power 253
Murder of Narayan Rao 255
Raghunath Rao Peshwa 255
His negotiations with the English 256
The Treaty of Surat 257
Battle of Adas 258
Intervention of the Bengal Government 259
Upton's mission 259
Treaty of Purandhar 260
St Lubin's intrigues 261
Renewal of war 262
The Convention of Wadgaon 264
The expedition from Bengal 265
Goddard's campaign 266
Capture of Gwalior 268
Negotiations with Nagpur 268
Goddard's negotiations 269
Treaty of Salbai 270

CHAPTER XV

THE CARNATIC, 1761–84

By H. H. DODWELL.

Position of Nawab Walajah 273
Grant of the Sarkars 274
Early relations with Hyder 'Ali 275
The first Mysore War 276
Political complications 277

	PAGE
Sir John Lindsay's mission	277
Walajah's occupation of Tanjore	279
Pigot's imprisonment	280
Sir Thomas Rumbold's government	280
The Guntoor sarkar	281
The alienation of Hyder 'Ali	282
Outbreak of war	283
Colonel Baillie's detachment destroyed	283
Coote's campaign	284
Hughes's actions against Suffren	285
Errors in the conduct of the war	285
Mathews in Bednur	286
Stuart's campaign against Bussy	286
Lord Macartney governor	287
Negotiations with Tipu Sultan	288
Macartney's relations with Hastings and Coote	289
The assignment of the Carnatic revenues	290
Difficulties about the command of the army	293

CHAPTER XVI

CHAIT SINGH, THE BEGAMS OF OUDH AND FAIZULLA KHAN

By P. E. ROBERTS.

Demands on Chait Singh	295
Hastings goes to Benares	296
Revolt of Chait Singh	296
Question of his tenure	297
Chait Singh's present to Hastings	298
Later condition of Benares	300
Hastings's defence	301
The nawab of Oudh's present to Hastings	302
Position of Faizulla Khan	303
Demands on him	304
Hastings's attempts to reform Oudh	305
Projected relations with Delhi	306

CHAPTER XVII

THE IMPEACHMENT OF WARREN HASTINGS

By P. E. ROBERTS.

Hastings's reply to Burke's charges	307
Pitt's motives in supporting the impeachment	307
The charges voted	309
The error of the impeachment	309
Burke's violence	311
Hastings's character	312

CONTENTS

CHAPTER XVIII

LEGISLATION AND GOVERNMENTS, 1786–1818

By H. H. DODWELL.

	PAGE
Disappearance of the Company's trade	313
Missionary activity	313
Relations of the Company and the Board of Control	314
Growth of a central power in India	316
The question of patronage	318
Correspondence with England	319
Governors, etc. chosen from outside the Covenanted service	320
The subordinate governments	321

CHAPTER XIX

THE EXCLUSION OF THE FRENCH, 1784–1815

By H. H. DODWELL.

French adventurers in India	323
French projects	324
Contemplated alliance with the Dutch	325
Tipu's embassies	325
The French Revolution	326
Napoleon's expedition to Egypt	327
Mornington's precautions	327
Baird's expedition to the Red Sea	328
Decaen's instructions	329
French privateers	330
Gardane's mission	331
Capture of the French islands	332

CHAPTER XX

TIPU SULTAN, 1785–1802

By the VERY REVEREND W. H. HUTTON, D.D.,
Dean of Winchester.

War between Tipu and the Marathas	333
Settlement of the Guntoor question	334
Tipu's attack on Travancore	335
Cornwallis's triple alliance	335
The third Mysore War	336
Treaty of Seringapatam 1792	337
Shore refuses intervention	338
Causes of the fourth Mysore War	339
Death of Tipu Sultan	341
Tipu's character	342
Wellesley's settlement	342
Re-establishment of the Hindu reigning family	344

CHAPTER XXI

OUDH AND THE CARNATIC, 1785–1801

By the DEAN OF WINCHESTER.

1. OUDH, 1785–1801.

PAGE

Condition of Oudh in 1787 347
Cornwallis's settlement 348
Shore and the succession question 348
Lucknow in 1794 349
Deposition of Wazir 'Ali 349
Oudh in 1798 351
Wellesley's views 352
Wellesley's negotiations 353

2. THE CARNATIC, 1785–1801.

Position and character of Nawab Walajah 355
His debts 355
Cornwallis's treaty 356
Lord Hobart's proposals 357
Wellesley's views 359
The Tanjore question 360
The Seringapatam papers 361
The assumption of the Carnatic 361

CHAPTER XXII

THE FINAL STRUGGLE WITH
THE MARATHAS, 1784–1818

By the late S. M. EDWARDES, C.S.I., C.V.O.

Mahadaji Sindhia 363
His position at Delhi 363
Rivalry of Nana Phadnavis 364
Ghulam Kadir seizes Delhi 365
Sindhia consolidates his position 366
Death of Mahadaji Sindhia 367
The Maratha confederacy 367
The pirate states 369
Intrigues and confusion at Poona 370
Wellesley's proposals to Baji Rao II 371
Holkar defeats Sindhia and Baji Rao 372
The Treaty of Bassein 373
War with Sindhia and Berar 373
War with Holkar 374
Barlow's settlement 375
State of Sindhia and Holkar 376
The Pindaris 377
The war with Nepal 377
Gangadhar Sastri's murder 379
Treaty of Gwalior 380
The last Maratha war 380
Lord Hastings's settlement 382

CHAPTER XXIII

MARATHA ADMINISTRATION

By the late S. M. Edwardes.

PAGE

Position of the raja of Satara 384
The powers of the Peshwa 384
The *Huzur Daftar* 385
The Deccani village 386
The *Mamlatdar* 387
Financial irregularities 388
Minor revenue divisions 389
The judicial system : *panchayats* 389
Criminal cases 390
Police 391
The army 393
General character of the administration 394
Division of the land revenue 394
Land tenures 395
Miscellaneous taxes 396
Customs, etc. 397
Total revenues 398

CHAPTER XXIV

THE CONQUEST OF CEYLON, 1795–1815

By Sir Montagu Burrows, C.I.E.

Early English relations 400
Cleghorn and the capture of Colombo 401
Portuguese and Dutch influence on the island 402
The Company's administration 402
Frederick North's government 403
His attempt on Kandi 404
The massacre of 1803 405
The Kandian war 406
Eheylapola 407
The occupation of Kandi 408

CHAPTER XXV

THE REVENUE ADMINISTRATION
OF BENGAL, 1765–86

By R. B. Ramsbotham, B.Lit.

Grant of the diwanni 409
Revenue agents in Bengal 409
The zamindar 409
The supervisors of revenue 411
The kanungo 412
Concealment of the land revenue 413

PAGE

Hastings as revenue administrator 413
The Committee of Circuit 414
Union of revenue and judicial powers 415
The rai-raian 416
Settlement of 1772 416
The collectors 417
The diwanni adalats 418
The changes of 1773: provincial councils 418
Criticisms of Francis, etc. 419
Interference of the Supreme Court 421
Krishna Kantu Nandi 421
Replies to the circular of 23 October, 1774 422
Discussions of 1775–76 423
The *Amini* Commission 424
Impey chief judge of the sadr 426
Annual settlements 426
Centralisation of 1781 427
Its defects 428
Macpherson's reorganisation 430
The chief *Saristadar* 431

CHAPTER XXVI

THE BENGAL ADMINISTRATIVE SYSTEM,
1786–1818

By Lilian M. Penson, Ph.D.

Cornwallis's instructions 433
His appointment 434
His advisers: John Shore 435
James Grant 435
Charles Grant 435
Sir William Jones 436
Cornwallis's character 437
The Board of Trade 438
The General Department 439
The Board of Revenue 439
The judicial system 440
The reform of the Board of Trade 441
The revenue reforms of 1787 442
The reform of criminal justice 444
The Secret Department of reform 446
The Secretariat 446
Further reforms of 1790 447
The decennial settlement 448
The permanent settlement 450
Reform of the police system 451
Separation of judicial and executive authority 452
The Cornwallis code 454
Changes introduced by Shore and Wellesley 456
The Select Committee of 1808 458
Lord Hastings's alterations 458
Importance of Cornwallis's work 460

CONTENTS

CHAPTER XXVII
THE MADRAS DISTRICT SYSTEM
AND LAND REVENUE TO 1818
By J. T. Gwynn, I.C.S. (Retd.).

PAGE

South Indian administration in the eighteenth century 462
Position of the poligars 463
Position of the ryots 463
Land and sair revenue 466
Early Company's administration 467
Lionel Place in the jagir 468
Colonel Alexander Read 468
Thomas Munro 470
Early ryotwari 471
Introduction of the permanent zamindari settlement 472
The Bengal judicial system 474
The poligar settlements 474
Village settlements 476
Munro and the Fifth Report 478
Results of the early period 480

CHAPTER XXVIII
AFGHANISTAN, RUSSIA AND PERSIA
By W. A. J. Archbold, M.A., LL.B.

Early history of the Kabul kingdom 483
Zaman Shah 485
Shah Shuja 485
English views on Central Asia 486
Missions to Persia, Kabul and Lahore 486
Rise of Dost Muhammad 488
Russian designs in Central Asia 489
Lord Auckland 490
Burnes's mission 491
The siege of Herat 493
The Tripartite Treaty 495
Preparation for the invasion of Afghanistan 497
The Simla Manifesto 498
Home policy 498
Keane's advance 499
The storm of Ghazni 501
Shah Shuja's position 502
The Russian expedition 502
Difficulties with the Sikhs 503
Troubles in Afghanistan 504
Surrender of Dost Muhammad 505
Situation in 1841 505
The revolt at Kabul 506
Macnaghten's negotiations 508
Retreat and massacre of the Kabul force 510
Auckland's measures 511
Sale's defence of Jallalabad 512
Ellenborough appointed Governor-General 513
Nott at Kandahar 515
Ellenborough's orders 516
Kabul reoccupied 518
The evacuation of Afghanistan 520

CHAPTER XXIX

THE CONQUEST OF SIND AND THE PANJAB

By W. A. J. Archbold.

I. SIND.

	PAGE
The Talpura Mirs	522
The navigation of the Indus	523
Sind and the Tripartite Treaty	525
Treaties with the Mirs	527
Ellenborough's early views	528
Napier's instructions	530
The Khairpur succession	533
Imam Garh	534
Outbreak in Lower Sind	536
Battles of Miani and Dabo	536
Annexation	538

II. THE PANJAB.

	PAGE
Rise of Ranjit Singh	539
The Cis-Satlej Sikhs	540
Expansion of Ranjit's dominions	541
The capture of Peshawar	543
Projects against Sind	544
Character of Ranjit	544
Intrigue and disorder after his death	546
Ellenborough's views	547
Further revolutions	548
The first Sikh War	548
Battles of Firozshah and Sobraon	550
Hardinge's settlement	552
Revision of the treaty	553
Murder of Agnew and Anderson	554
The second Sikh War	555
Annexation of the Panjab	556

CHAPTER XXX

BURMA, 1782–1852

By G. E. Harvey, I.C.S.

	PAGE
Early English intercourse	558
The first Burmese War	559
The Residents	560
The second Burmese War	561
Administration of Arakan	562
Administration of Tenasserim	565

CONTENTS

CHAPTER XXXI

THE INDIAN STATES, 1818–57

By the late Lt.-Col. C. E. Luard.

PAGE

Lord Hastings's settlement 570
Malcolm's work in Central India 571
Settlement in Rajputana 573
Hastings and Oudh 575
Hastings and the Nizam 575
The Bharatpur succession 577
Ellenborough and Gwalior 578
Annexation of Satara 581
Annexation of Nagpur 582
Dealings with Jhansi and Karauli 582
Annexation of Oudh 583
Dalhousie's policy 586

CHAPTER XXXII

THE DEVELOPMENT OF SOVEREIGNTY IN BRITISH INDIA

By H. H. Dodwell.

Dual origin of the Company's authority 589
Developments in the Carnatic 590
Developments in Bengal 591
The Crown and the Company 592
Language of statutes and treaties 592
Hastings's assertion of British sovereignty 597
Francis's views 599
French and English policy 600
Browne's mission to Delhi 601
The attitude of Cornwallis 603
Wellesley and Shah 'Alam 604
Lord Hastings's views 605
Amherst and Akbar II 606
Ellenborough's and Dalhousie's negotiations 606
Disappearance of the Moghul Empire 607

BIBLIOGRAPHIES

The Portuguese in India (Chapter I) 609
The Dutch in India (Chapter II) 613
The French Factories in India (Chapter III) 615
The East India Company, 1600–1740 (Chapter IV) 618
The Struggle with the French (Chapters V, VI, and VIII) . . . 620
The Conquest of Bengal (Chapters VII and IX) 623
Warren Hastings and Bengal, 1772–85 (Chapters X–XIII and XVI–XVII) . 625
The First Conflict of the Company with the Marathas, 1761–82 (Chapter XIV) 627
The Carnatic, 1761–84 (Chapter XV) 628
Legislation and Governments, 1786–1818 (Chapter XVIII) . . . 630
The Exclusion of the French, 1784–1815 (Chapter XIX) . . . 632
Tipu Sultan, 1785–1802 (Chapter XX) 633

	PAGE
The Carnatic, 1785–1801 (Chapter xxi)	635
Oudh, 1785–1801 (Chapter xxi)	635
The Final Struggle with the Marathas, 1784–1818 (Chapter xxii) .	636
Maratha Administration (Chapter xxiii)	638
The Conquest of Ceylon, 1795–1815 (Chapter xxiv)	638
The Revenue Administration of Bengal, 1765–86 (Chapter xxv) .	639
The Bengal Administrative System, 1786–1818 (Chapter xxvi) . .	641
The Madras District System and Land Revenue to 1818 (Chapter xxvii) .	642
Afghanistan, Russia and Persia (Chapter xxviii)	643
The Conquest of Sind (Chapter xxix)	647
The Conquest of the Panjab (Chapter xxix)	648
Burma, 1782–1852 (Chapter xxx)	650
The Indian States, 1818–57 (Chapter xxxi)	651
The Development of Sovereignty in British India (Chapter xxxii) . .	653
Chronological Table	653
Index	659

CHAPTER I

THE PORTUGUESE IN INDIA, 1498–1598

THE last decade of the fifteenth century witnessed the discovery of a new world by Columbus and of a new route to an old world by Vasco da Gama. Both discoveries were epoch-making, though in totally different ways. The latter, however, had the more immediate effect on the history of Europe; and perhaps no event during the middle ages had such far-reaching repercussion on the civilised world as the opening of the sea-route to India. Vast countries, hitherto visited only by rare travellers or not at all, and known by name only to the learned few, were suddenly brought into touch with the West; and the luxuries of the East, which had hitherto passed through so many hands before they reached the European market, could now be brought direct to Lisbon. As a result, the sea-borne trade of the Muslims in the Indian Ocean and the Red Sea was paralysed, and the prosperous houses of Genoa and Venice were faced with the ruin of half their trade in the Levant, while Portugal rose suddenly to such prosperity and fame that she was soon without a rival in Europe. Persia, too, was threatened with the loss of the heavy customs she had for centuries been levying on the wares which were carried westward through her territory. Nothing can better illustrate the revolutionary effect of the opening of the sea-route to India on the markets of Europe than the detailed statement of the payments made by merchants trading from India to Alexandria which is given by contemporary Portuguese writers. I repeat here the excellent summary given by Mr Whiteway:[1]

The profits on wares sent from the East to Europe were enormous to bear the cost of passage through so many jurisdictions and the expense of so many transhipments. There has come to us a detailed statement of the payments made by merchants trading from India to Alexandria, which is full of interest; it refers to a time when an independent Sultan ruled in Cairo, but under the Ottoman Turks the payments would certainly not have been smaller. The Red Sea merchants lived in Jedda and had their factors in Calicut. The regulations of the Sultan of Cairo required that one-third of the imports should be pepper, and this amount must be sold to him in Jedda at Calicut prices. Say a merchant brought goods from Calicut to the value there of £300, and among them no pepper. He would have to buy in Jedda, at Jedda prices, pepper worth in Calicut £100, and re-sell it to the Sultan at the Calicut price. On the balance of the goods he would pay 10 per cent. *ad valorem*, and again on the balance, after deducting this 10 per cent., 4 per cent. more. Instead, however, of getting the Calicut price of the pepper in money, he was compelled to take copper in Jedda from the Sultan at Calicut prices—that is, copper in Jedda was worth 7 cruzados the quintal, but this he was compelled to buy at 12 cruzados, the Calicut price. Practically, therefore, the Sultan of Cairo was, at no expense to himself, a partner to the extent of one-third in every voyage.

[1] *Rise of Portuguese Power in India*, pp. 7, 8.

In spite of these exactions the profits on the double journey would be very large indeed.

To continue, however, with the goods to Europe. Brought to Suez in smaller boats from Jedda, the importer had to pay 5 per cent. *ad valorem* in ready money; and to supply this money there were banks at Suez prepared to cash drafts. The journey to Cairo took three days; and a camel to carry about 450 lbs. cost about 37s. 6d. A mile out of Cairo the goods were registered. The value of pepper in the Cairo market was about 20d. the pound, and a merchant buying pepper had to buy an amount equal to one-third of his purchases. From Cairo the goods were taken down the Nile in boats, and were carried from the river to Alexandria on camels. At Alexandria they were registered again, and buyer and seller had each to pay 5 per cent. *ad valorem*. The shipper had also to pay 5 per cent. to frank him across the sea.

The Pope, Alexander VI, in view of the wonderful discoveries by the Spaniards and the Portuguese, had taken upon himself between 1493 and 1494 to issue no less than four bulls with the object of parcelling out the world between these two nations.[1] The Pope's delimitations, which with each bull showed greater advantages to Spain, were somewhat modified by the Treaty of Tordesillas (June, 1494), which gave Portugal all the lands which might be discovered east of a straight line drawn from the Arctic to the Antarctic Pole at a distance of 370 leagues west of Cape Verde, and to Spain all lands west of that line. And in 1502 the same Pope gave the king of Portugal permission to style himself "Lord of the Navigation, Conquest and Commerce of Ethiopia, Arabia, Persia and India".

It must not be forgotten that by the end of the fifteenth century the Portuguese had explored not only the whole length of the western coast of Africa but also a portion of the mainland beyond the Cape of Good Hope; and that Vasco da Gama was not sent to discover India, but merely to find the direct sea-route to that country. The original idea underlying this mission was to find spices and Christians. Factories were established without great difficulty, but the chief care of the Portuguese commanders was the attempt to drive all Muhammadan shipping from the Indian Ocean and the Red Sea in order to ensure the carrying of all Indian products in Portuguese vessels. The next hundred years are therefore occupied not only in establishing factories on the coast of India, but also in placing garrisons at a number of strategic points, i.e. at the entrance of the Red Sea and elsewhere outside India.

So long as their energies were mainly devoted to the control of the high seas and to the capture or defence of these strategic points, the Portuguese were pre-eminently successful, though thwarted of two of the prizes they most coveted, namely Aden and Jedda. But they showed themselves incapable of founding on Indian soil anything resembling an overseas empire; and although they have continued to hold a certain number of their Indian possessions down to the present

---

[1] See especially Van der Linden, "Alexander VI and his Bulls, 1493–1494", *American Historical Review*, XXI, No. 1, 1916.

day, they were not strong enough, when the time came, to defeat their European rivals in the East, and lost one by one those outlying bases which had once given them the command of the eastern seas.

Though, as has been so often observed, the predominance of the religious orders in civil affairs contributed greatly to the decline of the Portuguese power in India, the devoted labours in other spheres of the Jesuits at Goa must never be lost sight of. The contributions of their missionaries to the historical and geographical literature of the world constitute an inestimable treasure-house of knowledge, and have placed under a lasting obligation all students of the East. It is also a fortunate circumstance that, apart from the literary activity of the Jesuits, the Portuguese produced during this heroic age, in addition to a great epic poet, a number of fine chroniclers, who wrote minute and thrilling narratives of their progress in the East; notably Barros, Couto, Castanheda, Goes, Alvarez, Almeida, Duarte Barbosa, and last but not least the great Affonso d'Albuquerque himself, whose *Letters* and *Commentaries* will bear comparison with those of any other soldier-statesman.

Finally a word may be said regarding the Muhammadan sources for the history of the Portuguese in the Indian Ocean and the Red Sea, existing in Arabic, Persian and Turkish. Although these writers, like the Portuguese, are not free from prejudice nor above the suppression of incidents wounding national and religious pride, their narratives are usually in complete accord with those of their enemies, and bear striking testimony to the intelligent grasp which the Portuguese gained of the public affairs and private intrigues of the Musulmans.[1]

The principal states in Hindustan and Western India at the end of the fifteenth century were the Muhammadan kingdoms of Delhi, Gujarat, Berar, Bidar, Ahmadnagar and Bijapur: and the Hindu kingdoms of Vijayanagar, Kannanur, Calicut and Cochin.

It was actually the power of Vijayanagar which prevented the Muhammadan states of Northern India from making a coalition against the Portuguese when they first settled on the coast; and when in 1565 the power of Vijayanagar was broken and a coalition formed, the Portuguese were too strongly established to be ousted. As, during the first half of the sixteenth century, Vijayanagar was really the dominating power in Southern India, it is strange that the Portuguese never tried to conciliate that state, but on the contrary were at times openly hostile.

On 8 July, 1497, three vessels, varying from 60 to 150 tons burden, left Lisbon under Vasco da Gama, and on 17 May, 1498, they anchored off a small village eight miles north of Calicut. It is not without

---

[1] See *Journal of the Royal Asiatic Society*, October, 1921, and January, 1922, "The Portuguese in India and Arabia between 1507–1517; and between 1517–1538", by the present writer.

significance that the first landing of these men, whose main object was to usurp the spice trade, hitherto a monopoly of the Muhammadans, should have been on Hindu territory. One wonders what might have been the fate of da Gama and his companions if the landing had been attempted, say, in some part of the powerful Muslim kingdom of Gujarat. As it turned out, the Hindu ruler of Calicut, whose hereditary title was *Zamorin*, gave a friendly reception to these strangers, had them conducted by a pilot to a safer anchorage, and invited da Gama to pay him a visit in Calicut. In response to this invitation a party of fourteen set out for the Zamorin's capital; and so great was their ignorance of things Indian that they mistook a Hindu temple for a Christian chapel, imagining that what was not Muhammadan must be Christian. Though they cannot have found the Hindu idols very orthodox in type, they nevertheless entered the temple and prayed there.[1]

For the attainment of their immediate object these early Portuguese adventurers were poorly equipped. In the first place they had brought no presents for the local rulers with whom they would have to treat—a strange omission in view of their past experiences in Africa; and secondly their wares proved unattractive to the Indians, which in the circumstances was quite natural. In spite of the difficulties which the Muhammadan traders, in self-defence, put in their way, the adventurers achieved, thanks to the Zamorin, a certain measure of success and seem to have established quite friendly relations with the people of the country. When, however, on 29 August, 1498, da Gama set out on his return voyage, he carried with him five out of twelve inhabitants whom he had made prisoners as a reprisal for the detention of some of his goods, ultimately restored to him. This was the one injudicious act associated with the first expedition, and no doubt helped to confirm the stories, eagerly spread by the Muslim traders, of the high-handed methods of the Portuguese in Africa. As a reconnaissance, da Gama's voyage was of the utmost importance; for on his return to Lisbon after an absence of two years with two out of his three ships, and fifty-five survivors out of the original company of 170, he was able to show specimens of the articles obtainable in the Calicut market, and to tell the merchants of Portugal what wares met with the favour of the Malabaris. Of the religion and customs of that part of India he seems to have learnt surprisingly little. To judge by the instructions issued to the second expedition,[2] it would appear that da Gama's party had actually passed three months in a Hindu country without discovering the existence of the Hindu religion. All the inhabitants of India who were not Muslims were assumed to be Christians, but of course bad Christians as they were not Catholics; and we know how much time and how many lives the Portuguese

---

[1] See Whiteway, *op. cit.* p. 80.
[2] *Idem*, p. 89, n. 1.

afterwards devoted to the conversion to the Roman faith of the Ethiopians who were already Christians. Still it remains a mystery why they failed to discover that the Zamorin was neither Christian nor Muslim, seeing that they were for so long in daily intercourse with him.

After the return of da Gama, preparations were immediately made in Portugal to equip a new fleet on a far larger scale than the first, and, on 9 March, 1500, Pedro Alvarez Cabral set out from Lisbon in command of a fleet of thirteen vessels and 1200 men. Among his captains was Bartholomeu Dias, who had been the first sailor to round the Cape. After a series of amazing adventures, including the accidental discovery of Brazil and Madagascar, Cabral with six vessels reached Calicut on 13 September, 1500, and on the 18th he had an interview on shore with the Zamorin. Cabral was eminently unsuited for the diplomatic side of his mission, and showed no disposition to consider the sentiments and prejudices of those with whom he was sent to trade. Misunderstandings due to ignorance and mistrust arose after the first interview, and reached a climax with the seizure on 16 December of a ship belonging to the Arabs, which led to a riot in which forty Portuguese perished and their factory was levelled with the ground. In consequence of this it became impossible for Cabral to remain at Calicut, but, before leaving with only two ships laden, he put to death 600 innocent boatmen who had had nothing to do with the riot, and for two days bombarded the town. On 24 December they reached Cochin, where, though they did not actually meet the raja—who afterwards proved such a valuable ally to them—they succeeded in loading the remainder of their ships. Scarcely had they done so, however, when news came that a large fleet was sailing down the coast from Calicut to attack them. Cabral stole away on the night of 9 January, 1501, leaving in Cochin about thirty Portuguese, among whom was the famous Duarte Barbosa.[1] On the following day Cabral only escaped an encounter with the Zamorin's fleet by reason of a calm. It may be mentioned that when off Kannanur he was assisted by the local raja with supplies. Eventually Cabral reached Portugal with five vessels so richly laden that the expenses of the whole expedition were more than covered. But the most important result of this in many ways disastrous journey was the discovery of the Cochin harbour, which was greatly superior to Calicut as an anchorage, and the further knowledge of Indian politics, which taught them that in the raja of Cochin, the enemy of the Zamorin, they might find a constant ally.

In 1501 a fleet of four trading vessels went to Cochin and returned in safety, having been warned at Mozambique to avoid Calicut.

It is convenient here to review the new situation in which Portugal found herself as a result of these adventures. The Portuguese had now

[1] *Duarte Barbosa*, ed. by M. Longworth Dames (Hakluyt Society).

learnt that the Indians were not Christians, were capable of showing themselves formidable foes, and must consequently be treated with some consideration. They realised that the possibilities of trade were enormous, and that the rival they had to fear was the Arab trader. It could make no difference to the Hindus whether they traded with the Arabs or the Portuguese, though, as far as imports were concerned, the latter were able to introduce many commodities which were not brought by the Arabs from the Red Sea. The main business then of the Portuguese was to conciliate the local Indian rulers and drive away the Arab merchantmen. Although the Zamorin was an avowed friend to the latter, to whom Calicut owed its prosperity, the Portuguese had the great advantage of beginning their Indian enterprise at Hindu ports; and not until they moved further north along the west coast of India did they find themselves in conflict with a Muslim state whose sympathy with the Arabs was founded on something more binding than trade relations.

The object of the Portuguese was now not only to hinder as far as possible trade between India and the Red Sea and the Persian Gulf, but also to divert to Portugal all the trade of the East with Europe. To this end a fleet of twenty ships was dispatched in February, 1502, under Vasco da Gama, followed in April by five more vessels under Estavão da Gama. In September this combined fleet assembled off Anjadiva (south of Goa), where they perpetrated one of the most dreadful deeds in the annals of a not over-nice period. A rich Muslim pilgrim vessel on its way to India from the Red Sea was intercepted by da Gama's fleet, plundered and sunk; there were many women and children on board; but to these no mercy was shown; and we actually read that da Gama watched the horrors of the scene through a porthole, merciless and unmoved.

He reached Calicut on 29 October, 1502. His aim was to compel the Zamorin to turn the Muhammadans out of the country. This was an instruction previously issued to Cabral, but at a time when the powers in Lisbon imagined the Zamorin to be some sort of Christian. When da Gama arrived the second time, he found the Portuguese ostensibly at war with the Zamorin, and made the expulsion of the Muhammadans a preliminary condition to any peace. The Zamorin, of course, refused; and his refusal was followed by acts of wanton and revolting cruelty on the part of the Portuguese leader. It is needless here to enter into the details which are all too vividly described by the Portuguese historians; it is, however, quite evident that da Gama had no bowels of compassion, and that his only policy when opposed was one of frightfulness. On 3 November he sailed for Cochin, where he established a factory. From there he proceeded to Kannanur, where, after erecting a defensive palisade, he sailed for, and eventually reached, Lisbon on 1 September, 1503.

According to the original plan, Vincente Sodre had been left behind to patrol the coast with six vessels and a caravel. It cannot be supposed that the raja of Cochin bore any love to da Gama and his Portuguese, by whom he had been treated in a most high-handed manner, especially in regard to prices; but he was anxious to obtain the support of Sodre in the event of an attack by the Zamorin. Sodre, however, thought it would be more profitable to intercept vessels at the mouth of the Red Sea, and so sailed away from the Indian coast to the despair of the factors left in Cochin and Kannanur. He took several rich prizes, but perished with three of his ships at the end of April, 1503, in a bay in one of the Curia Muria islands. Meanwhile, as da Gama had foreseen, the Zamorin proceeded to revenge himself on Cochin, eventually succeeding in overrunning the raja's territory; and the raja himself was forced to retreat to an island sanctuary, taking the Portuguese with him. During 1503 the authorities in Lisbon, probably under the impression that the safety of the factories at Cochin and Kannanur was assured by the presence of Sodre with his patrol, did not send out a fleet. But in April of that year three small squadrons were dispatched under the respective commands of Affonso d'Albuquerque, his cousin Francisco d'Albuquerque, and Soldanha. Francisco was the first to arrive, and found the Zamorin and the Portuguese still at war. He drove the Zamorin's troops from the immediate vicinity of Cochin, and set about constructing the first fortress built by the Portuguese in India. On the arrival of Affonso, the rest of the Cochin territory was cleared of the Zamorin's men, and a treaty of peace was concluded between the two Hindu princes, by which the Zamorin agreed to pay upwards of 4000 cwt. of pepper. It was in connection with the late delivery of the second consignment that hostilities again broke out between Calicut and Cochin, provoked no doubt by the Portuguese. Nevertheless, on the last day of January, 1504, the two d'Albuquerques started for home; Francisco disappeared mysteriously on the voyage, and the great Affonso reached Portugal with only two vessels.

The famous Duarte Pacheco had been left with less than a hundred men to defend Cochin against the entire forces of the Zamorin, numbering some 60,000. Only about 8000 of the Cochin troops could be relied on to fight beside the Portuguese. Pacheco was not only a great soldier, but also a man of resource and intelligence. He quickly took stock of all the local resources, and in order to secure the regular provision of supplies during the siege of Cochin, which was self-supporting, he managed to conciliate the leading Muhammadan merchants on whom such supplies had always depended. The first assault was made on Palm Sunday, 31 March, and the siege dragged on for nearly four months, during which Pacheco showed himself the master of every situation, while the Zamorin's forces were daily reduced by gun-fire and sickness. Lisbon had, of course, no news of what was passing, and towards the end of 1504 Lopo Soares arrived in Indian waters with a fleet of fourteen vessels with orders to prevent any but Portuguese ships lading at Cochin. At the request of the Zamorin he visited Calicut, arranged a peace, and then, having taken in a cargo, he sailed for home carrying with him Duarte Pacheco, and leaving in his place a man who did everything to make the raja regret the departure of that brave soldier.

With the year 1505 begins a new era in the history of Portuguese India. The sending of an annual fleet, and the abandonment of a handful of men to their fate between the departure of one fleet and the arrival of the next, had proved a failure. One can picture the feelings of anxiety and desolation which must have possessed these little colonies of strangers without means of escape either by sea or land. Their only consolation can have been the thought that they were as safe in their isolated factories as they would have been on the high seas. It was now decided to appoint a viceroy who should remain at his post in India for three years. At the beginning of 1505 Francisco d'Almeida set out in command of a large fleet and 1500 soldiers, with orders to build fortresses at Kilwa, Anjadiva, Kannanur and Cochin.

It was a fortunate chance that led to the appointment of this man as viceroy, for in the first instance Tristão da Cunha had been selected, although owing to "temporary blindness" he had been unable to accept (just as the illness of Bobadilla who had been first proposed for the Eastern Mission by Ignatius Loyola, led to the dispatch of the great Francisco Xavier).

Almeida reached India in September, 1505, and at once began to build a fort at Anjadiva, which proved useless and was dismantled two years later. He next proceeded southwards to Kannanur and later to Cochin, where he arrived in time to settle in Portuguese interests a question of succession to the throne.

Now that the Portuguese fleet was continuously patrolling the Malabar coast, it became expedient for the Red Sea merchantmen to adopt a new route by way of the Maldives. Almeida sent his son Lourenço to patrol this route and to explore Ceylon; but nothing was achieved beyond a hasty visit to that island.

In March, 1506, an engagement took place between a large fleet of Muhammadan traders, armed and equipped by the Zamorin, and a Portuguese fleet of four vessels, resulting in the capture of the largest Muslim ships and a veritable massacre of their crews, with no casualties among the Portuguese. Later, owing to the unwarranted sinking of a Muhammadan vessel belonging to a well-known merchant of Kannanur, the ruler of that place, aided by the Zamorin, besieged the Portuguese garrison, who, after great suffering from shortage of food, were, at the end of four months, saved by the arrival of Tristão da Cunha (August, 1507).

Tristão da Cunha, having recovered his sight, left Portugal in April,

1506, with ten cargo vessels and a squadron of four ships under the famous Affonso d'Albuquerque, who was designated to succeed Almeida, though with only the lower title of Governor of India. Their instructions were that da Cunha, having captured and fortified Socotra, in order to block the entrance to the Red Sea as an answer to the Egypto-Venetian confederacy, should proceed to India, leaving Albuquerque with six ships and 400 men to attack Jedda and Aden. They finally reached Socotra, where they took the Arab fort by storm, and built a new fortress. On 10 August, 1507, Tristão left for India, and, as we have seen, was able by the end of the month to relieve the beleaguered garrison of Kannanur. At the end of November his own fleet and that of the viceroy completely destroyed the Zamorin's fleet; on 10 December Tristão set out for Portugal with a full cargo.

Albuquerque remained in Socotra until August, 1507, arranging for the defences and internal administration of the island. Perceiving, however, that Socotra was ill-placed for blockading the Red Sea, and further that with his slender forces he had no chance of successfully attacking Aden, he ignored his instructions and determined to attack Ormuz.

The second phase in the history of Portuguese India began in the middle of Almeida's viceroyalty. Till then the most northerly point touched by the Portuguese vessels had been Anjadiva, and not till 1508 did they venture nearer to what ultimately became the centre of their activities. But then begins their struggle with the Muhammadan powers, for on the Malabar Coast, though they had encountered Muhammadan merchants and their fleets, their political dealings had been only with Hindu rulers.

There were two motives which now induced the Muhammadans to take concerted action. On the one hand, the rulers of Arabia and Egypt were being deprived of the duties levied on Indian goods passing up the Red Sea and across Egypt on their way to Alexandria; and on the other hand the great Musulman kingdoms of Gujarat, Bijapur and the rest had begun to realise that the Portuguese must ultimately attempt at the northern sea-ports what they had so success-fully achieved at the southern. The news that the Portuguese had decided to appoint a resident viceroy and to keep a standing fleet in Indian waters impelled these Muslim rulers to negotiate with the sultan of Egypt for joint action against them. Even the Zamorin is said to have thought of inviting the help of the sultan of Egypt. So prompt was his response, that his fleet, specially equipped at Suez, was ready in May and reached Aden in August, 1507, under the command of Amir Husayn, whom Portuguese writers called Mir Hashim; and it was this fleet that the Portuguese encountered before they had tried issues with the Indian Muslims. Lourenço d'Almeida, the gallant son of the viceroy, set out for the north in January, 1508, and was anchored off Chaul when the Egyptian fleet arrived off that harbour; and in this, their first naval battle with the Muhammadans, they met with a severe reverse, and their young commander was killed (January, 1508).[1]

Meanwhile, Albuquerque had left Socotra with his own fleet in August, 1507, and, having systematically destroyed the chief ports belonging to the king of Ormuz, he then entered into negotiations. These led to nothing but a nominal treaty, and finally, in February, 1508, Albuquerque was compelled to leave for India, reaching Kannanur in December, 1508.

He arrived in India just as Almeida was setting sail to avenge the death of his son Lourenço. Almeida met the Muslim fleets off Diu and gained a signal victory, February, 1509. On his return to Cochin in March, a great quarrel arose about delivering the government to Albuquerque, and it was not until 5 November, 1509, that this was finally arranged.

The first expedition which the new governor undertook was against Calicut, but it achieved nothing beyond the destruction of a few buildings, and Albuquerque himself received two wounds in the shoulder. But as soon as he had recovered, he set to work to refit the whole fleet, and determined to set out for the Red Sea in search of the sultan of Egypt's fleet. On 10 February, 1510, he sailed from Cochin with twenty-three ships for Guardafui, but was diverted from his course by learning of the defenceless state of Goa, off which he anchored on 28 February. Only a slight resistance was offered, and on 4 March he received the keys of the fortress. His first care was to strengthen the fortifications in case Yusuf Adil Khan,[2] the ruler of Bijapur, should attempt to recover the place. Albuquerque had already contemplated making Goa the headquarters of the Portuguese in India; but, in spite of all his preparations and individual attention to every detail of defence, he was unable to resist Yusuf Adil Khan's attack, and after many misadventures he had at last to retire to Anjadiva on 16 August, much to the relief of his captains who had all along been opposed to the adventure. During the next two months he received important reinforcements in ships and men, and at the end of November he sailed back to Goa and recovered the place by storm. In reporting this victory to King Manoel, Albuquerque wrote: "My determination now is to prevent any Moor entering Goa, to leave a sufficient force of men and ships in the place, then with another fleet to visit the Red Sea and Ormuz".

Amir Husayn, who since his defeat in February, 1509, had been at Cambay awaiting reinforcements from Suez, then sailed back, to find the new fleet still in process of building.

Albuquerque now devoted all his energies to the strengthening of

---

[1] The story of his heroic death is told by Camoens in his *Lusiads*, Canto x, 29–32.
[2] Called by the Portuguese *Idalcão* or *Hidalcão*. He is also called by Albuquerque *Sabaio*. See Whiteway, *op. cit.* p. 133, note. See also Fonseca, *Hist. of Goa*, p. 131, note.

Goa, and to increasing its commercial importance. He dispatched several captains along the coast with orders to compel all the ships they met to put into that port. In the city itself every encouragement was given to trade, and vessels soon began to arrive there from Ormuz and elsewhere. Even Moors trading in spices were encouraged to settle there, and in order to secure a permanent population, Albuquerque did everything in his power to encourage his Portuguese to take Indian wives.

In April, 1511, Albuquerque set out for Malacca, at which point all traffic between India and China was concentrated. The first attack on Malacca (25 July, 1511) led to no definite result, and Albuquerque's captains were against making a further attempt. He, however, finally convinced them of the wisdom of his policy by pointing out that "if they were only to take Malacca out of the hands of the Moors, Cairo and Mecca would be entirely ruined, and Venice would then be able to obtain no spiceries except what her merchants might buy in Portugal". In August, 1511, a second and successful attack was made, and the Portuguese became absolute masters of the place. Great importance was attached to this triumph of Portuguese arms. King Manoel wrote to inform Leo X of the event, and the Pope made the news the occasion of a series of ceremonies of public thanksgiving of unusual pomp and splendour. Tristão da Cunha was head of the special mission sent to Rome, bearing magnificent presents to the pontiff, including an elephant of extraordinary size, which, as it passed the papal palace stopped, and kneeling down, bowed thrice to the Pope who was watching the procession from a window.

Albuquerque reached Cochin again in January, 1512, after an absence of less than twelve months, to find that affairs had everywhere fallen into disorder, while Goa was constantly alarmed by persistent rumours of the advent of the Turkish fleet. "The Rumes are coming" was the constant cry. In April, 1512, he wrote to King Manoel as follows: "I would respectfully submit to your Majesty that until we go to the Red Sea and assure these people that such beings as the Rumes are not in existence, there can be no confidence or peace for your Majesty's subjects in these parts". The security of Goa was not, however, yet assured: and at the end of 1512 Albuquerque was obliged to take a large force to attack the fort of Benasterim, six miles from Goa, which had been strongly fortified and garrisoned by the king of Bijapur. The reduction of this fort was one of Albuquerque's most gallant exploits.

Not till February, 1513, was Albuquerque able to set out for the Red Sea. He first attacked Aden. His force was composed of 1000 Portuguese and 400 Malabaris, who landed in small boats carrying with them scaling ladders. The Aden garrison, in order to avoid the fire of the Portuguese guns, enticed Albuquerque's men within the city walls, and, after four hours of fierce hand-to-hand fighting, the besieging force was obliged to withdraw to its ships. After this Albuquerque attempted to proceed to Jedda, but the winds were unfavourable, and he decided in May to anchor at Kamaran. Having destroyed all the fortifications on this island, he returned to Aden, but, finding it even stronger than when he left it, he set sail for India in August, 1513. The Portuguese historians tell us that Albuquerque lay ten days off Aden on his return from Kamaran,[1] but do not refer to any further attack on that city; but some Muslim historians speak of a second unsuccessful attack and assert that the guns of the fort did great damage to the Portuguese ships lying at anchor.[2]

In 1513 Albuquerque came into diplomatic contact with Persia. Ismail Safavi had sent ambassadors to the kings of Gujarat, Ormuz and Bijapur; and the ambassador sent to Bijapur visited Albuquerque at Kannanur, and invited him to send Miguel Ferreira to Ismail. Ferreira returned with the Persian via Ormuz, and at Tabriz had many interviews with the shah, who expressed a great desire for the destruction of the sultan and the house of Mecca. When he dismissed Ferreira, he sent with him an ambassador to Albuquerque with rich presents. While they were at Ormuz on the return journey, Albuquerque himself arrived there, but, instead of coming to terms, he established Portuguese suzerainty over Ormuz, thus denying Shah Ismail's claims in that quarter.

In November, 1515, Albuquerque, feeling his end was near, set sail for India, having just learnt that Lopo Soares had been appointed captain-major in India and that he himself had been recalled. The last letter he addressed to King Manoel, dated at sea, 6 December, 1515, must be quoted here:

This letter to your Majesty is not written by my hand, as when I write I am troubled with hiccoughs, which is a sign of approaching death. I have here a son to whom I bequeath the little I possess. Events in India will speak for themselves as well as for me. I leave the chief place in India in your Majesty's power, the only thing left to be done being the closing of the gates of the Straits. I beg your Majesty to remember all I have done for India, and to make my son great for my sake.[3]

He died on 16 December, 1515, having done more than any other Portuguese leader to establish the prestige of his king, and to make the name of his fellow-countrymen respected and feared. He realised that the three keys to the eastern trade were Malacca, Ormuz and Aden. He obtained complete control of the first two, and almost secured the third. He combined the most resolute determination with the greatest personal bravery. He was scrupulously loyal to his master; and the only blot on his character was his ruthless cruelty towards his enemies, the Muhammadans.

[1] Barros, II, viii, § 4.
[2] See J.R.A.S. Oct. 1921, p. 559.
[3] Cartas, I, 380, The Letters of Albuquerque, published by Royal Academy of Lisbon, 1884.

Had Albuquerque lived long enough to return to Aden from Ormuz, he would have found the governor of that town ready to submit, whereas owing to the stupidity of his successor, Lopo Soares, the chance of adding Aden to the Portuguese possessions was thrown away. In February, 1516, Lopo set out with a fleet of twenty-seven sail for the Red Sea in order to engage the fleet which the sultan of Egypt had been so long preparing at Suez. When he arrived unexpectedly before Aden, the governor, Amir Mirjan, who had been recently attacked by Rais Salman,[1] the commander of the Egyptian fleet, offered the keys of the citadel to the Portuguese general, but Lopo, instead of taking advantage of this surprising offer, continued his course in search of the Egyptian fleet, thinking to return and take possession of Aden when he had disposed of Rais Salman. Hearing that Salman and his fleet had been driven by stress of weather into Jedda, he followed him thither; but instead of bombarding the city, he sailed away two days later on the plea that he had instructions to fight the fleet but not to attack Jedda. On his return he destroyed the town of Zeyla, and, on reaching Aden, found Amir Mirjan in a very different mood, and the fortifications repaired. He returned to Goa in September, 1516, having achieved nothing. The remaining two years of his governorship were uneventful, saving that he succeeded in entering into relations with China.

In December, 1518, he was succeeded by Diogo Lopes de Sequeira, who in February, 1520, made a fruitless expedition into the Red Sea with a fleet of twenty-four vessels. On his way back he was entertained by Malik Ayaz at Diu, which the Portuguese had coveted ever since the time of Albuquerque, and which had once been offered them. Diogo Lopes in his conversations with Malik Ayaz must have shown his hand too clearly, for when he revisited the place in February, 1521, with a large fleet, its defences were so strong that the Portuguese refrained from attack.

Duarte de Menezes succeeded Diogo Lopes as governor on his arrival at Goa, September, 1521. His government was marked only by unpleasant happenings at Ormuz which reflected small credit on the Portuguese. King John III, who succeeded King Manoel in 1521, selected as viceroy Vasco da Gama, now a man sixty-four years of age. Vasco reached India in September, 1524, to die on Christmas Day of the same year. He was buried in Cochin, whence in 1538 his remains were carried to Portugal. He was succeeded by Henrique de Menezes, who held the office of governor from 1524 to 1526, mostly engaged in fighting on the Malabar Coast. The next governor was Lopo Vaz de Sampaya, who was in turn succeeded by Nino da Cunha.

---

[1] Not "Sulaiman"; Castanheda calls him correctly Salmão Rex. The Arabic historian Ibn ad-Dayba‘ says that Salman had been sent by Sultan Salim of Turkey to help the Egyptians against the Portuguese. See *J.R.A.S.* Oct. 1921, p. 549.

Nino da Cunha arrived in India in November, 1529. Early in 1530 the headquarters of the government were moved from Cochin to Goa, which from this date became, as it has ever since remained, the capital of Portuguese India. The next eight years were mainly occupied with the dealings of the Portuguese with Sultan Bahadur of Gujarat, and their acquisition of Diu. The history of this period is copiously illustrated by both the Portuguese and the Muslims; and on the whole the various narratives are convincingly consistent. In order the better to understand the local conditions with which the Portuguese had to cope, it is necessary to sketch briefly the state of affairs in Gujarat itself. In the year 1526 the emperor Babur had made himself master of Hindustan from the Indus to the borders of Bengal. He, however, died in 1530 before he could subdue the kingdoms of Bengal, Gujarat or the Deccan. His son and successor Humayun endeavoured to complete his father's work, and one of his first undertakings was an invasion of Gujarat and Malwa. The campaign opened with the battle of Mandasor at the beginning of 1535. The troops of Bahadur were in every engagement unsuccessful and in the early stages of the campaign he was deserted by his most valuable soldier, the famous master-gunner Mustafa Rumi Khan, who, aggrieved at the treatment he received at Bahadur's hands, offered his services to Humayun. In October, while Humayun was still pressing his conquest, Bahadur had made an appeal to the Portuguese for help, and had agreed to give them a footing at Diu in return for a contingent of 500 Portuguese. He had already, in 1534, made considerable concessions, ceding the island of Bassein with all its dependencies and revenues to the Portuguese. When at last, in 1537, Humayun suddenly withdrew, Bahadur, feeling that his troubles were over, regretted his promises, and set about negotiating with Nino da Cunha for his withdrawal from Diu. It may be mentioned incidentally that the 500 men had not been forthcoming. Long discussions took place with a view to a conference between Bahadur and Nino da Cunha, who had come up to settle the matter, Bahadur begging the Portuguese governor to visit him ashore, and the Portuguese insisting that the sultan should visit the fleet and conduct negotiations on board. Each thoroughly mistrusted the other; but eventually Bahadur consented to visit Nino on board, where a scuffle arose, and Bahadur was drowned endeavouring to escape. All Portuguese historians say that Bahadur had intended to murder the Portuguese governor on the occasion of his return visit. The exact circumstances which led to the drowning of Bahadur will probably never be known. The various narratives for the first time here come in conflict, each side blaming the other for the disaster, which occurred on 13 February, 1537.

Early in Bahadur's disastrous campaign with Humayun, the king of Gujarat had made plans for escaping from India with his belongings in the event of defeat. He had dispatched a certain Asaf Khan to

Mecca with his harem and treasure, and with rich presents for the sultan Sulaiman—the Ottoman sultans since 1517 had been in possession of Egypt—entreating him to come to his assistance.[1] The envoy had an audience with the sultan Sulaiman at Adrianople after the death of Bahadur; and by way of avenging the death of the Muslim king the sultan at once gave orders for the equipment of a powerful fleet in Suez to be sent to attack the Portuguese at Diu.

Among the small party that had accompanied Bahadur in his fatal visit to the Portuguese governor was a certain Khwaja Safar Salmani,[2] who played an important part in subsequent events. He at first was on friendly terms with the Portuguese, who put him in charge of Diu, but when he heard of the arrival of the Egyptian fleet under Sulaiman Pasha, he at once changed his tactics and attacked them. He reported to the pasha that there were 500 fighting men in Diu, and that all he required was guns and munitions. The siege began in October and came suddenly to an end on 5 November, 1538, when the pasha, hearing of the arrival of twenty Portuguese ships, sailed away without striking another blow. The defence of Diu by a tiny garrison commanded by Antonio da Silveira is one of the most heroic episodes in Portuguese history. The brunt of the first attacks fell on Gogala, a suburb of the island known to the Portuguese as *Villa dos Rumes* and to the Muslims as *Bandar-i-Turk*, which with its garrison of about eighty men had at last to capitulate. The main fort of Diu, however, continued to hold out, women and children working with the same devotion as the men. The besieged were also much favoured by the great differences which arose between the Turks and the Gujaratis.

In the meanwhile (September, 1538) Garcia de Noronha, nephew of the great Albuquerque, had reached Goa as viceroy, superseding Nino da Cunha, who had only held the rank of governor, and who died broken-hearted on the voyage home. In the fleet of eleven ships the new viceroy brought with him from Lisbon there also came the first bishop of Goa, which had been made a bishopric by a bull of Pope Paul III in 1534. Garcia de Noronha on his arrival in Goa had collected a powerful fleet and army for the relief of Diu, but seemed in no haste to lead them into action; so that, when news came of the departure of Sulaiman Pasha, his people were furious with the delay which had deprived them of an opportunity of engaging the Turkish fleet. The viceroy eventually reached Diu in January, 1539, and his first task was to rebuild the fort. He entered into negotiation with the new sultan of Gujarat, with whom a peace was signed in March of that year. Under its terms a high wall was to be raised between

---

[1] See *An Arabic History of Gujarat*, Indian Record Series, vol. II, Introduction.
[2] His name Safar has given rise to much confusion, as it has been variously corrupted by Portuguese and English writers into Ja'far, Ghazanfar, Suffy, Cofar and Sifr! See *J.R.A.S.* January, 1922, p. 17.

the fortress and the town, and one-third of the custom-house receipts were to be paid to the Portuguese.

In 1540 de Noronha, after a term of office characterised by gross corruption and cruelty, died, and was succeeded by Estavão da Gama (second son of Vasco), who had for five years been captain of Malacca. He immediately prepared for another expedition into the Red Sea. In February, 1541, with a large fleet of seventy-two sail he reached Massowah, where he left the greater part of his fleet and sailed with some lighter vessels to Suez, which he found so well guarded that he speedily withdrew, without having destroyed a single Turkish galley. One incident in connection with this fruitless expedition, however, deserves mention here. On his return to Massowah in June, 1541, urgent appeals for help were received from the Abyssinians who had been long engaged in hostilities with their Muhammadan invaders. In response to the call of these Christians, the governor landed his young brother Christavão da Gama with 400 men. The adventures of this handful of men form one of the most romantic tales in history.[1] Christavão was finally defeated and put to death in August, 1542; but at the beginning of the following year the king of Abyssinia, with 150 of da Gama's followers who had survived, attacked and defeated the Muhammadans, and recovered his country.

The next governor, Martim Affonso de Sousa, arrived in India in 1542, carrying with him the great Jesuit saint, Francisco Xavier, who had been selected by Ignatius Loyola and appointed papal nuncio by Pope Paul III. Affonso de Sousa was a bad and greedy governor. His successor, Dom João de Castro, who reached India in August, 1545, was the last of the great Portuguese governors in India. With his death, in June 1548, began the decline of Portuguese power and prestige in the eastern seas.

As soon as he had assumed the reins of government, an improvement became visible both in political and military affairs. There had been continued disputes with the king of Gujarat ever since the conclusion of peace in March, 1539, and finally the Portuguese pulled down the wall between their fortress and the town, built in accordance with the terms of peace. In April, 1546, Sultan Mahmud III, nephew of the sultan Bahadur, began to besiege the fortress of Diu, which was commanded by João Mascarenhas. Although he must have regarded this attack as inevitable, no preparations for a siege had been made, and the garrison numbered only about 200 men. In command of the besieging force was Khwaja Safar Salmani, who as governor of Surat had received the title of Khudawand Khan, and who had about 10,000 fighting men under him. On 18 May reinforcements reached the Portuguese from Goa, raising the garrison to about 400 men, but they remained inferior in artillery and

---

[1] The full narrative is given by Miguel Castanhoso. See also Whiteway, *The Portuguese Expedition to Abyssinia.*

musketry. In June Khwaja Safar had his head carried off by a cannon-ball and was succeeded by his son Ramazan Rumi Khan.[1]

At last in October João de Castro was able to send sufficient troops to relieve the garrison which by that time was reduced to a mere handful of wounded, sick and hungry men. In November the viceroy himself arrived in Diu and led an attack in which 3000 of the enemy, including Ramazan Rumi Khan, were killed and 600 taken prisoners. After this success de Castro was able to make a triumphant entry into Goa in April, 1547, but in May, 1548, he died and was succeeded by Garcia de Sa.

In the middle of the sixteenth century, when the Portuguese Empire in the East had attained the climax of its grandeur, it was divided into three sections: (1) from Guardafui to Ceylon, (2) from Pegu to China, and (3) all territories on the east coast of Africa.

Under the viceroy or governor of India, with his headquarters at Goa, were placed five governors or captains who ruled respectively over Mozambique, Ormuz, Maskat, Ceylon and Malacca. The viceroy or governor had entire control over the military, naval and civil administration. In civil suits his decision was final, and in criminal matters his power extended to sentence of death, except in the case of Portuguese nobles. He was assisted by two councils, the Council of State, and the Council of the Three Estates.

It will be evident from the brief narrative we have attempted that this history of one hundred years of Portuguese adventure in the eastern seas contains little or no indication of any effort to found an empire; never at any stage did the Portuguese captains assume the offensive on shore, nor did they actually come into contact with any of the great fighting races of India. They depended solely on their control of the high seas; their main objective was always the capture and occupation of the most important ports and their defence when occupied. For this purpose were needed, not administrators, but brave soldiers and sailors; and success was due, first, to the high military qualities and personal courage and endurance of most of the captains, and secondly, to the rich rewards which attracted so many to undertake perilous journeys (on an average not 60 per cent. of the men who left Portugal reached India, so great was the mortality on the crowded vessels) and face the countless risks which awaited them at the other end.

The ultimate decline of Portuguese power in India was due primarily to two causes: first, the encouragement of mixed marriages at home and abroad, and secondly, religious intolerance. The former policy had been adopted, as we have seen, by the great Albuquerque, who probably foresaw that the constant drain on the male population of a relatively small country like his own must ultimately lead to a shortage of man-power; the latter was pushed to its utmost

[1] See *Arabic History of Gujarat*, Indian Record Series, vol. II, Introduction.

extreme by the zealous fervour of the Jesuits who selected Goa as their second headquarters outside Rome, soon after the foundation of their order. The arrival of St Francisco Xavier in India in 1542 was an event of the most far-reaching importance and laid the foundations of that ecclesiastical supremacy in Portuguese India which sapped the financial resources and undermined the civil administration of its governor. Albuquerque and his immediate successors left almost untouched the customs of the people of Goa, only abolishing, as did the English later, the rite of sati. It may be recalled, however, that after the arrival of the Franciscan missionaries in 1517 Goa had become the centre of an immense propaganda, and already in 1540 by the orders of the king of Portugal all the Hindu temples in the island of Goa had been destroyed. The inquisition was introduced into Goa in 1560.

Garcia de Sa only held his high office for thirteen months, during which period little of importance is recorded. His general policy was one of conciliation with the Indian princes. In August, 1548, he concluded a formal treaty with the king of Bijapur, under which it was stipulated that Salsette and Bardas were to be the property of the king of Portugal in perpetuity, and that in the event of the Turks sending a fleet to attack the Portuguese, the Adil Khan should send men and supplies to help them, but at the expense of the Portuguese. Peace was also concluded with Sultan Mahmud of Gujarat.

Garcia de Sa was succeeded, on his death in August, 1549, by Jorge Cabral, who was immediately confronted with trouble in Cochin, where the safety of the king was threatened by a league formed against him by the Zamorin and the king of Pimienta. In spite of a rumour that the Turks were fitting out a new fleet at Suez, Cabral sent an armada of ninety sail to help the king of Cochin, and himself followed later with a large force of soldiers. The fighting was protracted and severe, and when Cabral was at last on the point of negotiating a peace with the enemy he had surrounded, a vessel arrived (November, 1550) with orders from the new viceroy, Dom Affonso de Noronha, to stay all proceedings, and the enemy were thus allowed to escape.

Affonso de Noronha's four years of viceroyalty were not marked by any very notable event, although Portuguese arms were often busily engaged in Malacca, Cochin and Ormuz, which nearly fell to the Turks. Two events of considerable interest, however, occurred during this period, namely the death of St Francisco Xavier (1552) and the arrival in India of Luiz de Camoens, the author of the *Lusiads* (1553), who, finding a new expedition was ready to sail to help the king of Cochin against the king of Pimienta, at once attached himself to it and, we are told, bore no inconsiderable share in the conquest of the Alagada Islands.

The next viceroy, Pero de Mascarenhas, who had been archbishop of Goa, only lived to hold office for ten months, and was succeeded in June, 1555, by Francisco Barreto with the title of governor. His three years of office showed him to be a man of courage and determination, but of exceptional cruelty even for those times. Being invited to come to the aid of the king of Sind, he went with a fleet and 700 men to Tatta. Finding on arrival that his help was no longer required, he demanded the payment of expenses incurred in fitting out the fleet, as had been previously agreed upon. "On this being refused, Barreto landed his men, entered the city and in his rage killed over 8000 people...and loaded his vessels with one of the richest booties ever taken in India."[1] It was during the governorship of Francisco Barreto that King John III of Portugal died, and with his death the fortunes of that country both in Europe and in the East began to decline. During the minority of Dom Sebastian, however, the regency selected for the viceroyalty Dom Constantino of Braganza, brother of the duke of the same name, who was one of the wisest and worthiest men ever entrusted with that great office. He arrived in India in September, 1558, and his first act was to recall a fleet which Barreto had dispatched to Malacca, which was threatened by the king of Achin. We have seen above how Affonso de Noronha on arrival in India put a stop to Cabral's proceedings in Cochin, and as Danvers says "it appears to have been a prevailing custom in India, that new governors never put into execution the plans of their predecessors".[2] During the governorship of Barreto the territory of Bassein had been granted to the Portuguese by the king of Gujarat, and one of the first aims of the new viceroy was to gain possession of the neighbouring port of Daman, which was only occupied after several fierce engagements with a rebellious Gujarat noble who had established himself there (1559). Now the king of Gujarat at that time, Ahmad II, was a mere puppet in the hands of two rival nobles, 'Imad ul-Mulk and I'timad Khan. The former of these nobles included among his officers the fief-holder at the port of Daman, a certain Sayf ul-Muluk Miftah (called by the Portuguese historians Cide Bofata). In order that he might devote his whole attention to combating I'timad Khan, he made an agreement with the Portuguese that in return for the services of 500 "Frankish" troops, he would hand over to them the port of Daman. Miftah, however, refused to surrender the port, even when the original mandate of 'Imad ul-Mulk had been sent to him. When, finally, the Portuguese got possession of Daman, they ignored their side of the bargain and sent no men to help 'Imad ul-Mulk, who then repented his action and resolved on the recapture of Daman. The Portuguese historians, who call 'Imad ul-Mulk "Madre Maluco, king of Cambay", relate that he was preparing for an attack in force on Daman, and the Portuguese governor of that port, feeling that he could not resist such a force, had recourse

[1] Danvers, *Portuguese in India*, i, 508.   [2] *Idem*, i, 510.

to stratagem. He persuaded Khudawand Khan Rajab, the son of Khwaja Safar (Portuguese *Cedeme*), lord of Surat, that his brother-in-law 'Imad ul-Mulk was in reality intending not to attack Daman but to drive him out of Surat. Khudawand Khan, believing this statement, invited his brother-in-law to a party, where on arrival he was foully murdered with all his attendants. The Muslim historians, on the other hand, tell us that 'Imad ul-Mulk marched on Surat in response to an appeal from the inhabitants of that town, who were grievously oppressed by Khudawand Khan, and make no reference to an attack on Daman. Chingiz Khan, the son of 'Imad ul-Mulk, at once resolved to avenge his father's murder and marched on Surat which he invested, but being able to produce no effect by this means, he called in the Portuguese to his assistance, who with ten ships blockaded the waterway by which provisions entered the port. It appears from the Portuguese accounts that both the besiegers and the besieged were given to suppose that the ships had been sent to help them, but the Muslim historians say that Chingiz Khan made definite promises of territory to the Portuguese in return for their help. However this may be, it appears that Chingiz Khan withdrew temporarily, and on his return to the attack was met by the Portuguese who put him to rout; for in the interval Khudawand Khan had promised to give Surat to the Portuguese if they would help him against Chingiz Khan. But no sooner had the Portuguese accomplished their task than Khudawand Khan was obliged to flee from his own people, who were incensed by his intention of surrendering the port. In making his escape he fell into the hands of one of Chingiz Khan's nobles who cut off his head and sent it to his master.

The next notable viceroy to be sent to India was Dom Luiz de Atayde, during whose viceroyalty (1568–71) the Portuguese were confronted by a danger which threatened their very existence in India. In 1569 three of the most powerful Indian princes concluded an offensive league against the Portuguese which, we are told, had been discussed among them with the utmost secrecy for the past five years. These princes were 'Ali II, the Adil Khan of Bijapur, Murtaza Nizam Shah of Ahmadnagar, and the Zamorin of Calicut. So great was the confidence of these princes in their ability to drive these unwelcome strangers out of India, that they had arranged beforehand exactly how the Portuguese possessions should be divided among them; the Adil Khan had gone so far as to nominate certain of his officers to posts in Goa, at the same time promising them certain Portuguese ladies, famous for their beauty, in marriage. Ignoring all treaties, the Adil Khan marched against Goa at the head of 100,000 men; and Murtaza Nizam Shah against Chaul. To protect Goa the viceroy had at his disposal 650 active troops and about 250 aged and infirm; having dispatched 600 to reinforce the commander of Chaul. He sent these troops to defend the most vulnerable points of attack, while the defence of the town of Goa was entrusted to Dominicans, Franciscans and other priests numbering some 300 in all. In addition to this he organised 1000 Christian slaves of various nationalities into four bands, and placed 1500 native Christians under selected Portuguese officers, with a sprinkling of reliable Portuguese soldiers. His council strongly urged the abandonment of Chaul and the concentration of all efforts on the defence of Goa, but the viceroy was resolved that the enemy should pay dearly for all they might take. The attack on Goa at the end of December, 1569, opened with the bombardment of the Pass of Benasterim, where the viceroy himself took command. The defence of Goa forms one of the most brilliant feats in Portuguese annals, and the courage and resource shown by Dom Luiz de Atayde in the face of such overwhelming odds entitle him to rank among the great soldiers of the world. Although during the siege, which lasted ten months, he received reinforcements in ships and men, it must be remembered that he was able not only to send troops to other threatened ports along the coast, but even to dispatch the trading ships with their annual consignments to Lisbon, as if nothing unusual were toward. Hardly less remarkable was the defence of Chaul by the small garrison of Portuguese against the superior forces of the king of Ahmadnagar which lasted all through the summer, and terminated in the signing of an offensive and defensive alliance between Murtaza Nizam Shah and Dom Sebastian of Portugal. The part played by the Zamorin was of little or no account, and it was not until the beginning of June, 1570, that he made an attack in force on the fort of Chale, near Calicut, where a small garrison was only saved from surrender by the arrival of reinforcements in September. Not until December, 1571, was a final treaty concluded between the new viceroy and the Adil Khan, whereby the local princes were compelled to recognise the rights of the Portuguese to their Indian possessions. Thus did Dom Luiz de Atayde, by his unflinching valour, his single-minded devotion and his military genius, succeed in re-establishing for a time the prestige of Portugal in the East, by withstanding the most serious confederacy that had ever taken arms against her. Dom Luiz returned in the same year to Portugal, where he was received with great honour.

The newly appointed viceroy, Antonio de Noronha, arrived at Goa in September, 1571, before the siege of that town had been raised. Chale, in the meantime, was holding out against desperate odds, and the reliefs sent by the new viceroy immediately after the conclusion of peace with the Adil Khan, arrived only to find that the garrison had surrendered conditionally to the Zamorin. With the appointment of Antonio de Noronha the administration of the Portuguese possessions in the East were divided, as we have seen above, into three governments, Noronha becoming viceroy of India, while governors were appointed to the other two provinces. This experiment led at once to disputes between the viceroy and Antonio Moniz Barreto, the governor of Malacca, and ultimately involved the viceroy's recall in 1573.

It is necessary at this stage to revert to the events which were passing in Gujarat. Ever since the invasion of that country by the emperor Humayun, and the tragic death of Sultan Bahadur in 1537, the kingdom of Cambay, as Gujarat was called by the Portuguese, had been in a state of almost continuous civil war, the nominal kings being merely figureheads at the mercy and disposal of whichever of the rival nobles was able to capture and hold them. Such a state of affairs was, no doubt, very greatly to the advantage of the Portuguese, who were able to play one chief off against another, as we have seen in the case of Surat. Although Humayun had virtually conquered Gujarat, he had withdrawn without making any arrangements for the incorporation of that country into the Moghul Empire; and not till 1572 did his son, the great Akbar, who had then been seventeen years on the Moghul throne, think fit to undertake the reduction of this rich province. The political situation in Gujarat at this moment has already been described.[1] It may here suffice to say that it was with two distinct classes of opponent that Akbar had now to contend. First, the Gujarat nobles, who were divided always into two or more factions, the one or the other having the person of the puppet king, and secondly, the so-called *Mirzas*, members of the royal house of Tamerlane, residing for their personal safety outside the Moghul Empire, who with the prestige of their descent were able to command a certain following wherever they went. The *Mirzas* were a constant source of trouble to their imperial cousin, especially in Gujarat, and it was due to them rather than to the Gujarat nobles that the final absorption of that country into the Moghul Empire was delayed.

The nominal king of Gujarat at this time was Sultan Muzaffar, and the leading noble was the I'timad Khan who has been mentioned above. It was at the invitation of the latter that Akbar, towards the end of 1572, entered Ahmadabad and received the submission of I'timad Khan and his partisans and later of Sultan Muzaffar, who was found lurking near Akbar's camp. It was after his entry into the capital that Akbar visited Cambay, where for the first time he saw the sea and made acquaintance with the Portuguese, receiving there certain of their merchants who came to pay their respects. Meantime, the *Mirzas*, headed by Ibrahim Husayn, had collected their forces in Broach and were plotting against Akbar; and when it reached the emperor's ears that they had murdered Rustam Khan, the lord of Broach, who had expressed his intention of obeying Akbar's summons, Akbar resolved on immediate vengeance and set out at the head of 200 men for Surat, which was occupied by Muhammad Husayn. On his way he encountered and defeated Ibrahim Mirza in superior force at Sarnal (December, 1572), but the *Mirza* escaped

[1] *Camb. Hist. of India*, III, chap. xiii.

to Delhi where he tried to stir up the common people in order to necessitate Akbar's withdrawal from Gujarat, only to perish shortly afterwards in Multan. In January, 1573, Akbar began siege operations against Surat. It was during this siege that Akbar first entered into negotiations with the Portuguese. The accounts are confusing, but it would appear from a collation of the narratives of Abul Fazl and Couto, that the besieged in Surat had offered to hand over that port to the Portuguese if they would help them against Akbar, but that, when the Portuguese contingent realised the strength of the Moghuls, they changed their rôle from that of enemies to ambassadors, and were well received by the emperor who "made enquiries about the wonders of Portugal and the manners and customs of Europe".

It was, no doubt, a source of great vexation to the emperor to find that important ports like Diu, Daman and Bassein, were in the hands of these alien merchants, but the failure of the triple alliance of 1569 had clearly shown that without the co-operation of a powerful fleet it would be impossible to dislodge the Portuguese from these coastal strongholds; and it was not within the competency of the Gujaratis, still less of the Moghuls, to build ships of the requisite strength. Akbar, therefore, confined his military activities to the reduction of the ports which still remained in the hands of the Gujaratis, notably Cambay, Surat and Broach.

To return to the Portuguese, in 1573 Antonio Moniz Barreto became governor in Goa, and it was during his term of office that a curious incident occurred which may be fitly recorded here. The annual pilgrimages of Muslim Indians to Mecca, whose route lay through Gujarat (which was called the Gate of Mecca) had been for some years interrupted by the domination of the Arabian Ocean by the Portuguese and also by the disorder prevailing in Gujarat. Now that order had been restored in this province and Akbar's relations with Goa were of a friendly nature, it was considered safe for the ladies of the imperial household to fulfil a long-cherished desire of performing this chief act of Muslim piety (for although Akbar himself in his religious experiments had almost abjured Islam, his family had remained devout Muslims). The party reached Surat in safety at the end of 1575, but it was not till the following season that satisfactory passes were furnished. The ladies, who included the famous Gulbadan Begum, performed the pilgrimage and returned safely in 1582.

In 1578, under the viceroyalty of Dom Diego de Menezes, Antonio Cabral (who had met Akbar at Surat in 1573) was accredited to the emperor's court as ambassador, and it was the conversations of Akbar and Cabral on religious matters which resulted in the dispatch of the first Jesuit mission to the Moghul court in 1580.[1] Like Kubilai Khan in the thirteenth century, Akbar was disposed to give Christianity a fair hearing, but he had to reckon with the spiritual forces of Islam

[1] See Payne, *Akbar and the Jesuits*.

which he was obliged to conciliate outwardly at least throughout his progress towards the new religion which was forming in his mind.

In the meanwhile, events of far-reaching importance for the history of India were passing in Europe.

In August, 1578, Dom Sebastian, then only twenty-five years of age, was killed in battle near Fez, fighting like a hero in a hopeless enterprise against the Moors. Philip II of Spain had long coveted the kingdom of Portugal, and on the death of the cardinal Dom Henrique, who had assumed the title of king, he invaded that country and totally defeated the Portuguese at the battle of Alcantara (1580), and in April, 1581, was crowned king at Tomar. Portugal thus became a part of the kingdom of Spain, but it was stipulated that the commerce of Africa, Persia and India should be reserved to the Portuguese, and carried only on their vessels.

The first viceroy sent to India under the new *régime* was Dom Francisco Mascarenhas, who had already considerable experience of India. Among the many happenings of his period of office may be mentioned the rebellion of the ex-sultan of Gujarat, Muzaffar, who, escaping from captivity, managed to raise an army of some 30,000 men and recovered a large part of his former kingdom (1583). In the confusion which ensued, the viceroy thought an opportunity possibly offered of "laying hands on Surat at small cost"[1], but his plans were frustrated by the sudden arrival of a Moghul army.

By reason of the assistance given by Queen Elizabeth to the Netherlands in their revolt against Spain, a declaration of war became merely a matter of time, and in 1584 diplomatic relations were broken off between England and Spain, and consequently Portugal. In 1586 six ships sailed from Lisbon for India. Off the Azores they fell in with Sir Francis Drake, who brought into Plymouth a cargo valued at over a hundred thousand pounds. This success taught the English and the Dutch that what the Portuguese had achieved in Indian waters was, no doubt, equally possible for themselves. Though the merging of Portugal into the kingdom of Spain may be said to have hastened the end of Portugal's monopoly of Indian trade, rival European adventurers were bound to appear in Indian waters sooner or later in an age which produced and encouraged such men as Francis Drake. The only wonder is that other seafaring nations allowed her to enjoy for so long the advantages she had gained. By the time she had recovered her independence after "sixty years' captivity", the Dutch had already deprived her of the greater part of her possessions and her trade.

The neighbouring island of Ceylon had been discovered by the Portuguese more or less by accident. It was during the viceroyalty of Dom Francisco d'Almeida that the Muhammadan merchants, in

[1] Couto, x, 6.

order to avoid their new rivals, began to make a detour by way of the Maldives when proceeding with their spice ships to the Red Sea. In November, 1505, the viceroy sent his youthful son Lourenço with a fleet of nine vessels to try and intercept these merchantmen, and while searching for them Lourenço was driven on to the coast of Ceylon in the neighbourhood of Galle, where he replenished his stores, and then proceeded to Colombo. According to some accounts a treaty was then concluded with the king of Ceylon, whereby the king agreed to pay tribute in cinnamon and elephants to the Portuguese, who, in return, undertook to protect Ceylon against all enemies. Seeing that the next official visit to Ceylon did not take place until 1518, when Lopo Soares actually secured similar terms from the local king, it would appear that the first treaty was not regarded very seriously, although we hear in the interval of Portuguese merchants trading in cinnamon at Colombo. The only evidence which remains of Dom Lourenço's visit is a stone, still standing, bearing the royal arms of Portugal surmounted by a cross, but marked with the unaccountable date of 1501.

The report sent to King Manoel from Cochin, dated 22 December, 1518, contains the following entry: "Lopo Soares has returned from Ceylon, where he has erected a fortress of mud, stone and clay, and obtained tribute of ten elephants and 400 *baharis* of cinnamon".

In 1520 Lopo de Brito, bringing with him 400 men, arrived in Colombo, and at once set about the rebuilding of the little fort, which had suffered badly from the torrential rains. He had scarcely had time to complete his defences when the inhabitants showed open hostility, which led to a siege of the little garrison, who were only saved at the end of six months by the timely arrival of a Portuguese galley. Hostilities ceased shortly after this and friendly relations were re-established. The Portuguese had, however, made themselves thoroughly disliked by the Sinhalese, and the constant exposure of the garrison to attack led them finally, in 1524, to dismantle the fort at Colombo, and to confine themselves to a factory under the protection of the Sinhalese king. In 1538 the Zamorin of Calicut dispatched a fleet of fifty-one vessels carrying 8000 men to attack Ceylon. A Portuguese fleet set out in pursuit, and inflicted a severe defeat on the Zamorin's forces after a very fierce engagement; the grateful king rewarded his allies with a handsome contribution towards the expenses of the expedition, but further assistance to meet a renewed attack by the Zamorin in alliance with the king's brother was not forthcoming as the Portuguese were at that time too busily engaged in and around Diu to spare any ships or men. In the following year, however, the required help was sent, and peace was restored in Ceylon. Shortly after this (1541) a Sinhalese embassy was sent to Lisbon carrying, among other gifts to the Portuguese king, an image of the child who had just been declared heir apparent to the throne.

The coronation of the image was celebrated with stately ceremony and the day was observed as a holiday throughout the land. The name of this child was Dharmapala, and on the death of his grand-father in 1550 he ascended the throne. In 1556, thanks mainly to the wave of religious enthusiasm kindled by the missionary activities of Francisco Xavier, Dharmapala and his queen were baptised and received into the Catholic Church. Had the priests by whom he was surrounded acted with moderation, or even with understanding, this conversion might have had momentous results; but, no doubt with the best of intentions, they did everything that was possible to offend the Buddhist inhabitants of the island; without making any effort to enquire into the nature of the Buddhist religion they determined to destroy it by every means in their power, and by their ruthless action only succeeded in undoing the labours of twenty years. It was at this time that we find introduced among the Sinhalese that curious medley of Portuguese names and the high-sounding title of *Dom*. From 1559 to 1565 the Portuguese were engaged in constant war with the Sinhalese by whom they were so much hated, and on more than one occasion were very near to being altogether ejected from the island. In 1560 matters became so serious that the viceroy, Dom Constantino of Braganza, himself led a great expedition against the Sinhalese. The headquarters of the Portuguese had hitherto been Kotte, but in 1565 it was decided to remove the garrison and factory and the native inhabitants to Colombo, and the ancient capital, thus abandoned, soon became the haunt of wild beasts. The rest of Ceylon remained in the undisputed possession of the Sinhalese monarch, the grand-uncle of Dharmapala, who was now a refugee under the protection of the Portuguese. In 1578 the old king, feeling he had no longer the strength to cope with the increasing aggressions of the Portuguese, abdicated in favour of his son, Raja Sinha, who, in the following year, laid siege to Colombo, but was driven off. In the meantime Dharma-pala executed a deed of gift, by which, after setting forth his own title to the throne, and explaining that nothing had been left him by his rivals but Colombo, he made over all his claims to the king of Portugal, Dom Henrique, and in 1583 executed another instrument by which Philip II, who was now lord of Portugal, was made heir to Dharmapala. Raja Sinha meanwhile devoted all his energies to raising an efficient army and to erecting strong forts, which became a source of much anxiety to the Portuguese, who on their side were engaged in strengthening the fortifications of Colombo. Constant appeals for assistance were sent to Goa, but seldom met with a satis-factory response. In 1587 Raja Sinha, with an army of 50,000 men, made his first great assault on Colombo. The carnage was terrible, but the half-clothed Sinhalese could not cope with the fully armed soldiery of Europe, and the assault was turned to a siege, during which large reinforcements in men and munitions arrived from Cochin, and later on from Malacca; and finally, in February, 1588, the Portuguese had acquired such superiority over the enemy that they were able to make a sortie in force, and Colombo was saved. In 1597 Dharmapala died and a convention of delegates was held, which, after two days spent in negotiations, agreed to recognise Philip II as the king of Ceylon, provided the Portuguese "would guarantee on his behalf that the laws and customs of the Sinhalese should be maintained inviolate for ever".

In considering the achievement of the Portuguese in the Indian Ocean, it is our duty to recognise the important part they played, having regard for the future history of India, in successfully frustrating all the attacks made on them by the Turks. Although we have no documentary evidence for believing that the Turks ever entertained the idea of establishing a naval, and still less a military base in India, it is quite conceivable that if one of their fleets had succeeded in driving the Portuguese out of their fortresses on the Indian coast, the establishment of the Christian powers in India might have been indefinitely postponed.

CHAPTER II

THE DUTCH IN INDIA

THE first Dutch vessels to sail round the Cape of Good Hope and to cross the Indian Ocean in search of trade left the Texel on 2 April, 1595. The owners were a group of Amsterdam merchants who had formed a company for Indian trade in 1592. The Netherlands had long been a most important centre for the European trade in the produce of the colonial world. The wares which the Spaniards and Portuguese transported from America and the Indies to Seville and Lisbon were carried further north very largely in Holland and Zeeland ships. Antwerp had been the great distributing centre for Northern and Middle Europe, but after its fall in 1585 and the consequent closure of the Scheldt by the more successful rebels of the northern provinces, the trading towns of Holland and Zeeland, and particularly Amsterdam, had inherited its position. The circumstances of the time made the use of the Iberian ports, all obeying Philip II after the conquest of Portugal in 1580, as centres of Mediterranean and colonial trade a perilous practice. Even though the economic dependence of Spain and Portugal on the Netherlands rebels was too great to permit the king to adopt a consistent policy of prohibition with respect to Netherlands trading, the embargoes of 1585 and 1595 served to create a sense of insecurity in Netherlands trading circles.

To venture out into the vast, unknown regions of the Indian world, however, was an enterprise not lightly to be undertaken. Knowledge of the route to India was of the vaguest, and ignorance exaggerated the power of the Spanish-Portuguese Empire to defend its claims. At first, therefore, attempts were made to reach the Indies by the north of Asia, although a plan for an expedition round the Cape of Good Hope had been conceived as early as any of the northern expeditions. But years of preparation preceded the execution. The first act of the Company formed in 1592 was to send Cornelis de Houtman to Lisbon to collect information about the conditions and methods of Indian trade, and in 1595 it was he who led the expedition. The famous geographer Petrus Plancius, a Reformed minister who had fled from Flanders, and who in 1592 had published a map of the world based, in so far as the Indies are concerned, on Portuguese data, was commissioned to instruct the skippers and mates who were to take part in the expedition in the newest discoveries of the science of navigation. And invaluable was the advice of Jan Huyghen van Linschoten, whose *Reysgeschrift van de navigatien der Portugaloysers*, a seaman's guidebook to Indian and Far Eastern navigation, appeared in 1595, while the *Itinerario, voyage ofte schipvaert van Jan Huyghen van*

Linschoten naer Oost ofte Portugails Indien, although published only in the next year, must have been printed earlier, since we know that de Houtman took a copy with him on his voyage.

The number of Netherlanders who made the voyage to India in the Portuguese period and served the Portuguese in some capacity or other must have been considerable. Some were engaged in trade out there, and many served on the Portuguese ships, particularly as gunners. Jan Huyghen van Linschoten in 1583, after some years spent in Spain and Portugal, accompanied the newly appointed archbishop of Goa to his post in the capacity of secretary. He was still a very young man, having been born in 1563. He stayed at Goa from September, 1583, to January, 1589. He came back to Holland in September, 1592, and settled at Enkhuizen. He became an active promoter of the plans for direct trading with the Indies which were already in the air. In 1594 and 1595 he took part in fruitless attempts to find the North-east Passage, yet in spite of that found time to work out the notes collected during his travels into the two works above cited.

Of the two, the *Reysgeschrift* was probably of the greater immediate use, but it is on the *Itinerario* that Linschoten's fame is chiefly founded. It is much more than the ordinary traveller's story. In fact, Linschoten's personal observation of India was practically confined to Goa, but in the *Itinerario* he gives an encyclopaedic account of the whole of the extensive area which the Portuguese looked upon as their special preserve. He describes towns and harbours, the political organisation, the social conditions and the religions of the various peoples, and the produce and industries of particular regions; through it all he traces the ramifications of the Portuguese Empire and of Portuguese trade, explaining how it works, where it is weak and where it is strong. One fact he stresses over and over again which must have stimulated the spirit of enterprise of his countrymen—and no doubt that was his intention—namely that the Portuguese system was vulnerable in the extreme, undermined by abuses and corruption, while Portuguese methods of navigation in particular were far inferior to those of Dutch seamen. At the same time Linschoten did not under-estimate the strength of the Portuguese fortified establishments, and he pointed to the Malay Archipelago as the most suitable area for Dutch enterprise on account of Sunda Straits being undefended: there was not a Portuguese fortress on either Java or Sumatra, which nevertheless offered great opportunities to the European merchant; Bantam in particular was the centre of a trading movement to Malacca on the one side and the Spice Islands, or Moluccas, on the other.

It was excellent advice and it was taken. Houtman set his course straight for Java, where he found the inhabitants quite willing to enter into commercial relations with rivals of the Portuguese, and although he spoiled his chances by injudicious behaviour and this first expedition yielded no profits, in August, 1597, Houtman, with three out of his four ships, reappeared before the Texel, and the mere fact of his having accomplished the voyage was encouragement enough. The pent-up enterprise of the Dutch commercial class burst forth as if a dyke had been cut. New companies for the Indian trade sprang up in several towns of Holland and Zeeland. Twenty-two ships left for the Archipelago in 1598, and about forty more in the next three years. Some of the so-called Pre-companies made enormous profits, but it soon became apparent that their keen competition would in the long run spoil the market both in the East and in Europe, while their jealousy made it impossible for them to co-operate in order to secure the new trade against the attempts of the Portuguese to enforce their monopoly. The foundation of the English East India Company (1600), which at once sent an expedition in the track of the Dutch, to Java, drove home the conclusion that unity was necessary. The Government, anxious lest a promising new source of wealth should dry up, and realising that the energies of commercial enterprise might be so directed as to help the country in its war with the Spanish Empire, took action. It was the Advocate of Holland, Johan van Oldenbarnevelt, who initiated negotiations for an amalgamation, on the basis of a national monopoly. For although public opinion in the Netherlands was strongly averse to monopolies, in this particular case it was realised that the amalgamated companies must be protected from further competition. In December, 1601, delegates of the various companies, at the invitation of the states-general, met at the Hague. It was far from easy to reach agreement, Zeeland interests in particular proving refractory. The Advocate, however, exerted all his influence and at last a scheme was evolved by which the Pre-companies consented to be merged into a monopolist chartered company and this was at once embodied in a resolution of the states-general (20 March, 1602).

The United Company was a very powerful organism. The directors of the Pre-companies, who now became directors of the United Company, had every time put up their capital for one expedition only. New capital was now invited from the general public—a total of 6,500,000 guilders (about £540,000) was subscribed—and that for ten years; the directors were to be liable only for the amount they subscribed as shareholders. In fact the return of the capital on the expiration of the period named in the charter never took place, nor had the shareholders ever any effective control over the direction of affairs. In its administrative organisation its origin as the result of an amalgamation appeared very clearly. It was composed of six "chambers" which traded each with its own capital, but profit and loss were pooled. The directors of the several chambers, who held office for life, were appointed by the government of the town in which the chamber was situated (by the Provincial States in the case of the

Zeeland Chamber) out of three persons nominated, on the death of a director, by his surviving colleagues. The Amsterdam Chamber was by far the most important and appointed eight of the seventeen general directors. "The Seventeen", who met three times a year, could only lay down general lines of policy, the execution of which rested with the several chambers. This complicated organisation, intended to reconcile the warring interests of various groups and political entities, particularly of Amsterdam and Zeeland, lasted as long as the company.

To this body the states-general by the charter of 20 March, 1602, delegated important sovereign powers. Not only was the Company given the exclusive right to trade in all countries between the Cape of Good Hope and the Straits of Magellan, but within that area it was empowered to carry on war, to conclude treaties, to take possession of territory, and to erect fortresses. The Pre-companies had had little thought of colonisation or of attacking the Portuguese, whom on the contrary they sought to avoid. Only on the outskirts of the Portuguese sphere of influence, in the Moluccas, had the desire to control the spice trade inspired attacks on Portuguese posts. The states-general, by their interference, set a new direction and made the United Company a great instrument of war and conquest.

The powerful fleets, of about a dozen large ships each, which the Company sent out annually during the first years of its existence, boldly attacked the Portuguese Empire at its vital points. Mozambique, Goa, Malacca, were all attacked, but in vain. The Dutch had the command of the seas, they hindered and interrupted communications between the Portuguese ports, they even prevented the sending of reinforcements from the mother country. But they failed to break Portuguese power ashore. Only in the Moluccas did they succeed in ousting the Portuguese and securing a foothold for themselves. Even there, however, the Portuguese, supported by the Spaniards from the Philippines, offered a strong resistance, and the determined attempt of the Company to become masters of the Moluccas —in an instruction of 1608, the directors described this as their principal aim—for a number of years claimed much of its energies. For a considerable period these were in any case concentrated on the Malay Archipelago. The spice trade of the Moluccas was looked upon as the great prize of the Indian world. Java, moreover, was proving as important as Linschoten had foretold. Factories were established at Bantam and Jacatra, and these insensibly became the centre of the trading movement which the Dutch were developing and which already embraced the Moluccas in the east, China and Japan in the north, and Coromandel and Surat in the west. In 1609 unity of command over the scattered ships and posts in the East was secured by the institution of a central authority, the governor-general and the council of the Indies. The first governor-general was Pieter Both and his instructions, endorsed by the states-general, ordered him to establish some fixed seat for the central government in the Indies, and suggested Johore, Bantam or Jacatra for that purpose. It was years before these instructions were acted upon, and it was done, not by Both, but by his second successor, Jan Pietersoon Coen, the real founder of the Dutch Eastern Empire. In 1619 Coen conquered Jacatra and founded Batavia on its ruins. At the same time his ruthless energy saved the Dutch from being superseded by the English, whose chances in the Archipelago were in the course of a few years effectually ruined, and who thenceforward concentrated their attention on India. Great exertions were still required of the Dutch, however, to defend their new capital against the Javanese themselves, and altogether it was not until the governor-generalship of Antonie van Diemen (1636–46) that the ruling powers at Batavia felt themselves sufficiently secure in the Archipelago to resume the earlier policy of aggression against the strongholds of Portuguese power in the Indian Ocean.

In 1633 the Dutch had already begun to blockade Malacca, which finally they took in 1641. Meanwhile from 1636 onwards a fleet had been sent every year to blockade Goa during the winter months, the only time when the port was accessible. In the spring of 1638 the fleet returning from that blockade attacked Batticaloa and a twenty years' struggle began in which the Dutch wrested from the Portuguese all they possessed on Ceylon and in the southern part of the mainland of India itself.

A long time before they made those conquests, the Dutch already had acquired factories on the Coromandel Coast, in Gujarat, and in Bengal. Except for the fortress Geldria at Pulicat, these settlements were merely unfortified trading posts, and the position of the Dutch in India for a long time remained essentially different from that in the Archipelago. And the Archipelago was not only the strategic and administrative centre of their system, it was also the economic centre. It was pepper and spices, the produce of Sumatra, Java and the Moluccas, then so much in demand for the European market, that had originally drawn the Dutch to the islands, and from the early years of the United Company they set themselves to obtain a monopoly in these articles. What took them to India in the first instance was rather the requirements of the Archipelago than of the European market; in other words, it was a distinctly subsidiary interest. The Dutch traders were not slow to discover that the system of paying in money for the pepper and spices had grave disadvantages. At the same time they saw that there was an active commercial movement in existence, with Bantam, and especially Achin, as its intermediary centres, by which the populations of the Archipelago exchanged their own products for cotton goods from Gujarat and from the Coromandel

Coast. The idea naturally arose of controlling that movement, eliminating the Arab and Indian middlemen, and paying for the spices by imported cotton goods.

As early as October, 1603, the Seventeen directed the attention of the admiral (Van der Haghen) of a fleet they were just then fitting out to the Coromandel Coast and particularly to Masulipatam as a place well fitted for the buying of cotton goods. Even before this, an attempt had been already made to start trade on the other side of the peninsula, at Surat and on the Malabar Coast, but it had ended in disaster. The two Zeeland merchants who had ventured out into those parts had fallen into the hands of the Portuguese and been hanged at Goa. So the United Company looked to the east coast, and a circumstance which especially recommended Masulipatam, was the weakness of the Portuguese in that northern region. Admiral Van der Haghen, from Calicut where he then was, while going on himself to Bantam with the main fleet, dispatched the yacht *Delft* to open up trade with the Coromandel Coast. Masulipatam belonged to the king of Golconda, and although there were Portuguese merchants in the town, their rivals were welcomed by the Indian authorities and the senior merchant Pieter Ysaac Eyloff remained behind with a small number of assistants to set up a permanent factory when the *Delft* left early in May, 1605, with the first cargo of cotton goods for Achin and Bantam.

The beginning was thus very easy, and another factory was founded at Petapoli (Nizampatam), also in the kingdom of Golconda, but many difficulties were still to be overcome before the new settlement could work smoothly and profitably. The governors of the two ports imposed crushing import and export duties in the most arbitrary fashion, and interfered in the intercourse between the factors and the native weavers and dyers. The export trade in textiles was highly technical, and the servants of the Dutch Company wanted to be free to instruct the native craftsmen as to the requirements of the Archipelago markets and actively to supervise their work. A mission to the Golconda court in 1606 secured farmans fixing import and export duties at 4 per cent., but the governors did not heed them much. In 1608, hoping that the fear of their going away altogether would check their tormentors, the Dutch factors sent out some of their subordinates to found a new settlement at Devenampatnam to the southward. A treaty guaranteeing the same tolls as in Golconda was obtained from the nayak of Jinji, in whose province the port was situated. After some trouble due to the influence which the Portuguese, themselves established at St Thomé and Negapatam, preserved at Vellore, the Dutch obtained permission to rebuild an old fort at Devenampatnam and to build a factory at Tirupapuliyur to be armed with four pieces of cannon, while the Portuguese were expressly forbidden access to either place. In 1610, by direct negotiations with the king, permission was obtained to found another factory at Pulicat, and again, in spite of their attempts to dissuade the king, the Portuguese were expressly excluded from the port. The Dutch were thus extending their position on the Coromandel Coast, although at the same time the main forces of their Company were so fully engaged in the Archipelago that no Dutch vessels appeared on the coast between October, 1608, and March, 1610. The king of the Carnatic began to doubt whether the Portuguese, whose trade the newcomers threatened with ruin, might not after all be the more valuable friends. But by means of a present of elephants from Kandi and other bribes the Dutch retained his favour, while the Portuguese, who made one or two fruitless attacks on the Dutch at Pulicat by sea from St Thomé, only displayed that inferiority in naval power which was the real cause of the ruin of their Indian Empire.

Meanwhile the Seventeen, before the news of the settlement at Pulicat had reached them, had realised the need for unity of administration on the Coromandel Coast. In December, 1610, the council at Bantam, acting upon their instructions, organised the administration of the Coromandel factories. The senior merchant of Masulipatam and Petapoli, Van Wesick (Pieter Ysaac had died), was appointed to be General Director. The Portuguese, however, had not yet learnt to acquiesce in the presence of their rivals. On 9 June, 1612, they carried out a successful raid on Pulicat from their neighbouring settlement of St Thomé. The Dutch factory was destroyed. Wemmer van Berchem, Van Wesick's successor as Director, was absent in Golconda; but some of the factors were killed and the senior merchant, Adolf Thomassen, carried off to St Thomé, whence he only escaped over a year later. Wemmer van Berchem realised that, if the factory at Pulicat was to survive, it would have to be fortified. The local authorities, as well as the raja at Vellore, professed great indignation at the action of the Portuguese; liberal presents secured freedom to proceed with the work; and with the aid of the crews of two ships, which happened to call in March, 1613, the fortress, called Geldria after Van Berchem's native province, was completed. In the very next month it had to withstand an attack by a native chief, Etheraja, behind whom Van Berchem naturally suspected the Portuguese. A direct attack by the Portuguese, both by sea and by land, soon followed, but was beaten off. For some time the Dutch still feared that, although the neighbouring Portuguese settlements had proved too weak to dislodge them, the viceroy at Goa might send an armada to restore Portuguese monopoly on the east coast. An attempt was actually made in 1615, when a Portuguese fleet sailed to Arakan to expel the Dutch; but the king of Arakan's ships, assisted by a single Dutch yacht, the *Duif*, compelled the assailants to return. Both in Golconda and in the Carnatic the native authorities and the Dutch factories prepared jointly to resist the Portuguese fleet, which sailed south along the coast; but at no point did it venture to attack. Portuguese prestige never recovered from this failure, and Geldria never again had to fear attack from them.

Fort Geldria, meanwhile, played a part of growing importance. For several years after 1614, the kingdom of the Carnatic was shaken by a disputed succession and civil war. The Dutch castle was a fixed point in the midst of turmoil, and many natives, and even many refugees from St Thomé, sought its protection, so that almost at once it became the nucleus from which a new territorial power might have sprung. When the anarchy in the Carnatic led to its falling under the sway of the kings of Golconda, conditions in that region were not greatly changed. The Dutch Company continued to coin its own gold pagodas at Pulicat, out of imported gold, as did the English later on at Madras. At Masulipatam, however, so much nearer the capital, no such developments took place. That town was ruled despotically by its havildar, while the Dutch factory, like the English one, remained a trading settlement pure and simple. The Company had soon obtained another farman by which the king of Golconda remitted the 4 per cent. duties for an annual payment of 3000 "old pagodas" (25,000 guilders). Even this did not save the Company from the exactions of the local authorities,[1] and embassies to Golconda were frequently needed to solicit the king's interference.

On the whole, however, the advantages of the new settlements far outweighed the drawbacks. The Coromandel Coast soon played a very important part in the life of the Company. As early as 1612, it was described as "the left arm of the Moluccas and neighbouring islands, since without the cottons from thence trade is dead in the Moluccas".[2] The export of textiles for the Archipelago market always remained the chief business of the Coromandel factories, although soon considerable quantities were exported to Europe as well, and the export of rice and vegetables and of slaves (for Batavia) became important;[3] diamonds also were exported; while the hinterland of Masulipatam supplied indigo. Both the indigo and the textile trades required considerable skill on the part of the Company's servants. As regards the latter, the requirements of the Archipelago market were exactly studied. Patterns were sent from Bantam or Batavia, and minute instructions were given to the weavers and dyers who worked for the Company in towns and villages within a wide radius of the factory.

The Dutch were able to carry on their trade to a large extent by importing other articles in exchange for those of the country. This

[1] *Daghregister gehouden int Casteel Batavia,* I, 229.
[2] E. Heeres, *Corpus Diplomaticum Neerlando-Indicum,* p. 154.
[3] *Daghregister,* I, 189, 221; II, 445 *sqq.*

was one of the great problems for the European Companies.[1] The Indian market could not absorb any considerable amount of European articles. Neither the English nor the Dutch Company could export an unlimited supply of money from their own countries. In India money could be borrowed only at an extortionate rate of interest. Two ways lay open to the European Companies who did not want to fall into the hands of the native moneylenders. They could raise money by trading in countries where imports were paid for with cash; the trade with China and Japan was the most fruitful in this respect, and here the Dutch had a practical monopoly. Secondly, they could escape the necessity of importing money by importing non-European articles for which there was a demand in India, and here again the Dutch were fortunate in their control of the supply of spices. Apart from spices, the chief articles which they imported on the Coromandel Coast were sandal wood and pepper from the Malay Archipelago, Japanese copper and certain Chinese textiles from the Far East.

In 1617 the directorate of the Coromandel Coast was raised into a *gouvernement*, its chief at Pulicat being given the title of governor as well as becoming an Extraordinary Councillor of the Indies. In 1689 the governor's seat was removed from Pulicat in the centre to Negapatam in the south, which as will be described in a subsequent paragraph, had been taken from the Portuguese in 1659. No doubt the decision to make it into the capital of the coast, which was adversely criticised by many who praised the situation of Pulicat as ideally central, was inspired by the consideration that in the troublous times ahead, now that Aurangzib was master of Golconda, Negapatam, close to the Company's new stronghold of Ceylon, was the natural strategic basis of the whole *gouvernement*. A new castle was at once constructed, at a cost, it was said, of 1,600,000 guilders, which far surpassed Fort Geldria in size and strength.

We possess a very vivid account of the conditions in the Dutch factories on the Coromandel Coast just about the time when this transfer was taking place in the travels of Daniel Havart.

The society into which Havart introduces his reader is purely official. The "Free merchants" whom early governors-general had wanted to encourage had been driven away by the severely monopolist policy on which the Seventeen insisted. There were only the servants of the Company left, who enriched themselves (although Havart does not say so) by infringing that very monopoly which was so dear to the directors' hearts. During the last years of Havart's stay on the coast this little society was shaken to its foundations by the appearance of a commissioner, Van Reede tot Drakensteyn, entrusted by the Seventeen themselves with extraordinary powers to put down corruption and reform abuses. Several officials, chiefs of factories among them, were broken by this ruthless reformer, whose social

---

[1] Moreland, *From Akbar to Aurangzeb*, pp. 58 *sqq*.

position (he was a member of the Utrecht nobility, a very unusual rank among the servants of the Company) added to the awe which he inspired.

By Havart's time some of the early factories, Petapoli and Tirupapuliyur, had been abandoned. On the other hand several new ones had been founded. Proceeding northward from Negapatam, Havart enumerates: Porto Novo, Devenampatnam, Sadraspatam, Pulicat, Masulipatam, Nagelwanze, Golconda, Palakollu, Daatzerom and Bimlipatam. Of these, Porto Novo, founded as late as 1680, was a prosperous centre for the collection of cottons. Sadraspatam and Palakollu were important on account of the especial excellence of the textiles to be had there. Devenampatnam and Masulipatam were the busiest factories, both for export and import, although Masulipatam had lost some of its importance since the establishment, in 1660, of a factory at Golconda, the chief of which, apart from his commercial duties, acted as the Company's resident with the king of Golconda, although special embassies continued still to be sent after as before 1660. Nagelwanze was the centre for the indigo trade. At Palakollu the Company had had a factory since 1613, and carried on a profitable dyeing industry. From 1653 the village was administered by the Company which held it from the king at an annual rent of 1000 pagodas.

In all these places the Dutch Company had buildings, more or less fortified, and large enough to accommodate the factors, their slaves, and sometimes a small body of soldiers. The number of factors varied a good deal. At Sadraspatam, although a very successful trading centre, there were only four; at Nagelwanze, at the time of its highest prosperity about 1680, eighteen. Many of the factors were married, and if the factory could not house their families, they lived outside. At Masulipatam eight or ten were married, when the Commissioner Van Reede strictly prohibited (except for the chiefs of factories) what was regarded as an abuse, and sent many families to Europe or Batavia. The factors in the Company's service were called merchants, and their ranks were assistant, junior merchant, merchant, and senior merchant. This nomenclature was preserved even in possessions where the duties of the Company's servants were not primarily commercial, but administrative, as in Ceylon. At the head of a factory there were as a rule two chiefs, the first and the second chief, who might be junior merchant, merchant, or senior merchant in rank. The Coromandel instructions of the Pulicat governors of 1649 and 1663[1] laid it down that the first chief presides over the council, on which the other factors also sat; he had the general supervision over the factory's affairs, kept the money, negotiated with native traders, contracting for textiles, etc., and corresponding with the central administration, with the director or governor, as the case might be, but consulting his *secundo*.

[1] Havart, *Op- en Ondergang van Cormandel*, III, 57.

The second himself kept the trading accounts and looked after the warehouses.

At Pulicat—Havart knew the place before Van Reede ordered the transfer of headquarters to Negapatam—the governor's house and those of some other high officials were within the castle. But in the town, there were "many streets where none but Dutchmen live, and among them one whole row of houses all built in the Dutch way, with three rows of trees in front of them". The governor, who had to consult his council about most matters of importance, corresponded, not with the directors in Europe, but with the government at Batavia. The Geldria fort, as Havart observes, was by no means so fine a castle as the English castle at Madras, and on the whole, the English factories surpassed those of the Dutch in size and beauty, if not in trade, all along the Coromandel Coast. Particularly after the reductions of 1678, when the Company ceased supplying chiefs of factories with horses and palanquins, and the number of servants in each factory was greatly cut down, Havart feared that Dutch prestige in the eyes of the natives would suffer irreparable damage.

In fact, bad times, but not only for the Dutch, were fast approaching. Relations with the court of Golconda had on the whole been very friendly. In 1676, on the occasion of a visit to Masulipatam, when the king insisted that the Dutch ladies should visit his wives, and when he himself attended service in the Dutch church, he remitted all the annual payments which the Company owed him in respect of freedom of tolls or possession of lands. In 1686, a quarrel broke out about a debt which the Company had outstanding at Golconda. It had just been settled after a display of vigour on the Company's part —the inland factories had been evacuated and Masulipatam occupied by a force shipped from Ceylon—when the army of Aurangzib appeared before Golconda; the king was deposed and the country overrun. The Dutch factory at Nagelwanze was destroyed, and altogether a time of dearth and insecurity began in which trade declined. The profits of the Coromandel *gouvernement*, which in the years 1684 and 1685 appeared in the Company's books as exceeding 1,200,000 guilders, fell to 445,000 guilders in 1686 and 82,000 in 1687.[1] Nor was the high water mark of the years before Aurangzib's conquest of Golconda ever reached again. Towards the middle of the eighteenth century there was an improvement, but it was not maintained, and the figures generally moved between 200,000 and 400,000 guilders profit, which indeed still made a good showing in the Company's books when, as will be shown in a subsequent paragraph, so many of its establishments were worked at a loss.

In the days before the amalgamation of the companies, two Zeeland

---

[1] Klerk de Reus, *Geschichtlicher Ueberblick der Niederl. Ostindischen Compagnie*, 1894, Beilage IX.

merchants, as has been briefly mentioned above, had tried to open up relations with the ports on the west coast of India, but had been hanged by the Portuguese at Goa. Their reports on Gujarat, however, had been most sanguine, and the United Company was anxious to follow up their pioneer work and secure Gujarat cottons for the markets of the Moluccas and the west coast of Sumatra and Jambi as well as for Europe. In 1604, and again in 1605, the admiral commanding the annual fleet was instructed to detach two ships to Surat; whether the order was carried out in 1604 does not appear; in the following year, at any rate, it was set aside because reports of an impending attack by the Portuguese made a concentration of all forces in the Archipelago seem imperatively necessary. A Dutch merchant was at Surat in 1606 and 1607, but, wrought upon by nervous fears that the Portuguese were succeeding in setting against him the mind of the Khankhanan, Jahangir's representative at Burhanpur, he committed suicide. The English soon were more successful, and, stimulated by their example, and urged moreover by the shahbandar of Surat, the Dutch governor of Coromandel in May, 1615, sent one of his officials, Gilles van Ravesteyn, to Surat, where he arrived after a six weeks' journey on horseback. Van Ravesteyn, who went to Burhanpur in the company of Sir Thomas Roe, on his return advised against the establishment of a factory. Political conditions in the Moghul Empire did not seem to him to promise security to foreign traders; in any case a farman signed by the Great Moghul himself would be required and would be very difficult to obtain.

Coen, however, who in the capacity of director-general of trade at Bantam was already the leading spirit among the authorities in the East, considered the cottons of Gujarat indispensable for the Molucca trade, the more so as the factory at Achin, where they could be obtained, if at much higher prices, was exposed to intolerable vexations and had soon to be withdrawn. Even before Van Ravesteyn's report had been received, therefore, Coen had dispatched a yacht under Pieter van den Broecke to Gujarat. After touching at Mokha, which became the usual practice, as cash useful for the purchases to be made at Surat could be obtained there, Van den Broecke arrived at Surat in August, 1616, and asked permission to establish a factory. Sir Thomas Roe did what he could to excite the Great Moghul's suspicions against the newcomers,[1] but the Surat merchants feared that in case of a refusal the Dutch might attack their shipping, and the governor of the town gave a provisional permission. The next year two senior merchants, Van Ravesteyn and Adriaan Goeree, were left in charge of the Surat factory, and they had to struggle through some very difficult years. Van Ravesteyn succeeded, to the mortification of Sir Thomas Roe, in negotiating, not it is true with Jahangir himself, but with his son Prince Khurram, a satisfactory treaty of

---

[1] *Embassy of Sir Thomas Roe* (ed. 1926), pp. 202 *sqq.*

commerce (1618), but all his and his colleague's efforts were in vain since no ships appeared to carry away their indigo and cottons. Van den Broecke, sent from Bantam for the third time in December, 1618, was immediately recalled on account of the outbreak of the war with the English, which necessitated the concentration of all available forces in the Archipelago. The two factors at Surat were driven almost to distraction by their false position until at last, in October, 1620, Van den Broecke, after having called at Aden, arrived at Surat. Coen had appointed him director of both Mokha and Surat, and he took up his residence at the latter place. A number of the Company's other servants arrived overland from Masulipatam later in the year, and factories could then be organised in the inland towns, explored during the preceding years, Broach, Cambay, Ahmadabad, Agra, and Burhanpur, where indigo and textiles of various kinds were to be had.

A more prosperous time now began for the settlement. There was a dangerous conflict in 1622 with the Gujarat authorities, especially with Asaf Khan, Prince Khurram's powerful father-in-law, over the activities of a Dutch ship which had sailed along the Arabian and Persian coast, seizing native craft belonging to Portuguese ports, and had confiscated property belonging—or so it was alleged—to that dignitary. The factor at Cambay, who was within the reach of Asaf Khan's resentment, nevertheless took a high tone and threatened Coen's vengeance in a way eloquent of the self-confidence engendered by the events of 1619. He was, however, arrested and sent to Agra, and Van den Broecke had to pay an indemnity before the Cambay factory could be recovered. Incidents like these were typical of trade in a strong but despotic empire like the Moghul's, and did not prevent the Gujarat factories from producing larger and larger profits. Coen was impatient with Van den Broecke for sending him indigo, when he wanted textiles.[1] In course of time, however, the indigo trade came to be as important as the trade in cottons. In 1624 the first ship sailed from Surat direct for Holland; its cargo consisted mainly of indigo. In those years three or four ships were sent annually from Batavia to trade with Gujarat and Arabia. The English Company, which, after its defeat in Java, was beginning to develop Gujarat as the centre of its eastern system, was still somewhat ahead of its rival here. But the advantages of the Dutch which have been mentioned in connection with their Coromandel trade told in Gujarat as well, and the directorate of Surat—the factories farther to the west were soon formed into a separate directorate—came to be one of the most profitable of all the establishments the Dutch Company possessed.

In 1627 the governor of Coromandel sent some of his subordinates to found a trading establishment in Bengal. At first the new post was kept within the jurisdiction of the Coromandel *gouvernement*, but

[1] Colenbrander, *Jan Pieterszoon Coen*, III, 184.

distance and its growing importance caused the government at Batavia in 1655 to give it a separate organisation as the Directorate of Bengal. Pippli, the first place where the Dutch had established themselves, was soon abandoned for Balasore. When in 1653 a firm footing was obtained at Chinsura up the Hugli river, Balasore was retained only for the convenience of the ships. Chinsura, Kasimbazar and Patna, however, became the centres of an exceedingly prosperous and profitable trade. Although the Dutch in Bengal never attained to the position of independence which they enjoyed in the Carnatic, they were given considerable liberties by the nawab of Bengal, from whom they held the villages of Chinsura and Bernagore in "perpetual fief", with wide jurisdiction even over natives. They were allowed to construct a fortress at Chinsura, called Fort Gustavus, which at any rate safeguarded them against any sudden attack by native forces. They were always exposed, nevertheless, to the exactions of native authorities, but the profits of the Bengal trade enabled them to suffer many losses and to pay many bribes with equanimity.

The articles of export were textiles and silk, saltpetre, rice, and particularly, opium. The opium, which was sent to Java and China, yielded enormous profits. Even when in the eighteenth century the Company's position in Bengal had become precarious, the establishments there continued to be among the most profitable in all the Company's domain.

Ceylon had attracted the Dutch from the early days of their colonial enterprise.

In 1602 Joris van Spilbergh, in command of three ships owned by Balthazar de Moucheron, called at Batticaloa, which was not occupied by the Portuguese, and travelled up to Kandi. Before the year was out, another three ships (detached from the first of the United Company's fleets) appeared at Batticaloa, and their commander, Sebald de Weert, followed Spilbergh's example and visited the "emperor". "Dom João" was eager to enlist the help of the Dutch against the Portuguese, and De Weert arranged with him to go to Achin for reinforcements with which to blockade Galle by sea while the Sinhalese attacked it by land. On 25 April, 1603, De Weert was back at Batticaloa with a fleet of seven ships, but before the expedition against Galle could be undertaken, a quarrel arose, and the Dutch commander was slain with a number of his companions.

This misfortune naturally had a discouraging effect on the Dutch Company, and for many years to come it devoted its energies to the strengthening of its position in the Malay Archipelago. Posts on the Coromandel Coast and Gujarat were a necessary corollary to the enjoyment of the monopoly of the Molucca trade, but the building up of a new monopoly in Ceylon could wait. Relations were not broken off altogether. When the Dutch had founded a factory at

Devenampatnam in 1608, the new king (Dom João had died in 1604) sued for their help again, and in 1610, and again in 1612, treaties were concluded. The man who had negotiated the latter treaty, de Boschhouwer, rose into high favour with the king and left Ceylon in 1615 full of zeal for the plan of an immediate attack on the Portuguese in the island. Both in Java and in Holland, however, he found the authorities immersed in their cares for the Moluccas. At last he persuaded the Danish Government to fit out an expedition to Ceylon, but he himself died on the way out, and without him the Danes achieved nothing at Batticaloa.

The Portuguese now woke up to the danger threatening their position, and closed the ring round the king of Kandi by occupying and fortifying both Trinkomali and Batticaloa. An attempt to take Kandi, however, failed disastrously.

Soon afterwards (1632), the throne of Kandi was occupied by an energetic young ruler, Raja Sinha, who resumed the policy of setting the Dutch against his arch-enemies the Portuguese. On 9 September, 1636, he wrote a letter to the Dutch Governor of the Coromandel Coast at Pulicat—it took his envoy six months to elude the watchfulness of the Portuguese and deliver the letter—in which he asked for a fleet of five vessels to blockade the Portuguese fortresses while he attacked them from the land side; he promised the Dutch leave to build a fortress of their own and the repayment of all the expenses of the expedition.

These proposals now found ready acceptance. The Company, securely established in the Archipelago, was thinking of expansion, and under the energetic leadership of the governor-general Van Diemen a determined attempt was being made to break down the Portuguese Empire. The main effort was directed against Malacca, but at the same time Goa, the nerve-centre of the Portuguese system, was paralysed by an annual blockade (this policy had been started in 1636), and the Dutch felt strong enough to try and wrest from the Portuguese the places which provided the valuable pepper and cinnamon, on the west coast of India and in Ceylon.

In January, 1638, the admiral of the fleet before Goa, Westerwolt, detached two yachts under the command of Coster to begin the siege of Batticaloa. When the south-west monsoon necessitated the break-up of the blockade, he himself appeared on 10 May with four ships and landed 300 men; Batticaloa surrendered after a bombardment without awaiting a storm.

The only importance of Batticaloa lay in that it established communications with the independent ruler of the interior. Westerwolt at once obtained Raja Sinha's consent to a new treaty prepared beforehand and which assured enormous advantages to the Company. By it the Company promised to supply the troops and ships required for the expulsion of the Portuguese from the island; the king was to make good all expenses thus incurred by deliveries of cinnamon, pepper, etc.; the Dutch were moreover to have complete freedom of commerce in the island to the exclusion of all other European nations. Clearly the king thought hardly any price too high that would help him to re-establish his authority over the coastal towns. By the third clause of the treaty, as Westerwolt sent it to Batavia, however, the king, on top of all this, consented that the Dutch should garrison the fortresses captured from the Portuguese. One wonders why he should have thought it worth his while to pay the Dutch so heavily merely to step into his enemies' place. But the mystery is solved when the Dutch copy of the treaty is compared with the Portuguese translation handed to Raja Sinha: in the only version known to the ruler of Kandi the clause in question contains an addition making the garrisoning of the fortresses by the Dutch dependent on his approval. The deception remained undetected for some time, as the king, pleased with his allies and conscious of his impotence against the Portuguese, made no objection to the Dutch retaining Batticaloa. When Westerwolt on 4 June, 1638, departed for Batavia, he left Coster behind him as governor of the town.

At about the same time another disaster befell the Portuguese, a fleet with reinforcements from Goa for Colombo being shipwrecked. Coster urged the authorities at Batavia to strike while the iron was hot, and the governor-general and council themselves wrote to the directors at home (22 December, 1638) that if they would only send some extra ships and troops, the time had come "to help the Portuguese out of India": the Malabar Coast with its rich trade, Ceylon and Malacca, all seemed within the grasp of the Company.

But quarrels with Raja Sinha supervened, and nothing was achieved in 1639 except the capture of Trinkomali, useless for the cinnamon trade, and the special effort which the Company made towards the end of that year, sending out a fleet of twenty-eight ships in order to blockade Goa and attack Ceylon simultaneously, still did not enable them to capture Colombo. But the command of the sea enabled the Dutch to attack the enemy where he was weakest. In order to provide for the defence of their capital, the Portuguese had reduced the garrison of Negombo, and on 9 February, 1640, that town was taken by the combined Dutch and Sinhalese forces. The first breach had been made in the strong places protecting the cinnamon country, but the immediate result was a quarrel between the allies over the right to occupy the captured town, and the discrepancy between the two versions of the treaty of 1638 now came to light. Raja Sinha's indignation can easily be understood, but the Portuguese were still the more formidable intruders, and Coster succeeded in bringing about a reconciliation on the basis of a compromise which assured to his masters the reality of power. Trinkomali and Batticaloa were to be surrendered to Raja Sinha in return for ten elephants and 1000 bahars of cinnamon; after the Portuguese had been driven out of Ceylon altogether, the Dutch were to be allowed to retain one fortress; they might, however, hold all they took as a pledge till their expenses had been paid; Colombo was in any case to be dismantled. This treaty was to take the place of the third clause of the treaty of 1638, which was reconfirmed as far as its other provisions went. Immediately after the conclusion of this arrangement, Coster sailed southward and laid siege to Galle, which after hard fighting was taken on 13 March, 1640. No Sinhalese troops took part in the siege.

The Dutch now held two ports in the cinnamon area and expected to have a good share in the trade. But Raja Sinha, although Trinkomali was given up to him in April when he paid the stipulated price of ten elephants, still suspected the intentions of his allies with regard to the captured fortresses. Thanks to their exertions, he now controlled part of the cinnamon fields, but he never delivered the quantities which the Dutch claimed under the treaty, preferring to deal with Arab merchants in spite of its provisions. Coster, who went from Galle to Kandi to remonstrate with the king, was murdered by his Sinhalese escort on his way back (August, 1640). Shortly afterwards the Portuguese were enabled by reinforcements from Goa, where an energetic new viceroy, d'Aveiras, had taken up the government, to make a determined attempt to retake Negombo, and although Galle, where Thijssen had assumed the command after Coster's death, held out, its position was difficult. The Portuguese now dominated all the surrounding area with their troops, and not only was no cinnamon to be obtained, but the town had to be provisioned from Pulicat.

The news of these events aroused the more disappointment at Batavia as developments had taken place in Europe which threatened to interfere with the Company's schemes of conquest. A rebellion against Spanish rule had for some time been brewing in Portugal; in November, 1640, the Duke of Braganza was proclaimed king. Portugal's colonial possessions had for forty years been fair game for the Dutch East India Company, because Portugal was part of the Spanish Empire, with which the states-general still continued at war. Now that Portugal had freed herself and had become Spain's enemy, peace between Holland and Portugal seemed inevitable. In fact negotiations with that object were begun at the Hague in April 1641,[1] and the Batavia government felt that no time was to be lost. The siege of Malacca, which had been taken in January, 1641, had exacted a high toll of life, and the forces at their disposal were small. Yet in September, 1641, they again, as in 1639, sent out a fleet capable of blockading Goa and attacking Ceylon simultaneously, but nothing was achieved, although the negotiators in Europe had taken care to allow as much latitude of time to the Company's arms as decency

[1] Prestage, *The Diplomatic Relations of Portugal with France, England, and Holland from 1640 to 1668*, p. 175.

would permit. On 14 February, 1642, news was received at Batavia of a ten-year truce signed at the Hague on 12 June, 1641; but it was only to come into force in the East a full year after the king of Portugal's ratification arrived at the Hague. War could go on, therefore, in spite of the attempts of the Goa government to arrange an immediate armistice. The ratification was not passed by the king of Portugal until 18 November, and news of this was only received at Batavia on 2 October, 1642. The delay had not been of any use to the Company. The Portuguese still kept Galle practically invested on the land side, and the Dutch had no access at all to the cinnamon fields. But the resources of the Company's diplomacy were not yet exhausted. A difference of interpretation as between Goa and Batavia of one important article of the truce arranged in Europe was used as a pretext to continue the war. It must be said that the Dutch interpretation seems the correct one, and that the Portuguese viceroy's attitude was most unyielding. The successes of the last two years in Ceylon had inspired the Portuguese with a new confidence.

The article in question, the twelfth of the treaty of truce,[1] arranged the affairs between the two nations on the basis of *uti possidetis*, with this proviso, however, that the *lati campi*, the countryside, between fortresses belonging to the contracting parties, were to be divided by the authorities on the spot in accordance with their dependence on these fortresses. Basing themselves on this article, the Dutch demanded that the Portuguese should evacuate the districts of Matturai and Saffragam, parts of the cinnamon country which had always been considered as falling within the jurisdiction of Galle. The Dutch Commissioner, appearing at Goa, which in spite of Portuguese protests was still being blockaded, on 1 April, 1643, proposed a provisional division of the cinnamon lands until the governments in Europe had settled the matter. When this was rejected, war was resumed.

It was not waged by the Dutch only to compel the Portuguese to accept their interpretation of the twelfth article of the truce. There still was a state of war between the Portuguese and Raja Sinha; the viceroy did not recognise the king's authority, in spite of the third article of the truce, which included all Indian rulers allied to either of the contracting parties. In Ceylon, therefore, the Dutch pretended to act on the king's behalf, which meant that they claimed to be free to extend their conquests. Reinforcements from home made it possible for the Batavia government to act with vigour. While in the autumn of 1643 the usual fleet sailed to blockade Goa, a second fleet of nine ships, manned by 1550 men and under the command of Caron, made straight for Ceylon. After a battle under the walls of Negombo, in which the Portuguese were entirely routed, the Dutch penetrated into the town in the wake of the flying army, and became masters of

---

[1] Dumont, *Corps Universel Diplomatique*, VI, 214.

Negombo once more (January, 1644). Without heeding Raja Sinha's requests that the town should be given up to him, the Dutch strongly fortified it.

The viceroy at Goa, regretting his uncompromising rejection of the offers made him the year before, now wrote to Batavia that he was willing to accept them. But the Dutch were no longer content with the cinnamon country near Galle, they also claimed Negombo with the surrounding area. They claimed it on behalf of Raja Sinha, to whom, however, they did not dream of surrendering it. Yet when in the autumn of 1644 the Batavia government once more sent a large fleet to blockade Goa, its commander, Joan Maetsuycker, was empowered to negotiate. The Seventeen, primed by the states-general, had been remonstrating with their servants in the Indies about the high-handed way in which they had made war on the Portuguese all over the Indian Ocean on account of some cinnamon fields in Ceylon, and it really was a relief to the Batavia authorities when Maetsuycker succeeded in obtaining from the viceroy a treaty (10 November,1644), by which both Galle and Negombo were ceded with the cinnamon lands divided at equal distances between those places and Colombo. The viceroy, however, only gave up Negombo under protest, and a treaty made between the home governments on 27 March, 1645, in ignorance of what had been done in the East, could still be interpreted by each party to suit its own interests.

At the same time, Negombo was the cause of serious trouble with Raja Sinha, whose men were ravaging the cinnamon lands in which the Dutch hoped to recoup themselves for their expenditure. The governor of Galle, Thijssen, rashly declared war on the king in May, 1645, and was at once recalled, but before Maetsuycker, who became his successor, could restore peace, a military disaster occurred; a Dutch encampment was surrounded, the troops sent to relieve it cut to pieces, and the king returned to Kandi with 400 prisoners (May, 1646). In the negotiations which now dragged on for years, Raja Sinha held a trump card, his prisoners. At last, in 1649, the Dutch consented to a treaty which restored the alliance of 1638, but on somewhat less favourable conditions; not even the monopoly of the cinnamon trade was to remain to them once Raja Sinha had paid off his debts, no doubt a somewhat unlikely contingency. In any case, the old scheme for the expulsion of the Portuguese was again being discussed between the king and the Dutch.

While the Portuguese claims to Negombo were still a matter of negotiation with Maetsuycker, news had arrived, in the summer of 1646, of the rebellion against Dutch rule that had broken out in Brazil. This settled the matter of Negombo; it served as a sufficient pretext for its indefinite retention by the Dutch. Relations between the Dutch Republic and Portugal were greatly strained and the East India Company's pretensions now had the support of the states-

general. Quite apart from the narrow issue of Negombo, it was clear
that the peace between the two countries was precarious. When the
ten years' truce ran out in 1652, the Company's servants in the East
were apprised that they were again to make war on the Portuguese.
During the next period, the affairs of the Dutch West India Company
kept the war between the Dutch Republic and Portugal alive, and
while the Portuguese were successful in Brazil, and could not make
peace on account of that very success, they lost nearly all they had
left in India, and the schemes of conquest of the Dutch East India
Company, which had been interrupted in 1642, were now to a large
extent realised.

It was not until 1655 that a serious effort was made. At the urgent
requests of the Batavia government, larger quantities of ships and men
had been sent from home: 13,500 men during the three years from
1653 to 1655. On 14 August, 1655, twelve ships, with 1200 soldiers
on board, left Batavia with orders to attack Colombo; Gerard Hulft,
director-general of India, was the commander. Towards the end of
September Colombo was invested. It was kept closely blockaded
both by land and by sea, and non-combatants trying to escape were
driven back. Famine and disease raged as the months wore on, and
still the Portuguese held out, hoping for relief from Goa. Early in
April a fleet of twenty-two small vessels trying to carry troops and
provisions to Colombo was scattered off Quilon by a single Dutch
ship. At last, on 7 May, after reinforcements had arrived from Batavia,
the town was stormed, and the north-east bastion captured. On
12 May Colombo capitulated, which did not save it from being sacked
by the Dutch soldiers.

Colombo was at once garrisoned and the ruined fortifications
rebuilt by the Dutch. Raja Sinha had not taken a very active part
in the siege. His army had most of the time been encamped near
Raygamwatte. Yet his help had been useful in the provisioning of
the Dutch troops, and his relations with Hulft had been most cordial.
The maharaja bravely kept up the fiction of the Dutch being merely
the humble auxiliaries of his august and all-powerful person. Of
Hulft he spoke as "my Director-General", and of the Dutch army
as "my army".[1] Hulft was killed during the siege, on 10 April, 1656,
and with Adriaan van der Meyden, who took his place, Raja Sinha's
relations soon grew less agreeable. When the capitulation of Colombo
was concluded, in his name and the Company's, but without his even
being consulted, and when it became clear that the Dutch had no
intention of giving up their conquest to him, the king's attitude
became frankly hostile. He closed the mountain passes and forbade
the delivery of cattle and other provisions to the Dutch. He tartly
reproached the Company with faithlessness. In November Van der
Meyden made an end of pretences. A little army was sent against the

[1] Aalbers, *Rijklof van Goens*, p. 53, note 4.

camp at Raygamwatte. Raja Sinha did not wait for it, but broke camp hastily and retired to his mountains. It was to be feared that he might be reconciled with the Portuguese, who were still in possession of two strong places on the north of Ceylon, Manar and Jaffnapatam, and held Tuticorin and Negapatam on the mainland. The Dutch could not feel safe in the possession of the cinnamon lands, therefore, until they had expelled the Portuguese from those last strongholds and "cleaned up that whole corner".[1]

In September, 1657, Rijcklof van Goens, an Extraordinary Member of the Council of India, who had already served the Company in many capacities and in many lands with striking success, was instructed to effect this. Having expelled the Portuguese from the open town of Tuticorin, Van Goens dispatched a mission to the *thever*, the nayak's vassal, and to the nayak of Madura himself, and continued on his way. On 19 February, the fleet crossed from the island of Rammanakoil along Adam's Bridge to Manar, where a number of Portuguese vessels with great obstinacy tried to prevent a landing. When it was nevertheless effected, on the 22nd, the fortress surrendered at once, most of the garrison having hurriedly evacuated it and made for Jaffnapatam. Thither, Van Goens, with 850 men, followed overland; 200 more soldiers, brought from Colombo, joined him before the town. On 9 March the Dutch troops fought their way into the town, the Portuguese retiring into the citadel, which as Van Goens put it, "deserved that name more than any one I ever saw in India". The Portuguese garrison numbered about 1000, and in addition there were 700 or 800 native soldiers. But some thousands of refugees from the town created confusion and accelerated the consumption of provisions. After having captured (26 April) the fortress on the islet of Kays in the mouth of the channel between Ouratura (afterwards Leyden) and Caradiva (afterwards Amsterdam), Van Goens could use the cannon of the fleet which was now assembling before Jaffnapatam, and ten batteries were constructed round the fort. Famine and disease, however, were the most potent weapons of the besieger, and at last, when all hope of relief from Goa had vanished, the Portuguese commander capitulated (23 June, 1658).

As soon as the difficult problem of the great number of prisoners and of the occupation of the fort was settled, Van Goens sailed for Negapatam. The garrison of 367 men was too small to hold that large fortified town, and capitulated at once. Negapatam at first remained under the governor of Ceylon, but, as has already been stated, in 1689 the Dutch made it the seat of their administration on the Coromandel Coast. Portuguese power was definitely broken in the whole of Southern India. The only remaining task was to expel them from the Malabar Coast, and this, too, was a few years later undertaken by Van Goens.

[1] Instruction for Van Goens, 5 September, 1657, *ap.* Aalbers, *Rijklof van Goens*, p. 66.

The Malabar Coast was the region on the mainland of India where the Portuguese had struck root most deeply. The small rulers between whom the country was divided had been unable to prevent the intruders from acquiring large political powers, which they used in the first place to secure for themselves the exclusive trade in the only important export of the region, pepper. In a number of towns there were considerable settlements of Portuguese, and Roman Catholicism had made many converts.

The Dutch, although they had never found time to obtain a firm footing on the Malabar Coast, had been repeatedly in communication with rulers unfriendly to the Portuguese in that region, particularly with the most powerful of the Malabar princes, the Zamorin of Calicut. In September, 1604, Admiral Steven Van der Haghen had concluded a treaty with the Zamorin[1] but, as we know, all available forces were needed for the establishment of Dutch power in the Archipelago in those early days. The piece-goods trade of the Coromandel Coast was moreover thought to be of greater importance than the pepper trade of Malabar, pepper being obtained in sufficient quantities at Bantam and at Achin. And so, although other fleets stopped at Calicut, and Van der Haghen's treaty was renewed, and once (1610) merchants were sent from Tirupapuliyur to conclude a fresh treaty of friendship and commerce, all these arrangements remained a dead letter, and in the days of Van Goens the only Dutch port on the west coast of India was Vengurla to the north of Goa. Here in 1637, when the policy of annually blockading the Portuguese capital had just been adopted, the Dutch had built a fort which served as a *point d'appui* for the blockading fleets and as a post of observation during the months when they were not there. The Malabar Coast proper was still controlled effectively by the Portuguese fortresses.

For some time after the conquest of Negapatam, the war with the Portuguese was carried on less energetically. The Company, exhausted by its effort, tried to obtain assistance from the states-general. But in 1661, although little assistance was forthcoming, it was decided to make a fresh effort to drive the Portuguese from the coast. The states were at last making up their minds to waive their claims to Brazil, and the Company was anxious to complete this new conquest before peace came to upset its schemes.

In October, 1661, a Dutch fleet of twenty-three sail, large and small, appeared under the command of Van Goens off Quilon. The town was taken after a fight with the Nairs, who here as elsewhere took the side of the Portuguese. A garrison was left behind, and the fleet sailed northward to Kranganur, which Van Goens desired to occupy before attacking the principal stronghold of the Portuguese at Cochin. Kranganur, which offered an unexpectedly vigorous resistance, was taken

---

[1] De Jonge, *Opkomst van het Nederlandsch gezag in Oost-Indië*, III (1865), 204.

by assault on 15 January, 1662, and now the Dutch making themselves masters of the island of Vypin, on which they built the fortress Nieuw Oranje, opened the attack on Cochin. The kings of Cochin had for a long time leant on the support of the Portuguese against their enemy the Zamorin of Calicut, and so again the Nairs had to be driven off, and the queen of Cochin to be made prisoner, before the Portuguese town of Cochin could be besieged. The difficulties of the marshy ground, however, were considerable. The army, weakened already by the garrisons left at Quilon, Kranganur and Nieuw Oranje, was further weakened by illness. The commander decided to raise the siege, and in the dead of night the 1400 men were successfully embarked before the Portuguese knew what was happening. The delay almost proved fatal. On 6 August, 1661, the treaty of peace between Holland and Portugal had actually been signed. It laid down that hostilities were to cease in Europe two months after signature and elsewhere on publication; each side to retain what it then possessed. Had this treaty been ratified at once, the Dutch East India Company would have been baulked of Cochin. But Portugal's new ally, Charles II, was unwilling to share with the Dutch in the remaining Portuguese possessions trading facilities which had hitherto been reserved to the English, and the Portuguese government was too dependent on English help not to seek an alteration of the terms. The Dutch East India Company possessed influence enough in the states-general to take advantage of these new negotiations, and so it was not until 14 December, 1662, that instruments of ratification were exchanged at the Hague, and only several months later was the treaty proclaimed—in Holland in April, in Portugal not before May.

Meanwhile in September, 1662 a large fleet had sailed from Batavia to attack Cochin. In November the siege was renewed. The town was subjected to a furious bombardment, but, fearing that peace might save it, the governor-general and his council had empowered the commander to offer unusually favourable conditions, particularly freedom of exercise for the Catholic religion. Only after repeated assaults had carried the Dutch into part of the town, were these conditions accepted (January, 1663), and Van Goens made his triumphant entry. The subjection of the king of Porakad and the capture of Kannanur completed the conquest of the Malabar Coast. In vain the Portuguese protested in Europe that Cochin and Kannanur, having been taken after the peace, ought to be restored. After protracted negotiations a settlement was arrived at in July, 1669. The Dutch promised to restore the two places on payment by Portugal of certain debts and of the costs incurred by the conquest and fortification of the two towns. As the sums in question far exceeded Portugal's financial capacity, the Company remained in possession.

The Malabar Coast, Kanara and Vengurla were organised as a separate administrative unit under a *commandeur* residing at Cochin. The title of *commandeur*, which was also borne by the chief officials at Galle and Jaffnapatam, who were subordinate to the governor of Ceylon, was not a very high one. The *commandeur* ranked after the director. In fact, the Malabar Coast never gave the Company all that had been expected.[1] The position here was quite different from that in the other establishments on the mainland of India, where the Company traded in open competition with European and native merchants. What had tempted it to conquer the Malabar Coast was the prospect of a monopoly in the pepper trade; and in the eyes of those who guided the Company's destinies, only a monopoly based on contracts at low prices with the native rulers could compensate the high cost of a political establishment. The first task of the *commandeurs*, therefore, was to make the pepper monopoly a reality, but this task proved more arduous than had been anticipated. English, Portuguese, and Gujarat competition enabled the native rulers to avoid dealing only on Dutch terms. It was impossible to prevent smuggling by way of Calicut and of the mountains. Towards the end of the Company's rule, however, the financial position was more satisfactory in this region.[2]

The Zamorin had preserved his independence, and relations with him were frequently strained. In 1717 there was a war, after which the Company attained greater influence over that potentate.[3] But Hyder Ali, who conquered the Zamorin's lands half a century later, was a far more dangerous neighbour, and under Tipu, his son, the Company was, very much against its inclination, drawn into the quarrels between that ruler and the English.

In Ceylon, as on the Malabar Coast, the Dutch had merely stepped into the position of the Portuguese. They held the coastal towns and controlled most of the cinnamon fields and of the regions where elephants were found. But the "emperor of Ceylon" still resided at Kandi, in undisputed possession of the mountainous interior, and the nobles and headmen of the plains, particularly of the south, never quite renounced their allegiance to him. The ancient organisation of society, under *disawas* and *mudaliyars*, was retained, and Dutch rule rested on a native officialdom, open to many influences of race and religion over which they had no control. It was the policy of the Dutch to maintain friendly relations with the court of Kandi, because whenever there was tension the king could stir up trouble for them among the Chalias, the cinnamon-peelers, or among the Sinhalese nobles and officials. Not only Raja Sinha, who lived until 1687, but

[1] *Selections from the Records of the Madras Government; Dutch Records*, No. 11 (1910), *Memoir of Commandeur Caspar de Jong*, 1761.

[2] *Dutch Records*, No. 2 (1908), *Memoir written in the year 1781 by Adriaan Moens*, p. 130.

[3] *Dutch Records*, No. 8 (1910), *Diary kept during the expedition against the Zamorin, 4th Dec. 1716–25th April*, 1717.

his successors as well, still claimed Colombo, and the Dutch, anxious above all to be left in peace so that the cinnamon might be safely collected, humoured their pretensions by paying them excessive honours and posing as their humble allies bound to aid them against the attacks of foreign powers. During Raja Sinha's lifetime this did not prevent frequent trouble, the king sometimes attacking Dutch posts and extending the cinnamon area directly under his control. Cinnamon-peeling was repeatedly prevented and the export of areca-nuts, the most important product of the king's own dominions, prohibited. Better relations prevailed under his immediate successors, although the Dutch maintained their pretension to keep the trade with the outside world completely in their own hands, and in 1707, in order the better to prevent smuggling, closed all ports except Colombo, Galle and Jaffnapatam. By placing ships at the disposal of the court for intercourse with Pegu, whence came Buddhist priests, and with Madura, whence the kings generally obtained their wives, the Company strove to make its control of overseas relations less galling. The kings of the Dravidian dynasty, however, who came to the throne in 1739 with Hanguraketa, and under whom all power at court was in the hands of nayaks from the mainland, were not so easily pacified. At the same time the Company's governors became more and more impatient of the humiliating conditions of their position in Ceylon. Particularly they disliked the annual embassy to the king's court, in order to secure with abject genuflections the right to collect the cinnamon-bark in the area under the king's sovereignty.

But the relations with Kandi did not constitute the only difficulty with which Dutch rule had to contend. Wide regions with populations of varying national and religious traditions and complicated social structures were brought under direct Dutch control. At the time of the conquest, material misery, after Portuguese misrule and protracted war, was the most pressing problem. The Dutch imported slaves from Southern India to restore irrigation works and cultivate the rice fields. They encouraged new crops, like cotton and indigo. They did their best to reduce the chaos which reigned in land tenure. In the Sinhalese country Maetsuycker's *Batavia Statutes*, a codification of the Company's laws, were introduced, but experienced Sinhalese were always members of the *Landraads* in order to see that the ancient customs of the country were observed. In the north, Tamil law, codified under Dutch auspices in 1707, was taken as the basis for legal decisions so long as it appeared consonant with reason, all deficiencies being supplied from Dutch law. The administration of justice left, however, a great deal to be desired. The governors never ceased complaining about the scarcity of officials with sufficient legal training and at the same time conversant with the conditions of the country.

On the whole, circumstances were not such as to favour the growth of a vigorous public spirit among the officials. The society in which they lived at Colombo and in the other coastal towns remained permeated with Portuguese influences. The same was true, to a greater or lesser extent, for all the places on the mainland of India and in the Malay Archipelago from which the Dutch had ousted the Portuguese, and it is to be explained by two characteristics of Portuguese colonisation, their marriages with the natives and their successful propagation of Catholicism. Under Dutch rule ministers of the Dutch Reformed Church at once took charge of the communities of Christians formed by the Portuguese ecclesiastics, but far into the eighteenth century complaints were frequent that the attachment of native Christians, then numbered in hundreds of thousands, to Protestantism, and even to Christianity, was purely nominal. The later historian owes a very real debt to some of the Dutch Reformed ministers. We mention only Philippus Baldaeus, whose description of Ceylon and the Malabar Coast was published in 1672, François Valentyn, whose encyclopaedic work on the possessions of the Company appeared from 1724 to 1726, Abraham Rogerius, probably the best scholar of them all, who was at Pulicat from 1631 to 1641, and whose *Gentilismus Reseratus* was described by A. C. Burnell in 1898 as "still, perhaps, the most complete account of South Indian Hinduism, though by far the earliest". The principal author, too, of the famous botanical work *Hortus Malabaricus*, which under the patronage of Van Reede tot Drakensteyn appeared in 1678 and following years, was a minister of the church—Johannes Casearius. But the Dutch *predikants* had little of the missionary zeal which distinguished the Roman Catholic priests, and they made far less impression on the native populations in whose midst they lived. In Ceylon, seminaries for the training of native missionaries were founded in 1690, but until the governorship of Baron van Imhoff, 1737–40, when only one at Colombo survived, they led a precarious existence.[1] Afterwards half-caste Malabar and Sinhalese pupils regularly passed from the Colombo seminary to Holland, and, after a course of theology at the universities of Utrecht or Leyden, returned to their native land fully qualified ministers of the Dutch Reformed Church. Their influence was never very deep however, and in spite of all repressive measures—no doubt greatly relaxed during the second half of the eighteenth century—Catholicism continued to show much vitality. Portuguese remained the language of the slave population and this, added to the deplorable failure to provide good education for them, had unfortunate effects on the children of the officials, who frequently entered the Company's service when they grew up. The number of Dutch free burghers who settled in Ceylon was never very great. There was, in short, no healthy

---

[1] Van Troostenburg de Bruyn, *De Hervormde Kerk in Nederl. Oost-Indië onder de O. I. Compagnie*, pp. 574 *sqq.*

public opinion to restrain corruption and loose living among the official class, and the efforts of several able and energetic governors to improve this state of affairs had little effect.

Nor could the Company's general policy be called inspiring. While conflicts with the native powers were anxiously avoided and the armed forces in the island lost all martial spirit, and fortresses were allowed to fall into ruin, the underpaid officials were everywhere urged to increase the financial profits. It was particularly private trading in areca-nuts with which they enriched themselves at the Company's expense, but the abuses which a reforming governor at the beginning of the eighteenth century (Hendrik Becker) discovered and tried to stamp out were of many other kinds besides.

It so happened that not long after Becker's governorship there were two governors in succession against whom the central authorities were constrained to take extreme measures.[1] The first was Pieter Vuyst, a man born in the East, and who behaved like the worst type of eastern tyrant. In 1732 he was arrested by a commissioner, specially sent over from Holland by the Seventeen, and, having been found guilty of the most revolting abuse of power, he was executed at Batavia. The commissioner, who became governor in his stead, Pieter Versluys, reduced the people to despair by speculating in rice. Again the home authorities interfered. A new governor was sent out, who had Versluys arrested and sent to Batavia, where after long delays he escaped with a fine. The misconduct of these men shook Dutch authority in the island. At the same time the cinnamon-peelers complained of undue exactions imposed on them, while agrarian unrest was rife in the Sinhalese districts. So in 1736 a very serious rebellion broke out in the cinnamon region, soon spreading over the whole south and south-west of the island, and secretly encouraged by the king of Kandi. The Dutch suffered some serious reverses and the situation might have taken a disastrous turn, had not in 1737 a vigorous governor appeared on the scene, Baron van Imhoff, who soon restored order.

The events of 1736 were a foretaste of the much more serious war that broke out in 1760, under the governorship of Jan Schreuder. It began with a rebellion in the district of Colombo, in which the Chalias, supported by the maharaja, soon joined. In 1761, the maharaja, who was especially aggrieved by the refusal of the Dutch to allow him freedom of trade from his last remaining ports of Chilaw and Puttalam, openly took the part of the rebels, and the deterioration of the Company's military forces soon became evident. The forts of Matara, Kalutara and Hanwella were captured by the Sinhalese, and although they could not long maintain their position in the plains, the Dutch were very greatly alarmed. The governor-general at Batavia tried to pacify the king by sending him a letter couched in

[1] Van Kampen, *Geschiedenis der Nederlanders buiten Europa* (1832), III, 19.

flattering terms and transmitted with the greatest ceremony. Fear of the English, from whom the Dutch had just suffered a severe humiliation on the Hugli and who were known to be in communication with the king, no doubt contributed to inspire this policy.When it failed, nothing remained but to make a military effort, and the suspicion of English intentions now served to drive home the necessity of carrying it through to a definite conclusion. A new governor, Van Eck, repeatedly attempted to invade the mountain kingdom. Troops were collected in Malabar, Coromandel and Java. In 1765, Van Eck succeeded in penetrating to the capital, which was plundered disgracefully. Van Eck died soon afterwards. The garrison of 1800 men left behind at Kandi could not maintain itself owing to lack of provisions. Its withdrawal became a disaster. In spite of this, such was the distress of the Sinhalese that, while the new governor, Iman Willem Falck, a young man of great ability, was making vigorous preparations for a new invasion, the king opened negotiations. On 14 February, 1766, a treaty was signed which restored peace and placed the relations between the Dutch and the king on a more satisfactory basis than that afforded by the treaties of 1638 and 1640. The Dutch Company's absolute sovereignty over the regions which they had held before the war was recognised. In addition, the sovereignty over a strip of land four miles in width from the sea coast round the whole of the island was expressly ceded to the Dutch, who had occupied Chilaw and Puttalam early in the war. For the rest the king's sovereignty was recognised, but he lost the power to permit or forbid the Company's trading in such produce of his dominions as experience had shown to be indispensable or profitable. The degrading ceremonies attending the annual embassy to the court were abolished. Finally, while the Company pledged itself to protect his dominions from all external aggression, he promised not to enter into any treaty with any European or Indian power, and to deliver up all Europeans coming within his territory.

The Dutch could congratulate themselves that the treaty of 1766 had consolidated their position in Ceylon. Falck, moreover, proved one of the best governors the island had ever known. Much was done during his term of office to improve the administration and to increase the economic prosperity of the people. But meanwhile the rise of English power constituted a menace against which nothing availed. In 1781, the king of Kandi appeared to be unwilling to support the English in their enterprise against Dutch rule on the island. In 1796, his aloofness no longer mattered: Dutch power, as we shall see, collapsed at the first touch.

In the seventeenth century, the Dutch Company's position in India rested on sea-power. While the English made of Surat, where they were dependent on friendly relations with the Moghul, the centre of their Indian system and obtained a footing at Goa itself by an amicable arrangement with the Portuguese, the Dutch broke down the Portuguese monopoly by the open and persistent use of force, capturing their ships and supplanting them as the actual rulers of one stronghold after another. Even in their relations with the Moghul they occasionally brought their naval superiority into play. So conscious were they of their naval supremacy that in 1652 the outbreak of war with both England and Portugal was welcomed at Batavia as likely to turn to the Company's advantage.[1] The advantage, as against England at any rate, was confined to the occasional capture of prizes. The factories of the English Company were protected by the Moghul's peace. In the third Anglo-Dutch War (1672-4) communications between Surat and the new English settlement of Bombay were constantly threatened, and three home-bound English ships were captured in the Bay of Bengal. France was England's ally in that war, and in 1671 Louis XIV had already dispatched to India a fleet of twelve sail under the command of Admiral de la Haye. Even before war had been declared in Europe, the French occupied some abandoned forts in the bay of Trinkomali. Van Goens, who was then governor of Ceylon, without losing time, collected such ships as were available and attacked the intruders. Soon reinforcements arrived from Batavia, and de la Haye was forced to leave Ceylon with the loss of several of his ships.[2] With the remainder he sailed for St Thomé and captured that town. Van Goens was soon on the spot and blockaded the town from the sea side, while the king of Golconda, its rightful sovereign, invested it by land. The English and the French were too jealous of each other to co-operate, and an English fleet of ten sail allowed itself to be beaten separately off Petapoli.[3] About a year afterwards, 6 September, 1674, de la Haye capitulated. He had lost all his ships, and the 900 men left to him out of the 2000 with whom he had started, were transported to Europe in Dutch vessels.

While the naval power of the Dutch was the despair of their rivals, they themselves often were inclined to envy the English, who were able to carry on their trade without incurring the vast expenses for the upkeep of a navy and of fortresses and garrisons which burdened the budget of the Dutch Company. The recollection that it was the Dutch attacks on the Spanish-Portuguese monopoly which had opened the Indian trade to their rivals as well as to themselves added bitterness to these feelings. In fact, the settlements where they had not taken up the responsibilities of sovereignty were by far the most profitable in the eyes of the Company, which never learnt to separate its purely trading accounts from its political budgets. In the years 1683-1757, therefore, the only period for which these figures are

[1] Aalbers, *Rijklof van Goens*, p. 81.
[2] De Jonge, *Geschiedenis van het Nederlandsch zeewezen*, II, 768.
[3] Shafaat Ahmed Khan, *Sources for the History of British India in the Seventeenth Century*, pp. 245-6.

available,[1] Surat, Bengal and Coromandel figure in the Company's books with annual profits of hundreds of thousands of guilders each, although Bengal, after 1720, very frequently shows a loss. Ceylon and Malabar on the other hand constantly showed heavy losses, although we know from other sources that Malabar ceased to be "a bad post" towards the end of the eighteenth century.[2] In these figures profit and loss made by commercial transactions are lumped together with the yield of taxation and tributes and the expenses of administration, and no account is taken of profits made in Holland by the sale of merchandise.

All through the eighteenth century the Company's commitments as a sovereign power increased: garrisons became more numerous, the expenses of administration grew. As a result, although its trade continued to prosper, the Company's finances became more and more involved. Something like 50 per cent. profit was regularly made on the Company's turnover even as late as the seventies of the eighteenth century, very largely owing to the enormously profitable trade of Surat, Bengal and Ceylon.[3] At the same time the general balance-sheet showed a steady decline. In 1700 there were still 21,000,000 guilders on the credit side; in 1724 the zero point was passed, and the deficit grew uninterruptedly until in the eighties of the eighteenth century it surpassed 100,000,000 guilders.[4]

Obviously the Company's system suffered from grave defects. Great as it had been as an empire-builder, able as it still was as a merchant, it failed as a colonial ruler. Its strict adherence, against the advice of all its ablest governors-general, to the policy of commercial monopoly was perhaps its gravest mistake. The settlement of "free burghers," which might have brought in its train a much more intensive economic development of countries like the Malay Archipelago and Ceylon, was consistently discouraged by the directors at home. Another defect, and one which more nearly concerns the Company's possessions in India, was the severe subordination of the whole of its system to the administrative and commercial centre at Batavia. Ceylon was the only place whence direct communications with Holland were more or less regularly conducted, and its governors were allowed to correspond with the Seventeen, while the chiefs of all other settlements could only correspond with the governor-general and his council. One unfortunate result of the distance of the central authority was the prevalence of corruption. No posts in the Company's employ were considered so lucrative as those in what were called "the Western Quarters".[5]

---

[1] G. C. Klerk de Reus, *Geschichtlicher Ueberblick*, Beilage IX.
[2] See above, p. 36, note 2.
[3] Klerk de Reus, *Geschichtlicher Ueberblick*, p. 193.
[4] Klerk de Reus, *op. cit.* Beilage VIII.
[5] This term in the early days was applied more particularly to Surat and the Persian and Arabian factories.

The commonest form of peculation was private trading. While the Company jealously suppressed the rise of a class of independent traders within its sphere of influence, it was powerless to prevent its own servants from infringing its monopoly to their own private advantage. As early as 1609 the directors bitterly complained of the prevalence of the abuse, but while they continued grievously to under-pay their employees, the constantly reiterated edicts prohibiting the practice, threatening penalties, prescribing oaths, remained entirely without effect. In 1626, the directors resolved[1] that all the establish-ments in the East were to be visited every year by two inspectors, to one of whom "the Western Quarters" were allotted; they were to report both to Batavia and to the Seventeen themselves. In spite of another resolution to the same effect in 1632, nothing came of this annual inspection, and even requests, made by the directors in 1650[2] and repeated afterwards, that an inspection should be held every two years had no result. The Batavia government excused themselves by the difficulty of finding suitable men for so arduous a task, but no doubt they were themselves lukewarm in the cause of integrity. Inspections were actually ordered only when there were special reasons to suspect mismanagement, but even then an energetic and honest man like Van Goens, who inspected Surat in 1654, had to confess[3] that it was difficult to bring the wrong-doers to book, as they knew well how to escape detection. In 1684 the Seventeen, de-spairing of ever getting the Batavia government to act with requisite firmness, themselves appointed a commissioner-general to inspect the Western Quarters, Hendrik Adriaan van Reede tot Drakensteyn, formerly *commandeur* of Malabar, whom we have met on the Coro-mandel Coast. For seven years Van Reede laboured at his herculean task; when he died in 1691, it was still far from being completed, and the results of the inspections actually carried out soon vanished. From then onwards no serious attempts were made to put down the evil, and it grew steadily. So much had it become an accepted thing that directors themselves began to traffic in appointments, and about 1720 an Amsterdam burgomaster accepted 3500 guilders for conferring on a candidate the post of under-merchant, the official salary for which was only 480 guilders a year.[4]

As in course of time the Company, from being a purely trading body, became the sovereign of many Eastern lands, its servants could enrich themselves in other ways than by infringing its monopoly or embezzling its money. Oppressions and exactions at the expense of the subject populations were no less lucrative and no less common. We have seen in the cases of Vuyst and Versluys that the supreme authorities were not prepared to countenance the worst excesses.

---

[1] J. A. van der Chijs, *Nederlandsch-Indisch Plakkaatboek*, I, 188.
[2] Aalbers, *Rijklof van Goens*, p. 30.   [3] *Op. cit.* p. 107.
Colenbrander, *Koloniale Geschiedenis*, II, 219.

Vuyst's judicial murders even caused them to introduce a general reform. Governors and directors had until then always presided over the Council of Justice in their governments. In 1738 this function was transferred to the second. Nor are these cases the only ones to show that the growth of humanitarian ideas during the eighteenth century occasionally inspired the authorities at Batavia or at home to energetic interference on behalf of the Company's wronged native subjects. In 1765, for instance, the Seventeen ordered action to be taken against the governor of Coromandel, Christiaan van Teylingen, on the strength of serious charges which a minister of the king of Tanjore, Paw Idde Naiker, had succeeded in bringing directly to their knowledge.[1]

If the directors occasionally exerted themselves to put down some crying abuse; if now and again an able and energetic man rose to some high executive post in the Indies; no radical reform of the Company's defective system was ever attempted. Van Imhoff, whom we have met as governor of Ceylon, became governor-general in 1743, and high expectations were founded on him, which were hardly realised. He attempted, among other things, to put down the illicit trade in Bengal opium by allowing officials to form an "Opium Society" among themselves, thus legalising private trade in this one instance. When, however, another generation of officials had arisen who did not own any shares in the "Society", matters were as bad as ever. In 1747, again, the Orangist restoration at home seemed to offer better prospects, but the new stadtholder, William IV, for whom in 1748, under the direct pressure of public opinion, the office of director-general of the Company was created, did not effect any essential or permanent changes.

At the same time circumstances had arisen which made the need for reform more urgent. Towards the close of the seventeenth century, the English Company, realising the insecurity of its position in the troubled Moghul Empire, had copied from "the wise Dutch" their policy of the strong arm. The first attempts ended in failure, but, as the eighteenth century proceeded, just when the Dutch had allowed their navy hopelessly to decay, and in their relations with native rulers trusted to flattery and presents, it became clearer that the position of the European nations in India had no solid basis except in naval and military power. The rise of French influence in the southern part of the peninsula caused the Dutch many alarms. Particularly obnoxious was Dupleix's capture of Masulipatam in 1750. In the War of the Austrian Succession, the Dutch Republic, although technically neutral, had in fact sided with England. In the Seven Years' War, on the other hand, its neutrality was real, with, if any-

---

[1] A. K. A. Gysberti Hodenpyl, De Gouverneurs van Koromandel: Christiaan van Teylingen (1761–65) en Pieter Haksteen (1765–71), *Bijdragen voor Vaderlandsche Geschiedenis*, v, x (1923), 136 *sqq.*

thing, a bias against England. Clive's successes in Bengal were viewed by the authorities at Batavia with deep suspicion. It was felt that the power to which the English, through their ally and tool Mir Ja'far, had now attained, threatened the prosperity, if not the existence, of establishments which were looked upon as constituting one of the Dutch Company's main supports. Immediately after Plassey, Dutch trade on the Hugli was reported to be suffering, and exactions on the part of the Indian authorities became more unbearable. So the governor-general and his council resolved to make an attempt to retrieve the position.[1] It only served to make it apparent to all the world how far the Dutch Company had left the days of Coen and of Van Goens behind it. The ships sent up the Hugli were captured, the troops cut to pieces. Nothing remained but to make a speedy submission, and the Dutch retained their factories, but had to promise not to garrison them with more than a small number of troops. They were now worse off than before, but the next crisis, in 1781, was to leave them even more helpless.

In the American War the Dutch Republic, tossed by violent party struggles, recklessly provoked England, and when England, at the end of 1780 declared war, the republic proved entirely incapable of defending its own interests. Its trade came to a dead stop. In the colonial world, the English took Negapatam, which in spite of its large garrison offered little resistance. Trinkomali was lost, and regained only by the efforts of the French. But at the peace congress Holland could not be saved from all loss by its ally. Negapatam had to be given up, and free access to the waters of the Archipelago had to be granted to English commerce.

The war, moreover, had revealed the Company's financial distress. The state had had to assist it when it proved unable to raise the money needed for its own armaments and for the reimbursement of the French. In 1783 only a public guarantee of the Company's shares enabled it to carry on. Everybody realised that the state must take in hand the reform of a body which had the care of such important national interests. Unfortunately, the state was too much shaken by internal dissensions to be capable of energetic action. When in 1787 the Orangist *régime* was restored by England and Prussia, still very little was done. In 1793 the republic was involved in the Revolutionary War, and only in 1795, when the Batavian Republic was established under French influence, did the state formally take over the administration of the Company's possessions. But at the same time these were exposed to the attacks of England, with whom the Batavian Republic found itself automatically at war.

[1] G. C. Klerk de Reus, "De expeditie naar Bengale in 1759", *De Indische Gids*, 1889 and 1890.

CHAPTER III

THE FRENCH FACTORIES IN INDIA

THE French appeared in India long before the time of Louis XIV. In the second quarter of the sixteenth century, about thirty years after the Portuguese had reached the Malabar Coast by way of the Cape, in July, 1527, a Norman ship belonging to the Rouen merchants appeared, according to the Portuguese João de Barros, at Diu. In the next year the *Marie de Bon Secours*, also called the *Grand Anglais*, was seized by the Portuguese, at the very time when one of Jean Ange's most famous captains was proposing to that famous merchant to sail to Sumatra and even to the Moluccas. In 1530 the *Sacre* and the *Pensée* actually reached the west coast of Sumatra; but they did so without touching at any intermediate point on the shores of Asia; and contemporary documents do not indicate the arrival of any other French ships in Indian harbours in the later years of the sixteenth century or the earlier ones of the seventeenth.

However, many facts show at the beginning of the latter a desire to open maritime and commercial relations with India. In 1601 we have the equipment by a company of St Malo merchants, de Laval and de Vitré, of the two ships, the *Croissant* and the *Corbin*, the voyages of which have been related by François Pyrard de Laval as far as the Maldives, and by François Martin de Vitré to Sumatra by way of Ceylon and the Nicobars; in 1604–9 came the attempts of Henry IV to set up a French East India Company, like those just established in the Netherlands and England; then in 1616 a fleet sailed from St Malo for the Moluccas, while in that year and 1619 the two so-called "fleets of Montmorency" sailed from Honfleur for Malaya and Japan. But the scanty success of these enterprises, and the violence of the Dutch, eager to keep for themselves the monopoly of that profitable trade with the Far East, soon checked these bold attempts of the French sailors. In 1625 Isaac de Razilly declared that "as regards Asia and the East Indies there is no hope of planting colonies, for the way is too long, and the Spaniards and Dutch are too strong to suffer it".[1] A little later Richelieu observes in his *Testament Politique* that "the temper of the French being so hasty as to wish the accomplishment of their desires in the moment of their conception, long voyages are not proper for them"; but nevertheless he admits that "the trade that could be done with the East Indies and Persia...ought not to be neglected".[2]

[1] Léon Deschamps, "Un Colonisateur au temps de Richelieu", *Rev. de Géographie*, XIX, 460, December, 1886.
[2] Ed. Amsterdam, 1708, pp. 154–5.

However, some captains, especially the Normans, attempted, though their accomplishment is on many points obscure, if not to reach India itself, at least to make it easier of attainment by securing near the Cape of Good Hope a place of refreshment, whence they could make their way to Arabia, Persia, the Deccan ports, Bengal, or the Malayan Islands. Such were Gilles de Rezimont and Rigault, the latter of whom obtained in 1642 from Richelieu for himself and his associates the privilege of sailing to Madagascar and the neighbouring islands, to establish colonies and trade there.[1] Indeed the French almost at once established themselves on the south-east coast of Madagascar, setting up their first post at Fort Dauphin, easily reached by ships coming from or going to India. Moreover, some of their ships or smaller vessels between 1650 and 1660 proceeded to the Arabian or Indian coasts. Thus was confirmed the opinion expressed some years earlier by the navigator, Augustin de Beaulieu, who had commanded one of the Montmorency fleets, in a memoir of 1631-2, still unpublished:

I find the said island [Madagascar] proper, once we are established there, for adventures to any place whatever in the East Indies...for from the said place at the due season Persia can be reached...where a very useful and important trade can be established.... And when the said trade with Persia is inconvenient, that with the countries of the Great Moghul, Ceylon, Masulipatam, Bengal, Pegu, Kedda, Achin, Tiku and Bantam, can easily be followed.

By way of Persia, which Beaulieu recognises as a valuable market, it was easy to reach India. While French sailors were exploring the sea-route by the Cape, various travellers and merchants were exploring the much shorter land-route, which leads from the shores of the Levant through Asia Minor right on to the valleys of the Indus and the Ganges. After the Italian, Pietro della Valle and the Englishman, Thomas Herbert (only to mention the most recent) several Frenchmen tried this way, such as Capuchin missionaries, including Father Raphael du Mans in 1643, inspired by the ideas of Father Joseph du Tremblay (the famous *Éminence Grise*), and before him the well-known traveller Tavernier who thus began in 1632-3 his numerous journeys in the East, and who on his return became controller of the household to the Duke of Orleans, brother of Louis XIII. Soon afterwards (1642-8) he returned eastwards, and reached India by way of Ispahan, followed speedily by the Angevin noble La Boullaye le Gouz, whose travels were so popular when they were published in 1653. Thus was heightened the eager desire felt in France on the eve and at the beginning of the personal reign of Louis XIV to share with Dutch and English in bringing to Europe the precious goods of India. Neither Fouquet, superintendent of finances, whose father had been

---

[1] Flacourt, *Relation de la Grande Île Madagascar*, ed. 1658, p. 193. Cf. "Les Documents inédits relatifs à la Constitution de la Compagnie des Indes de 1648", *Bull. du comité de Madagascar*, October, 1898, pp. 481-503.

concerned in all the maritime enterprises of Richelieu, nor Colbert, who had been employed in the private business of Mazarin before coming to play his great part under Louis XIV, were unaware of these travels, and sometimes even received direct reports. Thus the latter became the interpreter of the unanimous desire of the merchants and mariners of the kingdom, as well as of all those who desired its economic development, when he proposed to his master the creation of "a French company for the trade of the East Indies".[1]

His personal convictions even more than public opinion had led Colbert to regard the establishment of a company of this kind as likely to render the greatest services to and powerfully to aid the development of French maritime trade, on condition that it should be strong in a very different way from the numerous associations of a like nature that had formerly sprung up throughout the kingdom. Those had hardly been more than municipal, such as the Company of St Malo, the de Laval and de Vitré Company, or the coral companies of Marseilles; or provincial, such as the Company de Morbihan, and had never included more than a small number of shareholders. Their financial resources had always been limited, and their influence and prestige alike slight. No attempt had been yet made to create a national association, uniting the whole forces of the country. But that was just what Colbert desired the new *Compagnie des Indes Orientales* to do. He laboured therefore in every way before constituting it to educate public opinion, and, when it had been formed, to secure it full success. Hence the publication in April, 1664, of a *Discourse of a faithful subject of the King touching the establishment of a French company for the East India trade addressed to all Frenchmen*, prepared by François Charpentier, the Academician, and printed at the king's expense; hence a little later the formation of a company to which Louis XIV not only gave his full approval, but also advanced 3,000,000 *livres* free of interest, from which were to be deducted all losses that the company might incur for the first ten years; moreover he made the members of the royal family subscribe, and displayed his interest strongly enough to make the courtiers follow his example. Hence also Colbert's own subscription to the new *Compagnie des Indes Orientales*, and the campaign which he conducted throughout the country to induce the officials and merchants of the chief towns to prove their real interest in a project thus royally patronised.

By letters-patent in the form of an edict the *Compagnie* was placed under the management of a general chamber of twenty-one directors (twelve for the capital and nine for the provinces) and received for a term of fifty years an exclusive privilege of trade from the Cape of Good Hope to India and the South Seas. It also received a perpetual grant of Madagascar and the neighbouring islands, on condition of promoting Christianity there, a perpetual grant with all rights of

[1] Souches de Rennefort, *Histoire des Indes Orientales*, p. 2.

seigneurie of all lands and places conquered from its enemies, and ownership of all mines and slaves which it might take. The king was to supply the Company at cost price with all the salt required for its fleets, to pay it a bounty of fifty *livres* on every ton of goods exported from France and seventy-five on every ton imported into the country, to allow the Company to establish a free port on the French coast, with a reduction of duties on the articles of trade with France, and a special exemption of duties on all stores needed for the building of ships. The General Chamber, which was to be renewed one-third every year and to prepare accounts every six months, was entrusted with the duty of appointing governors of its possessions, and the king limited himself to giving them their formal investiture. The chamber was also to give account of its management every year to an assembly of shareholders each possessing at least six shares. The capital of the Company was divided into 15,000 shares of 1000 *livres* each.

The privileges thus granted were very considerable. But in order to form a complete idea of them it is necessary also to take account of certain other privileges, also of value, enumerated in the forty-eight articles of the charter establishing the Company as an official body and confirming at once its rights and duties. On his part the king promised to protect the new Company and to escort its ships with his own men-of-war; he allowed the Company to send ambassadors to make treaties with, and declare war on, the sovereigns of India; and, at the same time as he allowed it to fly the royal flag, he granted it arms and a motto—*Florebo quocumque ferar*—signifying the great hopes placed by both him and Colbert in the new association.

If the country had responded with enthusiasm to the appeals made to it, the Company would doubtless have realised those hopes and become that "mighty company to carry on the trade of the East Indies" anticipated in the preamble of the letters-patent. But nothing of the sort happened. For various reasons—lack of enterprise among the trading classes and the lesser *noblesse de robe* outside the ports and a few great cities; dislike of most wealthy men for distant expeditions; losses of the war with Spain still not made good; revival of the *frondeur* spirit in the face of an admittedly official propaganda; fear lest the subscription should be merely a device to tax the nobles and other exempt persons[1]—the king's appeal addressed to the mayors and bailiffs of the principal towns in the form of a *lettre de cachet*, was unheeded and the royal example followed by few. So that of the 15,000,000 *livres* of which the capital was to have consisted, only about 8,200,000 *livres* were actually subscribed, and of that only a third was called up when the letters-patent of August, 1664, had given legal existence to the new Company. Thus the *Compagnie des Indes Orientales*

---

[1] Unsigned letter to Colbert (Depping, *Correspondance administrative sous le règne de Louis XIV*, III, 476).

began its existence with a capital of about 5,500,000 *livres*, including the 3,000,000 advanced by the king.

Colbert in fact was in haste to secure for France a share in the considerable profits which foreigners were then drawing from the East India trade, and which were rendering the Dutch, as Charpentier said, the wealthiest people in Europe.[1] So from October, 1664, he sought to prepare the way for the traders whom the new Company was meaning to send as soon as possible to the most distant shores of the Indian seas. To the shah of Persia and to the Great Moghul he sent by way of Aleppo representatives of the king and agents of the Company with orders to secure the favour of those princes and to hold preliminary discussions for the conclusion of real treaties of commerce. At the same time he was busy with the preparation of the first fleet. After passing the Cape the Company's ships were to put into Madagascar to strengthen the position of the French colonists already settled on the east and south-east coasts of the Île Dauphine, as the island was now officially called, and to set up a post for victualling and refreshment for French vessels on their way to India; they would then push up the East African coast to Arabia, leaving it to a later fleet to reach the Deccan ports and establish factories there.

At first sight the plan seems wise and well concerted. Was it not wise in fact to secure to French vessels a good port of call on the long voyage to India, and to place it at a point from which the Company's ships could easily push on in all directions? By establishing themselves at Table Bay in 1652, by seeking to establish themselves at Mauritius from 1638, by trying to form a colony on the west coast of Madagascar at St Augustine's Bay, both the Dutch and English had in a way imposed this policy on Colbert, rendering it the more necessary by the jealousy which they displayed of the young French Company. His real error, explained, however, by his love for his country and his master, by the ambition of Louis XIV, and the devotion of France to the king at the outset of his personal rule, lay in not discerning sharply enough how the position of the French Company differed from that of the Dutch in the East; the result was that he imposed on the former from the first the task of conducting at the same time two distinct enterprises—a considerable colonising effort as well as the establishment of a commerce full of risks; perhaps also he reckoned too lightly the mishaps and successive disappointments of every new enterprise, especially in a field so remote from the seat of control. In point of fact the Company escaped no kind of misfortune, so that Colbert's elaborate plans were hardly realisable. Even if any of the five nobles and merchants who set out for the Middle East at the end of 1664 had been able to fulfil their instructions, none of the four ships that made up the first fleet sailing in March, 1665,

---

[1] *Discours d'un fidèle sujet du roi.*

got further than Madagascar. The second fleet of ten vessels that sailed a year later, made, like the first, a very long voyage to Fort Dauphin; so that, only at the beginning of 1668, nearly four years after the formation of the Company, did any of its qualified representatives arrive by the sea-route in the Swally Roads on the coast of Gujarat.

There one of the agents sent in 1664 had long been awaiting his chiefs. Béber (for so he was named), after accompanying La Boullaye le Gouz to Agra in August-September, 1666, had returned to Surat, where he proceeded to act on a farman of Aurangzib granting the French a site and factory at Swally and permission to trade in the neighbouring town on the same terms as the Dutch and the English. A man of zeal and ability, as one of his chiefs testifies, Béber had so well prepared for the new arrivals that they were able to establish themselves at once, purchase a certain quantity of goods, and send them back by one of the ships that had accompanied them from Madagascar.

Unluckily there, as at Madagascar, jealousies and misunderstandings between the directors themselves, and between them and their subordinates, led to disastrous results. A good beginning had been made; from Surat several of the Company's ships had sailed up the Persian Gulf, visiting Bandar Abbas (where Mariage, who had set out from France with Béber, had a short time before established a factory), and even reaching Basra; a footing had been also secured on the Malabar Coast as a stage on the way to Ceylon and Malaya. But François Caron, an old servant of the Dutch Company and a man of experience and intelligence whom Colbert had engaged in the French service, relying on his knowledge, tried to keep all business in his own hands, while he was also influenced by his personal sympathies and dislikes. Hence resulted many differences, of which the Dutch, irreconcilable enemies of the French establishment in India, took advantage the more easily because Caron had quarrelled with the Moghul governor of Surat.

Meanwhile many events had induced Colbert to modify his original project. In France what enthusiasm had at first been aroused by the formation of the Company had quite disappeared; many shareholders, who had only subscribed in order to pay their court to the king and minister, preferred to lose what they had already paid than to meet the demand for the second instalment, called up in December, 1665, and it was still worse with the demand for the remaining third a year later; so that the king had had to promise (September, 1668) two more millions to the company to enable it to carry on. Moreover, the reports from the Île Dauphine had shown Colbert that matters there were going ill, that, as he said, considerable sums had been absolutely squandered. Without yet deciding to give up the Madagascar project, the minister agreed for the present to relieve the

Company of the task of planting that great unsettled island, in order
to employ all its resources in the eastern trade, and, as the directors
demanded, go straight to India.[1] But on the advice of La Boullaye
le Gouz and Caron, who from their knowledge of the country had
urged him "to show a little sample of his master's power" to the
princes of Asia, Colbert resolved early in 1669 to send a considerable
fleet into the Indian seas. It was to display the *fleurs de lys*, to give the
native sovereigns "a high opinion of the justice and goodness of His
Majesty, at the same time that they learnt his power", and to disprove
the assertions of the Dutch who had never ceased attempting to ruin
the French reputation among the people of India. Accordingly a
squadron of ten vessels, under the command of Jacob Blanquet
de la Haye, "governor and Lieutenant-general for the King in the
Île Dauphine and in all India", sailed from La Rochelle 30 March,
1670.

The "squadron of Persia", as it was called to show the public, and
especially the shareholders of the Company, the new direction of
policy, took no less than eighteen months to reach Surat, instead of
the six or seven months Colbert had expected. When it arrived at
last, in the middle of October, 1671, Caron was no longer there. In
spite of the divisions among the tiny group of Frenchmen, he had
succeeded in the preceding months in founding certain factories on
the Malabar Coast and another at Masulipatam, and had then set
out to establish yet another at Bantam, in the extreme west of Java.
Thus the directors charged by Colbert with the restoration of amity
in the French factory, and de la Haye's great squadron, arrived during
his absence. De la Haye, who had taken the title of viceroy on his
arrival in India, had been instructed above all "to establish the
company so strongly and powerfully that it shall be able to maintain
itself and to increase and augment itself in the course of time by its
own power". Such was the "sole and single purpose" of this important squadron in Indian waters. De la Haye was to effect it by
establishing fortified posts at points reckoned most favourable for
trade, in Ceylon especially, and by force if necessary. Doubtless such
an enterprise would injure the European peoples already established
in India, especially the Dutch; but such a consideration would weigh
little with Louis XIV or Colbert, who could not forgive the United
Provinces for their manifestations of political and economic hostility.
Colbert wrote to de la Haye, "The Dutch, though powerful, will not
dare to prevent the execution of His Majesty's designs; but it will be
necessary to be on your guard against any surprise on their part".
And in this connection, as in all others, de la Haye was "to act in
concert with, and even follow the views and orders of, the directors
of the company who are in India;...and even though the Sieur de

[1] Dernis, *Recueil et collection des titres concernant la Compagnie des Indes Orientales*, I, 187.

la Haye knows that they are doing ill, [he should] after representing his opinions to them, exactly follow their judgment".[1]

In the face of instructions so formal and even imperative, what could de la Haye do but await the return of Caron, whom Colbert had mentioned by name as "having a profound knowledge, by reason of his twenty-two years' service with the Dutch, of all that can and ought to be done in India for the profit of the company"? He therefore awaited his return from Bantam. Hence followed a delay by which the Dutch profited, strengthening their defences, especially as at the end of 1671, in India as in Europe, war had been expected between France and the republic. To crown this, even when Caron and the newly arrived directors had met, they could not agree, which added to the delay in the sailing of the squadron. Not until the beginning of January, 1672, could de la Haye and his ships leave Swally Roads "to carry into the Indies the first knowledge of the arms and might of His Majesty".

The viceroy's instructions ordered him to neglect no means of attaining this end. He spent, therefore, six weeks sailing down the Malabar Coast, trying "to show it off, and to display to advantage its beauty, power, guns, and crews", firing numberless salutes in every port he visited—Daman, Bombay, Goa, Calicut, Kranganur, Cochin, etc. Just as he was about to quit the coast and make for Ceylon, he learnt of the approach of a Dutch fleet; on 21 February he sighted twelve ships out to sea off Cape Comorin. He desired to approach them, and even to attack; but "M. Caron was as displeased [de la Haye wrote to Louis XIV some months later] as if I had proposed to him a crime. How often [he adds with some bitterness and not a little reason] have I regretted my express orders to follow the opinions of the directors". He was indeed right; and Caron, overwhelmed as he had been with benefits by Colbert, was already beginning to exhibit a strange, dubious conduct, which later developments were to prove still more dubious.

Leaving then with great regret his enemies to sail away, de la Haye coasted round the south and west of Ceylon, where the Dutch were already established, and then ran up the east coast as his instructions directed. Soon he was off Trinkomali Bay, the one natural harbour of the island, which he entered at once, but only to find that the Dutch had been beforehand with him, and had improvised, if not solidly built, various defences. Thus the position reckoned on by Colbert in December, 1669, had totally changed by March, 1672.

Was he then to give up that considerable settlement on Ceylon, which the minister's instructions said was to open the cinnamon trade to the Company? Was he to disregard the king's view, that nothing could be more for the benefit of the Company? De la Haye thought not. Since then he was sent to choose a site, build a post

[1] Clément, *Lettres, instructions et mémoires de Colbert*, III (2), 461–70.

there, put it in a state of defence, and provide it with every necessity, he paid no heed to "the insolent orders" of the Dutch to leave the harbour. But he went no further. Once more at the repeated instances of Caron he abandoned his project, which was to fight the fleet of the Admiral Rijckloff van Goens, and contented himself with procuring from the king of Kandi a grant of the bay of Trinkomali, with the country of Kutiari and its dependencies, taking possession in the king's name, and building a little fort there. He did not know that the Dutch had told the natives that he had not dared to fight them, that they were isolating him, and that they were about to deprive his crews and sick of victuals. A victory would have established the prestige of the "squadron of Persia", and made the French undisputed masters of Trinkomali, if not of India; but on 9 July de la Haye quitted the bay without having given battle, merely leaving on one of the little islands within it a handful of men whom the Dutch seized a few days later, thus justifying in the eyes of all the assertions of his enemies.

A little later, on his arrival before St Thomé (or Mailapur, as the Indians called it) on the Coromandel Coast, de la Haye reaped the fruits of his error; the officers sent to ask for victuals met with an unreasonable refusal from the Muhammadan officials and insults from the populace.[1] On the advice of Caron, who was certainly the evil genius of this campaign, and who may with cause be suspected of treason, the viceroy resolved to strike a blow; on 25 July, 1672, five days after dropping anchor before the place, he carried it by escalade, to the great alarm of the Muhammadans and even of the Europeans scattered along the coast in the various factories.

Ten years earlier the king of Golconda had conquered St Thomé from the Portuguese, and had also occupied the neighbouring part of the Carnatic. The loss of the place irritated this sovereign; he at once set to work to recover it, and quickly surrounded it with horse and foot, elephants, and work-people with everything needed for a blockade.[2] In spite of the diligence with which he had sought to consolidate his position, de la Haye had had no time in which to lay in provisions; and from the beginning of October he had to revictual himself by sea. As yet the Dutch had not joined the Muhammadans, although they had learnt a month earlier of the outbreak of war between France and England on the one side and the Netherlands on the other. By dint of his own energy, the bravery and spirit of his troops, the zeal and intelligence of his subordinates, volunteers or agents of the company, the French leader held St Thomé for two years against the king of Golconda and the Dutch, with no help from the English. But courage and good will themselves are not always enough; and even after Caron's departure for France (October,

---

[1] *Mémoires de Bellanger de Lespinay*, p. 143.
[2] Carré, *Voyage des Indes Orientales*, f. 289.

1672), de la Haye failed to make the most of his opportunities. Even when he had obliged the Muhammadans once to raise the siege (March, 1673), he failed either to make peace with the king or to prevent him from allying with his European enemies; so that his position became entirely unfavourable when the Muhammadans and the Dutch joined against him. Little by little his army had melted away, and his ships had either been captured by the enemy or become unserviceable for want of repairs. De la Haye sadly admits this when, after a few weeks' absence, the Muhammadans began to press him again, and especially when the Dutch admiral, Rijckloff, lent them help ashore and blockaded the place by sea (September, 1673). His stubborn spirit still prolonged resistance for another year. In fact he did not sign the capitulation till 6 September, 1674, and then the honour of the defenders was fully safeguarded, for the town was only to be occupied by the Dutch in case the French received no succour within the next fifteen days.

Among the causes permitting this prolonged resistance to be made must be set in the front rank the activity displayed by several of the French Company's agents—François Baron, one of the directors in India and formerly French Consul at Aleppo; and François Martin, director of the Masulipatam factory. Bellanger de Lespinay, one of the volunteers who accompanied de la Haye, should also be mentioned. Sent in November, 1672, to Porto Novo to seek from the governors of the rival kingdom of Bijapur the provisions needed by the defenders of St Thomé, the young *Vendômois* had performed his mission with much skill. It is true that the governor of Valikondapuram had already sent to François Martin favourable proposals, to which Caron, the misguided or, more probably, treacherous adviser of de la Haye, had prevented him from replying. But the latter's departure now left Bellanger de Lespinay free to act. He obtained from the governor, Sher Khan Lodi, not only munitions and victuals, but also a site for a factory. Just as Lespinay was about to take leave, 2 January, 1673, an agent of the Dutch Company arrived in order to prejudice Sher Khan Lodi against the French. But he received a sharp answer. The other said "loudly that merchants were not soldiers, and that he knew the difference between the Dutch and the French". He concluded, to the great surprise and joy of his guest, by declaring that "as the Dutch and French were neighbours in Europe, so they should be in India, and therefore he gave us Pondichery as a place where our nation might settle".[1]

Sher Khan Lodi's gift was a little village near the borders of the hostile kingdom of Golconda, on the coast, and well placed for the assistance of the besieged in St Thomé. "Indeed it was a most convenient place for me", wrote Lespinay in his *Mémoires*. By order of his leader, he established himself there on 4 February, 1673, and, as

[1] *Mémoires de Lespinay*, pp. 203–4.

long as his countrymen held out, he did not cease to send them, with the constant help of Sher Khan, supplies of victuals, munitions, and even men. Thus began in modest fashion the historic rôle of Pondichery.

When on the morrow of the capitulation Bellanger de Lespinay quitted the few fishers' and traders' huts that surrounded the French factory, he did not suspect what a future awaited the tiny place. But he left there François Martin, the man whose great courage, intelligence, and perseverance were to develop it, transform it, and render it the capital of the French settlements in India.

At the beginning of 1674 Martin had been sent by the viceroy to second Lespinay, and this he had done effectively, thanks to his intelligence, knowledge of affairs, and patriotism. From 21 September, 1674, he was left at Pondichery with six Frenchmen "to act as affairs may require". At first, together with Baron, he sought to obtain from Golconda the grant of St Thomé. But though under pressure from Dutch and English alike the place was demolished, neither lost heart. Perceiving clearly that the Company could drive a profitable trade with two well-established factories, one on the Malabar and one on the Coromandel Coast, and deeming that Surat would serve for one of the two, they set to work to procure the other, though they had to surmount many difficulties merely to secure the maintenance of a French factory at Pondichery, while in Europe the war between the Great King and his enemies was going forward. Sivaji's defeat of Sher Khan Lodi, the persistent jealousy of the Dutch, the Company's neglect of its agents in India, all added to their difficulties. Martin however maintained the position. When Baron recalled him to Surat, he convinced Colbert of the commercial value of Pondichery, and, after the Peace of Nimweguen, succeeded in carrying through a little business for the Company. But would he be able to secure all that was needed, and make good the complete lack of goods and money in which he was left by the Company, at a time when the Company was in great straits and obliged to abandon not only Caron's factory at Bantam but also its new factory in Tonkin? Or would he be able with so few people to survive the political and economic crisis through which the Moghul Empire was passing in spite of Aurangzib's early conquests? Pondichery was, indeed, falling into that stagnation which precedes decay, but though Martin knew it, he did not hesitate to return thither in 1686 and to make it again the centre of his activities.

At that moment Colbert's son and successor at the ministry of marine, the Marquis de Seignelay, had just procured for the Company new capital, reorganised its directorate, and restored it to greater activity than it had long known. As, besides, there was peace in Europe, there was at least officially peace also among the European nations in India. Of these favourable circumstances, though counteracted by war, famine and pestilence in the country itself, Martin made good use. Not content with enlarging the trade of Pondichery and its dependencies, he laboured to consolidate and extend the French factories. The re-establishment of the French at Masulipatam, the dispatch of Deslandes to Bengal, where a French agent had appeared so early as 1674, and co-operation with the great Siam enterprise which was for a while at this time the pet scheme of the royal government, form the chief evidences of Martin's activity, though they were not all equally successful.

But soon again the outbreak of war in Europe threatened the fruit of his labours. Though the trade of Pondichery was not much hurt by the complete failure of the Siam expedition, it was brought into grave danger by the war between the French and Dutch, and soon after by the close union between the Dutch and English resulting from the Revolution of 1688.

The decay of trade and the abandonment of the project to set up a factory near Cape Comorin were the first fruits of the renewal of the war, although the English governor of Fort St David expressed his desire to maintain peace in India. But soon Dutch hostility took shape in action. When in January, 1691, the French squadron sent out by Seignelay the year before quitted the Bay of Bengal, for lack of a port where the vessels could be repaired, the enemies of France, who had been much alarmed, sought at once to crush this rivalry which they deemed a political danger and an economic injury. Martin had long been endeavouring, in the face of great difficulties, to fortify Pondichery, to make up a little garrison for it, and had procured, though at a high rate, from the court of Jinji the grant of almost all rights of sovereignty; but with all his efforts he could not repel the attack of the Dutch when (23 August, 1693) they besieged the place both by land and sea. Deserted by the natives, and unable to answer the fire of the enemy, on 6 September he had to sign a capitulation, honourable indeed, but one article of which seemed to rob him of all hope of ever making the place a French settlement.

But the event turned out otherwise. Inspired by their Indian servants, the Company desired the king, in the negotiations ending in the Treaty of Ryswick (21 September, 1697), to procure the rendition of "the fort and settlement of Pondichery"; and with some difficulty it was secured. Further negotiations, patiently followed, in the next year ensured to the Company the restoration of the place with "all the additions and improvements made by the Dutch company both in the place and in the neighbourhood". But in India Martin only obtained full execution of this agreement after long discussions, and had to wait till 3 October, 1699, for the Dutch garrison to take its departure.

But thenceforward he was free to act and possessed the base of operations, without which, since 1693, the French had been reduced to a state of complete impotence. Since the Company, radically reformed once more in 1697, had recovered some activity, and was able to send one after another several fleets into the Indian seas, to which indeed its privileges were now limited, Martin took advantage of this appearance of French vessels to demonstrate to all how brief had been the duration of Dutch naval supremacy; and when a final attempt at diplomatic intervention in Siam had met with a final failure, he sought to develop and strengthen the Company's position at Pondichery, at Chandernagore, where Deslandes had established himself in 1690, and even at Surat, the importance of which factory was, however, daily declining.

For now he saw clearly the situation of the country and discerned the essential conditions for the complete success of the French enterprise, foreseeing the approaching decadence of the Moghul Empire, and planning for the French the acquisition of a political predominance as the essential condition of free commercial development. "Prosperous settlements and a few well-fortified places will give [the Company] a great position among these people", he wrote on 15 December, 1700, to Jérôme Pontchartrain, the new minister of marine. Martin therefore surrounded Pondichery with the solid walls that had hitherto been wanting; and at the same time under his vigorous lead the company's trade made real progress in Bengal, while even the Surat factory itself seemed about to shake off its ever-growing torpor.

Unluckily this promising situation did not last. In 1701 the War of the Spanish Succession broke out, and round the Grand Alliance grouped themselves all who disliked the thought of a son of Louis XIV succeeding to the throne of Spain. The effects of the new war were soon felt in India. Trade was once more interrupted; the factories of Bengal and Surat fell back into inactivity; while at Pondichery the preparation for defence (now completed by the building of Fort St Louis), and the need of checking Dutch intrigue, fully occupied the aged but still active Martin, left to his own resources without the least help from Europe.

Long after the death (31 December, 1706) of the founder of the first French settlements in India, this wretched situation continued and actually grew worse, more owing to the distress of the Company than the events of the war or the worthless nature of Martin's successors. The failure of a fleet sent in 1706 to the western coasts of South America in defiance of the monopoly granted to another Company in 1697 for the trade of the South Seas, the difficulties of meeting the Company's obligations, and at last the cession of its privileges to the Malouins in 1712, were the real, essential causes of the languor of the French factories in India in the early years of the eighteenth century. That condition persisted until the death of Louis XIV (1 September, 1715), or rather till May, 1719, when a

famous edict united the Company of the East Indies and China with
the Company of the West founded by Jean Law a little earlier (August,
1717), giving to the united body the name of the *Compagnie des Indes*
and confiding to it the whole of French colonial trade.

In Law's mind it was to have been even more than that—the single
trading body of the kingdom, and perhaps the most important of the
institutions by means of which he hoped to restore French finance.
Thus the privileges granted to the great Company which it had just
absorbed were extended for fifty years; and besides this it received
so many other privileges and so wide an extension of its domain that,
as has been said with truth, it became not so much a colonial enterprise as a sort of farm general of the state.[1]

But could even so powerful a *Compagnie des Indes* transform into
realities the fair dreams of Colbert? By no means. In fact the speedy
bankruptcy of the System ruined all hopes. In order not to burden
the state with the shares issued on different occasions, first by the
Company of the West, and then by the Company of the Indies itself,
the liquidators named by the king (10 April, 1721) had to re-establish
the Company in its original form. Two years later (23 March, 1723)
its administration was confided to a council of the Indies consisting
of a chief, a president, and twenty councillors nominated by the
crown; but, soon after, to enable shareholders to have representatives,
there were introduced, besides twelve directors and four inspectors
named by the crown, eight syndics appointed by the shareholders.

Such was in its main lines the home administration of the Company
which, as in the time of Louis XIV, held the exclusive privilege of
trade from the west coast of Africa round the Cape up to the Red Sea,
the islands of the Indian seas of which two had already been occupied
by the French (the Isle of Bourbon in 1664 and the Isle of France in
1721), and finally India itself and the Further East.

For various reasons deriving from the general history of the time
and the particular history of the Company, the French had made no
progress in India since 1706. No doubt the governors who succeeded
Martin were less able than he; but it must also be remembered that
from 1707 to 1720 no less than five governors ruled in succession at
Pondichery. Each in turn adopted a line of policy different from that
of his predecessor, until, in 1720, the new *Compagnie des Indes* put an
end to this series of conflicts and inconsistencies by taking possession
of the existing factories and imposing an active and coherent policy.
Masulipatam, Calicut, Mahé, and Yanam were occupied between
1721 and 1723. Although the attempt to found a settlement on Pulo
Kondor—the *Îles d'Orléans*—south of the Mekong delta failed altogether, the Company was able to take vengeance for the insult of the
prince Bayanor in driving the French from Mahé. It re-established
itself there by force, for ten months its troops victoriously met the

[1] Cultru, *Dupleix*, p. 2.

attempts of Bayanor and four other rajahs to expel them, and obliged them to make peace, first in 1726,[1] and later, after a blockade of eighteen months, in 1741. Clearly there was a change in the attitude of the *Compagnie des Indes*.

It must, however, be observed, that the two governors who held office from 1720 to 1742 (Lenoir till 1735 and then Benoist Dumas[2]) had none but commercial objects in mind. It was with a purely commercial object, the protection of a factory expected to yield a profitable pepper trade, that the Company in 1724 built a fort at Mahé, which was long a source of great expense; it was with a purely commercial object too that Dumas brought to reason by a show of force the governor of Mokha where the French had a factory,[3] and occupied in February, 1739, Karikal, at the request of a native prince. There was nothing in this exclusively interested conduct that allows us to credit the Company with political views and still less ideas of conquest; its factories were more or less fortified, but for motives of simple security; and although it enlisted troops, it used them only for purposes of police. In 1664 perhaps Louis XIV and Colbert dreamt of securing conquests in the Indies; but in 1730 none of the Company's servants dreamt of supplying funds for trade out of the regular revenues of territorial possessions, or conceived the idea of obtaining them by interfering in the lawless conflicts that arose out of the decadence of the Moghul Empire, or attempted to interfere in any persistent, methodical way in the affairs of native princes. Only in the period that begins in 1740 does this notion first germinate and then begin to develop in the admirable brain of Dupleix.

---

[1] Martineau, *Les Origines de Mahé*. Cf. *Les Mémoires du Chevalier de la Farelle sur la prise de Mahé*.
[2] Martineau, "Benoist Dumas", *Rev. de l'hist. des col. fr.* IX, 145 *sqq.*
[3] Martineau, "La politique de Dumas", *Rev. de l'hist. des col. fr.* XIV, 1 *sqq.*

CHAPTER IV

THE EAST INDIA COMPANY, 1600–1740

THE success of the Portuguese in establishing a lucrative commerce with the East naturally excited a desire among the other nations of Western Europe to follow so tempting an example. The Portuguese, however, had a long start, and it was nearly a century before any rival made an effective entry into the field. The reasons for this were largely political. The papal bulls of 1493, and the subsequent agreement with Spain at Tordesillas, prevented any attempt on the part of the Catholic powers to infringe the monopoly claimed by Lisbon; and if the union of the crowns of Spain and Portugal in 1580 exposed the latter to the attacks of the revolted Netherlands, on the other hand it deterred the cautious Elizabeth of England from countenancing too openly the audacious schemes of her subjects for ventures into the forbidden area. For a time, therefore, English merchants concentrated their attention upon the discovery of a new sea-road to the East, either through or round America on the one side or by the northern coasts of Europe and Asia on the other; and either route had the additional attraction that it would bring the adventurers to Northern China, which was out of the Portuguese sphere and would, it was hoped, afford for English woollens a market hardly to be expected in the tropical regions to the southward. The story of these attempts to find a north-eastern or north-western passage to the Indies belongs rather to the general history of exploration than to our special subject, and no detailed account of them is necessary. Their failure directed attention afresh to the Portuguese route by the Cape of Good Hope, especially when in 1580 Francis Drake returned that way from his voyage round the world. New energy was infused into the project by the defeat of the Spanish Armada, by the return (1591) of Ralph Fitch from some years of travel in India and Burma, and by the riches found in Portuguese carracks captured by English privateers. At last in 1591–3 a ship under James Lancaster succeeded in penetrating the Indian Ocean and visiting the Nicobars and the island of Penang. Three years after Lancaster's return another fleet started under Benjamin Wood, but the enterprise ended in disaster. The Dutch, who had already imitated the English in endeavouring to discover a north-east passage, now joined in the attempt to force the Portuguese barrier; and in 1596 a squadron under Houtman reached Java, returning in safety a year later. As a result, in 1598 over twenty ships were dispatched from Holland to the East by way of the Cape.

The merchants of England were in no mood to see the prize they had so long sought snatched away from them by their Dutch rivals.

Preparations were therefore commenced in the autumn of 1599 for a fresh expedition to the East; but this had to be abandoned owing to Queen Elizabeth's fear of prejudicing her negotiations with King Philip for a peace. In the following year, however, these negotiations having failed, the scheme was revived, and early in 1601 a fleet sailed for the East under the command of Lancaster. In the meantime, by a charter dated 31 December, 1600, those interested in the venture had been incorporated under the title of "The Governor and Company of Merchants of London Trading into the East Indies", and the monopoly of English commerce in eastern waters (from the Cape of Good Hope to the Straits of Magellan) had been granted to them and their successors for a term of fifteen years.[1]

England being still at war with Spain and Portugal, and the immediate aim being the acquisition of the spices and pepper of the Far East, the First (1601–3) and Second (1604–6) Voyages[2] were made, not to India, but to Achin (in Sumatra), Bantam (in Java), and the Moluccas. However, in August, 1604, peace was at last concluded, though without any recognition of the English claim to share in the commerce of the Indian seas; while it was becoming evident that English manufactures—which it was particularly desirable to export, in order to avoid carrying out so much silver—could find no satisfactory market in the Malay Archipelago. When, therefore, a Third Voyage was under preparation (1606–7), it was resolved that the fleet should, on its way to Bantam, endeavour to open up trade at Aden and Surat. For this purpose the post of second in command was given to William Hawkins, a merchant who had had considerable experience in the Levant and could speak Turkish; and he was provided with a letter from King James to the emperor Akbar (whose death was as yet unknown in London), desiring permission to establish trade in his dominions.

The *Hector*, which was the vessel commanded by Hawkins, anchored off the mouth of the Tapti on 24 August, 1608, and her captain at once proceeded up the river to Surat, the principal port of the Moghul Empire. Early in October the ship departed for Bantam, and four months later Hawkins set out on his long journey to the court. He reached Agra in the middle of April, 1609, and was graciously received by the emperor Jahangir. For some time he was in high favour, and was admitted to share the revels of that jovial monarch, who went so far as to take him into his service and marry him to an Armenian damsel. But the Portuguese, alarmed at the prospect of English competition, were working hard to displace him, both at Agra, where they found willing helpers among the courtiers, and in Gujarat. Their arguments and threats prevailed upon the timid officials and merchants of that province to make representations against the admission

---

[1] Patent Rolls, 43 Eliz. pt VI.
[2] Narratives of the early expeditions will be found in *The Voyages of Sir James Lancaster*.

of the English; and in the end these representations were successful. It was unfortunate for Hawkins that in September, 1609, the *Ascension*, which had been dispatched from England to second his efforts, was wrecked in the Gulf of Cambay, while her crew, escaping to land, created a bad impression by their disorder. But this and other obstacles might have been surmounted, had not the chief merchants of Surat declared that commerce with the English would mean a rupture with the Portuguese and the consequent ruin of their trade. Thereupon Jahangir reluctantly ordered the exclusion of the new-comers. After making vain efforts to induce him to reverse this decision, Hawkins left Agra in November, 1611, and journeyed down to the coast.[1]

Meanwhile the East India Company, encouraged by the grant of a fresh charter in May, 1609,[2] extending its privileges indefinitely (subject to revocation after three years' notice), had sent out in the spring of 1610 three ships under Sir Henry Middleton, with orders to go first to the Red Sea ports and then to those of Gujarat. At Mokha, Middleton was seized by the Turkish governor and imprisoned for nearly six months. Escaping by a stratagem, he blockaded the port until compensation was paid, and then proceeded to India. He reached the mouth of the Tapti in September, 1611, but only to find it occupied by a squadron of Portuguese "frigates" (light country-built vessels, fitted to row or sail), which effectually cut off access to the shore. After some time information was obtained from a friendly Indian official of a pool or harbour among the sandbanks to the northward of the river mouth, where ships might ride close to the shore; and the discovery of this haven—known to succeeding fleets as "Swally Hole"—enabled the English to berth their vessels where their guns could command the shore, and to communicate freely with the country people. Some trade resulted, and the Governor of Surat held out hopes that a permanent settlement would be allowed; but fresh threats on the part of the Portuguese produced a reaction, and the English, who had meanwhile embarked Hawkins and his companions, were roughly bidden to be gone. They sailed accordingly in February, 1612. Middleton was not disposed to put up calmly with this rebuff. He determined to show that the power of the English was not less to be dreaded than that of the Portuguese, and that, if the latter could close the Gujarat ports, the former could do equal injury to the Red Sea traffic—the main dependence of the Surat merchants. Sailing to the Straits of Bab-ul-mandab, he there rounded up the Indian trading vessels and forced them to exchange their goods for his English commodities; while, in addition, the ships from Diu and Surat were obliged to pay a heavy ransom before they were

---

[1] His own narrative may be read in *Early Travels in India*, p. 60.
[2] Patent Rolls, 7 Jac. I, pt XI. There is a contemporary copy at the India Office (Parchment Records, No. 5).

released. He made no further attempt to trade with the Indian ports, but proceeded straight to Sumatra.

The news of the revenge taken by Middleton produced consternation at Surat. Besides the damage likely to be done to the trade of the port should such reprisals continue, there was a possibility that the large pilgrim traffic to the holy places of Islam might be diverted to other routes. When, therefore, in September, 1612, two ships from England, under the command of Thomas Best, anchored at the bar, unaware of what had happened in the Red Sea, they found a respectful reception and were readily promised full trading privileges. The news of this roused the Portuguese authorities at Goa to vigorous action, and in November a strong fleet appeared to try conclusions with Best's two vessels. The latter put boldly to sea and repelled their assailants with heavy loss, thus greatly raising the reputation of the English. A farman arrived from the emperor early in 1613, confirming the agreement already concluded with the local authorities,[1] and a permanent factory (i.e. a group of merchants, living together) was now established at Surat under Thomas Aldworth, a merchant being also sent up to Agra with presents, to watch over English interests at court.

Disappointed in his endeavours to destroy Best's ships, the viceroy of Goa decided to bring fresh pressure to bear upon the Indians to exclude the English; and with this object in view a Surat vessel of great value, returning from the Red Sea, was captured, although she was duly provided with a Portuguese pass. Jahangir was very indignant at this affront, and dispatched a force to besiege Daman. The arrival (October, 1614) of four ships under Nicholas Downton led the Moghul authorities to expect the active co-operation of the English in a war largely occasioned by the favour shown to them; and Downton's unwillingness to engage in hostilities, without express authority from home, caused much resentment. At this point, however, the viceroy himself unwittingly helped his enemies. Gathering together a powerful fleet, which he filled with soldiers, he sailed in person to crush the English and then punish the Indians for having harboured them. He found Downton's ships snugly ensconced in Swally Hole, where his own larger vessels could not reach them; an attack made by his frigates was smartly repulsed; and in the end he had to retire discomfited. In March, 1615, one of Downton's vessels, the *Hope*, laden chiefly with indigo and cotton goods, sailed for England —the first vessel to be sent home from an Indian port. Not long afterwards the Portuguese, finding their commercial interests suffering from the war, made overtures to the Moghul emperor for peace, offering compensation for the vessel they had seized, but requiring the expulsion of the English as an essential condition. To this Jahangir replied that the latter were too powerful at sea for him to interfere

[1] See Best's journal among the India Office Marine Records (No. xv).

and that, if their recourse to his ports was to be prevented, the Portuguese themselves must undertake the task. In the end, towards the close of 1615, an agreement was reached, without any stipulation on this point.

The position of the newcomers was, however, still precarious, owing to the certainty that the Goa authorities would continue their efforts to induce the emperor to forbid further trade; while, as they well knew, mercantile interests in Gujarat were greatly disturbed by the resultant bickerings, and the Indian officials were asking themselves whether it was worth while, for the sake of the small trade brought by the English, to risk the large and well-established commerce between their ports and Goa. It was, therefore, with much joy that the English factors greeted the arrival (September, 1615) of a new fleet, bringing out an ambassador from King James, in the person of Sir Thomas Roe. The East India Company had decided to make a great effort to establish permanent relations with India, and the surest way of effecting this seemed to be the dispatch of a royal envoy to the Moghul, for the purpose of concluding a treaty which should put the trade between the two countries on a regular footing. This plan had, moreover, the advantage of refuting the allegations of the Portuguese that the Company's attempts to trade in Eastern waters were not authorised by the English sovereign, while it threw the aegis of the latter over his subjects at Surat and thus discouraged further attacks from Goa.

Roe reached the court, which was then at Ajmir, in December, 1615; and for nearly three years he followed in the train of the emperor, striving diligently to carry out the objects of his mission. He found, however, that the conclusion of any form of treaty for commercial purposes was entirely foreign to Indian ideas. Moreover, his demands included concessions for trade in Bengal and Sind, which Jahangir's advisers opposed on the ground that the struggle between the two European nations would thereby be extended to other parts of India; while most of the remaining demands were looked upon as matters coming under the jurisdiction of the emperor's favourite son, Prince Khurram (Shah Jahan), who was then viceroy of Gujarat and was not disposed to brook any interference in his administration of that province. In the end Roe had to content himself with concluding an arrangement with the prince, who willingly conceded most of the privileges desired. The ambassador thus failed in achieving the particular end for which he had been sent; yet he had done all that was really necessary, and indirectly had contributed greatly to the establishment of his countrymen's position. His own character and abilities raised considerably the reputation of the English at court; while his success in obtaining the punishment of the local officials when guilty of oppression taught them and their successors to be circumspect in their dealings with the English traders. His sage advice to the Company did much also in guiding the development of its commerce along safe and profitable lines, particularly in regard to the commerce with Mokha and Persia.

By the time Roe embarked for home (February, 1619) there were regular English factories at Surat, Agra, Ahmadabad, and Broach. All these were placed under the authority of the chief factor at Surat, who was now styled the President,[1] and who in addition controlled the trade which had been opened up with the Red Sea ports and in Persia. These trade developments led to trouble; the first with the Surat merchants who had so long enjoyed this commerce; and the second with the Portuguese, who, if now hopeless of excluding the English from India, were determined to keep them, if possible, from interfering with the commerce of the Persian Gulf, from which they derived a considerable revenue. In this, however, they failed to take sufficiently into account the attitude of the Persian monarch, Shah Abbas, who had already extended his dominions to the sea and was by no means pleased to find the trade of Southern Persia controlled by the Portuguese fortress on the island of Ormuz. He was desirous of developing the new port of Gombroon (the present Bandar Abbas), which was situated on the mainland opposite to Ormuz; but little headway could be made in this respect while the Portuguese compelled all vessels to pay dues at the latter place. Naturally, too, he welcomed English overtures for a seaborne trade with Europe, since the raw silk of his northern provinces was largely in his hands and he was anxious to divert the trade as much as possible from its ordinary channel through the dominions of his hereditary enemies the Turks. The Portuguese, on their side, far from endeavouring to conciliate him, dispatched an envoy to demand the restitution of Gombroon and other territory conquered from their vassal, the titular king of Ormuz, together with the exclusion of all other Europeans from trade in his country. Both demands were firmly refused, and the shah declared his intention of supporting English commerce in his dominions.

The determination of the Company's factors to take full advantage of the Persian monarch's friendship quickly led to fresh hostilities with the Portuguese; and at the end of 1620 a fight took place off Jask, in which the English ships gained a fresh success. Their opponents once more committed the error of driving an Asiatic power into alliance with the English, for they now declared war against Shah Abbas and sent a fleet to destroy his port towns. The enraged monarch in his turn dispatched an army to turn the Portuguese out of Ormuz and the neighbouring island of Kishm; but this was impossible without the aid of naval power, and when in December, 1621, a strong English fleet arrived to cover the embarkation of the Company's silk, its commanders were practically forced, by threats of exclusion from

[1] *English Factories in India*, 1618–21, p. ix.

further trade, to take part in the operations. The Portuguese castle on Kishm was easily captured, but Ormuz itself only yielded after a siege of over two months (April, 1622). The reward of the English was a small share in the plunder of the place and the grant for the future of half the customs revenue of the port, the Company's own goods being freed from toll in addition.[1] As a matter of fact, though the Persians garrisoned Ormuz, the trade itself was transferred to Gombroon. However, the claim of the English to share the customs of the latter place was recognised and, though the full amount due to them was seldom paid, they for long drew a considerable revenue from this source, in addition to the privilege of exemption from customs.

Whether an English trading company, operating from so distant a base and governed by men who were consistently averse from using any but peaceable methods, would ever have managed to overcome the opposition of Portugal is, to say the least, doubtful; but, fortunately for our fellow-countrymen, during the whole of the struggle their opponents were being increasingly harassed by the Dutch, whose armaments and commerce alike were on a much larger scale than those of any of their European competitors. From the beginning of the seventeenth century the Hollanders had determined to take full advantage of the weakness of the Portuguese and to oust them from their eastern trade; and this object was pursued with all the tenacity and thoroughness of the Dutch character. Though organised, like the English, in the form of a trading company, the Dutch merchants had behind them practically the whole power of the state, and their commerce with the East was recognised as a most important national asset; while the vigorous war which their fellow-countrymen were waging with King Philip gave a special sanction to their attacks upon his Portuguese subjects. These attacks were at first directed mainly to the Spice Islands, the source of the cloves and nutmegs so much in demand in Europe. Here, until their hands were stayed by the conclusion of a truce with Spain in 1609, they made great progress in capturing the Portuguese forts and in concluding agreements with the native chiefs, by which the latter were guaranteed protection against the Portuguese in return for a monopoly of the trade in spices. Naturally this policy aroused much resentment among the English, who found themselves in danger of being excluded from a valuable commerce with a thoroughness that would never have been attained under the Portuguese. On the other hand the Hollanders argued that it was unfair for the English, who contributed in no way to the defence of the Spice Islands against the common foe, to expect a share in the benefits of the trade, under conditions which really gave them an advantage, since they were spared the heavy expenses of garrisons and ships of war. The dispute led to much negotiation between

[1] *English Factories*, 1622–3, p. 13.

London and the Hague, and to actual hostilities in the Far East, confined at first to the Bandas but soon extending over a wider area, though the English settlements in India were not involved. The news of these conflicts roused the governments of both nations to action, and under pressure from them an agreement[1] was concluded (1619) in London between the Dutch and English Companies, which really pleased neither party. By its terms the two bodies were to share in certain proportions the trade of the eastern islands and jointly to bear the cost of defending their interests against the Portuguese; English factors were to be admitted to the Dutch settlements, including Batavia; and each Company was to furnish ten ships for purposes of the common defence.

This agreement did not extend to Western India, Persia, or the Red Sea, except as regards united naval action against the Portuguese; but it embraced the English settlements on the east coast of India, concerning which a few words must now be said. The first attempt to open up communication with this part of the peninsula was made in 1611, when the Company, acting in conjunction with two Dutch merchants who provided a share of the capital and themselves took part in the voyage, sent out the *Globe* to visit the Coromandel Coast and the countries adjacent. An endeavour was made to settle a factory at Pulicat (a little to the north of where Madras now stands), but this was foiled by the Dutch, who had obtained an exclusive concession from the king of the Carnatic for trade in his dominions. The vessel then passed on to Masulipatam, the chief port of the Golconda kingdom, and here a factory was established in September, 1611. The chief object in view was the provision of chintzes and calicoes for use in the Far Eastern trade; and, accordingly, from the beginning the factories on the Coromandel Coast were placed under the superintendence of the president at Bantam, and had little in common with those in Western and Northern India save the geographical tie.

The Dutch notion of defence proved to be much the same as vigorous aggression; for as soon as the Truce of Antwerp had expired (1621) they proceeded to push home their attacks on the remaining Portuguese possessions. Accordingly, in the autumn of that year the joint Anglo-Dutch "Fleet of Defence" left Batavia for the Malabar Coast, to intercept the Portuguese carracks in their passage to and from Goa. In July, 1622, they inflicted much damage on a squadron that was bringing out a new viceroy; and they followed up this success by blockading Goa during the cold weather of 1622–3, thus preventing all intercourse with Lisbon. Before long, however, the co-operation of the two Protestant powers broke down. The English were by no means pleased to find themselves dragged by their allies into a series of warlike operations that brought them much expense and little benefit; disputes arose as to the fairness of the financial charges and

[1] *Calendar of State Papers, E. Indies*, 1617–21, nos. 679–81.

the amenability of the English to the Dutch tribunals at Batavia and elsewhere; while soon money was lacking to pay the English share of the military and naval charges. The result was that the English president and council resolved to withdraw their factors from the various Dutch settlements, since they could no longer carry out their financial engagements. Before this could be effected occurred the famous "Massacre of Amboina" (February, 1623), ten members of the English factory there being tortured and put to death by the Dutch authorities, after an irregular trial, on a charge of conspiring to seize the fortress. This virtually put an end to the alliance, in spite of the fact that at home, after protracted negotiations, a fresh agreement had been concluded (January, 1623),[1] which removed a few of the causes of friction. Early in 1624 the English quitted Batavia and proceeded to form a new head settlement of their own upon an uninhabited island in the neighbouring Straits of Sunda. This, however, proved so unhealthy that a return had to be made (with Dutch assistance) to their former quarters at Batavia; and there they remained until 1628, when they removed once again to their old station at Bantam, the king of which was unfriendly to the Dutch and powerful enough to maintain his independence.

As we have seen, the treaty of 1619 did not extend to Western India, Persia, or the Red Sea, being in fact intended only for the regulation of the spice and pepper trade. But the Dutch had now important interests in those parts, having established themselves at Surat (1616), Ahmadabad and Agra (1618), Mokha (1620), and in Persia (1623); and they were quite aware that the surest way to inflict a damaging blow on their enemy was to attack him in Indian and Persian waters. The war which broke out in 1625 between England and Spain, together with the efforts the Portuguese were making to retrieve their position in those waters, induced the Company's servants at Surat to join the Hollanders in active hostilities. Early in 1625 an Anglo-Dutch fleet defeated a Portuguese squadron near Ormuz, and in the following year a similar joint expedition destroyed the small Portuguese settlement on the island of Bombay. Some desultory fighting took place during the next few years, culminating in an attack on shore at Swally (1630); but here the Portuguese were easily routed by a small force of English sailors, to the surprise of the Indians, who had hitherto deemed the former invincible on land.

In this same year peace was concluded between King Charles and King Philip. It was expected in London that the Portuguese would recognise the futility of their opposition to English trade in the East and would agree to admit its continuance; but the Lisbon authorities proved unyielding on the point, and the Treaty of Madrid left matters

---

[1] British Museum, Add. MSS, 22866, f. 466 b; also *Hague Transcripts* (India Office), series 1, vol. 57, no. 2. The version given in *Cal. S.P., E. Indies*, 1622-24, no. 263, is incorrect.

as they were in the East Indies. However, the viceroy of Goa and his councillors soon began to listen to suggestions of accommodation. Hard pressed by the Dutch and involved also with various Asiatic foes, with ever-dwindling resources in Portuguese India itself, they thought it wise to remove at least one source of difficulty and danger by making a truce with the English. The latter, on their side, were eager for the cessation of a warfare which hampered their commercial operations (already suffering greatly from the effects of the severe famine of 1630–1) and necessitated the employment of costly fleets in maintaining communication with their other settlements and with Europe; and, moreover, they were well aware of the advantages which would result from the opening of the Portuguese harbours to their ships and the Portuguese settlements to their trade. The negotiations extended over a considerable period; but at last, in January, 1635, William Methwold, the English president at Surat, who had been the moving spirit, had the satisfaction of signing at Goa (on his way home) an accord[1] with the viceroy, which established a truce for an indefinite period—as it proved, a lasting peace. The accord was extended by the Anglo-Portuguese treaty of 1642, which also provided for the appointment of commissioners to settle outstanding questions; but it was not until the conclusion of Cromwell's treaty in July, 1654, that the right of the English to trade freely with the Portuguese possessions in the East (with the exception of Macao) was formally recognised.

The Dutch on their side continued the war with increased vigour and almost unvarying success. Year after year they blockaded Goa during the season for the arrival and departure of shipping; allying themselves with the king of Kandi, they captured several of the Portuguese strongholds in Ceylon; and in 1641, aided by an Achinese force, they made themselves masters of the city of Malacca, which controlled the traffic between India and China. By this time Portugal had regained her independence of Spain (December, 1640) and had opened up negotiations with Holland, which resulted in a treaty suspending hostilities for ten years and leaving the Dutch in possession of their conquests (June, 1641). The authorities at Batavia, however, were unwilling to halt in their victorious career, and it was not until sixteen months later that the truce was proclaimed there. Even then there were disputes, and the peace did not become effective until November, 1644. Troubles over Brazil brought about a renewal of the war in 1652, upon the expiration of the truce. Colombo fell in May, 1656, and Jaffna (the last Portuguese stronghold in Ceylon) two years later; while on the coast of India Negapatam and all the Portuguese possessions on the Malabar littoral to the southward of Goa were taken between 1658 and 1663. Peace between the two countries had been concluded in 1661; but the news of this did not come in time to save Cochin and Kannanur. The only consolation

---

[1] *English Factories*, 1634–6, p. 88.

for the Portuguese was that Dutch schemes for the conquest of their remaining settlements were thus foiled; while the danger of attacks in the future was warded off by an English guarantee, as related below.

Meanwhile England had in 1652 become involved in a war with Holland. At home the Commonwealth fleet proved victorious, after a hard struggle, and Cromwell was able to dictate practically his own terms when peace was made in 1654. In the East, however, the interests of the English had suffered considerably, owing to the preponderance of Dutch naval power in those waters. Though the Company's settlements were not attacked, for fear of offending the monarchs in whose dominions they were situated, ship after ship fell into the hands of the Hollanders, with the result that not only was heavy loss inflicted upon the Company but English prestige suffered greatly, both in India and in Persia. There was, however, some compensation in the outcome of the war; for the commissioners appointed under the Treaty of Westminster to assess damages awarded the English Company £85,000[1] in settlement of its claims against its Dutch rival, decreed the restitution of the island of Pulo Run[2] (in the Bandas), and provided for the payment of damages to the representatives of those Englishmen who had suffered at Amboina in 1623. Of these decisions the most unpalatable to the Dutch was the second, since to allow the English a footing in the Spice Islands meant a serious breach in the Dutch monopoly of cloves. Every mode of evasion was therefore practised; and although the surrender was again stipulated in a fresh treaty concluded in 1662, it was not until March, 1665, that the island was actually made over—only to be retaken in the following November, on the receipt of the news of the outbreak of the Second Dutch War. The long-standing dispute was finally settled by the peace of 1667, which assigned the island to Holland.

A further consequence of the hostilities with the Dutch in 1652–4 was a tendency on the part of both English and Portuguese in the East to draw together for mutual support; and also an increased desire on the part of the former to find some defensible spot on the western coast of India, where they could be secure against both the exactions of Indian officials and the attacks of European foes. The provision of such a retreat came, however, not from any action on the part of the East India Company but from the turn of events upon the accession of Charles II. By a secret article of the marriage treaty with Portugal (1661) England guaranteed the Portuguese possessions

---

[1] Of this amount the Commonwealth government at once borrowed £50,000, and the loan was never repaid (*Court Minutes of the E. India Co.*, 1655–9, p. v).

[2] This island had been made over to the English by its inhabitants in 1616, in hopes of protection against the Dutch, who, however, took advantage of the subsequent hostilities to effect its capture. By the Anglo-Dutch accord of 1623 it was recognised as English property, but the weakness of the East India Company was such that no serious attempt was made to take over so distant a possession, though proposals to that effect were mooted from time to time.

in the East against the Dutch, and to facilitate this the island of Bombay was included in the dowry of the new queen. Owing to difficulties placed in the way by the local officials, to whom the arrangement was distasteful, the island was not made over to the king's representatives until February, 1665. Experience soon showed that the outlay on the maintenance and development of the new possession would make too heavy a demand upon the royal purse; and on 27 March, 1668, in consideration of a temporary loan of £50,000 at 6 per cent., Charles transferred it to the Company at a quitrent of £10 per annum.[1] The actual date of the handing over was 23 September in the same year.

It is time now to turn our attention to more peaceful topics and to note the progress made by English commerce in India and the neighbouring countries. The friendly relations established with the Portuguese by the convention of Goa (1635) much improved the position of the East India Company's servants in those regions. It became possible to dispatch ships singly to and from England and to develop unhindered the port-to-port traffic, using for this purpose mainly small India-built vessels in lieu of the cumbrous and expensive ships built for the long sea-voyage out and home. The Malabar Coast, too, was opened to English trade, with the result that saltpetre, pepper, cardamoms, and cassia lignea (wild cinnamon) from those parts figured largely in the cargoes of the homeward-bound vessels. The tightening of the Dutch monopoly over the pepper and spice trade of the Far East and Ceylon drove the English to rely chiefly on the Malabar trade for these products. In Gujarat agriculture and the textile industry had not yet recovered from the terrible famine of 1630–1, and the Company's factors were forced to look for fresh sources of supply to make good the deficiency. Now that the menace of the Portuguese flotilla at Maskat was removed, trade was extended to Lahribandar and Tatta in the Indus delta (1635), and to Basra (1640); while at the same time the commerce with Gombroon was largely developed, partly owing to the eagerness with which Asiatic merchants availed themselves of the English and Dutch vessels for transporting their goods between India and Persia, especially during the long war between those two countries over the possession of Kandahar. Ventures were even made to Macao and Manilla; but these were discouraged by the Portuguese and Spaniards respectively, as soon as it was found that the English were not willing to risk trouble with the Dutch by carrying contraband of war; and so no permanent trade resulted. Further, we may reckon among the consequences of the Anglo-Portuguese *entente* the establishment of an English settlement at Madraspatam, on the Coromandel Coast; for, had hostilities continued, it would scarcely have been prudent to settle so near the

---

[1] The payment of this rent has been traced down to the year 1730. After that the treasury seems to have neglected to apply for it.

Portuguese fortress of St Thomé. Regarding this development something must now be said.

We have already noted that as early as 1611 the English had followed the example of the Dutch in starting a factory at Masulipatam, the chief port of the kingdom of Golconda. The trade here was valuable, particularly in piece-goods for export to Persia and to Bantam; while the grant in 1634 of freedom from all duties gave the Company a considerable advantage over their competitors, including the Dutch. It had already been discovered, however, that most of the piece-goods wanted for the trade of the Far East were procurable at cheaper rates in the Hindu territory to the southwards, under the dominion of the raja of the Carnatic, the shrunken remnant of the once extensive kingdom of Vijayanagar; and in 1626 the factors at Masulipatam established a subsidiary settlement at Armagon, a little to the northward of the Dutch fortress at Pulicat. This place proved to have many disadvantages, especially in the shallowness and exposed nature of the roadstead; and so in 1639 an agreement was made with a local ruler a little further south, by which permission was obtained to erect a fortified factory close to the little town of Madraspatam. Thither the English removed from Armagon in February, 1640; and in September, 1641, Fort St George (as the new station was named) superseded Masulipatam as their headquarters on the Coromandel Coast. In thus acquiring a fortified settlement—a privilege which would never have been granted in Golconda territory—the factors were only just in time; for the Hindu kingdom of the Carnatic was already tottering under the attacks of its Muhammadan neighbours, and in 1647 the district round Madras fell into the hands of Mir Jumla, the leader of the Golconda forces. The English, however, were on good terms with him and easily procured his confirmation of their privileges, which included the government of Madraspatam, subject to sharing with the royal treasury the customs paid by strangers.[1]

By this time English trade on the eastern side of India had been extended from Masulipatam to the seaports of Orissa, and factories had been started (1633) at Hariharpur (in the Mahanadi delta) and at Balasore. In 1650–1, following the example of the Dutch, this commerce was carried into Bengal itself and a settlement made at Hugli. Before long factories were planted at Patna and Kasimbazar; but for some years little benefit resulted to the Company, owing to the large amount of private trade carried on by its servants. However, the commerce on the eastern side of India grew steadily in importance as the merits of the Coromandel piece-goods came to be recognised at home and as Bengal sugar and saltpetre were likewise found to be

---

[1] This division of the customs continued until 1658, when it was agreed that an annual sum of 380 pagodas should be paid as the royal share. After much dispute, the agreement was revised in 1672 and the amount was raised to 1200 pagodas per annum. For eighty years that sum was regularly paid, and then it was remitted altogether by Muhammad 'Ali, nawab of the Carnatic.

in demand; and a considerable trade was consequently established between the coast and England. In 1652, under the stress of the war with the Dutch, the seat of the eastern presidency was removed from Bantam to Fort St George. Three years after, however, came the partial collapse of the Company described on a later page. Orders were sent out for the abandonment of the factories in Bengal and the reduction of those on the coast to two, viz. Fort St George and Masulipatam, with a corresponding diminution of staff. From a presidency the coast became once more an agency, though Greenhill, who had succeeded to the post of president before the Company's orders arrived, was generally accorded the higher title until his death at the beginning of 1659. The period of his administration was the low-water mark of the Company's trade in those parts, owing to the financial weakness at home and the competition of private ventures. The revival that followed the grant by Cromwell of a new charter will be the theme of a later page.

Meanwhile we must look back to 1635 and follow the course of the Company's affairs at home. The Convention of Goa, which produced such beneficial results in the East, had in England the unexpected result of arousing a dangerous competition. Financially the success of the Company had by no means answered expectations. The earliest voyages, it is true, had proved very profitable; but when the full burden of maintaining so many factories was felt, to say nothing of the losses caused by Dutch competition and the resulting quarrels, the profits fell off and the capital required to carry on the trade was raised with ever-increasing difficulty. The system adopted—that of terminable stocks—each of which was wound up in turn and its assets distributed, had many drawbacks. The plan was perhaps the only practicable one; but it tended to prevent the adoption of any continuous or long-sighted policy, and it concentrated attention on immediate profits; while, since it necessitated a fresh subscription every few years, it exposed the Company to the effects of any stringency prevailing in the money market. Owing largely to political troubles, the period from 1636 to 1660 was one of general depression of trade, especially towards the end of the Commonwealth; and this depression, together with the practical loss of its monopoly, went perilously near to extinguishing the Company. During the twenty years following 1636 the capital raised for four successive Stocks aggregated only about £600,000, whereas in 1631 a single subscription (that for the Third Joint Stock) had produced over £420,000, while further back still (1617) no less a sum than £1,600,000 had been subscribed for the Second Joint Stock.

These financial difficulties, and the small amount of profit earned in comparison with the Dutch East India Company, evoked much criticism of the Company's general policy, together with some impatience that so large a sphere of possible commercial activity should be monopolised by a body that was apparently incapable of dealing with more than a portion of it. The colonising movement—stimulated by the success of the plantations on the American seaboard and in the West India islands—produced suggestions that something more was required than the leaving of a few factors here and there in the East Indies, and that English trade in those regions would never flourish until it was based, as in the case of the Dutch and the Portuguese, upon actual settlements independent of the caprice of local rulers and strong enough to resist their attacks. The prospect of a considerable extension of commerce as the result of the Convention of Goa, and the apparent inability of the existing Company to take full advantage of this opportunity, provided a plausible excuse for those who were eager to engage in the trade on their own lines; and by the close of the same year (1635) a rival body—commonly known as Courteen's Association, from the name of its principal shareholder—was formed in London to trade with China, Japan, the Malabar Coast, and other parts in which the East India Company had not yet established factories. Endymion Porter, one of the royal favourites, was an active supporter of the project, and it was doubtless owing in great part to his influence that King Charles lent his countenance to the new association by issuing a royal commission for the first voyage and by granting to Courteen and his partners letters-patent which practically established them as a rival East India Company (1637). The promoters of the new venture, however, soon found their expectations disappointed. The result of the first voyage was a heavy loss, for the leaders, Weddell and Mountney, disappeared with their two vessels beneath the waves of the Indian Ocean on their homeward way in 1639. Sir William Courteen had died shortly after the departure of that fleet, and his son had succeeded to a heritage much encumbered by the cost of the venture; still, he struggled hard to maintain the trade, with the assistance of friends and of other merchants anxious to compete with the regular Company. Factories were established at various places on the Malabar Coast—Rajapur, Bhatkal, Karwar; and Courteen's captains did not hesitate, in spite of the limitations in his patent, to visit Surat, Gombroon, Basra, and other places within the sphere of the East India Company. But what was gained in one direction was lost in another; money was wasted in ill-judged enterprises, such as the attempt to establish a colony at St Augustine's Bay in Madagascar (1645-6);[1] and supplies from home were both irregular and inadequate, with the result that one factory after another had to be abandoned. About 1645 Courteen himself withdrew to the continent to escape the importunities of his creditors; and although other merchants continued to send out ships under licence from him, their interference with the operations of the East India Company became almost negligible.

[1] For this see Foster, "An English settlement in Madagascar," in the *English Historical Review*, XXVII, 239.

However, the monopoly of the latter, once broken, was not easily re-established; especially as, after the outbreak of the Civil War, the Company was no longer able to invoke the protection of its royal charter, and the efforts made to induce the parliament to grant a fresh one proved fruitless. An attempt in 1649 to raise capital for a new joint stock was frustrated by the appearance of another rival body (consisting partly of those who had acted with Courteen), headed by Lord Fairfax, with a scheme for establishing colonies in the East, particularly on Assada (an island off the north-western coast of Madagascar), on Pulo Run (when it should be recovered from the Dutch), and on some part of the coast of India—all these being intended to serve as fortified centres of commerce, after the pattern of Goa and Batavia. Under pressure from the Council of State, both bodies agreed to a modified scheme under which the trade was continued by a "United Joint Stock" for five years, much on the previous lines. The attempt to colonise Assada proved an utter failure, and the chief outcome of the new stock was the establishment of trade at Hugli and other inland places in Bengal. In 1653–4 (as already noted) the position of the English in the East was severely shaken by the successes of the Dutch in the war that had broken out between the two nations; and when the five years for which the United Joint Stock had undertaken to send out ships came to an end, it was found impossible, in the disturbed state of England, to raise further capital. Private merchants took advantage of the situation to dispatch a considerable number of ships and, although the Company did not altogether cease its operations, they were on a much diminished scale. The retrenchments made in consequence on the eastern side of India have been already noted; in the Moghul's dominions Agra and other inland stations were ordered to be abandoned; and English trade was practically confined to a few seaports. Such was the state of things when the grant of a fresh exclusive charter by Cromwell in 1657 put new life into the Company and enabled an effective trading stock to be raised.

The commerce of the English in India, though temporarily at a low ebb, was by this time firmly established; and it may be well to examine briefly its general character and the conditions under which it was carried on.[1] When the English commenced to trade in the dominions of the Moghul, they found there a voluminous and valuable commerce and a well-developed mercantile system. Expert merchants, often commanding large supplies of capital, were established in all the principal centres; money could be remitted readily between the chief towns by means of bills of exchange; and marine insurance is mentioned as early as 1622. The chief trend of trade was westwards, either by land through Kandahar to Persia or else by sea through the

---

[1] For a detailed account see Foster, "English commerce with India 1608–58," in the *Journal of the Royal Society of Arts*, 19 April, 1918.

ports of Gujarat and Sind to the Red Sea or the Persian Gulf; but there was also, until the Dutch monopolised the traffic, a considerable commerce between Surat and Achin and other parts of the Eastern Archipelago. In Western and Northern India the chief areas with which the Company's servants at first concerned themselves were Hindustan proper (the valleys of the Jumna and of the upper Ganges) and the fertile province of Gujarat. Bengal and Bihar were too remote from the headquarters at Surat; and although in 1620 some factors were dispatched from Agra to open up trade at Patna, in order to procure the local piece-goods and Bengal raw silk, the experiment proved a failure. The factors were withdrawn in the following year and (as we have seen) it was not until a later period that English trade was established in Bengal, this time by way of the Coromandel Coast. Of the Indian products purchased in the earlier years for the European markets the most important were indigo and cotton goods; though from 1625 onwards we note a growing demand in England for saltpetre and Malabar pepper. The indigo was procured mainly from Sarkhej (near Ahmadabad) or from Biana (near Agra), and its extensive use in Europe for dyeing purposes made it at first the most valuable article of the Company's trade. Soon, however, cotton goods, both the plain and the patterned, came into favour at home, the former displacing for household use the more expensive linens imported from Holland and Germany, the latter finding great acceptance for hangings and other decorative purposes; insomuch that in 1624 the governor of the Company declared that England was saved annually a quarter of a million sterling by the substitution of Indian calicoes for foreign linens. Of miscellaneous exports to England may be mentioned cotton yarn (largely used for fustians and other cloth manufactures), drugs, lac (for dyeing), carpets, and (later) sugar. Raw silk formed also an important item in the lading of the earlier ships; this, however, was almost entirely of Persian origin. The chief commodities brought from England were broadcloth, which was chiefly in demand at court; tin and lead, though after a time the competition of supplies from the Malay Peninsula made it unprofitable to import the former; quicksilver and vermilion; Mediterranean coral, for which there was a constant demand; ivory, of African origin; tapestries; gold and silver embroideries; and other articles of European manufacture. In the main, however, the factors were forced to rely, for the purchase of Indian commodities, on the importation of bullion or specie, the favourite form of the latter being the Spanish rial of eight. Most of the silver thus imported was at once coined into rupees at the Indian mints. Gold was occasionally brought out, either in bar or in coin, but not at first to any great extent. Subsidiary supplies were obtained from the Far East, and later from Guinea (in the form of gold dust). In providing funds for lading the returning ships, the English merchants were helped by the

profits made on intermediate voyages in Eastern waters, especially
to Mokha and Gombroon; as also by the sums earned by carrying
native merchants and their goods to and from those ports. Nor did
they hesitate to borrow freely from Indian merchants and bankers to
fill their ships, though these loans went far to reduce the profits on the
trade, owing to the high rates of interest prevailing. The volume of
English trade with India was by no means large. In the first fifteen
years (1615–29) twenty-seven vessels, averaging rather more than
500 tons apiece, were dispatched from Surat to London; while in the
next fifteen (1630–44) the number was only twenty-one. The cost of
the cargoes (which generally included goods from Persia and Bantam)
is only occasionally given, but it seems to have averaged during the
second of these two periods about £50,000 per annum. To this figure
must be added the value of the goods sent home from the Coromandel
Coast, though as regards this not even an estimate can be framed.
Obviously the commerce carried on by the English was only an insignificant proportion of the total seaborne trade of India; and it was
not by any means equal to that of the Dutch in the same region. The
Company's servants had many difficulties to contend with, even when
the land was at peace and no extraordinary obstacle presented itself,
such as the attempt made in 1633 to constitute the indigo trade a
royal monopoly, or the embargo laid thirteen years later by Prince
Aurangzib upon the sale of saltpetre to the English, for fear lest, as
an ingredient of gunpowder, it might be used against Muslims. In
the purchase of goods the factors were hampered by the intricacies of
the monetary system and the varying weights and measures; and these
difficulties, combined with their slight knowledge of the various
languages—in which few of them attained much proficiency—
necessitated the employment of brokers, who fleeced both sides
impartially. Again, the producers of the goods were intensely conservative, and when the Company wrote for piece-goods of special
sizes or indigo unmixed with sand, great trouble was experienced in
persuading the weavers or indigo-makers to depart from their customary practices. There were also difficulties of transport. Goods
from up-country had to be carried down to the port either in ox-carts
or on the backs of camels or oxen. The roads were mostly mere tracks,
impassable in bad weather, and often infested with robbers. The
exaction of petty duties on the way, in spite of imperial farmans,
proved a constant source of dispute; while in the cities, and especially
at the ports, the officials were apt to be overbearing and extortionate.
It is true that the European trader suffered no worse treatment than
the Hindu or the Armenian; indeed, his position was often strong
enough to enable him to resist with success. It was usually easy to
make friends at court by the presentation of Western curiosities, and
the mere threat of appealing to the emperor was sometimes sufficient
to render the local authorities compliant. Above all, the knowledge

that the English and Dutch were mighty at sea and could easily stop the commerce of a port—thereby injuring the customs revenue—formed a powerful restraint. As President Blackman explained in 1652 to the governor of a Malabar port that was undergoing disciplinary treatment in this way, "God hath given us power on the sea that, if wee bee wronged on the land, wee may right ourselves there"; and although such action involved serious risks, neither the English nor the Dutch hesitated to take it when more peaceable methods failed.

One great hindrance to the Company's trade, both outwards and homewards, was the competition of goods brought out or taken home by its own servants. For some time attempts were made to suppress this private trade by requiring the factors and ships' officers to sign penalty bonds and by confiscating their goods when they offended; later on, lists were drawn up of commodities in which the Company's employees might legitimately speculate, while leaving to their masters the trade in the more valuable items. But all was in vain. The articles which the Company wished to engross were naturally those most in demand and yielding the highest profits. Men went to the East to make money—for their meagre wages offered no temptation—and though some refrained from trenching upon their employers' monopolies, most had no scruple in taking advantage of every opportunity that presented itself. Capital was easily procured from friends at home or from Indian merchants, who were only too glad to share thus in the benefits of the privileges accorded to English goods, including favourable terms of freight and freedom from customs at Gombroon, Fort St George, Masulipatam, and elsewhere. At last, finding it hopeless to suppress such competition in the port-to-port trade (which the factors could carry on, if necessary, under the names of Indian merchants), the Company in 1661 resolved to confine itself to the direct trade between England and India. Another step in the same direction was taken in 1664, when the trade, outwards and homewards, in jewels, musk, civet, ambergris, etc., was thrown open, subject to registration and the payment of a small percentage for "permission and freight". After this the Company's efforts were mainly devoted to preventing at home the exportation or importation of forbidden goods, seizing them when found and inflicting penalties on those responsible. Even then its success was by no means great; and at home, as in the East, its profits suffered considerably by this illicit traffic.

Cromwell's hesitation to grant a fresh monopoly of Eastern trade on the lines of previous charters was largely due to an acute difference of opinion amongst those concerned as to the advisability of continuing the joint-stock system. A strong party, including several merchants whose influence with the Protector was considerable, preferred the "regulated system" followed by the Levant and certain other companies, permitting members to trade independently. The controversy lasted long enough to give the system of more or less open trade a trial; for since the United Joint Stock virtually ceased to send out capital after 1654, while the charter restrictions were quite inoperative, for about three years the markets of the East were free to all comers. As we have seen, advantage was taken of this by a number of merchants, including many members of the Company, to dispatch ships to the Indies; but the results were far from satisfactory to those responsible for the ventures. In India itself there ensued a ruinous competition among their agents, both in the sale of their cargoes and in the purchase of goods for the return voyage; while at home the rush to dispose of the latter produced a disheartening drop in prices. The merchants concerned soon realised that after all there were advantages in the old system, under which such competition was eliminated. A further sobering influence was exerted by the continued successes of the Dutch and their evident intention of ousting the Portuguese from their remaining possessions in India. The most likely method of countering such schemes seemed to be to oppose to them a united front such as could scarcely be expected from a "regulated" company; and it may be added that the spectacle of the prosperity attained by the Dutch East India Company—itself working by means of a joint stock—probably went far to remove the prejudice which had been inspired against the system by the poor results secured by the English Company in recent years. It is therefore not surprising to find that by February, 1657, the principal merchants engaged in the trade, including many of the chief "interlopers", were agreed in desiring the continuance of the joint-stock system. At the same time the existing Company resolved to endure no further delay, but to dispose by auction of all its rights and privileges and to withdraw from the trade. This quickly produced a decision on the part of the Protector and his advisers to grant a charter substantially on the lines of those of Elizabeth and James I; and on 19 October, 1657, this document passed the great seal.[1] Thereupon a new joint stock of nearly £740,000 was subscribed, though as a matter of fact only one-half of the capital was ever called up. The new stock, it is important to note, was to be a permanent one, with the proviso that periodical valuations (the first being fixed for 1664) were to be made, when shareholders were to be allowed to withdraw their proportionate shares of the assets. For the first time, therefore, the Company acquired a fixed capital, in lieu of successive stocks raised and distributed at short intervals.

Cromwell's charter of course lost its validity upon the restoration of the monarchy. King Charles, however, made no difficulty about granting a fresh one (3 April, 1661), which repeated with certain modifications and additions the grant of 1609. Power was given to

---

[1] For its terms see *Court Minutes*, 1655–59, p. xvii.

the Company to seize and send home interlopers: to wage war and conclude peace with non-Christian princes: and to appoint governors, who, in conjunction with their councils, were to exercise civil and criminal jurisdiction at the various settlements. Under this authority the agent at Madras was in 1666 created governor of Fort St George; while on the acquisition of Bombay the Company in like manner appointed the Surat president to be governor of that island. In view of later controversies, it is worth noting that the Company begged the king to get the new charter confirmed by parliament. Some steps were taken in that direction, but nothing was achieved. Similarly, in the case of Cromwell's charter, the Protector had promised to obtain parliamentary sanction for the Company's privileges, but had failed to do so.

The East India Company now entered upon a period of great commercial prosperity, due chiefly to the increasing demand for calicoes, tea, and coffee. Although for some years it prudently refrained from distributing its profits, using them instead to strengthen its position, a dividend of 20 per cent. on the paid-up capital was distributed in each of the years 1662–4, and one of double that amount in 1665. The losses sustained in the two wars with Holland (1665–7 and 1672–4) caused a temporary set-back; but in the main a satisfactory rate of dividend was maintained, and in 1682 the Company was able not only to pay 50 per cent. in money but also to declare a bonus of double that figure, crediting each shareholder with the half-payment still due on the original subscription. John Evelyn, who had been one of the subscribers in 1657, records in his diary that he now sold his share of £500 (on which he had paid £250) to the Royal Society for £750. Had he retained it until 1691, it would have given him an annual average of nearly 22 per cent. on his original outlay.

The prosperity enjoyed by the Company throughout the reign of Charles II excited some dissatisfaction among the general body of English merchants, who felt themselves aggrieved that this profitable commerce should be confined by royal charter within so narrow a channel. In the East there were not wanting interlopers who boldly defied the Company's authority; while at home the right of any power other than parliament to impose such restrictions upon foreign trade was continually questioned. Some attempts were made within the Company itself to widen its membership and give greater elasticity; but these had little result, as the majority held firmly to their rights of monopoly. In 1683–5 the issue was fought out in the law courts, with the result that Chief Justice Jeffreys upheld the legality of the Company's privileges and confirmed its claim to seize interlopers. The victory seemed complete. Sir Josia Child, who was the dominant figure in the Company's administration, had secured the favour of both King Charles and his brother James; and the latter, a year after his accession, gave the Company a fresh charter confirming all its privileges. Then came an unexpected blow in the shape of the Revolution. The new government was largely dependent on the Whig party, and the hopes of the opponents of monopoly rose high. A vigorous campaign was organised in support of the demand for a revision of the existing system; while the press teemed with pamphlets for and against the Company, to whose enemies were now added the various traders who were affected by its importation of printed calicoes and manufactured silks. The battle was long and furious. The Company defended itself ably and at times unscrupulously; but the arguments of its opponents made a great impression, and public feeling was on the whole in favour of their claims. Early in 1690 a parliamentary committee recommended that the trade should be granted to a new joint-stock body, to be established by act; and two years later the House of Commons, after the failure of a bill intended to widen the existing Company by increasing its capital to £1,500,000, presented an address to King William, praying him to withdraw the current charter and grant a fresh one on such terms as he might see fit. This could not be done without three years' notice; but while discussion was proceeding, the Company itself, by omitting to pay punctually a tax recently imposed, forfeited its charter.[1] A new grant was made in October, 1693, which practically carried out the wishes of parliament by doubling the capital, restricting the amount of stock that could be held by any one member, and providing that any merchant might join on payment of £5. This arrangement, however, though it considerably increased the number of shareholders, did not pacify the Company's opponents. Attempts were still made to disregard the charter by sending out private ships; and, upon the Company endeavouring to stop one of these (nominally bound for a Spanish port), the matter was carried to the House of Commons. A committee was appointed which reported that the detention was illegal, and in January, 1694, the House passed a resolution "that all the subjects of England have equal right to trade to the East Indies, unless prohibited by Act of Parliament". This naturally caused much exultation among the Company's enemies, who were now able to allege parliamentary authority for trading in the forbidden area.

In 1695 competition was threatened from an unexpected quarter. Seventy-eight years earlier James I had granted a patent for a Scottish East India Company, but had soon cancelled it under pressure from his English subjects. Now the project was revived, and the Scottish Parliament passed an act incorporating a company for the purpose of trading to Africa and the East and West Indies. By the terms of the act half the capital might be held outside Scotland; and when it was

---

[1] Sir William Hunter has suggested (*History of British India*, II, 310) that this was done of set purpose, Child being convinced that his lavish bribery at court would enable him to secure a fresh charter on favourable terms. It seems, however, unlikely that the Company would in this way put itself at the mercy of the government, and the actual outcome was that it had to concede many of the demands it had so long resisted.

found that £300,000 had been secretly subscribed in London, the English Company in alarm brought the matter before both Houses of Parliament. National jealousy came at once into play, with the result that the Commons resolved to take drastic action against the subscribers and to impeach the promoters of the scheme. This deterred the English members from paying up their subscriptions, and so the financial position of the new venture was seriously weakened. The dreaded competition in the East Indies never eventuated, for the new Company's energies were exhausted in a disastrous attempt to found a settlement at Darien, in Central America; yet the opposition of England rankled long in Scottish breasts, despite the fact that one of the articles for the union of the two kingdoms provided for the repayment to the shareholders of their capital with interest.

In England the uncertainty prevailing as to the validity of the East India Company's privileges led that body to apply in 1696 for parliamentary sanction to its trade; but this proved unsuccessful. However, two years later the financial needs of King William's government brought the matter to an issue. The monopoly was virtually put up to auction between the contending bodies. The existing Company, which, owing to great losses during the war with France, was not in a position to make a high bid, offered to increase its capital to £1,500,000, and out of this to make a loan to the government of £700,000 at 4 per cent. interest; while its competitors undertook to form a new company which would lend £2,000,000 at 8 per cent. The latter terms, despite the higher rate of interest, proved the more attractive, and a bill providing for a loan on these conditions was introduced. Thereupon the East India Company offered to find the £2,000,000 required, since its privileges could not be saved on any other terms; but the proposal came too late, and the bill received the royal assent in July, 1698. It provided for a subscription of £2,000,000 sterling as a loan to the state, which in return would grant to a "General Society", made up of the subscribers, the exclusive right of trading to the East Indies, with a saving clause allowing the existing Company to continue its operations until the expiry of the three years' notice required by its charter, i.e. until September, 1701. The concession made to the new body was to last until the government repaid the loan, and this was not to be done until after 1711. The members of the "General Society" might either trade separately, to the value each year of the amounts they had severally subscribed, or they might unite in a fresh joint-stock company to which His Majesty was empowered to grant a suitable charter. The great bulk of the subscribers chose the latter alternative, and on 5 September, 1698, they were accordingly incorporated by royal charter under the style of "The English Company Trading to the East Indies". The management was entrusted to twenty-four directors, who were to appoint from among themselves a chairman and deputy-chairman; and we may note in passing that the shareholders were not required, as in the earlier Company, to pay a separate sum for admission to the freedom.

The new body set to work with energy. Ships and factors were dispatched to the East; while a special ambassador, Sir William Norris, was sent to obtain from the Moghul emperor the grant of all necessary privileges. However, it soon became apparent that to oust the older Company from its well-established position was a task beyond the strength of the new corporation. Its original capital having been lent to the government and the interest received thereon being insufficient to maintain the trade, fresh money had to be raised from the members, and this proved difficult of accomplishment. Moreover, the "Old Company" (as it was now termed) had taken the precaution to subscribe, in the name of its treasurer, £315,000 to the loan, thereby obtaining the right to trade in his name each year to that amount, even after the expiration of its privileges; while the difficulty that the Company would cease to be a corporate body when its notice expired was surmounted in April, 1700, by obtaining an act permitting its continuance under its own name until the repayment of the £2,000,000 loan. This astute move decided the issue. The "New Company" had already made tentative proposals for an amalgamation, and as time went on this was seen on both sides to be the only possible solution. Under pressure from the government, an agreement was reached early in 1702. The actual direction of the trade during the process of amalgamation was entrusted to a body of "Managers", half to be appointed by each Company, the annual exports being provided in equal proportions by the two bodies. This arrangement was to last for seven years, during which the servants of both Companies in the East were to clear all debts and wind up the separate stocks sent out before the union. At the end of the time the Old Company was to surrender its charter and make over the islands of Bombay and St Helena to the New Company, the charter of which was to be henceforth the basis of "The United Company of Merchants of England Trading to the East Indies". Further, the Old Company was to purchase from the New sufficient stock to equalise their respective shares; while the latter was to pay to the former half the difference between the values of the respective "dead stocks" (i.e. buildings, etc.) in the East.

This agreement still left room for disputes, to settle which an act was passed in March, 1708, under which the Earl of Godolphin was appointed arbitrator; the term of the Company's privileges was extended by another fifteen years; and it was given the right of buying out those members of the "General Society" who had elected to trade on their own account. In return for these concessions the United Company was required to lend the exchequer a further sum of £1,200,000 without interest—thus reducing the rate of interest on the whole debt to 5 per cent. Godolphin's award was issued in September, 1708, and the union was consummated in the following March. The struggle was now at an end; and it is interesting to note that its result was to confirm the monopoly of the trade to a chartered joint-stock company, though on an improved basis. The right of parliament to control the conditions of this concession had, however, been established; also the principle of requiring in return some assistance towards the national finances.

Having thus reviewed the course of events at home, we must now follow the development of English trade in India during the same fifty years, a period which synchronised roughly with the long reign of the Emperor Aurangzib. Soon after the Restoration the Company withdrew from the port-to-port trade; and as the factories in Upper India (Agra, Lucknow, etc.) had been abandoned, the English settlements were now in groups centring at Surat, Madras, and Hugli respectively. It will therefore be convenient to deal with them more or less as separate entities.

In Western India the outstanding feature of the period is the gradual rise of Bombay, which had been ceded by the Portuguese to King Charles II in 1661, taken possession of on his behalf in 1665, and made over by him to the East India Company three years later. That its development was slow is no matter for surprise. The island was far from healthy; the neighbouring mainland produced little of commercial value, and the barrier of the Western Ghats—to say nothing of the insecurity resulting from the constant warfare between the Moghuls and the Marathas—precluded any regular communication in that direction with Indian trade centres; while the depredations of the bold pirates of the Malabar Coast were a perpetual menace to shipping. For nearly twenty years, therefore, Surat retained its position as the headquarters of English commerce and the seat of the presidency. Bombay, however, could afford to bide its time. It possessed a magnificent harbour; its security, thanks to its position and its fortifications, afforded a striking contrast to the experience of Surat, which was sacked by the Maratha chief, Sivaji, in 1664 and again in 1670; while the mild and impartial rule of the English proved an attraction to traders who had suffered from the tyranny of the officials on the mainland. Its potentialities did not escape the keen eye of Gerald Aungier, who in 1669 succeeded Sir George Oxenden as president at Surat and governor of Bombay; and he made it the main task of his administration to put the new settlement on a satisfactory basis. Courts of judicature were established; the local revenue was settled on equitable terms; a suitable currency was introduced;[1] and inducements were held out to merchants and craftsmen to settle on the island. As the result of all this, by the time of Aungier's death

[1] The first suggestion for this was made in 1668 (*English Factories*, 1668-9, p. 52). See also Foster, "The first English coinage at Bombay," in the *Numismatic Chronicle*, 4th series, vol. VI.

(June, 1677) Bombay was on the high road to prosperity, and its population (according to the estimate of Dr John Fryer) had risen to 60,000, three times the number of its inhabitants under Portuguese rule.

The one desire of the English merchants was to be left to pursue their calling in peace; but this was impossible in the conditions of the time. The perennial warfare between the imperial forces and the Marathas was quickened in 1681 by the arrival in the Deccan of Aurangzib himself, who thus entered upon the long campaign which was to engross his attention until his death. Unhappily for Bombay, the war was not confined to the land but was carried on at sea as well, the Sidi of Janjira (about 45 miles south of Bombay) acting on behalf of the emperor against his inveterate foes the Marathas. The Sidi claimed the right to make Bombay harbour a place of refuge for his fleets, and this could hardly be gainsaid without offending Aurangzib; but the effect of the concession was to make the neighbouring waters a scene of continual warfare. In 1679 Sivaji seized the island of Khaneri at the mouth of the harbour; whereupon the Sidi fortified its neighbour, Underi, with the result that all vessels entering the bay were liable to attack from one or the other. With the Marathas themselves the relations of the English were on an uncertain footing; while further south the Malabar pirates were a constant source of trouble. Even at Surat, which was distant from the scene of action, the strain imposed upon the Moghul finances was felt in the increased exactions of the local officials and their arbitrary disregard of the protests of the Company's factors.

In these conditions of turmoil it became more and more evident that only by being strong themselves could the English secure the continuance of their commerce; and a few months before his death Aungier, himself no lover of war, wrote to his employers that the trade could only be carried on sword in hand. In earlier times the home authorities had always turned a deaf ear to counsels of vigorous action, and any outlay on fortifications had been looked upon with the greatest repugnance. Now, however, came a change, mainly under the influence of Sir Josia Child, who, after seven years' service in the directorate, became governor in 1681, and continued to be the dominant force in the Company until his death (1699). He held firmly the view that the true line of action was to follow the example of the Dutch, by building up a power on the Indian coast-line which should be sufficiently strong to repel all attacks and to enforce respect from its neighbours, even the Moghul emperor himself. In this scheme Bombay was to be the counterpart of the Dutch settlement at Batavia. It was to be strongly fortified and provided with sufficient military and naval strength to protect English trade; while the cost of all this was to be met from increased rents, customs dues, and municipal taxation. Similar measures were to be taken at Madras; and it was in a letter to that place (December, 1687) that the aims of the Company were defined, in an oft-quoted passage, as being "to establish such a politie of civill and military power, and create and secure such a large revenue to maintaine both...as may bee the foundation of a large, well-grounded, sure English dominion in India for all time to come".

In the promotion of these designs Sir Josia found a willing agent in his namesake,[1] John Child, who in 1682 became president of Surat and governor of Bombay. The firstfruits of the new policy were, however, disconcerting. The endeavour to raise the revenue and cut down the expenditure at Bombay caused a revolt of the garrison in 1683 under its commandant, Richard Keigwin, who until November in the following year governed the settlement in the name of King Charles, submitting only on the appearance of a naval force with a royal mandate for the surrender of the place. The rebellion having been quelled, the Company proceeded to develop its schemes. Already President Child had been appointed captain-general of the Company's sea and land forces on that coast; and in October, 1686, when the Company, goaded by the injuries received in Bengal (as described later), had resolved to make a firm stand against the exactions of the Moghul officials, whatever the consequences might be, a further step was taken. Child (who had been created a baronet in the preceding year) was given the imposing title of Captain-General,[2] Admiral, and Commander-in-Chief of the Company's forces throughout its possessions, as well as Director-General of all mercantile affairs; and he was authorised to proceed to Madras and Bengal to regulate matters in those parts, should he see fit. Ordinarily he was to reside at Bombay, which in consequence (May, 1687) superseded Surat as the headquarters of the western presidency. To complete the organisation of the English possessions (and especially to check the interlopers who were making such inroads upon the Company's trade) a court of admiralty was erected at Bombay in 1684, and another at Madras two years later, both under letters patent

---

[1] It has been generally stated that the two Childs were brothers; but Mr Oliver Strachey has shown that this was not the case (*Keigwin's Rebellion*, pp. 20, 162).

[2] This designation—usually shortened to "General"—was explained in a letter of August, 1687, as being intended to give to its holder "the same preheminence and authority which the Dutch confer upon their Generall at Batavia". Its subsequent history is worth noting. After the death of Sir John Child, Sir John Goldsborough was sent out (1691) as commissary and supervisor; and two years later he was made captain-general and commander-in-chief, with Madras as his headquarters, while Sir John Gayer was to act as his lieutenant-general and governor of Bombay. On the death of Goldsborough, Gayer succeeded to the post of "General" (1694), remaining at Bombay; while Higginson, the Madras president, became lieutenant-general. Ten years later (Gayer being kept in prison at Surat by the Moghul authorities) Sir Nicholas Waite, the new governor of Bombay, assumed the title of "General"; and upon his dismissal in 1708 his successor, Aislabie, laid claim to the same designation. The title was abolished in 1715, when the new post of president and governor of Bombay was created, with Boone as its first occupant. The title of lieutenant-general had lapsed in 1698, when Thomas Pitt was appointed governor of Madras.

obtained from the king in 1683. Further, in 1688 a municipality was established at Madras, with a mayor and twelve aldermen, including several Portuguese and Indians—a concession intended to reconcile the inhabitants to a system of local taxation.

Into the war with the Moghuls which resulted from the troubles in Bengal the English on the western coast entered only after a long hesitancy and in a feeble manner. The seizure of some Moghul vessels brought about a rupture towards the end of 1688, with the consequence that the factors at Surat were imprisoned. Child in retaliation captured a number of richly freighted ships.[1] Thereupon ensued a siege of Bombay by the Moghul forces, until in 1690 the English put an end to the war by a humiliating submission, involving the payment of a considerable sum. Child, whose dismissal was one of the conditions of peace, died just as the negotiations were reaching a conclusion.

The remainder of the period was filled with trouble, owing largely to the depredations of the English pirates who were swarming in the Indian Ocean and capturing Indian vessels. For these their peaceful compatriots were held responsible, with the result that for some time all the factors at Surat and Broach were kept in prison by the Moghul authorities. On top of all this came the bitter rivalry between the servants of the Old and New Companies, elsewhere alluded to. Before leaving the subject mention should be made of the settlements established during the half-century on the Malabar Coast, mainly in order to obtain a supply of pepper. The chief of these were at Rajapur, which factory was plundered by Sivaji in 1661, subsequently re-established, but abandoned in 1679; at Tellicherri, where the English settled in 1683; at Anjengo, first established about 1694; and at Karwar, where a factory was maintained (with some intermissions) from 1660 until the middle of the eighteenth century and was then withdrawn, leaving Tellicherri and Anjengo to supply the needs of the pepper traffic.

On the eastern side of India the new start, made upon the grant of Cromwell's charter, separated the Coast factories (Fort St George, Masulipatam, etc.) from those in Bengal and Bihar (centring at Hugli), each of these two groups forming an agency, under the presidency of Surat; but this arrangement lasted only till 1661, when Madras became once more the seat of government for all the factories on that side of India. The domestic history of the agency for the next quarter of a century was on the whole one of peaceful progress. The capture of the Portuguese settlement at St Thomé by the forces of the king of Golconda in 1662 drove a considerable number of its inhabitants to the shelter of Fort St George; and about 1670 the population of

---

[1] In 1693–4 the Company paid into the royal exchequer £16,638 as the king's tenth share of the value of prizes taken during the war (W. R. Scott's *Joint Stock Companies*, III, 537).

Madras was estimated roughly at 40,000. The Second Dutch War (1665–7) produced much disturbance of trade, especially as it synchronised with internal trouble. Sir Edward Winter, who had been superseded in 1665 by a new agent from home (George Foxcroft), in the same year seized and imprisoned his successor, charging him with treason, and reassumed the government in the name of King Charles. For nearly three years Madras remained under his control; then (August, 1668) the arrival of a fleet with a royal mandate induced him to yield his place to Foxcroft, on an assurance that the persons and property of himself and his adherents should be respected. The war of 1672–4 between Holland on the one hand and England and France on the other brought fresh cause of alarm. In 1673 the Company's fleet was defeated and dispersed by a Dutch squadron off Petapoli; while on land there was much fighting round St Thomé, which had been occupied by the French in 1672 but recaptured by the Golconda forces, assisted by the Dutch, in the following year. The incursions of the Marathas into Southern India gave an excuse for strengthening the fortifications of Madras under Sir William Langhorn (agent, 1672–8) and his successor, Sir Streynsham Master (1678–81); while the administration of the latter is also memorable for the reorganisation of the judicial system and the erection of St Mary's church in the fort—the first Anglican church built in India. In 1681 permission was obtained from the Maratha ruler at Jinji for English settlements at Porto Novo, Cuddalore, and Konimedu; while in the following year a factory was established at Vizagapatam. A few years later the kingdom of Golconda was finally subjugated by the Moghul forces, and Aurangzib became the nominal overlord of the English factories on the Coromandel Coast. Negotiations ensued with his general, Zulfikar Khan, who in 1690 confirmed the existing grants for Madras, Masulipatam, and other stations; while in the same year a fort at Devenampatnam (close to Cuddalore) was purchased and made into a new stronghold named Fort St David. In 1693 the boundaries of Madras were enlarged by the grant of three adjoining villages; and during the administration of Thomas Pitt (1698–1709) five more were added, though these were resumed by the Moghul officials in 1711 and were not recovered until six years later, under the grant obtained by Surman from the emperor Farrukhsiyar.

As in the case of the western presidency, Madras suffered much from the rivalry caused by the establishment of the New East India Company; and this is perhaps the most convenient place to narrate briefly the struggle between the two bodies, so far as it affected the settlements in India. The mission of Sir William Norris, to which allusion has already been made, proved a fiasco, and the hopes built thereon by the directors of the New Company were entirely disappointed. After much trouble and delay he reached the camp of

Aurangzib in April, 1701, and was graciously received; but the emperor was irritated by the depredations committed by European pirates upon Indian vessels carrying pilgrims to the Red Sea ports, and the wazir, whom Norris had unwisely offended, threw all sorts of obstacles in his way. The ambassador found that he could only obtain the farmans he desired by undertaking to make compensation for all Indian ships taken by the pirates; and thereupon he quitted the court abruptly and returned to Surat. He died on the homeward voyage in 1702.

Meanwhile the presidents appointed by the New Company had added to the difficulties of their position by quarrelling violently with the representatives of the older body. All three of these new presidents were discharged servants of the Old Company, and this fact added acrimony to the disputes, which were further embittered by the fact that the newcomers had been given the rank of "King's consul", and were not slow to claim jurisdiction over all Englishmen resident in India. This pretension was indignantly repudiated by the servants of the Old Company, who maintained that the privileges of the latter remained intact until 1701 at least. The Indian authorities, while taking little interest in the controversy, were naturally inclined to support the representatives of the older body; and when at Surat the New Company's president, Sir Nicholas Waite, tore down the flag that floated over the rival factory, it was at once replaced under a military guard sent by the Moghul governor. It is true that Waite's charges against the Old Company, of complicity in the piracies from which the Indian traders were suffering, bore fruit in the seizure, by the emperor's orders, of Sir John Gayer and other servants of the older body; but the blow recoiled on the New Company, whose factors in Bengal were also arrested under the same instructions. Most of the Old Company's servants in that province secured themselves in the recently erected Fort William at Calcutta; while Madras successfully resisted the troops sent to occupy it. In the latter presidency John Pitt, the New Company's representative, had established his headquarters at Masulipatam, whence he carried on a violent controversy with his relative Thomas Pitt, the governor of Madras, much to his own discomfiture. The distractions caused by these disputes, and Norris's failure to obtain authority for new settlements, formed powerful arguments for an amalgamation of the two companies; and when once this was effected, the first task of the court of managers was to heal the dissensions in India. Accordingly the grant of consular powers was rescinded; at Madras Governor Pitt was confirmed in his post; in Bengal a curious experiment was tried for a time of a council of four members who were to preside in turn; while on the western side Gayer was to be governor of Bombay and Waite president at Surat. A proviso that, in the event of Gayer's continued imprisonment, Waite was to act for him enabled the latter to take possession of the post, which he continued to hold until his dismissal in 1708.

It now remains to trace the progress of the English in Bengal, Bihar, and Orissa. Under the arrangements made upon Cromwell's grant of a charter, an agent was appointed, with Hugli as his headquarters, having under his control the factories of Patna, Kasimbazar, and Balasore, the last named being the port at which all cargoes were received or shipped.[1] This arrangement was, however, short-lived, for in 1661 the agency was abolished and the factors were replaced under the agent at Madras. The importance of Dacca, both as the seat of government and as a centre for the purchase of fine cotton goods, led the Company in 1668 to sanction the formation of a factory in that city; while a few years later others were opened at Rajmahal and at Malda. The trade of the English in these parts grew steadily both in volume and in value. The Company looked to Bengal for its regular supply of saltpetre, for which there was an ever-increasing demand in Europe; while great quantities of silk and silk goods were also purchased, artisans being brought from England to improve the methods of manufacture. Sugar and cotton yarn were further articles of export, and by 1680 the annual investment in Bengal had risen to £150,000.[2] In hopes of further development, the Company in 1681 determined to make the settlements there independent of Madras; and accordingly in the following year William Hedges, one of the "committees", was sent out as "Agent and Governor of all affairs and factories in the Bay of Bengal". The experiment did not prove a success. In 1684 Hedges was dismissed and the Bengal factories were once again placed under Fort St George, the agent at which was given the new title of President and Governor for the Coast and Bay.

Now came a time of serious trouble. For many years there had been friction with the local officials over the question of way-dues and customs. From the beginning the English had aimed at securing complete exemption from such imposts, in consideration of an annual present of 3000 rupees; and in 1656 they had obtained from Shah Shuja, who was then governing the province, a grant freeing them from all demands on this score.[3] Such an arrangement was much to the benefit of the factors themselves, since their private trade passed free as well as the Company's, while the necessary presents went down to the account of the latter; and accordingly they made strenuous efforts to secure its continuance. On the other hand the Moghul officials saw no reason why the fast-increasing commerce of the English should escape the tolls levied upon other merchants, nor did they recognise that the nishan of Shah Shuja was binding upon his

---

[1] The establishment at Hariharpur (in Orissa), the earliest English settlement in those parts, had been withdrawn in 1642.

[2] Bruce's *Annals*, II, 451.

[3] For grants relating to Bengal, 1633–60, see the appendix to *English Factories*, 1655–60.

successors. The factors made several attempts to settle the matter by obtaining an imperial farman in their favour, but without success; and although Shaista Khan, then governor, gave them in 1678 a fresh nishan, with the approval of the emperor, freeing them from dues, these were soon again demanded. Two years later a farman was at last obtained from Aurangzib, which seemed to settle the dispute in favour of the English; but the wording was ambiguous, and the Indian officials declared that it really authorised them to demand the same dues as were paid by the English at Surat. The factors were powerless to resist any exactions the authorities chose to make, since it was easy to enforce the demand by stopping the saltpetre boats on their way down the Ganges or by preventing the native merchants from dealing with the English; and full advantage was taken of both methods to extort money from the factors. Gradually the latter came to the conclusion that force was the only remedy and that it was essential for their security to establish, at or near the mouth of the Ganges, a fortified settlement similar to those at Madras and Bombay. This they might make the centre of their trade, and thither they might withdraw when threatened; while from such a base they could at any time exert pressure upon the viceroy by stopping the sea-borne trade of the province. The home authorities, who (as we have seen) were already persuaded of the necessity of adopting a bold policy, readily fell in with this view, and in 1686 they sent out orders that the Bengal factories should be withdrawn and an attempt made to seize Chittagong, for which purpose they dispatched several ships and a small force of soldiers. At the same time on the western side of India the Moghul coast was to be blockaded and the local shipping seized; while the Coast settlements were to assist with the full strength of their resources. The enterprise was a rash one, though all might have been well if the Company had left the control of affairs entirely in the hands of Job Charnock, its experienced agent in Bengal; not that fighting would have been entirely avoided, but an accommodation would have been reached more speedily and nothing would have been done as regards the absurd plan of attacking so distant a port as Chittagong. In point of fact a rupture was forced by the Moghul governor of Hugli, who in October, 1686, made an attack upon the factory there.[1] The assault was repelled, but Charnock deemed it wise to abandon the place and drop down the river to Sutanati (on the site of the modern Calcutta), from whence he carried on some negotiations with the viceroy. These failing, the English withdrew further down the Hugli river and fixed their headquarters on the island of Hijili, at its mouth; while, in reprisal for the injuries sustained, their ships sacked and burnt the town of Balasore. In their new station they were blockaded by the Moghul forces, while fever made great havoc among

[1] For a detailed account of the operations see the introduction to C. R. Wilson's *Early Annals of the English in Bengal*, vol. 1.

the small garrison; but timely reinforcements enabled Charnock to
effect an agreement under which, in the autumn of 1687, the English
returned to Sutanati, where they remained for a year unmolested.
The home authorities, however, were obstinately bent upon the plan
of a fortified settlement in Bengal; with the result that in September,
1688, a fresh naval force arrived under Captain William Heath, who
had plenary powers to carry out the projected attack upon Chittagong. Despite the opposition of Charnock the new settlement was
abandoned, and in January the fleet arrived at Chittagong, only to
find it much too strong to be assailed with any chance of success;
whereupon Heath decided to retreat to Madras. However, the conclusion of peace in the early part of 1690, on the initiative of the
Bombay authorities, paved the way for the return of the English to
Bengal; and the new viceroy, uneasy at the loss of trade resulting
from the disturbances, wrote to Charnock at Fort St George, inviting
him back. To these overtures the agent would not listen until a
specific promise was added that the grievance over customs should
be redressed—a promise that was redeemed in February, 1691, by an
imperial grant of freedom from all dues, on condition of the payment,
as before, of 3000 rupees *per annum* in lieu thereof. It was in August,
1690, that the English once more settled at Sutanati and erected a few
huts that were destined to grow into the capital of their Indian empire. The site had disadvantages, for it was girdled on the land side
by swamps which rendered it unhealthy; but its position on the eastern
bank of the river gave it security, while it was accessible from the sea
and had good anchorage close inshore. In 1696 a local rebellion
provided an excuse for fortifying the factory; and two years later
permission was obtained to rent the three villages of Sutanati,
Calcutta, and Govindpur for 1200 rupees a year. The fortified factory,
which was named Fort William in honour of King William III, was
made in 1700 the seat of a presidency, Sir Charles Eyre becoming
the first president and governor of Fort William in Bengal.

The domestic history of the East India Company from the time of
the union in 1709 to the middle of the century was one of quiet
prosperity. The value of its imports rose from nearly £500,000 in
1708 to about £1,100,000 in 1748; while its exports increased from
£576,000 (of which £375,000 was in bullion) in 1710 to £1,121,000
(including £816,000 in bullion) forty years later. An act of parliament
obtained in 1711 extended the period of exclusive trade until 1733.
As the latter date approached, a body of merchants made a fresh
attempt to oust the Company from the trade by offering to find the
necessary money to enable the government to pay off the existing
debt, the new loan to bear only 2 per cent. interest; it was proposed
then to organise a new company on a "regulated" basis, open to all
merchants but subject to the payment of a percentage on imports.[1]

---

[1] *Historical MSS. Commission's Reports: Diary of Lord Percival*, p. 65.

The proposal found many supporters, and the East India Company in alarm offered to pay £200,000 to the treasury and to reduce its rate of interest on the government debt to 4 per cent. These terms were accepted, with the result that in 1730 an act was passed prolonging the Company's privileges to 1769. A further extension until 1783 was granted in 1744, at the cost of the loan of a further sum of one million to the government at 3 per cent. An act of 1750 reduced the interest on the earlier loan of £3,200,000 to 3½ per cent. up to Christmas, 1757, and 3 per cent. thereafter. Thus the interest paid by the government on its total indebtedness to the Company was placed on a general level of 3 per cent. The £1,000,000 lent in 1744 was not added to the Company's capital, which remained at £3,200,000 down to 1786, when another £800,000 was raised at a considerable premium. The capital was further increased in 1789 and 1793 by two sums of £1,000,000 each, likewise raised at a high premium; thus making a total of £6,000,000, a figure that was not varied down to 1858.

During the period under consideration the dividend paid by the Company rose rapidly from 5 per cent. in 1708–9 to 10 per cent. in 1711–12. After continuing at that rate till 1722, it dropped to 8 per cent., and in 1732 to 7 per cent. In 1743 it rose again to 8 per cent., and remained at that figure till 1755.

The parliamentary sanction under which the Company's monopoly was exercised effectually debarred other British subjects from any open competition; but there were not wanting enterprising spirits who sought to make profit by taking service with its foreign rivals, particularly the Ostend East India Company. To check this practice the English Company in 1718 obtained an act authorising the seizure of any British subject found trading under such auspices; and further enactments for the same purpose were passed in 1721 and 1723. Owing, however, to the pressure brought to bear by the several governments concerned, this danger was soon after removed (as related elsewhere) by the suspension of the charter of the Ostend Company.

The steady development of the East India Company's trade is shown by the fact that, whereas for the five years 1708–9 to 1712–13 on an average eleven ships were dispatched annually to the East, for the similar period between 1743–4 and 1747–8 the number was twenty per annum, of much larger tonnage. It may be mentioned that at this time, whatever the size of the vessel, the tonnage chartered by the Company was never more than 499 tons. The reason is a curious one. By a clause in the 1698 charter the Company was bound to provide a chaplain for every ship of 500 tons or over; and it would seem that, rather than incur this expense, the directors chose to engage a larger number of vessels, though in effect the cost must have been greater. The obnoxious clause was not repeated in the act of 1773; whereupon the Company began to charter ships at their full measurements, and later on considerably increased its requirements in regard to the size of vessels.

One feature of importance in the Company's history during the closing years of the seventeenth and the first quarter of the eighteenth century was the agitation excited amongst English manufacturers by the competition of the cotton and silk fabrics imported from India. During the early years of the trade the piece-goods brought into the country competed, as we have seen, mostly with linens from the continent, and the greater cheapness of the former ensured them a general welcome, whether they were plain or printed. About 1676, however, calico-printing works were started near London, and the industry quickly became one of importance, with the result that soon protests began to be heard against the importation by the Company of printed Indian calicoes which undersold those produced in England itself. Similar objections were raised by the silk weavers against India-wrought silks, as being detrimental to another rising industry; while behind both parties stood the woollen manufacturers, who alleged that the growing use of these foreign silks and cottons was ruining the staple manufacture of the country. In the spring of 1696 a bill was introduced to restrain the wearing of Indian silks, printed calicoes, etc.; but the opposition of the East India Company resulted in such vital amendments that the bill was allowed to drop. A fresh measure was then brought in, only to be abandoned owing to a disagreement between the two Houses; and as a consequence serious riots on the part of the artisans affected occurred in November, 1696, and the following spring. The agitation was continued until an act was passed (1700) forbidding the use of Asiatic silks and printed and dyed calicoes, though these goods might still be brought in for re-exportation. This legislation has been represented as a wrong done to India; but it must be remembered that the latter was then in no closer relation to England than any other country, while the encouragement of home industries was looked upon as a primary duty. Moreover, the effect upon the trade of the two countries was not so detrimental as had been feared, for the demand for raw silk, plain calicoes, and cotton yarn was considerably increased. In 1720 came a fresh turn; violent protests from the woollen and silk manufacturers induced Parliament to forbid the use (with certain exceptions) of calicoes dyed or printed in England. This prohibition, though modified in 1736 by permission to print on cotton stuffs having a linen warp, was maintained until 1774, when the British calico printers were once more allowed to dye and print stuffs wholly made of cotton, provided these were manufactured in Great Britain. The rapid rise of the English cotton industry, based upon Arkwright's inventions, soon removed all fear of Indian competition, though as a matter of fact the prohibitory enactments lingered on the statute book until the nineteenth century.

One special feature of the Company's operations during the period under survey was the development of the trade in tea from China and coffee from the Red Sea ports. Both articles came into use in England about the middle of the seventeenth century, and by 1686 the consumption of tea had increased to such an extent that the Company decided to remove it from the list of articles open to private trade and to reserve the commerce to itself. Supplies were at first procured from Bantam; and after the withdrawal of the English factors from that port in 1682, Surat and Madras became the intermediaries. From the beginning of the eighteenth century attempts were made to establish a regular trade with China to meet the increasing demand for tea, and by 1715 these efforts had proved successful. Some idea of the growth of the trade, and of the gradual reduction in the price of the commodity, is afforded by the fact that, whereas in 1706 the sales amounted to 54,600 lb., fetching £45,000, the amount sold in 1750 was 2,325,000 lb., which realised about £544,000. Coffee made its first appearance in the Company's sale lists at the beginning of 1660. This commodity was easily procurable at Surat, whence there was a constant trade with the Red Sea ports; but later it was found worth while to reopen for the purpose the factory originally started at Mokha early in the seventeenth century. In 1752, however, this arrangement was abandoned and the trade was left to be managed by the supercargoes of the ships employed in the traffic.

As in the preceding section, the history of the period 1700–50 may best be treated by examining in succession the records of the groups forming the respective presidencies of Bengal, Madras, and Bombay. Each of these had its peculiar difficulties, but surmounted them with more or less success; and each went on its way without heeding overmuch what was happening elsewhere. The one exception occurred early in the century, when all three presidencies were concerned in an embassy sent to Delhi to obtain a comprehensive grant from the Moghul emperor. The idea originated with Governor Pitt of Madras in 1708, when the emperor Shah 'Alam I was in Southern India; but before the matter could be put in train the court had returned to Delhi. Further delay was caused by the death of that monarch and the subsequent contest for the crown. When, however, the struggle ended in the accession of Farrukhsiyar, who had shown himself well disposed towards the English, it was resolved to go forward with the project; and the mission, which was under the charge of John Surman, reached Delhi in the summer of 1714. The negotiations were so protracted that it was the middle of July, 1717, before Surman was able to quit the capital, carrying with him the farmans he had obtained. His efforts had been largely aided by the services rendered by William Hamilton, the doctor attached to the mission, in curing the emperor of a painful disease; but the story that the concessions were granted as a reward for Hamilton's assistance is one that will not stand examination. The three farmans brought back by Surman were addressed to the officials of the three provinces—Hyderabad, Gujarat, and Bengal (including Bihar and Orissa)—in which the English were settled. The right of the latter to trade in Bengal free of all dues, subject to the customary payment of 3000 rupees *per annum*, was confirmed: they were to be allowed to rent additional territory round Calcutta and to settle where else they might choose: their long-standing privilege of freedom from dues throughout the province of Hyderabad was continued, the only payment required being the existing rent paid for Madras: certain neighbouring villages, which had long been in dispute, were added to that city: a rearrangement of the Company's land round Vizagapatam was sanctioned: a yearly sum of 10,000 rupees was accepted in satisfaction of all customs and dues at Surat: and the rupees coined by the Company at Bombay were allowed to pass current throughout the imperial dominions. Though Surman had not obtained all for which he had asked, he had secured a great deal, and his embassy stands out as a landmark in the history of the Company's settlements.[1]

The Bengal factors soon discovered that it was easier to obtain an imperial farman than to induce the local officials to obey it, in the disorganised state of the kingdom. Ja'far Khan, the governor of Bengal, openly declared that the English should never enjoy the additional villages round Calcutta specified in the grant; and although possession was obtained of some of them in an indirect manner, it was not until Clive's treaty with Siraj-ud-daula in 1757 that the territory was entirely brought under British control. Nevertheless Calcutta continued to grow in importance and wealth, and by the middle of the century its population was estimated at over 100,000 as compared with the 15,000 of 1704. This, it is true, was partly owing to a great influx about 1742, caused by the invasion of the province by the Marathas. The approach of these raiders created great consternation, for Fort William (finished in 1716) was of little real strength, and moreover its defensive capabilities had just been seriously reduced by the erection of warehouses against its southern face. However, the inhabitants dug a broad ditch round a great part of the town, while batteries placed at various points assisted to secure it from sudden attack. Fortunately these defences were not tested, for the Nawab 'Ali Wardi Khan managed, with the aid of a rival body of Marathas, to clear his province of the invaders; and although the latter returned in 1744, they were then defeated and driven back to their own territories. The general insecurity led to the consideration of many plans for the improvement of Fort William, but the expense, and the natural unwillingness of the owners to consent to the clearing away of the houses that crowded around it, prevented action being taken until

[1] The full story will be found in C. R. Wilson's *Early Annals*, vol. II, pt II.

it was too late. Had greater prevision been exercised, the story of the Black Hole might never have been written.

The domestic history of Calcutta for this period includes also the erection of a church (St Anne's, consecrated in 1709): the building of a fine house for the governor in the fort: and the organisation of a judicial system under a charter granted by George I in September, 1726, which also provided for the appointment of a mayor, sheriff, and aldermen. The courts thus established were similar to those erected at Madras under the same charter, as described later, but they did not come into full operation.

Concerning the subordinate settlements in Bengal there is little to record, save constant quarrels with the local functionaries, who, being now practically uncontrolled from Delhi, made the most of their opportunities to extort money. The trade of the English was very prosperous, alike as regards the regular operations of the Company and the private trade of its servants (which was sheltered under its privileges); and naturally the officials did their best to take toll of it for their own advantage. It was equally to be expected that such exactions should be resisted as far as possible; and hence a lengthy story of disputes and reconciliations.

During this half-century the English settlement at Madras likewise grew and prospered, though its history affords few events that call for notice in the present rapid survey. The absorption in 1717 of five additional villages (originally granted in 1708) has been mentioned already. Twenty-five years later a grant was obtained of Vepery and four other hamlets. The territory occupied by the British was still, however, quite small, comprising a space of about five miles by three; while their only other footholds on the Coromandel Coast were Fort St David at Cuddalore and factories at Vizagapatam and Masulipatam. In 1727 a new charter (this time from the crown, not from the Company) remodelled the Madras corporation, reducing the number of aldermen and appointing a sheriff, to be chosen annually by the governor and council. The mayor and aldermen were authorised to try all civil cases, with an appeal to the governor and council, whose decision was to be final up to 1000 pagodas; when that amount was exceeded, an appeal might be made to the King in Council. The governor and the five senior members of his council were to be justices of the peace for the town and were to hold quarter sessions for the trial of criminal cases.

On the western side of India the commerce of Bombay steadily increased, in spite of the disturbances caused by disputes with the Portuguese and the Marathas, and hostilities with the Malabar pirates, notably the Angrias, who dominated the coast-line between Bombay and Goa and attacked all vessels that offered a reasonable chance of capture. Boone, who was president and governor from 1715 to 1722, not only built a wall round Bombay, to guard against sudden raids, but also constructed a number of fighting ships for the protection of commerce. During the next forty years several expeditions were fitted out against the pirates; but it was not until the capture of Suvarndrug in 1755 by Commodore James and the destruction of Gheria[1] in the following year by Clive and Admiral Watson that the power of the Angrias was broken. In these operations the English were much aided by the cordial relations that had been established with the Peshwa, whose troops co-operated on both occasions. A much less welcome outcome of Maratha prowess was their capture of Bassein from the Portuguese in 1739, which brought them unpleasantly near to Bombay itself.

Of the internal organisation of that town the most noteworthy developments were the establishment of a bank in 1720: the erection of a mayor's court (similar to that at Madras, and created under the same charter) in 1728: and the formation of a large dockyard a few years later, under a Parsi shipbuilder from Surat. By 1744 the population had risen to 70,000, while the revenues amounted to about sixteen lakhs of rupees. Grose, who arrived on the island in 1750, records that the draining of the marshes had materially improved the healthiness of Bombay, while "the mildness of the government and the toleration of all religions" had drawn thither large numbers of artificers and merchants from Surat and other places on the mainland.

Concurrently with the growth and consolidation of the English settlements came increased competition from other European powers. Of the rivalry of the French, Dutch, and Portuguese nothing need here be said, as the subject is dealt with elsewhere in the volume; but some account must be given of the efforts made by other nations of the West to establish themselves in India and secure a share of the profitable trade resulting. The Danish East India Company was established in 1616, and four years later a settlement was made at Tranquebar, on the south-eastern coast. From thence commerce was soon extended to Masulipatam, and later to Bengal; but adequate support from home was wanting, and for a long time the exiguous trade of the Danes consisted chiefly in carrying goods from India to Macassar and other parts of the Malayan Archipelago. In fact more than once they were on the point of yielding Tranquebar to either the English or the Dutch and relinquishing the trade. A fresh company, however, was started in 1670, and to this body a new charter was granted about thirty years later; but its operations met with so little success that in 1714 the factories in Bengal were withdrawn. On the suspension of the Ostend Company (mentioned later), an endeavour was made to attract its shareholders into the Danish body, though without success, owing to representations made by the English,

---

[1] Better known as Vijayadrug. Upon its capture it was handed over to the Marathas in exchange for Bankot (renamed Fort Victoria), which thus became the earliest British possession on the mainland of Western India.

Dutch, and French governments. A new company was started in 1729, which in 1732 obtained a charter confirming its privileges for forty years—a term afterwards extended to 1792. In 1755 a fresh settlement was made in Bengal, this time at Serampur (on the Hugli), besides others in the Nicobar Islands and on the Malabar Coast. The principal trade of the Danes was, however, with China for tea, which was largely smuggled from Denmark into Great Britain, until a reduction in the duty on that commodity made this illicit commerce unprofitable. On the outbreak of hostilities between the two countries in 1801 Serampur and Tranquebar were captured by the English, but they were immediately restored under the treaty of Amiens. Six years later, on the renewal of the war, both places were again taken possession of, and they were retained until the general peace restored them to their former owners. Finally, in 1845, all the territory in India belonging to the Danes, viz. Tranquebar, Serampur, and a piece of ground at Balasore, was sold to the English East India Company for twelve and a half lakhs of rupees.

The treaty of Utrecht (1713), which transferred the Spanish Netherlands to the House of Austria, was indirectly the means of adding another competitor for the trade between Europe and Asia. The merchants of Flanders were not slow to seize the opportunity thus presented, and after several private ventures the emperor, in spite of remonstrances from England and Holland, granted (1723) a charter to an association generally known as the Ostend Company. This quickly established a prosperous commerce with Bengal and China, its success being largely due to the extensive smuggling into England that ensued from the proximity of Ostend to our south-eastern ports. The London Company was much exercised at this illicit competition; while the other European nations concerned in the Eastern trade also felt themselves aggrieved. As a result the matter was pushed to the forefront of politics, and when in 1727 a treaty was negotiated for securing to Maria Theresa the inheritance of her father's dominions, the emperor was obliged to agree to suspend for seven years the privileges of the Ostend Company; while the treaty of 1731, by which Great Britain guaranteed the succession of Maria Theresa, contained a clause which stipulated for the definite suppression of that body. Its chief settlement in India, Bankibazar (on the Hugli, three miles north of Barrackpore), hoisted the flag of the Austrian emperor, and trade was continued under its protection; but in 1744 the place was besieged by the faujdar of Hugli (at the instigation, it was alleged, of the Dutch and the English), and the garrison, finding the position hopeless, embarked in their trading ships and departed. Many of them were killed in Pegu, whither the chief, Schonamille, led them; the remainder took to piracy until they fell in with an English man-of-war, when they preferred joining that ship to standing their trial as pirates.

The gap caused by the disappearance of the Ostend association was filled to some extent by a Swedish East India Company, chartered in 1731 and trading almost exclusively with China. Its privileges were renewed from time to time, but it slowly perished when the reduction of the English duties on tea extinguished the profits made by smuggling that commodity into Great Britain. The project of an Austrian East India Company was revived in 1775, when, at the instigation of William Bolts, a discharged servant of the English Company, a charter was granted by the empress Maria Theresa to "The Imperial Company of Trieste". However, after experiencing many vicissitudes during the ensuing ten years, this association became bankrupt. With the mention of two Prussian ventures—the China Company, founded in 1750, and the Bengal Company, started three years later—neither of which proved a success, we may bring to a conclusion the story of the attempts made by the mid-European powers to share in the trade with the East.

CHAPTER V

THE WAR OF THE AUSTRIAN SUCCESSION

THE War of the Austrian Succession, though in appearance it achieved nothing and left the political boundaries of India unaltered, yet marks an epoch in Indian history. It demonstrated the overwhelming influence of sea-power when intelligently directed; it displayed the superiority of European methods of war over those followed by Indian armies; it revealed the political decay that had eaten into the heart of the Indian state system; and its conclusion illustrated the resultant tendency of European treaties to intrude into a world that had previously altogether ignored them. In short, it set the stage for the experiments of Dupleix and the accomplishments of Clive.

The only part of India affected by the war was the Carnatic. On the coast lay three important European cities—Negapatam under the Dutch; Pondichery under the French; and Madras under the English. Each was a place of large trade; each was inhabited by some 20,000 or 30,000 Indians who had gathered themselves round the small group of Europeans, 400 or 500 in number, who formed the dominant element; each was a place of reputed strength. They had sprung into existence for purposes of trade; and had attracted their Indian population, in part by the opportunities of wealth, in part by the certainty of protection offered by their walls and ships. Behind them the country was divided out between Hindu and Muslim. At Arcot, dependent on the subahdar of the Deccan, was the nawab of the Carnatic. He was busy trying to convert what had in origin been a mere official appointment into an hereditary rule, for his superior, Nizam-ul-mulk, was old, and constantly occupied with his aggressive Maratha neighbours or with the troubled affairs of Northern India. The nawab's territories formed a narrow strip along the coast stretching from Ongole on the north to Jinji on the south, and bounded westwards by the hills that buttress the Deccan. Up these he never attempted to spread his dominions; but southward lay a number of small, feeble states that invited his attack. The first of these was Trichinopoly, which, in 1736, was ruled by a Hindu princess, widow of the last nayak, whose family had established itself there on the break-up of the Vijayanagar Empire at the end of the sixteenth century. This had been conquered by Nawab Dost 'Ali's son, Safdar 'Ali, and his son-in-law, Chanda Sahib, in 1736 or 1737, and this success was followed by the occupation of Madura by Chanda Sahib's brother.[1] Tanjore, however, which had been established as a result

---

[1] Cf. Orme MSS, Various, xv, 10–15.

of the Maratha invasion of the Carnatic in the previous century, did not fall so readily. It was small, but it was rich and fertile; and although on several occasions Chanda Sahib and his brother-in-law, Safdar 'Ali, besieged the capital and plundered the country round, they never succeeded in mastering it.[1] Their attempts led to the expulsion of their own family from Arcot.

Although the Maratha armies had not set foot in the Carnatic for over a generation, the Peshwa had a standing pretext for intervention whenever it suited Maratha policy. This was the claim to a quarter of the revenues known as *chauth*. In 1740 Fateh Singh and Raghuji Bhonsle, two of the principal Maratha generals, were sent with a large army of horse to levy the largest contribution that circumstances would permit. Their expedition was probably suggested by the complaints of their fellow-Maratha, the raja of Tanjore; but the common rumour was that they had been invited by Safdar 'Ali in jealousy of Chanda Sahib's designs,[2] or that they had been abetted by Nasir Jang, son of Nizam-ul-mulk, in order to get them out of his father's territories. In any case their sudden movement southwards from the neighbourhood of Cuddapah took Dost 'Ali by surprise. He marched with what troops he had at hand to meet them at the Damalcheri Pass, a valley about 800 yards wide, defended by a wall running across it. But the Marathas did not attempt to storm this obstacle. Guided by a local Hindu chief, Chikka Rayalu, they moved by another route eastwards of the nawab's position, and then fell upon him from the rear. His army was destroyed, and he himself with his chief people killed. Moving at once upon Arcot, where was Safdar 'Ali, the Marathas obliged him to come to terms. He is said to have agreed to pay a crore of rupees and to restore to the Hindus their old possessions.[3] After this the Marathas moved westward towards Bangalore as if to return to Poona, where Balaji Rao was finding obstacles in securing the succession to his father Baji Rao. But early in the next year, 1741, they reappeared and attacked Chanda Sahib in Trichinopoly. After a short siege the place capitulated, and Chanda Sahib, being unable or unwilling to pay the ransom that was demanded of him, was carried off prisoner to Satara.

These events shook the rule of Dost 'Ali's family at Arcot to its foundations. Maratha plunder hindered the collection of the revenue and thus prevented Safdar 'Ali from replenishing his treasury. Moreover, he did not receive the formal investiture from his superior Nizam-ul-mulk, so that the bazaars were full of rumours of his impending removal.[4] In the autumn of 1742 he was at Vellore,

---

[1] Orme MSS, Various, xv, 89–90.
[2] Madras Country Correspondence, 1740, p. 12.
[3] *Lettres édifiantes et curieuses* (ed. Martin), ii, 701.
[4] Madras to the Company [   ], February, 1742; Pondichery to the French Company, 1 October, 1741.

demanding a contribution from his cousin Murtaza 'Ali, who was the commandant of the place. Murtaza 'Ali thought the time ripe for the transfer of power into his own more crafty hands. He first attempted to poison his cousin; that failing, he put him to death by violence, and attempted to seize the government of Arcot. But he lacked the nerve to carry through what he had begun. Alarmed by the attitude of the people and troops, he suddenly abandoned the capital and disguised as a woman made his way hurriedly back to Vellore with its crocodile-defended moat. For the moment Safdar's young son, who had been left for safety's sake by his father at Madras with the English, was recognised as nawab, and the administration was carried on by his father's ministers. But these disorders had attracted the attention of Nizam-ul-mulk. He appointed a nawab, and early in 1743 entered the Carnatic in person to restore order. He expelled the garrison which the Marathas had left in Trichinopoly; and finally, his first nominee having died, he appointed an old servant of his, Anwar-ud-din Khan, to the government of Arcot. But the task of restoring order was beyond any but the most vigorous. Relatives of the old family still held most of the chief fortresses and enjoyed large jagirs; and although Safdar 'Ali's son was opportunely murdered at Arcot,[1] Anwar-ud-din's position seemed hardly more secure than Safdar 'Ali's had been. The whole country was in a state of uncertainty, expecting some great event, though none knew what.

Following on these ominous events came the news of the declaration of war between France and England. Four years earlier it would have opened very much to the advantage of the French in the eastern seas. At that time, when war seemed close at hand, La Bourdonnais, the governor of Mauritius, had been sent out with a squadron intended to operate against the English trade; but when the crisis passed, the squadron was recalled; and so it happened that, when war really broke out, the French had no ships of force in Indian waters, and the small squadron equipped by the English immediately after the declaration of war[2] found nothing on its arrival at the close of the year capable of resisting it. Dupleix, who had become governor of Pondichery in 1742, had hoped to be able to arrange one of those irregular understandings such as had been reached between Madras and Pondichery in the previous war, for a neutrality in India. He addressed the three English presidencies in this sense before any news of the English squadron had been received. In this he was following the policy of his masters, the French directors, who had announced their willingness to enter into an understanding with the English Company. But a proposal so calculated to favour the interests of the weaker naval power had been rejected; and the English in India, while willing enough to disclaim hostile designs, which indeed they

[1] Madras Consultations, 26 June, 1744. Cf. Orme MSS, Various, xv, 74.
[2] Minute of 22 March, 1743/4 (Brit. Mus. Add. MSS, 33004, f. 78).

had not the power to execute, warned Dupleix that they would have no control over any king's ships that might arrive. His sanguine mind interpreted this answer as an acceptance of his proposals; and when the news came that English ships under Barnett had not only captured the Company's China fleet but also some richly laden country vessels in which he was largely interested, he felt very unreasonably that he had been tricked by the English.[1]

But if the French had thus lost the first hand in the game, they still had something in reserve. It might be impossible to fit and equip ships on the harbourless coast of Coromandel; but at Mauritius they had an excellent harbour, and a governor of genius. Dupleix had at first desired a policy of neutrality because it was well adapted to the interests of himself and of his settlement. But since neutrality could not be had, the next best thing was to call on La Bourdonnais to come to the rescue. There were a number of French Company's ships at Port Louis; and these, though not swift sailers, were stout vessels quite capable of taking their place in a line of battle. The deficiency of men was made good by sending a number of *coffrees* from Madagascar on board; and with one or two country ships to act as frigates, La Bourdonnais, after some delay and one or two mishaps, succeeded in reaching the coast with his improvised squadron. He found the English ships weakened by their long absence from the dockyard, with their crews depleted by the climate, and above all with their original leader dead and succeeded by his senior captain, Peyton, the most unenterprising of seamen. Moreover, one of his four ships of the line, the *Medway*, which had been leaky even before she left England,[2] had to keep her pumps perpetually going. Against them La Bourdonnais could place eight ships in the line. But the odds were not nearly so heavy as that. The English ships were the better sailers and more heavily armed. The French thus might have been out-sailed and out-ranged. But Peyton failed to use his advantages. After an indecisive action on 25 June, 1746, he made off for Ceylon, partly in the hopes of refitting, partly in the hopes of meeting with reinforcements and perhaps a senior captain to take the responsibility. In August he returned to the coast, and again sighted La Bourdonnais's squadron. The latter had taken advantage of the interval to increase his armament from the stores of Pondichery; and this so alarmed the English commodore that after a hasty visit to Pulicat, which he made in error for Madras, he left the coast and sailed for safety to the Hugli, where he lay until the arrival of reinforcements took the command out of his hands.

His departure delivered Madras into the hands of the French. A besieging force could only be collected by taking a large number of men out of the ships; so that had Peyton even resolved to remain

---

[1] Dodwell, *Dupleix and Clive*, pp. 5 *sqq.*
[2] Orders to Sir Charles Hardy, 19 March, 1743/4 (P.R.O. Adm. 2–61, f. 103).

upon the coast without coming to action, his presence would have prevented the French from making any considerable attempt. But his absence freed them from all apprehensions. La Bourdonnais appeared with his ships and a part of the Pondichery garrison before Madras on 4/15 September; it surrendered to him, after two English-men and four others had been killed by the fire of the besiegers,[1] on the 10/21. Thus the military conduct of the English on this occasion was about on a level with their conduct at sea. But it should be added that the defences of Madras were built rather to protect the place from incursions of horse than to resist a siege in form; and the garrison was weak, untrained, and commanded by officers who did not know their business.[2]

This resounding success led immediately to disputes between the two French governors, Dupleix and La Bourdonnais, about the dis-posal of the place. It had surrendered under an informal promise of ransom; and in the discussions about the sum that should be paid, mention had certainly been made of a present to La Bourdonnais; but if that scheme were carried out, Dupleix and his friends at Pon-dichery would reap no advantages from the assistance they had given to the expedition. They therefore put forward a proposal that the place should be kept. Although the matter has often been argued as though national interests had been at stake, the question was really, Who was to make money out of Madras?[3] La Bourdonnais insisted on carrying out his original plan, and concluded a ransom treaty with the Madras council. Dupleix, after trying to seize the captured city by force, appeared to give way. But their discussions had prolonged the stay of the French vessels at Madras. On 2/13 October, a hurri-cane broke on the coast, crippling La Bourdonnais's squadron, and obliging him to leave behind him a considerable number of men who thus passed under the command of Dupleix. On his departure Dupleix denounced the treaty which had been made; and the garrison and company's servants of Pondichery secured the opportunity for which they had hoped of plundering Madras from top to bottom.[4] Meanwhile, on his arrival in France, La Bourdonnais was imprisoned on the charges which Dupleix had sent home against him; and seems at last to have secured his release by the influence of the Pompadour.[5]

The nawab Anwar-ud-din had not regarded these events with un-concern. Indeed, his interference had been asked by each of the two nations in turn. At first it was Dupleix who wanted him to prevent the English from seizing French ships at sea; and in order if possible to scare their men-of-war into inaction, he procured permission for a country ship in which he was interested to sail under the nawab's flag. Barnett,

[1] Love, *Vestiges of Old Madras*, II, 425.
[2] Barnett to Anson, 16 September, 1745 (Brit. Mus. Add. MSS, 15955, f. 113).
[3] Dodwell, *op. cit.* pp. 15 *sqq.* [4] *Idem*, pp. 18–19.
[5] *Correspondance de Mme de Pompadour*, p. 5.

of course, treated such devices as they deserved. The nawab addressed letters of complaint to the Madras council, who explained that they had no power to control the conduct of the commander of the king's ships. After a while the matter was dropped; and, as Dupleix had no more ships to send to sea, it could not recur. Then, when the French had secured control of the sea, and were preparing to attack Madras, it was the turn of the English to invoke the help of Arcot. It has been said that their application failed because they neglected to send a proportionable present with their request; but I have elsewhere shown that that account is not warranted by the facts.[1] The nawab sent a warning to Dupleix which he ignored. When La Bourdonnais was still before Madras, the nawab demanded that the French troops should be recalled; and Dupleix coolly replied that he was only conquering the place in order to put it into the nawab's hands. When La Bourdonnais had just entered Fort St George, the nawab again demanded his withdrawal, and finally sent troops to compel obedience to his commands. It was as vigorous and prompt action as could have been expected by the most sanguine; and had Madras made a good defence, the French would still have been lying before the walls when the nawab's troops arrived. As it was they found the French flag flying, and all they could do was to attempt to starve the French into evacuation. But as soon as the latter found themselves inconvenienced by the blockade, a sally was made under La Tour, who scattered his assailants and made them retire to St Thomé. Similar success was obtained by Paradis, who was marching up with reinforcements. The nawab's troops, still in St Thomé, tried to bar his way on the little Adyar river; but were hustled out of the way as unceremoniously by Paradis as they had been by La Tour. By this time musketry and field artillery had developed so far that cavalry could make no impression on troops that kept their ranks and reserved their fire. The terror of Asiatic armies had disappeared.

The capture of Madras marked the limit of French achievements in the course of this war. For eighteen months after the fall of Madras Dupleix tried in vain to capture Fort St David, only a few miles south of Pondichery, and certainly no more capable of defence than Madras had been. But he tried in vain. On one occasion even the French troops broke and fled on the apprehension that the nawab's horse, sent to assist the English, were moving to threaten their retreat. Dupleix came to terms with the nawab; he gave him considerable presents, and even agreed to allow the nawab's flag to fly for a week over Madras in token of his submission.[2] But even then when the nawab's sons had retired from the neighbourhood of Fort St David, Dupleix still could not take the place. The fact was, that with the departure of La Bourdonnais the command of the sea had returned

---

[1] Dodwell, *op. cit.* p. 13.
[2] *Diary of Ananda Ranga Pillai*, III, 394.

to the English; a new commander, Griffin, had arrived; and as soon as Dupleix approached the English settlement, his topmasts were sure to appear above the horizon, and the French would hurriedly retreat lest he should make an attempt on Pondichery in their absence.

But for such fruitless episodes the year 1747, and the first half of 1748, passed away without incident. In June, however, affairs began to move. First there appeared a French squadron, under Bouvet, which lured Griffin from before Fort St David, where he was lying, only to disappear altogether from the coast after landing treasure for the French at Madras, while the English ships lay before Pondichery to prevent the enemy from landing there. Then early in August came in gradually the large expedition which had been fitted out in England in order to avenge the capture of Madras. It was commanded by Rear-admiral Boscawen, and consisted of not only six ships of the line and as many smaller vessels, but also of land forces some 1000 strong. Together with the vessels already in the East Indies this was ample on the naval side; but the land forces were of inferior metal. They had been hastily got together for the occasion; the companies into which they were divided had been raised in part by drafts from regiments in Ireland, in part by officers specially commissioned on condition of raising a certain number of men in Scotland. These had found it very difficult to comply with their promises; and in the long-run their companies had to be completed by deserters, criminals, or rebels pardoned on condition of enlistment, so that, although by landing his marines and parties of his sailors, Boscawen could assemble a large force of men, they were not trained military material.[1]

It was decided to begin operations by besieging Pondichery; and had the siege been skilfully conducted, it should have succeeded. But it was managed with a singular want of skill. Unluckily the only officers of experience were disabled or taken prisoner before the siege itself was formed; and the survey made by the engineers was conducted from so safe a distance that they could not judge the strength of the works or the nature of the ground. So it came to pass that the besiegers formed their camp on ground westward of the city, whither all the stores had to be carried with great labour, instead of beginning their approaches on the shore where they would have been covered by the guns of their own squadron. Then also they began their trenches at so great a distance from the town that they were unable to batter the walls, and on ground separated from it by a swamp, so that their works could not be advanced near enough to begin to batter in breach. The attack on Pondichery was scarcely managed with more skill than the defence of Madras. The French on the other hand defended themselves with vigour. Their sorties harassed the besiegers. Their fire remained stronger everywhere than that brought to bear on them.

[1] Fox to Pitt, 6 June, 1747 (P.R.O., W.O. 4–43); same to Capt. Forbes, 7 July, 1747 (*idem*); same to Calcraft, 21 September, 1747 (*idem*).

Finding the land siege progress so slowly, Boscawen resolved to try the effect of bombarding the place with his squadron. But his fire was ineffective; the weather was evidently breaking up for the monsoon; many of his men were in hospital; and at last, at the beginning of October, he decided to raise the siege and return to Fort St David, where his men could be placed under cover. It was a conspicuous success for Dupleix, and a conspicuous failure for the English.

While Boscawen was lying at Fort St David waiting for the weather to allow his recommencing operations, news arrived that the preliminaries of peace had been signed in Europe. This naturally brought all operations to an end; all prisoners were released on their parole; and when at last copies of the Treaty of Aix-la-Chapelle arrived with the necessary papers and instructions, Madras was solemnly handed back to the English, and Boscawen sailed back to Europe. But in spite of this trivial ending affairs were in a very different state from that in which they had been at the beginning of the war. The English, for instance, held Madras under the terms of a treaty, and never again paid for it the stipulated quit-rent of 1200 pagodas a year, of which they speedily procured a discharge from the claimant to the Carnatic whose cause they espoused. The French had secured a high and deserved reputation for their military conduct. They had defied Anwar-ud-din, and he had been unable to coerce them into doing as he demanded. So that while the events which had just preceded the war showed how uncertain and unsettled the Indian government of South India had become, the events of the war itself showed that the Europeans were quite equal to taking a decisive part in Indian affairs, and that they had little to fear from any armies that Indian princes were likely at that time to bring against them. The power which was preponderant at sea might thus become preponderant on land. And the fertile and ingenious mind of Dupleix had for the first time been set to the serious consideration of the Indian political problem. Moreover, the storm which had obliged La Bourdonnais to leave behind him a considerable body of his men had in that manner augmented the forces at the disposal of Dupleix. So that the war did indeed set the stage for the great projects which he began to develop in the very year in which he gave back Madras to the English.

CHAPTER VI

DUPLEIX AND BUSSY

ALTHOUGH by the terms of the peace Madras had been handed back to the English, it did not become once more the seat of their government until 6/17 April, 1752. Till then their affairs continued to be directed from Fort St David, close to Pondichery. One would have thought that so exhausting a war would have imposed on both the neighbours an equal need of living well together; the necessity of reviving trade must have been felt as much by the English governor Floyer as by the French governor Dupleix, and Floyer was not the man to seek quarrels for their own sake. But good will is not always enough to avoid or prevent conflict. Blind forces, which we sometimes call chance and sometimes destiny, may suddenly produce new causes of rivalry that seem innocent until the future has proved their venom. The English had not even re-entered Madras before both governors had each on his own account engaged in relations with Indian princes closely similar in nature but quite distinct, and which were with little delay to bring them into direct collision.

Quite independently Floyer and Dupleix had taken sides in local quarrels at almost the same moment and in common defiance of the policy laid down with similar emphasis alike at Paris and at London. Peace had left both with unemployed bodies of troops who were expensive to maintain but who could not be sent back to Europe because the shipping season had not arrived. Neither governor therefore was sorry to relieve himself of heavy charges by temporarily placing these troops at the disposal of princes who would contribute to their maintenance.

It was Floyer who in all seeming led the way. Early in 1749 Shahji, a dispossessed claimant of the throne of Tanjore, offered the English Devikottai on condition of their helping him to recover the throne.[1] Devikottai was a little place of small importance at the mouth of the Coleroon. The English fancied that its possession would make them masters of the navigable part of the river and enable them to control the inland trade. A first expedition sent in April under Captain Cope failed; the troops of the legitimate sovereign, Pratab Singh, offered an unexpected resistance. But a second, better prepared and led by Major Lawrence in person, succeeded; after a few days of siege Devikottai surrendered (23 June). The English kept it with the country belonging to it; and as for Shahji no one thought of restoring him to his throne. This occupation of Devikottai was nothing more than a

[1] Fort St David Consultations, 10 April, 1749.

belated and rather futile reply to the occupation of Karikal by Governor Dumas some ten years earlier. It restored in that part of the Carnatic the balance which had inclined in the favour of the French.

Quite other was the importance of the expedition that Dupleix was contemplating and preparing to execute at the same time. In the month of March he had learnt that Chanda Sahib, who had been a prisoner with the Marathas for the last seven years, had just been set free and was preparing to recover the possessions of his family in concert with Muzaffar Jang (grandson of Nizam-ul-mulk who had died in 1748) who laid claim to the succession of his grandfather. The two princes were making common cause, and Chanda Sahib had sent his son, Raza Sahib, to Pondichery to obtain from Dupleix the assistance of troops whom the confederates agreed to pay. Dupleix had a grievance against the actual nawab, Anwar-ud-din Khan, who had assisted his enemies during the siege of Pondichery. He therefore accepted with the utmost secrecy the offers made to him on condition of not taking the field until the two princes were themselves prepared to begin hostilities. At last, on 13 July, matters reached the point at which a public agreement could be made, and three days later the troops under d'Auteuil began their march on Vellore, where the allies were to concentrate. Dupleix hoped to conclude matters quickly enough to be able to confront the Company with fortunately accomplished facts, so that there would be room for nothing but praise of his initiative.

All at first went well. The French having joined their allies defeated and slew Anwar-ud-din Khan at the battle of Ambur, south-east of Vellore, on 3 August. After this victory Muzaffar Jang and Chanda Sahib, grateful for the help accorded them, came to offer their thanks to Dupleix at Pondichery, and granted him in full right the territories of Villiyanallur and Bahur, which more than doubled the French Company's possessions round Pondichery, and they added to this on the Orissa Coast the province of Masulipatam and the island of Divy.

In indirect answer to these grants Admiral Boscawen took possession of St Thomé, where he suspected Dupleix also meant to establish his authority. St Thomé is not four miles from Madras, so that its possession was a vital matter for the English. Already men were not paying too much attention to the question, who was the rightful owner of desirable territory? Dupleix held that St Thomé belonged to Chanda Sahib; Boscawen to Muhammad 'Ali, son and heir of Anwar-ud-din Khan, though he had inherited little power enough. After the battle of Ambur, he had taken refuge at Trichinopoly, where he was preparing to oppose Chanda Sahib and his allies. The English, feeling that it was in their interest to support him, from October onwards sent him help. Dupleix too understood that he would never be the real master of the Carnatic under Chanda Sahib's name until

he had got rid of Muhammad 'Ali. In November, therefore, he sent
troops against Trichinopoly under the command of his brother-in-law
d'Auteuil; but instead of finishing the war by reducing that town as
quickly as possible, the French, at the suggestion of their allies, turned
off against Tanjore, whence they hoped to draw a large tribute for
the maintenance of their forces—a consideration not lacking importance. That town, the capital of the kingdom of the same name,
resisted all attacks, and kept the allies before it for three months. The
English openly encouraged the king in his resistance, and led him to
expect prompt help from Nasir Jang, the rival subahdar of the
Deccan.

Nasir Jang was Nizam-ul-mulk's son and so Muzaffar Jang's uncle.
As at the time of his father's death he had been able to seize the
treasury, he had also been able to secure his accession, and was preparing to dispute his nephew's claims, both of them resting their rights
on a real or alleged investiture by the Moghul. Nasir Jang had not
at first understood all the importance of the battle of Ambur, and, in
spite of the English invitations, had hesitated to take part in a war
which after all was not being fought in the Deccan. He only made
up his mind when the danger seemed to threaten himself, and at the
beginning of 1750 he appeared on the borders of the Carnatic. His
approach compelled the French and Chanda Sahib to raise the siege
of Tanjore and to retire on Pondichery; while the English took
advantage of this retreat to occupy Tiruvendipuram, which adjoins
Cuddalore.

The opposing armies found themselves face to face at the end of
March, on the banks of the Jinji river, near Valudavur. Nasir Jang
had been joined by a few English under Captain Cope, and a battle
seemed inevitable, when thirteen French officers, struck with panic,
fled to Pondichery on the night of 4 April, and Muzaffar Jang cast
himself on the generosity of his uncle, who made him prisoner. The
French army was also obliged to withdraw, but nevertheless Dupleix
was able to offer his enemy an unbroken front at the bounds of Pondichery. After some short and fruitless negotiations, Dupleix suddenly
decided on a night attack on Nasir Jang's camp, which was thrown
into panic. That prince, having secured his nephew, thought nothing
more was to be gained by fighting with the French, and so quietly
retired to Arcot, where for the next six months he lay inactive. In
vain did the English and Muhammad 'Ali implore him again to take
the field. He only decided to do so when he learnt that Dupleix had
occupied Tiruviti, Villupuram, and Jinji, and was moving towards
Arcot. The capture of Jinji, thought impregnable but which Bussy
took by a brilliant feat of arms, 12 September, 1750, profoundly
disquieted him. The English, as they had already done at St Thomé
and Tiruvendipuram, replied to the occupation of these places by
procuring for themselves a more or less regular cession of Poonamallee

near Madras. As for Nasir Jang, after having painfully set out, he was surprised on the night of 16 December by the French army under La Touche. To this had contributed the treachery of the nawabs of Karnul, Savanur, and Cuddapah, and certain other nobles. Abandoned by some of his troops, Nasir Jang was slain on the field of battle, and Muzaffar Jang, who had been brought prisoner with him, was at once recognised as subahdar. Legitimacy had once more changed sides.

Muzaffar Jang returned to Pondichery as if to receive a sort of investiture from Dupleix, whose power increased daily. To the grants already made was added the province of Nizampatam on the Orissa Coast; Dupleix was recognised as governor of all India south of the Krishna; and, certain of not being allowed to reign over his own states in peace, Muzaffar Jang demanded a few Europeans to accompany him to his capital and aid him to consolidate his power. Dupleix reckoned that his triumphs permitted him now to ignore Muhammad 'Ali, whom he could settle with either by treaty or by force, and so consented. On 15 January, 1751, Bussy, his best officer, set out for the Deccan, with orders to support at any cost the prince to whom the French owed the titles on which they relied for the legitimate possession of the country. Dupleix thought, with a certain *naïveté*, that the English and Muhammad 'Ali would bow before his claims and allow him to regulate the affairs of the Carnatic at his pleasure. Unluckily for him Floyer was no longer governor of Fort St David. He had been replaced (28 September, 1750) by Saunders, formerly chief of Vizagapatam. Saunders was a man cold, silent, and reserved, a man of action rather than of speech. Like his predecessors he had orders to keep aloof from political affairs; but he felt that, if he left Dupleix free to act, it would be all over with British trade. Having adopted a formal resolution in council, he encouraged Muhammad 'Ali not to accept the proposals then being made to him from Pondichery, and on his advice that prince conducted himself with such seeming frankness that he deceived Dupleix himself while the English were making ready their men and munitions.[1]

At last in May, 1751, before the French had made any movement, Captain Gingens set out with 800 or 900 Europeans to support Muhammad 'Ali. Dupleix, understanding that he had been tricked, as indeed he had half suspected, dispatched in his turn a little army with orders to capture Trichinopoly. Then began a long, fatiguing, and commonly monotonous war for the possession of that town, before which the French wasted their strength. The two European armies of course did not appear as principals, but only as auxiliaries, the one of Chanda Sahib, the other of Muhammad 'Ali; but that concession to appearances did not prevent them from killing one another or taking one another prisoners. At first neither side displayed great

[1] Madras County Correspondence, 1751, p. 4.

qualities. D'Auteuil, the French leader, had gout and could not maintain discipline; the English troops were still more unruly, and Gingens himself was not worth much. The march towards Trichinopoly was extremely slow. The English, having been beaten at Valikondapuram, crossed the Kavari on 28 July, and it was only on 25 September that the French, having in turn crossed the river, found themselves before the city.

The English and Muhammad 'Ali once more sought to amuse their opponents with negotiations, in the sincerity of which Dupleix once more seems to have believed. But the fact was that Muhammad 'Ali wanted to gain time. In the course of these discussions the English claimed that their ally had mortgaged Trichinopoly to them in July, 1750, careless of the fact that, were the act authentic, it could have had no value, as he was not the subahdar of the Deccan. At last the siege began. The French were no longer commanded by d'Auteuil, whose health compelled his resignation, but by a young captain, great in name if not in action, Jacques Law, nephew of the famous financier of the Regency. But he did not justify his selection. If the town did not yield to his summons, he had only two courses open— to take it by assault or to subject it to a strict blockade. Neither was easy to execute, for the town was large and the French troops, even with their allies, few in number. Law never attempted more than to prevent provisions from being brought into the town by cutting off convoys. He never completely succeeded; light parties were always bringing in victuals by some unexpected route; and nothing more serious took place than actions of scouts and outposts. Then allies who had been secured by clever negotiations came to strengthen the English position. At the end of the year Muhammad 'Ali secured the help of the raja of Mysore by promising the cession of Trichinopoly, and of the famous Maratha chief Morari Rao by taking him into pay; and soon afterwards the king of Tanjore joined the coalition. Moreover, the English had struck a serious blow at French prestige by Clive's bold seizure of Arcot, the capital of the Carnatic, the defence of which (September-October) first brought him into prominence. All the efforts of Dupleix to recover the place had been checked by a carefully organised resistance, and in the four or five following months his troops, without encountering an actual disaster, failed to obtain any appreciable success. In that area fortune was evidently turning against him.

This change of situation, though not as yet alarming, nevertheless made an impression on Law, and struck him with a sort of paralysis. He dared not make the smallest movement. Profiting by this timid inaction, the English in April brought into Trichinopoly a large convoy which secured that place for several months, and then, as Law had crossed the Coleroon and taken refuge in the island of Srirangam, they set to work to block him up there. This plan was proposed by

Clive, who had returned from the northward, and warmly approved by Lawrence. Dupleix, seeing the danger of leaving his army besieged in Srirangam, sent reinforcements, but d'Auteuil who led them was forced to surrender (9 June) at Valikondapuram, and three days later Law, demoralised and helpless, became a prisoner with all his troops, 600 according to Lawrence, 780 according to Orme. At the same time Chanda Sahib, trusting to the generosity of his enemies, gave himself up, but was beheaded by the Tanjorean general, Lawrence not caring to interfere. This disaster, news of which reached Europe early in the following January, largely contributed to determine the French court to recall Dupleix and reverse his Indian policy. But in India nothing could shake Dupleix's energy and confidence, or change his resolute attitude. He was indeed at his best amid calamities; he never admitted defeat, and found within himself unexpected resources for the continuance of his struggle with misfortune.

On the morrow of Srirangam, when by a sudden return to the coast the English and their allies could have threatened the French settlements, the Mysoreans and Morari Rao, already sounded by Dupleix, withdrew from the coalition, and Tanjore returned to neutrality. Meanwhile the English, after hesitating a month about their future course, returned to the coast, leaving only a small detachment as a precaution against the defection of the Mysoreans whom they already suspected. They easily took Tiruviti and Villupuram, but failed before Jinji (6 August), and Major Kineer, who was commanding while Lawrence was disabled by sickness, was beaten at Vikravandi by Kerjean, Dupleix's nephew. But this led to nothing. Lawrence recovered, reassumed the command, and pursued the enemy as far as the Great Tank, some eight miles west of Pondichery, in French territory. There an indecisive action was fought; but five days later (5 September) the over-confident Kerjean was surprised and completely defeated beyond Aryankuppam, losing some hundred European prisoners and himself being severely wounded. But for the state of peace between the two nations, the English might then have attacked Pondichery; but, being restrained by the national treaties and not daring to confide the task to Muhammad 'Ali, they went into winter quarters, the rainy season having arrived, at Tiruviti and Fort St David.

Elsewhere, too, the French had encountered checks which, though less striking, had greatly contributed to weaken their authority and prestige. After the affair of Arcot, and when Dupleix perceived that he could not recover the place, he attempted a diversion against Madras, and in January, 1752, Brenier in command of a French force camped at Vandalur; but he only succeeded in plundering the country round St Thomas Mount and Poonamallee; some trifling engagements took place near Conjeeveram; but at last, 12 March, the French force underwent complete defeat at Kavaripak; and all hope of seriously threatening Madras had to be given up. Law's surrender further weakened the French forces; and while Lawrence took advantage of his success to threaten Pondichery, Clive cleared the country round Madras by seizing Covelong and Chingleput, which the French had occupied as advance posts beyond the Palliar. Clive, fortunate as ever, took these places on 21 September and 1 October, and then the French held in the Carnatic only Pondichery and Jinji with their limited territories.

In these grave but not desperate circumstances, Dupleix still found means of counteracting the English success. After five or six months of laborious discussions, Morari Rao passed over to the French service, and less than two months later Mysore agreed to join the French, pay their troops until Trichinopoly had been taken, and then pay Dupleix thirty lakhs of rupees in return for the possession of the town. Dupleix re-opened operations, 31 December, 1752. But du Saussay, who was placed at the head of the troops, was not the right man for the conduct of war, and at the end of a month Dupleix replaced him by Maissin, on whom he placed the greatest reliance. The new chief besieged Tiruviti, but could not carry the place until 7 May. Meanwhile the Mysoreans had tried to invest Trichinopoly. In mid-April Lawrence suddenly learnt that the town was threatened by lack of provisions. Abandoning Tiruviti, he marched at once. A party of French troops followed him and on 8 May appeared before the place under Captain Astruc. Financial difficulties hindered close co-operation between him and the Mysorean commandant, Nandi Raja; while Morari Rao, making war in his own fashion, was rather plundering on his own account than helping the French; and the new siege of Trichinopoly dragged on as in the time of Law, with futile attack and counterattack. In July, Dupleix replaced Astruc first by Brenier, a conscientious leader but self-distrustful and unenterprising, who was beaten on 9 August, and then by Maissin, already discouraged by his campaign round Tiruviti and by the failure of his two predecessors. He soon fell sick, and Astruc, who succeeded to the command during his illness, was in turn beaten on 21 September, being himself made prisoner with 111 Europeans. But these were fruitless victories for the English. The French did not repeat the mistake of shutting themselves up in Srirangam and continued to face their enemies. At last on 14 October a new leader arrived. This was Mainville, lately returned from the Deccan.

Mainville was a man of resolution. He believed in Dupleix's plans and was prepared to execute them. After restoring discipline he prepared to carry Trichinopoly by surprise. The attack was prepared with the greatest secrecy for a month, and took place on the night of the 27–28 November. The French easily secured the outer wall; but aroused the English by an act of imprudence and were driven back as they attempted to climb the inner rampart. A large part of them became prisoners. But instead of being discouraged by this series of misfortunes, luckily discounted by the steady success of Bussy in the Deccan, Dupleix resolved to sacrifice something to ill-luck and agreed to discuss with Saunders terms of peace. Indeed, the authorities at home were weary of this unceasing war, and every packet contained advice and even orders to bring these troubles to an end. A conference was therefore held at Sadras 21–25 January, 1754. As a preliminary the English commissaries, Palk and Vansittart, demanded that their French colleagues, Lavaur, Delarche, and du Bausset, should recognise Muhammad 'Ali as nawab of the Carnatic. The French did not choose thus to derogate from the authority of the subahdar of the Deccan; and after three meetings full of chicane over the validity of the titles of Muhammad 'Ali and those of Dupleix, the negotiations were broken off and war was renewed. It had, indeed, never been actually suspended, but had slackened down as if peace were near. Under Mainville the French troops experienced no further checks. On 15 February they even secured a conspicuous success over the English, taking 134 European prisoners. But like the English victories, this, too, led to nothing. The French still found themselves before Trichinopoly, with too small an army to invest or storm it, and with auxiliaries too unskilled or timid to afford material help. All they could attempt was to cut off the town from the neighbouring country which supplied it with victuals. Mainville therefore carried the war into Tanjore and the Pudukottai country; but achieved no more than fruitless raids, as the enemy declined action. Moreover, the conduct of Mysore gave rise to grave anxiety. By failing to pay the promised sums, Nandi Raja was exposing the French commander to the danger of finding himself one pay-day deserted by his troops. Mainville was thus busier soothing the discontent of his own men than attacking the enemy. He could never rely on the morrow. The coalition was evidently breaking up. Nandi Raja talked of returning to Mysore; and in June Morari Rao quitted the French camp though he did not positively break with them. Mainville met all these difficulties with great firmness, and, like Dupleix, never despaired of taking Trichinopoly, when news came that Godeheu had landed at Pondichery on 1 August.

That meant the recall of Dupleix and the reversal of his policy. Godeheu replaced Mainville, whom he thought over-anxious to continue the war, by Maissin, less self-willed and more pacific. Soon after he concluded a truce, followed by a provisional peace, which ruined all French hopes in the Carnatic. But the whole of Dupleix's policy was not condemned. As we shall see, in spite of their desire for peace, neither the Company nor the ministry at Paris was willing to sacrifice the decisive advantages that had been obtained in the Deccan. But before turning to that region, in which the French fortunes had shone with their greatest lustre, we will attempt to disengage in a few lines the causes of Dupleix's failure in the Carnatic.

It has been seen that Dupleix espoused the cause of Chanda Sahib and Muzaffar Jang without consulting the Company, convinced doubtless that it would not authorise him any more than his predecessors to engage in the politics of the country. Swift success would have relieved him from the necessity of embarrassing explanations. And when he saw that event deferred, he concealed the facts by saying that the war cost nothing and would leave plenty of money free for the purposes of trade. The French Company, though with some scepticism, accepted these roseate prophecies, and sent no money, since Dupleix asked for none. But finance was his stumbling-block from first to last. His reverses, which began in September, 1751, prevented the collection of the revenues he had reckoned on; and he was hard put to it to maintain his army. Each month he could only just secure enough to prevent his troops from disbanding. To meet these urgent needs he used over £350,000 of his own money and that of his friends. It was not, however, lack of money alone that hindered his success; in this respect the English were not much better off than he. What ruined him was his excessive belief in the justice of his cause. Full of the belief that, as Muhammad 'Ali was a rebel, the English government could not support him, he really thought that the English Company would disavow Saunders and leave him free to carry out his policy. All his letters show a confidence that is almost disconcerting.[1] He should have remembered that men do not sacrifice too much to theory and ideals, and that, in view of their threatened trade, the English were justified in resisting his plans. Trusting too much to legal formulas, he did not accommodate himself to the facts; and, while he displayed marvellous skill in negotiating with Indian princes, in his relations with the English he showed an unaccommodating spirit which did much to provoke opposition in Europe quite as much as in India.

Whether the Company ought to have supported him is quite another matter. In truth it could not do so without understanding his plans; but Dupleix, who at first had perhaps been uncertain of being able to carry them through, began by half-concealing them, and did not until 16 October, 1753, formally expound the advantages of possessing extensive territories in India, yielding a fixed, constant and abundant revenue that would relieve the Company from sending funds. But when he was developing this doctrine, which till then he had only sketched, Godeheu already was about to embark for India. No doubt if the Company had entered into the ideas of Dupleix, it could have established at the necessary cost in men and money the empire which he hoped to found; but besides the hesitation always felt before novel and daring ideas—*ignoti nulla cupido*—the Company, or rather the king, had other motives for caution. Disputes were already arising between French and English on the Ohio and Missis-

[1] Dupleix to Saunders, 16 February, 1752 (French Correspondence, 1752, pp. 1–41).

sippi; the preservation of that region seemed more important than hypothetical conquests in India, and this constituted another motive for not endangering the peace for the sake of Asiatic domains which after four years of war Dupleix had not succeeded in subduing. And if a more distant future is taken into consideration, perhaps the king and Company were right.

But in the Deccan affairs wore a different appearance. Peace is usually discussed on the basis of accomplished facts, not of those hopes which the war has either destroyed or realised. The French position at Hyderabad was too strong in 1754 for the English to insist on the ruin of Bussy's work, however much they might desire it. I have already mentioned the terms on which Dupleix had lent his help to Muzaffar Jang; by protecting the legitimate ruler of South India, he hoped above all to secure the rights he had acquired in the Carnatic. Bussy's activities did not lead to direct competition with the English; but his achievements are too important to be neglected. When shortly after setting out a conspiracy of dissatisfied nawabs cost Muzaffar Jang his life (14 February, 1751), Bussy's prompt action avoided any break in the succession and danger to public order; Salabat Jang, uncle of the dead prince and brother of Nasir Jang, was recognised as subahdar; but he needed even more than his predecessor the support of French troops to establish his power, thus born of disorder, and Bussy, who was to have gone only to Hyderabad, in the centre of the Deccan, accompanied him to Aurangabad at its extremity. There he was more than 900 miles from Pondichery. It was a magnificent raid, accomplished with hardly a shot. From the first Bussy had understood how to manage Indian princes, showing due deference and doing nothing without permission. His manners gave no hint of his power; he never seemed to despise the weak or the vanquished. In his hand was armed force; but he always thought that gentleness was better than severity, negotiation than battle, human life than the laurel of victory. As he himself said, he was more of a statesman than a soldier; he was a born diplomatist. But his resolutions were firm, his action bold. When a decision had to be taken, Bussy saw straight to the heart of things, and carried his purpose into effect though without brutality or offence. More than anything else these rare and happy talents established French supremacy at Hyderabad, which reacted on the work of Dupleix by setting up a counterpoise to those sometimes unlucky but always indecisive events of the Carnatic. Dupleix could not sufficiently express his gratitude to his lieutenant. Most of his letters to Bussy are full of thanks and admiration. In order to cement the friendship and confidence between them, Dupleix had hoped to marry Bussy to one of his wife's daughters familiarly known as *Chonchon*; they were actually betrothed; but Bussy's remoteness and Dupleix's sudden departure prevented the completion of the marriage. Thus the administration of affairs in the Deccan was peculiar, being treated on both sides as a family business quite as much as an affair of state. Bussy, however, was independent enough not to approve blindly all the projects of Dupleix, and he could oppose them when they sacrificed too much to ideals or conflicted too sharply with facts.

After the French reached Aurangabad (18 June), Dupleix dreamt for a moment of pushing his successes in the north, and planned by Bussy's means to place Salabat Jang at the head of the subah of Bengal.[1] He would thus have dominated the greater part of India. But, just when this bold plan was to have been put into action, the Marathas attacked the Deccan, and Bussy had to march against them. In less than a month he had driven them back; a night attack on 4 December, which threw the enemy into confusion, has become famous. Balaji Rao, the Peshwa, at once entered into negotiations, and peace was made at Ahmadnagar, 17 January, 1752. Dupleix then thought of bringing a part of the subahdar's troops against Trichinopoly, and Bussy was to co-operate by attacking Mysore in the rear. But the diwan Ramdas Pandit, who was murdered at that time (4 May), proved to have been in communication with Muhammad 'Ali and the English; and it was believed that the nobles, no longer fearing the Marathas, were seeking the expulsion of the French. The subahdar, whose influence was small, alone was interested in keeping them. Bussy was inclined to recognise this state of things by abandoning the Deccan. What use could be made of people so ungrateful and a prince so powerless? Dupleix thought otherwise. To him the Deccan meant the protection of his rights and authority; and he implored Bussy not to forsake the work which he had begun. At this moment news arrived that Ghazi-ud-din, the eldest son of Nizam-ul-mulk and holding high office at Delhi, was claiming his father's territories and marching thither with a large army and the expectation of support from Balaji Rao. Bussy remained to encounter this invasion; but had no need of fighting. Ghazi-ud-din was poisoned by one of his father's wives, and Salabat Jang's throne was thus secured. But that prince was always exposed to underhand attacks from his nobles, who disliked his dependence on the French. The new diwan, Saiyid Lashkar Khan, constantly intrigued against Bussy's influence, and had agreed with Balaji Rao in some mysterious plan in which the interests of his master can have had little part. Bussy, who followed closely all these Indian intrigues, succeeded in avoiding a new war which in November was on the point of breaking out with the Marathas, and having, under the guise of mediator, come to terms on his own account with Balaji Rao, he prepared to enter Mysore in order to assist in Dupleix's plans against Trichinopoly; but now he was checked by the refusal of the subahdar's troops to move; they were tired of fighting without pay; no advance was possible and the army fell back on Aurangabad. Bussy then renewed his proposals to

[1] Dupleix to Bussy, 4 August, 1751 (Archives de Versailles, E 3748).

quit the Deccan and offered his resignation. Ghazi-ud-din was dead, the disputes with the Marathas settled, and the French could withdraw with honour.[1] Dupleix did not have time to answer these proposals. Bussy had scarcely written before he fell seriously ill; and decided to retire to Masulipatam to recover his health (February, 1753). He had not intended to return; but Dupleix's appeals to his affections and his patriotism decided him to continue their common work, and he came back in the following May.

During his absence affairs had gone grievously wrong. Goupil, who had succeeded to the command, had been overpersuaded by Saiyid Lashkar Khan to divide his troops, the smaller part remaining with the subahdar at Aurangabad, and the rest being scattered over the country, after the Muslim fashion, to collect the revenues. The object was to make them hated; and then they were to be ordered to leave the country. In this passive opposition the saiyid was encouraged by Saunders, who was prevented by the state of the Carnatic from playing a more active part. On his arrival at Hyderabad Bussy restored order, and, as the need of money was almost as great as in the Carnatic, he skilfully arranged that each governor was to pay his share towards the maintenance of the troops. He then secured an invitation from the subahdar himself to proceed to Aurangabad, where he arrived at the end of November. There he laid down his terms, and obtained a personal grant of four sarkars—Mustafanagar, Ellore, Rajahmundry, and Chicacole—for the payment of his troops, so that he should have to make no more demands on the subahdar or his officials. The revenues of these districts were reckoned at thirty-one lakhs of rupees; whereas the cost of the army was twenty-five and a half lakhs a year. This was a masterly stroke. Bussy ceased to be at the mercy of the subahdar and his ministers and, having secured the grant in his own name for a specific purpose, he was able to tell the Dutch and English that nothing had been changed in that part of India and that the French had no more than they had had before, although through his control the sarkars had really passed into the hands of the French Company. The English at Ingeram and Vizagapatam did their best to annul the effects of these grants, by making friends with discontented renters and governors, especially with Ja'far 'Ali, governor of Rajahmundry; but they lacked the means of offering a serious opposition.

Bussy consolidated his advantages by reforming the ministry. Saiyid Lashkar Khan was replaced by Shah Nawaz Khan, and the principal posts were filled by nobles friendly to the French. Trouble with Raghuji Bhonsle in Berar (March-April, 1754) was quickly settled, and then, feeling himself secure, he set out for the new provinces, of whose revenues he had never had greater need. He had to maintain 900 Europeans and 4000 sepoys.

[1] *Réfutation des faits imputés au sieur Godeheu*, pp. 41–9.

Arriving at Bezwada, 5 July, Bussy was about to start for Chicacole when he learnt of the arrival of Godeheu at Pondichery. He had been expecting this for six weeks, and, although he felt a certain anxiety, he was not unduly alarmed. Dupleix and Godeheu had been very friendly of old, when in 1738 the latter had visited Chandernagore.

Let us pause to consider the affairs of the Deccan which till then had developed in accordance with French interests, because Dupleix had entrusted them to a man of consummate capacity and wisdom. He himself declared that had he had another Bussy in the Carnatic, affairs there would have gone quite differently. It was not, perhaps, extraordinary that the little French army should have reached Aurangabad without difficulty; but it was extraordinary that it should have been able to maintain itself there. When the new *régime*, resulting from the unexpected accession of Salabat Jang, had consolidated itself, a real national sentiment arose among the nobles of the subah, aiming at the expulsion of the French. That called into play all Bussy's skill. Not strong enough to impose his authority, he maintained it nevertheless by his remarkable tact and his personal prestige. Without seeming to notice the intrigues by which he was surrounded, he contrived to turn them all to advantage. The greatest source of anxiety was the weakness of Salabat Jang. How could he trust a prince whose mind was like a child's? But for Dupleix's gratitude for the grant of the Carnatic, and his need of a subahdar to legitimate his rights, Salabat Jang would, perhaps, have been replaced by one of his brothers, or even by Balaji Rao. Both solutions were considered, and the second was not entirely laid aside. Without previous concert, both Dupleix and Bussy independently recognised that the French would be strengthened in their struggle with the English by an alliance with a nation remote from their frontiers and of proved power and solidity. Bussy was even instructed to lay the foundation of an agreement which in the first case would be aimed only at Trichinopoly but which might be extended to the Deccan. It is impossible to estimate the consequences had Dupleix sacrificed the point of honour and thrown over Salabat Jang.

However that may be, at the moment of his recall the position of the French appeared impregnable; and it would have been so but for the division of their forces, which had already hindered the capture of Trichinopoly, and which might lose them the Deccan if some necessity obliged them to recall their troops. Indeed, this division of his forces was the weak point of Dupleix's policy; and although in the Deccan he secured unrivalled glory and almost incredible territorial possessions, he was disabled from securing the Carnatic, and thus afforded the English both time and opportunity of making that breach by which they were to overthrow the whole structure. It is, indeed, unwise to pursue two objects at once and to attempt more than one has the means of accomplishing. The French Company shared this intoxication of success, for it did not condemn the policy followed in the Deccan as it did that followed in the Carnatic. Instead of repudiating the conquests of Dupleix and Bussy, it accepted them. Godeheu himself did not wish to leave Salabat Jang without support, for fear that the English would establish their influence with him, and abandoned only conditionally part of the French possessions on the Orissa Coast. The war which broke out two years later between the French and the English prevented his agreement being carried out, and at the end of 1756 the position of the French and English in India was much the same as three years earlier. The French were again threatening Trichinopoly, and the English were devising means of driving Bussy out of the Deccan.

The latter, after some months' stay on the coast, where he reached an agreement with Moracin, chief of Masulipatam, about the establishment of a regular administration, returned to Hyderabad in January, 1755. He found that feelings had changed since his departure. The recall of Dupleix had revealed the weakness of French policy; and the subahdar talked of nothing but asking the English for that military help which he could not do without. Bussy had great difficulty in re-establishing his waning confidence without condemning the policy of his country. An invasion of Mysore, under the plea of arrears of tribute, at once raised French prestige and filled the treasury. Bussy succeeded in obtaining a voluntary payment of fifty-two lakhs of rupees on condition of preventing an invasion by the Marathas, which would have completed the ruin of the country. Thus, in the phrase of Duval de Leyrit, the heir of both Dupleix and Godeheu, the position of Bussy was as brilliant as ever. He was in correspondence with the wazir, and received flattering letters from the Moghul. But the national sentiment was by no means extinct. Like Ramdas Pandit and Saiyid Lashkar Khan, Shah Nawaz Khan from the end of 1755 desired above all else to get rid of Bussy and the French. An expedition against Savanur and Morari Rao gave occasion for the rupture. Morari Rao had acquired extensive territory round Gooty, whence he defied both Salabat Jang and Balaji Rao. The two therefore united to suppress him. Bussy brought the expedition to a successful end, but by reason of the services Morari Rao had formerly rendered to Dupleix was unwilling entirely to crush him. But when he gave him easy terms, Shah Nawaz Khan cried treason and dismissed Bussy.

His position was critical. Though Bussy had few troops, he disliked retreating; and instead, therefore, of marching to the coast as had been expected, he calmly made his way to Hyderabad, where he entrenched himself in the *Chahar Mahal*, a garden on the outskirts of the town belonging to the subahdar. There he awaited reinforcements. Luckily Law, who was sent with 160 Europeans and 700 sepoys, besides five guns, showed more decision than before Trichinopoly. He overthrew the enemy barring his way, and about 15 August, 1756, joined Bussy. Thus Shah Nawaz Khan's plans were upset. But it was not altogether his fault. Bussy's dismissal had been concerted with the English, who were to have sent a detachment to take the place of the French, but who were prevented from doing so by news that on June 21, Calcutta had fallen into the hands of Siraj-ud-daula. The victorious Bussy thus quietly resumed his place in the subahdar's councils as if nothing had happened. He did not even take the trouble to dismiss Shah Nawaz Khan; though he was hostile, would another be more sincere and friendly? He therefore did no more than keep an eye upon him. It was, indeed, a fixed principle with him to avoid as much as possible all appearance of interfering with internal matters and to leave to the subahdar all the forms of independence. Not to labour the point, his ideas are summarised in the following passage of a letter to Dupleix of 26 February, 1754:

What I can, and think I should, assure you, is that it is of the greatest importance to manage these provinces [the sarkars] at first according to the Asiatic manner and only to substitute a French government for that of the Moghuls gradually and by degrees. We certainly must not begin on the first day of our rule. Experience and practical acquaintance with the country, and with the nature and manners of its inhabitants, show that we should not hasten the assertion of absolute authority, but establish it gradually, instead of exposing it to certain failure by claiming it at our first appearance. I attribute the successes I have gained hitherto principally to my care on certain occasions to observe Asiatic customs.[1]

The remainder of 1756 passed without incident. It was at this time that news arrived of the declaration of war with England; but the war had begun six months or more earlier, if we take into account the events that had occurred in America. Bussy returned to the coast, less to look after the administration than to watch the English, who had important factories at Ingeram, Madapollam, Bandarmalanka, and Vizagapatam. These he took one after the other. For a moment he thought of sending Law up to Bengal to the assistance of Chandernagore, attacked by Clive and Watson; but the fall of the place (March, 1757) made such a plan useless.

All that year Bussy remained on the coast. He desired to accustom the Deccan to his absence, in order one day to abandon it. It no longer mattered, as in the time of Dupleix, that the subahdar was the legitimate ruler of Southern India; circumstances had judged that fiction of legality. But the subahdar could not yet be abandoned. If he and his court were not secured, there was a danger of seeing them fall into the arms of the English, and the war in progress between the two powers would now enjoin the use of every weapon. Bussy knew that the danger had grown during his absence. Shah Nawaz Khan, who had never renounced his design of expelling the French, had by degrees transferred the powers of government from Salabat

[1] Bib. Nat., Nouvelles Acquisitions, 9158, f. 157.

Jang to his brothers, Nizam 'Ali and Basalat Jang, and had secured
for himself a place of refuge in Daulatabad, while he was negotiating
with the Marathas for external help. The English, in accordance with
their interests, gave him good advice until such time as they should
be able to do more. All this disappeared with Bussy's return. Without
employing force, he found once more within himself the patient
powers of persuasion which enabled him to restore order. He secured
Daulatabad by surprise; and re-established Salabat Jang in all his
rights. But he needed more vigilance than of old. The English
successes in Bengal had their reaction in the Deccan. One day his
diwan, Haidar Jang, was murdered; and Shah Nawaz Khan was
killed in the tumult which followed. These were not propitious omens;
no one doubted that a crisis was at hand.

On the declaration of war, the king of France had sent Lally to
India to drive the English out. After taking Fort St David, Lally
prepared to attack Madras; for the success of this enterprise he considered he had need of all the national forces, even of those in the
Deccan. By a letter of 15 June, 1758, he recalled Bussy with his
detachment. Salabat Jang felt that this meant his own destruction,
as was indeed the case; but Lally's orders were formal; Bussy obeyed,
like a disciplined soldier, and set out at once to join him. This did not
necessarily signify the ruin of French hopes, even in the Deccan, if
Lally triumphed in the Carnatic. In 1758 the position of the French
on the coast was as strong as in the best days of Dupleix, and the
Carnatic itself with Trichinopoly might have been secured, had
fortune favoured the new general. But the check before Madras, then
the battle of Wandiwash where Bussy was taken prisoner, destroyed
the work of the previous nine years, and left of the work of Dupleix
and Bussy only memories on the one side, and hopes on the other.
It was by learning from these two great Frenchmen that Clive was
enabled to lay the British Empire in India on secure foundations.
Their success showed him the weakness of the Indian princes; that
the walls of their power would fall at the first push. Frenchmen will
ever regret that Dupleix did not confine his efforts to the Carnatic;
with united forces he might have triumphed over Trichinopoly before
the patience of the Company was tired out, and then, if it was resolved
to go farther, the way was open. He lost everything by wishing to
hasten the work of time, and by forgetting the certainty of English
resistance in India and of public disapproval in France, where men
did not know his plans and were alarmed at the endless wars into
which he was leading them.

CHAPTER VII

CLIVE IN BENGAL, 1756–60

ON 9 April, 1756, died 'Ali Wardi Khan, subahdar of Bengal and Bihar. He had established himself by force of arms as ruler of those provinces after a severe struggle with the Marathas; and when his position was no longer assailable, the Moghul emperor had recognised him as his lieutenant on condition of his paying fifty-two lakhs of rupees a year. Apparently this condition was never fulfilled; but he went on ruling none the less, and in 1752 designated as his successor his great-nephew, Siraj-ud-daula, then a young man of twenty-three. Of the latter neither his English nor his Indian contemporaries have the least good to say; and his conduct confirms their words. Having been proclaimed as nawab at the capital, Murshidabad, he marched almost at once against his cousin, Shaukat Jang, the governor of Purnia, whom he suspected rightly of intriguing against him. On 20 May, when he had reached Rajmahal on his march against Purnia, he suddenly changed his mind, ordered an immediate return to Murshidabad, and directed the English factory at Kasimbazar to be seized. This was carried out on 4 June, three days after the nawab's return to Murshidabad; and on the 5th his army began its march against Calcutta. On the 20th he captured the place.

This extraordinary series of events took everyone by surprise; and when they came to offer explanations to their friends and superiors, personal feeling ran so high, and each member of the Calcutta Council was so visibly anxious to throw the blame elsewhere than on himself and his friends, that little weight can be attached to their evidence. Some declared that Omichand had instigated this attack in revenge for having been excluded from his former share in the Company's business; others attributed it to the reception of a fugitive who was alleged to have eloped with large sums of money, and to the expulsion of the messenger whom the nawab had sent to demand him. Others again asserted that on his deathbed 'Ali Wardi Khan had solemnly warned Siraj-ud-daula against the dangers of European aggression. All these are vigorously asserted and as vigorously denied in the letters describing that eventful twelvemonth which elapsed between the capture of Calcutta and the battle of Plassey[1]. But there is reason to think that fear of European aggression was the main predisposing cause of the attack. Holwell, to whom we owe a detailed account of 'Ali Wardi's deathbed warning, may have been drawing on his imagination or may have been indebted to mere rumour; but it is certain that those who like Watts, the head of the Kasimbazar factory,

---

[1] Holwell to Company, 30 November, 1756; Watts to the same, 30 January, 1757.

dismissed the story on the ground that orientals were too incurious and indolent to trouble about what happened in distant provinces, had chosen to forget at least two incidents which should have taught them better. We know that when the news of Nasir Jang's death reached Bengal, 'Ali Wardi Khan had threatened to seize the goods belonging to the French.[1] We know, too, that a short time before 'Ali Wardi's death Siraj-ud-daula had accused the English of preparing to resist the government; the English had been repeatedly questioned, and though they had convinced 'Ali Wardi of their innocence they had not succeeded in convincing Siraj-ud-daula; he had ordered his spies to keep a close watch on their doings, and it was common talk at Murshidabad that the vast wealth of the English might easily be captured.[2] The day on which Siraj-ud-daula turned back from his march against Purnia he had received a letter from Drake, the English governor, explaining recent additions to the defences of Calcutta as intended to protect the place against a French attack. That letter has not been preserved in any form, and we cannot tell whether in any other way it was calculated to irritate the nawab; but there was certainly an uneasy feeling in his mind that unless he took precautions the Europeans would turn Bengal upside down as they had done the Carnatic and the Deccan. It is very possible that this feeling was accentuated by other imprudences on the part of Drake, who was at best but a short-sighted mortal. But the main reason for the nawab's attack was the idea that the English had taken advantage of 'Ali Wardi's illness to strengthen their military position, and that he had better check them before they became dangerous.

This idea, as the event was to prove, was ludicrously false. Drake had indeed mounted some guns along the river front, in case French vessels should sail up the river and attempt a landing when war broke out again; but that was no protection against any attack which the nawab might deliver, for that would come from the land, not from the water. Nor, indeed, was any attack anticipated. The common view held by Europeans in Bengal was that expressed in a letter of 4 June, 1743, written by Dupleix and his council at Pondichery to his successor at Chandernagore. The latter, alarmed by the expulsion of Schonamille and his Ostenders, had planned a large and powerful fortress. Dupleix rejoined: "So long as Europeans trade in Bengal, we do not believe that the Moors will directly attack them; they have surer means of making them pay the unjust contributions which they exact".[3] Their river-borne commerce could be stopped at any point; and no fortifications would enable them to carry on trade against the will of the nawab. That was also the view of the English. At the beginning of the century they had built Fort William; but they had

---

[1] Law, *Mémoire*, p. 52; Cultru, *Dupleix*, p. 353.
[2] Forth to Drake, 16 December, 1756.
[3] *Correspondance...de Pondichéry à Bengale*, ii, 288.

been at no pains to make it defensible from the land, or to maintain its original strength. So early as 1725 the timbers of the bastions had become so rotten that they had had to be shored up. In 1729 the south curtain was rendered defenceless by the building of outhouses which masked the flanking fire of the bastions. They had built a church close at hand which commanded the gorges of all four bastions. Private persons had been allowed to build solid brick houses almost adjoining. Then the fort had been found stuffy, and so great windows had been cut in its walls. No soldier or engineer who saw it but foretold that it could never be defended against attack. A captain of artillery in 1755 reported that there was not an embrasure fit to hold a gun or a carriage fit to mount one; on which the council reprimanded him for not sending his letter through the commandant.[1] Nor even was the garrison at its full strength. During those alarming years when Madras and Pondichery were at unauthorised war, many recruits intended for Bengal had been detained at Madras; and this deficiency had not been made good.[2] Finally the officers who commanded the garrison were of the same poor quality, with no more experience of war, and hardly more military spirit, than had been displayed by their brothers-in-arms at Madras in 1746. So far from being prepared to disturb the peace of Bengal, the place was not even capable of defence. Few events have had a more ironical conclusion than Siraj-ud-daula's attack upon Calcutta.

The short interval between the first warning and the appearance of Siraj-ud-daula's troops served no better purpose than to display the lack of military talent in the settlement. All the available Europeans, Eurasians, and Armenians were embodied in the militia; a body of Indian matchlockmen was taken into pay; and plans were made for the defence of the town. But there was no leadership. The projected line of defence was larger than could be held by the numbers present; and nothing was done to render the fort itself defensible. On 16 June, the nawab's troops appeared before the place, and were repulsed in an attack they made on the northern side of the town; but on the 17th they entered the town limits from the east; on the 18th they drove the defenders from their outposts; and on the 19th the fort was deserted by the governor, the commandant, and several of the members of council, who took refuge with a number of women on board the ships in the river. When their desertion was known, the remainder placed the command in the hands of Holwell, the junior member of council; and the defence was prolonged for one more day. But the soldiers, exhausted with their efforts, got out of hand, and broke open the liquor godowns, as had happened at Madras; the enemy's fire from the church and neighbouring houses rendered the bastions untenable; and in the afternoon the place surrendered. After

[1] Wilson, *Old Fort William*, II, 25.
[2] Bengal to Madras, 25 May, 1756 (Madras Letters received, 1756, no. 95).

anxious enquiries about the treasure which the fort was thought to contain, the prisoners were shut up for the night in the military prison generally known as the Black Hole. This was a room 18 feet long by 14 feet 10 inches wide, from which only twenty-three survivors emerged next morning.[1]

The news of this disaster arrived piece-meal at Madras. First, on 14 July, came news of the seizure of Kasimbazar. It was decided to send reinforcements at once; and on the 20th Killpatrick sailed with 230 men. He arrived on 2 August, and found a number of refugees at Fulta, where he was obliged to encamp amidst the swamps of that unhealthy place. Not till 16 August did news come of the fate of Calcutta. At the moment the council was actively preparing an expedition which was to have joined Salabat Jang in the Deccan and replaced French influence there by English. Luckily it had not marched. Admiral Watson, who had come out two years earlier with a squadron and a King's regiment in case the French could not be brought to terms, was called into council, and Clive was summoned up from Fort St David where he was now deputy governor. There was a strong and natural feeling in the council against the dispatch of a large force to Bengal, based partly on the local advantage of expelling the French from the Deccan, partly on the evident approach of war with France with its consequent dangers to Madras. This was overcome, mainly owing to the firm and prudent arguments of Robert Orme, supported by the governor Pigot and by Clive.[2] But there still remained the problems of who was to command the expedition and what were to be his powers. The command was claimed by Colonel Adlercron, the commander of the royal regiment that had come out with Watson. But he refused to agree to the division of the prospective plunder in the shares laid down in the Company's instructions, or to promise to return on a summons from the Madras Council;[3] and so the command was finally entrusted to Clive. As regards his powers, there were obvious objections to entrusting the direction of the Madras forces to persons who had proved themselves so wanting in conduct and resolution as the council of Fort William. At the same time it was contrary to the Company's practice to entrust uncontrolled power to a military officer. It was, therefore, first decided to send two deputies with Clive, who were with him to constitute a council with power to determine the political management of the expedition. But then arrived a member of the Calcutta Council who protested so loudly against this supersession of the Calcutta authorities that that plan was laid aside and Clive was invested with complete military independence, while the funds—four lakhs of rupees—sent

---

[1] See note at the end of the chapter.
[2] Orme to Payne, 3 November, 1756 (Orme MSS, Various, 28, p. 58).
[3] Madras Public Consultations, 21 September, 1756; Adlercron to Fox, 21 November, 1756 (India Office, Home Misc. 94, p. 210).

with the expedition were consigned to him personally. In fine the Madras council came to the best conclusion possible. In part this was due to luck. It was a miracle of fortune that Colonel Adlercron was so unaccommodating. But the decision to dispatch a large expedition instead of a small one showed high qualities of courage and insight.

These discussions took up a long time. The expedition did not actually sail till 16 October, after the north-east monsoon had set in. Their passage was therefore long and stormy. One of the vessels was driven into Vizagapatam, whence she put back to Madras; so that when Clive reached the Hugli a few days before Christmas and was joined by Killpatrick and the remains of his detachment, he had only about the same number of troops as he had set out with—800 Europeans and 1000 sepoys. He marched up the eastern bank of the river, occupied Baj-baj, recovered Calcutta (2 January, 1757), and plundered Hugli. This brought Siraj-ud-daula once more upon Calcutta. He refused to listen to the embassy which Clive sent to him; but a night attack, though far from a complete success, so disquieted him that he retired and sent offers of terms. Within a week the treaty had been completed and signed. It confirmed the English privileges, promised the restoration of the Calcutta plunder in the nawab's hands, and granted the power of fortifying Calcutta and coining rupees.[1]

This treaty came at a timely moment. News of the outbreak of the Seven Years' War had arrived at almost the same time as Clive had reached Calcutta, and the English were not strong enough to fight the nawab and the French together. Indeed had the French followed the English example, and thrown every available man into Bengal, the immediate course of events must have been very different. But they were entangled in the Deccan. They had already sent all the forces they could spare to assist Bussy in his crisis at the Chahar Mahal; and now had no one to send for the crisis in Bengal. Just as in 1751 the dispatch of Bussy to the Deccan had disabled Dupleix from completing his designs in the Carnatic, so now in 1757 the need of maintaining Bussy's position prevented them from interfering with effect in Bengal. Law, the French chief at Kasimbazar, and the author of an illuminating memoir on the events of 1756–7, had urged the *directeur*, Renault de St Germain, either to agree with the English for a neutrality or at once to join Siraj-ud-daula. "If he makes peace without having received any help from you, you cannot expect help from him should you be attacked."[2] Renault tried to adopt the first alternative. On Watson's arrival he had sent deputies to propose a neutrality; but Watson had replied that he would accept nothing short of an alliance against the nawab. Then when the nawab was

[1] Treaty of February, 1757.
[2] Law, *Mémoire* (ed. Martineau), p. 93.

marching on Calcutta, the English offered to relax this stipulation, and Clive fully expected them to accede to his proposals, unless indeed they "should not be vested with powers to enter into engagements of such a nature, which I somewhat suspect".[1] But no answer was returned to this offer until 21 February, when peace had been made with Siraj-ud-daula. Then they sent deputies again, and a draft treaty was drawn up. But when the question of their powers was raised, it proved that they could bind neither the Pondichery council nor any royal officers who might come out to India. Thus negotiations were broken off on 4 March.

Meanwhile Watts, that "helpless, poor, and innocent man" as Siraj-ud-daula had called him,[2] had been sent up to Murshidabad to act as English resident there and watch over the execution of the treaty. There ensued a duel between him and Law, in which the latter had the advantage of the nawab's sympathy. He was by no means disposed to acquiesce in his defeat, and could not speak of the English without blazing eyes. But the durbar was on the whole inclined to the English and against the French. Then too came news that the Durani Afghans, who had invaded Northern India, were likely to advance on Bengal. Under the alarm caused by this, Siraj-ud-daula wrote to offer the English a lakh a month if they would aid him against the Afghans. This was on 4 March, the day on which the Anglo-French negotiations were broken off and on which also Watson had written to the nawab a very angry letter, demanding the complete execution of the treaty within ten days, or else "I will kindle such a flame in your country as all the water in the Ganges shall not be able to extinguish".[3] In these circumstances, on the 10th, a letter was written by the nawab's secretary, bearing the nawab's seal, permitting the attack on Chandernagore. Law asserts that this letter was not written by the order of the nawab.[4] However, it was enough to authorise Watson to move. On the 14th Chandernagore was attacked, though not closely, from the land; on the 23rd the ships appeared off the place and after a day's severe fighting it surrendered.

This deprived the nawab of his natural allies against the English; and nothing can extenuate his folly in allowing their destruction. Indeed, after his reluctant consent had been given, he seems to have changed his mind, and ordered Rai Durlabh to march with a considerable force to relieve the town. But then, on hearing from Nandakumar, the faujdar of Hugli, that the French would not be able to resist the English, the nawab changed his mind again, and in the end did nothing. No conduct could have been feebler or more unwise. He gave open display to his hostile feelings against the

---

[1] Clive to Secret Committee, 1 February, 1757.
[2] Siraj-ud-daula to Pigot, 30 June, 1756.
[3] Watson to the nawab, 4 March, 1757.
[4] Law, *op. cit.* pp. 121–2.

English while allowing them unmolested to destroy the French. And then as if to emphasise his errors he proceeded to protect Law at Murshidabad together with the fugitives who joined him from Chandernagore, and to write to Bussy to come to his help from the Deccan. These facts are established by the evidence of Law[1] as well as by the assertions of the English.

Although then the English had recovered Calcutta, although they had secured from the nawab promises of privileges which they had long desired, and although they had succeeded in depriving the French of their principal stronghold in Bengal, they were still far from a position of safety. At any time might come news that the French had arrived in strength upon the coast, and then Clive would be obliged to abandon either Madras to the French or Calcutta to the nawab. It was also becoming apparent that many persons besides the English had cause to fear Siraj-ud-daula, and desired a revolution in the government. The chief people in this movement were Hindus. 'Ali Wardi Khan had favoured them, and had promoted many of them to high places in his administration. Siraj-ud-daula did not share his predecessor's feelings, and he succeeded in alienating all the principal men of the durbar. The great Hindu bankers, the Seths, who had contributed largely to the establishment of 'Ali Wardi Khan, had been threatened with circumcision; Rai Durlabh, who had held the office of diwan, had been placed under the orders of a favourite called Mohan La'l; Mir Ja'far, who had held the office of bakshi, had been dismissed with insult, and cannon had been planted against his palace. The first hint of intrigues against the nawab had come to the English through Omichand, when they were still lying at Fulta waiting the arrival of help from Madras. Warren Hastings, who was employed in this first affair, thought poorly of it; and for the moment it came to nothing, partly, it seems, because the English lacked forces and a leader, partly because the Hindus had no suitable candidate to propose. But after the fall of Chandernagore the idea was again brought forward. The nawab, having defeated and slain his only dynastic rival, Shaukat Jang, in the previous October, had lost at once all stimulus to self-restraint in his government and the protection afforded by the hope that he would be overthrown without the trouble and danger of private action. The Seths were at once the persons specially concerned and specially active. Law, who was well placed to view the position with considerable accuracy, says that without them the revolution of 1757 would never have been accomplished.[2] That view is probably correct. The English policy had never been adventurous. They had rather supported existing princes than replaced them by new. In Bengal they would not have attempted a revolution without the certainty of a large Indian

[1] Law, *op. cit.* pp. 112, 131.
[2] *Idem*, pp. 108 *sqq.*; Gleig, Warren Hastings, I, 41; Elliott and Dowson, VIII, 426.

backing; and the Seths' intrigues created the situation, bringing the discontent to a head and the discontented into active contact with one another, without which the English would never have stirred at a time when a French war was visibly impending. The Select Committee declared no more than the truth when it recorded among its other reasons for participating in the plot that

The Nabob is so universally hated by all sorts and degrees of men; the affection of the army is so much alienated from him by his ill-usage of the officers; and a revolution so generally wished for, that it is probable that the step will be attempted (and successfully too) whether we give our assistance or not. In this case we think it would be a great error in politics to remain idle and unconcerned spectators of an event, wherein by engaging as allies to the person designed to be set up we may benefit our employers and the community very considerably, do a general good, and effectually traverse the designs of the French and possibly keep them entirely out of these dominions....[1]

This matter first came to a definite form when on 20 April Scrafton wrote to Clive that the Seths through Omichand had proposed to set up Yar Lutf Khan as nawab. This man was a protégé of the Seths who had employed him in command of a body of troops to protect them against attacks from the nawab or anyone else. On the 23rd Scrafton's letter was read in committee and Clive was authorised to sound the principal people in Murshidabad about their willingness to co-operate. On the 26th Watts wrote that Mir Ja'far had informed him through Khwaja Petrus, an Armenian, that he and other important persons were willing to assist the English in overthrowing the nawab. This proposal was obviously much more attractive than engaging to support an unknown man such as Yar Lutf Khan. The question was considered in committee on 1 May and at once accepted on the following conditions: an alliance offensive and defensive; the surrender of all French fugitives and factories; restitution of all English losses, public and private, caused by the capture of Calcutta; the admission of all farman rights; liberty to fortify Kasimbazar and Dacca; no fortifications to be erected on the river below Hugli; the recognition of English sovereignty within the bounds of Calcutta; the grant of territories for the maintenance of a proper military force; extraordinary expenses while the troops were on campaign for the nawab to be paid by him; and the residence at the nawab's durbar of one of the Company's servants. Four days later to these terms was added the additional stipulation that "Omychund in consideration of his services should have all his losses made good by an express article in the treaty". But by the time that these proposals had reached Murshidabad, Omichand had fallen into disfavour with the other conspirators. Watts might write on 6 May, "I will conclude nothing without consulting Omichand", but on the 14th he had learnt that the latter had procured from the nawab orders for the restoration of his property, and, when he was shown the proposed articles, he not

[1] Bengal Select Committee, 1 May, 1757.

only insisted on his receiving 5 per cent. on the nawab's treasure, but also demanded many other alterations, "in which his own ambition, cunning, and avaricious views were the chief motives".[1] In consequence of these intrigues both the English and Mir Ja'far resolved to have nothing more to do with the greedy Sikh; but the matter was not so simple as that. Omichand had unwisely been let into the secret, and the immediate problem was to keep his mouth shut until the preparations were more complete. For this purpose the Calcutta council decided on the expedient of a double treaty, in one copy of which Omichand's claims were to be inserted, but which was not to be regarded as the valid copy. In order to make the trick pass, Watson's signature was added by some person, probably Lushington, to the false copy.

Meanwhile, the final terms had been concerted with Mir Ja'far. They were rather more favourable to the English than had been at first put forward; and on 5 June, Watts visited Mir Ja'far in secret and obtained his oath to the treaty. But already doubts had arisen regarding the amount of assistance that might be expected from him and his friends. In words which proved true in the event, Watts wrote:

We can expect no more assistance than that they will stand neuter and wait the event of a battle. If we are successful they will reap the benefit, if otherwise they will continue as they were without appearing to have been concerned with us.[2]

Nevertheless, the march of events was not suffered to pause. On 11 June the treaty was delivered to the Select Committee; on the 12th Watts and his companions fled from Murshidabad; and the day after Clive began to march towards the nawab's capital.

The matter had not been kept so secret as it should have been. We shall never know whether Omichand revealed the plot to Siraj-ud-daula, or who broke silence at Calcutta; but it was openly discussed at the English capital on 5 June; two days later it was known at Murshidabad; and on the 8th the Frenchman, Sinfray, warned the nawab of what was impending. But he was too irresolute by nature to take advantage of his knowledge. He seems also to have so distrusted his army that he would not venture on the decisive step of seizing Mir Ja'far. Instead of that he visited the latter in person, and accepted, though presumably he did not place much trust in, the conspirator's protestations of fidelity. Meanwhile Clive set out with 3000 men. Of these 2200 were sepoys and topasses; 800 European infantry and artillerymen. The sepoys were men whom he had brought up with him to Bengal; they had been raised and trained under Lawrence in the south and had served well against the French. After a momentary hesitation he reached Plassey at midnight 22–23 June,

---

[1] Watts to Clive, 14 May, 1757.
[2] Watts to Clive, 3 June, 1757.

and found himself within striking distance of Siraj-ud-daula's army, consisting of some 50,000 men.

His knowledge of the situation was slight and disquieting. He had received letters from Mir Ja'far promising co-operation; but he was by no means certain how far the latter would keep his word. In the first draft of Orme's famous history we find a passage which was afterwards omitted, probably in deference to the susceptibilities of his hero:

Colonel Clive...saw the morning break with increasing anxiety; at sunrise he went with another person upon the terras of the hunting-house, from whence having contemplated the enemy's array, he was surprised at their numerous, splendid and martial appearance. His companion asked him what he thought would be the event; to which he replied, "We must make the best fight we can during the day, and at night sling our muskets over our shoulders and march back to Calcutta". Most of the officers were as doubtful of success as himself; but the common soldiery, being mostly tried men, who had served under Major Lawrence on the plains of Trichinopoly, maintained the blunt spirit of genuine Englishmen, and saw nothing in the pomp or multitude of the Nabob's army either to admire or to fear....[1]

In view of the spirit of his men Clive seems to have resolved to remain on the defensive during the day, but when night fell to try the effect of a surprise attack upon the nawab's camp. Accordingly, till 2 o'clock in the afternoon nothing was done but reply to the cannonade opened by the enemy. But when the latter ceased fire and began to fall back on their own camp, Killpatrick on his own responsibility ordered an advance. The enemy were soon driven from the mound near the British camp which they had occupied; the next point of attack was another mound close to the nawab's entrenchments. Apparently at about the time when Clive ordered his men to advance to storm this post, the nawab sent word to the small party of Frenchmen with him that he was betrayed, that the battle was lost, and that they should save themselves; immediately after this he fled on a swift camel, and himself brought to Murshidabad the news of his overthrow. All this time Rai Durlabh and Mir Ja'far had been as inactive as the Pathan nawabs with whom Dupleix had concerted the destruction of Nasir Jang. They had hung on the right flank of the English forces, without attacking, but also without giving any sign of their holding other intentions. Not till the next morning did Mir Ja'far venture into the English camp, and even then he was apparently very uncertain of his reception. Scrafton noted that he started when the guard turned out to receive him, and his face did not brighten till the colonel came out and embraced him.[2] That day the new nawab hastened to Murshidabad, of which he took possession; on the 28th Clive entered and conducted him to the *masnad* on which he had not yet ventured

---

[1] Orme MSS, Various, 164 A, p. 115.
[2] Scrafton, *Reflections*, p. 90.

to seat himself; and on 2 July Siraj-ud-daula was brought back by Mir Ja'far's son Miran, and put to death that same night. So this revolution was completed. Clive wrote of it to Orme, "I am possessed of volumes of materials for the continuation of your history, in which will appear fighting, tricks, chicanery, intrigues, politics, and the Lord knows what".[1] It offers a strange mingling of the admirable and the mean. No series of events could have thrown into stronger relief Clive's insight and the way in which he saw "things and their consequences in an instant"; nothing could have afforded a better illustration of his resolute conduct as soon as his swift mind had been made up; nothing could have better displayed his extraordinary gift of leadership. If once or twice he hesitated in the course of affairs, he was after all but man; and his hesitation took place when there was no immediate call for action. In attacking Siraj-ud-daula he was amply justified not only by the standards of his own time but also by those of our own. But the deception of Omichand has thrown an ugly air over the business. As has been well said, had Omichand sought it he could not have devised a more bitter revenge than the stain which he brought upon the name of Clive.[2] And the large presents with which Mir Ja'far rewarded those who had given him Bengal add the touch of sordidness. It is true that in this Clive and his companions were only following the example of Dupleix and Bussy; that their motives were not corrupt; that they might have had more for the asking; that they were only doing what any of their contemporaries would have done in their place. Here our judgment must fall upon the age rather than upon the individuals; but none the less the acceptance of the presents was of evil example; and could Clive have looked on to 1765 perhaps he would have refrained from laying up for himself untold bitterness.

Clive now found himself installed in the same position and exposed to the same dangers as Bussy in the Deccan. In character Mir Ja'far was much like Salabat Jang—weak and irresolute. The principal people of his durbar were as likely to be jealous of the English as the nobles of the Deccan had proved themselves to be of the French. Intrigue and hostility were certain. In these circumstances, though without any formally declared intention, we find Clive adopting as a definite policy the protection of those prominent Hindus who had assisted in bringing about the revolution, and whom Mir Ja'far wished to despoil as soon as it was accomplished. The two chief persons concerned were Rai Durlabh, who had been diwan and had received repeated promises of being continued in that office, and Ramnarayan, the deputy of Bihar, who was thought unlikely to support the new régime. Before the end of 1757 the nawab was already accusing Rai Durlabh of intending to set up a new nawab. On this pretext the

---

[1] Clive to Orme, 1 August, 1757.
[2] Hill, *Bengal in* 1756–57, I, p. clxxxix.

unfortunate brother of Siraj-ud-daula was put to death; and Rai Durlabh was on the verge of being attacked.[1] Watts, who was still resident at the durbar, interfered and brought about a reconciliation for the time being, which was the more necessary because Ramnarayan was reported to be allying himself with the wazir of Oudh against Mir Ja'far. However, when the nawab took the field to march against Bihar, Rai Durlabh refused to march with him, on the pretext of ill-health, but really because he was afraid to trust himself in the nawab's camp. Clive, who had decided to accompany Mir Ja'far to Patna, visited the diwan at Murshidabad in connection with the Company's claims for payment which were overdue. At first he secured nothing but promises. But when the diwan was warned that he was risking the loss of English protection, an agreement was reached under which the Company was to receive orders on the collectors of the various districts (30 December).[2] Clive and Mir Ja'far now moved towards Patna. At first Clive had been decidedly hostile towards Ramnarayan. Immediately after the battle of Plassey he had sent Coote up with a detachment in order to seize Law and any other Frenchmen whom he could find; and he also issued orders to dispossess Ramnarayan of Bihar.[3] These orders were never carried out, because Coote was dissuaded by Mir Ja'far's friends, who probably thought that the plunder of the deputy had better be left for their own hands. Six months later Clive's attitude had changed. In December he had received protestations of the deputy's fidelity; and on 1 January he had with the approval of the nawab written giving that guarantee of personal safety without which Ramnarayan refused to trust himself within the nawab's reach. Relying on this, Ramnarayan at once came down the river to meet the nawab; and then ensued a pretty trial of strength between the nawab and Clive, the first bent on the spoliation of the deputy, the second on the maintenance of his promise. Clive won, although at one time after his arrival at Patna he had certainly speculated on the possibility of being attacked by the nawab's forces,[4] as Bussy had been at the Chahar Mahal. Ramnarayan received investiture of his office, for which he paid nine lakhs of rupees; and he received a definite promise that so long as he did not intrigue with foreign powers and provided his due share of the revenues, he should not be dismissed. The net result was that the two principal servants of the state depended for their personal security not upon their ostensible master but upon the influence of Clive.

Down to this time Clive had no definite position among the English at Bengal, and still remained a servant of the governor and council

---

[1] Clive to Secret Committee, 23 December, 1757.
[2] Clive to Secret Committee, 18 February, 1758.
[3] See Coote's correspondence and journal ap. Orme MSS, India, VII, pp. 1608-50, and 1673-91.
[4] Clive to Select Committee, 7 February, 1758.

of Madras. On the receipt of the news of the fall of Calcutta, after some deliberation the Company had resorted to that absurd plan, which had been attempted before in the period of confusion at the beginning of the century, of establishing a rotation government. On this occasion there were to be four governors, who were to have succeeded to the chair in successive periods of a month. But the Calcutta Council refused to put this plan into operation; Clive was invited to act as governor till orders should arrive subsequent to the news of the revolution. This sensible decision was taken in June, 1758; and later in the year a dispatch arrived by which the Company appointed Clive to the position which he was already occupying.

Meanwhile the policy of protecting the Hindu servants of the nawab was further developed by the attack made by Miran upon Rai Durlabh. The resident had once more to intervene in order to prevent his house being plundered; and then an intrigue was started with a view to ruining him with the English by accusing him of a conspiracy against the nawab. Clive with great probability on his side refused to credit the accusation, and the minister was allowed to retire to Calcutta. The support of persons whom he wished to plunder must have done much to alienate the nawab; but almost immediately afterwards came a reminder that he depended upon the English for military support. In 1759 appeared on the borders of Bihar 'Ali Gauhar, better known under his later title of Shah 'Alam II, who, flying from the confusion of Delhi, had found a refuge in Oudh and was now hoping to strengthen his position by the occupation of Bihar and Bengal. He laid siege to Patna, but Ramnarayan proved staunch; after temporising as long as he could, he defended the place until succour arrived, on which the wandering prince withdrew into Oudh. This support was the occasion of that great gift of the jagir, which involved Clive in such animated disputes with the Company at a later time. It consisted of the quit-rent which the nawab had withheld when he granted the 24-Parganas to the Company, and which was till Clive's death and later paid to him instead of to the nawab, though he had much ado to secure his rights from the Company when control of the direction passed for the time being out of his hands.

The last striking incident of his first government in Bengal was the attempt of the Dutch to supplant English influence with the nawab. Although the centre of Dutch power and wealth lay not in India but in the islands to the eastward, they had watched with growing disfavour first the French and then the English establishing themselves in a position of political predominance. When Masulipatam had been granted to the French in 1751, the Dutch, who had long had a factory there, made several attempts to assert their independence. On more than one occasion they attempted to hoist their flag—a thing which the French would in no wise permit; and they constantly scrupled to pay the duties which the French imposed on the trade within their grants.[1] But Dutch interests in the Northern Sarkars were trivial compared with their interests in Bengal. Not only were the piece-goods of Bengal exported in great quantities to Batavia on the account of the Dutch Company, but the Dutch servants enjoyed a most lucrative though secret monopoly of the export of opium to Batavia; and though this never appeared in the forefront of their disputes with the English, we may be sure that it was never far from their minds. On the establishment of Mir Ja'far they had attempted to obtain a price for recognising him as nawab; and as a penalty had seen their trade stopped and their agent seized.[2] Then when Pocock left the Hugli for the Coromandel Coast, the Dutch had been invited to concert measures to prevent French vessels from entering the river; they had not been able to concur; and so the English took their own measures, which consisted in subjecting all foreign vessels coming up the river to a strict search.[3] Then too, Clive had obtained for the English Company a monopoly of the saltpetre produced in Bengal, with a view to preventing that article from reaching the French, and the Dutch protested against this measure, although they had themselves applied for a similar privilege to Siraj-ud-daula. The duties on the export of opium were also raised and workmen were said to have been prevented from working for the Dutch Company. The Dutch were in fact in the same position as the English would have occupied on the Coromandel Coast had Saunders done nothing to counteract the schemes of Dupleix. Bisdom and Vernet, the Dutch leaders, have therefore the same moral justification for attempting to overthrow the English supremacy as Saunders and Clive have for overthrowing that of the French in the south. They committed, however, so many errors of conduct as entirely to destroy any chances that they may ever have had against so wary and resolute a leader as Clive.

The Dutch authorities at Batavia had already resolved to increase their Indian garrisons by some 2000 men, but, before they had put this design into execution, they received news from Chinsura that Vernet had entered into relations with Miran, taking advantage of the disputes over Rai Durlabh, with a view to the introduction of a large force into Bengal; and early in 1759 Vernet had interviews with Mir Ja'far, in which he expressed hatred of the English and a desire to be done with them. In the following June the Dutch governor-general dispatched a small fleet of seven vessels with 300 Europeans and 600 Malay troops, with orders to proceed to Negapatam and follow such orders as they should receive there. The Dutch evidently felt that they could not take decisive action from so remote a station as Batavia; but it was the first of many gross mistakes. The ships lay

---

[1] Pondichery to Negapatam, 5 August, and 11 and 27 September, 1750, Pondichery Records, No. 15, pp. 424, 442, 443.
[2] Klerk de Reuss, De expeditie naar Bengale, p. 6.
[3] Bengal Select Committee, 2 March, 1758.

at Negapatam for a month, during which the English had time to assemble their men to repulse the threatened invasion. Even when at the beginning of October the Dutch reached the entrance to the river, they still had not made up their minds what they would do. They were confronted with a prohibition, in the name of the nawab, of introducing troops into Bengal. They were simple enough to attempt to induce the nawab to withdraw his orders, which were, indeed, the orders of Clive. They evidently did not understand that, as in the days before Plassey, Mir Ja'far could not be expected to show his hand till he saw how things were going. More than a month was thus wasted; and then the Dutch resolved to force their way in. They seized various small English craft near the mouth of the river, thus giving their enemies a better *casus belli* than they could have hoped for; and finally made their attempt, landing the troops on the night of 21–22 November. But they met with complete failure. On the 24th their vessels were all captured by three Company's ships that Clive had equipped for the purpose of defending the river. On the same day Forde, who had returned from Masulipatam in the nick of time, but who, had the Dutch been less supine, would have been too late, routed a party of 400 men marching from Chinsura to meet the new troops; and on the next day he met and completely overthrew the latter body. It is curious to note that the Malay troops were armed with the old plug-bayonets which had been disused in Europe for some sixty years.[1]

These repeated disasters brought the Dutch to their knees. Indeed they had no choice. Their garrison had been destroyed, and now that the issue had been decided Miran had suddenly appeared before Chinsura with a large body of horse, eager to punish them for having lured him on with the hope of changing one master for another. The Dutch acknowledged that they had begun the hostilities, submitted to a demand that the forces they maintained in Bengal should be limited, and promised to pay ten lakhs damages. Thus Clive, taking warning by the events of the Carnatic, had a second time, by his prompt action, crushed the danger of war in Bengal with another European power. The province was not to be fought over, and its revenues destroyed, as had happened in the Carnatic.

He had thus been singularly successful in establishing the English in a position of predominance and had skilfully avoided for three years the various dangers that arose to threaten their position. But he had only done so by virtue of his astounding mastery over weaker minds and his promptitude in crushing each enemy as he arose. But the general position was still uncertain. The English had no moral position in the province. Their power was a matter of personal influence and military force. Clive's dexterity might maintain the

---

[1] Klerk de Reuss, *op. cit.*; Malcolm, *Clive*, II, 74–90; Price to Pocock, 25 December, 1759 (P.R.O. Adm. 1–161).

balance; had he continued governor of Fort William, he might have continued to maintain it; but it was unlikely that any lesser man would succeed in doing so. Leaving matters in this uncertain position, though no external danger was at the moment to be feared, Clive delivered over the chair to Holwell, and embarked for England on 25 February, 1760.

NOTE ON THE BLACK HOLE. In *Bengal Past and Present*, July, 1915, and January, 1916, will be found an attempt to discredit the accepted version of the Black Hole tragedy by Mr J. H. Little. His principal arguments are (1) that Holwell's narrative contains numerous demonstrable errors; (2) that it lacks contemporary corroboration. He concludes that Holwell, Cooke, and the other persons who vouch for the event concocted the story, and that those who are supposed to have perished in the Black Hole really were killed in the storm of the place. At a later stage in the controversy he even asserted that there was no evidence for the existence of the monument in memory of the Black Hole which Holwell erected. Everyone who has studied the records of the time must have come to the conclusion that Holwell was not a virtuous man; it is even likely that he touched up his story so as to make the part he played as conspicuous as possible. But even when we have made all allowance for this sort of thing, the main outlines of the story still remain. The small divergences which distinguish the story of Cooke from that of Holwell, for instance, are such as constantly occur in the independent accounts of contemporary witnesses; and, so far from throwing suspicion on the whole story, suggest that Cooke and Holwell did not combine to foist a false version of events on the public. Mr Little labours to prove that there could not have been so many survivors in the fort as Holwell says were shut up in the Black Hole; but the truth is that we have not the material to decide what may have been the exact number of persons remaining after the capitulation. His first argument thus casts doubt over certain details only. As regards the silence of contemporaries, he is in more than one respect entirely mistaken. It was natural that the Calcutta Council should avoid mention of the Black Hole which threw such a lurid light over the circumstances of their desertion of the place. It is not the fact that neither Clive, nor Watson, nor Pigot, refers to the Black Hole. Clive does so in some of his published correspondence; Watson does in his declaration of war; Pigot does so in a letter dated 18 September following. But, says Mr Little, the acceptance of the story by uncritical contemporaries proves nothing. However, Holwell's contemporaries were exceedingly critical. Watts, for instance, who disliked Holwell so much, and criticised his assertions so sharply, makes no attack upon this. Drake and the other fugitive councillors could have cast off a load of obloquy had they proved Holwell's story of the Black Hole to be the imposture Mr Little supposes it to have been. Altogether the controversy seems to have arisen from the perplexities of a student unaccustomed to the conflicts of evidence which the historian has perpetually to encounter; and his negative arguments do not seem to me capable of bearing the weight he would lay upon them.

CHAPTER VIII

THE SEVEN YEARS' WAR

DURING the negotiations in Europe which finally resulted in the conclusion of Godeheu's provisional treaty with Saunders, Admiral Watson had been sent out to the Coromandel Coast with a small squadron and Adlercron's regiment of foot, in case the French should refuse to come to terms; and in the next year, 1755, Clive returned to India, after a two years' rest at home, with additional troops and rank as lieutenant-colonel in the king's service. His dispatch was connected with a project that had been formed in London in case, as was shrewdly suspected, the French refused to evacuate the Deccan. This project contemplated an alliance with Balaji Rao and an attack on Bussy's position either from Bombay or from some point on the east coast.[1] But this scheme fell through, partly because the dispatches to Madras were delayed by the loss of the *Doddington* conveying the originals, partly because the Bombay Presidency was reluctant to co-operate.[2] The result was that the naval and military forces assembled at Bombay early in 1756 were employed on an affair of mere local interest—the capture, in co-operation with the forces of Balaji Rao, of the pirate stronghold of Gheriah, after which the English and Marathas fell out over the division of the plunder. Clive proceeded to take up his post as deputy-governor of Fort St David, and then, as we have seen, sailed with all the forces that could be spared at Madras for the recovery of Calcutta.

The new war that was opening in 1756 differed much from the preceding struggle. The successes of Dupleix and Bussy had been obtained during an interval of peace between France and Great Britain, that is to say at a time when the French in India did not have to trouble about their sea-communications with Europe, and when there was no possibility of hostile interference with the arrival of munitions and reinforcements. But that favourable situation had disappeared; and success now meant the control of two elements instead of one. Further it was fought out almost exclusively in the Carnatic. First Madras was besieged, and then Pondichery. The only extension of the war into Bengal consisted of Clive's seizure of Chandernagore early in 1757. So that all the advantages which the English had secured by Clive's extraordinary successes remained unimpaired. When funds ran short at Madras, Calcutta could supply the need. In this sense the Seven Years' War may be considered as the attack

[1] Military dispatches to Madras and Bombay, 26 March, 1755.
[2] Madras Record Office, Military Sundry, No. 9.—Private Committees.

and defence of the outworks of Bengal.[1] Had Lally conquered the Carnatic, he would speedily have appeared before Fort William. It was exceedingly lucky for the English that the war should have been fought out in an area of minor financial importance. They stood to gain everything and to lose little.

For the first eighteen months after the news of war had been received in November, 1756, the only outstanding event was the capture of Chandernagore, which has already been described. The English squadron was still lying in the Hugli, and Madras and Pondichery were both too bare of troops to attempt hostilities. Leyrit, governor of Pondichery, had sent all the troops he could spare to assist Bussy at Hyderabad; Pigot, governor of Madras, had sent the major part of the English forces to recover Calcutta. It had, however, been definitely understood that on the outbreak of war Clive was to return to the south with the Madras troops; and as no one in Fort St George knew what momentous designs he was revolving, much annoyance was felt and expressed at his failure to carry out his promises.[2] The French were the first to receive reinforcements. In September, 1757, a squadron of ten vessels arrived under the command of Bouvet, who had made a fugitive appearance on the coast nine years before; and he brought a battalion of the *régiment de Lorraine* under the Chevalier de Soupire. But the season was too advanced for active operations. Within a month or so the north-east monsoon might be expected to set in with the storms which made the harbour-less coast so dangerous to ships at that season, and deluges of rain that rendered all military movements impossible. Bouvet therefore made haste to return to Mauritius whence he had come, and Soupire did little except send some troops against Trichinopoly and seize the little fort of Chetpattu.

Operations really began in 1758. In February Pocock, who had succeeded to the naval command on the death of Watson in 1757, sailed from the Hugli and assembled his whole squadron of seven ships of the line at Madras. He then cruised down the coast in order to intercept any fleet that might be making for Pondichery. On 28 April he sighted a French fleet of nine ships of the line a little to the northward of Pondichery. After an action lasting from 3 to 5 in the afternoon, the French bore away, and the English were too crippled to pursue; but the former had lost 400 killed and wounded as against 118 among the English.

This fleet had convoyed the second portion of the French reinforcements, with its leader, Lally. He brought with him his own regiment, and had been invested with the fullest civil and military powers. He was syndic for the company, commissary for the king, and commandant-general of the French settlements in India; and he was

[1] Madras (Military) to the Company, 28 June, 1759.
[2] Madras Military Consultations, 28 April, 1757.

charged with the two-fold task of reforming the French administration and driving the English out of India. However, the control of the squadron was reserved for the commander d'Aché, so that Lally might find himself unexpectedly deprived of its co-operation.

The instant his troops were brought ashore, he hurried them off to besiege Fort St David. He was naturally and properly anxious to lose nothing by delay. Accordingly all the available troops were dispatched and the siege formed on 1 May. After some delay, while the material was being collected, Lally was able to break ground on the 17th. The same day he carried the outworks of the place by storm. On the 27th he began to batter in breach; and on 2 June the place capitulated. This was a disagreeable surprise for the English, who had expected it to hold out much longer. But the place was not really strong. Its extensive outworks demanded more men for their defence than the place could accommodate; there was no bomb-proof shelter for the men off duty; above all the commandant, Major Polier, distrusted and was distrusted by his men.[1] But though the issue was not flattering to English hopes, there were ugly omens on the French side too. Lally had shown great vigour and resolution, but it was something of that *vis consilii expers* which does not lead to victory. When the mortars or fascines were delayed beyond expectation, he would hasten to Pondichery and tell off Leyrit and the councillors, who retained their offices, much as he would tell off a private who appeared dirty on parade.[2]

Fort St David taken, Lally desired to proceed at once against Madras. But d'Aché refused to sail against Pocock; and without his assistance the siege was impossible until the approach of the north-east monsoon should have driven the English squadron off the coast. Meanwhile, therefore, Lally resolved, mainly on the advice of the Jesuit, Père Lavaur, to raise money by attacking Tanjore. In 1749 the raja, when besieged by Chanda Sahib and the French, had given them his bond for seventy lakhs of rupees on condition of their raising the siege. Later developments had relieved him of the need of paying any part of it; Lally decided to demand payment of the bond, sword in hand, and he might doubtless have secured a considerable sum of money had he gone to work a little less ferociously, and with a little more forethought. But he displayed the same inconsiderate haste with which he had marched against Fort St David. He marched his men off down the coast without adequate arrangements for feeding them, and without sufficient quantities of military stores. On entering Tanjore, he seized the seaport of Nagur and sold the plunder of the place to his colonel of hussars. Then turning inland he reached Tiruvalur, a place with a temple famous for its sanctity. Here Lally expected to find great plunder, but got nothing and displayed such

---

[1] Dodwell, *Dupleix and Clive*, p. 162.
[2] Cf. *Diary of Ananda Ranga Pillai*, xi, 278.

severity, executing six of the temple Brahmans whom he took for spies, that, when he marched on, the inhabitants abandoned the country through which he passed. When he arrived before the city of Tanjore (18 July), he could not begin the siege for want of powder and shot. He therefore opened negotiations, in the hope that with the assistance of the raja he might be able to attack the English force at Trichinopoly. The raja sat comfortably behind his walls, content to negotiate till famine drove away the enemy. At last Lally grew tired of fruitless discussions. He improvised batteries and opened an attack upon the place. Then on 8 August he heard that Pocock had beaten d'Aché off Karikal; he lacked material to carry through his attack; and at midnight 10–11 August he raised the siege and marched for the coast, having dispirited his men by useless hardships and inflicted a deep wound on his own reputation.[1]

The action at sea, too, had serious consequences. After the first battle d'Aché had been prevented with difficulty from sailing back to the French islands, and only remained on the coast in consequence of the urgent demands of Lally and every other Frenchman in Pondichery. He lay there till 27 July, and then put to sea on the news of Pocock's approach. An action followed on 3 August, which lasted for about an hour, during which the French squadron lost over 500 men while the English did not lose 200. This time d'Aché refused to remain longer on the coast or again to encounter the English ships. After embittered discussions in a council consisting of the chief naval, military, and civil officers, d'Aché called another council consisting of his naval officers only, who resolved with one accord that the squadron could not remain longer upon the coast. Having landed a body of seamen under the Chevalier de Poëte to reinforce Lally's land forces, he set sail from Pondichery on 3 September, and did not reappear for a twelvemonth all but a day.[2]

All that Lally could do for the moment was to wait until the change in the season should compel Pocock likewise to depart, when he might, if the rains were favourable, have a couple of months free in which to besiege Madras. He was still very superior to the English in numbers. The latter were still waiting for their reinforcements, and had received only a detachment of Draper's regiment, together with its commander, an amiable and not unskilful soldier, whose main claim to memory, however, is his courage in venturing to cross pens with Junius. But though their numbers were few, a different spirit reigned in the place from that which had so meekly submitted to La Bourdonnais. The governor, George Pigot, was irascible but resolute; he had the old veteran Colonel Lawrence to command the forces; he had John Call as engineer. The works had been entirely new-drawn; and though they were but earth, faced with turf, and

---

[1] Cf. Duteil, *Une famille militaire*, pp. 131 *sqq.*
[2] Dodwell, *op. cit.* p. 168.

needed constant repair, they were skilfully designed to frustrate attack. Ever since Lally's arrival Pigot had been busy gathering great stores of munitions and food; and orders had come from the Company that, if ever an enemy sat down before the place, the council was to deliver its authority over to the governor and the four principal military officers. Moreover, they were united, whereas Lally and the French council hated each other worse than they hated the English.

Early in October the French marched to take possession of various posts lying between Pondichery and Madras. This was successfully carried out, with the exception of Chingleput, which remained in English hands. For the moment that place, Madras, and Trichinopoly were the only spots in the Carnatic left to them. Then, when the rains were over, the French advanced and formed the siege (14 December). No attempt was made to defend the Black Town, which was at once occupied, though an unsuccessful sally was made on the news that the besiegers had got drunk on stores of arrack which they found there on their arrival. After this the siege dragged on with few incidents. As usual Lally had been unable to co-ordinate his efforts. The preparation of stores for the attack and their transport to Madras took longer than he had expected; and he was not able to open fire until 2 January, 1759. After a month's steady fire a breach was made, but the fire of the place was still unsubdued, and the breach itself so steep and so commanded by the fire of the neighbouring works that it was deemed impracticable. Neither had the besiegers been able to carry on their work unmolested. While all the French forces were lying before Madras, a detachment of the English had marched up from Trichinopoly to join the Chingleput garrison, and these troops had harassed the besiegers, threatening their convoys and posting themselves near St Thomas Mount, until Lally had been obliged to send out strong detachments against them. The French army was worn out between its work in the trenches and the pursuit of this elusive enemy. Lally hesitated, but did not venture to attempt a storm. Finally, on 16 February, a squadron of ships hove in sight. It proved to be English; and Lally at once quitted his trenches and abandoned the siege. This was the second great blow to his reputation and a proportionate encouragement to the English. Indeed their defence had been gallant. The whole of the garrison off duty as well as on had been exposed, for want of bomb-proof shelter, to the enemy's shell which he threw perpetually into the fort, and many were thus killed in their sleep; but in spite of everything they held on with admirable determination.[1] Indeed their failure would have imperilled Clive's work in Bengal.

This severe check to the French arms was speedily followed by another. Clive, well aware of the importance of keeping the French

---

[1] The official narrative of the siege is Madras Public Sundry, no. 13.—Diary of the siege of Fort St George, 1758–59 (*Records of Fort St George*, 1915).

at a distance, and yet having no troops that could be permanently spared, decided to help Madras by sending a detachment under Colonel Forde against the French in the Northern Sarkars. Lally, as has been said in a previous chapter, had resolved to recall Bussy and his troops from the Deccan. But he had not fully carried out his first intention. He had insisted on the return of Bussy and Moracin; but he had allowed a body of troops to continue under other and incapable commanders. Lally had urged with great truth the need of drawing together the whole force of the French; and there he had been right. But he had not persisted in his purpose. Bussy joined him without a man of his northern troops, who had been left behind to guard what were probably private interests. The French troops were still separated, and the Deccan detachment was now in incompetent hands. Forde had landed at Vizagapatam early in October, 1758, and was joined by Ananda Razu, the important zamindar of Vizianagram. After a pause spent in collecting provisions and coming to exact terms with his ally, Forde marched south, and completely defeated the French under Conflans at Kondur, a little to the north of Rajahmundry, the capital of the province (7 December). That place was occupied, and there a long delay occurred, owing to the difficulty of getting the promised funds from Ananda Razu, without which the men would not advance. In February, 1759, Forde renewed his march and appeared (6 March) before Masulipatam. There he lay for a month, distressed by news of the approach of Salabat Jang, by shortage of gunpowder, and by a mutiny of his Europeans.[1] But on the night of 7–8 April he carried the place by escalade, capturing a greater number of regular troops than he had under his own command.[2] On 14 May a treaty was signed with Salabat Jang, and Forde remained in undisturbed possession till the following October, when he returned to Bengal just in time to meet and defeat Roussel and his Dutchmen.

The siege of Madras and the capture of Masulipatam marked the turning-point in the war. In the Carnatic the English took the field, although they still could only bring 1000 Europeans against Lally's 2000; nor had they at first a leader able to carry them to victory. Draper went home for reasons of health; Lawrence was too old and worn to take the field, so that the command fell to Major Cholmondely Brereton, who had never had any experience of war as a subaltern.[3] He made a rash attack on Conjeeveram in September, where he was beaten off with considerable loss; but the French were unable to use their strength to press this advantage home because their men were thoroughly discontented with the lack of pay, and in the next month their discontent broke out into a very alarming mutiny, which com-

---

[1] Forde to Madras, 19 March, 1759, *ap*. Madras Military Consultations, 28 March, 1759.
[2] Forde to Madras, 10 April, 1759, *loc. cit.* 20 April, 1759.
[3] Call to Speke, 30 October, 1759 (Brit. Mus. Add. MSS, 35917, ff. 40 *sqq*.).

pelled the principal people of Pondichery to part with their plate in order to provide a proportion of the arrears.

Shortly before these events took place d'Aché had reappeared for the last time in Indian waters. He had not been able to revictual his ships at Mauritius, which, with its sister island, Bourbon, did not produce enough food for their joint consumption; and consequently he had been obliged to send to the Cape, where he had to pay heavily, thus using up a large part of the funds that had arrived from France for the use of Lally. When at last d'Aché made the Coromandel Coast (2 September), he fell in at once with Pocock who was on the watch for him. Several days were spent in manœuvres. But on the 10th a stubborn battle was joined. D'Aché managed to catch the English at a moment when their ships were widely strung out, so that two of them could take little or no part. For two hours the squadrons continued their action within musket shot. The English suffered severely. Two ships had all their sail shot away, and over 500 men were killed or wounded. But at last the French rear gave way and broke the line, then the flagship was put about by her pilot at the moment when d'Aché himself fell wounded, and the French took refuge under the guns of Pondichery. They had lost nearly 900 men and, though their fleet was still intact, it had been too severely handled to encounter the English again. In that way the action had been decisive. D'Aché lay for a fortnight off Pondichery, patching up his vessels, then on 1 October he sailed never to return.[1] Nothing more would break the blockade of the English squadron before Pondichery.

Meanwhile, at the end of October, Coote had arrived with his regiment, which, even when a detachment had been sent up to Bengal, made up the English forces to 1700 men. With these he took the field as soon as the rains were over, and began reducing the numerous little forts which studded the Carnatic. But his great object was to bring Lally to an action. With this in view, he looked on while Lally invested the fort of Wandiwash which the French had lately lost; and then, when Lally was fairly committed to the siege, Coote advanced swiftly on him. The result was a battle (22 January, 1760) as decisive on land as Pocock's late action had been at sea. Lally was routed, and it was the last pitched battle of the war. The remaining posts in the Carnatic were soon reduced, and in the course of March the French were reduced to Pondichery, Jinji, and Karikal, of which the last surrendered on 5 April.

There remained the reduction of Pondichery. For the moment Coote judged his forces too few to enable him to form the siege of the place. Meanwhile Lally attempted to retrieve his position by means of help from Hyder 'Ali, the rising general in the service of Mysore. A treaty was made by which Hyder was promised certain forts, French assistance to conquer territories to the southward as soon as the English

---

[1] Dodwell, *Dupleix and Clive*, p. 182, and references there cited.

had been beaten, and two lakhs of rupees a month. On this Hyder
sent his brother-in-law with a detachment to Pondichery; but he
brought no provisions, he suggested no feasible plans for the destruction of Coote and his army, and after a month's hesitation he departed,
giving up the fort which had been delivered to him. Meanwhile
Coote had captured the fort of Villiyanallur, and induced the admiral
to land a body of marines to reinforce his troops. With them he
prepared to drive the French within their bound-hedge.

At this moment the command changed hands. Dispatches arrived
with a commission giving Monson rank over Coote who till then had
been the senior alike in service and in position. The latter therefore
retired to Madras, and prepared to proceed with his regiment to
Bengal, whither indeed he had been ordered. That would have meant
the abandonment of the siege of Pondichery. Monson offered to
leave the army till the place had been captured, and Coote then
agreed to leave his regiment behind. Monson drove the French within
the bound-hedge, but was severely wounded in the operation, and
Coote then resumed the command on the understanding that the
other should not rejoin the army before the fall of Pondichery.[1] This
was on 20 September.

Pondichery had now been blockaded for several months, and the
condition within the place was miserable. Lally and the Company's
servants were on the worst possible terms. No money was to be had.
Attempts to wring money out of either the European or the Indian
inhabitants of the place had proved singularly fruitless; and endeavours to fetch up supplies from the neutral settlements on the
coast had been frustrated by the vigilance of the blockading ships.
The enemy without pressed nearer and nearer. In December they
opened fire on the defences; in the first days of January a storm
scattered the English squadron lying in the roads, and for an instant
the way lay open for supplies, but before advantage could be taken
of this the men-of-war were back at their old posts; the position of
the town was hopeless; and on 16 January, 1761, it surrendered at
discretion. Jinji surrendered after some weeks of blockade; Mahé,
on the west coast, surrendered to an overpowering force which sat
down before it, and the French were left without a foot of ground in
India.

The principal cause which had contributed to this complete victory
was certainly the relentless pressure of sea-power. Although the
French fleet was never destroyed, yet the cumulative effect of the
three actions which were fought established an irresistible superiority,
such as later in 1783 Suffren had just established when the news of
peace robbed him of the fruits of victory. While the English received
supplies of food and money from Bengal, recruits of men from Europe,
and grain from their northern settlements, the French could receive

---

[1] Dodwell, *op. cit.* pp. 186–7, and references there cited.

nothing but what came to them laboriously by land. The first were constantly strengthened, the second as constantly weakened. And this enabled Coote to establish his military superiority over Lally in the field and to hem him in within the walls of Pondichery. And in this connection we may doubt whether the possession of Mauritius was an unmixed blessing to the French. It possessed an excellent harbour where their squadrons could refit; but it was remote from the decisive area of the war, and was a constant temptation to a faltering commander to abandon the coast to the enemy.

Next to the pressure of sea-power we must set the influence of superior finance. From first to last Lally was embarrassed for means of paying his troops; of obtaining material; of paying work-people. He came out with scanty supplies, nor could the war-ravaged Carnatic make good this crushing disadvantage. But here the control of the Bengal nawab, established in 1757, was a strong help to the English. At more than one critical moment, when our men were on the point of mutiny, Bengal sent down supplies which enabled Madras to carry on. The one good thing which can be said for the revolution of 1760 is that it enabled the siege of Pondichery to be continued to its conclusion. It has been said that had Lally retained Bussy in the Deccan he might have been able to secure funds thence; but I cannot accept that view. The Deccan had never been able to remit money to the south. Whatever had been got there, or from the Sarkars which had been ceded to Bussy, had always been eaten up by the establishments which were maintained there, and, except the lakh and a half of rupees which Bussy sent to Lally in 1758, the place had never provided any resources for the public treasury of the French.

Thirdly, we must place the personal character of Lally among the causes of the French failure. His hastiness, his violent temper, his uncontrolled and cutting speech, his habit of threatening without punishing, were all strong obstacles in his way. Nor was his task made easier by the orders which he received to carry into execution a reform of the Pondichery administration in a time of war. The two things were incompatible. Against such difficulties and such defects his personal gallantry fought in vain.

CHAPTER IX

BENGAL, 1760–72

WHEN Clive quitted Bengal early in 1760, the position of affairs was still very unsettled. 'Ali Gauhar was still lingering on the borders of Bihar, financial relations with Mir Ja'far were still unsatisfactory, and the share which the nawab had taken in the recent attempts of the Dutch, though as yet unknown in detail, was strongly suspected. Moreover, Clive's successor, Holwell, was a man of greater talent than character; he only held his office temporarily and by accident till Clive's permanent successor arrived; and he was not capable of imposing his will, as Clive had done, either on the Company's servants or on the nawab. Consequently the unstable political situation, which had grown up in the last three years as the result of the military power of the Company and the personal character of Clive, was not likely to remain unshaken when the control passed into weaker hands.

The command of the troops had fallen to Caillaud, who had been brought up from Madras at the particular request of Clive. He was a skilful soldier, and under his command the English forces were not likely to undergo defeat; but, like Holwell, he was not a man of any moral vigour or capable of making good the deficiencies of the temporary governor. At the moment he was on campaign against the shahzada, with a battalion of Europeans and another of sepoys, together with a large body of cavalry under the nawab's son, Miran. He succeeded by the action of Sirpur (22 February) in relieving Patna, which had been attacked by the shahzada, but Miran's men did not follow up their success, mainly, Caillaud thought, owing to the inertness of their leader; and then for a week Miran insisted on nursing some slight wounds he had received, while the shahzada, having collected his scattered troops, raided into the province of Bengal. Caillaud followed him so closely that he had little opportunity of doing anything effectual, and again withdrew; but the nawab's horse had again proved unserviceable, and the nawab entered into correspondence with the shahzada, declaring, it was believed, that his resistance was solely due to the insistence of the English. However, when Caillaud had once again relieved Patna, the shahzada finally retired from Bihar.[1] Caillaud and Miran then set out to chastise the zamindars who had afforded him help during his raid into Bengal. But in the course of these operations, on 3 July, Miran perished, probably killed by lightning.[2]

---

[1] Caillaud's Journal, *ap.* Orme MSS, India, vi.
[2] India Office, Home Miscellaneous, 456 D.

The death of Miran was in itself no great loss. From the Indian historians we gather a conception of his character much resembling that which they attribute to Siraj-ud-daula.[1] But the event at once brought up the question of succession, and placed in a position of great prominence a man of consummate political skill, connected with the nawab by marriage, and generally well-reputed among the English. This was Mir Kasim. He sought at once to obtain a promise of being named either the diwan or the successor of Mir Ja'far; and for the moment Mir Ja'far seems to have acquiesced in his plans. But for some time before this occurrence Holwell and Caillaud had been discussing the political future of the provinces. Holwell had taken up an attitude strongly opposed to the maintenance of the present nawab. He argued that he had betrayed the English both with the Dutch and with the shahzada, that he had failed to make the payments that he had promised the Company, that the country was going to ruin under his government, and that the sooner he was removed the better for the English and for the country. Caillaud, to whom these views were communicated, did not agree with them. He thought the Company was bound to support the nawab and that a revolution would be fraught with ill consequences. Hastings held the same ideas.

"Mr Holwell's censures on the Nabob's conduct," he wrote, "are but too just; but I dread the consequences he seems to draw from them. Let the Nabob be ever so bad, we are bound if not in justice, in honour and policy to support him through these troubles, now we are so far engaged. I do not suppose he is grown a worse man since the commencement of this war....That he is a usurper is certain, and one of our making...."[2]

Caillaud replied with a long letter traversing Holwell's arguments. The latter rejoined:

Had it ever been my wish or intention to have taken our support from the present Nabob and transfer it to any other, your arguments in that case would have all the weight with me they so greatly merit....But my views for the Company went much higher. That the country will never be in a settled peaceful state whilst this family is at the head of it, is a position I lay down as incontestable, and that until the country enjoys that state the Company's affairs must be daily approaching to certain ruin: I therefore judge we could never be possessed of a more just or favourable opportunity to carry into execution what must be done, I plainly see, one time or other, if the Company have ever a secure footing in the provinces, to wit, take this country into their own hands....The situation of the Prince at present is such that I am sure he would readily and thankfully hearken to an overture from us, and without hesitation grant a phirmaund appointing the Company perpetual subas of the province....[3]

Holwell already knew that his term of office was limited, and in those circumstances he could not press views which he knew found little support with his councillors.[4]

---

[1] *Jami-ut-tawarikh, ap.* Elliott and Dowson, VIII, 429.
[2] Hastings to Caillaud, 4 June, 1760.
[3] Holwell to Caillaud, 14 June, 1760.
[4] The correspondence between Holwell and Caillaud will be found in Holwell's *India Tracts* and *Vindication*, and in the Orme MSS, India, XII.

On 27 July arrived the new governor, Henry Vansittart. He was
a Madras servant of some fourteen years' standing. He possessed a
good knowledge of Persian, and had transacted with success the
business between the Madras Council and Nawab Muhammad 'Ali;
his tact and dexterity had won him very favourable notice at Madras,
and Clive had urged his appointment on the Company in the strongest
terms. It proved, however, to be singularly unfortunate. He encountered the sharp jealousy of all the Bengal servants whom he had
superseded; and though always well-intentioned, the policy which
he adopted proved to be the source of many misfortunes. He was
one of that large body of men who can execute the orders of their
superiors much better than they can frame a policy of their own. In
the present case he adopted the policy suggested to him by Holwell,
who by this time had abandoned his original plan in favour of
appointing Mir Kasim heir-apparent. It is more likely that Holwell
yielded to the material arguments of Mir Kasim than to the reasons
which Caillaud and others had produced against the establishment
of the Company as subahdar.[1] After prolonged discussions Mir
Kasim was invited down to Calcutta. The negotiations with him were
confided to Holwell in person; and on 27 September an agreement
was reached by which Mir Kasim was to receive the office of deputy
subahdar, with a guarantee of succession to the subahdari, while the
English were to receive the three districts of Burdwan, Midnapur,
and Chittagong for the maintenance of their troops. Mir Kasim also
agreed to pay off the outstanding debts of Mir Ja'far to the Company.[2]

He then returned to Murshidabad. Vansittart and Caillaud
reached the same place in order to carry the agreement into effect
on 14 October. But they then found that Mir Ja'far refused absolutely
to place his person and government in the hands of his kinsman.
After five days' discussion, Caillaud was ordered to occupy the palace
of Motijhil, where the nawab was. In the face of superior force, the
latter at last decided to resign his office, on which Mir Kasim was
immediately seated on the *masnad*, and the revolution of 1760 was
completed. Mir Ja'far went down to reside at Calcutta under an
English guard which he demanded, and Mir Kasim grudgingly agreed
to allow him 15,000 rupees a month.[3]

Thus the matter ended by pulling down one nawab only to set up
another. Nothing was done to reconcile the essentially opposed interests of the nawab and the English. Nor was the agreement with
Mir Kasim so full and explicit as to exclude future causes of misunderstanding. In that respect the settlement was most unsatisfactory, and
Vansittart merits the severest criticism for having adopted it. It was
also followed by the grant of presents which cast a sordid air over

---

[1] Dodwell, *Dupleix and Clive*, p. 205.
[2] Bengal Select Committee, 11, 15, 16, and 27 September, 1760.
[3] *Calendar of Persian Correspondence*, 1, 43, 130, 135, 138 and 140.

the whole business; but except in the case of Holwell, these do not seem to have been stipulated beforehand, as had been the case with the presents that were bestowed after Plassey; nor is it likely that they formed an element in the motives of Vansittart and his followers. There were, as Grant said, "many easier avenues to irregular emolument than the troublesome, hazardous, and...public road of a general revolution".[1]

The unstable nature of the settlement quickly manifested itself in three principal affairs—the question of the shahzada, the question of Ramnarayan, and the question of the internal trade. The shahzada, whose father the emperor 'Alamgir II had been murdered in the previous year, was still in Bihar, while the nawab's troops in that region were mutinous for want of pay. In spite of this, Carnac, who had just arrived as commander of the Company's troops in Bengal, defeated him (15 January, 1761) on the Son, taking Law and most of the other Frenchmen with him, and on 6 February the shahzada, who had assumed the title of Shah 'Alam II, was induced to confer with Carnac at Gaya, and then to accompany him to Patna. Before Mir Kasim had become subahdar, he and the Select Committee had agreed on a project to make peace with and assist the shahzada in marching to Delhi and establishing himself as emperor.[2] The design proves the political imbecility of Vansittart. It mattered nothing to the English who called himself emperor, and it would have been the height of folly to dissipate their unconsolidated power in interfering in the affairs of Upper India. In fact, however, the project came to nothing, because when Mir Kasim had been safely installed, he offered a persistent, though half-concealed, opposition to the design. He was clearly obsessed with the fear that the English would obtain from Shah 'Alam a grant for the provinces on their own account, as Holwell had at first intended and as Rai Durlabh, who had been consulted, had advised.[3] There had, indeed, been from the first a party strongly opposed to Vansittart and therefore to any policy which he advocated; and the substitution of Carnac for Caillaud had strengthened this party. When in April Coote arrived from Madras, and took over the command from Carnac, the change emphasised the opposition, for Coote entertained as his diwan Nandakumar, whom Mir Kasim regarded as pledged to the restoration of Mir Ja'far.[3] When Mir Kasim went up to Patna, more than one misunderstanding arose between him and the military commander; Mir Kasim refused to proclaim Shah 'Alam as emperor till after his departure, and even then was only brought to do so by Coote's threat of doing it himself if Mir Kasim delayed any longer.[4] When the emperor departed in

---

[1] Grant, *Sketch*, p. 187.
[2] Letter to McGwire and Carnac, *ap.* Bengal Select Committee, 13 February, 1761; letter to Mir Kasim, 2 February, 1761 (*Calendar of Persian Correspondence*, I, 63).
[3] Vansittart to Mir Kasim, 27 October, 1761 (*Calendar of Persian Correspondence*, I, 130).
[4] Coote's Journal, Orme MSS, India, VIII.

June, the nawab evidently felt that he had narrowly escaped seeing power transferred over his head to the English by Shah 'Alam. Although there was not a shred of truth in the nawab's suspicions, Vansittart's policy was already beginning to break down under the stress of circumstances and lack of union among the English.

Ramnarayan's case was to demonstrate this even more clearly. In Mir Ja'far's time the English had steadily protected him from the nawab, and his conduct had justified their protection. He had resolutely and at times skilfully resisted the inroads of the shahzada; and the new governor was resolved to continue the protection which Clive had given. Coote's instructions, when he was proceeding to Patna in April, contained a clause directing him to secure Ramnarayan from injustice and at all events to maintain him in his government.[1] However, the tone of the Calcutta government gradually cooled. On 18 June the committee agreed to Ramnarayan's suspension and Vansittart wrote to Mir Kasim that he could do what he liked about the deputy. Coote and Carnac were recalled from Patna. In August Vansittart approved of the appointment of a new deputy, and in September he ordered Ramnarayan to be delivered into the nawab's hands.[2] When as much money as possible had been extracted from him, he was put to death. In this matter Vansittart had acted in plain opposition to the policy of Clive. The latter had desired above everything to strengthen the English position; Vansittart desired to strengthen that of the nawab. The first had therefore made a point of protecting the principal Hindu ministers; the second deliberately desisted from protecting them. He failed to see how far his policy would lead him and how strong a reaction it would provoke.[3]

Having succeeded in getting rid of the emperor and in getting the chief English protégé into his hands, Mir Kasim now proceeded to raise the third question, that of the internal trade of the province. This was a matter which neither Clive nor Vansittart had ever fairly faced. Its history goes back to the days before the battle of Plassey, when the imperial farmans conferred on the English complete liberty of trade exempt from the imperial transit dues. The Company's servants had always interpreted this as authorising them to trade in articles such as salt, betel and tobacco, without paying the tolls imposed on those articles. The nawab had always insisted on their doing nothing of the sort. The Company, having no interest in this matter, had prohibited its servants from following the internal trade, for fear of their provoking troubles with the nawab on that account. The Company's servants felt that they had been kept out of their rights by the strong hand; and when the strong hand was at last on their side

[1] Bengal Select Committee, 21 April, 1761.
[2] Vansittart to Mir Kasim, 18 June and 21 September, 1761 (*Calendar of Persian Correspondence*, I, 108 and 122).
[3] Cf. Scrafton, *Observations on Mr Vansittart's Narrative*, p. 32.

they resolved to exercise their supposed rights to the full. Clive in
1757 was instructed to procure an express authorisation from Mir
Ja'far for their participation in the internal trade free of duties. No
such article appears in the treaty; but the parwanas issued by the
nawab in execution of the treaty were phrased in such wide terms
and included such definite instructions as show that Clive carried out
this part of his orders.

> Whatever goods the Company's gumastahs may bring or carry to or from their
> factories, the aurungs or other places, by land or by water, with a dustuck from
> any of the chiefs of their factories, you shall neither ask nor receive any sum,
> however trifling for the same. Know they have full power to buy and sell; you are
> by no means to oppose it....Whoever acts contrary to these orders, the English
> have full power to punish them.[1]

As the Company's servants had always been thought entitled to enjoy
the same privileges as the Company itself, they proceeded to take
advantage of their new freedom from control to trade in the articles
so long prohibited. Clive on the whole seems to have set his face
against this practical extension of English privileges; but it seems
clear that under his government it went on, though perhaps not in
any great volume, and that at the end of his government Mir Ja'far
complained of it. On that occasion, Clive, who was on the eve of his
departure, refused to give any decided answer, but the council seems
to have decided in favour of the fullest interpretation of English rights;
the practice grew; and when Vansittart arrived at Calcutta it was in
full swing. In the discussions which preceded Mir Ja'far's removal,
the matter never seems to have been mentioned. Indeed, had Mir
Kasim proposed its abolition, he would almost certainly have received
not a shred of English support. But he was too wise to raise such a
thorny matter at a time when the favour of the English meant everything to him. He therefore waited till the emperor had departed, till
Ramnarayan had been delivered over to him, and the Hindus could
no longer look to the English for countenance and support, and then,
in December, 1761, came the first complaints that the nawab's
officers were obstructing the trade of the Company and its dependents.[2] In May, 1762, came the first recorded complaint from the other
side, Mir Kasim alleging misconduct on the part of the English traders'
Indian agents.[3] Vansittart still thought the nawab was making
himself uneasy about small matters, and that the whole question
could be cleared up by a personal interview; but in fact complaints
doubled and redoubled. The officers of the nawab obstructed English
trade; the English "did themselves justice"; the nawab claimed the
right of himself administering justice. Such different persons as

---

[1] Dodwell, op. cit. pp. 214 sqq.
[2] Vansittart to Mir Kasim, 18 and 19 December, and to Mir Sher 'Ali, 19 December,
1761 (Calendar of Persian Correspondence, I, 137).
[3] Idem, I, 161.

Scrafton and Hastings both accord in testifying not only that the
words of the nawab's parwana quoted above had been steadily acted
upon, but also that such privilege was necessary.[1] It had constantly
been exercised during the government of Mir Ja'far; it had not been
mentioned when Mir Kasim succeeded his father-in-law, any more
than had been the question of the internal trade; but now he suddenly
discovered that these practices were incompatible with the proper
exercise of his powers and complained of them as new and unbearable
usurpations. It is, indeed, clear that they were incompatible with
Vansittart's policy of strengthening the nawab; but no engagements
seem to have been sought or given in 1760; and, indeed, Vansittart
had probably not realised what a difficulty they offered.

Out of them sprang the war of 1763 and the restoration of Mir
Ja'far as nawab. At the close of 1762 Vansittart visited the nawab
at Mongir, where he had established his capital, and made a treaty
with him on the subject of the internal trade. In future English
merchants were to pay 9 per cent., whereas Indian merchants paid
40 on salt carried up to Patna, but, as against this, disputes were to
be heard and determined by the nawab's officers. This agreement
was not to have been announced until Vansittart had procured the
assent of the council; but Mir Kasim published it at once. It is
doubtful whether the council would in any case have accepted it;
but the news of the abandonment of the right of "doing themselves
justice", received as it was through the nawab's officers, excited a
blaze of anger. This was exaggerated by various other news that came
in about the same time. One was that Vansittart had been imprudent
enough to accept seven lakhs from the nawab, in part as a refund
of advances he had made, but in part as a present, and of course
everyone declared that the money was the price of abandoning
English rights; it is curious that Mir Kasim had instructed his deputy
at Dacca to show special favour to Vansittart's agents;[2] perhaps he
expected to strengthen his position by setting the English quarrelling;
if so, the event must have disappointed him. Ellis, the chief at Patna,
had been in constant disputes with the nawab's servants, who had
neglected to visit him on his arrival as chief; many of the council
were deeply suspicious of Mir Kasim, who had recently entered into
relations of an unknown character with the nawab of Oudh. All
these things combined to produce a revolt against the authority of
Vansittart and the policy with which he was associated. His agreement was rejected; all the absent members of council were called
down to Calcutta; and it was resolved that in future the English
should trade duty-free except for $2\frac{1}{2}$ per cent. on their salt, and that
English agents should be subject to none but English control. When

---

[1] Scrafton, *op. cit.* p. 34; Hastings to Holwell, 19 February, 1760 (Brit. Mus. Add. MSS,
29096, f. 223 verso).
[2] Mir Kasim to the Naib of Dacca, n.d. (Select Committee Report, 1772, I, (2), App. 34).

the nawab resolved to abolish the duties, the council refused to assent and deputed Amyatt and Hay, two of their members, to insist on large preferential terms for the English trade. These Mir Kasim refused to concede. At the same time affairs at Patna had greatly exasperated feelings on both sides. Ellis, the chief, a man of violent temper, and a bitter enemy of Vansittart, had insisted on the English privileges without any heed to appearances; while Mir Kasim had begun to prepare against those events which evidently drew nearer every day. He closed and stockaded the Patna gate close to the English factory; he assembled troops in Patna; and in June he sent emissaries to seduce the Company's European and sepoy troops stationed there. On 21 June he sent a fresh body of troops from Mongir towards Patna; and on this news Ellis attempted to seize the city; after a temporary success he failed to retain it; his garrison was destroyed; and the war had begun.

Blameworthy as were individuals, it was a war of circumstances rather than intentions. Vansittart had failed to realise that a strong nawab would inevitably desire to reduce the extraordinary privileges which the English claimed, and he had made no allowance for the fact that the English councillors would become uncontrollable if their material interests were attacked. In short he lacked the insight and vigour which his position demanded. The councillors with the exception of Hastings allowed their material interests to colour and distort their policy. Mir Kasim had displayed great political dexterity but little wisdom. But the dominating fact of the situation was that the interests of the English and of the nawab were irreconcilable. There could be no stability in affairs so long as the nawab fancied himself an independent governor and the English claimed privileges wholly inconsistent with that independence.

The war which thus began in 1763 was destined to end this uncertain position. On 10 June Major Adams, an officer of Coote's, took the field at the head of 1100 Europeans and 4000 sepoys against Mir Kasim's army of 15,000 to 20,000 men. Between that date and 5 September he won four considerable victories in the course of his advance upon the nawab's capital of Mongir. Mir Kasim had now lost all confidence in his troops and their leaders. He fled to Patna, where he put to death all the English who had fallen into his hands; and he had already murdered his commander-in-chief, who had been guiltless of any crime but that of failure, and the Seths, who had been guiltless of any crime at all. He was, indeed, displaying that same weak violence which the English councillors had already displayed, though in a less bloody fashion. He then fled into Oudh, where he hoped to find assistance with which to recover the provinces from the English. The nawab of Oudh, Shuja-ud-daula, agreed to assist him, and the emperor Shah 'Alam joined the confederates. But at this point the war came to a pause. On the one side the Oudh troops were not ready for attack; on the other, the English commander, Adams, retired to Calcutta to die; he was succeeded by Carnac who was hampered, not only by lack of conspicuous military talent in himself, but also by mutiny among his men, by disputes with the council, and by counteraction on the part of the restored nawab, Mir Ja'far, who had been sent back from Calcutta to reign once more at Murshidabad.[1] After a series of very inconclusive events on the borders of Oudh and Bihar, which occupied the first half of 1764, Major Hector Munro, of the 89th, arrived and took command of the army. He spent August and September in restoring the discipline of the army. After executing twenty-five mutineers by blowing them from his guns, and breaking one sepoy battalion with all possible ignominy,[2] he invaded Oudh, and on 22 October, after a stubborn contest, completely defeated the enemy at Baksar. There was no more resistance. Oudh was overrun by Fletcher, who succeeded Munro in the command. Shah 'Alam joined the English camp once more; Shuja-ud-daula fled into the Rohilla country; while Mir Kasim, stripped of his treasure and deserted by his followers, escaped into obscure poverty.

Meanwhile the old nawab had been restored. On 10 July, 1763, was signed a new treaty, by which he agreed to limit the forces he kept up, to receive a permanent resident at the durbar, and to levy no more than $2\frac{1}{2}$ per cent. on the English trade in salt. Advantage was also taken to secure a promise of compensation for all losses, public and private, caused by the war with Mir Kasim. These stipulations regarding private interests were severely criticised by the Company. Nor even were the other provisions found to concede all that was required. The nawab appointed Nandakumar as his chief minister; and in the course of the war the latter was believed to have betrayed the English plans, and in various ways to have obstructed their operations. Accordingly when Mir Ja'far died early in 1765 his son Najm-ud-daula was only recognised on condition of his appointing a minister nominated by the English, and agreeing not to displace him without their approval. The minister held the title of deputy subahdar, and was to have under the nawab the chief management of all affairs.[3] By this agreement the long struggle between the English and the nawab was brought to an end. The nawab survived as a figurehead, in whose name administration was conducted by a nominee of the English, but who of himself could do nothing. Clive, whose appointment as governor of Fort William had already been announced, was very indignant with the council in thus determining an affair of importance before his arrival; but, venal as

---

[1] Besides the proceedings of the Bengal Select Committee, see also Champion's Journal, ap. India Office Home Miscellaneous, no. 198.

[2] Munro's reports, ap. Bengal Select Committee, 24 September, 1764.

[3] Bengal Select Committee, 14 and 28 February, and 16 March, 1765.

the council were, in this case their action from the point of view of policy was irreproachable. It would have been very unwise to have left the matter of the succession hanging over until Clive's arrival, and still more so to have invested the new nawab with powers which it afterwards would have been found expedient to diminish. Unfortunately the council marred their conduct by making this settlement the occasion of taking large presents in defiance of the orders of the Company which had already been received.

Clive's victories in Bengal had transformed not only the position of the English in India but also the proceedings of the Company in England. Violent political discussions succeeded to the dull and decorous statements of the course of the trade in the East. Control of the Company and of its policy became a thing worth paying for. Clive on the one side and Laurence Sulivan on the other, entered into a series of campaigns to secure a dominant interest, buying up stock, and subdividing it so as to create if possible a majority of secure votes. The right to Clive's jagir had been the great bone of contention, and the preservation of that valuable property had cost Clive great sums of money. Sulivan, the great friend of Warren Hastings, was a man without an idea in advance of the low level of his time. He almost ruined himself in his struggle with Clive, while his friend Vansittart did so completely; and he then took advantage of his position and following at the East India House to seek to retrieve his position by procuring lucrative posts for his sons and relatives in the East.[1] In 1764 Clive succeeded for the time being in obtaining the control of the Company; and the fact was marked by his acceptance for a second time of the office of governor of Fort William. He went out in order to set right the errors that had evidently been committed by his successors. The revolution of 1760 had been bitterly attacked in England, and so had the war which followed with the new nawab. It was generally felt that unless the Company set its house in order, it would be impossible to prevent the ministry from interfering in Indian affairs, and perhaps abolishing the Company itself.

Clive reached Calcutta in May, 1765, and found two problems awaiting his solution—one political, the future relations of the English with the emperor, the nawab of Oudh, and the nawab of Bengal; and the other administrative, the reform of the swollen profits from illicit or quasi-illicit sources, and the re-establishment of order and subordination, which had disappeared in the revolt of the council against Vansittart. On his arrival the new governor found that Vansittart had promised Oudh to the emperor. It seemed to Clive a foolish step. There was no ground for thinking that Shah 'Alam would be able to maintain himself there without English help, so that the

[1] *Palk MSS*, pp. 91, 126 and 188; Sulivan to Hastings, 6 June, 1781 (Brit. Mus. Add. MSS, 29149, f. 244).

settlement contained within itself all the elements of future complications. Clive therefore sent up Carnac to reopen negotiations until he himself should be able to visit Oudh in person. Carnac soon found himself in communication with the fugitive Shuja-ud-daula, with whom Clive decided to come to terms, restoring to him his old dominions with the exception of Allahabad, on condition of a payment of fifty lakhs of rupees. Allahabad with the surrounding districts was bestowed on the emperor. The settlement has been attacked on both sides—as a breach of faith with the emperor in taking away from him what had been promised, and as bestowing territory on one who would not be able to protect it. As regards the first no formal treaty had as yet been arranged, so that Clive's hands were still free; as regards the second, some sort of provision had to be made for the emperor, and the one which Clive adopted cost the Company nothing, and committed it to nothing. Indeed the grant of Allahabad marks the end of those foolish dreams which had been cherished by almost everyone in Bengal, of restoring the empire to its legitimate holder. Any such attempt would have strained the Company's resources beyond their power. It would have united the princes of India against the English. At the same time the restoration of the nawab of Oudh placed on the frontiers an ally who at the moment was too grateful to attack them, and who afterwards was much too severely threatened by other powers to think of doing so. Clive's settlement was a middle course, which afforded more advantage and threatened fewer dangers than any other that could have been adopted at the time. In Bengal itself Clive decided on a long step forward towards the assumption of ostensible power. He demanded from the emperor as the price of Allahabad and its districts a farman granting the diwanni of Bengal to the Company. That involved the complete control of the finances of the province, and carried to its completion that process of the extrusion of the nawab's power which had been almost secured by the arrangement of February, 1765. The disadvantages of this plan are obvious enough; but they were such as counted for less in those days than they would now. Power was separated from responsibility. But no one at the moment thought of undertaking the administration of large tracts of India, and the fact of bad and corrupt administration appeared one of those natural and inevitable evils which are beyond possibility of reform. As against this the plan offered certain immediate advantages. It secured that control over the nawab which was regarded as the most pressing need of the time; it also promised some protection against the complaints of foreign powers and the demands of the home government. Clive still remembered how the too-ostensible assumption of power contributed to produce the unyielding opposition of the English to the schemes of Dupleix; and farmans of the emperor or parwanas of the nawab, though valueless without the support of English power, could not be fully discounted at Paris or the Hague without a serious breach of diplomatic etiquette. It was thought too that something short of the assumption of full dominion would be less likely to excite legal difficulties in England or provoke the interference of parliament. In short the grant of the diwanni was designed to secure the full control of Bengal affairs so far as the Company's interests went without incurring the inconvenience of formal and avowed dominion.

The administrative questions that demanded settlement were much more difficult than these political questions. First there were the Company's covenanted servants. They had been demoralised by the conditions under which they had been working and the facility with which wealth could be acquired through the English privileges in the internal trade of Bengal; while a tradition had arisen that each change of nawab should be the occasion of large presents, open or concealed. The accession of Najm-ud-daula had been a particularly bad case, because the succession was normal, and because the precedent of presents from the nawab had been extended to the minister as well. Further, this extension of a bad practice had been made in the face of specific orders from the Company prohibiting the acceptance of presents and requiring its servants to sign covenants agreeing not to accept such in future. Instead of announcing their orders the councillors had quietly left them over for Clive to deal with on his arrival. Indeed they seem to have thought that his previous practice and present influence would have led him to procure the abrogation of the orders before he came out again as governor. But they were mistaken in their man. Clive feared nothing, not even his own past; and he was as fully bent on enforcing the orders of the Company as if he himself had never made a rupee by the revolution of 1757 or were not still in enjoyment of a jagir of £30,000 a year. One of his earliest acts on his arrival at Calcutta was to require the covenants to be signed by civil and military servants alike. That was done, but Champion, and probably many others as well, did so with the idea that this reforming zeal could not last and that their signature was a mere matter of form.[1]

Clive, however, saw as clearly as did Cornwallis twenty years later that if illicit gains were to be abolished, considerable regular advantages had to be provided. On his arrival he found that there was a great lack of senior servants. Since everyone had been held entitled to passes for the internal trade, it had been possible for even junior servants to make fortunes by selling their passes to the Indian merchants of Calcutta. The result was that Clive found the secretary's department in charge of a writer of three years' standing, the accountant was a writer yet younger than the secretary, while the paymaster of the army, with balances of twenty lakhs in his hands

[1] Champion's Journal, 6 August, 1765.

for months together, had also been a writer.[1] Clive resolved therefore
to reorganise the internal trade, to place it on a wholly new basis,
and to employ the profits so as to secure handsome salaries for the
senior servants of the Company; and meanwhile to call up from
Madras a small number of covenanted servants to fill the immediate
vacancies in council. This last measure produced the sort of uproar
that was to be expected. An association was formed; Clive's entertainments were boycotted; memorials were framed. But when the
malcontents found that they were promptly deprived of every lucrative
office, refused passes, and sent hither and thither very much against
their liking, they concluded at last that they had better put up with
Clive's tyranny, and the opposition died down. Meanwhile Clive
went on with his salt scheme. That had always been a government
monopoly, and as such Clive decided to administer it and employ
the profits arising out of it in the payment of allowances to the
principal civil and military servants. He did so under the form of a
trading company, under the close control of the council, and the
allowances took the form of shares in the company. This was contrary
to the orders of the Company; but Clive considered that those orders
had been issued before he had taken over the revenue administration
of the provinces, that his new plan could not possibly rouse difficulties
with the nawab, and that consequently the main objections of the
Company did not apply to his present proposals. In this respect
he was guilty of a miscalculation. When the news of what he had
done reached England, the Company at once ordered the internal
trade to be entirely abandoned; these orders were again suspended,
and Clive hoped to procure their reversal on his return to England;
but the directors insisted on their views being carried out; and so at
last the trading company was wound up. In this matter Clive has
been unduly blamed. His proposals amounted in reality to the
continuation of the monopoly which had been customary and the
assignment of the revenues so raised to the payment of establishment.
Although in form his plan seemed to continue the vices of the Vansittart *régime*, in essence it was wholly different and amounted to just
that measure of reform for which Cornwallis has received such high
praise. The mistake which Clive made was apparently one of tactics.
He thought the Company would be less likely to oppose the scheme
so long as the payment of the extra allowances did not appear to
come out of its own revenues. He forgot that the apparent similarity
between his plan and the abuses of the past might lead to its condemnation.

With the military officers Clive had even more trouble than with
the civilians. This was natural, because in the latter case he had had
only to deal with illicit gains whereas in the former he was required
to cut down regular and acknowledged allowances. For some years

[1] Bengal Select Committee to the Company, 24 March, 1766.

the Company had been endeavouring to cut down the batta or field-allowances of the Bengal officers. These allowances were designed to make good the extra cost of living in the field as compared with living in garrison. They originated in the Carnatic, where both Chanda Sahib and Muhammad 'Ali had paid batta to the French and English officers respectively in their service; and difficulties had arisen when Muhammad 'Ali had transferred lands to the English Company in lieu of this batta, and the question of its regulation had arisen between the officers and the Company. Affairs had followed the same course in Bengal, where batta had at first been paid by the nawab and then became a charge upon the Company, who desired to reduce it to the more moderate level paid at Madras. Orders to this effect had reached Bengal when the war with Mir Kasim had been on the point of breaking out; their immediate execution had thus been impossible. But when they were repeated, in 1764, they met with the same fate as those other unpleasant orders prohibiting presents, and obedience was deferred until Clive's arrival. He accordingly prepared regulations on the subject. Officers in cantonments at Mongir or Patna were to draw half batta, as did officers at Trichinopoly; when they took the field they would draw batta while within the limits of Bengal and Bihar, but if they crossed into Oudh they would then become entitled to double batta. For a captain these rates amounted to three, six, and twelve rupees a day. These orders led to a combination among the officers, just as the appointment of covenanted servants from Madras had led to a combination among the civilians. It was agreed that they should simultaneously resign their commissions. In this step they seem to have been encouraged by the commander of one of the brigades, Sir Robert Fletcher, who was not only the friend of Clive's opponents in England, but also thought himself injured by decisions of Clive regarding pecuniary claims which he had put forward.[1] The agitation coincided in time with the trouble with the civilians, and there was talk of a subscription for the benefit of those who should suffer through Clive's conduct. In this matter as in the other Clive overbore all opposition with a bold front. Every resignation was to be accepted; supplies of officers were requested from Madras; everyone displaying the least inclination to mutiny was to be sent down at once to Calcutta. Clive visited the headquarters of the three brigades in person, to assure himself that the men were under control; and the officers gradually fell out among themselves. Those who had already made their fortunes were careless of what might come out of the affair, but those who still had their fortunes to make were more timid, and, when it came to the point, were reluctant to forgo their prospects. In these circumstances the mutiny broke down. Those who were considered the least guilty were allowed to return to duty on condition of signing

[1] Dodwell, *Dupleix and Clive*, p. 266.

a three years' agreement, which under the East India Mutiny Act would bring within the penalty of death any who so conducted themselves in future. Of the rest Fletcher and six more were cashiered.

At the same time Clive resolved to apply to the use of the Company's officers a sum of five lakhs which Mir Ja'far was alleged to have desired on his deathbed to be delivered to him. One of the great lacks of the service was some provision for those who were compelled to retire from the service by wounds or ill-health while their circumstances were still embarrassed. Being a legacy the sum was deemed not to come within the Company's prohibition; it was therefore accepted, vested in trustees, and under the name of Lord Clive's Fund did much to bridge over the interval until the Company adopted the practice of pensioning its servants.

Clive quitted India for the last time in February, 1767. It is not necessary to dilate upon the greatness of his character or the results of his work. He had a supreme faculty for seeing into the heart of a situation, undistracted by side-issues, for compelling the obedience of others, and for finding an immediate expedient for the needs of the moment. His principal defect was a certain bluntness of moral feeling which enabled him to perform and defend actions which did not commend themselves even to his own age. But there was nothing small or petty about him. Though he made an enormous fortune, he was not mercenary; though he tricked Omichand, he was trusted implicitly by Indians of every class. His unfaltering will and uncompromising vigour took the fullest advantage of a peculiarly happy concourse of events firmly to establish the Company's power in the wealthiest province of India.

Between him and Warren Hastings come two governors who were hardly more than stop-gaps. Verelst succeeded Clive, and at the end of 1769 Cartier succeeded Verelst. But their combined five years of rule were little more than an introduction to the period of Hastings. The stage was being set for new performers. The Marathas, recovering from their overthrow at Panipat, were beginning once more to interfere in Northern India; the emperor quitted Allahabad, where Clive had settled him, and went off to Delhi under their protection; misunderstandings arose with Shuja-ud-daula, but they did not break the alliance which Clive had established; the English in Bengal began to take a share in the administration which they had so long regarded with suspicion; attempts were made to enter into communication with the Himalayan states and to come to terms with our Maratha neighbours on the south. But in all these ways the time was preparatory only for the time of growth and formation which Hastings was to inaugurate.

CHAPTER X

THE EAST INDIA COMPANY AND THE STATE.
1772–86

THE period 1772–86 is the formative epoch of British Indian History. During these years three important questions had to be dealt with: firstly, the relation of the East India Company to the state; secondly, the relation of the home to the Indian administration of the Company; and thirdly, the relation of the supreme government in Bengal to the subordinate presidencies. In this chapter we are concerned with the first of these questions, and it may be pointed out that the fourteen years of our period witnessed all the great statutes which definitely subjected the Company to the control of the crown and parliament, and converted it into a quasi-state department. Between 1786 and 1858 we feel that the constitutional changes are not really fundamental. Even the taking over of the Company's powers by the crown in 1858 was less a revolution than a formal and explicit recognition of facts already existing. Again, this was the period which saw the Company subjected to minute and severe inspection at the hands of parliamentary commissions, the Select and Secret Committees of 1772, and the Select and Secret Committees of 1781. Each occasion was followed by a great statute and an attack upon a great individual. In 1772 we have the attack upon Clive, followed by the Regulating Act of 1773. After 1781 we have Pitt's Act of 1784, followed by the impeachment of Warren Hastings. Lastly, as a result of these inspections a reformation of the civil service was carried through, partly by Hastings himself, and in fuller measure by Lord Cornwallis.

At no time was the question of British dominion in India so closely interwoven with political and party history at home. In Cobbett's *Parliamentary History* a very large space from 1767 to the end of the century is devoted to Indian debates. "The affairs of the East India Company", wrote the editor in 1768, "were now become as much an object of annual consideration, as the raising of the supplies."[1] The Indian question was entangled with a serious constitutional crisis and with the personal rivalry and political ambitions of the two greatest statesmen of the time. It caused the fall of the notorious Coalition Government of Fox and North, gave George III the opportunity to effect a daring *coup d'état*, doomed Fox to almost a lifetime of opposition and put Pitt in power practically for the rest of his life. From 1772 to 1795 Indian affairs were constantly before parliament in both its legislative and its judicial aspect.

[1] *Parliamentary History of England*, XVI, 402.

Now all this was inevitable and, when everything is taken into consideration, not to be regretted. It is easy to paint the interference of parliament as mischievous and misinformed, and to complain that India was made a pawn in the party game; but there was—as some of the most clear-sighted of contemporary statesmen saw—a serious risk of a great empire being created and ruled by Englishmen outside the sphere and control of the British cabinet. "The East India Company", as Burke said, "did not seem to be merely a Company formed for the extension of the British commerce, but in reality a delegation of the whole power and sovereignty of this kingdom sent into the East."[1] No national government could be expected, or indeed ought, to tolerate such a dangerous shifting of the centre of political gravity. Some action on the part of the state was necessary; the question had to be tackled even at the cost of strife, dislocation, and possibly some injustice to individuals. "In delegating great power to the India Company", wrote Burke, "this kingdom has not released its sovereignty. On the contrary, its responsibility is increased by the greatness and sacredness of the power given."[2]

This bringing into relation of the Company and the state was from the nature of the case a very difficult problem. It had to be worked out experimentally, for there were no precedents. We cannot be surprised that many mistakes were made.

"The British legislature", says Malcolm, "has hitherto but slowly followed the progress of the power of the Company in India. It had legislated for factories on a foreign shore, when that Company was in the possession of provinces; and when the laws were completed to govern these, it had obtained kingdoms."[3]

This was entirely true, but it was inevitable. The rapid developments in the East out-distanced the efforts of parliament to comprehend and to deal with them. According as men visualised the position from the eastern or the western point of view, authority in the East seemed dangerously circumscribed or perilously unhampered. Hastings describes the sphere of his administration as "a dominion held by a delegated and fettered power over a region exceeding the dimensions of the parent state, and removed from it a distance equal in its circuit to two-thirds of the earth's circumference".[4] Its remoteness postulated the necessity of semi-independence, "distant as it is from the reach of more than general instruction from the source of its authority, and liable to daily contingencies, which require both instant decision, and a consistency of system".[5] Burke, on the other hand, from the home aspect, declares, "It is difficult for the most wise and upright government to correct the abuses of remote, delegated

---

[1] *Speeches...in the trial of Warren Hastings* (Ed. Bond), I, 15.
[2] *Idem*, p. 13.
[3] Malcolm, *The Political History of India*, I, 8.
[4] *Selections from the State Papers of the Governors-General of India. Warren Hastings.* Ed. by (Sir) G. W. Forrest, II, 92.
[5] *Idem*, p. 93.

power, productive of unmeasured wealth, and protected by the boldness and strength of the same ill-got riches";[1] and he puts his finger on the crux of the whole matter, though no doubt he here inculcates a counsel of perfection, when he says, "I think I can trace all the calamities of this country to the single source of our not having had steadily before our eyes a general, comprehensive, well-connected and well-proportioned view of the whole of our dominions, and a just sense of their true bearings and relations".[2] The question then before the statesmen of the eighteenth century was: How was the Company's quasi-sovereignty in the East to be reconciled with the necessary subordination to the imperial parliament? There were three possibilities. The first was that the Company's privileges and powers should remain untouched, with the hope that some practical *modus vivendi* would in time be worked out. But this was felt by the majority of the nation and even by the more far-sighted of the Company's own servants to be no longer feasible. Both Clive and Warren Hastings suggested tentatively to the prime ministers of their time that it might be advisable for the state to take over the Company's powers. There seemed a danger not only that misgovernment in India might tarnish the name of Great Britain as an imperial state, but that the Indian interest in England, supported by huge revenues and corrupt parliamentary influence, might gain a preponderating and improper power in home affairs.

The second possibility was that the state should take over in full sovereignty the territorial possessions in India and convert the Company's servants into a civil service of the crown. But this was felt to be too great and drastic a change. It was opposed to all eighteenth-century notions of the sacredness of property, and the problem was complicated by all kinds of delicate legal and political questions. It might even be plausibly contended that the Company had no considerable territorial possessions at all. It administered Bengal, Bihar and Orissa merely as the diwan of the Moghul emperor. That was a tenable position for a private corporation; it was not a tenable position for the government of Great Britain. If the "territorial" possessions were annexed by the crown, the act might be represented as sheer usurpation against the Moghul Empire, and Great Britain might be embroiled with the representatives of other European nations in the East.

It remained that the state should take the Company into partnership, assuming the position of controlling and predominant partner in all matters relating to the higher branches of government, but leaving to the Company the monopoly of the trade, the disposal of its valuable patronage under crown sanction, and the details of the administration. What we see going on during the period 1772–86 is

---

[1] *Works of Edmund Burke*, III, 193–4.
[2] *Idem*, p. 125.

the gradual realisation of this conception. It must be remembered that some attempts in this direction had already been made before 1772. A little band of members of parliament, prominent among whom were Beckford, Barré and General Burgoyne, had long been urging that conquests in India should pass to the crown. Their persistent efforts met with some success in 1767 when five separate acts were passed. These measures amongst other things interfered in the regulations for voting in the General Courts of the Company, regulated the amount of dividends to be paid and the manner of paying them, and, most important, obliged the Company to pay the exchequer an annual sum of £400,000 for two years from February, 1767, for the privilege of retaining their territorial acquisitions (the payment was afterwards extended to 1772). "Thus", says Sir Courtenay Ilbert, "the state claimed its share of the Indian spoil, and asserted its rights to control the sovereignty of Indian territories."[1] These changes were only carried in the teeth of a strong opposition. The protests of the dissentients in the House of Lords showed how strong as yet were the barriers of the rights of property, and the sanctity of contract.

A legislative interposition controlling the dividend of a trading Company, legally voted and declared by those to whom the power of doing it is entrusted...is altogether without example.[2]

The solution, it may be admitted, was not particularly logical. It was on the face of it absurd that a British chartered company should pay the crown of England an annual sum of money for permission to hold certain lands and revenues of an eastern potentate, and the friends of the Company did not hesitate to describe the payment as mere political blackmail.

But for five years at any rate the attack against the Company was stayed. Then again in 1772 troubles gathered round it, arising from the following circumstances. In March, 1772, a dividend at the rate of 12½ per cent. was declared. In the same month the Company, obviously endeavouring to forestall a drastic reformation from outside, attempted through Sulivan their deputy-chairman to introduce a bill for the better regulation of their affairs. Lord Clive, being assailed, defended himself by taking the offensive and roundly attacked the Company. In the debate some interesting points were raised as to the relations between the Company and the state. Clive had in 1759 proposed to Chatham that the crown should take over the Company's dominions. Chatham, probably because he had no leisure to face the practical and exceedingly thorny difficulties, contented himself with an oracular answer that the scheme was of a very nice nature and, as Clive's agent reported, "spoke this matter a little darkly".[3] Clive

---

[1] Ilbert, *The Government of India*, p. 39.
[2] *Parliamentary History*, xvi, 356.
[3] Malcolm, *The Life of Clive*, ii, 126.

had resented this treatment and now with an imprudence amazing in a man, around whom his enemies were closing, struck out in all directions as though his one aim was not to leave himself a single partisan. With a magnificent recklessness he included the government, the directors, the proprietors and the servants in the East in one comprehensive condemnation:

"I attribute the present situation of our affairs", he said, "to four causes: a relaxation of government in my successors; great neglect on the part of administration; notorious misconduct on the part of the directors; and the violent and outrageous proceedings of General Courts."[1]

The Company had acquired an empire and a revenue of £4,000,000.

It was natural to suppose that such an object would have merited the most serious attention of administration; that in concert with the Court of Directors they would have considered the nature of the Company's charter, and have adopted a plan adequate to such possessions. Did they take it into consideration? No, they did not.... They thought of nothing but the immediate division of the loaves and fishes....They went so far as to influence a parcel of temporary Proprietors to bully the Directors into their terms.

They ought to have forced the directors to produce a plan, or with the aid of Parliament to have made one themselves.

If administration had done their duty, we should not now have heard a speech from the throne, intimating the necessity of Parliamentary interposition, to save our possessions in India from impending ruin.[2]

One of those who took part in the debate, Governor Johnstone, maintained views of some interest. He declared that:

The British legislature should not move in the affairs of Asia, unless she acts with dignity and effect....I am clear we hold those lands by conquest. I think the conquest was lawfully made by the Company and a small part of the King's forces in conjunction. I deny that conquest by a subject, lawfully made, vests the property in the state, though I maintain it conveys the sovereignty.[3]

He went on to advocate that the crown under certain conditions should grant the lands to the East India Company as was done in the case of New England and several other of our chartered colonies. He did not accept the theory that we need consider the susceptibilities of other European nations.

Does any man believe that foreign nations permit us virtually to hold these territories under the magic word Devannee? Can it be supposed they are not equally sensible of the imposition as ourselves, or will it be believed they would not be much better contented to hold their different privileges under the confirmation of a British legislature, than of a cypher of a Nabob, directed by a Governor and Committee whom they can never trace?[4]

In the end leave to introduce Sulivan's bill was refused, and in April, 1772, Burgoyne carried a motion to appoint a select committee

---

[1] *Parliamentary History*, XVII, 361. [2] *Idem*, pp. 363–4.
[3] *Idem*, pp. 376–7. [4] *Idem*, p. 378.

of thirty-one to enquire into the affairs of the East India Company. The debate testifies to the intensity of feeling against the Company. Burgoyne declared that:

> The most atrocious abuses that ever stained the name of civil government called for redress...if by some means sovereignty and law are not separated from trade... India and Great Britain will be sunk and overwhelmed never to rise again.

Any bill based upon the present state of the Indian Government must be "a poor, paltry, wretched palliative". The committee was to enquire into

> that chaos where every element and principle of government, and charters, and firmauns, and the rights of conquests, and the rights of subjects, and the different functions and interests of merchants, and statesmen, and lawyers, and kings, are huddled together into one promiscuous tumult and confusion.

He ended with an impassioned peroration:

> The fate of a great portion of the globe, the fate of great states in which your own is involved, the distresses of fifteen millions of people, the rights of humanity are involved in this question—Good God! What a call—the native of Hindustan born a slave—his neck bent from the very cradle to the yoke—by birth, by education, by climate, by religion, a patient, submissive, willing subject to eastern despotism, first begins to feel, first shakes his chains,...under the pre-eminence of British tyranny.[1]

It is interesting to note that Burke, who was himself to write some of the most condemnatory reports in the 1781 enquiry, spoke against any investigation at all.

The Select Committee was presided over by General Burgoyne himself, and included among its members Lord George Germain, Barré, Lord Howe, Sir Gilbert Elliot, Pulteney, and Charles James Fox. But the Company's troubles were not yet over. In August, 1772, though it had recently been helped by the bank, it was obliged to apply to government for a loan of £1,000,000. There was a storm of opposition, for this application seemed to show that there was no justification for the dividend declared in March. Parliament was especially summoned. Lord North moved for a committee of secrecy on the ground that complaints had been made of the disclosure of confidential information by the Select Committee. North was careful to state that he himself believed that, however closely pressed the Company might be by present exigencies, it was nevertheless in point of external strength and vigour in full health. Burgoyne rose in defence of the Select Committee, and in the end, though a new secret committee of thirteen was set up, the old Select Committee was continued in being. The Select Committee produced twelve, and the Secret Committee six, reports, all highly condemnatory. Tremendous feeling against the Company was aroused. Horace Walpole records the popular impression: "Such a scene of tyranny and plunder has

---

[1] *Parliamentary History*, XVII, 454–9.

been opened up as makes one shudder....We are Spaniards in our lust for gold, and Dutch in our delicacy of obtaining it".[1] Responsible statesmen took a view hardly less grave. Lord Shelburne writes to Chatham: "Every man of every party acknowledges a blow to be impending in that part of the world, which must shake to its foundations the revenue, manufactures, and property of this".[2] As the reports continued to appear, Chatham's indignation rose, and we find him writing in 1773, "India teems with iniquities so rank, as to smell to earth and heaven".[3] But mere abuse of the servants in India was of little avail. We have Warren Hastings's authority for the statement that Shelburne was "better informed in India affairs than almost any man in England",[4] and the latter, in a further letter to Chatham, distributed the blame pretty impartially. He declared that though the crimes and frauds of the servants in India were enormous, yet the directors appear to be accomplices throughout, while the proprietors seem to be the most servile instruments of both, "nor", he continues, "has there been found as yet, to speak impartially, anywhere in the House of Commons that firm, even, judicial spirit, capable of administering, much less originating, that justice which the case requires".[5]

The Company now made feverish efforts to conduct its own reformation and, following the precedent of 1769, nominated six supervisors, who, with plenary powers and salaries of £10,000 each, were to proceed at once to India to overhaul the whole system there. But this was more than parliament could stand, and, on the advice of the Committee of Secrecy, a bill was passed in December, 1772, prohibiting the Company from sending out the supervisors. Burke, still as yet the stalwart friend of Leadenhall Street, opposed the bill; Clive, on the other hand, supported it. "I could wish", he said, "the Company had met this house half-way instead of petitioning and quarrelling with the mouth that is to feed them", then, in reference to the supervisors and thinking of his own past history, he added, "had they, Sir, known the East Indies as well as I do, they would shudder at the bare idea of such a perplexing and difficult service".[6] In March the Company again petitioned parliament for a loan of £1,500,000. In May, Burgoyne developed his attack upon Clive in the Commons, and amongst the resolutions accepted by the House was one "That all acquisitions, made under the influence of a military force, or by treaty with foreign princes, do of right belong to the State".[7] This was in one sense a definite declaration of sovereignty over the Company's territories, but it might be asked first, what is the exact validity of a resolution of the House of Commons, and

[1] Paget-Toynbee, *Letters of Horace Walpole*, VIII, 149.
[2] *Correspondence of Chatham*, IV, 210.
[3] *Idem*, p. 276.
[4] Gleig, *Memoirs of Warren Hastings*, II, 557.
[5] *Correspondence of Chatham*, IV, 271.
[6] Malcolm, *Life of Lord Clive*, III, 313.
[7] *Parliamentary History*, XVII, 856.

secondly, could the claim apply to the anomalous system created in Bengal by the grant of the diwanni? The curious form of the expression used, "under the influence of a military force", instead of some simpler phrase such as "by conquest", was no doubt intended to cover the *de facto* position in Bengal. Burke in various speeches still resisted all attempts to extend state control over the Company. He disbelieved in the motives of the government: "The pretence of rectifying abuses, of nourishing, fostering and protecting the Company was only made with a design of fleecing the Company". The pretext for interfering was the same in 1773 as in 1767, but "Have these evils been rectified? Have any of the criminals been summoned before you? Has their conduct been enquired into? Not one single suspected person has been examined". If these evils really existed, it could only be concluded that ministers

sanctified this bloodshed, this rapine, this villainy, this extortion...for the valuable consideration of £400,000....This crime tax being agreed to, we heard no more of malpractices. The sinners were arrayed in white-robed innocence; their misdeeds were more than atoned for by an expiatory sacrifice of the pecuniary kind....

And again:

I have studied, God knows; hard I have studied, even to the making dogs' ears of almost every statute book in the kingdom, and I now thus publicly and solemnly declare that all you have been doing and all you are about to do, in behalf of the East India Company, is impolitic, is unwise, and entirely repugnant to the letter as well as the spirit of the laws, the liberties, and the constitution of this country.[1]

Two acts of parliament were now passed. The first granted the Company a loan of £1,400,000 at 4 per cent. on certain conditions. The second was the important Regulating Act. The latter did three things. It remodelled the constitution of the Company at home, it remodelled the constitution of the Company in India, and it tentatively and incompletely subjected the Company to the supervision of the ministry and the subordinate presidencies to the supervision of the supreme government in Calcutta. The bill was fiercely opposed by the Company and its friends. The Company's own petition declared that the bill "will destroy every privilege which the petitioners hold under the most sacred securities that subjects can depend upon in this country". The act "under the colour of Regulation, will annihilate at once the powers of the...Company, and virtually transfer them to the Crown".[2] The City of London also petitioned against the bill on the ground that "the privileges the City of London enjoy stand on the same security as those of the East India Company".[3] One of the directors in the House of Commons stigmatised the bill as "a medley of inconsistencies, dictated by tyranny, yet bearing throughout each line the mark of ignorance".[4] Burke described the principle of the measure as "an infringement of national right, national faith, and national justice".[5] But the bill was passed by

---

[1] *Parliamentary History*, XVII, 819—21, 835.   [2] *Idem*, pp. 889–90.
[3] *Idem*, p. 889.   [4] *Idem*, pp. 890–1.   [5] *Idem*, p. 902.

131 to 21 votes in the Commons and by 74 to 17 in the Lords. Its main provisions were as follows: The qualification for a vote in the Court of Proprietors was raised from £500 to £1000 and was restricted to those who had held their stock for at least twelve months. Measures were taken to prevent the collusive transfer of stock, and the consequent multiplying of votes. The directors were henceforth to be elected for four years, and one-fourth of their number must retire every year, remaining at least one year out of office. There was to be a Governor-General of Bengal assisted by four councillors. The vote of the majority was to bind the whole, the governor-general having merely a casting vote when there was an equal division of opinion. The governor-general and council were to have power to superintend the subordinate presidencies in making war or peace. The directors were to lay before the treasury all correspondence from India dealing with the revenues; and before a secretary of state everything dealing with civil or military administration. The first governor-general and councillors, Warren Hastings, Clavering, Monson, Barwell and Philip Francis, were named in the act. They were to hold office for five years, and future appointments were to be made by the Company. The act empowered the crown to establish by charter a Supreme Court of Justice, consisting of a chief justice and three puisne judges. Liberal salaries were granted, £25,000 to the governor-general, £10,000 to each councillor and £8000 to the chief justice.

Something by way of detailed criticism may now be attempted on these clauses. The alteration in the voting qualification of the General Court was introduced with a view to prevent the Company's servants, when they returned from the East, from gaining an excessive influence over the directors. The raising of the qualification meant that 1246 of the smaller holders of stock were disqualified. It was generally held that the clause failed to attain its object.

"The whole of the regulations concerning the Court of Proprietors", said the authors of the Ninth Report of the Select Committee of 1781, "relied upon two principles, which have often proved fallacious, namely that small numbers were a security against faction and disorder, and that integrity of conduct would follow the greater property."[1]

There was certainly a good deal of point in the argument of those who held that, by abolishing the vote of the £500 stock-holders, the act punished the small proprietors, who could not split votes, and rewarded those who could.

The change in the constitution of the court of directors was made with the view of giving the members of the court greater security of tenure, lessening the temptation to secure votes by a corrupt dispensation of patronage, and encouraging a more continuous and

[1] *Reports from Committees of the House of Commons*, VI, 46.

consistent policy at home and abroad. Hitherto the twenty-four directors were elected each year, and might have been completely changed at each election. As Clive once averred, they spent the first half of their year of office in discharging the obligations by which they had purchased their seats, and the other half in canvassing and preparing for a new election. At the first election after the bill passed, six directors were to be chosen for one year, six for two years, six for three years and six for the full term of four years. In practice the six who retired each year were always re-elected for the following year and the effect therefore was as Kaye notes, "to constitute a body of thirty directors, of whom six, forming a sort of non-effective list, go out every year by rotation".[1] It was of course possible for the proprietors at each election to have chosen six new members, but in practice they never did so.

It was unfortunate that the governor-general was not given in the last resort power to override his council. After 1786 this was found to be necessary, and it has ever since remained a prerogative of the governor-general. Hastings always felt deeply the restrictions on his power and more than once declared that experience would prove the governor-general must have this privilege in reserve. After five years' experience of the working of the act, he writes in 1779:

> I would not continue the pageant that I am...for all the rewards and honours that the king could give me. I am not Governor. All the means I possess are those of preventing the rule from falling into worse hands than my own.[2]

And again:

> What I have done has been by fits and intervals of power, if I may so express it, and from the effects, let a judgement be formed of what this state and its resources are capable of producing in hands more able and better supported.[3]

It was not perhaps the fault of the framers of the act, for the matter was very difficult to define, but the clause giving Calcutta control over the subordinate presidencies worked badly. Calcutta was given powers of superintending and controlling the subordinate governments so far that the latter were not to commence hostilities or make treaties without its consent, but then followed two exceptions of disastrous latitude; namely, unless the case were one of such imminent necessity as would make it dangerous to await the arrival of orders, or unless the local government had received orders direct from home. But the main reason probably was that the other presidencies had been so long independent that it would take some time before a tradition of loyalty to the supreme government could grow up. Hastings records his disappointment at the result of the act in this respect.

---

[1] Kaye, *The Administration of the East India Company*, p. 123.
[2] Gleig, *op. cit.* II, 274.   [3] *Idem*, p. 309.

The act gives us a mere negative power and no more. It says the other presidencies shall not make war nor treaties without the sanction of this government, but carefully guards against every expression which can imply a power to dictate what the other presidencies shall do.... Instead of uniting all the powers of India, all the use we have hitherto made of this act of Parliament has been to tease and embarrass".[1]

The clause empowering the crown to establish a Supreme Court of Justice by charter was unhappily vague. It left undefined the field of jurisdiction, the law to be administered and, above all, the relations between the council and the court.

It is interesting to note, in view of what happened afterwards, that when the names of the governor-general and councillors were inserted in the act, Lord North recommended the name of Hastings "as a person to whom nobody would object".[2] For the post of councillor General Monckton's claims were advocated against Clavering's, but the other names were accepted without any opposition. The dissentient Lords recorded a protest against the appointment of executive officers in parliament as plainly unconstitutional.

The Regulating Act was in operation for eleven years till it was superseded by Pitt's act of 1784. Warren Hastings was the only governor-general who had to administer India under it. After 1784 we have, as Sir Alfred Lyall has pointed out, a series of parliamentary governors-general with wider powers and a more independent position. The act was probably on the whole an honest attempt to deal with a difficult problem, but it was open to many criticisms. A speaker in the Commons in 1781 said of it not unfairly, "In the mode of applying a reform, Parliament was precipitate and individuals were intemperate".[3]

Certain remedial and supplementary legislation followed on the Regulating Act. It will be remembered that the governor-general and council were appointed for five years. Their period of office would therefore normally lapse in 1779. It also happened that by the act of 1744 the Company's privileges were to determine in 1780 unless definitely extended. The position was a curious one; there was a possibility of the government in India and the existence of the Company at home coming to an end almost simultaneously. North, to call attention to the legal position, moved in 1780 that the state debts to the Company should be paid off (they amounted to £4,200,000) and that formal notice should be given to the Company of its dissolution. The motion was made the excuse for an acrimonious attack from the opposition. Fox asked "whether the Noble Lord was not content with having lost America? Or was he determined not to quit the situation in which he stood, till he had reduced the dominions of the Crown to the confines of Great Britain"?[4] Burke, with characteristic violence, stigmatised the proposal to give notice to the

[1] Gleig, *op. cit.* ii, 41-2.   [2] *Parliamentary History*, xvii, 896.
[3] *Idem*, xxi, 1194.   [4] *Idem*, p. 310.

Company as "the most wicked, absurd, abandoned, profligate, mad, and drunken intention that ever was formed".[1] North replied coolly that his motion was meant merely "as putting in a claim on the behalf of the public, to the reversion of a right which undoubtedly belonged to them, at that moment when it was especially proper that it should be formally made".[2] By acts of 1779 and 1780 the Company's privileges were extended for a year and it was enacted that no changes were to take place in the offices of governor-general and council at Calcutta. As North had now for some time shown himself hostile to Hastings, the reason for this reappointment is undoubtedly that given by Gleig: "the Minister who had lost America, did not care to risk the loss of India likewise, and therefore sought to represent matters as great and prosperous there".[3] A more permanent act was passed in 1781. This act, besides other less important regulations, extended the Company's privileges to three years' notice after 1 March, 1791, and obliged it to submit to a secretary of state all dispatches proposed to be sent to India relating to political, revenue and military matters. The Company was also to pay £400,000 to the state in discharge of all claims up to 1 March, 1781, to pay dividends out of its profits of 8 per cent., and out of the remainder of its profits, if any, three-quarters were to go to the state.

The year 1781 saw also the appointment of two more committees of enquiry, one select, on the administration of justice in India, presided over by Burke, and the other secret, on the causes of the war in the Carnatic, presided over by Dundas. The first committee resulted in the act of 1781 amending the constitution of the Supreme Court, which will be dealt with later. Both committees poured forth voluminous reports. Twelve were issued by the Select and six by the Secret Committee. The ninth and eleventh reports of the Select Committee were written by Burke himself. The friends of the Company naturally did not like them. Lord Thurlow in the House of Lords said contemptuously that he paid as much attention to them as he would do to the history of Robinson Crusoe. Johnstone in the Commons on a motion for the printing of one of the reports declared that he did not object to the publication of what was "frivolous, ridiculous, and absurd, and fit only to be presented on such a day as this" (it happened to be 1st April). He accused the majority of the committee of "heat and violence,...passion and prejudice".[4] Burke angrily defended the committees; "their conduct", he said, "had been an instance of the most extraordinary perseverance, and the most steady and patient assiduity, that perhaps ever had occurred".[5] Though the reports undoubtedly display a certain amount of prejudice, yet they have often been unduly neglected by the historian, and their value as a storehouse of facts and documents is considerable. At any

---

[1] *Parliamentary History*, xxi, 313.   [2] *Idem*, p. 312.   [3] Gleig, *op. cit.* ii, 469.
[4] *Parliamentary History*, xxiii, 715–16.   [5] *Idem*, p. 717.

rate their effect at the time upon parliament and the nation was very great. In April, 1782, Dundas moved that the reports of the Secret Committee should be referred to a committee of the whole house and followed this up by a long series of forty-five resolutions condemning many of the principles and practices of the Indian administration as censured in the reports. But the attempt of the Commons at disciplinary action proved a dismal failure. Bills of pains and penalties were introduced against Sir Thomas Rumbold and Whitehill, ex-governors of Madras, but these bills after long discussion were finally dropped in 1783 because it proved impossible to keep a quorum in the House to discuss them. Mill says most unfairly that Rumbold "consented to accept of impunity without acquittal".[1] Rumbold, on the contrary, had repeatedly urged that it was unfair to him not to come to a definite verdict, and as late as June, 1783, implored the House in God's name to "put an end to the business speedily, and either send him to condemnation or acquittal".[2] But a stroke was now aimed at greater game. On 30 May, 1782, the Commons resolved that it was the duty of the directors to pursue all legal and effectual means, i.e. by representation to the crown, to recall Hastings and Hornby, governor of Bombay, for "having, in sundry instances, acted in a manner repugnant to the honour and policy of this nation, and thereby brought great calamities on India, and enormous expenses on the East India Company".[3] According to the Regulating Act, Hastings was only removable by the crown on representation from the court of directors. The Commons therefore could only constitutionally adopt the roundabout course of calling upon the directors to approach the crown. An extraordinary concatenation of events followed, illustrating the cumbrousness of the state's semi-control of the Company. In reply to the House of Commons the General Court on 19 June, 1782, passed a resolution of contemptuous defiance against the recall of Mr Hastings merely in compliance with a vote of one house of the legislature. The directors, however, who naturally in their position of greater responsibility did not find it so easy to flout the government, decided on 2 October reluctantly by a small majority after holding eleven meetings that they would approach the crown for his recall. Scott told Hastings that the governor and deputy-governor carried the vote against him, "the two chairs are against you",[4] and declares that the Company's solicitor had shown him the draft of a resolution by which the directors hoped to soften the blow as much as possible. The resolution, after acknowledging Hastings's many very great and meritorious services, declared

that in no one act of his government hath he been actuated by a corrupt motive, nor is he suspected of peculation; but it is resolved by this court that Warren

---

[1] Mill, *The History of British India*, IV, 532.
[2] *Parliamentary History*, XXIII, 985.
[3] *Idem*, p. 75.   [4] Gleig, *op. cit.* II, 485.

Hastings Esq. hath formed wrong opinions upon points of great political importance, and that he hath acted upon those opinions so as to bring great distress upon this Company.[1]

But the letter of recall was never sent, for the General Court by a large majority rescinded the resolution of the directors. The government upon this refused to pass for transmission to India the dispatch drawn up by the directors informing Hastings of this series of occurrences, though of course everyone was aware that unofficially he would be cognisant of the whole of them. This strange imbroglio showed three things: first that the hold of Hastings on the allegiance of the proprietors, whom indeed he was wont to call his constituents, was very strong; secondly, that the Company still possessed a large measure of practical independence; and thirdly, that the clause in the act of 1781 making it necessary to submit outward dispatches to the secretary of state was liable to result in a rather ludicrous deadlock.

Things could obviously not be left in this inconclusive and unsatisfactory state. The Regulating Act had clearly broken down. It had neither given the state a definite control over the Company, nor the directors a definite control over their servants, nor the governor-general a definite control over his council, nor the Calcutta Presidency a definite control over Madras and Bombay. The whole question was reopened in 1783, for the Company in March was again obliged to petition for financial relief, and the country as a whole was inclined to agree with Burke that "the relief and reformation of the Company must go together. The Company had flown in the face of Parliament".[2]

Three successive proposals were put forward, those namely of Dundas, Fox and Pitt. Dundas introduced his bill in April, 1783. Its main provisions were: That the crown should have power to recall the principal servants of the Company (the power was thus no longer to be consequent on representations from the directors); that the control of Bengal over the other presidencies should be increased; that the governor-general should have the power of acting on his own responsibility in opposition to the opinions of his council, and also be empowered, if necessary, to hold the office of commander-in-chief; that the displaced zamindars in Bengal, i.e. those displaced by the results of the quinquennial settlement, should be restored. The bill was obviously aiming everywhere at centralisation. It strengthened the power of the crown over the governor-general and the control of the governor-general both over his own council and the subordinate governments. It is from this aspect that Malcolm called it a

Bill for appointing a person who, under the high title of Governor-General and Captain-General, should exercise in his own person (under certain checks) complete authority and control over British India.[3]

---

[1] Gleig, *op. cit.* II, 493.   [2] *Parliamentary History*, XXIII, 647.
[3] Malcolm, *Political History of India*, I, 37.

In his introductory speech Dundas already pointed to the desirability of appointing Cornwallis governor-general by a strong panegyric on his character:

that man, of whom all men and all parties were lavish in commendation. A man of family, of fortune, and the most unsullied reputation....On the virtues of this man the late ministry built, and justly built, all their hopes of the salvation of our dying interests in Asia. Here there was no broken fortune to be mended, here was no avarice to be gratified. Here was no beggarly mushroom kindred to be provided for—no crew of hungry followers gaping to be gorged.[1]

But as Dundas was now in opposition there was no chance of his bill becoming law, and after its introduction it was allowed to drop.

On 18 November, 1783, Fox introduced his two famous bills. The first dealt in detail with matters of administration and may not unfairly be said to have definitely forbidden in future most of the characteristic acts of the Hastings administration. The second and better known bill gave the Company a new constitution. In the preliminary debates Pitt himself had clamoured for a bill "not of temporary palliation or timorous expedients; but vigorous and effectual, suited to the magnitude, the importance and the alarming exigency of the case". The bill was in some respects vigorous and effectual enough. It proposed entirely to sweep away both the court of directors and the court of proprietors and to set up two bodies: (1) seven commissioners, or directors, to administer the revenues and territories of India and to appoint or dismiss all persons in the Company's service. They were to be named in the act and were irremovable except on an address from either house of parliament. Vacancies were to be filled by the crown. Fox's reason for this last provision was

that he felt already the inconvenience of Parliamentary appointments; for at present the Governor-General of Bengal, deriving under an Act of Parliament, seemed to disavow any power in the Court of Proprietors, Directors, or the King himself to remove him.[2]

The board was to sit in London and parliament was to have opportunity to inspect the minutes of its proceedings. This was no doubt to meet the criticism that the commissioners were given too independent a power. (2) Nine assistant directors (eight in the original draft) were to be nominated in the act from the proprietors with the largest holdings in the Company. They were to be appointed for five years, and vacancies were filled by the court of proprietors.

The debates on the bills took up a very large measure of parliamentary time and are of great interest. The bills were bitterly opposed by the Company and all the Indian interest. Fox, with his usual lack of political astuteness, had failed to make any terms with the Company, or to take it into his confidence. He avowedly based the necessity for the measure upon the Company's "extreme distress and

---

[1] *Parliamentary History*, XXIII, 759.   [2] *Idem*, p. 1201.

the embarrassed state of their affairs", his bill "was the only possible means of averting and preventing the final and complete destruction of the Company's interests".[1] It was patent to all the world, as Malcolm says, that Fox's seven commissioners were "to act like trustees to a bankrupt house of commerce",[2] and it was this charge of insolvency that the Company and its friends particularly resented. It was indeed clear that Fox, who never really understood finance, had largely failed to grasp the pecuniary position of the Company, which, as one of its supporters in parliament declared, "so far from being bankrupt, had but a very trifling mortgage on a very fine estate".[3] In contrasting his bill with that of Dundas, Fox declared the latter "aimed at lodging an absolute and despotic power of government in India. This provided a controllable government; but it was a powerful government, and it was at home".[4] He admitted that his bill "was a child not of choice, but of necessity".[5] He was willing at present to leave the question of the right to territorial possessions undecided. The measure was to set up "a mixed system of government, adapted...to the mixed complexion of our interests in India".[6] He met the charge of giving patronage to the crown, or rather to ministers, by the pertinent question, "What great officer had been appointed, but by the advice and influence of Ministers? And ought they to have been otherwise?"[7] But he did nothing to smooth the passage of the bill by his fierce onslaught on the existing government of India, which he described as "a system of despotism unmatched in all the histories of the world".[8] Nor could he refrain from fierce invective against the governor-general,

a man who, by disobeying the orders of his employers, had made himself so great as to be now able to mix in every question of State, and make every measure of government a personal point in which he had a share.[9]

Both the virulence and the honesty—however mistaken—of his detestation of Hastings shine out clearly in his final speech on the bill.

The Indian people, he cried, "in spite of every exertion both of the legislature and Court of Directors, groan under the scourge, the extortion, and the massacre, of a cruel and desperate man, whom in my conscience and from my heart I detest and execrate".[10]

Burke delivered one of the greatest of all his speeches in support of the bill. Wraxall, who was no particular friend of his, declared that it was the finest speech delivered in the House of Commons while he was a member of it.[11] Indeed, though the orator's language was

---

[1] *Parliamentary History*, XXIII, 1188.   [2] Malcolm, *Political History of India*, I, 40.
[3] *Parliamentary History*, XXIII, 1212.
[4] *Idem*, p. 1276.   [5] *Idem*, p. 1262.   [6] *Idem*, p. 1200.
[7] *Idem*, p. 1277.   [8] *Idem*, p. 1407.   [9] *Idem*, pp. 1274–5.
[10] *Idem*, XXIV, 221.   [11] Wraxall, *Historical memoirs*, IV, 567–8.

surcharged with passion and emotion, there is no doubt that he struck some shrewd blows at the defects of the Company's administration and testified his own sincere if unbalanced devotion to what he conceived to be the wrongs of the Indian peoples. He spoke of himself with a certain proud humility as

a member of Parliament, who has supplied a mediocrity of talents by the extreme of diligence, and who has thought himself obliged, by the research of years, to wind himself into the inmost recesses and labyrinths of the India detail.[1]

And again:

Our Indian government is in its best state a grievance. It is necessary that the correctives should be uncommonly vigorous; and the work of men sanguine, warm, and even impassioned in the cause.[2]

As long as he remains on the abstract plane of political philosophy, his treatment of his subject is lofty and unimpeachable:

If we are not able to contrive some method of governing India well, which will not of necessity become the means of governing Great Britain ill, a ground is laid for their eternal separation; but none for sacrificing the people of that country to our constitution....I am certain that every means, effectual to preserve India from oppression, is a guard to preserve the British constitution from its worst corruption.[3]

He would have none of the doctrine that it was impossible to act owing to the chartered rights of the Company. Monopolistic rights, granted by a legislature, are something very different from natural rights. The Company's rights were indeed "stamped by the faith of the King...stamped by the faith of Parliament", but if abuse was proved, they must be recalled:

All political power which is set over men, and all privilege, claimed or exercised in exclusion of them, being wholly artificial, and for so much a derogation from the natural equality of mankind at large, ought to be some way or other exercised ultimately for their benefit...such rights, or privileges...are all, in the strictest sense, a trust; and it is of the very essence of every trust to be rendered accountable; and even totally to cease, when it substantially varies from the purposes for which alone it could have a lawful existence....[4]

But his indignation too often hurried him into invective. The Company's government was "one of the most corrupt and destructive tyrannies, that probably ever existed in the world".[5]

There is not a single prince, state, or potentate, great or small, in India, with whom they have come into contact, whom they have not sold;...there is not a single treaty they have ever made, which they have not broken;...there is not a single prince, or state, who ever put any trust in the Company, who is not utterly ruined.[6]

---

[1] *Parliamentary History*, XXIII, 1313.   [2] *Idem*, pp. 1334–5.
[3] *Idem*, p. 1314.   [4] *Idem*, pp. 1316–17.   [5] *Idem*, p. 1376.
[6] *Idem*, p. 1322.

The speech contains the famous passage on the Company's servants, how

animated with all the avarice of age, and all the impetuosity of youth, they roll in one after another; wave after wave; and there is nothing before the eyes of the natives but an endless, hopeless, prospect of new flights of birds of prey and passage, with appetites continually renewing for a food that is continually wasting....Their prey is lodged in England; and the cries of India are given to seas and winds, to be blown about in every breaking-up of the monsoon, over a remote and unhearing ocean.[1]

It is the fashion to discount such a passage as mere rhetoric and prejudice, but it is after all its universality and its total want of relief that makes it misleading. To prove the large residuum of truth behind the burning words, we need only cite the evidence of Warren Hastings himself. In the first year of his governor-generalship he wrote:

Will you believe that the boys of the service are the sovereigns of the country, under the unmeaning title of supervisors, collectors of the revenue, administrators of justice, and rulers, heavy rulers of the people?[2]

and eight years later, after all his attempted reforms, he speaks in a moment of unwonted candour of the sphere of his administration as:

a system charged with expensive establishments, and precluded by the multitude of dependents and the curse of patronage, from reformation; a government debilitated by the various habits of inveterate licentiousness. A country oppressed by private rapacity, and deprived of its vital resources by the enormous quantities of current specie annually exported in the remittance of private fortunes....[3]

Are these admissions of the administrator at all at variance with the terrible invective of the orator?

It is, however, clear that what really ruined the bill was the tremendous unpopularity of the Fox and North coalition. Most of the speakers hardly made any attempt to discuss it on its merits at all, but were never tired of reflecting obliquely on the recent amalgamation of the two statesmen. One member suggested that Hastings and Francis should be associated in the government of India, "and thus make a new coalition".[4] Fox at last was stung into a protest:

The coalition is...a fruitful topic; and the power of traducing it, which the weakest and meanest creatures in the country enjoy and exercise, is of course equally vested in men of rank and parts, though every man of parts and rank would not be apt to participate in the privilege.[5]

Generally speaking, the language of Fox's opponents seems to modern ears grotesque and insincere. Grenville, for instance, said that the aim of the bill was "no less than to erect a despotic system which might crush the free constitution of England".[6] Pitt's attack was the most effective, though he, too, when he described the bill as "one of the boldest, most unprecedented, most desperate and alarming attempts at the exercise of tyranny, that ever disgraced the annals of

---

[1] *Parliamentary History*, XXIII, 1333–4.   [2] Gleig, *op. cit.* I, 234.   [3] *Idem*, II, 329.
[4] *Parliamentary History*, XXIII, 1308.   [5] *Idem*, p. 1422.   [6] *Idem*, p. 1225.

this or any other country",[1] was yielding to the unreal histrionic atmosphere of the debate. Apart from this, he dwelt mainly on the danger of conferring the patronage of India on the nominees of a party, and the want of co-operation between the seven commissioners and the cabinet. The former were

a small *junto*, politically connected, established in a manner independent of the crown, by whom India was to be converted into one vast political engine, an engine that might be brought to bear against the independence of this house.[2]

Jenkinson put the same point more temperately when he objected to the bill as "setting up within the realm a species of executive government, independent of the check or control of the Crown".[3] There was undoubtedly some truth in this, and seven commissioners did not appear to be properly subordinated to the imperial government; but it must be remembered, first, that there was no easy solution of the problem, and if Pitt afterwards succeeded in solving it, he was able to profit by Fox's errors and experiments.

The government found it difficult to meet the charge that they were destroying the East India Company. Burke declared that their aim was to cure not to kill. In sly allusion to this metaphor, Wilberforce compared the seven directors and eight assistant directors to seven physicians and eight apothecaries come to put the patient to death *secundum artem*.[4]

The commissioners nominated were Lord Fitzwilliam, F. Montague, Sir Henry Fletcher, R. Gregory, Colonel North, Viscount Lewisham and Sir Gilbert Elliot. Professor Holland Rose declares that all these were partisans of Fox or North. "If Fox and North", he says, "had chosen the seven commissioners fairly from among all three parties, the mouths of gainsayers would have been stopped."[5] This seems inherently reasonable and probable, but it would not appear from the parliamentary debates that this particular point was made by any one of the opponents of the bill. In his final speech Fox answered his critics and ended by declaring:

I risk my all upon the excellence of this Bill; I risk upon it whatever is most dear to me, whatever men most value, the character of integrity, of talents, of honour, of present reputation and future fame; these, and whatever else is precious to me, I stake upon the constitutional safety, the enlarged policy, the equity and the wisdom of this measure.[6]

The words proved true in a sense perhaps other than he had intended. He had indeed risked—and lost—almost the whole of his future career upon his ill-fated measure.

The bill was passed in the Commons by 208 to 108, but was defeated in the Lords by nineteen votes through the daring intervention of George III, who was determined to stick at nothing in his

[1] *Idem*, p. 1279.   [2] *Idem*, xxiv, 411.   [3] *Idem*, xxiii, 1238.
[4] *Idem*, p. 1247.
[5] G. Holland Rose, *Life of William Pitt*, Part i, p. 146.
[6] *Parliamentary History*, xxiii, 1433.

efforts to free himself from the hated control of the Coalition. He had consulted Lord Temple and commissioned him to show to the peers a letter in which he stated that he would regard anyone who voted for the bill as "not only not his friend, but his enemy". The ministry was dismissed on 18 December.

Pitt came into office and brought in his India bill, January, 1784. It was treated contemptuously by the opposition, who still had a large majority in the Commons. But Fox made his terrible tactical mistake of opposing a dissolution; his only chance was to appeal to the country as soon as possible in the hope that popular disapproval of the king's unconstitutional action might counteract the unpopularity of the Coalition. Instead of this he resisted every suggestion of such a course, and so enabled Pitt to display to the world his wonderful skill and adroitness in holding his enemies at bay. At the right moment Pitt dissolved parliament, came back with a triumphant majority, re-introduced his bill with some slight modifications and passed it in August, 1784. The act established six "Commissioners for the Affairs of India" popularly known as the Board of Control. They were to consist of the chancellor of the exchequer, a secretary of state and four privy councillors appointed by the king and holding office during pleasure. They were unpaid, for Pitt hoped that "there could be found persons enough who held offices of large emolument, but no great employment, whose leisure would amply allow of their under-taking the duty in question".[1] The secretary of state was to preside; failing him the chancellor of the exchequer, and failing him the senior of the four privy councillors. Urgent or secret orders of the com-missioners might be transmitted to India through a secret committee of directors, and the court of proprietors was deprived of any right to annul or suspend any resolution of the directors approved by the board. The government of India was placed in the hands of a governor-general and council of three, and the subordinate presi-dencies were made definitely subject to Bengal in all questions of war, revenue and diplomacy. Only covenanted servants were in future to be appointed members of council. The experiment of appointing outsiders had been too calamitous.

It is interesting to note how largely Pitt had profited both by the experience under the Regulating Act and by the criticism directed against Fox's India bills. In his introductory speech he compares his own bill with that of his rival, as

affording as vigorous a system of control, with less possibility of influence,—securing the possessions of the East to the public, without confiscating the property of the Company; and beneficially changing the nature of this defective government without entrenching on the chartered rights of men.[2]

The Board of Control obviously represented Fox's seven com-missioners, but there is a fundamental difference. They do not stand

---

[1] *Parliamentary History*, XXIV, 1093.   [2] *Idem*, pp. 319–20.

apart as an independent executive body, they are linked up with the government of the day, for the two most important members at least change with each ministry. Further, they had no patronage, and did not appoint or dismiss the Company's servants in India. In other respects, though their power was veiled, it was nearly as extensive as that of Fox's commissioners, for they had access to all the Company's papers and their approval was required for all dispatches relating to other than commercial business. In case of emergency they could send their own drafts to the secret committee of the directors, to be signed and sent out in the name of the Company. This secret committee was a curious device by which the court of directors kept a show of independence, though liable to the complete control of the board. According to the act, it was to consist of not more than three directors. In practice, it nearly always consisted of two, the chairman and the deputy chairman of the court. Clearly the ultimate direction had passed to the cabinet, and when Pitt was pressed to the point, he frankly and openly acknowledged it, the public control of India "could not, with safety or propriety, be placed in any other hands than those of the genuine and legitimate executive power of the constitution".[1] The directors were mainly satisfied, because they were left with the patronage and the right of dismissing their servants. They had recognised that something would have to be sacrificed, and they might well be satisfied with what they had been allowed to retain. For, though Fox declared that "if ever a charter was completely and totally annulled, it was the charter of the East India Company by the present bill",[2] and that "it worked upon the Company's rights by slow and gradual sap",[3] yet, besides the patronage, the directors were left with considerable powers of revision and initiation. As Mill says:

The power is considerable which appears to remain in the hands of the directors ...whenever there is not a strong motive to interfere with business of detail, there is always a strong motive to let it alone. There yet has never been any great motive to the Board of control to interfere....Of the power which the directors retain, much is inseparable from the management of detail.[4]

In any case Pitt had taken the wise precaution of neutralising, as far as possible, opposition from the Company.

"In proposing", he said, "a new system of government and regulation, he did not disdain to consult with those, who, having the greatest stake in the matter to be new-modelled, were likely to be the best capable of giving him advice. He acknowledged the enormous transgressions of acting with their consent, rather than by violence;....He had not dared to digest a bill without consultation."[5]

In January he had a conference with representatives from Leadenhall Street. The act in the end was based on resolutions which were drawn

---

[1] *Idem*, p. 322. [2] *Idem*, p. 1124. [3] *Idem*, pp. 1127–8.
Mill, *Histor of India*, IV, 396. [5] *Parliamentary History*, XXIV, 318–19.

up and accepted by a General Court. Pitt was therefore able to claim that the bill came forward "fortified and recommended by the consent of the Company".[1]

The act was drafted with great skill. Burke admitted that it was "as able and skilful a performance for its own purposes, as ever issued from the wit of man".[2] Pitt, as Sir Courtney Ilbert has pointed out, had done two things; he had avoided the charge of conferring patronage on the crown, and also the appearance of radically altering the constitution of the Company. He himself declared "that to give the Crown the power of guiding the politics of India with as little means of corrupt influence as possible, is the true plan for India, and is the true spirit of this Bill".[3] He had linked up the East India Company and the imperial government. "Sir", he said in the House, "I do wish the persons who shall rule India to maintain always a good understanding with administration". Fox had compared the powers of the Board of Control to those of a new secretary of state, and had lamented that such an office should be created. "I accept of his comparison", said Pitt, "and I say that the power of government over India ought to be in the nature of that of a Secretary of State". Fox's bill, he averred, only ensured a permanency of men, his own act meant a permanency of system.[4]

The most questionable and ineffective clauses in the act were those requiring the Company's servants to declare on oath the amount of property they had brought back from India, and establishing a special court, consisting of three judges, four peers and six members of the House of Commons for trial of offences committed in India. The greatest opposition was raised to this clause. "The tribunal", said Fox, "might fairly be called a bed of justice, for justice would sleep upon it."[5] It was attacked as inquisitorial and as violating the Englishman's right of trial by jury.

On the whole we may admit that it was a great bill. It did in spite of all defects answer the main questions as propounded by Erskine in the House of Commons in 1783: "Was it fit that private subjects should rule over the territories of the state without being under its controlling powers"?[6] Pitt never pretended that his solution was a perfect one.

"Any plan", he said, "which he or any man could suggest for the government of territories so extensive and so remote, must be inadequate; nature and fate had ordained in unalterable degrees, that governments to be maintained at such a distance, must be inadequate to their end."[7]

Scott, Hastings's agent in London, believed that the passing of the bill heralded a change for the better in his patron's fortunes. He tells Hastings that Dundas has now become his friend, that Lord Thurlow

---

[1] *Parliamentary History*, XXIV, 412.   [2] *Idem*, XXV, 206.   [3] *Idem*, XXIV, 408.
[4] *Idem*, pp. 409–10.   [5] *Idem*, p. 1135.   [6] *Idem*, XXIII, 1293.
[7] *Idem*, XXIV, 321.

is anxious to make him an English peer by the title of Lord Daylesford, that Burke and Francis are entirely discredited. He only regrets that the lack of opposition in the Lords prevented Lord Thurlow from "giving Mr Francis a precious trimming".[1] A little later he writes that, though Pitt has pronounced Hastings to be a very great, and indeed a wonderful man who has done very essential service to the state, "and has a claim upon us for everything he can ask", yet the resolutions of the House of Commons, standing upon the Journals, are at present a bar to the granting of an honour "until the sting of those resolutions is done away by a vote of thanks for Mr Hastings's great services".[2] But Hastings himself, writing and watching with anxiety and expectancy in the East, came to a very different conclusion. He read the bill and the speeches in the debates with the deepest disgust.

"I have received and studied Mr Pitt's bill", he wrote, "and receive it as so unequivocal a demonstration that my resignation of the service is expected and desired, that I shall lose no time in preparing for the voyage."[3]

He was perhaps too apt to regard all the attacks upon the Indian system as directed against himself personally:

It has destroyed all my hopes, both here and at home....What devil has Mr Pitt dressed for his exemplar, and clothed with such damnable attributes of ambition, spirit of conquest, thirst of blood, propensity to expense and troubles, extravagance and improvidence...disobedience of orders, rapacity, plunder, extortion....And am I this character? Assuredly not; but most assuredly was it the declaimer's intention to fix it upon me.[4]

The logical supplement to Pitt's act was contained in three short measures passed in 1786. The first repealed the provisions requiring the Company's servants to disclose on oath the amount of property they brought home from India. The special court to try in England offences committed in India was remodelled, but it was in fact never constituted. The second act made the approval of the crown for the choice of the governor-general unnecessary, though the king of course had still the power of recall. The third empowered the governor-general in special cases to override the majority of his council—the dissentient councillors having the privilege of recording written protests—and enabled the governor-general to hold also in emergencies the office of commander-in-chief. Lord Cornwallis had made this measure a condition of his acceptance of the post of governor-general. The bill was fiercely opposed by Burke, who declared that the principle of it was

to introduce an arbitrary and despotic government in India...the preamble of the clause which laid it down...that arbitrary power was necessary to give vigour and dispatch, was a libel on the liberties of the people of England, and a libel on the British constitution.[5]

[1] Gleig, op. cit. III, 107, 170, 172. [2] Idem, p. 174.
[3] Idem, p. 217. [4] Idem, pp. 224, 226.
[5] Parliamentary History, xxv, 1274.

Pitt argued that the bill was only the logical development of the act of 1784. He always thought that the power of the governor-general ought to be put on a different footing:

in the former Bill, therefore, his powers had been enlarged by diminishing the number of the Council,...and in the present Bill the same principle was still adhered to and farther followed up.[1]

[1] *Parliamentary History*, xxv, 1290.

CHAPTER XI

THE EARLY REFORMS OF WARREN HASTINGS IN BENGAL

IN 1772 Warren Hastings was appointed governor of Bengal. He had already been twenty-two years in India. Born at Churchill in Oxfordshire on 6 December, 1732, he had been educated at Westminster School and reached Calcutta in 1750 as a writer, the lowest grade in the Company's service. In the troubles in Bengal, 1756–7, he was imprisoned at Murshidabad by Siraj-ud-daula, but was soon released. After Clive's reconquest of Calcutta he was made Resident at Murshidabad. In the revolutions in the Muhammadan government in 1760 and 1763 he seems to have played an entirely honourable part. Burke is wrong and unjust when he says: "He was co-existent with all the acts and monuments of that revolution, and had no small share in all the abuses of that abusive period".[1] Lord North declared more truly that at this period Hastings "though of flesh and blood, had resisted the greatest temptations".[2]

Hastings returned to England in 1764. His hands were clean, but it is unnecessary to speak of his conduct as a miracle of self-denial. He did indeed bring home an amount of wealth honourably moderate in comparison with that of some of his contemporaries, and every credit should be given to him for it; yet at the age of thirty-two he had acquired by legitimate means in fourteen years a competence of £30,000—a rather striking commentary on the normal emoluments at this time of an Indian career. Of this sum he soon lost £25,000 in an unwise and thoroughly characteristic investment, for he was incurably imprudent in the conduct of his own money matters.

In 1766 the directors were impressed by the ability with which he gave evidence before a committee of the Commons, and in 1769 he was sent back to India to be second of council at Madras. There he won further favour by the skill with which, as export warehouse-keeper, he improved the plan for the Company's investments. At the end of 1771 he was appointed governor of Bengal, "a station", as he said himself, "of more éclat, but of more trouble and difficulty".[3] We cannot wonder that Hastings felt no undue elation at his prospects. He would have a council of twelve or thirteen members, and all questions would be decided by a majority of votes. The governor's chance of controlling his colleagues depended on his own personality, on his being the sole executive official when council was not actually sitting, and on an undefined but traditional influence over the exercise

---

[1] *Burke's Works*, VII, 55. [2] M. E. Monckton Jones, *Warren Hastings in Bengal*, p. 104.
[3] Gleig, *op. cit.* I, 225.

of patronage. He had in fact, as he himself declared, "no other pre-eminence beside that of a greater responsibility".[1] Hastings, however, almost dominated his council. The truth is that as long as a majority of votes could decide all questions, the governor-general was more secure against unreasonable opposition in a large, than in a small, council, for in the former there was more chance of finding a certain number of men of good will, and a wider sphere within which his personal powers might exert themselves. In the smaller council the governor-general's position was insecure till the state in 1786 reluctantly consented to grant him in the last resort the power to override a hostile majority. We must add that Hastings's control over foreign relations was strengthened by the fact that they were managed by a select committee of himself and two others. It is evident that down till October, 1774, he was allowed almost unhampered control.

What was the exact position of the British in Bengal in 1772? The British dominions consisted of a curious conglomeration of territories, held by a curious variety of titles. We may divide them into three classes. The first class consisted of Burdwan, Midnapur, Chittagong, acquired in 1760, which were held free of all revenue tax. The second class was made up of Calcutta itself, won in 1698, and the 24-Parganas, acquired in 1757. The Company held these territories on a zamindari title paying an annual revenue to the nawab. But by a curious legal fiction the 24-Parganas would after 1785 pass into the first class. This came about as follows: The revenue paid for them by the Company was assigned by the Moghul emperor in 1759 to Lord Clive as a jagir. The directors stopped payment of it to him in 1763, but in 1765, wishing to make use of his services again, they made an agreement with him by which he or his representatives were to enjoy the revenue of the jagir for ten years, after which time it would lapse to the Company. When, however, he returned home in 1766, they granted to him or to his representatives another period extending to 1785. In the third class we must place Bengal, Bihar and Orissa, over which provinces the Company held the diwanni, or right to collect and administer the revenue, which had been granted to them in 1765. They paid at this time twenty-six lakhs of rupees to the emperor for the right to administer the diwanni, and thirty-two lakhs to the nawab of Bengal for the expenses of government, retaining the surplus for themselves.

From 1765 to 1772 the actual administration was in the hands of two Indian officials known as naib diwans, or deputy finance ministers —the Company itself being the actual diwan—Muhammad Reza Khan in Bengal and Shitab Rai in Bihar. Their activities were to a limited extent regulated by British supervisors who were to have "a controlling though not an immediate, active power over the collections",[2] first appointed in 1769. The holders of this office must

---

[1] Monckton Jones, *Warren Hastings in Bengal*, p. 200.   [2] *Idem*, p. 89.

of course be distinguished from the three eminent ex-servants of the
Company, also called supervisors, who were sent out this same year
with almost autocratic powers to reform the whole administration
of the Company, but whose ship after leaving the Cape sank some-
where in mid-ocean. This system of Indian executive officers under
a vague British control was the famous dual system. It was now
in ill repute, for while the Company itself was in serious financial
straits, its servants were returning to England with great fortunes.
For its failure in India we have to go no further than the admissions
of some of the Company's servants who were endeavouring to administer it.

"It must give pain to an Englishman", wrote Becher, Resident at Murshidabad
in 1769, "to have reason to think, that since the accession of the Company to the
Diwani, the condition of the people of this country has been worse than it was
before; and yet I am afraid the fact is undoubted....This fine country, which
flourished under the most despotic and arbitrary government, is verging towards
its ruin, while the English have really so great a share in the administration."[1]

And again:

I well remember this country when Trade was free and the flourishing state it
was then in; with concern I now see its present ruinous condition....[2]

Furthermore, the directors strongly suspected that the naib diwans
were intercepting a great part of the revenue that ought to have
reached the Company's exchequer.

Such was the state of things with which Hastings was called upon
to deal. He was definitely appointed to put an end to the dual
system. He was, in fact, selected to take the place of the three supervisors, Scrafton, Forde and Vansittart, to whose tragic end we have just
referred. "We now arm you with our full powers", wrote the Company, "to make a complete reformation."[3] The responsibility therefore was very great. Though he was given definite instructions on
most points, it is to a certain extent true, as Lord Thurlow says, that
he was ordered "to destroy the whole fabric of the double government
...he was to form a system for the government of Bengal, under
instructions so general, that I may fairly say the whole plan was left
to his judgment and discretion".[4] So, too, Hastings claimed for
himself: "The first acts of the government of Bengal, when I presided
over it, were well known at the time to have been of my formation,
or formed on principles which I was allowed to dictate".[5] For good
or ill, then, the internal reforms in Bengal prior to 1774 are mainly
in their details at any rate the work of Warren Hastings and bear the
stamp of his personality.

[1] *Idem*, p. 85.   [2] *Idem*, p. 83.   [3] *Idem*, p. 145.
[4] *Debates of the House of Lords, on the evidence delivered in the trial of Warren Hastings....*
London, 1797, p. 132.
[5] *Selections from the State Papers of the Governor-General...Warren Hastings*, Ed. Forrest,
II, 63.

He had great difficulties to confront. Something like an Indian Empire had grown up, but it had no administrative framework. "The new government of the Company consists of a confused heap of undigested materials, as wild as the chaos itself."[1] "Our constitution is nowhere to be traced but in ancient charters, which were framed for the jurisdiction of your trading settlements, the sales of your exports, and the provision of your annual investment."[2] "I found this government in possession of a great and rich dominion, and a wide political system which has been since greatly extended, without one rule of government, but what descended to it from its ancient commercial institutions."[3]

He had to attack strong vested interests, and, what is more, he had to try to strengthen an overweakened central government against a too-powerful exterior ring of provincial powers. The political centre of gravity had got seriously displaced. The government of the country, he wrote, consisted of the supervisors, the boards of revenue at Murshidabad and Patna, the governor and council at Calcutta. Hastings is, of course, naming these powers in exactly the reverse of their theoretical position in the hierarchy of administration, but, as he says, "the order in which I have named them is not accidental, but consonant to the degree of trust, power and emolument which they severally possess".[4] In the government of Bengal "all trust, power and profit are in the hands of its deputies, and the degree of each proportionate to their want of rank in the service".[5] He tells us elsewhere that "every man capable of business runs away to the collectorships or other lucrative stations....At the Presidency, where the best assistance is required, the worst only can be had...".[6]

The reforms themselves fall under three heads, first the commercial reforms, secondly, the reform of the judicature and the settlement of land revenue, dealt with elsewhere, and thirdly, all those measures which followed on the abolition of the dual government in pursuance of the Company's professed intention "to stand forth as Diwan".

Hastings's commercial reforms involved the following changes. He abolished in March, 1775, the fraudulent use of the dustuck or free pass under which the goods of the Company's servants or their agents were exempted from dues. Thus the old problem which had haunted so disastrously the administrations of Vansittart and Verelst was at last settled. He suppressed the custom-houses (or chokeys) in the zamindaris, which were a great impediment to the free circulation of goods. Only five central custom-houses were henceforth maintained, at Calcutta, Hugli, Murshidabad, Patna and Dacca. Lastly, he carried out a uniform lowering of the duties to $2\frac{1}{2}$ per cent. on all goods, except the monopolies of salt, betel-nut and tobacco, to be

---

[1] Gleig, op. cit. I, 317.   [2] Idem, p. 368.   [3] Idem, II, 148.
[4] Monckton Jones, Warren Hastings in Bengal, p. 148.
[5] Idem, p. 146.   [6] Gleig, op. cit. I, 300.

paid by all Europeans and Indians alike. These reforms were entirely beneficial. It is true they were all ordered by the court of directors, but Hastings entirely assented, carried out the details with expert knowledge and adroitness, and smoothed away all opposition by his tactful methods. They did much to revive the decaying internal trade of Bengal. Hastings could with some justice boast that "goods pass unmolested to the extremities of the province".[1]

Hastings's modification of the land revenue system and the reform of the judicature will be dealt with elsewhere. But something must be said of the abolition of the dual government. Formally it meant no more than that the Company should henceforth collect the revenues through the agency of its own servants. But in reality, and in the peculiar political and economic position of Bengal, it meant becoming responsible for the whole civil administration. Hastings hardly exaggerated when he described it as "implanting the authority of the Company, and the sovereignty of Great Britain, in the constitution of this country".[2] The first step was the abolition of the offices of naib diwan of Bengal and Behar, and the prosecution of Muhammad Reza Khan and Shitab Rai for peculation. After undergoing a long trial and being kept in custody for rather more than a year they were both acquitted. Shitab Rai was entirely cleared, and Hastings declared he scarce knew why he was called to account. He was reappointed to high office in Patna as rai-raian of Bihar, but died soon afterwards, largely it was supposed from illness brought on by the anxieties and discredit of his imprisonment. Hastings recorded his epitaph and revealed his own regret for the whole proceeding when he wrote:

He ever served the Company with a fidelity, integrity and ability which they can hardly expect to experience in any future officer of government, whom they may choose from the same class of people.[3]

Muhammad Reza Khan was also acquitted, but Grant held that he had for years intercepted much of the revenue due to the Company. Hastings believed that he was culpable but that it was impossible in view of his wide connections and past precautions to bring him to account. The whole incident is a curious one and not very easy to understand. The least reputable feature of it was the expedient of using "the abilities, observation and active malignity of Maharaja Nandakumar" to attack Muhammad Reza Khan, but the responsibility for that lies with the court of directors and not with Hastings. It is clear that the latter looked upon the whole business with the greatest distaste. "These retrospections and examinations", he wrote, "are death to my views".[4] He was eager to get on with his work of reformation, and he could foresee clearly enough that he

---

[1] Gleig, op. cit. I, 304.   [2] Idem, II, p. 30.
[3] Monckton Jones, *Warren Hastings in Bengal*, p. 199.   [4] Gleig, op. cit. I, 283.

would not escape censure for having brought the trials "to so quiet and unimportant an issue".[1] In this he was not mistaken. Among the charges afterwards brought against him by Nandakumar was one that the two accused men had offered Hastings and himself enormous bribes for an acquittal.

A third reform was the reduction from thirty-two to sixteen lakhs of rupees of the sum paid to the nawab from the revenue of Bengal. This was the third reduction of this tribute; originally in 1765 it had been fifty-three lakhs, in 1766 it had been reduced to forty-one, and in 1769 to thirty-two. As this change was carried out under direct orders of the court of directors, neither credit nor discredit can fairly be attributed to Hastings for the principle involved, but the skill with which he so reformed the administration that the nawab actually received more than before for his personal requirements, is all his own.

Fourthly, we have a reform which in the eyes of Hastings was of the greatest importance, namely, the removal of the treasury or *khalsa* from Murshidabad to Calcutta. This was the method taken by Hastings to rectify that displacement of the political gravity of the British administration which has been already referred to.

"The Board of Revenue", wrote Hastings, "at Murshidabad, though composed of the junior servants of the Company, was superior before this alteration, to the governor and council of the presidency. Calcutta is now the capital of Bengal, and every office and trust of the province issues from it."[2]

Again:

The seat of government [is] most effectually and visibly transferred from Murshidabad to Calcutta, which I do not despair of seeing the first city in Asia, if I live and am supported but a few years longer.[3]

Fifthly, we come to an expedient which is much more difficult to judge. In reorganising the household of the nawab of Bengal, who was still in his minority, Hastings decided to appoint as his guardian not only a princess, which considering the secluded position of women in the East was itself unusual, but one who was not even the nearest relative to the nawab. He passed over the prince's mother and he appointed the widow of a former nawab, Mir Ja'far, who was known as the Munni Begam. Rajah Gurdas, son of Nandakumar, was at the same time appointed steward of the household. For these appointments Hastings was afterwards vehemently censured, and indeed they do seem to require justification. The princess was said, apparently with truth, to have been originally a dancing girl in the court. Burke stigmatised Hastings's act as "violent, atrocious and corrupt",[4] and one of Hastings's own justifications—that the begam's "interest must lead her to concur with all the designs of the Company, and to solicit their patronage"[5]—may itself be described as of a highly questionable

---

[1] Gleig, *op. cit.* I, 391.   [2] *Idem*, p. 271.   [3] *Idem*, p. 285.
[4] Bond, *Speeches in the Trial of Warren Hastings*, II, 32.   [5] Gleig, *op. cit.* I, 254.

nature. Lord Thurlow afterwards protested against the attacks on the princess:

"Whatever situation", he said, "she may have filled in her very early life,... she held the rank of the first woman in Bengal for near forty years, the wife of one prince, the mother of another and the guardian of two other princes."[1]

It may be said at any rate that Hastings's choice received the approval of the court of directors. The evidence is conflicting as to the begam's treatment of the young nawab. When in 1775 the majority of the council divested the begam of her guardianship and appointed Muhammad Reza Khan, the British officer who carried out the change reported that the nawab was rejoiced to recover his freedom, and complained that he had been stinted of his proper allowance, and debarred from all opportunity of learning the work of administration. The officer expressed his personal belief in the truth of these statements, but the facts and the deductions from them were disputed by the Resident at Murshidabad.[2]

Before pronouncing a final verdict on the work of these two years, 1772–4, we may for a moment consider the question how far Hastings secured for the future a real purification of the British administration in Bengal—how far the *moral* of the Company's servants was raised and improved. Undoubtedly he effected much. Recent writers have maintained that, when Hastings returned to England in 1785, the whole system of administration had been purified, clarified and reorganised, and, to support this contention, we have on record an early letter of Sir John Shore, then a junior servant of the Company, written in 1782, in which he says:

The road to opulence grows daily narrower, and is more crowded with competitors ...the court and directors are actuated with such a spirit of reformation and retrenchment, and so well seconded by Mr. Hastings, that it seems the rescission of all our remaining emoluments will alone suffice it. The Company's service is in fact rendered an employ not very desirable.[3]

But we can only accept the theory that Hastings purified the administration with considerable qualifications. In contrast to such a contention we must set the fact that the nearer we get back to Hastings's own time, the less belief do we find in this theory of the entire reformation of the Company's service. Sir John Malcolm is probably much nearer the truth when he writes that Hastings's "most strenuous advocates... while they defend his personal integrity, are forced to acknowledge that the whole system of the government over which he presided was corrupt and full of abuses".[4] Had

---

[1] *Debates of the House of Lords in the Evidence...*, p. 145.
[2] Forrest, *Selections from Letters, Despatches and other State Papers preserved in the Foreign Department of the Government of India*, 1772–1785, ii, 381, 385.
[3] Lord Teignmouth, *Memoirs of the Life and Correspondence of John Lord Teignmouth*, i, 39.
[4] Malcolm, *Sketch of the Political History of India*, ed. 1811, p. 40.

there been a complete purification of the service, there would surely have been nothing for Lord Cornwallis to do, when he came to India in 1786, but we know that there was abundant material for his reforming hand. The quotation from Sir John Shore proves, if any proof were needed, that a vigorous attempt at reform was made, but as regards results, it probably records the exaggerated apprehension of a junior servant of the Company, rather than an actual fact. Certainly we may say that the effects anticipated by Shore did not follow.

All this, however, is consistent with the assumption that Hastings made a strenuous and loyal endeavour, as far as in him lay, to amend and purify the service. Probably, short of staking his retention of office upon the question, he did as much at first as was humanly speaking possible. He may well have argued that to quarrel with the court and to throw up his office, because more power was not allowed him, would merely have ruined his own career without improving the service. The trouble was that he got no consistent support from home. One party among the directors were genuinely desirous of a reform, but there was always another party from time to time in the ascendant, who were prepared to connive at misconduct in their servants, provided that the value of their own patronage was not diminished. The plunder was to be had, and, as Cornwallis said, they hoped in their struggle with Hastings to secure the greater part of it.[1] Hastings in 1772 gives as one reason for abandoning his desire to remove the collectors altogether, that,

there were amongst them so many sons, cousins, or *élèves* of Directors, and intimates of the members of the Council, that it was better to let them remain than provoke an army of opponents against every act of administration....They continue, but their power is retrenched.[2]

In the end, therefore, Hastings seems to have compromised to a certain extent with evil, and to bind men to his interests, he freely used the means of patronage at his disposal. To some extent he gave up the struggle for reformation.

"I will neither be responsible", he wrote in 1772, "for the acts of others, nor stand forth as the general reformer, and make every man whose friendship and confidence are necessary for my support my inveterate enemy."[3]

Again we find him writing of Wheler in 1781: "I have made it a rule to give him the first option in most vacant appointments, and have provided handsomely for all his friends".[4] It seems likely, too, that having been obliged, if he wished to retain his power, in the days of Francis's ascendancy in the council, to use questionable means to win support, his finer feelings became blunted. His carelessness in money matters and his incapacity to keep any kind of accounts, or

---

[1] Ross, *Correspondence of...Marquis Cornwallis*, I, 306.
[2] Gleig, *op. cit.* I, 269. [3] *Idem*, p. 319. [4] *Idem*, II, 384.

to recognise the need of doing so, were proverbial, and amounted to a grave fault. His own regulations had strictly forbidden that the banyan (or agent) of a collector should "be allowed to farm lands or directly or indirectly hold any concern in any farm". Yet his own banyan was found, with his knowledge and consent, to be farming the revenues on a large scale. In regard to contracts and commissions, Hastings undoubtedly entangled himself in financial transactions of so questionable a nature, that it taxed the abilities of his counsel to the utmost to defend him at the impeachment. There can be no doubt, too, that by the end of his administration many of his supporters among the Company's servants were enjoying emoluments entirely disproportionate to the services they rendered. Francis pointed out in parliament in 1785 that the cost of the civil establishment of Bengal had risen from £251,533 in 1776 to £927,945 eight years later. There can be no possible doubt about these figures, for Major Scott, who rose later in the debate to answer Francis, was not able to call them in question, and, if it had been possible, he would surely have done so. The rise was largely due to the enormous emoluments of many of the Company's servants. The chief of the board that controlled the salt office received £18,480 a year. The salaries of five other members ranged from £13,183 to £6257. Again, salaries at the Board of Customs amounted to £23,070 among three persons, and at the Committee of Revenue to £47,300 among five persons.[1] These statements are corroborated by a later speech of Pitt in which it is mentioned that among the offices which were at that time open to the servants of the East India Company, apart from the governor-generalship and the office of councillor, were one place of £25,000 a year, one of £15,000, five of £10,000 and five of £9000.[2] Now Hastings's defence in the case of the salt office was that down to 1780 the Company had gained no profit from its salt monopolies, but that after he had hit upon the expedient of allowing 10 per cent. on the profits, the Company in spite of the huge commissions paid to its servants acquired a net revenue of £540,000. It seemed to him that these facts were a complete answer to Francis's charge, but there was surely reason in the latter's contention that before the commissions had risen to this height they ought, while still being fixed at a generous scale, to have been retrenched. Apart from this, it may well be asked at what cost to the ryots were these enormous revenues derived from one of the prime necessities of life.

To return to the reforms of 1772-4. In judging them it is not always easy to specify how many were due to the initiative of Hastings himself, how many to the suggestions of others, and how many to the direct orders of the court of directors. It is certainly clear that the majority of them were enjoined from home. "I am little more",

---

[1] *Parliamentary History*, xxv, 146.
[2] *Idem*, p. 538.

said Hastings on one occasion, "than the compiler of other men's opinions."[1] But what is also clear beyond any doubt, is the immense ability, the tact, the urbanity with which they were carried. In every period of history any notable political or social improvements, if carefully investigated, will be found to be largely derived from a common stock of enlightened contemporary opinion. Many of them are in the air of the time. But to argue from this that credit must be withheld from the statesman who finally carries them into actuality is extremely unfair. The general impression forced upon any enquirer by a perusal of the innumerable minutes, letters, consultations and dispatches of these two years is that Hastings carried along parallel lines, and contemporaneously, a great series of reforms, economic, fiscal, judicial and social. They form a fine record of devoted and laborious work and reveal in their author administrative capacities of a unique kind. He is master of every branch of the enquiry, endlessly fertile in resource, convincing in argument, reasonable in discussion. He toiled ceaselessly and encountered all opposition dauntlessly. Yet the bitter tragedy of the whole thing was that, before the work could be completed, power and authority were snatched away from him, and years that would naturally have been devoted to the further development of his great task were spent in a desperate and sometimes almost a despairing effort to protect his position, career and honour against a vindictive and cruel assault. He speaks of his work by the metaphor of an unfinished building, "a great and weighty fabric, of which all the parts were yet loose and destitute of the superior weight, which was to give them their mutual support and their...collateral strength".[2]

[1] Monckton Jones, *Warren Hastings in Bengal*, p. 151.
[2] *Selections from the State Papers of the Governors General...Warren Hastings*, ed. Forrest, II, 64.

CHAPTER XII

EXTERNAL RELATIONS AND THE ROHILLA WAR

HAVING abolished the dual government set up by Clive, Hastings had next to overhaul the system of relations established with Indian princes. Clive's policy in this field had worked well for five years, but changing circumstances had made revision necessary. At the time of Clive's settlement northern India had been temporarily free from the Maratha terror. It was the imminent renewal of that menace which entirely altered the whole situation. The Marathas, who in 1761 had been driven headlong into the Deccan after their terrible rout at Panipat at the hands of Ahmad Shah, once more recrossed the Narbada in 1769, and came surging northward again to occupy Delhi in 1771. They offered to restore Shah 'Alam to his throne and make his imperial title a reality. The emperor consulted the English, who implored him to reject so dangerous and deceptive a proposal. In spite of this, he agreed to the Maratha terms, and left Allahabad in May, 1771. Though the English had protested, they parted with him amicably. It was to prove a momentous and calamitous decision, and the misguided emperor was never again to return to British territory. For thirty-two years he was practically a state prisoner in the hands of the Marathas or the Afghans. A year after his restoration, the Marathas forced upon him a minister of their own choice, and obliged him to make over to them the districts of Kora and Allahabad. A new and delicate problem now confronted the Company's servants. To continue to pay the tribute was practically to subsidize its most formidable enemies. The Company was bound to suffer for its own quixotic generosity. It had bound itself to pay tribute, as Hastings said, to an idol of its own creation, "not one of his natural subjects offered any kind of submission to his authority, when we first fell down and worshipped it".[1] With regard to the districts there were four possible courses; to let the Marathas occupy them, to take them ourselves, to keep them for Shah 'Alam, or to give them back to Oudh. It was finally decided to discontinue paying the tribute of twenty-six lakhs to Shah 'Alam on the ground that "his desertion of us, and union with our enemies, leaves us without a pretence to throw away more of the Company's property upon him",[2] and to restore Kora and Allahabad to the nawab of Oudh (by the treaty of Benares) for fifty lakhs of rupees.

[1] Strachey, *Hastings and the Rohilla War*, p. 59.
[2] Gleig, *op. cit.* I, 360.

Hastings had no doubts and no reservations as to the desirability of this course: "I am not apt to attribute a large share of merit to my own actions, but I own that this is one of the few to which I can with confidence affix my own approbation".[1] He thus sums up the advantages of his policy:

By ceding them to the [Nawab of Oudh], we strengthen our alliance with him, we make him more dependent upon us, as he is more exposed to the hostilities of the Marathas; we render a junction between him and them, which has been sometimes apprehended, morally impossible, since their pretensions to Korah will be a constant source of animosity between them; we free ourselves from the expense and all the dangers attending either a remote property, or a remote connection; we adhere literally to the limited system laid down by the Honourable Court of Directors...we provide effectually for the protection of our frontier, and reduce the expenses of our army, even in employing it; and lastly we acquire a nett sum of 50 lacs of rupees most seasonably obtained for the relief of the Company's necessities.[2]

This solution met with the support both of the council and the directors, and it is difficult to see what other course was possible. Yet it has been condemned, and was opposed by Sir Robert Barker. Burke described it as a "shocking, horrible, and outrageous breach of faith".[3] Mill says:

Generosity, had it any place in such arrangements, pleaded with almost unexampled strength in behalf of the forlorn Emperor,...the representative of so illustrious a race, who now possessed hardly a roof to cover him. Justice too, or something not easily distinguished from justice, spoke on the same side.[4]

But Hastings and his council clearly require no defence. The districts and the tribute, which was purely eleemosynary, had only been granted to Shah 'Alam to support his imperial dignity while under the protection of the British. When he handed them over to the Marathas, morally—if not legally—he forfeited his right to retain them. The Company's course would no doubt have been clearer, and its case stronger, if it had definitely warned the emperor, as it might well have done, when he marched away to Delhi, that it would not continue to pay tribute or allow him to retain the districts, should he become dependent upon its enemies. It should also be remembered that, before the decision to withhold the revenues was taken, Shah 'Alam was asked to send representatives to Benares to state his case, but that he omitted to do so.

The only other question worth consideration is whether there was any possible alternative. Might not the Company have retained Kora and Allahabad for itself? To this Hastings had two objections; in the first place, it would be unwise to retain in our own hands the administration of provinces entirely separated from the rest of our territories. Secondly, as he afterwards said before the

[1] Gleig, op. cit. I, 355.
[2] Forrest, Selections from State Papers in the Foreign Department of the Government of India, I, 50.
[3] Bond, Speeches in the Trial of Warren Hastings, IV, 759.
[4] Mill, History of India, III, 397.

House of Commons, we should then have excited the jealousy of the nawab of Oudh, to whom the districts had formerly belonged, and so have endangered our alliance with him. It is always worth while to remember that the central pillar of Hastings's foreign policy was the alliance with Oudh.

The other important problem of foreign affairs before the arrival of the new council was the Rohilla War. Rohilkhand, a fertile country lying along the base of the Himalayas, marched with the north-west frontier of Oudh. Its area was about 12,000 square miles and its population about 6,000,000. The bulk of the people were Hindus, but the ruling race were Rohillas, that is mountaineers, or Pathans, or Afghans, the words signifying much the same thing. The country was governed by a loose confederacy of chiefs under the headship of Rahmat Khan, generally known as Hafiz Rahmat Khan because he had been guardian (hafiz) of the sons of the late ruler 'Ali Muhammad and had ultimately usurped their rights. The Rohillas had established their power early in the eighteenth century.

The events leading up to the war must be briefly summarised. In 1772 the Marathas invaded and ravaged Rohilkhand. The Rohillas thereupon appealed to the nawab of Oudh. They did so reluctantly, for there was no cordiality between him and them. The nawab had long notoriously coveted their territory. They knew that if it paid him to do so, he would not hesitate to combine with the Marathas against them, just as they in their turn had considered the possibility of making peace with the invaders, by giving them a free passage through their territory into Oudh. But both parties for the moment dreaded a Maratha invasion more than anything in the world, and this drove them into an uneasy alliance. In reality, as Sir John Strachey observes, "The Vizier, the Rohillas and the Marathas were all utterly unscrupulous and each knew that no trust could be placed in either of the others".[1] We find, for instance, that the nawab asked Hastings "whether he should persuade the Rohillas to attack the Marathas...and take his advantage of both when they should have weakened each other by mutual hostilities". British officers of a later date would probably have improved the occasion by a homily on political rectitude, and it is rather typical of Hastings—both of his cynicism and his frankness—that, in his own words, "I commended the project, but expressed my apprehension of the consequences".[2]

Finally, after the usual interval of intrigue and finesse, during which the advice of Sir Robert Barker just availed to prevent the nawab from joining the Marathas, a treaty of alliance was made 17 June, 1772, between the Rohillas and Shuja-ud-daula. The Rohillas agreed to pay him forty lakhs on his obliging the Marathas to retire from their country "either by peace or war". The treaty was really due to the initiative and intervention of Sir Robert Barker, the British

[1] Strachey, *Hastings and the Rohilla War*, p. 49.   [2] *Idem*, p. 113.

commander-in-chief, an intervention not at first welcomed by Hastings and the Select Committee, and was signed in his presence. Almost before the signatures were appended, the Marathas evacuated Rohilkhand, and the Rohillas reoccupied the country.

The *casus foederis* arose in 1773. In the spring the Marathas re-entered Rohilkhand at Ramghat. The nawab of Oudh, with a British brigade in support under Sir Robert Barker, advanced to repel the invasion. After some manœuvring and counter-marching the detachments of the Marathas which had crossed the Ganges (the main body seem to have remained on the other bank) recrossed the river on 28 March. In May the revolution at Poona, which broke out on the death of the Peshwa, Madhu Rao, caused the Marathas to return to the Deccan, leaving only a few small garrisons in Northern India. The nawab of Oudh now demanded from the Rohillas the sum due to him, but they refused to pay. They claimed that the Marathas had really retired of their own accord, and that there had been no collision with the allies.

It seems clear that the nawab and the British protected Rohilkhand mainly by their presence on the spot, for Hastings on one occasion acknowledged that "the Marathas (i.e. the main body) lay during the whole campaign of 1773 in the neighbourhood of our army, but without daring either to cross the river or to approach the borders of Kora".[1] It was claimed—and technically no doubt the claim was indisputable—that the Rohillas still owed the forty lakhs, for the treaty stipulated that they were liable if the Marathas retreated "either by peace or war". The Rohillas, however, fell back upon a second line of defence by questioning whether the Marathas had really been driven out at all: "they might return the next year, when our joint forces were not in the Rohilla country to defend them: that we had done little, meaning that we had not destroyed the Maratha armies". Legally no doubt the Rohillas were in the wrong, but it must be admitted that European nations have often evaded treaty obligations on no better grounds.

Nothing further was done till Hastings held his conference with the nawab of Oudh at Benares in August and September, 1773. There he concluded a public treaty which made no direct mention of the Rohillas. By it Kora and Allahabad, as already mentioned, were ceded to the nawab in return for fifty lakhs of rupees, and it was stipulated that, whenever he employed a British brigade, he should pay a subsidy of 210,000 rupees a month. At the same time a secret agreement was made by which the British were to furnish a brigade, to help the nawab punish the Rohillas for their evasion, and conquer the country for him. In return the nawab was to bear all the expenses of the campaign and to pay a sum of forty lakhs. Almost as soon, however, as the treaty had been concluded, the nawab began to doubt

[1] *Selections from the State Papers of the Governors General... Warren Hastings*, ed. Forrest, II, 311.

whether he could bear the pecuniary burden involved, and since Hastings had some heart-searchings as to its expediency, they mutually agreed to postpone the expedition. The thought came to the governor-general, as he said years afterwards in his defence before the House of Commons in 1786, that:

all my actions were to be viewed through a very remote medium, with a thousand refractions of private interest, secret misrepresentation, general prejudice, and the precipitation of unformed judgement.[1]

In November, 1773, the nawab having, with his usual fickleness, changed his mind, asked for the aid stipulated in the treaty. Hastings laid a minute before the council in which he pointed out the advantages of intervention and among them that "our ally would obtain by this acquisition a complete state shut in effectually from foreign invasions by the Ganges, all the way from the frontiers of Behar to the mountains of Tibet". On the other hand he expressed doubts as to its expediency:

arising from the circumstances of the Company at home, exposed to popular clamour, all its measures liable to be canvassed in Parliament, their charter drawing to a close and...ministers unquestionably ready to take advantage of every unfavourable circumstance in the negotiation for its renewal.[2]

Accordingly he proposed to agree to the expedition but on terms which were likely to make the nawab relinquish the design. The council, which, through Hastings and his Select Committee, had been committed to the whole business without much choice on their part, declared: "We concur heartily in wishing to avoid the expedition proposed, without entering into the discussion of the propriety of such an enterprise on general principles".[3] They added rather meaningly that they were sensible of the embarrassment that Hastings was under "from what passed on the subject between him and the Vizier at Benares".[3] The upshot was that the nawab on 10 January, 1774, declined the conditions laid down. But on 3 February, 1774, a letter arrived from the vacillating nawab agreeing to everything and asking that the brigade should be sent. So after all the policy of bluff had broken down, and the Bengal government found themselves committed to the expedition.

The British army under Colonel Champion marched into Rohilkhand supported by the forces of Oudh on 17 April. Six days later a battle took place at Miranpur Katra, called by the victors the battle of St George because of the date on which it was fought. Hafiz Rahmat Khan was killed fighting bravely at the head of his troops. The valour of the Rohillas extorted the admiration of the British commander. They showed, he said:

great bravery and resolution...they gave proofs of a good share of military knowledge by showing inclinations to force both our flanks at the same time and

---

[1] Strachey, *Hastings and the Rohilla War*, p. 112.
[2] *Idem*, p. 121.   [3] *Idem*, p. 123.

endeavouring to call off our attention by a brisk fire on our centre...it is impossible to describe a more obstinate firmness of resolution than the enemy displayed.[1]

The action was entirely decisive. About 20,000 Rohillas were driven out of the country, which was incorporated in the dominions of the nawab of Oudh, a small portion only, together with Rampur, was left in the possession of Faizulla Khan, son of 'Ali Muhammad, the founder of the Rohilla power, whose sons had been dispossessed by their guardian, Hafiz Rahmat Khan, and a treaty was made with him 7 October, 1774, before the campaign was over. Champion brought serious charges against the nawab of Oudh and his troops for cruelties inflicted on the peasantry and the family of Hafiz Rahmat Khan.

The Rohilla War was the subject of the first attack on Hastings in Parliament in April, 1786, but as the Commons refused to accept the charge, it was not made one of the articles in the impeachment. The war has earned the strong condemnation of all the older school of Indian historians. Their view, in its extreme presentment, was that Hastings deliberately sold the lives and liberties of a free people and condoned horrible atrocities on the part of the armies of the nawab of Oudh. Sir John Strachey in his *Hastings and the Rohilla War* has put forward a complete and elaborate defence. He contends that the Rohillas were a plundering Afghan tribe who had only established their power over the Hindu population of Rohilkhand for about a quarter of a century. The Rohillas, he says, were as much foreigners in Rohilkhand as Frenchmen in Spain or Russians in Poland in the time of Napoleon; that the aim of the nawab of Oudh and the English was to "exterminate" the Rohillas only in the literal sense of the term, that is, to drive them over the frontier, not to massacre them; that Champion failed to substantiate his serious charges against the conduct of the allies by definite details; that he began the campaign in a thoroughly discontented frame of mind, and that he was extremely jealous of the plunder acquired by the soldiers of his ally; that, since the Rohillas declined to pay the forty lakhs they had promised in the treaty of 1772, the nawab of Oudh had a good legal and moral case against them; that Hastings can be entirely defended from the charge of callousness and brutality, for he took prompt measures to make a serious protest to the nawab; that as a matter of fact, the campaign in Rohilkhand "had been carried on with an absence of violence and bloodshed and generally with a degree of humanity altogether unusual in Indian warfare";[2] finally, that Hastings's motives in the war were statesmanlike and defensible. They were first, to punish the Rohillas for a serious breach of a treaty, secondly to protect Bengal by giving the nawab, the Company's ally, a scientific and natural

---

[1] Forrest, *Selections from the...State Papers in the Foreign Department of the Government of India*, I, 97.
[2] Strachey, *Hastings and the Rohilla War*, p. 233.

frontier; thirdly, to acquire for the Company the valuable pecuniary benefit of a subsidy for the maintenance of one-third of our army. Summing up generally, Strachey asks the question:

Is a British Governor justified in making war upon a confederacy of barbarous chiefs, who, not long before, had imposed their rule on a population foreign to themselves in race and religion; through whose country the only road lies open for attacks by savage invaders upon a British ally, whose security is essential to the security of British possessions; who are too weak and too treacherous to be relied on to close this road; and who have injured that ally by breaking a treaty with him, negotiated and attested by the British general, and approved by the British Government?[1]

Clearly he assumes an answer in the affirmative, and we may certainly admit that we have fought many wars on grounds far less adequate.

But though Sir John Strachey makes good most of his points, it is absurd to say that either the policy leading up to the war or the actual conduct of operations was beyond temperate criticism. Hastings was obviously himself doubtful about the expediency of the whole transaction, and his council still more so. He seems to have allowed himself to be drawn into the matter without having carefully thought it out. The whole question in its initial stages was weakly handled. For a statesman to commit himself to a course of action while hoping that the need for it may not arise, is not the happiest or the most efficient kind of political expedient. The truth is Hastings was always tempted by novel and daring schemes. We shall frequently encounter the same characteristic in his later history. Sir Alfred Lyall speaks truly of "the hardy and self-reliant spirit of political enterprise that is so strongly diffused through his whole career and character".[2]

It is no less true that Mill and Macaulay wasted a good deal of sentiment, and falsified a good deal of history, in painting a picture of the Rohillas as an ancient people long inhabiting a peaceful and happy valley, but the fact that the Rohillas had only established themselves for about twenty-five years has really nothing to do with the justice or injustice of the war. Their rights were quite as good as that of most of the ruling powers of India at this time, and quite as good as those of the East India Company itself. The more important question is whether the rule of the nawab of Oudh, which we were now imposing over the peasantry of Rohilkhand, was better or worse than that of the chieftains we were dispossessing. The evidence as to the condition of the country under Rohilla sway is conflicting, but the weight of it is undoubtedly in their favour.

The only writer hostile to them is Charles Hamilton, who depends mainly on sources inimical to Hafiz Rahmat Khan, and even he only condemns their *régime* when their control was relaxing. As Hafiz Rahmat Khan's power weakened, he says, "the Hindu farmers, and

---

[1] Strachey, *Hastings and the Rohilla War*, p. 260.
[2] Sir Alfred Lyall, *Warren Hastings*, p. 174.

other inhabitants of the country, groaned under the worst species of military vassalage".[1] There seems to be no other corroboration of this view. Hafiz Rahmat Khan was a ruler of ability, courage and considerable culture. Sir John Strachey himself concludes that under his strong personal rule and that of his brother chiefs, "the mass of the Hindu population were treated with greater consideration and received better protection than was the case in any of the neighbouring provinces, excepting those in the possession of Najib-ud-daula"[2]— himself, be it noted, a Rohilla. Elphinstone declares that their kindness to their Hindu subjects cannot be denied, and that the state of improvement to which they had brought their country excited the admiration of our troops. In 1781 the British Resident at Rampur described that district as "what the whole of Rohilkhand was under the government of the Rohillas, a garden without an uncultivated spot".[3] Major Hannay in evidence given before the council in 1774 said that "the country appeared to be in good cultivation....It is in general one of the best cultivated countries I have seen in Hindostan". In any case, whatever the rule of the Rohillas had been, it was better than that of the nawabs of Oudh, which, especially in the time of Shuja-ud-daula's successor, was unspeakably bad and vile.

As regards the alleged atrocities perpetrated by the nawab and his army, there is little doubt that Champion greatly exaggerated them, partly out of pique that he was not allowed to control the political relations, which were left in the hands of Middleton, partly from envy of the booty that fell into the hands of his allies. At the same time there was probably a modicum of truth in the strong statements to which he committed himself, that the nawab did not "cease to overspread the country with flames till three days after the fate of Hafiz Rahmat Khan was decided";[4] that "the whole army were witnesses of scenes that cannot be described";[5] and that "I have been obliged to give a deaf ear to the lamentable cries of the widow and fatherless, and to shut my eyes against a wanton display of violence and oppression, of inhumanity and cruelty".[6] Middleton too, who was friendly to the nawab, admitted that he could not acquit him of severe treatment of Hafiz Rahmat Khan's family or of wanton ravages of the country. But Champion was curiously loth to give details when Hastings demanded them, and when twelve years later he was interrogated on the matter before the House of Commons, though he repeated his allegations, he declared that his memory was too much weakened by long illness to recall any definite instances of cruelty. In any case there can be no doubt that as soon as the reports and complaints of the commander-in-chief reached him, Hastings took

[1] C. Hamilton, *An historical relation of the origin, progress and final dissolution of the Government of the Rohilla Afghans*, p. 209.
[2] Strachey, *Hastings and the Rohilla War*, p. 30.
[3] *Reports from Committees of the House of Commons*, VI, 30.
[4] Strachey, *Hastings and the Rohilla War*, p. 196.   [5] *Idem*, p. 203.   [6] *Idem*, p. 191.

all possible measures by strong representations to the nawab to ensure that this conduct should cease. Hastings afterwards was inclined to speak of the Company's honour as "pledged implicitly by General Barker's attestation", but this is not accurate. Barker had merely witnessed the signatures, though it is probably true enough, as Sir John Strachey says, that without his "active interference and persuasion"[1] no treaty would have been made. But even supposing that it was the duty of the British to coerce the Rohillas into payment, was so drastic a method as the conquest of the whole country necessary? Surely, as Fox suggested, a lesser penalty might have sufficed.

It must be admitted that there is something rather repellent about the finance of the whole operation. Hastings himself was frank enough to avow that the question of money was one of his main motives.

"The absence of the Marathas", he wrote, "and the weak state of the Rohillas, promised an easy conquest of them, and I own that such was my idea of the Company's distress at home, added to my knowledge of their wants abroad, that I should have been glad of any occasion to employ their forces, that saves so much of their pay and expenses."[2]

There is a certain truth in the acrid comment of the majority of the council: "The expectation in sharing in the spoils of a people who have given us no cause of quarrel whatsoever, is plainly avowed to be a motive for invading them".

It seems unlikely that it was really within the power of the Rohillas to produce the original sum of forty lakhs for the nawab, and the weight of evidence goes to show that in the end Shuja-ud-daula was demanding two crores, or five times that sum. Their country had recently been ravaged by the Marathas. The Rohilla War was condemned in mild terms by the court of directors, and it was the one occasion on which Hastings lost the support of the proprietors. The fact that even they felt bound to record a reluctant disapproval, testifies clearly that disapproval was very widespread:

"Notwithstanding", they said, "this court hath the highest opinion of the service and integrity of Warren Hastings, and cannot admit a suspicion of corrupt motives operating on his conduct without proof; yet they are of opinion with their Court of Directors, that the agreement made with Shuja-ud-daula for the hire of a part of the Company's troops for the reduction of the Rohilla country, and the subsequent steps taken for carrying on that war, were founded on wrong policy, were contrary to the general orders of the Company, frequently repeated, for keeping their troops within the bounds of the provinces, and for not extending their territories...."[3]

Even Sir John Strachey admits that his policy was somewhat cynical, and there was a certain substratum of truth in Francis's comment: "we do not enquire into, nor think ourselves concerned in,

---

[1] Strachey, *Hastings and the Rohilla War*, p. 55.
[2] *Idem*, p. 113.
[3] *Idem*, p. 273.

the justice of the cause in which the troops are to act".[1] Sir Alfred Lyall notes that the war was the last occasion upon which British troops have joined in a campaign with Indian allies without retaining control of the operations, and his final verdict seems not unreasonable that "the expedition against the Rohillas was wrong in principle, for they had not provoked us, and the Vizier could only be relied upon to abuse his advantages".[2] But it was at its worst an error in judgment, which could only be proved to be such after all the consequences had developed.

[1] Forrest, *Selections from the...State Papers in Foreign Department of the Government of India,* I, 127.

[2] Lyall, *Warren Hastings,* p. 49.

CHAPTER XIII

WARREN HASTINGS AND HIS COLLEAGUES

THE Rohilla War was the last important event in Hastings's first period of office prior to the Regulating Act. The judges of the Supreme Court arrived on 17 October, 1774, the councillors two days later. The new council began badly by quarrelling with the governor-general on some petty detail of their reception, which merely exemplified the spirit with which they approached their work. They embarked from the very outset, in Barwell's words, upon "a predetermined, pre-concerted system of opposition".[1]

The six years' struggle which now ensued between Hastings and the majority of the council can hardly be paralleled in history. There was room, no doubt, for reasonable criticism of the administration; there should have been no room for the personal vindictiveness which was designed to hound the governor-general from office. "Every page of our public records", wrote Barwell, "teems with matter of private and personal discussion which neither directly nor remotely bear relation to the interests of the country."[2] Such was the lamentable result of the policy embodied in the Regulating Act of sending out as councillors men without Indian experience. It should be remembered that Hastings was the only governor-general who was subjected to this regulation. It need not, however, be supposed that parliament could have expected that such dire results necessarily followed from such a policy. Had the councillors been men of reasonable goodwill and of reasonable modesty—had, we might almost say, Philip Francis not been one of them—they would have found a way either of agreeing with Hastings, or at least of disagreeing with him with sanity and moderation. They came out imbued with a self-righteous conceit and a fixed determination to overthrow the government, which they had condemned before examination. Something must now be said about their individual characters. Philip Francis has been described once and for all by Lord Macaulay as

a man clearly not destitute of real patriotism and magnanimity, a man whose vices were not of a sordid kind. But he must also have been a man in the highest degree arrogant and insolent; a man prone to malevolence and prone to the error of mistaking his malevolence for public virtue.

The first part of this verdict may appear to some to err on the side of generosity. Sir James Stephen, while he quotes it with approval,

---

[1] *Bengal, Past and Present*, xii, 74.
[2] *Idem*, xiii, 78.

adds that Francis was capable "not only of the faults of undying malignity and ferocious cruelty, but also of falsehood, treachery, and calumny".[1] Francis himself, it may be added, soon after his arrival in Bengal, acknowledged to a friend that his aims were flagrantly personal. "I am now", he wrote, "I think, on the road to be Governor of Bengal, which I believe is the first situation in the world attainable by a subject."[2]

Sir John Clavering has been described as "an honest, straightforward man of passionate disposition and mediocre abilities". Hastings' first impression of him was that he was honourable, but brought strong prejudices with him. His opinion, however, gradually changed for the worse, and after his death he could only write: "May God forgive him all the injuries which he has heaped upon me, and me, as I forgive him".[3]

Monson had served in southern India from 1758 to 1763. Impey described him as "a proud, rash, self-willed man, though easily misled and very greedy for patronage and power".[4] Again, in this case also, Hastings had to modify unfavourably his first impression. At first he wrote, "Colonel Monson is a sensible man",[5] but afterwards he came to believe that Monson was almost his worst enemy. In March, 1775, he says of him: "Colonel Monson, with a more guarded temper, and a more regular conduct, now appears to be the most determined of the three".[6]

Richard Barwell, the only one of the new councillors already resident in India, was the regular type of the Indian official of those days. His family had been connected with the East for some generations. His father had been governor of Bengal and a director of the Company. He himself had been in India since 1758. He was a man of many merits and considerable, though not pre-eminent, ability. He made a great fortune in India, and, as Sir James Stephen says, this fact of itself raises a presumption against his official purity. His letters show that in the year 1775 alone he remitted £40,000 to England. Barwell probably acted up to his lights, but his standard was low. We find him, for instance, writing to his sister in 1769: "I would spend £5,000 to secure to myself the chiefship of Dacca, and to supervise the collection of the revenues of that province".[7] In another letter he states that he considers himself justified in evading the law which prohibited the Company's servants from trading, by engaging in salt contracts under the names of native Indians. Barwell, as we know, became Hastings's staunch supporter, but at first they

---

[1] Stephen, *The Story of Nuncomar and the Impeachment of Sir Elijah Impey*, I, 30–31.
[2] *Dictionary of National Biography*.
[3] Gleig, *op. cit.* II, 179.
[4] Parkes, and H. Merivale, *Memoirs of Sir Philip Francis*, I, 376.
[5] Gleig, *op. cit.* I, 477.
[6] *Idem*, p. 517.
[7] *Bengal, Past and Present*, X, 233.

were by no means in sympathy. Hastings found him tedious and punctilious. He wrote in 1772:

There is a gentleman of our Council who seems to think that every subject that comes before the Board, or that he can obtrude upon, ought to go through a long discussion.[1]

And again:

Mr Barwell has made it necessary to declare that although I have the justest deference for his abilities, I have not yet had an opportunity of experiencing their effects but in points of controversy or opposition, nor derived any benefit from his assistance.[2]

The distrust was reciprocated. Barwell wrote in 1773:

I think there is a probability of our continuing friends, or more properly speaking upon good terms, for it certainly is prostituting a name for the most sacred tie to say Mr. Hastings is my friend, which he never was, and I verily believe, never will be. A duplicity of character once detected and known, as his is by me, proves an insuperable bar to any cordial intimacy ever taking place.[3]

Gradually, however, the two men drew together and Barwell was entirely won over by the tact, and impressed by the capacity, of his chief. We find Hastings writing in 1777: "Francis...must be grossly misinformed indeed if he entertains any hope of change in Barwell's conduct, after the proofs which he has given of his steadiness and fidelity".[4] Again he writes in 1778: "I owe much to Barwell, and to his steady friendship",[5] and a little later he pays him a generous tribute by saying: "He possesses much experience, a solid judgment, much greater fertility of official resources than I have, and his manners are easy and pleasant".[6]

Before dealing in detail with the disputes between Hastings and the council after 1774, it may be useful to sketch in outline his relations with his councils generally till the end of his period of office. For two years, 1774–6, he was steadily outvoted and overruled, and for all practicable purposes he had ceased to be governor-general. His position is best described in his own vivid words:

My situation is truly painful and mortifying, deprived of the powers with which I have been invested by a solemn Act of the Legislature,...denied the respect which is due to my station and character, denied even the rights of personal civility by men with whom I am compelled to associate in the daily course of official business, and condemned to bear my share in the responsibility of measures which I do not approve, I should long since have yielded up my place in this disgraceful scene, did not my ideas of my duty to you and a confidence in your justice animate me to persevere; and if your records must be dishonoured and your interests suspended by the continuance of such contests as have hitherto composed the business of your present Council, it shall be my care to bear as small a part in them as possible.[7]

---

[1] Monckton Jones, *Warren Hastings in Bengal*, p. 201.
[2] Forrest, *Selections from...State Papers in the Foreign Department of the Government of India*, I, 39.
[3] *Bengal, Past and Present*, XI, 51. [4] Gleig, *op. cit.* II, 185.
[5] *Idem*, p. 224. [6] *Idem*, p. 243.
[7] Forrest, *Selections from...State Papers in the Foreign Department of the Government of India*, II, 279.

Yet he held on his way with marvellous fortitude and tenacity, and at last came relief. In September, 1776, Monson died, and Hastings now held the mastery though only by his casting vote, he and Barwell opposing Clavering and Francis. In 1777 came the curious and confused incident of Hastings's conditional resignation. The facts were as follows: Hastings had first given, on 27 March, 1775, and then on 18 May withdrawn, discretionary powers to his agent in England, Colonel McLeane, to signify to the directors his intention to resign. McLeane came to the conclusion that Hastings could not long hope to withstand the opposition growing up against him at home, and, having obtained the promise of certain conditions from Lord North, signified to the court of directors the intention of his chief to resign. The court accepted the resignation. By the terms of the Regulating Act, Clavering, as senior councillor, would normally succeed till the five years of the original appointment were over. Wheler was appointed to fill the place in council that would be vacated by Clavering's succession, but before he sailed the news came of Monson's death and he was now appointed to fill that vacancy. Soon after these events, McLeane, owing to the granting of a knighthood of the Bath to Clavering without any corresponding honour to the governor-general, came to the conclusion that Lord North did not really intend to fulfil the conditions of the agreement, and he therefore wrote to Hastings advising him not to resign. The position apparently was that Hastings, through the action of his agent, and though he himself had recalled his original instructions two months after they were sent, had signified his intention to resign, but had fixed no date. When the news came to Bengal in June, 1777, Francis and Clavering at once assumed that Hastings had resigned; Clavering claimed the governor-generalship, took his seat in council at the head of the table, demanded the keys of the fortress and the treasuries, and in general acted with the greatest precipitation and violence. Hastings was stung into a flat resistance, and declined to vacate the seat of authority, though he declared that, but for Clavering's presumptuous and absurd haste, he would have held himself bound by his agent's action. The deadlock was so hopeless that both sides agreed to refer the question to the Supreme Court, who decided "that Mr. Hastings had not resigned". Not content with this decision, which saved him from ruin, Hastings next contended that Clavering by his action had forfeited even his seat in council, but here the Supreme Court decided against him. Thus ended what Hastings himself called the "convulsion of four days, which might have shaken the very foundation of the national power and interests in India".[1]

Clavering died on 30 August, 1777, and Hastings's control over the council was greatly strengthened, though Wheler at first was inclined to act with Francis, the usual division being Hastings, Barwell and

[1] Gleig, op. cit. II, 159.

the casting vote against Francis and Wheler. Clavering was succeeded in 1779 as commander-in-chief by Sir Eyre Coote, who, though often intractable and difficult, acted quite independently of Francis. Hastings, therefore, was still able by the exercise of his casting vote to make his views prevail, and it is at this period that he writes of his rival: "Francis is miserable, and is weak enough to declare it in a manner much resembling the impatience of a passionate woman, whose hands are held to prevent her from doing mischief".[1] In 1779 Barwell retired. Hastings had prevailed upon him to stay till he had made, as he supposed, an accommodation with Francis that the latter would not oppose measures for the prosecution of the Maratha War or for the general support of the present political system of government. In July, 1780, he accused Francis of violating this compact, and in a minute laid before the council, said: "I judge of his public conduct by my experience of his private, which I have found to be void of truth and honour":[2] he accepted the inevitable challenge from Francis to a duel, and wounded him rather severely. Though Hastings spoke of this incident with a certain compunction, writing: "I hope Mr. Francis does not think of assuming any merit from this silly affair. I have been ashamed that I have been made an actor in it",[3] yet he had forced on the meeting with great deliberation and most clearly intended to disable his adversary. As regards the accommodation a few words must be said. Francis, as we have seen, was not over-scrupulous, but he always hotly declared that he had never been party to any such engagement as Hastings pretended.

> The agreement I meant to enter into, with respect to the Maratha War, was to prosecute the operations actually existing on the Malabar coast, which, since the campaign was begun, and General Goddard had already taken the field, I thought should be pushed as vigorously as possible.[4]

He flatly denied that he had ever promised any general support. It is probable that Francis's account of the matter is mainly correct. Hastings seems to have been far too easily content with a vague acceptance of his proposal, and it was surely the height of folly, if he really wished for a compact, after his experience of Francis's character, not to get a definitely signed agreement from him. It almost appears as though Hastings, despairing of any other method of freeing himself from his opponent, was purposely content with a mere verbal promise, intending afterwards to force a quarrel upon Francis for not fulfilling it. Whether this were true or not, he had at last attained his object.

[1] *Idem*, p. 263.
[2] Forrest, *Selections from... State Papers in the Foreign Department of the Government of India*, II, 712.
[3] Gleig, *op. cit.* II, 310.
[4] Forrest, *Selections from... State Papers in the Foreign Department of the Government of India*, II, 715.

Francis left India in November, 1780, and Hastings wrote in exultation:

In a word, I have power, and I will employ it, during the interval in which the credit of it shall last, to retrieve past misfortunes, to remove present dangers, and to re-establish the power of the Company, and the safety of its possessions.[1]

Hastings's position was now indeed much easier and his chief tribulations were over; for some time the council was reduced to three, and as Sir Eyre Coote was generally absent from Calcutta on military expeditions, Wheler was practically the governor-general's only colleague, and he found him very amenable to guidance. At first, as we have seen, Hastings had formed a poor opinion of him. He wrote in 1777: "He is now, and must be, a mere cipher and the echo of Francis, a *vox et praeterea nihil*, a mere vote".[2] But his opinion of him gradually improved: "I treat him", he writes to a friend, "with an unreserved confidence, and he in turn yields me as steady a support as I could wish",[3] and again: "I cannot desire an easier associate, or a man whose temper is better suited to my own".[4] It is clear that Wheler was gradually won over by the dominant personality of the governor-general; and it is during this time that Hastings, uncontrolled by opposition, enters upon those proceedings in regard to Chait Singh and the begams of Oudh which have done so much to blemish, fairly or unfairly, his reputation. The truth seems to be that Wheler was an honest and conscientious man, who tried to view each question on its merits. As Sir Alfred Lyall says: "Wheler feebly tried to do his duty, and was rewarded by a sentence in one of Burke's philippics against Hastings, where he stands as 'his supple, worn-down, cowed, and, I am afraid, bribed colleague, Mr. Wheler'".[5]

Two new councillors appeared in due course, John Macpherson in September, 1781, and Stables in November, 1782. Macpherson first came to India nominally as purser of an East-Indiaman and entered the service of the nawab of the Carnatic. He returned to England on a secret mission and was sent out to India again, this time in the East India Company's service, in 1770. Seven years later he was dismissed the service, and returned to England. He sat in parliament from 1779 to 1782 for Cricklade, and he was supposed to be in receipt of a salary from the nawab of the Carnatic. In January, 1781, the Company reinstated him in its service—an appointment which was severely criticised. Macpherson was a shrewd and worldly man, endowed by nature with extreme good looks and with pleasant manners. At first Hastings found in him "every aid and support that I expected, and an ease with a benevolence of disposition ...far exceeding my expectations".[6] With Stables he was far less pleased, and he complains of "his coarse and surly style".[7] For a time Hastings found his relations with his later council easy and pleasant, but we cannot but see that his approval or disapproval of

[1] Gleig, *op. cit.* II, 330–1.   [2] *Idem*, p. 186.   [3] *Idem*, p. 384.   [4] *Idem*, p. 387.
[5] Lyall, *Warren Hastings*, p. 168.   [6] Gleig, *op. cit.* II, 450.   [7] *Idem*, III, 151.

his colleagues varied accordingly as they were prepared, or refused, to sink their individuality in his. Towards the end of his administration he found them inclined to oppose him on certain questions, as for instance—and it must be added most properly—when he proposed in 1784 to intervene in the troubled affairs of the Moghul Empire. "You will wonder", he writes, "that all my Council should oppose me. So do I. But the fact is this: Macpherson and Stables have intimidated Wheler, whom they hate, and he them most cordially."[1] Hastings acknowledged at this time that "I have not that collected firmness of mind which I once possessed, and which gave me such a superiority in my contests with Clavering and his associates."[2] As time went on he railed against them more and more bitterly: "I in my heart forgive General Clavering for all the injuries he did me. He was my avowed enemy. These are my dear friends, whom Mr Sulivan pronounced incapable of being moved from me by any consideration on earth".[3] Again he complains that the councillors have received a hint from their friends not to attach themselves to a fallen interest. Even Wheler for a time fell into disfavour.

These unfortunate dissensions led Francis in a speech in the House of Commons to claim with a certain amount of superficial justification that "the opposition to Mr. Hastings has not been confined to General Clavering, Colonel Monson, and myself. His present colleagues... have exactly the same opinion that we had of him and of his measures".[4] But this of course is untrue. The opposition now was at times vexatious, but it was occasionally justified, and it was very different from the persistent, unremitting and bitter hostility of the old *régime*. The truth is that, as Sir Alfred Lyall said: "It would have puzzled any set of Councillors to hit off the precise degree and kind of opposition that Hastings was disposed to tolerate".[5] Like all men of pre-eminent ability and dominating personality, he could not bear to have his purposes thwarted; and there is probably a substratum of truth in the verdict of Barwell—friend of Hastings though he was—written in 1774:

> The occasions of difference between us that did exist were not sought for by me, but proceeded wholly from the jealousy of his own temper, which cannot yield to another the least share of reputation that might be derived in the conduct of his Government. Unreasonable as it may be, he expects the abilities of all shall be subservient to his views and [that all shall] implicitly rely upon him for the degree of merit, if any, he may be pleased to allow them in the administration of Government.[6]

It must be remembered of course that none of the councillors appointed under the Regulating Act were in any sense men of first-rate ability except Philip Francis. Barwell probably stood next to him in capacity; Clavering, Monson, Wheler, Macpherson and Stables were all thoroughly mediocre men. But the fact remains that, while Hastings

---

[1] *Idem*, p. 121.   [2] *Idem*, p. 122.
[3] *Idem*, p. 129.   [4] *Parliamentary History*, xxiv, 1175.
[5] Lyall, *Warren Hastings*, p. 164.   [6] *Bengal, Past and Present*, xii, 71.

was capable of inspiring the most intense affection and fidelity from
some with whom he came into close personal contact, it is also true
that he had a certain propensity to fall foul of men—and they were
sometimes men of ability and repute—with whom he was called upon
to work in public life. Sir Robert Barker, Sir Eyre Coote, Charles
Grant, Lord Macartney, and even Sir Elijah Impey all were at times
seriously at variance with him. Hastings himself never doubted that
he was in the right and his contemporaries in the wrong, and through
every disappointment and defeat he still clung with characteristic
tenacity to a defiant approval—generally, it must be added, entirely
justified—of his own actions.

> I have now held the first nominal place in this Government almost twelve years.
> In all this long period I have almost unremittedly wanted the support, which all
> my predecessors have enjoyed from their constituents. From mine I have received
> nothing but reproach, hard epithets and indignities, instead of rewards and en-
> couragement....Yet under all the difficulties which I have described, such have
> been the exertions of this Government, since I was first placed at the head of it,
> that in no part of the Company's annals has it known an equal state, either of
> wealth, strength, or prosperity, nor, let it not be imputed to me as a crime if I add,
> of splendid reputation.[1]

The points upon which the new council at once came to grips with
the governor-general were the Rohilla War and the measures to be
taken for terminating it, the conclusion of the Treaty of Faizabad,
and the charges brought against Hastings by Nandakumar.

> "Upon our arrival", they wrote, "the first material intelligence that came before
> us, concerning the state of the Company's affairs, was, that one third of their
> military force was actually employed, under the command of Sujah Dowlah, not
> in defending his territories against invasion, but in assisting him to subdue an
> independent state."

Without waiting for any reasonable investigation, they condemned
the war as

> carrying, upon the face of it, a manifest violation of all those principles of policy
> which we know have been established by the highest authority, and till now uni-
> versally admitted...as the basis of the Company's counsels in the administration
> of their affairs in India.[2]

They inflicted upon Hastings, in his own words, "a personal and
direct indignity"[3] by recalling Middleton from Lucknow, and
demanding that the whole of his correspondence, some of which was
confidential, should be laid before the council. They ordered Champion
to demand at once the forty lakhs, which the nawab had promised,
and to withdraw from Rohilkhand. "They denounced", it has been
well said, "the Rohilla War as an abomination; and yet their great
anxiety now was to pocket the wages of it."[4] Hastings in vain

---

[1] Forrest, *Selections from...State Papers of the Foreign Department of the Government of
India*, III, 902–3.
[2] *Idem*, I, 120–1.   [3] Gleig, *op. cit.* I, 474.
[4] Beveridge, *A Comprehensive History of India*, II, 365.

endeavoured to set up some kind of barrier against this wild flood of censure and criticism. He claimed with good reason that, whatever the rights or wrongs of the matter, since the Rohilla War was begun and all but concluded by the past administration, the new councillors should have been satisfied with recording their formal disapproval of it, and should not have attempted to prevent its conclusion. He declined to produce the correspondence between himself and Middleton, though he offered to submit all passages dealing with public policy to the council, and to send the whole of it for inspection to Lord North, the Prime Minister.

If the conduct of the majority seemed unreasonable on the question of the Rohilla War, it appeared still more perverse on the occasion of the death of the nawab of Oudh, which took place on 26 January, 1775. Their one aim seemed to be to press hard upon the Company's ally. They decided that the existing treaty was personal to the late ruler, and they took the opportunity to conclude a new treaty—the Treaty of Faizabad—by which all his successor's liabilities were increased. He had to pay a heavier subsidy for the use of British troops; the tribute paid by the zamindar of Ghazipur passed to the Company; and the sovereignty of Benares was also ceded to it. Hastings opposed the treaty, but was outvoted. In view of what was to follow it is interesting to note that on his suggestion it was made a condition of the treaty that the raja of Benares should exercise a free and independent authority in his own dominions subject only to the payment of his tribute. On 11 March, 1775, Nandakumar brought against Hastings his charge of having received from the begam a bribe of 354,105 rupees for appointing her guardian of the young prince. There followed the famous scene, in which the majority of the council welcomed the accusation, and Hastings withdrew in fierce anger, refusing to be arraigned at his own council board "in the presence of a wretch, whom you all know to be one of the basest of mankind".[1]

What are the facts of the allegations against Hastings? It is best perhaps to begin with everything that can possibly be said in his disfavour. Hastings at once drew up a long minute, which according to Burke and Gilbert Elliot bore every sign of conscious guilt. Even Sir James Stephen admits that it suggests that there was something to explain. Hastings never at any time actually denied in so many words the truth of Nandakumar's statement. In his written defence, read to the House of Commons, he "entered upon a kind of wrangle equally ill-conceived and injudicious".[2] In a letter to Lord North he uses the curious expression: "These accusations, true or false, have no relation to the measures which are the ground and subject of our original differences".[3] We must assent to Sir James Stephen's comment that "Hastings's character would no doubt have stood better,

---

[1] Stephen, *Nuncomar and Impey*, I, 53.   [2] *Idem*, p. 72.
[3] Gleig, *op. cit.* I, 518.

if he had boldly taxed Nandakumar with falsehood". The begam acknowledged that she had given 150,000 rupees, and Hastings admitted that he had received the sum as entertainment money, but it is not clear why so much mystery was made about the transaction.

On the other hand, for Hastings, it must be said that he had every right to object to the whole procedure of the majority: "I could not yield [to their claim to investigate the charge at the council board] without submitting to a degradation to which no power or consideration on earth could have impelled me".[1] He saw with bitter scorn that his enemies were hot upon the despicable trail, and he had no doubt as to the master hand.

At the impeachment, the Lord Chancellor, who was not favourable to Hastings, commenting upon the whole of the evidence, admitted that the managers had failed to prove that Hastings had ever received any part of the 354,105 rupees except the 150,000. There is no question that he had accepted that sum, but there is no ground for holding that it was a bribe for the appointment of the begam. He contended that, when he received the money, the act prohibiting presents was not yet passed; the allowance was customary, and he could show that it had been received by Clive and Verelst when they visited Murshidabad. This was in reality the weak part of Hastings's case. The Company had forbidden presents long before the Regulating Act. It was really a monstrous abuse that, when the governor of Bengal, whose salary and allowances amounted to between £20,000 and £30,000, visited Murshidabad, he should receive from the nawab an allowance amounting to £225 a day. That it had been taken by Clive and Verelst was very little justification, and in any case it must be noted that at least in their day the nawab received a revenue of fifty-three lakhs, while it had now been reduced to sixteen. There can be little doubt that we have here the reason for Hastings's failure to deny the charge; he could not deny that he had received part, and therefore preferred to deny nothing. Even Sir James Stephen admits that the transaction, "if not positively illegal was at least questionable",[2] and we cannot wonder that in the impeachment the Lord Chancellor, while acquitting Hastings of corruption, said: "He hoped that this practice, which however custom might have justified in some degree, no longer obtained in India".[3] The whole incident illustrates the exactions made upon Indian powers at this time by the Company's servants, whenever opportunity offered.

When Hastings had withdrawn from the council, the majority resolved that "there is no species of peculation from which the Governor-General has thought it reasonable to abstain". They declared that he had received the sums specified, and ordered him to

---

[1] Gleig, op. cit. I, 515–16.
[2] Stephen, Nuncomar and Impey, I, 72.
[3] Debates of the Lords on the Evidence..., p. 147.

refund the money into the Company's treasury. Owing to the dramatic series of events that followed, and the fall of Nandakumar, the charges were never proceeded with. Ultimately the information and papers of Nandakumar were submitted to the Company's legal adviser in Calcutta. He did not advise a prosecution in India, but gave it as his opinion that the evidence should be sent home. There the Company's law officers declared that the statements could not possibly be true.

We must now return to the events that brought about the ruin of Nandakumar and the stay of all proceedings against Hastings. On 23 April, Hastings, Barwell and Vansittart prosecuted Fowke, Nandakumar and another Indian on a charge of conspiracy. The charge was that they had endeavoured to coerce a certain Indian, named Kamal-ud-din, to accuse Hastings and Barwell of having received other bribes. At the assizes in July all the defendants were acquitted of conspiracy against Hastings; Fowke and Nandakumar were convicted as against Barwell, Fowke was fined; no sentence was passed on Nandakumar since he was by that time lying under sentence of death for forgery. Meantime, on 6 May, before Justices Lemaistre and Hyde, sitting as magistrates, Nandakumar was committed for trial on a charge of forgery brought against him by the executor of an Indian banker. His trial took place 8 to 16 June; he was found guilty, sentenced to death, and executed 5 August, 1775. The sequence of events was curious, and it was long believed that the unhappy man was put to death, nominally for forgery, but really for having dared to accuse the governor-general. Burke epigrammatically summed up the popular view when he said in his speech on Fox's India Bill:

The Raja Nandakumar was, by an insult on everything which India holds respectable and sacred, hanged in the face of all his nation, by the judges you sent to protect that people, hanged for a pretended crime, upon an *ex post facto* Act of Parliament, in the midst of his evidence against Mr. Hastings.[1]

In considering the question, it is important to remember that there were two distinct charges against Nandakumar; the charge of conspiracy in which Hastings and Barwell were the avowed prosecutors; the charge of forgery, in which the prosecutor was an Indian, Mohan Prasad, though it was alleged that the real initiative came from Hastings.

The whole question has been examined by Sir James Stephen in his *Nuncomar and Impey,* and he claims to have shown that Nandakumar had a perfectly fair trial, and that in his summing up Sir Elijah Impey gave full weight to any point that could possibly tell in favour of the accused. This is certainly corroborated by the statements of Farrer, Nandakumar's counsel in the famous trial, who was called to give evidence at Impey's impeachment. He was examined at great length, and, though during the trial he had sometimes come into collision with the Chief Justice, he declared that all the favour in the power of

[1] *Parliamentary History,* XXIII, 1369.

the court had been extended towards his client, and particularly from Sir Elijah Impey. Stephen points out that all four judges were upon the bench, and therefore, if there was a conspiracy between the Supreme Court and the governor-general, we have to assume, either that the whole bench was privy to it, or that they were entirely dominated by Impey's personality. The jury consisted of twelve European or Eurasian inhabitants of Calcutta, and the prisoner had, and exercised, the right to challenge. Stephen maintains that the charge of forgery developed in a natural way out of long-standing litigation which had begun in December, 1772. A civil suit against Nandakumar having failed, his adversary had determined to prosecute him criminally, and the first steps in this process had been taken six weeks before Nandakumar produced his charges against Hastings at the council board. As it has been said, "that charge would, in the natural course of law, have been made at the very time when it was made, though Nandakumar had never become a willing tool in the hands of Messrs Clavering, Monson and Francis".[1] Against this it must be mentioned that Mr H. Beveridge, in his *Trial of Maharaja Nanda Kumar*, denies that there was any real attempt at a criminal prosecution till May, 1775, and he gives some shrewd reasons for his conclusion. Stephen rightly contends that Hastings' subsequent reference to Impey as one "to whose support I was at one time indebted for the safety of my fortune, honour and reputation",[2] which Macaulay supposed to refer to the trial of Nandakumar, almost certainly refers to the incident of the resignation of 1777. Quite apart from every other reason, it is of course inconceivable that, if Macaulay's supposition had been true, Hastings would have been indiscreet enough to use the words quoted.

There seems, on a careful review, to have been only two incidents in the trial to which exception may be taken. First, the judges cross-examined—and cross-examined rather severely—the prisoner's witnesses. Their reason was that this was done to prevent the ends of justice from being defeated, counsel for the prosecution being incompetent. The reason seems strangely inadequate; it can never be proper for judges to act the part of advocate. When Farrer protested, Justice Chambers was obviously uneasy on the point, but the protest did not stop the practice. Secondly, Impey, from lack of Indian experience, told the jury that if Nandakumar's defence was overthrown, the fact condemned him; but, as Stephen points out, this rule cannot be applied in the East, where a perfectly good case, should proof be otherwise lacking, is often bolstered up by flagrant perjury.

It is certain that there was no conspiracy between Hastings and Impey to murder Nandakumar. It is possible, as Sir Alfred Lyall hints,

---

[1] Beveridge, *A Comprehensive History of India*, II, 378.
[2] Gleig, *op. cit.* II, 255.

that Hastings, knowing that Nandakumar was liable to a serious charge and was probably guilty, conveyed to Mohun Prasad the intimation that it was a favourable opportunity to bring forward the case, and "the fact that Impey tried the man with great patience, forbearance, and exact formality, might prove nothing against an intention to hang him, but only that he was too wise to strain the law superfluously".[1] There is, however, absolutely no evidence for such a supposition. If it is entertained, it must depend for its justification upon certain evidences of implacable enmity, which it may appear to some that the conduct of Hastings displayed after the trial.

The question of Nandakumar's guilt is a different one from the fairness of the trial, and it is probably impossible at this distance of time to come to any definite conclusion. Sir James Stephen is extremely cautious here. He says that, if he had to depend upon the evidence called for the prosecution, he would not have convicted the prisoner—a notable admission on his part. It was the mass of perjury on the other side and the statements of Nandakumar's own witnesses that tipped the scale against him. There is a further doubt whether the English law making forgery a capital crime ought to have been considered at this time as applicable to India. The question is very technical and abstruse. Impey held that the act under which Nandakumar was tried, and which was passed in 1729, was extended to India in 1753, and that therefore a forgery committed, as his was, in 1770, fell under it, for which he had the precedent of Govinda Chand Mitra; but Stephen admits that the rule afterwards universally accepted by the courts was that the English criminal law as it existed in 1726 was what was in force in India at the time. On that reasoning the act of 1729 could not have applied.

There is a further question apart from those of the fairness of the trial, the guilt of the prisoner and the question of jurisdiction. There can be no doubt that the infliction of the death penalty was so excessively severe that it amounted to a miscarriage of justice, and for this at any rate the court, and possibly other persons, may justly be condemned. Stephen himself admits that fine and imprisonment would have met the case,[2] and Impey and Hastings have only themselves to blame if their conduct in the matter suggested to the world that they were determined to put Nandakumar out of the way. The Supreme Court by their charter had authority "to reprieve and suspend the execution of any capital sentence, wherein there shall appear, in their judgment, a proper occasion for mercy".[3] They could have hardly had a more convincing case for the exercise of this discretionary power. Forgery was universally regarded by Indians as a mere misdemeanour, carrying with it hardly any moral condemnation. Hastings himself had written a few years before—and

---

[1] Lyall, *Warren Hastings*, p. 71.
[2] Stephen, *Nuncomar and Impey*, II, 35.   [3] *Idem*, I, 19.

the words sound almost prophetic—"there may be a great degree of injustice in making men liable at once to punishments with which they have been unacquainted, and which their customs and manners have not taught them to associate with their idea of offence".[1] There was the additional reason that the execution of a man who was the accuser of the governor-general might be misunderstood by the Indian population. Impey afterwards declared that, if this ground had been put forward in any petition, he would have reprieved the prisoner, and Stephen agrees that he could have taken no other course. To this we may perhaps reply by the question: Was it really necessary, or ought it to have been necessary, to call the attention of the Chief Justice to the fact?

The judges therefore were responsible for the harsh decision to carry out the death penalty. Yet we must not necessarily assume that their motives were corrupt. They were very jealous of their prerogative, pedantic in their legal interpretations, and too self-opinionated to recognise that they had not been long enough in India to understand the necessity of adapting the jurisprudence of the West to the environment of the East. "I had", said Impey afterwards, "the dignity, integrity, independence and utility of that Court to maintain."[2] He held that the prevalence of forgery in Bengal required that very strong measures should be taken to suppress it, and that to have reprieved a man of such wealth and influence as Nandakumar would have created a suspicion that the Supreme Court was subservient to the executive. "Had this criminal escaped, no force of argument, no future experience, would have prevailed on a single native to believe that the judges had not weighed gold against justice."[3]

As for Hastings, he had constitutionally no power to reprieve the prisoner. He had therefore a perfect right to leave the matter to the judges, but he could undoubtedly have exerted himself in the cause of mercy, and perhaps it may be said that his character would have stood far higher if he had done so. He here showed that streak of relentlessness in his otherwise kindly nature which appeared on one or two other occasions. He was without pity, and glad that Nandakumar was being removed from his path. "I was never", he wrote, "the personal enemy of any man but Nandakumar, whom from my soul I detested, even when I was compelled to countenance him."[4] Hastings, we have said, failed to exert himself to procure a reprieve, but it must be added that there is some reason for thinking that one of his dependents, an Italian named Belli, exerted himself to prevent Farrer from presenting a petition for a reprieve.

[1] Monckton Jones, *Warren Hastings in Bengal*, p. 158.
[2] Stephen, *Nuncomar and Impey*, I, 260.
[3] *Idem*, p. 257.
[4] Gleig, *op. cit.* III, 337–8.

Farrer persisted in his efforts to procure petitions. One was to be signed by the jury, but only a single juryman would lend his name. The second was to come from the council. Only Francis approved of it; Monson and Clavering declined to have anything to do with it, on the ground that it "had no relation whatever to the public concerns of the country"—a reason that did not usually influence them—and that they "would not make any application in favour of a man who had been found guilty of forgery".[1] It is difficult to understand why the majority of the council did not petition for a reprieve. They owed it to their wretched dupe Nandakumar, and they might have seriously embarrassed Hastings and the court. The theory of Hastings's enemies afterwards was that the execution had struck such terror into the hearts of all men, that no one dared henceforward to cross his path; but it seems impossible to believe that such motives could affect men in the position of Monson and Clavering. There is the less reason for the supposition, since the contemptuous and heartless way in which they answered Farrer seems to show that they had given up believing in Nandakumar, if they had ever done so, and were ashamed of their connection with him. What of Francis? Although he had given a perfunctory approval of the proposed petition, he made no other effort. He entirely disregarded the piteous letter written to him by Nandakumar from prison, and, as Stephen says, "left him to die, when he could have saved him with a word".[2] However much the death of Nandakumar reflects upon the mercy of Hastings and the judges, it casts the darkest and most sinister shadow over the reputation of the men who used him for their own purpose and then callously and contemptuously flung him to the wolves. To Francis no doubt came the dastardly consolation that Nandakumar dead would be an even more potent weapon than Nandakumar living, for his future campaign of persecution against the governor-general.

Nine days after the execution, Clavering laid before the council a petition from Nandakumar, which he had received the day before that event, in which for the first time the doomed man suggested that he was the victim of a conspiracy between the judges and the governor-general. Francis seems to have seen the use that might be made of this document, but for the moment he took the lead in reprobating it. He described it as "wholly unsupported and...libellous",[3] and proposed and carried his resolution that it should be burnt by the common hangman. When, in after years, he was confronted with his action at the time, he declared that it was due to the fact that he "feared for Clavering's safety, not knowing to what length those judges, who had dipped their hands in blood to answer a political purpose, might proceed on the same principle".

[1] Stephen, *Nuncomar and Impey*, I, 233.
[2] *Idem*, p. 235.
[3] *Idem*, II, 94.

All the circumstances in regard to this document are somewhat mysterious. When it was presented, Hastings proposed that it should be sent to the judges, but the majority opposed him and accepted Francis's resolution that it should be destroyed with all copies. All this took place in the secret department of the council on 14 August. On 28 August the judges asked to be furnished with a copy of the libel. The council declined their request, and on the motion of Francis a letter was sent to them asking them to say "from whom you receive the imputed information, which appears to have been conveyed to you on this and other occasions, of the proceedings of this Board in our secret department".[1] The judges were also informed that the petition and all copies had been destroyed. In spite of this, Hastings gave a copy of the document to Impey under an oath of secrecy that he should not disclose it except to his fellow-judges. This fact was revealed twelve years later, when Impey produced a copy at the time of his impeachment. Three deductions follow from this incident. In the first place, it is clear that Hastings went behind the decision of the council, a highly unconstitutional act, and also violated his oath of office. In regard to this his staunch defender Stephen can only say:

Oaths of such a nature never bind closely, and it is one of the great objections to their use that, if they are rigidly enforced they often do cruel injustice, and that, if tacit exceptions to them are admitted, they not only become useless for the immediate purposes for which they are imposed, but are also snares to the honesty of those who take them. Whether in the particular case there was any moral guilt in the breach of the oath of secrecy, and whether its terms were, or were not, subject to exceptions express or implied, are points on which I express no opinion.[2]

Secondly, the facts reveal a certain lack of straightforwardness, which, however much we may excuse it, owing to the fiendish persecution to which he was often subject, sometimes characterises Hastings's conduct. As Stephen admits, he was "a curiously cautious secret man"—"of his conduct to his colleagues I will only say that, if he had acted openly, he would have done better than he did".[3] Lastly, we cannot shut our eyes to the fact that the incident implies, as Francis noted and Stephen agrees, a very strong intimacy between Hastings and the Chief Justice, and "it greatly weakens Impey's argument that he had no means of knowing the particulars of Nandakumar's accusations against Hastings, because they were made in the secret department under an oath of secrecy".[4]

No part of Lord Macaulay's essay is so prejudiced as the famous passage on the terror in Bengal caused by the action of the Supreme Court, and the corrupt nature of the bargain or sale by which in the end Hastings is alleged to have bought or bribed the Chief Justice. The question is a very difficult one and much of the evidence is

---

[1] Stephen, *Nuncomar and Impey*, I, 251.   [2] *Idem*, II, 115.
[3] *Idem*, p. 116.   [4] *Idem*, p. 115.

contradictory. Before considering it in detail, we may perhaps lay down the following points:

(i) A conflict of jurisdiction was inevitable; it was inherent in the charter establishing the court and in the clauses of the Regulating Act. The framers of that act shrank from the logical course of proclaiming the king of England sovereign in Bengal, but that sovereignty was really implied in the very constitution of the court. And, as Macaulay said, they "had established two independent powers, the one judicial, and the other political; and with the carelessness scandalously common in English legislation, had omitted to define the limits of either".

(ii) It cannot be denied that the court caused much disturbance and discontent by exercising its powers too rigidly and too pedantically. But the point is, what classes were aggrieved and offended? If it can be shown that the zamindar class and the European inhabitants of Bengal objected to the court because it restrained oppressive practices against Indians, then the agitation is highly honourable to the judges, and this is as a matter of fact the claim put forward by Impey's son and largely accepted by so impartial and exact an enquirer as Sir James Stephen.

(iii) We must in any case entirely discard the overcharged and overheated language of Macaulay. All we know of Sir Elijah Impey's life makes it impossible that he could ever have been the monster of iniquity described by Macaulay. We must remember that the worst charge against Impey—and it may not be true—is that he harried and distressed the population by exercising too meticulously the legal powers given him, and that, in accepting the new office offered him by Hastings, he was not careful enough to think out all the consequences, or to visualise the manner in which the affair would strike hostile observers. The whole incident casts a serious slur on the literary and historical integrity of Macaulay.

There were many points in dispute as between the council and the court; for instance, the court admittedly had jurisdiction over British subjects but the words had not been carefully defined.

"In one sense", says Stephen, "the whole population of Bengal, Behar, and Orissa were British subjects. In another sense, no one was a British subject who was not an Englishman born. In a third sense, inhabitants of Calcutta might be regarded as British subjects, though the general population of Bengal were not."[1]

Secondly, had the court jurisdiction over the provincial councils? Thirdly, had it jurisdiction over the zamindars?

Something must now be said of the progress and gradual growth of the dispute. Hastings obviously looked forward to the advent of the court with dread, but hoped that his friendship with Impey might prevent the worst consequences. In 1774 he wrote to a friend: "The court of justice is a dreadful clog on the government, but I thank

[1] *Idem*, p. 126.

God, the head of it is a man of sense and moderation".[1] Clearly, if the question had only lain between the governor-general and the Chief Justice, a *modus vivendi* would have been arrived at.

Hastings, therefore, did everything in his power to smooth the path for the judges, and was determined if possible to put the best construction on all their actions. He would, of course, in writing to Lord North, naturally avoid speaking ill of the court, but we find him definitely committing himself to the statement that the protection which it affords to the weak against oppression had already been felt by many. In 1776 he wrote:

> The conduct of all the judges has been directed by the principles of moderation, and a scrupulous attention to the just authority of government, and to the laws and customs of the people. I am afraid that to this prudent caution alone it must be ascribed, that the undefined state of the powers of the Governor-General and Council and of the Supreme Court of Judicature have not been productive of ill consequences both to the company and to the country.[2]

He foresees difficulties, because it will scarcely be found possible in practice "to make the distinction intended by the Act and Charter, between such persons as are employed in the service of the Company, or of British subjects and other native inhabitants". He suggests, to further a good understanding between court and council, that the Chief Justice should have "a fixed or occasional seat" at the council board, and that the Company's courts should subsist by delegated powers from the Supreme Court and be dependent upon it.[3]

In 1776 he worked out and sent home a plan for amalgamating the Supreme and the Company's courts—a scheme which would have in part anticipated that which he effected less constitutionally on his own initiative in 1780. His plan was, first, to extend the Supreme Court's jurisdiction to all parts of the province, that is, to do away with the nawab's shadowy authority and ensure "that the British sovereignty, through whatever channels it may pass into these provinces, should be all in all".[4] Secondly, to unite the judges of the Supreme Court with members of the council in control of the Sadr diwanni adalat, or the Company's chief civil court of appeal. Thirdly, to give the provincial councils a legal authority in the internal government of the country and in the collection of revenue. Of this plan Hastings writes: "All the judges approve of it, and I like it myself, which is not always the case with my own productions".[5] The plan was of course opposed by the majority of the council, who showed their usual controversial ability and lack of real statesmanship (for it was impossible to act as though a *tabula rasa* lay before them), saying:

> It is proposed to give the Supreme Court a complete control over every part of the country....The complaint is that they have assumed more than they have a right to; the redress proposed is to set no limits to their power.[6]

---

[1] Gleig, *op. cit.* I, 471.   [2] *Idem*, II, 16.   [3] *Idem*, I, 541–2.
[4] *Idem*, II, 14, 50.   [5] *Idem*, p. 35.
[6] Forrest, *Selections from...State Papers in the Foreign Department of the Government of India*, II, 540.

At first Hastings attributed the disputes, when they came, mainly to the majority on the council: "It seems to have been a maxim of the Board to force the court into extremities for the purpose of finding fault with them", and he admits that there have been "glaring acts of oppression committed by the Board, which would have produced the ruin of the parties over whom they were exercised, but for the protection of the court". At this time, too, Hastings agreed that it was necessary to bring before the court persons who were eventually excluded from its jurisdiction in order to establish their exemption: "their right to this exemption must be tried to be known".[1] Of himself he says with truth: "On every occasion which was likely to involve the Board in contests with the court, I have taken a moderate and conciliating part".[2] But the plan of 1776 not having been accepted, the position gradually became worse and Hastings and Impey drifted apart.

The trouble centred round two famous cases. The first was the Patna case, 1777–9. The question at issue was the right of the Supreme Court to try actions brought against the Indian judicial servants of the Company for acts done in their official capacity. The Supreme Court cast in heavy damages the Muhammadan law officers of the Patna council. Sir James Stephen has exhaustively analysed the whole case, and shows pretty conclusively that the Supreme Court was mainly in the right. The provincial councils were worthless bodies and had allowed their Indian officials far too much power:

If the Patna council was a fair specimen of the rest, the provincial councils, considered as courts of justice, were absolutely worthless, and no system for the administration of justice, which deserved the name, existed at that time out of Calcutta.[3]

The second case was the Kasijora case, 1779–80. The question at issue here was whether the Supreme Court had the right to exercise jurisdiction over everyone in Bengal, Behar and Orissa, and especially over the zamindars. Hyde had issued a writ against the raja of Kasijora, a zamindar of the Company. The council told the raja he was not subject to the jurisdiction of the Supreme Court, and, when the Supreme Court sent sheriff's officers to apprehend him, the council sent some companies of sepoys to arrest the sheriff's officers and bring them back to Calcutta. Hastings might well say: "We are upon the eve of an open war with the court".[4] Even now he did his best to look at the question fairly. He still felt doubtful about the legal point, though he was convinced of the practical inconveniences arising from the court's action. Referring to the danger to the public revenues and to the quiet of the provinces, and to the irregular and illegal nature of the writ, he says: "God knows how far we are right on the last conclusion. I am sure of the former".[5] But he now came to agree

---

[1] Gleig, *op. cit.* II, 36.   [2] *Idem*, p. 248.   [3] Stephen, *Nuncomar and Impey*, II, 178.
[4] Gleig, *op. cit.* II, 244.   [5] *Idem*, p. 245.

with the majority of his council, that zamindars were neither British subjects nor the servants of British subjects, and that the court could not be allowed to drag "the descendants of men who once held the rights of sovereignty in this country, like felons, to Calcutta on the affidavit of a Calcutta banyan or the complaint of a court serjeant".[1]

The justice of the whole matter is very difficult to decide. It has generally been assumed that Hastings was in the right, especially as he was normally so loth to infringe the powers of the court. But Sir James Stephen declares that in the Kasijora case "the council acted haughtily, quite illegally, and most violently".[2] There could, at any rate, be no doubt that Impey was acting in good faith and he felt bitterly the burden of taking on his shoulders all the unpopularity. He felt bound to protect, as he thought, the peasant and the poorer classes against the European magistrates, "who never appeared themselves" but oppressed the ryots through native agents.[3] We find him saying in a private letter at this time: "We are beginning to make the vultures of Bengal to disgorge their prey".[4]

At the same time it must be admitted that the position in Bengal was rapidly becoming deplorable. The proceedings of the court were extremely vexatious to a large class of people, and there was no doubt that the judges were becoming very unpopular. The memory of this long lingered in Bengal. Cornwallis, who was one of the most tolerant of men and who could never be induced to speak against his colleagues or predecessors unless it were necessary, wrote in 1786: "I trust you will not send out Sir Elijah Impey. All parties and descriptions of men agree about him".[5] Further, though the evidence from this source is probably largely vitiated by partiality, the ninth report of the select committee of 1781 declared that they had been able to discover very few instances of relief given to the natives against the corruptions or oppressions of British subjects. "So far as your committee has been able to discover," they wrote, "the court has been generally terrible to the natives, and has distracted the government of the company without substantially reforming any one of its abuses."[6]

In any case Hastings naturally and rightly desired to put an end to the deadlock, and in 1780 he hit upon the ingenious scheme of offering Impey the presidency of the Sadr diwanni adalat. It is important to realise exactly what this meant. Impey was already at the head of the Supreme Court, sent out in the name of the king to exercise jurisdiction over all British subjects, and especially to deal with complaints against the Company's servants. He was now placed at the head of the judicial system of the Company, which was largely

---

[1] Gleig, op. cit. II, 248.　　　　[2] Stephen, Nuncomar and Impey, II, 220.
[3] E. B. Impey, Memoirs of Sir Elijah Impey, p. 134.　　　　[4] Idem, p. 148.
[5] Ross, Correspondence of...Cornwallis, I, 238.
[6] Report from Committees of the House of Commons, VI, 48.

staffed by those very servants. Macaulay's accusation is that Impey accepted a bribe, compromised the independence of the Supreme Court and finally became "rich, quiet, and infamous".[1] Contemporary opinion in England, especially after Francis had returned home to fan the flame, was not much more favourable. In May, 1782, the court of directors and the House of Commons petitioned the crown for Impey's recall. He left India in 1783 to answer the charge

of having accepted an office granted by, and tenable at the pleasure of, the servants of the East India Company, which has a tendency to create a dependence in the said Supreme Court upon those over whose actions the said court was intended as a control.[2]

It is difficult to understand the warmth of feeling aroused. The practical advantages of the plan were great. A real control was now exercised by a trained and expert judge, through an appeal court which was at last a reality, over weak provincial courts which badly needed guidance. The old Sadr diwanni adalat had been a shadowy body, and, in practice, says Sir James Stephen, never sat at all because the governor-general, its nominal president, had no time to undertake judicial duties. Hastings himself could describe it in 1776 as "having been long since formally abolished".[3] The plan also did away with the friction between the judicature and the executive. It enabled Impey to introduce his code of procedure at the cost of eight months' severe labour—that code of which Sir James Stephen writes: "It is not a work of genius like Macaulay's penal code...but it is written in vigorous, manly English, and is well arranged".[4]

At the same time some tactical mistakes were undoubtedly made. It was an unfortunate circumstance that the salary attached to the new office was revocable at the will of the governor-general and council, but it was almost certainly inevitable in the conditions. The Company's government had no power to create an office independent of itself. Still, it enabled the East India Company's legal adviser to say: "Impey is found one day summoning the Governor-General and the council before his tribunal for acts done as council, and the next accepting emoluments nearly equal to his original appointment to be held during the pleasure of the same council".[5] All this, unhappily, gave the impression that Impey was compromising his dispute with the council for a money consideration. Secondly, since the Supreme Court had been especially created to be independent of the council, it looked as though the spirit of the Regulating Act was being violated. Sir James Stephen himself,

[1] Lord Macaulay, *Essays*, p. 624.
[2] *Parliamentary History*, XXII, 1411.
[3] Gleig, *op. cit.* II, 29.
[4] Stephen, *Nuncomar and Impey*, II, 246.
[5] *Reports from Committees of the House of Commons*, V, 422.

Impey's strenuous champion, thinks that the Chief Justice had put himself in an invidious position.

He did undoubtedly weaken, if it is too much to say that he forfeited, his judicial independence....He exposed himself to a temptation to which no judge ought to expose himself....[His action] was wrong, though I do not think it was actually corrupt.[1]

Thirdly, it is perhaps reasonable to ask whether such sweeping changes ought to have been made without approval first gained from home.

We have, however, to remember certain further circumstances in Impey's favour. He wrote at once to the Attorney-General in London, offering to refund the salary, if ministers thought the acceptance of it improper; and apparently he did afterwards refund it. He claims to have told Hastings that his assumption of the office would not in the least affect his conduct in regard to the question at issue between the council and the court. He wrote in 1782 with some truth:

I have undergone great fatigue, compiled a laborious code, restored confidence to the suitors and justice and regularity to the courts of justice, and settled the internal quiet of a great empire...and for my recompense shall have lost my office, reputation, and peace of mind for ever.[2]

Finally, to some extent, as Impey declared in his speech at the bar of the House of Commons, the judges reaped all the odium of the violent struggle of parties. One faction bitterly attacked the judges

as being partisans of the opposite faction. That opposite faction, cautious to avoid the imputation of undue connection with the judges, found it in their interests not to defend them. Neutral men (if such there were) took no part, and the judges, who really were (as they ought to have been) of no party, were left undefended.[3]

Impey on his return to England was left undisturbed for four years, but in 1787 he was impeached by Sir Gilbert Elliot, afterwards Governor-General of India and Earl of Minto. Six charges were brought against him, namely Nandakumar's case, the Patna case, the illegal extension of the jurisdiction of the Supreme Court, the Kasijora case, the acceptance of the office of judge of the Sadr diwanni adalat, and the taking of the affidavits in Oudh in relation to the Chait Singh business. The impeachment was frankly made a party affair. Almost all the prominent Whig leaders were associated with it. It broke down completely and humiliatingly. Only the first charge was proceeded with. Summoned to the bar of the House of Commons, Impey made an eloquent and triumphant defence. He spoke extemporaneously and without the aid of notes. His speech, which lasted two days, gives a striking impression of his ability. No one can read it without feeling that it is the work of a capable and sincere man. It is far franker and more spontaneous

---

[1] Stephen, *Nuncomar and Impey*, II, 238.   [2] *Idem*, p. 245.
[3] *Parliamentary History*, XXVI, 1347.

than the laboured and confused paper read as an *apologia* by Hastings.

The thorough unfairness of the Whig attitude is shown by the fact that Burke and Fox made it a matter of complaint that Impey had delivered an unprepared speech and had not submitted a written document, whereas, when Hastings presented a written defence, it was alluded to contemptuously by Burke as that "indecent and un-becoming paper which lies on our table".[1] Impey's masterly speech really shattered the case. Pitt declared that, after hearing it, he could say that he never gave any vote with less hesitation than the one he was going to give against the impeachment. The division on the first charge was 73-55 against the impeachment. A half-hearted attempt was made later to raise the second charge, the Patna case, but it was negatived without a division. It would seem that few men have met with less justice from history and the verdict of their own contem-poraries than Sir Elijah Impey.

In the meantime the question between the council and the court had been definitely settled by statute, and, as Sir Courtney Ilbert says, the decision of parliament was substantially in favour of the council and against the court on all points. Two petitions had been sent home, one by the governor-general and council, and the other by 648 British subjects resident in Bengal. The first dealt mainly with the Kasijora case. The council claimed that it was bound to protect the people against "the control of a foreign law, and the terrors of a new and usurped dominion".[2] If the court prevailed, "these provinces, and the British dominion in India, must fall a certain sacrifice to the ultimate effects of the exercise of an impolitic, unnatural and law-less authority".[3] Finally, they declared that they had no alternative but public ruin, if they submitted to the jurisdiction assumed by the Supreme Court, or personal ruin, if they opposed it.[4] The second petition protested against the danger of "giving to the voluminous and intricate laws of England a boundless retrospective power in the midst of Asia".[5]

These petitions were the real cause of the appointment of the Select Committee of 1781, to which reference has been already made, and the result was the act of that year amending the constitution of the Supreme Court. The most important of its provisions was that the governor-general and council were not to be subject to the court for anything committed, ordered, or done by them in their public capacity, but this exemption did not apply to orders affecting British subjects. The Supreme Court was to have no jurisdiction in matters of revenue or its collection. No Indian was to be liable to the court's jurisdiction by reason of being a landholder or a farmer of rents. The

---

[1] Bond, *Speeches in the Trial of Warren Hastings*, i, 6.
[2] *Parliamentary History*, xxi, 1170.   [3] *Idem*, p. 1173.
[4] *Idem*, p. 1174.   [5] *Idem*, p. 1178.

court was again definitely given jurisdiction over all inhabitants of
Calcutta, but Hindu or Muhammadan laws were to be administered
in cases of inheritance, contract and successions.

We must on the whole then conclude that the verdict of the British
in India, of Lord Cornwallis and of parliament, was a triumph for
the council's view of the controversy as against the court, on the
question of fact, and by fact is meant the vexatious and harassing
nature of the court's procedure. But, turning from the objective to
the subjective aspect of the case, and considering the motives of the
parties concerned, we can only conclude that hard measure was
dealt out both to Impey and his colleagues.

CHAPTER XIV

THE FIRST CONFLICT OF THE COMPANY WITH THE MARATHAS, 1761–82

FROM 1750 to 1761 it was an open question whether the Marathas or the Afghans would become the masters of India. The answer was given by the battle of Panipat fought in January, 1761, between the Marathas and the Durani, Ahmad Shah, which resulted in the total defeat of the Hindu confederacy, and the end of the Moghul Empire, save as a mere name. It is worthy of note, that contrary to the ordinary sequence of events in Asiatic countries, no change of dynasty occurred at Delhi, where the effete descendant of the house of Timur remained seated on the throne. Had Ahmad Shah retained his hold on Northern India, the consolidation of the English power would have been far less easy of accomplishment. For the Maratha confederacy, although it had the great binding force of a common racial origin as its foundation, was rent by internal jealousies, while it depended for its aggrandisement on a system of brigandage, which ultimately drove many other Indian states into the arms of the English.

The very growth of its power, indeed, carried in it the seeds of dissolution. As the area in which the confederacy operated expanded, its military commanders, prosecuting campaigns far from headquarters, rapidly lost much of their respect for the central power at Poona, a respect which the characters of the Peshwas who succeeded Madhu Rao did nothing to maintain. Holkar, Sindhia, the Gaekwad, the Bhonsle and others, in consequence, worked more and more in their own private interests to the neglect of those of the Peshwa and of the Marathas as a whole.

The Peshwa, Baji Rao, his spirit broken by the defeat at Panipat, died in June, 1761, his son Madhu Rao being installed Peshwa in September by the raja at Satara, whither he proceeded for the ceremony accompanied by his uncle Raghunath Rao. For the transfer of power from the descendants of Sivaji to the family of one of the ministers did not displace the occupant of the throne at Satara or abolish his nominal rule. Madhu Rao was, however, only seventeen years of age and his uncle kept the reins of the administration in his own hands.

The Nizam of Hyderabad, who saw the chance of profiting by the changes at Poona, prepared to attack the Marathas, upon which Raghunath Rao made overtures to Crommelin, then governor at Bombay. The Bombay Council were most anxious to strengthen the defences of their harbour by securing possession of Bassein Fort,

Salsette and the islands in that neighbourhood, and were quite ready to negotiate. Raghunath Rao, however, anxious as he was to obtain military assistance, was not as yet prepared to surrender such important places. At this juncture the Nizam's Maratha troops deserted him and obliged him to come to terms, whereupon Raghunath Rao promptly broke off his negotiations with Bombay. The incident is important. It deliberately introduced the English as arbiters in Maratha affairs, and, as later events will show, brought them into that personal association with Raghunath Rao which was to become a deciding factor in the consolidation of the British power in Western India.

So far Raghunath Rao had kept all the power in his own hands. But his nephew was not of the metal long to brook control, and early in 1762 insisted on asserting his independence. His uncle and his diwan Sakharam Bapu thereupon resigned and the young Peshwa appointed his own officers. Among them was one who played a conspicuous part in the history of Western India, Balaji Janardhan, better known as Nana Phadnavis, from the office of *phadnavis* or chief accountant which he held from 1763. His family came from the Ratnagiri district. His grandfather had been employed by the Peshwa Balaji Vishvanath, whose son, Nana's father, was appointed *phadnavis*, a post that became hereditary in the family.

The changes at Poona did not make for peace. Raghunath Rao and his officials were annoyed at the loss of power, and this jealousy was fanned by the strong personal animosity which existed between Gopika Bai, the Peshwa's mother, and Anandi Bai, the wife of Raghunath Rao. Anandi Bai, to whom Raghunath Rao was devoted, was a woman of very violent character, and exercised absolute control over her husband, much of whose subsequent misfortunes were due to the sinister influence of his wife.

At her instigation Raghunath Rao now proceeded to make overtures to the Nizam, who readily responded, and, rapidly gathering a body of Maratha and Moghul troops, they advanced together on Poona, an unfortified city, defeating a force sent to oppose them. Madhu Rao, driven into a corner, in order to save the situation and preserve the integrity of the Maratha state, went personally to his uncle and submitted. He was placed in confinement but was treated with all respect.

Assumption of control by Raghunath Rao inevitably led to a spread of discontent. The Nizam, ever on the watch for such opportunities in hope of reducing the Maratha power, in 1763 adopted the cause of Janoji Bhonsle of Berar who claimed to act as regent for the young Peshwa. Raghunath Rao was wholly unprepared, but his nephew, by using his great personal influence, induced Holkar and the Gaekwad to assist his uncle. The Maratha army, avoiding an encounter with the Nizam, ravaged the Bhonsle's districts in Berar and then entered Hyderabad territory. The Nizam, finding he could not stop the Marathas, marched to Poona, which he plundered. Raghunath Rao in the meantime had contrived to buy off Janoji Bhonsle, who agreed to desert the Moghuls when occasion offered. At Rakshasbhavan, on the Godavari river, the two armies met; the Bhonsle quietly withdrew and the Nizam was defeated with severe loss. But the Nizam, always a consummate actor, went personally to Raghunath Rao, and by working on his feelings and appealing to their old friendship, induced his conqueror to pay him ten lakhs of rupees. This curious arrangement was characteristic of Raghunath Rao's vacillating disposition.

Madhu Rao again offended his uncle by insisting in commanding the army which was sent, in 1764, against Hyder 'Ali of Mysore, but the offence was to some extent mitigated by the completion of the campaign being left to Raghunath Rao. Nephew and uncle were now on friendly terms and possibly might have continued so, for some time at least, but for Anandi Bai's violent conduct which induced Gopika Bai to advise her son to place his uncle under some restraint, a step which Madhu Rao, who could easily control his uncle when away from his wife's influence, was most averse to taking.

The English, although not as yet definitely drawn into the intrigues and squabbles of Maharashtra, were fully aware of the trend of events. Lord Clive had, in 1765, restored to Shuja-ud-daula, the nawab of Oudh, the territories taken from him after the battle of Baksar (October, 1764) except the two districts of Kora and Allahabad assigned to the emperor Shah 'Alam, who was at that time dependent on British charity. His reason for adopting this policy was his aversion to adding to the Company's territory, as he clearly foresaw that the Company must either confine its activities to the area it already possessed, or go forward as a conqueror, which, in his opinion, was a scheme so extravagantly ambitious and absurd that it could not be considered for a moment, unless the whole system of the Company's interest was entirely remodelled.[1] It was, therefore, not because the directors and administrators of the Company failed to see whither events were leading them, that constant attempts were made to limit the area of activities, but because the inevitable results of such expansion were only too fully appreciated. The collapse of the house of Timur had opened the road of conquest to any strong integral power, a position the English alone could claim, but it meant exchanging the rôle of a merchant for that of a military adventurer.

Clive, writing in 1765, summed up the situation in these words:

We have at last arrived at that critical conjuncture, which I have long foreseen, I mean that conjuncture which renders it necessary for us to determine whether we can, or shall, take the whole to ourselves...it is scarcely hyperbole to say, that the whole Mogul empire is in our hands. The inhabitants of the country...have no

---

[1] Forrest, *Clive*, II, 176.

attachment to any Nabob whatever, their troops are neither disciplined nor commanded nor paid as ours are. Can it then be doubted that a large army of Europeans would effectually preserve to us the sovereignty not only by keeping in awe the ambitions of any country prince, but rendering us so truly formidable that no French, Dutch or other enemy will presume to molest us?[1]

Although the English had in 1766 made a treaty with the Nizam against Hyder 'Ali they had not yet definitely entered into the struggle in Maharashtra, but the events which took place there between 1765 and 1772 paved the way for the *dénouement* of 1782.

The Peshwa in 1766 decided to punish Janoji Bhonsle of Berar, who was intriguing against him, and in order to do so formed an alliance with the Nizam, an instance of the kaleidoscopic interchanges between friends and foes which is so characteristic of the history of Western India.

It must be mentioned that Malharji Holkar, the founder of the present Indore ruling family, who had accompanied the force under Raghunath Rao, died on his way home at 'Alampur on 20 May, 1766. He had been one of the Peshwa's foremost adherents, and his death, which left Indore under the rule of his daughter-in-law Ahalya Bai, with Tukoji Holkar as her military commander, considerably weakened the support obtainable from the house of Holkar, while it finally gave Sindhia an ascendancy which his house has retained ever since.

In 1767 Madhu Rao, fearing the rapidly rising power of Hyder 'Ali in Mysore, attacked and defeated him. The growing power of Madhu Rao, whose strong personality had now fully asserted itself, soon engaged the attention of the Bombay Council and they began to court the Peshwa officially, Mostyn being sent to Poona to ascertain and report on the actual state of affairs there, and to endeavour, without committing himself to a treaty, to prevent the Peshwa from contracting an alliance with the rulers of Mysore or Hyderabad. This increasing power of the Marathas under Madhu Rao's direction was indeed a matter of so much concern to the council that in their orders to Mostyn they laid stress on the fact that no means should be omitted to check it. But nothing resulted from this embassy.

Raghunath Rao had, in pursuit of his own ends, for some time been gathering a force together with the assistance of the Gaekwad and Holkar. He now marched to the Tapti river where he hoped to be joined by Janoji Bhonsle. But Madhu Rao gave him no time, attacking him and making him prisoner. The Peshwa then advanced against Janoji (1769), forced him to come to terms, and also made overtures of friendship to the Nizam.

A force was this year sent into Hindustan under the command of Visaji Kishan, accompanied by Sindhia and Holkar, to operate against the Rajputs, Rohillas and Jats.

---

[1] Forrest, *Clive*, ii, 256.

In 1770 the Peshwa's health began to fail. He was consumptive, and the severe strain of the last few years had told upon him. He was unable to take command in a campaign against Hyder 'Ali, who was attacked and defeated by Trimbak Rao. This defeat was viewed with alarm by the councils of both Bombay and Madras, as the territory of Mysore formed a barrier against Maratha aggression into the southern presidency, but Hyder would not listen to any overtures from Bombay, while the Madras authorities were prevented from acting by the ill-advised interference of Sir John Lindsay.[1]

The Peshwa's illness increased and he died on 18 November, 1772, at the age of twenty-eight. His death had long been expected and caused no immediate upheaval; but the ultimate effect was tremendous, and it has been truly said that the battle of Panipat was scarcely more fatal to the solidarity of the Maratha Empire than the early death of Madhu Rao. He was a man of unusually fine character, an invariable supporter of the weak against the strong, of the poor against the tyranny of the rich; he stood for justice and equity in all things, and fought vigorously, if with but little result, against the rampant corruption of his day. His death swept away the only barrier which restrained the floods of political intrigue, and they now rushed forward to undermine what was left of the foundations of Maratha ascendancy laid by the great Sivaji.

Mention was made of the expedition sent into Hindustan, under Visaji Kishan, in 1769. After exacting tribute from the Rajput princes, the Rohillas and the Jats, the Marathas removed the aged emperor from Allahabad, where he had been residing since 1764 under British protection, and installed him once more at Delhi, at the end of December, 1771. Further exploits were prevented by Madhu Rao's death, and the force returned to the Deccan.

From 1772 onwards the English began to find themselves drawn more immediately into Maratha affairs, and rapidly assumed the rôle of a protagonist.

The events from 1772 to 1782 are apt to be rendered confusing by the number of actors who appear upon the scene, and by the kaleidoscopic interchanges between friend and foe. It is, however, possible to grasp the trend of events if attention is concentrated on the protagonists, and upon the central figure in the drama, that of Raghunath Rao.

Raghunath Rao, more familiarly known by the shortened form of his name as Raghoba, or, as he is almost invariably styled by Indian writers, Dada Sahib, was the second son of the Peshwa Baji Rao Balal (1720–40), and was thus brother of Balaji Baji Rao (1740–61); uncle of the two Peshwas Madhu Rao and Narayan Rao; great uncle of Madhu Rao Narayan; and father of the last of the Peshwas, Baji Rao.

Round Raghunath Rao, a man of great personal bravery but of weak vacillating character, the events of this period revolve.

[1] Cf. p. 297, *infra*.

Occupying at the outset a position of some importance as a claimant to the Peshwaship, he at length became a mere puppet, to be used for political ends, and he finally passes, almost unheeded, off the stage, before the conclusion of the Treaty of Salbai, stricken by disease and disappointment, to die a few months later.

The two protagonists were the English and the ministers at Poona, for after Madhu Rao's death, the succeeding Peshwas counted for little. The dominating personality at Poona was Nana Phadnavis.

The directing hand in the case of the English was that of Warren Hastings, who, in spite of the continuous opposition in his council, the imbecility of the local authorities in Bombay and Madras, serious complications in Oudh, and continuous financial straits, guided events with a consummate courage and skill that placed the English ten years later in a position to dominate the situation throughout the future. Others who played important but subordinate parts, sometimes on one side and sometimes on another, were the Nizam of Hyderabad, Hyder 'Ali of Mysore, the Gaekwad of Baroda, the Bhonsle of Berar and the great Maratha sardars, Tukoji Holkar and especially Mahadji Sindhia, whose rivalry with Holkar became a deciding factor in Maratha party squabbles. The last by his astute manœuvring emerged, after the Treaty of Salbai, as the leader in Indian politics, a position he retained until his death in 1794.

This period from 1772 to 1782 is one of the most important in history of the British in India. The defeat of the nawab of Oudh at the battle of Baksar (1764) had brought peace to Bengal, and the Deccan became the new theatre for the struggle. The Marathas were at this time the most important power in India, having practically displaced the Moghul emperor in all but name.

To return to events at Poona, the restraint to which Raghunath Rao had been subjected by his nephew was not very rigorous, and no sooner did he perceive that the Peshwa's days were numbered than he commenced to intrigue with the Nizam and Hyder 'Ali for support in his claims to the Peshwaship. But Madhu Rao, fully alive to the weak character of his younger brother, just before his death, summoned his uncle to his bedside and confided his successor to his care. Narayan Rao, a weak man given over to sensuality, was duly invested as Peshwa at Satara, and Sakharam Bapu became minister, with Nana Phadnavis in his hereditary position. The implacable enmity that existed between the Peshwa's mother, Gopika Bai, and Anandi Bai soon led to a rupture between nephew and uncle, and Raghunath Rao was again placed under restraint and confined in the Peshwa's palace at Poona.

On 30 August, 1773, symptoms of discontent manifested themselves amongst the Peshwa's infantry, and Hari Pant Phadke, the army commander, was warned to take precautions, which unfortunately he omitted to do. While the Peshwa was resting at mid-day a commotion arose and a body of men from the regiment burst into the palace led by one of the officers, Sumer Singh. Narayan Rao fled to his uncle's apartments for safety, where Raghunath Rao appears indeed to have interceded for his life, but Sumer Singh then threatened Raghunath Rao also, and he withdrew, while the conspirators murdered the young Peshwa with their swords.

There is no doubt that Raghunath Rao was fully cognisant of the rebellion, but he was attached to his nephew, as far as so egotistical a nature was capable of affection, and it is probable that the confinement of Narayan Rao was all he had intended, the tragic ending being due to the sinister intervention of Anandi Bai.

It was agreed that Raghunath Rao's claim to the Peshwaship must now be recognised, and he was duly invested. But it was fated that whenever Raghunath Rao was placed in a position of command troubles should at once commence. He proceeded to appoint as his ministers new men who were lacking in the necessary qualities, while his own excessively suspicious nature made him distrust even his own nominees.

His first troubles arose with the Nizam who, always ready to profit by events at Poona, prepared to attack the Marathas. Raghunath Rao, however, defeated him, but once more surrendered any advantages he might have obtained, and characteristically yielding to the Nizam's flattery and cajolery restored all that was to have been taken from him.

Raghunath Rao was turning his attention to Hyder 'Ali and the nawab of the Carnatic, when the dislike with which he was universally regarded developed into concerted opposition, conducted by Sakharam Bapu and Nana Phadnavis, and he hastened back to Poona. At length the plan was made public. A trump card had been placed in his opponents' hands, for it was found that Ganga Bai, the Peshwa's widow, was pregnant. On her husband's death she had proposed to become sati, but Anandi Bai, knowing her own part in the tragedy of Narayan Rao's death, contrived to confine her until her husband's cremation was complete, as she feared a sati's curse. Now Nemesis was satisfied. The confederates removed Ganga Bai to safety in Purandhar Fort where she was placed in charge of Parvati Bai, the widow of Sadashiv Rao Bhao, who had been killed at Panipat. On 18 April, 1774, a son was born to Ganga Bai, and Raghunath Rao's claims to the Peshwaship were finally extinguished. The confederates at once formed a council of regency.

Raghunath Rao was in the middle of the campaign against Hyder 'Ali when he received news of the imminent birth of a child to the late Peshwa, and hastened back to Poona, defeating a force under Trimbak Rao Mama sent out by the regency to oppose him. In consequence of this victory troops, as usual, flocked to his standard, and consternation reigned in Poona, when, with typical indecision, he suddenly abandoned his advance on the capital and turned in the direction of Burhanpur. It was at this moment that the birth of Ganga Bai's son was publicly announced. The child was at once formally invested as Peshwa. From this time Raghunath Rao becomes, in fact, a mere pawn in the complicated intrigues and consequent struggles, in which the Maratha leaders gradually played more and more for their own individual aggrandisement and but little for the cause of the Maratha state, thus facilitating the ultimate supremacy of the English.

Raghunath Rao, finding himself in this desperate case, turned once more to the English, with whom he had coquetted in 1761. The Bombay Council had never lost sight of the necessity for acquiring Bassein, Salsette and the islands in Bombay harbour. Indeed the directors in London, in their dispatch of April, 1772, had instructed the council to appoint a regular envoy at Poona, who would endeavour to secure such rights and privileges as might be beneficial to their commerce and the safety of their possessions, and in particular these coveted places.

On receiving overtures from Raghunath Rao, therefore, although averse from an alliance with the Marathas, they seized this opening to renew their demands for Bassein, Salsette and the islands. Raghunath Rao, however, marched away to Indore soon after, in the hope of enlisting Holkar and Sindhia on his side, but finding that, if not actually hostile, they were at any rate indifferent to his cause, he returned. On his return, Gambier, the Company's agent at Surat, was asked by Raghunath Rao if the English would provide him with a force sufficient to carry him to Poona and establish him in the government, in return for which he would defray all costs and make substantial grants to the Company.

The Bombay Council were uncertain, in view of the passing of the Regulating Act, whether they had powers to make a treaty without sanction from Bengal, but, as they had not been notified of the arrival of the new councillors at Calcutta, they decided to act. Raghunath Rao, however, positively refused to cede Bassein and Salsette. While this matter was still under discussion news arrived that the Portuguese were about to endeavour to recover Bassein, taken from them by Chimnaji Appa in 1739. The council, faced with this new danger, decided to obtain possession of Salsette at all costs. An attack was made on Thana Fort, the key to the district, and it was captured on 31 December, 1774.[1]

The council defended this attack in a letter to the governor-general on the grounds that it would have been fatal to allow the Portuguese to acquire Salsette, as they would have

had it in their power to obstruct our trade, by being in possession of the principal passes to the inland country...which, of course, would have been of infinite

[1] Forrest, *Bombay Selections, Maratha Series*, i, 179–208.

prejudice to the trade, revenue and interests of the Company in these parts, in so much that we should in great measure have been subject to the caprice of the Portuguese.[1]

The council at Calcutta, except Warren Hastings himself, expressed their disapproval of the capture of Salsette, which they held had seriously damaged the Company's reputation for good faith. The Poona ministers had in the meantime contrived to bribe Holkar and Sindhia away from Raghunath Rao, who retired into Gujarat towards Baroda, leaving his wife Anandi Bai, who was enceinte, in Dhar Fort, where she gave birth in January, 1775, to Baji Rao, destined to be the last of the Peshwas. Raghunath Rao's object in moving into Gujarat was to get into touch with the English and also to obtain the assistance of Govind Rao Gaekwad, who was engaged in besieging his brother Fateh Singh in Baroda.

This quarrel, into which the English were drawn, arose in 1768 on the death of Damaji Gaekwad. Damaji left four sons, Sayaji who was imbecile, Govind Rao, Manaji and Fateh Singh. Govind Rao was the son of the senior wife and claimed on that basis. Fateh Singh, who was manager for Sayaji, supported him. After the murder of Narayan Rao Peshwa, Govind Rao obtained the support of the Poona ministers for his cause and was granted the hereditary family title of *Sena Khas Khel*.

Negotiations continued between the English and Raghunath Rao and finally on 7 March, 1775, the Treaty of Surat,[2] as it is called, was signed. It consisted of sixteen articles of which the most important provisions were that the earlier treaties of 1739 and 1756 be confirmed; that the English would assist Raghunath Rao with a force of 2500 men, he defraying the cost, and undertaking not to side with enemies of the Company; Salsette, Bassein and the islands were to be ceded in perpetuity with a share of the revenues of the Broach and Surat districts; Maratha raids into Bengal and the Carnatic were to cease; any peace made with Poona was to include the English. As security Raghunath Rao deposited six lakhs. Such was the treaty which, as Grant Duff says, occasioned infinite discussions amongst the English in India and in Europe, and led to the first Maratha war.

Before the treaty was completed the Bombay Council had assembled troops under Colonel Keating who arrived at Surat, by sea, on 27 February, 1775.[3]

Raghunath Rao had, however, been forced to fly from Baroda owing to defection amongst his own troops, and the arrival of an army from Poona under Hari Pant. He first made his way to Cambay where he was assisted by Charles Malet to reach Surat. Here he met Colonel Keating, who describes him as "a man of sound judgment and of quick and clear conceptions", an estimate of Raghunath Rao's

---

[1] Forrest, *op. cit.* I, 205.   [2] *Idem*, pp. 211–15; Aitchison, *Treaties*, VI, 21.
[3] Forrest, *op. cit.* I, 217.

character, which it may be safely said, was not generally held. The view ordinarily taken of Raghunath Rao's disposition is often alluded to by Ahalya Bai Holkar in her letters, where she refers to his entire lack of judgment, which, she adds, was well known to the English, who in consequence invariably acted without consulting him and merely used him in furthering their own designs. It is clear that the Bombay Council, perhaps influenced by events in Bengal, imagined that their small force could easily account for the whole of the Maratha army, and Colonel Keating was, therefore, instructed to assist their ally against all his enemies, as well as against the ministerial party and their adherents, and to do everything to bring the war to a speedy and happy conclusion.

The first difficulty that arose was Raghunath Rao's lack of funds and the consequent disaffection in his army. Colonel Keating was obliged to advance money before they would even march.[1] The allies advanced and after a minor engagement or two encountered on 18 May, 1775, the ministerial army on the plain of Adas [Arras], which lies between the town of Anand and the Mahi river. This was the first direct encounter between the Maratha forces and the English since Sivaji's attack on Surat in 1664. At one time the allies were in serious trouble but the steadiness of the English troops and the coolness of Colonel Keating secured the complete discomfiture of the enemy.[2] This victory decided Fateh Singh Gaekwad to make an alliance with the English, with whom he had for some time been playing fast and loose. The destruction of the Maratha fleet by Commodore John Moore, at almost the same time, drove the ministers at Poona to desperation. Raghunath Rao's affairs were now in the ascendant, and important members of the Maratha community were preparing to join him when the whole situation was suddenly changed by the action of the council at Calcutta.

On 3 February, 1775, the governor-general and council at Calcutta wrote to Bombay expressing surprise that the capture of Salsette had never been reported to them,[3] and later, on 8 March, intimated their alarm at the support offered to Raghunath Rao, which was wholly inconsistent with their traditional friendly relations with Poona and with Sabaji Bhonsle. Divided as the Calcutta Council were in most things, they were united in condemning this act of the Bombay government. On 31 May, 1775, the Supreme Government again addressed[4] the Bombay Council, pointing out that their action was not merely impolitic but directly contrary to the Act of Parliament; and they concluded, "we...peremptorily require you to withdraw the Company's forces to your own garrison, in whatsoever state your affairs may be in, unless their safety may be endangered by an instant retreat".

---

[1] Forrest, op. cit. I, 220–5.   [2] Idem, p. 226; Forbes, Oriental Memoirs, II, 95.
[3] Forrest, op. cit. I, 232.   [4] Idem, p. 238.

Warren Hastings was not in favour of these orders but was outvoted by his council. The Bombay Council, convinced that they had acted for the best, if unconstitutionally, fought to the end for their policy. They pointed out the immense advantage they had obtained in securing Salsette and the fairness of the terms come to with Raghunath Rao, who was, in their opinion, the rightful heir to the Peshwaship. They added, with some reason, that if at that distance they were always to await confirmatory orders from Calcutta it must be fatal to any policy, a fact, it may be remarked, that had not escaped Hastings, who in a minute on this question expresses his doubts as to the action which should be taken in view of the impossibility of their knowing what the actual state of affairs at Bombay might be by the time their orders arrived. So eager were the Bombay Council, however, to carry their point that they sent one of their members, Taylor, to Calcutta. He submitted a very able, clear, and on the whole fair and accurate report on Maratha affairs, past and present, to the governor-general, explaining the methods followed in Maratha politics.[1] He laid stress on the importance to the very existence of Bombay, in having control, through Salsette, of the passes by which goods travelled inland, and of Bassein and the islands for the protection of the harbour. By supporting Raghunath Rao these safeguards were being secured. The Bombay Council, he said, had never intended to flout the authority of the governor-general and, in their opinion, the new act even supported their position, inasmuch as it exempted them from referring to Calcutta cases in which they had received direct orders from England, and they had received repeated and special orders regarding the safeguarding of Bombay. Moreover, success had attended Colonel Keating's operations, and any desertion of Raghunath Rao at this juncture would throw him into the arms of the Nizam and Hyder 'Ali, or of Holkar and Sindhia, and the trouble would recommence. Indians also did not in the least understand this sudden limiting of the powers of the Bombay Council, and the abandonment of Raghunath Rao would be considered a deliberate breach of faith. Parliament, Taylor said, when it armed the Supreme Government with controlling power over the other presidencies, had never intended, "that they should appear so degraded and so contemptible in the eyes of the native governments as the Presidency of Bombay must be, unless you will commit the treaty of peace to their management".

But the Supreme Government was adamant and sent its own officer, Lt.-Colonel Upton, from Calcutta to Poona with full powers to negotiate a treaty. The dispatches of this date from Calcutta clearly show the Bengal Council's ignorance of conditions in Western India, even on the part of Hastings himself, who frankly expressed his surprise at the vigour of the Maratha confederacy. Hastings wrote

[1] Forrest, *op. cit.* i, 247–68.

personally, at the same time, to Sakharam Bapu, at Poona, explaining the new controlling powers vested in him as governor-general and the illegality of the Bombay Council's action in supporting Raghunath Rao without his sanction, and intimating the dispatch of his envoy; he concluded, "I have heard of your wisdom and capacity from everywhere, therefore trust in your person that you will not fail to get the business done through your interest".[1]

Although the Bombay Council were not free from blame, this action on the part of the Supreme Government meant playing directly into the hands of the Poona ministers, and they at once saw the advantage it gave them.

As Taylor had pointed out, the first effect of this interference was to lower the prestige of the Bombay authorities in the eyes of all Maharashtra, while it simultaneously exalted, for the time being, the prestige of the ministers.

In accordance with these orders from Calcutta, Colonel Keating was at once made to withdraw his forces, the Bombay Council in conveying these orders to him sincerely lamenting "that these gentlemen have so unluckily taken upon themselves to interfere as they have done, at this juncture". He retired to the neighbourhood of Surat.

Colonel Upton proceeded to Purandhar, where he arrived in December, 1775, and commenced his negotiations. But he was in no sense a match for the astute Brahman ministers, who, while they loudly extolled the far-sighted statesmanship of the governor-general, proceeded to seize every possible advantage of the new turn in affairs. They refused to consider for a moment the cession of Salsette or Bassein or of the revenues of Broach, taking their stand upon the ground that the governor-general could not claim to draw advantages from a war which he had condemned as unjust. On the other hand they demanded the surrender of Raghunath Rao and the restoration of all territory acquired since hostilities commenced. Colonel Upton on 7 February, 1776,[2] reported the deadlock to Calcutta on which the governor-general and his council determined to resume hostilities. Troops were prepared and Raghunath Rao, the Nizam, Hyder 'Ali, the Bhonsle, Holkar and Sindhia were all addressed and desired to join the English, or at least to remain neutral.

This unexpected *volte face* brought the ministers to their knees and they at once conceded practically all that Colonel Upton demanded, and on 1 March, 1776, the Treaty of Purandhar was signed.[3] The gist of the treaty was: the establishment of a general peace with the Marathas; the retention of Salsette, if the governor-general so desired; the cession of the Broach revenues; twelve lakhs of rupees to be paid to defray expenses incurred in the war; the Treaty of Surat to be

[1] Forrest, *op. cit.* I, 246.   [2] *Idem*, p. 274.
[3] *Idem*, p. 277; Gleig, *Warren Hastings*, II, 194 ff.; Aitchison, *Treaties*, VI, 28.

formally annulled; and Raghunath Rao's army to be disbanded within a month, he himself retiring to Kopargaon in Gujarat on a pension of 25,000 rupees a month, with a retinue consisting of a body of 1000 horse and certain domestic servants. The Bombay Council rightly condemned this treaty as highly injurious to the interests and reputation of the Company.

Raghunath Rao was wholly bewildered by these transactions and imagined that they were due to the insufficient liberality of the terms he had offered, and he at once proposed others, which could not of course be considered. He then decided to refuse the terms agreed upon and to continue fighting, an attitude in which he was encouraged by the friendly overtures of Mahadaji Sindhia, who was now commencing to work out the policy which was, a few years later, to make him independent of Poona. But Raghunath Rao, whose character invariably alienated those who might have assisted him, found that none of the Maratha leaders would give him any practical help. The Bombay Government, on their part, would not lift a hand in support of a treaty which they considered grossly unfair to themselves, but they readily afforded asylum to Raghunath Rao at Surat, in spite of the protests of Colonel Upton, who considered it as a direct breach of the treaty. But they held that they were well within their rights in protecting their late ally from personal danger at the hands of his enemies. Hastings, although he felt bound to ratify the Treaty of Purandhar, disapproved of it.

While affairs were in this uncertain state a dispatch, dated 5 April, 1776, came from the directors in England approving the Treaty of Surat and directing that the territory obtained from Raghunath Rao should be retained. On this the Bombay Government threw the Treaty of Purandhar to the winds and Raghunath Rao was invited to Bombay, where he arrived in November and took up his residence on Malabar Hill. The Peshwa at once objected to the asylum thus given to the ex-Peshwa.

Colonel Upton was recalled to Bengal (1777) and Mostyn was then sent to Poona to superintend the carrying out of the treaty. But nothing resulted, as he was suspected by the ministers, who believed that he was the person responsible for the capture of Salsette, while dissensions between the aged Sakharam Bapu and Nana Phadnavis tended to complicate matters still more.

These negotiations were dragging on when an entirely fresh turn was given to events by the unexpected appearance of a French adventurer, called St Lubin. He landed at Chaul from a French ship and stated that he was an accredited ambassador from the French king Louis. He was in fact, as Mr Farmer reported,[1] "a most perfect adventurer" who had previously lived at Pondichery and had some connection with the Madras authorities. He had contrived to

---

[1] Forrest. *ob. cit.* I, 296.

ingratiate himself with Sartine, the French minister of marine, alleging that he was an intimate friend of the raja at Satara, whose children he had taught to ride. He soon disgusted his colleagues by his arrogance, and the mission came to nothing. Nana affected, at any rate, to credit his story, as he was not prepared to lose such an opportunity of opposing the English, and St Lubin was received with a respect and ceremony never shown to the British resident, being met personally, as he alighted from his elephant, by Sakharam Bapu and Nana. The idea of a French intrigue in India was sufficient to stir up the resentment of every Englishman in the country. At the same time a dispatch dated 7 April was received from the directors regretting the sacrifices made by the Treaty of Purandhar, but stating that it must be adhered to unless any attempts were made by the ministers to evade its conditions, in which case the Bombay Government would be at liberty to form a fresh alliance with Raghunath Rao on the basis of the Treaty of Surat. As the ministers had never carried out the stipulations of the Treaty of Purandhar the Bombay Government at once formed a fresh alliance with Raghunath Rao.

In 1778 Sakharam Bapu, whose quarrel with Nana had reached an acute stage, with Holkar's assistance commenced intriguing to support Raghunath Rao, and enlisted Moroba Phadnavis, a cousin of Nana, on his side. Moroba appealed to the Bombay Council who agreed to assist him, informing Hastings of their action, which met with his approval and that of Mr Barwell, though strongly opposed by the rest of the council, and he agreed to send a force to aid them. The force assembled at Kalpi, Colonel Leslie being put in command with orders to march across India to Bombay.[1] This feat had never before been attempted and was stigmatised by Dundas as one of Hastings' "frantic military exploits", exploits, nevertheless, which fully justified their inception and proved the governor-general's courage and understanding of Indian psychology. Events were becoming insistent, and fully established the truth of Hornby's opinion, expressed in a minute written at the time, that we were fast verging on a period which must compel the English nation either to take some active and decisive part in events or relinquish for ever all hopes of bettering their situation on the west of India.

Moroba Phadnavis soon proved to be a broken reed, while Sakharam Bapu, always a trimmer, declined specifically to announce his support of Raghunath Rao. The Bombay Council were deliberating how to effect a change in the control at Poona when Nana, who had been driven temporarily to take refuge in Purandhar Fort, managed to cajole Moroba into deserting Raghunath Rao, and soon after, with the connivance of Sindhia, seized his cousin and imprisoned him at Ahmadnagar, Holkar, who had been supporting him, being easily bribed, with nine lakhs, to stand aside. Nana was now again in

---

[1] Forrest, *op. cit.* I, 327.

power, but he had miscalculated the effect of the change at Poona on the English, who at once called upon him to state whether he was prepared to carry out the Treaty of Purandhar, and dismiss St Lubin, with whom he was still coquetting, and to whom it appears he had made certain promises, though probably with no intention of fulfilling them. Nana was in a dilemma. It was impossible for him to conciliate the ex-Peshwa, towards whom his enmity was too well known, while on the other hand he had no desire to fulfil the conditions of the Treaty of Purandhar and so come to terms with the English.

This evasion was enough for the Bombay authorities and they felt that they might now act under the instructions conveyed to them by the dispatch of 23 March, 1778, from the Supreme Government, which empowered them to take any step necessary to subvert a hostile party in the Maratha state.[1] The Bombay Council thereupon decided that Raghunath Rao should be installed at Poona as regent for the young Peshwa, Madhu Rao Nayaran, since he could no longer claim the Peshwaship.[2]

Nana, fully cognisant of their intentions, took immediate steps to oppose them. He removed the aged Sakharam Bapu from all voice in affairs and collected troops. Sindhia and Nana held complete control, Holkar, whose leaning towards Raghunath Rao made him suspect, being employed at a distance. Luckily the Bombay Government had a most able agent, Lewis, at Poona who kept them fully informed of Nana's activities.

The Bombay forces were weak, and Draper urged caution, but was outvoted by the rest of the council, though Colonel Leslie's force, on which they relied for support, was still far distant in Bundelkhand. Hastings remarked, when criticising these proceedings, that the passions of the Council were enlisted on Raghunath Rao's side because in supporting him they were carrying out their own personal wishes.

The council placed their forces under the command of Colonel Egerton, an officer whose health was bad, and whose purely European training and entire ignorance of Indian conditions wholly unfitted him for the post. Thus, with a mere handful of troops under an inefficient commander, and most ill-considered preparations for hostilities, the Bombay Council set out to defy the whole strength of the Maratha Empire; that they in fact suffered comparatively lightly was due to good fortune and not to any action of their own.

The campaign started in November, 1778, the force consisting of 3900 men, of whom 592 were Europeans. Owing to jealousies in the Bombay Council a curious and fatal arrangement was adopted, by which the control of the troops in the field was vested in a committee of three, consisting of the commanding officer and two civilians. The

---

[1] Forrest, *op. cit.* I, 314.　　　　　[2] *Idem*, p. 334.

movements of the troops were in fact controlled by Colonel Carnac acting as civil commissioner, in spite of Colonel Egerton's protests. He was by profession a soldier, who had distinguished himself in Bengal, but he failed lamentably on this occasion. Governor Hornby afterwards admitted that the powers granted to the committee were far too comprehensive and had escaped his notice when they were issued. Raghunath Rao, in his usual vacillating way, now began to raise various objections and insisted on being granted certain concessions before he would move. The force, encumbered with an enormous baggage-train of 19,000 bullocks, was scarcely able to march two miles a day.

Raghunath Rao at length appreciated that he was being used as a mere pawn in the game. In December, 1778, he sent an envoy to Dom José da Camara, the captain-general at Goa, asking for assistance in troops and munitions and offering in return to cede Bassein and other forts as well as territory in the neighbourhood of Daman. The envoy said that Raghunath Rao had become suspicious of British intentions in regard to his affairs and feared that their real object was to place him in the same position of subjection as that in which they had placed the nawab of Bengal; hence he was most anxious to become an ally of the king of Portugal. The captain-general commended the proposal to his superiors, but nothing came of it.[1]

In January, 1779, Colonel Egerton had to resign the command through ill-health and Colonel Cockburn took over the force. Raghunath Rao and his adopted son Amrit Rao now joined the army which proceeded up the ghats. On 9 January the army reached the village of Talegaon, twenty miles north-west of Poona, to find it destroyed and themselves confronted by a large Maratha army. Colonel Carnac was seized with panic and instead of boldly pushing on to Poona, most fatally counselled retreat, his panic being augmented by Raghunath Rao who assured him that until a substantial victory was gained no influential Maratha would join his standard. Colonel Cockburn considered he could reach Poona with the troops, but that he could only do so by abandoning the enormous baggage-train. Raghunath Rao begged them not to retire, but in vain, and on 11 January all the heavy guns were thrown into a tank, the stores were burnt, and the force started on its return journey, as it fondly believed unbeknown to the enemy, some 50,000 strong.

On 12 January, 1779, the force encamped at Wadgaon, twenty-three miles north-west of Poona. The retreat was at once known to the enemy who attacked continuously. On the 13th further retreat was held to be impossible, and Farmer, secretary to the committee, was sent to negotiate terms. As a preliminary Nana demanded the surrender of Raghunath Rao, and this would have been perforce

---

[1] Letter from the captain-general to Martinho de Mello e Castro of 22 December, 1778 (unpublished).

agreed to, but luckily the ex-Peshwa decided the matter for himself by taking refuge with Sindhia. The action taken by Colonel Carnac was inconsistent, for while Farmer was instructed to point out that no treaty could be made without the sanction of the Supreme Government, Holmes was at the same time deputed with full powers to negotiate with Mahadaji Sindhia. Sindhia was delighted at this mark of distinction as it assisted him to attain the position he had so long coveted, that of acting as an independent arbiter between the two Maratha parties.

Finally terms were settled: that all acquisitions of territory made since 1773 should be restored; that the force advancing from Bengal should be stopped; that Sindhia was to obtain the share of the Broach revenues; and that a sum of 41,000 rupees and two hostages were to be surrendered as security for performance. Such was the disgraceful Convention of Wadgaon, fatal alike to the interests and good name of the Company. The army retired but the order countermanding the advance of the Bengal force was suspended.[1]

This ill-starred venture of the Bombay army was at once repudiated by Hastings who felt the disgrace acutely, and wrote: "We have already disavowed the Convention of Wargaum. Would to God we could as easily efface the infamy which our national character has sustained".[2] He considered, however, that the promise in the treaty made to Sindhia should be carried out, in return for his support. The directors, on receiving the report of the convention, ordered the dismissal of Colonel Carnac, Colonel Egerton and Colonel Cockburn from the Company's service. The scheme deserved, indeed, no better fate in view of the impolitic lines on which it was conceived and the lack of care devoted to its execution. It was in fact born of pique, pique at the control exercised by the Supreme Government, and of the insane desire to show what Bombay could do on their own initiative, combined with a greater consideration for private interests than for the general good of the Company, the limited views of the commercial adventurer obscuring the wider outlook required by statesmanship.

Hornby, however, rose to the occasion. He also disavowed the convention,[3] which Carnac had, indeed, no power to make, and at once took steps to recruit and improve his army. He believed, moreover, that Sindhia, who was known to be inimical to the French, would be open to an alliance, and he urged the payment to Mahadaji of the sum of 41,000 rupees settled under the Convention of Wadgaon.

Colonel Leslie, who had been instructed to march with all speed to Bombay, had wasted time embroiling himself with the chiefs in Bundelkhand. When the detachment started, Nana had been asked to grant passports for the march. He objected, on the ground that

---

[1] Forrest, *op. cit.* I, 333–6; Aitchison, *Treaties*, VI, 39.
[2] Forrest, *Selections from the State Papers in the Foreign Department*, II, 672.
[3] Forrest, *Maratha Series*, I, 385.

as the force was sent to counteract French machinations, its advance was now unnecessary, since St Lubin had gone. But Holkar and Sindhia, who feared that their possessions in Malwa might suffer, agreed to allow the detachment a passage. Nana ultimately also granted permission, but secretly told his officers and the Bundelkhand chiefs to oppose the advance. Hastings, in view of Leslie's incompetence, had decided to replace him by his second-in-command, Colonel Goddard, and letters had been issued to the Bundelkhand chiefs, disavowing Colonel Leslie's acts. At this moment, however, news arrived of Leslie's death on 3 October, 1778. Goddard was a man of very different calibre. He used the utmost tact, and advanced with great rapidity through Bhopal, where Nawab Hayat Muhammad Khan assisted him to the utmost in spite of Maratha threats.[1] On 2 December he reached the Narbada where, in accordance with Hastings's instructions, he awaited a communication from Mudaji Bhonsle, with whom Hastings hoped to form an alliance thus detaching him from the Peshwa's party. But Mudaji declined, and informed Colonel Goddard that he could not negotiate.

The Bombay Council now sent urgent appeals to Colonel Goddard to expedite his march, and although, by Hastings's express orders, Goddard was independent of Bombay control, he considered it was incumbent on him, in the interests of his country, to comply.

He reached Burhanpur on 30 January, 1779, and Surat on 26 February. Thus by his tact and skill did Goddard bring this "frantic military exploit" of Hastings to a successful conclusion, and as Hastings had foreseen, immensely increase the prestige of the British arms throughout India. Writing to Laurence Sulivan[2] (1779) Hastings says that the precipitate and miserable enterprise of the Bombay Presidency had blasted his political plans, but that Goddard's march had gained no trivial or speculative advantage as it had shown the people of India the difference between the powers of the capital government of the British nation and the feeble efforts of an inferior presidency, and had done far more than military victories to confirm our ascendancy. On reaching Bombay Goddard was given a seat on the council and the position of commander-in-chief.[3]

Mahadaji Sindhia had not as yet responded, as Hornby had hoped he would, and hence nothing remained but to continue the war, a somewhat alarming situation, in view of the fact that the Bombay Council had no funds for the purpose. Hastings had instructed Goddard, who remained directly under his orders,[4] to endeavour to make peace with the ministerial party at Poona on the lines of the Purandhar Treaty, adding a clause specifically excluding the French from acquiring any settlements in Maratha territory. He refused, however, to agree to Hornby's proposal to intervene and settle the

---

[1] *Bhopal State Gazetteer*, p. 16.   [2] Gleig, *Warren Hastings*, II, 272.
[3] Forrest, *Home Series*, II, 368.   [4] Forrest, *Maratha Series*, I, 386.

quarrel between Govind Rao and Fateh Singh Gaekwad. As regarded Sindhia, Goddard was to wait until he showed a desire to form an alliance before approaching him. At this time, however, Sindhia was secretly instigating hostilities against the Company while simultaneously sending his agents to talk platitudes at Bombay.

Sindhia now saw that nothing was to be gained by supporting Raghunath Rao, whereas his hold over Nana would be strengthened if the ex-Peshwa returned to the English. He used his influence, therefore, to get Nana to grant the ex-Peshwa a jagir in Bundelkhand, and then connived at his escape from custody while proceeding there.[1] Raghunath Rao at once fled to the protection of Goddard, who made him an allowance of 50,000 rupees a month, which Hastings considered excessive. No treaty was, however, arranged for him, and from this moment he drops out of practical politics, the support of one so unpopular with the whole of his compatriots being too obvious a mistake to be continued. The English now became in name, as well as in fact, a principal in the struggle which ensued.

Negotiations continued between Nana and General Goddard without any definite result until, at the end of the rains, Goddard learnt of the formation of a confederacy of the Marathas, the Nizam and Hyder 'Ali, which was to make a series of simultaneous attacks on the English possessions. A final request to Nana for a definite reply elicited a reiteration of the demand for the surrender of Raghunath Rao and the restoration of Salsette, as preliminaries.

Without sending an answer to this demand, General Goddard proceeded to Bombay, where he expedited the dispatch of a force under Colonel Hartley, and obtained sanction to make a treaty with Fateh Singh Gaekwad. At the same time Hastings, in order to create a diversion in the north, entered into a treaty with the rana of Gohad, who had always been a thorn in the side of the Marathas.

On his return to Surat Goddard dismissed the vakils of Nana Phadnavis and opened negotiations with Fateh Singh who, however, gave no definite reply until Goddard, crossing the Tapti on 1 January, 1780,[2] captured Dhaboi, on which he signed a treaty (26 January) agreeing to assist General Goddard with a force of 3000 horse and cede the revenues of certain districts as soon as he was put in possession of Ahmadabad, the Peshwa's possessions north of the Mahi river being also made over to him.

Goddard at once marched on Ahmadabad, which was carried by assault by Colonel Hartley on 15 February, eighty-one Europeans being killed and wounded including ten officers.[3] Sindhia and Holkar now advanced in support of the Peshwa, though how far Sindhia was in earnest seems doubtful, as on reaching Baroda he released Farmer and Captain Stewart, the hostages for the Convention of Wadgaon,

---

[1] Forrest, *Maratha Series*, I, 387.   [2] *Idem*, pp. 392–96.
[3] *Idem*, pp. 397–99.

and also sent his agent, who assured General Goddard of his master's friendly feelings towards the English and of Nana's enmity. Goddard made no overtures, merely replying in the same vein, but requiring Sindhia, if he wished to treat, to send definite proposals within three days, thus defeating any intention of the Maratha leader to keep him inactive until the dry season was over. Nothing came of these pourparlers, while Sindhia began to negotiate with Govind Rao Gaekwad, the rival of Fateh Singh.

Goddard, finding negotiation useless, proceeded to attack. He advanced against the Marathas and drove them back with severe loss, but without any material gain as the enemy following their usual tactics, merely encamped at a short distance, in an endeavour to lead the English into a long fruitless pursuit.

In spite of protests from Bombay, where the council were urging the need for capturing Bassein, General Goddard refused to leave Gujarat, as it would have meant abandoning his ally Fateh Singh Gaekwad.

The approaching summer found the fortunes of the English at a somewhat low ebb. Funds were exhausted, in all three presidencies; the Nizam, and Hyder 'Ali, who had swept over the Carnatic up to the gates of Madras, were supporting the Marathas; and fears were entertained of the co-operation of a French fleet on the east coast. But numerous successful engagements of minor importance took place, including the seizure of Kalyan (October, 1780).[1]

Amidst all these difficulties Hastings never lost his head. He created a diversion in Central India by dispatching Captain Popham from Bengal to support the rana of Gohad. Captain Popham after capturing the fort of Lahar, fifty miles from Kalpi, advanced to Gwalior which he carried by a brilliant night escalade on 3 August, 1780.[2] This, an achievement of great merit in itself, was of far greater importance in its political effects. This fort had always been looked upon throughout India as impregnable, and its capture raised the prestige of the English enormously. Warren Hastings writing to Laurence Sulivan on 27 August, 1780,[3] thus refers to this episode: "I shall begin by reciting to you an event of the greatest importance ...an enterprise...[of which] in this country the effect is not to be described...it is the key of Indostan". But it also had another, and perhaps even more important, result. Sindhia, to whom the fort belonged, was dismayed at its loss and at once hurried northwards, abandoning his colleagues.

To turn for a moment to the other members of the confederacy. Hyder 'Ali had attacked the Carnatic, and Mudaji Bhonsle had sent his son Chimnaji against Cuttack, but as he had no real intention of seriously aiding the cause, he was easily bought off by Hastings.[4]

---

[1] Forrest, *Maratha Series*, I, 413-15.   [2] *East Indian Military Calendar*, 1823, II, 93.
[3] Gleig, *Warren Hastings*, II, 311.
[4] Forrest, *Selections from the State Papers in the Foreign Department*, II, 707.

Mudaji had, in fact, himself originally informed Warren Hastings of the confederacy formed between Nana Phadnavis, the Nizam, and Hyder 'Ali, also intimating that the obligation to attack Bengal had been laid upon him, and that he could not refuse to obey. His son Chimnaji was, however, instructed to delay his march as much as possible. This he effectually contrived to do, reaching the Bengal border in May, 1780, instead of in October, 1779, as he might have done. Hastings, well aware of the enmity which existed, the alliance notwithstanding, between the Poona ministers and Hyder 'Ali, asked Mudaji if he would act as mediator between the English and Nana Phadnavis, and even sent him a draft treaty. But these negotiations came to nothing. Hastings then deputed David Anderson to interview Chimnaji and inform him that a force, under Colonel Pearse, was marching from Bengal to Madras,[1] and to ask for his assistance for the detachment. This was granted, and the promise most faithfully kept. Anderson then went to Cuttack where he induced Mudaji to recall his forces on the payment of fifteen lakhs. The Nizam took no active part in the proceedings of the confederacy.

In October General Goddard advanced on Bassein and, starting operations against the fort in November, captured it on 11 December. The fall of Bassein was a very serious blow to Nana, as besides the loss of a stronghold the moral effect of the victory was almost as great as that caused by the capture of Gwalior, owing to the fact that it had been taken from the Portuguese in 1739 and thus represented a victory over Europeans.

Goddard in 1781 received orders to conclude peace if he saw any chance of effecting it. The Madras Presidency, in particular, was anxious for a cessation of hostilities, ascribing the attacks made on them by Hyder 'Ali to the support of Raghunath Rao and the consequent war. Sir Eyre Coote, at this time in Southern India, wrote to Goddard in the strongest terms pointing out that he must impose upon him as a duty he owed to his king, his country and his employers to leave no means untried to effect a peace.[2] He also wrote in similar strain to the Bengal Council (March, 1781). He says,

I have frequently declared it to you, gentlemen, as my firm opinion that we are altogether unequal to the difficult and dangerous contention in which we are now engaged...and I must once more call upon you...to apply the least dangerous and least expensive means whereof a change may be speedily brought about on a system of policy so ruinous in itself and so destructive to their [the Company's] interests.[3]

After the capture of Bassein Goddard moved up and forced the Bhor Ghat pass. But he allowed himself to be delayed in negotiations, which Nana began in order to give himself time to bring up more

[1] Forrest, *Selections from the State Papers in the Foreign Department*, II, 749.
[2] Forrest, *Maratha Series*, I, 445–7.
[3] Forrest, *Selections from the State Papers in the Foreign Department*, III, 760.

troops. Holkar and Hari Pant advanced with a large force and when Goddard, seeing that the negotiations were leading to nothing, tried to retire on Kalyan and Bombay, he was attacked fiercely and lost 400 men killed and wounded. This it may be noted was the only reverse Goddard ever suffered.

Sindhia who had hastened northwards on the fall of Gwalior was defeated on 16 February, 1781, at Sipri (now Shivpuri) by Major Camac, who had been sent in June, 1780, to support the rana of Gohad. The effect of the fall of Gwalior and of Bassein, his own defeat and the enhancement of his rival Holkar's reputation by the victory at Bhor Ghat, convinced Sindhia that his real advantage lay in coming to early terms with the English, and he never again took up arms against them. He opened negotiations with Colonel Muir and signed a treaty on 13 October, 1781.[1] By this treaty Sindhia agreed to retire to Ujjain while Colonel Muir recrossed the Jumna. But the really important clause in the agreement was that by which Mahadaji undertook to effect a treaty between the ministers and the English and so stand guarantee for its observance.

Hastings, on receiving this news, deputed David Anderson, in January, 1782, with full powers to conclude a treaty.[2] His instructions to Anderson are contained in a letter dated 4 November, 1781, from Benares. The points which Anderson was to bear in mind were: to make an alliance with the Peshwa through Sindhia's mediation against all enemies, but in particular against Hyder 'Ali; otherwise simply peace, on the condition that we restored all territory gained during the war, except the city of Ahmadabad and lands granted to Fateh Singh Gaekwad; adequate provision to be made for Raghunath Rao; Bassein to be kept if possible, even if all the lands obtained by the Treaty of Purandhar had to be restored, except Salsette and the islands and revenues of Broach; but if the retention of Bassein hindered the settlement of the peace, it must be given up; nothing was to be done hostile to the raja of Berar; Fateh Singh Gaekwad was to be included in the treaty; the treacherous rana of Gohad was to be left to make his own terms; all other European nations were to be prohibited from founding new settlements; and if possible the Marathas were to be induced to attack Hyder 'Ali.

Hastings, when he learnt of Colonel Muir's negotiations, was at Benares, surrounded by rebels, almost in their hands, yet, wholly undisturbed, he issued these instructions to his envoy. Well might he refer to this transaction with pardonable pride in one of his letters as having "conducted a successful negotiation of peace with Mahdajee Sindia in the most desperate period of my distresses".[3] Anderson

---

[1] Forrest, *Selections from the State Papers in the Foreign Department*, III, 813; Aitchison, *Treaties*, IV, 33.

[2] Forrest, *Selections from the State Papers in the Foreign Department*, III, 821–2.

[3] Gleig, *Warren Hastings*, II, 453.

joined Mahadaji Sindhia, who was acting as our intermediary, and on 17 May the Treaty of Salbai was signed.[1]

The Treaty of Salbai contains seventeen clauses, the chief stipulations being: that the whole of the territory conquered since the Treaty of Purandhar (1776) should be restored, together with three lakhs' worth of revenue at Broach; the Gaekwad's possessions to be restored to what they were before the war, in 1775; Raghunath Rao, within three months from the signing of the treaty, to fix on a place of residence, receiving no further help from the English, the Peshwa undertaking to pay him an allowance of 25,000 rupees a month, if he would of his own accord repair to Sindhia; Hyder 'Ali to return all territory recently taken from the English, and the nawab of Arcot; and the Peshwa and the English undertook that their several allies should remain at peace with one another.

Anderson writing about these negotiations (27 February, 1783) remarks on Sindhia's difficulties as intermediary owing to differences among the ministers at Poona, the opposition of his rival Holkar, who was supported by Hari Pant, and the Nizam's intrigues.[2] The treaty was ratified on 20 December, 1782, but the final adjustments were delayed by Nana till the next year, as he was still striving for the restoration of Salsette and was, in fact, secretly intriguing with Hyder 'Ali in hopes of being able to reject the treaty altogether.

But on 7 December, 1782, Hyder 'Ali had died. In any case his support would have been unlikely, as he was said to be convinced of the futility of opposing these new forces which had entered the arena of Indian politics, and to have left a written message for his son Tipu enjoining him to make peace with the English on any terms, and so avoid ruining himself, advice which Tipu did not follow. Hyder 'Ali's death obliged Nana to ratify the treaty, which he did not do until 20 February, 1783.

The importance of this treaty, which placed the political relations of the English and the Marathas on an entirely new and definite footing, cannot be over-estimated. It formed the turning-point in the history of the English in India. It secured us peace with the Marathas for twenty years, and, without the acquisition of any fresh territory, it established, beyond dispute, the dominance of the British as controlling factor in Indian politics, their subsequent rise in 1818 to the position of the paramount power, being an inevitable result of the position gained by the Treaty of Salbai.

No greater vindication of Hastings's policy can be asked for than this successful termination of seven years of constant struggling, no finer monument be raised to his courage, talents and amazing powers of organisation—for it was he, single-handed, who found money and men, and steered the political course which led to victory.

[1] Gleig, op. cit. II, chap. xii; Aitchison, Treaties, IV, 41.
[2] Forrest, Selections from the State Papers in the Foreign Department, III, 929.

It forms the turning-point in Mahadaji's career. Mahadaji and Nana were both desirous of forcing Tipu to conform to the Treaty of Salbai in order that he should figure as a tributary, but each of them wished to claim the whole credit for doing so and Sindhia was not prepared to abrogate his newly-established independence of Poona by sharing that credit with Nana. Hitherto, though he had often disregarded orders, Mahadaji had considered himself a vassal of the Peshwa, and had generally acted in conformity with the wishes of his chief. During the next twelve years, however, assured that the English would leave him a free hand, he becomes the most prominent actor on the stage of Indian history, pursuing with quiet tenacity, but without ever forgetting, as his successor did, the limits of his strength, his policy of personal aggrandisement, a policy, moreover, which, to a very large extent, determined the general course of events in India, up to his death in 1794.

CHAPTER XV

THE CARNATIC, 1761–84

IN the Carnatic the course of events was very different from that in Bengal. In both provinces the English had attained military supremacy; but in the south they did not follow this up by the almost immediate assumption of political control. The reasons for the difference seem to be that with the overthrow of the French the Carnatic had become a secondary area not rich enough to provoke direct administration or to bring the interests of the nawab and the Company's servants into direct conflict. The pet vice of the latter in the Carnatic was indeed quite different from that which prevailed in Bengal. In Bengal they had sought to trade untaxed; in the Carnatic they found their easiest advantage to lie in lending money to the nawab. Muhammad 'Ali had from the first found himself in embarrassed circumstances. The war with the French had been carried on at his expense though largely with the Company's funds; so that the fall of Pondichery found him with a debt of 22,25,373 pagodas owing to the Company. In 1766 this had been reduced to 13,65,104 pagodas; but in reality his financial position had grown worse instead of better, for at the later date he owed private creditors a sum exceeding that which he had owed the Company in 1761. These private loans had been borrowed at the high rates of interest prevailing in the country—at first from 30 to 36 per cent.; then 25 per cent.; and then on the intervention of the governor, Palk, to 20 per cent. When questioned, the nawab stated, probably with truth, that he would have had to pay higher rates to Indian lenders. In 1766 the interest was reduced by the Company's orders to 10 per cent. The existence of this large private debt, which so far from being liquidated went on increasing throughout the whole of Muhammad 'Ali's government, branching out into all those divers funds which Burke enumerated with such passionate emphasis, affected the whole of the relations between the English and the Nawab Walajah, as he became after Clive's Treaty of Allahabad. Having the control of so large a portion of the private savings of the settlement, the nawab was able to exercise a most unwholesome influence over the policy of the council, particularly in regard to Tanjore; and was sure of a following even when the Company or the governor was positively opposed to his designs. Not a governor but was corrupted by his bribes or calumniated by his hatred. For a time at least the financial interests thus created dominated Madras in the person of Paul Benfield, who, though probably not quite deserving all the strictures of Burke, undoubtedly subordinated public affairs to the exigencies

CHI V

18

of private concerns. The true history of the period will perhaps never be written. The persons principally concerned did not entrust their designs to the publicity of the Company's records; and though a certain number of private papers have come to light, many others have been destroyed or concealed; so that we are often left to guess at what actually happened.

While the French war was still continuing, there was a strong inclination on the part of the council to take over the direct administration of the territory secured by the Company's arms. But the nawab's protests and perhaps more solid arguments induced the council to abandon that idea;[1] nor, even under the pressure of circumstances, did it in fact proceed to that extremity. Probably the financial help which was received from Bengal saved the nawab's independence. At the fall of Pondichery he found his nominal power undiminished. He had granted to the Company the district immediately surrounding Madras, and mortgaged other parts of his dominions, but the English displayed no desire to take any part in the administration of these areas; and even in the Company's jagir the revenue was ultimately leased out to the nawab himself.

In the south the first ostensible exercise of power resulted from Clive's Treaty of Allahabad. Among the other grants which he secured from Shah 'Alam was one exempting Walajah from his traditional dependence on the Deccan and another for the Northern Sarkars, which in the time of French greatness had been granted by the Nizam to Bussy, and which after the expulsion of the French had lapsed into the hands of that prince. By this time the feeble prince, whom Bussy had had such difficulty in maintaining at Hyderabad, had been replaced, and put to death, by his more vigorous brother, Nizam 'Ali. The latter had already made more than one offer of the sarkars to the English on condition of military help; but these had not been accepted, in view of the Company's strong desire to limit its responsibilities; and offers, the origins of which are obscure, to set up Walajah in the Deccan instead of Nizam 'Ali, had also been rejected under English dissuasion.[2] However, the English now took steps to carry the grant of 1765 into effect. Caillaud was sent up into the sarkars, and succeeded in occupying them practically without resistance. But it was not to be expected that Nizam 'Ali would silently acquiesce in this dismemberment of his dominions. In the end Caillaud was sent to Hyderabad to settle the dispute, and on 12 November, 1766, he concluded a treaty with Nizam 'Ali on the following terms: in return for a grant of the five sarkars the Company agreed "to have a body of troops ready to settle the affairs of His

---

[1] Madras Mil. Consultations, 1754, p. 145; 1755, pp. 146 *sqq.*; 29 August and 1 September, 1757.
[2] Bengal Select Committee to Madras, 27 April, 1768; R. J. Sulivan, *Analysis of the Political History of India*, p. 104.

Highness's government in everything that is right and proper, whenever required", but it retained liberty to withdraw the troops if demanded by the safety of the English settlements, and it was to pay a tribute of nine lakhs a year in each year in which its military assistance was not required. By a final article the Nizam was to assist the English when needed.[1] This agreement was pointed directly at Hyder 'Ali, against whom the Nizam had already entered into an alliance with the Marathas, and with whom now the English were inevitably embroiled. The Company condemned the negotiations as showing great lack of firmness.

Hyder 'Ali, who had very recently established his power in Mysore, was the son of a soldier who had risen to the post of commandant of the fortress of Bangalore. During the Seven Years' War he had coquetted with the idea of assisting the French, but had judged the situation too correctly to involve himself in their failing fortunes. Instead, he had succeeded in placing himself in the position of the chief minister—the *dalavay*—seizing the person of Khande Rao, the last holder of that post, and keeping him imprisoned in an iron cage until he died. The raja was kept a prisoner in his palace, and shown to the people once a year; but altogether ceased to enjoy power or influence. The new ruler of Mysore was an unlettered soldier, but a man of great energy and talent. His main preoccupation was the extension of his dominions. He quickly extended his rule to the Malabar Coast; but when he turned his attention to the north he found his way blocked by the Marathas and the Nizam. Meanwhile his conquests on the Malabar Coast had brought him into contact with the English factories there. At first the Bombay Presidency was in favour of an agreement. It decided to afford Hyder facilities for building fighting vessels in the Marine Yard at Bombay; and hoped that Madras would be able to accommodate the disputes subsisting between Hyder and Walajah. Hyder also hoped for advantages from supplies of arms and gunpowder from the English, and offered his alliance, both parties affording military help to the other in case of need. This was in 1766, just before Caillaud's treaty with the Nizam. But by then Hyder's conquests of the petty Nair chiefs with whom the English were in alliance had on the whole indisposed the Bombay Government to any formal alliance with its restless neighbour, though it was at the same time anxious to avoid hostilities if possible.[2] In the meantime, as has been seen, the Madras Government had agreed to assist the Nizam against Hyder as the price of the cession of the Northern Sarkars, rather than face the probable alternative of an alliance between Hyder 'Ali and the Nizam against Walajah.

---

[1] Caillaud's proceedings on this mission are recorded in two volumes (*Military Sundries*, 31–32) in the Madras Record Office.
[2] Forrest, *Bombay Selections*, II, 123–31.

English hopes rested on the triple alliance of themselves, the Nizam, and the Marathas. But the Marathas, who were first in the field, were quickly bought off by Hyder. The Nizam, accompanied by a detachment under the command of General Joseph Smith, invaded Mysore, and advanced within sight of Bangalore. But the attack was not seriously pressed home; the invaders entered Mysore on 29 April, 1767, but all the time Mahfuz Khan (brother and rival of Walajah) remained in the Nizam's camp as Hyder's agent; many letters passed between the enemies; and a secret understanding was reached, probably while the Nizam was still before Bangalore.[1] Thus the English were abandoned by the allies on whose assistance they had relied, and left by themselves to encounter the full brunt of Hyder's attack. They had indeed managed matters with a great want of skill.

The war which followed (August, 1767, to April, 1769) was one of tactical success and strategic failure in the Carnatic. At Changama and Tiruvannamalai Smith succeeded in driving Hyder off the field of battle; and after the severe lessons which he received on those occasions, Hyder was careful how he ventured within the reach of the English infantry; but these successes led to nothing. The English leaders had not at their disposal sufficient bodies of cavalry to keep the enemy's horse out of the Carnatic. They were further distracted by personal jealousies between Smith, the senior commander, and Colonel Wood, the favourite of the council. And they were harassed by the appointment of "field-deputies" sent by the council to keep watch over their movements. On 23 February, 1768, the Nizam made peace with the English in the same irresponsible manner as he had broken with them; confirming his previous treaty engagements, consenting to a limitation of the forces which the English were obliged to send to him on demand to two battalions and six guns, and ceding to the Company the diwanni of Mysore when that country should have been conquered from the enemy. About the same time the Bombay forces managed to capture the town of Mangalore; but the place was not defended when Hyder appeared to recover it, and the peace with the Nizam made little difference to the course of the war. The Carnatic lay still open to the ravages of the enemy horse, so that the principal sources of English finance were dried up; and, finally, when in the month of March, 1769, Hyder appeared before Madras at the head of a body of cavalry, and when Smith had conspicuously failed to expel the enemy from the nawab's country, the Madras Government resolved to make peace. But it had to do so on Hyder's terms. These were generous enough, but included the burden of a defensive alliance, so that the Madras Council was still far from free of the political difficulties in which it had become involved. In the

---

[1] Smith's Narrative, *ap*. Orme MSS, Various, 10; and Cosby's Journal (Brit. Mus. Add. MSS, 29898).

following year a further treaty was concluded between Hyder and the Bombay Government, which thereby secured further commercial privileges.[1]

The general conduct of the war, incompetent as it had been, was a small evil compared with the purposeless, undecided policy by which it was preceded and followed. At this time the interests of Southern and Western India were closely connected; the Marathas, the Nizam, Hyder 'Ali, and the English at Bombay and Madras, were in close and intimate association from which they could not escape. Moreover, the interests of the three Indian powers were mutually destructive. The one certain thing about the situation was that an alliance between any two of them against the third would be only temporary, and would be dissolved by its own success. In these circumstances the obvious course for the English was to avoid entanglements with any of the parties. But what they did was to ally themselves first with the Nizam, then with Hyder, and then with a party of the Marathas, without any clear idea of the responsibilities to which they were pledging themselves, and without the vigour to carry out the responsibilities which they had undertaken. But we must remember that they had certain excuses for the imbecility of their policy. In the first place their interests were divided between the rival presidencies of Madras and Bombay; and when under the Regulating Act the government of Bengal tried to impose on the subordinate presidencies a common policy, its action was neutralised by the jealousies of the minor governments for each other and for the Supreme Government. In the second place the action of the Madras Presidency was hampered by the conduct of its *protégé* the nawab Walajah. He was jealous of the superior rank of the Nizam; he was jealous of the assumed and (in his eyes) illegitimate rank of Hyder; he was jealous of the influence which the English claimed to exercise in his councils in virtue of the military power which alone preserved his position in the face of an enemy incomparably his superior in vigour and talent. So that while the English had imposed on themselves the impossible duties of assisting both the Nizam and Hyder in their various policies, the nawab was always seeking to impose on them the further duty, hardly more inconsistent with their treaty obligations, of assisting the Marathas. In the third place the local governments were always liable to the interference of the home authorities, sometimes ill-informed, sometimes ill-authorised, but at this time generally incalculable.

In 1770 this was illustrated by the arrival of a small naval squadron in Indian waters, under the command of Sir John Lindsay, who proceeded to take an active, authorised, but illegitimate part in the politics of Madras. His appointment was the result of a series of intrigues in England in which the ministry was on the whole

[1] Dupré to Orme, 10 June, 1769 (Love, *Vestiges*, II, 599); Auber, I, 266.

discreditably concerned. The discussions of 1766–7 had left the ministry decidedly inclined to interfere in the conduct of Indian affairs; and occasions were not wanting to provide it with excuses. In 1768, on the news that the government of Bengal had allowed the French at Chandernagore to mount cannon on their walls contrary to the treaty of Paris, Shelburne had written with some justification:

I cannot conceal from you His Majesty's surprise that so extraordinary a trans-action with a foreign power, by which the articles of a treaty of peace have been dispensed with, should have passed in India by the sole authority of the Company's servants and have received your approbation at home, without your having previously attempted to know His Majesty's opinion or receive his commands upon so hazardous a concession....[1]

In the following year complaints were received from the ambassador at Constantinople about the conduct of the Company's servants in the Persian Gulf;[2] and at the same time, the Company gave an opening to the ministry by asking for naval assistance on an alarm of French preparations. At this moment the Company was pro-posing to send three supervisors to India with extraordinary powers. Grafton, who was now secretary of state, seized the occasion to try to secure some controlling share in the proposed commission; he suggested that the commander of the naval force which the Company had asked for should be joined with the supervisors.[3] This proposal was rejected by the Company. About the time that these affairs were in progress there arrived from Madras John Macpherson on a mission from the nawab of Arcot. He had gone out as purser on an East-Indiaman, and had got access to the nawab on the pretext of showing him "some electrical experiments and the phenomenon of the magic lanthorn".[4] He appears to have persuaded Grafton that the nawab was a much ill-used person. The result was that, as the Company would not agree to giving Lindsay the powers that the ministry demanded, he was sent with a secret commission, which was not communicated to the Company, empowering him not only to act as plenipotentiary on behalf of the crown with all the princes of India, but also to enquire into the relations between the nawab and the Company's servants on the Coromandel Coast.

"As there is great reason to fear", his secret instructions ran, "that the Nabob of Arcot has been treated in a manner by no means correspondent to the friendly stipulations which His Majesty procured in his favour at the Company's request [in the Treaty of Paris]...it is therefore His Majesty's pleasure that you make the strictest enquiry into their conduct towards the Nabob of Arcot since the last peace in order to judge how far it has coincided with His Majesty's friendly declara-tions."[5]

[1] Shelburne to the Company, 21 January, 1768 (Lansdowne House MSS, No. 99).
[2] Michell to Wood, 17 March, 1769 (P.R.O., C.O. 77–21).
[3] Wood to the Chairs, 26 July, 1769 (loc. cit.).
[4] Harland to Rochford, 1 September, 1772 (I.O., Home Miscellaneous, 110, p. 495).
[5] Weymouth to Lindsay, Secret, 13 September, 1769 (P.R.O., T. 49–1).

Lindsay arrived at Bombay early in 1770 and after some preliminary enquiries into the position of the Marathas, sailed for Madras. His secret mission naturally involved him in disputes with the council, which knew nothing of it, and had received no instructions to admit him to a part in its political deliberations. The result was that the commodore was thrown into the nawab's arms and adopted his political views. He advocated an alliance with the Marathas and the abandonment of the treaty with Hyder; and interfered at Bombay to prevent the council there from entering into a treaty promising Hyder the same friendship and support that had been promised by the Treaty of Madras. In the course of the war between Hyder and Madhu Rao in 1770-1 Lindsay did his utmost to bring the Company in on the side of the Marathas; and his successor, Harland, in 1771, actually threatened to enter into negotiations and frame a treaty with Madhu Rao on his own account. When the council objected that that would be a violation of its treaty with Hyder, Harland replied:

Should it be found expedient to enter into an alliance with any Indian power for the preservation of the Carnatick, for the security of the possessions of the East India Company in it, and to give a probability of permanency to the British interests in this country, which may be incompatible with the agreement you made with Hyder Ally, in 1769, it would be so far from a breach of national faith that even as private persons you stand exculpated.[1]

The threatened treaty was indeed avoided. But backed by the plenipotentiary on the one side, and the corrupt influences of the private debt on the other, the nawab became irresistible and exacted from the council its agreement to the attack and capture of the little kingdom of Tanjore. Its relations with the nawab were regulated by a treaty of 1762 which Pigot, the governor, and the council of that time had forced upon the nawab. It was alleged that the raja had violated its terms partly by neglect to pay the stipulated tribute, and partly by hostile intrigues with Hyder 'Ali and with Yusuf Khan, the sepoy commandant who had rebelled at Madura and whom it had taken the English long months and considerable efforts to reduce. The first attack took place in 1771; but on that occasion the raja was allowed to remain on terms. But two years later he was again attacked, and this time his kingdom was annexed to the nawab's possessions. About the same time English expeditions were sent to reduce the two great southern poligars of Ramnad and Sivaganga.

These acquisitions caused much stir in England. By some, and by the Burkes in particular, they were attributed to the corrupt intrigues of the Company's servants. A whole pamphlet literature sprang up on the subject, fathered by the Burkes and their friends on the one side, and by the two Macphersons on the other. The truth of the matter, as distinguished from the mere external facts, remains very

[1] Harland to Dupré, etc., 25 December, 1771 (P.R.O., C.O. 77-22).

obscure. It is certain that the presidents, Bouchier and Wynch, were exceedingly averse to these extensions of the nawab's power; and these events were associated with and followed by furious disputes between the nawab and the Madras authorities. Matters became worse when the Company sent orders that Tanjore was to be given back to the raja. George Pigot, who had so distinguished himself in the Seven Years' War and had bought himself an Irish barony, returned as governor for a second term to put these orders into execution. This brought him into violent collision not only with the nawab but also with the creditors, Benfield at their head, who had acquired interests in Tanjore which were injured by the orders for its retrocession. They were supported by a majority of the council and by the commander-in-chief, Sir Robert Fletcher, who had formerly displayed his talent for intrigue in the officers' mutiny in Bengal. Pigot claimed, as did Hastings in like case, to have the power of adjourning the council at his pleasure and of refusing to put motions of which he disapproved. But unlike Hastings, he attempted to establish his claims by moving the suspension of his principal opponents, and thus excluding them from the council. This measure was countered by a conspiracy, in which Benfield and the nawab were much concerned, having for its object the seizure of his person and the overthrow of his government.[1] The conspirators were assisted by the second-in-command, Colonel James Stuart, who condescended to act as their decoy; and Pigot was seized as he drove from the fort to the governor's garden house one evening in August, 1776, and hurried off into military confinement at the Mount. He died in the following year while still in confinement.

This event marked the apogee of the nawab's power. He had not only evaded all attempts to establish the Company's influence in his territories or to control his administration, but he had also brought to condign punishment a governor who had ventured to thwart his will, even though that governor was acting under the explicit orders of the Company. Indeed this series of events at Madras illustrates quite as clearly as the simultaneous events in Bengal how far the ill-judged interference from England had weakened the stability of the English government in India. Nor was the balance to be restored until Pitt's India Act had re-established one effective control over Indian affairs. In the present case although the guilty members of the council were recalled and tried before the Court of King's Bench, their punishment was limited to fines of £1000 each; and although for the moment Benfield was recalled, he was allowed to return to the scene of his intrigues in 1781.

After a short interregnum Sir Thomas Rumbold was appointed governor and sent out to Madras, with Sir Hector Munro, the hero of Baksar, as commander-in-chief. Rumbold, against whom at a later

[1] See Palk MSS, p. 289.

pany's servant, was sent with a similar intention; but Hyder refused to accept the presents with which he was charged.[1] In ordinary circumstances this would have been warning sufficient. But unluckily about this time a regiment of king's troops—Macleod's Highlanders—arrived at Madras; and the council easily persuaded itself that Hyder would not dare to attack the English now that they had received this accession of strength. Early in April Rumbold, whose health had been for some time but indifferent, sailed for England, without any real apprehensions of the storm that was overhanging the presidency. After the event his contemporary enemies accused him of having known of Hyder's intentions and fled from the dangers which he had brought about. But in fact he does not seem to have displayed more than that very ordinary degree of blindness which all but men of extraordinary gifts display in the face of the future.[2] Rumbold's own talents were not such as to make his presence or absence a matter of great concern. But unhappily he left the chair to a man, John Whitehill, who in many ways recalls the character of Foote's *Nabob*, Sir Matthew Mite. To mediocre talent he joined a passionate acquisitive temperament, impatient of opposition, incapable of cool judgment. He was believed to have shared in the corruption which had distinguished the revenue collections in the sarkars, and to have been concerned in the equipment of a French privateer. Unluckily too the commander-in-chief, Munro, was a man whose best days were long past; personally honest, he was also slow-minded, irresolute in an emergency, unable to profit by the ideas of other people. He could see no reason for opposing the governor so long as the latter did not interfere with his military plans. Rumbold's departure left the Select Committee, to which was entrusted the conduct of political affairs, reduced to four members; so that the governor and commander-in-chief, so long as they agreed, had full control of the situation. At an earlier time the disputes between those high personages had almost brought Madras to ruin; but now their agreement went nearer still to produce the same unhappy end. Despite the warnings they received of Hyder's preparations, they were united in a foolish optimism which they did not abandon till they received the news (23 July) that his horse was already ravaging the Carnatic.

Even then they did not realise the seriousness of the position. With that contempt of the enemy, which, as Macleod observed, generally leads to "a damned rap over the knuckles",[3] Munro resolved to concentrate his forces at Conjeeveram instead of near Madras, with the result that the active Hyder intercepted and destroyed at Polilur a detachment marching under Colonel Baillie from the northward.

[1] Grey's Journal, I.O., Home Miscellaneous, 250, pp. 1–19.
[2] Rumbold's minute, *ap.* Madras Mil. Consultations, 1 April, 1780, p. 440.
[3] Hook, *Life of Baird*, I, 17.

The action passed so close to the main body of the English that they heard the guns firing, and, had Munro moved resolutely towards Baillie, the courage and confidence of his troops might have carried the day even against Hyder's superiority of force. But the campaign had been begun hastily, without due preparation, and without the necessary supplies or transport. That, and Munro's blind confidence in the English success, prevented him from making any decisive movement. On learning what had actually occurred, his confidence gave way to panic, and he retired hurriedly, losing much of his baggage, to Chingleput, and then to Madras.

The material loss had been considerable, but it was unimportant compared with the loss of *moral* which accompanied this disastrous opening of the war. The nawab's garrisons at Arcot and elsewhere surrendered, as they had done in the last war, after but the feeblest of defences, except at Wandiwash, where Lieutenant William Flint, of the Company's service, arrived just in time to take the command out of the hands of the nawab's killadar and inspire the garrison with such confidence in his leadership as secured a long and successful defence. At Madras, meanwhile, Whitehill and the Select Committee could find no prospect of successfully carrying on the war but in obtaining help at the earliest moment from Bengal. The news reached that presidency on 23 September. Hastings rose to the occasion. On 13 October the commander-in-chief, Coote, sailed to assume the command, with nearly 600 Europeans and fifteen lakhs of rupees; a considerable body of sepoys set out overland; and orders were issued for the suspension of the governor, Whitehill, on the ground of disobedience to the orders of the Supreme Government in the matter of Guntoor. The monsoon months were occupied in putting these orders into execution and preparing to take the field, and at last on 17 January, 1781, Coote marched from St Thomas Mount.

The campaign which followed closely resembled that of Joseph Smith in the First Mysore War. Coote lacked cavalry to meet that of the enemy; he lacked transport, partly owing to the lack of preparations before war broke out, partly owing to the systematic ravaging of the country by Hyder; and his movements were further hampered by a great train of artillery, which he probably needed to keep the enemy horse at a respectful distance, and by enormous hordes of camp-followers, whom he would not take adequate measures to reduce. In these circumstances, due partly to the inefficient government which had been in control, partly to the defects of the military system which had grown up, and partly to the vigorous conduct of his adversary, Coote never succeeded in commanding a greater extent of territory than was covered by his guns. He won a considerable tactical victory at Porto Novo (1 July, 1781), where Hyder committed himself more closely to action than he ventured to do again; and at Polilur, the scene of Baillie's destruction (7 August), and Sholinghur (27 September) he drove the enemy from the field of battle; but although these successes restored the English confidence in themselves and their leader, such a war of attrition would exhaust them sooner than the enemy; and neither in this year nor in 1782 did Coote make the least progress towards driving Hyder out of the nawab's possessions, while the English resources and finances steadily decayed.

Meanwhile a French squadron had appeared in the Indian waters, under the command of a leader of transcendent abilities. Early in 1782 Suffren, who had succeeded to the command of the French squadron by the death of d'Orves, announced his arrival by the capture of grain vessels bound for Madras from the northward. At this time the English men-of-war were under the command of Sir Edward Hughes, a stout fighter, but without the spark of genius. In the previous year he had actively co-operated in the capture of Negapatam from the Dutch, and had then sailed to Ceylon, where he had taken Trinkomali. He had under his command nine ships of the line, of which six had been in the East for some time, with the result that their bottoms were foul and their crews depleted. Against them Suffren could place twelve ships in the line. In the course of 1782 four actions took place between the two squadrons—17 February, 11 April, 5 July, and 3 September. From the first the English began to get rather the worst of it, in consequence of the superior numbers and superior tactical skill of the French leader. Twice he succeeded in bringing the greater part of his squadron to bear on a small part of ours, but on the whole the English held their own by a stubborn resistance against superior concentrations. In February the French landed some 2000 men under the command of Du Chemin; but luckily he proved not nearly so competent a leader as Suffren, and his junction with Hyder led to no change in the military situation. On 31 August Trinkomali surrendered to Suffren, Hughes having failed to refit himself in time to relieve it.

On the whole the campaign against Hyder in the Carnatic seems to have been conceived on false lines. The easiest way to drive him out was not to accept battle in the nawab's territory but to carry the war into the enemy's dominions, which lay exposed to attack from the sea all along the Malabar Coast. Then he would have been obliged to decide whether to ravage his own country or to allow the enemy to make war in it at ease. In either case he would early have become disgusted with a war carried on to his own evident detriment. This was self-evident, and, as soon as Bombay had been relieved by the progress of Hastings's negotiations from the pressure of the Maratha War, the Supreme Government urged upon that presidency the necessity of taking measures for an expedition against Hyder's western provinces.[1] The Madras Government had constantly urged

[1] Bengal to Madras, 16 May, *ap.* Madras Mil. Consultations, 5 June, 1782, p. 1710.

the same point, much to Coote's indignation, who thought that the principal forces should be concentrated in the Carnatic under his own command.[1]   However, a body of reinforcements from Europe had been landed at Calicut, and the royal officer in command, Colonel Humberstone, had assumed command of the Bombay troops there and moved inland, a threat which had compelled Hyder to send his son Tipu with a part of his army to repulse the invaders.   Humberstone had been too weak to do more than make a demonstration and had had to fall back before Tipu's advance; but in the beginning of 1783 the Bombay Government equipped an expedition, under the command of one of its own officers, Brigadier Mathews, to attack Mangalore and the province of Bednur.   His success was unexpectedly rapid.   Mangalore was carried, the passage up the ghats was forced with ease; and the capital of the province surrendered almost at once. But this success was due rather to the weakness of the enemy than to the skill of the English.   The Mysorean commander, Aiyaz Khan, was disaffected to Tipu, who had then just succeeded his father, and surrendered the capital of the province, Bednur, on condition of retaining the management of the country under the new masters. But these swift successes were quickly followed by complete over-throw.   Mathews scattered his scanty forces in detachments all over the country, and neglected to concentrate them or secure his communications with the coast on the news of Tipu's approach.   Then, too, the army had been distracted by quarrels over the Bednur prize-money, and disputes between the king's and the Company's officers. So that when Tipu appeared, as he speedily did, having for that purpose withdrawn most of his troops from the Carnatic, he was able to re-establish his power as quickly as he had lost it.   Mathews and all his men fell into the enemy's hands; and small garrisons in the sea-ports of Mangalore and Honawar alone remained to keep up the struggle.

In the autumn of 1782 Coote had returned to Calcutta, leaving the command with Stuart, the officer who had played so dubious a part in the Pigot business of 1776.   Like Munro he had lost all the talent he had ever had; and he had, moreover, lost a leg at the second battle of Polilur, so that he was not only unenterprising but also immobile.   During the monsoon of 1782 he failed to get the army ready to take the field again; so that when Hyder died early in December, he was unable to take advantage of the three weeks that elapsed between Hyder's death and Tipu's arrival from the Malabar Coast where he had been opposing Humberstone.   He did not actually take the field until the short successes of Mathews had summoned Tipu with the bulk of his army to the other side of India. This was the first piece of good fortune that had befallen the English since the beginning of the war.   It was lucky that Stuart did not have

[1] Coote to Madras, 21 June, *ap.* Madras Mil. Consultations of same date, 1782, p. 1893.

to encounter Hyder in the field; it was supremely lucky that he did not have to encounter Hyder reinforced with the large body of French troops under Bussy who arrived on the coast in the month of April, only to find that their expected allies were elsewhere. In these circumstances Bussy established himself at Cuddalore. In May Stuart reluctantly marched south to oppose him. After a march of extraordinary languor he arrived before Cuddalore on 8 June. On the 13th followed a stubborn action in which the English secured only a very incomplete success. Stuart's movement had been covered by Hughes's squadron; but on the 20th in action against Suffren the latter was so severely handled that he had to abandon his position and put back to Madras to refit. On the 25th Bussy attacked Stuart's position. The French were repulsed; but Hughes's retreat had placed the English army in a most dangerous situation. Stuart at this crisis wrote that he could not answer for the consequences if Hughes had really gone to Madras.[1] But luck still was on the side of the English. On the 23rd Benfield received news by a special messenger that the French and English had signed the preliminaries of peace. The news was communicated at once to Bussy who agreed to a suspension of arms, and the English army was saved.

The Madras army was thus set free to renew the struggle with Tipu; it had been already decided to try a complete change of operations and commanders; Colonel Fullarton, though far from being the next senior officer to Stuart, was selected to attack the southern possessions of Mysore. A beginning had already been made earlier in the year by the capture of Dindigul. On 1 June, Fullarton captured Dharapuram, and was preparing for a further advance when he received orders to suspend operations until the issue of peace proposals to Tipu should be known.

Ever since 1781, when Lord Macartney arrived as governor of Madras, in succession to a series of Company's servants who had clearly fallen short of the demands of their position, the Madras Council had eagerly desired the conclusion of peace. In September, 1781, Macartney, in conjunction with Coote, Hughes and John Macpherson, who was passing through Madras on his way to take his seat in the council of the governor-general, took it on themselves to address the Maratha ministry at Poona, assuring it of the sincerity of the English proposals for an accommodation.[2] This measure Hastings had naturally and bitterly resented. Later on the Madras authorities had repeatedly asked the Bengal Government for powers to negotiate a peace with Hyder; a request which Hastings had evaded, preferring to entrust the negotiations to Coote. Coote's discussions,

---

[1] Stuart to Madras, 28 June, *ap.* Madras Mil. Consultations, 4 July, 1783, p. 2903.
[2] Letter of 11 September, 1781, *ap.* Madras Mil. Consultations, 30 January, 1782, p. 243. Cf. Macartney to the Chairs, 31 July, 1781 (I.O., Home Miscellaneous, 246, p. 16) and Macartney, Coote and Macpherson to Hastings, 11 September, 1781 (Brit. Mus. Add. MSS, 22454, f. 25).

however, had come to nothing; so also did informal overtures which were made to Tipu by Macartney, without sanction from Bengal, early in 1783. But the preliminaries concluded in Europe contained stipulations (Article XVI) to the effect that all allies should be invited to accede to the present pacification. On the strength of this, Macartney reopened conversations with Tipu, thinking it likely that the loss of his French allies, following on the peace which Hastings had made with the Marathas, would permit of effective negotiations; and on applying to Bengal, he received a guarded permission, not to enter into a separate treaty with Tipu, but to negotiate for a cessation of hostilities and a release of prisoners. In other words, Hastings relied on the provisions of the Treaty of Salbai to secure a settlement. Macartney, however, was bent on making peace, being confident that that would serve the interests of the Company better than waiting indefinitely for Sindhia to take action against Tipu. He dispatched commissioners to confer with Tipu, who was still lying before Mangalore. The commandant of the English garrison, Colonel Campbell, had accepted very disadvantageous terms for a suspension of hostilities. He had agreed for instance to receive no supplies of victuals by sea—the only way by which he could possibly receive supplies.[1] Each occasion on which the Company's vessels revictualled him occasioned therefore sharp disputes; and Tipu seems to have considered himself warranted by his acquiescence in continuing work on his entrenchments, which was also a contravention of the suspension of arms. At last on 29 January, 1784, Campbell preferred giving up the place to continuing longer to hold it, being driven to this by the rapidity with which the garrison was falling sick. The situation before Mangalore had produced more than one report that hostilities had broken out again. As a result, in December, 1783, Brigadier Macleod had seized Kannanur, belonging not indeed to Tipu but to one of his allies; while Fullarton also had renewed his attack on the southern possessions of Tipu, capturing Palghaut and Coimbatore before his movements could be countermanded by the deputies on their way to Mangalore.

The latter reached that place shortly after it had surrendered and immediately opened negotiations. On 7 March terms were agreed to which completely ignored the Treaty of Salbai. However, they were not unreasonable. Both parties were to give up their conquests; all prisoners were to be released; certain specified allies were included. In short, much the same terms were obtained from Tipu as Hastings had managed to get from the Marathas. But men's minds were irritable with defeat and the treaty became the object of a host of legends. Tipu was said to have treated the deputies with unparalleled indignity, erecting a gallows by their encampment, and keeping them in such a state of panic that they contemplated flight to the English

[1] Articles dated 2 August, *ap.* Madras Mil. Consultations, 27 September, 1783, p. 4232.

ships lying off the town. There is reason to think that these stories had their origin in the excitable imagination of Brigadier Macleod. They seem to have passed to Calcutta by way of Bombay, along with extraordinary versions of the ill-treatment accorded to the prisoners by Tipu. The facts seem to have been that the commissioners of their own accord pitched their tents near a gallows which had been set up before the surrender of Mangalore for the execution of one of Tipu's officers who had entered into communication with the English garrison; and that, while the prisoners were not well treated, there are no grounds for believing that any of them were deliberately murdered. In one respect Tipu certainly violated the treaty. He did not release all the prisoners in his hands. This was made a very serious charge against Macartney. But we must remember that in 1792, after a successful war, Cornwallis did not succeed in getting Tipu to release all the prisoners whom he had taken; and it is clearly unfair to condemn Macartney for failing to do what Cornwallis himself after a successful war could not effect. The probability is that in each case the persons detained were those who had submitted to circumcision and accepted Tipu's service; and who, though kept under a guard, were considered by Tipu as on a different footing from those who had consistently rejected his offers and defied his threats. These matters, along with the fact that the treaty was distinct from, and independent of, the treaty of Salbai induced Hastings to condemn it with extraordinary asperity, and to move Macartney's suspension for having disobeyed the orders of the Supreme Government. But he can hardly have judged the matter with an unbiassed mind. The episode of the treaty came at the end of a long series of disputes between the Bengal and Madras Governments in which Hastings displayed something less than the serene and balanced judgment of which at one time he had given such striking evidence.

At the close of 1780 Lord Macartney had been appointed governor of Madras at the moment when Hastings's friends, with Laurence Sulivan at their head, had contracted a short-lived alliance with the ministry under North. Macartney was therefore pledged to the support of Hastings, and indeed came out with the full intention of so doing. But on his arrival he found himself unable to adopt the measures which Hastings had recommended to the southern presidency. Hastings had urged an alliance with the Dutch, in order to obtain from them a force of European infantry in return for the cession of the district of Tinnevelly by the nawab. But Macartney had brought out with him orders to seize the Dutch factories, since the United Provinces had just joined the French and the Americans in the war against Great Britain. In the second place Hastings had advised the cession of the sarkars to the Nizam on condition of substantial assistance from him against Hyder. Macartney had no specific orders from the Company on this head; but none the less he

stoutly refused to dismember the Company's possessions; he urged
that such a cession would not produce effects commensurate with the
cost, and in that he was very likely right. A third cause of difference
between the two was fortuitous. Hastings, on Macartney's arrival,
had written to him advising that the raja of Tanjore should be
required, and if necessary compelled, to contribute his share to the
cost of the war. Macartney was in agreement with this view; and
forwarded an extract from Hastings' letter to the chairman and
deputy chairman of the Company in support of his own arguments.
Unfortunately the letter arrived in England when Sulivan and
Hastings's friends had lost control of the directorate; and led to severe
and unmerited reproaches directed against Hastings by the new
chairs. Hastings accused Macartney of having betrayed him to his
enemies; and does not seem to have been convinced by Macartney's
temperate and candid explanation.[1] Gleig, it may be noted, was
mistaken in supposing that no answer was returned to Hastings's
letter of accusation. Besides these occasions of difference in which
Macartney was in the right there was that unfortunate letter to the
Marathas, which has already been mentioned, in which he was
decidedly in the wrong. The result was a strong tendency in each to
suspect and question the opinions of the other.

At the same time Macartney was involved in disputes with Coote
and with the nawab. In sending Coote to Madras the Bengal
Government had invested him with separate and independent powers,
as the Madras Government had done with Clive, in not dissimilar
circumstances in 1756. Coote interpreted them in the widest possible
sense, neglecting to attend the meetings of the Select Committee and
declining to explain his plans for the conduct of the war, while he
harassed the committee with ceaseless complaints regarding the
shortness of transport and supplies. Both sides complained to Bengal;
and Bengal preferred to support Coote, without seriously considering
the Madras assertions that the financial management of the army,
as distinguished from the military conduct of the war, was wasteful
and extravagant. Underlying these disputes were intrigues in which
Paul Benfield took a considerable part, exasperating Coote's irritable
mind against the unfortunate governor.

From the first the resources of Madras had been wholly unequal to
the maintenance of the war. Bengal had contributed largely, sending
no less than 265 lakhs of rupees, in specie, bills, and supplies, in the
course of the four years that the war continued. But the government
had frequently and loudly declared that it was incumbent on the
Madras Government to do everything in its power to increase its own
resources, particularly the contributions from the nawab's revenues.
But that spring had completely dried up. Twenty years of financial

[1] Macartney to Hastings, 10 May, 1783 (Brit. Mus. Add. MSS, 22455, f. 47
verso).

mismanagement had exhausted the nawab's treasury, never very full. In the crisis which resulted from Hyder's invasion, he had sought to evade payment rather than to provide with funds the only power that would protect him. To the demands of the Madras authorities he had returned blank refusals. Foreseeing that this course could not be continued indefinitely, he had sent a mission to Calcutta where terms were settled between him and the Supreme Government, which proceeded to dispatch to Madras a special agent, chosen with singular lack of tact from among the Madras covenanted servants, to watch over the performance of the treaty. This was in 1781, before Macartney had arrived. In so doing Hastings and his council had clearly overstepped the limits of their statutory powers; but they had not doubted their power of coercing the Madras Government into obedience. It was as discredited as had been that of Drake in 1756 But Macartney's arrival had changed the situation altogether. He soon made this clear. He and the Select Committee declared that they could not acquiesce in the appointment of an agent to perform the functions with which they were specially charged by the Company. But though they refused to recognise the agent whom Hastings had appointed, they did adopt the Bengal treaty as the basis of a new agreement which Macartney proceeded to negotiate with the nawab. On 2 December, 1781, the latter executed an assignment of his revenues to Macartney in person for a fixed term of five years, reserving to his own use one-fifth of what amounts should be collected. This agreement was formally approved by the Bengal Government. But it soon was evident that it was no more genuine than had been all the previous promises of the durbar. The revenues which were collected were not paid in to the Company, but secretly transmitted to the nawab. When it was proposed to appoint inspectors to watch over the revenue officials, the nawab refused to grant them the necessary powers; when it was proposed to lease out the country to renters, the nawab refused to sign the documents appointing them. In these circumstances Macartney resolved no longer to give way, but to exercise himself the power of appointing the renters. In this conduct he was confirmed by a letter from Bengal, written indeed without knowledge of the crisis that had arisen at Madras, but strongly and pointedly urging the absolute necessity of making the assignment a reality in order that all the resources of the country might be made available for the conduct of the war. In this course Macartney persevered with considerable success. The Committee of Assigned Revenue, which he appointed to manage the business, introduced great reforms into the nawab's disordered administration. The gross revenue levied from the cultivators was reduced from 14·4 to 13·8 lakhs of pagodas in the six districts which remained under effective control, while at the same time by the abolition of a host of needless charges the net revenue was increased from six to twelve lakhs, and the total collections of assigned revenue amounted between the end of 1781 and September, 1784, to over thirty-three lakhs of pagodas, or over one hundred lakhs of rupees, not a fanam of which would have been secured for the Company's use but for Macartney's insistence on making the assignment a reality instead of a mere bit of window-dressing.

The nawab, however, was untiring in his endeavours to secure the abolition of the grant which he had made but had not intended to make effectual. First he offered to Coote the management of the revenues which he had already granted to Macartney; and then he sent another mission to Bengal to induce the government to cancel a measure of which it had repeatedly and formally approved. At first the mission met with no success. But in the autumn of 1782, just about the time of the return of Coote, Hastings changed his attitude. The reasons remain obscure, but were almost certainly connected with the necessity under which he thought he lay of preserving the support of Benfield's friends in London. At the moment he, Macpherson, and Coote were united on the need of annulling the assignment. But when the matter came up for final decision in the early part of 1783, though it was resolved that the assignment should be annulled, yet, when Hastings proposed to give Coote provisional powers to suspend Macartney in case he failed to obey the orders of Bengal, he failed altogether to carry the council with him. He and Coote alone voted for the proposal; so that when Coote at last did return to Madras, he lacked the orders to coerce Madras into obedience to most unpalatable resolutions. That government, however, being privately informed of Hastings's intentions, had resolved no longer to recognise the special powers which Coote had formerly enjoyed, nor to render up the assignment until the orders of the court of directors should be received. Coote died immediately on landing at Madras, otherwise a fierce struggle must have resulted from the decisions of the Bengal and Madras Governments respectively. As it was the matter did not pass beyond the stage of controversy, the Madras Government obstinately refusing to obey the orders of Bengal until in 1785 the matter was settled by orders from the Company requiring the assignment immediately to be cancelled. On this Macartney at once resigned and went home rather than carry out a policy which he was convinced, and rightly, could lead to nothing except misgovernment.[1]

These disputes with the Bengal Government did not exhaust the difficulties which Macartney had to encounter. His controversy with the commander-in-chief continued after Coote's departure to Bengal and even after Coote's death. The military talents of Stuart, Coote's successor, were too slender in any way to warrant the continuance of

[1] Dodwell, "Hastings and the Assignment of the Carnatic", *English Historical Review*, XL, 375-96.

the special powers which the commander-in-chief had been exercising; and the Select Committee assumed the control of military affairs. Stuart, however, paid it but an unwilling obedience and in some points departed from its actual instructions. As soon as news of peace with France was received, he was therefore summoned to hand over the command of the army and return to Madras. There the dispute developed with vigour and threatened to merge itself with the dispute over the assignment. There appeared that same ominous conjunction, the nawab, Benfield and Stuart, which had produced the arrest of Pigot just seven years before. Macartney arrested Stuart, and sent him off to England, while Benfield was ordered down to a small station at a considerable distance from the presidency, where he could do no harm. It is impossible to say with certainty to what extent Macartney was justified in his belief of impending violence. But there were many suspicious circumstances, and he cannot be blamed for keeping on the safe side. Unluckily the matter involved him in further disputes with the military authorities. Coote had been commander-in-chief of the king's troops in India as well as of the Company's and had been succeeded in this dual office by Stuart. When the latter was dismissed in 1783 no difficulty arose over the command of the Company's forces, but the command of the king's was a very different question. The officer next in succession was Sir John Burgoyne, who honestly, and, in the circumstances, justly, doubted Macartney's power of removing the commander of the king's troops. The two men failed to reach any agreement on the point; and the outcome was that Macartney and the Select Committee nominated Colonel Ross Lang, of the Company's service, to the command-in-chief, with the rank of lieutenant-general, which placed him in command of all the king's general officers on the coast. This was a measure of very doubtful prudence. But for the sober conduct of Burgoyne, it might have led to open disorder. At first all the general officers withdrew from the army, directing their subordinates to obey the orders issued by Lang. The object of this was to permit the commands of government to be obeyed without giving up the principles of the service which were regarded as sacrosanct. But Macartney instead of accepting this compromise in the spirit in which it was offered was bent on triumph at any price. Burgoyne was placed in arrest; the other general officers were struck off staff allowances until they submitted. In the early part of his struggles with the military he had on the whole been in the right; but in the concluding part of his contest, with the king's general officers, he showed much want of tact; and owed his success to the public spirit of his adversaries rather than to his own wisdom. Finally the matter was regulated by a decision from home that in future king's officers holding commands under the East India Company should receive letters of service authorising them to exercise their rank only so long as they continued in the Company's service, so that dismissal from the latter automatically ended their authority in India.

It must be remembered that Macartney was placed in a position of extraordinary difficulty owing to the lack of definition of powers as between the Bengal and Madras Governments, and between the civil government and the military commanders. The first was due to the neglects of those who drew the Regulating Act; the second in part to the anomalous position of the king's officers in India, in part to the decision of Hastings in the crisis of 1780 to free Coote from dependence on the civil government at Madras. Only a man of very extraordinary gifts could have overcome such difficulties with complete success.

CHAPTER XVI

CHAIT SINGH, THE BEGAMS OF OUDH AND FAIZULLA KHAN

THE Company's exchequer had been seriously drained by the Maratha War, and the outbreak of hostilities with France in 1778 warned Hastings that he must consider new methods of raising money.

He had recourse to the rather harsh and discreditable policy which brought upon him the impeachment and which, when every possible excuse has been made for it, remains the one serious stain on his administration. Was there no other alternative? Would it not have been possible to raise a loan as would have been done in modern times? The answer is that Hastings was very unwilling to contract another bonded debt, for he had received much credit with the directors for having paid off that which he found existing when he came to India. He decided that he was justified in demanding from Chait Singh, the raja of Benares, a special sum of over £50,000 in addition to his regular tribute, or rent, of £225,000. The council agreed, and were therefore equally responsible with Hastings for the exaction. Francis, it is true, was inclined to demur and suggested— a suggestion which was not accepted—that Chait Singh should be assured at the same time that the demand was entirely exceptional, but in the end he acquiesced in Hastings's policy. The same demand was made in the two following years. Chait Singh naturally, following the invariable practice in the East, protested against these exactions, but after slight delay he paid the money.

The British methods of enforcing payment were certainly harsh. In 1779 Chait Singh asked that the payment should be limited to that year, and his "contumacy" was punished by an order to pay the whole in one sum instead of in instalments. When again he asked for an indulgence of six or seven months, he was told that if he failed to meet the original demand he would be treated as though he had refused altogether. He urged that his agreement with the Company should have exempted him from all contributions beyond the normal tribute. Troops were then ordered to march into his territory, and an extra charge of £2000 was made against him for their expenses.

In 1780, on the same day that he paid the last instalment of the third £50,000, an entirely new demand was made upon him that he should provide the Company with 2000 cavalry, although when the Company took over the sovereignty of Benares in 1775, he had been merely recommended to maintain a body of that number of horse, and was told that there would be "no obligation on him to do it".[1]

[1] *Reports from Committee of the House of Commons*, v, 489.

Chait Singh replied that he was unable to spare so large a number. The demand was then reduced to 1000. He mustered 500 horse and 500 infantry and sent a message to Hastings that these troops were ready for his service. Chait Singh declared that he never received an answer to this message, a statement which is almost certainly accurate, for Hastings in his *Narrative of the Insurrection* practically admits it: "I do not know but it may be true. He had received positive orders, and those had been repeated. It was his duty to obey them, not to waste my time with letters of excuse".[1]

Hastings now made up his mind to inflict upon Chait Singh the immense fine of half a million sterling: "I was resolved to draw from his guilt the means of relief to the Company's distress....In a word I had determined to make him pay largely for his pardon, or to exact a severe vengeance for his past delinquency".[2] Hastings was by this time entirely his own master, for Wheler was the only councillor left at Calcutta. An arrangement was made by which Hastings himself was to go to Benares and settle the question as he deemed best, while Wheler was to remain on duty in Bengal. The governor-general went northward in July. Chait Singh met him at Baksar and abjectly humbling himself, asked for pardon. Hastings refused to give him any answer till his arrival at Benares. There he again refused to grant him a personal interview and merely transmitted his demand in writing. He received a letter from the raja, which to an impartial judge would seem to err, if at all, in the direction of servility, but which Hastings described as "Not only unsatisfactory in substance but offensive in style".[3]

Though Hastings had taken with him only a weak escort, he ordered Chait Singh to be put under arrest. The raja humbly submitted but the troops, infuriated by the indignity placed upon their ruler in his own capital, suddenly rose and massacred a company of British sepoys with their officers. Chait Singh, fearing for the consequences, escaped in the turmoil and joined his rebellious army. Hastings was in the most imminent danger and had to fly for safety to Chunar. There he showed his customary coolness and presence of mind, rallied all available forces to his aid and drove back his enemy. Chait Singh, maintaining his innocence of the massacre, was hunted over the Ganges and fled to Gwalior. His dominions were sequestrated and were conferred upon a nephew, the tribute at the same time being raised from £225,000 to £400,000. The council at Calcutta, now consisting of Wheler and Macpherson, were obviously embarrassed in their attempts to defend and ratify these proceedings of their chief. They felt bound to ask themselves certain questions, first, "Where were the Governor-General's particular instructions for such extra-

---

[1] Warren Hastings, *A Narrative of the Insurrection which happened in the Zamindary of Benares*, p. 27.
[2] *Idem*, p. 9.   [3] *Idem*, p. 19.

ordinary demands upon Chait Singh?" To this they replied that "he was fully authorised by the general tenor of his instructions" and that in not requiring more particular injunctions "there was a delicacy in the mode he preferred and it imposed a greater responsibility." Their second question was, "Why was Chait Singh put in arrest when he offered to make every concession?" to which they replied that nothing but arrest could have convinced Chait Singh of Hastings's determination. Their third question was "Whether there was not a compact between him and the Company which specified that he was only to pay them a certain annual tribute?" They agreed that this "involves much argument", but they accept Hastings's own version of the sanad or original agreement with Chait Singh given in his *Narrative*. They admit that his actions "certainly precipitated the storm from the cloud in which it had gathered", and that these acts "judges at a distance, judges unoppressed with the actual embarrassments of this government, may with great speciousness of argument condemn".[1] Their attitude suggests a certain uneasiness, together with an obvious desire to defend the governor-general. We must deal here very shortly with certain technical and legal points which were discussed at immense length in the impeachment. The first is whether Chait Singh was an independent raja or a mere zamindar. The fact was that though he undoubtedly had a zamindari status, he had a very real measure of independence and quite an exceptional position. Hastings had committed himself in the past to the view that he was far more than a zamindar, but this question clearly does not affect the main point at issue, which is whether Chait Singh, whatever his exact degree of dependency upon the British, was treated with fairness and mercy. In any case, as Grey pointed out in the impeachment, Hastings's defenders were impaling themselves upon the horns of a dilemma, if they maintained that Chait Singh was a mere zamindar and at the same time that the demand made upon him was justifiable. In that case the exaction ought to have taken the form of a general universal tax levied on all the zamindars under the Company's rule; but it was directed only against Chait Singh. Hastings had admitted that "there was no other person in the situation of Chait Singh",[2] which was really fatal to the "mere zamindar" theory. The second question is whether the Company had not bound itself to levy no contribution upon him beyond his normal tribute or rent of £225,000. It would take too long to discuss this question in all its detail, but there is no doubt of the technical point that such a promise had been definitely given in 1775. A later grant, it is true, of 1776, contained the words that "all former sanads had become null and void", and it was upon this fact that Hastings tried to base a technical defence; but it is clear that Chait Singh had

---

[1] Forrest, *Selections from the State Papers in the Foreign Department*, III, 830–2.
[2] Bond, *Speeches in the Trial of Warren Hastings*, I, 328.

objected, as he had every right to do, to the insertion of these words, and that the grant was altered accordingly. Hastings also claimed that:

it [is] a right inherent in every government to impose such assessments as it judges expedient for the common service and protection of all its subjects; and we are not precluded from it by any agreement subsisting between the Raja and this government.[1]

These Asiatic views naturally exposed Hastings to the attacks of Burke.

A third question whether Chait Singh was in rebellion against the Company hardly deserves examination. It is perfectly certain that, until his troops broke out in detestation of the treatment to which their ruler was subjected, the idea of rebellion had never dawned upon the raja. The truth is that Hastings in his desperate need for supplies allowed himself to depart from his usually generous and kindly attitude towards Indian powers. Whatever the legal rights and wrongs of the matter, no sane person can deny that Hastings's treatment of the unfortunate raja was merciless and vindictive. This can be illustrated by one incident which occurred in the year 1780. In that year after the demand for a third sum of £50,000 had been made, Chait Singh sending a confidential agent to Calcutta offered Hastings a present of about £20,000. Hastings at first refused it, which was of course the only proper course to take, for the sum was meant as a bribe to save Chait Singh from the larger amount of £50,000. If it was right to levy the latter sum, it was unquestionably most improper to receive the former. But Hastings after a few days, being in serious need of money to equip an expedition against Sindhia, accepted the money. We need not here consider the unconstitutional nature of his act in taking such sums without the knowledge of his council, the difficulties in which he involved himself by representing the money as a gift from his private estate or the unfortunate view of money transactions which the whole affair implies; but it is difficult to understand how any man of ordinary feeling and consideration for his fellow-creatures could accept the proffered gift of £20,000 and then immediately exact the larger sum of £50,000, confront his suppliant with a further demand for troops, and, on the ground that the demand was not met, proceed to levy a fine of £500,000. There seems no doubt, as Sir Alfred Lyall points out and as Hastings' own language shows, that the governor-general had never quite forgiven Chait Singh for having in the crisis of 1777 sent an emissary to make favour with Clavering.

Quite apart from the morality of the transaction, Hastings lies open to criticism in regard to the policy of it. He has been justified, after all other defences have been surrendered, on the ground that the

---

[1] *Reports from Committees of the House of Commons*, v, 463.

political situation was so serious as to justify any means of obtaining money. The answer to this is that he obtained none, and, what is more, placed his own valuable life in the utmost peril. By his imprudent action in arresting Chait Singh he was responsible for the uprising of the people of Benares; the raja escaped with part of his wealth—the amount he took with him was in all probability grossly exaggerated—and the rest of it amounting to twenty-three lakhs of rupees was seized by the troops at Bijaigarh who promptly proceeded to divide it up amongst themselves. This was largely due to an indiscreet letter of Hastings himself which encouraged the army to claim the prize money. The immediate result therefore on the financial side was that the Company incurred the expense of the military operations that ensued. For the moment they got nothing, and it was an immediate subvention that was required. Hastings afterwards boasted, "I lost the zemindari with the rent of 22 lakhs; I recovered it with a revenue of 40".[1] But this only applied of course to the future, and as a matter of fact for a long time the augmented revenue (partly owing to the simultaneous occurrence of a famine) could not be raised. Two successive ministers of finance were dismissed because they failed to produce it. All the evidence shows that it was a very long time before Benares recovered from the heavy exactions made upon it. Hastings, with a curious detachment which often prevented him from seeing, or at any rate from acknowledging the consequences of his own actions, himself bears witness to the desolation of the country without apparently the least apprehension that he was in any way responsible for it. In June, 1784, he wrote that he would avoid Benares on his way back to Calcutta, "for I underwent the persecution of mobs of complainants from Buxar to Joosee in my way thither, and there is now a little mob parading even at my gate".[2] In 1788 Lord Cornwallis sent Jonathan Duncan as a commissioner to report on the condition of Benares. His report dealt one by one with the districts of the province and is a most serious indictment of the treatment meted out to Benares. In one district it is said that a third of the land is uncultivated. In another for about twelve or fourteen miles, "the whole appeared one continual waste as far as the eye could reach". In a third in a stretch of about twelve miles "not above twenty fields of cultivated ground are to be seen: all the rest being as far as the eye can reach,...one general waste of long grass". The report adds significantly that this falling off in cultivation is said to have happened in the course of a few years, that is, since the late raja's expulsion.[3]

Hastings having failed, as we have seen, to obtain any money from Chait Singh had to seek for another source of supply. The nawab of Oudh, Asaf-ud-daula, owed the Company at this time, for arrears of

[1] Gleig, op. cit. II, 421. [2] Idem, III, 185.
[3] Minutes of the Evidence in the Trial of Warren Hastings, pp. 261-2.

subsidy, about fifteen lakhs of rupees, and he professed that he had no means of discharging the debt. His mother and grandmother, the begams or princesses of Oudh, had inherited from the late nawab large jagirs or landed estates and a treasure amounting it is said to about £2,000,000. The nawab had long desired to get control of this wealth and claimed that it was unjustly withheld from him. The will had never been produced and it was claimed that by the Muhammadan law the begams had no right to inherit so large a proportion of the late ruler's property. In any case, it was said, this property was really part of the wealth of the sovereign of the country and the first claim upon it ought to have been the late nawab's debt to the Company. All this was no doubt largely true, but in 1775 the widow of Shuja-ud-daula, on the urgent representation of the British Resident, agreed to pay her son £300,000 in addition to £250,000 already given to him, on condition that he and the Company guaranteed that no further demand should ever be made upon her. The guarantee was given. In 1781 Asaf-ud-daula, urged on thereto by the Resident, as is clear from the private correspondence between Hastings and Middleton, asked that he might be allowed to resume the estates and seize the treasure of the begams. Hastings in sore need of money agreed to the proposal and withdrew the Company's protection from the begams. At this point the nawab, who had probably never desired to seize the treasure, and was afraid, as the Resident said, of the "uncommonly violent temper of his female relations", began to hang back, and had henceforward to be steadily driven on by the British authorities to avail himself of the opportunity thus given him. In December, 1781, Hastings wrote to Middleton, "You must not allow any negotiations or forbearance, but must prosecute both services until the begams are at the entire mercy of the nawab".[1] In January, 1782, he writes to say that he had hoped the nawab would have immediately entered upon the measures agreed upon, but "after having long waited, with much impatience, for this effect, I was apprised...that the nawab, from what cause I know not, had shown a great reluctance to enter on this business". He tells the council that if the Resident cannot carry out the instructions, "I would myself proceed to Lucknow, and afford the nawab any personal assistance for carrying them into execution...I dread the imbecility and irresolution, which too much prevail in the nawab's councils". Hastings refers to "the pressing letters which I have written to the nawab, the strong injunctions which I have repeated to the Resident".[2] Middleton replied that "the temporising and indecisive conduct of the nawab seem to promise an issue very different from that expected in your commands".[3] Hastings, however, was not to be deterred from his object by the unwillingness of

---

[1] Forrest, *Selections from the State Papers in the Foreign Department*, III, 950.
[2] *Report from Committees of the House of Commons*, VI, 537.   [3] *Idem*, p. 538.

the nawab or the shrinking from strong measures of his representative, and in February we find him writing to Scott that he had been compelled to rouse Middleton's activity "by letters written in a style of the greatest severity".[1]

Middleton, not having satisfied Hastings as sufficiently energetic in applying coercion, was superseded as Resident by Bristow, and Bristow wrote in June:

> The begam complains that having no pension or jagir she now subsists, her family and herself, with the greatest difficulty....Previous to my arrival her eunuchs were kept for many months in confinement, and led out to corporal punishment....These measures failed, and you have before you the opinions given by Major Gilpin...that all that force could do has been done.[2]

The above quotations are perhaps sufficient to meet the theory that Hastings was not responsible for what his agents were doing at Faizabad and that the latter were merely carrying out the wishes of the nawab. As a matter of fact the nawab was a reluctant party throughout, and Hastings asks that a very severe rebuke should be given to his minister for having assumed "a very unbecoming tone of refusal, reproach and resentment in opposition to measures recommended by me and even to acts done by my authority".[3] As to the actual treatment inflicted on the begam's two ministers, they were imprisoned from January to December, 1782, and they were for a time deprived of food and put in irons. It seems doubtful whether flogging was actually inflicted.

Finally in December, 1782, they paid over large sums of money and were released. The British officer who had charge of them wrote: "I wish you had been present at the enlargement of the prisoners. The quivering lips, the tears of joy stealing down the poor men's cheeks was a scene truly affecting".[4]

The justification put forward by Hastings for tearing up the Company's guarantee was that the begams had supported the rising of Chait Singh and were in rebellion against the British Government. The answer to this appears to be that, even if it were entirely true, the proper course would have been to confront the begams with the charge, produce the evidence and demand proofs of innocence, not to cancel the treaty and cast them to the tender mercies of the nawab, or rather to those of the British Resident.

The evidence for the alleged rebellion is conflicting. It depends upon the affidavits taken by Sir Elijah Impey, in his injudicious attempt to support the governor-general, the statements of Colonel Hannay and his officers, and those of Wheler and others. The affidavits are worthless. Sir James Stephen points out that only ten

[1] Gleig, *op. cit.* II, 449.
[2] Forrest, *Selections from the State Papers in the Foreign Department*, III, 969.
[3] *Idem*, p. 982.
[4] Bond, *Speeches in the Trial of Warren Hastings*, I, 707.

of them mention the begams and then only on hearsay, and if they are to be accepted at all, most of them equally inculpate the nawab himself—an awkward fact which was ignored by Hastings and the council. The evidence of Colonel Hannay can only be accepted with many reservations; he was in the service of the nawab and acquired a large fortune by questionable means. The country was no doubt in a state of disturbance and Hannay and his colleagues would be interested, as Mill suggests, in finding for these disturbances some cause other than their own malversations. The third piece of evidence, and the strongest, is the statement of Wheler, an honest man, that he believed the begams were really stirring up a rebellion. Against the theory of the defection of the begams, is, first of all, the extreme improbability of their taking any part in any serious movement against the British Government. Even those who afterwards adopted the charge, wrote and spoke during the events as though such a thing were impossible. For instance, in a letter from Middleton to Hastings on 18 January, 1782, the phrase occurs, "The reliance which not-withstanding the part I have avowed and acted with respect to her she probably placed in the support and mediation of our Govern-ment".[1] Further, in all the correspondence that passed between Hastings and Wheler at the time, there is no mention at all of any rebellion. The only question is how soon the money could be exacted from the begam and her ministers. In the private correspondence too between Middleton, Impey and Hastings there is nothing to lead one to suppose that the money was being levied as a fine for an in-surrection. It seems probable that the charge of rebellion was *ex post facto*, made when it was found necessary to present a justification for the whole business. It was easy enough to do this, because under the wretched government of the nawab there was always an endemic insurrection going on in Oudh, the unfortunate rajas who owned him as their suzerain being frequently in revolt against his oppressions. In any case we must be fair enough to admit that the treatment meted out to Chait Singh, whatever its justification, was sufficient to make any Indian power adopt measures for its own protection. The truth is that, making every possible allowance for Hastings's financial difficulty, and granting for purposes of argument that the begams were quite willing to stir up every kind of trouble for him, we must yet agree that it was a sordid, shabby and sorry business. Before we leave the subject a curious episode must be mentioned. We have seen that Hastings in 1780 took a present of £20,000 from Chait Singh while engaged in pressing him for money. In almost exactly the same way in 1781, he was offered and accepted £100,000 from the nawab of Oudh. He employed it in the Company's service and then after a considerable delay and some amazing manipulation of the accounts, he reported the matter to the directors and made the

---

[1] *Minutes of the Evidence*, p. 820.

astonishing request that they should present it to himself as a token of their approval. We need not concern ourselves here with the decency or taste of his suggestion to the directors—the suggestion we must remember of a man whose official salary with allowances was about £30,000—but the transaction throws a vivid light on Hastings's laxity of view on all monetary transactions. The money was undoubtedly offered by the nawab as a bribe to Hastings to release him from the disagreeable task of coercing the begams. Hastings accepts it but continues his policy nevertheless, an exact parallel to his conduct in the Chait Singh case. The whole proceeding was kept secret from the council, a most unconstitutional act. If the money had been taken at all, it ought to have been accepted as a mere instalment of the debt due to the Company. In truth there is no defence at all for the acceptance of these sums. Modern historians sometimes write as though the practice was defensible, if it can be proved that Hastings spent the money in the public service. But the Regulating Act had forbidden presents absolutely, for the sake of Indian princes. The whole theory underlying them was highly objectionable. Either the giver obtained some special favour from the government, which means corruption, or he did not, which implies deception. The Select Committee of 1781 said with justice that the generosity of the donors "is found in proportion, not to the opulence they possess or to the favours they receive, but to the indigence they feel, and the insults they are exposed to",[1] and Burke for once was surely fully justified when he described presents from Indian rulers as "the donations of misery to power, the gifts of wretchedness to the oppressors".[2] Hastings we must admit seems to have had a blind spot in his mind as regards money matters.

A third case of Hastings's financial operations with an Indian ruler must be mentioned as it throws considerable light on the other two. We have explained how at the end of the Rohilla War the only chieftain of that race left in possession of territory was Faizulla Khan of Rampur. A peace had been made between him and the nawab of Oudh. By it he was to retain not more than 5000 troops and if the nawab was at war he was to "send two or three thousand men according to his ability".[3] Faizulla Khan proved himself an able and vigorous ruler, as Hastings some years later freely admitted. Under him the country prospered and the people were contented. In February, 1778, there were some rumours that he was maintaining an unnecessarily large army. Middleton, Resident in Oudh, said that he might well have acted in this way owing to the injustice and oppression of the nawab, but the commissioner who was sent down to Rampur to investigate reported that Faizulla Khan had "preserved

[1] *Reports from Committees of the House of Commons*, VI, 585.
[2] Bond, *Speeches in the Trial of Warren Hastings*, I, 70.
[3] *Reports from Committees of the House of Commons*, VI, 22.

every article of his treaty inviolate".[1] Faizulla Khan was, as a matter of fact, one of the very small band of Indian rulers like Ranjit Singh, who formed a great admiration for the British nation and recognised once and for all the advantage of trusting them. It is rather a lamentable reflection that he was very nearly entangled and ruined in the policy of Hastings. He asked that the treaty which Champion had made between him and the nawab might now receive the Company's own ratification, on the ground that it was "the only power in which he had confidence, and which he could look up to for protection".[2] The council agreed to his proposal and a special treaty was presented to him. Soon afterwards Faizulla Khan, whose treaty only bound him to assist the nawab, on a hint from Middleton offered to lend the Company 2000 horse. He was formally thanked for this mark of his faithful attachment to the Company and the English nation.

In November, 1780, Hastings obliged the nawab of Oudh to write to Faizulla Khan requiring him to furnish "the quota of troops stipulated by treaty...being 5000 horse".[3] It is charitable to assume that in the original demand Hastings had simply made a mistake about the terms of his treaty. But this excuse could not be made for his subsequent action, for Faizulla Khan replied civilly and moderately pointing out that he was only bound to furnish 2000 or 3000 troops, not necessarily horse, "according to his ability", and offering to discharge his liabilities to the full by sending 2000 horse and 1000 foot. It has been well pointed out that if he had been able to provide 5000 horse he might have been charged with breaking the other article in the treaty which prevented him from maintaining more than that number as his total army. Hastings recorded a minute that Faizulla Khan had "evaded the performance of...the treaty"[4] which was of course a direct falsehood. He then in March, 1781, slightly mitigating his demand, sent a deputation requiring the delivery of 3000 cavalry. As Faizulla Khan firmly but politely maintained his former position, Hastings made a formal protest against him for breaking the treaty and gave the nawab of Oudh permission to resume his lands. That Hastings knew perfectly well that the treaty had not been broken is proved by the amazing minute which he laid before the council at Calcutta:

The conduct of Faizulla Khan, in refusing the aid demanded, though not an absolute breach of treaty was evasive and uncandid...so scrupulous an attention to literal expression, when a more liberal interpretation would have been highly useful and acceptable to us, strongly marks his unfriendly disposition, though it may not impeach his fidelity.[5]

Even at this distance of time the thought that a British administrator could have written such words arouses a flush of shame and it may

---

[1] *Reports from Committees of the House of Commons*, VI, 24.   [2] *Idem*, p. 24.
[3] *Idem*, p. 27.   [4] *Idem*, p. 29.   [5] *Idem*, p. 31.

safely be surmised that such a justification for charging a ruler with disaffection has never been offered before or since. Faizulla Khan escaped ruin partly because Hastings, it is to be hoped with a sense of compunction, postponed for a time the execution of the decree against him, and partly because before it was put into force the directors of the Company much to their honour sent a stern dispatch condemning the whole business and forbidding Hastings to go any further in the matter.

Hastings's final activities in India were devoted to an attempt at reconstruction in Benares and Oudh. Bristow had not succeeded in recovering the Company's balances from that incorrigibly insolvent debtor, the nawab of Oudh, and his own financial transactions seem to have been open to serious criticism. The nawab himself desired, or more probably had been ordered by Hastings to ask for, the recall of the Resident, and the abolition of the residency. Hastings may have been right in demanding a complete change of system in Oudh, but it must be confessed that his action in the matter was curiously tortuous, and no quite adequate explanation of his conduct has ever been offered. He had himself given Bristow the strictest orders to obtain a complete control over the government of Oudh. Soon afterwards he proposed to the council that Bristow should be recalled for having attempted to tyrannise over the nawab, and that the nawab himself, and his minister, Haidar Beg Khan, whom he had in the past severely criticised, should jointly be security for the Company's debts. The council at first defended Bristow on the ground that he had only been endeavouring to carry out his instructions, and that Haidar Beg Khan had consistently opposed all reforms. Finally, however, with great reluctance they accepted Hastings's proposal and agreed that he should proceed to Lucknow to carry out the change. Hastings arrived at the nawab's capital on 27 March, 1784, and attacked his new task with characteristic courage and buoyancy. "It is my ambition", he wrote, "to close my government with the redemption of a great government, family, and nation from ruin...it is the boldest enterprise of my public life, but I confidently hazard the consequences."[1] It is generally said that he was very successful, but there is not much evidence of it; he merely won a respite for the time by a heavy mortgage on the future. He conciliated the nawab by his dominating personality, by removing the residency, and by restoring the jagirs to the begams—an act of restitution which had been ordered by the court of directors. He also claimed to have "adjusted all the disputed accounts between the Nabob Vizier and the Company".[2] The position in Oudh was no doubt easier for the moment, but as soon as Hastings had departed, the hollowness of his reforms was revealed. It then appeared that, if the residency was removed, there had been established in its place an "agency of the governor-general", which

[1] Gleig, op. cit. III, 153.   [2] Idem, p. 184.

interfered quite as drastically in the affairs of Oudh, and was a still greater burden on its revenues. Whereas the expense of Bristow's residency had been £64,202 *per annum*, the cost of the new agency was over £112,000, of which £22,000 was the salary of the agent. As soon as Cornwallis came out, the nawab approached him with exactly the same complaint that he had addressed to Hastings, that the burden upon his country was insupportable. As for the alleged reform of the finances, Cornwallis writes: "I cannot express how much I was concerned...to be witness of the disordered state of his finances and government, and of the desolated appearance of the country. The evils were too alarming to admit of palliation".[1]

In regard to Benares, Hastings laid before the council a scheme for securing the revenues, for removing incapable and oppressive officials, and for safeguarding the tenancy rights of the ryots; but even his unremitting defender Gleig admits, that in the regeneration of Benares he was not so immediately successful as in the case of Oudh.[2] No real reformation was possible, so long as the British Resident was allowed to amass, exclusive of his official salary, an income of £40,000 a year, and Cornwallis could only describe the whole position there as "a scene of the grossest corruption and mismanagement".[3]

While he was at Lucknow, Hastings had an interview with the eldest son of the Moghul emperor, who, a fugitive from the warring factions in Delhi, implored the aid of the British to re-establish his father's throne. It was thoroughly typical of Hastings—typical both of the defiant hardihood, which formed so strong an element in his character, and of the wilful blindness to obstacles lying athwart his path—that he was willing to engage upon this enterprise. Any other man in the face of an imminent retirement, would have been glad enough to disentangle himself from old responsibilities, let alone incur new ones. But Hastings urged upon the council as a reason for taking up the prince's cause "our relaxation from every other external concern"; and had the political effrontery to maintain: "I am not sure, but I believe, that we shall be applauded at home, if we take the generous side of the question".[4] The council very wisely would have none of it, and Hastings, though he felt that their action went some way to save his own interests and peace of mind, could not resist the temptation of flinging a gibe at them for their want of courage and for their propensity to turn from the setting to the rising sun.

---

[1] Ross, *Correspondence of...Marquis Cornwallis*, I, 300.
[2] Gleig, *op. cit.* III, 194. [3] Ross, *op. cit.* I, 253.
[4] Gleig, *op. cit.* III, 191.

CHAPTER XVII

THE IMPEACHMENT OF WARREN HASTINGS

HASTINGS left India in February, 1785, and arrived in England in June, unconscious of the tremendous attack on his life and work that was being prepared by the vindictive enmity and foiled ambition of Francis and the more honourable but misguided zeal of Burke. He was at first well received, especially at court, for George III was one of his firmest supporters. But in January, 1786, Scott, Hastings's agent, challenged Burke to produce his charges. Scott has been severely blamed for this, and contemporary observers, like Wraxall and Fanny Burney, declared that the prosecution was really due to him. Scott was undoubtedly an impetuous and injudicious man, yet, as Professor Holland Rose points out, he would scarcely have acted without Hastings's consent; and since the vote of censure of 28 May, 1782, still remained on the records of the House, the question would have had some day to be raised and settled. Burke moved for papers on 17 February, 1786, and in April brought forward his charges; at first eleven in number, they were afterwards increased to twenty-two. On 1, 2 and 3 May Hastings was granted permission to read a defence at the bar of the House. The actual reading was done partly by himself, partly by Markham, son of the archbishop of York. The step was a serious error in judgment; it would have been better for Hastings to have reserved his defence. The *apologia* was too long and wearied his hearers. It was badly put together and was not always consistent, for parts of it had been drawn up by different hands: by Scott, Shore, Middleton, Markham and Gilpin. It was combative and defiant in tone, for Hastings not only defended himself against censure, he claimed positive merit for all his actions. There was a certain moral splendour in such a demeanour, but in the present temper of the House it was not diplomatic. As one member said: "I see in it a perfect character drawn by the culprit himself, and that character is his own. Conscious triumph in the ability and success of all his measures pervades every sentence". On 1 June parliament refused to accept an impeachment on the charge of the Rohilla War by 119 votes to 79, Dundas and Pitt voting with the majority. On the 13th, the House accepted the charge on the Chait Singh case, and on this occasion Pitt and Dundas voted against Hastings. From that day to this an extraordinary amount of ingenuity has been exercised in the attempt to find some motive, recondite or unworthy, for this action. It has been suggested that Pitt was jealous of Hastings and his favour with the king; that he was over-persuaded by Dundas, who feared that Hastings might succeed him at the Board of Control; that Pitt was not sorry to see the energies of a powerful and able opposition directed to a quarry other than His Majesty's Government. The first of these reasons seems only worthy of the author, Gleig, from whence it sprang. That Hastings, whose career rightly or wrongly had been subject to so much controversy, should ever become President of the Board of Control was entirely impossible. The third suggestion loses sight of the fact that though the trial lasted over seven years, the court only sat in full session 118 days out of that time, and there is not the least reason to suppose that the energy of the opposition in the ordinary work of parliament was in any way diminished.

All this subtlety is beside the mark, and overlooks the fact that there is a very simple and adequate explanation. It must be remembered that, till a full and elaborate defence was put forward at the trial, the evidence in the Chait Singh case looked extremely damaging. There is no reason to suppose that Pitt acted otherwise than as an honest man, that he weighed the evidence carefully, defended Hastings when he could conscientiously do so, as in the matter of the Rohilla War, and reluctantly voted against him where the evidence appeared to be *prima facie* strong. Above all, it often seems to be forgotten that he was only voting for a trial not for a condemnation. Apart from the inherent probabilities of the business, there is plenty of evidence to support this view. We have first the letter of Dundas to Cornwallis, 21 March, 1787:

> The proceeding is not pleasant to many of our friends; and of course from that and many other circumstances, not pleasant to us; but the truth is, when we examined the various articles of charges against him, with his defences, they were so strong, and the defences so perfectly unsupported, it was impossible not to concur.[1]

There is, secondly, a still more important piece of evidence that has we think generally escaped notice, namely a letter of George III to Pitt which is, it may be said, equally creditable to king and minister. George III was always a thorough-going believer in Hastings, and Pitt naturally desired wherever he could to meet the king's wishes. After the adverse vote on the Chait Singh charge, George III wrote:

> Mr. Pitt would have conducted himself yesterday very unlike what my mind ever expects of him if, as he thinks Mr. Hastings' conduct towards the Rajah was too severe, he had not taken the part he did, though it made him coincide with the adverse party. As for myself, I own I do not think it possible in that country to carry on business with the same moderation that is suitable to a European civilised nation.[2]

It may be added that Wilberforce entirely believed in Pitt's integrity; he tells us that Pitt paid as much impartial attention to the case "as if he were a juryman". It is important to remember that there was

---

[1] Ross, *Correspondence of... Marquis Cornwallis*, i, 281.
[2] Stanhope, *Life of William Pitt*, i, 480.

no attempt to constrain men's opinions by the application of party discipline. The colleagues of the prime minister were left free to vote as they chose, and Grenville, Lord Mulgrave and the attorney-general opposed their chief in debate. There is a final argument which will only appeal to a limited class but will appeal with irresistible strength—we should have to alter our whole conception of the serene, pure and lofty mind of Pitt, if we believed that on such a question he were capable of being swayed by mere motives of the lowest political expediency.

On 7 February, 1787, the charge relating to the begams of Oudh was introduced by Sheridan in a speech, which was said to have eclipsed all previous displays of eloquence ever heard in the House of Commons, and the debate was adjourned that members might not vote till their minds were freed from the spell of the orator. On 8 February, the charge was accepted by 175 votes to 68, and finally in May the decision was made to impeach on twenty-two articles. These articles attempted to cover the whole of Hastings's administration. He was charged with having violated treaties made with the nawab of Oudh, with having interfered in that ruler's internal affairs, with having unrighteously sold to him Kora and Allahabad, with oppression and cruelty in the case of Chait Singh and the begams of Oudh, with an arbitrary settlement of the land revenues of Bengal, with fraudulent dealings in contracts and commissions and the acceptance of presents and bribes. The managers for the Commons were Burke, Fox, Sheridan, Pelham, Windham, Sir Gilbert Elliot, Charles Grey, Sir James Erskine and twelve others. The House most properly refused to allow Francis to be one of them. Hastings's counsel were Law (afterwards Lord Ellenborough), Plumer (afterwards Master of the Rolls), and Dallas (afterwards Chief Justice of the Common Pleas).

The impeachment was a calamitous mistake and before it had gone very far it developed into something like a cruel wrong. It was not unreasonable that some enquiry should be held; indeed, after the vote of censure of May, 1782, it was perhaps essential. The fair course would have been to hear Hastings's case and then parliament might have expressed a temperate disapproval of some of the methods he had employed in the case of Chait Singh and the begams of Oudh, and might well have commented severely upon the laxity of his ideas of account-keeping. Having ensured that these unhappy features of his period of office should not be allowed to become precedents for British policy in the East, they should have recognised the immense difficulties that confronted Hastings and acknowledged his magnificent services to his country. A grant of some high honour from the crown would naturally have followed, and the energies of the reformers might have been devoted, with Hastings's aid and co-operation, to amending the whole system of the Indian government.

The impeachment of Hastings was an anachronism, a cumbrous method of inflicting most unmerited suffering on one of the greatest Englishmen of his time, something very like a travesty of justice.

For this there were several reasons. The trial was intolerably lengthy. It lasted from February, 1788, to April, 1795, through seven sessions of parliament and 148 sittings of the court. The *personnel* of the judges was constantly changing—during the seven years there were 180 changes in the peerage. There was a great inequality between the defence and the attack. Hastings's counsel consisted of trained lawyers—all of them afterwards rose to high judicial office—men who used, and rightly used, all the technical devices of the law to protect their client. His accusers were parliamentary orators and debaters, masters of invective and controversy, but men unused to weigh testimony, to substantiate their charges in the cold and dry atmosphere of a court of law or to be guided by the rules of evidence. Lord Thurlow, Hastings's friend, and Lord Loughborough, who was on the whole hostile, agreed in reprobating the "looseness and inaccuracy" with which the articles were drawn up. They formed indeed an absurd hotchpot of charges, some involving, had they been proved, heinous guilt, others mere errors of policy or pardonable miscalculations. Over the whole trial there lies the false and histrionic glitter of an elaborate and self-conscious display. Sheridan's speeches were dramatic entertainments for connoisseurs of oratorical invective. The Whig party made the occasion a manifesto for their humanitarian sentiments and an exercise in vituperation. Burke, whose motives were the most reputable, for he was entirely sincere, was the worst sinner of all, in his utter surrender to a violent animosity against the accused and his refusal to accord to him even those rights and facilities which it would have been unrighteous to deny to the worst of criminals. Through constant disputes as to the admissibility of evidence and through the lack of technical juridical skill on the part of the prosecution the trial lasted just over seven years. Gradually it was found necessary to drop most of the charges. In 1791 it was resolved to proceed only with those dealing with Chait Singh, the begams of Oudh, fraudulent contracts, presents and bribes; the verdict was finally given on 23 April, 1795. Hastings was acquitted on all the articles on which a verdict was recorded. The highest minorities against him were on the charges relating to Chait Singh and the begams of Oudh, where the voting was 23 to 6.

The Lords reviewed the evidence with the greatest care. Though the trial had opened before 160 peers, only 29 recorded their votes. This was due to the fact that, by an informal understanding honourably observed, only those Lords actually voted who had either attended the trial from its commencement, or had been present during a majority of the days when the court was sitting. Lord Carnarvon had suggested that the House should itself determine "what lords had, and what lords had not, a right to vote".[1] But in the end it was resolved to accept the opinion of Lord Thurlow "that every lord must draw the line for himself; his own conscience and his own sense of honour must determine how many days' attendance entitled him to vote".[2] In the discussion Lord Thurlow and the bishop of Rochester were strong supporters of Hastings. Loughborough, the lord chancellor, was on the whole against him; Lord Mansfield, though a former friend, felt himself bound to censure some of his acts. It is clear that even Hastings's warmest allies were hard put to it to defend some parts of his financial administration and in the last resort could only do so on the plea that his difficulties were great and that "he was a man uncommonly regardless of money". It seems fairly certain that some votes were given for an acquittal, not because the judges condoned every act of the accused, but because they held that the long torture of the trial was a more than adequate punishment for some errors of judgment, financial irregularities and even acts of unjust severity committed in circumstances of supreme crisis and peril. For long it had been clear that this was the only possible issue. The curious thing is that Burke to the last refused to see it. He seemed determined to reach the acme of unreason and folly:

The crimes with which we charge the prisoner at the bar are substantial crimes. ...They are crimes which have their rise in the wicked dispositions of men...in avarice, rapacity, pride, cruelty, ferocity, malignity of temper, haughtiness, insolence; in short, my Lords, in everything that manifests a heart blackened to the very blackest—a heart dyed deep in blackness—a heart corrupted, vitiated and gangrened to the very core.[3]

It is not surprising that men revolted from such a monstrous position.

The defence, on the other hand, did their best to build a golden bridge for the retreat of the managers, and perhaps showed, by the reasonableness of their attitude in this respect, that they recognised that there was a case to meet and to defend.

"The Commons", they said, "have well exercised their honour by preferring a charge and bringing it here to be discussed, to know whether it is true or not; and it is no dishonour or disgrace to the House of Commons to say, ultimately, that upon that inquiry, it turns out that the charge is not well founded....Their object is not the individual, but the crime. If the crime does not exist, they have no resentment against Mr. Hastings...the House of Commons and every individual member of it has no other wish but that the charge should be fairly sifted and examined, to see whether their suspicions are well or ill founded; and...every member of the House of Commons will rejoice if it should turn out, in the event, that Mr. Hastings is able to exonerate himself from these imputations that have been cast upon him and upon the nation."[4]

But the sentiments thus described had no place in the heart of the leading manager. Burke would have none of it:

"No", he cried in answer to Plumer, "we never would, nor can we conceive that we should, do other than pass from this bar with indignation, with rage and

---

[1] *Debates of the House of Lords on the Evidence...*, p. 11.   [2] *Idem*, p. 13.
[3] Bond, *Speeches in the Trial of Warren Hastings*, I, 6–7.   [4] *Idem*, II, 692–3.

despair, if the House of Commons should, upon such a defence as has here been made against such a charge as they have produced—if they should be foiled, baffled and defeated in it. No, my Lords, we never should forget it. A long, lasting, deep, bitter memory of it would sink into our minds; for we have not come here to you in the rash heat of a day, with that fervour which sometimes prevails in popular assemblies and frequently misleads them. No; if we have been guilty of error, it is a long deliberate error; an error the fruit of long labourious inquiry.... We are not come here to compromise matters at all. We do admit that our fame, our honours, nay, the very being of the inquisitorial power of the House of Commons are gone, if this man is not guilty. We are not come here to solve a problem, but to call for justice.....I, for myself and for others, make this deliberate determination, I nuncupate this solemn and serious vow—that we do glow with an immortal hatred against all this corruption."[1]

It is not surprising that when a motion of thanks was made to the managers of the impeachment, one member declared that he would be willing to agree, if the leading manager were excepted, "who had by his conduct disgraced and degraded the House of Commons". But Burke's errors were the errors of a noble, if utterly misguided soul. He never recovered from the verdict. The day after it was given he left the House of Commons for ever.

Throughout the trial—in the darkest hour of his fate—Hastings had borne himself with the same dauntless courage which had enabled him to hold his head high under the cruel "bludgeonings of chance" in scenes far distant from Westminster Hall. Nothing, not even the scorching invective of his accusers, nor the long mental agony of the seven years' ordeal, had been able to break that indomitable spirit. As in the council chamber at Calcutta, so at the bar of the House of Lords, treatment that would have crushed most men to the earth seemed only to brace him to a stubborn, heroic and provocative defiance. For his most questionable acts he claimed not pardon or indulgence but full justification and unmeasured praise. In facing his accusers he showed in every gesture and every inflection of his voice that icy yet burning scorn which sprang from his unconquerable belief in his own rectitude and which drove his adversary, Burke, into frenzies of impotent anger.

And so perhaps the greatest Englishman who ever ruled India, a man who with some ethical defects possessed in superabundant measure the mobile and fertile brain, the tireless energy and the lofty fortitude which distinguishes only the supreme statesman, was left with his name cleared but his fortunes ruined, and every hope of future distinction and even employment taken from him. The East India Company came not ungenerously to his assistance, and Hastings passed from the purview of history to spend the long-drawn evening of his arduous life, surrounded by a circle of devoted friends, in the peaceful seclusion of his recovered ancestral home at Daylesford.

[1] Bond, *Speeches in the Trial of Warren Hastings*, IV, 332, 334, 345.

CHAPTER XVIII

LEGISLATION AND GOVERNMENTS, 1786–1818

THE legislation of 1784–6 was developed and in some respects extended when the Company's privileges were reviewed by parliament in 1793 and 1813. On each occasion the principal object of attack was the commercial monopoly of the eastern trade, and on each occasion the Company had to give up something of its rights. In 1793 it was obliged to allow a certain amount of tonnage for private merchants' goods both outward and homeward; in 1813 it lost its monopoly of the Indian though not of the China trade. In this respect legislative action merely anticipated by a few years the consequences of economic developments. The application of machinery and power to the cotton manufacture and calico printing would in any case have soon brought to an end its main commercial activity in India—the export to Europe of cotton piece-goods. After a period of abnormal activity during the wars with France, this rapidly declined, and expired about the end of the third decade of the nineteenth century, just before the commercial powers of the Company were finally abolished by the act of 1833.

In the field of general policy the main tendency was to develop and emphasise that consciousness of moral obligation in administering the Company's possessions which had marked the act of 1784. In 1793 Wilberforce had striven, though in vain, to procure the insertion in the act of provisions for the admission and encouragement of missionaries in India. In that he had been defeated; but in 1813 section 33 declared that "it is the duty of this country to promote the interest and happiness of the native inhabitants of the British dominions in India", and section 43 empowered the government to expend not less than a lakh of rupees on the revival and encouragement of learning. At the same time, although missionaries were not specifically named, a section, which clearly had them in view, empowered the Board of Control to give licences of residence in India to persons improperly refused them by the court of directors; and another section set up a bishop and archdeacons in India.

So far as political institutions went, Pitt's India Act and the supplementary acts of 1786 had already defined the outlines of the Anglo-Indian constitution, which, though developed by subsequent legislation, was not fundamentally altered so long as the Company continued to exist. However, a good many changes in detail took place, and the actual working of the superior institutions then set up demands statement and illustration. This is particularly necessary as regards the Home Government, although the only formal changes of any moment were the establishment of a paid board by the Charter Act of 1793 in lieu of the unpaid board set up in 1784, and the declaration of British sovereignty over the Company's eastern possessions in the Charter Act of 1813—which continued the administration in the Company "without prejudice to the undoubted sovereignty of the Crown of the United Kingdom...in and over the same".

Meanwhile the board rapidly lost its powers, which were concentrated in the hands of a single person, the president. This change was not effected without some ill-feeling. Henry Dundas had from the first been the moving spirit, to the great indignation of some of his colleagues, especially Lord Sydney, who protested against the way in which Dundas pushed the interest of Scotsmen in India.[1] In 1786 it was intended to make the change formal; "In which case", wrote Dundas, "I suppose your humble servant not only in reality but declaredly will be understood as the cabinet minister for India".[2] But although this idea was ultimately carried out by the withdrawal of the *ex-officio* members from attending at the board, to the last the president required the formal assent, first of two and then of one of his colleagues to legalise his proceedings. The position of the president as regards the cabinet varied. It depended on the position of the person holding the office. So long as Dundas continued to hold it, his intimacy with Pitt ensured his inclusion in the cabinet; but others, Minto for example, held it without a seat in the cabinet.[3] Relations with the court of directors also varied. Dundas almost invariably took a high hand with the court. At one time he had even contemplated taking all the administration out of the hands of the Company and leaving it with nothing but the conduct of the East India trade.[4] But this probably seemed to Pitt too near an imitation of the bills of Fox, and even the hints which Dundas had let fall revived something of the language which had resounded through the country in 1783. When the negotiations for the renewal of the charter in 1793 had been completed, a member of the Company, in moving a vote of thanks to the directors and the ministry,

hoped by Englishmen it would be long remembered that an administration in the meridian of power, well knowing that the patronage of India would render that power immortal, and almost urged by the people to grasp it,...had had the magnanimity to refuse it and assign as reason to the House of Commons...that such an accession of power to the executive government was not compatible with the safety of the British constitution.[5]

But though in this project Dundas was foiled, in lesser matters he had his own way. When, for instance, in 1788 the Company protested against the dispatch to India of four royal regiments, and declined

---

[1] Sydney to Pitt, 24 September, 1784, *ap.* Stanhope, *Life of Pitt*, I, 227.
[2] *Cornwallis Correspondence*, I, 244.   [3] *Minto in India*, p. 3.
[4] *Cornwallis Correspondence*, II, 13.
[5] *Debates at the East India House in* 1793, p. 120.

to provide the funds for their payment, a Declaratory Act was promptly passed, legalising the ministerial view of the question.[1] In the appointment of governors to the subordinate presidencies, too, he used the power of the board relentlessly to enforce his own wishes on the directors. But later presidents certainly exercised a less complete control. Castlereagh, for instance, wrote to Wellesley:

Your lordship is aware how difficult and delicate a task it is for the person who fills my situation (particularly when strong feelings have been excited) to manage such a body as the court of directors so as to shield the person in yours from any unpleasant interference on their part.[2]

The fact was that each part of the Home Government could make the position of the governor-general intolerable if it pleased; so that despite the superiority of the Board of Control and its access to the cabinet, and despite its power of sending orders through the Secret Committee of the directors, which the latter could neither discuss nor disclose, policy in general was determined, when disputes arose, on a basis of compromise; just as in the matter of appointments both sides had in effect a power of veto, so also, in discussions about policy, neither body cared to provoke the other overmuch save in exceptional circumstances. There were two recognised methods by which the orders to be transmitted to the governments in India might be prepared. In matters of urgency the president himself might cause a dispatch to be prepared, which was then sent to the Secret Committee, which could only sign it and send it off. Dispatches from India in like manner might be addressed to the Secret Committee, in which case they would only be laid before the court of directors if and when the president desired. But this was not the procedure generally adopted. Usually the chairman of the court would informally propose a course of action to the president; and the matter would be discussed between them, either in conversation or by private letters. The chairman would then informally propose a dispatch, which would be prepared at the India House, and sent to the Board of Control together with a mass of documentary information on which the dispatch was founded. This was technically called a Previous Communication. It was returned with approval or correction to the Company, and after reconsideration sent a second time to Westminster—the document on this second submission being called a Draft. This double submission—informal and formal—resulted from the clause in the act of 1784 by which amendments had to be completed by the board within fourteen days. After 1813 the term was extended to two months. If the court concurred with the amendments, the dispatch would then be sent off; but if they did not, the discussions might continue, in the last resort the board securing obedience by a *mandamus* from the Court of King's Bench. The

[1] 28 Geo. III, c. 8. Cf. *Cornwallis Correspondence*, I, 349, 354.
[2] *Wellesley Despatches*, III, 92.

procedure renders it exceedingly difficult without the information afforded by private correspondence to define the actual part played by the various presidents of the board in the determination of policy; the Previous Communications have seldom been preserved; and so one seldom knows to what extent a Draft was influenced by the preliminary discussions between the president and the chair.[1] The system was certainly slow and clumsy. But the importance of such a defect was largely neutralised by the length of time that communications took to reach India, and the large degree of discretion which the Indian governments necessarily enjoyed. With all its defects it was a vast improvement over the ruinous system which had preceded it, when the ministry was seeking to control Indian policy by a system of influence, and when there was no certain link between the cabinet and the head of the Indian administration such as was now provided by the ministry's share in the appointment of the governor-general, and the possibility of sending direct orders from the ministry to the governor-general through the president of the board and the Secret Committee of the court of directors. In the last resort and in matters of real importance the ministry could enforce its will on the most factious court of directors or on the most independent of governors-general; while no governor-general was now exposed to the shocking danger which had confronted Warren Hastings of having to determine policy without even a probability of support from either side of the House of Commons.

In other ways, too, the government of Bengal had been strengthened. Previous chapters have illustrated the fatal manner in which the limited powers of the governor-general and the limited control of the Bengal Government over the subordinate presidencies had worked. Under the new system the governor-general could enforce his will over refractory councillors if he were convinced of the need of doing so. Nor was he longer exposed to the opposition of Madras or Bombay without adequate powers of repressing it. The act of 1773 only gave a superintending power, and that with exceptions and limitations, with regard to the declaration of war and the making of peace; so that it still lay within the powers of the subordinate governments by their previous conduct of policy to render war or peace inevitable. But Pitt's India Act gave power of control over "all transactions with the country powers or the application of the revenues or forces...in time of war, or any such other points as shall be referred by the court of directors to their control". And, further, to prevent disputes regarding the extent of the powers of the government of Bengal, orders from the latter were to be obeyed in every case except only where contrary orders had been received from England and were still unknown to the superintending government.[2] The supplementary act

[1] Foster, *John Company*, pp. 246 *sqq.*
[2] Sections 31 and 32.

of 1786 had permitted the union in the same hands of the offices of governor-general and commander-in-chief; so that no effective opposition was now to be expected from the military as distinct from the civil power. But in spite of all these extensions, one serious limitation still remained—that imposed by the distances and the slow communications of India. Calcutta was a long way from Madras and Bombay; and what would be the position of the governor-general if he quitted Bengal and went to one of the subordinate presidencies to supervise or conduct affairs in person? The question emerged during the government of Cornwallis, when he went down to Madras to assume the command against Tipu Sultan. He was formally granted separate powers by his council; but as it was held in England that the council had no authority so to do, an act was passed[1] validating what had been done under such defective authority; and in the Charter Act of 1793[2] provision was made for the appointment of a vice-president during the governor-general's absence from Bengal, and the governor-general himself was empowered (1) to act with a local council in all things as with the council of Bengal, and (2) to issue orders to any of the Company's servants without previously communicating them to the local council. By virtue of these alterations the governor-general was enabled to proceed to either of the subordinate provinces and assume the full control of affairs there. The result was seen in the swift overthrow of Tipu, when Wellesley, following Cornwallis's example, proceeded to Madras in 1798 in order to control the preparations for the war with Mysore. Thus the later governors-general were freed from the restraints which had so disastrously hampered the action of Warren Hastings, and which he had vainly tried to overcome by the futile expedient of nominating residents on behalf of the Supreme Government at Madras and Bombay.

Nor were these statutory provisions more than was actually needed to keep the control of policy under one hand. Even Cornwallis had had to meet counteraction on the part of the governor of Madras, the unworthy John Hollond, who, mainly, it appears, owing to his concern in the nawab's debt, not only dispatched military expeditions without informing the Bengal Government, but also, when ordered to afford assistance to the raja of Travancore against Tipu, tried to bargain with the raja for the assistance it was his duty to give. Lord Hobart, governor of Madras, would order the naval squadron about without reference to the governor-general, Sir John Shore, and at last quarrelled so violently with his official superior that he preferred to return to England and forfeit his ultimate succession to the post of governor-general rather than continue under Shore's orders.[3] Even Wellesley was, or thought he was, opposed in the

---

[1] 31 Geo. III, c. 40. [2] Sections 52–54.
[3] Teignmouth, *Life of Shore*, I, 372; *Cornwallis Correspondence*, II, 307.

preparations which he ordered for the war against Tipu, and used very direct language on the subject of his superior powers not only to the subordinate officers of the government of Bengal, but also to the subordinate presidencies. "The main-spring of the government of India", said he, "can never be safely touched by any other hand than that of the principal mover."[1]

In another way also a great change for the better was made. Before the act of 1784 patronage was exercised in a peculiarly demoralising way. The home authorities, not content with having the nomination of the persons who were to enter the Company's civil and military services, had also sought to control their promotion. Covenanted servants and military officers would take a trip to England in order to gain admission to council, appointment to some lucrative office, or the command of a regiment or an army out of their turn. The relatives of directors expected special promotion without regard to their seniority or talents. Laurence Sulivan, for example, looked to restoring the fallen fortunes of his family by employing his influence in favour of his son. Men with powerful connections were constantly appearing in India—the illegitimate half-brother of Charles Fox, for instance—expecting to be provided for. The necessary result was that the government in India lacked that most salutary power of rewarding merit by promotion. Hastings in particular had found this a most grievous tax. But Dundas's legislation cut at the root of these pernicious practices. In the first place the India Act forbade vacancies in the councils to be filled by other than covenanted servants except in the case of the governor-general, the governors, and the commanders-in-chief, and confined promotion to due order of seniority except in special cases when full details were immediately to be sent to the court of directors. Then the act of 1786[2] limited the nomination to vacancies to the Company's servants on the spot and prescribed terms of service as the minima for offices carrying more than certain rates of pay. The Charter Act of 1793 went a step further and decreed that

all vacancies happening in any of the offices, places, or employments in the civil line of the Company's service in India (being under the degree of councillor) shall be from time to time filled up and supplied from amongst the civil servants of the said company belonging to the presidency wherein such vacancies shall respectively happen....No office, place or employment, the salary, perquisites, and emoluments whereof shall exceed £500 *per annum* shall be conferred upon or granted to any of the said servants who shall not have been actually resident in India as a covenanted servant of the said company for the space of three years at the least in the whole....

Six years' service was the minimum for posts of £1500 a year, nine years for those of £3000, and twelve years for those of £4000. The net results of these enactments were (1) that the flood of adventurers into India

---

[1] *Wellesley Despatches*, I, 290, 528.
[2] 26 Geo. III, c. 16, sections 13–14.

was checked; (2) that the jobs of the directors were curtailed; and (3) that after 1786 the civil and military services, and after 1793 the civil service, secured a monopoly of well-paid administrative employment in the old provinces, though not in new acquisitions. The policy of Cornwallis in confining employment in the higher ranks to Europeans had thus a legislative basis which has often been forgotten. Even had he wished to do so, it would not have been legal for him to nominate an Indian to any post carrying more than £500 a year, for no Indian was a Company's servant within the meaning of the acts.

And while the recruitment to the higher administrative posts was thus being limited to the members of the Company's service, the practice of appointment from home to special posts was also curtailed. "The system of patronage, which you so justly reprobated", wrote Shore to Hastings in 1787, "and which you always found so grievous a tax, has been entirely subverted."[1] Cornwallis put the matter to one of the directors very bluntly.

"I must freely acknowledge", he wrote, "that before I accepted the arduous task of governing this country, I did understand that the practice of naming persons from England to succeed to offices of great trust and importance to the public welfare of this country, without either knowing or regarding whether such persons were in any way qualified for such offices, was entirely done away. If unfortunately so pernicious a system should be again revived, I should feel myself obliged to request that some other person might immediately take from me the responsibility of governing...."[2]

A little later difficulties arose from the directors' nominations to posts on the board of revenue at Madras and their refusal to confirm Wellesley's nomination to the post of Political Secretary. But these were due rather to the directors' distrust of Wellesley's policy than to any revival of the old system. Save as regards the highest posts of all, the tendency was for the directors to be limited to the recruitment of their services by the nomination of writers and cadets, while the executive governments in India determined their promotion and employment.

On the whole the covenanted servants benefited by these changes. The old system had been exceedingly unhealthy, promoting intrigue, and that most vicious practice of private correspondence between subordinates and members of the direction in England on matters of public concern, in which the officials sought to secure favour in England by communicating news that they had learnt in the discharge of their official duties. This custom was prohibited (though not suppressed) in 1785. Burke expressed great indignation at the prohibition,[3] but it was in fact the natural and necessary concomitant of the introduction of a modern system of administration, under which it neither is, nor is thought desirable to guard against the misconduct of the heads of the government by such indirect and devious means.

[1] Teignmouth, *Life of Shore*, I, 136. [2] *Cornwallis Correspondence*, I, 421.
[3] *Life and Letters of Sir G. Elliot*, I, 100.

In one direction, however, the covenanted servants lost ground. With the appointment of Cornwallis they became practically ineligible for the highest post in India. It is true that he was immediately succeeded by Shore, who was a covenanted servant; but his appointment was already regarded as somewhat exceptional in nature.[1] In 1802, in discussing the selection of Wellesley's successor, Castlereagh, who inclined strongly to the nomination of another Company's servant, Barlow, nevertheless wrote, "I am aware that there is the strongest objection on general grounds to the governments abroad being filled by the Company's servants, but there is no rule which is universal".[2] But having heard what Wellesley had to say on this head, and in view of the renewal of war in Europe, Pitt and Castlereagh decided to try to find a suitable man in England.[3] It will be remembered that Cornwallis was sent out, only to die; and so Barlow succeeded to the chair. But his succession only proved, even more strikingly than the government of Shore had done, that under the new *régime* the Company's servants were apt to shirk responsibility and yield too ready a compliance with the wishes, right or wrong, of their honourable masters, the court of directors. Nor was the experiment repeated until the time of Lawrence, although the directors made a strong push in favour of Metcalfe in 1834, in opposition to the president of the board, Charles Grant, who had (it seems) proposed himself. But on that occasion Melbourne's ministry rejected the recommendation, founding its opposition on principles which had been laid down by George Canning during his short tenure of the presidency of the board.[4] The system of appointing the governor-general from England must on the whole be considered to have worked well. The persons selected were in fact of very various character and talent; two indeed were failures outright; but in general their rank and standing secured for them a more ready and willing obedience than the Company's servants would have accorded to one of themselves; moreover, these English noblemen brought with them a wider experience of affairs, a broader knowledge of politics, a higher standard of political ethics than were likely to be found in India; nor should it be forgotten that they carried much more weight, and that their representations were treated with greater respect by the home authorities than would have been the case with the Company's servants.

The same system was extended to the governorships of the two subordinate presidencies. The earliest example of this was the appointment of Lord Macartney to the government of Madras in 1780. He was succeeded by a soldier, Sir Archibald Campbell, who

[1] *Cornwallis Correspondence*, II, 219.
[2] *Wellesley Despatches*, III, 91.
[3] *Idem*, IV, 533.
[4] Kaye, *Life of Tucker*, p. 449; Kaye, *Life of Metcalfe*, II, 237 n.; and *Wellesley Papers*, II, 248, 259.

had had experience of administration in the West Indies. Lord Hobart and Lord Clive (son of the hero of Plassey) filled the same office before the end of the century. But in the case of the subordinate presidencies the line was less firmly drawn and exceptions made less reluctantly. At almost the same time Elphinstone and Munro received the governments of Bombay and Madras, in recognition of their services in the last Maratha War.

"The more general practice of the court", Canning wrote during his short tenure of the Board of Control, "is to look for their governors rather among persons of eminence in this country than among the servants of the Company; and when I profess myself to be of opinion that this practice is generally wiser, it is, I am confident, unnecessary to assure you that such an opinion is founded on considerations the very reverse of unfriendly to the Company's real interest; but the extraordinary zeal and ability which have been displayed by the Company's servants civil and military in the course of the late brilliant and complicated war, and the peculiar situation in which the results of that war have placed the affairs of your presidency at Bombay, appear to me to constitute a case in which any deviation from the general practice in favour of your own service might be at once becoming and expedient."[1]

On the whole the system was less advantageous in the case of the provincial governors than in that of the governor-general. The men willing to accept these second-rate posts were mostly second-rate men. Lord William Bentinck is the only man of real eminence who can be named among them; and Dalhousie was probably justified in advocating the abandonment of the practice.[2] The main advantage that can be fairly claimed for this extension of the recruitment from the English political world is that it multiplied contact between it and India and increased the number of persons in the British parliament who really knew what India or a part of it was like.

In form these subordinate governments were framed on the same plan as that of Bengal. The governor had a council of two civil members with the commander-in-chief when that post was not joined to his own. He enjoyed the same power of overruling his council as the governor-general. Under the Governor in Council were three boards—the Board of Trade, the Board of Revenue, and the Military Board—which conducted the detail of the administration, and normally were presided over by a member of council. Under the Board of Revenue there was at Madras, where large territories had come under the Company's control in the decade 1793–1802, a complicated district system (described in chapter xxv). At Bombay, where the great accession of territory only came with the peace of 1818, the district administration was on the whole of later development, and will be described in the succeeding volume.

The main defect in the organisation thus established under the legislation of the period was the union of general responsibility for

---

[1] Colebrooke, *Life of Elphinstone*, II, 100.
[2] Lee-Warner, *Life of Dalhousie*, II, 252.

the whole of British India and the special administration of Bengal in the hands of the governor-general and council. It meant almost certainly that the whole influence of the supreme government would be devoted to the imposition of the Bengal system on the other provinces, irrespective of its suitability, and that the Supreme Government would find itself with much more work to do than could be done by any one set of men. The first of these evils was that principally evident in the period here dealt with; the second that of the period which succeeded.

CHAPTER XIX

THE EXCLUSION OF THE FRENCH, 1784–1815

THE French rivalry must be reckoned in that series of lucky events and fortunate conditions which did so much in the second half of the eighteenth century to enable the English East India Company to rise to a position of predominance in India. Without intending it, French adventurers played the part of *agents provocateurs*. Indian princes were encouraged by their sanguine estimates of French co-operation to entertain designs against the English, while the impossibility of effective French support, from European considerations in time of peace and from lack of the necessary naval superiority in time of war, ensured that they would take up arms without the assistance on which they had reckoned. Since the previous century there had always been a certain number of adventurers in the service of the Indian states; and after the great period of Dupleix various causes combined to increase their numbers, activity and influence. The career of Dupleix, like that of Clive, had served to attract great attention in his country to India. It seemed to Frenchmen, as to Englishmen of the time, the land of easy wealth, so that the number of those who sought fortunes there rose. At the same time the decay of the Moghul Empire, and the rise of the numerous military states on its ruins, enlarged the demand for military leaders and organisers; while the resounding victories won by European arms, whether French or English, raised the value set upon all who could pretend to any knowledge of European tactics and discipline; so that the adventurers found themselves no longer mere artillerymen but commanders of regiments and brigades, personally consulted by the princes whose pay they drew. Finally the ideas of Dupleix and the Anglo-French rivalry which had sprung out of them had opened out new possibilities promising personal gain and national aggrandisement.

The result was that from the government of Warren Hastings down to that of Wellesley the Indian courts were full of Frenchmen, commanding large or small bodies of sepoys, and eager for the most part to serve their country by the exercise of their profession. A typical example of them is afforded by René Madec, who, after serving in the ranks under Lally and then joining the English service for a while, deserted and passed from court to court, serving now a Jat chief, now Shah 'Alam, and now Begam Samru, until in 1778 he retired and went home to his native Brittany. With him and others in a like condition Chevalier, head of French affairs in Bengal, was in constant communication, discussing schemes, now for the march of Madec into Bengal, now for the cession and occupation of Sind, whence a

French army was to march to Delhi, and then drive the English into the sea. Chevalier's policy was to spread great ideas abroad regarding French power, and he had no hesitation in offering to the emperor in 1772 the services of two or three thousand Frenchmen from the Isle of France. Madec in 1775 writes from Agra that when war breaks out with the English he will march down the Ganges and ravage the upper provinces of Bengal, holding the towns to ransom and doing his utmost to destroy the English revenues.[1] A little later we find St Lubin and Montigny at Poona, making treaties which neither party attempted to carry out, and venting large promises which the Marathas were much too astute to trust.

On the whole these political activities were more harmful than advantageous to the French cause, for they achieved nothing beyond a reputation for big words. Nor did Bussy's expedition of 1782 add much to the French position. It arrived too late. Before it had accomplished anything, it was paralysed by the news of peace, and that too of a peace which merely put the French back where they had been before. It was difficult for their agents to persuade Indian princes of the great successes they claimed to have won in America when they still remained in their old position of inferiority in India. Souillac might write assuring Sindhia that the English had been driven out of all their American possessions and declare that now the great object of the king of France was to compel the English to restore the provinces which they had stolen from the princes of India;[2] but Sindhia simply did not believe him. Bussy, who viewed the position with tired and disappointed eyes, wrote nevertheless with great truth to the minister, de Castries (9 September, 1783), that the terms of peace had produced an unfavourable impression, and that impossible hopes of Indian co-operation had been raised in France by the fables sent home inspired by vanity and self-interest. He actually advised the recall of the various parties serving with Indian princes, as being nothing but a lot of brigands—*un amas de bandits*.[3]

As regarded the future, too, the French plans were quite indefinite. It was proposed, for instance, to remove the French headquarters from Pondichery, as too near the English power at Madras, and too remote from the possible allies of France—Tipu and the Marathas. For a while the minister thought of removing it to Mahé on the other side of India, where perhaps Tipu would cede a suitable extent of territory, or else to Trinkomali, if it could be obtained from the Dutch, or to some point on the coast of Burma.[4] But either of the last two presupposed the maintenance of a large naval force. Bussy again went to the heart of the matter. All this consideration of possible allies, he said, was beside the mark. Pondichery was suitable enough if the ministry would find the money to fortify it and garrison it with

---

[1] Barbé, *René Madec, passim*.   [2] Gaudart, *Catalogue*, I, 321.
[3] *Idem*, p. 137.   [4] *Idem*, p. 183.

1800 Europeans and 2000 sepoys; the French should do like the English
—depend on themselves alone.[1] The only way to get allies, he says
again a year later, is to send out large military and naval forces with
plenty of money, and "everything to the contrary that you will be
told on this point will be derived from that charlatanry that has so
long obscured the facts".[2]

As regards possible allies against the English in India the views of
the ministry were frankly hostile. In 1787 de Castries resolved to
recall one Frenchman, Aumont, who was then with the Nizam, and
to replace the French agent, Montigny, at Poona by a Brahman
vakil, since nothing was to be got out of the first, while with the second
no common interests could be discovered. But Tipu was to be informed
of the French desire to co-operate with him in hindering the English
from remaining the masters of India. The king's intention, de Castries
went on, is to

tâcher de conserver les princes de l'Inde dans la tranquillité entre eux jusqu'à ce
qu'il soit en mesure de les secourir, et comme nous parviendrons sans doute à
combiner un jour nos forces avec celles de la Hollande, il faut attendre que cet
arrangement soit fini pour pouvoir poser quelques bases avec cette puissance.[3]

Indeed at this moment, when Holland was sharply split into French
and Orangist factions, the French seem to have counted on being
able in a time of war to employ Dutch naval power and naval bases
against the English, as partly came to pass in the Revolutionary and
Napoleonic Wars, though even then the French were to find that the
lukewarm assistance which they received from the Dutch was a poor
counterpoise to the overwhelming force of the English navy and an
incomplete compensation for having to protect the Dutch possessions
as well as their own. In 1787, when these proposals were being
considered, the Orangists were urging the adoption of an exactly
opposite policy, that of an alliance with Great Britain. Neither treaty
was formally concluded; but the eyes of both French and English
seem to have been fixed upon the same points—Dundas declaring that
the only thing which would make the alliance useful to us was the
cession of Trinkomali, while de Castries issued orders that in the event
of war with England Pondichery was to be evacuated and all troops
and munitions of war removed to Trinkomali, which harbour seems
to have been promised them by the French party in Holland.[4]

It was while these matters were under discussion that Tipu sent to
France the first of the embassies by which he tried in vain to secure
material assistance against the English in the event of war. The
ambassadors proceeded by a French vessel, the *Aurore*, and were
received with every courtesy; but beyond that they obtained nothing,
for, as has been seen, de Castries did not, and indeed with any degree

[1] Gaudart, *Catalogue*, I, 142.   [2] *Idem*, pp. 157 *sqq.*
[3] *Idem*, p. 361.
[4] *Cornwallis Correspondence*, I, 357; Wilks, *Historical Sketches*, II, 124.

of financial prudence could not, desire so soon to renew the struggle. But they must have received a good deal of encouragement in view of future contingencies, and that must have contributed to stiffen Tipu's attitude. However, with the usual English good fortune, Tipu selected as the time for his provocative attack upon Travancore the time when the French were much too engrossed by their domestic affairs to spare a thought to India; so that he was left to meet Cornwallis's attack alone, and had already been reduced to sign away half his kingdom and surrender much of his treasure before the year 1793 renewed war in Europe.

Indeed French intrigues had been somewhat interrupted by the outbreak of the Revolution. In the French settlements in India the latter produced more excitement than bloodshed; and as soon as war broke out Pondichery was immediately besieged and quickly taken, and the other factories could offer no resistance; so that the revolutionary spirits soon found themselves under a foreign and military control, while of their possible allies Tipu was crippled, and the Marathas were looking rather to the conquest of their weaker neighbours in the north and south than to the attack of the powerful East India Company. So the Revolutionary War brought no immediate troubles on Indian soil. At sea, indeed, French privateers, fitted out at the Isle of France, captured many prizes; but though these losses weighed heavily on private merchants, they scarcely affected the resources of the East India Company, while at the same time the naval squadron under Rainier accompanied by an expedition equipped at Madras in 1795 occupied Ceylon, Malacca, Banda and Amboina, not unassisted by the partisans of the Orangist party, indignant at the establishment of the republic in Holland. An expedition from England occupied the Cape. The position in India, however, was thought too uncertain to launch enterprises against the French islands, which would have made a stouter resistance and required a considerable proportion of the English forces in India for their subjugation.

Although the French settlements in India had all been occupied, there still remained considerable forces under French control. At Hyderabad Raymond had built up a body of sepoy troops under French instruction and leadership; under Sindhia Perron had done the same; and although these armies were in the pay of Indian princes, no one could say when they might not be marched against the Company's possessions, with or without the consent of their ostensible masters. The appearance of a French expedition would almost certainly set them in movement. But such an expedition by the ordinary route was hardly practicable in view of the English superiority at sea and the absence of stations at which provisions or protection could be found. In these circumstances the French pressed into realisation a scheme which had long floated in their minds, that, namely, of establishing themselves in Egypt, and thence preparing an attack on India.

A quarter of a century earlier Warren Hastings had attempted to open a trade with Suez. He had probably been impelled by considerations of imperial policy; the traders whom he supported may have been influenced by hopes of evading the regulations which confined the English trade to Europe to the East India Company itself. At a later time George Baldwin, under the influence of both motives, for a time succeeded in convincing ministry and Company of the need of a British consul in Egypt and the advisability of naming him to the office. But his efforts had come to nothing under the persistent opposition of the Turks to a policy which would have placed the half-independent ruling beys in intimate association with a European power. These ideas of the importance of Egypt had not been confined to the English. The French had shared them; and from about 1770 onwards many *mémoires* had been submitted to the ministers urging the importance of Egypt upon their attention. The trade between Alexandria and Marseilles was active; the French had maintained a consul in Egypt; and after the war of the American Revolution, de Castries's eastern projects had included the occupation of Egypt in case Austria and Russia combined to partition Turkey. In 1785 a French agent succeeded in concluding treaties with the leading beys; and these would have reopened the Red Sea route for Indian trade had not the Porte at once resolved to vindicate its authority and sent an expedition which overthrew the beys and for the moment re-established Turkish authority.[1] When therefore in 1798 Napoleon decided on the expedition to Egypt as a stroke aimed against the English, he was carrying into effect plans laid long before. But though he was locally successful, this partial success did the French cause more harm than good. Napoleon himself accurately appreciated the situation when he wrote: *La puissance qui est maîtresse de l'Égypte doit l'être à la longue de l'Inde.* Time was needed to concert measures with Tipu or the Marathas, to prepare and organise transport, whether by way of the Red Sea or by the route of Alexander.[2] Establishment in Egypt did not and could not lead at once to an attack on India; so that while in March, 1800, Napoleon was still talking of appearing on the Indus, Tipu had fallen and the French force at Hyderabad had been broken up.

The immediate effect of the French appearance in Egypt was to set all the English authorities in India on the alert; and at their head was a man of exceptional energy, of keen insight, of great organising power, Lord Mornington, better known by his later title of the Marquess Wellesley. On arriving at Calcutta in May, 1798, he was struck by the diffusion of French influence, and resolved not to allow

[1] Charles-Roux, *Autour d'une route*, *passim*; Brit. Mus. Add. MSS, 29210, ff. 341 *sqq.*
[2] Charles-Roux, *L'Angleterre et l'expédition française*, I, 227–9.

it to gather to a head. At almost the same time he learnt that Tipu had recently sent an embassy to the Isle of France, seeking military help, that the governor, Malartic, had issued a proclamation calling for volunteers, and that the embassy had returned to Mangalore with a small party thus collected. Mornington regarded, and rightly regarded, this as a sign of Tipu's reviving hopes. Then came news of Napoleon's success in Egypt, impelling the governor-general to meet the danger before it grew greater, and inspiring Tipu with the hope that help was nearer than it really was. As a first measure Mornington entered into negotiations with the Nizam, who in 1795 had suffered a severe defeat by the Marathas followed by considerable loss of territory. He was willing enough to sacrifice his French-led troops who had been beaten, though not by any fault of theirs, at Kharda, if thereby he could secure the services of a body of the Company's forces. Thus was signed the first of that group of treaties which contributed so much to establish the Company's dominion in India; and then Mornington demanded of Tipu that he should expel all Frenchmen from Mysore. Tipu, encouraged by the apparent approach of the French, could not bring himself to answer these demands till the English troops had already crossed his frontiers and the last Mysore war had begun. Once more French attempts had gone far enough to involve their friends in trouble without going far enough to afford them material aid.

As soon as the danger from Mysore had been overcome, Mornington contemplated three further objects. One was the conquest of the French islands, as the only effective measure that could be taken to stop the privateers from preying on English vessels; the second was the capture of Batavia; and the third was an expedition directed against the French in Egypt. With these alternatives in view, he assembled troops at Trinkomali. But the last of these was a project which the governor-general perceived could not be prudently undertaken except in co-operation with an expedition from England; and the first was prevented by the refusal of Commodore Rainier to co-operate, as he had received no specific instructions to that end. At first, therefore, Mornington's views were limited to his design against Batavia. But various circumstances deferred the dispatch of the expedition till at length on 6 February, 1801, dispatches arrived announcing Abercromby's expedition to Egypt, and desiring the assistance of a force from India.[1] Mornington's reluctance therefore to send the expedition so far to the east as Batavia was rewarded by his now being able to send it to the Red Sea with a minimum of delay. Baird, to whom the command had been entrusted, landed at Kosseir, marched across the desert to Thebes, and on 10 August reached Cairo, six weeks after it had surrendered to Hutchinson, Abercromby's successor, but in time to impress Menou at Alexandria

---

[1] *Wellesley Despatches*, ii, 436.

with a full consciousness of his inability to continue the struggle.[1] The first French attempt to establish themselves on the overland route to India had been defeated.

The Revolutionary War thus came to an end in 1802 with a marked advantage to the English in the East. Nor did the brief breathing-space which followed last long enough to permit the French to regain a positive foothold in India. The treaty which had closed the war merely stipulated for the retrocession of the French and Dutch factories in India and of the Cape and the spice-islands to the Dutch. Ceylon remained permanently in English hands. But before Decaen, the newly appointed captain-general of French India, could reach Pondichery, the English ministry was already doubtful of the duration of peace. A dispatch (17 October, 1802) received by Wellesley 30 March, 1803, directed him to delay the restitution of the French factories; and though these instructions were cancelled by later orders of 16 November (received 8 May),[2] yet even then the Indian government was warned against the possibility of French attempts upon the Portuguese possessions in Asia.[3] Soon after came news of the critical situation in Europe; and on 6 July the governor-general learnt that the renewal of war was officially thought very probable. In the first week of September he learnt that diplomatic relations had been broken off, and a few days later that war had been declared. It was what with his usual discernment he had expected. At the close of the previous year, more than four months before Decaen had sailed from Brest, Wellesley had directed the governor of Madras not to deliver up the French possessions without specific orders from Bengal. On 15 June, 1803, Binot, Decaen's chief of staff, arrived at Pondichery in the frigate *Belle Poule* with authority to take over the place. He was allowed to land, and his dispatches were sent up to Calcutta, arriving there 4 July. Wellesley resolved at once not to hand over the French possessions until receiving further orders from Europe; and accordingly deferred answering the dispatches from Decaen until that officer should actually arrive in India. This event took place on 11 July, and was known at Calcutta on the 23rd, together with the further news that a French packet had come in the day after Decaen's arrival, and that Decaen's squadron had quitted the Pondichery roads that night. The packet was the *Belier*, sent out after Decaen with orders that if war had broken out by the time of his arrival in Indian waters, he was to proceed, not to Pondichery, but to the French islands. Binot and his party, being ashore, were left behind, and when the news of war arrived, were obliged to surrender.[4]

But though the French flag was thus excluded from India, French intrigue was active. Binot had employed his brief sojourn at Pondi-

---

[1] Charles-Roux, *op. cit.* II, 213-4. [2] *Wellesley Despatches*, III, 72, 98.
[3] Prentout, *Decaen et l'île de France*, p. 437.
[4] Gaudart, *op. cit.* II, 460 *sqq.*; Prentout, *op. cit.* pp. 39 *sqq.*

chery in sounding the rulers who seemed likely to welcome his overtures. Thus he opened relations with the rajas of Tanjore and
Travancore, and sent to visit the Marathas an officer who obtained
an English passport under the assumed guise of a German painter.
Decaen took up the quest for allies. He had agents at Tranquebar
in the south, and Serampur in the north, until, after the breach
between England and Denmark, these places passed temporarily into
English keeping. These men, with their spies constantly coming and
going, deemed all India ready for revolt against the English. They
represented the Vellore mutiny as having spread to every cantonment
in the south. The lesser southern chiefs were all ready, and only
needed a small sum of money, for a rising. To them the English cause
was maintained (as one of them wrote) by nothing but violence and
corruption.[1] A manifesto, addressed by Decaen to the chiefs of
Hindustan, urged them to attack the Company with their united
force if they would save themselves from the fate of Oudh, Arcot and
Mysore.[2] But all this, as Prentout has justly remarked, served the
English cause better than the French. It assisted the English to recognise
their enemies, without providing the latter with anything more serviceable than encouragement in what was to prove a suicidal policy.

The fact was that the French, now as in the Revolutionary War,
could not get within reach in India. "It is painful", wrote Decaen
commenting on the sanguine reports of his agents in India, "to learn
of all these good dispositions and to be unable to support them."[3]
But his military forces were barely enough to garrison the islands;
the French squadron—one ship of the line and three frigates—under
the unenterprising leadership of Admiral Linois was not even able
to take the China convoy under the protection of the Company's
armed vessels (14 February, 1804); and the only serious means of
attack in Decaen's power was the encouragement of the privateers,
which again covered the Indian seas in all directions, capturing a
great number of private merchantmen and even a few Company's
ships. The two Surcoufs, in the *Caroline* and the *Revenant*, were perhaps
the boldest and most enterprising of the privateers; and after Linois'
departure from Indian waters in 1805 (to fall in with an English
squadron off the Canaries 13 March, 1806) the frigates which then
came under Decaen's control vigorously seconded the efforts of the
privateers. Obstinate conflicts took place on many occasions when
these met armed English vessels, as when the *Psyche* was taken by
the English frigate *San Fiorenzo*. But all these efforts did nothing
beyond inflicting heavy private losses, and left the Company's
position in India untouched, while the reoccupation of the Cape by
the English in 1805 deprived the French islands of their nearest
supplies of foodstuffs.

---

[1] Prentout, *op. cit.* pp. 374–7.   [2] *Wellesley Despatches*, III, 663.
[3] Prentout, *op. cit.* pp. 460 *sqq.*

In Europe Napoleon planned eastern expeditions—in 1805 three squadrons and 20,000 men;[1] in 1807 a triple plan which was to have combined land expeditions through Central Asia and Egypt with a sea expedition round the Cape[2]—but these fell through, in part because of the English command of the sea, in part because of Napoleon's continental preoccupations. It was in preparation for the second of these that the embassy of General Gardane to Persia was arranged. In 1803 war had broken out between Persia and Russia; and in 1805 the latter power had joined England in the Third Coalition. Persia naturally turned to France for help, and on 4 May, 1807, was signed the Treaty of Finkenstein, by which Napoleon guaranteed the integrity of Persia, engaged to use every effort to compel Russia to evacuate Georgia, and promised supplies of field guns and small arms; while the shah engaged to break off all relations, political and economic, with the English (thus subscribing to the Continental System) and to give all facilities and assistance to French military and naval forces on their way to attack the British in India. On this agreement, Gardane was sent to Teheran, to promote Persian hostility against England and Russia, and to collect information about routes and resources for the projected expedition. But Gardane's mission, like Decaen's, was foredoomed to failure. When the Treaty of Finkenstein was signed Napoleon was already contemplating peace and even alliance with Russia; and when he realised these ideas by the Treaty of Tilsit and the entente with Alexander, he was no longer willing to do anything to support the Persians against his new ally. Here was one more example of the way in which the interests of a world power are apt to diverge and become irreconcilable. So long as the Persians could hope for French support in the recovery of Georgia, they remained willing to exclude the English from Persia, as Malcolm found in 1808, when he was sent by Minto to counter the French mission but failed even to get a footing in the country, although backed by an armed force; but when in the autumn of that year the Persians perceived that they would have to negotiate with Russia direct, and that the French would not even act as mediators, they concluded naturally that the advantages of the French alliance were all on one side; on the arrival of Harford Jones to replace Malcolm, not even Gardane's threats of departure could prevent the reception of the new English mission; and so, early in 1809, Harford Jones replaced Gardane at Teheran, while Napoleon, involved in continental interests, abandoned his schemes of emulating the exploits of Alexander the Great.[3]

The time had now come also for the complete expulsion of the

---

[1] Prentout, *op. cit.* pp. 402 *sqq.*

[2] Gardane's Instructions, 10 May, 1807, *ap.* Gardane, *Mission du Général Gardane*, pp. 81 *sqq.*

[3] Gardane, *Mission du Général Gardane*; Kaye, *Life of Malcolm*, I, 395, etc., *Minto in India*, pp. 55 *sqq.*

French from the East. The English squadrons at the Cape and in India were strengthened. The French islands were blockaded by English vessels; and although over-rashness on the part of their commanders led to the loss of two sunk and two taken, in the course of 1810 both the Isle of France and the Île Bonaparte (as Bourbon had been renamed) were compelled to surrender to Admiral Bertie and General Abercromby; while in the next year another expedition occupied Java, to which island a French regiment had been sent some time before by Decaen. These captures brought to an end the activities of the privateers, who thus lost the bases at which they had refitted, revictualled, and sold their prizes; and wiped out the French reputation in India. The settlement brought by the treaties of 1814 and 1815 confirmed the position established by force of arms. The French and the Dutch recognised for the first time British sovereignty over the Company's possessions; the French agreed to maintain no troops and erect no fortresses; and so the Company was at last completely freed from European menace just at the moment when it was, under the leadership of Lord Hastings, about to establish an unquestioned predominance in India.

CHAPTER XX

TIPU SULTAN, 1785–1802

B Y that "humiliating pacification" (as Hastings called it), the Treaty of Mangalore, Tipu appeared as a conqueror. Grant Duff, years afterwards, asserted that the governor-general was

only prevented from disavowing and annulling it by the confusion which mus have resulted to the Company's affairs in consequence of the fulfilment of a part of the terms, before it could have been possible to obtain their ratification.[1]

There is no doubt, indeed, that Hastings regarded it with the dislike and disapproval with which he viewed almost the whole of the policy and actions of the rulers of Madras; but, on the other hand, when he wrote his *Memoirs relative to the State of India* during the long journey home which began on 5 February, 1785, he seemed not to anticipate any immediate consequences of danger.

It is not likely that Tipoo should so soon choose to involve himself in a new war with us, deprived of all his confederates, and these become his rivals; nor that, whenever he shall have formed such a design, he will suffer it to break out in petty broils with our borderers.[2]

None the less it was quite evident that war was pending between Tipu and the Marathas. The Nizam and Nana were known to be in negotiation if not in alliance: the power of Sindhia cast its mantle of supremacy over the Moghul. The claim which Tipu, as it seemed with unjustifiable audacity, advanced upon Bijapur—which mean-while Nana had promised to surrender to the Nizam—may have been based on an imperial grant to Hyder of a portion of the Deccan, and was certainly not one which in 1785 could be confirmed or made effective. But, while wisdom would have persuaded Tipu to be content with the successes he had won, his inherent passion and restlessness urged him to new aggression. Thomas Munro, when he summed up his career in 1799, said "a restless spirit of innovation, and a wish to have everything to originate from himself, was the predominant feature of his character".[3] Upon the success of the war which ended in 1784 he formed the designs first of crushing the Nizam and the Marathas and then turning, flushed with victory, upon the English. This project he avowed to the French.[4] Early in 1785 he attacked the hill-post of Nargund, belonging to a Brahmin desai, with whom he had already had unfriendly relations, the one making extravagant

---

[1] Grant Duff, II, 469.
[2] Forrest, *Selections from the State Papers of ... Warren Hastings*, II, 54.
[3] Gleig, *Life of Munro*, I, 233.
[4] Wilks, *Historical Sketches of Southern India*, II, 535 *sqq.*

demands, the other claiming tribute.[1] In vain the Marathas intervened to save Nargund and Kittur: by guile as well as force Tipu
made a successful conquest. Nana, alarmed, looked for help from
the English in the conquest which he foresaw. He appealed to the
Treaty of Salbai and asked for aid against Tipu: Macpherson, in the
cautious spirit of the non-intervention policy which was now ascendant
in the counsels of the Company, replied that the treaty

did not stipulate that the friends and enemies of the two States should be mutual,
but that neither party should afford assistance to the enemies of the other, and that
by the treaty of Mangalore the English were bound not to assist the enemies of
Tipu.

Thus he gave the sultan of Mysore reason to think that he could
proceed undisturbed.

But Nana was not going to fall without a struggle. He applied
to Goa for alliance: a step which alarmed Macpherson into establishing a resident (C. W. Malet) at Poona.

By the fifth month of 1786 the Marathas were in alliance with the
Nizam and ready to move. Their forces joined on 1 May, and on
20 May they took Badami. Against Tipu also were Holkar and
Mudaji Bhonsle: Kittur was recovered: the victors returned home
flushed with success: Hari Pant advanced, and relieved Adoni, while
Tipu captured Savanur. The end was a peace which hardly modified
the *status quo*. The Marathas retained important districts (Nargund,
Kittur, Badami) and Tipu recovered others. His brother-in-law
regained Savanur, and a kinsman of the Nizam Adoni. On the whole
the treaty of 1787 was a rebuff for Tipu. He had begun to perceive
that the English were more dangerous than he had thought. Malet
at Poona and the military preparations of Cornwallis gave him pause.

Hardly had Cornwallis arrived in India when his attention was
turned to Tipu. His knowledge of international politics made him
consider India as a vital point in the enduring rivalry between
England and France: perhaps he was the first English statesman in
India who fully grasped its importance. A letter of March, 1788,[2]
shows that he had considered the situation in all its bearings.

"I look upon a rupture with Tipu as a certain and immediate consequence of
a war with France", he wrote to Malet, "and in that event a vigorous co-operation
of the Marathas would certainly be of the utmost importance to our interests in
this country."

The settlement of the Guntoor Sarkar affair caused a new settlement
with the Nizam, and this, embodied in a curiously disingenuous
message—which kept the non-intervention order of the act of 1784
in the letter but broke it in the spirit—brought about the war which

[1] See Kirkpatrick's *Letters of Tipu*, referred to by Wilks, *Historical Sketches*, II, 535.
[2] *Cornwallis Correspondence*, I, 345.

Cornwallis had foreseen. Wilks,[1] the historian of Southern India at this period, sardonically remarks that

it is highly instructive to observe a statesman, justly extolled for moderate and pacific dispositions, thus indirectly violating a law, enacted for the enforcement of these virtues, by entering into a very intelligible offensive alliance.

Cornwallis, of course, knew well what he was doing, and was convinced that he could do nothing else with any regard for the safety of the English in Madras: he expressed himself strongly to Malet[2] on the danger of having to make war without efficient allies.

The actual ignition of the flame (foreseen by Tipu, who had long ago promised the French to attack the English, as well as by Cornwallis) was caused by Tipu's attack on Travancore, 29 December, 1789. The ostensible reason for this was the sale of Jaikottai and Kranganur to the raja by the Dutch, Tipu asserting that they belonged to his feudatory the raja of Cochin. The raja of Travancore said that the Dutch had held them so long ago as 1654 and acquired them from the Portuguese, and he applied to Hollond, the governor of Madras, for aid. It seems probable that Hollond was already warned of what was about to happen, and had taken a bribe from Tipu; he certainly delayed preparations and endeavoured to persuade the governor-general that they were unnecessary.[3] Then when Tipu attacked Travancore, the raja, though included by name among England's allies in the Treaty of Mangalore, was left to his fate. Tipu carried all before him till Cornwallis, indignant at the disgraceful sacrifice "that had been made of British honour", intervened in person, preluding his action by a letter condemning the conduct of the Madras Government in the most vigorous terms.[4] Orders had been disobeyed, preparations not made, and allies betrayed. Now the resources of the Carnatic must be exploited: even the sums set apart for the payment of the nawab's enormous debts must be seized; at the same time the necessary alliances with the Marathas and the Nizam must be immediately stabilised; Cornwallis hoped, that "the common influence of passion and the considerations of evident interest" would draw them to his side. And so it proved. On 1 June, and 4 July, 1790, treaties were made with the Marathas and the Nizam in view of the imminent war with Tipu. These formed "the Triple Alliance"; and the war began in May, 1790.

Briefly the objects may be expressed as follows. Tipu was continuing his father's attempt to win supremacy in Southern India. The Nizam and the Marathas were in greater fear of him than of the English. Cornwallis saw danger near and far, to all British interests in India, and in the wider international spheres of Europe and America. His experience had accustomed his mind to world-wide maps.

---

[1] Wilks, *op. cit.* III, 38.   [2] *Cornwallis Correspondence*, I, 496.
[3] Cf. Malcolm, *Political History of India*, I, 72.   [4] *Cornwallis Correspondence*, I, 491.

The war lasted for nearly two years, and the result was both disastrous to Tipu and the prelude to greater and final disaster. It fell into three campaigns. The first was commanded by General Medows, whose devotion to duty and universal popularity were contrasted by Cornwallis[1] with the qualities and estimation of the late governor of Madras. Transferred from Bombay (where Ralph Abercromby replaced him) to Madras, this gallant but precipitate officer was to lead the principal force of the Carnatic to seize the Coimbatore district and then to penetrate through the Gazzalhatti pass to the heart of Mysore. Colonel Kelly was to watch over the safety of the Carnatic and the passes that led into it most directly from Mysore. To General Abercromby with the army of Bombay was given the task of subjugating the territory of Tipu on the Malabar Coast, a task which he accomplished in a few weeks. Medows was less immediately successful. A chain of forts stretched from the Coromandel Coast to the Gazzalhatti Gorge; all these were eventually captured and by July, 1790, Medows stood at Coimbatore sixty miles from his nearest support and ninety from the farthest. Then Tipu suddenly descended the famous pass and with rapidity and skill inflicted sharp blows on the British troops in different quarters. On 10 November he was narrowly prevented from destroying the force of Colonel Maxwell, successor to Kelly; six days later Medows came up and the British force was saved. But Tipu, moving rapidly, was still a source of considerable danger, and it was thought well that Cornwallis himself should come to the scene of action. The Marathas and the Nizam, however, were giving useful aid, and the capture of Dharwar added greatly to the allies' security and power.

The year 1791 found Cornwallis in command, and in politics the project broached of deposing the usurper Tipu in favour of the heir of the old Hindu rajas of Mysore. The governor-general recovered in India not a little of the military reputation he had lost in America; it is not insignificant that the favourite portrait of him shows a background of eastern tents and turbaned soldiery. Taking a new point of attack he moved by Vellore and Ambur to the capture of Bangalore, which he achieved on 21 March, 1791; and by 13 May he was within nine miles of Seringapatam. But the campaign ended in disappointment. Tipu showed unexpected generalship, and Cornwallis when the rains came was compelled to retreat by the utter failure (as Wilks reports) of all the equipments of his army: Madras, incompetent and sluggish, again at fault. It seemed necessary to open negotiations with Mysore, but Cornwallis was not disposed to yield, and when Tipu sent a propitiatory offering, it was with delight that "the whole army beheld the loads of fruit untouched and the camels unaccepted returning to Seringapatam".

When the fighting was resumed, though Tipu succeeded in cap-

---

[1] *Cornwallis Correspondence*, i, 429.

turing Coimbatore (3 November, 1791), which had been most gallantly defended, the troops of Cornwallis, gradually removing all obstacles, and after arduous efforts (recounted with enthusiastic vigour by Wilks), occupying the chain of forts which was interposed, drew near to the capital; and on 5 February, 1792, the lines were drawn round Seringapatam. Cornwallis's letters give graphic descriptions of the attacks which followed. Tipu displayed much military and diplomatic skill, the native allies were urgent with Cornwallis to conclude the war by negotiation, and the governor-general was never keen completely to crush an enemy. Three days before peace was signed he wrote to Sir Charles Oakeley, governor of Madras, that "an arrangement which effectually destroys the dangerous power of Tipu will be more beneficial to the public than the capture of Seringapatam, and it will render the final settlement with our Allies, who seem very partial to it, much more easy"; and the Secret Committee had anticipated such an arrangement with approval.[1] Half Tipu's territory was surrendered,[2] and a large portion of this went to the Nizam (from the Krishna to beyond the Pennar river with the forts of Ganjkottai and Cuddapah) and to the Marathas (extending their boundary to the Tungabhadra); while the English secured all his lands on the Malabar Coast between Travancore and the Kaway, the Baramahal district and that of Dindigul, and Tipu was obliged to grant independence to the much persecuted raja of Coorg. At home great interest was aroused by one provision: two sons of Tipu were surrendered as hostages for his good faith. A popular picture represents them being presented to Cornwallis amid an assemblage of perturbed Muhammadans. They were nurtured carefully at Calcutta: their portraits, not uninteresting, are still at Government House. In England also the treaty seemed a most satisfactory example of "our old and true policy",[3] presumably one of deliberate avoidance of territorial acquisitions beyond the necessities of safety—for it was on this ground in his letters home that Cornwallis justified his seizures; but he was utterly deceived in thinking that Tipu recognised defeat or ceased to plan renewed aggression. Yet the English alliance with the Nizam undoubtedly received a new accession of strength; it may be said to have now reached something of the traditional stability which in Europe linked Portugal and England in unbroken alliance. The jealous Poona Marathas "saw with regret the shield of British power held up between them and the Nizam": new seeds for future war were planted though they did not grow up for some years. Cornwallis was not blind either, though he did not go much beyond declaring[4] (to Sir C. Malet at Poona) that the allies were bound mutually to guarantee what each had won from Tipu. But before he left India a cloud was beginning to rise on the horizon towards

---

[1] *Cornwallis Correspondence*, II, 159. [2] *Idem*, p. 537.
[3] *Annual Register*, 1792. [4] *Cornwallis Correspondence*, II, 176 *sqq*.

Mysore.[1] Early in October, 1793, the governor-general returned to England, and his successor had none of his military interests or international experience, and little of his political sagacity.

The war between the Marathas and the Nizam (1794–5), in which Shore not unnaturally avoided intervention, ended in the Nizam's defeat and in Sir John Shore's belief that he was a less valuable ally than his conquerors, with the inept anticipation that there was "no immediate probability that we shall be involved in war".[2] He had, says his biographer,[3] anticipated no danger from the union of the Marathas and Tipu against the Nizam, and contemplated without apprehension the total collapse of the latter's government. It is sufficient comment on Sir John Shore's political wisdom that it, alone of the three, survives to-day.

The results of Shore's non-intervention were speedily seen. The Nizam dismissed his English troops and increased the French, and but for his son's rebellion, which the English had remained long enough to suppress, would have thrown himself entirely on the French side, and thus have come inevitably into alliance with Tipu. Shore returned to England in 1798. A very careful and conscientious administrator, he was succeeded by a man of genius, who became one of the makers of British India. Himself without Indian experience, Richard Wellesley, Earl of Mornington (who arrived on 26 April, 1798), approached the problems of the East with a mind unbiassed though not uninformed. He was already on the Board of Control and had studied the history, politics and government of India assiduously. He had accepted the governorship of Madras, and had therefore observed the difficulties of Southern India particularly, on Lord Cornwallis being appointed governor-general a second time (1 February, 1797); but when Cornwallis accepted the lord-lieutenancy of Ireland a few months later, Wellesley was sent on instead to Calcutta. His earliest letters to Dundas,[4] on his way out to India, evince a remarkable knowledge of Indian affairs, and on 28 February, 1798, though he did not know of Tipu's recent negotiations with France, he saw that in the power of Mysore lay the key to the whole position. Since Cornwallis had left India the fruits of his successes had disappeared.

"The balance of power in India", he wrote, "no longer exists upon the same footing on which it was placed by the peace of Seringapatam. The question therefore must arise how it may best be brought back to the state in which you have directed me to maintain it."

But he soon saw that the balance of power, if such there were to be, must stand on a very different footing from that on which Cornwallis, or Shore, or even Dundas, believed that it would rest securely.

[1] *Cornwallis Correspondence*, II, 219.
[2] See his state papers, Malcolm's *History*, II, App. II, XLIV *sqq.*
[3] The second Lord Teignmouth, *Life*, I, 320.
[4] From Cape of Good Hope: *Despatches*, I, 25. Cf. *The Wellesley Papers*, vol. I.

An admirable paper written years after by the Duke of Wellington —Mornington's younger brother Arthur, who arrived in India in January, 1797—describes the condition of the country when the new governor-general arrived. To Wellesley, actively though he intervened in the affairs of other countries, especially those of the Nizam, the centre of interest was Mysore. He landed on 26 April, 1798, and immediately learnt of the negotiations of Tipu with France and her dependency Mauritius.[1] Tipu had sent envoys to Versailles (where they were received with almost as much mirth as satisfaction), called himself "Citoyen", and addressed the most urgent and flattering applications to Malartic, the governor of Mauritius, for alliance and aid. In the name of the French Republic one and indivisible, the governor of the Isles of France and Bourbon issued a vigorous proclamation to the "citoyens de couleur libres", announcing Tipu's desire for an offensive and defensive alliance, and welcoming his assistance to expel the English from India. Tipu's ambassadors returned home and landed at Mangalore accompanied by a small French force on the very day (26 April, 1798)[2] that Sir John Shore received a letter from him desiring "to cultivate and improve the friendship and good understanding subsisting between the two states and an inviolable adherence to the engagements by which they are connected". The new governor-general was not deceived. He addressed a friendly letter to Tipu and received an effusive reply; but he left no ground for doubt as to the seriousness of his intentions, of which he desired the sultan to be aware. On 18 October he heard of Bonaparte's landing in Egypt, and two days later he ordered Lord Clive, governor of Madras, to prepare for war. He was now secure on the side of Hyderabad[3], and he began a series of exploratory operations (as surgeons might say) in the direction of Mysore. He wrote: Tipu replied: more than once: the governor-general courteous with a touch of imperiousness, the Muhammadan despot evasive and deceitful. At first Mornington's plan was merely to require a repudiation of the French alliance; it developed, through increasing requirements of territory, into a determination utterly to annihilate the power of the usurper of Mysore.

The Mysore War with the destruction of Tipu has often been criticised as unjustifiable and unjust, precipitate and unwarranted by the conduct of the vanquished. The great majority of contemporary opinion is entirely against this view. Indeed it may be said that hardly a single writer or speaker who had personal knowledge of India doubted that the war, and its object, were absolutely necessary. England was already in danger from France, and the danger for several years grew greater; how much greater would it have been had the life and death struggle been carried on in India as well as in Europe! Already a French force was in Egypt. Did not the classical

---

[1] *Wellesley Despatches*, I, 213. [2] *Idem*, I, App. pp. viii–xi. [3] Cf. p. 328 *supra*.

models which the ambitious pedants of the Revolution delighted to follow point towards the creation of a new western dominion in the East? The armies of Tipu, daily growing in numbers and efficiency, were ready implements to make this achievement possible. "His resources", said the Madras Government to Mornington, "are more prompt than our own." Yet war was embarked on by the English only after serious attempts at negotiation, and it seemed to the governor-general that it needed the vindication which the course of events would afford.

"It will soon be evident", he said, "to all the powers of India that the fundamental principle of our policy is invariably repugnant to every scheme of conquest, extension of dominion, aggrandisement or ambition either for ourselves or our allies."

It may be wondered whether the serious attempts at negotiation were ever regarded by Tipu as anything but endeavours to gain time. His letters to Lord Mornington were no doubt amusing from their fulsome professions of sincerity and friendship mingled with denunciations of the French, to one who already possessed authentic information of all that had happened in the Isle of France. They continued all through the winter of 1798–9, and were in no way influenced by the vigorous letter sent from Constantinople by the sultan, Selim III, urging the necessity of opposing the faithless French, enemies of the Muhammadan faith. Mornington suffered them to continue, for, as early as 12 August, 1798,[1] he had drawn up a minute in the Secret Department sketching measures necessary for "frustrating the united efforts of Tipoo Sultaun and of France". Yet he was still anxious to defend himself against any charge of aggressiveness. "The rights of states applicable to every case of contest with foreign powers", he asserted,[2] "are created and limited by the necessity of preserving the public safety." This necessity was now obvious. By the beginning of 1799 both sides were ready for the contest. Tipu retorted to Constantinople the charges made against his allies (10 February): Mornington issued to General Harris at Madras his instructions for the political conduct of the inevitable war (22 February). A commission was appointed to negotiate with any neighbouring chiefs, to conciliate the population and to watch over the family of the ancient Hindu rajas, whom the governor-general already thought of restoring to the throne of Mysore. On this commission Colonel Arthur Wellesley served. It was the first important political work of one who was to become England's prime minister as well as commander-in-chief. On the same day there was issued from Madras a declaration by the Governor-General in Council of the causes of the war, and Mornington addressed from Fort St George an order to General Harris not to delay the march of the army one hour, but to enter Mysore and march upon Seringapatam.

[1] *Wellesley Despatches*, I, 159.   [2] *Idem*, p. 171.

The circumstances were favourable. The armies of the Nizam and the Peshwa might be useful, and relations with the Nizam at least were cordial. But the chief dependence was on the British troops. The army of the Carnatic was believed to be

the best appointed, the most completely equipped, the most amply and liberally supplied, the most perfect in point of discipline, and the most fortunate in the acknowledged experience and abilities of its officers in every department which ever took the field of India,

and the Malabar force was also efficient. The object of the war was plain: the general in command had full powers, and the country was well known from the experience of the earlier war. British ships were at sea, successfully scouring it of French vessels. The governor-general himself was at Madras masterfully directing every step in advance, and acting in cordial association with the governor, the son of the great Clive. On 3 February General Harris moved from Vellore, and General Stewart from Kannanur. On 8 March Stewart defeated Tipu at Sedasere, and on the 27th he was again defeated at Mallavelly, by Harris. The raja of Coorg,[1] Tipu's bitter enemy, witnessed the achievements of Stewart with enthusiasm. Arthur Wellesley was in command of the contingent from Hyderabad, largely troops of the Nizam. Tipu was utterly out-generalled, and could do no more than turn to bay in his capital. The English armies met before Seringapatam early in April, and on 17 April the siege began. The English were compelled to hurry operations owing to the lateness of the season and the inadequacy of supplies—then a common fault in the organisation of all South Indian campaigns. A letter of General Harris dated 7 May describes the siege, and the assault and capture on 4 May. By the evening of the 3rd the walls were so battered that a practicable breach was made, and the assault was decided on for the 4th in the heat of the day. At one o'clock the English troops, with two hundred men from the Nizam's forces, crossed the Kavari under very heavy fire, passed the glacis and ditch and stormed the ramparts and the breaches made by the artillery; Major-General David Baird, who had been a prisoner of Tipu's till the Treaty of Mangalore, was in command. Tipu's body was found in a heap of hundreds of dead. His son, formerly a hostage, surrendered himself, and the Muhammadan dynasty was at an end.

Tipu was regarded by ignorant pamphleteers in England as a martyr to English aggression, and James Mill in later years attempted to vindicate his ability if not his character. But his Indian contemporaries rejoiced at his fall. He was a man of savage passions and vaulting ambition, whose capacities were not equal to his own estimation of his powers. He ruled, as a convinced Muhammadan, over a population of Hindus, whose ancient sovereigns his father had

---

[1] See Wilks's *Sketches*, III, 493.

dispossessed and whom he had bitterly persecuted. The district around Mysore abhorred him, and though the English found signs of prosperity within his dominions these were certainly due to no inspiration of his own. His character was a contrast to that of his father, who was wise and tolerant.

"Hyder", says Colonel Wilks,[1] "was seldom wrong and Tipu seldom right in his estimate of character....Unlimited persecution united in detestation of his rule every Hindu in his dominions. In the Hindu no degree of merit was a passport to his favour; in the Mussulman no crime could ensure displeasure....Tipu in an age when persecution only survived in history revived its worst terrors....He was barbarous where severity was vice, and indulgent where it was virtue. If he had qualities fitted for Empire they were strangely equivocal; the disqualifications were obvious and unquestionable, and the decision of history will not be far removed from the observation almost proverbial in Mysore, 'that Hyder was born to create an Empire, Tipu to lose one'."

In a letter from Thomas Munro to his father[2] facts are given which support a judgment fully as severe. It is shown that through the means Tipu had taken to strengthen his power, by employing men of different races and being himself responsible for their payment, and by keeping the families of his chief officers as hostages at Seringapatam, he had made the stability of his government depend entirely upon himself, and with him it collapsed; and "also he was so suspicious and cruel that none of his subjects, none probably of his children, lamented his fall".

At the fall of Seringapatam practically the entire sovereignty of Mysore fell into the English hands. How was this power to be exercised? Mornington was not disposed to annex the whole, as he might well have done. Nor did he desire to add to obligations which it was not easy either to estimate or to discharge. He wrote that

owing to the inconveniences and embarrassments which resulted from the whole system of government and conflicting authorities in Oudh, the Carnatic and Mysore, I resolved to reserve to the Company the most extensive and indisputable powers.

Thus the family of Tipu was swept into obscurity but with ample provision and dignity. Then came provision for all the territory that had been conquered. Mornington set himself at once to the serious task of providing for the future government of the country. He decided

that the establishment of a central and separate government in Mysore, under the protection of the Company, and the admission of the Marathas to a certain participation in the division of the conquered territory, were the expedients best calculated to reconcile the interests of all parties, to secure to the Company a less invidious and more efficient share of revenue, resources, commercial advantage and military strength than could be obtained under any other distribution of territory or power, and to afford the most favourable prospect of a general and permanent tranquillity in India.

[1] Wilks, *op. cit.* III, 464.
[2] Gleig, *Life*, I, 228 *sqq.*: a most interesting and valuable letter.

Thus Tipu's territory was divided, leaving only a small and compact possession for the descendants of the ancient Hindu rajas, of which the Company was to undertake the defence, occupying any forts it might choose. Beyond that, the division of territory had results of considerable political as well as geographical importance. To the English dominions were added the province of Kanara, the districts of Coimbatore, Wynad and Dharapuram, and all the land below the Ghats between the coast of Malabar and the Carnatic, "securing", said Wellesley, "an uninterrupted tract of territory from the coast of Coromandel to that of Malabar, together with the entire sea-coast of the kingdom of Mysore". The fortresses commanding all the heads of the passes above the Ghats were also secured, and, in addition, the fortress of Seringapatam. Thus it was made certain that no ruler should arise in Mysore like Tipu who could intervene in a contest of sea-power, or hold out a hand to European enemies of England to give a landing for troops which might threaten British power in the south of India, as it had been threatened in the days of La Bourdonnais and Dupleix.

This rearrangement greatly increased the responsibilities of the presidency of Madras, a fact which the directors of the East India Company did not at once appreciate. The governors and the council were not generally men of wide vision or practical sagacity. Lord Clive was a useful subordinate to the governor-general; not so much could have been said of all his successors. Nor was the military organisation of Madras satisfactory; it took a long time to provide a permanent system of recruiting, commissariat, and command. Sir Hilaro Barlow, afterwards governor-general, had a difficult task with regard to the army, and it may at least be said that he discharged it with greater wisdom than several of his contemporaries. In Sir Thomas Munro, however, the Company soon found a servant of the very highest ability, and so long as he was in authority in the province of Madras the improvement was rapid and continuous.

"Perhaps there never lived a European more intimately acquainted", says his biographer, Gleig,[1] "with the characters, habits, manners and institutions of the natives of India, because there never lived a European who at once possessed better opportunities of acquiring such knowledge, and made better use of them."

It was not till twenty years later than the conquest of Mysore that he became governor of Madras, but his growing influence over Southern India can be traced in all the years which intervene. On the acquisition of Kanara he was its governor, and he made a deep impression on the inhabitants of that rugged and wild district which stood between the Portuguese, the Marathas, and the sea. It was a time when the power of the Marathas began visibly to decline. The share of Tipu's territory which was offered them they refused, the Peshwa already scheming for an occasion of attack upon the English;

---

[1] Preface to *Life*, p. xii.

the land then was divided between the English and the Nizam. As the Marathas became more clearly alienated from the English—though, as will be seen later, the process was not continuous, the Nizam—again with interruptions—became more definitely their ally. The Treaty of Hyderabad, Mornington's first achievement in constructive statesmanship, had brought the Nizam close to the English government in India; his aid in the Mysore War had not been inconsiderable and now his position was consolidated by the acquisition of the districts of Gurramkonda and Gooty and the land down to Chitaldrug, and other border fortresses of Mysore. Thus the process begun in the Treaty of Hyderabad was continued after the overthrow of Tipu, and the Nizam was established as a strong and independent support of the English in the south. In the words of Arthur Wellesley a few years later, "our principal ally, the Nizam, was restored to us"; and affairs in the south were placed "on foundations of strength calculated to afford lasting peace and security".

Towards this security the settlement of Mysore was an essential factor. Mornington had for some time considered the wisest course to adopt. He felt that a native state must remain; but that it should be unable to embroil itself and its neighbours with the Company. When Mornington announced the results of the war and the peace to the directors of the Company, he said:

Happily as I estimate the immediate and direct advantages of revenue and of commercial and military resources, I consider the recent settlement of Mysore to be equally important to your interests, in its tendency to increase your political consideration among the native powers, together with your means of maintaining internal tranquillity and order among your subjects and dependents, and of defending your possessions against any enemy whether Asiatic or European.

And the settlement was this. The family of the ancient Hindu rajas was searched for, discovered, restored. There was a story years before of how Hyder selected the fittest child of a baby family to be its head, though he had never given him real power. Among the children he threw a number of baubles, of fruits and ornaments, and among them concealed a dagger: the child who chose this was to be the chief.

"In 1799 the future raja", says Colonel Wilks,[1] "was himself a child of five years of age, but the widow of that raja from whom Hyder usurped the government still remained, to confer with the commissioners and to regulate with distinguished propriety the renewed honours of her house."

By the change of dynasty the sentiments of the Hindu people of Mysore were attached to the British power which had restored to them the representatives of their ancient religion and government, and the stability of the new government was secured by

the uncommon talents of Purniya (the very able financial minister of Hyder) in the office of minister to the new raja, and that influence was directed to proper objects by the control reserved to the English Government by them in the provisions of the treaty.

[1] Wilks, *Historical Sketches*, III, 470.

By the treaty of Seringapatam, 1 September, 1798, between the Company and "Maharaja Mysore Krishnaraja Udayar Bahadur, Raja of Mysore" the raja was to pay an annual subsidy, and if this were unpaid the Company might order any internal reforms and bring under its own direct management any parts of his country; and the raja undertook to refrain from correspondence with any foreign state and not to admit any European to his service.

The Earl of Mornington, for this achievement, was created Marquis Wellesley in the peerage of Ireland, an honour which he described as a "double-gilt potato". He was indeed highly indignant at so slight a recognition of such considerable services.

The settlement of the territory newly acquired by the British, and the establishment of the government of Krishnaraja, the new ruler, a child of seven, proceeded apace. On 24 February, 1800, the governor-general sent Dr Francis Buchanan to make an extensive survey of

the dominions of the present raja of Mysore, and the country acquired by the Company in the late war from the Sultan, as well as that part of Malabar which the Company annexed to their own territories in the former war under Marquis Cornwallis.[1]

Drawn up by the Marquis Wellesley himself, who during all his rule was keenly interested in Indian agriculture, the instructions show the care with which the governor-general provided for his successors full information as to the condition of the country. Agriculture was the chief subject investigated, in such detail as "esculent vegetables" and the methods of their cultivation, including irrigation, the different breeds of cattle, the farms and the nature of their tenure, the natural products of the land, the use of arts, manufactures, medicine, mines, quarries, minerals, the climate and the ethnology of the country. The record of the investigation is a work of very great value and extraordinary minuteness, and throws considerable light on the cruel and erratic government of Tipu as well as on the just and well-organised system introduced by Colonel Close, the British Resident at Seringapatam. The thoroughness of the investigation, with the large tracts of country it covered, shows the spirit in which the English rulers entered on their task, and justifies the statement made by Arthur Wellesley[2] six years later.

The state in which their government is to be found at this moment, the cordial and intimate unity which exists between the Government of Mysore and the British authorities, and the important strength and real assistance which it has afforded to the British Government in all its recent difficulties, afford the strongest proofs of the wisdom of this stipulation of the treaty,

namely, "the most extensive and indisputable powers" which the governor-general had reserved to the Company by the provision "for the interference of the British Government in all the concerns" of

---

[1] The results were published in 1807 in three volumes.
[2] Mem. by Sir A. Wellesley 1806, ap. Owen's edition of *Wellesley Despatches*, p. lxxxii.

the Mysore state "when such interference might be necessary". This satisfactory result, however, was not achieved immediately or without a period of difficult guerrilla warfare. Accounts of this are to be found in the letters of Arthur Wellesley and Thomas Munro.

Though Tipu's sons remained in retirement and Seringapatam was tranquil under the wise government of Colonel Close, the districts at a distance from control were soon overrun by freebooting bands. The chief of these was led by Dundia Wagh, a Maratha by birth but born in Mysore. This vigorous and savage personage had been trusted by Hyder, but degraded, compulsorily converted to Islam, and imprisoned, till the very day of the capture of Seringapatam, by Tipu. When he escaped he collected a band of desperate men and thought to establish for himself, as Hyder had done, a kingdom in the south. Arthur Wellesley pursued him, step by step, taking and destroying forts, clearing districts, endeavouring to force the bandit into the open field. The private letters of Colonel Wellesley to Thomas Munro show the difficulty of the task which he at last successfully accomplished, and the determined sagacity with which he achieved it. Dundia had almost established a kingdom: he was extraordinarily energetic, capable, and acute. But he was no match for the persistent vigilance of Wellesley. Employing troops from Goa, the pledge of the firm alliance with Portugal which he was afterwards to vindicate and cement, Wellesley pursued the foe till he was defeated and killed. Alike in the personal letters to his friends and in the official dispatches Wellesley showed the calm unbroken perseverance which was to make him the greatest English general of his age. The tranquillity of the Mysore kingdom, which has been practically unbroken for a century, was due to him, it may well be said, more than to any other man. Without the brilliancy and the political genius of his elder brother, Arthur Wellesley had qualities which endured longer and which brought him at length to the highest place in his country's service. When he became famous in the Spanish Peninsula the portrait painted of him as a young general in India was early sought for reproduction; and this in a figure represented the beginnings of his great military career. The rough work of Indian warfare supplied lessons which he never forgot, and a study of it is indispensable to the understanding of his later achievements.

The governor-general as a statesman, David Baird and Harris as soldiers, Close as administrator, played great parts in the story of conquest and settlement, but Arthur Wellesley is the real hero of the re-establishment of Mysore as a Hindu state.

CHAPTER XXI

OUDH AND THE CARNATIC, 1785–1801

I. OUDH, 1785–1801

THE condition of Oudh under Sir John Macpherson very speedily aroused the suspicion and then the indignation of Cornwallis. Corruption was rife, perhaps even more flagrantly than in the Carnatic. Cornwallis vented his anger in a letter to Dundas.[1] "His government", he said, was "a system of the dirtiest jobbing—a view shared by Sir John Shore[2]—and his conduct in Oudh was as impeachable, and more disgusting to the Vizier than Mr Hastings'." To Lord Southampton he wrote a year later[3] that as soon as he arrived in India he had in Macpherson's presence tied up his hands "against all the modes that used to be practised for providing for persons who were not in the Company's service, such as riding contracts, getting monopolies in Oudh, extorting money for them from the Vizier, etc.". Of his honest determination there could be no question, but he did not find it easy to carry out. Asaf-ud-daula was as corrupt as any native prince of his time could possibly be, and, so far as it was possible for foreigners to judge, as popular. He was certainly as cunning and as determined. In 1787[4] Cornwallis wrote a description of him to Dundas as extorting

every rupee he can from his ministers, to squander in debaucheries, cock-fighting, elephants and horses. He is said to have a thousand of the latter in his stables though he never uses them. The ministers on their part are fully as rapacious as their master; their object is to cheat and plunder the country. They charge him seventy lacs for the maintenance of troops to enforce the collections, the greater part of which do not exist, and the money supposed to pay them goes into the pockets of Almas Ali Khan and Hyder Beg.

It was with no favourable ear, therefore, that the governor-general listened to the request of the wazir for the alteration of the arrangements made by Hastings. The claim was that the temporary quartering of the British (Fatehgarh) brigade should be withdrawn, leaving only one brigade of the Company's troops in Oudh, and that his "oppressive pecuniary burdens" should be reduced. Cornwallis had a conference with the wazir's minister, Haidar Beg, and then (15 April, 1787) addressed a letter to him in which he offered to reduce the tribute from seventy-four to fifty lakhs, if this should be punctually paid, but he refused to withdraw the troops from Fatehgarh. The

---

[1] *Cornwallis Correspondence*, I, 371.
[2] *Life of Lord Teignmouth*, I, 128.
[3] *Cornwallis Correspondence*, I, 445.
[4] *Idem*, p. 247.

condition of the nawab's own troops was a standing menace to the security of the British territory; Cornwallis demanded that they should be greatly reduced.

"I was obliged", wrote Cornwallis to the Directors,[1] "by a sense of public duty to state to him my clear opinion that two brigades in Oudh would be indispensably necessary for the mutual interest and safety of both governments. The loss of Colonel Baillie's and several other detachments during the late war has removed some part of that awe in which the natives formerly stood at the name of British troops. It will therefore be a prudent maxim never to hazard, if it can be avoided, so small a body as a brigade of Sepoys with a weak European regiment at so great a distance as the Doab; and from the confused state of the upper provinces it would be highly inadvisable for us to attempt the defence of the Vizier's extensive territory without a respectable force."

His minute on the subject, rightly regarded by Sir John Malcolm[2] as a very clear view of the connection between the Company and the wazir, states his opinion that it "now stands upon the only basis calculated to render it permanent". He relied for the continuance of the condition of affairs, which he viewed so optimistically, upon the fidelity and justice of the nawab's very able minister, exposed though he was "to the effects of caprice and intrigue". Sir John Malcolm regarded the arrangement "as happy as the personal character of Asaf-ud-daula admitted of its being". So it remained in outward tranquillity at least, unshaken by an insurrection by the Afghans still—in spite of the first Rohilla War, so greatly exaggerated in England—remaining in Rohilkhand. There was a sharp contest, in which British forces supported the nawab. The end was the restoration of their possessions to the Afghans under Hamid 'Ali Khan. The restoration of tranquillity tended to the maintenance of the nawab's administration undisturbed by the very necessary intervention of the Company; but Sir John Shore was fully aware of the condition of affairs. He wrote to Dundas (12 May, 1795)[3] that the dominions of Asaf-ud-daula were

in the precise condition to tempt a rebellion. Disaffection and anarchy prevail throughout; and nothing but the presence of our two brigades prevents insurrection. The Nawab is in a state of bankruptcy, without a sense of his danger, and without a wish to guard against it. The indolence and dissipation of his character are too confirmed to allow the expectation of any reformation on his part;

and the death of Haidar Beg in 1794 had put an end to all hopes of reform. In 1797 Asaf-ud-daula died. Early in the year Sir John Shore had paid a visit to Lucknow, of which a letter of his aide-de-camp and brother-in-law preserves a vivid impression.[4] The nawab seemed still to be "the most splendid emanation of the Great Mogul now remaining", but he had "an open mouth, a dull intellect, a quick propensity to mischief and vice", and "the amusements of Tiberius at Capua must, in comparison with those of their feasts, have

---

[1] *Cornwallis Correspondence*, i, 276.   [2] *History of India*, i, 110.
[3] *Life*, i, 332.
[4] *Bengal Past and Present*, xvi, pt ii, 105 *sqq.*

been elegant and refined". He had still an able minister who acted for him at Calcutta, had translated Newton's *Principia* into Arabic, was a great mathematician, and if he had had sufficient influence with the nawab could have "made his country a paradise".

Lucknow at the time Shore visited it contained at least two persons of peculiar interest. The nawab himself, Asaf-ud-daula, with all the faults of idleness and luxury, in many respects ignorant, and in all subtle, cruel and unsound, was yet, after the fashion of his age, a man of cultured tastes. The remarkable building, the great Imambarah, whose stucco magnificence still, after long years and many dangers, remains impressive, was built by him in 1784, its great gate after the model (it is said) of the gate of the Sublime Porte at Constantinople, which it far surpasses in dignity. In the great hall the remains of the nawab still lie under a plain uninscribed slab. Another memorial of that time is the Martinière, the college founded by General Claude Martin, which was his own house till he died and for which Asaf-ud-daula is said to have paid him a million sterling. Martin from 1776 had been in the service of the nawabs of Oudh; he had made a fortune out of their necessities; he had been a maker of ordnance and a speculator in indigo, and he still retained his position in the Company's military service; he lived till 1800, and was buried, with plainness equal to the nawab's, in the house he had built.

The nawab died a few weeks after Shore's visit, which might seem to have been in vain. At first the governor-general recognised Wazir 'Ali, in spite of some doubts as to his legitimacy, as his successor. Asaf-ud-daula had acknowledged him as his son; there was also the sanction of the late nawab's mother, and appearance of satisfaction among the people. But it was not long before all these appearances were reversed. Shore re-examined the question of right, and came to an opposite conclusion. "Ali", his biographer says, "was surrounded by a gang of miscreants." Other and more important old ladies shrieked their protests into the governor-general's ears. The good man was terribly confused.

"In Eastern countries", he said, "as there is no principle there can be no confidence. Self-interest is the sole object of all, and suspicion and distrust prevail under the appearance and profession of the sincerest intimacy and regard."

General Craig, who had for some time commanded the British forces in Oudh, and Sir Alured Clarke, the commander-in-chief, warned him of the danger he was in if he changed his decision, and Tafazzul Hussain Khan, with agitated emphasis, told him "this is Hindustan, not Europe: and affairs cannot be done here as there". Lucknow showed every sign of an outbreak, and in the city were "many respectable families who live under the protection of British influence". But Shore took the risks, declared the deposition of 'Ali and the substitution of his uncle, Sa'adat, and escorted him through the

city mounted on his own elephant. Not content with declaring the
spuriousness of 'Ali, he included in the same disgrace all the other sons
of Asaf-ud-daula. On 21 January, 1798, Sa'adat 'Ali, now on the
masnad, entered into a treaty which considerably strengthened the
English power. This seemed to be necessary through the recurring
threats of an invasion from Afghanistan by Zaman Shah, of whose
power and ferocity the English letters of the time are full. He had
already occupied Lahore, and, though this had not been followed up,
it showed the weakness of the northern frontier. At home as well as
in India the danger was thought to be grave. Dundas, writing on
18 March, 1799, regarded it as of the first importance to guard
against it, and proposed to encourage and foment "distractions and
animosities" in his own territory to keep Zaman Shah employed, and
was tempted, he said, to direct that our own forces and those of the
wazir should never go beyond his territories and our own, so as to be
ready to repel any attack.

The treaty may have been necessary and just; but it was certainly
a departure from the policy, if not the principles, associated with its
author. Yet the directors evidently approved it, and the ministry
gave Shore an Irish peerage, as Lord Teignmouth—a precedent
followed, and bitterly resented, in the case of his successor. The terms
of the treaty included an increase to seventy-six lakhs of the annual
payment to the Company by the wazir of Oudh; the placing of an
English garrison in the great city of Allahabad; the increase of British
troops to 10,000, who were given the exclusive charge of the defence
of the country, and the strict limitation of the wazir's own troops; and
finally the nawab agreed to have no dealings with other powers without
the consent of the English.

The praise of the treaty was not universal. Burke seemed for a
while to be taking the war-path again. There was a threat of impeachment; and, indeed, Shore seemed to have been at least as autocratic
as Hastings. "I am playing, as the gamesters say, *le grand jeu*", he
said, "and with the same sensation as a man who apprehends losing
his all." But nothing came of it. Wazir 'Ali had undoubtedly been
overawed by force: a proceeding against which, in the case of the
Carnatic, Shore had himself piously protested, and Sa'adat, equally
under pressure, agreed to pay for any increase of English troops
that might be necessary. It was the last act of Lord Teignmouth
as governor-general, and certainly the most vigorous, but it was no
more effective than his less emphatic actions.

When Mornington arrived in India the condition of Oudh was
represented to him as tranquil. The directors in May, 1799, thought
that Shore's settlement bade fair to be permanent. They were not
disturbed by the subsidy, during the first year of Sa'adat 'Ali, being
in arrear; yet this was the very eventuality for which Shore's treaty
had provided a remedy. They were ready even to counter-order the

augmentation of the English force. Shore had infected them with his roseate confidence. Mornington very soon saw more clearly. He had in 1798 found it necessary to station an army of 20,000 men in Oudh under the command of Sir J. Craig, to be ready for the anticipated invasion by Zaman Shah. The new wazir had complained that his own troops could not be trusted and had demanded an English force as a security against them. For this an increase of the subsidy of fifty lakhs was considered necessary. This was a heavy burden but the protection could not be had for nothing, and Mornington's keen eye saw that the internal dangers of Oudh were pressing. There was the Doab: what was to become of it? There was the danger that would come on the death of Ilmas, its possessor; how was it to be guarded against? And there was the state of the nawab's own troops, which it soon became a fixed custom to describe as a "rabble force": there was no other way to meet this but by an increase of the British contingent. But more than this: there was the civil disorder, still unremedied, in every branch of the nawab's administration.

With respect to the Wazir's civil establishments, and to his abusive systems for the extortion of revenue, and for the violation of every principle of justice, little can be done before I can be enabled to visit Lucknow. (December, 1798.)

Mornington had no misconception of the character of oriental sovereigns. Shore seemed satisfied that Sa'adat would be a great improvement on the nephew whom he had dispossessed. But Amurath to Amurath succeeds; and a leopard cannot change his spots.

Mornington's gaze, like that of Cornwallis, was concentrated also on the English locusts in Oudh. Shore, almost as much as Macpherson whom he so sternly condemned, had seemed to be content to leave them alone. Mornington regarded their presence as "a mischief which requires no comment". And he determined "to dislodge every European except the Company's servants". Nor was his anxiety at this time restricted to the Englishmen in the country. The deposed Wazir 'Ali, residing near Benares, with a handsome pension from his uncle, apparently on a momentary impulse, but more probably by a premeditated scheme, murdered Cherry, the British Resident, and soon received "active and general support": it needed a British force to pursue and capture him. He was kept at Fort William in captivity and lived till 1817. The confusion with which Mornington had to deal was even more entangling than that of the Carnatic, and, for the moment at least, more actively dangerous. Whether Sa'adat 'Ali had a better right to rule than his nephew or not, he certainly was no more capable of doing so. He was as incompetent as he was inconsistent: at one time crying for protection against his own troops, at another refusing to disband them. He protested that he could not rule: he volunteered to abdicate: he withdrew his offer. It was impossible from a distance to understand his manœuvres and tergiversations. Mornington supplemented the Resident by a military negotiator, Colonel Scott, who came to Lucknow in June, 1799. He did not act precipitately: he made as careful an investigation of the country and the circumstances as time would permit. He found that the wazir was unpopular to an extreme degree: the durbar was deserted: the administration was hopelessly corrupt. The nawab's object was only to temporise and delay. Colonel Scott soon convinced himself that what he really wanted was to obtain entire control of the internal administration and the exclusion of the English from any share in it. Then corruption would grow more corrupt, and the English would be responsible for the maintenance of a system which was thoroughly immoral, inefficient and dangerous. And the wazir assured the envoy that he had a secret and personal proposal in reserve. What was it? Ultimately it appeared to be his resignation, which was offered, accepted, and, as soon as it was accepted, withdrawn.

To Mornington and his advisers the first necessity appeared to be military security, the second civil reform; and neither of these was possible under a vicious and incompetent government. The establishment of a strong military force was essential, as strong in peace as war. Mill,[1] thirty years afterwards, considered that "a more monstrous proposition never issued from human organs". The fact is that the ceaseless oriental procrastination increased the external danger and the internal oppression day by day. Coercion at last became the only remedy. The condition of Oudh, then and for fifty years afterwards, proves that the action of the governor-general was neither precipitate nor unwise.

On 12 November, 1799, the wazir announced to Colonel Scott his intention to abdicate. He desired that one of his sons should succeed him. On the 21st the governor-general expressed his satisfaction with the decision.

The proposition of the Wazir is pregnant with such benefit, not only to the Company, but to the inhabitants of Oudh, that his lordship thinks it cannot be too much encouraged; and that there are no circumstances which shall be allowed to impede the accomplishment of the grand object which it leads to. This object his lordship considers to be the acquisition by the Company of the exclusive authority, civil and military, over the dominion of Oudh.

The cat was out of the bag.

But then there was the most tedious and exasperating delay. Sa'adat would and he would not. Wellesley could with difficulty restrain his irritation. Colonel Scott had a difficult task, between the two, to carry out any arrangement which should secure the prosperity of the country.

Mornington's proposal was similar to that arrived at in the south, at Tanjore: that is, the establishment of a native ruler with a fixed income and all the paraphernalia of sovereignty, the administration being placed in the hands of British officials. But this by no means

---

[1] *History of India*, VI, 142.

suited Sa'adat. The control of the internal administration, with the fruits of peculation and oppression, was the apple of his eye. He withdrew his abdication and retired, metaphorically, into his tent. He thought, like the nawab of the Carnatic, that he could sit tight and wait. But Wellesley had now full experience of this process, and he would no longer endure it. He ordered several regiments to move into the north of Oudh and required the nawab to maintain them. The wazir replied that this was contrary to the treaty with Shore, that the British force should only be augmented in case of necessity, and that the nawab should have control of his household treasure. Sir John Malcolm[1] rightly rejects this argument, which English critics of Wellesley have accepted. As to the wazir's consent being necessary, he says that

if this assertion had not been refuted by the evidence of the respectable nobleman who framed the treaty, it must have been by its own absurdity; for the cause of the increase is said to be the existence of external danger—of which one party—the English Government—can alone be the judge, as the other, the Wazir, is precluded by one of the articles of this treaty from all intercourse or communication whatever with foreign states.

In a masterly letter to the wazir from Fort William, 9 February, 1800, Mornington exposed the inconsistencies of his conduct, and sternly told him that the means he had taken to delay the execution of all reform were calculated to degrade his character, to destroy all confidence between him and the British Government, to produce confusion and disorder in his dominions, and to injure the important interests of the Company to such a degree as might be deemed nearly equivalent to positive hostility. It was a long, severe, eviscerating epistle. But a year passed and nothing happened that pointed to a conclusion. On 22 January, 1801, Wellesley wrote to Colonel Scott, exonerating him from any responsibility for the delay, analysing the condition of the country and the government, and insisting that the time had now come for "the active and decided interference of the British Government in the affairs of the country", and that the wazir must now be required

to make a cession to the Company in perpetual sovereignty of such a portion of his territory as shall be fully adequate, in their present impoverished condition, to repay the expenses of the troops.

The treaty was to be drawn up on the same terms as those already concluded with the Nizam and with Tanjore. And so within ten months it was.

Wellesley associated in the drawing up of the treaty his brother Henry, the astute diplomatist afterwards famous as Lord Cowley. The date of the treaty was November, 1801. The required territory was ceded. It "formed a barrier between the dominions of the Wazir and any foreign enemy". And the wazir promised to establish such an administration in his own dominions as should conduce to the

[1] *History of India*, I, 275–6.

happiness and prosperity of his people. From Wellesley's explanation of the treaty to the directors, and from the Duke of Wellington's justification of it, may be drawn the grounds on which it was considered necessary and effectual at the time. The subsequent history of Oudh up to the Sepoy War shows that it did not fully meet the intentions of its framers. But at the moment there was the obvious advantage of getting rid of a useless and dangerous body of troops ready at all times to join an enemy of the Company—the extinction indeed of the nawab's military power. Obviously important, too, was the obtaining responsibility by the Company for the general defence of the nawab's dominions. By the renewed security for the payment of the subsidy the continual disputes with the court of Lucknow were ended. Commerce grew, in consequence of the new security, enormously. The Jumna was made navigable for large vessels: Allahabad became a great emporium of trade, and indeed started on its modern career of prosperity. A real improvement in the condition of the people was soon evident. Wellesley had seen elsewhere the enormous benefits of the British rule in the "flourishing and happy provinces" which he had already visited, and Wellington a few years later pointed to "the tranquillity of those hitherto disturbed countries and the loyalty and happiness of their hitherto turbulent and disaffected inhabitants". The settlement of the ceded districts was managed by a commission under Henry Wellesley. His appointment was the subject of severe criticism. The bitterest charges of nepotism were launched against the governor-general. But there can be no doubt that, in entrusting such important work to his brothers Arthur and Henry, Wellesley chose the best means at his command, and materially benefited the people who were entrusted to their protection.

It has been said that the Oudh assumption was the most high-handed of all Wellesley's despotic actions. He would hardly have denied this, but he would have justified it. The tangle of conflicting interests could only be cut by the sword: and he did not hold the sword in vain. Honest administration turned the ceded districts from almost a desert to a prosperous and smiling land.

But in this, and the other subsidiary treaties, it must be observed that there were grave defects. The Company was made responsible for the maintenance of a government which it was impossible for its representatives, as foreigners, entirely to control. The Carnatic no doubt had a new and happy future: but in Oudh the snake of oppression was scotched, not killed. The progress of amelioration under English rule—often stern as well as just, and unpopular because not fully understood—was always slow, often checked, often incomplete. But of the great aims, the high conscientiousness, the keen insight, and the impressive wisdom, of the Marquis Wellesley, in these, the most characteristic expressions of his statesmanship, there can be no doubt.

II. The Carnatic, 1785–1801

The condition of the province of Madras had been a constant anxiety to succeeding governors-general, and indeed a danger to the British position in India. So far back as 1776 the Tanjore question had been complicated by the gravest disagreements between the governor and his council, leading up to the arrest of Lord Pigot and his removal from the government of Fort St George. The numerous papers, published in two large volumes in 1777, are concerned not a little with the affairs of the nawab of the Carnatic, and form indeed an indispensable preliminary to the understanding of his position in 1785. A smaller volume published in the same year deals more directly with this subject, and claims to explain fully the right of the nawab to Tanjore and to refute all the arguments of Lord Pigot's adherents "and the authors of the unjust and impolitic order for the restoration of Tanjore". It was declared by those who were in favour of Muhammad 'Ali, nawab of Arcot, "the old faithful and strenuous ally of the British nation", that the raja of Tanjore was the hereditary enemy of the nawab and of the British, "destitute of morality, but devoted to superstition", and that the nawab was heart and soul in English interests, and "without power to emancipate himself from English control even if he wished to do so".

Are not his forts garrisoned with our troops? His army commanded by our officers? Is not his country open to our invasion? His person always in our power? Is not he himself, are not his children, his family, his servants, under the very guns of Fort St George?[1]

This argument was repeated as strongly in 1785. But it was urged, in reality, on behalf of the British creditors of the nawab, of whom the notorious Paul Benfield, now caricatured as "Count Rupee" with a black face riding in Hyde Park on a stout cob, was, if not the great original, at least the most successful and the richest. It was the nawab's creditors, some at least of whom were actually members of the Madras Council, who kept him so long in possession of his throne and with the trappings of independence. A crisis, it may be said, was reached when the English legislature endeavoured to deal with the nawab of Arcot's debts. But such crises were recurrent. Dundas's bill, Fox's bill, Pitt's bill, took up the matter, and the Act of 1784 ordered, in regard to the claims of British subjects, that the Court of Directors should take into consideration "the origin and justice of the said demands"; but the Board of Control itself intervened, divided the loans into three classes and gave orders for the separate treatment of each. This was challenged by the Company.

There was a motion by Fox and a famous speech by Burke, February, 1785, in which the ministry was denounced as the

[1] *Original Papers relative to Tanjore*, p. 40.

submissive agent of Benfield, a "coalition between the men of intrigue in India and the ministry of intrigue in England". The orator threaded his way through a network of intrigue: he could not disentangle it. He used it as an instrument for belabouring the English ministry. It was to form another scourge for the back of Hastings. The governor-general had ordered the assignment of all the revenues of the Carnatic during the war with Hyder to British control, and the government of Madras had negotiated it. This plan left the nawab with one-sixth of the whole for his own maintenance and thereby made him richer than before. The creditors were determined to obtain more: they raised vehement cries of protest: they partially convinced Hastings: they wholly convinced the Board of Control; and Dundas ordered restitution of the entire revenues to the nawab. In vain Lord Macartney, in a letter from Calcutta (27 July, 1785), proclaimed that the assignment was "the rock of your strength in the Carnatic", and on his return to England, after declining the government of Bengal, he pressed his views very strongly upon Pitt and Dundas. In vain. Restitution was ordered. There was no provision in Pitt's Act which could prevent new loans, and so the nawab plunged deeper than ever into debt.

Thus Cornwallis found the relations of the Company with the nawab more complicated than ever. The new governor of Madras, Sir Archibald Campbell, made a new arrangement with him, moved it would seem by his crocodile tears and "a very pathetic remonstrance" that he could not live on what was left him after contributing to the payment of his debts and the expense of the state. A treaty, 24 February, 1787, assigned nine lakhs of pagodas to the state and twelve to the creditors: and the nawab was supposed to be "more sincerely attached to the prosperity of the Honourable Company" than "any prince or person on earth". Special provisions were made in view of possible war, and the sole military power was placed in the hands of the Company. But the conditions were no better fulfilled than others. When war came in 1790 Cornwallis was obliged to take possession of the Carnatic,[1] in order, says Sir John Malcolm,[2] "to secure the two states [the Carnatic and Madras] against the dangers to which he thought them exposed from the mismanagement of the Nawab's officers". It was quite clear that it was impossible to leave the "sword in one hand, the purse in another". By the control now assumed the success of the war with Tipu was made much more easy, and it became obvious that a new treaty to stabilise this condition of affairs had become necessary. In 1792 this was concluded. By this the Company was to assume entire control of the Carnatic during war, but to restore it when war ended. It was to occupy specified districts if the nawab's payments should fall into arrear; the

---

[1] See *Cornwallis Correspondence*, II, 2, 3.
[2] *History of India*, I, 94.

poligars of Madura and Tinnevelly, whose resistance to the feeble government of the nawab rendered the collection of revenue impossible, were transferred to the rule of the Company; and the nawab's payments, for which these terms were a security, were to be nine lakhs for the peace establishment and four-fifths of his revenues for war expenses, his payment to his creditors being reduced from twelve to six lakhs. From this treaty Cornwallis hoped for a new and stable settlement of the most puzzling, if not the most dangerous problem, with which successive representatives were confronted. In nothing did he show more clearly his lack of political sagacity than in this hope. The fact that the moment any war broke out the control of the country should change hands made confusion worse confounded, and an efficient native administration became impossible. The nawab too was left exposed to all the schemes and intrigues which had enmeshed him of old. The pavement of good intentions left Paul Benfield and his companions more secure than before. English management for a limited period gave no opportunity for the detailed knowledge which is essential to good government, and the people naturally preserved their allegiance to the rule to which they were soon to return. The Board of Control saw the weakness of the scheme and soon determined that new arrangements must be made: but nothing was done, perhaps nothing could have been done, so long as Muhammad 'Ali lived. He died 13 October, 1795, at the age of seventy-eight, an astute intriguer, never a serious foe, but always a serious trouble, to the Company. He had played on ruler after ruler with the skill of an expert, and he had continually succeeded in obtaining terms much better than he deserved, if not always all that he desired.

The time of his death seemed propitious. A year before, 7 September, 1794, Lord Hobart, an honourable and intelligent personage, had become governor of Madras; and in a minute immediately after the nawab's death recording the ruinous results of the policy of the past and tracing all to the usurious loans which had been effected by Europeans for mortgages on the provinces of the Carnatic, he declared that the whole system was "destructive to the resources of the Carnatic and in some degree reflecting disgrace upon the British Government". In the letter appears an early expression of English concern for the welfare of the poorest class, a protest against that oppression of the ryots which the misgovernment and financial disorder inevitably produced. British power, it seemed, had actually increased the capacity for evil-doing which native governments had never been slow to exercise. The Europeans to whom control of this mortgaged district was allowed came to terms with the military authorities, and enforced their claims by their aid: the cultivators had recourse to money-lenders, who completed their ruin.

The accession of 'Umdat-ul-Umara determined Lord Hobart to press his views of needed reform on the new nawab and on the English

Government. He proposed to assume the whole military and civil administration of the districts pledged for the payment of the tribute, and the cession of the sovereignty over the poligars and of some specified forts. He declared that the treaty of 1792 was a total failure. But he found the new nawab immovable. He "sat tight" and appealed to the dying injunctions of his flagitious parent. Hobart felt that he could wait no longer. He proposed to annex Tinnevelly. Sir John Shore, now governor-general, considered such a course impolitic, unauthorised and unjust. He wrote[1] to his predecessor declaring that nothing could be more irreconcileable than Lord Hobart's principles and his own. The governor of Madras seemed to him to be "pursuing objects without any regard to the rectitude of the means or ultimate consequence". Shore's principles, regarded by many as the cause of future wars, could not be better expressed than in one sentence of this letter[2]—

> That the territories of the Nawab of Arcot...may be mismanaged in the most ruinous manner, I doubt not; that he [Hobart] should be anxious to correct those evils which, from personal observation, may be more impressive, I can readily admit; but the existing treaties propose limits even to mismanagement, and let it be as great as is asserted, which I do not deny, these people are not to be dragooned into concessions.

In fine, let the nawab go on, and let us hope that our goodness, without pressure, will make other people good. The Evangelical idealist lost all touch with fact, and thus all power to succour the oppressed. So, as James Mill, for once not too severe, expresses it,[3]

> by the compound of opposition of the Supreme Government and of the powerful class of individuals whose profit depended upon the misgovernment of the country, no reform could be introduced.

A change in the directing principle was necessary; and it came. Lord Hobart, defeated and discouraged, resigned his post. Lord Clive, his successor, arrived at Madras on 21 August, 1798. Meanwhile Lord Mornington had succeeded Sir John Shore. The new governor-general had not only studied Indian affairs in general with more industry and insight than any of his predecessors before their arrival in the country, but as the intimate friend of Pitt was well acquainted with the bitter criticisms directed against the India Act in its bearing upon the affairs of the Carnatic. He saw the condition of the country from much the same point of view as was described by his brother Arthur in 1806. The evils of the alliance, begun[4] "in the infancy of the British power in the peninsula of India", centred on the non-interference of the Company in the nawab's internal affairs, the prominent feature in the policy of the directors, while such interference was constantly proved to be absolutely necessary, and in the necessity of borrowing

---

[1] To Cornwallis, *Life of Lord Teignmouth*, I, 371 *sqq.*   [2] *Idem*, p. 373.
[3] *History of India*, VI, 49.   [4] *Wellington Supplementary Despatches*, IV, 893.

money to pay the tribute from those who had given assignments of territory and had no interest in anything beyond the security of their own interests. Thence came, as Arthur Wellesley said,

a system which tended not only to the oppression of the inhabitants of the country, to the impoverishment of the Nawab, and to the destruction of the revenues of the Carnatic, but was carried into execution by the Company's civil and military servants, and by British subjects.

It had become an evil of enormous magnitude. Arthur Wellesley acutely observed that, apart from its other results, it created in Madras a body of men who, though in the Company's service, were directly opposed to its interests; and these men gave advice to the nawab which was necessarily contrary to the requirements of the British Government and encouraged him in his maintenance of a condition of affairs which, though it kept him in wealth and nominal power, tended directly to the impoverishment of his country. The payment of interest to private persons at 36 per cent. meant ruin even in India; and in order to discharge it assignments had been given on the districts especially secured to the Company, in case of failure to pay the subsidy due to the government. This was in direct contradiction to the terms of Cornwallis's treaty of 1792.

Not a month elapsed that did not afford matter of speculation as to whether he could continue to pay his stipulated subsidy; and not one in which [the Nawab] did not procure the money on loan at a large interest by means which tended to the destruction of the country.

In vain did Hobart, Mornington, and Clive endeavour to win the nawab's consent to a modification of the treaty: persistent immobility and trickery had been displayed to the full by Muhammad 'Ali, and 'Umdat-ul-Umara, his son, followed in his steps. It is more than probable that Mornington, masterful, determined, and impartial though he was, might have failed like his predecessors to cleanse the Augean stable if the nawab's rash treachery had not delivered him into the governor-general's hands.

Impartial and uninfluenced by underground intrigue was Mornington: the directors can hardly be said to have deserved this praise. Though not personally corrupt, as were not a few of their representatives in India, they were obsessed with the idea that it was necessary to maintain treaties in permanence which were proved to have been drawn up on inadequate knowledge. They thought that Cornwallis had established this "honourable principle". They declared to Mornington that, while they agreed with the proposals of Hobart, they could not authorise the use of "any powers than those of persuasion" to induce the nawab to form a new arrangement. Mornington replied, 4 July, 1798, that he had taken immediate steps to negotiate but that there was no hope at present of obtaining the nawab's consent. His father's injunctions and his usurers' disapproval were the ostensible and the real reasons of his obduracy.

Then came the war with Tipu, in which the nawab behaved rather as an enemy than a friend. Negotiations were conducted with scrupulous courtesy but no success. Then suddenly the whole position changed. The Home Government had begun to see through the nawab's disguises: the government of Fort St George still hesitated: Mornington thought that the rapid progress of the war made the seizure of the pledged territories, though ordered by the directors, unnecessary. He was soon to discover that it was pressingly urgent.

For the moment he was turned aside from what was already his object, as it had been that of Cornwallis and Hobart, to assume entire control of the Carnatic, by affairs in the district about which Lord Pigot and Muhammad 'Ali had been embroiled—Tanjore. There in 1786 Amir Singh had been appointed regent for Sarboji, the nephew by adoption of his late brother the raja. A council of pandits to whom the question of right was referred by the Madras Government decided against the claims of the nephew. Sir John Shore was as usual conscientious and dissatisfied. He found that the pandits had been corruptly influenced. He summoned more pandits, especially those of Benares—a body, it might be thought, not less amenable to monetary influence. They decided in favour of Sarboji. It was clear that the land was grievously oppressed by Amir Singh's minister, Siva Rao, and that the districts, mortgaged, like those in the Carnatic, for debt to the Company, were on the verge of ruin. Hobart persuaded the raja to surrender his territory. But Shore would none of it. His biographer[1] says that the prize did not tempt him to forget what he conceived to be the undue pressure by which it had been won.

He observed that the raja had been intimidated into compliance by the repeated calling out of British troops, even after he had consented to the dismissal of his minister—that the employment of Mr Swartz, the avowed protector of the raja's competitor and public impeacher of his life, as interpreter in the transaction, had been injudicious—that the punctuality of the raja's payments had precluded all pretext for taking possession of his territory—that if maladministration of mortgaged districts could justify the forfeiture of them the British Government might lay claim equally to Oudh and Travancore; and he concluded by declaring that justice and policy alike prescribed the recission of the treaty and the restoration of the ceded district to the Nawab, whatever embarrassments might result from the proceeding.

Lord Hobart, the man on the spot, naturally protested, and Shore, writing to the omnipotent Charles Grant[2] at the Board of Directors, was equally emphatic on the error of Madras, which he attributed to want of judgment and to ignoring his opinion "that honesty is, in all situations, the best policy". But that same honesty made him temper his criticism by a warm eulogy of the missionary, Swartz, one of the greatest of the men whose services were at that time given unreservedly to Southern India. Shore was indeed, one cannot but

[1] His son, the second Lord Teignmouth, *Life*, 1, 356.
[2] *Idem*, pp. 374 *sqq*.

feel as one reads the documents, completely muddled over the affair. It needed a Wellesley to straighten out the problem.

In October, 1797, the directors requested Lord Mornington to "make a short stay at Madras". He did so, and he studied the cases of Tanjore and Arcot on the spot. On 21 March, 1799, Dundas wrote hoping that in the former case a settlement might be made by which there could be expected from the raja "a pure and virtuous administration of the affairs of his country".[1] Mornington went into all the questions involved most thoroughly, and brought "the several contending parties to a fair discussion (or rather to a bitter contest)" in his own presence. Finally, 25 October, 1799, a treaty drawn up by him was signed by which Sarboji was recognised as raja, but the whole civil and military administration of the country was placed in British hands, and the raja was given an allowance of £40,000, and Amir Singh £10,000. The arrangement was undoubtedly beneficial to English interests, but it

was far more beneficial to the people of Tanjore. It delivered them from the effects of native oppression and European cupidity. It gave them what they had never before possessed—the security derived from the administration of Justice.[2]

From this settlement we pass to one much more difficult to achieve, which was, as we have said, secured by the discovery of the treachery of the nawab of Arcot.

At the capture of Seringapatam a mass of secret correspondence, hitherto entirely unknown, between Muhammad 'Ali and his son and the ruler of Mysore, fell into British hands. It was investigated by Colonel Close and Mr Webbe and submitted to the Board of Control and the Court of Directors. Wellesley would run no risk of again being the victim of ingeniously manufactured delays. This investigation was thorough. Witnesses as well as documents were most carefully examined and a report[3] was signed at Seringapatam, 18 May, 1800. The conclusion was—and it is reiterated in calm judicial terms by Arthur Wellesley—that by their correspondence with the Company's enemies the rulers of the Carnatic had broken their treaties with the English and forfeited all claim to consideration as friends or allies. The timely death of 'Umdat-ul-Umara, 15 July, 1801, gave further facilities for the change of system which the English had long believed to be necessary and inevitable. The succession was offered to the "son, or supposed son" of the nawab, 'Ali Husain, if he would accept the terms offered—a sum sufficient for his maintenance in state and dignity and the transference of the government to the Company. He rashly refused. Accordingly the nephew of the late nawab, 'Azim-ud-daula, was approached. He was the eldest legitimate son of Amir-

[1] *Wellesley Despatches*, II, 110.
[2] Thornton, *History of India*, III, 103-4.
[3] *Wellesley Despatches*, II, 515.

ul-Umara, who was the second son of Muhammad 'Ali and brother of 'Umdat-ul-Umara.

"This prince", in Wellington's words, "having agreed to the arrangement, a treaty was concluded by which the whole of the civil and military government of the Carnatic was transferred for ever to the Company, and the Nawab, Azim-ud-daula, and his heirs were to preserve their title and dignity and to receive one-fifth of the net revenues of the country."

An arrangement was also made for the gradual liquidation of the long-standing and enormous debt.

Wellesley's justification of the treatment of 'Ali Husain[1] falls into four divisions, which sum up the whole history of the last fifty years. The nawabs were not independent princes but the creatures of the Company, established and maintained by their assistance. Muhammad 'Ali and 'Umdat-ul-Umara had by their treachery forfeited all claim to consideration for themselves or their line. The condition of the Carnatic was a standing menace to the British position in Southern India, and a scandalous blot on the principles of peace, justice and prosperity which English rulers had endeavoured to introduce. A definite settlement was absolutely demanded. And no injustice was done to 'Ali Husain, for he rejected the terms offered which his successor accepted. Thus a stable and honest government was at last given by Wellesley to the land which had been the earliest to enter into close association with England. And the political errors of earlier statesmen were put aside. The nawab of Arcot was in truth no independent prince.[2] He was merely an officer of the subahdar of the Deccan of whom he had been rendered independent, ignorantly or generously, by the English. A political error had been committed in ever treating him as independent; and political errors, however generously originated, are often as dangerous as intentional crimes. Wellesley, in the annexation of the Carnatic, vindicated political justice as well as political wisdom.

---

[1] Declaration of the Annexation of the Carnatic.   [2] *Idem.*

CHAPTER XXII

THE FINAL STRUGGLE WITH THE MARATHAS, 1784–1818

THE Treaty of Salbai, which was signed 17 May, 1782, and was ratified by the Peshwa in February of the following year, assured peace between the East India Company and the Maratha power for the next twenty years, and marked a stage in the acquisition by the English of a controlling voice in Indian politics. The treaty left Mahadaji Sindhia, through whom it was negotiated, in a virtually independent position, and the history of the decade preceding his death in 1794 is largely the story of his efforts to re-establish Maratha control over Northern India and to outwit the design of Nana Phadnavis, who sought to maintain the Peshwa's hegemony over the whole Maratha confederacy. While the mutual jealousy of these two able exponents of Maratha policy and power prevented their acting wholeheartedly in unison, they were restrained from overt antagonism by a natural apprehension of the growing power of the English, this apprehension in Mahadaji Sindhia's case being augmented by his experience of the military ability displayed by the English in 1780 and 1781. These views and considerations determined their attitude towards the transactions of the English with Mysore. An attempt to force Tipu Sultan to comply with the terms of the Treaty of Salbai ended with the unfortunate Treaty of Mangalore, concluded between the English in Madras and the sultan in March, 1784, which provided for the mutual restitution of conquests and left Tipu free to mature fresh plans for the expulsion of the English from India. The Marathas, who wished Tipu Sultan to be regarded as their dependent and tributary, disapproved of the terms of the treaty quite as strongly as Warren Hastings, who had no little difficulty in persuading Sindhia and other leaders that he was in no way responsible for the compact. But, desirous of prosecuting their own policy and intrigues in other parts of India, the Marathas gave a grudging assent to the *fait accompli* and reverted for the time being to matters of more immediate importance.

Sindhia's political influence in Northern India synchronised with an enhancement of his military power, which resulted from his employment of Count Benoît de Boigne and other European military adventurers to train and lead his infantry.[1] With these forces, drilled and equipped on European lines, he obtained the surrender of the fortress of Gwalior, made an incursion into Bundelkhand, and secured complete control of affairs at Delhi, whither he had been invited in

[1] Compton, *European Military Adventurers in Hindustan*, pp. 15 *sqq.* and 223 *sqq.*

the name of the emperor, Shah 'Alam, to assist in quelling the revolt of Muhammad Beg, governor of the province of Agra. Chaos reigned in the Moghul capital in October, 1784; and the emperor, powerless to assert his will and anxious to secure by any means the tranquillity to which he had long been a stranger, permitted Sindhia to assume full control of affairs at Delhi, appointed him deputy of the Peshwa, who was formally honoured *in absentia* with the title of *Wakil-i-mutlak* or vice-regent of the empire, and bestowed upon him the command of the Moghul army and the administrative charge of Agra and Delhi provinces. In return for these official honours, which gave him executive authority over Hindustan and a rank superior to that of the Peshwa's other ministers, Sindhia undertook to contribute 65,000 rupees monthly towards the expenses of the imperial household, and subsequently such additional amount as the increasing revenues of the two provinces might justify. By the close of 1785 Sindhia had secured the submission of Muhammad Beg and had recovered by force of arms the Doab, Agra, and Aligarh, which had flouted the authority of the titular emperor.[1] In the first flush of his success and emboldened, perhaps, by the disappearance of Warren Hastings, who had retired from office in February, 1785, Sindhia demanded, in the name of the Moghul, the tribute of the British provinces in Bengal. But he met with a flat denial of the claim from Sir John Macpherson, who endeavoured to counteract Sindhia's influence by making overtures through the Bombay Government to Mudaji Bhonsle, raja of Berar, and by suggesting to Nana Phadnavis the substitution for Sindhia of a British Resident as representative of the Company's interests at the court of the Peshwa.

Meanwhile Nana Phadnavis, who viewed Sindhia's ascendancy in Northern India with disfavour, had been prosecuting his designs against Mysore, as part of his policy of recovering the territories south of the Narbada, which once formed part of the Maratha possessions. After issuing a formal demand upon Tipu for arrears of tribute, he concluded a general treaty of alliance with the Nizam in July, 1784, to which Tipu replied by overt preparations for the invasion of the Nizam's territory south of the Krishna. Hostilities were, however, postponed by mutual agreement, as Tipu was conscious of his own incapacity to support a lengthy campaign and the Nizam was unable to count for the moment on the active support of the Marathas. Nana Phadnavis's attention was wholly engaged in countering a plot to depose the Peshwa, Madhu Rao Narayan, in favour of Baji Rao son of Raghunath Rao, who had died in retirement at Kopargaon on the Godavari a few months after the Treaty of Salbai. The minister succeeded without difficulty in quashing the movement, which had possibly been secretly fomented by Mahadaji Sindhia, in pursuance of his general policy of restricting Nana's influence.

[1] Francklin, *The History of the Reign of Shah-Aulum*, pp. 119–37.

Nana Phadnavis was thus free to commence hostilities, when Tipu made an unprovoked attack in 1785 on the desai of Nargund, and aroused Maratha anger still further by forcibly circumcising and otherwise maltreating many Hindu inhabitants of the districts south of the Krishna. Believing that the Mysore troops were superior to those of the Peshwa and the Nizam, and being doubtful of the aid of the latter, Nana sought the help of the English, but without success; and consequently the Maratha army, which left Poona at the close of 1785 under the command of Hari Pant Phadke, had to depend upon the co-operation of Tukoji Holkar and the raja of Berar, and on the dubious assistance of the Nizam. After a series of comparatively futile operations, which were rather more favourable to the Marathas than to Tipu, the latter, assuming that the appointment of Charles Malet as Resident at Poona and certain military preparations in Bombay and elsewhere betokened the intention of the English to intervene, persuaded the Marathas to conclude peace in April, 1787. By this pact Tipu agreed to pay forty-five lakhs of rupees and to cede the towns of Badami, Kittur, and Nargund to the Peshwa, who on his side restored to Mysore the other districts overrun by the Maratha forces.[1]

During the progress of these events in the south, Mahadaji Sindhia found his position in Northern India far from secure. His decision to organise a regular standing army on the European model necessitated the sequestration of many of the jagirs bestowed in the past for military service—a course which alienated their Muhammadan holders; while his pressing need of money obliged him to demand a heavy tribute from the Rajput chiefs, who resisted the claim and, aided by the disaffected Muhammadan jagirdars, drove his forces from the gates of Jaipur. His difficulties were aggravated by the faction in Delhi, which supported the invertebrate emperor, and by the hostility of the Sikhs. When he finally gave battle to the united Rajput forces, he witnessed the desertion to the enemy of a large contingent of the Moghul forces under Muhammad Beg and his nephew Ismail, and was consequently obliged to beat a hasty retreat to Gwalior. His flight emboldened a young Rohilla, Ghulam Kadir, to renew the claims of his father, Zabita Khan, upon the Moghul emperor and obtain for himself the dignity of Amiru'l-umara. Having seized Aligarh and repulsed an attack by Sindhia and a Jat army under Lestineau[2] near Fatehpur Sikri, the Rohilla took possession of Delhi in June, 1788, plundered the palace, and treated the wretched Shah 'Alam, whom he blinded, and his household with barbaric cruelty. His crimes, however, were speedily avenged. Nana Phadnavis, who had no wish to see a permanent diminution of Maratha influence in Hindustan, dispatched reinforcements from Poona under 'Ali Bahadur and Tukoji Holkar. With these and his own battalions

---

[1] Grant Duff, *History of the Mahrattas*, chap. xxxii.   [2] Compton, *op. cit.* p. 368.

under de Boigne and Appa Khande Rao, Sindhia succeeded in recovering Delhi in 1789, and, after taking a bloody revenge upon the usurper, reseated the blind emperor upon the throne.[1]

These events resulted in the jagir of Ghulam Kadir, the greater part of the Doab, and the provinces of Delhi and Agra being annexed to the Maratha dominions; while Sindhia had leisure to organise his army with the help of de Boigne, who ultimately commanded three brigades of eight battalions each, equipped in European style and composed of both Rajputs and Muhammadans, with the necessary complement of cavalry and artillery. With these forces Sindhia finally defeated Ismail Beg at Patan (Rajputana) in 1790, and the Rajput allies of that chief at Mirtha (Mairta) in Jodhpur territory in the following year. Sindhia's supremacy in Northern India still suffered, however, from the hostile intrigues of Holkar, who declined overtures of conciliation and, in sympathy with the secret policy of Nana Phadnavis, showed little inclination to assist his rival to impose his authority upon the Sikhs and Rajputs. The veiled enmity between the two Maratha chiefs burst into open hostilities after Ismail Beg's submission to Perron, Sindhia's second-in-command, at Kanund Mohendargarh. Their armies, which at the moment were jointly devastating Rajput territory, suddenly attacked one another and fought a battle at Lakheri (Kotah) in September, 1792, which ended in the complete defeat of Holkar's troops under the command of a French adventurer named Dudrenec.[2] This success finally assured Sindhia's predominance in Northern India.

At the close of December, 1789, war between the Company and Mysore was precipitated by Tipu Sultan's attack upon the lines of Travancore. Hostilities had been preceded by curious negotiations between Lord Cornwallis and the Nizam, which resulted in the cession to the Company of the Guntoor district and in a promise by Cornwallis that in certain future circumstances he would sanction the restoration to the Nizam and the Marathas of the Carnatic uplands (*balaghat*), which were at that date included in the Mysore state. On the outbreak of hostilities with Tipu, Nana Phadnavis made immediate overtures to the governor-general, and in the names of both the Peshwa and the Nizam concluded an offensive and defensive alliance with the Company against Tipu in June, 1790. The support afforded by the Marathas and the Nizam was, however, of little value; and it was not until March, 1792, that Lord Cornwallis succeeded in forcing Tipu to sign the Treaty of Seringapatam, which gave the Company possession of districts commanding the passes to the Mysore table-land, and handed over to the Nizam and the Marathas territory on the north-east and north-west respectively of Tipu's possessions. This policy of partial annexation, in lieu of the complete subjugation of

---

[1] Francklin, *Shah-Aulum*, pp. 141–86; Scott, *History of Dekkan*, II, 280–307.
[2] Malcolm, *A Memoir of Central India*, I, 171–2.

Mysore, was forced upon Lord Cornwallis by the desire of the directors for immediate peace, and by a disinclination to displease the Nizam and the Marathas, neither of whom were wholly loyal to their alliance with the Company.[1]

Mahadaji Sindhia had offered to join the confederacy against Tipu on terms which the governor-general was not prepared to accept, and he therefore seized the opportunity of this enforced neutrality to pursue his private object of establishing his authority at the Peshwa's capital against all rivals, including the English, and of checking Holkar's interference with his position and plans in Hindustan. Shortly after his defeat of Ismail Beg, he obliged Shah 'Alam to issue a fresh patent, making the Peshwa's office of *Wakil-i-mutlak*, as well as his own appointment as deputy, hereditary. The delivery of the imperial orders and insignia of office to the Peshwa gave him the desired excuse for a personal visit to Poona, where he duly arrived with a small military escort in June, 1792. His arrival caused great dissatisfaction to Nana Phadnavis, who made every effort to prevent the investiture of the Peshwa. Sindhia, however, while avoiding an open rupture with the minister, won his object, after obtaining the formal consent of the raja of Satara to the Peshwa's acceptance of the honour; and then directed all his efforts towards ingratiating himself with the young Peshwa, Madhu Rao, allaying the antipathy shown against himself by the Brahman entourage of Nana Phadnavis and the leading Maratha jagirdars, and securing open recognition by the Poona Government of his paramount position in Northern India. The rivalry between Sindhia and Nana Phadnavis was, however, summarily terminated by the sudden death of the former at Poona in February, 1794, and the Brahman minister was thus left in practically sole control of Maratha policy and affairs. A thirteen-year-old nephew, Daulat Rao, succeeded to the possessions of Mahadaji, who left no direct male issue.[2]

The constitutional position of the Maratha confederacy at this date has been described as "a curious and baffling political puzzle". While the powers of the raja of Satara, the nominal head of the confederacy, who was virtually a prisoner in his palace, had long been usurped by the Peshwa, the subordinate members of the confederacy had thrown off all but the nominal control of the Brahman government in Poona. Among these virtually independent leaders, who ranked as hereditary generals of the Peshwa, was Raghuji Bhonsle, raja of Berar, whose possessions stretched in a broad belt from his capital Nagpur to Cuttack on the Bay of Bengal. After the death of his father Mudaji in 1788, Raghuji and his younger brothers quarrelled about the succession; but the death of one of the latter and the bestowal upon the other of the Chanda and Chattisgarh districts enabled

---

[1] Grant Duff, *History of the Mahrattas*, chap. xxxiv.
[2] *Idem*, chap. xxxv.

Raghuji to secure public recognition of his claim to rule Berar, and by the date of Mahadaji Sindhia's death he was in undisturbed possession of his inherited fief. Holding, as he did, the hereditary post of *Sena Sahib Subah* of the Maratha army, Raghuji should have complied with the Peshwa's orders to participate in the operations against Tipu in 1791, but on his personal representation that the intrigues of his brother Khanduji obliged him to remain in Nagpur, he was permitted by Nana Phadnavis to purchase exemption from the campaign by a contribution of ten lakhs to the Maratha war-chest.[1]

Another important member of the confederacy was the Gaekwad, whose ill-defined territories roughly included Gujarat and the Kathiawad peninsula. The ruler, Sayaji, being imbecile, the territory was administered from 1771 to 1789 by his younger brother Fateh Singh, who died in the latter year. A conflict for the regency then ensued between his brothers Manaji Rao, whose claim was admitted by the Peshwa, and Govind Rao, who secured the support of Mahadaji Sindhia. In 1792, while the dispute was still undecided, the imbecile Sayaji Rao died, and Govind Rao, who had been allowed by the Peshwa to purchase the title of *Sena Khas Khel*, sought the approval of the Poona Government to his succession to the throne. His rival, Manaji, also died in 1793; but, despite this fact, the price of his recognition, demanded by the Peshwa, was so heavy that the British Government was compelled to intervene, in order to prevent the dismemberment of Baroda territory. Eventually, in December, 1793, owing to the representations of the British Resident, the Peshwa waived his demands and assented to Govind Rao's assumption of full authority over the state. His rule, which terminated with his death in 1800, was disturbed by the rebellious intrigues of his illegitimate son, Kanhoji, and by the hostility of Aba Selukar, who had been granted by the Peshwa the revenue management of the Ahmadabad district. After several engagements Aba was captured and imprisoned, and in 1799 the Peshwa consented to lease Ahmadabad to the Gaekwad.[2]

The territories of Holkar, which embraced the south-western part of Malwa, were ruled at this date by the widow of Malhar Holkar, the famous Ahalya Bai, who assumed the government as sole representative of her husband's dynasty in 1766 and ruled with exceptional wisdom until her death in 1795. Tukoji Holkar, who was no relation of the reigning family, though a member of the same class, was chosen by Ahalya Bai to bear titular honours and command her armies, and in that capacity co-operated loyally with the queen and established the first regular battalions with the help of the Chevalier Dudrenec, the American soldier, J. P. Boyd, and others. Ahalya Bai's internal

---

[1] Grant Duff, *History of the Mahrattas*, chap. xxxvi.
[2] *Idem*, chap. xlii.

administration of the state was described by Sir John Malcolm as "altogether wonderful". During her reign of thirty years the country was free from internal disturbance and foreign attack; Indore, the capital, grew from a village to a wealthy city; her subjects enjoyed in full measure the blessings of righteous and beneficent government. It is not surprising, therefore, that she was regarded by her own subjects as an *avatar* or incarnation of divinity, and by an experienced foreigner as "within her limited sphere one of the purest and most exemplary rulers that ever existed". She was succeeded by the aged Tukoji, who strove to administer the state according to her example until his death two years later (1797) at the age of seventy-two. With his departure chaos and confusion supervened, which lasted until the final settlement imposed by the British power in 1818.[1]

Among the minor figures of the Maratha confederacy were the piratical chiefs of Western India. When Raghuji Angria, who held Kolaba fort as a feudatory of the Peshwa, died in 1793, he was succeeded by an infant son, Manaji, who was deposed and imprisoned four years later by Daulat Rao Sindhia. His place was usurped by Baburao Angria, the maternal uncle of Sindhia.[2] The Company suffered considerable annoyance from the piratical habits of both Angria and the Sidi or Abyssinian chief of Janjira. On the death of Sidi Abdul Rahim in 1784, a dispute for the succession arose between his son Abdul Karim Khan *alias* Balu Mian and Sidi Johar. Lord Cornwallis, to whom the matter was referred, was at first disposed to leave the task of settling the dispute to the Peshwa, who had already befriended Balu Mian; but a premature attempt on the part of the Maratha Government to seize Janjira by stealth caused him to reconsider the matter. A compromise was not reached until 1791, when the Peshwa, in return for the grant to Balu Mian of a tract of land near Surat—the modern Sachin state—was recognised as superior owner of the Janjira principality.[3] His rights over the island, however, were never acknowledged by Sidi Johar, who, repelling all efforts to oust him, was still master of the principality at the date of the Peshwa's downfall. The third principal instigator of piracy was Khem Savant of Wadi, who had married a niece of Mahadaji Sindhia and was on that account created Raja Bahadur by the Moghul emperor in 1763. His rule, which lasted till 1803, was a tale of continuous piracies by his seafaring subjects in Vengurla and of conflict with the British, the Peshwa, and the raja of Kolhapur. Eventually in 1812 the Bombay Government forced his successor to enter into a treaty and cede the port of Vengurla.[4] They also in the same year obtained the cession of the port of Malwan, an equally notorious stronghold of pirates, from the raja of Kolhapur. Owing

---

[1] Malcolm, *A Memoir of Central India*, i, 156–95.
[2] *Bombay Gazetteer*, xi, 157.   [3] *Idem*, pp. 448–9.
[4] *Idem*, x, 442–3.

to the constant losses inflicted on British vessels, the Company had dispatched an expedition against the raja in 1792 and forced him to pay compensation and to permit the establishment of factories at Malwan and Kolhapur; and during the following decade internal dissension and wars with neighbouring territorial chiefs so weakened the Kolhapur state that in 1812 the raja was glad to sign a permanent treaty with the British, under the terms of which his territory was guaranteed against foreign attack, in return for the cession of several strong places and an undertaking to refer all disputes with other powers to the Company's arbitration.[1]

Mutual distrust and selfish intrigue effectually prevented the leaders of the Maratha confederacy from offering a united front to their opponents, though they were not averse from temporary combination for any special object which offered a chance of gratifying their personal avarice. In 1794 the renewal by the Peshwa of Maratha claims upon the Nizam for arrears of *chauth* and *sardesmukhi*, in which all the chiefs expected to share, offered them an occasion for acting in concert with the Poona Government. The Nizam, alarmed at the imminence of the combined Maratha attack, appealed to the governor-general, Sir John Shore, for the military assistance which he had been led to expect, and had certainly earned, by his cession of Guntoor. But Sir John Shore, who dreaded a war with the Maratha confederacy, sheltered himself behind the words of the act of parliament of 1784 and declared his neutrality, leaving the Nizam to bear the whole brunt of the Maratha attack.[2] The issue was not long in doubt. In March, 1795, the Nizam's army, which had been trained by the Frenchman Raymond, was overwhelmed by the Marathas and their Pindari followers at Kharda, fifty-six miles south-east of Ahmadnagar, and the Nizam was forced to conclude a humiliating treaty, which imposed upon him heavy pecuniary damages and deprived him of considerable territory.

This victory, coupled with the spoils distributed among the Maratha chiefs, restored for the moment the prestige of the Peshwa's government and placed Nana Phadnavis at the height of his power. It was, however, the last occasion on which "the chiefs of the Mahratta nation assembled under the authority of their Peshwa", and the inevitable domestic dissensions, which shortly followed, resulted in the Marathas forfeiting much of the results of their victory. The young Peshwa, Madhu Rao Narayan, tired of the control of Nana Phadnavis and disheartened by the latter's refusal to countenance his friendship with his cousin Baji Rao Raghunath, committed suicide in October, 1795, by throwing himself from the terrace of the Sanivar Wada at Poona. Baji Rao at once determined to secure for himself the vacant throne, and had no sooner overcome Nana's profound and instinctive opposition by false professions of friendship and loyalty

---

[1] *Bombay Gazetteer*, xxiv, 236.   [2] Malcolm, *Political History of India*, i, 127–47.

than he was faced with the hostility of Daulat Rao Sindhia and another faction, bent upon opposing Nana's plans. This faction contrived to place Chimnaji Appa, the brother of Baji Rao, on the throne at the end of May, 1796, whereupon Nana took refuge in the Konkan and there matured a counter-stroke, which ended in Baji Rao's return as Peshwa and his own restoration as chief minister in the following December. In preparing his plans, Nana secured the goodwill of Sindhia, Holkar, the Bhonsle raja, and the raja of Kolhapur, and also obtained the approval of the Nizam by promising to restore to him the districts ceded to the Peshwa after the battle of Kharda and to remit the balance of the fine imposed by the Marathas.

The return of Baji Rao to Poona was the signal for grave disorder, engendered by his determination to ruin Nana, to whom he owed his position, and to rid himself of the influence of Sindhia, who had financial claims upon him. Nana was arrested, and his house plundered, by a miscreant named Sarji Rao Ghatke, father-in-law of Sindhia, who was also given *carte blanche* to extort from the citizens of Poona by atrocious torture the money which Sindhia claimed from the Peshwa. The confusion was aggravated by open hostilities carried on in the Peshwa's territories between Sindhia and the widows of Mahadaji Sindhia, by the growing inefficiency of the Peshwa's army, whose pay was seriously in arrears, and by the continuous intrigues and counter-plotting of Baji Rao and Sindhia. The confirmation by Baji Rao of the arrangement made between Nana and the Nizam, which the latter demanded as the price of his assistance against Sindhia, was immediately followed by Sindhia's release of Nana Phadnavis, who once again acquiesced in a hollow reconciliation with his avowed enemy and resumed his old position at Poona.[1]

In 1798 Lord Wellesley arrived in Calcutta, determined to shatter for ever all possibility of French competition in India. The political outlook was far from favourable, for, largely in consequence of Sir John Shore's invertebrate policy of non-interference in Indian politics, Tipu Sultan had regained his strength; French influence, supported by troops under French commanders, had become paramount at the courts of Sindhia and the Nizam; the raja of Berar had indulged in intrigues against British interests; and the Carnatic was in a condition bordering on anarchy. Wellesley's first step was to persuade the Nizam to accept a form of "subsidiary alliance"; and he then proceeded to deal with Tipu. The Peshwa was invited to send troops in support of the British and promised to do so; but, true to his character, he carried on secret intrigues with Tipu up to the last and gave the English no appreciable help. Surprised by the rapid and complete downfall of the ruler of Mysore, he endeavoured to excuse his inactivity by putting the blame upon Nana Phadnavis.[2]

---

[1] Grant Duff, *op. cit.* chaps. xxxviii–xl.
[2] Malcolm, *Political History of India*, I, 196–236.

The state of his own territories would have served as a more valid excuse. The contest between Sindhia and the ladies of his family was still being hotly pursued on both sides; the ruler of Kolhapur, a lineal descendant of Sivaji, who had always been in more or less permanent opposition to the Peshwa, was laying waste the southern Maratha country, and was aided for a time by Chitur Singh, brother of the raja of Satara; while, more dangerous and violent than the rest, Jasvant Rao Holkar, who had escaped from confinement in Nagpur during the feud of 1795 between the legitimate and natural sons of Tukoji Rao Holkar, was carrying fire and sword through Sindhia's territory in Malwa, with a large force composed of Indian and Afghan freebooters.[1]

Such was the state of affairs in March, 1800, when Nana Phadnavis died. "With him", remarked the Resident, "has departed all the wisdom and moderation of the Mahratta government." He had controlled Maratha politics for the long period of thirty-eight years, and his demise may be said to mark the commencement of the final *débâcle*. Nana being beyond his reach, Baji Rao, who was the personification of treachery and cowardice, sought revenge upon Nana's friends and agreed to support Sindhia against Holkar, in return for a promise by Daulat Rao to assist his policy of vengeance. While Sindhia was absent from Poona, endeavouring to protect his lands from Holkar's devastations, Baji Rao, giving free rein to his passions, perpetrated a series of atrocious cruelties in Poona, which alienated his subjects and brought upon his head the implacable wrath of the savage Jasvant Rao. Among those whom he barbarously murdered in 1801 was Jasvant Rao's brother, Vithuji; and it was to avenge this crime that Jasvant Rao invaded the Deccan in the following year. The English endeavoured to set a limit to this internecine warfare by offering terms and treaties to both parties. But their efforts were of no avail.

In October, 1802, Holkar defeated the combined forces of Sindhia and the Peshwa at Poona, placed on the throne Amrit Rao, brother by adoption of Baji Rao, and then plundered the capital. Baji Rao, as pusillanimous as he was perfidious, fled to Mahad in the Konkan and thence to Bassein, whence he besought the help of the English and placed himself unreservedly in their hands. On the last day of the year (1802) he signed the Treaty of Bassein, which purported to be a general defensive alliance for the reciprocal protection of the possessions of the East India Company, the Peshwa, and their respective allies. The Peshwa bound himself to maintain a subsidiary force of not less than six battalions, to be stationed within his dominions; to exclude from his service all Europeans of nations hostile to the English; to relinquish all claims on Surat; to recognise the engagements between the Gaekwad and the British; to abstain from

[1] Malcolm, *Central India*, I, 197–225.

hostilities or negotiations with other states, unless in consultation with the English Government; and to accept the arbitration of the British in disputes with the Nizam or the Gaekwad. Having thus persuaded Baji Rao to sacrifice his independence, the Company lost no time in restoring him to the throne. By a series of rapid forced marches, General Arthur Wellesley saved Poona from destruction, obliged Holkar to retire to Malwa, and reinstalled the Peshwa in May, 1803

The Treaty of Bassein gave the Company the supremacy of the Deccan. Although it was regarded askance by some authorities in England and by the directors, as likely to involve the government in the "endless and complicated distractions of the turbulent Maratha empire", it entirely forestalled for the moment a combination of the Maratha states against the Company, and by placing the Peshwa's foreign policy under control, it made the governor-general really responsible for every war in India in which the Poona Government might be engaged. In short, "the Treaty by its direct and indirect operations gave the Company the empire *of* India", in contra-distinction to the British Empire *in* India, which had hitherto existed. On the other hand, while the support and protection of the English power saved the Peshwa from becoming the puppet of one of the other Maratha leaders, they averted the fear of a popular rebellion, which alone restrains an unprincipled despot from gratifying his evil passions, and inevitably inclined his mind to substitute intrigue against his foreign defenders for the military excursions which had formed the principal activity of the Maratha state since the seventeenth century. The period of fifteen years between Baji Rao's restoration and his final surrender is a continuous story of oppressive malad-ministration and of shameless plotting against the British power in India.

The other Maratha leaders regarded Baji Rao's assent to the treaty with open alarm and anger. Jasvant Rao Holkar declared that the Peshwa had sold the Maratha power to the English; Sindhia and the raja of Berar, who disliked particularly the provisions regarding British arbitration in disputes between the Peshwa and other Indian rulers, realised that at last they were face to face with the British power, and that Wellesley's system of subsidiary alliances would reduce them to impotence as surely as the Maratha claim to *chauth* had ruined the Moghul power. With the secret approval of the Peshwa, the leading Marathas, therefore, addressed themselves to the problem of a joint plan of defence. But a general combination was frustrated by the neutrality of the Gaekwad and the withdrawal of Holkar to Malwa. Sindhia and the raja of Berar, who had crossed the Narbada with obviously hostile intent, were requested by the English to separate their forces and recross the river; and on their refusal to comply, war was declared in August, 1803, with the avowed object of conquering Sindhia's territory between the Ganges and

Jumna, destroying the French force which protected Sindhia's frontier, capturing Delhi and Agra, and acquiring Bundelkhand, Cuttack and Broach. General Wellesley and General Lake commanded the two major operations in the Deccan and Hindustan respectively, while subsidiary campaigns were planned in Bundelkhand and Orissa, in order to secure the southern frontier of Hindustan and the districts lying between the boundaries of Bengal and Madras.

The operations were speedily successful. Wellesley captured Ahmadnagar in August, 1803, broke the combined armies of Sindhia and the Bhonsle raja at Assaye in September, and then, after forcing on Sindhia a temporary suspension of hostilities, defeated the raja decisively at Argaon in November, stormed the strong fortress of Gawilgarh, and thus forced the raja to sign the Treaty of Deogaon, 15 December, under the terms of which the latter ceded Cuttack to his conquerors and accepted a position similar to that assigned to the Peshwa by the Treaty of Bassein. Equally decisive were the results achieved by Lake. Marching from Cawnpore, he captured Aligarh at the end of August, causing Perron to retire in dejection from Sindhia's service. He then defeated Perron's successor, Louis Bourquin, at Delhi in September; took possession of the old blind emperor, Shah 'Alam; made a treaty with the raja of Bharatpur; and finally in November vanquished Sindhia's remaining forces at Laswari in Alwar state. Sindhia was thus rendered impotent; his regular troops, commanded by French officers, were destroyed; and he was consequently obliged to accept a "subsidiary alliance" and sign the Treaty of Surji Arjungaon, 30 December, 1803. In the course of the subsidiary campaign, Broach was captured and all Sindhia's territories annexed.[1] Thus within five months the most powerful heads of the Maratha confederacy had been reduced to comparative harmlessness.

Holkar alone remained unpacified. At the end of 1803 Lord Lake opened negotiations with him without avail; and on his preferring extravagant demands and plundering the territory of the raja of Jaipur, war was declared against him in April, 1804. With Lake operating in Hindustan, Wellesley advancing from the Deccan, and Murray marching from Gujarat, it was hoped to hem in the Maratha chief. But the plan miscarried, owing to the failure of Colonel Murray and Colonel Monson, who was acting under Lord Lake, to carry out their instructions. Monson, who according to Wellesley "advanced without reason and retreated in the same manner", allowed himself to be overwhelmed by Holkar in the Mukund Dara pass, thirty miles south of Kotah, and beat a disorderly retreat to Agra at the end of August. This disaster gave fresh courage to the Company's enemies. Sindhia showed a disposition to fight again, and the Jat raja of Bharatpur, renouncing his alliance with the English, joined with Holkar in an attack on Delhi, which was successfully repulsed by

[1] Fortescue, *A History of the British Army*, v, 1–69.

Ochterlony. In November one of Holkar's armies was defeated at Dig, and another, led by Holkar himself, was routed by Lake a few days later at Farrukhabad. The most serious reverse suffered by the English was Lake's failure to capture Bharatpur early in 1805. He was eventually obliged to make peace with the raja in April of that year, leaving him in possession of the fortress, which had repulsed four violent assaults by the Company's troops.[1]

Monson's disaster and Lake's failure before Bharatpur caused grave apprehension to the authorities in England, who had watched the Company's debt increase rapidly under the strain of Wellesley's forward policy, and were disposed to think that England's conquests were becoming too large for profitable management. As a necessary preliminary to a change of policy, they determined to recall the governor-general and to entrust the task of making peace with the various Indian powers to Lord Cornwallis, now in his sixty-seventh year and physically infirm. They failed to realise that, despite the misfortune of Monson, Wellesley's operations had actually broken Holkar's power and had left no single Maratha chief strong enough to withstand the English. Moreover, as the resentment felt by every Maratha chief towards the English at this juncture was too deep to be assuaged by a policy of concession and forbearance, the abandonment of Wellesley's programme merely amounted to a postponement of the final hour of reckoning. The peace concluded with the Marathas in 1805 was unfortunately marked by a spirit of weak conciliation, which caused future embarrassment to the Company's government in India, handed over weak states like Jaipur, which relied on British support, to the mercy of their rapacious neighbours, and ultimately forced the Marquess of Hastings thirteen years later to consummate the task which Wellesley was forbidden by the timidity of the ruling party at the India House to bring to a successful conclusion. The arrangements made by Lord Cornwallis and his successor, Sir George Barlow, amounted practically to a renunciation of most of the Company's gains for the sake of a hollow peace and to the abandonment of the Rajput states to the cruelty of the Maratha hordes and their Pindari allies. Sindhia recovered Gohad, Gwalior, and other territory, while to Holkar were restored the districts in Rajputana, which had been taken from him by the Treaty of Rajpurghat. In two instances only did Sir G. Barlow refuse to traverse Wellesley's policy. He declined to allow the Nizam freedom to indulge in anti-English intrigue, and he rejected a suggestion from England to modify the position of the Peshwa under the Treaty of Bassein.

The Gaekwad of Baroda had taken no part in the struggle outlined above. On the death of Govind Rao in 1800, the inevitable feud about the succession broke out between Anand Rao, his legal successor, who was of weak mind, and his illegitimate brother Kanhoji,

[1] Fortescue, *op. cit.* v, 70–137.

who was supported by the restless Malhar Rao. In 1802 the Company sent a force from Cambay to support Anand Rao, and in return secured the cession of a good deal of territory and an acknowledgment of their right to supervise the political affairs of the state. A little later they frustrated an attempt by Sindhia and Holkar to meddle with the Gaekwad's rights in Gujarat, and in April, 1805, concluded a treaty whereby the Gaekwad undertook to maintain a subsidiary force and to submit to British control his foreign policy and his differences with the Peshwa. In 1804 the Peshwa renewed the lease of Ahmadabad territory to Baroda for four and a half years at a rent of ten lakhs per annum.

The decade following the hollow peace of 1805 was marked by increasing disorder and anarchy throughout Central India and Rajputana. Internal maladministration and constant internecine warfare had produced the inevitable result, and the leading Maratha states were forced to try and avert their impending bankruptcy by means of contributions extorted from reluctant tributaries. In Holkar's territories the peaceful progress, which had marked Ahalya Bai's wise rule, had vanished beyond recall. In 1806 Jasvant Rao poisoned his nephew Khande Rao and his brother Kashi Rao, who were suspected of intriguing with his disaffected soldiery, and died a raving lunatic at Bhanpura in 1811. His favourite concubine, Tulsi Bai, contrived to place his illegitimate son, Malhar Rao, on the throne, with Amir Khan, the leader of the Pathan banditti, as regent. Acute friction between this Pathan element and the Maratha faction under Tulsi Bai involved the state in chaos; revenue was collected at the sword's point from the territory of Sindhia, the Ponwars, and Holkar himself indiscriminately; the machinery of administration fell to pieces; and a semblance of authority only remained with a vagrant and predatory court, dominated by the profligate ex-concubine. The country had no respite from disorder, until the murder of Tulsi Bai by a Pathan, 20 December, 1817, and the failure of British overtures for peace obliged Sir Thomas Hislop to ford the Sipra river and extinguish at Mahidpur the last embers of anarchy and hostility.[1]

Sindhia's dominions were in no better plight. His troops, in default of pay, were forced to subsist on the peasantry, who were already impoverished by the mutual hostilities of their own ruler and Holkar. The intermingled possessions of these two chiefs in Malwa became the common hunting-ground of every band of marauders; Amir Khan and his Pathan followers overran the raja of Berar's territory; the Rajput states were swept by Sindhia, Holkar, the Pathans and the Pindaris.

"Never", in the words of a modern writer, "had there been such intense and general suffering in India; the native states were disorganised, and society on the verge of dissolution; the people crushed by despots and ruined by exactions; the

[1] Malcolm, *Central India*, I, 260–324.

country overrun by bandits and its resources wasted by enemies; armed forces existed only to plunder, torture and mutiny; government had ceased to exist; there remained only oppression and misery."

The one sentiment uniting the warring units was hatred of the English. All the Marathas, from the Peshwa downwards, realised that if they were to regain their independence and make their predatory power supreme in India, they must exterminate the foreign government. It was to Baji Rao they all looked for support in this desperate and ill-omened enterprise; and had the Peshwa shown any spark of courage and statesmanship, the final struggle of the Company for complete supremacy might conceivably have been more protracted. But, while from 1803 the Peshwa never ceased to court disaster by intriguing against his foreign supporters, he alienated the Maratha feudal nobility by his tyrannous behaviour, as illustrated by the overthrow and degradation of the Pant Pratinidhi. He also failed completely to protect his own territory from Pindari inroads and to check the hostilities of the raja of Kolhapur and the Savant of Wadi. In the case of the former, peace was not assured until 1811, when the English forced the raja to sign the Treaty of Karvir.

The hesitation of the Company's government to assert its authority as paramount power resulted between 1805 and 1814 in the rapid growth of the destructive spirit of the Maratha hordes and Pathan freebooters and a dangerous increase of the power of the Pindaris, who were closely related to the two former organisations.[1] The Pindaris, consisting of lawless persons of all castes and classes, originally attached loosely to the Maratha armies, developed, "like masses of putrefaction in animal matter out of the corruption of weak and expiring states", into a formidable menace to the whole of India. Under their leaders, Chitu, Wasil Muhammad, and Karim Khan, they made rapid raids across India, inflicting appalling devastation upon the countryside and committing most atrocious outrages upon all classes of the inhabitants. In 1812 they commenced to raid the Company's territory by harrying Mirzapur and the southern districts of Bihar; but it was not until 1816, when they attacked the Northern Sarkars, plundering, torturing and killing the peaceful inhabitants, that the directors in England, who still cherished an exaggerated dread of Maratha power, became alive to the need for action and authorised Lord Hastings in September of that year to extirpate the evil.

The Pindaris would have met their doom much earlier but that the governor-general had been obliged to postpone his measures for a while. A new power had been founded in the Himalayan regions by the Gurkhas, a warlike race of hardy hillmen. The only serious effort to check their progress had been made by the nawab of Bengal in 1762, but his army was severely defeated under the walls of Makwanpur. In 1768 they conquered the Nepal valley and established

---

[1] Prinsep, *A Narrative of the Political and Military Transactions of British India*, pp. 21–32.

themselves at Kathmandu. The hill chiefs were subdued one after another and the Gurkha kingdom expanded rapidly until it extended from Sikkim on the east to the Satlej on the west. In 1814 the Gurkha frontier was conterminous with that of the British over a distance of seven hundred miles and the border districts suffered terribly from their incessant inroads. The concessions of Barlow and the expostulations of Minto proved equally futile and Lord Hastings found it necessary to take strong measures. In April, 1814, he sent a small force to occupy the disputed districts but the Gurkhas suddenly fell upon the outlying stations and killed or captured the small garrisons. War was therefore declared in November of that year.

The campaign was planned by the governor-general himself. The main Gurkha army under Amar Singh Thapa was at that time engaged in an expedition on the Satlej. It was decided that Major-Generals Marley and Wood should advance upon the Gurkha capital from Patna and Gorakhpur respectively, while Major-General Gillespie from Saharanpur and Colonel Ochterlony from Ludhiana were to close upon Amar Singh Thapa's main body. A speedy and easy victory was expected. But the Gurkha country was yet unknown to the British generals; there was no good road and the difficulties of transport were exceptionally great. Most of the older generals, moreover, were unfamiliar with hill fighting.

In none of the Indian wars had British arms met with so many reverses. Marley and Wood fell back after some feeble demonstrations. Gillespie died in an assault on Kalanga, and his successor suffered a defeat before the stronghold of Jaitak. The news of these defeats spread widely in the country and offered no small encouragement to the Peshwa and his partisans in their anti-British designs, and the Gurkhas talked of invading the neighbouring provinces. Fortunately the genius of Colonel Ochterlony soon restored the lost prestige of his nation. By a series of masterly manoeuvres he compelled the Gurkha general to give up two strong positions and to withdraw his army to his last retreat, the fort of Malaon. Here he was closely besieged and the conquest of Kumaon in April, 1815, so demoralised the Gurkhas that they deserted in large numbers. The fall of Malaon on 15 May compelled the Gurkha Government to sue for peace. Lord Hastings at first demanded the permanent cession of the whole of the Tarai but afterwards reduced his demands and a treaty was signed. The Nepal Government, however, refused to ratify the treaty and prepared to renew the war. All the main passes were secured and strongly defended by stockades but their plans were again upset by Ochterlony who penetrated into the heart of Nepal and inflicted a severe defeat upon the Gurkhas at Makwanpur on 28 February, 1816. The English army was within easy reach of the Gurkha capital and there was no more time for hesitation. The Treaty of Sagauli was promptly ratified and a lasting peace was concluded. The Gurkhas ceded Garhwal and

Kumaon with the greater portion of the Tarai. They withdrew permanently from Sikkim and received a British resident at Kathmandu. The Gurkha country, it is true, has not yet been thrown open to the English, but the Nepal Government have faithfully adhered to their treaty obligations, and the British districts have never since been disturbed by the dreaded hillmen of the north.[1]

Meanwhile British relations with the Peshwa were moving towards the inevitable *dénouement*. When the old question of the Peshwa's claims upon the Gaekwad was again raised in 1814, the British Government, anxious to secure a final and peaceful settlement of the dispute, arranged for the dispatch to Poona, under a safe conduct, of the Gaekwad's minister, Gangadhar Sastri. The Peshwa, who had refused to renew the lease of Ahmadabad to the Gaekwad and had granted it to a vicious favourite, Trimbakji Danglia, connived at the murder of the Baroda envoy by Trimbakji during the course of the negotiations at Nasik.[2] After much prevarication, he was forced by Mountstuart Elphinstone, the Resident, to deliver the murderer to the British authorities in September, 1815. Trimbakji, however, effected a romantic escape from custody a year later, probably with the knowledge of Baji Rao, who was now engrossed in plans for a Maratha combination against British supremacy. The governor-general, confronted by the Pindari menace, the hostile intrigues of the Peshwa, and dangerous unrest among other Maratha chiefs, was glad to arrange a subsidiary alliance in May, 1816, with Appa Sahib of Nagpur, who on the death of Raghuji Bhonsle became regent for his imbecile successor, Parsaji.[3] This agreement by which the Company obtained security for three hundred miles of frontier, disconcerted for the moment the secret plans of the Peshwa and Sindhia, and secured a military position near the Narbada, whence it could, if need arose, attack Sindhia and intercept Pindari raids. That done, Lord Hastings turned his attention to the Peshwa, who with his usual perfidy openly disowned Trimbakji, concluded an agreement with the Gaekwad, and generally adopted a conciliatory attitude. Proof of his treachery, however, was shortly afterwards furnished to Elphinstone, who forced him by a hostile military demonstration in June, 1817, to sign a compact supplementary to the Treaty of Bassein. He thereby explicitly renounced his headship of the Maratha confederacy and ceded the Konkan and certain other lands and strongholds to the British. He also recognised the independence of the Gaekwad, waived all claims for arrears, and granted him a perpetual lease of Ahmadabad for an annual payment of four lakhs. To the British he ceded the tribute of Kathiawad.[4]

---

[1] Fortescue, *op. cit.* XI, 118–62.
[2] Forrest, *Official Writings of Mountstuart Elphinstone*, pp. 119–78.
[3] Prinsep, *op. cit.* pp. 125–34.
[4] *Idem*, pp. 186–203.

Sindhia, who had been invited to assist in suppressing the Pindaris, was naturally disposed to side with the ruffianly hordes who were partly under his protection. Lord Hastings, therefore, crossed the Jumna, marched on Gwalior, and taking advantage of the internal dissension and military disorganisation which had reduced Sindhia's offensive capacity, secured his signature in November, 1817, to the Treaty of Gwalior, which bound him to co-operate against the Pindaris and rescinded the clause in the Treaty of Surji Arjungaon restricting the British from negotiation with the Rajput and other chiefs. As a result, treaties were concluded at Delhi with Udaipur (Mewar), Jodhpur (Marwar), Bhopal, Kotah, Jaipur, Bundi and thirteen other Rajput states. Negotiations were also opened with the Pathan leader, Amir Khan, who was subsequently granted the principality of Tonk as the price of his neutrality and the disarmament of his followers.

Such was the position towards the close of 1817 when the process of exterminating the Pindaris commenced. Though outwardly friendly, every Maratha leader, including even Appa Sahib of Nagpur, was a potential enemy, prepared to take advantage of any reverse sustained by the British during the campaign. Thus it happened that "the hunt of the Pindaris became merged in the third Maratha war" and struck the final death-knell of the Maratha power. Lord Hastings's plan of campaign was to surround the Pindaris in Malwa by a large army of 113,000 men and 300 guns, divided into a northern force of four divisions, commanded by himself, and a Deccan army of five divisions under Sir Thomas Hislop, operating from a central position at Handia in Allahabad district. In order to divide the Deccan states from those of Hindustan and prevent the Marathas from assisting the Pindaris, a portion of the army was interposed as a cordon between Poona and Nagpur. The operations were completely successful. By the close of 1817 the Pindaris had been driven across the Chambal; by the end of January, 1818, their organised bands had been annihilated. Of the leaders, one was given land at Gorakhpur, another committed suicide in captivity, while the third and most dangerous of them all, Chitu, fled into the jungles around Asirgarh and was there devoured by a tiger.[1]

The Maratha danger alone remained and was finally precipitated by the folly of the Peshwa and Appa Sahib Bhonsle. On the day (5 November, 1817) that Sindhia signed the supplementary Treaty of Gwalior, the Peshwa rose in revolt, sacked and burnt the British Residency at Poona, and then attacked with an army of about 26,000 a small British force of 2800, which was drawn up under Colonel Burr at Kirkee (Khadki). He was heavily defeated and fled southwards from Poona, seizing as he went the titular raja of Satara. The British followed in hot pursuit, intending to prevent his escape into Berar, fought two brilliant and victorious engagements against

[1] Fortescue, op. cit. XI, 177–250.

heavy odds at Koregaon and Ashti, in the latter of which the Peshwa's general, Bapu Gokhale, was slain, and finally forced the hunted fugitive to surrender himself to Sir John Malcolm, 18 June, 1818. To the annoyance of the governor-general, Malcolm, whose political judgment was temporarily obscured by feelings of compassion for fallen greatness, pledged the Company to grant Baji Rao an excessive annuity of eight lakhs of rupees; and, the office of Peshwa having been declared extinct, Baji Rao was permitted to reside at Bithur on the Ganges, where he doubtless instilled into the mind of his adopted son, known later as Nana Sahib, that hatred of the English which bore such evil fruit in 1857.[1]

Meanwhile, Appa Sahib, emulating the example of the Peshwa, attacked the British Resident at Nagpur, who had at his command a small force of native infantry and cavalry and four guns. Taking up its position on the ridge of Sitabaldi, the British force won a brilliant victory on 27 November, and with the aid of reinforcements which arrived a few days later, it forced the Bhonsle to surrender and finally defeated his troops at Nagpur on 16 December, 1818. Appa Sahib, who fled to the Panjab and eventually died in Rajputana, was formally deposed in favour of a minor grandson of Raghuji Bhonsle; his army was disbanded; and the portion of his dominions which lay to the north of the Narbada was annexed to British territory under the style of the Sagar (Saugor) and Narbada Territories.[2]

The tactical arrangements of Lord Hastings, which prevented the Maratha states from combining at the moment when mutual assistance was vital to their plans, ensured the defeat of Holkar. The Indore Darbar openly sympathised with the Peshwa's bid for freedom and rejected all offers of negotiation; but deprived of external aid and handicapped by internal dissension, the state forces could not withstand Sir Thomas Hislop's advance. Holkar's defeat at Mahidpur was followed by the Treaty of Mandasor, signed on 6 January, 1818, under the terms of which the chief relinquished his possessions south of the Narbada, abandoned his claims upon the Rajput chiefs, recognised the independence of Amir Khan, reduced the state army and agreed to maintain a contingent to co-operate with the British, and acquiesced in the appointment of a British Resident to his court.

Sindhia, who failed to fulfil his promise of active help in the Pindari campaign and, in contravention of the Treaty of Gwalior, had connived at the retention of the great fortress of Asirgarh by his killadar, Jasvant Rao Lad, now saw that further opposition would be fruitless, and, therefore, agreed in 1818 to a fresh treaty with the Company. This agreement provided, *inter alia*, for the cession to the English of Ajmir, the strategical key to Rajputana, and for a readjustment of boundaries. The Gaekwad, Fateh Singh, who acted as regent for

---

[1] Fortesque, *op. cit.* xi, 180–247.
[2] *Idem*, pp. 189–97, 246–9.

Anand Rao, signed a supplementary treaty in November, 1817, whereby he agreed to augment his subsidiary force, ceded his share of Ahmadabad for a cash payment representing its estimated value, and received in exchange the district of Okhamandal, the island of Bet, and other territory. Fateh Singh, who died in 1818 a few months before the titular ruler Anand Rao, adhered scrupulously to his alliance with the British during the operations against the Pindaris and the Maratha states. In return he was granted full remission of the tribute annually payable to the Peshwa for the revenues of Ahmadabad.[1]

In accordance with the precedent set by Wellesley in the case of Mysore, the raja of Satara, who had been delivered from the clutches of Baji Rao by Colonel Smith's victory at Ashti, was provided with a small semi-independent principality around Satara, and was enthroned on 11 April, 1818. With a view to a pacific settlement of the Peshwa's conquered dominions, arrangements satisfactory to both parties were made by the Company with the Pant Pratinidhi, the Pant Sachiv, the raja of Akalkot, the Patvardhans, and the other Maratha nobles and jagirdars; while the piratical chiefs of the western littoral, who had been incompletely chastised in 1812, were completely reduced in 1820 and forced to cede the remainder of the coast between Kolhapur and Goa.

"The struggle which has thus ended", wrote Prinsep in his *Political Review*, published in 1825, "in the universal establishment of the British influence is particularly important and worthy of attention, as it promises to be the last we shall ever have to maintain with the native powers of India. Henceforward this epoch will be referred to as that whence each of the existing states will date the commencement of its peaceable settlement and the consolidation of its relations with the controlling power. The dark age of trouble and violence, which so long spread its malign influence over the fertile regions of Central India, has thus ceased from this time; and a new era has commenced, we trust, with brighter prospects,—an era of peace, prosperity and wealth at least, if not of political liberty and high moral improvement."

There can be no doubt that the English and Maratha Governments could not co-exist in India; for the practical working of the Maratha system, which was inspired more deeply than has hitherto been recognised by the doctrines of the ancient Hindu text-books of autocracy, was oppressive to the general mass of the people, destitute of moral ideas, and directly antagonistic to the fundamental principles of the Company's rule. Lord Hastings fully realised that, if India was ever to prosper, orderly government must be substituted for the lawless and predatory rule of his chief antagonists, and he brought to the achievement of his complex task a singular combination of firmness and moderation. Every chance was offered to the treacherous Peshwa and the raja of Berar of reforming their corrupt administration and living in amity with the English; consideration was shown

[1] Prinsep, *op. cit.* pp. 418–68.

to avowed freebooters like Amir Khan and even to the ruffians who led the Pindari raids across India; Sindhia's duplicity was treated with undeserved forbearance. And when the doom of Maratha rule had been sealed, the governor-general's prudence and knowledge framed the measures which converted hostile princes like Sindhia and Holkar into staunch allies of the British Government, caused new villages and townships to germinate amid the ashes of rapine and desolation, created new and permanent sources of revenue, and diffused from Cape Comorin to the banks of the Satlej a spirit of tranquillity and order which India had never known since the spacious days of Akbar

CHAPTER XXIII

MARATHA ADMINISTRATION

THE Maratha administrative system, in the eighteenth century and the opening years of the nineteenth, may be described as a compound of the principles embodied in ancient works on Hindu polity, such as the *Arthasastra* of Kautilya, of the arrangements instituted by Sivaji and followed to some extent by his immediate successors, Sambhaji, Raja Rama, and Shahu, and of the modifications introduced by the Peshwas from the year 1727. In the various branches of the state's activities, the main differences between the system originally perfected by Sivaji and that which obtained under the Peshwas resulted naturally from the change in the position of Sivaji's lineal descendant, the raja of Satara, whose powers and prestige rapidly declined from the moment when the appointment of Peshwa became hereditary in the family of Balaji Visvanath (1714–20). Although the raja continued after that date to be regarded as the head of the Maratha state, and in theory retained the right to appoint the Peshwa and other high officials, his powers gradually became little more than nominal, and he was subsequently deprived even of the right of appointing and dismissing his own retainers. His personal expenses, moreover, were closely scrutinised by the Peshwa's secretariat, and he was obliged to obtain sanction from Poona for all expenditure connected with public works, private charities, and the maintenance of his household.[1] Originally one of Sivaji's *Ashta Pradhan* and holding, like the other seven ministers, a non-hereditary appointment, the Peshwa gradually assumed a position superior to that of the other ministers, including even the pratinidhi who had originally been appointed by Raja Rama as his vice-regent at Jinji and continued to occupy the senior position on the board until the genius of Balaji Visvanath made the Peshwa's office both hereditary and supreme. The gradual transformation of "the mayor of the palace" of the raja of Satara into the virtual ruler of the Maratha state and the Maratha confederacy, thus initiated by Balaji Visvanath, was aided by Tara Bai's imprisonment of Raja Rama in the Satara fort and was completed by Raja Shahu's grant of plenary powers to the Peshwa Balaji Baji Rao on his deathbed.[2]

Thus from the first quarter of the eighteenth century until the final *débâcle* of the Maratha power, the Peshwa, though acting nominally as the vice-regent of the raja of Satara and showing him on public occasions the attentions due to the ruler, actually controlled the whole

---

[1] Sen, *Administrative System of the Marathas*, pp. 186–96.
[2] *Idem*, pp. 196–202.

administration and even usurped the raja's powers and prerogatives as ecclesiastical head of the state. This latter function was not consequent upon the Peshwa's social position as a Brahman, for the Chitpavan sect, to which the Peshwas belonged, was not accounted of much importance by other Brahmanic sects and by some, indeed, was considered ineligible for inclusion in the Brahmanic category. As was the case with Sivaji, the Peshwa's supremacy in the socio-religious sphere was the natural corollary of his position as head executive power or chief magistrate, and in that capacity he gave decisions in a large variety of matters, including the appointment of officiating priests for non-Hindu congregations, the remarriage of widows, the sale of unmarried girls, and arrangements for dowry and adoption.[1]

The Peshwa's predominant position was also recognised by the Maratha feudal nobility, composed of estate-holders and chiefs, who were expected to provide troops and render military service, as occasion demanded, in return for their *saranjams* or fiefs, and were practically independent autocrats within the boundaries of their own lands and villages. As the Peshwa himself was originally one of these feudal landholders, subject to the general control of the raja of Satara, he was not slow to realise that his assumption of supremacy might evoke combinations of the others against himself. This possibility was largely discounted by dividing the revenues of any one district between several Maratha chiefs, who generally considered it beneath their dignity as fighting men to learn the art of reading and writing their mother-tongue and were at the same time exceedingly resentful of any supposed infringement of their financial proprietary rights. This system of sub-division of revenues gave rise to great complications in the state accounts, of which the Peshwa and his Brahman secretariat were not slow to take advantage: and it also engendered among the Maratha chiefs perpetual feuds and jealousies, which prevented their combining whole-heartedly against a common enemy and were ultimately responsible in large measure for the downfall of the Maratha power. The Maratha respect for the maxim that "it is well to have a finger in every pie", and their constant search for opportunities of extortion and pillage, are well illustrated by the refusal of Sindhia, as recorded in the private journal of the Marquess of Hastings, to relinquish his share in certain lands included in the possessions of the chief of Bundi, although he was offered in exchange more valuable territory, contiguous to his own dominions.

The focus of the Maratha administration was the Peshwa's secretariat in Poona, styled the *Huzur Daftar*, which was composed of several departments and bureaux. It dealt, broadly speaking, with the revenues and expenditure of all districts, with the accounts

[1] Sen, *op. cit.* pp. 202–4, 397–417.

submitted by the district and village officials, with all alienations of public revenue in the form of *inams, saranjams*, etc., with the pay and privileges of all grades of the public service, and with the budgets of the civil, military and religious establishments. The daily registers (*roz kird*) of the various departments recorded all revenue transactions, all grants and payments, and all contributions and exactions levied on foreign territory. These records, which included state transactions of every kind, were maintained with great care and efficiency until the rule of Baji Rao II (1796–1818), when they became practically valueless by reason of the maladministration and political disorder of that period.[1]

The foundation of the Peshwa's administrative system was the self-contained and self-supporting village community, which had its roots in an almost prehistoric past. Each village had a headman, the *patel* (the *pattakila* of ancient lithic and copperplate records), who combined the functions of revenue officer, magistrate and judge, and acted as intermediary between the villagers and the Peshwa's officials. His office was hereditary and might form the subject of sale and purchase, and his emoluments, which varied slightly from village to village, consisted chiefly in the receipt from every villager of a fixed share of his produce. These receipts ranged from a daily supply of betel-leaves, provided by the dealers in *pan-supari*, to a tax on the remarriage of a widow; and in return for these emoluments and for his recognition as the social leader of the village community, the *patel* was expected to shoulder the responsibility for the village's welfare and good conduct. The *kulkarni*, or village clerk and record-keeper, who was always a Brahman, was second in importance to the *patel*, and like the latter was remunerated by a variety of perquisites. He was often expected to share the *patel's* responsibility for the good behaviour of the village community, and ran an equal risk of oppression and imprisonment by casual invaders or tyrannous officials. Excluding the *chaugula* who had custody of the *kulkarni's* bundles of correspondence, assisted the *patel*, and was frequently an illegitimate scion of the *patel's* family, the communal duties and wants of the village were performed and supplied by the *bara balute* or twelve hereditary village servants, who received a recognised share of the crops and other perquisites in return for their services to the community.[2] The *personnel* of the *bara balute* was not invariably the same in all parts of the Deccan, and in some places they were associated with an additional body of twelve village servants, styled *bara alute*. Up to the period of the rule of the Peshwa Madhu Rao I (1761–72), certain classes of village mechanics and artisans, like the carpenter and blacksmith, were liable to forced labour (*begar*) on behalf of the state—an exaction which had the express sanction of the most ancient

[1] Sen, *op. cit.* pp. 267–71.
[2] *Idem*, pp. 211–37, 503–21.

Hindu law codes and was certainly practised by previous governments in India.[1]

The backbone of the Maratha district administration, which perhaps drew its original inspiration from the principles laid down in Kautilya's *Arthasastra*, was supplied by the *mamlatdar*, who was in charge of a division styled *sarkar*, *subha*, or *prant*, and by the *kamavisdar*, his subordinate or deputy, who administered a smaller territorial area of the same kind, usually termed a *pargana*. This territorial nomenclature had, however, lost its significance by the beginning of the nineteenth century, and the revenue divisions—the *sarkar*, the *pargana*, and the smaller areas styled *mahal* and *tarf*, had been largely broken up as a result of internal changes and confusion. The *mamlatdar*, who corresponded roughly to the *subhedar* or *mukhya deshadhikari* of Sivaji's day, and the *kamavisdar* were directly subordinate to the Peshwa's secretariat in Poona, except in the case of Khandesh, Gujarat and the Karnatak, where a superior official, styled *sarsubhedar*, was interposed between them and the government. Originally the *mamlatdar* and the *kamavisdar* were appointed for short terms only, but in practice they managed frequently to secure renewals of their term of office in a district. As the direct representative of the Peshwa they were responsible for every branch of the district administration, including agriculture, industries, civil and criminal justice, the control of the *sihbandis* (militia) and the police, and the investigation of social and religious questions. They also fixed the revenue assessment of each village in consultation with the *patel*, heard and decided complaints against the village officers, and were responsible for the collection of the state revenue, which in cases of recalcitrance they were accustomed to recover through the medium of the *sihbandis*.[2]

It will be obvious that under this system there were many opportunities for peculation and maladministration on the part of the district officials, while the only checks upon the action of the *mamlatdar* were of a theoretical rather than a practical character. The first of these restraints was provided by the *desmukh* and *despande*, who had long ceased to hold any official status and had been relegated to a more or less ornamental position since the days of Sivaji.[3] In theory the *mamlatdar's* accounts were not passed by the secretariat at Poona, unless corroborated by corresponding accounts from these local anachronisms, and in all disputes regarding land the *desmukh* was expected to produce his ancient records, containing the history of all *watans*, *inams* and grants, and the register of transfer of properties, which he maintained in return for the annual fee or perquisites received from the villagers. The safeguards not infrequently proved illusory, for there was nothing to prevent the *mamlatdar* obtaining official approval of his returns by methods of his own, while the

[1] Sen, *op. cit.* pp. 532–4. [2] *Idem*, pp. 252–8.
[3] *Idem*, pp. 243–51.

desmukh's registers were irregularly written up and often very incomplete. The second check upon the *mamlatdar* was provided by a staff of hereditary *darakhdars* or office-holders, who were appointed to the various provinces or major divisions of the Maratha dominions, were directly subordinate to the Peshwa, and reported direct to the government in Poona. These officials were eight in number, viz. the *dewan* or *mamlatdar's* deputy, *mazumdar*, *phadnavis*, *daftardar*, *potnis*, *potdar*, *sabhasad*, and *chitnis*; and they were expected to act as a check, not only upon one another but also on the *mamlatdar*, who was not empowered to dismiss any one of them. A ninth official of this class, the *jamenis*, who apparently concerned himself with the land revenue of the villages, is mentioned in the reign of the Peshwa Madhu Rao I.[1]

With the object, doubtless, of preventing the wholesale malversation of public money, the Maratha Government was accustomed to demand from the *mamlatdar* and other officials the payment of a heavy sum (*rasad*) on their first appointment to a district, and careful estimates of probable income and expenditure were drawn up for their guidance by the *Huzur Daftar*. These precautions were of even less value than those mentioned above. The *mamlatdar* was at pains to recover his advance with interest and frequently made considerable illicit profits by concealment of receipts, non-payment of pensions, and the preparation of false bills and muster-rolls. A fruitful source of gain was the *sadar warid patti*—an extra tax intended to cover miscellaneous district expenditure not provided for by the government; and one of the chief items of this additional expenditure was the *darbar kharch* or fee to ministers and auditors, which, originally a secret bribe, developed eventually into a recognised scale of payments, audited like other items of account. These illicit claims showed a constant tendency to increase, and as it was obviously impolitic to recover more than a certain amount from the peasantry, who provided in one way or another a very large proportion of the public revenues, the *mamlatdar* did not scruple to pay himself and his superiors out of funds that should have been credited wholly to the government.[2] Under the rule of the last Peshwa, Baji Rao II, the peasantry were deprived of even this modified protection from extortion by the system of farming the district appointments, which had been in vogue under the preceding Muhammadan governments of the Deccan.

"The office of *mamlatdar*", according to Mountstuart Elphinstone, "was put up to auction among the Peshwa's attendants, who were encouraged to bid high and were sometimes disgraced, if they showed a reluctance to enter on this sort of speculation."

The *mamlatdar*, who had secured a district at these auctions, promptly

---

[1] Sen, *op. cit.* pp. 258–63.
[2] *Idem*, pp. 263–5; Forrest, *Official Writings of Mountstuart Elphinstone*, pp. 287–9.

rented it at a profit to under-farmers, who repeated the process until it reached the village officers. Under such a system the scale on which each peasant was assessed was based upon his ability to pay, not upon the area and quality of the land which he occupied; and as the demand was usually immoderate and constant resort was had to fictitious accounts, the villagers were steadily exhausted by the shameless exactions of the official hierarchy.[1]

The *kamavisdar*, whose official emoluments were often fixed at 4 per cent. of the revenues of the district in his charge together with certain allowances, e.g. for the upkeep of a palanquin, was provided, like the *mamlatdar*, with a staff of clerks and menials, who were generally paid ten or eleven months' salary in return for a full year's work. The reason for this short payment, which was also adopted in the military department, is not clear. Possibly it amounted to a tacit acknowledgment that an aggregate period of at least one or two months in every twelve would be spent on leave or otherwise wasted, or that petty illicit perquisites, which it would be fruitless to trace or expose, would probably total to the amount of a month's salary. The small territorial divisions, known as *mahal* or *tarf*, were administered on the same lines as the *mamlatdar's* and *kamavisdar's* charges by a non-hereditary official styled *havaldar*, assisted and checked by a hereditary *mazumdar* (accountant) and *phadnis* (auditor). In each *mahal*, as a rule, were stationed four additional officials of militia, viz. the *hashamnavis*, who maintained a muster-roll of the villagers, their arms, and their pay; the *hasham phadnis* and *hasham daftardar*, who kept the accounts and wrote up the ledger of the militia, and the *hazirinavis*, who maintained a muster-roll of those actually serving in the militia.[2]

The Maratha judicial system has been described as very imperfect, there being no rules of procedure, no regular administration of justice, and no codified law. In both civil and criminal matters decisions were based upon custom and upon rules or formulae embodied in ancient Sanskrit compilations, like those of Manu and Yajnavalkya. In civil cases the main object aimed at was amicable settlement, and arbitration was therefore the first step in the disposal of a suit. If arbitration failed, the case was transferred for decision to a *panchayat*, appointed by the *patel* in the village and by the *shete mahajan*, or leading merchant, in urban areas. An appeal lay from the decision of a *panchayat* to the *mamlatdar*, who usually upheld the verdict, unless the parties concerned were able to prove that the *panchayat* was prejudiced or corrupt. In serious or important suits, however, it was the duty of the *mamlatdar* to appoint an arbitrator or a *panchayat*, the members of which were chosen by him with the approval, and often at the suggestion, of the parties to the suit. In

[1] Forrest, *op. cit.* pp. 294–6.
[2] Sen, *op. cit.* p. 266.

such cases the *panchayat's* decision was subject to an appeal to the Peshwa or his legal minister, the *nyayadhish*. The system of *panchayats* left a good deal to be desired from the standpoint of modern legal administration. These bodies were slow in action and uncertain in their decisions: the attendance of the members was usually irregular, depending as it did entirely upon the individual's sense of duty or fear of public opinion. The powers of the *panchayat* were strictly limited; it was exposed to constant obstruction; and it possessed no authority to enforce its decisions, which were left to the *mamlatdar* to carry out or neglect, as he pleased. It had likewise no power to compel the attendance of parties and their witnesses, and depended upon the *mamlatdar* or other local official to supply a petty officer for this purpose. In cases where the members of a *panchayat* were nominated by the parties to a suit, they functioned rather as advocates than as judges; and, speaking generally, the system offered considerable scope for partiality and corruption, which became very marked under the rule of Baji Rao II. Yet, despite its primitive character and its liability to be improperly influenced, the *panchayat* was a popular institution, and the absence of a decision by a *panchayat* in any suit was almost always regarded as complete justification for a retrial of the issues. The fact must be admitted that among themselves, within the confines of the self-contained ancestral village, the peasantry did obtain a fair modicum of rude justice from the village *panchayat*. What they failed to obtain either from the *panchayats* or from the government was any measure of redress against the merciless oppression of their superiors.[1]

In criminal cases much the same procedure was adopted, though a *panchayat* was less frequently appointed than in civil disputes. The chief authorities were the *patel* in the village, the *mamlatdar* in the district, the *sarsubhedar* in the province, and the Peshwa and his *nyayadhish* at headquarters; and they administered a law which was merely popular custom tempered by the trying officer's own ideas of expediency. Ancient Hindu law in its criminal application had become practically obsolete by the end of the eighteenth century, and Mountstuart Elphinstone's opinion that "the criminal system of the Mahrattas was in the last stage of disorder and corruption" was fully justified by the state of the criminal law and procedure immediately prior to the downfall of the last Peshwa. No regular form of trial of accused persons was prescribed; flogging was frequently inflicted with the object of extorting confessions of guilt; and in the case of crimes against the state torture was usually employed. The punishment for serious offences against the person was originally fine, or confiscation of property, or imprisonment, the fine being proportioned to the means of the offender;[2] but after 1761 capital punish-

---

[1] Sen, *op. cit.* pp. 347–79.
[2] *Idem*, pp. 381–3.

ment and mutilation were inflicted upon persons convicted of grievous hurt, dacoity and theft, as well as upon those found guilty of murder or treason.[1] The usual methods of execution were hanging, decapitation, cutting to pieces with swords, or crushing the skull with a mallet, exception being made in the case of Brahmans, who were poisoned or starved to death.[2] Powers of life and death were originally vested in the ruler only, and in the principal feudal chiefs within the limits of their respective jagirs. In later times, however, these powers were delegated to the *sarsubhedar* of a province; while throughout the second half of the eighteenth century the *mamlatdar*, as head of a district, considered himself justified in hanging a Ramosi, Bhil, or Mang robber, without reference to higher authority. The punishment of mutilation consisted usually in cutting off the hands or feet and in the case of female offenders in depriving them of their nose, ears or breasts. False evidence must often have figured in criminal enquiries, as it still does to some extent; and the false witness and the fabricator of false documents were practically immune from prosecution under a system which prescribed no penalty for either perjury or forgery. The only notice taken of a case of deliberate and wholesale fabrication of false evidence consisted of a mild reproof from the *nyayadhish*.

The penalties imposed on convicted prisoners were aggravated by the knowledge that their families were not secure from oppression; for it was a common practice of the Maratha Government to incarcerate the innocent wives and children of convicts, as a warning to other potential malefactors. The prison arrangements were primitive, the only jails being rooms in some of the larger hill-forts. Here the prisoners languished in the gravest discomfort, except on rare occasions when they were temporarily released to enable them to perform domestic religious ceremonies such as the *sraddha*.[3] It is perhaps needless to remark that a prisoner had to pay heavily for such temporary and occasional freedom, as well as for other minor concessions to his comfort. Provided that he could command sufficient funds to satisfy the avarice of his gaolers, even a long-term convict could count upon a fairly speedy release. Even in the days of Sivaji the power of gold to unlock the gates of hill-forts had often proved greater than that of the sword, spear and ambush.

The district police arrangements under the Peshwas were practically identical with those that existed in the seventeenth centu y, and were apparently based largely on the doctrine of setting a thief to catch a thief. Each village maintained its own watchmen, who belonged to the degraded Mahar or Mang tribes, under the direct control of the *patel*, and remunerated them for their services with rent-free lands

[1] Sen, *op. cit.* pp. 393–6.
[2] Tone, *Institutions of the Maratha People*, pp. 15–16.
[3] Sen, *op. cit.* pp. 417–24.

and other perquisites. These watchmen were assisted in the detection of crime by groups or gangs of hereditary criminal tribesmen, like the Ramosis and Bhils, who were attached to each village, or to a group of villages, and resided on its outskirts. Each group was under the control of its own *naiks* or headmen, who were answerable to the *patel* for any theft or robbery committed in the village, and for any disturbance created by their followers.[1] The antiquity of the system is indicated by the fact that most of these village groups of Ramosis or Bhils received certain perquisites of long standing in return for their services to the village, in the same way as the recognised village servants, and they cherished their rights as ancillary watchmen and thief-catchers, particularly in respect of some of the hill-forts, as jealously as any village officer or village artisan.

The practical working of the system was as follows. Whenever a crime against property occurred in a village, the Mahars or Ramosis, as the case might be, were bound as a body to make good the value of the stolen property, unless they succeeded in recovering the actual goods or in tracing the offenders to another village. In the latter case the delinquent village was forced to indemnify the owners of the property. While this system afforded a moderate safeguard to each village against the anti-social propensities of its own particular group of criminal tribesmen, it failed to prevent crime and predatory incursions by the Ramosis of other areas or by Bhils from the forest-clad hills of the northern Deccan. It offered, moreover, unlimited chances of subterfuge and blackmail on the part of the tribesmen concerned. A striking example of the shortcomings of the system is afforded by the career of Umaji Naik, the famous Ramosi outlaw, who during the administration of Sir John Malcolm (1827–30) perpetrated a long series of crimes against person and property, while he was actually in receipt of a salary from the Bombay Government for performing police duties in the Sasvad division of the Poona collectorate.[2] His methods proved that there was nothing to prevent the village police and the Ramosis combining to escape responsibility by falsely saddling crimes upon the innocent. These watch and ward arrangements were also of no avail in cases where the petty chiefs and estate-holders of the Deccan plundered the villages of their rivals. For the payment of fees and perquisites to the Ramosis or Bhils, either by the village or by the government, was essentially a form of blackmail, designed to secure immunity, partial or complete, from the depredations of a body of professional criminals and freebooters, and it naturally could not influence the intentions or actions of the landed gentry, whenever its members chose to indulge in marauding excursions through the countryside. Consequently, whenever serious

---

[1] Sen, *op. cit.* pp. 425–7.
[2] Mackintosh, *An Account of the Origin and Present Condition of the Tribe of Ramossies* pp. 125–227.

epidemics of dacoity and other crime occurred, the government authorities usually strengthened the village police with detachments of *sihbandis*, or irregular infantry, from the neighbouring hill-forts. The *sihbandis* in every district were under the control of the *mamlatdar*, and were maintained on the proceeds of a general house tax imposed on the residents of the disturbed area. Their duty was to support the village police under the *patel* and to oppose violence by force of arms, but did not extend to the detection of crime. They were also deputed to assist the village police in maintaining order at festivals, fairs and other important social gatherings.

Under the misguided rule of Baji Rao II the district police system was modified by the appointment of additional police officials, styled *tapasnavis*, charged with the discovery and seizure of offenders.[1] These officials were independent of the *mamlatdar* and other district authorities, and their area of jurisdiction was not necessarily conterminous with that of the revenue and police officials. As a class they were shamelessly corrupt; they constantly extorted money by means of false accusations, and were often hand in glove with avowed robbers and outlaws. In the latter respect they were little less culpable than the Maratha jagirdars and zamindars, who frequently offered an asylum and protection to fugitive criminals wanted for serious crimes in other districts.

In urban centres magisterial and police powers were vested in a *kotwal*, who also performed municipal duties. He regulated prices, took a census of the inhabitants, investigated and decided disputes relating to immovable property, supplied labour to the government, levied fees from professional gamblers, and, generally speaking, performed most of the functions ascribed to the *nagaraka* or police superintendent in the *Arthasastra* of Kautilya.[2] The best urban police force at the close of the eighteenth century was unquestionably that of the capital, Poona. It was composed of foot-police, mounted patrols, and Ramosis, used principally as spies and trackers, and was described as efficient. Opportunities for nocturnal delinquency on the part of the inhabitants were, however, greatly lessened by a strict curfew order which obliged everyone to remain within doors after 10 p.m.[3]

The Maratha army, composed of the mercenary forces of the feudal chiefs and the regiments under the immediate command of the Peshwa, had undergone a radical change since Sivaji's day. Originally recruited from men who, though not invariably Marathas by race, were yet united by a common bond of country and language, the army tended, as the Maratha power spread across India, to assume a professional rather than a national character. The real Marathas

[1] Forrest, *op. cit.* pp. 305–6.
[2] Sen, *op. cit.* pp. 427–31; 522–4.
[3] *Idem*, pp. 431–2; Tone, *Institutions of the Maratha People*, pp. 54–5.

were gradually relegated almost entirely to the cavalry, in which their horse-craft and knowledge of horse-breeding proved of the highest value; the infantry was mostly drawn from Northern India; and the artillery, which offered little attraction to the Maratha freebooter, was manned and commanded by Portuguese and Indian Christians. As has been mentioned, the military services of the various Maratha chiefs and landholders were secured by the grant of *saranjams* (fiefs), care being taken by the Peshwa and his Brahman secretariat so to group the holdings of rival chiefs in the same area that the former might reap full advantage from their inveterate mutual jealousies.[1] A hegemony founded on internal strife and dissension was not calculated to give stability to the state; and ultimately the lack of cohesion induced by this policy, coupled with the personal unpopularity of the last Peshwa, contributed largely to the downfall of the Maratha confederacy.

The Maratha state did little towards the economic improvement of the country and the intellectual advancement of its inhabitants. Being essentially a predatory power, it regarded itself as always in a state of war, and a large proportion of its revenue was supplied by marauding expeditions into the territory of its neighbours. Unlike other ancient and contemporary Hindu governments, it constructed no great works of public utility, and its interest in education was confined to the annual grant of *dakshina* to deserving *pandits* and *vaids*.[2] In the days of Sivaji and his successors it had been one of the duties of the Pandit Rao to enquire into the merits and accomplishments of applicants for this form of state aid and to settle in each case the amount and character of the award. But the system had degenerated at the opening of the nineteenth century into a form of indiscriminate largesse to Brahmans, of whom some at least were probably unworthy of special recognition. Some writers on Maratha affairs have sought to discover the germ of modern postal communications in the system of intelligence maintained by the Maratha Government. The comparison has no value, in view of the fact that, although the *jasuds* (spies) and *harkaras* (messengers) did carry messages and letters with astonishing rapidity throughout India, they were primarily employed for political and military purposes, and not for the public convenience.[3] They represented, in fact, during the eighteenth century the official system of intelligence, which was originally described in the *Arthasastra* and was perfected by Chandragupta Maurya in the third century B.C.

A survey of Maratha administration must necessarily include some account of the principal sources of the state revenues. The most important items were the *chauth* (one-fourth) and *sardesmukhi* (the tenth), which originally were payments in the nature of blackmail

---

[1] Sen, *op. cit.* pp. 439–69.   [2] *Idem*, pp. 470–2.
[3] *Idem*, pp. 469–70.

made by districts under the government of other powers which desired protection from plunder. While the proceeds of both levies were reserved for the state treasury, the *chauth* from early days had been sub-divided into the following shares:

(*a*) *babti* or 25 per cent., reserved for the raja or ruler.

(*b*) *mokasa* or 66 per cent., granted to Maratha sardars and chiefs for the maintenance of troops.

(*c*) *sahotra* or 6 per cent., granted to the pant sachiv.

(*d*) *nadgaunda* or 3 per cent., awarded to various persons at the ruler's pleasure.

This sub-division of *chauth* continued under the *régime* of the Peshwas; and when the territories, which paid both the levies, were finally incorporated in the Maratha dominions, the remaining three-fourths of their revenues, after deducting the *chauth*, were styled *jagir* and were also granted in varying proportions to different individuals. As previously stated, this system was characterised by a multiplicity of individual claims upon the revenues of a single tract or village, and consequently in great complication of the accounts, which the Brahman secretariat in Poona was alone in a position to comprehend and elucidate. During the Peshwa's rule a somewhat similar sub-division was made of the *sardesmukhi*, which had originally been credited wholly to the raja, in accordance with Sivaji's fictitious claim to be the hereditary *sardesmukh* of the Deccan.[1]

The second important head of state revenue was the agricultural assessment upon village lands, which were generally divided between two classes of holders, the *mirasdar* and the *upri*.[2] The former, who is supposed to have been the descendant of original settlers who cleared the forest and first prepared the soil for agriculture, possessed permanent proprietary rights and could not be ejected from his holding so long as his rent was paid to the government. His property was hereditary and saleable; and even if he was dispossessed for failure to pay the government dues, he had a right of recovery at any time during the next thirty or forty years, on his liquidating all arrears. The *upri*, on the other hand, was a stranger and tenant-at-will, who merely rented and cultivated his fields with the permission and under the supervision of the Peshwa's district officers. He did not enjoy the same advantages and fixity of tenure as the *mirasdar*, but he was not liable, like the latter, to sudden and arbitrary impositions, and he bore a comparatively moderate proportion of the miscellaneous village expenses, which included such items as the maintenance of the village temple and the repair of the village wall. Theoretically the assessment on the village lands was supposed to be based on a careful survey of the cultivated area, the lands themselves being divided into three main classes. Allowance was also supposed to be

[1] Sen, p. 112.
[2] *Idem*, pp. 237–9.

made for the character of the crop and the facilities existing for irrigation, and special rates were imposed upon coconut and other plantations and also upon waste or permanently unproductive lands. The assessment was payable either in cash or in kind, and it was generally recognised that remission of the assessment and advances of money and grain (*tagai*) should be granted to the peasantry in seasons of drought and distress. Theoretically, indeed, the Maratha land revenue system was favourable to the interests of the cultivator, and under the rule of a Peshwa like Madhu Rao I the peasantry were probably contented and tolerably well off. But actually the *patel* was the only person who could champion the rights of the villager against the higher official authorities, and as the latter had usually to satisfy the demands of the government and fill their own pockets at one and the same time, the cultivator met with much less consideration than was due to his position in the economic sphere. Under a bad ruler like Baji Rao II, whose administration was stained by perfidy, rapacity and cruelty, the equitable maxims of land revenue assessment and collection were widely neglected, and the cultivator was reduced in many cases to practical penury by the merciless exactions of the Peshwa's officials. In addition to the regular village lands, there were certain lands which were regarded as the private property of the Peshwa. These fell into the four-fold category of pasture, garden, orchard, and cultivated land, and were usually let on lease to *upris* under the authority of the *mamlatdar* or *kamavisdar*, who was responsible for recovering the rental and other dues from the tenant.[1]

A third item of the Maratha revenues consisted of miscellaneous taxes, which varied in different districts. They included, *inter alia*, a tax of one year's rent in ten on the lands held by the *desmukh* and *despande*, a tax on land reserved for the village Mahars, a triennial cess on *mirasdar* occupants, a tax on land irrigated from wells, a house tax recovered from everyone except Brahmans and village officers, an annual fee for the testing of weights and measures, a tax on marriage and on the remarriage of widows, taxes on sheep and she-buffaloes, a pasturage fee, a tax on melon cultivation in river beds, a succession duty, and a town duty, including a fee of 17 per cent. on the sale of a house. There were several other taxes and cesses of more or less importance, as for example the *bat chhapai* or fee for the stamping of cloth and other merchandise; and some of these can be traced back to the Mauryan epoch and were probably levied by Indian rulers at an even earlier date. In theory such taxes were to be proportioned in their incidence to the resources of the individual; but on the not infrequent occasions when the Maratha Government was pressed for money, it had no scruple in levying on all landholders a *karja patti* or *jasti patti*, which was generally equivalent to one year's income of the individual tax-payer.[2]

---

[1] Sen, *op. cit.* pp. 277-307.   [2] *Idem*, pp. 308-14.

The fourth source of Maratha revenue was customs duties, which fell roughly into the two classes of *mohatarfa* or taxes on trades and professions, and *jakat* or duties on purchase and sale, octroi and ferry charges.[1] The *mohatarfa*, for example, included a palanquin tax on the Kolis, a shop tax on goldsmiths, blacksmiths, shoemakers and other retail dealers, a tax on oil mills, potter's wheels and boats, and a professional impost of three rupees a year on the *Gondhalis* or worshippers of the goddess Bhavani. The *jakat*, a term originally borrowed from the Muhammadans, was collected from traders of all castes and sects, and was farmed out to contractors, who were often corrupt and oppressive. It was levied separately in each district, and was divided into *thalbarit* or tax at the place of loading the merchandise, *thalmod* or tax at the place of sale, and *chhapa* or stamping-duty. In some places a special fee on cattle, termed *shingshingoti*, was also imposed. Remissions of *jakat* were sometimes granted, particularly to cultivators who had suffered from scarcity or from the incursions of troops; but, as a rule, every trader had to submit to the inconvenience of having his goods stopped frequently in transit for the payment of these dues and octroi. Elphinstone records that the system was responsible for the appearance of a class of *hundikaris* or middlemen, who in return for a lump payment undertook to arrange with the custom farmers for the unimpeded transit of a merchant's goods. Brahmans and government officials were usually granted exemption from duty on goods imported for their own consumption, just as they were exempted from the house tax and certain minor cesses.

A small revenue was derived from forests by the sale of permits to cut timber for building or for fuel, by the sale of grass, bamboos, fuel and wild honey, and by fees for pasturage in reserved areas (*kurans*).[2] Licences for private mints also brought some profit to the state treasury. These licences were issued to approved goldsmiths (*sonars*), who paid a varying royalty and undertook to maintain a standard proportion of alloy, on pain of fine and forfeiture of licence. At times spurious and faulty coins were put into circulation, as for example in the Dharwar division in 1760. On that occasion the Maratha Government closed all private mints in that area and established in their stead a central mint, which charged a fee of seven coins in every thousand.[3]

The administration of justice produced a small and uncertain amount of revenue. In civil disputes relating to money bonds, the state claimed a fee of 25 per cent. of the amount realised, which really amounted to a bribe to secure the assistance of the official who heard the case. The general inertia of the government effectually prevented the growth of revenue from legal fees and obliged suitors to depend for satisfaction of their claims on private redress in the form of *takaza* or

---

[1] Sen, *op. cit.* pp. 321–5.   [2] *Idem*, pp. 314–17.
[3] *Idem*, pp. 317–21.

dharna (dunning), or on patronage, which signified the enlistment of the aid of a superior neighbour or influential friend. In suits for partition of property worth more than 300 rupees in value, the parties were expected to pay a fee at the rate of 10 per cent. of the value of the property; fees were also charged in cases concerned with maintenance or inheritance, particularly in cases in which an applicant claimed to succeed to the estate of a childless brother.[1] It is not clear what proportion of the fines imposed in criminal proceedings was credited to the state; but during the ministry of Nana Phadnavis (1762–1800) the legal revenues included a considerable sum extorted from persons suspected or found guilty of adultery.

No definite estimate of the total revenue of the Maratha state can be given. Lord Valentia (1802–6) calculated the Peshwa's revenue at rather more than 7,000,000 rupees; while J. Grant, writing in 1798, estimated the total revenue of the Maratha empire at six crores, and the revenue of the Peshwa alone at not less than three crores of rupees, including *chauth* from the Nizam, Tipu Sultan, and the Rajput chiefs of Bundelkhand.[2] The revenue of a state which subsists largely on marauding excursions and blackmail, as the Maratha Government did in the time both of Sivaji and the Peshwas, must necessarily fluctuate; and the facts outlined in the preceding pages will serve to indicate that, though the general principles of the domestic administration may have been worthy of commendation, the practices of the Maratha Government and its officials precluded all possibility of the steady economic and educational advance of the country. Tone records that the Maratha Government invariably anticipated its land revenues.

These mortgages on the territorial income are negotiated by wealthy soucars (between whom and the Minister there always exists a proper understanding), and frequently at a discount of 30 per cent. and then paid in the most depreciated specie.

Owing to the unsettled state of the country, the Maratha Government preferred to raise a lump sum at enormous interest on the security of the precarious revenue of the next two or four years, and made little or no attempt to balance its revenue and current expenditure. The Maratha army was organised primarily for the purpose of plunder, and not so much for the extension of territory directly administered; and the people were gradually impoverished by the system of continuous freebooting, which the Marathas regarded as their most important means of subsistence. The general tone of the internal administration was not calculated to counteract to any appreciable extent the feelings of instability and insecurity engendered among the mass of the people by the predatory activities of their rulers. Indeed the constitution of the Maratha Government and army was "more calculated to destroy, than to create an empire";

---

[1] Sen, *op. cit.* pp. 371–3.　　　　　　　[2] *Idem*, pp. 342–3.

and the spirit which directed their external policy and their internal administration prevented all chance of permanent improvement of the country over which they claimed sovereign rights. There can be no doubt that the final destruction of the Maratha political power and the substitution of orderly government by the East India Company were necessary, and productive of incalculable benefit to India.

CHAPTER XXIV

THE CONQUEST OF CEYLON, 1795–1815

THE English had been nearly two centuries in India before Ceylon attracted their attention. They were too much occupied with, at first, establishing a precarious foothold, and then extending their conquests on the continent, to trouble much about a small island so far to the south. There had indeed been a curious attempt at intercourse as far back as 1664, which the Dutch historian, Valentyn, records. The king of Kandi at that period had a *penchant* for retaining in captivity any Englishmen he could capture—mostly castaways from merchant-ships wrecked on the coast, and an effort was made to negotiate with him for their release, but it was abortive, and the curtain fell for 100 years. But towards the end of the eighteenth century, the rivalry with the Dutch became acute, and the protection of our communications with our Indian possessions was a question of vital importance. Not only might the Dutch prey upon our commerce from their harbours in Ceylon, but there was a fear lest other nations, tempted by the tales of the fabulous wealth that poured into Holland from the Isle of Spices, might be induced to forestall us. Indeed the French, our dangerous rivals in India, had shown signs of this inclination a hundred years earlier, and had sent a fleet to attack Trinkomali. Though it was repulsed, a small embassy under de Laverolle was dispatched to Kandi to negotiate with the raja. But the ambassador was badly chosen: his unwise and intemperate behaviour resulted not only in the failure of the mission but in his own imprisonment.

The first serious attempt made by the English to gain a footing was in 1762, when Pybus was sent to Kandi to arrange a treaty with the raja, Kirti Sri. He has left an account of his mission—subsequently published from the records of the Madras Government—which gives a curious, if somewhat tedious, sketch of the state of affairs at the Kandian court. He was admitted to the audience hall at midnight, and ordered to pull his shoes off and hold above his head the silver dish containing the letter for the raja. Six separate curtains, white and red, were withdrawn, and the king was then discovered seated on his throne, which was a large chair, handsomely carved and gilt, which may now be seen in Windsor Castle. The envoy was forced upon his knees and had to make endless prostrations till at last his painful progress ended at the foot of the throne, where he presented his credentials. He describes the elaborate costume of the monarch, and the decorations of the hall, and adds:

I should have been well enough pleased with the appearance it made, had I been in a more agreeable situation. At the foot of the throne knelt one of the King's Prime Ministers, to whom he communicated what he had to say to me, who, after prostrating himself on the ground, related it to one of the generals who sat by me; who, after having prostrated himself, explained it to a Malabar doctor, who told it in Malabar to my dubash, and he to me. And this ceremony was repeated on asking every question.[1]

Whether or not this somewhat tortuous method of communication led to misunderstandings, the Madras Government took no steps to pursue the matter further then; but in 1782 war was declared against the Dutch, an English fleet under Hughes captured Trinkomali, and Hugh Boyd was sent to Kandi to solicit the raja's help against the Dutch. The failure of Pybus's mission had left a bad impression on the Kandian court; the raja curtly refused to negotiate; and Trinkomali was next year lost to the French and finally restored to the Dutch when peace was declared. However in 1795 the Dutch were involved in the European upheaval, and had also got into trouble with the Kandian court; and the English determined to strike. A force under Colonel James Stuart was dispatched to Ceylon by the governor of Madras, and accomplished its object with an unexpected rapidity. The Dutch had been firmly established for 140 years along the sea coast; they had built magnificent forts—the great fortress of Jaffna, which is little the worse for wear even to-day, was perhaps the finest specimen—and they were a sturdy and tenacious people. But the smaller sea-ports were easily occupied, and the garrison of Colombo marched out without a blow. The English historian asserts that the enemy was in a state of utter demoralisation. When the English entered the gates of Colombo, he says,

the Dutch were found by us in a state of the most infamous disorder and drunkenness, in no discipline, no obedience, no spirit. The soldiers then awoke to a sense of their degradation, but it was too late; they accused Van Angelbeck of betraying them, vented loud reproaches against their commanders, and recklessly insulted the British as they filed into the fortress, even spitting on them as they passed.[2]

On the other hand it is asserted that adequate preparations had been made for the defence, but that the surrender was due to the treachery of the governor, Van Angelbeck.[3] The facts were as follows. Early in 1795 an English agent, Hugh Cleghorn, induced the Comte de Meuron, *colonel propriétaire* of the Swiss regiment of that name, to transfer his regiment, then forming the chief part of the Ceylon forces, from the Dutch to the English service. Cleghorn and de Meuron arrived in India in the following September. Much seemed to depend upon the conduct of Van Angelbeck. He was believed to be an Orangist, but several of his council were strong revolutionaries, and it was feared that precipitate action might lead to the governor's arrest or murder. It was decided therefore to send

[1] Pybus, *Mission*, p. 79. [2] *Percival*, p. 118.
[3] Thombe, *Voyage aux Indes Orientales.*

him a copy of the capitulation regarding the de Meuron regiment, with a demand for its execution; but the news was also secretly communicated to the commandant of the regiment at Colombo. Van Angelbeck, who clearly did not intend more than a show of resistance, allowed the regiment to depart; and, when Stuart appeared before Colombo, surrendered it on terms. Indeed the withdrawal of the Swiss troops left him no alternative, whatever may have been his political views.[1] Accordingly the British flag flew over Colombo for the first time on 16 February, 1796, and the Dutch rule was over. Most of the wealthy folk filtered away to Batavia and elsewhere, but many of the officials were wisely kept on to finish up the judicial and other matters in which they were engaged.

It is open to argument whether the Portuguese or the Dutch left the stronger mark of their rule upon the island. The Sinhalese language was strongly affected by both. Nearly all the words connected with building are of Portuguese origin, for the ancient houses of the Sinhalese were rude and primitive structures. In the same way, most of the words connected with the household, domestic utensils, the kitchen, food, etc. come from the Dutch—the legacy of the *huisvrouw*.[2] In religious influences the Portuguese were far the more powerful, and the number of Portuguese names (bestowed at baptism) still surviving among the natives is most remarkable. The Dutch Reformed religion never got beyond the walls of the fortresses, but they taught the natives many lessons in town planning, sanitation, and the amenities of life.

"Within the castle [of Colombo]", says a Dutch writer[3] in 1676, "there are many pretty walks of nut-trees set in an uniform order: the streets are pleasant walks themselves, having trees on both sides and before the houses."

But it was by their magnificent bequest of Roman-Dutch law that they left their most abiding mark on the island; while their zeal for trade was a curious counterpart to the Portuguese zeal for conversion. Nor must it be forgotten that the "burgher" (the offspring of Dutch and native marriages) is probably the best outcome of mixed unions to be found in the East, and the colony has good reason to be grateful for the fine work they have accomplished in many official callings.

The transfer of power was effected without any great upheaval and with little bloodshed, and at first it seemed likely that the future course of events would be peaceful and prosperous. As the island had been taken by the troops, and at the expense, of the East India Company, it was only natural that it should claim the right to administer it; a right which it proceeded to assert, in spite of the opposition

[1] *The Cleghorn Papers*, pp. 14 *sqq.*, 202 *sqq.*
[2] *Census Report*, 1911, by E. B. Denham.
[3] Christopher Sweitzer's *Account of Ceylon*.

of Pitt and Melville, who wished it to be handed over to the crown. The results were lamentable. The Company selected as its representative a Madras civilian named Andrews, who was to negotiate a treaty with the king of Kandi, and, with plenary powers, to superintend the revenue arrangements. He was a man of rash and drastic measures, utterly ignorant of the people he was sent to govern, and blind to the fact that a newly, and barely, conquered country requires sympathy and tactful persuasion rather than revolutionary changes. He ruthlessly swept away all the old customs and service tenures, and introduced, without warning or preparation, the revenue system of Madras, which meant not only taxes and duties unheard of before, but the farming-out of those imposts to aliens from the coast of India, "enemies to the religion of the Sinhalese, strangers to their habits, and animated by no impulse but extortion" (Governor North).[1] They were under inadequate supervision, and it did not take many months to bring about the inevitable catastrophe. A fierce rebellion broke out; the forces at the disposal of the new rulers were few; the rebels held strong positions on the borderland between the low country and the hills; and it was only after fierce fighting and considerable loss of life that any headway was made against them.

This state of affairs was intolerable. Andrews was at once withdrawn; his outrageous crew of tax-collectors was sent back to the coast, and Pitt got his way earlier than he expected. The island was made a crown colony, and the first governor sent out to administer it was Frederick North,[2] who landed in October, 1798. He was at first placed under the orders of the governor-general of India; but after the Treaty of Amiens four years later, this arrangement was ended. He kept up a considerable correspondence with Lord Mornington (afterwards the Marquess Wellesley), preserved in the Wellesley MSS, and his letters throw a revealing light upon the questionable policy he adopted. He set to work at once to abolish the hateful taxes of his predecessor, eject the remaining Madras civilians, and change the fiscal policy of the government by reverting for the time to the system which the Dutch had worked upon; for, in spite of its obvious defects, it was at least familiar to the people. Unfortunately his attention was diverted from these peaceful efforts towards reform by a series of events at the capital of the island, Kandi; and his method of dealing with this crisis has undoubtedly left a stain upon his character. At the same time it may be urged that a man must to a certain extent be judged by the standard of his age; and it was not an age of extreme official probity or humanity. In 1787 we find Governor Phillip, before starting for New South

---

[1] Letter from Hon. F. North, Wellesley MSS.
[2] Afterwards fifth Earl of Guildford. He was remarkable for his love of Greece and the Greek language. He had a good deal to do with the foundation of the Ionian University at Corfu, of which he was the first Chancellor.

Wales, deliberately suggesting in an official memorandum that, for certain crimes,

I would wish to confine the criminal till an opportunity offered of delivering him as a prisoner to the natives of New Zealand, and let them eat him.[1]

It was not a nice age, from the modern point of view; but whether such instances as these can excuse North for the breach of faith he was guilty of, must be left to the judgment of the reader.

The king of Kandi died, or was deposed, in the same year as governor North landed, and the prime minister nominated a nephew of the queen's, Vikrama Raja Sinha, to succeed him. This was quite in accordance with Kandian custom, and the English Government accepted the arrangement, and prepared an embassy to the new king. The prime minister's name was Pilamé Talawé, and he was to bulk very large in the history of Ceylon for the next few luckless years. He was a traitor of a not unfamiliar oriental type, and had no sooner put his nominee on the throne than he began to conspire against him with a view to his own advancement to the kingly dignity. He sought a secret interview with North and explained his plans, his excuse for his treachery being that the reigning family was of alien (i.e. South Indian) origin, and that it was advisable to replace it by a family of native extraction. Unfortunately North listened to the tempter; he was anxious to get hold of Kandi, and thought he saw his chance. After much tortuous negotiation it was finally agreed that the prime minister should persuade the king to allow an ambassador to enter Kandi with an armed escort, which was to be far larger than was reported to the king; and North hoped that this "ambassador" (to wit, his principal general) would be able to secure and hold Kandi for the English, depose the unoffending monarch, and put Pilamé Talawé in his place as titular monarch.

The plot fell through; for though the raja at first fell into the trap and sanctioned the entry, the size of the escort leaked out, the other nobles got alarmed, the king was persuaded to cancel his permission, and the troops were mostly stopped at the boundary or led astray. The general did indeed arrive at Kandi, but with only a handful of men, and there was nothing for him to do but to return discomfited.

But this rebuff by no means diverted the prime minister (or adigar, as his real title was) from his intentions. After various fruitless endeavours, he at last, in 1802, managed to effect a breach between the Kandians and the English by causing a rich caravan, belonging to English subjects, to be robbed by Kandian officials. This was enough for North, who sent a large force under General Macdowall to seize Kandi—an easy victory, as the inhabitants and the king precipitately fled. A puppet king, Mutuswamy, with some claims to royal blood, was placed on the throne; but it was agreed with

---

[1] *Historical Records of New South Wales*, vol. I, pt II, p. 53.

Pilamé Talawé that this puppet should be at once deported and that he, the traitor, should reign in his stead. The English were sufficiently deluded to believe in the good faith of such a turncoat, and retired in triumph to the coast, leaving a very small garrison (only 300 English and some native levies) behind. They had their due reward. The *adigar* saw his chance, and was as ready to betray his allies the English as his master the monarch. He calculated that by destroying the tiny garrison and seizing the two kings, he could attain the summit of his desires without further tedious negotiations; and proceeded to carry out the former part of the programme. He surrounded Kandi with sufficient troops to make resistance hopeless; he attacked and killed many of the garrison, already decimated by disease, and called on the remnant to surrender. Their commander, Major Davie, was apparently not of the "bull-dog breed". He accepted the traitor's word that their lives should be spared, laid down his arms, and marched out of the town on his way to Trinkomali with his sickly following and the puppet king, Mutuswamy. But the *adigar* knew well that they could not cross the large river near Kandi, as it was swollen by floods. A party of headmen came up while they were waiting desperately by the bank, and explained that unless Mutu-swamy was given up, they would never be allowed to cross. Davie was base enough to entreat the prince to agree, as the envoys had promised that his life should be spared. The prince knew his countrymen and the *adigar* too well. "My god", he exclaimed, "is it possible that the triumphant arms of England can be so humbled as to fear the menaces of such cowards as the Kandians?"

Nevertheless, he was unconditionally surrendered; he stood a mock trial with heroic restraint, answering only, "I am at the king's mercy"; and within five minutes he met his death from the krises of the Malay guard. His relatives and followers were stabbed or impaled, and his servants were deprived of their noses and ears.

But this base act failed to save the English remnant. They were seized by the king's troops, Major Davie was taken back to Kandi, and the other officers and men were led two by two into a hollow out of sight of their comrades, felled by blows inflicted by the Caffres, and dispatched by the knives of the Kandians.[1] One man alone escaped from the carnage. He was found to be alive, and was twice hung by the Kandians, but each time the rope broke. He survived this trying ordeal, and struggled in the darkness to a hut, where a kindly villager fed him and tended his wounds, and eventually took him before the king, who spared his life, more probably from superstition than humanity.[2]

The scene of the massacre is still pointed out. "Davie's Tree"

---

[1] Emerson Tennent, *Ceylon*, II, 83.
[2] See *An Account of the Interior of Ceylon*, by Dr Davy, a brother of the celebrated Sir Humphry Davy.

is about three miles from Kandi, near the fatal river. The ill-starred Major Davie met with a lingering doom. His life was spared, says Mrs Heber in her journal, from a kind of superstitious feeling, as being the individual with whom the treaty was made. He was removed to Dumbara, but, owing to a plot by some Malays to carry him off and get a reward from the English Government, he was brought back to Kandi, suffering from ill-health, and died there in 1810. Several attempts were made by government to obtain his release, but the king demanded a sea-port on the coast as the ransom for his prisoner, and the negotiations broke down. He assumed the dress and habits of the natives, from whom he is said latterly to have been scarcely distinguishable, and if he had a defence for his conduct, he was never able to make it known. His apparent cowardice was in marked contrast to the heroism of two subordinate officers, whose names should be remembered. Captain Madge was in command of a small fort named Fort Macdowall, with a tiny force at his disposal. It was assaulted by swarms of Kandians simultaneously with the attack on the capital, and safe conduct was offered in return for capitulation. Captain Madge sternly refused, stood a blockade of three days, and then cut his way out and began a masterly retreat to Trinkomali, which he reached in safety, though his march lay through an almost unbroken ambuscade. Ensign Grant was in charge of a small redoubt called Dambudenia, slightly constructed of fascines and earth, and garrisoned by fourteen convalescent Europeans and twenty-two invalid Malays. He equally scorned the threats and promises of the enemy, strengthened his flimsy fortifications with bags of rice and provision stores, and sustained an almost incessant fire from several thousand Kandians for ten days. His force was then relieved from Colombo, and the place dismantled.

Such was the result of North's disastrous policy; yet he seems to have been fortunate enough to escape all official censure. Certainly his letters to Lord Mornington do not show much remorse for his crooked dealings; doubtless he had strong influence at home; and the date alone may explain his escape, for in 1803 England was far too deeply involved in her struggles with Napoleon to have much time to spare for the petty squabbles of a distant and hardly-known island.

The effects of the disastrous surrender at Kandi were immediate and widespread. The whole island hovered on the verge of revolt, or broke out into open hostilities; and the available British troops, thinned by death and sickness, could do no more than repel the attacks of the invaders; while the war between England and France made it impossible to send reinforcements from home. The king of Kandi, inflamed by hatred of the English, defied the wiles of Pilamé Talawé, and was backed by his whole people in his efforts to eject them from Ceylon. He sent emissaries throughout the low country, inciting the population to revolt, and led a large army to lay siege to Colombo. But the garrison was strong enough to repel him when he was eighteen miles from his objective, and he retired to his hill-fastnesses, where he felt himself secure. For it must be remembered that the country was then without roads of any kind; dense forests and steep hills and ravines guarded the approach to the capital; the damp enervating heat of the low country and the foot-hills, and the plague of leeches and mosquitoes, constituted an additional defence against English soldiers, whose dress and equipment at that period were not exactly of the kind best suited to warfare in near proximity to the equator.

An abortive attempt to attack Kandi from six different points in 1804 led to a very gallant action. The necessary orders had been issued to the six different commanders, but it was eventually decided that the difficulties were too great, and fresh orders were sent cancelling the whole scheme. But the countermand failed to reach Captain Johnston, whose original orders were to march from Batticaloa, join a detachment from Uva, and attack Kandi from the east. He set out accordingly, with a force of 82 Europeans and 220 native troops, failed to find any detachment from Uva, fought his way to Kandi through the thick, unhealthy jungle and unknown country, and took and occupied the capital for three days. As there was no sign of any of the supporting contingents, he evacuated the town and marched back to Trinkomali, with only sixteen British soldiers killed and wounded. His march was through a continuous ambuscade; and, besides his human foes, he had to contend with malaria, heavy rains, bad equipment, the plague of insects and the want of provisions. He has the credit of having performed the pluckiest military feat in the annals of Ceylon.

A long period of sullen inaction followed, during which the Kandian king gave way to all the worst excesses of an oriental tyrant. The traitor *adigar* was detected in an attempt to assassinate the king and met with a traitor's doom in 1812, and was succeeded by his nephew, Eheylapola. This minister, heedless of the warning of his uncle's fate, secretly solicited the help of the English to organise a general revolt against the despot of the hills. But his treason was discovered, and he fled for protection to Colombo, leaving behind him his wife and family. The tragedy which followed is thus described by Dr Davy:[1]

Hurried along by the flood of his revenge, the tyrant resolved to punish Eheylapola through his family, who still remained in his power: he sentenced his wife and children, and his brother and wife, to death—the brother and children to be beheaded, and the females to be drowned. In front of the Queen's Palace the wife and children were brought from prison and delivered over to their executioners. The lady, with great resolution, maintained her own and her children's innocence, and then desired her eldest child to submit to his fate. The poor boy, who was eleven years old, clung to his mother terrified and crying; her second son, of nine years.

[1] *An Account of the Interior of Ceylon.*

stepped forward and bade his brother not to be afraid; he would show him the way to die. By the blow of a sword the head of the child was severed from the body, and thrown into a rice mortar: the pestle was put into the mother's hands, and she was ordered to pound it, or be disgracefully tortured. To avoid the infamy, the wretched woman did lift up the pestle and let it fall. One by one the heads of the children were cut off, and one by one the poor mother—but the circumstance is too dreadful to be dwelt on. One of the children was an infant; it was plucked from its mother's breast to be beheaded. After the execution the sufferings of the mother were speedily relieved. She and her sister-in-law were taken to the little tank at Bogambara and drowned.

This extract has been given in full because the memory of the horror is still very vivid among the Sinhalese; and "The Tragedy of Eheylapola's wife" is told and retold by many a professional story-teller.

But the tyrant's punishment was fortunately near at hand, and the year 1815 equally witnessed the defeat of Napoleon and the extinction of the Kandian dynasty. He ventured to seize and disgracefully mutilate a party of merchants, British subjects, who had gone up to Kandi to trade, and sent them back to Colombo with their severed members tied round their necks.[1] This was the last straw: an avenging army was instantly on the march, led by Governor Sir R. Brownrigg in person, and within two weeks was well within reach of the capital. The king meanwhile remained in a state of almost passive inertness, rejecting all belief in our serious intentions to attack him. A messenger brought him news of our troops having crossed the frontiers: he directed his head to be struck off. Another informed him of the defeat of his troops in the Seven Korles: he ordered him to be impaled alive. At length he precipitately quitted Kandi, and (14 February) the English marched in and took possession. An armed party sent out by Eheylapola discovered the house to which the king had fled, pulled down the wall of the room where he was hiding, and suddenly exposed the crouching tyrant to the glare of the torches of the by-standers. He was bound with ropes, subjected to every obloquy and insult, and handed over to the English authorities, who eventually transported him to Vellore in India, where he died in January, 1832.[2]

Kandian independence was over; the whole island was in the hands of the English, and the new *régime* began.

---

[1] Emerson Tennent, *Ceylon*, ii, 89.

[2] *A narrative of events which have recently occurred in Ceylon*, by a Gentleman on the Spot, London, 1815.

CHAPTER XXV

THE REVENUE ADMINISTRATION OF BENGAL, 1765–86

IN May, 1765, Clive returned to India, and his forceful personality was soon at work. On 16 August, 1765, the emperor Shah 'Alam, from motives very foreign to those of Akbar, divested the nawab of his powers as diwan, and conferred that office on the British East India Company to hold as a free gift and royal grant in perpetuity (*altamgha*). The Company in turn appointed as its deputy or naib diwan the same officer who had been selected to act as naib nazim, viz. Muhammad Reza Khan, who now united in his person the full powers of the nizamat and diwanni which had been separated by Akbar and reunited by Murshid Kuli Khan. But the arrangement spelt failure from the beginning. The emperor was a ruler in name only: his diwan in Bengal was a mysterious being locally known as the *Kampani Sahib Bahadur*, represented by a victorious and masterful foreign soldier, assisted by men who were avowedly traders, whose interests were principally engaged in maintaining the Company's dividends, and who lacked completely the professional training essential to efficient administration. Confusion reigned both in the provinces of justice and revenue.

The revenue of Bengal as assessed in the reign of Akbar[1] varied little either in the amount or the mode of levying it until the eighteenth century, when increasing anarchy introduced fresh assessments and further exactions under the name of *abwabs* or cesses. The three main sources of revenue at the time when the Company assumed the diwanni were (a) *mal*, i.e. the land revenue, including royalties on salt; (b) *sair*, i.e. the revenue received from the customs, tolls, ferries, etc.; (c) *bazi jama*, i.e. miscellaneous headings, such as receipts from fines, properties, excise, etc. The land revenue was collected by hereditary agents who held land in the various districts, paid the revenue, and stood between the government and the actual cultivators of the soil; these agents were in general known as zamindars, and the cultivators of the soil as ryots.

The position of the zamindar gave considerable difficulty to the Company's senior officers. At first he was looked upon merely as a revenue agent, with an hereditary interest and privileges in certain districts; but later he was considered as owning land in fee simple. The controversy is too lengthy to be followed in this chapter; but it may be asserted that the zamindar, though not the owner of the land

---

[1] Report of Anderson, Croftes and Bogle, dated 28 March, 1778.

in fee simple, was by no means a mere revenue agent; it was practically impossible by constitutional methods to break his hereditary connection with the land of which he was the zamindar; and as long as he performed his duties he was far more impregnable in his position than the average English official. On the other hand, the position of the ryots was less enviable than that of an English cultivator of the soil at the same period. In each village there was a *mandal*, or chief ryot, who acted as their agent in dealing with the various petty officers employed by the zamindar in the collection of the land revenue. The result of the investigation ordered in 1776 was to give a sad picture of the lot of the ryot and of the zamindar's indifference to his welfare, especially during the chaotic fifty years that followed on the death of Murshid Kuli Khan, during which the zamindar's receipts, owing to anarchy and consequent lack of cultivation, diminished.

"Although", in the words of the 1776 report, "the increase of the assessment [in 1772] may have been the principal, or at least the original, cause of the various additional taxes imposed on the ryots it did not follow that a reduction in the assessment would produce a diminution in the rents. The prospect of contingent and future benefits from the cultivation and improvement of his country is hardly sometimes sufficiently powerful to induce a zamindar to forego the immediate advantage which he enjoys by rack-renting his zamindari and exacting the greatest possible revenue from the tenants and vassals. Were it necessary to support the truth of this position we could produce many proofs from the accounts which we have collected. The instances, especially in large zamindaris, are not infrequent where a reduction in the demands of Government have been immediately followed by new taxes and new impositions."

The proceedings contain frequent references from the districts in Bengal complaining of the exactions and harshness of the zamindars.

After so many years ought not Government [i.e. the nawab's government] to have obtained the most perfect and intimate nature of the value of the rents and will it be believed at this day, it is still in the dark?

So wrote Edward Baber, Resident at Midnapur, in a letter dated 13 December, 1772, to the Committee of Revenue in Calcutta.[1] We must now consider the efforts by the leading executive officers of the Company to pierce this fog of ignorance.

It has been alleged[2] that having accepted the diwanni the English deliberately adopted a policy of *festina lente* chiefly because they wished to avoid the expense and unpopularity of a general survey of the lands; but such a survey, unless conducted entirely under expert European supervision, was worthless, and such supervision was unprocurable. Moreover the existing revenue nomenclature had then been in use for nearly two centuries, the population was almost entirely illiterate, and the bulk of such revenue records as existed were in the hands of native registrars; these factors, combined with

---

[1] Revenue Board Proceedings, 15 December, 1772, pp. 417–26.
[2] Firminger, *Fifth Report*, etc. I, 167.

their own curtailed powers and the caprices of the directors, might well induce the Company's local authorities to move slowly. The directors commenced by attaching an enormous salary,[1] nine lakhs of rupees *per annum*, to the office of the naib diwan, hoping thereby to obtain uncorrupt and efficient service.

Meanwhile, under the governorship of Verelst, the president and Select Committee made as full an enquiry as they could, arriving at the well-known conclusions contained in their Proceedings[2] for 16 August, 1769, in which "certain grand original sources" of the unsatisfactory state of the revenue collection in Bengal were enumerated. At home, the court of directors in June, 1769, had sent orders to Bengal, appointing a committee "for the management of the diwanni revenue"; and three "supervisors" with plenary powers sailed from England in September, 1769, but after leaving the Cape of Good Hope were never heard of again.

Verelst and his committee made a correct diagnosis of the trouble. They realised that the Company's European servants were kept in complete ignorance "of the real produce and capacity of the country by a set of men who first deceive us from interest and afterwards continue the deception from a necessary regard to their own safety". The chaos and misrule caused by the venal officials and adventurers who had frequented Bengal since the death of Aurangzib, combined with the secretive methods which a continuous oppression of the ryot by the zamindar had produced, formed an impenetrable labyrinth of which the key was sought in vain.

Verelst's committee established supervisors of the collections; these supervisors received instructions to make a full and complete enquiry into the method of collecting the revenue in their respective districts and, in fact, into any customs, knowledge of which might assist to improve the condition of the people; the instructions breathe a warm and humane spirit and a real desire, not merely to collect revenue, but to assist the oppressed cultivator of the soil. The supervisors failed, as indeed they were bound to do. Their instructions ordered them to prepare a rent roll, and, by enquiry, to ascertain the facts from which a just and profitable assessment of the revenue could be made. Such instructions were impossible to carry out. The supervisors soon found themselves confronted by a most formidable passive opposition from the zamindars and kanungos which prevented any real knowledge whatever of the amount of revenue actually paid by the ryot to the zamindar from coming to the knowledge of the Company. By this conspiracy of two corrupt and hereditary revenue agencies all avenues of information were closed. Between them, the zamindars and the kanungos held all the essential information, but the kanungo was the dominant figure.

[1] Cf. letter from Hastings to the Secret Committee, 1 September, 1772.
[2] Cf. Verelst, *A View*, etc. pp. 224–39.

A full account of this officer and his duty was submitted in May, 1787, to the Board of Revenue by J. Patterson,[1] register, Kanungo's Office.

The kanungo comes into prominence in the reign of Akbar, who employed him, as the name implies, to keep the records of the pargana, a revenue sub-division. He was in fact a registrar of a district appointed to see that the crown received its dues and that the ryot was not oppressed; his duties were responsible and onerous; he had to

register the usages of a district, the rates and mode of its assessment, and all regulations relating thereto. To note and record the progress of cultivation, the produce of the land and the price current thereof, and to be at all times able to furnish Government with materials to regulate the assessment by just and equitable proportions.

The kanungos' duties also included

the keeping of a record of all events, such as the appointments, deaths or removals of zamindars, to preserve the records of the Tumar and Taksim Jama, and the record of the boundaries and limits of zamindaris, talukdaris, parganas, villages, etc.

They also preserved in their registers the genealogies of zamindars, records of all grants of land, copies of the contracts of the zamindars and tax-farmers with the government, and, in short, acted as general custodians for every description of record in the district. There were two main, or *sadar*, kanungos for Bengal, but in each pargana there was a deputy or naib kanungo; the office became hereditary at an early date. Murshid Kuli Khan is stated to have replaced the kanungos of his day by an entirely new set, but the evil was not checked, because the new kanungos passed on their office and their knowledge to their descendants in the same way as the evicted ones had done.

Thus the whole of the land registration, and the entire knowledge of the actual receipts of the land revenue, were in the hands of a hereditary close corporation, who were the only authorities on the real state of the revenue; their power was enormous; and only complete ignorance can explain Verelst and his committee's imagining that such knowledge would be surrendered to the Company on demand. Edward Baber, in his letter of 13 December, 1772, called the attention of the Board of Revenue to these facts, and to the great power which the kanungos had over the zamindars,

because it was in the power of the Kanungos to expose the value of their parganas. ...This power the Kanungos availed themselves of, and it was the rod which they held over them so that the apprehension of an increase of his rents kept the zamindar in very effectual awe of the Kanungo....In a word the Kanungos have an absolute influence over the Zamindars which they exercise in every measure that can promote their own interests....It now happens that the Kanungos manage, not only the zamindars, but the business of the province. There is not a record but

[1] Original consultations, no. 63, Revenue Dept. 18 May, 1787. Printed *ap.* Ramsbotham, *Land Revenue History of Bengal*, pp. 163–97.

what is in their possession and so much of the executive part have they at last obtained that they are now virtually the Collector, while he is a mere passive representative of Government. They are the channel through which all his orders are conveyed....Instead of being the agents of Government they are become the associates of the zamindars and conspire with them to conceal what it is their chief duty to divulge.

Baber drives home the argument by challenging the board to state how the last settlement (he is referring to the settlement made by the Committee of Circuit in 1772) was made; taking the example of Midnapur, his own district, he asks "on what information, on what materials was it made? was there a single instrument produced to guide the judgment of the board?"[1] It will be obvious that the supervisors appointed in 1769 were bound to fail. They were completely and wilfully kept in the dark by officials who had everything to lose and nothing to gain by giving the required information. The kanungos were only prepared to serve the state on their own terms; and those terms included a retention of the very information which their office was created to obtain for the state. Their action was utterly unconstitutional and involved the admission that a few families should hereditarily possess information which is the sole prerogative of the state, and that they should use that information for their personal and pecuniary profit.

The Company's government in India created in 1770 two Boards of Revenue, one in Murshidabad and one in Patna, to control respectively the Bengal and Bihar collections; but dissensions taking place in the council, John Cartier was ordered to hand over his office to Warren Hastings and several other alterations were made. Hastings assumed office as governor and president of Fort William on 13 April, 1772.

The outstanding result of the first seven years of the Company's administration of the diwanni is that the Company's officers in Bengal realised that they were face to face with the great problem of ascertaining the difference between the sum received as land revenue by government, and the sum actually paid by the ryot to the zamindar. This was the secret of the zamindar and kanungo which the Company never fathomed; it forms the burden of the collectors' reports to the Board of Revenue from 1772 onwards; and it is the basis of the great Shore-Grant controversy. When the revenue settlement was made permanent in 1793 this information was still wanting, and not a single revenue officer of the Company in 1793 could state with accuracy the entire actual amount which the zamindars in his district received from the ryots, or the proportion which it bore to that which the zamindar paid to the government; yet these were the conditions in which the revenue settlement was declared permanent.

Hastings brought to his work a sound experience of Bengal, a fluent

[1] Revenue Board Proceedings, 15 December, 1772, pp. 417–26.

and accurate knowledge both of Persian and of Bengali: moreover, he had the reputation of being a loyal and most efficient servant of the Company. It is still difficult to give an impartial verdict on his official career. In revenue work his ability was not remarkable, and on his own admission[1] he had no practical working knowledge of it; in fact, his influence on the actual conditions of the revenue was unfortunate, especially when contrasted with his administration and reorganisation of the judicature in the districts, which was a vigorous beneficial achievement. His masterful temperament often prevented him from using the advice of subordinates better qualified than himself to speak authoritatively on details of revenue administration. This inflexibility must share responsibility with the jealousy of Francis and the ill-temper of Clavering for the deadlock which occurred in the administration of Bengal between 1774 and 1776.

The directors' orders which confronted the new governor were of a disturbing nature. On 14 April, 1772, these dispatches containing the well-known proclamation arrived in Calcutta. On 11 May the information was made public:

Notice is hereby given that the Hon'ble the Court of Directors have been pleased to divest the Nawab Muhammad Reza Khan of his station of Naib Diwan and have determined to stand forth publicly themselves in the character of Diwan.

This announcement radically altered the existing system of the collections.

The new governor and his council, as a prelude to carrying out their orders, appointed a committee to tour through various districts of Bengal and to submit a report on their observations. Thus was formed the Committee of Circuit, consisting of the Company's most senior officers, including the governor himself, S. Middleton, P. M. Dacres, J. Lawrell, and J. Graham. Their terms of reference were based on the resolutions taken by the council on 14 May, 1772, viz.

(a) to farm the lands for a period of five years;

(b) to establish a Committee of Circuit to form the settlement;

(c) to re-introduce the supervisors under the name of collectors, assisted by an Indian diwan in each district;

(d) to restrict the officials of the Company from any private employment.

The Committee of Circuit realised the difficulty of their work.

The Hon'ble Court of Directors...declare their determination to stand forth as Diwan, and, by the agency of the Company's servants, to take upon themselves the entire care and management of the Revenue. By what means this agency is to be exercised we are not instructed....They have been pleased to direct a total change of system, and have left the plan of execution of it to the direction of the Board without any formal repeal of the regulations they had before framed and

[1] Cf. the evidence given by Hastings for the plaintiff in the case brought by Kamal-ud-din Khan against the Calcutta Committee of Revenue, Governor-General's Proceedings, 2 September, 1776, pp. 3367–89.

adopted to another system, the abolition of which must necessarily include that of its subsidiary institutions unless they shall be found to coincide with the new. The Revenue is beyond all question the first object of Government.[1]

The Committee of Circuit decided to place the revenue administration entirely under the direct control of the president and council, who were to form a committee of revenue; they also recommended that the *Khalsa*, or treasury office, should be removed from Murshidabad to Calcutta, making the latter town the financial capital of the province.

As the duties of the diwanni comprised the administration of civil justice, and as the business of the Committee of Circuit was to consolidate the Company's control over the diwanni, the important question of restoring the administration of justice in the districts came before them. The close connection between the land revenue and civil justice necessitates a brief mention of the committee's proposals recorded in their Proceedings.[2] They recommended in each district under a collector the formation of two courts, the diwanni adalat and the faujdari adalat, the former with civil, the latter with criminal jurisdiction; the matters cognisable by each court were strictly defined, and the diwanni adalat was under the direct charge of the collector. In addition to these *mufassil* or district courts, two similar *sadar*, or headquarters' courts, were to be established in Calcutta, the sadar diwanni adalat being presided over by the governor or a member of council. These courts were designed to remove the abuses in the administration of justice referred to by Verelst in his *Instructions to the Supervisors*. "Every decision", he writes of these native courts, "is a corrupt bargain with the highest bidder....Trifling offenders are frequently loaded with heavy demands and capital offences are as often absolved by the venal judge."[3]

The most objectionable feature of the proposed regulations, as is pointed out by Harington,[4] was that they vested in one person the powers of a tax-collector and of a magistrate. Hastings[5] himself made this complaint against Verelst's plan introducing the supervisors; but he was apparently forced to embody the same defect in his own regulation. Perhaps the best and most straightforward defence of this admitted defect was that made by Shore.[6]

...It is impossible to draw a line between the Revenue and Judicial Departments in such a manner as to prevent their clashing: in this case either the Revenue must suffer or the administration of Justice be suspended....It may be possible in course of time to induce the natives to pay their rents with regularity and without compulsion, but this is not the case at present.

[1] Committee of Circuit's Proceedings, 28 July, 1772, pp. 162–8.
[2] *Idem*, 15 August, 1772, pp. 234–48. Cf. also Colebrooke, *Supplement*, etc. pp. 1–8.
[3] Verelst, *op. cit.* pp. 229–30.
[4] Harington, *Analysis*, I, 34.
[5] In a minute printed in *India papers*, vol. VI, quoted by Harington, *Analysis*, II, 41–3.
[6] Letter to Sir G. Colebrooke, 26 March, 1772.

The Committee of Circuit's recommendations[1] were sent with a covering letter to the council at Fort William on 15 August, 1772, and received the council's approval on 21 August. They proposed that a large proportion of that land, known as *huzur zilla* land, because it paid its revenue direct to the *Khalsa*, should be converted into separate districts each under a collector. The whole council was to act as a committee of revenue, and to audit the accounts of the diwanni assisted by an Indian officer styled the *rai raian*. The latter was a most important person; his duties included the supervision of all the provincial diwans attached to the various collectorships,

to receive from them the accounts in the Bengali language and to issue to them a counterpart of the orders which the Board of Revenue shall from time to time expedite to the Collectors.

The salary attached to this important post was 5000 rupees a month. The first holder was Raja Rajballabh, a son of Raja Rai Durlabh, the old colleague of Muhammad Reza Khan. The business of the *Khalsa* was precisely defined; the post of accountant-general was created, the first holder being Charles Croftes; and the various departments of that office, and of the treasury in general, defined and organised. This completed the main work of the Committee of Circuit, and unquestionably the most successful portion was that which dealt with the administration of justice. They inherited from the Moghul government every evil that could afflict a judicial system: a disorganised and corrupt judicature and incompetent agents. Dacoity was rampant, and there was no ordinary security in the land. The new courts, although by no means perfect, brought great relief to the ryots and talukdars, and within a short time began to foster confidence in the Company's administration.

On 13 October, 1772, the new Committee of Revenue commenced its work by settling the revenue to be collected from Hugli, Midnapur, Birbhum, Jessore and the Calcutta zamindary lands. The settlement was for five years, and the lands were farmed out by public auction, in order better to discover the real value of the lands. This, in itself, is a comment on the board's revenue policy, for they must have known that to farm the land revenue by public auction would induce many people to bid from motives other than mere desire for profit; the gambling instinct, the desire for power, the opportunity of inflicting injury on an enemy or of humiliating a local zamindar, all powerfully contributed to raise the bidding beyond the value of the revenue. The board certainly expressed an opinion[2] that, *ceteris paribus*, it was preferable to accept the bids of established zamindars, but they had definitely placed both the zamindar and the ryot at the mercy of

---

[1] Committee of Circuit's Proceedings, pp. 248–58. Cf. Colebrooke, *Supplement*, pp. 8–14 and 194–200; also Harington, *Analysis*, II, 25–33.

[2] Letter of the President to the Court of Directors, 3 November, 1772. Cf. Harington, *op. cit.* II, 16–18.

speculating and unprincipled adventurers who, in many cases, ousted the old zamindars and thus severed an old-established link between government and the cultivator of the soil, for the zamindar, in spite of his shortcomings, had (in the words of Hastings himself) "riveted an authority in the district, acquired an ascendancy over the minds of the ryots and ingratiated their affections". Between 1772 and 1781 the connection between the zamindars and their tenants was seriously impaired by this unfortunate method.[1]

In justice to Hastings and his colleagues it must be remembered that they were suddenly called upon to administer the revenues of a country which for half a century had been in a state of increasing disorder, and to create an administrative service from young men who had come to the country at an immature age for a purely commercial career. Among their critics is Hastings himself, whose letters[2] in the early days of his governorship contain disparaging references to the collectors; yet many of those so criticised were almost immediately employed by him and rose to positions of comparative eminence; the majority came from good British homes. The record of their work, contained in the forgotten and unpublished minutes of perished boards, shows them to have been humane, if untrained, men genuinely anxious to relieve the distress in their districts.

A careful perusal of the proceedings of the Board of Revenue for the years 1772 and 1773 reveals that the most valuable suggestions for alleviating distress among the cultivators are to be found in letters from the district officers rather than in the resolutions of the board: in spite of the most determined passive resistance which zamindars, kanungos, and farmers of the revenue made to their enquiries, it was the collectors who enabled the voice of the oppressed ryot to reach the headquarters of government.

The collectors soon realised that the settlement had been seriously over-estimated, but the board refused to believe their district officers and added to the trouble by peremptory orders for the collection of deficits. This was done with undoubted harshness, for the collectors had no option[3] but to carry out their orders. Confinement of zamindars and farmers was freely used, but without any result except that of adding to the confusion; and the words with which Hastings, in his letter to the directors, dated 3 November, 1772, described the conditions of the revenue collections in Bengal on his assumption of the governorship, might be used with truth to describe the conditions in collecting the same revenue in 1773.

The entire system of revenue registration was still in the hands of an hereditary corporation and was still unknown to government, which

[1] In the matter of the public auction of the farms consult also the letter dated 17 May, 1766, para. 17 from the Court of Directors (Long, *Selections*, no. 893).
[2] E.g. to L. Sulivan, 10 March, 1774.
[3] Letter from the Council of Revenue at Patna, dated 17 October, 1774. Revenue Board Proceedings, 1 November, 1774, pp. 6395–8.

had no accurate working knowledge on which to base a general settlement, and which was, as several district officers testified, completely ignorant of the actual amount paid by the cultivator compared with that received by itself.[1] Over-assessment and wholesale farming had aggravated the mischief. Though government had established a business-like system for keeping the accounts of such revenue as was actually received, this was but a trifle compared with the weighty problem that was still unsolved.

The diwanni adalats relieve the sombre colours of the picture, and in them the cultivator found a real protection and assistance at the hands of those collectors whose work received such scanty acknowledgment: but the day of the collectors was to be short. In April, 1773, the court of directors sent orders to the governor and council to recall the collectors from their districts and to adopt other measures for collecting the revenues. These orders were similar to those issued in 1769 abolishing the supervisors; the directors apparently distrusted their junior officers, and were nervous lest private trade should engross their time. These orders were considered by the president and council on 23 November, 1773.[2]

The board drew up a detailed temporary plan in order to give effect to these instructions, to be "adopted and completed by such means as experience shall furnish and the final orders of the Hon'ble Company allow". (1) A committee of revenue at the presidency was formed consisting of two members of the board and three senior servants below council who were to meet daily and transact the necessary business assisted by the rai raian; (2) the three provinces were divided into six divisions, each under a provincial council consisting of a chief, assisted by four senior servants of the Company: in Calcutta the committee of revenue above mentioned was to carry out the duties of such a council; (3) each district, originally a collectorship, was placed under the control of an Indian revenue officer (diwan), except in districts entirely let to a zamindar or farmer, who was then empowered to act as diwan; (4) occasional inspections were to be made by commissioners specially selected by the board for their knowledge of Persian and "moderation of temper". The selection of these commissioners was to be unanimous;

an objection made by a single member of the Board to any proposed as wanting these requisites shall be a sufficient bar to his rejection without any proof being required to support it;

(5) the various collectors were to make up their accounts and hand over charge to Indian deputies who were empowered to hold the courts of diwanni adalat, but appeals in all cases were allowed to the provincial sadar adalat now constituted to form a link between the

---

[1] Letter from C. Bentley, collector of Chittagong, dated 10 July, 1773. Revenue Board Proceedings, 17 August, 1773, pp. 2620–39.
[2] *Idem*, 23 November, 1773, pp. 3453–77.

mufassal and headquarters diwanni courts; (6) with a view to checking private trade the chiefs of the provincial councils were given a salary of 3000 sicca rupees *per mensem*, and had to take an oath[1] not to engage in private trade.

The changes, necessitated by the directors' orders, were for the worse. The collectorship as a district unit of the revenue administration was retained, but the employment of Indian diwans instead of European collectors deprived the Company of an increasing knowledge among its European servants of the country, the state of the revenue, and the methods of collection; it checked the growth of a spirit of responsibility and of public service among the junior officers; and it diluted the European element in the district collections to such an extent as to render it negligible. The whole scheme, for which the directors must bear the responsibility, is tainted with the inference that, provided the stipulated revenue was received, the method of collecting it did not much matter.

The proceedings of the Board of Revenue from 1773 to 1776 record a monotonous list of large deficits, defaulting zamindars, absconding farmers, and deserting ryots. The provincial councils, like the collectors before them, protested that the country was over-assessed; the diwans proved incapable and unbusinesslike, and were the subject of a circular letter[2] of complaint issued by the board to the provincial councils.

The new system was only in force for six months before the Regulating Act made further changes, but its proceedings display all the signs of impending collapse. The council of Patna sent in a moving description[3] of the distress in their province. Anticipating Philip Francis, they definitely recommended a settlement in perpetuity, because no satisfactory collections could be made except on that basis of stability which only a lengthy tenure furnishes.

"It remains", they write, "that we should submit to you our sentiments on the measures calculated to produce a remedy. It has been successfully practised by the Hindostan Princes that where a particular district has gone to ruin to give it to a Zamindar or any other man of known good conduct for a long lease of years or in perpetuity at a fixed rent not to be increased should ever the industry of the renter raise an unexpected average to himself...."

The board in their reply considered the suggestion to be too hazardous for experiment.

Other events were now impending. On 19 October, 1774, Clavering, Monson, and Francis arrived in Calcutta. Of the three new members of council the ablest was Francis, whose malicious and petulant character needs no description here, but whose ability and grasp of the intricate revenue problem in Bengal, although not free from error,

---

[1] Revenue Board Proceedings, 16 March, 1774.
[2] *Idem*, 5 July, 1774, pp. 5425–6.
[3] *Idem*, 29 January, 1773, pp. 627–33.

was remarkable, even if due allowance is made for his alleged indebtedness to the "coaching" of John Shore.

The Supreme Council soon offered a most unfortunate example of disunion to all the subordinate officers of the Company, and the same spirit appeared in the provincial councils; thus was created a spirit of partisanship throughout the entire service, which encouraged in farmers, zamindars, and tenants the hope that profit might be obtained by supporting one side or the other; but in spite of these evils, the new council brought into the administration of the revenue a vigorous and, on the whole, healthy spirit of enquiry. Abuses were brought to light which under a more easy-going *régime* would have remained dormant. The most noticeable result of the new change was the position of the governor-general. Hitherto Hastings had exerted an overwhelming, almost dictatorial, control over his council, whose proceedings for the years 1772–4 show a general compliance with the governor's desires, and the greatest reluctance to oppose him. This authority was now openly disregarded. The new members of the council came out prejudiced, if not against individual servants of the Company, against the *personnel* and the Company's service in general; but allowing for their wholesale suspicion, it must be conceded that the time was ripe for a complete investigation into the methods of collecting the revenue, and for some radical changes in that administration.

On 21 October, 1774, the new Board of Revenue met for the first time and the governor-general explained in detail the mode of collecting the land revenue, and the lately introduced system of the provincial councils, and he recommended a continuation of the system, at any rate for the present, as the season of year was soon approaching in which the heaviest instalments of the revenue were due for payment. The board agreed to the suggestion, partly because they wanted to see the existing system at work, and partly because they realised the force of the argument for a temporary continuation of the existing system, but "they do not mean to preclude themselves from such future alterations as...some mature deliberation may suggest to them". In revenue matters, as in others, the new councillors soon displayed their intolerance, and the first difference was between the governor-general and Clavering over a complaint made to the former by the rai raian against Joseph Fowke. It is impossible to relate here in detail the many cases of friction and open quarrelling which occurred during the new administration; this was not always produced by the quarrelsome attitude of the new arrivals. Hastings and Barwell were also intolerant. The rejection of certain officers proposed by the governor-general for promotion drew a protest from Barwell who alleged that "good and zealous servants had been deprived of normal promotion"; a policy, he contended, that would create faction throughout the service and "involve the policy and connection of the state with the different powers of Hindostan". But Clavering was able to quote figures to prove that in the matter of revenue appointments the governor-general's choice had almost always been accepted by the council. In a letter to the court of directors dated 1 September, 1777, and embodied in proceedings for 1 October, 1777, Clavering states without contradiction that out of thirty-four officers recommended by the governor-general for appointment to seats on the provincial councils, only six were set aside by the vote of the majority; moreover, in 1777 there were on the provincial councils only three men who had not been recommended by Hastings himself: these three were John Shore, Boughton Rous, and Goring. This effective reply remained unanswered, and disposes very decisively of Barwell's insinuations.

In addition to the weekly reports from the districts of defaulting farmers and oppressed ryots, a new and serious problem was created by the interference of the Supreme Court in the revenue administration. This threatened to bring the collections to a standstill, because the Supreme Court, by issuing writs of *habeas corpus* in favour of persons confined by the orders of the provincial diwanni adalat courts for non-payment of revenue, paralysed the effective control exercised by these courts. Complaints and requests for instructions poured in from all the divisions: the Supreme Council became very restive but was induced to concur for the time being in the governor-general's advice "not to controvert the authority which the Supreme Court may think fit to exercise".[1] The judges of the Supreme Court acknowledged the caution displayed by the board in a letter[2] which conveyed their opinion on certain questions propounded by the board regarding the appellate jurisdiction of the sadar diwanni adalat and the Supreme Court. The matter rested there for a while.

The dissensions in the council encouraged unscrupulous people, hostile to Hastings, to bring accusations of corruption against the governor-general to which the majority in the council lent a greedy ear.

It must be admitted that the governor-general had shown much laxity in permitting his banyan Krishna Kantu Nandi (the well-known "Cantoo Baboo") to hold lucrative farms. The Committee of Circuit had laid down[3] that no banyan of the collector, nor any of his relations, should under any circumstances hold a farm or be connected with a farmer. Gleig's[4] shuffling defence that this order applied to collectors only is unworthy of serious consideration, for the chances of corrupt profit that might accrue to the banyan of a collector were insignificant compared to those which an unscrupulous

---

[1] Governor-General's Proceedings, January, 1775.
[2] *Idem*, 25 July, 1775. Cf. also Hastings's letter to Lord North, dated 10 January, 1776.
[3] Committee of Circuit's Proceedings, pp. 56–9.
[4] Gleig, *op. cit.* I, 529, 530 (ed. 1841).

banyan of the governor-general might receive. Kantu Babu held farms in his own name whose annual rental exceeded thirteen lakhs of rupees,[1] and, in addition, he held farms in the name of his son, Loknath Nandi, a child of twelve or thirteen years. The acquiescence of Hastings in this matter was contrary to the spirit of the regulations drawn up by the Committee of Circuit of which he himself had been the most prominent member. His statement that he had no personal interest in the affairs of his banyan does not alter the situation. In this case, and in his defence[2] of Bhawani Charan Mitra, diwan of Burdwan, whose sons and servants had been discovered in the possession of farms, no excuse can be offered for Hastings's inertness; but the majority of the council allowed their venom to poison their judgment in declaring that "there was no species of peculation from which the governor-general had thought fit to abstain". Certain transactions of Barwell, when chief of the Dacca provincial council, were also declared by the majority to be corrupt, but the real target was the governor-general who protested with unavailing logic that his would-be judges were also his accusers. Hastings, to preserve the dignity of his office, was forced on several occasions to break up the council. Such were the conditions in which the new government proceeded to administer the revenues of Bengal; conditions which lasted till Monson's death on 25 September, 1776. During this period some very valuable information was obtained from the senior servants of the Company in response to a circular issued on 23 October, 1774, to the chiefs of the provincial councils asking their views on the causes of the diminution of the land revenue and of the frequent deficits.

Middleton,[3] writing of the Murshidabad division which included Rajshahi, named the famine of 1770 as the first cause; he also considered that "the unavoidably arbitrary settlement made by the Committee of Circuit" and the public auction of farms contributed heavily to the distress, especially the last cause:

the zamindar being tenacious of her hereditary possessions, and dreading the disgrace and reproach which herself and her family of long standing as zamindars must have suffered by its falling into other hands.

He suggested that "a universal remission of a considerable amount of the revenue due" be granted, and the settlement in future be made with the zamindars: if farmers must be employed, they should be very carefully selected.

P. M. Dacres,[4] late chief of the Calcutta committee, also considered the public auction of farms to be largely responsible for much distress, instancing the bidding in the Nadia district; other causes were the great famine and the excessive assessment of 1772. He advocated a general remission of deficits and urged a permanent settlement with

---

[1] Governor-General's Proceedings, 17 March, 1775, 25 April, 1777, and 29 April, 1777.
[2] *Idem*, 23 January, 1776.   [3] *Idem*, 7 April, 1775.   [4] *Idem*.

the zamindars which "would fix the rents in perpetuity and trust to a sale of their property as a security for their payments": advice that was not lost on Francis.

G. Hurst,[1] from the council of Patna, shared Middleton's views and also referred to the wars that had ravaged Bihar from the days of 'Ali Wardi Khan until the assumption of the diwanni by the Company. Of these interesting comments, that of P. M. Dacres, advocating a permanent settlement of the land revenue, commands the most attention. This advice did not reach the board for the first time. Two years previously[2] the council of Patna had suggested it, and in January, 1775,[3] G. Vansittart, late chief of the Burdwan Council, had urged the board to adopt a lengthy settlement, for life at least. In July, 1775, G. G. Ducarel, lately in charge of the Purnia district, in his evidence given before the board[4], expressed the view that "a person of experience with discretionary power might render great service to the Company by effecting a permanent settlement in the most eligible mode". He even argued that it was desirable to effect a permanent settlement "with inferior talukdars or with the ryots themselves if possible", advice which implies that the speaker did not regard either the state or the zamindars as owners of the soil. At home the same idea was also finding expression. In 1772 Colonel Dow[5] had strongly advocated a settlement in perpetuity with the zamindars, and in the same year a pamphlet urging a similar course was published by H. Patullo.[6]

Meanwhile the results of the quinquennial settlement were proving more deplorable each year, and some fresh method was imperatively necessary. Accordingly, on 21 March, 1775, the governor-general invited the individual opinions of members of the council on the subject of settling and collecting the land revenue. On 22 April he and Barwell submitted a joint plan consisting of seventeen proposals in which they practically adopted the principle of a permanent settlement by recommending leases for life or for two joint lives. Beveridge[7] has shown that the concluding remarks of this scheme bear strong if unintentional testimony to the hardships inflicted on the ryots by the nawab's and, latterly, the Company's mismanagement of the collections. This plan was opposed by one propounded by Francis on 22 January, 1776, in which he definitely recommended a settlement in perpetuity with the zamindars, and he emphasised this opinion at meetings of the board in May, 1776[8], when a letter was

[1] Governor-General's Proceedings, 7 April, 1775.
[2] Revenue Board Proceedings, 29 January, 1773.
[3] Governor-General's Proceedings, 27 January, 1775.
[4] Idem, 15 July, 1775.
[5] Enquiry into the state of Bengal, affixed to vol. II, History of Hindostan, ed. 1772.
[6] Firminger, Fifth Report, etc. I, 309, note.
[7] Op. cit. II, 410–17.
[8] Governor-General's Proceedings, 17 May and 31 May, 1776.

considered from the provincial council of revenue at Patna describing the over-assessment and consequent poverty of the people. Francis published in 1782 his proposals, together with the plan of Hastings and Barwell and various extracts from the minutes of the board's proceedings[1], but he did not acknowledge the debt that he obviously owed to Dacres and other servants of the Company. The following comments from two distinguished writers are sufficient to reveal the defects of the scheme of Francis, who recognised only the zamindar and ignored the ryot. "We are left to infer", says Beveridge,[2] "that, after all, the best security for the ryot would be to throw himself on the zamindar's mercy." Mill[3] is even more trenchant.

Without much concern about the production of proof he [Mr Francis] assumed as a basis two things: first, that the opinion was erroneous which ascribed to the sovereign the property of the land; and secondly, that the property in question belonged to the zamindars. Upon the zamindars as proprietors he accordingly proposed a certain tax should be levied; that it should be fixed once and for all; and held to be perpetual and invariable.

The effect of Francis's pertinacity was to bring into prominence the question of the ownership of the land. It is sufficient to point out that while Hastings and Barwell assumed that the sovereign possessed the land, and Francis and his school were equally convinced that the zamindar was the real owner, no one thought, with the possible exception of Ducarel, of what might be the claim of the ryots to the possession of the land, and of the *khudkasht* ryot[4] in particular.

The settlement problem, though of the first importance, was not peremptory; the quinquennial settlement had still some time to run. At this juncture, Monson died, and the governor-general recovered his lost authority in the council. Almost the first use that Hastings made of his restored authority was to take up the business of the coming settlement, a duty which he had felt to be paramount, and which he could now approach with effect.[5] In August, 1776,[6] he had laid before the board certain proposals connected with the necessity of preparing for the approaching settlement, suggesting that all provincial councils and collectors should submit an estimate of the land revenue that might justly be expected from their districts. This idea was eventually agreed to and a circular letter to that effect issued.

On 1 November[7] the governor-general suggested that an "office" or, in modern parlance, a commission should be formed whose duty

---

[1] *The Original Minutes of the Governor-General and Council of Fort William*, etc., published in London, 1782.
[2] *Op. cit.* II, 417.
[3] Mill, *History of British India*, 5th ed. IV, 24.
[4] *The Zemindary Settlement of Bengal*, vol. I, para. 2, and appendix viii, vol. I, pp. 198–9. (Calcutta, 1879.)
[5] Letter to L. Sulivan, 21 March, 1776, also to John Graham, 26 September, 1776.
[6] Governor-General's Proceedings, 30 August, 1776.
[7] *Idem*, 1 November, 1776.

should be to tour throughout Bengal "to procure material for the settlement of the different districts". The reports from the various district officers had revealed the disastrous effect of an assessment based on faulty information, and Hastings was determined to avoid that evil, if possible, in making the approaching settlement. His proposals were strenuously, even violently, opposed by Clavering and Francis, who feared that the powers given to the *amins*, or Indian officers, of the commission to enable them to obtain the requisite information would be used in a method prejudicial to the good name of the Company. This fear, which was not without basis, was expressed in their usual intemperate fashion, and was made to serve as an attack on the governor-general's character; for he was accused of diverting the constitutional powers of the Supreme Council for his own gratification by means of the casting vote.

Hastings met these unfounded allegations with more than his wonted courtesy and self-control, entering into detailed explanations of the information required, and the necessity for it, but his determination was as inflexible as ever: on 29 November D. Anderson and C. Bogle, two of the most promising of the younger officers of the Company, were selected[1] as members of the commission: the accountant-general, C. Croftes, was shortly afterwards added, and the cost of the commission was estimated at something less than 4500 rupees *per mensem*. Thus was established that commission whose report, presented in March, 1778, is perhaps the most valuable contemporary document in the early revenue history of Bengal under the Company's administration.[2] The information collected and its style of presentment reflect the greatest credit both on the professional capacities of its authors, and on the choice and acumen of the governor-general. The report lost no force from the dispassionate and unassuming tone in which it recounted with studied moderation the wholesale alienation of lands and deliberate oppression of the ryots by the zamindars, who not infrequently continued to collect taxes which the indulgence of government had abolished. The report therefore exposed the inaccuracy of much that Francis had asserted: it also included a large collection of

the original accounts in the Bengal, Persian, and Orissa languages....If preserved as records they will be highly serviceable as references in settling disputes...and may lay the foundation of regular and permanent registers.

Meanwhile the court of directors wrote to express their displeasure with the governor-general, and their support of the minority; they censured the use which Hastings had made of the casting vote, and expressed surprise that "after more than seven years' investigation" further information about the collections was still required.

[1] Governor-General's Proceedings, 6 December and 27 December, 1776.
[2] Printed *ap*. Ramsbotham, *op. cit.* pp. 99–131.

No definite decision was taken in the matter of the new settlement. In the face of much conflicting evidence the directors decided to mark time; accordingly, on 23 December, 1778, they sent orders for the land revenue to be settled annually; it is not easy to say what else they could have done. In 1779 the trouble[1] between the Supreme Court and the Company's diwanni adalats, which had been simmering since 1774, boiled over. The Kasijora case, with its disgraceful incidents, compelled the immediate interference of the council. The Supreme Court refused to yield, and the quarrel threatened to split the entire administration. A solution was found by the chief justice in consultation with the governor-general. Sir Elijah Impey was offered and accepted the chief judgeship of the sadar diwanni adalat with an additional salary of about £6500: he thus united in his own person the authority of both jurisdictions. His action was severely criticised by Francis and Wheler at the time, and by later critics. But the law officers of the crown in England found nothing incorrect in Impey's action which "put an end to an intolerable situation… and anticipated by many years the policy which extended the appellate jurisdiction of the Supreme Court over the provincial courts".[2]

It will be remembered that the plan drawn up by the Board of Revenue in 1773, placing the collections under six provincial councils of revenue, was expressly declared by the governor and council to be temporary. No opportunity occurred for introducing a permanent scheme until Hastings had regained his control of the council, when a commission of enquiry was appointed to prepare the way for a permanent measure. In July, 1777, the governor-general and council promulgated to all the provincial councils except Patna a modified scheme for the settlement of the revenue for the current year. The scheme contained ten paragraphs and bore strong impress of the board's debates during the previous three years, in that it gave the zamindar a position of increased importance at the cost of the ryot. The councils were empowered to use their own discretion in making fresh settlements with those zamindars who refused to agree to a renewal of the existing terms, and where possible the zamindar was to be invited to co-operate in making the settlement. In April, 1778, a circular letter was sent to all provincial councils requiring a list of all defaulting zamindars to be posted at every district headquarters, while defaulters were warned that failure to meet obligations might result in the sale of the zamindari, or its transference to others who were willing to take over the existing arrangement and to pay the arrears. These instructions were repeated each May in 1778, 1779 and 1780.

In December, 1780, Francis sailed for Europe. The field was now

---

[1] Mill, *op. cit.* IV, 218–54; Beveridge, *op. cit.* pp. 436–40.
[2] Roberts, *History of British India*, p. 213.

clear; Hastings had an undisputed authority; his adversaries "had sickened, died and fled".[1] *Tenax propositi*, if ever man was, Hastings continued his endeavours to reorganise the collections, and shortly there was issued

a permanent plan for the administration of the revenue of Bengal and Bihar, formed the 20th February, 1781, by the Hon'ble the Governor-General and Council in their Revenue Department.[2]

The main alteration involved cannot be described better than in the words of the introductory minute. After recalling the temporary nature of the provincial councils, the easy prelude of another permanent mode, and referring to the Revenue Board's proceedings of 23 November, 1773, where the board's intention is "methodically and completely delineated", the alteration is stated to consist substantially in this: that

all the collections of the provinces should be brought down to the Presidency and be there administered by a Committee of the most able and experienced of the covenanted servants of the Company under the immediate inspection of, and with the opportunity of constant reference for instruction to, the Governor-General and Council.

"By this plan", wrote Hastings, "we hope to bring the whole administration of the revenues to Calcutta, without any intermediate charge or agency, and to effect a saving of lacs to the Company and to the Zamindars and ryots." He added complacently: "Read the plan and the minute introducing it; it will not discredit me, but the plan will put to shame those who discredit it".

Shore, after a year's experience of the plan in working, did not hesitate emphatically to condemn it.

The new scheme[3] consisted of fourteen paragraphs. Its object was to reduce the expense of the collections and to restore the revenue of the provinces as far as possible "to its former standard"; an indefinite reference. To this end a new committee of the revenue was created consisting of four members assisted by a diwan; the first members of this committee were David Anderson, John Shore, Samuel Charters, and Charles Croftes; Ganga Govind Singh was appointed diwan. The members of this committee took oath to receive "no lucrative advantage" from their office, except of course, from their salary which was made up of 2 per cent. on the monthly net receipts[4] and divided proportionally among them. The provincial councils and appeal courts were abolished, and collectors replaced in all the districts. The superintendentship of the *Khalsa* was abolished and its functions transferred to the Committee of Revenue; the office of the rai raian was placed under the Supreme Council and its holder was specifically forbidden to "interfere in the business transacted by the diwan of

---

[1] Gleig, *op. cit.* II, 329, 330.
[2] Governor-General's Proceedings, 20 January, 1781.
[3] Colebrooke, *op. cit.* pp. 213–16.　　　　[4] *Idem*, pp. 215, 216.

the Committee". Finally, the kanungos were reinstated "in the complete charge and possession of all the functions and powers which constitutionally appertain to their office".

The scheme bears all the signs of being prepared in a secretariat. On paper it possibly appeared extremely reasonable and efficient; in practice it broke down at every point. The information, valuable as it was, collected by the commission of 1776, could not, and, by its authors, was not intended to take the place of that information which only trained district officers could furnish, but Hastings was bent on concentration. In 1773, the result of his grouping the various districts into six divisions under provincial councils resulted in a loss to the Company's government of much valuable local knowledge and experience. His plan of 1781 carried concentration still further.

The re-appointment of Collectors appears to suggest an idea of decentralisation. This however was not the case. The collector was denied any interference with the new settlement of the revenue.... The new collectors were merely figureheads, and the distrust which the council showed in their appointment could lead to nothing but discouragement.[1]

The truth of this comment is exemplified by two quotations selected at random from the Committee of Revenue's proceedings for April, 1783. John David Patterson, collector of Rangpur, wrote on 3 April, 1783, to ask for instructions as to what action he might take in his district.

There is nothing but confusion; there is no Kanungo to be found, he is fled the country; the ryots wanting to withhold their payments; the Farmer seizing everything he can lay his hands upon and swelling up his demands by every artifice.... No pains shall be spared on my part to get at the truth altho' it is wading through a sea of chicanery on both sides....

On 13 March William Rooke, collector of Purnia, wrote with even greater detail to the same effect; he reported that the farmer

has repeatedly flogged those who preferred any complaint to me.... In the course of the last ten days a numerous body of ryots from all quarters have beset me on every side, uncommonly clamorous for justice. Their complaints exhibit an almost universal disregard and setting aside of their pottahs, an enormous increase exacted from them, etc.:

and the letter concludes with a request to be informed of "the degree of interference which is expected of me by you". The Committee of Revenue was accustomed to such letters. Within one month of the establishment of the new scheme it had pointed out that much of the work of the settlement should be left in detail to the collector. Shore had ruthlessly exposed, in his minute of 1782[2], the inefficiency of the whole scheme. Space unfortunately permits only of a small quotation from this illuminating criticism, in which he showed that there could be no check on oppression or extortion, that the real state

[1] Ascoli, op. cit. pp. 35, 36.
[2] Harington, op. cit. II, 41–3.

of any district could not be discovered, and that it was impossible to discriminate truth from falsehood.

> I venture to pronounce that the real state of the districts is now less known and the revenues less understood than in 1774....It is the business of all, from the ryot to the diwan, to conceal and deceive....With respect to the Committee of Revenue, it is morally impossible for them to execute the business they are entrusted with.

Shore concluded that the committee "with the best intentions and the best ability and the steadiest application, must after all be a tool in the hands of their Diwan" and that the system was fundamentally wrong. Shore's opinion was afterwards endorsed in 1786 when the Governor-General in Council, in instructing the Committee of Revenue to appoint collectors for certain districts, observed

> from experience we think it past doubt that situated as you are at the Presidency, you cannot without a local agency secure the regular realisation of the revenues, still less preserve the ryots and other inferior tenants from oppressions.[1]

The scheme of 1781 further restored to their old position and perquisites the sadar kanungos, whose claim to appoint their own deputies had been correctly contested by the collector of Midnapur,[2] who pointed out that the Committee of Circuit had ordered the registration of all deputy kanungos as servants of the Company. The collector of Rangpur in 1784 was similarly restrained from exercising any control over the deputy kanungos without the express orders of government. The claim of the kanungos to their arrears of fees was sanctioned to the extent of over 1,10,000 rupees, and they regained the full control of their deputies in the districts; their triumph was complete, and the evil situation exposed by Baber and others in 1772 was restored.

The picture, however, is not entirely black. In 1782 an office, known as the *zamindari daftar*[3], was established for the management of the estates of minor and female zamindars; it also afforded protection to zamindars of known incapacity. This was a wise and beneficent step which anticipated the work of the present court of wards. The growing influence of officers with district experience can be seen in the orders issued by the Committee of Revenue to all collectors in November, 1783, directing them to proceed on tour throughout their districts in order to form by personal observation an estimate of the state of the crops and their probable produce for the current year. In the past, district-officers had in vain sought permission to tour through their districts, but this had always been peremptorily refused by the board. The wholesome influence now exerted on the board by practical men who had served in districts

---

[1] Colebrooke, *op. cit.* pp. 243–4.
[2] Committee of Revenue's Proceedings, 12 September, 17 September, 8 November, 1781.
[3] *Idem*, May and September, 1782.

was to grow stronger. Anderson, Shore and Charters were men who had had a real *mufassal* training, and Croftes had been a member of the 1776 commission. They knew that "in every pargana throughout Bengal there are some district usages which cannot clearly be known at a distance", yet which must be known if the administration is to be just and efficient. In 1786 a great and beneficial change comes over the revenue administration of Bengal; it is not too much to attribute this to the district experience of the members of the committee appointed in 1781. For five years they laboured under the evils and difficulties of attempting to administer a system which was over-centralised, and which placed secretariat theories before district experience. In 1786 the district officer comes to his own. Before discussing these changes in detail some important facts must be briefly noticed. In 1784 Pitt's India Act was passed. Section 39 of this act directs that the conditions governing the collection of land revenue shall be "forthwith enquired into and fully investigated" and that "permanent rules" for the future regulation of the payments and services due "from the rajas, zemindars and other native land-holders" will be established. Thus the opinion of which Francis was the leading advocate, that the zamindar was a landowner, was adopted by the act and the permanent rules, which Lord Cornwallis was sent out to put into effect, were, to the great misfortune of the Bengal cultivators, founded on that assumption. Before the details of the act could reach India Hastings had resigned his charge; on 8 February, 1785, he delivered over charge to Macpherson and in the same month sailed for England. His influence on the collection of the land revenue in Bengal was unhappy. In 1772 he was mainly responsible for the defects which marked the quinquennial settlement; in 1781, his further attempt at centralisation reduced the collections to chaos. He possessed, as has been shown, very little first-hand knowledge of district revenue work. It has been claimed for him that

he adopted the principle of making a detailed assessment based on a careful enquiry in each district and...he conferred on the raiyats who were the actual cultivators, the protection of formal contracts.

Neither of these encomiums can be substantiated. The assessment of 1772 was summary and admitted by its authors to have been too high. The system of putting up the farms to open auction resulted in utterly fictitious values that were never realised and was soon afterwards forbidden by the Company. The system of *pattahs*, or leases, completely broke down, and failed, then as later, to protect the ryot.[1] Furthermore, the reinstatement of the kanungos, the abolition of collectors, the establishment of the provincial diwans, and lastly the excessive power placed in the hands of the diwan of the Committee of Revenue, all testify to the incapacity of Hastings in his administration of the

---

[1] Letter from the Burdwan Council, Governor-General's Proceedings, 18 April, 1777.

Bengal land revenue; it is not too much to say that in this respect his achievements compare unfavourably with those of Muhammad Reza Khan. But Hastings was not a civil servant of the crown. To judge him, therefore, by the crown standard of a later date is unjust and unhistorical. The Company's servants were imbued with one idea: they came to serve the Company first and last; their intensity of purpose made the East India Company master of India; and this purpose was not the less strong because it did not profess to be governed by the restrictions which are attached to an administrative service of the crown. Hastings gave his employers a service and devotion that was unflinching in its loyalty, that feared no difficulty, that shrank from no adversary; although he may have failed in his personal handling of the land revenue, he is entitled to the credit of having selected some most able officers to deal with this branch of the administration. Conspicuous among these were Shore, David Anderson, Samuel Charters, Charles Croftes and James Grant. In the same week as Hastings handed over charge of the government, a letter[1] from the court of directors was received calling for an accurate account of the administration at the precise period at which Hastings resigned his office; a foretaste, had he but known, of the anxious days ahead.

On 25 April, 1786, the new scheme was published: it spelt decentralisation. "The division of the province into districts is the backbone of the whole system of the reforms."[2] The collector becomes a responsible officer, making the settlement and collecting the revenue; the provincial diwans were abolished; and the districts were reorganised into thirty-five more or less fiscal units, instead of the previous "series of fiscal divisions over which the earlier collectors had exercised their doubtful authority";[3] these thirty-five districts were reduced in 1787 to twenty-three. These measures of the local government were reinforced by orders from the court of directors dated 21 September, 1785, which were published in Calcutta on 12 June, 1786; under them the Committee of Revenue was reconstituted and officially declared to be the Board of Revenue. The president of the board was to be a member of the governor-general's council. The special regulations drawn up for the guidance of the board may be read in the pages of Harington and Colebrooke. Its duties were those of controlling and advising the collectors and sanctioning their settlement. On 19 July the office of *Chief Saristadar* was instituted to bring the revenue records, hitherto the property of the kanungos, under the control of government. This measure was long overdue, and had been urged by the abler district officers since 1772, as being "no less calculated to protect the great body of the people from oppression

---

[1] Committee of Revenue's Proceedings, 14 February, 1785.
[2] Ascoli, *op. cit.* pp. 38–40.
[3] *Idem.*

than to secure the full and legal right of the Sovereign". James Grant was selected to be the first *Chief Saristadar*, being specially chosen for his interest in and research among the revenue records. For the first time since the assumption of the diwanni, government had made a resolute effort to reduce the kanungos to their constitutional position in the state.

The reforms of 1786 were, therefore, the work of men who desired to gain the confidence of and to co-operate with the local district officer. The authors of the reforms were convinced from their own district experience that the real work of the revenue must be carried out by trusted officers on the spot; they set themselves to create the conditions and atmosphere in which those officers could best work.

The period 1765–86 in the administration of the land revenue in Bengal by the Company's servants is a record of progress from the employment of untested theories to the establishment of an administration based on much solid knowledge. A careful perusal of the voluminous manuscript proceedings of the Committees of Revenue during those years reveals a fact too little known, namely, that this progress was largely the result of unrecognised work by the district officers of the Company in their own districts where, generally speaking, they laboured to establish a just and humane collection of the land revenue. Their advice, based on sound local knowledge, was too often rejected by their official superiors in Calcutta, by whom, as well as by the Court of Directors, they were regarded with suspicion and even hostility. Their persistence had its reward; twenty years after the assumption of the diwanni the first sound and just administration of the land revenue was established.

NOTE. The reader has doubtless found the various references to boards and committees of revenue confusing.

In 1769 the Council had delegated its authority in revenue matters to a "select committee" drawn from its own members. This select committee in 1772 appointed the Committee of Circuit to examine the conditions with a view to making a new settlement. The Committee of Circuit in August, 1772, proposed that the whole Council should compose a Board of Revenue—this was established in October, 1772, as the Committee of Revenue, and remained in existence till 1781, when it was reorganised and composed of members junior to and subordinate to the Supreme Council, but still retained its name "Committee of Revenue". The term "board" is used indifferently by contemporary writers up to 1781; after 1781 it indicates the Supreme Council when sitting to hear revenue appeal cases from the Committee of Revenue. The modern Board of Revenue dates from 1786, when it replaced the second Committee of Revenue.

CHAPTER XXVI

THE BENGAL ADMINISTRATIVE SYSTEM, 1786—1818

THE Select Committee of 1781 had been directed to find means for gaining not only "security and advantage" for Britain but "the happiness of the native inhabitants," and from the discussions of the years 1781–4 certain maxims of local government had clearly emerged. There must be a reform of abuses among the Company's servants; the methods by which they grew rich must be watched; they must no longer take presents. Their trading activities must no longer operate to destroy the trade of native merchants and bankers. The system of monopolies must be restricted. The rights of zamindars and land-holders must not be superseded in order to increase the revenues. There must be even-handed justice for Europeans and Indians alike.

The instructions to Cornwallis embodied the principles thus described. In relation to local government three main subjects were discussed. First, there was the land revenue. It was to be handled leniently: "a moderate *jama*, regularly and punctually collected" was to be preferred to grandiose but unrealised schemes. It was to be settled "in every practicable instance" with the zamindars. Ultimately the settlement was to be permanent, but at present it was to be made for ten years. Secondly, there was the question of administration. This was to be organised upon a simple and uniform basis. The frequent changes of recent years had produced injury and extravagance, and made "steady adherence to almost any one system" a preferable policy. The higher officers should be Europeans; and the subordinates Indians, as being more suited to the detailed work of the province. These higher officers were to be chosen carefully from the principal servants of the Company; men "distinguished for good conduct and abilities, and conversant with the country languages". They should be adequately paid, partly by salary, partly by commission. Their districts were to be large; there should not be more than twenty, or at most twenty-five, in the whole province. In the settlement of the revenue, and in the administration of justice, they were to have wide authority.

Thirdly, there was the judicial system. The instructions contemplated the continuance of the existing system of civil justice, under European judges. In the districts the collectors of revenue were to be, also, judges of the civil courts; for this would "tend more to simplicity, energy, justice and economy". In criminal jurisdiction, too, the existing system was to be maintained. Indian control was to continue. Although the collector was to enjoy magisterial powers of arrest, "the power of trial and punishment must on no account be exercised by any other than the established officers of Mahomedan judicature". The judicial system indeed was to be informed with European ideas of justice, but to be governed by Indian usages.[1] One point recurred frequently throughout the instructions. There was to be a general movement for purification and economy. Abuses of all kinds were to be swept away; peculation was to cease; useless offices were to be reduced, and the interests of economy and simplicity were to regulate the various branches of the administrative system. Such was the task of Cornwallis.

The proposal to make Cornwallis the first instrument of the new policy was first mooted in 1782 during the administration of Shelburne;[2] and his appointment had been one feature of the scheme for Indian reform proposed by Dundas in the report of the Secret Committee of 1781. The Fox-North coalition rejected the idea, but Pitt revived it on their defeat. The negotiations began in April, 1784;[3] at the end of the year they seemed to have failed completely; a renewal in February, 1785, was again a failure; and it was not until February, 1786, that Cornwallis accepted. Then the union of the military command with the governor-generalship, and the promise that the governor-general should be independent of his council, induced Cornwallis to accept.[4] He finally landed at Calcutta in September, 1786.

Cornwallis was a man of middle age with extensive military experience. He had taken part in the campaigns of the Seven Years' War, and had gained sufficient reputation to secure his appointment in 1776 to command in America. There, his ultimate failure, after some brilliant preliminary successes, did not suffice to ruin his career. Even his opponent, Fox, paid homage to his abilities in 1783, and his employment under Pitt on the mission of 1785 to Prussia was sufficient evidence of the trust in which he held him. Of the affairs of India, he had little knowledge and no experience. He is distinguished as the first governor-general who did not climb to power from the ranks of the Company's service. Appointed by the Company, he owed his nomination to the ministry. His selection was one more evidence of the new spirit in Indian affairs. It brought India a stage nearer to incorporation in the overseas empire of Britain.

Inexperience made Cornwallis largely dependent on advisers both in framing his policy, and, still more, in working it out. The broad

---

[1] The instructions are in a series of dispatches dated 12 April, 1786. They are to be found in I.O. Records, Despatches to Bengal, vol. xv. One of the most important of these is printed as Appendix 12 to the Second Report from the Select Committee of the House of Commons on the Affairs of the East India Company. *Parliamentary Papers*, 1810, v, 13.

[2] Cornwallis to Pitt, 8 November, 1784. Ross, *Correspondence*, i, 179.

[3] Ross, *op. cit.* i, 167.   [4] *Idem*, p. 208.

lines of his action were laid down by the administration; the instructions of the court of directors gave more detailed guidance. But much was left necessarily to the men on the spot, and hence the servants of the Company by their practical knowledge had great influence on the result. Cornwallis acknowledged plainly his debt to them. Perhaps the chief of them was John Shore, chosen especially by the directors to supply the local knowledge which Cornwallis lacked. "The abilities of Mr Shore", Cornwallis wrote a month after his arrival, "and his knowledge in every branch of the business of this country, and the very high character which he holds in the settlement, render his assistance to me invaluable."[1] And again in 1789 in connection with the revenue settlement, he said, "I consider it as singularly fortunate that the public could profit from his great experience and uncommon abilities".[2] In revenue matters Cornwallis trusted mainly to Shore. He was by far the most experienced of the Company's servants in this branch, for he had been in its service since 1769, and had held important revenue offices since 1774. Francis had brought him to the front, but Hastings also had recognised his merit.

James Grant is indeed as famous as Shore in connection with the revenue settlement. But Grant had but little practical experience. His reputation has come from his wide study of the revenue system, and the series of published works in which he stated the results of his learning. He was an expert rather than a man of affairs. As *saristadar* he had unrivalled opportunity for studying revenue records, and Cornwallis retained the office of *saristadar* till Grant went home in 1789. But in making important decisions he preferred men of experience to men of learning. After Shore, Cornwallis therefore put Jonathan Duncan, another experienced collector, and later governor of Bombay. He was little known in England when Cornwallis arrived, but "he is held in the highest estimation by every man, both European and native, in Bengal", wrote Cornwallis in 1787, "and, next to Mr Shore, was more capable of assisting me, particularly in revenue matters, than any man in this country".[3] He had, said Cornwallis in 1789, "besides good health...knowledge, application, integrity, and temper", the last "not the least useful".[4] Although a junior, he was recommended by Cornwallis for a seat on the council as early as 1788.[5] And in the last stages of the revenue settlement Cornwallis found consolation in the approval of Duncan for his differences with Shore over the question of permanence.

The final decision in that matter was due, however, largely to Charles Grant. When Dundas decided to support Cornwallis against

---

[1] Cornwallis to Dundas, 15 November, 1786. Ross, *op. cit.* I, 227.
[2] Cornwallis to Court of Directors, 2 August, 1789. Ross, *op. cit.* I, 545.
[3] Cornwallis to Dundas, 14 August, 1787. Ross, *op. cit.* I, 271.
[4] Cornwallis to N. Smith, 9 November, 1789. Ross, *op. cit.* I, 449.
[5] Dundas to Cornwallis, 20 February, 1789. Ross, *op. cit.* I, 410–11.

the advice of Shore, it was partly at least owing to the representations of Charles Grant. He had no personal knowledge of revenue matters, but he received the greatest share in the confidence of Cornwallis, and had given him invaluable help during the years 1786–90. When Grant sailed for home in 1790 Cornwallis recommended Dundas "to converse with him frequently upon every part of the business of this Country",[1] and his zeal for the governor-general's interests gave him considerable influence over Dundas during the years 1790–3. James Grant (a cousin of Charles),[2] like Shore and Duncan, specialised on the revenue side. But Charles Grant was the chief adviser in matters of trade. His loss "in the commercial line", wrote Cornwallis when he left India, "is irreparable". He had been secretary to the Board of Trade in the time of Hastings and had been appointed by the board in 1781 commercial resident at Malda. He was outstanding both in experience and integrity. At first, at least, Cornwallis thought him the only honest man on the commercial side[3], and trusted very largely to him in his attempt to reform that branch of the administration. In this work Cornwallis had also the help of Charles Stuart, member of council and president of the Board of Trade (1786–9). Stuart, however, never gained in the same degree the confidence of Cornwallis, and he lacked the wide commercial experience of Charles Grant.

In his judicial work Cornwallis had also an invaluable adviser. Here the Company's servants could be of but limited use. Cornwallis took full advantage of their experience in judicial business, but their experience was relatively small and they lacked expert knowledge. Some of them—Charles Grant among them—were of great value in carrying out reforms: but only the judges could help in devising them. Cornwallis was, therefore, fortunate in the aid of Sir William Jones, an oriental scholar of reputation unrivalled in his own time, and a man of great practical ability, who had devoted many years to the study and practice of the law. In 1783 he had come to India as judge of the Supreme Court of Judicature at Calcutta, and he brought to his task the zeal of an enthusiast, and the knowledge of an expert. "A good system of laws" seemed to him the first necessity of India; and, following the lead of Hastings, he set himself to this end to codify the existing Hindu and Muhammadan laws. But he realised also the need for "due administration" and a "well-established peace". He gave, therefore, full aid to Cornwallis in his reform of the judicial administration and in the regulation of the police.

Although the policy that Cornwallis came to enforce in 1786 was new, it was not wholly new. In every direction Cornwallis built

---

[1] Cornwallis to Dundas, 12 February, 1790. Ross, *op. cit.* I, 480.
[2] Firminger (ed.), *Fifth Report...on the Affairs of the East India Company...* 1812, II, p. xiv.
[3] Ross, *op. cit.* I, 306.

on foundations already laid or begun to be laid by his predecessors, and especially by Hastings. It was the emphasis rather than the principle that was new; but the principles were now clearly stated, and the strength of the home government was used to enforce them. Every aspect of reform was foreshadowed in the work or in the projects of Hastings, and hence the solidity of the work of Cornwallis.

Yet even when all allowance has been made, much credit must be given to Cornwallis himself. Certainly no man of genius, he contributed no new ideas to the work he undertook. He was not an expert like Jones or Grant, nor a man of wide experience like Shore. He was not a doctrinaire like Francis, nor an inventive genius like Hastings. He was content, as Hastings had never been, to plead a command from home as a final cause for decision, and this respect for authority was his outstanding characteristic. But in spite of this he possessed great qualities and stood for important principles. Above all, he was, beyond reproach, upright and honest. He had not to fear a sudden decline in favour; he had no pettiness of ambition; he was not a time-server; and he left behind him a tradition of service which was of lasting value in Indian administration. Loyalty and integrity there had been before, but it was a loyalty to the Company and an integrity in the Company's affairs. Cornwallis was a public servant who upheld national and not private traditions. His service was to the Crown and to the people over whom he ruled, and he thus embodied fitly the new spirit of Indian rule.

To this invincible honesty and desire for the public good, he added a soldier's sense of duty to his superiors. The command of Dundas or Pitt, or even of the court of directors, was decisive to him. He had a belief in the possibilities of justice, a faith in the standards by which conduct would be judged at home. He was determined that these standards should not be lowered in India, nor overlaid by native practices. To secure this he gave the higher administrative posts to Englishmen, and he was always loth to leave real responsibility in native hands. Yet he was wise enough to see that this was not enough: these Englishmen must maintain the English standards. They must be appointed and promoted for merit, not by patronage. In the interests of this maxim he was prepared to resist the recommendations of all, even of the Prince Regent or of the directors. Lastly, every deviation from honesty must be rigorously punished.

This is the system Cornwallis set out to establish, and no doubt because it was practical rather than ideal, he came much nearer than most reformers to a realisation of his aims.

When Cornwallis landed in Bengal in September, 1786, important changes in administration had just taken place. More than twenty years of experiment had gone to make them, and the recent innovations were rather a further stage in experiment than a final reorganisation.

Much of the work of Cornwallis also was experimental in character, but his greatest claim to importance is that he permanently established some features of administration.

It is necessary to go back more than twenty years to explain the character of the system with which Cornwallis dealt. The main work of the Company in India had at one time consisted, like that of any other company for overseas trade, in import from England and export home. The import had from early times consisted mainly of specie, so that the most burdensome duty of the Company's servants was the provision of the cargoes for England, cargoes for the most part of raw silk, wool, cotton, or indigo; in other words the "investment". In the mid-eighteenth century the import of specie ceased: the import of English goods, never large, was still comparatively small, and the main source from which the investment was provided —and the local expenses paid—was the territorial revenue of Bengal.

The result was a dual system of administration. The management of this revenue and the exercise of responsibilities arising from it, was one branch of the Company's work; the provision of the investment the other. Hastings in 1785 had written of the division between "the general and commercial departments". The Company's servants in all parts of Bengal wrote to Cornwallis on his arrival describing their years of experience in the "revenue" or the "commercial line". The commercial was the senior branch, but the revenue line was already becoming the more important.

Since 1774 the investment had been under the supervision of the Board of Trade. Originally a body of eleven members, very imperfectly controlled by the Supreme Council, the Board of Trade had been reorganised in May, 1786. It was now definitely subordinated to the Supreme Council, and reduced to five members. One of them, the president, was Charles Stuart, a member of council. Under the board, the investment was in the hands of the Company's servants stationed at scattered centres in Bengal. The chief "residents" at the various stations were responsible to the board for such share of the investment as had been assigned to them. In dealing with it they had great opportunities for good or evil in coming into contact with the people, and especially they had valuable and recognised facilities for private trade.

From the time of the board's first appointment in 1774 it had been increasingly the practice to obtain the investment by a series of contracts. At first these contracts were generally direct with Indian manufacturers or agents, the residents merely exercising supervision over them. Since 1778, however, the contracts had been made more frequently with the Company's servants themselves. So a resident at one of the Company's stations contracted with the Board of Trade, and then obtained the goods from the Indian manufacturers at as great profit as he could get. This system, though a direct breach of their covenants and of an order of the Company of 1759, was none the less the general rule. The directors were so complaisant of the breach that even in their reform proposals of 1786 they did not think that it was "necessary to exclude our servants from entering into contracts". Their criticism was not one of principle, but of practice. The prices paid were high, the quality of the goods was poor, and there was a general feeling that corruption and oppression were frequent. The reform of the Board of Trade and the commercial establishment generally was one of the first tasks of Cornwallis.

The "general department" was more complicated if less corrupt in its management of local administration. It had come into existence slowly during the eighteenth century, and bore still a few marks of its piecemeal origin, though broadly speaking in 1786 there was one system for the whole province. It is in this sphere that those frequent changes had taken place which the directors deprecated. The changes were really a series of attempts, on the "rule of false" extolled by Hastings, to reach some satisfactory system for a most complicated and varied work.

In the "general department", it may be said without question, the chief concern was the revenue, and the second the administration of civil justice. As diwan the Company was responsible for both these branches of administration. Criminal justice was outside the scope of the diwan, although the Company here also had obtained a large measure of control. One of the results of the work of Cornwallis was that before he left, in 1793, this side of the administrative system had definitely bifurcated. There was the management of revenue on the one side: the administration of civil and criminal justice on the other. But this involved a breach with historical origins, and it was not achieved until 1793.

In 1786 the chief machinery in the sphere of revenue was the Board of Revenue. This body was stationed at Calcutta, and before Cornwallis landed, had just undergone change, like the Board of Trade. In July, 1786, at the instance of the court of directors it had received an addition to its existing membership. There were to be, as previously, four members; but a president was added, who must be a member of the Supreme Council. The president appointed in 1786 was John Shore.

The work of the revenue administration concerned certain main sources of revenue. By far the most important was the revenue from land, and the machinery for revenue administration had grown up mainly in connection with this. There was also, however, the *sair* revenue—from customs and excise—and the revenues from the opium contract and the monopoly of salt. In 1786 the *sair* revenue was managed by the same agencies as the revenue from land. The opium revenue had been managed ever since 1773 by a contract with certain Indians, who paid a royalty to the Company. In 1785 the contract had been disposed of to the highest bidder on a four-years' agreement. This system was, therefore, in force when Cornwallis arrived. In connection with the opium, the duties of the Company's servants, when once the contract had been let, were limited to a general right of enquiry to prevent the oppression of the cultivators. The monopoly of salt was another source of revenue. Here again the system in force was at one time one of contract. But in 1780 Hastings had substituted a system of European agency. A number of the Company's servants were employed to superintend the manufacture and sale of salt, the price being fixed annually by the Supreme Council. Whereas, therefore, work in connection with the *sair* revenue and the opium contract was undertaken by the same officers as those of the land revenue, a small separate establishment, responsible directly to the Supreme Council, dealt with the monopoly of salt.

The land revenue organisation consisted, under the Board of Revenue, of a number of the Company's servants, known already as collectors. Here also reorganisation had taken place.[1]

In addition to the collection of revenue, and of the information upon which the assessment was made, the collectors, like the zamindars, had originally judicial functions. The judicial system, however, like the revenue administration, had been the subject of repeated experiments, and as a result, when Cornwallis arrived, the work of collecting the revenue was almost wholly divorced from that of administering justice. Civil justice was administered in local civil courts (diwanni adalat) presided over by Company's servants; from them appeal lay to the governor-general in council in the capacity of judges of the sadr diwanni adalat. For criminal cases there was again a separate organisation. Magisterial powers were indeed vested in the judges of the civil courts; but the power of trial and punishment lay in district courts for criminal cases, presided over by Indian judges. Appeal lay from them to the nizamat adalat, now under the supervision of the governor-general in council. The final power, therefore, in civil cases directly, and in criminal cases indirectly, lay with the Supreme Council, but the local courts were almost everywhere outside the control of the Company's collectors. In most districts then there were collectors of revenue, judges of the diwanni adalat, and in some also commercial residents, all of them Company's servants, with functions in many particulars defined rather by tradition than by regulation; all of them in the minds of critics at home suspected of too great concentration on "private interests".

In 1786, Bengal contained all the pieces that were to form the administrative mosaic of British India, but the pattern had not yet been decided; and even the collector was not yet established as the centre-piece. The system was complicated, illogical, wasteful and

[1] Cf. pp. 417 *sqq. supra.*

suspected of being corrupt. Cornwallis had justly received instructions to simplify, to purify and to cheapen the administrative system.

In a letter to Cornwallis of 12 April, 1786, the Secret Committee pressed on him the urgency of removing abuses and corruption in the Company's service. The reforms were most needed in the commercial administration. The Board of Trade, which should have acted as a check, was suspected of collusion; and fraud and neglect went alike unpunished. Cornwallis was directed that suits should, if necessary, be instituted against defrauding officials, and that they should be suspended from the Company's service.

In fact the task of Cornwallis here, as in the question of revenues, was two-fold. He had to cleanse the establishment from corruption, and to revise the system into which the corruption had grown. It needed only a few weeks to convince him of the need for cleansing the establishment; there would be no lack of "legal proofs" of both "corruption" and "shameful negligence". As the weeks passed, information poured in upon him as to the methods and difficulties of the trade. Requisitions were sent to the commercial residents for accounts, stretching back in some cases over twenty years. In October, Cornwallis summoned Charles Grant from Malda to Calcutta, to obtain his information and advice.

In January, 1787, Cornwallis was ready to act. He informed a number of contractors and members of the Board of Trade that bills in equity would be filed against them; pending judgment the suspected persons were suspended from office.[1] The result was the dismissal of several of the Company's servants, including members of the old Board of Trade. The directors urged further enquiries,[2] but Cornwallis had confidence in the effect of these examples, and a stricter system of surveillance for the future.

Meanwhile he was taking measures to build up the system anew. In January, he had appointed Charles Grant as fourth member of the Board of Trade, and with his help set himself to collect information upon which to base a revision of the commercial system. Already he had decided on a change. Instead of contracts with the commercial residents and others, he revived the system of agency by the commercial residents. It was possible, as yet, to introduce the new plan only partially, but "in all practicable instances" it was adopted even for the 1787 investments. By the end of 1788 Cornwallis thought the trial had been sufficiently long, and definitely adopted the agency system. The decision was typical of the early period of Cornwallis's reforms. His experience of the culpability of the Company's servants did not prejudice him against their employment. He did not feel justified, he told the directors, in laying down "at the outset as a

---

[1] Ross, *op. cit.* 1, 242.
[2] P.R.O., *Cornwallis Papers*, Packet XVIII. Charles Stuart to Cornwallis, 18 August, 1787.

determined point, that fidelity was not to be expected from your servants". He preferred to try the effect of "open and reasonable compensation for honest service", and believed that many would prefer this to "concealed emolument", if it could be obtained. So in the new system he made the commercial residents the representatives of the Company in the direct control of the investment. They were responsible to the Board of Trade, but even so, their own responsibilities were great. They were to arrange the prices with the manufacturers, to make the necessary advances to them, to receive from them the goods produced, and to supervise the carrying out of the work. The residents were to be paid adequately by a commission on the investments passing through their hands. There was to be no prohibition of private trade, for it could not be enforced, and in such circumstances "to impose restraints...would not remove supposed evils, but beget new ones".

The new system was enforced by strict regulations issued as early as March, 1787. There was to be no oppression of the Indian producer, or the Indian or foreign trader. It had been the former practice to prevent weavers, working for the Company, from undertaking any other work. This system, which had tended to squeeze out all Indian trade, was now revoked, and it was required only that work should be executed in the order of the advances received for it. Cornwallis, indeed, looked to the resident for the protection of the Indian workers. These commercial servants came into closer contact with the people than did the collectors of revenue, and, therefore, acted as "useful barriers" to the oppression of Indian farmers or zamindars.

The bad season of 1788–9 was a severe trial to the new system, but Cornwallis held that it had "stood the test". From this time he made no material change in its organisation. The investment, he wrote in 1789, "is now reasonably and intelligently purchased, and delivered to the Government at its real cost". From the commercial standpoint, this was what had so long been wanted. Characteristically, he went further, and foresaw the spread downwards, "through the wide chain of the natives" connected with trade, of the new "principle of integrity"; and, as he said, "the establishment of such a principle must...be regarded as a solid good of the highest kind".[1] If the system did not prove to have so wide an effect as this, it was justified in its more immediate results, and the system for conducting the Company's trade which Cornwallis set up was not materially altered after him. These reforms, therefore, were among the lasting achievements of Cornwallis.

While Stuart and Grant on the Board of Trade were reforming the commercial side, a similar process was being applied to the administration of revenue and justice. Here the chief instrument and adviser

[1] I.O. Records, Bengal Letters Received, xxviii, 310. Letter dated 1 August, 1789.

of Cornwallis was John Shore. Already a member of the Supreme
Council and the Board of Revenue, he was appointed president of the
Board of Revenue in January, 1787, and was largely responsible for
the character of the changes.

The preceding reforms, under Macpherson, had created thirty-five
revenue districts, each under a European collector. This officer was
the real authority in revenue matters in the district. For a post of
such importance his salary was ludicrously small, only 1200 rupees
per month. The collectors were "almost all", Cornwallis said, "in
collusion with some relative or friend engaged in commerce", and it
was suspected that even less honourable means were sometimes used.
The reforms in relation to the collector aimed at three things:
economy, simplification and purification. In the interests of economy,
the number of districts was to be reduced; in the interests of both
economy and simplification, the divorce of revenue from justice was
to cease; in the interests of purification adequate payment was to
obviate the need for illicit gains.

Rumours of these changes were current as early as January, 1787,
but it was not until March (the end of the Bengal year) that definite
steps were taken. Then, in accordance with a scheme drawn up by
the Board of Revenue, the number of districts was reduced to twenty-
three; a reduction that brought down upon Cornwallis the protests
of the dispossessed. At the same time, preparations were made for a
second change: the union of revenue and judicial duties. In February
a preliminary investigation was made. By June it was complete, and
regulations were issued to enforce it. The collectors were given once
more the office of judge of the courts of diwanni adalat. In this
capacity they dealt with civil cases, appeal lying for the more important to the sadr diwanni adalat. To relieve the collector, an Indian
"register" was attached to each court to try cases up to 200 rupees.
The courts were prohibited from dealing with revenue cases, these
being reserved for the Board of Revenue. At the same time (27 June,
1787) the collectors were also given powers in criminal justice. The
authority of the magistrates was increased and conferred on the
collectors. They now had power, not merely of arrest, but of hearing
and deciding cases of affray, and of inflicting punishments up to
certain prescribed limits. The trial of more important cases lay still
with the Indian courts, and appeal lay with the nizamat adalat at
Murshidabad.

The new collectors had, therefore, larger districts and far greater
powers, for with the exception of the fifteen commercial residents they
were the only instruments of the Company's authority in the districts.
It was an essential feature of the scheme that they should be adequately paid. "For if all chance of saving any money...without
acting dishonestly, is removed, there will be an end of my reformation." And so, instead of the 1200 rupees per month formerly received,

they were now to have a salary of 1500. But this was to be regarded as "the means of subsistence". "In the nature of reward" they had a commission on the revenue they collected. Fixed at an average rate of "rather short of 1 per cent. on the actual collections", it varied according to the size of their charge. For the largest collector-ship—Burdwan—the amount expected to be realised was 27,500 rupees *per annum*. The collectors were provided further with adequate assistance. Two European assistants were given to each district: the first to receive 500 rupees per month and the other 400. Where a third was necessary he should receive 300. So rewarded, the collectors were forbidden, by letter of 18 July, 1787, directly or indirectly to enter upon trade. In their case, unlike that of the commercial residents, breach of this rule could easily be detected; and Cornwallis, therefore, did not hesitate to assert it.

With these changes the more fundamental reforms in the administrative system were for the time complete, and Cornwallis was able to issue detailed regulations covering all sides of the collectors' work. By the regulations of July details of establishment and procedure were prescribed and rules laid down to govern the action of the collectors in their judicial and magisterial functions.

Later changes elaborated and extended what had already been done. Instructions to collectors in November, 1788, further defined their duties, and finally these were consolidated in a code of 8 June, 1789. It was required that henceforth all the Company's servants must belong definitely either to the revenue or the commercial line. At the time this aimed at greater efficiency, but it was important later as facilitating the change that came when the Company lost its monopoly of trade.

In May, 1790, still more functions were added to the collectors. The trial of revenue cases took up too much time at the Board of Revenue and arrears and delays resulted. New local courts were instituted—courts of mal adalat—presided over like the local civil courts by the collector. From these new courts appeal lay to the council. This change marks the culmination of the collector's power. Later Cornwallis realised that he had gone too far; hence the revolution of 1793.

In the years 1788–90 the most important work lay in the sphere of criminal justice. Here it was soon clear that the reforms of 1787 had removed only part of the abuses. In this matter Cornwallis proceeded cautiously, being far less certain, than in the case of revenue administration and civil justice, that he knew the cause of the defect. An enquiry from the magistrates set on foot in November, 1789, confirmed the rumours of defective justice. The reports suggested two main causes for the evils. There were defects in the Muhammadan law, as judged by English ideas of justice; and there were defects in the constitution of the courts. Both must be remedied. The first was a difficult matter. Upon the question of authority Cornwallis had no misgiving. The difficulty was one of knowledge, and it was necessary to go forward slowly. Certain changes were embodied in the resolution of 3 December, 1790; others were left over until further advance had been made in the researches of Sir William Jones.

Upon the side of administration (the remedying of the defects in the constitution of the courts) the reforms of 3 December, 1790, proceeded on the principles which Cornwallis followed in other matters. The system of 1787 left the control of criminal justice largely, though not wholly, in Indian hands. From Muhammad Reza Khan, who presided over the chief criminal court (nizamat adalat) at Murshidabad, to the judges of the provincial courts, the administration of justice lay in Indian hands. The ultimate control of the governor-general in council (an authority difficult to exercise) and the magisterial functions of the collectors alone represented the European share in this branch of administration. "I conceive", Cornwallis wrote on 2 August, 1789, "that all regulations for the reform of that department would be useless and nugatory whilst the execution of them depends upon any native whatever...."[1] "We ought not, I think", he wrote in his minute of 3 December, "to leave the future control of so important a branch of government to the sole discretion of any Native, or, indeed, of any single person whosoever." To remedy this Muhammad Reza Khan was deprived of his office. The nizamat adalat was again moved from Murshidabad to Calcutta. In the place of Muhammad Reza Khan as sole judge, the governor-general and the members of his Supreme Council presided over the court, expert knowledge being provided by Indian advisers.

The same distrust of Indian agencies was seen in the reorganisation of the provincial courts. In the place of the local courts in each district, with their native *darogas*, four courts of circuit were established. Over each of them two covenanted civil servants presided, assisted again by Indian advisers. These courts were to sit at Calcutta, Murshidabad, Dacca, and Patna, but they were to make tours twice a year through their divisions. Lastly, the magisterial duties of the collectors were increased. These duties were again set forth in detail: the most important additions to them being the custody of prisoners confined under sentence or for trial and the superintendence of the execution of sentences passed by the courts of circuit.

The reforms of criminal, like those of civil justice, then, added new powers to the collector. This was, however, only one aspect of the general principle underlying a number of the changes of Cornwallis, the substitution of an English for an Indian agency. Despite the need for purification in all branches of the Company's service, and the candid recognition which Cornwallis gave to it, he seems to have been persuaded of the need for further encroachments by Europeans. In

[1] I.O. Records, Bengal Letters Received, xxviii, 274. Letter of 2 August, 1789.

the sphere of criminal justice he had, indeed, an important justification. Although the actual changes were cautiously made, there seems no doubt that he aimed ultimately at bringing the law administered into line with that of England. Such an aim was irreconcilable with the continuance of Indian administration. The appointment of English judges, therefore, paved the way for the modification of the laws, and this intention is clearly revealed in Cornwallis's minute of 3 December, 1790.

The work of reorganising the district system of the province was in part accomplished piece by piece during the reform of 1786–7, and was systematically reviewed after that reform was complete. This systematic examination embraced all parts of the service, central and local. The greatest changes were those carried out at headquarters' offices. Even here, however, a measure of reform had already taken place before Cornwallis arrived. Business had been divided between the public, secret and commercial departments, and the secretarial work and correspondence reorganised accordingly. In the secret department there was already a section engaged on the reform of the establishment, and early in 1786 this had been regularised as a sub-department of reform. Its work was to carry out the decisions of the Supreme Council, when it met to deal with reform business.

This system was continued unchanged by Cornwallis until the beginning of 1788. Then the "Secret Department of Reform" was reorganised as the "Secret and Separate Department of Reform", and it was required that the Supreme Council should set aside one day a week for the examination of the state of the public offices. The result was a thorough overhauling of the machinery, completed by January, 1789. The most business-like procedure was followed. Before the actual changes were prescribed, rules upon which they were to be based were drawn up. The number of offices was to be as few as possible; the establishment proportionate to the work done; the salaries paid were to be adequate, but no unauthorised gains should be made; all principal offices were to be held by Company's servants, and no servant should hold office under two different departments. So far as was compatible with these principles there was to be the strictest economy.[1]

Considerable changes were necessary to enforce these principles. There were at the time three main departments, the general (or public) department (i.e. civil, military and marine), the revenue department, and the commercial. Within these the duties of all authorities were prescribed. In some cases all that was required was a restatement of reforms already carried out. The secretariat had been

---

[1] An account of the reforms is given in I.O. Records, Home Miscellaneous Series, vol. ccclix. See also the report of Cornwallis to the directors, Bengal Letters Received, vol. xxvii; letter of 9 January, 1789.

reorganised in July, 1787, there being henceforth one secretary-general with three assistants, instead of two joint secretaries. The establishment of the revenue department had already been the subject of a number of changes, and that of the commercial had been thoroughly overhauled. The changes made, therefore, in departments were of minor importance. In the revenue department regulations were issued regarding the treatment of Company's servants when out of employment, and the office of *saristadar* was marked out for abolition when James Grant should cease to hold it. In the commercial department little change was made, save a regulation that henceforth the posts of export and import warehousekeepers should no longer be held by members of the Board of Trade. In other branches the changes were more radical. The treasury, the paymaster's office, and the accountant-general's office were all reformed; the duties of the *Khalsa* (the exchequer) defined; the establishment of the customs reduced. New regulations were prescribed for the postal service. A detailed examination was made of the inferior servants employed on the staffs of all the headquarters' offices, and the whole system regulated. For each department a special list of rules for the conduct of business was drawn up, defining the duties to be carried out and the restrictions placed on the actions of their members. The regulations on these matters were among the lasting achievements of Cornwallis. For, although the increase in business of later years necessitated further elaboration of the machinery, the later changes did not affect the main structure.

By January, 1789, much of the preliminary work of Cornwallis was over. He was still, it is true, in the midst of overhauling the systems of civil and criminal justice. The end of the first stage of reform in these departments did not come until his resolutions of 3 December, 1790. But the system of the investment was settled, and the purification of the civil service complete. In 1789–90, side by side with the completion of the judicial reforms went the revenue settlement. In this he had been most cautious, despite the definite orders from home. A year of experiment sufficed to decide the method of the investment, but, in the matter of land revenue as in that of the administration of justice, it was desirable to go warily, and to examine fully the evidence before any irrevocable step was taken. Hence the annual settlement of 1787 was followed by another in 1788 and yet another in 1789; it was not until the end of 1789 and the first weeks of 1790 that the final decision was made.

When Cornwallis landed in 1786 the question was already the subject of vigorous debate. The land system of Bengal was a difficult one for Europeans to understand; and under the alternative influence of Grant and Shore, the old Committee and the new Board of Revenue had taken opposite views on its character. The old Committee of

Revenue, under the influence of Grant, argued that the state was in legal conception the owner of the land. It was, therefore, open to the government to use either the zamindar or any other farmer as the agent for collecting revenue. Nor were they bound to definite limits in the amount of their exactions. The zamindar was an official rather than a landowner. The opposing theory, which was maintained by the new Board of Revenue under the influence of Shore, was that the zamindar was the legal owner of the land, and the state was entitled only to a customary revenue from him. If this was right, a settlement through the zamindar was the only right one. But although the debate was vigorous, the issue, from the point of view of Cornwallis, was already settled. The act of parliament of 1784 and the instructions of the directors had decided for the zamindar. This indeed Grant himself had recognised before the arrival of Cornwallis; for the office of *saristadar* which he had accepted had no meaning save under a zamindari system.

The rival views, however, influenced materially the question of the amount and duration of the settlement. On Grant's theory the amount of the revenue was limited only by the productivity of the land. As a result of his investigations he had concluded that this limit had never been approached since the Company obtained the diwanni. He recommended, therefore, that the basis taken should be the assessment of 1765; but insisted that considerable further examination of local conditions must be made before any settlement was concluded. This with less learning but more experience, and with far greater clarity, was refuted by Shore in his minutes of 18 June and 18 September, 1789. According to Shore, not only was Grant wrong in his conception of the status of the zamindar (to Cornwallis, if not to Shore and Grant, only of theoretic interest) but in his estimate of the yield of the land. Against the Moghul assessment, of 1765, Shore proposed as a basis the actual collection by zamindars and farmers in recent years. Only by careful examination could this be ascertained.

From the beginning, Cornwallis preferred Shore to Grant as his adviser in revenue matters. While their discussions were taking place, he was making experiments in revenue assessment with the help of Shore, and collecting materials upon which a lasting system could be based. In January, 1787, Shore took his place as president of the Board of Revenue: in February the board began its work of making preparation for a revenue settlement "for a long term of years".[1]

The board passed on its instructions to the collectors. The work took longer than Cornwallis expected, and it was not until the end of 1789 that all the required reports were received. It was at this point that Cornwallis left his wise caution, and threw aside the counsel both of Grant and Shore. Unlike them he held that there was now

[1] Ross, *op. cit.* I, 541.

sufficient information to warrant a settlement not merely for ten years but for perpetuity. Against this Shore and Grant protested. Permanence was unjustified, according to Shore, without a survey, or, according to Grant, without an exhaustive study of the records. Cornwallis, however, had the approval of Duncan, and the support of Shore's fellow-counsellor, Stuart. He had, further, his instructions to justify him, and with him these were final. He decided therefore provisionally for perpetuity, referring the matter home for ultimate decision. At the end of 1790, in Bengal, the collectors were circularised with instructions to carry out the settlement. A proclamation of 10 February, 1790, announced the ten-years' settlement with zamindars and other landholders; the settlement to be made perpetual if the home government should authorise it.

The settlement gave great and undefined powers to the zamindars, and Cornwallis has been criticised severely for his disregard of the interests of the ryots. But he was not indifferent to the possibilities of oppression. The lesser landholders, the talukdars, were to be dealt with separately whenever they were "the actual proprietors of the lands". Whereas in many cases formerly the zamindars had collected revenue from them, henceforth they were to be exempt from such control, and pay their revenues immediately to the public treasury of the district. In some districts of Bengal where the number of petty landholders was great the collectors were directed to appoint Indian assistants, *tahsildars*, as was already the practice in Bihar. The zamindars, therefore, were to be confirmed in the tenure of what was looked upon as their own land: but not in their position as collectors for other landholders. The principle of settlement with the "actual proprietors of the soil" enjoined by the directors was thus observed, in accordance with their interpretation of the term proprietor.

For the protection of the ryots Cornwallis looked to the local control of the collectors, reinforced by information from the commercial residents. No specific measures for their protection accompanied the Decennial Settlement, save the abolition of the *sair* duties of 1790. These incidents were collected by the zamindar, and it was held that the only way to avoid oppression was to abolish all duties so collected. In 1792 by resolution of the Supreme Council, and in 1793 by regulation, the zamindar's authority over his under-tenants was further limited.

The settlement thus completed was, it is clear, in the mind of Cornwallis a means to an important end. Until such a settlement was made "the constitution of our internal government in the country will never take that form which alone can lead to the establishment of good laws, and ensure a due administration of them". The Supreme Council and the Company's servants must alike be set free from the "unremitted application" to revenue business. Henceforth it would be possible for the servants "of the first abilities and the most established integrity" to attend first to other work.[1] In the mind of Cornwallis the administration of justice was of greater importance than that of revenue. Perhaps he did not realise how closely revenue administration, like that of trade, was bound up with the welfare of the people. Other reasons also were advanced—above all the encouragement it would give to the development of the land and the reclamation of the waste—but the fact that it would make possible better judicial administration seems the final factor. With such explanations, therefore, the ten-years' settlement was sent home for the decision of the point of difference between Cornwallis and Shore. At the end of 1789 Shore left Bengal for England, so the authorities at home could consult him if they wished.

The completion of the Decennial Settlement took longer than Cornwallis had expected. It was not until the autumn of 1791 that a full code of regulations could be issued: and in some districts the system did not come into force until nearly two more years had passed.

By the end of 1790, however, the final arrangements were in sight, and Cornwallis fully intended to return home at the beginning of the next year. He was well satisfied with his work. He had laid the basis of a sound system by his administrative purification; his reforms of justice, of revenue, and of trade had gone far enough to show the character of the structure which he had planned. What was now needed was to carry out schemes already started; and to maintain the principles of no patronage, and no corruption: and further to develop the judicial and administrative systems. But from the autumn of 1790 until June, 1792, he was absorbed in the Mysore War. Then he had fifteen months of peace, till he left for home in October, 1793.

These last years, however, saw the culmination of his work in several directions. They were the years of the proclamation of the Permanent Settlement of the land revenue, and of the promulgation of comprehensive regulations regarding the police system.

Of the first it is not necessary to say much. The minute of 10 February, 1790, announcing the Decennial Settlement, had contemplated its transformation into one for perpetuity. A perpetual settlement had formally been promised "provided such continuance should meet with the approbation of the...court...of directors... and not otherwise". The decision lay therefore with the Court of Directors and the Board of Control. The answer came in a letter from the court of 29 August, 1792. But the decision had been reached by the board. Dundas waited for a year, fully conscious of the importance of the matter, and in the end he went to Pitt for the decision. At Pitt's house in Wimbledon they went into the details and the principles of the plan, for ten days, and Charles Grant (the commercial adviser of Cornwallis) was with them "a great part of the time".

[1] Minute by Cornwallis, 10 February, 1790. Printed *ap.* Ross, *op. cit.* II, 459–74.

They decided in favour of permanence. In principle the matter was prejudged; for the idea of permanence lay behind the agitation of the 'eighties. But respect for Shore made Dundas hesitate; and he and Pitt seem to have been genuinely undecided in 1791.

The authorisation reached Cornwallis in 1793, and the change was immediately announced by proclamation (22 March). All that remained therefore was to watch the working out of this contested system. So far the full effect had not been seen. Some of the dangers of the system were, however, apparent in the frequent sales of zamindari estates and in the oppressions of sub-tenants by the zamindars. Regulations in 1793 attempted to deal with these, but without much effect.

One accidental result followed the settlement. In 1793, Cornwallis was about to leave Bengal: and at last a successor had been found for him. The choice was Shore. The man who was to see the first results of the Permanent Settlement, was the man who had opposed its permanence. And the decision was deliberate. Cornwallis had written home in 1789 that their differences had been marked by great good humour. Dundas and Pitt, in their discussions with Shore, were struck with his "talents, industry and candour". And so Shore was appointed to take the lead at Calcutta, expressing himself characteristically as ready to step aside and "become second in Council" if on further enquiry someone else seemed more suitable. It is the best defence of the administration which Cornwallis "purified" that it contained such men as Shore and Grant, who were willing to do their best to ensure the good working of schemes of which they disapproved in principle. If not perhaps the qualification best suited to a governor-general, the humble-minded zeal for duty that characterised Shore was an excellent testimony to the Bengal service.

The authorisation of the Permanent Settlement reached Cornwallis in time to head the list of great reforms that mark the year 1793. It is regulation 1 of the long series of regulations passed by the Supreme Council on 1 May, and known collectively as "the Cornwallis Code".

For by this time Cornwallis had prepared the series of changes that mark his second period of reform. Some, indeed most, of them were the result of his earlier work: either elaborating or reversing what had been done. The chief new reform was the reorganisation of the system of police. Cornwallis had long realised that the police system of Calcutta was defective, and he had drafted a scheme for reform as far back as 1788. He thought, however, at this time that his legislative powers were not sufficient for this, and he proceeded therefore by drafting an act to be laid before parliament. As this, however, involved considerable delay, he decided at the end of 1788 to appoint a committee to enquire into the complaints that had been made. As the result, a scheme was drawn up, and it was published in October, 1791. The regulations were said to be provisional, pending the reply from home relative to the passing of an act of parliament.

The regulations applied only to the town of Calcutta. By the new system, superintendents of police were appointed, with functions confined to the maintenance of order and to the arrest of suspected persons. They were no longer to share the attention of the superintendents with magisterial and judicial functions. By subsequent regulations of December, 1791, duties were defined and salaries fixed.

The next stage was the application of the new system to the whole province. This, the work of April to December, 1792, involved a further exemplification of the principle of employing Europeans in the place of Indians. The zamindars were relieved of their responsibilities for maintaining the peace and were ordered to disband their local police forces. In each district small areas were to be portioned off, and placed under the control of a *daroga* or superintendent, under the supervision of the Company's representative in the district. These regulations were issued provisionally in December, 1792. They were accompanied by a project for the erection of gaols in all the collectorships of the province. The police regulations were provisionally confirmed from home early in 1793, and were embodied in the general restatement of the regulations, the Cornwallis Code of May, 1793.

The regulations of 1 May, 1793, covered the whole field of administration. In many respects they were of importance merely as defining the existing system. This work of definition Cornwallis and the directors agreed was of first importance. His reforms were in a precarious position if they depended only upon personal support. One year of negligence would destroy the whole system. The exhaustive regulations of 1793 aimed at stereotyping the rules which Cornwallis had introduced. They dealt with the commercial system, with civil and criminal justice, with the police and with the land revenue. While restating the existing position, they contemplated further changes, for by regulation xx special procedure was laid down for the proposal of new regulations by the officials charged with working the present system. And, even where in substance the regulations restated former rules, minor alterations showed a readiness to profit by experience.

Among the changes effected by the code one of the most important was the separation of the judicial from the revenue administration. The junction of the two, which had given unprecedented power to the collector from 1787 to 1790, had been due to the need both of economy and of simplification. In the hierarchy of the administration the collector had become by 1790 the bottle-neck through which all lines of control must pass. Though in all his functions responsible to some superior authority, he was in practice virtually independent. As early as 1790 Cornwallis realised the dangers of this position, even though he was then making it still more powerful. As it stood, nothing but the character of the collectors was a real safeguard to the subject. He had long been of opinion, he wrote, that this was a mistake.

...No system will ever be carried into effect so long as the personal qualifications of the individuals that may be appointed to superintend it, form the only security for the due exercise of it.

In his view the conclusion of the Permanent Settlement was a necessary preliminary to change: and it was not therefore until 1793 that change could be made. In the regulations of May detailed instructions prescribed the action of the Company's servants, and a system of check and counter-check was substituted for the quasi-independence of 1787. By regulation II of 1793 the Board of Revenue and the collectors were deprived of all judicial powers. The new courts of 1790—of mal adalat—for the trial of revenue causes were abolished. These causes were transferred to the other district courts, those of diwanni adalat. These, too, had hitherto been presided over by the collector. But now the offices of judge and collector were separated. Judges were to be appointed to preside over the courts, renamed *zillah* or district courts, responsible for all civil cases. From them appeal was to lie to four provincial courts of appeal, situated, like the criminal courts, at Patna, Dacca, Murshidabad and Calcutta. From them in the larger causes appeal lay to the Supreme Council in its capacity as a court of sadr diwanni adalat. Over each of these provincial courts were three English judges. And these judges, it was provided, were also to preside over the criminal courts of circuit stationed at the same towns. The administration of justice, both civil and criminal, was therefore vested in the same hands. To make the system of checks upon the revenue administration more complete, it was provided that

the collectors of revenue and their officers, and indeed all the officers of Government, shall be amenable to the courts for acts done in their official capacities, and that Government itself, in cases in which it may be a party with its subjects in matters of property, shall submit its rights to be tried in these courts under the existing laws and regulations.[1]

In the reforms of the early period the chief aims had been economy, purification and simplification. Cornwallis had come to India assured that to purify the Company's service it was essential that the holders of office should be Englishmen, adequately remunerated, and not foisted on the Company by influence. In the interests of economy and simplification he had given to these Englishmen almost unparalleled powers. It seems to have been felt that while he was in office no great danger would result. But now in this second period of reform the outstanding aim was the safeguarding of the Indian from oppression. Cornwallis himself had completed the process by which Bengal swarmed with Englishmen in commercial or administrative

[1] Ross, *op. cit.* II, 558.

offices; he seems to have reflected that it was at least necessary that they should not be free to add to the oppression of Indians the old practice of making a fortune. So the Company's servants and all other English residents were to be subject to the courts. The revenue and judicial systems were separated, and the collector of revenue confined rigidly to the position suggested by his name

Such a change operating without delay might well be expected to rouse discontent in the Company's service. But Cornwallis was able to allay this. The new district courts required judges, and it was part of his scheme that the collectors of the district, chosen formerly as being "of the first abilities and most established integrity", were transferred to this office. As judges of the *zillah* courts they exercised jurisdiction in revenue and other civil causes: upon them was conferred the magisterial power of the collector. The revenue duties, which they left, devolved upon the assistants in the various districts. Thus, under the new system, judicial administration was marked as separate from, and as of much more importance than, revenue and the executive functions associated with it.

The new system then created three branches of the service, instead of two. The "commercial line" remained unchanged: the commercial residents lived still at the various factories or stations, responsible to the Board of Trade, and ultimately to the Supreme Council. The revenue service, shorn of the important duty of the assessment, was now the sole function of the new collectors of revenue. They were responsible as before to the Board of Revenue, and then to the Supreme Council. The district judges exercised civil jurisdiction and the petty criminal jurisdiction of the magistrate. They were responsible to the judges of the provincial courts in civil causes, and to those same judges in the courts of circuit in criminal causes. The system did not lack simplicity. It was not extravagant and it observed the important principle of responsibility towards the inhabitants which had been one of the chief characteristics of the new policy Cornwallis came in to enforce.

With the Cornwallis Code the work of Cornwallis in India was ended. But he was fully aware that it was only a beginning. He had set up the machinery: established the recognition of certain principles: but there was still no provision of a code of law. The resolutions of December, 1790, and the regulations of 1793, had done something to amend what seemed the greatest deficiencies of the existing system. The law administered remained, however, in its main features unchanged. The regulations of 1793 improved the position a little by defining the qualifications of the Indian interpreters of the law, who were attached to the various courts. But Cornwallis judged rightly that no greater innovation was possible at present. "A good system of laws" was a thing more hard to come by even than "a due administration of them, and a well-established peace". Sir William Jones was preparing the way by his treatise on Indian laws. Cornwallis hoped that something would be done by the building up of a case-made law on the findings of judges of the courts. The developments of the future alone could fulfil the aim of Cornwallis. He had created the machinery: upon the spirit that informed it depended its success.

For twenty years after the retirement of Cornwallis, the system of his code remained substantially unaltered. The periodical renewal of the Company's Charter was due in 1793, but it took place without any of the close scrutiny of administration which had heralded the acts of 1773 and 1784. Cornwallis himself was of the view that little real change was necessary; and the Company kept for another twenty years its dual character as a commercial monopolist, and an instrument of administration. It is in the events of this period that the strength and weakness of the Cornwallis Code are most clearly seen.

The continued observance of Cornwallis's principles of administration was due to some extent to the pressure of political cares. But the lack of revolutionary change was in large measure a deliberate policy. The preference for "steady adherence to almost any one system" had become an accepted tenet: and the rulers of British India did not attempt either a reversion to older ideas or the formulation of new ones. The permanent settlement of the land revenue, the severance of judicial from revenue administration, and the restriction of Indians to offices of lesser responsibility were faithfully observed by Cornwallis's successors. In the first half of the period, indeed, the respect for the Cornwallis Code was so great that it was introduced to the furthest degree possible into the new lands of the Ganges basin, and even applied to Madras. Yet even the greatest reverence could not hide the defects of the code, nor the utmost piety avoid some attempt to correct them. The regulations of the period 1793 to 1813 are filled with amendments. Some were necessitated by the faulty wording of the code, for which Barlow rather than Cornwallis was responsible; but many were due to the defects and the rigidity of Cornwallis's own principles. In the last three years of his rule he had added distrust of the covenanted servants of the Company to his initial dislike of Indian agency. He deliberately placed confidence in the system rather than in individuals, and he seems to have ignored the fact that systems, like individuals, are bound to be faulty. The great fault of his system was that he confounded courts of justice with justice itself. In a land where the laws were still vague and unknown, and the new system of administration was alien to the ideas of the natives, the multiplication of court-made justice was no advantage in itself. In theory, the Indians were protected by courts of justice from the oppression of officials: zamindars and talukdars against revenue collectors, ryots against zamindars. But the courts were both unsuited and inadequate for the task. Delays were so serious that suits, it was said, were not decided in the normal course of a lifetime. Protection of this kind was not of much value, and, without the gravest unconcern for the welfare of the people, it was impossible to disregard the need for reform.

The changes of the period 1793 to 1813 were mainly in two directions, in connection with the Permanent Settlement, and with the speeding up of civil and criminal justice. The reform of the system of police was left over to the next period, but measures, on the whole successful, were taken to deal with dacoits.

The general approval of the Permanent Settlement by the authorities in India and at home did not hide the defects that resulted from the system. It was soon found that the evil of "balances" continued as before: that the efforts made to prevent the oppression of tenants and ryots led only to the complete blocking of the courts of justice: that the attempts made to realise the revenue without personal coercion of the zamindars resulted in frequent sales of estates. Moreover the provision that talukdars could claim exemption from the zamindars' control increased the business before the courts, and led to the cutting up of estates.

The measures taken by Shore were in two directions. A regulation of 1795 modified the rules as to the actions of zamindars in collecting rents from their tenants and ryots. In effect, their powers of coercion were increased. Secondly, additional civil courts were established, and additional powers granted to the Indians who were responsible for deciding minor causes. By these two measures it was hoped that the "balances" would diminish and sales become less frequent. Above all, they would remedy the existing state of affairs by which "the determination of a cause could not...be expected...in the ordinary course of the plaintiff's life". Despite these measures, however, the delays in the settlement of suits continued; and so did sales and the dismemberment of estates. The latter were due to the numerous claims of exemption from the control of zamindars on the ground of talukdari rights, and, in 1801, Lord Wellesley met this by a regulation giving a date after which no such claim could be recognised. The evil of sales was not so soon settled. A regulation passed by Wellesley in 1799 gave still further powers of coercion to the zamindars, and over them the former practice of arrest was reinstated. The latter measure was a return to the procedure of Cornwallis, the regulation of 1793 making the zamindar liable to arrest as well as to the sale of his land having been amended by Shore. Now, in 1799, the practice of personal coercion was restored, again with the object of checking the flood of sales. Even so, Lord Minto found the same defect, and attempted further to restrict sales by a regulation of 1807. In fact the position was intrinsically difficult, and no mere regulation would alter it. By Lord Minto's time the difficulties were beginning to grow less, but this was due more to the greater goodwill of the zamindars than to the revised regulations. So long as the system was regarded with suspicion the difficulties continued. In fact it is clear that in the years following its establishment the Permanent Settlement was neither profitable to government nor popular with the people. Such advantages as it had did not begin to operate until a later time.

In his advocacy of the Permanent Settlement, Cornwallis had put high among the advantages the freeing of the Company's servants from their absorption in revenue matters. In fact the difficulties in the working out of the system made the task of a collector much less simple than had been intended. Moreover, the mass of revenue suits filled the *zillah* courts beyond measure, and the old collectors who were now judges in these courts were certainly no freer than before to concern themselves with the interests of the people. One of the first and most pressing changes was therefore the limitation of suits. Various regulations with this object date from the years 1795–1802. They start with the reimposition of a fee upon registering a suit. This was the work of Shore, as was also the increase in the number of courts, and of Indians qualified to settle minor suits. Then, under Wellesley, the regulation as to appeals was stiffened, and assistant judges were appointed. The seriousness of the pressure extended even to the sadr court, and Lord Wellesley thought it undesirable that the governor-general and council should continue to act as its judges. A reorganisation therefore took place in 1805, and three judges took over the responsibilities of the court. The reforms of Wellesley, like those of Shore, did not stop the evil of delay. Lord Minto attempted further to remedy it. In 1807 the number of judges in the sadr court was increased to four: in 1811 it was enacted that the number of district judges should be increased as necessity occurred. Another expedient for remedying the congestion of business was the reorganisation of the system of circuit. According to the regulations of 1793 the provincial court of appeal was necessarily closed while the three judges went on circuit in their capacity of circuit judges. A regulation of 1794 provided for the unbroken session of the court. A further change of 1797 made possible the trial of appeal cases during the absence of the judges on circuit. Similar congestion in the trials of criminal cases was met by the increase in the power of magistrates in petty cases, and by conferring on them the right of delegating power to their assistants. Special rules for the punishment of dacoits were enacted in 1807.

None of the changes, however, did more than palliate the evils of the system. These evils were still formidable when they were submitted to the clear scrutiny of the next few years.

The unhesitating acquiescence in the Cornwallis system ended in 1808, and the work of reform started in earnest five years later.

Unlike the act of 1793 the Charter Act of 1813 made important changes in the position of the Company; and, again unlike that act, it was the result of the careful examination of several years. This new reform movement started on 11 March, 1808, when Robert Dundas moved the appointment of a select committee to enquire into the affairs of the Company. The committee issued five reports, and the fifth, issued in 1812, contained a detailed analysis of the Bengal system. Together with its appendices (and with some of the material contained in the second report of 1810), it is a valuable exposition of the history and the results of the Cornwallis Code. Above all, it makes clear some, if not all, of its defects.

The period of the Select Committee saw also the beginning of an enquiry in Bengal. The defects of the early system forced themselves especially on the judges of the courts, and in the summer of 1809 Lord Minto set on foot an enquiry as to the best lines of change. The investigation, however, was not completed by him. In 1813 he was succeeded by the Marquess of Hastings and it was in the ten years of his rule that the most thorough enquiry was made. In 1813 the Charter Act embodied one aspect of the new reform movement. On 9 November, 1814, a dispatch of the court of directors[1] emphasised the other.

The act of 1813 abolished the Company's monopoly of trade in India. The change in administration involved was not at first of much importance, since the monopoly and not the trade was abolished. The Board of Trade continued its work until 1835: the commercial residents remained at their factories, although their number decreased as the trade diminished. The most immediate alteration was at the presidency offices, for the act required a rigid separation of the commercial and administrative accounts.

The instructions of 9 November, 1814, prescribed a far more radical change. The pressure on the civil courts dictated a resumption by the collector of his powers in civil justice: the difficulties found in administering criminal justice and in the regulation of the police demanded that the collectors should once more have magisterial powers, and be responsible for the superintendence of the police. With the same object of improving the administration of justice, additional powers were to be given to Indian agents: and by increasing the criminal jurisdiction of the *zillah* judges the pressure on the higher courts would be relieved. At the same time the judicial interference of the collector would serve to increase the protection of the ryots; and with the latter object in view the Board of Control added a clause to the directors' dispatch urging the observance "in all possible cases" of "the principle of realising the revenues from the ryots themselves".

The recommendations of the dispatch were a denial of Cornwallis's principles in several respects. If they were carried out, the separation

---

[1] I.O. Records, Bengal Despatches, vol. LXVII, Judicial Despatch of 9 November, 1814.

of revenue from judicial administration would once more disappear. The collector would resume in some measure his position of 1790 as the bottle-neck through which all administration must pass. It was impossible to set back the Permanent Settlement as fully as this, but the dispatch showed at least that the authorities at home were alive to its dangers. Even the prejudice of Cornwallis against the employment of Indians was set aside. Such revolutionary measures did not commend themselves to the government of Bengal. The mistake of Cornwallis in carrying out his reform without sufficient investigation was not repeated. The new instructions were referred for opinion to all the boards and courts in Bengal, and to the principal servants of the Company. The repeated pressure of the court of directors did not obtain an answer to their dispatch until 22 February, 1827, and then in several respects the attitude of the government of India was more conservative than that of the authorities at home.

In the meantime, however, much had been done to modify the existing system. The period of Hastings's rule saw a number of regulations which improved the working and loosened the rigidity of Cornwallis's Code, while still paying rather more than lip-service to his principles.

The first changes were already accomplished when the reforming dispatch arrived.[1] Regulations of 1813 and 1814 had provided a fairly efficient police system for the large towns. In 1813, in the cities of Dacca, Murshidabad and Patna, and in 1814 at the headquarters of every district, police chowkidars were appointed under the control of the superintendents of police. The system was said to be working well in 1816. In 1817–19 the system of village watch was reformed. These police reforms were regarded by the government as the most urgent and the most satisfactory of the reforms.

The necessity for lessening the burden of the civil courts was met by a series of measures. The powers of Indian *munsiffs* and *sadar amins* in civil justice were defined in 1814 and extended in 1821. The doctrine that no class of Indian officers should be vested with final powers was, however, maintained, and other measures were necessary to remedy the position. The procedure in appeal was laid down by a regulation of 1814; and steps were taken to relieve the pressure in the higher courts. The burden of the Calcutta appeal court was diminished by the establishment of a separate court for the Western Provinces, but the most important steps were the appointment of a fifth judge and the systematic division of labour between the judges. The difficulties of the lesser courts were met partly by the establishment of special commissions to administer justice in the new parts of the province. But the more effective measures for relief were the increase in the number of *zillah* judges, and the transfer of certain

---

[1] I.O. Records, Bengal Letters Received, vol. LXX, Judicial Letter of 29 November, 1814.

judicial functions to the revenue authorities. The latter expedient was adopted very slowly, the proposal for the re-establishment of *mal adalats* being disregarded. In unsettled districts the judicial powers of the collectors were fairly extensive, but they were still slight in Bengal. There, the new powers were chiefly in connection with the sale of liquor and the manufacture and sale of opium. Even in Bengal, however, the collectors had some judicial business in connection with the land revenue. In 1819 the collectors were authorised to deal with cases relating to claims to freedom from assessment, and in 1822 to rectify errors committed at the time of sales.

Closely connected with the measures to facilitate civil justice, are those for the protection of the ryot. One of the chief reasons asserted by the directors (and emphasised by the Board of Control) for conferring power of civil justice on collectors had been the greater protection that would be given to the ryot. The increased function of the collectors would not be enough to secure this, and further measures were urged. What was done was rather to prevent further encroachment than to reverse what had already taken place. The offices of kanungo and patwari were re-established in the years 1816-19, and the institution of the *mufassal* record committees aimed at stabilising the position of the various classes concerned in land. This was furthered also by the comprehensive definition of the rights of the various classes concerned in land by regulation VIII of 1819. That more was not done was due to the fact that the Permanent Settlement made a satisfactory system impossible.

The aspect of the directors' instructions to which least observance was secured, was that which was concerned with criminal justice. The principles of Cornwallis here died hard. As late as 1827 the separation of the administration of criminal justice from the work of the revenue officers was looked upon with respect as the chief "principle on which the civil administration framed by Lord Cornwallis" was founded. The length of time that that system had been in force made in itself a substantial argument against reversing it, since the collectors of the 1820's were practically all without experience in judicial affairs. Another principle also was involved. The collectors were assisted in most districts by Indian *tahsildars*, and to entrust magisterial powers to them would be to abandon Cornwallis's refusal to vest real power in Indian hands. What was done in this direction was therefore of a tentative character. In criminal justice, as in civil, pressure of cases necessitated an increase in the number of *zillah* judges and the addition of a fifth member in the appeal court. But all that was done to meet the instructions to reunite justice and revenue was the permissive regulation of 1821. In 1818 the first step in this direction had been taken when three collectors were specially empowered to act as magistrates. Now by regulation IV of 1821 such power might be granted to any collector at the discretion of the Supreme Government. In the following years a few collectors and sub-collectors were granted power under the regulation.

When Hastings left India in 1823, despite his absorption in political affairs, considerable changes had taken place in the system of Cornwallis. The chief need as Cornwallis estimated it was still no nearer completion. "A good system of law" was not yet established, for Sir William Jones had died in 1795, and little had been done to continue his work. It is true that the code which Cornwallis had promulgated had been simplified, and redrawn where its ambiguities were greatest. But a vast body of new regulations had followed, and the courts had piled up judicial precedents. No comprehensive code had been issued: what had really been done was to follow up the reforms of Cornwallis by further changes and experiments. In criminal and civil justice, perhaps above all in the police system, many improvements had been made. The position of the collector had once more been changed: for if he had not recovered the overwhelming power of 1790, the degradation of 1793 had been considerably mitigated. The collector was climbing back to his position as the state's man of all work; and was well on his way to reach it in time to be the chief instrument of the next reform movement. Yet much of the work of Cornwallis was still standing. The building had been extended and improved, and the original plans had been modified; but all the early work had not been destroyed. The reforms of the civil service had not needed to be done again. By his cleansing of the administrative system, Cornwallis had established a lasting tradition. After thirty years the best of his work, the result of his uprightness and zeal for the public service, was still in being. In spite of his mistakes, therefore, Cornwallis, like Warren Hastings, had left a lasting impression on the system of government: and it was one of the merits of his successors that they were slow to experiment in change.

CHAPTER XXVII

THE MADRAS DISTRICT SYSTEM AND LAND REVENUE TO 1818

THROUGHOUT the eighteenth century up to the last decade no power in South India felt itself secure enough to spare serious attention for the improvement of the territories under its authority. The more energetic rulers found their time fully occupied with the task of suppressing rivals and rebels and raising the armies and revenues necessary for this end. The rest were content to make hay while the sun shone. Thus in time of peace the chief concern of every ruler was the collection of the revenue and especially of the land revenue, which usually produced more than nine-tenths of the total state income. The insecurity of the ruler's position compelled him to raise his demand as high as possible and to take the quickest and easiest means of collecting what he claimed without thought for the future. Checks and precautions were relaxed and abuses sprang up on all sides. A strong ruler like Hyder of Mysore preferred to collect through officers of his own appointment, amildars having jurisdiction over large areas containing some hundreds of villages. The amildar usually dealt with the village through the village headman and the village accountant, whose records were supposed to show what the villagers should by custom pay. As it was difficult to prevent the village accountant from falsifying his accounts the amildar frequently struck a bargain with the village headman, or, if he would not rise to the amildar's terms, rented the village to a powerful outsider who was left to collect what he could.

If the amildar could not trust the village officers, neither could the ruler trust the amildar, who took presents and levied extra cesses for which he rendered no account, securing the acquiescence of the villagers partly by terror, partly by lowering the public demand on the plea of a failure of the crop. Hyder met the difficulty by allowing the amildars to grow rich and then flogging them till they disgorged. Milder-mannered princes, such as the nawab of Arcot, tended to supplant the amildars by renting out whole districts to rich or influential speculators. Where this was done, all the authority formerly exercised by the amildar in practice devolved upon the renter, since any restriction upon his proceedings was made an excuse for withholding the sum contracted for. Neither the amildar nor the renter enjoyed any security of tenure. As a rule they looked only for immediate profit regardless of longer views.[1]

But South Indian rulers were not everywhere strong enough to

---

[1] Srinivasaraghava Aiyangar, *Memorandum*, App. pp. xx *sqq.*

collect the revenue on the system which suited them best. Half the Northern Sarkars and elsewhere many of the less accessible tracts were under local chiefs who had never been completely subdued, feudal nobles who had succeeded in retaining their feudal status, local officials and adventurers with local influence who had seized power and asserted a partial independence. These poligars and zamindars exercised within their own territory all the functions of a sovereign, even making war on their own account upon their peers. But they acknowledged an obligation to pay tribute or *peshkash* to the sovereign and to serve in his campaigns with a certain number of armed retainers. The *peshkash* was sometimes fixed, sometimes it varied from year to year with the state of cultivation. But its amount and the regularity with which it was paid depended less upon the resources of the poligar's territory than on the ease with which he could be coerced.

Unlike the renters and the amildars the zamindars and poligars had an hereditary interest in the territories under their control. But their traditions and upbringing were as a rule essentially martial. "Eat or be eaten" was the condition of their existence. Their grand aims had always been to extend their territories at the expense of their neighbours and to strengthen themselves to resist the central power. Many of them were too spirited to exchange uncontrolled if precarious authority for the assured income of a peaceful landlord, and very few of them were capable of believing that the central power would continue to allow them to intercept a share of the land revenue once they had been disarmed. The central power usually aimed at extirpating these territorial chiefs, as opportunity offered. Hyder and Tipu of Mysore were especially active in pursuing this policy. It is unlikely that the cultivators often regretted their poligar when he was hanged. For he had to consider first the interests of his armed retainers and he was often under the necessity of satisfying their demands for arrears of pay by giving them authority to collect the land revenue direct from the villages.[1]

The workers of South India, the agriculturists and the artisans, living for the most part in villages, hoped little and feared much from their rulers. So narrow was the margin on which the cultivators were living that advances of seed-grain had often to be made to enable them to raise a crop. In many South Indian villages the land revenue depends upon the upkeep of the irrigation works and some amildars spent pains and money on this account. But as a rule the works seem to have been neglected or maintained only by the villagers. Even for protection the villagers relied chiefly on their own mud walls or thorn fences which could be defended by stone-throwing against the predatory horse and the camp followers of the period. Whether these owed allegiance to an invading power or to the country's prince made little difference in the feelings which they inspired among the

[1] *The Fifth Report of* 1812, pp. 80 *sqq.*

villagers. There were no made roads, no bridges, and no wheeled vehicles outside a few large towns. Trade was carried on by pack cattle. There was no code of law generally recognised as being in force; and even where Hindu or Muhammadan law-books were supposed to have authority, there were no regular courts in existence to interpret or give effect to them, or to solidify custom and precedent into law. Petty crime was dealt with by the village headman and most civil disputes were settled in the village by the award of arbitrators or by the decisions of village *panchayats* or juries. Caste offences were punished by caste headmen or caste *panchayats*, the state only interfering to raise revenue by leasing out the right to levy fines. Grave crimes could be brought before the amildar, who might inflict any punishment short of death. There were no gaols, and imprisonment was not a recognised form of punishment. Mutilation for the poor and fines for the rich were the order of the day. The proceedings of the amildar were controlled not by law, but by his sense of equity. The powers of the amildar were also exercised not only by zamindars and poligars, but also by renters and military officers, and indeed by any person who had at his command the force necessary to give effect to his decision. The same authorities could sometimes be induced to appoint arbitrators for the decision of important civil disputes. There was always the possibility of an appeal to the sovereign, but access to him was difficult, and the chance of a careful enquiry small.[1]

For police in the more orderly tracts the villagers relied chiefly on the hereditary village-watchman. But where criminal tribes or the retainers of a poligar lived in the neighbourhood, they usually found it expedient to invite one of their tormentors to become their *kavalgar* or guard, and to pay him to save the village from theft, or at least to obtain restitution of the stolen property for a reasonable consideration. A poligar or other person of local influence often had himself recognised as a *head-kavalgar* controlling the village *kavalgars* throughout his sphere of influence and sharing their emoluments. In one or two districts this system was reported to work well, but in general it seems to have been a convenience to the criminal classes rather than to the cultivators.

But if the sovereign concerned himself little with most aspects of his subjects' lives, his interest in the produce of their agriculture was close and persistent. Everywhere a share in the produce of the land was claimed either by the sovereign, or by a grantee of the land revenue deriving his right from the sovereign, or by a zamindar or poligar who claimed this among other rights of sovereignty. In the absence of any court of law, the nature of the sovereign's rights and the cultivators' tenure was determined not by law but by the interplay of three forces—the power of the sovereign, the custom of the village, and the economic condition of the district. The Hindu family system and the lack of stock tended to divide up the land into small holdings.

[1] Cf. Gleig, *Munro*, 1, 405 *sqq.*

In many villages, especially in the irrigated tracts, there was a tradition of a joint settlement and a common ancestry, and the whole village was owned in shares, the lands in some of them being periodically redistributed[1]. In such villages there was a habit of common action which enabled the villagers to oppose a certain resistance to the sovereign and his agents. Elsewhere rights were derived from the individual occupation of waste land, and the power of resistance was very small. Almost everywhere there was more cultivable land than could be cultivated by the labour and stock of the inhabitants. The ruler therefore had seldom any reason to assert a claim to the land itself or to oust a cultivator from it. His anxiety was to find cultivators for the land and to secure the largest possible share of the product of their industry. The share of the crop which he succeeded in obtaining was usually so high as to leave the cultivator no more than a bare subsistence. This, taken together with the presence of land waiting to be brought under cultivation, prevented the land from acquiring any saleable value except in Tanjore and in a few other specially favoured localities. The cultivator therefore had all the security of tenure that he desired. Hereditary rights were seldom in question. The ryot was more concerned to assert his right to relinquish a holding—a right which the amildar was at pains to deny. To the ruler's demands for an increasing land revenue the cultivator could oppose an ill-defined village custom and sometimes the records of an old assessment which showed what the cultivator ought to pay. But the state's admitted share was itself very high, amounting often to more than half the whole crop; and the cultivator was unable to resist the imposition of all manner of extra cesses to meet the needs of the ruler, the amildar and the village officers.[2] It was said that in practice the ruler and his agents took all that they could get, sometimes even the whole crop, and that the cultivator often kept no more than he could conceal. But it must be remembered that, in the circumstances of the time, it was easy for the cultivators to conceal the extent of cultivation and to misrepresent the out-turn of their crops. The village accountants and the revenue underlings who estimated or measured the out-turn could usually be propitiated at no very extravagant cost. At the opening of our period the uncertainty and the inequality of the incidence of the demand was probably at least as great an evil as the magnitude of the total sum collected.

To prevent fraud, it was clearly in the interest of the ruler that his claim should be commuted for a fixed sum of money or a fixed quantity of grain payable annually in good and bad seasons alike, and in some districts there were in the hands of the village accountants records of old surveys in which the sum payable on each field or on each holding was defined. Elsewhere attempts had been made to

[1] Ellis, Mirassi Paper, ap. Rev. and Jud. Sel. i, 810.
[2] Graeme's Report on N. Arcot, 31 March, 1818, ap. Rev. and Jud. Sel. i, 959.

fix the sum payable by each village. But so long as the state's demand in average years left the cultivators little more than a bare subsistence, it could not be paid in bad years. The revenue underlings and the village officers opposed a system which tended to curtail the sources of illegitimate gain; and the cultivators feared that the fixed demand might operate merely as a minimum and would not protect them against extra cesses.

The most important crop in South India was the rice crop cultivated on the irrigated lands. The state's share of this crop was usually calculated each year in grain. The villagers were sometimes required to buy back the state share at a price fixed at the discretion of the sovereign's agent. Sometimes the state's share was stored in granaries to be consumed by the state servants, or sold when prices rose.[1] To eliminate competition the villagers were often forbidden to sell their grain till the state had disposed of its stock. The unirrigated lands of South India were far more extensive than the irrigated. A great variety of crops was raised and many of these crops were harvested piecemeal. To assess, collect, store and market the state's share in all these crops would have been an impossible task. It was therefore commuted for a money payment. This was sometimes fixed on each field, sometimes for each kind of crop cultivated; and sometimes it varied with the state of the season.

The net result was that every year saw a struggle between the state's agent and the villagers to raise or lower the assessment, and a good crop well cultivated might cost the village dear. When the demand on the whole village had been fixed for the year, the apportionment of it among the villagers was usually left to the discretion of the village headmen, or other principal inhabitants, who might or might not be charitably disposed to the poor, but were very unlikely to encourage exceptional enterprise, industry, or thrift. There was thus everything to discourage improvement and the cultivator lost all interest in his land. So much was this the case that there had grown up among the revenue officers a tradition that the cultivator was idle, and that it was their duty to drive him and to force him to cultivate more land than he was willing to be responsible for.[2] The cultivator on his side was often on the look-out for an opportunity to relinquish old land in order to take up waste that happened to be more leniently assessed. He would even leave his village for this purpose. Indeed the most effective check on the activities of the revenue officers was the readiness of the cultivator to fly to some adjoining district where the administration was less exacting.

Beside the land revenue there were a host of miscellaneous taxes, licences and monopolies, designed to secure the sovereign a share in

---

[1] Revenue letter from Madras, 6 February, 1810, *ap. Rev. and Jud. Sel.* I, 502.
[2] Cf. Moreland, *India at the death of Akbar*, p. 97.

the income arising from every source. Thus there were taxes on houses, on looms, on oil presses, on stonemasons, on dancing girls, and on most petty industries; taxes on forest produce; monopolies of salt, of liquor, and of ghee, and duties on the transport of goods. The revenue derived from these sources was small, partly because of the prevailing poverty, partly because the machinery for collection was neither trustworthy nor efficient. By far the most important of these miscellaneous taxes were the duties levied on the transport of goods. The right to levy these taxes was usually farmed out. The rates of duty and the location of the stations at which they were levied were governed partly by custom, partly by the discretion of the farmer. The stations were very numerous. On some routes they were on the average not more than ten miles apart, and duties had to be paid at each one. But trade is more easily killed or frightened away than agriculture, and the farmers of the transit duties were therefore less oppressive than the land revenue officials.[1]

In European eyes the three radical evils in South India were the insubordination of the zamindars and poligars, the lack of recognised laws and law courts, and the uncertainties of the land revenue system. Since 1775 the court of directors had been pressing the Madras Government to take steps towards correcting these evils in the territories under their control, that is in the Northern Sarkars and the jagir.[2] But when Lord Cornwallis came to India, there was as yet little to distinguish the administration of these territories from that of the adjoining native states. A blank ignorance of the people, their customs, and their languages, inclined the Company's servants to give unlimited discretion to the persons whom they chose to exercise authority in their stead. All business was transacted through interpreters.[3] There was no incentive to exertion. Money was the chief consideration, and it could only be acquired by corrupt means. But a new spirit was soon to be infused. In 1792, the defeat of Tipu Sultan and the annexation of the Baramahal and Dindigul to the Madras Presidency made it plain that the administration of the Company's territories would henceforth be the chief duty of the Company's servants, and that there was a career for those who equipped themselves for this work. A stimulus to industry was supplied by the fact that for lack of civil servants with a knowledge of the languages and customs of the people, Captain Read with three military assistants was appointed to take charge of the land revenue administration of the Baramahal. A central Board of Revenue had been set up in 1786, and the working of the new spirit led it to fall foul of the corrupt and inefficient chiefs and councils in the Northern Sarkars, who had allowed their territories to go from bad to worse,

---

[1] Cf. *Baramahal Records*, section VII.
[2] *Fifth Report of* 1812, pp. 78 *sqq.*
[3] Arbuthnot, *Selections*, p. xxxvii.

obstructing every effort towards reform. In 1794, the governor of Madras, Lord Hobart, was induced to abolish these authorities and to substitute district collectors, subordinate to the Board of Revenue.[1] In the same year the whole of the jagir was put under a single collector, Lionel Place. The district collector, having an interest in his work and exercising a wide discretionary authority much the same as that which was vested in the amildar under native rulers, soon showed himself far better fitted to overawe opposition and to obtain information than the councils and committees that had preceded him.[2] Light began to flow in on the foundations of the land revenue system, the land tenures, and the customs of the villages. These things had hitherto been regarded as impenetrable mysteries, but the district officers now began to understand them, and to see that it was possible and advantageous to work through the indigenous institutions, reforming and adapting them to suit their ends.

In the jagir, Place found the villages owned in heritable shares by *mirasdars* who exercised the right of disposing of their shares by mortgage, gift, or sale. This discovery upset the then accepted theory that the state was the owner of the soil, and that the cultivator was little more than a tenant-at-will with at most a preferential right to cultivate on the terms which the state chose to offer. The principal *mirasdars* had been accustomed to act together on behalf of the village, and it was found convenient and profitable to abandon the old practice of renting out the jagir in parcels to speculators, and to settle instead with the *mirasdars* of each village for a lump sum calculated to be equivalent to the state's share of the crop. Place exerted himself to restore the efficiency of the village accountants, and he acquired a close knowledge of the affairs of the villages under his control. The system, therefore, worked smoothly enough and gave an increasing revenue during the four years of his administration. A similar system was applied in the government villages in the Northern Sarkars. But the results there were less satisfactory, partly because the villagers were less capable of joint action, partly because the collectors had not Place's knowledge.

The conditions with which Read had to deal in the Baramahal were widely different from those which Place had found in the jagir. In the latter was a tradition of an original colonisation, and the *mirasdars* of each village traced their titles to a joint-occupation of its lands. The main crop was rice, which was threshed on a common threshing-floor. The state's share was calculated in grain on the total produce of the village, and its amount or its equivalent in cash was demanded in the lump from the village, the apportionment of the demand being left entirely to the *mirasdars*. But in the Baramahal the rice crop was of minor importance. The majority of the cultivators

---

[1] *Fifth Report of* 1812, pp. 89–90, and App. 14.
[2] *Idem*, App. 16; cf. *Wellesley Despatches*, I, 230.

drew their living from the unirrigated lands. The population was sparse, the waste lands extensive, and titles were derived from the individual's occupation of waste. The ties which bound the villagers together were therefore comparatively weak, and the habit of joint action less highly developed. Instead of a committee of the principal *mirasdars*, there was a village headman who collected the state's dues, sometimes in his capacity as a state servant, sometimes as the renter who had leased the village from the amildar. In either case he dealt separately with each individual cultivator, and each cultivator's dues were assessed and paid in cash. Read was a man of extraordinary integrity and industry. He studied the history and the details of the land revenue system in force in his district, and observed its effect on the cultivators. The scheme which he devised for its reform based itself on existing practice and deviated but little from the lines marked out by the best Indian administrators in dealing with such tracts. He determined to dispense with all renters and middlemen, and to deal direct with the individual cultivator through his own servants, among whom he included the village accountant and the village headman. To relieve the cultivator from all uncertainty, to give him confidence, and to protect his improvements, he wished to fix the land revenue due from each field once for all in terms of money, and to leave the cultivator free to take up or relinquish such fields as he chose. For this purpose a detailed survey field by field was necessary, and such a survey was undertaken and carried through.[1] Read actually published a proclamation outlining his scheme of land revenue administration, and promising the cultivators an assessment fixed in perpetuity. His proclamation was neither confirmed nor cancelled by superior authority. He was left in the district and tried to give effect to his plan. But he had made certain miscalculations. In proposing to fix a money assessment in perpetuity he had ignored the chance of a permanent change in the price of grain. In fact the fall in the price of grain during the next fifty years would have converted even a moderate money assessment into an intolerable burden. But the standard of assessment which Read took for his guidance was far too high for the success of his scheme; he took into consideration the theoretic claim of the state, which in this district was usually about half the crop, and the actual collections made by Tipu; he aimed at fixing rates that would be a little below the average collections made by Tipu. But by discovering concealed cultivation and improving the machinery of collection he actually drew from the country as much as Tipu and his officers had drawn to prepare for war and to satisfy private greed. To maintain taxation at such a level would have been a fatal obstacle to improvement, and,

[1] Arbuthnot, *Selections*, pp. xxxix–xl; cf. Munro to his father, 21 September, 1798, *ap.* Gleig, *Munro*, 1, 204.

even if improvement had been no object, it was simply impossible to collect such an assessment in bad seasons from cultivators who had no capital. Again, the agency which Read had at his disposal was neither sufficiently trustworthy, nor sufficiently experienced, to make a survey which could be accepted as final. The assessment was very unequal, and required to be revised as mistakes came to light. The result was that the plan of a fixed assessment was never rigidly adhered to. Remissions had to be allowed on account of poverty, loss of crops, loss of cattle, death of working members of the family, and such like reasons. Nor did Read succeed in fulfilling his intention to protect the cultivator's improvements and give him full freedom to relinquish the land he did not want. Half a century had to elapse before the obvious wisdom of Read's ideas could overcome the bad traditions of the revenue administration.

But though Read's plan could not be carried into effect in its entirety, it was worked in a modified form and gave good results. Among Read's assistants was another soldier, Thomas Munro, who was Read's equal in industry and integrity, and had besides a clear head and a reflective disposition. After the fall of Seringapatam, Munro was transferred to the newly annexed district of Kanara to take charge of the land revenue administration there. Kanara was in many respects very unlike the Baramahal, but the native land revenue system had been even more definitely ryotwari. A money assessment had been fixed on each holding centuries before and, though extra assessments had been superimposed upon this, the original assessment was still known and recorded. Munro was thus confirmed in the belief that the ryotwari system was the indigenous system of South India, and therefore presumably the system best suited to the needs of the country. Under his direction it gave good results in Kanara. There, too, Munro found surviving a strong sense of private property in land, of which he had seen no trace in the Baramahal. He traced the existence of this sense of property to the original low level of the land assessment. He held that the development of this sense of property was the only road to the improvement of the country. He argued that it could not exist where, as in the Baramahal and through-out the Carnatic districts, the assessment was so high as to swallow up the whole of the economic rent, and thus became a steady advocate of a policy of lowering the assessment. But he held that it was for government to decide whether the standard of assessment should be lowered to promote improvement, and that his duty as collector was to be guided by the standard set up by previous rulers, taking care only to see that his demand was not so high as to discourage the cultivator or encroach upon his stock, and thereby occasion a future deterioration of the revenue. Acting on this principle, he allowed at once a small remission on his own responsibility, and recommended government to grant a further remission later, though he gave reason to believe that the government's demand in Kanara was lower than that usual on the east coast.[1]

From Kanara, Munro was transferred in 1800 to the Deccan districts newly ceded by Hyderabad. These districts were overrun by poligars and extraordinarily lawless, but otherwise conditions were not unlike those with which Munro had been familiar in the Baramahal. The ryotwari system was clearly applicable. Starting with four surveyors, and training his men as he went along, Munro surveyed and assessed the tract field by field. As elsewhere the standard assessment fixed was intended to be a little below the average actual collections made under the native rulers. But the tract had suffered from a decade of anarchy under the Nizam, and Munro won the Board of Revenue's applause by the patience with which he nursed its revenue, keeping the demand low at first and raising it gradually to the standard as the ryots accumulated stock, gained confidence, and extended their cultivation.[2] Munro himself was not wholly satisfied. He still held that a general lowering of the standard of the assessment was the crying need of the country, and he was alarmed by the pressure from above for increased revenue. He obeyed this pressure, but when he left the district in 1807 he put on record a recommendation for a 25 per cent. reduction in the standard assessment.

In 1799 Tanjore and Coimbatore, and in 1801 Malabar and the territory of the nawab of Arcot, were annexed to the Madras Presidency. The ryotwari system of management was as a rule found easily applicable, but in some tracts, notably in Tanjore, the village organisation resembled that which Place had found in the jagir, and village settlements were customary. But the Board of Revenue was at this time much impressed by the tyranny exercised by the principal inhabitants under the village settlements. Preference was therefore given to the ryotwari system, and in 1805 it was at least nominally in force in all these districts, and surveys had been or were being carried out in most of them. Many of the collectors of districts had been trained under Read or Munro, but not all of them showed equal discretion in adapting the system to the circumstances of their districts. In Malabar, Macleod provoked a fresh outbreak of rebellion by trying to raise the land assessment nearer to the standard recognised on the east coast, ignoring the peculiar history of Malabar where the land tax was an innovation introduced after the Mysore conquest.[3] In South Arcot the Board of Revenue supported the collector in demanding a share in the crop which the government later condemned as "excessive beyond measure and we hope beyond example

---

[1] Cf. Munro to Cockburn, 7 October, 1800, and to Read, 16 June, 1801, ap. Gleig, Munro, I, 288, and III, 161.

[2] Cf. Munro to Board of Revenue, 30 November, 1806, and 15 August, 1807, ap. Rev. and Jud. Sel. I, 94 sqq., and 115 sqq.

[3] Logan, Malabar Manual, p. 540.

in other parts of the Company's territory". Nowhere was it found possible to give full effect to Read's original plan. Annual settlements had everywhere to be made not only because cultivation extended and shrank with the rainfall, but because the survey assessment could only be treated as a maximum. Collectors had to exercise their discretion freely in granting remissions in view of the poverty of the cultivator or the failure of his crop. Still the system did work. If the state demand was not rigidly fixed the collector had a standard for his guidance in making the annual settlement. The cultivator at least knew his maximum liability before he began to sow, and later on he could get a bill under the collector's signature showing the details of the demand upon him for the year. It was thus easier for him to distinguish between authorised and unauthorised exactions, and to explain his grievance when he had been wronged. Above all, the system had in itself the seed of improvement. The government and the collector felt a direct responsibility for all that was done or left undone in the assessment and collection of the land revenue. They were therefore impelled to reform abuses rather than to treat them as inevitable. The collectors were brought into close touch with the affairs of the village. They learnt to know something of the cultivator's needs, his rights, and the wrongs he suffered. They had to make frequent reports to the Board of Revenue, and a store of experience and information thus accumulated steadily year after year.

Where the ryotwari system was in force, civil and criminal justice usually continued to be administered much as it had been under the native rulers, the collector taking the place of the amildar. But the authority of poligars and *kavalgars* in police matters was no longer recognised, and the fees formerly paid to them were claimed by government. Reliance was placed instead on the village headman and the village watcher, who was restored to his emoluments where these had been encroached upon by the *kavalgar*. The work that could not be done by village police was entrusted to the collector's revenue subordinates assisted where necessary by armed irregulars locally levied. This concentration of all authority in the collector's hands was useful not only in enabling him to overawe poligars and protect the cultivator against their retainers, but also because it made it easier to brush aside a rank growth of inconvenient customs such as that by which the same village office might be shared among different members of a family.

But before Place, Read, and Munro had had time to show what could be done by working along the lines of indigenous systems, the Bengal Government was pressing for the introduction into Madras of the exotic revenue and judicial systems it had recently planted in Bengal.[1] The Madras Government wished to move slowly, but in 1798 the governor-general, Lord Wellesley, ordered the Madras

---

[1] Malcolm to Lord Hobart, *ap.* Kaye, *Malcolm*, I, 176; and *Wellesley Despatches*, II, 121.

Government to introduce the Bengal system without delay. The Board of Revenue was accordingly asked to report how this could be done. Now one main object of the Bengal Permanent Settlement had been to promote the cultivation of the land. In Bengal almost the whole country was in the possession of great zamindars whose position bore at least a superficial resemblance to that of English landlords. It was therefore possible to suppose that the object in view could be attained by giving them a guarantee against any future enhancement of the state's demand from the land. But there were no zamindars in the greater part of the territories then included in the presidency of Madras. Even in the Northern Sarkars hardly half, and that not the richer half, was in their possession. Elsewhere there were only a few unimportant poligars. It was evidently good policy to confirm the zamindars and poligars in their existing possessions if that would induce them to acquiesce in the extinction of their military power. But there was nothing to suggest that they would make good landlords, or that it was desirable to extend their control over neighbouring villages. Neither in the jagir nor in the Baramahal was there any landlord class or any other class which seemed capable of supplying good landlords. To achieve the object in view, to encourage the improvement and extension of cultivation, there was no need to set landlords over independent villages. The end could more easily be attained either by making a permanent settlement with each village or by fixing a moderate assessment on each field. But the Board of Revenue was very anxious to get rid of the uncertainties of the existing system as soon as possible. It still felt itself to be groping hopelessly in the dark, and it doubted whether its officers could ever acquire sufficient knowledge to enable them to deal successfully with the villages. It was therefore glad to follow the beaten path and to rid itself of responsibility by a zamindari settlement.[1] To meet the difficulty caused by the non-existence of zamindars the board proposed the simple expedient of grouping villages to form estates of convenient size, and selling them by auction to the highest bidder. The original object of the Permanent Settlement had almost dropped out of view. No one can seriously have supposed that the purchasers would or could promote the improvement or extension of cultivation. The argument pressed by the champions of the Permanent Settlement in Madras was that it would relieve government of the duty of assessing and collecting the land revenue, a duty which government officers were judged incompetent to perform. The Madras Government accepted the board's proposals, and in 1800 it received authority from Bengal to effect a permanent settlement on those lines throughout the presidency. In the following year the court of directors concurred, but warned the Madras Government that the work should be done well rather than quickly, and that the military establishments

---

[1] Cf. Minute of the Board of Revenue, *ap.* Kaye, *Administration*, p. 225.

of the zamindars and the spirit of insubordination should first be suppressed.[1] A special commission was appointed in 1802 and between 1802 and 1804 the Northern Sarkars, the jagir, the Baramahal, and Dindigul were settled on the lines prescribed. The zamindars were forbidden to keep up a military establishment, and were deprived of their police authority and their control over the miscellaneous sources of revenue. They were declared to be proprietors of their estates with the cultivators for their tenants. They were given the power of distraint and were authorised to collect rent at the rates which prevailed in the year preceding the Permanent Settlement. In return they were required to pay yearly a *peshkash* fixed in perpetuity; if the *peshkash* fell into arrears their estate could be attached and sold. The *peshkash* was usually calculated to be the equivalent of one-third of the gross produce, or two-thirds of the gross rental, of the estate; but deviations from the standard were allowed in special cases.

Simultaneously with the introduction of the zamindari system in each district came a new judicial system and a code of regulations modelled on those of Bengal. The collector ceased to exercise civil or criminal jurisdiction or to be concerned with the police. A *zillah* (or district) judge was appointed with a jurisdiction in all civil cases. Attached to him was a native commissioner empowered to try and decide petty suits. Appeals lay from the *zillah* judge to a provincial court. Serious criminal cases were tried by judges of this court touring as a court of circuit. The *zillah* judge was also district magistrate, and in this capacity he controlled the new police force of *thanadars* and *darogas* who were posted at selected stations throughout the district, the village watchmen being put under their authority. The new courts and the new code of regulations were intended to protect the cultivator's existing rights against the landlord whom the zamindari settlement had set over him. But the courts were fettered by British rules of procedure and evidence, and litigation was tedious and costly. Ignorant, illiterate, and poverty-stricken cultivators could rarely venture to challenge their landlords' proceedings before an unfamiliar and distant authority. The protection given them by the courts was in fact little more than an illusion.[2]

The principles of the permanent zamindari settlement were at the same time applied in dealing with the *palayams* of the Carnatic. The armed force which the Carnatic poligar had at his disposal was often formidable, the *peshkash* due from him was small, and it was rarely paid except under duress. By the treaty of 1792 Lord Cornwallis had made the Company responsible for the collection of the *peshkash*; but the nawab's sovereignty continued, and the Madras Government

---

[1] General letter from England, 11 February, 1801, *ap. Rev. and Jud. Sel.* 1, 601.
[2] Report of Board of Revenue, 18 December, 1815, *idem*, II, 391; Bengal to Madras, 19 July, 1804 (*idem*, IV, 924); Gleig, *Munro*, I, 413 *sqq.*, especially Munro's letters to Cumming.

found themselves thwarted in their efforts to reduce the poligars to subordination. The court of directors insisted that the military power of the poligars must be suppressed and their *peshkash* raised to a level at which it would absorb the resources that had formerly been applied to secure the allegiance of hordes of armed retainers. It was impossible to give effect to these orders while a war with Mysore was in prospect; but after the fall of Seringapatam a military force was sent to overawe the poligars of Tinnevelly, who were particularly formidable and refractory. Most of the poligars chose to fight. Two severe campaigns and some executions and forfeitures were necessary before their spirit could be broken, but by the end of 1801 the work was done. A permanent settlement was then made with twenty-four poligars. Of the six forfeited estates, three were sold by auction and three went to reward poligars who had rendered service to the Company. Elsewhere less difficulty was experienced. Ramnad was in the Company's possession and the poligar of Sivaganga was under the district collector's influence. There was some trouble in Dindigul, and an expedition had to be sent to reduce the small poligars of Chittur; but the four great western poligars acquiesced in the arrangements proposed to them. In the Ceded Districts the poligars had defied the Nizam's officers, but they were quickly brought to order by Munro who had a military force at call. As in the Carnatic they were forbidden to maintain any armed force and were deprived of their police authority; and Munro further took the opportunity to fix definitely the rents which they were entitled to demand from the cultivators. The *peshkash* which they were required to pay was calculated to leave them sufficient to support their dignity.

Regarded as a measure designed to induce the existing zamindars and poligars to acquiesce in the loss of their military power and to become quiet subjects of the Company, the Madras zamindari settlement was on the whole a success. The *peshkash* fixed on the old zamindaris and *palayams* was usually paid punctually, and even when the collector found it necessary to attach or sell the estate, there was rarely any reason to fear a disturbance. But the scheme for creating new zamindaris had only bad results. The speculators who bought the newly-formed estates proved, as might have been expected, thoroughly unsatisfactory, whether they were regarded as landlords or as farmers of the land revenue. Some extorted what they could from the cultivators and defaulted, leaving government to recover the arrears from an impoverished estate; but what wrecked the scheme was less the character of the purchasers than the level at which the *peshkash* had been fixed. Though the standard set up left the proprietors only a narrow margin of profit, the tendency in Madras at this time was against leniency, and in calculating the actual *peshkash* the collectors were inclined to err in favour of government and to anticipate improvements which were long in coming. Few of the purchasers had the capital necessary to meet the loss in a bad year. From the first many of the newly-created estates in the jagir and the Baramahal began to fall into arrears. 1806–7 was a bad season. Many estates came to sale and the trouble spread even to the old zamindaris in the Northern Sarkars which had been assessed on more favourable terms. Bidders were few; and when estates began to lapse into government management, it was often found that the villages had deteriorated under the exactions of the late proprietor. Meanwhile the whole theory and practice of the Bengal system had come to be challenged, and men now doubted the wisdom of thrusting an exotic system on Madras where two indigenous systems had already been made to work tolerably, and seemed capable of being adapted to give still better results. In 1804 the court of directors again warned the Madras Government of the danger of concluding permanent settlements in haste. Munro and the assistants trained under him had by this time gained much influence, and Lord William Bentinck, who was governor of Madras from 1803 to 1807, was attracted by their doctrine. Further progress with the zamindari settlement was stayed; but, instead of working along the lines of the ryotwari system, the Board of Revenue in 1808 sought and obtained from Lord William Bentinck's successor permission to experiment again with village settlements.

The ryotwari system found its champion in Munro, whose experience had been gained in districts where the corporate life of the village was comparatively undeveloped, and the revenue officers had been in the habit of dealing with individual villagers rather than with the village as a whole. But the leading spirit in the Board of Revenue at this time was Hodgson. The district with which he was best acquainted was Tanjore, where the corporate life of the village was vigorous, and the leading *mirasdars* had been accustomed to settling with the revenue officers on behalf of the village. Hodgson succeeded in persuading his colleagues that the village system might be made the foundation of a satisfactory land revenue system for the whole presidency. The average produce or the average collections of each village could be estimated or calculated and a fair demand arrived at from those data. The right of collecting the government share of the crop could then be leased to the principal inhabitants at that sum for a term of years. Later a lease in perpetuity might be substituted for the temporary lease. Where there was no body of *mirasdars* accustomed to act on behalf of the village, the lease could be given to the village headman. It was true that at an earlier date the board had been impressed by the manner in which headmen and principal inhabitants had abused the powers which these village settlements gave them. But the new judicial system had in 1806 been extended to the ryotwari districts, and the oppressed could now seek protection from the courts. A variety of motives induced the board to prefer the village system to the ryotwari. Hodgson was influenced by the belief that it would keep alive and stimulate the habit of village self-government, a habit which the ryotwari system tended to destroy. He also realised that it was not only principal inhabitants who could be oppressive. All collectors were not Munros. Some were corrupt and many were lazy. The Indian agency at their command was by tradition high-handed, extortionate, and venal. Under a corrupt or slack collector the ryotwari system gave these men ample opportunities and government would share the discredit of their misdeeds. The board also hoped for some saving in expenditure under the village lease system, since the task of assessing and collecting the dues of each cultivator would be left to the villagers.

But the decisive motive seems to have been the fear of the newly-established courts of judicature. It appeared a hopeless task to train the petty agents of government, long accustomed to be a law unto themselves, to observe the elaborate procedure laid down in an unfamiliar code. It was doubtful whether the provisions of a code drawn up *à priori* would prove workable when applied to existing conditions, and there was reason to fear that an inexperienced judicature would show little respect for the practical necessities of administration. The board, therefore, thought it desirable to throw the responsibility for the apportionment and the collection of the land revenue on to the villagers, and the government accepted the board's view.[1]

Accordingly, in 1808–9 the collectors of most districts were required to lease out all villages not included in a permanently settled estate to the principal inhabitants or headmen for a term of years. The lease amounts were to be fixed with reference to the actual collections of the past, with a view to maintaining the land revenue at the level then reached. Full effect could not be given to the board's scheme, because many villages feared to bind themselves to pay a fixed sum for three years. They had little credit, and the risk of loss in a bad year far outweighed the hope of gain in a good. Even where the leases were accepted, the scheme did not always work smoothly. In some villages the lessees were too weak to collect their dues. Elsewhere they were strong enough to throw an unfair share of the burden on to their weaker neighbours. But the most serious obstacle to the success of the scheme was the same as that which had already upset Read's plan for a permanent ryotwari settlement, and wrecked the permanent zamindari settlement. The state demand had been fixed too high to be collected every year without regard to the state of the season and the circumstances of the individual cultivator. Munro knew this, and had in 1807 submitted a new scheme for a permanent ryotwari settlement, the essential feature in which was a reduction of 25 per cent.

[1] Revenue letter from Madras, 24 October, 1808, *ap. Rev. and Jud. Sel.* i, 475; Minute of Board of Revenue, 5 January, 1818, *ap.* Kaye, *Administration*, p. 222.

in the survey assessment. Government ruled out the possibility of such a reduction, and preferred the board's village lease scheme, not seeing that a reduction was more necessary under this scheme than under the ryotwari system. For without a general reduction seasonal remissions could not be dispensed with, and, except under the ryotwari system of dealing separately with each cultivator, it was rarely possible for the revenue authorities to ensure that the remissions given were such as the season required or that they reached the cultivator who stood in need of them.

Though the reports of the district collectors on the working of the village leases were generally unfavourable, the government decided to try new leases for a period of ten years, and even proposed that they should be made perpetual;[1] but the court of directors had prohibited the conclusion of any arrangement in perpetuity without the court's specific sanction. Reductions were made in the lease amounts demanded, but they were generally inadequate. It was still found necessary to allow remissions in bad seasons and a door was opened for fraud. Having been relieved of the duty of a detailed scrutiny of the village accounts, which the ryotwari system had imposed on them, the collector and his staff were relapsing into their former state of ignorance, and the village accountants found themselves masters of the situation.

But hardly had the ten-year leases begun to run when the affairs of the Madras Presidency were reviewed in the fifth report of the Select Committee of the House of Commons. The committee was impressed by the doctrine and achievements of Munro and his school. They doubted the wisdom of forcing zamindars on districts where no zamindars were found. They saw that Munro had made his system work smoothly and bring in an increasing revenue in regions so disturbed, so distant, and so dissimilar as Kanara and the Ceded Districts. They did not consider that the theoretic advantages claimed for the village lease system justified the substitution of that experiment for a system which had given good results under trial. They saw that a sound land revenue system was the chief need of South India, and concluded that, if it was incompatible with the new judicial system, it was the latter and not the former that should be modified.

The report was thus decisively in favour of the ryotwari system and Munro henceforward had the ear of the court of directors and made use of this advantage to remodel the Madras administrative system in accordance with his own ideas.

Though the policy of forcing Cornwallis's zamindari settlement upon Madras had been discredited since 1804, the Cornwallis judicial system had been allowed to establish itself and the ideas of the Cornwallis school had still numerous and influential champions. To prevent oppression, reliance was placed on codes and courts adminis-

[1] Revenue letter from Madras, 5 March, 1813, *ap. Rev. and Jud. Sel.* I, 556.

tering law on British lines. Magisterial and police work could best be supervised by a judicial officer both because of his legal knowledge and because he would act as a check on the executive activities of the revenue department. The administration of justice was to be kept as far as possible in the hands of British officers, Indian agency being assumed to be incorrigibly untrustworthy. Since the new judicial courts had been allowed to banish the ryotwari system, these ideas had begun to dominate the Madras administration. Munro criticised them with great effect. The men who stood in need of protection were poor and illiterate cultivators, accustomed to acquiesce in oppression. They would never seek, nor, if they did seek, could they obtain, protection from the complicated and costly procedure of strange and distant courts. Our British judges had not and could not through their court work acquire a real knowledge of the life of the villages which they had no occasion or leisure to visit. They were therefore unfit to be magistrates or to control the police. The Company could not supply British judges in numbers adequate to the business arising in so wide and populous a country. If it could the expense would be ruinous. Further, the systematic exclusion of Indians from all offices of trust was a cruel policy calculated to destroy all vestiges of self-respect and to crush the springs of improvement.[1]

Munro's own view was that the incidence of the land revenue more than anything else decided the cultivator's fortune. The collector should, therefore, take direct responsibility for its assessment and collection. To enable him to fulfil his responsibility, and because his revenue duties gave him an intimate knowledge of the life of the people, magisterial power and the control of the police should be concentrated in his hands. This was the native system, and in governing the country we should make the greatest possible use of native institutions and native agency. Even in apportioning the land revenue the collectors should aim at ascertaining and acting upon the genuine opinion of the villages, and for determining civil disputes the village *panchayat* should be kept active. Such disputes as could not be dealt with by the *panchayat* should go in the first instance before Indian judges, little but the appellate work and the trial of grave criminal cases being reserved for British judges.

This view was now to prevail. In 1812 the Madras Government received orders to revert to the ryotwari system, and in 1814 the court of directors required them to make certain other administrative changes which went a long way towards meeting Munro's views. Munro himself was sent out as a special commissioner to see that the orders were carried out, and in 1816 the Madras Government sanctioned a series of regulations giving effect to the changes proposed. The office of district magistrate and the control of the police were transferred from the *zillah* judge to the collector. The new police

[1] Cf. Judicial letter to Madras, 29 April, 1814, *ap. Rev. and Jud. Sel.* II, 236–56.

force of *darogas* and *thanadars* was disbanded, and the police work was left to be carried out by the village watchmen and the collector's revenue servants. Native district *munsiffs*, with jurisdiction to decide civil suits of value up to 200 rupees, were appointed in adequate numbers and stationed at convenient centres; and a suitable remuneration was attached to the office. Power was given to village headmen to try petty civil suits and to summon village *panchayats* which were authorised to determine all suits without limit of value if the parties agreed to submit to their jurisdiction. In 1817 the Board of Control concurred with the court of directors in pronouncing the creation of artificial zamindars highly inexpedient. Thus all idea of extending the zamindari system was finally abandoned, and in 1818 the Board of Revenue issued instructions to the collectors for the introduction of a revised ryotwari system. This was admittedly based on that of Read and Munro, and such changes as were introduced were not in practice important. It had been proposed to give the force of law to these instructions by embodying them in a regulation, but Munro advised against this in pursuance of his policy of reserving for government the power of controlling the collector's discretion and limiting the opportunities for the interference of the courts.[1]

Looking back across the interval traversed in this chapter we see that by the year 1818 the administration of the Madras Presidency had come to be quite unlike anything that could be found in the South India of 1786. The government possessed a military force which was without any external rival and their territories were all but completely immune from invasion. In all districts they had agents who were capable of supplying information and could be trusted to carry out the instructions sent them. No inferior authority was in a position to question their orders. The zamindars and poligars had been reduced to subordination and their military organisation broken up. This last was a most beneficial change. It was estimated that at the end of the eighteenth century the southern poligars alone maintained 100,000 armed retainers, who were employed in resisting the central power, in making war upon one another, and in plundering peaceable cultivators. By 1818 the poligars' retainers were hardly anywhere a serious menace. Most of them had settled down to cultivate the land in earnest. Those who belonged to criminal tribes could not forsake their traditions so readily, but their activities were no longer public and unrestrained. Though no regular police force was in existence, the military power of the government made it easy for the collector to maintain order by means of his revenue servants and the village watchmen. Regular judicial courts had been set up and were freely resorted to by those who could afford the cost of litigation. Indeed so popular were these innovations that Munro failed in his attempt to give new life to the village *panchayat*, which

[1] Cf. Baden-Powell, *Land Systems*, III, 32.

could hardly survive in competition with professional lawyers and judges. The uncertainties of the land revenue system continued but had become less alarming. In many districts there was a fixed maximum assessment on record. The cultivators no longer ran the risk of being handed over to a stranger who had rented a district for a short term of years and was anxious to see what could be made out of it in the time allowed him. The collector was now almost as free from legal restraint as the renter had been. But he was influenced by longer views and feared the future effect of his current demands. And even where the collector was too severe, there was a chance of redress. As early as 1804 the government had overridden the Board of Revenue and removed a collector whose assessments were injudiciously high. But with the strengthening of the administration had come a great increase in the efficiency of the assessing and collecting agency. This had its danger, since the recognised standard of assessment was still that which had been sanctioned by the practice of Indian rulers. If the proportion of the annual crop actually taken by the state agents was not higher than it had been in 1786, certainly it was usually too high to allow the cultivator to accumulate stock. There was a persistent pressure for revenue to meet the heavy military and administrative expenses of the presidency, and no attention had been paid to Munro's plea for a substantial reduction in the standard assessment. Turning to the miscellaneous sources of revenue we find that some of the most vexatious and unprofitable imposts had been swept away but others were unnecessarily retained. The inland transit duties had been replaced by the hardly less objectionable town duties. The new salt monopoly was a far more powerful instrument for raising money than the medley of systems which it replaced, and the new stamp tax produced very considerable sums. The Company's subjects suffered less from vexatious methods of taxation but more money was drawn from them.

The subjugation of the poligars, the establishment of judicial courts, and the improvement of the revenue system had absorbed the chief of the government's energy. Little thought or money could be spared for other matters. It was during our period that India was converted from an exporter to an importer of cotton cloth. A French missionary has left us a vivid description of the ruin which that revolution brought upon the cloth weavers of South India, but this aspect of the matter hardly attracted the attention of the Madras Government. Information was gathered about the prevalence of slavery in the Tamil country and on the west coast, but no action was taken. It was not till 1822 that an enquiry into the state of education was set on foot. Munro seems to have been almost the only Madras official who had considered the advisability of employing Indian officers in positions of trust. Famines were dealt with when they came by opening relief works and granting remissions, but the government had not yet learnt to regard them as recurring visitations against whose coming preparations should be made in advance. Even Munro supposed that they could only arise from war or gross misgovernment, and that there was never likely to be a succession of crop failures bad enough to produce a famine. Some collectors, notably Place in Chingleput, had shown great activity in repairing the irrigation works; and for this purpose, and for the improvement of the roads, the nucleus of a public works organisation had been brought into being. But its activities were narrowly restricted, because no adequate funds were placed at its disposal. Much less was there any serious thought of providing money for the construction of great new irrigation works, though the existence of so many ancient works was recognised as a challenge inviting honourable emulation.

CHAPTER XXVIII

AFGHANISTAN, RUSSIA AND PERSIA

THE student of Indian history hardly needs the caution that the British India of the earlier part of the nineteenth century was vastly different in size and in environment from that of to-day. The boundary to the north-west was the Satlej for but a very short distance; Bahawalpur and the desert bordering Rajputana lay further south; whilst beyond the frontier were two great states, of one of which at least little was known, the Panjab and Sind. The frontier problems were necessarily different from those of our own time, different and much more important. In the eighteenth century the French had been the great rivals of the English in the East; but their place was now taken by Russia, a power which had natural connections with Central Asia, and one whose mission and intentions were dreaded and much misunderstood for the rest of the century. It is one of the few claims to statesmanship which can be urged on behalf of Auckland that he refused to be frightened of Russia, and that almost alone of the men of his time he took a moderate view of what she could do that might harm the Indian Empire.

The modern kingdom of Kabul came into existence on the break up of the great empire of Nadir Shah, the Persian. That famous adventurer himself came from Khorassan and when he was, perhaps owing to Persian jealousy of the Afghans, assassinated in 1747 Ahmad Khan of the Abdali tribe, chief of the sacred Sadozai clan, the most important in Afghanistan, was chosen king by the revolting nation. He changed the name of his tribe from Abdali to Durani, and after the change was always known as Ahmad Shah Durani. Having been crowned at Kandahar he proceeded to build up a state, understanding, what it would have been well if the English had remembered, that he who would maintain any hold upon the Afghans must keep them busy with constant warfare. He resolved that wherever there were Afghans there should his rule extend, and so when he died in 1773 he left his family firmly established in a kingdom which, as defined by Ferrier, was bounded on the north by the Oxus and the mountains of Kafaristan; on the south by the sea of Oman; on the east by the mountains of Tibet, the Satlej, and the Indus; and on the west by Khorassan, Persia, and Kirman; and if this empire was to some extent what Sir Henry Maine would have called a tributary empire, there was present a strong national feeling which would keep the centre at any rate vigorous and independent.

Ahmad Shah left eight sons, of whom he had designated the second, Taimur Mirza, as his successor. He was governing Herat when his father died, and his elder brother, Sulaiman Mirza, at once proclaimed himself king at Kandahar. Sulaiman had married the daughter of Shah Wali Khan, wazir of Ahmad Shah, and this gave him confidence. Shah Wali Khan, however, when Taimur approached, at once deserted to him, and together with others of his party was promptly executed. Sulaiman finding himself without sufficient support fled to India. Taimur was now crowned, and having learned to distrust the Duranis, though one himself, he decided to move the seat of government from Kandahar, their city, to Kabul. Kandahar was placed under his son, Mahmud Mirza, and his general policy is described as one designed to curb the powers of the tribal chiefs. Near the throne was Payandah Khan, the chief of the Barakzai tribe, whose father had given way when Ahmad Shah was chosen king.

But Taimur though able was indolent, and his vast dominions were, perhaps, too great a tax upon his energy. He had great difficulty in crushing a revolt in Khorassan, which had hitherto acknowledged the overlordship of Afghanistan, and he exercised but nominal control over Balkh and Akhshah. In Sind he was even less successful. Ahmad Shah had had difficulties in that country and had given the title of Amir of Sind to one of the chiefs. This man, the head of the Kalora tribe, was attacked in 1779 by Mir Fath 'Ali Khan, the head of the rival tribe, the Talpura. Taimur, on being appealed to, wasted the country round Bahawalpur and restored the Kalora amir, but the conflict began again when he left the province; his generals were unable to reduce the Talpuras, who were secretly helped by the khan of Kalat, and in the end Mir Fath 'Ali Khan was made governor of Sind on promising tribute. This was in 1786. Three years later he threw off his allegiance and Sind was independent when Taimur died in 1793. Afghanistan then consisted of the principalities of Kashmir, Lahore, Peshawar, Kabul, Balkh, Kulu, Kandahar, Multan, and Herat. Kalat, Balochistan, and Persian Khorassan acknowledged overlordship, and there was still a claim on Sind though, as has been said, tribute had not been paid for some years.

As Taimur left twenty-three sons there was ample scope for ambition; especially as they were born of many different mothers and divided, therefore, into corresponding groups. Nearly all the mothers were Afghans, but three princes were by a great-granddaughter of Nadir Shah, and two were by a Moghul princess whom Taimur had married. Several of the sons were governors of provinces; Humayun Mirza was at Kandahar, and Mahmud Mirza, the second son, who supported his elder brother, was at Herat. Abbas Mirza, the fourth, was at Peshawar, and seemed the most popular candidate for the throne. Zaman Mirza, the fifth, who actually secured it, had on his side Payandah Khan, the chief of the Barakzais. Shuja-ul-Mulk was at Ghazni, and Kohan Dil was in Kashmir. But the outstanding factor in the situation was the influence of Payandah Khan, because to him and to the Barakzais the people looked to maintain their privileges as against their kings. When, therefore, he pronounced for Zaman Mirza he drew with him the chief Afghan families and, what was not to be expected, the mercenary Kizilbashis of Kabul, and decided the preliminary election.

Zaman Shah had constant difficulties in the Panjab east of the Indus, although he placed Lahore under Ranjit Singh, formally, in 1799; but whenever he came down to Peshawar trouble broke out in Afghanistan, most of it of his own making. He had chosen his wazir badly and the result was the long and tragic conflict between the Durani chiefs, and of them principally the Barakzais and the royal house or Sadozais, which continued for the next half century.

Payandah Khan, the head of the Barakzais, took part in a conspiracy in favour of Shuja-ul-Mulk, Zaman's brother, and with other important men was executed in 1799. This was the period of Zaman Shah's glory when his descent upon India, improbable as it seems now, was considered as a national peril by the English authorities. Indeed it was to prevent any such movement that they turned anxiously towards Persia, knowing that the Rohillas had invited Zaman Shah to come in 1796 and fearing combinations of the Indian Muhammadans in his favour. Zaman Shah had, however, work enough at home. The Barakzai brothers, the sons of Payandah Khan, were no less than twenty-one in number and the eldest, Fath Khan—the kingmaker—fled into Khorassan, joined Prince Mahmud Mirza there and persuaded him to revolt. The result was that Zaman Shah, who was troubled with risings in Peshawar and Kashmir at the same time, was overthrown and blinded. He fled to Herat and later to India where he lived, a striking and pathetic figure, for many years.

Mahmud Shah who thus became the monarch of Afghanistan (1800) soon sank into ease and indifference, forgetting that the throne was easier to get than to keep. He sent his son Kamran Mirza to take Peshawar from Shuja Mirza, whom Zaman Shah had made governor, and who had now proclaimed himself king. In 1801 Shuja Mirza was defeated by Fath Khan when marching on Kabul, and thus Mahmud secured Peshawar, though he had the mortification of knowing that it was only by the will of the all-powerful Barakzai that he remained on the throne at all. A revolt of the Ghilzais, a turbulent tribe, was suppressed in 1801. But a peaceful prince could never hold Afghanistan, and the Kizilbashis on whom Mahmud relied were unpopular as Shias; the annexation of Khorassan by the Persians in 1802 weakened him; and in 1803 Shuja Mirza defeated his army and secured the throne.

Shah Shuja was merciful and yet always unpopular. He loved pomp, and throughout the course of his long life, which cost the English so dear, he showed himself singularly incapable either of understanding his own people or of attaching them to him. His great difficulty, that of every Afghan monarch, was with the powerful chieftains. He made the mistake of pardoning without trusting the great Barakzai, Fath Khan, with the result that Fath Khan stirred up Prince Kaysar, son of Zaman Shah, who had been made governor of Kandahar, but who was easily persuaded to try for more. This revolt was crushed with some difficulty, Prince Kaysar being forgiven and Fath Khan flying to Kamran Mirza, the restless son of Mahmud, at Herat. And though Sind was reduced to obedience in 1805, new revolts followed, Dost Muhammad Khan, afterwards so famous, aiding his brother Fath Khan and appearing for the first time prominently. Things, however, looked a little brighter in 1808, though there was no hope of recovering the southern provinces; the Barakzais had been checked if not conquered.

Up to the day of the Treaty of Tilsit the attention of the English in India had had perforce to be concentrated on the Marathas, and it was not till the early months of 1818 that the power of the confederacy was broken by Lord Hastings. But the direction that things were taking was well understood and the people of Sind as well as the Sikhs were aware that they would both sooner or later come under British rule unless they made a very strong attempt to prevent it. This steady policy of concentration and annexation was interrupted, but not for long, by the course of western events. The Persians were not really strong enough to threaten India, but memories are long in the East; Nadir Shah had been murdered in 1747, but a movement eastward might restore some of the territory that had been lost since his day. In 1799 Lord Wellesley sent Malcolm, one of the ablest men of his time, to Fath 'Ali Shah who had been on the throne at Teheran for about a year; and Malcolm arranged the two famous treaties signed on 28 January, 1801.[1] The first was commercial and provided for the establishment of factories in Persia; it also spoke of the cession of islands in the Persian Gulf to the East India Company. The second was political, and was directed against the aggressions of Afghanistan and the extension of French influence in Persia. But events were more powerful than treaties. Georgia was annexed by Russia in 1801, and the proclamations of the Russians indicated further advances. The Persians suffered heavily in Armenia in 1804, and the shah appealed to the French for help in 1805, as England and Russia were for the moment on the same side. Hence we get French influence and French officers in Teheran. Very little resulted of a positive kind, for the Treaty of Tilsit in 1807 changed the whole position and France and Russia were now in alliance.

The government of Bengal had not cared much for Malcolm's treaties, but its sense of the importance of the states on the frontier to the west had increased, especially as Afghanistan became more

[1] Aitchison, *op. cit.* XII, 38.

and more distracted. Their policy was represented by a series of missions, those of Seton to Sind, Metcalfe to the Sikhs, Elphinstone to Afghanistan, and Malcolm once more to Persia.

As Malcolm set out from Bombay Sir Harford Jones reached India on a mission from the court of St James's to Teheran. Finding how things were, he wisely waited till Malcolm had failed to oust the French and then started. He was more successful than his predecessor, reaching Teheran late in 1808 and satisfactorily combating French influence; helped no doubt by the fact that the Russians remained in Georgia, and by the certainty that if any expedition came through Persia to India it would be Persia that would suffer first. By the treaty of 12 March, 1809,[1] the shah promised that he would not allow any European force whatsoever to pass through Persia towards either India or its ports. If India were attacked by Afghanistan or any other power the shah would help, and if Persia were attacked by a European power the English would provide either troops or a subsidy and a loan of officers. The projected attack on the Island of Karrak—a foolish business—was disowned. From this time the relations with Persia were chiefly in the hands of the Foreign Office. The only treaty that needs notice in a brief summary is that of Teheran concluded in 1814 which, *inter alia*, in return for a promise of protection, bound the Persians to attack the Afghans if they invaded India.[2]

Meanwhile the missions to the Sikhs and the Afghans had also set out. Elphinstone's object was to try and get the help of the Afghans against the French, and if necessary against the Persians, but action was to be limited to the occasion and no troops were to be promised. It came to very little and Elphinstone never got further than Peshawar. A useless treaty against an imaginary Franco-Persian combination was made on 17 June, 1809,[3] but by that time Shah Shuja had trouble to face nearer home and the mission was hurriedly sent away.

While Shah Shuja lingered at Peshawar he sent his best army under Akram Khan into Kashmir where it was defeated. This was a fatal blow as news arrived that Mahmud Shah and Fath Khan had taken Kandahar. Shah Shuja was now defeated at Nimula near Gandammak (1809) and began his years of wandering intrigue. In 1812 he was a prisoner in Kashmir; later he was at Lahore, where Ranjit Singh took the great Durani diamond, the *Koh-i-nur*, from him, and made various promises of help which he did not intend to fulfil. After more adventures and much journeying he reached Ludhiana in 1816 and there he remained for the time under British protection.

Mahmud Shah owed everything to the Barakzais and for a time he left matters in the strong hand of Fath Khan, who in turn confided most of the governorships to his brothers, Herat only remaining in

---

[1] Aitchison, *op. cit.* XII, 46. [2] *Idem*, p. 54.
[3] *Idem*, XI, 336.

the hands of Firoz-ud-din, the brother of Mahmud Shah. His great helper now was his brother Dost Muhammad who, as the son of a Kizilbashi mother, was until his talents became known but little regarded by the Barakzais. Fath Khan asserted the Afghan supremacy over Sind and Balochistan. In alliance with Ranjit Singh he reconquered Kashmir, which had rebelled, and made his brother Muhammad Azim the governor there. But when he tried to avoid paying the promised reward to the Sikhs, Ranjit Singh seized Attock and defeated a force under Dost Muhammad.

Fath Khan, however, now entered on a disastrous undertaking. He resolved to lead an expedition to Khorassan to clear out the Persians there; his real motive doubtless was to obtain possession of Herat. Dost Muhammad managed by a stratagem to get hold of the city, killed some of its guards, and insulted the ladies of Firoz-ud-din's harem. This roused the feelings of their relatives to madness and Kamran Shah (son of Mahmud Shah) with the consent of his father seized Fath Khan, blinded him and finally hacked him to pieces with savage cruelty. This was in 1818. Dost Muhammad, who had fled to Kashmir, raising an army with the aid of Muhammad Azim Khan, marched against Kabul which was held by Jahangir the son of Kamran Shah. Mahmud Shah fled to Ghazni, and Dost Muhammad obtained possession of the capital by the treachery of Atta Muhammad, whom the Barakzais promptly blinded. Soon all the country was in Barakzai hands save Herat where were Shah Mahmud and Prince Kamran, who acknowledged the suzerainty of Persia. There Mahmud lived till 1829 when he died and was succeeded by Kamran.

Thus fell the empire of the Sadozais. But at first the Barakzais were too much divided to assert any claim for themselves. Dost Muhammad put forward Sultan 'Ali of the royal line. Muhammad Azim Khan brought forward Shah Shuja and later Ayyab Khan, another son of Taimur Shah. The foreign situation was serious and after a short time Ranjit Singh acquired the right bank of the Indus and the lordship over Peshawar, of which Sultan Muhammad (one of Muhammad Azim's brothers) was governor, and for which he paid tribute. The position at home seemed clearer, Muhammad Azim holding Kabul; Dost Muhammad, Ghazni; Pir Dil Khan, Kohan Dil Khan, and their brothers, Kandahar; Jabbar Khan, the Ghilzai country; and over all was the puppet king Ayyab Khan. But there were further struggles between the brothers and with Ranjit Singh, in the course of which Muhammad Azim Khan died broken-hearted in 1823 after Ranjit Singh's victory at Nawshahra. The leading feature of these confused struggles was the gradual rise to power of Dost Muhammad. He drove his brother, Sultan Muhammad, in 1826 back to Peshawar, secured Kabul, holding also Ghazni and later Jallalabad. In considering the future policy of England in the matter we have to remember that this man, no worse if little better than his contemporaries, had secured the throne by his own abilities; that Shah Shuja with all the advantages that descent could give had lost it; and that Dost Muhammad ruled for the next twelve years with vigour and ability. He was strong enough to defeat with ease Shah Shuja's attempt to recover the throne in 1834, and the struggles of that time revealed in Muhammad Akbar Khan a soldier who was to prove of great help to his father in years to come. He strengthened himself by crushing the Durani chieftains, and taking away their immunities. But he had to suffer one result of the treachery of his brothers which had been so manifest in the attempt of Shah Shuja. Peshawar was lost for ever to the Afghan state in 1834, and even the successful expedition of 1837, in which Dost Muhammad's son won the battle of Jamrud (1 May), failed to retake it.

Meanwhile Russia's Eastern ambitions, shown by the annexation of Georgia in 1801, led to a war between Russia and Persia in 1811, ending in the Treaty of Gulistan (1813). By this Russia gained very important additions to her territory on the shores of the Caspian on which Persia was to keep no more armed vessels. Persia hoped by the aid of English officers to strengthen her army, and a certain number were lent for the purpose; England thought that by the Treaty of Teheran (1814) she had made Persia into a buffer state for the defence of India. Neither result was, however, attained.

After the death of Alexander I, Shah Fath 'Ali was driven by the fanatical excitement of his subjects to go to war again, and hostilities began afresh in 1826. The Persians were very unfortunate; they were defeated by the Russians at Elizabethpol and elsewhere, and Paskievich crossed the Araxes, secured Erivan and Tabriz, and forced the shah to conclude the humiliating Treaty of Turkomanchai in 1828. From this time Russian influence grew in Persia, while English influence declined.

The strength of Russia received great addition in Europe by the conclusion of the Treaty of Adrianople. The opinion which regarded Russia as a danger to our Indian Empire found expression in much vague talk in England and the East; it is represented by the pamphlets (1829) of Sir De Lacy Evans, a man of restless and enquiring mind, which, however, secured at least one careful answer. Of similar tendency were the writings of Dr J. McNeill, afterwards minister at Teheran.

Lord William Bentinck left a valuable minute for Lord Auckland on the subject of Russia's designs. At this time she was working through Persia which seemed easier than herself trying to reduce Khiva and Bokhara. In 1831 Abbas Mirza with (it was thought) Russian encouragement planned an expedition against Khiva, and though this was abandoned for the moment he overran Khorassan by the end of 1832. The Khivan scheme with possible extensions was then taken up again, and in 1833 Muhammad Mirza, son of Abbas

Mirza, the heir apparent, led an army which in the first instance was to reduce Herat. However, in the autumn of this year Abbas Mirza died at Meshed, and Muhammad Mirza had to withdraw to secure his own recognition as heir to the throne. Scarcely had this been settled by the aid of England and Russia, when Fath 'Ali Shah died (1834) and Muhammad Mirza, who was now a close friend of Russia, became shah of Persia. Count Simonich, the Russian agent, became all powerful, and Ellis, who was soon to be succeeded by McNeill, the English representative, sent home disquieting reports of the young king's Eastern projects, including, as they did, not only the capture of Herat but that of Kandahar also. The whole matter was very complicated. The Russians were encouraging the idea of an expedition against Herat and the English were trying to curb the shah's ambition. Kamran, however, led on by Yar Muhammad, his minister, had given ground of offence, especially by asserting a claim to Sistan which Persia could not allow. The Barakzai sirdars of Kandahar, against Dost Muhammad's wish, intrigued with the shah, and the English at one time even thought of giving active assistance in training the amir of Afghanistan's army.

The situation in 1835 when Lord Auckland was appointed governor-general was thus very difficult. He had been chosen instead of Lord Heytesbury by Lord Melbourne's ministry, and was regarded as a safe man who would devote himself to the internal development of the country rather than to the pursuit of a vigorous foreign policy. But we must never forget in judging him that he was not his own master. He came out as the exponent of the views of others, and the study of his correspondence gives one the impression that, while he undoubtedly made mistakes, his own opinions, had he dared to assert them, were in the main more sensible and acute than those which were dictated from home or pressed upon him by men whom he trusted, too much in some cases, in India. The dispatch of 25 June, 1836, which was sent to him by the Secret Committee has sometimes been forgotten, and yet it was the guide of his conduct throughout, even perhaps when he questioned its wisdom. Attention was first drawn to it by Sir Auckland Colvin's *apologia* for his father.[1]

Dost Muhammad already had a grievance against the English for countenancing Shuja in 1834. Ranjit Singh, too, the ally of the English, still kept Peshawar; the wish of the Afghan king to recover this city is often considered unreasonable, but it was a natural object of Afghan ambition, and Dost Muhammad had sent a protest on the subject to Lord William Bentinck. It was no doubt this too which induced him to send his agent to St Petersburg, whose visit subsequently resulted in the mission of Vitkevich.

It must be remembered that we had an agent named Masson at Kabul in 1836, though his position was not publicly recognised.

[1] Sir Auckland Colvin, *John Russell Colvin*, p. 86.

Information that he gave is preserved in the India Office. Dost Muhammad, however, in May, 1836, sent a formal letter to Auckland congratulating him on his arrival, speaking frankly of his difficulties with the Sikhs, and saying that he would be guided by what Auckland advised.[1] In reply Auckland said that he hoped that Afghanistan would be a flourishing and united nation; he mentioned the project for the navigation of the Indus; and while he spoke of his intention to send some one to discuss commercial questions at Kabul he asserted his neutrality as to the Sikh dispute. The idea of a commercial mission (proposed by the Secret Committee) was not new. Kaye thinks it was suggested to Lord William Bentinck by Sir John Malcolm, and in February, 1836, it had been mentioned at Ludhiana. As long before as 1832 Alexander Burnes, an Indian officer of great intelligence and enterprise, had made a famous journey through Afghanistan and Persia, and on his return to India had been sent on a mission to the amirs of Sind whom he persuaded to agree to a survey of the Indus. While busy about this matter he was instructed to undertake the commercial mission to Afghanistan.

In November, 1836, Burnes started from Bombay on his mission. He passed through Sind and at Dehra Ghazi Khan he heard of the battle of Jamrud, which made the task of the English more difficult owing to their relations with Ranjit Singh; Dost Muhammad, as we know by a letter of 30 January, 1837, had begged for English intervention. Burnes journeyed through the Khaibar and on 20 September, 1837, the mission arrived at Kabul and lodged in the Bala Hissar, a combination of palace and fortress afterwards to become so famous. How far the idea of a commercial mission was sincere may be judged from the correspondence that has come down to us. For instance Auckland's letter of 6 January, 1838, is purely political, and on 26 July, 1837, Colvin had written to Burnes warning him as regards peace between the Sikhs and the Afghans not to enter into any negotiations which would commit the government after the death of Ranjit Singh or Dost Muhammad, and he adds in strange contrast to Auckland's recent letter:

A consolidated and powerful Mahommedan State on our frontier might be anything rather than safe and useful to us. The existing division of strength seems far preferable, excepting as it adds to the risk of Herat's being attacked by Persia.

Auckland's real views are to be found in a letter of 8 February, 1838, where he favours the then divided state of Central Asia, though he would like to see Kandahar and Herat on friendly terms.[2] It is only fair to add that Colvin had written to Burnes on 13 September, 1837,

---

[1] Kaye, *Afghan War*, I, 170.
[2] *Parliamentary Papers*, 1859 (2), xxv, 283 (I, 273).

to the effect that Auckland entirely approved of Burnes' determination not to allow Dost Muhammad to play off any other power against the British.

But Burnes could not get very far. Dost Muhammad was anxious to recover Peshawar with the aid of the British, and this Auckland would not hear of; Burnes could only offer help in making peace. He said that he thought that Ranjit Singh intended to make some change in the arrangements for the control of the city; that this change would be the work of Ranjit Singh and not of the British; and that it would probably take the form of the city being given over to Sultan Muhammad, Dost Muhammad's brother, to be held under the control of the Sikhs. But, as he frankly wrote, the Afghan king would as soon have Peshawar in the hands of the Sikhs as in those of his brother. What he wished was to hold it himself even if he held it nominally by paying tribute under Lahore.[1] The British, however, were certainly not going to support Dost Muhammad as against Ranjit Singh, and the importance of this attitude when a Russian agent arrived in December, 1837, can readily be realised. We must not forget Burnes' opinion expressed in his letter of 26 January, 1838, that Dost Muhammad was merely acting on the defensive, and that his views deserved serious consideration. The whole letter is full of wise foresight.[2] There was another matter. Mr Moriarty has suggested that it was as a counterstroke to Russian activity in Teheran that Auckland sent Burnes to Kabul[3], and on his way Burnes had written to the British minister in Persia to the effect that he would try and stop the intrigues between the Kandahar chieftains and the Russians; he soon found it necessary to threaten Kohan Dil Khan on the subject. Here he had the support of Dost Muhammad, who really would have preferred the British alliance to any other. Burnes showed this in his letter of 23 December, 1837.[4]

As Kohan Dil Khan altered his attitude and grew afraid of the Persians Burnes hoped for a more friendly relation. So he wrote and offered British help, to the extent of money at least, in case of attack by the Persians, who were now, it must be remembered, besieging Herat. Dost Muhammad was in a difficult position with regard to Herat. The blood feud prevented his going to the rescue of Kamran, who on the other hand talked of recovering Afghanistan if he were successful. The Persians, too, made no secret of regarding Herat as the first step towards the acquisition of the domain of Nadir Shah. Burnes also said that in case of need he would go with Dost Muhammad to the rescue of Kandahar, and he sent over Lieutenant Leech who had accompanied him about the end of December, 1837.

To all this Auckland could not agree, and Macnaghten, on

---

[1] *Parliamentary Papers*, 1859 (2), xxv, 43. [2] *Idem*, p. 130.
[3] *Cam. Hist. For. Pol.* II, 204. [4] *Parliamentary Papers*, 1859 (2), xxv, 99.

20 January, 1838, told Burnes so.[1] He was to get out of his difficult position in the best way he could, and if necessary, he was to tell the chiefs that he had exceeded his instructions; and Colvin's letter of the following day explains the position.

In the end it is said that Auckland thought that Burnes was right, and Hobhouse, it would appear from one of his letters, thought the same. But the result of the policy of the government of India was to alienate all parties in Afghanistan. Dost Muhammad said that if Sultan Muhammad held Peshawar it meant his own ruin, for he knew that the latter was trying to arrange a combination with Shah Shuja and the Kandahar chiefs against him. A proposal that was put forward with the amir's consent that there should be joint rule on the part of the amir and Sultan Muhammad over Peshawar was rejected. Peshawar must be left to the Sikhs. And all that Auckland had to offer in the way of restraining Ranjit Singh from attacking Afghanistan was regarded as worth little in exchange, as it was, for a request that Dost Muhammad would promise not to connect himself with any other state. On 5 March, 1838, a list of demands from the amir including a promise to protect Kabul and Kandahar from Persia, the surrender of Peshawar by Ranjit Singh, and the protection by the British Government of those who might return there, supposing it were restored to Sultan Muhammad Khan, was declined by Burnes, and after further fruitless talk Burnes left on 26 April, 1838.[2] This threw the amir into closer relations with the Russians with whom the Kandahar brothers had agreed on terms assuring them Ghorian as well as Herat. The Russian envoy even hoped to open negotiations with Ranjit Singh. But Dost Muhammad was far from satisfied.

For the moment things looked gloomy, for McNeill had found the Russian agent, Simonich, too strong for him, and had not been able to prevent or stop the siege of Herat. Muhammad Shah's expedition had started with the approval of the sirdars of Kandahar, and many of the people of Herat, being Shiahs like the Persians, might have welcomed a change of masters on religious grounds. The ruler, Kamran Shah, was the last of the Sadozai princes to retain a throne; but he was old and degraded, and the power was in the hands of the wazir, Yar Muhammad Khan, one of the vilest wretches in Asia. In the summer of 1837, then, the forces of the state had to hurry back from Sistan because it was reported that, far from helping in the conquest of Kandahar and Kabul for the Sadozais, the Persians were going to begin by taking Herat for themselves. Ghorian fell into their hands on 15 November, 1837, and on the 23rd of the same month the famous siege of Herat began.

Eldred Pottinger, who had been sent by his uncle, the well-known resident in Sind, was in the city, and by his energetic assistance the

---

[1] *Parliamentary Papers*, 1859 (2), xxv, 121.   [2] For Auckland's account see *idem*, p. 293 *sqq.*

defence was maintained for many months. McNeill, the English envoy, reached the camp on 6 April, 1838, and said that this war was a violation of the treaty between England and Persia. His mediation proved useless and the promises from Russia and Kandahar raised the Persian hopes. McNeill's influence declined, and Herat was all but taken on 24 June. Meanwhile, on 19 June, a British naval force appeared before Karrak in the Persian Gulf and landed troops there. McNeill at once sent word to the shah that the occupation of Herat by the Persians would be considered as a hostile act by the English. Colonel Stoddart, who arrived in the Persian camp on 11 August, 1838, bore the message, and the siege was raised, and by 9 September the Persian army was on its march westward. The Russian agents had encouraged the shah in this undertaking, but they were duly disowned, and one of them committed suicide when he reached St Petersburg. On 20 October, 1838, Count Nesselrode in a dispatch to Count Pozzo di Borgo, the Russian ambassador in London, dealt with the Persian question and the English apprehensions as to the part Russia was playing in the matter.[1] And Palmerston sent a very characteristic dispatch to him on 20 December, 1838,[2] followed by a note on the whole question, to be presented to Nesselrode by Lord Clarendon. It has been urged with some force that it was rather difficult for England to claim the monopoly of intrigue in Central Asia.

In India there was general unrest. Auckland was worried; he grumbled that he had to manage affairs which ranged from Canton to Suez, and though he was a man of peace he made the unfortunate choice of a strong forward policy. How much the fault lay with Macnaghten, Torrens and Colvin, whom he chiefly relied upon, will probably never be settled, but he slowly came to a decision. Though in 1837 he had written to Metcalfe that he had not a thought of interfering between the Afghans and the Sikhs, by 12 May, 1838, he had come to hold very different views. If Persia should succeed before Herat and advance upon Eastern Afghanistan he thought that there would be three possible courses open to him:[3]

The first to confine our defensive measures to the line of the Indus, and to leave Afghanistan to its fate; the second to attempt to save Afghanistan by granting succour to the existing chiefships of Caubul and Candahar; the third to permit or to encourage the advance of Ranjit Singh's armies upon Caubal, under counsel and restriction, and as subsidiary to his advance to organise an expedition headed by Shah Shooja, such as I have above explained. The first course would be absolute defeat, and would leave a free opening to Russia and Persian intrigue upon our frontiers. The second would be only to give power to those who feel greater animosity against the Sikhs, than they do against the Persians, and who would probably use against the former the means placed at their disposal; and the third course, which, in the event of the successful resistance of Herat would appear to be most expedient, would, if the State were to fall into the hands of the Persians, have yet more to recommend it, and I cannot hesitate to say that the inclination of my opinion is, for the reasons which will be gathered from this paper, very strongly in favour of it. . . .

[1] *Parliamentary Papers*, 1839, XL, 501.　　[2] *Idem*, p. 512.　　[3] Kaye, I, 320.

With these views, as their dispatches of 24 October and 9 November, 1838, show, the home authorities were in accord, and though there is little enthusiasm in their letter of 27 October to the governor-general, they speak of the necessity of his recovering his influence. Three days later than the date of Auckland's minute,[1] Macnaghten on proceeding to Lahore received instructions which suggested two alternative courses as possible. The one was that the Sikhs should advance on Kabul accompanied by British agents, whilst a demonstration should be made by a division of the British army occupying Shikarpur with the Shah Shuja in their company; the British Government advancing him money and lending him officers. The other was that the maharaja should take his own course against Dost Muhammad, only using Shah Shuja if success seemed certain, and if Shah Shuja was agreeable. The governor-general thought the former plan the more efficient, but the second the simpler, and on the whole the more expedient.

There was a good deal of reconsideration, but in the end Ranjit Singh seems to have got the better of Macnaghten. He agreed to recognise the independence of the amirs of Sind, and withdrew his claim to Shikarpur on receiving a money compensation. The independence of Herat as a principle was also agreed to. But he clearly showed that as to Afghanistan he wished to act with the British Government and not independently. But while it seems clear that Auckland had never contemplated taking the leading part in the proceedings which were to follow, it is equally clear that Ranjit Singh gradually forced him to do so; thus the Sikh secured the greatest advantage from the bargain. We do not know all that Macnaghten did say, but he gave it to be understood that the English would in certain circumstances advance with their own troops in support of Shah Shuja. The point is a very delicate one, but it seems that Macnaghten told Ranjit Singh, not that if Ranjit Singh would not co-operate with Shah Shuja the English would restore him themselves, but that they might find it necessary to do so. This brought Ranjit Singh round, and when he ceased to press for Jallalabad, which he did not really want, the way was open for the famous "Tripartite Treaty", signed by the maharaja on 26 June, 1838.[2]

This treaty, which was a new and enlarged version of that made between Ranjit Singh and Shah Shuja in 1833, confirmed the maharaja in the possessions which he held on the banks of the Indus with their dependencies, thus assuring to him Kashmir, Peshawar, Bannu, Dehra Ismail Khan, Dehra Ghazi Khan, and Multan. No one was to cross the Indus or the Satlej without the maharaja's permission. As to Shikarpur and the Sind territory lying on the right bank of the Indus, Shah Shuja would agree to what might be determined between the maharaja and the British. Should the maharaja require any of the shah's troops to carry out the object of the treaty they were to

[1] 12 May, 1838.　　　　[2] Aitchison, *op. cit.* VIII, 154.

be sent, and in the same way Muhammadan troops were to be sent by the maharaja as far as Kabul. The shah was to give up all claim on Sind, which was to belong to the amirs for ever, on such money payment being made by the amirs as should be decided by the British and handed over to the maharaja. Payment was to be made by the shah to the maharaja of two lakhs a year under the guarantee of the British Government in return for the assistance furnished. When the shah should have established his authority in Afghanistan he would not molest his nephew in Herat. The shah bound himself and his successors not to enter into any negotiations with any foreign state without the consent of the British and the Sikh governments.

Such was the treaty. Auckland before signing it sent it to Shah Shuja at Ludhiana by the hands of Macnaghten, Wade and Mackeson, who arrived there on 15 July, 1838. The shah objected to various articles. He secured, however, various assurances from the British Government, and on 17 July, 1838, the mission left Ludhiana with the signed treaty.

Kaye has pointed out that there were three different ideas as to the projected invasion. Auckland originally wished it to be undertaken by the Sikhs, aided perhaps by some Afghan levies. Even in the negotiations with Shah Shuja the project only took the form of an alliance which the British guaranteed, Shah Shuja and the Sikhs each marching into the country his own way. And Shah Shuja evidently thought that he would take the leading part himself. But when the matter was finally deliberated at Simla, it was settled, possibly against the better judgment of Auckland, that the British should do the work. There was to be a great army employed and it was to be the force that would set Shah Shuja on the throne. Probably Macnaghten knew that the maharaja wished to do as little as possible in the matter; Auckland did not want to displease the maharaja. We do not know what Burnes advised. He joined Macnaghten at Lahore when it was too late to oppose the policy of the treaty, and he certainly told Ranjit Singh that the restoration of Shah Shuja would be to his advantage. His real opinion is probably to be found in his well-known letter of 2 June, 1838:

> It remains to be reconsidered why we cannot act with Dost Mahomed. He is a man of undoubted ability, and has at heart high opinions of the British nation; and if half you must do for others were done for him, and offers made which he could see conduced to his interests, he would abandon Persia and Russia tomorrow. It may be said that that opportunity has been given to him; but I would rather discuss this in person with you, for I think there is much to be said for him. Government have admitted that at best he had but a choice of difficulties; and it should not be forgotten that we promised nothing, and Persia and Russia held out a great deal.[1]

And on 22 July he wrote to his brother, "I am not sorry to see Dost Mahomed ousted by another hand than mine". He was not like

---

[1] *Parliamentary Papers*, 1859 (2), xxv, 251.

Wade in favour of a turbulent Afghanistan where tribe constantly fought with tribe:

"*Divide et impera*", he wrote, "is a temporising creed at any time; and if the Afghans are united, we and they bid defiance to Persia, and instead of distant relations we have everything under our eye, and a steadily progressing influence all along the Indus."

Sir Henry Fane, the commander-in-chief, had given very sensible advice in 1837:

Every advance you might make beyond the Sutlej to the Westward in my opinion adds to your military weakness....If you want your Empire to expand, expand it over Oudh or over Gwalior, and the remains of the Mahratta Empire. Make yourselves completely sovereigns of all within your bounds. But let alone the far West.

The selection of Shah Shuja overlooked the claims of Kamran Shah and made it certain that if Afghanistan was to be a buffer state of any value we should have to help in reducing Herat also. And there were not wanting far-seeing critics who realised that active interference in Afghanistan must necessarily involve the taking of the Panjab, at all events on the death of Ranjit Singh if not earlier. However, the decision was taken; it was justified to the directors in the dispatch of 13 August; and orders were issued for the assembling of a great army to march upon Kandahar in the ensuing cold weather. Auckland's frame of mind may be judged from his letter to Hobhouse of 23 August, 1838:

I am sensible that my trans-Indus arrangements are in many points open to objection but I had no time to pause, there was no choice but between them and the more objectionable danger of remaining passive—and a friendly power and intimate connection in Afghanistan, a peaceful alliance with Lahore and an established influence in Sinde are objects for which some hazard may well be run.[1]

In the important letter of 13 August, 1838, Auckland gives a long and clear account of the negotiations with Ranjit Singh.[2]

The army of the Indus, which was to rendezvous at Karnal, was to consist of a brigade of artillery, a brigade of cavalry, and five brigades of infantry. It was to assemble under Sir Henry Fane with whom were to serve many officers of great distinction. Another army under Sir John Keane was to proceed *via* Bombay and Sind. The shah's army was being raised at Ludhiana, and it was rapidly losing its importance. The Sikh force was to move by Peshawar. Macnaghten, an unfortunate choice, was the political officer, and under him, not wholly to his own satisfaction, was Burnes, who now went away to arrange for the passage of troops through Sind, for the main army as well as that from Bombay was to go that way. It ought to be remembered that Macnaghten wished Pottinger to be appointed and only accepted the post himself under pressure.

---

[1] Brit. Mus. Add. MSS, 37694, f. 21.
[2] *Parliamentary Papers*, 1859 (2), xxv, 294.

On 1 October, 1838, the governor-general issued from Simla a long manifesto dealing with the origin and causes of the war and the policy of the British Government in regard to the whole business. It was a clever attempt to justify the action of the government, but it was open to serious criticism. Its greatest fault was that it made out no sort of case for attacking Dost Muhammad and did not do justice to the difficult position in which that ruler was placed. Perfect frankness would have been better, and Auckland seems to have felt this as he says to Hobhouse (13 October, 1838) in writing about the manifesto:

It will be for others to judge of my case and I will say nothing of it except that I could have made it stronger if I had not had the fear of Downing Street before my eyes, and thought it right to avoid any direct allusion to Russia. But I have no want of sufficient grounds of quarrel with Persia, etc....[1]

But however ill-advised Auckland may have been, he was carrying out, in part at least, the wishes of the home authorities. His letters to them (e.g. that to the Secret Committee in August, 1838) were perfectly clear, and they evidently approved of what he was doing; not, however, without reflections and comments which have hardly perhaps received sufficient attention. Their letter of 10 May, 1838, was not quite decisive;[2] the dispatch quoted by Sir Auckland Colvin[3] of 24 October, 1838, sanctions indeed armed intervention but seems to see possibilities of avoiding it. Their memorandum of 27 October, 1838, where they lay down general conditions, ought to be carefully studied. There were many outspoken critics. Elphinstone and Sir Henry Willock pointed out the difficulties of distance and climate, and the unwisdom of employing Sikhs whom the Afghans hated and feared, and then asked how, even if Shah Shuja got the throne, he could keep it. Hobhouse minuted on Willock's letter that its details were founded on presumption and that he did not think much of it. The Duke of Wellington, however, said that the consequences of the advance into Afghanistan would be a "perennial march into that country". The directors of the East India Company would no doubt have been glad to have been out of the business,[4] but they, and most Englishmen who thought about the matter, looked at it as a question of Central Asian policy, and they were under an entirely false impression as to the power of Russia and Persia to injure British interests in the East. It has been said that Auckland's council formally disclaimed responsibility for the manifesto, but the evidence against such a protest is strongly martialled by Sir Auckland Colvin,[5] and the probability seems to be that most of them agreed with him. A more serious point is that the siege of Herat was abandoned nearly a month before the manifesto appeared. Auckland did not know this

---

[1] Brit. Mus. Add. MSS, 37694, f. 69, verso.
[2] *Parliamentary Papers*, 1859 (2), xxv, 292.
[3] Colvin, *op. cit.* p. 124.
[4] *Parliamentary Papers*, 1859 (2), xxv, 267
[5] Colvin, *op. cit.* p. 122.

at the time, but when the knowledge came, and one of the chief reasons for the expedition had vanished, there was time to have abandoned it. This course strangely enough, considering what we know of his character, Auckland decided not to adopt, and by a proclamation (8 November, 1838), in which the raising of the siege was announced, he declared that he would continue to prosecute with vigour

the measures which have been announced, with a view to the substitution of a friendly for a hostile power in the Eastern provinces of Afghanistan, and of the establishment of a permanent barrier against schemes of aggression against the North West Frontier.

In the same sense on 9 February, 1839, he writes to Hobhouse.

Those at the India House were not without misgivings, but public opinion at home, and to some extent in India, was misled by the issue of the dishonest blue book in 1839, known as "the garbled dispatches". This gave an entirely false impression of the views of both Dost Muhammad and of Burnes. No defence worth considering has ever been offered of such an extraordinary performance.[1] The *naïveté* with which Broughton condemns the "rascality" of the Burnes family in trying to correct the impression made by the government's own action is almost as incredible as his and Palmerston's denials of garbling in the House of Commons. A revised edition of the letters was published in 1859, long after the exposure.

By this time the great expedition was well under weigh. At the end of November, 1838, the army of the Indus was assembling at Firozpur where a meeting took place between the governor-general and Ranjit Singh. Owing to the retreat of the Persians the force was somewhat reduced, and Sir Henry Fane, who was old and ill, decided to retire from the command, his place being taken by Sir John Keane from Bombay. The Bengal column now consisted of some 9500 men of all arms; Shah Shuja's contingent numbered about 6000; the Bombay column would add another 5600. It had been decided for political reasons (Ranjit Singh did not wish it to traverse the Panjab) that the march of the force from Firozpur should be by way of Bahawalpur and Sind, the amirs not having been behaving too well from Auckland's point of view. Burnes, as has been seen, had gone ahead, and it appears from his correspondence that it had been already decided to annex Bukkur where the Indus was to be crossed. The route then to be followed was by Shikarpur and Dadur to the Bolan Pass and so *via* Quetta to Kandahar. A large money claim was also to be made upon the amirs, though this claim had been long abandoned; and it must be remembered that a promise had been given that no military stores should be conveyed along the Indus. But Auckland treated the situation as a new one,

[1] Cf. C[abell]'s minute, 14 February, 1839 (Hobhouse MSS); Vernon Smith to Melvill, 13 April, 1839 (India Office); and Lord Broughton to Fox Maule (Hobhouse MSS). Cf. Hansard, CLXI, 38 *sqq.*

and threatened the amirs that serious consequences would follow if they did not co-operate. This course of proceeding can hardly be defended, and Colonel Pottinger, the resident at Hyderabad, said that we were in the wrong, and that the communications with Persia alleged on the part of one of the amirs hardly justified our action. Burnes secured unwilling co-operation in Upper Sind, but the Talpur amirs were very reasonably alarmed at the restoration of Shah Shuja, and at the passage of troops through their territory, largely at their expense.

However, the great force managed to enter Sind on 14 January, 1839. Burnes had obtained Bukkur, and thus the passage of the Indus, for as long as was necessary. And meanwhile Keane had landed at Vikkur at the end of November, and after long delays was marching up the bank of the Indus; his men grumbling that they were treated as though they were in an enemy's country. Further delay occurred while the question of the attitude of the amirs was settled at Hyderabad, and the Bengal column could not advance because Sir Willoughby Cotton came down the Indus with unnecessary reinforcements for Sir John Keane. Macnaghten, who was with Shah Shuja, was much annoyed and naturally asked as February advanced what was to become of the expedition when it got to Afghanistan. However, the amirs gave way, Cotton returned on 20 February, and four days later the march to Kandahar began; without, however, the shah's contingent, which remained behind for lack of transport.

In spite of great difficulties as to provisions and much loss of transport, Sir Willoughby Cotton pushed on at a fair pace. On 16 March he entered the Bolan Pass and on the 26th after considerable suffering his force reached Quetta. Rations had to be reduced, and Burnes was sent off to the khan of Kalat who signed a treaty in return for a subsidy, promised help in the way of supplies and transport, recognised Shah Shuja, and gave Burnes plenty of good advice which came too late to be of any practical use.

Keane, the shah, and the Bombay army were moving through Sind under great difficulties. The advance of the columns had caused great dissatisfaction and the Balochis complained bitterly of the damage to their crops. By 4 April the force was near Quetta. From Cotton they heard nothing but the most dismal forebodings, as well they might, for his men were on quarter rations, and he saw, what Macnaghten refused to see, that Shah Shuja was not likely to be popular amongst his own people. On 6 April, 1839, Sir John Keane took over the command of the expedition at Quetta and wisely decided to push on the next day. Macnaghten thought that we ought to punish the khan of Kalat by annexing Shal, Mastung and Kachhi to Shah Shuja's dominions; his letter is almost comic in its fury:

The Khan of Khelat is our implacable enemy, and Sir John Keane is burning with revenge. There never was such treatment inflicted on human beings as we have been subjected to on our progress through the Khan's country.

Meanwhile the Barakzai sardars in Kandahar were giving up the game. When the expedition with the shah at its head entered Afghan territory they fled from the city, and the money Macnaghten expended did the rest. On 25 April, 1839, Shah Shuja entered Kandahar. In a letter, written a month later (25 May, 1839) to Hobhouse, Auckland describes the scene and reviews the situation from a defensive point of view.[1]

Once in Kandahar the task of the British was but commenced. Shah Shuja was not popular, and his character was not such as to win men to his side. The Afghans displayed curiosity but little more, and the fact that their new ruler came in with English aid, and obviously under English control, prevented them from regarding his arrival even as a party, much less as a national, triumph. The Barakzai sardars were far away across the Helmund, but, as Dost Muhammad had yet to be conquered, Shah Shuja did his best to conciliate the Durani leaders who might be expected to give him their support. Dost Muhammad, seeing that the army paused in Kandahar, thought it was going against Herat, and therefore sent his son Akbar Khan against Shah Shuja's son Taimur, who was advancing with Captain Wade by way of Jallalabad. Things were in a bad way certainly at Herat, where Eldred Pottinger was continually obstructed and even insulted by the adherents of Yar Muhammad Wazir. But for the moment Macnaghten had no idea of doing more than send a mission to Shah Kamran, and Major Todd left Kandahar on that errand on 21 June, 1839, reaching Herat about a month later.

On 27 June, 1839, the army, considerably thinned by sickness and other misadventures, set out for Ghazni which was reached on 21 July. The heavy guns had strangely enough been left behind but, seemingly by treachery, a weak point was discovered, the Kabul gate was blown up, and the fortress hitherto regarded as invulnerable was taken by storm. It was a notable feat and the names of Dennie, Thomson, Durand, Macleod, and Peat will live in connection with it.[2] Sale was cut down in the great struggle at the gate but managed to escape with his life. Haidar Khan, the son of Dost Muhammad, who was in command of the fortress, was captured, and the amir's brother, the Nawab Jabbar Khan, then came to try and make terms. A remark he made might well serve as a commentary on the tragedy that was to follow:

"If", he said, "Shah Shuja is really a king, and come to the kingdom of his ancestors, what is the use of your army and name? You have brought him by your money and arms into Afghanistan, leave him now with us Afghans, and let him rule us if he can."

Negotiation was fruitless and Dost Muhammad marched out to meet the invaders. Finding, however, that he could not rely upon his troops, after a last despairing and not ignoble appeal, he rode away

[1] Brit. Mus. Add. MSS, 37696, f. 31.
[2] H. M. Durand, *Life of Sir Henry Durand*, I, 52.

from Arghandab to the country near the Hindu Kush. This was on 2 August, 1839; on the 7th Shah Shuja entered the capital, and the Barakzai monarchy for the time had perished. The arrival on 3 September of Prince Taimur and the Sikh contingent who had come through the Khaibar seemed to complete the triumph. Those chiefly concerned were duly rewarded, Auckland being made an earl, Sir John Keane a baron, and Macnaghten a baronet; these amongst others. Burnes who had already been knighted was annoyed that no further honour came to him, and it took all Auckland's tact to comfort him.

Auckland's minute of 20 August, 1839, made it certain that a considerable force was to be left in Afghanistan, and what was finally decided upon was larger than what had at first been thought sufficient. It had become abundantly clear that though the Afghanistan to which Shah Shuja returned was much smaller than that over which his father had ruled, it was larger than he could manage unaided. So though the Bombay column left on 18 September, nearly all the Bengal troops under Sir Willoughby Cotton remained. Keane returned with those of the Bengal force who were not required. The main garrisons were at Kabul, Jallalabad, Ghazni and Kandahar, but the forces were too widely scattered. A detachment followed Dost Muhammad, and occupied Bamiyan in the hope of his appearing there.

The country was distracted, the ministers were worthless, and the native army which was to support the throne and to which Auckland looked with almost pathetic hope and eagerness proved equally unsatisfactory. So that a double system of government, Afghan and English, was inevitable. The natural result, the only possible result, was constant sporadic insurrection, or looting that might become such, at any turn of events. The road to India through the Khaibar was never safe, and communication that way was only kept up by force and bribery. Kalat was taken by General Willshire on 13 November, 1839, as he was marching home, because the English terms were not accepted. The khan himself, Mihrab, was killed and the new khan, Shah Nawaz, who was set up in his place was anything but popular, the less so as the provinces of Shal, Mastung and Kachhi were now handed over to Afghanistan. It may be doubted whether these proceedings were wise, and it seems certain that they were unjust.

The news now began to filter through of a Russian expedition under General Peroffsky from Orenburg into Central Asia and particularly against Khiva. The provocation was the slave trade in Russian subjects which, there, as at Herat, was actively carried on and had been so for over a hundred years; this and the constant plundering of caravans. If proof were needed of the general nervousness as to Russia, it could be found in a letter from Burnes written in November, 1839. He writes: "Ere 1840 ends, I predict that our frontiers and those of Russia will touch—that is, the states dependent upon either of us will—and that is the same thing". Kaye has shown the difficulties of this winter—the Russian scare; trouble at Herat; trouble with the Uzbegs; trouble in Bokhara where Colonel Stoddart, the Resident, had been imprisoned under the most humiliating conditions, and where Dost Muhammad had now found at once a refuge and a prison; troubles in Kandahar, in Kohistan, and at Kalat; trouble with the Sikhs who were ceaselessly intriguing with the disturbing elements in Afghanistan. The tendency in all such cases is to try and crush the symptoms rather than eradicate the causes of the mischief. The English officials thought only of expeditions, and Macnaghten planned one to the Hindu Kush. It is only fair to Auckland to say that he consistently resisted all such proposals, and a letter written by him to Macnaghten on 22 March, 1840, shows what his views were;[1] there are others of the same nature.

The wisdom of his attitude was shown when, about the middle of March, 1840, the failure of the Russian expedition was announced. Auckland had made proper preparations, and he was far from being blind to the seriousness of the situation, had Russia obtained a hold on Khiva and still more on Bokhara. But it must be recalled that the difficulties of the Afghan position had been increased rather than diminished by the death of Ranjit Singh (27 June, 1839) and the confusion in the Lahore state which followed it. The matter is alluded to by Lord Auckland in a letter of 11 May, 1840, to Hobhouse.[2] It was even suggested that various Sikh magnates were engaged in treasonable intrigues with various rebels in Afghanistan, and there is no doubt that the *Khalsa* and the heir to the throne, Nao Nihal Singh, were strongly opposed to the passage of British troops through the Panjab, at which, considering the language of Macnaghten, one can hardly be surprised. Colvin had written to William Butterworth Bayley on 23 January, 1840:

There never was a time when the Sikh Durbar was more dependent upon us than at present. They are conscious of their many dissensions and real weakness and are, I imagine, surprised and in some measure distrustful at our self-denial in taking no advantage of them. A serious quarrel with us at the present time on the part of the Sikhs I look upon as an impossible thing.[3]

With this may be compared his letter to Macnaghten on the following 13 June, which is impressive in its seriousness. There was soon to be plenty of proof of the correctness of Colvin's suspicions.

The position at Herat was what might have been expected. Major Todd and his associates did their best to put down the slave trade there, and Captain Abbot was sent to Khiva with the same end in view. The latter arranged a treaty which was disavowed, but his successor, Captain Shakespeare, managed to get 400 Russian slaves

---

[1] Brit. Mus. Add. MSS, 37698, f. 89, verso.
[2] *Idem*, 37699, f. 76, verso.
[3] *Idem*, 37698, f. 6.

set free. Much money was advanced to the ruler of Herat, but he was far from loyal, and Macnaghten would have annexed the little state to Afghanistan had Auckland, who was supported by the commander-in-chief, Sir Jasper Nicolls, agreed. Major Todd we learn afterwards came round to the same view.

The Ghilzais gave constant trouble; their chiefs had taken refuge during the winter of 1839 in Peshawar, but, when the warm weather came, they were in arms again between Kandahar and Kabul, and took a good deal of repressing. There was failure in Kalat, which, the same summer, was recaptured by Nasir Khan, the son of the chief who fell when the British took the place. And when later he was driven out he was not conquered. Quetta was besieged; and everywhere there were indications that Shah Shuja inspired no sort of fear or respect. Yet strangely enough Macnaghten wrote to Colvin: "I have nothing more to say about His Majesty's character than I have already said. I believe him to be the best and ablest man in his Kingdom". Auckland in one of his letters to Hobhouse, when speaking of the suppression of the Ghilzais, throws a little light on the causes of the trouble:

But the business was ill and discreditably done. Blunders were made and harshnesses committed. Our officers quarrelled with, and as is too often the case counteracted, each other, and what as it appeared to me might have been a business of ease and graciousness, has been very much the reverse.

Macnaghten could not prevail upon the Indian Government to go to war with the Sikhs or to annex Herat, but he continued to dream of the further extension of British influence in Central Asia. In September, 1840, he sent Captain Arthur Conolly—something of a visionary but a very gallant one—on a mission to Khiva and Kokand. He subsequently proceeded to Bokhara where he and Colonel Stoddart were cruelly murdered.

The brightest circumstance of this uncomfortable summer was the assurance given by Russia that there would be no further attack on Khiva. And equally important perhaps was the surrender of Dost Muhammad. In July, 1840, the Nawab Jabbar Khan gave himself up to the small force stationed at Bamiyan. Dost Muhammad, having escaped with some difficulty, had taken refuge with his old ally the wali of Khulum. He soon had a considerable force under him and drove back the British outposts, a most distressing feature of the business being the desertion to the enemy of some of the new national levies raised to support Shah Shuja. There was evidence, as Torrens wrote to the Resident at Lahore on 1 October, that the Sikhs were not altogether neutral in the matter, and the government of India promised considerable reinforcements as soon as possible. Macnaghten still thought the remedy to be a forward policy, and characterised as "drivelling" Auckland's sensible suggestion that we could hardly expect co-operation from potentates whose territory we were always talking of annexing.

On 18 September, 1840, however, Brigadier Dennie defeated the forces under Dost Muhammad and the wali of Khulum near Bamiyan, and though Dost Muhammad and his son, Afzal Khan, escaped, the wali came to terms on the 28th and promised not to give refuge or help to the ex-amir or any member of his family. Dost Muhammad, therefore, fled to Kohistan, where he was followed by Sale and Burnes. There was some hard fighting in which Edward Conolly, Lord and others were killed, but Dost Muhammad, after winning an important if small success at Parwandurrah on 2 November, 1840, galloped to Kabul and gave himself up to Macnaghten. He was treated honourably and taken to India.

The few months that followed were restless. Macnaghten was still anxious for movement and for the break-up of the Tripartite Treaty, to which Auckland, though he had Hobhouse against him, would not consent. As he once said to the chairman of the East India Company, the country was one of clans and tribes, and there was war and lawlessness in one district whilst there was peace and contentment in another. The Ghilzais were seldom quiet, and the Duranis about Kandahar strongly resented taxation. Shah Shuja showed no signs of becoming either a capable or a popular ruler, and the cost of Afghanistan to the Indian Government was becoming unbearably great. Todd could no longer put up with the demands of Yar Muhammad at Herat and broke up the mission there in February, 1841; but this could not draw Auckland into an attack upon the little state, though it produced a very bad impression both in India and in England. Expeditions quelled the Duranis and the Ghilzais, but only for a time.

Thus the situation as 1841 wore on was critical. No proper system of government had been established. The native army was unreliable and the only form of executive action, that of the tax-gatherer, increased the tension. The English were the only real authority and they practically retained their hold by force and by the distribution of money amongst the chiefs. Macnaghten was now appointed governor of Bombay and Burnes was designated his successor. The forces were under the command of General Elphinstone, who in April, 1841, succeeded Cotton, and his appointment, made against his own wishes, constitutes one of the most serious mistakes that Auckland committed. In a position requiring above all things activity and physical energy, was placed an elderly invalid, personally brave, but, as he himself stated, hardly able to walk. Nott, a man of will and resource, if of strong temper, would have been a better choice. But those who spoke of the dangers of the situation, like Brigadier Roberts, had no chance of promotion. There were no doubt many men in the various garrisons of talent as well as courage. All they required was capable leading, and that they never got. There was another mistake. The troops at Kabul had now been moved to the ill-constructed and ill-fortified cantonments outside the city next to the mission compound but very badly placed; whilst the commissariat stores were placed separately and some distance away. It has always been maintained that the placing of the troops in this wretched position instead of in the Bala Hissar was the chief cause of the subsequent disaster, and for that Cotton, and to some extent Macnaghten, must bear the blame.

As has been indicated one great difficulty was obviously finance. Afghanistan was going to cost at the lowest estimate a million and a quarter a year, and the views of the home authorities on the subject reached India early in 1841. They were beginning to feel that Shah Shuja was not worth the money he cost. It was decided in consequence that economies must be effected, and it was unwisely thought best to retrench the stipends paid to the various Afghan chiefs by which alone their adherence was secured. This misplaced economy produced its natural results. The Ghilzai chiefs left Kabul and took up their stand in the country near Jallalabad, plundering those who came by and entirely preventing regular communication with India proper. Auckland seems to have understood what was happening better than Macnaghten, but he hoped for the best; he was misled and made the most of any trifling success. Sale, who was soon afterwards wounded, was directed to clear the passes; troops were hurried out, and Macnaghten hoped that Macgregor, who had been serving in the district near Jallalabad, would soon have the rising in hand. The disaffection was, however, spreading and Kohistan was beginning to be disturbed. There was plenty of fighting before Sale reached Gandammak at the end of October, 1841, but by that time events of a far more important and tragic nature were preparing in the capital.

It seems to have been known at Kabul that some sort of outbreak was coming, and warnings were given but not heeded; we must not press responsibility too far on that account, as wild rumours were sure to be running round the bazaar. Still it seems extraordinary that more should not have been known of a conspiracy which included the heads of nearly all the important tribes in the country. The actual outbreak seems to have been premature as, had the conspirators waited a little, Macnaghten and a considerable body of troops would have left Kabul. On 2 November a revolt broke out in the native quarter; and, in Burnes' house in the city, Alexander Burnes, his brother Charles, and William Broadfoot were murdered. The shah's treasury was looted and the guards killed. Shah Shuja sent a regiment of Hindustani soldiers to suppress the tumult, but they did nothing, and were with difficulty brought into the Bala Hissar by Brigadier Shelton who had been sent by Elphinstone. The movement in force which might have restored order never came, and the question, as Kaye truly says, is: "How came it that an insurrectionary movement, which might have been vanquished at the outset by a handful of men, was suffered to grow into a great revolution?" The responsibility clearly seems to rest with Macnaghten and Elphinstone, who did not consider the outbreak as serious when they first heard of it, and took no proper steps to quell it. Even the next day but a trifling attempt was made and that ended in failure. Hurried messages were sent to Sale and Nott for help, and the position became more serious than ever when all the commissariat stores fell into the enemy's hands. Day after day there was the same helpless story. Almost at once the general took the heart out of everyone by suggesting the possibility of negotiation, and Macnaghten began to give and to promise money. By this time Muhammad Akbar Khan, the son of Dost Muhammad, had reached Bamiyan on his way from Turkestan.

Elphinstone was worse, far worse, than useless, and on 9 November, 1841, he was persuaded to bring over Brigadier Shelton from the Bala Hissar to give him charge of the cantonment. But even then the general would not allow him to be independent; the two did not agree, and no improvement resulted. Trifling successes at a fearful cost in valuable lives—there were many brave men in the army of occupation—brought no relief, and even they ceased about 13 November. On the 15th Pottinger came in from Kohistan, bringing news of the loss of Charikar, the destruction of a Gurkha regiment, and the march of Kohistanis to join the Kabul rebels. To add to this Macnaghten now learned that Sale had gone to Jallalabad. Some step had to be taken, so he wrote a formal letter on 18 November to the general recommending that they should hold out in the cantonments as long as possible. He was not in favour of a removal to the Bala Hissar, agreeing in this with Shelton. Both seem to have been wrong; for though the change would have been attended with loss and danger, the same could be said of any course decided upon, and the move there would have been a better plan of action than the retreat to Jallalabad. On 23 November the Afghans won a victory, which Eyre thought decisive,[1] over a force sent out to hold the Bemaru hills, and it was evident from the conduct of the troops that they were losing heart. Hence on the 24th it was decided to try negotiation. When, however, the Afghans demanded unconditional surrender the conference broke up.

From 25 November, 1841, onwards news of these terrible events began to reach Auckland. He saw at once the real difficulty of the situation. On 1 December he wrote to the commander-in-chief:

It is however I fear more likely that the national spirit has [been] generally roused and in this case the difficulty will not be one of fighting and gaining victories but of supplies, of movement, and of carriage.[2]

He approved of the sending of reinforcements, but feared that they would be too late. Sale, he thought, would have to fight his way to

[1] Eyre, *Kabul Insurrection*, p. 163.   [2] Brit. Mus. Add. MSS, 37706, f. 197.

Peshawar. In a letter of the 2nd he asked Anderson at Bombay how all this could have come about when he had received nothing but favourable reports; alluding, no doubt, to the letters, remarkable enough, which Macnaghten had written just before the outbreak. On 4 December, when he knew of course of the death of Burnes, he wrote to Macnaghten:

And yet under the most favourable events I would have you share in the feeling which is growing strongly upon me—that the maintenance of the position which we attempted to establish in Afghanistan is no longer to be looked to, and that after our experience of the last few weeks it must appear to be if not vain, yet upon every consideration of prudence far too hazardous and too costly in money and in life for us to continue to wrestle against the universal opinion, national and religious, which has been so suddenly and so strongly brought in array against us. And it will be for you and for this government to consider in what manner all that belongs to India may be most immediately and most honourably withdrawn from the country.[1]

A bolder, even a wiser man would have struck a fiercer note, but Auckland seems to have come to a decision, perhaps one that he afterwards regretted, but to which he adhered in principle for the few sad months which remained to him in India. On 8 December Colvin wrote to Clerk that the policy of the government would be:

in the event of a reverse at Kabul to maintain indeed a high tone, and to speak of plans of punishing the Afghan, but in reality to content ourselves with remaining in collected strength along the line of the Satlej and Indus.[2]

Meanwhile Muhammad Akbar Khan had arrived in Kabul, and provided a recognised leader for the rebellious Afghans. He was a young man of daring and energy, but with all the wild characteristics of his savage race. He saw that the easiest way to deal with the English was to starve them out, and that, as provisions became scarce, the rank and file would become demoralised. This truth was equally clear to the besieged, and they realised, if there was to be a retreat, the sooner it began the better. On 8 December, 1841, it was decided to renew negotiations, and on the 11th Macnaghten's articles were drawn up and in the main accepted by the Afghans. They provided for the complete evacuation of Afghanistan by the English. The troops were to leave as soon as possible and to be allowed to go in safety. Shah Shuja was either to remain on an allowance or to go to India with the British troops, and as soon as the British troops reached Peshawar in safety Dost Muhammad and all the other Afghans were to be allowed to return. When this had been effected the family of Shah Shuja should be permitted to join him. Four British officers were to be left as hostages, and Afghan chiefs were to accompany the British army. Friendship was to be maintained between the Afghans and the English, and the Afghans were not to ally themselves

---

[1] Brit. Mus. Add. MSS, 37706, f. 202, verso.
[2] *Idem*, 37707, f. 14.

with any other foreign power without the consent of the English. A resident should be received in Kabul if the two nations so wished.

It is perfectly obvious that the Afghans never dreamed of carrying out these articles, but on behalf of Macnaghten it has been said that he was bound to make some such agreement because he realised that no sort of reliance could be placed on the military forces. And this no doubt is true. But the further and more serious question remains as to how far the whole position of affairs was not due to his own previous folly, and to his want of prompt action when the revolt began. On the whole he was at least as much to blame as the soldiers, for whose leaders no excuse can be offered. Their plain duty, as Wellington told Greville, was to have attacked the rebels in the city the moment they realised what was going on, and those who refused or neglected to give orders to that effect involved the many brave men who served under them, and who asked for nothing better than to die sword in hand, in undeserved blame.

The evacuation was to begin in three days, and those troops that were in the Bala Hissar left on the 13th, not without difficulty and humiliation. The forts round the cantonment were ceded, and now, amid every circumstance of discouragement and dishonour, the retreat towards Jallalabad must commence. While the force delayed the snow began to fall, and on 19 December the last chance of help vanished when it was known that the force which had set out from Kandahar had returned there. The departure was fixed for the 22nd. But useless, complicated, and not too honourable negotiations still continued, for Macnaghten never lost the hope, a vain one, of dividing the enemy. The result of this policy came on the 23rd when he was murdered by Akbar Khan while at a conference. Shelton accidentally escaped the same fate; but Trevor was killed and others present were taken prisoners. It does not seem that Akbar Khan meant at first to kill Macnaghten; but it is one more token of the envoy's essential unfitness for the post he occupied that with his experience of the character of the Afghans he should have trusted them as he did. As Burnes said, he was an excellent man, but quite out of place in Afghanistan. When at the end he descended to a policy of intrigue, he followed the course which has usually led to failure in the East. As to the murder, he must have known what a trifle a man's life was in the eyes of an Afghan, and how many of those near at the moment were thirsting for the blood of every Englishman in their country. The event then, while a tribute to Macnaghten's courage, cannot do anything to clear his memory from the serious mistakes of which he had been guilty. On 24 December it was known for certain in the cantonments that he was dead, and yet nothing was done. Fresh conditions were sent in, more and more humiliating; money, guns, ammunition, and hostages were demanded, and though Pottinger in vain protested, there seemed to be no depth of humiliation to which the general would not descend. On 1 January, 1842, the final treaty was ratified. English ladies were not to be left as hostages; otherwise the Afghans had all they wished.

And now the march through the snow, looked forward to with dread, was to become a reality. On 6 January the soldiers, refusing to wait any longer for the promised safeguard from the Afghan chiefs, marched out of the cantonments. Their leaders would not fight, and they had to do their best at running away. Sixteen thousand men, brave men too, were to be sacrificed to the utter incapacity of their commanding officers; already they had become a disorderly rabble. The sick and wounded were left behind in the Bala Hissar.

Sale has been criticised for not coming, as ordered, to help Elphinstone, and it is certainly difficult to understand how anyone in his position could refuse to do so; but there seems no reason to doubt his statement that his brigade could not reach Kabul, and certain it is that with things as they were his force would have been of little use. He probably could not realise that matters were in such a desperate condition. Hence he took what he thought was the wisest course, and fell back on Jallalabad which he surprised on 13 November, 1841, and where he prepared to hold out indefinitely. Broadfoot especially distinguished himself in the laying out of the fortifications. On 9 January a message was received from Pottinger, who was now in political charge at Kabul, and Elphinstone, ordering the evacuation of the fortress, but Macgregor and Sale declined to obey. On the 13th as the men were at work on the fortifications they saw a solitary horseman approaching along the Kabul road. It was Dr Brydon, almost the sole survivor of the army which had left Kabul.

The exact composition of the force which had disappeared is known from Lady Sale's journal:

The advanced guard consisted of the 44th Queens, 4th Irregular Horse, and Skinner's Horse, two horse artillery six-pounder guns, Sappers and miners mountain train, and the late Envoy's escort. The main body included the 5th and 37th Native Infantry, the latter in charge of the treasure; Anderson's Horse, the Shah's 6th Regiment, two horse artillery six-pounder guns. The rearguard was composed of the 54th Native Infantry, 5th Cavalry, and two six-pounder horse artillery guns. The force consisted of about 4500 fighting men, and 12,000 followers.[1]

It left hurriedly without, as has been said, the Afghan escort, herein acting against the advice of friendly Afghans. The progress was slow, the suffering was intense, and pillage on the part of the Afghans began from the start. Soon too the semblance of order was abandoned and discipline vanished. The Afghan horsemen continued to hang upon the rear, taking what they could get hold of. It is significant that in two days only ten miles were covered. In the terrible pass of Khurd Kabul, which runs for five miles between high mountains, the attacks on the retreating force became more serious, and three thousand at least are said to have perished here. Akbar Khan appears

[1] Cf. Eyre, *Kabul Insurrection*, pp. 256–7.

to have been unable to check the Ghilzais who were mad with fanatical rage. The wives and widows of officers and the married officers were now given into his charge, partly for protection, partly as hostages. But the murders continued and increased as the march was resumed, and on 10 January not more than a quarter of the force was left. Soon Elphinstone and Shelton were in the hands of Akbar Khan, and at Jagdallak, where there was a barrier, the final stage of the massacre began. A small number reached Gandammak only to perish there, and of half a dozen who had pushed on to Fatehabad only Dr Brydon, as has been said, got to Jallalabad. It is computed that more died from cold than from the knives of the Afghans—but who can say? The prisoners who had been taken by the way numbered 120: men, women, and children.

It is easy to gather from his correspondence that Auckland's first feelings were those of utter astonishment. He had been entirely misled, and that fact prevented him at first from thinking that matters were as serious as they really were. But events told their own tale and as the terrible details reached him he realised to the full the responsibility which attached to him personally. He seems to have given way to despair and at first only wished that one brigade with artillery, which was placed under Brigadier Wild, should be sent to Jallalabad. All that he desired now was to get out of Afghanistan as best he could. And as Sir Jasper Nicolls, the commander-in-chief, had always been opposed to the Afghan occupation, and thought it dangerous to move more troops out of British India, he was not likely to want support in his views. Fortunately, however, the initiative was taken by men of determined character acting on their own responsibility. Troops were hurried up by Clerk, the agent at Peshawar, and Robertson, the lieutenant-governor of the North-West Provinces. Aiding them were men like Henry Lawrence, who knew what to do in a crisis; and on 4 January, 1842, the second brigade, just over 3000 strong, crossed the Satlej on its way to Peshawar. And when later in the same month the command of the whole relief force was given to General Pollock, everyone felt that at last a step had been taken in the right direction.

It is needless to follow Auckland's varying thoughts as disaster followed disaster. The letter of 23 January, 1842, written by Colvin to his father before the fate of the Kabul army was known, illustrates the views of the official world of Calcutta. It shows at once extra-ordinary penetration and a corresponding lack of statesmanship, but its closing sentences in which he speaks of his own position and prospects will ever be read with pride by the members of the great service of which he was so distinguished an ornament.

At the end of the month of January came the definite news of the loss of the Kabul army and a proclamation couched in spirited language was at once issued. But Auckland, doubtful as ever and anxious not to embarrass his successor who was opposed to the Afghan war,[1] had not really made up his mind. On 3 February he wrote to the commander-in-chief that Jallalabad might have to be abandoned, but that a strong force ought to be kept at Peshawar.[2] On the same day on fresh information he spoke in an undecided way of retiring to Firozpur. This confirmed what he said in his letter home of 18 February.[3] Meanwhile Brigadier Wild had hurried from Firozpur with four regiments of native infantry; guns he was supposed to get from the Sikhs through the political agent. When he got to Peshawar, however, at the end of December, 1841, he found the Sikhs not at all disposed to lend guns, and what they had were hardly worth borrowing. He managed to procure four very inferior guns on 3 January, but he had difficulties about transport and very little ammunition. The Sikhs under General Avitabile would only promise at first to go as far as 'Ali Masjid. The importance of holding this, the key to the Khaibar, was obvious, so, on 15 January, 1842, half the brigade moved on there. When Wild followed on the 19th with the rest, the Sikhs who were to have accompanied him refused to go; and though he pushed on himself he was decisively beaten with the loss of a gun at the entrance to the pass. The net result was that on 24 January 'Ali Masjid was given up and the four regiments fell back on Jamrud. All that could be done was to wait for the arrival of Pollock, who reached Peshawar on 5 February, and by that time so many of the troops were sick that an immediate advance could not be thought of. So all through February and March, 1842, the brigades remained at Peshawar, and Pollock resisted every temptation to move, though Sale and Macgregor wished him to do so. We must not forget too that headquarters was strongly of opinion that any movement should only be designed to relieve the garrisons.

At Jallalabad there was considerable anxiety. Sale knew that he could not help those in Kandahar and Ghazni, and he felt under no obligation to help Shah Shuja. And if Auckland, as seemed obviously the case, did not wish him to go to Kabul, it was not much use staying in Jallalabad, especially as he was bound under the treaty, as Shah Shuja reminded him, to leave the country. There was of course the question of the prisoners, but Sale knew that their position was not likely to be improved by the movement of a small force to rescue them. The heroic conduct of Broadfoot, backed by Havelock, prevented a surrender in February, 1842; and though an earthquake on the 19th of that month did great damage to the fortifications, the garrison was not disheartened. Akbar Khan was close by, and on 11 March a successful sortie was made. It was not, however, till 31 March, 1842, when dragoons and horse artillery had reached him, that Pollock began his famous march. His difficulties of transport were great,

---

[1] Law, *India under Lord Ellenborough*, p. 1.
[2] Brit. Mus. Add. MSS, 37707, f. 145.   [3] *Idem*, 37707, f. 187.

and, though he had secured at last some sort of co-operation from the Sikhs, it was not till 5 April that he advanced to attack the Khaibar. This was successfully managed. 'Ali Masjid was abandoned by the Afghans. Pollock, leaving the Sikhs to guard the pass, well or ill, pushed forward and marched into Jallalabad on the 16th. Meanwhile Sale had on the 7th attacked and burnt Akbar Khan's camp and all danger for the moment was over.

On 8 October, 1841, the post of governor-general of India in succession to Auckland was offered to and accepted by Lord Ellenborough. He had long been closely connected with Indian affairs, as he had been appointed president of the Board of Control in 1828.

Lord Ellenborough reached Calcutta on 28 February, 1842. His general policy as regards Afghanistan is indicated in the well-known dispatch of 15 March to the commander-in-chief. It has been the subject of much criticism, and yet it is difficult to see that he could have said anything better. Sir Henry Hardinge has recorded that he desired no stronger proof of Ellenborough's ability and soundness of judgment than it afforded, and we can certainly add that it supplies extraordinary evidence of his rapid grasp of the essential features of the situation. After a brief historical review it continues:

All these circumstances, followed as they have been by the universal hostility of the whole people of Afghanistan, united at the present moment against us in a war which has assumed a religious, as well as national character, compel us to adopt the conclusion, that the possession of Afghanistan, could we recover it, would be a source of weakness, rather than of strength, in resisting the invasion of any army from the west, and therefore, that the ground upon which the policy of the advance of our troops to that country mainly rested, has altogether ceased to exist.

After saying that the British can be no longer bound to support the cause of Shah Shuja it proceeds:

Whatever course we may hereafter take, must rest solely upon military considerations, and have, in the first instance, regard to the safety of the detached bodies of our troops at Jellalabad, at Ghuznee, at Khelat-i-Ghilzye, and Candahar, to the security of our troops now in the field from all unnecessary risk, and finally, to the re-establishment of our military reputation by the infliction of some signal and decisive blow upon the Afghans, which may make it appear to them, to our own subjects and to our allies, that we have the power of inflicting punishment upon those who commit atrocities, and violate their faith, and that we withdraw ultimately from Afghanistan, not from any deficiency of means to maintain our position, but because we are satisfied that the King we have set up, has not, as we were erroneously led to imagine, the support of the nation over which he has been placed.

Very significant are the paragraphs of Lord Ellenborough's dispatch to which most attention has been directed. They run:

We are of opinion that it would be erroneous to suppose that a forward position in Upper Afghanistan would have the effect of controlling the Sikhs, or that a forward position above the passes of Lower Afghanistan would have the effect of controlling the Beloochees, and the Sindians, by the appearance of confidence and strength. That which will really, and will alone control the Sikhs, the Beloochees, and the Sindians, and all the other nations beyond and within the Indus, is the knowledge that we possess an army, perfect in its equipment, possessed of all the means of movement, and so secure in its communications with the country from which its supplies and its reinforcements are drawn, as to be able at any time to act with vigour and effect against any enemy.

In war, reputation is strength; but reputation is lost by the rash exposure of the most gallant troops under circumstances which render defeat more probable than victory; and a succession of reverses will dishearten any soldiers, and most of all, those whose courage and devotion have been mainly the result of their confidence that they were always led to certain success. We would, therefore, strongly impress upon the commanders of the forces employed in Afghanistan and Sind the importance of incurring no unnecessary risk, and of bringing their troops into action under circumstances which may afford full scope to the superiority they derive from their discipline. At the same time, we are aware that no great object can be accomplished without incurring some risk; and we should therefore consider that the object of striking a decisive blow at the Afghans, more especially if such blow could be struck in combination with measures for the relief of Ghuznee—a blow which might re-establish our military character beyond the Indus, and leave a deep impression of our power, and of the vigour with which it would be applied to punish an atrocious enemy,—would be one for which risk might be justifiably incurred, all due and possible precaution being taken to diminish such unnecessary risk, and to secure decisive success.

The commanders of the forces in Upper and Lower Afghanistan will in all the operations they may design, bear in mind these general views and opinions of the Government of India. They will, in the first instance, endeavour to relieve all the garrisons in Afghanistan, which are now surrounded by the enemy. The relief of these garrisons is a point deeply affecting the military character of the army, and deeply interesting to the feelings of their country; but to make a rash attempt to effect such relief, in any case, without a reasonable prospect of success, would be to afford no real aid to the brave men who are surrounded, and fruitlessly to sacrifice other good soldiers, whose preservation is equally dear to the government they serve. To effect the release of the prisoners taken at Cabool is an object likewise deeply interesting in point of feeling and of honour. That object can, probably, only be accomplished by taking hostages from such part of the country as may be in, or may come into, our possession; and with reference to this object, and to that of the relief of Ghuznee, it may possibly become a question in the event of Major-General Pollock's effecting a junction with Sir Robert Sale, whether the united force shall return to the country below the Khyber Pass, or take a forward position near Jellalabad, or even advance to Cabool.[1]

The conditions of such further advance are then stated. This long extract (with which may be compared Lord Ellenborough's memorandum to Queen Victoria of 18 March and his letter home of 21 March, 1842)[2] is sufficiently complete to show Lord Ellenborough's real meaning. What he obviously intended to convey was that, as soon as it was possible safely to do so, everyone must retire from Afghanistan, that before they did so some decisive blow must be struck if possible, and that those on the spot, subject to certain general conditions of caution, must make the decision. How necessary caution was is evident enough; even so well informed an officer as Major Rawlinson had suggested that Kandahar should be handed over to Shah Kamran and that we should give him our general support, though the attitude of Persia was uncertain.

On 6 April, 1842, the governor-general left Calcutta and no one can accuse him of want of activity. We must look at the situation

---

[1] Ellenborough MSS (P.R.O.), 83.
[2] Colchester, *Indian Administration of Lord Ellenborough*, pp. 17 and 176.

from his point of view. At Kandahar was Nott, who had been asked in the early days of the trouble at Kabul to send Maclaren's brigade to Elphinstone's assistance. It was sent but returned, because unable to advance, on 8 December, 1841. Its return has been criticised on several grounds, but Nott at all events was glad enough to see it back again. The country round Kandahar was in a state of insurrection, and after much tortuous negotiation an army of insurgents settled down about five miles from the city on 12 January, 1842. Nott went out and scattered them, but this victory only seemed to bring the surrounding Durani chiefs into more open hostility, and under Mirza Ahmad they gave active resistance to the enemy. On 21 February Nott received the belated message from Elphinstone and Pottinger ordering the evacuation of Kandahar and Khilat-i-Ghilzai, the latter a fort under Leech about half way to Ghazni. He felt under no obligation to obey this command, for the position of the English in the country, as was pointed out by the Durani chiefs, was now somewhat anomalous, and required independent consideration. Nott decided, therefore, to stay where he was. On 10 March the city was wellnigh captured by a stratagem. On the 31st news came of the fall of Ghazni; Khilat-i-Ghilzai was still holding out. But where was the rescue party from Sind? About the close of February, 1842, Brigadier England approached the Bolan Pass. He left Dadur on 7 March and reached Quetta on the 16th. But on the 28th he was beaten at Hakulzai and retreated, with some discredit, to Quetta. At last, on 30 April, aided by Nott's men from Kandahar, he got through the Khojak Pass and the two brigades entered the city on 10 May.

The position was now somewhat clearer, and it had been simplified still further by what had happened at the capital. Shah Shuja, who had continued to reign as the nominal king at the Bala Hissar, on 5 April was shot down by men posted by Shuja-ud-daula, son of Zaman Shah, as he set out for Jallalabad. There is much uncertainty as to the cause of the murder, but it was doubtless the inevitable outcome of Barakzai feeling whatever the immediate occasion.

We have therefore now this position. A strong force on the west at Kandahar, with very uncertain means of communication with its base, and a strong force at Jallalabad in an even worse position as regards supplies and reinforcements. Both forces, as things were, were unable to move forward. When, therefore, Lord Ellenborough on his march up-country heard of General England's repulse and the fall of Ghazni he gave the instructions which have been the subject of so much controversy. On 18 April he wrote to the commander-in-chief:

I cannot think that Major-General Pollock will under his instructions of the 15th ult. remain at or near Jellalabad. Your Excellency is so much nearer to Peshawar than I am that I depend upon your giving any instructions upon that head to

Major-General Pollock which you may think necessary. His position is far from satisfactory, even during his operation; with an active enemy in his front and a large force of Sikhs in his rear he is placed almost in the fauces caudinae if there should be treachery. Then this horrible climate, so much more destructive than any battle, which in three days may deprive him of two thirds of his force....[1]

On the 19th he reviewed the whole position, allowing the commander-in-chief to decide as to General Pollock, but pointing out the advantages of the force remaining at Jallalabad during the hot weather on the ground of health and on account of the influence which the presence of this force might have upon negotiations for the exchange of prisoners. On the other hand he spoke of the decision which had been taken in favour of ultimate retirement to the Indus and the difficulties in which the force would find itself "at one end of a long and difficult pass with an enemy in front and an ally not to be entirely depended upon, in its rear".[2] The orders to Nott were as follows. The letter is dated Benares, 19 April, 1842:

1. I am directed by the Governor-General to instruct you to take immediate measures for drawing off the garrison of Kelat-i-Ghilzie. You will effectually destroy all such guns as you cannot conveniently bring away. You will destroy the fort likewise unless, at the time at which the operation shall be effected which is hereinbefore enjoined, Prince Timur having remained faithful to the British interests shall possess sufficient force to be reasonably expected to be able to maintain that fort upon your giving it into his charge.

2. You will evacuate the city of Candahar giving that too into the charge of Prince Timur under the circumstances above mentioned. You will otherwise ruin its defences before you abandon it.

3. You will then proceed to take up a position at Quetta until the season may enable you to return upon Sukkur.

4. The object of the above directed measures is to withdraw all our forces to Sukkur at the earliest period at which the season, and other circumstances, may permit you to take up a new position there. The manner of effecting this now necessary object is, however, left to your discretion.

5. You will understand that, in the event of Prince Timur having continued faithful, it is the desire of the Governor-General to afford him the means of preserving by his own native troops or any other troops in his pay the city of Candahar and the fort of Khelat-i-Ghilzye, but no British guns must be left which you can carry away, and no British officer must remain in his service retaining his commission in the British army.[3]

It has often been stated that Lord Ellenborough at this period was in a state of panic, but a letter to Peel of 21 April, 1842, does not give any such impression; it runs:

At last we have got a victory, and our military character is re-established. Sir Robert Sale has completely defeated the Afghans under the walls of Jellalabad. Major-General Pollock has forced the Khyber Pass and is in march on Jellalabad. These events took place on the 6th and 7th of this month. The garrison of Khilat-i-Ghilzye is safe, but is not yet drawn off. Candahar has been nearly lost by the error of General Nott. Brigadier England was repulsed in a movement he should never have made towards Candahar with an insufficient force.

I am satisfied that the momentary success of Sale and of Pollock must not lead us to change our view of what ought to be our permanent policy. We must draw

---

[1] Ellenborough MSS, 83.
[2] *Idem*, 83.   [3] *Idem*, 95.

back our forces into positions in which they may have certain and easy communication with India. You will see all I think in my letters to the Commander-in-Chief and the Secret Committee. The victory of Jellalabad does not change my opinion. Send us every man you can. We want them all, as you will see when you read the letter to the Secret Committee. I am making the most of my victory with the troops here and everywhere....

The commander-in-chief did not give the suggested instructions to Pollock till 29 April, 1842, and even then he specified conditions under which retirement might be delayed. But on 28 April a letter had been sent by the governor-general informing Pollock that:

The aspect of affairs in Upper Afghanistan appears to be such according to the last advices received by the Governor-General, that his Lordship cannot but contemplate the possibility of your having been led by the absence of serious opposition on the part of any army in the field, by the divisions amongst the Afghan chiefs, and by the natural desire you must, in common with every true soldier, have of displaying again the British flag in triumph upon the scene of our late disasters, to advance upon and occupy the city of Cabool.

Those who have criticised this letter have often forgotten that it was sent just when the news had reached the governor-general that Shah Shuja had been assassinated. Hitherto Lord Ellenborough had had to resist those who were pressing for a fresh occupation of Afghanistan. A letter which he wrote to the Duke of Wellington on 17 May, 1842, has often been misunderstood because only partially quoted; it runs:

But I must tell you that in not ordering the army to Ghuznee and Cabul without the means of movement or supply, and in giving up the irrational schemes of extending our dominions to the westward, I stand alone and have to withstand against the whole monstrous body of political agents. I have acted altogether in all that I have done upon my own judgment.[1]

But that he contemplated considerable exercise of individual judgment even at this early stage is evident from the letter to Nott of 13 May, 1842:

Your position when supplied with treasure, ammunition, and medicines, will be more favourable than the Governor-General had reason to suppose it would be when the instructions of the 19th ultimo were addressed to you, but this improvement of your position is not such as to induce his Lordship to vary the instructions, in as far as they direct your retiring upon Sukkur.

That movement you will make at such period and with such precautions as may best conduce to the preservation of the health of your troops and the efficiency of your army.

The Governor-General understands that consistently with the necessary regard to these objects of primary importance you cannot retire below the passes till October.

Neither does the decease of Shah Shoojah induce the Governor-General to vary those instructions as far as they relate to the measures you were directed to adopt on evacuating the fort of Khelat-i-Ghilzye and the city of Candahar.

In the present divided state of Afghanistan the Governor-General is not prepared to recognise anyone as the governor of that country; but the fidelity of Prince Timour would justify his being so put in possession of those places and of Giriskh on your returning to the Indus.[2]

[1] Colchester, op. cit. p. 196.   [2] Ellenborough MSS, 95.

In the same general sense is the letter from Ellenborough to the commander-in-chief of 14 May.

What no doubt Lord Ellenborough was really afraid of, and with some reason, was action on the part of the Sikhs. On 23 May, 1842, he wrote to the commander-in-chief:

I have removed, I trust, by the declaration I have made, the apprehension which appears to have been entertained that the British Government desired to have possession of Peshawur. This apprehension in Mr Clerk's opinion led to the congregating of so large a Sikh force there.[1]

Pollock had hitherto delayed on the question of carriage, and he gladly welcomed the idea of a forward movement; on 1 June, 1842, a very wide discretion was allowed him. Nott's position was quite different, and in any case depended largely on that of Pollock. On 1 June a letter was written to him directing his retirement as soon as the season would permit.

So Nott busied himself with maintaining his position and with the withdrawal of the Khilat garrison. But by a letter of 4 July he too received full discretionary powers which allowed him to go back *via* Ghazni and Kabul. It was now for the first time that he had sufficient transport and that Lord Ellenborough, with many natural misgivings, was able to sanction his advance.

It was in this letter that the instruction was contained which afterwards excited so much ridicule. It ran:

If you should be enabled by a *coup de main* to get possession of Ghuznee and Cabool, you will act as you see fit, and leave decisive proofs of the power of the British army, without impeaching its humanity. You will bring away from the tomb of Mahmood of Ghuznee, his club, which hangs over it; and you will bring away the gates of his tomb, which are the gates of the Temple of Somnaut. These will be the just trophies of your successful march.

But as regards this direction those who know the East will hesitate to condemn Lord Ellenborough; and they will also be pretty sure that the idea was either suggested or approved by those around him. It is a trifling affair in any case, but Wade attests the fact that the Gates had been demanded by Ranjit Singh in 1831.[2] The Duke of Wellington approved of Lord Ellenborough's conduct in this matter. The discretion as to the route was again fully allowed to Nott in a letter of 10 July. On the 6th of that month Lord Ellenborough summed up the matter in a letter to the Duke of Wellington:

The case is one in which, at this distance, I could not direct an advance, but, at the same time, I should hardly be justified in continuing to prohibit it. It is entirely a question of commissariat.

By the end of June, Pollock had sufficient transport but it was not till the middle of August, 1842, that he heard that Nott was going to Kabul. He started from Jallalabad on the 20th of that month,

[1] Ellenborough MSS, 83.   [2] Cunningham, *Sikhs*, pp. 196–7.

reaching Gandammak on the 23rd and scattering a body of the enemy near by. On 1 September Fath Jung, the puppet king, gave himself up, and, having heard that Nott had started, Pollock set off for the capital on the 7th, defeated the Ghilzais at Jagdallak on the 8th, and on the 13th won a great final victory over Akbar Khan at Tezin near the fatal pass of Khurd Kabul. The hope of the Barakzais fled, and on the 15th Pollock was in Kabul.

Nott had made preparations for moving his force from Kandahar to Quetta when on 20 July, having received sufficient transport and the governor-general's letter of the 4th, he decided to march to Ghazni and Kabul with a portion of his army. The rest of the force was to return under the appropriate care of Brigadier England, and with him went Prince Taimur Shah (Shah Shuja's eldest son), who had no sort of authority in the country. They left Safdar Jung, the younger son, in possession, a move which shows how little the actual significance of events in Afghanistan had been realised even then. There was no trouble till Nott's army reached Mukur, 160 miles from Kandahar, on 27 August, 1842, and there irregular fighting began. Ghazni was occupied on 6 September and the fortifications destroyed. The army marched away, carrying with them the gates of Somnath, and on 17 September they camped outside the city of Kabul.

Lord Ellenborough had been very careful to state that all he wished, once the garrisons were relieved and the prisoners restored, was to leave Afghanistan as soon as possible, but Pollock thought it necessary for the time being to enthrone Fath Jung in the Bala Hissar, without of course any hope of future help from the English. There was not entire sympathy between Nott and Pollock, but fortunately this did not interfere with the release of the prisoners, who had been carried off in the direction of the Hindu Kush, and who, after the most extraordinary adventures, rescued themselves and on 17 September joined a relief party which had been sent under Sir Richmond Shakespeare.

All that remained was to break up the gathering forces of the Barakzais which Aminullah Khan was bringing together and which might have annoyed the army on its way back to India. This was effected by General McCaskill who won a battle at Istalif in Kohistan on 29 September. The Great Bazaar of Kabul was, rather unfortunately, selected for destruction as a reminder of the evil that had been done by those accustomed to stream through its arcades, and on 12 October the army marched away from the city. On the same day Fath Jung having abdicated, Prince Shapur, another son of Shah Shuja, was declared king.

Meanwhile Lord Ellenborough issued a proclamation at Simla, dated 1 October, 1842, which is open to little criticism beyond this, that he might well have left unnoticed the faults, sufficiently obvious, of those who were responsible for the disasters which had occurred. It annoyed Auckland, who made the ridiculous remark, to a party of friends of whom Greville was one, that he had been convinced that Lord Ellenborough was mad from the moment of his landing. Ellenborough's defence of his proclamation and of his orders as to the Somnath Gates, which is to be found in a letter to the Secret Committee of 28 March, 1843, has much to recommend it.

The most important part of the proclamation was that in which it was stated that the governor-general would willingly recognise any government approved by the Afghans themselves, which should appear desirous and capable of maintaining friendly relations with neighbouring states. The opportunity was soon given. Those Afghans who had been detained in India were allowed to return and the most important of them all was Dost Muhammad, a wooden spoon which could be thrown anywhere, as he described himself. Early in 1843 he returned to Afghanistan and to its throne, for poor Prince Shapur had long since fled for his life to Peshawar.

The armies of Pollock and Nott returned through the Khaibar without any great difficulty, though they suffered occasionally from the depredations of freebooters. They destroyed the defences of Jallalabad and 'Ali Masjid as they passed, thus perhaps happily rendering useless a scheme for handing over Jallalabad to the Sikhs. Then they passed through Peshawar and across the Panjab and were welcomed in December, 1842, very magnificently, by the governor-general and the army of reserve which he had assembled at Firozpur, with the idea of overawing the Sikhs. But although there was great rejoicing, and although rewards were deservedly given to those chiefly concerned, there is no doubt that the errors of the first part of the war cast their shadow over the triumphs of the second. It suited the politicians who were really responsible for the first invasion of Afghanistan to treat the whole war as one connected incident; whereas in reality it consisted of four distinct operations. That Auckland's invasion of Afghanistan was a terrible mistake is obvious; the government of the country under Macnaghten was a failure; the conduct of the authorities when the revolt of November occurred is open to the gravest criticism, and forms perhaps the most painful episode in our military history; but the work of Pollock, Sale and Nott reflects nothing but credit on the British and Indian troops whom they led and who displayed the highest courage and endurance.

Lord Ellenborough's conduct throughout a most difficult time still awaits detailed and candid examination, but in spite of the careless censures which one text-book after another has repeated from his own day to ours, his reputation has the powerful support of the Duke of Wellington and Lord Hardinge. The Duke's letter of 9 October, 1842, in which he gives a carefully considered and generously expressed approval of Lord Ellenborough's conduct in regard to the relief operations, is perhaps the most important testimony in his favour. It concludes:

These observations just tend to show that it is impossible for anybody at a distance, even informed as you must be, to dictate the exact course of a military operation. This must be left to the officers on the spot. And you have acted most handsomely by yours. You have stated clearly your objects. You have afforded them ample means and you have suggested the mode of execution with all the reasons in favour of and against your suggestions, the latter formed upon the knowledge acquired by experience. You could not do more. You might have done less. I concur in all your objects. I think your generals ought to be successful in carrying into execution your views.[1]

Equally valuable and conclusive are the marginal comments by the Duke on the letter of Lord Ellenborough to the Secret Committee of 17 May, 1842.[2]

[1] See the whole letter *ap.* Law, *op. cit.* pp. 42 *sqq.*   [2] *Idem,* pp. 33 *sqq.*

CHAPTER XXIX

THE CONQUEST OF SIND AND THE PANJAB

I. SIND

THE conquest of Sind and the subjugation of the Sikhs, though
no doubt often contemplated as possible before the invasion of
Afghanistan, were very closely connected with it; almost to the extent
of cause and effect, as can be seen from Lord Ellenborough's memorandum of 23 April, 1839.[1] Sind has a long interesting history which
has been dealt with in previous volumes of this work, so that it will
suffice to refer to it very briefly. The province was theoretically
subject to Afghanistan but the tribute due was often withheld. In
1783 Mir Fath 'Ali Khan overthrew the last of the Kaloras and
established himself as Rais of Sind, the first of the Talpura mirs. His
family divided the country between them, and so we have the
Hyderabad or Shahdadpur family ruling Central Sind from the
capital; the Mirpur or Manikani family at Mirpur; and the Sohrabani
line at Khairpur. Mir Fath 'Ali Khan died in 1802, leaving a son,
Subudar Khan; but his three brothers Ghulam 'Ali, Karam 'Ali,
and Murad 'Ali shared the sovereignty. Of these Ghulam 'Ali left a
son Mir Muhammad Khan; Karam 'Ali left no issue; and Murad 'Ali
left two sons, Mir Nur Muhammad Khan and Mir Nasir Khan, who
with their cousins just named, Subudar Khan and Mir Muhammad
Khan, were ruling, if ruling it could be called, in 1838; and of these
Subudar Khan was a Sunni and the other three were Shiahs, which
affected their several relations with Persia. Mir Nur Muhammad
Khan held a nominal superiority in position.[2] In 1841 he died
leaving two sons, Shahdad and Husain 'Ali, and it was the latter of
these that he confided on his deathbed, together with Nasir Khan,
to the care of Outram. The Khairpur family was very numerous,[3]
but they were all more or less subject in 1838 to Mir Rustam Khan,
an aged chief who had taken part in the original establishment of his
family in the country. At Mirpur, Shir Muhammad, known as the
Lion of Mirpur, was the ruler, though he was supposed to be to some
extent controlled by the mirs of Hyderabad.

The East India Company had re-established its factory at Tatta
in 1758; it was abandoned in 1775; but the idea of trade remained,
though a commercial mission to the Talpura mirs in 1799 ended
abruptly and without result. Negotiations at the beginning of the
nineteenth century were directed against the French, and a treaty

---

[1] Law, *op. cit.* pp. 1 *sqq.*   [2] *Parliamentary Papers*, 1843, xxxix, 316.   [3] *Idem,* p. 260.

with the amirs in 1809 provided that they should not allow that "tribe" to establish itself in Sind. Similarly, a treaty of 1820 said that no European or American settlements should be allowed, and that raids on British or allied territory should be restrained;[1] with regard to the latter matter a raid of the Khosas upon Cutch forced the Company to send a field force there in 1825, and with this little expedition went James Burnes, brother of the more famous Alexander, who was invited, after the military operations had finished, to visit the amirs of Sind at Hyderabad. His published account of his journey is still valuable as an early description of a practically unknown country. It may have been this connection which led to the sending of Alexander Burnes to visit Ranjit Singh by way of the Indus.[2]

The course of that river was now for the first time known to the English; and exaggerated ideas seem to have been entertained, both in India and in England, as to its future as a highway of commerce. Colonel Pottinger, therefore, recently appointed Resident in Sind, arranged a treaty on 20 April, 1832 (supplementary articles were added two days later), with Mir Murad 'Ali in Hyderabad, which was afterwards confirmed by Mir Rustam Khan in Khairpur, some of the articles of which had importance in the future. Such were:

II. That the two contracting Powers bind themselves never to look with the eye of covetousness on the possessions of each other.

III. That the British Government has requested a passage for the merchants and traders of Hindoostan by the rivers and roads of Sinde, by which they may transport their goods and merchandise from one country to another; and the said Government of Hyderabad hereby acquiesces in the same request, on the three following conditions:—

1. That no person shall bring any description of military stores by the above river or roads.

2. That no armed vessels or boats shall come by the said river.

3. That no English merchants shall be allowed to settle in Sinde, but shall come as occasion requires, and having stopped to transact their business, shall return to India.

It was also provided that a tariff of tolls should be drawn up and mutually agreed upon, and the details of this tariff were settled by a treaty of 1834.[3] The next year Colonel Pottinger obtained leave to survey the coast of the delta of the Indus. In view of what followed it is important to remember that there was considerable probability (as can be seen from Lord Auckland's correspondence) of the invasion of Sind by Ranjit Singh in 1836. He had demanded a heavy tribute from the amirs, had actually captured a fort near Shikarpur, and was making preparations for further operations. This led the governor-general to try to come to a closer arrangement with the amirs on the one hand, and to induce the Sikhs to give up their designs on Sind

---

[1] Aitchison, op. cit. VII, 351, 352.   [2] Ellenborough, Political Diary, I, 275.
[3] Aitchison, op. cit. VII, 353 and 357.

on the other. The dispatch to Pottinger of 26 September, 1836, contains the following significant paragraphs:

You will in treating with the Amirs communicate with them, without reserve, in reference to the dangerous position in which they stand, and you will apprise them, that this Government is sensible how essential it is, not to their interests only, but to their very existence, that the ties by which they are connected with the British Empire should be strengthened.

It is difficult at this distance immediately to prescribe to you the conditions upon which the British Government should agree to enter into a closer alliance; but you will avow its readiness, under such circumstances as are likely to arise, and upon such conditions as may be reasonable, to enter more ostensibly, than has hitherto been the case, into alliance with the Ameers of Sinde.

Whether the communication which you may make to the Ameers, in pursuance of these instructions, shall end in no new result, or in the mere reception, at the Court of Hyderabad, of a British Agent, or in the advance of a subsidiary force, for the protection of the Sinde territories, will probably depend upon the conduct of the Maharajah, and the course of events.

The Governor-General in Council sincerely desires, that the extension of British influence in the direction of the Indus, should be effected by the pursuit of commercial and peaceful objects alone. In interposing for the protection of Sinde from imminent danger, the British Government may justly expect to receive, in return, some corresponding advantages. His Lordship in Council would not, without your deliberate advice, and a very careful consideration of all the circumstances of the position of Sinde, enter into a general engagement to defend that country from all external enemies; but he does not hesitate to authorise you to promise his mediation in all disputes between the Ameers and the Government of Lahore, if a reasonable equivalent be assented to. As one condition of this mediation, and with a view to enable this Government readily to give effect to it, it would be advantageous if the Ameers would consent permanently to receive a body of British troops, to be stationed at their capital, the expense of the detachment being paid from the Sinde revenues. His Lordship in Council would not insist upon this, as an indispensable part of any arrangement, but he empowers you (reserving all points of detail) to agree to it on his part, should the Ameers not persist in opposing it under any circumstances. Short of this the present mediation of the British Government with Maharajah Runjeet Singh, may be promised, on the condition of the reception of a British agent at Hyderabad, and, of course, of all the relations between Sinde and Lahore being conducted solely through the medium of British Officers....[1]

Although Lord Auckland wrote on 27 December, 1837, that he was disappointed with the progress of negotiations, he certainly helped Sind greatly in regard to Ranjit Singh, and though it was unwillingly done, Pottinger concluded on 20 April, 1838, a treaty with the amirs of Hyderabad by which the governor-general promised his mediation in the matter and the amirs consented to receive an accredited British minister.[2] No doubt the main idea in the minds of Lord Auckland and his advisers was the security of the trading privileges on the Indus, but this soon gave way to larger schemes connected with the Afghan War. When that struggle became probable, Lord Auckland considered the whole position as altered; and though it may be argued with some justice that Sind was no longer part of Afghanistan, that Shah Shuja had already freed the amirs from any claims he might have upon them, and that treaty obligations stood

---

[1] *Parliamentary Papers*, 1843, XXXIX, 15.
[2] Aitchison, *op. cit.* VII, 363.

in the way of military movements through their country, there is something, though perhaps not very much, to be said for the governor-general's contention that what had now arisen was a larger question, one of the defence of India, an Asian not only an Indian question, and one in which Russia and Persia were concerned as well as the frontier of the Indian states.

The Tripartite Treaty of 26 June, 1838, between the government of India, Ranjit Singh and Shah Shuja contained important references to Sind:

IV. Regarding Shikarpoor and the territory of Sinde lying on the right bank of the Indus, the Shah will agree to abide by whatever may be settled as right and proper in conformity with the happy relations of friendship subsisting between the British Government and the Maharajah, through Captain Wade.

XVI. Shah Shooja-ool-Moolk agrees to relinquish, for himself, his heirs and successors, all claims of supremacy, and arrears of tribute, over the country now held by the Ameers of Sinde (which will continue to belong to the Ameers and their successors in perpetuity) on condition of the payment to him by the Ameers of such a sum as may be determined under the mediation of the British Government; 15,00,000 of rupees of such payment being made over by him to Maharajah Runjeet Singh.

A copy of the treaty was sent to Pottinger on 26 July, 1838, and he was instructed to press its lesson home on the amirs:

"You will", he was told, "in the first place state to the Ameers that, in the opinion of the Governor-General, a crisis has arrived at which it is essentially requisite for the security of British India, that the real friends of that Power should unequivocally manifest their attachment to its interests; and you will further apprise them that a combination of the Powers to the Westward, apparently having objects in view calculated to be injurious to our Empire in the East, has compelled the Governor-General to enter into a counter-combination for the purpose of frustrating those objects."[1]

If the amirs co-operated and consented to the abrogation of the article in the former treaty as to the use of the Indus for the con- veyance of military stores—well and good. They would secure independence from Afghanistan at a comparatively cheap rate. If they did not do so, Shikarpur would be occupied and the amirs would be left to the vengeance of Shah Shuja. If the amirs were found to have entered into any engagements with the shah of Persia, Pottinger might request the immediate advance of a British force from the Bombay army, sufficient to occupy the capital, and announce the breaking off of friendly relations with such of the amirs as had taken part in the Persian alliance.

With reference to this last point there is some difficulty. Pottinger wrote on 13 August that the Amir Nur Muhammad Khan had sent an 'arizat to the shah and that possibly the Amirs Nasir Khan and Muhammad Khan had done the same. Mir Subudar Khan had not taken part, possibly because he was a Sunni. Pottinger's words show

---

[1] *Parliamentary Papers, ut supra*, p. 65.

his opinion and are worth repeating because those who use them in controversy often quote one part without the other:

5. I do not myself ascribe any immediate political object to this Ureeza. I feel almost certain that it proceeds solely from the bigotry of Sheeaism, of which intolerant sect all the Ameers, with the exception of Sobdar, are rigid followers. It is not, however, to be concealed that the allusion to the messages with which the Hajee is charged will authorise a much more extended and important interpretation of the Ameer's address; and, as a matter which seems already known to so many individuals (for the scribe was sent to copy the letter at the house of Mirza Bakir Goorgian, where several persons likewise met to discuss the proper style) can hardly be considered a secret, I propose to take an early occasion, after reaching Hyderabad, to introduce the topic to the Ameers, and to demand a categorical declaration of their intentions.

6. The important political events and arrangements which are now pending will do even more than my observations, to open the eyes of any of the Ameers who may be wavering between our alliance and that of Persia, to the precipice on which they stand; but I shall not fail to tell them distinctly, that the day they connect themselves with any other Power will be the last of their independent authority, if not of their rule, for that we have the ready power to crush and annihilate them, and will not hesitate to call it into action, should it appear requisite, however remotely, for either the integrity or safety of our Empire, or its frontiers.[1]

Pottinger was under no illusions as to what might be expected from the amirs in the way of help. He knew that the danger would be greatest when the troops had passed through, and hence, on 20 December, 1838, he urged the hurrying up of the reserve force from Bombay.[2] He saw that the amirs valued very slightly the promise of freedom from Afghanistan, because they were free already, and because, as has been already said, they held releases from tribute given by Shah Shuja. Lord Auckland could, however, only push on. Burnes was sent into Sind to try and arrange matters regarding the passage of the troops to Afghanistan, and he wrote on 11 November to Pottinger that Mir Rustam Khan had heard from Mir Nur Muhammad Khan in favour of resistance to the English army, and that the mir of Khairpur had refused to take part in any such scheme. "I could only tell him", adds Burnes, "that if a shot was fired in the country against the English, Sinde would become a province of British India."[3] Pottinger showed courage and discretion, but supplies were withheld as long as possible. On 2 December, 1838, he writes:

I also sent a moonshee to Nur Mahomed Khan to inform him that part of the troops had arrived; that if grain was not sold to them the general officer commanding would take it by force, paying its price, and would make a signal example of Gholam Shah and all others who might oppose the people disposing of their property to us.[4]

And even when he is more hopeful there is evidence of distrust:

"My intelligence from Hyderabad", he writes on 15 December, 1838, "up to the 13th instant, leads me to believe that the Ameers there, excepting Sobdar, are now really exerting themselves to obtain carriage for this army, as the only means

---

[1] *Parliamentary Papers, ut supra*, p. 67.
[2] *Idem*, p. 160.   [3] *Idem*, p. 127.   [4] *Idem*, p. 150.

that offer of getting rid of it. At the same time, they are adopting all sorts of precautions, which evince a total distrust of our designs, and have already assembled a considerable body of their rabble of troops at the capital. They have also written to all the chiefs, whether Beloochees or not, to be in readiness with their quotas in case of necessity, etc."[1]

It is clear that events were altering men's minds as to the future, for, although Pottinger characterised Burnes's notions and proposals as rash and embarrassing, that officer hit the mark when on 17 December, 1838, he stated that the government had determined on fixing a subsidiary force in Sind permanently, this being one of the suggested results of the Persian intrigues. On 24 December, 1838, Burnes signed a treaty with Mir Rustam Khan.[2] Its chief clauses provided for the protection by the British of the principality of Khairpur, the submission of all external relations to British control and the furnishing of such troops and assistance by the state as were necessary during the war. A separate article authorised the English to occupy for the time being the island of Bukkur, thus securing the passage of the Indus.

It would be useless to enter into the details of the negotiations with the amirs of Hyderabad. They wished to prevent the passage of the British troops, but they could not prevent it, and the advance of Sir John Keane's force on their capital obliged them to accept the new treaty, which was finally signed on 11 March, 1839.[3] Lord Auckland on 13 March summarised its effects as follows:

The main provisions of the proposed engagements are, that the confederacy of the Amirs is virtually dissolved, each chief being upheld in his own possessions, and bound to refer his differences with the other chiefs, to our arbitration; that Sinde is placed formally under British protection and brought within the circle of our Indian relations; that a British force is to be fixed in Lower Sinde, at Tatta, or other such point to the Westward of the Indus as the British Government may determine; a sum of three lacs of rupees per annum, in aid of the cost of this force, being paid in equal proportions by the three Amirs, Mir Noor Mahomed Khan, Mir Nusseer Mahomed Khan, and Mir Mahomed Khan; and that the navigation of the Indus, from the sea to the most northern point of the Sinde territory, is rendered free of all toll. These are objects of high undoubted value, and especially so when acquired without bloodshed, as the first advance towards that consolidation of our influence, and extension of the general benefits of commerce, throughout Afghanistan, which form the great end of our designs.[4]

It is clear that one step led to another. On 2 January, 1839, Lord Auckland wrote to Hobhouse:

I have rejected propositions for the forfeiture of territory, for it would give a character of grasping to our enterprise which would be very injurious to us, and the establishment of our dominion at the north of the Indus would excite alarm and jealousy up to the very source of the river.

And yet on 3 February, 1839, Karachi passed into the hands of the English. On 2 September the same year Pottinger was informed:

It is not in contemplation to maintain permanently a large military force at that place [Karachi] but a small detachment will always remain there....The question

[1] Parliamentary Papers, ut supra, p. 157.   [2] Aitchison, op. cit. VII, 363.
[3] Idem, p. 369.   [4] Parliamentary Papers, ut supra, p. 237.

of the number and the stations of any force which may after the return of the army of the Indus be left in Sind, is still under the consideration of his Lordship, and under discussion with you, and with other political and military authorities....[1]

Thus the unfortunate amirs found themselves when the Afghan War was in progress saddled with a general liability to help the British forces; parts of their territory had been taken from them, obviously for ever; they had to contribute in varying proportions a large amount of money, instead of the old tribute, in order to maintain troops in their midst whom they did not want; and their independent position was gone for ever, because they had now come definitely within the sphere of British influence. There was obvious injustice in these arrangements, though one can easily see how difficult it was for the authorities to have acted otherwise than as they did. In this connection it must be noted that Outram took the place of Pottinger on 24 February, 1840, and the part that he took in all that happened between that date and the battle of Miani does not seem to have received sufficient attention. Macnaghten would have liked some scheme that would have handed over Sind, wholly or in part, to the Afghans. But Lord Auckland wrote to him on 15 June, 1839:

I do not agree with you in your views with regard to Sind. I consider Afghanistan and Sind to be absolutely severed by the Tripartite Treaty, and any further reckoning for new offences must be between us and the Amirs.

It is important to remember that the home authorities were with the governor-general, or, we might say, were behind him, in support of this policy. In a letter to Macnaghten of 8 January, 1840, Lord Auckland says that the directors

attach with the Governor-General the utmost importance to the complete maintenance of the British superiority in Sind and the navigation of the Indus not only during the occupation of Afghanistan but permanently.

From this to the acquisition of territory was but a step, and when a treaty was ratified in July, 1841, with the only remaining amir, the amir of Mirpur, binding him to certain payments, guaranteeing him in the possession of his territory and against foreign aggressions, but placing his foreign relations under British control,[2] Sind may be said to have passed under British authority to a very considerable extent.

The difficulties with the amirs continued for the rest of Lord Auckland's term of office, and the Sind problem was one of the many he left to the unfortunate Lord Ellenborough. But it does not seem that Lord Ellenborough was unduly anxious to take possession of the country in the first instance. On 27 April, 1842, in a minute written at Allahabad, he speaks in the following cold and sensible strain:

It may be expedient with a view to the navigation of the Indus to retain our new relations with Sinde even after the cessation of military operations in that

[1] *Parliamentary Papers, ut supra*, p. 278.   [2] Aitchison, *op. cit.* VII, 371.

quarter shall have rendered the continuance of those relations no longer indispensable; but the more recent reports as to the river Indus and our improved acquaintance with the populations on its banks, and the countries with which it communicates, certainly lead to the conclusion that the hopes originally entertained of extending our commerce were to a great degree exaggerated.... It is now 77 years since the first acquisition was made of the Dewannee. During a large portion of the period which has since elapsed, we have been extending our dominions, but we have not equally increased our revenue while we increased our charges. The acquisitions which have been made may, some of them, have been necessary in order to secure what we already possessed, some of them may have more than repaid in revenue the cost of governing and protecting them. The consequence of extended dominion has necessarily been a more extensive employment of British-born subjects in military and civil capacities, but the general revenue of the State has not been improved, and the government has diminished means of improving the condition of the people.[1]

Still, as the government made no secret of its intention to hold Karachi, Bukkur and Sukkur at least, it is not surprising that Outram discovered ample evidence that the amirs were intriguing with the enemies of Great Britain, and there was little doubt that they were ready to take advantage of any opportunity that might arise. In a letter of 14 May, 1842, to the commander-in-chief, Lord Ellenborough said:

I see everywhere the effect of the reverses sustained at Cabul. The late successes of which I have made the most may have checked the feeling that was growing up that we had no longer our former power, but within the last few weeks there have been strong indications that we were no longer considered to be what we were. Major Outram has observed a commencing change in the Ameers of Sinde.... [This in connection with the formation of an army of reserve.][2]

And in a letter to General Nott of 21 June, 1842, he spoke in the same sense:

Whenever you retire upon the Indus, some portion of the Bengal Troops will remain at Sukkur, and there may possibly be two brigades against the Ameers of Hyderabad unless their conduct should be more loyal than it is represented to have been of late. Currachie will continue to be occupied by Bombay Troops. An army of reserve of 15,000 men will be assembled in the Sirhind Division in November, etc....[3]

When, however, on 21 June, 1842, Outram sent a draft of a new treaty by which he wished to bind the amirs down to cession of territory,[4] Lord Ellenborough, though he forwarded letters of warning to be used in case of need, told him (10 July, 1842) that he did not see any occasion for precipitate negotiation; and he added that it would be a matter for consideration before the final instructions were issued to Outram on the subject whether any probable benefit to be ever derived from the treaty could compensate for the annual expenditure which would be brought upon the government of India by the maintenance of a large force at Sukkur and Karachi.[5] It is only fair

---

[1] Law, *op. cit.* p. 28.
[2] Ellenborough Papers, 83. Cf. Law, *op. cit.* p. 63.
[3] Ellenborough Papers, 95.
[4] *Parliamentary Papers, ut supra,* p. 397.
[5] *Idem,* p. 404.

to add that Sir George Arthur, governor of Bombay, in a minute of 2 September, 1842, stated that:

> There can be no doubt that most of the Ameers of Upper and Lower Sinde, have for some time past, been engaged in intrigues against us; in fact that they only want the power, not the will to make an attempt, in imitation of the tribes of Afghanistan, to expel us from their country.[1]

Sir Charles Napier had arrived in Bombay on 12 December, 1841, and in the following March we find him, in answer to a request from Lord Ellenborough, giving his views as to the best way to deal with the situation in Afghanistan.[2] Lord Ellenborough did not feel, and seemingly he was right, that he could adopt Napier's suggestions, and on 23 April, 1842, Napier writes in his journal: "My fear is that they will send me to Sinde, where there is no honour to be gained".[3] On 26 August following he was formally given command of all the troops of Upper and Lower Sind and Balochistan, and was empowered to exercise control over all civil and political as well as military officers within his command. This of course placed Outram under his orders, but it was part of a general scheme, not without justification from recent experience, and Outram had already been placed under the control of Nott. Napier reached Karachi on 9 September, 1842, and prepared to meet the difficulties of the situation. The English were in possession of Karachi, Sukkur, Bukkur, Rohri, Shikarpur, and a number of posts leading to the Bolan Pass. But as the general advanced through Sind to meet England, who was returning from Kandahar, he found that the amirs, though full of professions of loyalty, were constantly breaking the treaty in small points and anxious to throw off British ascendancy altogether. There is some excuse for Lord Ellenborough's letter to him on 25 September, 1842:

> Your first political duty will be to hear all that Major Outram and the other political agents may have to allege against the Ameers of Hyderabad and Khyrpore, tending to prove the intention on the part of any of them to act hostilely against the British army. That they may have had hostile feelings there can be no doubt. It would be impossible to believe that they could entertain friendly feelings; but we should not be justified in inflicting punishment upon the thoughts.
>
> The British army being withdrawn from Afghanistan it will be for the authorities at home to decide whether we shall retain the position we now hold upon the Lower Indus. For the present it must be retained in order to enable the home government to exercise a full discretion upon the subject.
>
> With a view to the maintenance of this position hereafter it will be necessary to have various diplomatic transactions with the Ameers especially with relation to Karachie and Bukkur and Sukkur. My impression is that for some period at least it would be desirable to hold those places, and if Bukkur and Sukkur be held they should be held in force, and their artificial defences made such as to render them not liable to insult....

The latter paragraphs of this letter have not perhaps been given due weight in considering Lord Ellenborough's attitude towards the

---

[1] *Parliamentary Papers, ut supra*, p. 408.
[2] Sir William Napier, *Life of Sir Charles Napier*, II, 162.
[3] *Idem*, p. 169.

conquest of Sind. With them may be taken his opinion that the ports on the Indus would never repay their cost, which is alluded to in a letter from Napier of 20 October following.

The amirs were frightened by Napier's plain speaking at Hyderabad. On 25 October he sent off his famous letter to the governor-general containing his "Observations on the occupation of Sind" with many illustrative documents, in the preparation of which he had been assisted by Outram.[1] Outram was then on the point of leaving; the Lower Sind agency closed on 14 November, 1842; and it is noteworthy, in view of the unsatisfactory controversy that followed, to remark that the two seem to have been in cordial, if not complete, agreement on general questions of policy up to this point. This is confirmed by Napier's subsequent choice of Outram as commissioner to help him a few months later (at a time when Outram, for reasons in no way connected with Napier or Sind, was not in favour with the governor-general) and by entries in Napier's diary.

On 14 October, 1842, the government of India directed Napier to threaten the amirs that he would compel them to execute the treaty by force. He was at the same time instructed to treat with them for a revision of the treaty.[2] And it is significant that on the 17th of the same month before he received these instructions Napier had written that the amirs were quite ready to attack us. Shadows of what was coming are to be found in Lord Ellenborough's letter of 23 October, 1842:

I am inclined to think that the Ameer Nusseer Khan will be so wrong-headed or so ill-advised as to persist in refusing to observe the conditions of the Treaty; in which case he must at once be compelled to do so; and, if the Government is obliged to incur any expense for the purpose of so compelling him, the least punishment which can be inflicted upon him is that of defraying the expense. But I should prefer depriving him of territory; and you will understand that, if you are under the necessity of making any movement of troops towards Hyderabad, the Ameer Nusseer Khan will forfeit all his property and right in Kurachee, Tatta, Shikarpore, Sukkur, the pergunnas adjoining the Bahawulpore country and Subzulkote; and all the property and rights in these two last districts, whatever they may be, shall be immediately transferred to the Khan of Bahawulpore.[3]

Consequent on the infractions of the old treaty by the amirs came the new treaty, different in several important respects, which was sent off on 4 November, 1842. It relieved the amirs from the payment of all tribute due to the British Government from 1 January, 1843. It settled the currency of Sind from 1845, the British Government providing the coins (one side of which was to bear the Queen's head) that alone were to be legal tender. With regard to territory it contained the following provisions:

7. The following places and districts are ceded in perpetuity to the British Government: Kurachee and Tatta, with such arrondissement as may be deemed necessary by Major-General Sir Charles Napier, and moreover, the right of free

---

[1] *Parliamentary Papers, ut supra*, pp. 418 *sqq.*   [2] *Idem*, p. 415.
[3] *Idem*, p. 361.

passage over the territories of the Amirs between Karachee and Tatta, along such line, and within such limits on either side thereof, as Major-General Sir Charles Napier may prefer; and, within such limits, the officers of the British Government shall alone have jurisdiction.

8. All the right and interest of the Ameers, or any one of them, in Subzulkoti and in all the territory intervening between the present frontier of Bahawalpore and the town of Roree, are ceded in perpetuity to his highness the Nawab of Bahawalpore, the ever faithful ally and friend of the British Government.

9. To the Meer Sobdarkhan, who has constantly evinced fidelity to his engagements, and attachment to the British Government, is ceded territory producing half a lakh of annual revenue, such cession being made in consideration of the loss he will sustain by the transfer of Kurachee to the British Government, and as a reward for his good conduct.

The necessary adjustments of the territory and revenue between the amirs were to be made by a commissioner appointed by Sir Charles Napier, and it was for this purpose, as noted above, that, with the approval of the governor-general, he brought back Outram. A similar treaty of the same date, designed to be made with the amirs of Khairpur, provided, as regards territory, that:

1. The pergunna of Bhoong Bhara, and the third part of the district of Subzulkoti, and the villages of Gotkee, Malader, Chaonga, Dadoola, and Uzeezpore, and all the territories of the Ameers of Khyrpore, or any of them, intervening between the present dominions of his highness the Nawab of Bahawalpore and the town and district of Roree, are ceded in perpetuity to his Highness the Nawab.

2. The town of Sukkur, with such arrondissement as shall be deemed necessary by Major General Sir Charles Napier, and the Islands of Bakkur and the adjoining islets, and the town of Roree, with such arrondissement as may be deemed necessary by Major General Sir Charles Napier, are ceded in perpetuity to the British Government.

Here again the currency was to be managed by the British Government, and arrangements were made for the necessary adjustments as between the various amirs. A provision was inserted making it clear that the amirs of Khairpur, in the same measure as those of Hyderabad by the treaty of 1839, were to promote the freedom of navigation of the Indus. Subject to these provisos the British Government renounced all claim to tribute.[1] Oddly enough, the amir of Mirpur, as Napier pointed out in a letter of 8 December, 1842, seems to have escaped notice, though by no means friendly to the British. Napier suggested that he might go on paying his old tribute of half a lakh annually, and Lord Ellenborough said that he had designedly left him under the older treaty.

Lord Ellenborough threw the responsibility for the decision as to the guilt of the amirs on to the local authorities. This is distinctly stated in his letter to Sir Charles Napier of 4 November;[2] and indeed, after the previous correspondence, he could hardly do otherwise. Napier in his diary takes another view of the matter and says, that given the proof of treason Lord Ellenborough ought to decide. On

[1] Aitchison, *op. cit.* VII, 374.
[2] *Parliamentary Papers, ut supra*, p. 496. Cf. *idem*, 1844, XXXVI, 611, and Law, *op. cit.* pp. 72–3.

18 November he says that the amirs had collected in various places about 20,000 men, and on the 30th, in answer to a definite enquiry from Lord Ellenborough, he says that he is convinced of the guilt of the amirs. Napier now knew, and Lord Ellenborough knew, for he offered more troops, that there would be fighting, but the treaty had to be considered first. On 2 December, 1842, it was sent to the amirs of Hyderabad and on the 4th it was sent to Khairpur. Just before this, on 1 December, Napier issued a proclamation to the amirs of Upper and Lower Sind. It ran:

I have received the draft of a treaty between the Ameers of Khyrpore (and Hyderabad) and the British Government, signed by His Excellency the Right Honourable Lord Ellenborough, Governor-General of India, whose commands I have to present it to your Highnesses, for your Highnesses' acceptation and guidance.

In obedience to the commands of the Governor-General of India I shall proceed to occupy Roree, and the left bank of the Indus, from the latter town up to the Bhawulpore frontier, including the whole of the districts of Bhong Bara and Subzulkote, as set forth in the said Treaty.[1]

It is not necessary to go into a minute description of the various intrigues which were in progress, but it may be well to touch on one that was the subject of much comment at the time. The amir of Khairpur was, as has been seen, a very old man. Once inclined to throw in his lot with the English, he had long since joined the other amirs, and the misfortunes of our troops in Afghanistan had affected him as they had affected them. He had given evidence of this by taking part in various schemes directed against the English, and the new treaty was one of the results. But the question of the moment was that of his successor. The choice lay between his brother 'Ali Murad, who professed attachment to the English interest, and his son. The claims of the former to the "Turban", as it was termed, had been placed before the governor-general by Outram on 21 April, 1842, and again by him to Napier on 30 October. On 23 November Napier had an interview with 'Ali Murad and promised him, provided he continued to act loyally towards the British Government, that the governor-general would prevent the nomination of old Mir Rustam's son, Mir Muhammad Husam, either during Mir Rustam's life or at his death. His reasons for this step are worth recording:

1. It is just. Ali Moorad has the right to the "Turban" for his own life, after the death of Meer Rustim, and it promises to protect him in this right.

2. It detaches Ali Moorad from any league among the Ameers, and, consequently, diminishes the chance of bloodshed.

3. It lays a train to arrive at a point which I think should be urged, viz., that we should treat with one Ameer, instead of a number. This will simplify our political dealings with these princes, and gradually reduce them to the class of rich noblemen, and their chief will be perfectly dependent on the Government of India, living as he will do so close to this large station (Sukkur) and I have no doubt that it will quickly be a large town.[2]

---

[1] *Parliamentary Papers*, 1843, xxxix, 518.   [2] *Idem*, p. 513.

Napier's letters now breathe the calm confidence of the experienced soldier. He writes on 1 December, 1842: "I am perfectly confident in the troops under my command being equal to any emergency". On the 4th the governor-general wrote:

As long as you have six regiments ready to support your just demands, I am inclined to think they will be acceded to, as they have been in this instance [a case of tolls on the Indus]; and I am willing to hope that, with these aids to your negotiation, you may be able to make a settlement now without the use of force; but I very much fear that, until our force has been actually felt, there will be no permanent observance of the existing treaty, or of any new treaty we may make.[1]

The various amirs now agreed verbally to be bound by the new treaty, but they continued to collect troops. The British could only count upon the support of 'Ali Murad at Khairpur, and Mir Subudar Khan and Mir Husain 'Ali at Hyderabad. The chiefs of Khairpur decided at the end of November that Mir Rustam Khan should abdicate in favour of his son on 5 December. Napier now began pushing his troops across the Indus to take possession of Rohri, and the plan was that Brigadier Wallace was to march towards the ceded districts on 20 December, 1842, whilst Napier moved on Khairpur. On 18 December he wrote to Mir Rustam:

My own belief is that personally you have ever been the friend of the English. But you are helpless among your ill-judging family. I send this by your brother His Highness Ali Moorad; listen to his advice; trust yourself to his care; you are too old for war; and if war begins how can I protect you?[2]

We know that Mir Rustam, who wished, or pretended to wish, to come to Napier's camp, went to his brother for a short time, and thus Murad 'Ali became the chief in reality if not in name. Napier wrote on 23 December:

The whole of Upper Sinde is now in the hands of Meer Ali Moorad. There are no armed bands but his, and his interest is synonymous with our friendship. I consider therefore that Upper Sinde is perfectly settled.[3]

Wallace now started for Firozpur, taking possession of and handing over to Bahawalpur the ceded districts en route, and Napier proceeded in force to Mangni. But he now found that many of the family and followers of Rustam had fled to Imam Garh, a desert fortress some way to the eastward beyond the Nara river about half way between Khairpur and Hyderabad. Here Napier resolved to follow them and so he told 'Ali Murad on 26 December; his decision was in no way altered by 'Ali Murad's wishing to go against the fortress himself, and by the fact that there had been no declaration of war. On 23 December, 1842, Napier advised 'Ali Murad not to assume the turban, but, when he heard of the flight of Mir Rustam, which took place on the 28th, he at once (1 January, 1843) issued a proclamation mentioning the facts, and stating that he would now support

---

[1] *Parliamentary Papers, ut supra*, p. 519.
[2] *Idem*, 1844, XXXVI, 518.   [3] *Idem*, 1843, XXXIX, 535.

'Ali Murad as chief in his various rights. Napier, however, thought that the flight was either due to fear or that 'Ali Murad drove him to it so as to strengthen his own position. Lord Ellenborough, while he approved of what Napier was doing, saw difficulties in the way of making one of the amirs responsible for the others, which would, he felt, mean taking the rule into British hands. Napier's letter, however, to 'Ali Murad of 14 January[1] shows that the governor-general considered 'Ali Murad as the legitimate possessor of "the Turban". What Napier was really anxious to effect was the striking of a convincing blow; he saw that the amirs were merely trifling with him, seeking to gain time. Imam Garh was said to be the Sind Gibraltar, and he would show that he could march across the desert, and take it. So, though detained near Khairpur by rain, he reached Daji, a strong fortress, on 4 January, 1843; near there on the 6th he heard of Mir Rustam whom Outram, who had now rejoined Napier, visited and found submissive. At Daji he left the main body of the force and mounting 350 men of the Queen's Regiment on camels and adding 200 horse and a couple of howitzers he set off on his memorable expedition. At the end of the first march there was so little fodder that he had to send back 150 of the horse, but he pushed on and camped near Imam Garh on the 12th. The fortress which was surrounded by walls forty feet high offered no resistance, and Outram with the consent of 'Ali Murad blew it up. This desert march of Napier's, however irregular it might be, had no greater admirer than the Duke of Wellington, who spoke of it as one of the most curious military operations he had ever heard of.

Napier now sent off Outram to Khairpur where he was to meet the amirs of Upper and Lower Sind or their representatives, and arrange with them the details connected with the new treaty. He carried a letter dated 15 January to Mir Rustam, saying that the past was all forgotten, and with regard to the amirs he was given considerable latitude, at all events so far as suggestion was concerned, provided that the spirit and the principle of the treaty were preserved. The amirs were ordered to attend, and threatened with the occupation of their territories if they did not. But though Outram fixed a date, the 20th, for the meeting at Khairpur, only the amirs of Hyderabad sent vakils, and the odd thing is that Outram, as we see from his letters to Napier of 22 January, had no idea of what was going on. He wrote to Napier objecting to the retention of Tatta, where Napier agreed with him, and also wished to modify the coinage clause, which Napier had no power to alter, but he did not see how unreal the whole business was.[2] Napier, who now moved near to the Indus, sent a strong proclamation to the amirs of Upper Sind on the 27th giving them till 1 February to come in.[3]

---

[1] *Parliamentary Papers*, 1843, XXXIX, p. 549.   [2] *Idem*, 1844, XXXVI, 530.
[3] *Idem*, 1843, XXXIX, 556.

At Outram's request also he, on the 28th, ordered that officer to move to Hyderabad where Outram thought that all could be satisfactorily arranged by personal influence. Napier read the East far more correctly than Outram, and knew how little words counted in a country filled with armed men who were stirred by the fear that their national independence was at stake. Napier also saw that, whatever the amirs might say, they had but little control over the bands who were moving rapidly about the country near the capital. Nor was the fact that Wallace towards the end of January handed over Sabzalkot and Bhung Bara to the nawab of Bahawalpur likely to make for peace.

While Outram was dreaming and talking, the two sides were acting. The amirs were collecting large masses of troops; of this Napier knew, and he prepared accordingly, although he extended the period of peace till the 6th. On that date he wrote to Outram, ordering him to tell the amir of Khairpur that he was directed to disperse their troops and would do so. Outram had also to tell the amirs of Hyderabad not to allow troops from Khairpur to come into Lower Sind. Outram reached Hyderabad on the 8th and managed before the end to get all the amirs but one to sign. He thought more of this willingness than it deserved. He wrote to Napier that he did not believe that the amirs would begin hostilities; on two occasions he urged Napier not to bring his troops any nearer; he said that there was not an armed man in Hyderabad, and on the 12th added the crowning absurdity of suggesting that Napier should come alone to the capital. That evening Outram was insulted in the streets and wrote, simply enough, that he did not think Napier would wish to come now. The general had no intention of doing so and wrote on the 15th from Hala ordering Outram not to pledge himself to anything, and telling him that he was marching on Hyderabad. The same day Outram was attacked in the Residency, and, after a gallant defence against several thousand armed Balochis, took refuge on a steamer and rejoined his commanding officer. He ceased henceforth to count in Napier's calculations, and the great controversy between them is best left in obscurity. Those who wish to enter further into the question of the negotiations with the amirs between the 8th to the 13th will find an interesting criticism of Outram's notes by Lord Ellenborough in a letter to the Secret Committee of 23 June, 1843.[1]

Napier knew that the amirs were at Miani with over 20,000 men; he had but 2800 himself with twelve pieces of artillery. But he was ready, even anxious to fight, and the thought of the odds only stimulated him. At 4 a.m. on the morning of 17 February, 1843, he marched, and at 9 o'clock he attacked. The great mass of the enemy were in the dry bed of the Fulaili river, and the scene, as described

[1] *Parliamentary Papers*, 1844, xxxvi, 609. Cf. Holmes, *Sir Charles Napier*, pp. 43 *sqq.*

by Sir William Napier from his brother's accounts, has rarely been equalled for picturesque detail:

Then rose the British shout, the English guns were run forward into position, the infantry closed upon the Fullailee with a run, and rushed up the sloping bank. The Beloochs, having their matchlocks laid ready in rest along the summit, waited until the assailants were within fifteen yards ere their volley was delivered; the rapid pace of the British, and the steepness of the slope on the inside deceived their aim, and the execution was not great; the next moment the 22nd were on the top of the bank, thinking to bear down all before them, but they staggered back in amazement at the forest of swords waving in their front! Thick as standing corn, and gorgeous as a field of flowers, stood the Beloochs in their many coloured garments and turbans; they filled the broad deep bed of the Fullailee, they clustered on both banks, and covered the plain beyond. Guarding their heads with their large dark shields, they shook their sharp swords, beaming in the sun, their shouts rolled like a peal of thunder, as with frantic gestures they rushed forwards, and full against the front of the 22nd dashed with demoniac strength and ferocity.... Now the Beloochs closed their dense masses, and again the shouts and the rolling fire of musketry and the dreadful rush of the swordsmen were heard and seen along the whole line, and such a fight ensued as has seldom been known or told of in the records of war. For ever those wild warriors came close up, sword and shield in advance, striving in all the fierceness of their valour to break into the opposing ranks; no fire of small arms, no push of bayonets, no sweeping discharges of grape from the guns, which were planted in one mass on the right, could drive the gallant fellows back; they gave their breasts to the shot, they leaped upon the guns and were blown away by twenties at a time, their dead went down the steep slope by hundreds; but the gaps in their masses were continually filled up from the rear, the survivors of the front rank still pressed forward, with unabated fury, and the bayonet and the sword clashed in full and frequent conflict.

Such was the fierce battle of Miani in which Napier gained a victory —a victory important out of all proportion to the loss of life. 5000 Balochis fell as against 256 of the British force. Six of the amirs at once came into camp and surrendered, giving up Hyderabad which was immediately occupied. But crushing though the blow was, Sind was not yet conquered, for the Lion of Mirpur, Shir Muhammad, was still in command of considerable forces, and Napier's little army, wasted by sickness, was surrounded by hostile tribesmen. Lord Ellenborough sent prompt reinforcements, but Napier wisely waited, entrenching himself, and hoping that he would be attacked in a position of his own choosing. In March, hearing that the Balochis were concentrating, he prepared to move, though in great difficulties, owing to the heat of the weather and the intrigues of the captive amirs. So that he was glad to be able to strike a final blow at Dabo, six miles from Hyderabad, where on 24 March, 1843, he defeated Shir Muhammad. The victory was not achieved without difficulty, and Shir Muhammad fled to the desert. Hurrying onwards it was a race against summer. Napier secured Mirpur on 27 March, and Umarkot on 4 April, movements through a desert country which prove capacity and resolution of no common order. The annexation of Sind had been decided upon as early as 13 March (dispatch of 26 June, 1843[1]) and Napier was made its first governor. Khairpur, however, was as

[1] Law, *op. cit.* pp. 68 *sqq.* Napier, *Conquest of Scinde*, 334.

a reward handed over to 'Ali Murad. The next four and a half years were occupied in the organisation and development of this important addition to the British Empire. There was still fighting to be done, but when Jacob on 14 June, 1843, defeated Shir Muhammad finally and drove him out of Sind, the main war was at an end.

Napier's own view of the conquest of Sind has been perhaps best expressed in a letter to Outram of January, 1843, of which a few sentences may be quoted:

> Lord Auckland began by a great act of injustice, political injustice, which produced the treaties. Lord Ellenborough then came and had his line of policy, viz., to abandon all beyond and maintain all on the Indian side of the Indus. He found existing treaties with Scinde to maintain, but the only part of his predecessor's policy in which he appears to agree is the maintenance of free traffic on the Indus, with possession of certain towns on its banks, the seizure of which was Lord Auckland's act; to keep them has been Lord Ellenborough's in compliance with treaties which no man of sense will say were well drawn up....Now I do not agree with you in thinking the Amirs are fools. I think them cunning rascals to a man if measured by our standard of honesty; but assuredly Lord Auckland's policy was not calculated to make them form a higher estimate of us. Well, they saw our defeat and that encouraged them to break existing treaties, it gave them heart, and that they hoped to have a second Cabool affair is as clear to me as the sun now shining....Now what is to be done? That which is best for the advancement of good government and well-being of the population; and we must not sacrifice all this to a minute endeavour, utterly hopeless, I may say impossible, to give to these tyrannical, drunken, debauched, cheating, intriguing, contemptible Ameers, a due portion of the plunder they have amassed from the ruined people they conquered sixty years ago. They are fortunate robbers one and all, and though I most decidedly condemn the way we entered this country (just as honest, however, as that by which the Talpoors got it from the Kalloras) I would equally condemn any policy that allowed these rascals to go on plundering the country to supply their debaucheries after we had raised the hopes of every respectable man in the country. This I consider to be Lord E.'s view and in that sense I act. If I thought Lord E. was acting on an unjust plan I would of course obey my orders, but should deeply regret my position. But I do no such thing: the whole injustice was committed by Lord Auckland, and such a course of injustice cannot be closed without hardship on someone. It is likely to fall on the Ameers, and on a crew more deserving to bear it hardly could it alight. It falls heaviest on Roostum, an old worn debauchee, a man drunk every day of his life, breaking his own religious ordinances, and even the habits and customs of his country.[1]

The judgment that has held the field hitherto has been hostile; from 1844 when a writer in the *Calcutta Review* said: "The real cause of this chastisement of the Ameers consisted in the chastisement which the British had received from the Afghans", till the recent verdict in the *Cambridge Modern History*. But the truer view will be more like that of Outram's great apologist: "In the light of subsequent history it may even be argued that Outram's policy of trust in the Ameers would have proved less wise than Napier's policy of vigilant coercion": assuming for the moment that such were the respective policies of the two men.

The conquest of Sind, however, cannot be said to be the fault of any one man. Lord Auckland looking on the country as a portion

[1] Napier, *Life...of Sir C. J. Napier*, ii, 300.

of the older Afghanistan treated its liberties—or rather the liberties of its conquerors—as subsidiary to the general Afghan policy, for which again he can hardly be held altogether responsible. He left the Sind problem in a desperate condition to his successor, but neither of them seems to have wished to annex the country; circumstances were too strong for both of them. As to Sir Charles Napier, who came fresh to the country, he acted a soldier's part and acted it extraordinarily well. He illustrated the extreme value of common-sense and directness, and there is an element of profound, as well as kindly, truth in his remark that "Outram is a clever fellow, but he seems to have been so long accustomed to Indian tricks that he thinks them of real importance". In any estimate of Napier's conduct the instructions he received must always be remembered; and in particular those of 26 August, 1842:

It may be convenient that you should at once be informed that, if the Ameers or any one of them, should act hostilely or evince hostile designs against our army, it is my fixed resolution never to forgive the breach of faith and to exact a penalty which shall be a warning to every chief in India.[1]

And yet the whole transaction has been thought to bear a colour of injustice which may rightly be ascribed to some of its parts, and the plea of the happiness of the people, who gained enormously by the change, has not been held sufficient to justify what happened.

II. THE PANJAB

At the beginning of the nineteenth century Ranjit Singh, the greatest of the Sikh rulers, had consolidated a powerful kingdom north-west of the Satlej, and seemed likely to extend his empire as far as the Jumna; he was aided on the one hand by the weakness of the Afghans and on the other by the policy of the English, who seemed disinclined at first to interfere owing to the more serious responsibilities of their great struggle with the Marathas. Lake, it will be remembered, and Wellesley defeated Sindhia and Holkar in a series of great battles the result of which was to increase the importance of the English in the north-west, and so to make the relations between them and the Sikhs more vital. The Cis-Satlej chiefs fought against the English in the battle of Delhi, and in 1805 Holkar fled to Amritsar. Ranjit Singh was too clever to help him against Lake, and the resulting treaty of Lahore of 1 January, 1806, kept the Marathas out of the Panjab, secured the friendship of the English, and left the Sikhs free from English interference for the time being north of the Satlej. This state of affairs, however, was not to last.

The Cis-Satlej states had risen to virtual independence owing to the gradual decline of the Muhammadan power, but they were engaged in constant strife, and the unsettled state of the country they inhabited invited the ambition of any freebooting adventurer.

[1] *Parliamentary Papers*, 1843, XXXIX, 408.

A quarrel between the chiefs of Nabha and Patiala gave Ranjit Singh an excuse to cross the Satlej (26 July, 1806) and to capture Ludhiana which was at once transferred to his uncle Bhag Singh of Jind. The English, under Lord Lake, had had considerable connection with Sirhind and it was natural that the idea of the establishment of Ranjit Singh's power in this wild and desolate country, for such it was then, was viewed with some concern. And when he had crossed the river a second time in 1807, the chiefs of Sirhind became sufficiently alarmed to send and ask for British protection. This was in 1808, at a time when the possibility of a French invasion of India was much discussed, and though there was no definite answer at once, the result was the sending in September of that year of Metcalfe to Ranjit Singh with the purpose of arranging a treaty; at the same time assurances of protection were given to the frightened chiefs. For the moment it seemed likely that the negotiation would fall through; Ranjit Singh crossed the Satlej for the third time, seized Faridkot and Ambala, and would have taken Patiala had he not feared English intervention. But the advance of Ochterlony with a detachment, the adroitness of the young diplomatist who is said to have assured the Sikh chieftain that he could make conquests in other directions without British interference, and it has been conjectured the weakening of the danger from the West owing to the improved relations between England and Mahmud II, the new sultan of Turkey, caused Ranjit Singh to pause. On 9 February, 1809, Ochterlony issued a warning proclamation to the effect that any further aggressions south of the Satlej would be forcibly resisted; and this coupled, as Cunningham suggests, with the fear that some of the Panjab chiefs might also seek British protection, brought the great Sikh to terms. He therefore signed the treaty of 25 April, 1809. This guaranteed him against interference on the part of the English north of the Satlej, and as to the left bank, it was stated (in the second article) that the raja would never maintain, in the territory which he occupied there, more troops than were necessary for the internal duties of that territory, nor commit or suffer any encroachments on the possessions or rights of the chiefs in its vicinity.[1] The transaction was completed by a proclamation of 3 May, 1809, of which the important articles ran as follows:

1. The country of the chiefs of Malwa and Sirhind having entered under the British protection, they shall in future be secured from the authority and influence of Maharaja Ranjit Singh, conformably to the terms of the treaty.

2. All the country of the chiefs thus taken under protection shall be exempted from all pecuniary tribute to the British Government.

3. The chiefs shall remain in the full exercise of the same rights and authority in their own possessions which they enjoyed before they were received under the British protection.

4. Should a British army on purposes of general welfare, be required to march

[1] Aitchison, *op. cit.* VIII, 144.

through the country of the said chiefs, it is necessary and incumbent that every chief shall, within his own possessions, assist and furnish, to the full of his power, such force with supplies of grain and other necessaries which may be demanded.

5. Should an enemy approach from any quarter, for the purpose of conquering this country, friendship and mutual interest require that the chiefs join the British army with all their force, and, exerting themselves in expelling the enemy, act under discipline and proper obedience.[1]

The idea was that Ranjit Singh's Cis-Satlej conquests made before the last campaign were to remain his, but that he was to have no claim to allegiance from Cis-Satlej chiefs. Still, this was a very important negotiation. On the one hand it directed Ranjit Singh's energies elsewhere than southwards; he gave up Faridkot and Ambala. On the other it has been said to have moved the British frontier from the Jumna to the Satlej. The relations of the protected chiefs among themselves took a good deal of arranging. It was necessary to protect the weak against the strong, when the fear of Ranjit Singh was removed, and a proclamation had to be issued on 22 August, 1811, to the effect that while the independence of the chiefs would be respected and their states duly protected, they would not be allowed to usurp the rights of others.[2] But it was long before all the various claims were settled and rights established.

Ranjit Singh was thus free to devote his attention elsewhere. He got the better of the Gurkhas from 1809 to 1811, taking the Kangra district, and when the English war in 1814–15 with the same people brought the English and Sikhs together in the mountains, there was excellent reason for their remaining friends. Another similar reason was supplied by the Afghan question. Shah Shuja had been driven from Afghanistan in 1809–10. Ranjit Singh sought to prevent him from getting aid from the English, in view of his own project against Multan which he unsuccessfully endeavoured to seize in February, 1810. However, Shuja was soon carried off to Kashmir, and after various adventures in the course of which Ranjit Singh secured the *Koh-i-nur* from him, he returned to Ludhiana in 1816. Meanwhile the Sikhs, though they secured Attock, defeating the Afghans at Haidaru in 1813, did not manage to secure Kashmir. More important during this period was their reduction of the northern plains and lower hills by which they gradually strengthened themselves for further efforts. The first of such was the capture of Multan, which had been attempted more than once before, and which was effected in 1818. In the same year, by taking advantage of the troubles which followed Fath Khan's death, Ranjit Singh entered Peshawar, though he relinquished it to the Barakzai governor Yar Muhammad Khan. 1819 saw him master of Kashmir. In 1823 he again took Peshawar, and this time he left Yar Muhammad Khan to rule in his name. Thus by 1824 he had added to his dominions the three Muhammadan

---

[1] Cunningham, *History of the Sikhs* (ed. 1918), p. 382.
[2] *Idem*, p. 383.

states of Kashmir, Multan and Peshawar. A small Sikh minority ruled a vast kingdom almost equally divided as regards inhabitants between Hindus and Muhammadans, the latter more numerous towards the north-west. The older organisation of the *misls* or confederacies, each following a chief or group of chiefs, had given place to an organised military despotism, although the phrases used by Ranjit Singh disguised the fact. The whole strength of the state was devoted to war. The system suited the Sikh people who were excellent soldiers, and it was not disliked by the military Muhammadans of the Panjab, whom Ranjit Singh slowly reduced to obedience. The material at his disposal, recruits obtained by the feudal system of land tenure, was rendered more formidable by the European methods of discipline which he adopted; he used men who had deserted from the British service to train his troops, and soon Frenchmen and other European officers like Allard, Court, Ventura and Avitabile joined his service.

Sir Lepel Griffin has truly said that the conquest of the frontier was a matter beyond the Sikh strength; it was inevitable that the subjection of so much territory in the Himalayan region should involve constant struggles and constant loss. The events of Ranjit Singh's later years often made him wish that he had not had the trouble of maintaining such expensive conquests. With the English he became more friendly, especially as his relations with them were in the hands of Captain Wade at Ludhiana. In the discussions as to the districts south of the Satlej, the English gave way on some points but secured Firozpur. But it required all Wade's skill until the end of the Burmese War and the capture of Bharatpur to keep the Sikhs quiet. After a troublesome religious revolt under Saiyid Ahmad Shah Ghazi, who for a time (1830) held Peshawar, had been suppressed, Ranjit Singh's position in India was very strong. It was now, therefore, when the idea of counteracting Russian influence by the formation of buffer states was in favour, that Lord William Bentinck arranged the famous meeting with the Sikh ruler at Rupar on the Satlej in October, 1831, when an assurance of friendship with the English was given which satisfied both parties for different reasons. Much discussion took place about Sind and about the navigation of the Indus, Ranjit Singh agreeing that that river and the Satlej should be open to commerce. He also gave up for the time being his designs on Shikarpur (1832) on which he had fixed his mind.

Hence the attitude of the English in regard to Shah Shuja in these years is easily understood. They looked upon his efforts to regain the Afghan throne with benevolent neutrality, and left him to make his own bargain with the Sikhs and the amirs of Sind. But the Sikhs got the advantage. The negotiations fluctuated from time to time. The amirs feared the approach of the English, and in 1832 they offered help if Shah Shuja would give up his claims on their country. He agreed in case he succeeded. But he reopened the question with the maharaja, and, finding that he was the only potentate whom he had to conciliate, he entered into an alliance with him in August, 1833. This treaty was the basis of the Tripartite Treaty of 1838, and provided that the districts beyond the Indus in possession of the Sikhs should be formally ceded to them. The Sindians were abandoned and Shah Shuja was allowed to proceed towards his native land by way of Shikarpur where he defeated the Sindians, who had finally decided to oppose him, on 9 January, 1834. He then passed on towards Kandahar, near which city he was routed by Dost Muhammad and his brothers on 1 July, 1834, and later after much wandering and various attempts to secure aid he reached Ludhiana again. Ranjit Singh resolved to make what he could out of the affair, and accordingly he sent Hari Singh, his general, and Nao Nihal Singh, his grandson, who secured the town and citadel of Peshawar on 6 May, 1834, thus finally establishing Sikh power there. Dost Muhammad, who had been so perplexed when Shah Shuja entered Afghanistan that he had offered his submission to the government officials as a dependent on Great Britain, now plucked up courage, calling himself ghazi as well as amir, and advanced as he thought to retake Peshawar. He still wished to secure English help, and tried to do so through his nephew Abdul Ghiyas Khan, who was at Ludhiana. The English, however, who had their attention still directed to the question of the navigation of the Indus, declined to interfere. The result was that Dost Muhammad came to the eastern end of the Khaibar and having, on 11 May, 1835, been almost surrounded by the Sikhs, was glad to retreat hurriedly enough with considerable loss of prestige. About September in the same year he commenced negotiations with Persia though still hoping for English aid. Hearing, however, that the Sikhs had sent home some of their forces, he sent Muhammad Akbar Khan, his son, who, though he failed to secure the Sikh position, won a doubtful battle near Jamrud on 30 April, 1837, Hari Singh the great Sikh leader being killed. Reinforcements, however, arriving, Muhammad Akbar Khan had to retire without having taken either Peshawar or Jamrud.

The defeat of the amirs of Sind by Shah Shuja frightened them and they would probably have gladly allowed Ranjit Singh to have taken Shikarpur if he would have protected them against further attempts of the same kind. This did not please the English who, as Cunningham points out, were beginning to have political as well as commercial schemes in those directions. Ranjit Singh did not really wish to be friendly with the amirs, and kept a representative of the exiled Kaloras in his state; he even began negotiating with Shah Shuja once more. There was a good deal of local friction and the fortress of Rojhan, the stronghold of a robber tribe called Mazaris, who indeed gave trouble to the Sikhs but could hardly be termed subjects of the amirs, was taken by the governor of Multan in August, 1836. Soon afterwards the Sikhs went south to Ken. As there seemed every likelihood of further aggression, Lord Auckland decided to mediate, especially as both parties were ready to declare open war. In December, 1836, Ranjit Singh yielded, though unwillingly, and agreed to let things be on their own footing, retaining however Rojhan and Mazari territory while he destroyed the fortress of Ken. It was on this occasion that he asked the famous question of those who were trying to dissuade him from peace what had become of the 200,000 spears of the Marathas.

There was then a feeling of intense hostility at this time between the Afghans and the Sikhs. Both had considerable dread of the English and the last thing they wished for was British interference. Unfortunately this state of feeling, which might otherwise have passed naturally away, occurred at a time when the fear of the Russians was the mainspring of Indian foreign politics. There were also numerous French designs, and the story of Allard's diplomatic character at the court of Lahore aroused suspicion; Wellington afterwards (4 February, 1843) warned Lord Ellenborough of the French connection. In such circumstances the English could please no one. Ranjit Singh did not like to be restrained from action in Sind and elsewhere; and Dost Muhammad would have gladly welcomed English aid against the Sikhs. The English chose perhaps the worst possible way out of their difficulties.

The weakness of the scheme of the Tripartite Treaty of 1838 was obvious. The English could not trust Shah Shuja to the Sikhs for fear that the war of restoration should become a war of aggression on their part. Ranjit Singh disliked the final passing of all hopes of gaining Shikarpur, and although the march of a Sikh force through the Khaibar with Shah Shuja's son was decided upon, the Sikhs not altogether unnaturally decided to do as little as they could and to gain the utmost advantage. At the end of 1838 Ranjit Singh met Lord Auckland at Firozpur, where the British force was assembled, but his health had failed. He heard of the fall of Kandahar, and died on 27 June, 1839.

Ranjit Singh's power was personal and as he founded no permanent institutions which could live apart from himself his death was the signal for the beginning of anarchy. Cunningham, the sympathetic historian of the Sikhs, has thus estimated his claims to greatness:

Ranjit Singh found the Punjab a waning confederacy, a prey to the factions of its chiefs, pressed by the Afghans and the Marathas and ready to submit to English supremacy. He consolidated the numerous petty states into a kingdom, he wrested from Kabul the fairest of its provinces, and he gave the potent English no cause for interference. He found the military array of his country a mass of horsemen, brave indeed but ignorant of war as an Art, and he left it mustering fifty thousand disciplined soldiers, fifty thousand well armed yeomanry and militia, and more than three hundred pieces of cannon for the field. His rule was founded on the feelings of a people, but it involved the joint action of the necessary principles of military order and territorial extension; and when a limit had been set to Sikh dominion, and his own commanding genius was no more, the vital spirit of his race began to consume itself in domestic contentions.[1]

Sir Lepel Griffin admits his private vices:

"He was selfish, false and avaricious; grossly superstitious, shamelessly and openly drunken and debauched", and continues: "We only succeed in establishing him as a hero, as a ruler of men, and as worthy of a pedestal in that innermost shrine where history honours the few human beings to whom may be indisputably assigned the palm of greatness, if we free our minds of prejudice and, discounting conventional virtue, only regard the rare qualities of force which raise a man supreme above his fellows. Then we shall at once allow that, although sharing in full measure the commonplace and coarse vices of his time and education, he yet ruled the country which his military genius had conquered with a vigour of will and an ability which placed him in the front rank of the statesmen of the century."[2]

Ranjit Singh when dying was said to have declared his imbecile son, Kharak Singh, his successor; but, though acknowledged in the main, his claims were disputed by Shir Singh, a reputed child of Ranjit Singh; while his own son, Nao Nihal Singh, a bold but vicious youth of eighteen, wished to obtain the ascendancy. The wazir, Dhian Singh, hated the able Resident, Wade, who supported Kharak Singh, and Dhian Singh and Nao Nihal Singh both hated the imbecile monarch's favourite, Chet Singh. Chet Singh was murdered on 8 October, 1839. Wade was replaced by Clerk as British agent at the beginning of April, 1840, Wade's Sikh enemies persuading Auckland that this step would secure easier communication between British India and the forces in Afghanistan; Lord Auckland further imagined that the long-cherished schemes for the opening of a valuable commerce with Afghanistan by way of the Indus were now about to take shape. The only real and tangible result of these intrigues was the increase of the power of Nao Nihal Singh who hoped by the reduction in the strength of the rajas of Jammu, and then probably by the destruction of Raja Dhian Singh, to make himself supreme. He was, however, interrupted in his ambitious schemes by disputes with the English as to the favouring by the Sikhs of Afghan rebels against Shah Shuja and even treacherous communication with Dost Muhammad himself; and there was a very strong feeling on the part of men like Macnaghten in favour of taking away much of the Sikh territory, that part of it at all events which had once been held by Afghanistan. Kharak Singh died on 5 November, 1840, and on the same day his more brilliant son, passing homewards from the funeral rites, was crushed by the fall of the gateway in the Lahore fort, and so seriously injured that he died the same night. How far his death was accidental was disputed; the rajas of Jammu had every reason to wish for it.

[1] Cunningham, op. cit. p. 222.
[2] Griffin, Ranjit Singh, p. 95.

The question now was as to the succession. Shir Singh was preferred by the British agent, but he was not certainly legitimate. After much intrigue the widow of Kharak Singh, Mai Chand Kaur, who was supported by various Sikh chiefs, notably the Sindhianwala family, which included men of note such as Atar and Ajit Singh Sindhianwala, and like many other Sikh families of importance was opposed to the rajas of Jammu, came forward and secured the regency. She was to hold it till it was seen whether Nao Nihal's widow bore a son. Shir Singh was to be a kind of viceroy, and Dhian Singh the wazir. This temporary arrangement was nominally in force when Dost Muhammad surrendered, but the factions soon came to blows. Shir Singh attacked Lahore in January, 1841, and was proclaimed maharaja on the 18th of that month, the Sindhianwala family taking refuge in flight. Shir Singh, however, though he might like to be king, could not rule, and the obvious result followed that the army became all powerful. The discussion of projects for armed intervention on the part of the British Government, while it did not make things easier for what authority there was in the country, enabled the Sikh army to regard itself more and more as the representative body of the Sikh people; its position resembled that of the Ironsides of the seventeenth century without there being any Cromwell in control. Another source of difficulty lay in the activity of Zorawar Singh who, as deputy of the rajas of Jammu, after taking Skardu, seized Garo, and seemed likely to conquer much of Chinese Tibet. When, however, the English found him established near Almora they decided to interfere, and ordered Garo to be restored by 10 December, 1841. By this time the Chinese arrived and defeated the Sikhs in a wonderful campaign in the mountains, one of the most awful perhaps in the history of warfare, and peace was made in the autumn of 1842, matters between China and the Sikhs being placed on their old footing. About the same time the English managed to prevent Gulab Singh, the brother of Dhian Singh, from being made governor of the Afghan province, which would have placed an enemy of the British at Peshawar instead of the Italian Avitabile.

During the troubles connected with and following the insurrection at Kabul in November, 1841, the English were in the unpleasant position of distrusting the Sikhs, and yet not being able to do without their aid; this was added to the fact that the English had no decided policy. They could claim help under the Tripartite Treaty, but the Sikhs, as has been seen, helped but grudgingly, rather because the authorities had little control over the army than for other reasons, though such reasons were doubtless present. Some part, however, they took, and it was suggested to give Jallalabad to them. But its destruction by Pollock relieved them from taking what they really did not want. That Ellenborough at this time viewed the prospect of a Sikh war with disfavour can be seen from his dispatch of 15 May, 1842.[1]

---

[1] Ellenborough Papers, 102.

In June, 1842, the murder of Mai Chand Kaur altered the state of things at the court, but it did not relieve the difficulties of Shir Singh, and, when the Sindhianwala chiefs came to an agreement with the rajas of Jammu, his fate was sealed. On 15 September, 1843, he was assassinated by Ajit Singh, who proceeded to kill his son Pertab Singh also. But Dhian Singh also reaped the reward of his treachery, and was murdered by his Sindhianwala allies. He left, however, a son, Hira Singh, who, in spite of the hatred of the people for his family and the Jammu rajas, managed to raise enough troops to kill Ajit and Lahna Singh, the two Sindhianwalas, and to proclaim Dalip Singh, a supposed son of Ranjit Singh by a woman afterwards notorious enough, Rani Jindan. Hira himself took the post of wazir much to the vexation of Suchet Singh, youngest of the Jammu rajas, who now becomes prominent.

These struggles were intricate and not very important, the one fact that mattered being that as they became more and more intense they brought the army into ever greater prominence and importance. Clerk had given way as Resident to Colonel Richmond, whose letters have furnished the world with an account of what happened. The maternal uncle of Dalip Singh, Jawahir Singh, having tried conclusions with the Jammu rajas in 1843, was cast into prison. Then Kashmira Singh and Peshawara Singh, adopted sons of Ranjit Singh, seized Sialkot, possibly with the connivance of Raja Suchet Singh, who may also have procured the release of Jawahir Singh about the same time, and who was killed while attempting an insurrection against his nephew in March, 1844. The same fate overtook Atar Singh Sindhianwala in the following May; he had fled to British territory the year before and now returned, joined a religious fanatic, Bhai Bir Singh, of some popularity, and managed to gain Kashmira Singh to his cause. It is noteworthy that Hira Singh managed to secure the adherence of the army by telling them that the Sindhianwalas were relying upon English help. Kashmira Singh and Bhai Bir Singh both shared Atar Singh's fate. This same feeling of resentment against the English Hira Singh made use of about the same time when he pretended that the English reliefs for Sind were directed against the Sikhs.

Serious grounds of dispute between the two peoples were bound to arise. The central government of the Sikhs was no doubt a scene of confusion and crime, but the nation was strong enough. Gilgit had been annexed to Kashmir towards the end of 1843, and the Sikh army was at once anxious for active service and also intensely superstitious. "Our position", wrote Lord Ellenborough on 11 February, 1844, "with respect to the Punjab can now be viewed only in the light of an armed truce."[1] The comparatively recent events in Afghanistan and the news of a mutinous disposition in some of the Sepoy regiments had lessened their respect for their powerful neighbour, whom also they believed to be preparing to annex their territory. There was a

[1] Law, *India under Ellenborough*, p. 113.

35-2

dispute as to a village in the Nabha state where both had interests, and the action of the English in retaining the treasure of Suchet Singh, which had been brought by him to Firozpur before his death, was neither liked nor understood. Colonel Richmond too was succeeded by Major Broadfoot as Resident on 1 November, 1844, and, as he was suspected by the Sikhs, his appointment did not ease matters.

When things were in rather a critical state, another revolution took place by which Hira Singh was overthrown and slain on 21 December, 1844. With him fell his tutor, Pandit Jalla, who had acquired much influence over him. For some time there was confusion, but the power was secured by Jawahir Singh, the brother, and Lal Singh the lover of Rani Jindan; Lal Singh, a Brahmin, had once been an adherent of the Jammu rajas. They had, however, to reckon with Gulab Singh, and sent the army against Jammu early in 1845. Gulab saw that there was nothing for it but submission, so he parted with vast sums of money and much territory and came to Lahore with the army, with whom he became more or less a favourite. Jawahir Singh became wazir on 14 May, 1845, and Gulab Singh retired to the mountains again. In the same way Mulraj, who had succeeded to the governorship of Multan when his father was assassinated in 1844, and who had shown some vigour, was forced to pay a fine and to promise to surrender territory, when he heard that the army had agreed to march against him. Peshawara Singh, who had taken refuge in British territory the year before, also rebelled and was put to death at Attock in September of this same eventful year. But Jawahir's time was at hand. The all-powerful army distrusted him as a friend of the English, even when he talked of making war against them. The regimental *panchayats*, therefore, decided that he must die, and he was shot on 21 September, 1845. Lal Singh now became wazir, an unworthy ruler, but the power was not with him but with Sardar Tej Singh, the commander-in-chief, and the *panchayats* of the army.

The direct causes of the Sikh war with the English are obscure. The English seeing the confusion which followed the death of Ranjit Singh no doubt made preparations of a defensive kind; as the event showed they would have been very foolish if they had not done so, though there was some point in the words of a hostile critic: "To be prepared is one thing; to be always making preparations another". The Sikhs, seeing more men placed in the neighbourhood of their frontier, at a time when they knew that their own power was weaker than before, drew the natural but erroneous inference that the English wanted their country. And this impression was strengthened by the fact that they knew that some of the Sikh chiefs would gladly have seen the English come. There was the object lesson of Sind before their eyes; they had always been an aggressive people themselves, and they could not understand that a powerful nation could be otherwise. They remembered, long after the English had ceased to think about such matters, projects for sending troops to Lahore and for handing Peshawar over to the Afghans; men had talked, too, in the days of the Afghan occupation of "macadamising" the Panjab. The actual changes in recent years, so far as troops are concerned, have been summarised thus:

Up to 1838 the troops on the frontier amounted to one regiment at Sabatha, and two at Ludhiana, with six pieces of artillery, equalling in all little more than 2500 men. Lord Auckland made the total about 8000, by increasing Ludhiana and creating Ferozepore. Lord Ellenborough formed further new stations at Ambala, Kasauli and Simla, and placed in all about 14,000 men and 48 field guns on the frontier. Lord Hardinge increased the aggregate force to about 32,000 men, with 68 field guns, besides having 10,000 men with artillery at Meerut. After 1843, however, the station of Karnal, on the Jumna, was abandoned, which in 1838 and preceding years may have mustered about 4000 men.

But Lord Hardinge has shown that his father deserved even greater credit than this account, believed to be from the pen of Lawrence, would allow. The strength on the frontier, exclusive of hill stations which remained the same, at the departure of Lord Ellenborough was 17,612 men and sixty-six guns: at the outbreak of war it was 40,523 men and ninety-four guns. This comprises the garrisons of Firozpur, Ludhiana, Ambala and Meerut.[1]

Cunningham thinks that the Sikhs distrusted Major Broadfoot because of angry proceedings on his part when passing through their territory with Shah Shuja's family in 1841, and because of the strong line he took when British agent with regard to the relations between the Cis-Satlej states and the British Government. In the latter connection various small incidents occurred, trifling in themselves but magnified by bazaar gossip in a land where there are but few topics of conversation. More important was undoubtedly the fact that many of the chiefs of the Panjab had, or thought they had, everything to gain if the army with its system of *panchayats* dashed itself to pieces against the English, and among these were such men as Lal Singh, the wazir, and Tej Singh, the commander-in-chief; their interests or their wishes coinciding with those of the soldiers on widely different grounds. Cunningham has mentioned, too, the story of two Sikh villages having been sequestrated because they harboured criminals, but, whether this is true or not, it probably had little to do with the matter. The soldiers were determined, although their commander knew that they were mistaken, and although Gulab Singh and many others were entirely opposed to the war. The Sikh army then, hoping to surprise the English and march to Delhi, crossed the Satlej on 11 December, 1845, between Huriki and Kasur.

The governor-general, Sir Henry Hardinge, and the commander-in-chief, Sir Hugh Gough, were both old and tried soldiers. They had available forces of between 20,000 and 30,000 men and they had to meet (the exact number is uncertain) over 50,000 well-armed

---

[1] Lord Hardinge, *Viscount Hardinge*, pp. 74 *sqq.*, and Burton, *Sikh Wars*, pp. 10 *sqq.* Cf. Rait, *Lord Gough*, I, 371 *sqq.*

opponents. The governor-general on 13 December issued a formal declaration of war. He stated that the British Government had ever been on friendly terms with that of the Panjab and had continued to be so during the disorganised state of the government which had followed the death of Shir Singh in spite of many unfriendly proceedings on the part of the Sikh durbar. The Sikh army had now invaded British territory without a shadow of provocation and the governor-general must, therefore, take steps necessary to protect the British provinces, to vindicate the authority of the British Government, and to punish the violators of treaties and disturbers of the public peace. He therefore declared the possessions of the maharaja on the left bank of the Satlej confiscated and annexed to the British territories.

As there was a strong striking force of the Sikhs to contend with, it was wisely decided to bring as many troops together as possible; the garrison of Ludhiana was therefore transferred to Basian where it served the admirable purpose of protecting a great grain depot of the forces. The Sikhs took up a position within a few miles of Firozpur. It is unnecessary to discuss the alleged treachery of Lal Singh and Tej Singh, it suffices to follow what happened. The English under Gough pushed forward by way of Wadni and Charak to Mudki which they had no sooner reached than they were attacked by the Sikhs (18 December, 1845). The enemy were, however, defeated with a loss of seventeen guns. How men who had marched so far under such difficult conditions, and who had but the short remnant of a winter's day to fight in, could have done better is hard to see, but more than one critic has expected it. Sale, amongst other brave men, fell here.

The English army was now only twenty miles from Firozpur, where was General Littler, and if his force could join that of Gough and Hardinge, who had now placed himself as a volunteer under the orders of the commander-in-chief, they would have about 18,000 men with which to attack the large body of Sikhs who were encamped round Firozshah. Gough was anxious not to wait, but the governor-general obliged him to do so; they were joined by Littler a few hours later on the 21st, and they attacked at four in the afternoon, both sections of the army having been many hours under arms. This was a very different affair from Mudki, and on the night of 21 December "the fate of India trembled in the balance". The enemy's camp was indeed taken, but much remained to be done, and the two leaders were equally resolved to fight things out to a finish in the morning. So the next day the wearied troops renewed the battle; again the governor-general and the commander-in-chief led the attack; and finally with a magnificent bayonet charge the fight was won. But this two days' battle had been a terrible risk; there had been some confusion and the loss of life (Broadfoot fell amongst many less known men) had been great; he hesitated and on 30 December requested Gough's recall.[1]

Fortunately Gough was a man of iron who never hesitated for a moment as to what he had to do. It was far otherwise with the British public and the cabinet which represented them. It was at once resolved that the governor-general should take the command and to get over the technical difficulty a "Letter of Service" was sent out to him from the queen which would enable him as a lieutenant-general on the staff to command in person the troops in India. Happily conditions had altered so much that the letter owing to the generous spirit of Sir Henry Hardinge was never published; nor indeed was its existence generally known till fifty years later.[2]

Seventy-three guns had been taken and several thousand Sikhs killed at Firozshah, but there was still a formidable army to reckon with, and the British force was sadly reduced. Fresh Sikh troops kept pouring across the Satlej, more guns were brought, and every day became of importance especially as an attack on Ludhiana was threatened. Under these circumstances, reinforcements having arrived from Meerut, Sir Harry Smith was sent to Ludhiana, and, after being joined by the troops under General Wheeler, he attacked on 28 January, 1846, a strong enemy force. The Sikhs in this neighbourhood, afraid of being taken on both sides by the two bodies of English troops, had fallen back to an entrenched position at Aliwal. The result was a brilliant victory. The Sikh position was entirely destroyed and over fifty guns were captured. It was valuable on its own account, but it also vastly encouraged the main body of the British troops who were preparing for the far more serious ordeal of an attack on the great Sikh army posted near Sobraon Ghat on the Satlej, a few miles from Firozpur.

In sanctioning the attack on the Sikh entrenchments on the memorable 10 February, 1846, Hardinge made the attempt conditional on the artillery being able to be brought into play. But it was soon evident that the Sikh guns could not be silenced by artillery, and Gough, so the story goes, rejoiced when the ammunition gave out and he could "be at them with the bayonet". This, the glory of Sobraon, was what happened, for the infantry carried all before them in their onrush and proved once more what Napier has said, "with what a strength and majesty the British soldier fights". With such a leader, ever anxious to lead the charge himself, everything was possible, and at his side there were men of great distinction and promise: the two Lawrences, Havelock, Robert Napier; these amongst others. Never was a victory more decisive. The Sikhs fled across the river losing at least 10,000 men and all their guns. The fighting was over at 1 o'clock on the 10th and by the 13th almost the whole

---

[1] Rait, op. cit. II, 88 sqq.
[2] Lord Hardinge, op. cit. pp. 104–5.

British army was across the Satlej and well on its way to Lahore. By the 18th they were close to the city. On the 20th it was occupied and the only question was that of terms.

There were, it has often been pointed out, at least three possible courses open to Lord Hardinge. He might have annexed the Panjab. But this was contrary to his own ideas, contrary to the policy of the Company, and would have required the services of a much larger force than he had at his disposal, even had Sir Charles Napier joined him with 12,000 men from Sind. He might again have established a "subsidiary alliance", that is to say he might have kept the existing government on foot, with troops under the Company's command but paid for by the state, and a Resident representing the wishes of the outside authority. This was the system which commended itself to the Lahore durbar. It had, however, other disadvantages than that of keeping on foot the rule of a selfish body of time-serving intriguers. It would have introduced a divided authority in the state, and was certain to lead to disturbance and possibly to further interference in the future. The third plan was that which he followed. It had much to be said for it, as all compromises have, but it did not really settle the problem, and was open to many of the same objections as that to which reference has just been made. Perhaps, however, as things were it was unfortunately the only possible course open to him. It was in the main that which was represented by the treaty concluded at Lahore on 9 March, 1846.[1]

All the territories lying to the south of the Satlej were handed over to the British Government. The Jalandhar *doab* between the Bias and the Satlej was also ceded, and, in substitution for the war indemnity of one and a half crores of rupees, the hill countries between the Bias and the Indus, including Kashmir and Hazara. The Sikh army was limited to twenty-five battalions of infantry and 12,000 cavalry, and thirty-six guns in addition to those already captured were surrendered. Two other important articles prevented the maharaja from employing any British, European, or American subject without the consent of the British Government, and provided that the limits of the Lahore territory should not be changed without the concurrence of the British Government. Kashmir was transferred to Gulab Singh, a man of humble beginnings indeed, for he had been a running footman to Ranjit Singh, but of talent and address. He knew and feared the Sikhs, he was a Rajput, and was glad to be finally, as the reward of a life of service which included no inconsiderable amount of cruelty and self-seeking, separated from the state to which he owed everything, but to which it is difficult to regard him, in spite of Lord Hardinge's defence, as other than a traitor. What was clear was that the Lahore state must be reduced in size, that Kashmir was the easiest limb to lop off, and that such being the case Gulab Singh was the only man to whom it could be well handed over.

[1] Aitchison, *op. cit.* VIII, 160.

The treaty had recognised Dalip Singh as maharaja, but the governor-general was careful to state that the British Government would not interfere in the internal administration of the Lahore state. It was, however, agreed that a force sufficient to protect the person of the maharaja and to secure the execution of the treaty should be left in the capital until the close of the year 1846, and Henry Lawrence was appointed as British agent. It was, however, soon clear that this arrangement would have to be prolonged. In October an insurrection under Shaikh Imam-ud-Din, directed against the transfer of Kashmir to Gulab Singh, took place in that country, and a considerable British force, assisted by 17,000 of the Sikhs who had fought against us, was necessary to put it down. And as it was proved at a formal court of enquiry that Lal Singh the wazir had been at the bottom of this movement, his deposition was demanded from the durbar and agreed to. The favourite of the rani was accordingly deported to British territory notwithstanding her protests; and as the remaining members of the durbar saw nothing but anarchy ahead of them if the English retired, they asked for and obtained a revision of the treaty. It was a distinct march in the direction of annexation, a solution which Hardinge disliked and wished to avoid, but of which he saw even then the possibility.

The revised treaty only modified the previous one in respect of the extent and character of British interference. It provided for the appointment by the governor-general of a British officer with an efficient establishment of assistants to remain at Lahore and to have full authority to direct and control all matters in every department of the state. There was to be a council of regency composed of leading chiefs and sardars, acting under the control and guidance of the British Resident. The members of this council were named, and the consent of the governor-general, expressed through the Resident, was necessary for any change in its composition. Such British force as the governor-general thought to be necessary should remain in Lahore and should occupy all forts in the Lahore territory that the British Government deemed needful for the maintenance of the security of the capital or the peace of the country. The Lahore state was to pay twenty-two lakhs a year in respect of the expenses of the occupation. An allowance was to be granted to the maharani and the new arrangements to last till the maharaja attained the age of sixteen years (4 September, 1854), or till such period as the governor-general and the durbar might agree on.[1]

This treaty marked the downfall of the rani's ascendancy (she was finally deported to Benares), and the beginning of the control of the famous Resident, Henry Lawrence. He chose men whom he knew and could trust and distributed them over the province, allowing them as much freedom of action as he could. Their names are an undying testimony to Lawrence's capacity as a ruler: John and

[1] *Idem*, p. 166.

George Lawrence, Nicholson, Herbert Edwardes, Lake, Lumsden, Hodson; these and others like them. But this is not the place to deal with the details of administration. Unfortunately Henry Lawrence sailed for England with Lord Hardinge on 18 January, 1848, and his successor, after a brief interval, was Sir Frederick Currie, a different type of man indeed, but it would be unjust to hold him responsible for what followed.

For the second Sikh War must be regarded as inevitable. It was clear that the arrangements made were temporary in their nature, and they could only result either in the annexation of the country or in a resumption of its independence. That the Sikh people who had fought with determination in the war just over, and who had a long record of successful achievements behind them, were likely to settle down without a further struggle was not to be believed. It needed but an event of sufficient general interest to excite a national rising, and that event was supplied by the city of Multan, long a storm centre.

The governor of Multan, the Diwan Mulraj, whom we have already noted as a man of some force and ability, was in trouble about money matters, and probably for this reason wished to resign his post. A successor, one Sardar Khan Singh, was appointed in his place and two officials, Vans Agnew of the Civil Service and Lieutenant Anderson, on being sent to arrange the matter were murdered at Mulraj's instigation on 20 April, 1848. Mulraj strengthened the defences of the town and proclaimed a general revolt in the surrounding country; the troops of the considerable escort which had come with the officials joined him and thus there was open warfare.

The question was, what to do. Detachments of troops were moved against Multan as soon as the urgent message sent by Vans Agnew had been received. But when it was known that the two British officers were dead, Lord Gough, to whom Sir Frederick Currie had written, decided against sending large masses of troops just before the beginning of the hot weather, and Lord Dalhousie agreed with him. This decision, though approved by the home authorities including the Duke of Wellington, was much criticised at the time; especially by those who did not know what the troops available were, and the difficulties attending large military movements during the hot weather and the rains. But politically there was much to be said for delay. Lord Gough knew that the whole country was really at the back of Mulraj. Had an expedition been hurried forward, and if it had been successful, it would have narrowed the issue down to the punishment of the governor of Multan, and the inevitable struggle would have been postponed. It is certain too that for such a small object as the reduction of Multan the loss of life would have been very great. If proof were wanted of the widespread nature of the movement it could be supplied by the movements of Chatter Singh, father of Shir Singh, who was busy raising a revolt in Hazara and who succeeded in winning over Peshawar to the rebel cause. By holding out that city as a bait he was able to draw in Dost Muhammad, who afterwards sent troops, though to small purpose.

And Lord Gough resolved that when done the work should be finished. He estimated for and prepared a large striking force with all its necessary auxiliaries and transport; it was to assemble at Firozpur in November. It is not necessary to describe the movements which took place in the interval, especially as they have been the subject of controversy. Edwardes and Currie made heroic but mistaken efforts to deal with the rising on a small scale, the results being that Shir Singh came out into open hostility on 14 September, that the siege of Multan had to be abandoned, and that the second Sikh War, as a national rather than a local movement, began in earnest, as it had promised to do sooner or later in any case. The importance of the siege of Multan has been exaggerated. It was begun again with reinforcements in December and the fortress fell on 22 January, 1849. Lord Gough had held the sound view of Multan from the first, but Lord Dalhousie took some time to come round to it.

On 13 October, 1848, the secretary to the government of India wrote to the Resident at Lahore that the Governor-General in Council considered the state of Lahore to be, to all intents and purposes, directly at war with the British Government; and Lord Dalhousie in a letter to the Secret Committee of 7 October, 1848, spoke of a general Panjab war and the occupation of the country.[1] The real war as a whole may be said to date from 9 November when Lord Gough crossed the Satlej, though on the 15th he rather petulantly said he did not know whether he was at peace or at war or who it was he was fighting for. The situation soon cleared. On the 13th his force of over 20,000 men reached Lahore. On the 16th he crossed the Ravi and advanced to Ramnagar. On the 22nd he drove the Sikhs across the Chenab, and himself crossed that river, Shir Singh, who was in command of the Sikhs, having been forced by a flanking movement by part of the troops under General Thackwell[2] higher up the river to retire on the Jhelum. Gough was anxious to wait as long as possible so as to be strengthened by the forces before Multan, but the fall of Attock and the consequent reinforcement of the Sikhs on the Jhelum made it necessary for him to risk an engagement. So he moved to Dinghi on 12 January, and found himself almost due east of Shir Singh who was just beyond the village of Chilianwala, between it and the river. Gough now had with him about 14,000 men and sixty-six guns. On the 13th, after a march of four hours, he fought and won the glorious but expensive action of Chilianwala. He had been anxious to wait until the next day, and it was only because the Sikhs advanced their positions somewhat, making it impossible for the

---

[1] *Parliamentary Papers*, 1849, XLI, 374.
[2] Wylly, *Thackwell*, pp. 243 *sqq.*, and *Calcutta Review*, XII, 275 *sqq.*

British army to encamp, that he was forced into an action under such disadvantageous conditions. But it was a dangerous and difficult affair, marked, too, by a certain amount of confusion and mistake[1]; marked also, however, by an amazing number of heroic deeds on the part of individuals. The British losses were over 2000, and the impression made both in India and in England, when it was also heard that four guns and the colours of three regiments had been taken by the enemy, was very great. The news of the battle inspired the first poem of George Meredith, which well represented the general melancholy felt. But Chilianwala was a very important victory. Large numbers of Sikhs had been killed; many guns had been taken or destroyed; and a very strong position had been carried. But the general public knew even less than the poet of the real facts and called for a victim, and the directors were forced to supersede Lord Gough as commander-in-chief by Sir Charles Napier. Fortunately the former had the opportunity of taking the noblest revenge before the news of his disgrace reached India.

The drawing on of night prevented Chilianwala from being a complete victory. The Sikhs could not at once retire on their position at Rasul, but they had not been driven into the river and they stationed themselves at Tupai on its banks. The British army was prevented by rain from following up their victory, and large reinforcements joined the Sikhs. On 2 February they moved deliberately towards Gujrat near the Chenab; Lord Gough slowly following by way of Sadullapur. By the 20th the Multan army had joined him, and he felt strong enough, especially as regards artillery, to strike a crushing blow. From his camp at Shadiwal on the 21st he moved out to attack the Sikh position, a strong one, to the south of Gujrat with the Chenab on its left. In a few hours the battle of Gujrat was over; a brilliant victory was won; and the enemy were in rapid flight. A body of 12,000 men pursued them across the Jhelum; on 12 March they surrendered at discretion, and the capitulation of Peshawar and the hurried escape of the Afghan auxiliaries ended the war.

The Panjab was formally annexed by a proclamation in full durbar on 30 March, 1849, the maharaja being pensioned and required to reside outside the state. Henry Lawrence was the obvious man to carry out the difficult work of organisation, but Lord Dalhousie did not agree with his views. Hence as a compromise a "Board of Government" was appointed consisting of Henry and John Lawrence and Charles E. Mansell. The three all pulled in different directions and yet the results were satisfactory. But the three would never have achieved the mighty task that was set before them, that of transforming one of the ancient military autocracies, where revenue was the chief interest of the government after warfare, into a modern state, had it not been for the work of those who assisted them, and

---

[1] Cf. Rait, *op. cit.*, Wylly, *op. cit.*, and *Calcutta Review*, xv, 269 *sqq.*

to whom reference has been made. In 1853 Henry Lawrence went to Rajputana, and John, whose views were nearer to those of Lord Dalhousie, became chief commissioner.

Various opinions have been held and will be held as to the annexation of the Panjab. But it is quite clear that if the British were to hold the controlling power in India it was inevitable. We may even go further than that. After the death of Ranjit Singh the state of the Panjab was such that the Sikhs, a small minority, could not have long continued to hold the country; it was bound either to split up into various independent states, or, as was more probable, to become in whole or in part the prey of some external conqueror. Dost Muhammad would no doubt have annexed most of the old Afghan portions, and the rest might have relapsed into the condition of the Cis-Satlej states at the time when they passed under British protection. From such a fate the interference of the English delivered the country. But there was a wider influence and a greater question. The English did not wish to invade the Panjab, they were anxious to avoid doing so; but once the challenge was given they were bound to accept it, and what was really fought out at Sobraon and on the other great Sikh battlefields was the continuance of British power in India.[1] It was here that Lord Dalhousie was right, and he expressed in rough but spirited language the only feeling that a conquering race could have, the only answer that such a race could make when the question was put: "Unwarned by precedents, uninfluenced by example, the Sikh nation has called for war, and, on my word, sirs, they shall have it with a vengeance".

[1] Cf. Ellenborough's language *ap*. Lew, *op. cit.* p. 113.

CHAPTER XXX

BURMA, 1782–1852

THE conquests of the Alaungpaya dynasty were completed under King Bodawpaya, 1782–1819. On the east, the Burmese had long received tribute from the Shans, to the south they had annexed the Talaing country (Irrawaddy Delta and Tenasserim) in 1757, on the north they had repelled the great Chinese invasions of 1765–9. They now conquered Arakan in 1785, Manipur in 1813, Assam in 1816. Thus brought into contact with the English, they felt no fear: Ava was the centre of the universe, its arms invincible, its culture supreme. In 1818, as successors to the crown of Arakan which in mediaeval times had received tribute from the Ganges Delta, they summoned the governor-general to surrender Chittagong, Dacca and Murshidabad under pain of war.

Fifty thousand Arakanese fled into Chittagong; the more spirited, under Nga Chin Pyan, used British territory as a base; the English seized most of the principals, but Nga Chin Pyan was still at large when he died in 1814. In Assam the Burmese diminished the population by half in 1816–24, partly by massacre, partly by driving 30,000 in slave-gangs to Ava; Chandrakant, an insurgent prince, procured muskets and men in British territory, bribing subordinates not to tell their English superiors. Burmese commanders started violating the Chittagong frontier in 1794, the Goalpara frontier in 1821, and were amazed at their own moderation, since, as Burmese customary law made no distinction between crime and rebellion, the English refusal to surrender political refugees was a hostile act.

European intercourse with Burma had centred at Syriam and its successor Rangoon. Teak was the principal product, shipbuilding the industry; but disorder was endemic, export of most commodities was interdicted, and the volume of trade was not great. The Dutch came in 1627 and left in 1680. The French came in 1689, built ships for Dupleix, and decayed. The English East India Company founded a factory at Syriam in 1647 which lasted a decade, and private traders, chiefly from Masulipatam, continued to use the factory buildings and dockyard for many years. In 1680 the demand for Burmese lac led Fort St George, Madras, to begin a series of negotiations for reopening official trade, and several missions visited Ava, notably those of Fleetwood and Leslie in 1695 and Bowyear in 1697, but these resulted only in the regulation of private trade, which continued till 1743 when the Talaings, alleging complicity with the Burmese, burnt the Syriam factory. In 1753 a factory was opened on Negrais Island but in 1759 the Burmese, alleging complicity with the Talaings, massacred the staff, and the protest of Captain Alves in 1760 resulted merely in the Company being permitted to return to Rangoon. Thus commercial relations alone had so far existed between the English and Burma, and in the eighteenth century barely four Englishmen had reached Ava. Bodawpaya's conquests created a frontier situation which necessitated political intercourse. The governor-general sent envoys—Captain Symes, 1795, 1802; Captain Cox, 1797; Captain Canning, 1803, 1809, 1811. Though expensively equipped, they failed. English officers were accustomed to kneel unshod in the presence of Indian kings, but at Ava they were expected to unshoe before entering the palace, and to prostrate themselves at gateways and spires; they were ignored for months and segregated on a scavengers' island. Symes did indeed obtain a treaty, but Burmese thought had not evolved such a concept; the king was above contractual obligations and anything he signed was revocable at will. An inland race who regarded Rangoon as a foreign garrison, the Burmese had no international relations, they never thought of sending an ambassador to England or knew its whereabouts, yet they rejected the envoys, saying that their king could receive only an ambassador from the king of England.

So little was known of Burma that it was almost a "mystery land", responsible officers entertained exaggerated ideas of its strength, and Burmese victories once caused a panic in Calcutta; Symes in 1795 estimated the population at 17,000,000, although King Bagyidaw's Revenue Inquest of 1826 gave only 1,831,467. The governor-general had no desire to be involved in Indo-China, but in the dry season 1823-4 his outposts from Shahpuri Island to Dudpatli were driven in by Burmese commanders whose orders were to take Calcutta. General Sir Archibald Campbell with 11,000 men, mostly Madras sepoys, and ships under Captain Marryat, R.N. (the novelist), occupied Rangoon, 11 May, 1824. The Talaings were expected to rise in their favour, but the Burmese deported the population, leaving the delta a waste whence the invader could get no intelligence, supply, or transport; till the end of the rains the English could not move two miles. The Burmese withdrew from the north, attacked Rangoon in December, 1824, and retreated to Danubyu where Bandula, their greatest leader, was killed. There were operations in Tenasserim and in Arakan, but it was round Rangoon that the Burmese armies were broken. Lack of transport persisted, and only on 24 February, 1826, was Campbell able to dictate the Treaty of Yandabo, whereby Ava yielded Arakan, Tenasserim, Assam, Cachar, Jaintia, and Manipur, paid £1,000,000, received a Resident at Ava and maintained one at Calcutta.

The Burmese host was the greatest in their history—600 guns, 35,000 muskets, and a cadre of 70,000. Except 4000 household troops they were a mass levy, and even the household troops had not sufficient training to fight in the open; but their musketry and jingal fire was good, their sapper work admirable, and their jungle fighting of the highest order; they tortured prisoners, and practised a species of head-hunting, but Englishmen respected their courage and physique. As Henry Havelock, who served as deputy assistant adjutant-general, pointed out, the direction of the English forces was indifferent—stormers were left to take stockades, among the most formidable in history, without scaling ladders; sepoys, sent into action without a stiffening of British infantry, were so often routed that their *moral* declined and they were obsessed with a belief that Burmese warriors had magical powers. Administration was discreditable—medical precautions were lacking, and, in expectation of Talaing aid, no arrangements had been made for commissariat supply from India. Campbell sometimes had only 1500 effectives. The original contingents of European troops were 3738 at Rangoon, 1004 in Arakan; at Rangoon their hospital deaths (scurvy and dysentery) were 3160, their battle deaths 166; in Arakan their hospital deaths (malaria) were 595, battle deaths nil—4 per cent. battle deaths, 96 per cent. hospital; 40,000 men passed through the cadres, 15,000 died, and the war cost £5,000,000.

The Residency, held successively by Major Burney (Fanny's brother) and Colonel Benson, lasted from 1830 to 1840. Few have served their fellow-men better than Burney during his seven lonely years at Ava; trusted by both sides in civil wars, he stayed several executions; he supported the Burmese against the governor-general, winning them the Kabaw Valley on the disputed Manipur frontier; and when he left, an invalid, the parting was full of mutual regrets; but, urge as he might that Siam and Persia recognised the governor-general, that the very greatest powers found permanent embassies the only way of avoiding friction, even he could not induce the Burmese to maintain a Resident at Calcutta. None of the ministers, he noted, was the equal of a *gaunggyok* in Tenasserim, the character of King Bagyidaw, 1819–37, being such that he would have no other type near him. Bagyidaw became insane and was put under restraint. His brother King Tharrawaddy, 1837–45, said:

The English beat my brother, not me. The Treaty of Yandabo is not binding on me, for I did not make it. I will meet the Resident as a private individual, but as Resident, never. When will they understand that I can receive only a royal ambassador from England?

In repudiating the treaty, Tharrawaddy was within the Burmese constitution, whereby all existing rights lapsed at a new king's accession until he chose to confirm them. The governor-general, who had disapproved previous withdrawals, now sanctioned final withdrawal. Becoming insane, Tharrawaddy was put under restraint by his son King Pagan, 1845–52.

Rangoon stagnated, and even its shipbuilding industry was inter-

mittent. Its British community (five Europeans and several hundred
Asiatics) periodically complained of ill-usage after the withdrawal of
the Resident, but government refused to intervene, saying that anyone
who went to live under Burmese rule did so with his eyes open.
Finally a governor, appointed in 1850, used, when tipsy, to threaten
to torture and behead the whole population, and among his acts of
extortion were three dozen committed on British subjects, culminating in the cases of Sheppard and Lewis. Sheppard's 250-ton
barque from Moulmein ran aground near Rangoon; the Chittagong
pilot, a British subject, fearing she would become a total wreck,
jumped overboard and swam to safety; Sheppard brought his ship
into Rangoon and was promptly accused by the governor of throwing
the pilot overboard; he and his crew were imprisoned, detained eight
days, and had to pay 1005 rupees. Lewis sailed his 410-ton vessel
from Mauritius, and one of his lascars, a British subject, died the
day he anchored off Rangoon; the governor accused him of murdering
the lascar and threatened to flog and behead him; he was made to
attend court daily for three weeks and had to pay 700 rupees.

Dalhousie sent H.M. frigate *Fox*, Commodore Lambert, R.N., to
ask that the king remove the governor and compensate Sheppard and
Lewis. The king replied courteously and sent a new governor empowered to settle the matter; but the old governor was given a
triumphal farewell, the new governor brought an army, and when
Lambert sent a deputation of senior naval officers to greet him, they
were refused admission on the pretext that the governor was asleep.
Lambert forthwith declared a blockade and seized a king's ship; the
governor retorted that the naval officers who had been turned away
were drunk, and his batteries opened fire on the *Fox*.

The Burmese mobilisation was only the usual precaution; in
removing the former governor, and in writing to the governor-general,
thereby recognising his existence, the court of Ava showed a desire
to avoid war. The miscarriage was at Rangoon. Had Lambert been
accustomed to orientals, he would have warned his officers against
riding their horses into the governor's courtyard, a breach of Burmese
manners, and he would have accompanied them himself, as a Burmese
governor could not receive assistants, however senior. The governor,
a backwoods mandarin, failed to reflect that Lambert had in person
received even the humblest Burmese emissaries on the deck of his
frigate; and the reports he sent to his chiefs at Ava were alarmist
and false. Dalhousie regarded the annexation of yet another province as a calamity, and had misgivings over Lambert's precipitancy.
But the court of Ava accepted their governor's every act. Dalhousie's
ultimatum received no reply, and on the day it expired, 1 April,
1852, the forces of General Godwin (a veteran of the First Burmese
War) and Admiral Austen (Jane's brother) reached Rangoon.

The Shans refused to send levies, the Delta Burmese welcomed the

English, the Talaings rose in their favour. Dalhousie had studied the records of the First Burmese War as a precedent to avoid; thanks to his insistence—he now visited Rangoon himself—the commissariat and medical arrangements were such that the health of the troops in the field was better than that of many a cantonment in India. Martaban and Rangoon fell in a fortnight, Bassein a few weeks later; Prome, to intercept the rice supplies of Ava, and Pegu, to please the Talaings, were captured in the early rains, but were not held till the dry season. The Burmese numbered 30,000; the invaders, 8000, of whom 3000, including sailors, were English; the gross battle casualties throughout were 377, and the campaign cost under £1,000,000. The Secret Committee gave Dalhousie a free hand; but he would not advance into Upper Burma, saying that though welcomed in Lower Burma, the population of which was only partly Burmese, we should be opposed by the Burmese in their homeland and could not administer them without undue expense. He annexed Pegu by proclamation 20 December, 1852; he left the king to decide whether he would accept a treaty or not, and wrote to him that if he again provoked hostilities "they will end in the entire subjection of the Burmese power, and in the ruin and exile of yourself and your race".

The government of Bengal administered Arakan through joint commissioners, Hunter and Paton, till 1829; through a superintendent, successively Paton and Dickinson, under the commissioner of Chittagong, till 1834; thereafter through a commissioner—Captain Dickinson, 1834-7; Captain (later Sir Archibald) Bogle, 1837-49; Captain (later Sir Arthur) Phayre, 1849-52. Assistant commissioners (three on 1000 rupees monthly, two on 500 rupees), one for each district—Akyab, An (headquarters at Kyaukpyu), Ramree, Sandoway —and one for Akyab, the capital, were usually recruited from officers of the Bengal regiment at Kyaukpyu seconded to the Arakan local battalion.

Before them lay a kingdom devastated by forty years of Burmese rule, without records showing the system of administration. Pencil notes in Burmese were indeed found, and one of these, part of a revenue inquest of 1802, gave the population of Akyab district as 248,604: the English found under 100,000 in the whole province. The rainfall was 225 inches; in 1826 it was proposed to abandon the interior and administer it indirectly from Cheduba Island, and, even later, of seventy-nine English officers who served in Akyab, eighteen died and twenty-two were invalided; on returning from the bloodless pursuit, in January, 1829, of an insurgent in Sandoway district, three English officers died, and all their sepoys died or were invalided; a four years' attempt to establish a district headquarters at An was abandoned in 1837 because the three assistants successively sent there died. Till 1837 the commissioner had no ship, and officers were invalided on native craft where they had to lie either on deck, exposed to the monsoon, or in the cargo hold, suffocating amid scorpions and centipedes.

And yet by 1831 the administrative system was complete. It was imposed ready-made from above, not built up from below; the Bengal acts and regulations were applied by rule, and lithographed forms followed. There was a daily post from Calcutta, and district officers, compiling returns sometimes a year in arrears, had little leisure for touring; their letters were of such length that each had to be accompanied by a précis. The commissioner could not buy a cupboard, create a sweepership on five rupees monthly, or pay three rupees reward for killing a crocodile, without previous sanction from Calcutta, and in 1832 the assistant at Ramree was censured because, during an outburst of dacoity, he had, on his own initiative, hired some villagers as temporary constables. Assistants could imprison for two years, the commissioner for fourteen years, submitting records to Calcutta for heavier sentence. Forty-nine per cent. of persons tried were convicted, and 66 per cent. of sentences appealed against were confirmed; appellate interference sometimes proceeded from the desire of seniors to display their impartiality. Till 1845, when Persian was abolished, the trial record was threefold, the vernacular deposition being accompanied by Persian and English translations. The only native entrusted with judicial functions was a judge on 150 rupees monthly appointed in 1834 for Akyab district, which contained 57 per cent. of the population and 66 per cent. of the cultivation; he tried most of the original civil suits, but had no criminal powers.

A district assistant's executive staff consisted of a *myothugyi* (principal revenue clerk), an Arakanese on 150 rupees monthly; civil police stations, under Bengalis or Arakanese on eighty rupees; and *kyunok* or *thugyi* (circle headmen). The circle headman, an Arakanese, paid by 15 per cent. commission on his revenue collections, resided among his villages, numbering sometimes forty, each under its *yuagaung* (village headman); the principal revenue and police officer of the interior, the *thugyi* tried petty civil suits; he was, on showing capacity, transferred to a larger circle; although family was considered he was not hereditary, and he was sometimes styled a *tahsildar*.

Arakan's contribution to her governance was an admirable ryotwari system evolved by officers of whom Bogle was the survivor. Hunter and Paton were superseded for imagining circle headmen to be zamindars and letting them collect, at Burmese rates, revenue of which little reached the treasury. By 1831 rates fell three-quarters and extortion ceased, for each cultivator had his annual tax bill, and in Burma each cultivator can read; the circle headman submitted the assessment roll, the *myothugyi* checked it, and the assistant issued a tax bill, initialled by himself, for each villager by name. Save for *thathameda* (household tax, in the roll of which each inmate of a house was entered), the Indo-Chinese system of a lump sum assessment on the village community, apportioned by the elders, was displaced by land revenue, at one rupee four annas to two rupees four annas an acre of cultivation, which after 1835 was roughly surveyed by circle headmen.

Native rule had professed prohibition and it was reluctantly, on finding the Arakanese as addicted to intoxicants as any race could be, that the commissioner in 1826 introduced liquor and opium licenses; held by Chinese, they produced little revenue but acted as a check. Kyaukpyu exported salt, 300,000 maunds annually, to Chittagong, but rice soon became the main industry of the province, and its export, prohibited under native rule, now averaged 70,000 tons annually; its production caused seasonal migration from Chittagong and there was a steady trickle of settlers from Burma, but the main source of population was remigrant Arakanese. The following figures include cultivated acreage of all kinds, tonnage cleared from Akyab port, and revenue from all sources:

	Cultivation (acres)	Tonnage	Total revenue (rupees)	Population
1830	78,519	—	371,310	131,390
1840	204,069	69,038	629,572	226,542
1852	351,668	80,630	904,501	333,645

Although Akyab was the greatest rice port in the world, no jetty existed till 1844. It was largely to build this jetty that Arakan received an executive engineer in 1837, but under a system which forbade him even frame an estimate without sanction from Calcutta, he took seven years to build it; usually a subaltern unacquainted with engineering, he was transferred five times a year, and his energies were confined to Akyab town where he built thatched wooden offices. There were gaols at Akyab, Ramree, and Sandoway, and in the intervals between mutinies, each district assistant used convicts to lay out his headquarters and drain the marshes in which it lay. Outside the towns roads and bridges were non-existent.

The Arakan local battalion, two-thirds Arakanese, one-third Manipuris, were military police who in 1851 took over the province from the regulars; in 1852 they clamoured to be led against their hereditary foes the Burmese, and captured the Natyegan stockade in the An Pass. Hardy and mobile, they had from their foundation in 1825 played a leading part in suppressing the insurgency which broke out when the English, hailed as deliverers who would restore Arakanese rule, were found to be introducing a direct administration of their own; Arakanese officers who had served the Burmese were then displaced, for they were found to be trained in little but extortion and intrigue; émigrés, returning from Bengal to their ancestral villages, found themselves no longer lords but peasants under an alien administration which reserved high office to itself and regarded all men as equal. Arakanese of birth and spirit found English conceptions of justice and efficiency intolerable, and they soon took the measure of their new masters—under native rule, to escape torture, a dacoit confessed as soon as caught, and was beheaded then and there; but the English ruled confessions inadmissible and held prolonged trials during which the witnesses, fearing reprisals, resiled. They never united, but until 1836, when they burned Akyab town and police station, dacoity, accompanied with murder, rape, and arson, averaged annually 290 per million people. Thereafter the incidence per million was dacoity thirty-seven, murder twenty-six, and these were mainly on the frontier; the decrease was attributed to preoccupation with expanding cultivation and to the growth of a propertied class. In 1850 stabbing appeared, and was attributed to excessive prosperity unbalancing the passions.

Government had no vernacular schools but in 1838 founded Anglo-vernacular schools at Akyab and Ramree to teach Arakanese boys Roman and Greek history and to produce clerks and surveyors; in 1845 Bogle discovered why they were apathetic—there were not sufficient clerkships, whereas circle headmanships, the largest cadre, were vernacular. Two-thirds of the population spoke Burmese, but the remainder, especially in the towns, spoke Bengali and Hindustani; and when, in 1845, at the instance of Phayre, who alone knew Burmese, the government finally prescribed Burmese, Bogle protested that Arakan should be assimilated to Bengal and that Burmese was the language of an enemy country, it was too difficult a language for English gentlemen, its literature contained nothing but puerile superstitions, he had served eighteen years without learning it and the people were entirely satisfied with his administration.

Only the ignorant can doubt the disinterestedness of the men who gave Arakan the most benevolent and businesslike government she had ever seen; yet though, being English gentlemen, they instinctively appreciated the external side of the native character and respected its prejudices, they were out of touch with its inner and probably finer side. Nor did any of them question the fact that the great administrative machine they built up was so alien that its higher offices could not be held by natives, and that, once having gained initial impetus, it must expand with increasing complexity and require an ever-increasing European staff.

The government of Bengal administered Tenasserim through a commissioner, Maingy, jointly with Sir Archibald Campbell, 1826–8; Maingy, 1828–33; Blundell, 1833–43; Major Broadfoot, 1843–4; Captain (later Sir Henry) Durand, 1844–6; Colvin, 1846–9; thereafter Major Archibald Bogle. Assistant commissioners—one for each district (Amherst, Tavoy, Mergui), one for Moulmein, the capital, and after 1844 one additional for Amherst, which contained all the timber, 57 per cent. of the population, 58 per cent. of the cultivation—were usually recruited from the Madras regiments at Moulmein. Mails were infrequent, and references to Calcutta sometimes remained unanswered for months because the retention of Tenasserim was doubtful. Arakan was strategically part of Bengal; Tenasserim was isolated, needed an expensive garrison, cost at first 22,00,000 rupees against a revenue of 2,40,000 rupees, and there was little prospect of increase as it had no Chittagong whence to draw population. In 1831 the Resident was instructed to discuss its retrocession with the ministers, but their only reply was triumphantly to demand Arakan as well; considerations of humanity also prevailed—the governor-general remembered the fate of Pegu at the evacuation. In 1842 King Tharrawaddy, hearing of the Afghan disasters, camped with 40,000 men at Rangoon; finding the Moulmein garrison promptly strengthened, he withdrew, convinced that he had brought Tenasserim, through garrison charges, one stage nearer retrocession.

A district assistant's staff consisted of an *akunwun* (principal revenue clerk) on 200 rupees monthly; a *sitke* (native judge) on 300 rupees, who tried most of the civil suits and criminal cases requiring only two months' imprisonment; and six *gaunggyok* (township officers) on twenty-five to 100 rupees. The revenue and police officer of the interior, the *gaunggyok*, also tried petty civil suits and criminal cases requiring only twenty rupees fine; he supervised the *thugyi* (circle headman) who was paid by commission on revenue collections, such commission seldom exceeding five rupees monthly whereas a coolie earned twelve rupees. There were no police stations outside the towns, and little information existed as to events in the districts.

Burmans and Talaings were so mixed that the population was homogeneous; all assistants knew Burmese; and the first translations and vernacular text-books were printed at Moulmein, where the American Baptist Mission possessed Burmese and Siamese founts. But education was mainly European, for the climate was healthy, Moulmein was styled a sanatorium, there was always a European regiment in the garrison, and the 40,000 townspeople included one of the largest domiciled communities in India. Juries were prescribed for trials requiring over six months' imprisonment, but in practice were empanelled only at sessions. After 1836 there was always at least one newspaper at Moulmein; its columns were full of per-sonalities, and in 1846 the commissioner sentenced Abreu, editor of *The Maulmain Chronicle*, to two years' imprisonment and 3000 rupees fine; the judgment was immediately reversed at Calcutta. Officials quarrelled among themselves in interminable letters, and, after perusing some of these, the government removed Durand from his commissionership, sent Major McLeod, district assistant, Amherst, out of Tenasserim, and transferred others.

The main industry lay in the magnificent forests. In 1847 a staff from Pembroke Dockyard arrived to buy Admiralty teak, and 109 ships

(35,270 tons), including a 1000-ton steam frigate for the Royal Navy, were built at Moulmein in 1830–50. Barely half the fellings were extracted, yet the annual teak export was 12,000 tons. Dr Wallich in 1827 was the first to visit the forests and urge the need of conservation, yet no teak was planted, no check imposed on waste. There was indeed a Superintendent of Forests, 1841–8, but when he asked for power to prevent felling of unselected trees, the court of directors replied that such power was not for local officers. Logs reaching Moulmein were taxed 15 per cent. *ad valorem*; through fraud and neglect, three-quarters of them escaped payment in 1834–44, and even subsequently timber provided only 18 per cent. of the total revenue. The timber traders—discharged warrant officers and ship's mates—never visited the forests but sent out Burmans who made the jungle-folk, timid Karens, extract timber for little or nothing; the Karens burned several forests to discourage such visitations. In 1842 better firms appeared but as these had the ear of government the result was to accelerate exploitation—Durand's removal placated Calcutta firms whose leases he had cancelled. By 1850 the forests were ruined.

In 1827, immediately on the evacuation, the Burmese, despite the Treaty of Yandabo, executed eleven circle headmen between Yandabo and Rangoon, searched out every woman who had lived with the English and every man who had served them, and wreaked vengeance. The Talaings rose, failed, and fled, 30,000 of them, into the Amherst district. Otherwise, apart from seasonal labour, there was little immigration, as for long taxation was not lighter, or property more secure, than in Pegu, where criminal administration was effective and governors, wishing to retain their subjects, now requisitioned less forced labour. The Talaing Corps, which lasted from 1838 to 1848, was intended to raise the Talaings against the Burmese, but failed because its commandant was not a whole-time officer, and, in Broadfoot's words, Talaings as well as Burmans could rise to the highest offices in Ava, whereas in Tenasserim both were on low pay only augmented by bribes.

Until 1842 the village revenue demand, distributed by elders, was paid in kind; government had no information regarding tenures or crop yields. By 1845 money payment was substituted, and assessment was on each villager's field, surveyed by the village headman; reductions by 72 per cent. in 1843–8 left the rates at four annas to two and a quarter rupees per acre; thereafter cultivation increased and yielded 37 per cent. of the total revenue:

	Cultivation (acres)	Total revenue (rupees)	Population
1826	?	240,131	? 66,000
1835	?	339,370	84,917
1845	97,515	517,034	127,455
1852	144,405	570,639	191,476

Attempts to attract European planters by large grants of land failed. The difficulty was lack of population, for immigration, sometimes amounting to thousands annually, from the Coromandel Coast, was usually confined to the towns; it began in 1838 with imported commissariat labour, and increased in 1843 when debtor slavery ceased and convicts were withdrawn from private employment. Cattle were imported from the Shan states, but the visits of Dr Richardson in 1830, 1834, 1835, 1837 to Chiengmai and Mong Nai and of Major McLeod in 1837 to Kenghung, failed to open up general trade because, though the people were friendly, jealousy between the overlords, Ava and Bangkok, stifled intercourse.

The terrible system of frontier raids ceased in 1826–7 when Major Burney visited Bangkok and obtained the return of 2000 persons whom the Siamese had enslaved. Internal slavery, abolished by the great Act V of 1843, was usually of the same mild type, debtor and domestic, as in Arakan. But in Tavoy, noted for the comeliness of its women, Muhammadans, exploiting ignorance and poverty, bought girls for the Moulmein brothels and these debtor-bonds were enforced in English courts; under Blundell's rules, abolished by Broadfoot in 1844, brothels were recognised, paying revenue in proportion to their size. Liquor and opium licenses which, in spite of Chinese rings, yielded 16 per cent. of the revenue, were introduced in the towns with Madras and European garrisons; Maingy, after seeing the effect on Burmans and Talaings, regretted their introduction. Gambling, also prohibited under native rule, was licensed until 1834 when the protests of the Buddhist clergy prevailed.

Crime was rare save on the Burmese frontier. Burmese governors were unpaid, they suppressed crime because brigandage was the perquisite of their retinue, and the daily sight of prosperous Moulmein was too much for the governor of Martaban. Warnings having failed, the commissioner burned Martaban in 1829, and gained several years respite. But in 1847–50, of thirty-three traced dacoities in the Amherst district, twenty-five were traced to Martaban; dacoits came in racing canoes, posted pickets in Moulmein high street, looted houses within two furlongs of the garrison, and vanished into the darkness. Until 1844 most assistants never left their headquarters, revenue accounts for the whole year covered only a single sheet, and statistics of cultivation and population were rare. Criminal law was the Muhammadan law of Bengal, but no copy of it existed; civil law was Burmese, but until Dr Richardson, assistant, translated and printed it in 1847, nobody knew what it was. Gaols were inefficient, and in 1847 Sleeman protested against thugs being transported to Moulmein, where they escaped at the rate of one a month.

Irregularities were of a type unknown in Arakan. In 1843 Corbin, district assistant, Mergui, misappropriated grain revenue received in kind, and his native mistress purchased girl slaves to weave cloth for sale. In 1844 De la Condamine, district assistant, Amherst, drew the pay of vacant clerkships, and kept no account of timber revenue received in kind, while his clerks traded in timber and usury with capital attributed to himself and Maingy. In 1848 the adjutant, Talaing Corps, recovered from his sepoys money lent them by his native mistress. Captain Impey, district assistant, Amherst, submitted no treasury accounts for nine months, misappropriated 21,880 rupees, refunded two-thirds on detection in 1850, and disappeared into the Shan states.

Control from Calcutta was so slight that the commissioner might have evolved a system of indirect government which allowed native institutions proper scope. But even had that functionary been creative, such native institutions as survived Burmese misrule and Siamese devastation showed little vitality. Freedom from Calcutta thus ended simply in an undeveloped copy of the non-regulation model.

CHAPTER XXXI

THE INDIAN STATES, 1818–57

THE period 1818 to 1857 is important as that in which our relations with the Indian states were finally placed upon practically that basis on which they still rest. This policy, initiated by Lord Wellesley, but abandoned by his successors, Cornwallis, Barlow and Minto, was revived by Lord Hastings who carried it on to its logical conclusion. When Lord Wellesley left India in 1805 our military superiority had been proved beyond question; the huge state armies, led in great measure by European officers, had melted away; while a series of treaties defined our relationship with all the important rulers in India. The foundations of the system which obtains to this day had thus been laid, and Wellesley himself wrote in 1804:

A general bond of connexion is now established between the British Government and the principal states of India on principles which render it the interest of every state to maintain its alliance with the British Government...and which secure to every state the unmolested exercise of its separate authority within the limits of its established dominion, under the general protection of the British power.[1]

The earlier system, of treating the states as if they stood on an equal footing with us, was finally abandoned; and our political, as well as our military supremacy, was specifically recognised. It is, of course, unquestionable that this supremacy would ultimately have been attained, probably only after conflict, but it is also beyond doubt, that the policy followed by Lord Wellesley during the seven years of his office simplified its establishment, and shortened the period required for its attainment.

Lord Moira, afterwards Marquess of Hastings, landed in India in 1813, in avowed opposition to the policy pursued by Lord Wellesley, but, as he himself remarks, he soon changed his views. Writing in 1815 he says: "It was by preponderance of power that those mines of wealth had been acquired for the Company's treasury, and by preponderance of power alone would they be retained". The policy of non-interference with the Indian states was, he saw, a futile policy; for no highly civilised state, placed in the midst of less civilised or less developed states, can ever hope to pursue it without disastrous results. In 1817, four years after his assumption of the governor-generalship, the Maratha confederacy was again intriguing actively against us, and Central India was overrun by hordes of plunderers. By May, 1818, however, Sindhia had been forced to make terms, these hordes had been dispersed, and Holkar defeated, while the Peshwa's power had been extinguished. Other important Indian states, though in

[1] Dispatch of 13 July, 1804, *Despatches*, IV, 177.

no sense enthusiastic on our behalf, had welcomed our change of policy and signed treaties of friendship and subordinate alliance with the Company. The British Government thus became the acknowledged suzerain, though the Moghul emperor still sat upon the throne of Delhi. A period of reconstruction now commenced, directed by Lord Hastings and carried out by a group of men whose names are still household words in the areas in which they worked; Malcolm in Central India, Elphinstone in the Deccan, Munro in Madras, and Metcalfe, Tod and Ochterlony in Rajputana.

The chief centre of disturbance had been in Malwa, the high level tract comprising the group of states which now forms the "Central India Agency", with the addition of the Gwalior state. To understand the process of reconstruction initiated by Sir John Malcolm, in Central India, it is essential to grasp the conditions prevailing in this tract. The territories of the Indian states and estates in this area were then, and are indeed to this day, mixed in inextricable confusion as regards their boundaries, while they are at the same time linked together by political agreements which enormously complicate administrative procedure. The settlement of the great Maratha generals in Malwa at the close of the eighteenth century led to the subjection of the Rajput landholders, who were ousted from the greater part of their possessions, by the formation of the Maratha states of Gwalior, Indore, Dhar and Dewas, such lands as they were allowed to retain being held on a tributary or feudatory basis. These tributaries included the more important Rajput states such as Ratlam, as well as a large number of small estate-holders belonging to the same class. This subjection to Maratha overlords had always been strongly resented and in early days tribute was never paid except under compulsion. Disputes, moreover, were continuous and boundaries were constantly changing, as one or other party temporarily predominated. During the Pindari War the Rajputs tried to make all they could out of the disturbed conditions prevailing. Then came our intervention, the rapid sweeping aside of the marauding hordes and the sudden imposition of peace, which resulted in the crystallisation of the territorial distribution as it chanced to be at that moment. The effect of this sudden termination of hostilities was to leave the whole of Malwa parcelled out, in a very haphazard way, among the various owners, and the territorial patchwork thus created persists, in spite of some adjustments, to this day. The territories of the various landowners appear, indeed, to have been shaken out of a pepper-box, so that, when travelling in this region, it is difficult to say whose property you are traversing.

When Sir John Malcolm took up the task of settling Malwa he found that, besides the payment of tribute demanded by the great Maratha overlords, the Rajput thakurs, as the smaller landholders are termed, claimed certain payments, called *tankha*, from these same overlords, payments which were in origin a form of blackmail, paid in order to induce them to abstain from raiding and pilfering. Those who received such payments were called *grasias*, or those receiving a *gras* or "mouthful". Owing to the distracted condition of their own administrations, after the late struggle, the Maratha rulers were quite incapable of maintaining order or enforcing payment of their demands and, in consequence, welcomed the assistance offered by us in asserting their claims, and "unfeignedly resorted to us for aid".[1]

Malcolm at once took up the task of adjusting these claims and while securing to the Maratha rulers the tribute due to them also secured to their tributaries the *tankha* they demanded, at the same time guaranteeing them in the permanent possession of the land they then held, so long as they kept the peace and carried out the conditions in their *sanads*, or deeds of possession. These agreements were mediated by Sir John between the Maratha overlord and the Rajput ruler or thakur. They were drawn up in the names of the Maratha suzerain and his Rajput feudatory and bore the overlord's seal, but carried in addition an endorsement, signed by Sir John or one of his assistants, usually over the words "Confirmed and guaranteed by the British Government".

The basis on which these agreements were drawn up is thus enunciated by Lord Hastings. It was, he says, therefore,

easy, when no acknowledged usages stood in the way, to establish principles between the sovereign and the subject advantageous to both, giving these principles a defined line of practical application, a departure from which would afford to either party a right of claiming the intervention of our paramount power. While the Sovereign had his legitimate authority and his due revenue insured to him, the subject was protected against exaction and tyrannical outrage.[2]

The effect of these agreements was immediate and the most distracted population in India became in a few months a comparatively law-abiding community. It may be of interest, however, to mention briefly the subsequent history of the "guarantee" system. As has been pointed out above, the agreements thus "guaranteed" were made out as between the Maratha ruler and his feudatory, the British Government merely undertaking to see that each side carried out its part, intervening only if the conditions were disregarded. Actually, however, the confusion which existed for many years after peace was introduced prevented the Maratha overlords from exercising any real supervision and, in consequence, the Rajput feudatories fell directly under the control of the British residents and political agents in a way never contemplated by Lord Hastings, or in any sense warranted by the terms of the *sanads*. They, in fact, were treated by these officers as if in all respects under their direct charge, and not simply as regarded adherence to the conditions laid down in the

---

[1] Hastings, *Summary*, p. 48.   [2] *Idem.*

agreements. A form of political practice thus grew up which became very galling to the Maratha overlords, and especially to the Gwalior durbar, in which state by far the greater number of "guaranteed thakurs" held their estates. Remonstrances were continually made and a good deal of irritation was displayed until finally in 1921 the government of India admitted the correctness of the Gwalior durbar's contentions. The thakurs were then officially informed by the viceroy, in a special durbar held at Delhi on 14 March, 1921, that they would in future be wholly under the control of the Gwalior state, which would exercise full suzerainty over them, the government of India, however, reserving the right to intervene should the conditions of the "guarantee" be in any way disregarded by either side.

Two Musulman states exist in the same area, Bhopal and Jaora. The former, which had loyally supported us since 1778, was rewarded with a grant of territory, while Jaora was created a separate entity by the twelfth article of the Treaty of Mandasor[1] made with Holkar, certain lands in that state being granted on service conditions to Ghafur Khan, son-in-law of Amir Khan, nawab of Tonk, in return for assistance rendered to Sir John Malcolm.

Of the two important Maratha states, Gwalior and Indore, Sindhia had very reluctantly come to terms in 1817, while Holkar, defeated in the battle of Mahidpur (December, 1817), had been obliged to accept the terms offered to him.

In Rajputana the process of settlement was far simpler, as the Marathas, though claiming tribute from the rajas, had never settled in that area which, being mainly arid and uninviting in comparison with Malwa and the Deccan, did not attract them as a place of residence. Moreover, the states were fewer, larger and more compact in form and more homogeneous in character.

The conditions obtaining in each state were carefully examined, and arrangements made in accordance with those conditions. Considerable objections were raised at the time to our assuming this responsibility, the freeing of the Rajput lands from marauding bands being considered the utmost we should engage to do for them, while our undertaking to see that the tribute claimed by the Marathas was punctually paid was held to be inconsistent with our general policy and indefensible in principle, in view of the fact that this tribute was nothing but blackmail levied by force, without any real overlordship to support the claim. The alternative would have been to leave these states to settle their own disputes on the Utopian theory of non-interference, which had invariably plunged them in disaster. The pages of Tod but too clearly show how hereditary jealousies, family feuds, not to mention ordinary motives of ambition and avarice, would have made a peaceful settlement impossible except under the aegis

---

[1] Aitchison, *Treaties*, IV, 199.

of our strong controlling authority. The result of Lord Hastings's policy fully justified its adoption.

This payment of tribute to the Marathas was continued on the grounds that we accepted the *status quo* at the time when we first entered Rajputana and Central India, as we could have no concern with conditions obtaining before the war. Adherence to this principle had also insured the co-operation of the Marathas and facilitated arrangements at the outset of the campaign. Payment of tribute was in future made through the British authorities. Secondly the payment of the tribute was a recognised mark of fealty, exacted by all suzerains, including the Moghul emperor, whose place we had taken, while it was also a fair return for the obligations we had assumed in protecting the states from aggression: the amount, moreover, was henceforth fixed in perpetuity and this, together with the financial advantages of peace, rendered these payments in no way burdensome. At the same time each state was recognised as a separate unit, independent internally but prohibited from forming any relations with another state in India or any outside power. The settlement was effected without difficulty except in Jaipur where internal dissensions were rife.

Apart from these two great groups of states in Rajputana and Central India there remained the Peshwa, the nominal head of the Maratha confederacy, and the more important states of Nagpur, Satara, Mysore, Oudh, Hyderabad, Baroda, Travancore and Cochin.

After very careful consideration Lord Hastings decided

in favour of the total expulsion of Baji Rao from the Dekhan, the perpetual exclusion of the family from any share of influence or dominion and the annihilation of the Peshwa's name and authority for ever.

This was an important step, as it removed even the nominal head of the Maratha confederacy. It was, moreover, thoroughly justified by Baji Rao's conduct. By nature timid, indolent, suspicious, and fond of low companions, Baji Rao had proved himself uniformly untrustworthy. He had never adhered to the Treaty of Bassein (1802), sending out his agents to intrigue against us in every state that would receive them. The lesson was sharp but salutary.

In Nagpur the crimes and perfidy of Appa Sahib met with their just reward in his deposition and the confiscation of the Sagar and Narbada districts of his state. Later on, in 1853, when Lord Dalhousie was governor-general, Nagpur was finally extinguished, for lack of direct heirs, and became the nucleus of the present Central Provinces.

The effete descendant of Sivaji at Satara was, as a concession to Maratha sentiment, given a small estate round his hereditary capital.[1] In 1848, however, Lord Dalhousie abolished the arrangement.

The Mysore state, restored to its Hindu rulers in 1799, on the defeat of Tipu Sultan, supported us with troops in the Pindari War. But the raja was a spendthrift and destitute of ability.

[1] *Parliamentary Papers*, 1847-8, XLVIII, 327-31.

The state of Oudh calls for more detailed notice. Lord Hastings, whose experience in England with the prince regent had, as it was said, inclined him to "sympathise with royalty in distress," treated the nawab wazir with unusual consideration. Nawab Sa'adat'Ali, who, by severe exactions and parsimonious expenditure, had amassed a hoard of thirteen millions sterling in eleven years, was averse to all reforms, badly as his administration needed them, but Lord Hastings abstained from pressing him. In July, 1814, Sa'adat 'Ali died and was succeeded by his son Haidar-ud-din Ghazi. The new wazir interviewed the governor-general at Cawnpore in October, 1814, and, in consideration of the sympathetic attitude of Lord Hastings, and his own anxiety regarding a Gurkha invasion across his northern border, was induced to lend the British Government a crore (£1,000,000) of rupees, for the prosecution of the war against Nepal. When this was expended by the governor-general's council on other objects a second crore was lent, but only under great pressure.

Differences arose between the Resident and the nawab on the subject of administrative abuses, but Lord Hastings recalled his officer and left the nawab to his own devices. The inevitable result of non-interference followed, the administration rapidly going from bad to worse. In 1818, however, Lord Hastings, somewhat inconsistently, urged the nawab to assume the title of king, and so formally break his allegiance to the emperor of Delhi, to whom his family owed its elevation. In the governor-general's opinion this act would benefit the British Government by causing a division between these important leaders of the Muhammadan community. The change was, however, regarded with the greatest contempt and aversion by the Indian princes and unfavourably contrasted with the conduct of the Nizam of Hyderabad who had refused to accede to a similar suggestion made to him, as being an act of rebellion against the emperor. It also met with the disapproval of all experienced British officials, Sir John Malcolm freely expressing the opinion that it was most impolitic and a deliberate reversal of our previously well-considered treatment of the imperial house of Taimur, and very likely to nullify the sentiments of gratitude entertained for us by the princes of this family, owing to our generous assistance in their distress. From his subsequent behaviour it is clear that our support of his assumption of this new honour evoked no sense of gratitude in the newly-created king.

The Baroda state, which had benefited materially by the Treaty of Poona (1817) and gained certain acquisitions of territory in 1818, lost its minister, Fateh Singh, who had long managed its affairs during the lifetime of the imbecile Anand Rao Gaekwad. A new treaty was made in 1820, and no difficulty was experienced in connection with this state.

Serious trouble soon arose in Hyderabad. The Nizam and his

minister Munir-ul-mulk took no interest in the administration, which was left in the hands of a Hindu, Chandu Lal. He was capable but extravagant, his extravagance being left unchecked by the Resident. The Nizam's sons, moreover, were entirely out of hand and committed many atrocities. Chandu Lal was at length forced to borrow and contracted a heavy debt with Palmer and Co., a British firm in Hyderabad. By the act of 1796[1] no European could enter into financial transactions with an Indian prince without the express sanction of the governor-general. It was understood that Palmer and Co. were prepared to lend money at a lower rate of interest than Indian bankers and, therefore, in 1816, Lord Hastings sanctioned the transaction on the understanding that his government would not be responsible for the repayment of any sums lent. In 1820, when sanction for a further sum was asked for, the directors demurred, became suspicious of these loans and cancelled permission for them.[2] Sir Charles Metcalfe, who had succeeded Mr Russell as Resident, went very carefully into the matter and found that nearly a million sterling had been lent and then wasted in highly irregular expenditure, including even the grant of pensions to members of the firm, while as much as 24 per cent. was being charged as interest. Lord Hastings, who had relied on the former Resident's recommendation and was entirely ignorant of the details of the transactions, no sooner learned the truth than he condemned the whole arrangement.[3] Unfortunately an entirely unjustifiable colour was placed on the affair because one of the partners in Palmer and Co. was married to Lord Hastings's ward, for whom he had a great affection. The correspondence on the subject with the directors shows that, though they condemned the policy followed, they exonerated the governor-general.[4] But Lord Hastings, disgusted with the implied censure, resigned in January, 1823.

Except in Cutch, where we had to intervene on account of a dispute over the succession, no other state gave cause for interference.

To summarise Lord Hastings's work. His greatest claim rests upon the pacification and opening out of all India (except the Panjab) to British access, for Central India, Rajputana and the Deccan had, to all intents and purposes, remained hitherto sealed areas to us, the Marathas interposing a compact barrier between the three presidencies. To Lord Hastings must be assigned, therefore, credit for the consolidation of our empire, which completed the work of Lord Wellesley. This policy he had pursued indomitably in spite of great opposition from the directors. Arriving in India to find marauding

---

[1] Act 37, Geo. III, Cap. 142, S. 28.
[2] Letter to Bengal, 24 May, 1820, *Hyderabad Papers*, p. 6.
[3] Letter of governor-general to Resident, 13 September, 1822, *Hyderabad Papers*, p. 186.
[4] Letter from Palmer and Co., 19 May, 1820, to Resident, and letters from directors, 24 May and 16 December, 1820, *Hyderabad Papers*, pp. 42 and 70. Mill and Wilson, *History*, VIII, 344–57.

bands sweeping across Central India, Nepal arrogant, the Marathas conspiring against us and the Rajput states divided by internal feuds and depressed under the Maratha yoke, he left India, with Nepal an ally, and one that has never since receded from that position, the Maratha power broken, Central India pacified and self-respect restored to the states of Rajputana. Above all it is to Lord Hastings that we owe the founding of that policy of partnership and friendly co-operation which now determines the relations of the government of India with the Indian states.

Lord Amherst (1823–8), who succeeded Hastings, initiated no new policy and most of his time was occupied by the war with Burma. This war did, however, react on the states, the view that our downfall was near being freely circulated. As a result of this some disturbances took place in Alwar, in the Sondhwada tract of Central India, and at Bharatpur.

The Bharatpur disturbance alone was important. In 1823 Sir David Ochterlony had sanctioned the succession to the Bharatpur *gaddi* of Raja Baldeo Singh, a minor. His cousin, Durjan Sal, opposed him and Sir David ordered troops to move from Delhi to support his nominee. But Lord Amherst, who was very nervous about the effect of a Burmese War, countermanded these orders, denouncing the Resident's action as premature and enunciating the principle that the mere fact of recognising Baldeo Singh during his father's lifetime imposed no obligation on our government to support him against the wishes of his subjects. Ochterlony, considering this as a censure on his conduct, resigned, dying not long after. He was succeeded by Sir Charles Metcalfe, who soon proved that Durjan Sal was, in fact, plotting against us with the neighbouring Rajput and Maratha states, and he pointed out the impolicy of allowing a small unimportant state to flout the paramount power.[1] On this, troops were sent up under the commander-in-chief, Lord Combermere, and after a desperate resistance the Bharatpur fort was captured on 18 January, 1826. Durjan Sal was deported.

When, in July, 1828, Lord William Cavendish-Bentinck succeeded Lord Amherst, the inevitable reaction had set in in England, and Bentinck came out with instructions to revert to the fatal non-interference policy of Cornwallis and Barlow, a policy already, in the last thirty years, conclusively proved to be disastrous in its results. Once more, the fallacy of adhering to this policy was proved and the governor-general was driven to interfere far more drastically than he would have had to do had steps been taken in time.

The administration in Hyderabad and Oudh continued to deteriorate. In Indore the death of Tantia Jogh, the minister who had introduced a regular administration into that state, left its control

---

[1] Kaye, *Life of Metcalfe*, II, 140.

in the weak hands of Maharaja Malhar Rao, and disturbances at once commenced. In Gwalior the death of Daulat Rao Sindhia in 1827, and the succession of the youthful Jankoji Rao, led to the formation of antagonistic parties and the fomentation of endless intrigues. Bentinck visited the states and announced his support of the young maharaja, but his remonstrances had no effect in the face of the regent maharani Baiza Bai's ill-advised policy, and troubles continued to augment till they led to the *dénouement* of 1843. The Supreme Government, however, contented itself with enunciating the policy that it was immaterial to it who held the reins of power in a state, provided that hostilities did not break out.

The Gaekwad of Baroda had become openly hostile, while the Rajputana states, left wholly to their own devices, were in a condition of ferment, the good work done by Tod and his colleagues being rapidly undone. Finally, attention was forcibly drawn to the conditions obtaining in this tract by an attack at Jaipur on the Resident and his assistant, in which the former was wounded and the latter killed. This actually took place just after Bentinck had embarked for England in 1835. In Mysore the governor-general was obliged to take over the administration owing to the incompetence and extravagance of Raja Krishna Udaiyar and the consequent outbreak of disturbances. The administration remained in our hands until 1881.

Some absorption of state territory also took place. The raja of Jaintia in Assam sacrificed three British Indian subjects to the goddess Kali, for which act his lands were annexed, while those of the raja of Cachar, in the same province, were taken over for gross maladministration. Coorg, near Mysore, where the raja openly declared his hostility towards us and plotted to seize the station of Bangalore, while at the same time murdering his relatives wholesale, was also annexed.

Bentinck handed over temporary charge to Sir Charles Metcalfe, who acted as governor-general until the arrival of Lord Auckland in March, 1836.

Most of Lord Auckland's energies were taken up by the Afghan War and he devoted little attention to the states.

However, when the debauchee king of Oudh died in 1837, advantage of this was taken to conclude a new treaty, further mention of which is made below.

The raja of Satara, to whom Lord Hastings had given a small area in 1816, was deposed for intriguing, his brother being elevated to the *gaddi* in his place.[1] The territory of the nawab of Karnul, in Madras, was annexed for attempting to make war.

Lord Ellenborough succeeded as governor-general in 1842. Only one case of importance arose in connection with an Indian state, but

[1] *Parliamentary Papers*, 1844, XXXVI, 351–453.

that was of the first importance. The troubles in the Gwalior state, referred to in Bentinck's time, had continued to increase and now came to a head. Jankoji Rao Sindhia died in 1843, to be succeeded by an adopted son, a minor, Jayaji Rao. Intrigues multiplied and the army, some 40,000 strong, became all powerful. The minority was in the hands of Krishna Rao Kadam, the Mama Sahib, or maternal uncle of the late ruler. He was opposed to Dada Khasgi-wala (the administrator of the family estates of the maharani), who succeeded in engineering his downfall. Dada was, indeed, expelled from the state on the demand of the governor-general, but this step failed to put an end to the intrigues.

Lord Ellenborough's remonstrance fell mainly on deaf ears, while the few sardars who were prepared to assist us in restoring order were powerless in the face of the army, which had complete control of affairs. The governor-general, therefore, decided to act and accompanied by the commander-in-chief, Sir Hugh Gough, crossed the Chambal and advanced on Gwalior. To their surprise (for no proper reconnaissance had been made) the British troops suddenly found themselves face to face with the state forces, and after two simultaneous battles at Maharajpur and Panniar, the state army was broken up.[1] A fresh treaty was made and a council of regency appointed to conduct affairs during the minority of the maharaja, then nine years old. Lord Ellenborough's action in the Gwalior case was the object of much criticism, and the main reason for his recall. But whatever criticism may be levelled at his methods, there can be no doubt as to the correctness of the policy pursued. When he landed in India, Lord Ellenborough inherited, as a legacy from his predecessor, the Afghan War. In addition, the assembly of a menacing army of Sikhs, some 70,000 strong, just across the Satlej river, made him nervous, and he felt that it would be courting disaster to leave a hostile, undisciplined force in his rear, close to the important town of Agra, especially in view of the weakness of our own army.[2] The best reply to the strictures levelled at him is to be found in his own letter to Lord Ripon, written on receiving the news of his recall.[3] He refers to the criticism passed on him by the court of directors in which his conduct was stigmatised as "wanting in decision and inconsistent with itself", and says in reply, that he is unable to controvert this opinion because he has not "the remotest idea to what supposed facts it can possibly refer". He then turns to the two objections raised by the court, firstly that he should have supported the regent, who was appointed with our approval, and secondly that he should not have crossed the Chambal river against the expressed wishes of the maharani and the sardars of the states. The Mama Sahib (the regent), he points out, was offered military support but refused

[1] *Calcutta Review*, 1844, I, 535.   [2] *Parliamentary Papers, loc. cit.* pp. 143–344.
[3] Law, *India under Lord Ellenborough*, p. 28.

it, and, when his fall came, it was so sudden as to preclude any possibility of such assistance reaching him. On 19 May (1843) he was in full control of the administration, on the 21st he was removed from the regency and by 5 June had left Gwalior, a fugitive. It would, moreover, have been impossible to carry out military operations at the end of May, with the rains imminent and many streams to cross, including the great Chambal river.

With regard to the second point, the crossing of the Chambal in December against the wishes of the durbar, he remarks that at that season the winter rains were expected which would have made the river difficult, if not impossible, to cross; provisions were not obtainable for the troops at his encampment; while the deep ravines which surrounded his position made it dangerous. To have withdrawn the troops would have led to an immediate cessation of all negotiations, as the Gwalior army, which was *de facto* ruler of the state, would never have submitted quietly to disbandment, even if the durbar had really intended to assist us. The court's view was, he notes, too limited, in regarding

the movement as an insulated transaction, which with an army in the field the Governor-General could deal with at his leisure. . . . It should rather be considered as a movement upon a field of battle extending from Scinde through the Punjab even to the frontiers of Nepaul.

Delay in dealing with the situation would have induced the Sikhs to advance, and to have left a hostile force of 40,000 men within a few marches of Agra would have been the height of folly. He concludes by saying that no negotiations would ever have been effected without the presence of a force and it had always been apprehended that its use would be necessary.

The weak point in Lord Ellenborough's procedure was his reliance on the Treaty of Burhanpur,[1] of 1804, which, though never denounced, had been objected to by Lord Cornwallis, and treated as a dead letter when new compacts were made with Gwalior in 1805 and 1817. By article 6 of this treaty we undertook to support the maharaja, should necessity arise, with a subsidiary force; and the governor-general, in view of the maharaja's youth, construed the disturbances of 1843 as falling under the spirit of this article.

In July, 1844, Lord Ellenborough was recalled and Sir Henry Hardinge succeeded him. The Sikh War engaged most of the governor-general's attention but he visited the king of Oudh in a fruitless endeavour to induce him to overhaul his administration, informing him that unless reforms were introduced at an early date, the British Government would be obliged to take over the state. The warning, however, fell on deaf ears. Hardinge also urged the abolition of sati in the Indian states, following the lines of Lord W. Bentinck's enactment in British India.

[1] Aitchison, *op. cit.* IV, 53; *Parliamentary Papers, loc. cit.* p. 146.

In January, 1848, Lord Dalhousie assumed the governor-generalship. His name is, even now, apt to be invidiously coupled with the
so-called "annexation policy" in connection with the Indian states.
But, indeed, in all probability, no criticism would have been roused
by his action had not the Mutiny, following so closely on his retirement, called for a scapegoat.

The cases on which this adverse criticism is mainly based are the
absorption of Satara (1848); Nagpur (1853); Jhansi (1854) and
Oudh (1856). There were also some other but less important instances. Of all these only that of Oudh was strictly speaking a case
of deliberate annexation; in every other case Lord Dalhousie based
his decisions on the fact that no direct heir existed to inherit the state,
which was, moreover, "dependent", that is created by ourselves or
held on a subordinate tenure. In each case, also, a decision was only
arrived at after infinite pains had been taken to ascertain the facts,
and was invariably carried out with the full approbation of the court
of directors.

The Satara state was created by Lord Hastings in 1818, the treaty
on which it rested (1819)[1] containing no clause conferring the right
of adoption, while Sir James Rivett-Carnac in installing the raja
had warned him that, being childless and no longer young, the
state would lapse at his death, unless as a mark of special favour
he was permitted to adopt a successor. Lord Dalhousie left no stone
unturned to arrive at a just decision; no argument for or against
adoption escaped his scrutiny. His policy was based on the well-
established Hindu doctrine, still followed by the ruling princes of
India, which denies the right of succession by adoption in a subordinate state or estate unless the previous sanction of the suzerain
has been obtained, a rule applying equally to old-established or
recently-created holdings. Thus, in Central India it is followed by the
big Maratha durbars with respect to Rajput feudatories, who were
established much earlier than their masters. This permission to adopt
must in every case be given by the suzerain before the ceremony
of adoption is carried out, otherwise the adoption is not legal. On
the other hand it is not, in Indian states, customary to enforce an
escheat, so that the actual absorption of an entire holding is very
rare, although the terms of the tenure are often modified by the area
being reduced, the tribute raised or some new conditions imposed.
A succession fee called *nazarana* is invariably levied, amounting often
to one year's revenue or even more.

This well-known principle was disregarded by the raja of Satara,
who, just before he died, in 1848, adopted a son without informing
the British Resident or obtaining the permission of the governor-
general. Hence Lord Dalhousie would have been fully within his
rights in ordering escheat, simply on the basis of this omission,

[1] *Parliamentary Papers*, 1849, xxxix, 267.

especially as the court of directors had, in 1841, enunciated the principle, that the right to political succession was an indulgence which should be the exception and not the rule, and be granted only as a mark of special favour and approbation, adding that the Company should "persevere in the one clear and direct course of abandoning no just and honourable accession of territory or revenue, while all existing claims of right are at the same time scrupulously respected".[1]

Lord Dalhousie consulted all his most experienced colleagues and found that he was supported by the majority of them in refusing to recognise the adoption. But before passing orders he referred the case to the court, which agreed with his view, as "being in accordance with the general law and custom of India".[2]

The Nagpur case was in many ways similar. The raja died heirless in 1853. He had not adopted any one and no lineal descendant in the male line survived. In a long, careful minute[3] Lord Dalhousie pointed out that the original state was of recent creation and was founded on usurpation and conquest; its ruler had always been hostile to us, and after the campaign which ended in his defeat it had lain entirely with us to deal with this territory as we thought fit. Lord Hastings had then, as a concession to Maratha sentiment, recreated the state from the conquered territory, after deducting a considerable portion of it. Nagpur, like Satara, was thus a state of our own making. In this minute Lord Dalhousie classed the Indian states as being tributary and subordinate, of our own creation, or independent. In the first case he considered that our assent was necessary to an adoption, in the second case that adoption should not be allowed, while in the third case we had no right to interfere.[4]

Lord Dalhousie found, however, that in the Nagpur case many of his advisers were against him, especially Colonel Low,[5] who quoted the views of Lord Hastings, Elphinstone, Munro, and Metcalfe, all of whom considered that the adoption of heirs to states by Indian princes should be recognised by us. The main grounds of dissent were, that our rule was generally unpopular; that the absorption of a state invariably meant that the aristocracy ceased to find employment and became a discontented body; that the rigorous enforcement of the doctrine of lapse would only lead to misgovernment, as every childless raja, feeling that his state must come to an end, would oppress his subjects, extorting the last penny from them for his own use. The case was referred to the court, which upheld the escheat.

The Jhansi case (1854) stood on quite a different footing. The subhedar of Jhansi had originally been a provincial governor under

---

[1] Minute of 30 August, 1848, *Parliamentary Papers, loc. cit.* pp. 224–8.
[2] *Parliamentary Papers, loc. cit.* pp. 272–98.
[3] *Parliamentary Papers,* 1854, XLVIII, 317 *sqq.*
[4] Minute of 28 January, 1854, *idem,* pp. 337–53.
[5] Minute of 10 February, 1854, *idem,* pp. 355–67.

the Peshwa, and was in no sense a ruling chief. When in 1818 all the Peshwa's lands fell to us the province of Bundelkhand passed with them, and the subhadar with it. In submitting the case to the court the governor-general laid stress on this aspect of the affair.[1]

One case which Lord Dalhousie took up cannot well be brought into the same category as the three just mentioned, and that is the case of Karauli. This state lies in Rajputana and was founded in the eleventh century. Sir Frederick Currie in his minute on the case points out how Karauli, an old Rajput state, differed entirely from "Satara the offspring of our gratuitous benevolence". Lord Dalhousie, however, recommended the escheat, but the directors decided that their policy was inapplicable to Karauli, which was not a dependent state but a "protected ally".[2] It may be remarked here that the absorption of Satara, Nagpur and Jhansi caused no real alarm amongst the Indian princes.

The crowning act of Lord Dalhousie's administration was the annexation of Oudh, a genuine case of annexation, and undoubtedly one which did stir the hearts of the princes of India. It is only fair to the governor-general to show how averse he was to the procedure he was ordered to follow.

Our relations with the state of Oudh were governed by the treaty of 1801 which required the nawab to reform his administration and follow the advice of the Company's officers. Succeeding governors-general had warned him that unless he reformed his administration we should be obliged to interfere, but, though abuse increased year by year, we took no steps to enforce our admonitions. Wellesley,[3] when granting the treaty of 1801, had remarked prophetically that our support of the nawab only protected the vile and that no effective security could be provided against the ruin of the province of Oudh until we took over the administration. In 1837 Lord Auckland made a new treaty with the nawab by which we were empowered to intervene in case of misrule and put our own officers in charge. The king accepted, but the directors refused to ratify it. Lord Auckland, however, never informed the king that the treaty was a dead letter, though he did report to the directors that he had not done so.[4] Lord Hardinge, nevertheless, when he warned the king, in 1847, that he must reform, cited this treaty in his memorandum as if it was still in force and confirmatory of the treaty of 1801.[5]

Convinced by the reports of Sleeman and Outram of the need for immediate action, Dalhousie, although his term of office was just expiring, and he might well have left this unpleasant duty to Lord Canning, investigated the case with his usual minute care. He was

---

[1] *Parliamentary Papers*, 1854-5, XL, 87-103. [2] *Idem*.
[3] Wellesley, *Despatches*, II, 426—Despatch of 22 January, 1801.
[4] *Parliamentary Papers*, 1857-8, XLIII, 307-65.
[5] *Idem*, p. 368, para. 8.

informed by Mr Dorin and General Low, members of council, that though the treaty of 1837 was a dead letter, this fact was unknown to the king of Oudh. Mr Grant, another member, urged that the king should be informed of this fact. Dalhousie referred the point to the directors who replied that the best course to take was to leave things as they were until circumstances arose necessitating the disclosure.[1]

Long afterwards, writing to Sir George Couper on 6 January, 1858,[2] Dalhousie refers to this question. He remarks that it was really a matter of indifference to the king and the people of Oudh, when we actually took over the state, whether it was done under the treaty of 1837 or by the strong hand: "for every human being knew the assumption would be permanent", and so the degree of their knowledge could not have affected the result. But he held that the authorities had no right, at the time, to withhold the information.

In a long and careful minute[3] the governor-general discussed the whole case. He put the treaty of 1837 aside as being a dead letter, and pointed out that "for tolerating so long this total disregard of the obligation of a solemn Treaty [of 1801]...the British Government is heavily responsible". We had warned and counselled but never acted, abuses had grown, while our own troops in Oudh protected the king from justifiable revolt on the part of his subjects. He then suggested four courses:

(a) that the king should abdicate, Oudh being incorporated in British India;

(b) that the king should be allowed to retain his titles but should vest the administration in us in perpetuity;

(c) that the administration should be made over to us for a time;

(d) that the Resident should take over general control of the state administration.

Lord Dalhousie declared that he believed the first course would lead to the happiest issue, but added:

yet I do not counsel the adoption of this measure. The reform of the administration may be wrought and the prospects of the people secured without resorting to so extreme a measure as the annexation of the territory and the abolition of the throne and I for my part do not advocate the advice that the province of Oudh be declared British territory.

He held that in spite of maladministration the consistent loyalty to us of successive nawabs of Oudh precluded annexation. So he urged the second course that the king should vest control in us but retain his titles and rank, as this course would be "perpetual in duration as well as ample in extent"; but the king must himself do this, not be forced to do it. Different views were held by the members of his council but the general opinion was against Lord Dalhousie and in

---

[1] *Parliamentary Papers*, 1857–8, XLIII, 307–65.   [2] Dalhousie, *Letters*, p. 393.
[3] Minute of 18 June, 1855, *Parliamentary Papers*, loc. cit.

favour of the king's abdication. The case was sent to the court, and the directors rejected Dalhousie's proposal, ordering annexation and the abolition of the throne.[1]

Dalhousie undertook to carry out this thankless task, although Lord Canning had just arrived in India to succeed him as governor-general. Outram, the Resident, was asked to induce the king to sign a document voluntarily transferring the kingdom to us. Outram was confident that he could do so, but the king refused in tears, and the proclamation annexing Oudh was at once issued. No disturbance arose. Minute directions were also given to Outram as to disarming the province but these were, at his suggestion, not carried out, owing to the approach of the hot season, and the order was later on cancelled by Lord Canning. Had it been carried out, Oudh with an unarmed population would have been a less formidable factor in the disturbance of 1857. Lord Dalhousie refers to this in a private letter to Sir George Couper of 5 February, 1858;[2] he says: "Lord Canning's Government made a fatal blunder in not disarming Oude in 1856, when it might have been done easily and completely". He adds that no official record exists of his determination to carry this out because it was a task for his successor, and hence it only appears in his confidential demi-official correspondence with Outram, in these words:

It is my intention that not a single fortified place should be left in Oude, with the exception of those that belong to Government. It is further my intention that the whole population should be disarmed...as was done with such excellent effect in the Punjaub in 1849.

It is thus clear that Lord Dalhousie, while he deprecated half-measures, was strongly opposed to the policy of annexation, though he was convinced that, so far as the people of Oudh were concerned, it would be far the best course to take.

In a letter to Sir George Couper written on 15 December, 1855,[3] before the orders of the court had arrived, he says:

I understand that they [the Directors] mean to *force* the King to form a new treaty or to assume the government of his country. This is all very well for the home authorities but it was not for me to suggest it....The course proposed by the Court is not warranted by international law. It would be either conquest or usurpation of the power of government by force of arms.

This argument of international law would not in these days be raised in connection with the Indian states.

Sleeman, however, Outram's predecessor as Resident at Lucknow, expressed the opinion that the annexation was a political blunder, holding that we should have acted under the treaty of 1837, abrogated though it was. The confiscation of the state would, he said, "cause our good name to suffer", and "that good name is more valuable

---

[1] *Parliamentary Papers,* 1857, XI, 109–17.
[2] Dalhousie, *op. cit.* p. 399.
[3] *Idem,* p. 363.

to us than a dozen Oudes". We had used our giant's strength like a giant, he said, and had injured our reputation in the eyes of all India. This opinion was largely instrumental in leading to the grant of "Adoption sanads" in 1862. But any such step would have been impossible in Dalhousie's day as it would have savoured of interfering with the "independent" states.

The other cases with which Lord Dalhousie had to deal were the extinction of the pension granted to Baji Rao, the last Peshwa, the disappearance of the Carnatic and Tanjore titles, and the question of the Hyderabad contingent.

Baji Rao died in 1852 leaving no heir, and the governor-general ruled that the pension, being personal, terminated with his death, though the large private fortune accumulated by Baji Rao would pass to his adopted son, Dhondu Pant, who later on became notorious in the Mutiny, as Nana Sahib.

Trouble arose in regard to payment of the Hyderabad contingent force by that durbar, and in 1853 the Nizam under pressure placed the administration of the Berar province of his state under our control so that its revenues might be devoted to the up-keep of that force. This arrangement, made with such reluctance in the first instance, has since been the cause of much contention and is likely to remain so.

The nawab of the Carnatic, in 1855, died leaving no son and, on the ground that his state was created by us in 1801, and on the fact that his title was personal, his estate escheated and the title did not descend to his successors, who have since then been styled Princes of Arcot.[1] A similar case arose on the death of the raja of Tanjore.

Reviewing Lord Dalhousie's administration in so far as it affected the Indian states, it is clear that the policy of absorbing them in cases of failure of direct heirs was not of his making but was inherited by him, and, whether right or wrong, was at that time the avowed policy of the Company, whose one anxiety was to consolidate its possessions.

Lord Dalhousie was careful to confine action under this policy to the "dependent" states. Thus, when he was urged by the directors, soon after he reached India, to take a strong line and interfere in Hyderabad, he threatened to resign; while in Bahawalpur, when the newly-installed ruler was ousted by his brother, he refused to support the fugitive nawab, although we had recognised his succession, in view of the fact that the people of the state did not wish to have him as their ruler, and it was for them alone to decide. These two cases occurred in "independent" states. Lord Dalhousie was one of the most scrupulous and conscientious governors-general who ever guided the destiny of India; he was absolutely incapable of doing an injustice. On the other hand, a sincerely religious man, he was convinced of the desirability of substituting our rule for that of the Indian princes,

[1] *Parliamentary Papers*, 1860, LII, 531–78.

whenever it could in fairness be effected. He says himself, writing on 21 July, 1857, to Sir George Couper:[1]

I never advised annexing any principality unless it lapsed naturally for want of heirs or was forfeited for misconduct. But when a principality does so fall to our disposal it does seem to me to be cruel to hand over its inhabitants to be squeezed and skinned by a native despot, merely that our own subjects may be able to compare their own lot favourably with that of those whom we have abandoned....

His unflagging warfare against abuses of all kinds and his desire to extend to all the benefits of the new era he had introduced into British India certainly dimmed his perception of other points of view; as for instance that of the hereditary ruling princes themselves, that of their subjects with the innate reverence for their natural rulers which then did (if it does not now) distinguish the people of India, and by their preference, in spite of abuses, for the less rigid government of an Indian state. Never did his administration justify the fancifully fierce condemnation levelled at it as being "more like counting out the spoil of brigands...than...the acts of English statesmanship",[2] nor did any man ever merit less the stigma of being called the "very worst and basest of rulers".[3] We must not judge those days by these. Besides an entire change of policy on our side, the Indian states have themselves, for the most part, travelled far administratively since 1856, and, though still in the main autocratic, have reached a much higher standard than they then possessed, while they are now subjected to the glare of criticism and the antiseptic of publicity to a degree impossible in those days of a limited public press and very inadequate communications.

The sudden upheaval which followed so soon after his departure was quite unforeseen by Lord Dalhousie who in his farewell minute[4] considers that he is justified in saying that he leaves India "at peace without and within".

To summarise the results of the policy pursued towards the Indian states between 1818 and 1856.

This period is by far the most important in the history of the relationship of the states to the British Government. It witnessed their metamorphosis from a congeries of quasi-independent units, some openly hostile, most, at heart, antagonistic to us, and all doubtful and resentful of our intentions towards them, into a body with so complete an acquiescence in our paramount position that even the shock of the Mutiny could not subvert it. This result we owe mainly to Lord Hastings, who built so carefully on the foundations laid by Lord Wellesley, the structure being completed by the generous policy adopted when India came directly under the crown. For Lord

---

[1] Dalhousie, *op. cit.* p. 381.
[2] Edwin Arnold, *The Marquis of Dalhousie's Administration of British India*, p. 199.
[3] Major E. Bell, *The Empire in India*, p. 26.
[4] *Parliamentary Papers*, 1855-6, XLV, 107-52.

Hastings introduced those distinct relations of supremacy and sub-ordination which still fundamentally control the position between us and the states. In his time those parts of India not directly under our administration passed equally under our sovereignty; and our ascendancy, as also our indefeasible right to interfere if the peace and security of India was menaced, became henceforth unquestioned. Step by step, sorely against its will, the Company had been driven, by inexorable fate, to abandon its policy of the ring-fence and of non-interference, and so we passed through the system of subordinate alliance to the wise and generous policy of co-operative partnership which holds at the present day.

CHAPTER XXXII

THE DEVELOPMENT OF SOVEREIGNTY
IN BRITISH INDIA

"BRITISH authority in India", says Ilbert, "may be traced to a two-fold source. It is derived partly from the British crown and parliament, partly from the Great Mogul and other native rulers of India."[1] The development has been slow and at times obscure. It has lent itself to much misinterpretation, and has involved strong contrasts between facts and theories. One of the great difficulties has arisen from the fact that in the East public law has not been subject to the same scrutiny and definition that it has undergone in Europe. Technical terms, such as sovereignty, and their Persian equivalents, seem to have been used with the greatest laxity, both by Indians and by Englishmen in India; while in most of our documents the needs of current controversies are predominant, and one is seldom sure whether Hastings and Clive were laying down general principles which they were prepared to support in every case or only drawing temporary arguments from an ambiguous position in order to defend a particular action.

It is clear that from the first the position of the English in India was variable and uncertain. The fact may be illustrated by the different positions held by the English in the seventeenth century in their principal settlements of Bombay, Madras and Calcutta respectively. In the first the Company exercised sovereign powers under the English crown, to whom the island had been ceded by the Portuguese. The right to fortify and defend the place, to maintain troops there, to administer justice, to levy taxes, to coin money, was clear, full and indisputable. All inhabitants, whether English or Indian, were presumably subjects of the English crown.

Madras fell in another category. That place was held under a grant of the chief of Wandiwash, who empowered the English Company to build a castle and fortress, to mint money, together with

full power and authority to govern and dispose of the government of Madraspatam for the term and space of two years next insueing after they shall be seated there and possesst of the said fortifications; and for the future by an equal division to receive half the custom and revenues of that port.[2]

After the Hindu power had been overthrown by the Muslim kingdom of Golconda, the grant was in effect continued; but, as complaints perpetually arose over the division of the customs, a new grant was

---

[1] *The Government of India*, p. 1.   [2] Love, *Vestiges*, I, 17.

made in 1672, which commuted the share of the customs for a quit-rent of 1200 pagodas; the grant continues:

Neither shall any avaldare or any of the diwan's people ever be kept or placed in the town of Chinapatam, and, as I have done, that no person whatsoever shall have to do in the least with the town of Chinapatam, but that it shall remain wholly and for ever under the English, where they may accordingly act all the command, government and justice of the said town as they shall think necessary and most convenient to be done.[1]

When, in 1687, Golconda was conquered by Aurangzib, no change seems to have been made in the English status. Here then was a position quite different from that at Bombay. The English exercised all the powers of sovereignty subject however to Indian superiority shown by the payment of quit-rent. Here too it should be noted, that as the local coinage bore no superscription, but only the figures of Hindu deities, it did not carry with it the same implications that it would have done in Northern India; and when the Moghul authorities permitted the coinage of rupees at Madras, those coins bore the usual marks of Moghul supremacy.

At Calcutta the position was again different. There the English had been allowed to purchase the zamindari of the three villages that grew into the capital of British India. Their jurisdiction, as at Madras, was therefore two-fold. Over Englishmen the Company relied upon its chartered powers; but over Indians, and especially over Muslims, in whom alone the local government took any great interest, its authority was that of a minor zamindar under the local faujdar. The position is shown with special clearness by the fact that the Company could not, till the treaty of 1757, obtain the right of minting coin at Calcutta, and by the jurisdiction of the law courts there. The Company's criminal court, established by the royal charters of 1727 and 1753, was limited to Europeans. Indians were tried in the zamindar's court. In theory all sentences of death should have been submitted to the faujdar of Hugli and the *Nazim* at Murshidabad before being put into execution.[2] In practice this does not seem to have been done; but the Calcutta Council was clearly very cautious of putting Muhammadans to death. We must discount Bolts's story, that they were flogged to death instead of being hanged, out of deference to Muslim opinion;[3] but one case at least is on record, where the Muhammadan members of a party of criminals were spared for fear of the nawab's interference.[4]

This position at Madras and Calcutta was profoundly changed by the course of events which may be dated from the War of the Austrian Succession. Madras was the first to be affected. During the war it passed into the hands of the French by right of conquest, in defiance

---

[1] Love, *op. cit.* I, 345. "Chinapatam" is Madras.
[2] Committee of Secrecy, 1773, Sixth Report, pp. 2 and 11.
[3] Bolts, *Considerations*, I, 80.　　　　　　　　　　[4] Long, *Selections*, p. 51.

of the prohibitions of the nawab; it remained in French hands during the war, although Dupleix agreed to make a formal recognition of the nawab's position by flying his flag over the place for a week.[1] At the end of the war it was restored to the English by the Treaty of Aix-la-Chapelle. From that time the English might have claimed to hold it independently of any Indian prince. However, they were on the best of terms with Muhammad 'Ali, whom they were seeking to establish as against the French nominee; and so, in 1752, as a mark of gratitude the quit-rent was abolished, and with it went the last fragment of dependence upon an Indian prince at Madras.[2]

That, however, only applied to Madras itself and a very narrow strip of land round its walls. The rest of the country lay within the undisputed control of the nawab under the nominal sovereignty of Delhi. When, in 1780, the nawab applied to Hastings to secure a settlement of outstanding questions, he was specially eager to secure declarations from the English that he was hereditary prince of the Carnatic, with full power over the administration of his country and the right to nominate his successor, under the general protection of the Company and the English nation.[3] It is apparent that all thoughts of the Moghul emperor have disappeared, although doubtless his name was still recited in the Friday prayers at Arcot, and for that matter at Madras. In fact the very application shows that the Company, and not the emperor, was now suzerain. In 1792 the old nawab died and was succeeded by the son whom for so many years he had striven to disinherit; but the succession took place with the approval of the Company. Finally, ten years later, for reasons which have been explained in a previous chapter, on the next demise of the nawabship, the Company intervened decisively. Its representative refused to recognise any succession except on terms which at a stroke reduced the nawab to the same position to which the nawab of Bengal had only fallen after a term of years.[4] He became a pensioner. On this occasion we hear no mention of Delhi or the emperor. Sovereign powers over the Carnatic passed to the Company, not indeed by conquest, but in virtue of a long-established political situation, in which the Company was in fact, though not in name, the overlord. For three generations the old title and dignity were allowed to survive; but in 1855, in the time of Dalhousie, they were deliberately extinguished, as a "semblance of royalty without any of the power is a mockery of authority which must be pernicious".[5]

The case of Bengal was much more complicated, partly because of the inferior status from which the Company set out, partly because

[1] P. 122 *supra*.   [2] Madras Public Consultations, 31 August, 1752.
[3] Requests of the Nawab Walajah of the governor-general, Madras Military Consultations, 22 August, 1781, p. 2280.
[4] P. 361 *supra*.
[5] Lee-Warner, *Dalhousie*, II, 140.

it offered the first example of something like territorial acquisitions on a large scale, and partly because of the conflicts and hesitations of the crown and Company in England. The status of zamindar persisted at Calcutta until the year 1756. But when at the close of that year Clive recovered the place, we may suppose that the logic of events had already begun to modify the position. It was recovered by force; and we may infer that when the English returned, they returned no longer as humble dependents of the nawab. The change is clearly indicated in the treaty which Clive made with Siraj-ud-daula on 9 February following. In future the place might be fortified as the English thought proper; the privilege of a mint was granted; and the English nation and Company agreed to live on good terms with the nawab so long as he observed the treaty.[1] The theory of Moghul sovereignty still stood, but a large breach had been made in it. The breach was further enlarged when the English proceeded to overthrow the ruling nawab and set up another. In the treaty with Mir Ja'far, although the sovereignty over the country, in whosesoever hands it lay, was not formally impaired, the English were nevertheless established as an *imperium in imperio* with the right of doing themselves justice.[2] The revolution of 1760 was designed to strengthen the nawab and led, as we have seen, to a conflict between the person invested with the sole rights of administration in the province, and the corporation controlling the only efficient military force therein. Again the nawab was overthrown and Mir Ja'far restored, not as had formerly been the case, with the aid and concurrence of his friends and supporters, but by the mere act of the Calcutta Council. In 1765 this *de facto* power assumed the right of nominating the nawab's principal minister, and in the same year, under Clive's Treaty of Allahabad, it was invested with the right of revenue administration. The formal sovereignty still lay where it had; but alongside of the emperor and nawab there had sprung up a body which not only possessed the sole military force in Bengal, but also had conquered the province in 1763, had assumed the power of nominating the nawab's chief officer, and was now invested with the right of collecting the revenues. It was an indefinite situation which could not readily be brought within the scope of any western formulae.

The situation, perplexing as it was, was prolonged by the hesitation of the English authorities to assume formal sovereignty over the territories which in fact they controlled. Neither the crown nor the Company was prepared, though for very different reasons, to lay claim to territorial sovereignty in India. The Company feared that any such claims would provoke or hasten interference by the ministry;[3] the crown was unwilling to assail the legal rights of the Company.[4]

---

[1] Hill, *Bengal in* 1756–7, II, 215 *sqq.*   [2] P. 171 *supra.*
[3] Verelst, *op. cit.* p. 81.
[4] E.g. Chatham to Shelburne, 24 May, 1773 (*Chatham Correspondence*, IV, 264).

Indeed, the establishment of such a position was the precise motive with which Clive seems in 1765 to have desired the diwanni of Bengal rather than any territorial cession, which could have been obtained just as readily. It placed the Company in a strong tactical position alike as regards foreign powers and as regards the government at home.

This had not always been Clive's aim. After Plassey he had sought to induce Pitt to take over the government of the Company's possessions, in despair of ever seeing that body establish good government.[1] But Pitt had then been reluctant to intervene in so complicated a position. How complicated it was may be seen from an opinion delivered by the law-officers on 24 December, 1757, on the Company's memorial praying for the grant of all booty and conquests made in India.

"In respect to such places", they say, "as have been or shall be acquired by treaty or grant from the Mogul or any of the Indian princes or governments, your Majesty's letters patent are not necessary, the property of the soil vesting in the Company by the Indian grants, subject only to your Majesty's rights of sovereignty over the settlements as English settlements, and over the inhabitants, as English subjects who carry with them your Majesty's laws wherever they form colonies.... In respect to such places as have lately been acquired or shall hereafter be acquired by conquest, the property as well as the dominion vests in your Majesty by virtue of your known prerogative, and consequently the Company can only derive a right to them by your Majesty's grant...."[2]

But although the Company could not acquire territory by conquest, it could nevertheless "cede conquests made upon Indians", since by its charters it had power to make war and peace with them. In 1765 the legal view undoubtedly was that British sovereignty was established in Calcutta, in the 24-Parganas, and in the districts of Burdwan, Midnapur and Chittagong ceded by Mir Kasim, but not in the diwanni districts, a result which accorded well with the Company's policy of that time. The question as to where and at what point Indian inhabitants of places subject to English sovereignty became English subjects does not seem to have been considered, as is clear enough from the uncertain and ambiguous language of the Regulating Act. It was declared at Calcutta in 1773 that Sepoy officers were "not...subjects of Britain, but aliens and natives of Hindustan".[3]

From the point of view of the ministry the question was clearly two-fold: internal as regarded the Company, external as regarded the French and other foreign nations. It will be most convenient to sketch the development of policy under these two heads, and finally to describe the relations between the Company's government in India and the Moghul emperor—the *de facto* and the *de jure* wielders of Indian dominion.

[1] Malcolm, *Life of Clive*, II, 119 *sqq.*; Williams, *Life of Chatham*, II, 28–9.
[2] Public Record Office, C.O. 77–19; cf. an undated and unsigned minute, *ap.* Chatham MSS, I, 99.
[3] Forrest, *Selections from the State Papers of the Foreign Department*, I, 89.

The first direct exercise of sovereign power in India by the crown since the cession of Bombay to the Company resulted from an international document, the Treaty of Paris of 1763, in which both the French and the English governments recognised Muhammad 'Ali as nawab of the Carnatic and Salabat Jang as subahdar of the Deccan. No one seems to have considered how far these stipulations were consistent with the structure of the Moghul Empire. Indeed they were at the time intended only to secure the peace between the two European nations in India by preventing them from continuing to support rival princes in those regions. At a later time, however, the clauses were put to a new use. The disputes between the crown and the Company which came to a head in 1766–7 made the ministry anxious to find some means by which it could learn how matters were actually going in India. There was reason to distrust the execution which the Company's servants had given to the treaty in the East; and the upshot of the matter was that when the Company sent out its supervisors to reform its Indian administration, the ministry sent out in command of the squadron an officer vested with plenipotentiary powers from the king to the princes of India. About the commission of this officer there was much underhand work that ill became the dignity of the ministry; the commission, for instance, was not communicated to the Company; and so when the commodore arrived in India he found that the Company's governments knew nothing about the powers that had been granted to him. The natural result was the outbreak of violent disputes between the representative of the king's majesty and the councils which exercised the powers of the Company. These divided and undefined powers were bound to weaken and impede, rather than to strengthen the conduct of affairs, and the time had not yet come when the ministry was prepared to take a decisive part in determining Indian policy. However, it is curious to note that among the other duties of the plenipotentiary was included a mission to the Moghul emperor, who had sent presents to George III by the hands of Clive, and these, by some oversight, had never been acknowledged. Commodore Lindsay was entrusted with a letter of thanks from the king, whose titles were for the occasion strangely modified, obviously with a view to impressing the court of Delhi with a due sense of the king's importance. "George III", the letter is headed, "King...Defender of the Christian faith...and Sovereign of the Seas, etc."[1] A generation later the same style was employed in a letter addressed to the emperor of China.

The next step after this ill-concerted effort to interfere in the Company's Indian administration was the Regulating Act of 1773. That act takes for granted the existence of British sovereignty in Calcutta and its immediate neighbourhood, but not apparently

[1] Weymouth to Lindsay, 14 September, 1769, and George III to the Moghul, of the same date (Brit. Mus. Add. MSS, 18020, ff. 46 verso and 50 verso).

beyond. At best its language is hesitating and uncertain. A distinction appears between British subjects and the native-born inhabitants. The India Act of 1784 leaves the question still untouched, although it legislates for the full exercise of all sovereign powers in territory that in 1773 was clearly not yet a part of the dominions of the crown. The act of 1793 merely declared that all territorial acquisitions and their revenues were to remain in the possession of the East India Company for the next twenty years, thus leaving the question of sovereignty still open. Not until 1813 do we find the claim to sovereignty formally asserted. In the act renewing the Company's privileges in that year the territorial acquisitions were continued under its control "without prejudice to the undoubted sovereignty of the crown of the United Kingdom, etc. in and over the same". But at what moment that sovereignty came into being still remained a riddle.

Much the same attitude is displayed by the treaties concluded in this period. At first the question of sovereignty is not raised except in regard to the factories possessed by the European nations, and which it was taken for granted formed part of their respective territories. Thus Article 11 of the Treaty of Paris declares,

Dans les Indes Orientales la Grande Bretagne restituera à la France...les différents comptoirs que cette couronne possédait...Et sa majesté Très Chrétienne renonce à toute pretention aux acquisitions qu'elle avait faite sur la côte de Coromandel et d'Orixa depuis le dit commencement de l'année 1749....Elle s'engage de plus à ne point ériger des fortifications et à ne point entretenir des troupes dans aucune partie des états du soubah de Bengale....

It is clearly implied that the English enjoyed a special position in Bengal by the limitations which the French engaged to observe; but neither then nor till long after was the least attempt made to define the position by the use of any of the political terms employed in Europe. The article in the Treaty of Versailles of 1783 even more obviously evades the matter. After providing for the restoration of the French factories in Bengal, it continues:

Et sa Majesté Britannique s'engage à prendre les mesures qui seront en son pouvoir pour assurer aux sujets de la France dans cette partie de l'Inde, comme sur la côte de Coromandel, et de Malabar, un commerce sûr, libre et indépendant....

In 1786–7, when troubles with the French in Bengal produced renewed discussions in Europe, leading to the convention of 1787, the most inconsistent language was used, showing that the English still had not been able to make up their minds as to their position in India. Thus the Committee of Secrecy writes to the Governor-General in Council, 19 July, 1786, stating that the French could hardly expect the benevolent intervention of the Company so long as they assumed a position of independence and did not "acquiesce in the general controuling power existing in the English Company as Dewan of the provinces".[1] But in Paris, on 6 February, 1787, Eden, who was negotiating the convention, took up a very different position in an *explication confidentielle* which he delivered to Montmorin. His proposals, he said, were intended,

> sans rien faire qui soit censé déroger à la souveraineté possessoire et exclusive dont l'Angleterre jouit dans l'Inde, de donner à la France toutes les facilités praticables, dans la vue de former un traité de commerce....C'est un fait incontestable que l'Angleterre possède tous les droits substantiels de la souveraineté dans les provinces de Bengale, Bahar, et Orixa....C'est en supposant cette qualité effective de la souveraineté que les deux cours ont formés l'article 11 de traité de Paris et l'article 13 de celui de Versailles....[2]

The French, however, did not accept this doctrine, which can hardly be read into the treaties mentioned without vigorous interpolation. The position is clearly summed up in an unpublished letter of Cornwallis to the Committee of Secrecy, dated 16 November, 1786. "From this complicated system", he says, "founded on grants conferred and powers assumed, of sovereignty exercised though not avowed, many difficulties arise in all negotiations with foreign nations."[3]

The Treaty of Amiens only dealt with India under a general article, but the Treaty of Paris of 1814, and the convention with the Netherlands of the same year, both place the position of the English Government in India beyond question internationally. Both refer specifically to the British sovereignty in India, which was then for the first time acknowledged by the French and the Dutch. In this connection, and as displaying the contrast which this treaty displays with previous diplomatic language, a sentence from Article 12 of the Treaty of Paris may be quoted:

> Sa Majesté Britannique s'engage à faire jouir les sujets de sa Majesté Très Chrétienne relativement au commerce et à la sûreté de leurs personnes et propriétés dans les limites de la souveraineté britannique sur le continent des Indes, des mêmes facilités, privilèges et protection, qui sont à présent ou seront accordés aux nations les plus favorisées.

Thus the claim put forward by the legislation of 1813 was in the following year formally announced to the diplomatic world of Europe and recognised by the two powers principally interested in the East.

We must now turn to see how in India itself the position of the East India Company gradually developed. The obvious point of departure is the Treaty of Allahabad, by which Clive secured for the Company a grant of the diwanni, agreeing in return to pay to the emperor twenty-six lakhs of rupees a year besides giving him possession of Allahabad and the revenues of the neighbouring country. The emperor at the time when he made the grant was a fugitive from his capital, without money, without troops, dependent on the English for his daily bread. His grant gave them nothing which they could

---

[1] India Office, *French in India*, vol. XIII.   [2] *Idem.*
[3] *Idem.*

not very well have taken for themselves had they been so minded, and Clive's reason for his generosity, as has been pointed out above, referred not to the position of affairs in India but to the Company's relations with the crown and the French. The grant was, Hastings said, "a presumptuous gift of what was not his to give",[1] and

The sword which gave us the dominion of Bengal must be the instrument of its preservation; and if...it shall ever cease to be ours, the next proprietor will derive his right and possession from the same natural charter.[2]

Holding these views Hastings was inevitably opposed to Clive's settlement so far as it concerned the action of the governments in India. Indeed, he had hardly taken over the government in Bengal in 1772 before an opportunity arose for him to give effect to his ideas. The emperor, Shah 'Alam, having quitted English protection at Allahabad for Maratha protection at Delhi, Hastings decided to stop payment of the Bengal tribute. "I think I may promise", he wrote, "that no more payments will be made while he is in the hands of the Mahrattas, nor, if I can prevent it, *ever more*."[3] The refusal was diplomatically placed to the account of the Bengal famine of 1769–70. There followed an unceasing stream of letters from Delhi, in which the emperor or one of his ministers called upon the English to withdraw from their position, or at the least to lend the emperor troops who might be paid out of the arrears. Hastings at last wrote, "I must plainly declare that until the safety and welfare of these provinces will admit of it, I cannot consent that a single rupee be sent out of them which it is in my power to retain".[4] The payment of tribute was the one really crucial element in the relations between the emperor and the rulers of the provinces. A governor might strike coin and have the Friday prayers read in the emperor's name; he might pay handsomely to obtain the imperial confirmation of his succession, and offer large sums for the continuance of his predecessor's titles; but these things meant little except when they were accompanied by the regular remittance of the annual tribute, which alone signified a real, living allegiance to the imperial power. Hastings's refusal of tribute was in effect a declaration of the practical independence of Bengal.

It was accompanied by another act which in its way was equally significant. The districts of Kora and Allahabad were ceded to the nawab of Oudh. Clive's arrangement by which they had been given to the emperor might conceivably have been represented as obedience to the monarch's commands. Not so the decision which dispossessed the imperial revenue-officers and transferred the districts back to the nawab of Oudh in return for fifty lakhs paid into the Company's

---

[1] Minute, *ap*. Bengal Select Committee, 4 October, 1773.
[2] Minute, *loc. cit.* 12 October, 1772.
[3] Hastings to Purling, 22 March, 1772 (Monckton Jones, *op. cit.* p. 147).
[4] Hastings to Shah 'Alam, 13 September, 1773 (Forrest, *op. cit.* 1, 58).

treasury. As if in order to make the position clearer still, Hastings declined the title which the emperor offered him.[1] In another way, too, Hastings aimed at introducing English sovereignty, though circumstances did not allow him to carry it into execution. He advocated the replacement of alliances between Indian princes and the Company by alliances between them and the crown. The first occasion on which he placed these ideas on paper seems to have been in a letter to North of 26 February, 1775;[2] but from a later letter to Elliot of 12 January, 1777,[3] it appears that the subject must have been discussed between him and Shuja-ud-daula when he visited Benares in 1773. He states that the nawab was desirous of alliance with George III and even offered to coin money in the name of the English monarch. Hastings was still in favour of this project in 1777, and thought it might be applied not only to Oudh but also to Berar. Had this policy been carried into effect, it would have led to a formal assertion of English paramountcy in India. But the directors, had it even been proposed to them, would have objected to it as lessening their importance, while the ministry of the time had no clear-cut conception of its own purposes. The plan thus came to nothing, and survives only as a project, foiled, like so many of Hastings's plans, by the opposition or the inertia of others.

While Hastings was thus bent on repudiating the emperor's authority over Bengal, he was equally active in reducing even the ostensible part played by that phantom the nawab in its internal management—implanting, as he said, the authority of the Company and the sovereignty of Great Britain in the constitution.

"The truth is", he wrote to the Secret Committee on 1 September, 1772, "that the affairs of the Company stand at present on a footing which can neither last as it is nor be maintained on the rigid principles of private justice. You must establish your own power, or you must hold it dependent on a superior, which I deem to be impossible."[4]

In these ideas he was encouraged by the Company's decision "to stand forth as diwan". One of the guiding principles which inspired the reforms of the period 1772–4 was to make Calcutta the visible capital of the province. Thither was moved the chief revenue-office, and thither went the appeals from the courts which he established. "In a word", he claimed in 1773, "the sovereign authority of the Company is firmly rooted in every branch of the state."[5]

But in this he had out-run the intentions of his masters, the directors, and their masters, the parliament and crown. Lawyers like Thurlow might with brutal directness declare that in India existed no powers

---

[1] Hastings to Shah 'Alam, 1 August, 1773 (*Calendar of Persian Correspondence*, IV, 77).
[2] Gleig, *op. cit.* I, 508.
[3] *Idem*, II, 136.
[4] *Idem*, I, 254.   [5] *Idem*, p. 332.

or rights but force, and that it was "a country with no public moral or faith".[1] But no one in England was yet ready to accept the idea of filling with British sovereignty the void created by the dissolution of the Moghul power. The vagueness of the Regulating Act corresponded in its own way with the vagueness of the directors' orders. They might resolve directly to administer the Bengal revenues on reports that their Indian deputy was playing them false; but though they enjoyed the powers they were not prepared to assume the position of the masters of Bengal. When they received complaints, for instance, that the French were refusing to obey the orders issued in the nawab's name, they replied:

We direct that you afford the Country Government all necessary assistance in the execution of such equitable laws as are or may be framed for the protection of the natives....If the French persist in their contempt of the Nabob, it is our order that you decline as much as possible entering into a discussion of such of their complaints as shall be cognizable by the Nazim of the province, for so long as the English pay attention to His Excellency, it cannot be expected that other Europeans should be allowed to disregard him....[2]

So when Clavering and his followers arrived in India, and found that Hastings had adopted a different policy, and above all when they found the Supreme Court taking the same line, calling the nawab "a man of straw", and demanding that the majority should make oath that he was a sovereign independent prince, conducting his own affairs independently of their government and capable of making war and peace with Calcutta, though they were unable to make the required affidavits they were strongly inclined to adopt, support, and enforce the Company's views, reviving the phantom which Clive had summoned up. Not impossibly the latter had urged this course on Francis in some of those meetings which took place at Walcot shortly before the majority sailed from England and which were full of evil omen for the relations between the governor-general and his new colleagues. Hence their endeavour to maintain the fiction of the dual government and to hide the authority of the East India Company. Accordingly they insisted on re-establishing Muhammad Riza Khan as deputy nazim and supported their decision by taunting Hastings with neglect of the Company's intentions.[3]

"The Governor roundly insists", we read, "on the futility of attempting to maintain a country government.....An old servant of the Company might at least have treated their deliberate and invariable opinion with greater respect. With regard to us, if our ideas on this subject had not entirely concurred with theirs, and if we had not been convinced that in their circumstances it was the only rational system they could pursue, we should still have thought it our duty...to have adopted their doctrines."

[1] Thurlow's Opinion on Clive's Jagir Case.
[2] Company to Bengal, 3 March, 1775, paras. 59 *sqq.*
[3] Bengal Secret Consultations, 29 February, 1776.

Beside these thin and hollow declarations should be placed Hastings's vigorous and (in this case) accurate language.

All the arts of policy cannot conceal the power by which these provinces are ruled, nor can all the arts of sophistry avail to transfer the responsibility of them to the Nabob, when it is as visible as the light of the sun that they originate from our own government, that the Nabob is a mere pageant without so much as the shadow of authority, and even his most consequential agents receive their appointment from the recommendation of the Company and the express nomination of their servants.[1]

Absolute as the opposition appears, it is nevertheless deceptive. The majority were ready to use any stick to beat Hastings with, even if it was not one of their own growing; and although under the stress of controversy they found themselves committed to the views set down above, they had not always considered the dual system of government that best adapted to the situation of Bengal. In a letter written early in 1775 Francis had pointed out that under the system which in the next year the majority advocated so heartily, the people of Bengal had either two sovereigns or none, and that the only course to follow was to declare the sovereignty of the king of Great Britain over the whole of the provinces; and at this time his criticisms of Hastings's conduct seem confined to the fact that in abolishing the Moghul sovereignty he had not formally declared the British.[2] Francis had recorded similar sentiments in a minute of 8 March, 1775. After this it is odd to find him, in a private, unpublished letter to Lord North, declaring that the English should set about giving or restoring an active constitution to the Moghul Empire. "The authority of the Emperor should be in a considerable degree restored and means given him to support it."[3] The revival of the empire would have been wholly inconsistent with English authority in Bengal.

It is worth noting that in this respect the policies of the English and the French had been, and continued to be, diametrically opposed. Dupleix and Bussy had consistently acted within the theory of the empire. They had based their claims in Southern India on the authority of Salabat Jang, as legitimate subahdar of the Deccan. Even in the Seven Years' War, when matters were going ill for the French, Bussy advocated summoning the subahdar's brother, Basalat Jang, into the Carnatic, on the ground that the authority of his name and connection with the subahdar would enable the French to collect revenues where without him they could not raise a rupee. All their intrigues of a later date included schemes to secure the influence of the imperial name, as if that could give them a man more in the field or a rupee more in the treasury. Down to the time of Wellesley they continued to dream of reviving the empire in order

---

[1] Hastings's Minute, *ap*. Bengal Secret Consultations, 7 December, 1775.
[2] Francis to North, February, 1775 (Parkes and Merivale, II, 27).
[3] Same to same, 21 November, 1775 (Public Record Office, T 49-8).

thereby to establish their own supremacy; and so obsessed were they with this idea that some of them even attributed it to their English rivals.[1]

But Jean Law, the coolest head among them, saw better and more clearly into the heart of things. In a *mémoire* composed in 1777 he pointed out with incisive force that English security depended on the existence of many independent princes, certain to be divided among themselves, and so incapable of a united attack on the foreigner; but, if the government of Calcutta set to work to increase its power under cover of re-establishing the Moghul Empire, it would be following the only policy which would give every prince of India an urgent motive for attacking it.[2] The ideas with which Francis dallied had occurred to many Englishmen before him—to Clive, who had resolutely put them aside; to Vansittart, who had been willing to put them into action but luckily had been prevented by circumstances. Here the Company was in complete agreement with its servants' actual policy. An attempt to restore the emperor at Delhi, the Company had written, "might bring on the total ruin of our affairs; and we add that, should you be persuaded into so rash and dangerous a measure, we shall deem you responsible for all the consequences".[3]

Hastings, however, was never adverse to modifying his policy, if it seemed desirable, with all that freedom from the shackles of a formal consistency which is the peculiar privilege of the despot. Not that he ever weakened on the point of English sovereignty in Bengal, but in 1782 he thought it desirable to re-enter into relations with Delhi, and with that object had appointed Major James Browne to be his agent at that place. Browne was first to visit the nawab of Oudh and ascertain his views, since Hastings desired "to second and assist his views [rather] than to be the principal or leader in any plan that may be undertaken". Aware that the emperor might take advantage of the agent's appearance to raise once more the old question of the tribute and Allahabad, Hastings instructed him to avoid if possible the discussion of such unpleasant topics, "since it is not in my power to grant either one or the other". The purpose of the mission was rather to secure information than anything else. "Hitherto we have known nothing of the political state of the court but from foreign and suspected channels. Your first care must be to collect the materials for a more complete and authentic knowledge," not only of Shah 'Alam's court but also of "the independent chiefs and states whose territories border on his".[4] This was then no revival of the schemes of Vansittart, merely an extension of political relations to

[1] Cf. Modave's Memorandum of 1774, *ap.* Barbé, *Madec*, p. 65.
[2] Law, *État politique de l'Inde en* 1777, pp. 76-7.
[3] Company to Bengal, 16 March, 1768.
[4] Hastings to Browne, 20 August, 1782, *ap.* Bengal Secret Consultations, 10 September, 1783. A collection of papers bearing on the British relations with Delhi forms Home Miscellaneous volume no. 336 at the India Office.

a prince of exalted dignity and pretensions but of definitely circumscribed territorial power, and whose sovereignty, as Hastings observed on a later occasion, "is universally acknowledged though the substance of it no longer exists".

Browne's mission led to no action of any kind; but on the occasion of Hastings's final visit to Benares in 1784, he was brought into contact with a fugitive prince, Mirza Jiwan Bakht, who had fled from Delhi and was anxious for English or any other intervention to procure his return. At this time Hastings was regarding with a speculative eye the rise of the Sikh power in Northern India, whence he predicted the emergence of new dangers to the Company's possessions "if this people is permitted to grow into maturity without interruption". He seems to have contemplated the possibility of affording assistance to the prince with a view to checking the advances of the Sikhs; but preferred that Mahadaji Rao Sindhia should be committed to this enterprise; indeed very shortly after this, on the occasion of the murder of Afrasiab Khan, Sindhia did assume control of affairs at Delhi; and this was the position of affairs when Hastings quitted India early in 1785.

The degree in which the decay of the Moghul Empire was apparent to and recognised by the people of India, and the aspect under which the rising power of the East India Company appeared to them, must have varied widely according to the class and the interests of the observer. Princes such as the nawab of Oudh or the Nizam of Hyderabad still made haste on their accession to obtain a formal confirmation in their offices and the grant of titles; and for these they were willing to pay in hard cash. They still struck coin in the emperor's name; in his name were still read the prayers in the mosques; and the seals which they used to authenticate their public documents still declared them the humble servants of the emperor. But, in strong contrast to the observance of these forms, none thought of obeying his orders, of remitting to him the surplus revenues of the provinces, of mustering troops for his support. Shah 'Alam himself with his immediate courtiers doubtless regarded them all as rebels whom he would duly chastise had he the power; but in view of his complete impotence he could only acquiesce. To the common people these affairs were too remote to concern them in any way. They had suffered in silence the establishment of Muslim rule; they had watched with unconcern one Muslim dynasty replace another; and now they watched unmoved the last of these falling into decay and dishonour, while they paid their taxes to whatever power appeared with armed force to demand them, whether it were Muslim, Maratha, or European.

Among the princes of India two policies emerged as alternatives to that policy of drift to which most of them were inclined. One was to declare their independence of the empire, as Tipu did when he proclaimed himself *padshah* in his own right;[1] the other was to espouse the imperial cause and extend a personal dominion under the shadow of the imperial name, as Mahadaji Rao Sindhia sought to do. Of these the first was generally reprobated by Muslims, to whom even the later Moghul emperors, as in an earlier century even the later Abbasid Khalifs, symbolised religious as well as political sentiments, though no longer capable of transforming them into effective action; while the second of the two could only commend itself to able and ambitious individuals, like Sindhia, who perhaps dreamed of ultimately transforming the empire from Muslim to Hindu.

When matters were in this state of flux, Cornwallis arrived in India and a new period begins in the development of the East India Company's position. Cornwallis and the later governors-general could not be expected to and in fact did not display that sympathy with Indian ideas which made the Company's servants not unwilling to perpetuate traditional forms, even though they might obscure the essential facts of the situation. To Cornwallis the customary diplomatic language was a "pompous, unmeaning jargon".[2] The tone of the Calcutta government rises.

"I expect", writes Cornwallis, "that all the princes of the country except those of the royal family shall habituate themselves to consider the English residents at their respective courts as the representatives of a government at least equal in power and dignity to their own."[3]

When Shah 'Alam fell into the hands of the cruel Rohilla Ghulam Kadir Khan, Cornwallis, though horrified at the torture inflicted on him, could see no political reason for interference. "If we should now free him," he said, "unless we could give him an army or a permanent fund for the payment of it, he would immediately again become the slave and perhaps the prisoner of some other tyrant."[4] Casual interference would thus be useless; and practical statesmen could not be expected to employ their resources in restoring a vanished empire.

"I have received several melancholy [letters] from the King", Cornwallis writes to Shore, "calling on me in the most pressing terms for assistance and support. This morning I wrote him a letter, perfectly civil and respectful, but without all that jargon of allegiance and obedience, in which I stated most explicitly the impossibility of our interference."[5]

This was not Cornwallis's only assertion of the Company's independence. In 1790 the Bombay Government proposed that advantage should be taken of the death of the nawab of Surat to obtain a farman from Shah 'Alam for the country in the Company's name. Cornwallis rejected the proposal. For one thing the nawab had left a son whose claims should not be overlooked; and for another, "I am...unwilling

[1] Wilks, *Historical Sketches*, ed. 1867, II, 110.
[2] *Cornwallis Correspondence*, I, 418.
[3] *Idem*, p. 558.   [4] *Idem*, p. 352.   [5] *Idem*, p. 295.

to lay much stress on a sannud from the King, as a formal acknowledgment of its validity might be turned to the disadvantage of the
Company upon some other occasion".[1] Accordingly the nawab's
son was recognised as his successor by the Company, and there the
matter was left. The same procedure was adopted in 1793 when
Nasir-ul-mulk was recognised as nawab of Bengal. Sindhia in the
name of Shah 'Alam protested; but his protests were disregarded.
Similarly too when Sindhia indirectly sought to revive the demand
for Bengal tribute in 1792. Sindhia was at once informed that any
such claim would be warmly resented, on which he hastened to assure
Cornwallis that he regarded the British as supreme within their own
territories.

The government of Shore displays no change in the Company's
position; and, indeed, if circumstances had demanded of him any
important decision, he would hardly have borne the Company's
banner so high. He was much more careless of the political deductions
that might be drawn from a compliance with forms, and actually
submitted to be invested with a *khil'at* or dress of honour by the
princes whom he visited at Benares in 1797.[2] But when in the
following year he was succeeded by Mornington as governor-general,
a change of tone rapidly became apparent. In the course of the war
with Sindhia, Lake defeated the enemy before Delhi in 1803, and
the capital and the person of the emperor fell into English hands.
This was an object which, on account of French intrigues, Mornington, now become Lord Wellesley, had much at heart. A French
paper, written by one of Decaen's officers, had fallen into his hands,
stating that Shah 'Alam

ought to be the undisputed sovereign of the Mogul empire....The English
Company by its ignominious treatment of the Great Mogul, has forfeited its rights
as dewan and treasurer of the empire...; thus the Emperor of Delhi has a real
and indisputable right to transmit to whomsoever he may please to select, the
sovereignty of his dominions, as well as the arrears due to him from the English.[3]

Wellesley concluded that the English interests demanded the removal
of Shah 'Alam from the reach of such dangerous suggestions. The
emperor might confer on the French an independent sovereignty in
the French possessions and factories, and that, in a time of peace in
Europe, might produce most embarrassing consequences. Accordingly
when Sindhia's troops fled from Delhi, the person of the emperor
was reckoned among the most precious spoils of victory. In Maratha
hands the imperial name and prestige had not counted for much, as
was demonstrated clearly enough by the events of this same war, for,
though Sindhia was as deputy *wakil-i-mutlak* master of all the resources
of the empire, and on the outbreak of war had caused the emperor to
declare that he had erected his conquering standards and entered his

---

[1] *Cornwallis Correspondence*, II, 22.   [2] Teignmouth, *Life of Shore*, I, 404.
[3] *Wellesley Despatches*, IV, 652 *sqq.*

tents in order to settle the points at issue, it is certain that Sindhia neither strengthened himself nor weakened the Company by his use of the imperial name. But it might have been very different if a French army had taken the field, or if French diplomatists in Europe could have fortified their pretensions with imperial grants.

The situation created by Wellesley's occupation of Delhi can hardly be expressed by the technical language of the West, which carries with it too sharply defined ideas to be appropriate to such vague relations as were established. The facts were these: Shah 'Alam blandly acquiesced in the defeat of his lieutenant. He received Lake in his palace, conferred on him a *khil'at* and a title; and shortly after it was decided to continue the jagirs assigned by the Marathas for his maintenance, but they were to be administered by the Company's Resident at Delhi who was also in charge of the administration of the city; these functions were to be discharged under orders from Calcutta in the emperor's name, and the only area in which the imperial orders were really effective was the palace and its precincts. No written engagements of any sort were given; no grants of any kind were requested; everything that was done was done by the authority of the Company's government at Calcutta; but it was intimated that the latter did not intend "to interdict or oppose any of those outward forms of sovereignty to which His Majesty has been accustomed. His Excellency is desirous of leaving His Majesty in the unmolested exercise of all his usual privileges and prerogatives", and the Resident was directed to use all the forms of respect "considered to be due to the emperors of Hindustan".[1] Wellesley's view of the matter was that the emperor had passed under the protection of the British Government. The palace view possibly was that the Company had returned to its obedience; but in the eyes of India the fortune of war had transferred Shah 'Alam from the custody of Sindhia into that of the Company.

Down to this time the British assertion of sovereignty within the Company's possessions had been spasmodic and incomplete. But from the arrival of Lord Moira in 1813 it was definite and full. The date corresponds with the statutory assertion of the king's sovereignty and only precedes by a year the diplomatic acknowledgment of the claim by France and Holland. Moira was persuaded of "the expedience (and indeed necessity) of extinguishing the fiction of the Mogul government".[2] His seal, therefore, no longer bore the phrase proclaiming the governor-general the servant of the emperor. The *nazars*—gifts offered by an inferior to his lord—were no longer presented in the name of the governor-general.[3] Akbar II, who had succeeded his father Shah 'Alam in 1806, desired an interview with Moira, but the latter declined unless the other waived all ceremonial

---

[1] *Idem*, pp. 153, 237, 542 and 553.
[2] Hastings's *Private Journal*, I, 78.   [3] *Idem*, p. 323.

implying supremacy over the Company's dominions. "Nothing", Moira wrote in his journal, "has kept up the floating notion of a duty owed to the imperial family but our gratuitous and persevering exhibition of their pretensions." He encouraged the nawab of Oudh to assume the title of king, and declared the expediency of granting titles of honour. And while he thus refused to acknowledge any supremacy but that of his own master, he established the Company's power on a new and broader basis by his decisive overthrow of the Marathas and the network of protective alliances which he cast over Northern India.

Probably these developments had their share in deciding Akbar II to receive his successor, Amherst, in 1827, without that ceremonial to which Hastings had objected. The two entered the Diwan-i-khas at Delhi from opposite sides at the same moment; they met in front of the throne, exchanged embraces, and then took their seats, the emperor on his throne, the governor-general on a state-chair placed on the right; no *nazar* was offered; and on Amherst's departure, the emperor presented him with a string of pearls and emeralds.[1] Amherst also modified the style of letters addressed to the emperor, using forms which recognised the other's superiority but excluded allegiance or vassalage on the part of the British Government.[2] In 1835 the coinage, which ever since 1778 had purported to have been issued in the nineteenth regnal year of Shah 'Alam, was replaced by the Company's rupee bearing the English monarch's image and superscription.

With this change the absolute disappearance of the old style and titular dignity came in sight. Ellenborough, an enthusiast for the direct government of India by the crown,[3] cherished a scheme for inducing the Delhi family to quit the palace that had been built by Shah Jahan, and to resign the title which was, by voluntary request of the chiefs, to be offered to the queen,[4] despite the oddity—had his ideas been carried into effect—of her figuring as *Padshah Ghazi*, the imperial champion of Islam, which would have made a queer pendant to the *Fidei defensor*. Dalhousie shared Ellenborough's dislike of such survivals of the past world of India. Under his reformatory rule the titles of nawab of the Carnatic and raja of Tanjore were allowed to lapse along with the pension which had been granted to the Peshwa on his surrender in 1818. He proposed that with the death of the existing emperor, Bahadur Shah II, the imperial dignity too should be allowed to lapse. In this matter the Court of Directors was strongly opposed to him, and though the president of the Board, Sir John Hobhouse, obliged it to sign a dispatch formally sanctioning such action, he also wrote to the governor-general, informing him that there was strong feeling against his plan, and hinting that it would

[1] *Selections from the Panjab Records*, I, 337.   [2] *Idem*, p. 343 *sqq.*
[3] Colebrooke, *Elphinstone*, II, 266.
[4] Durand, *Life of Sir H. Durand*, I, 84.

be well to reconsider matters, while the chairman of the Court, General Sir A. Galloway, strongly urged the impolicy of any measures that had not the assent of the heir to the title. In these circumstances Dalhousie decided not to carry out the original plan, but to negotiate. Prince Fakr-ud-din was therefore approached with proposals offering recognition as emperor on his father's death, provided he would consent to meet the governor-general at all times on equal terms, and to remove the imperial family from the palace in Delhi to the Kutb, some miles to the southward of the modern city. To these terms the prince assented, so that it seemed that the principal purpose which had inspired all these manoeuvres, securing possession of the palace not only as a symbol of sovereignty but also as the ideal site for the principal military depot in Upper India, would be accomplished within a few years.[1] This, it may be noted, explains how it came to pass that the vigorous Dalhousie took no action regarding the famous magazine at Delhi beyond removing the powder magazine to a point outside the city walls.

But on the death of Fakr-ud-din in 1856 the question was raised once more. Bahadur Shah urged that another son, Jiwan Bakht, should be recognised as heir, but Canning, who had by then replaced Dalhousie, was more obstinately determined than had been his predecessor on the abolition of the dignity. In this decision he seems to have been supported by all the Company's servants in a position to be consulted—the Resident at Delhi, the lieutenant-governor of the North-West Provinces, and the members of the governor-general's council; the court of directors either changed its mind or was over-ruled; and nine months before the outbreak of the Mutiny it was decided that the imperial rank should no longer be recognised after the death of Bahadur Shah.[2]

But at last circumstances precipitated the crisis. After the fall of Delhi the old emperor was tried for complicity in the Mutiny, and ended his days in exile in Rangoon, while the direct government of the Company's possessions by the British crown was at last established. That the course of events, the gradual stripping of the imperial house of all the emblems of royalty, and the final resolve to terminate its honours, created a furious resentment within the walls of the palace, and was represented as a blow at their faith by the more fanatical Muslims in India, may be accepted as certain. But to regard it as the main, or one of the main, causes of the outbreak involves the absurdity of attempting to explain a complex movement by viewing it from one only of its many aspects. The hostility of the Moghul court had been a constant factor from the day, eighty odd years earlier, when Warren Hastings had refused to continue the tribute due from Bengal as a Moghul province; it had

---

[1] Lee-Warner, *Dalhousie*, II, 135 *sqq. Selections from the Panjab Records*, I, 405 *sqq.*
[2] *Idem*, p. 456 *sqq.*

inspired Akbar II when he saw the Company's government assuming the marks of eastern sovereignty; and it was in itself no more formidable in 1857 than it had been any time in the previous eighty years.

If this shadow-king had had influence enough to make the Company's sepoy forces mutiny, he would have used it many years before.

Finally, it should be noted that such survivals of vanished power were by no means uncharacteristic of eastern history. The khalif of Baghdad was visited by embassies bearing gifts and seeking titles long after the provinces of the Abbasid Empire had become independent, and ceased to send their tribute to the imperial treasury. A nearer parallel may be found in India itself. When the Peshwas founded their power at Poona, they did not overthrow the Maratha monarchy. The descendants of Sivaji continued to reign at Satara while for a century their ministers ruled from Poona, and each Peshwa solemnly sought investiture from the king, although the king could only do as he was directed. At Mysore Hydar and Tipu preserved the old Hindu kingly family, and showed its representative periodically to the people; and at Nagpur the Bhonsles preserved a Gondh prince, to whom they left the title of raja and in whose name they issued their orders. The relations between the East India Company and the Moghul, the one exercising and the other claiming the attributes of sovereignty, the one possessed of material power and the other of mystic superiority, the one obeyed and the other revered, were by no means extraordinary. The peculiar factor in this case was not the separation of right and power, but the fact that the East India Company was not a purely Indian body, that it represented the sovereign of Great Britain and brought with it a European impatience of pretensions that had ceased to have a basis in fact.

BIBLIOGRAPHY

CHAPTER I

THE PORTUGUESE IN INDIA

A. ORIGINAL MATERIALS

(1) *PORTUGUESE SOURCES*

MANUSCRIPT

The official records are contained in the Archivo da Torre do Tombo and the Bibliotheca Nacional at Lisbon, and in the archives at Goa. The records in the Torre do Tombo are described in P. A. de Azevedo and A. Baiao, *O Archivo da Torre do Tombo*, Lisbon, 1905; A. Mesquita de Figueiredo, *Archivo Nacional da Torre do Tombo*, Lisbon, 1922; and F. C. Danvers, *Report on the Portuguese Records*, 1892.

In this country the India Office Records include an important series of transcripts and translations from the Lisbon records made under the direction of F. C. Danvers. They are drawn chiefly from the *Livros das Monções*, the *Corpo chronologico*, the *Gavetas Antigas*, and the *Conselho Ultramarino*. A full list is printed in the India Office *List of General Records*.

A number of Goa Records were purchased by William Marsden. Part of these were presented to the British Museum (Add. MSS, 9390–9397, and 9852–9861) during Marsden's lifetime, the remainder were presented to King's College in 1835 and transferred to the School of Oriental Studies with the whole of Marsden's Library in 1917. The MSS of Almeida, *Storia de Etiopia a alta*, were in Marsden's possession; one of these, which was used by Beccari for his printed edition, is now in the British Museum (Add. MS, 9861); the other, which seems to bear the corrections of Almeida himself, is in the School of Oriental Studies. (See *Bulletin School of Oriental Studies*, II, 513–38.)

The British Museum possesses a large collection of official documents relating to the Portuguese possessions in India ranging from 1518 to 1754 (Add. MSS, 20861–20913), also the Resende MS (Sloane, 197).

Notes on the Goa archives will be found in Surendranath Sen, *Historical Records at Goa*, Calcutta, 1925, and *A Preliminary report on the historical records at Goa*, Calcutta, 1925.

PRINTED
Periodicals

O Oriente Portugues. Revista da Commissão Archeologica da India Portuguesa. Nova Goa, 1904– .
Archivo Historico Portuguez. Vols. II and III. Lisbon, 1904–5.
Boletim da Sociedade de Geographia de Lisboa. Lisbon, 1875, etc.
Royal Asiatic Society. Journals of the Ceylon Branch. Colombo.

Chronicles and contemporary documents

ALBUQUERQUE. Cartas de Affonso de Albuquerque. (Collecção de Monumentos ineditos para a historia das conquistas dos Portuguezes em Africa, Asia, e America. Tom. x–xvi. Lisbon, 1884–1915.)
—— Commentarios do Grande Afonso d'Albuquerque. 4 vols. Lisbon, 1774.
—— The commentaries of the Great Afonso Dalboquerque. Translated from the Portuguese by Walter de Gray Birch. (Hakluyt Society.) 1875–7.
Alguns documentos do archivo nacional da Torre do Tombo acerca das navegações e conquistas portuguezas. Lisbon, 1902.

BARBOSA, DUARTE. Libro dell' Indie Orientali. Sommario di tutti i regni, città, e populi dell' Indie Orientali. (Ap. Ramusio.)
—— The book of Duarte Barbosa. Translated by M. Longworth Dames. (Hakluyt Society.) 1918–21.
BARROS, JOÃO DE. Decadas da Asia. Lisbon and Madrid, 1563–1615.
BIKER, J. F. Collecção de tratados. 14 vols. Lisbon, 1881–7.
BOCARRO, ANTONIO. Decadas 13 da historia da India. (Academia Real das Sciencias.) Lisbon, 1876.
BOTELHO, SIMÃO. O Tombo do estado da India feito em 1554; Cartas de Simão Botelho; Lembranças das cousas da India em 1525. (Academia Real das Sciencias.) Lisbon, 1868.
CABRAL, PEDRO ALVAREZ. Navegação. (Ap. Ramusio.)
CASTANHEDA, FERNÃO LOPEZ DE. Historia do descobrimento. 1552–61. Reprinted 1833.
CASTANHOSA, M. DE. Dos feitos de D. Christovam da Gama em Ethiopia. Ed. by F. M. Esteves Pereira. Lisbon, 1898.
Corpo diplomatico portuguez. 14 vols. Lisbon, 1862–1910.
CORREA, GASPAR. Lendas da India. 4 vols. (Monumentos ineditos, para a historia das conquistas dos Portuguezes. Lisbon, 1858–64.)
COUTINHO, LOPE DE SOUSA. Livro primeyro do cerco de Dio. Coimbra, 1556.
COUTO, DIOGO DE. Decadas da Asia. (Continuation of the work of Barros.) 15 vols. Lisbon, 1778–88.
CUNHO RIVARA, J. A. DA. Archivo portuguez oriental. Nova Goa, 1857–77.
DU JARRIC, PÈRE. Histoire des choses plus memorables advenues tant ez Indes Orientales que autres pais de la découverte des Portugais. Bordeaux, 1608–14.
—— Thesaurus rerum Indicarum. Cologne, 1615.
—— Akbar and the Jesuits. Ed. by C. H. Payne. 1926.
Documentos remettidos da India. (Academia Real das Sciencias.) 1880–93.
FALCÃO, L. DE FIGUEREDO. Livro em que se contem toda a fazenda e real patrimonio dos reinos de Portugal, India, e ilhas adjacentes de sua corôa e outras particularidades, dirigido ao rey Philippe III. Lisbon, 1859.
FELNER, R. J. DE LIMA. Subsidios para a historia da India Portugueza. (Academia Real das Sciencias.) 1878.
FIGUEROA, CHRISTOVAL SUAREZ DE. Historia y anal relacion de las cosas que hizeron los padres de la Companhia de Jesus...los annos passados de 607 y 608. Madrid, 1614.
GAMA, VASCO DA. Journal of the first voyage of ——. Ed. Ravenstein. (Hakluyt Society.) 1898.
GODINHO. Relação do novo caminho que fez por terra e mar vindo da India para Portugal no anno de 1663 o padre Manoel Godinho de Companhia de Jesu enviado a Magestade del Rey N. S. Dom Affonso VI. Lisbon, 1665.
GOES, DAMIÃO DE. Dienisi oppugnatio.
—— Commentarius rerum gestarum in India citra Gangem a Lusitanis. Louvain, 1539.
—— Chronica do felicissimo rey Dom Manoel. Lisbon, 1566–7.
GUERREIRO, FERNÃO. Relaçam annual das cousas que fizeram os padres da Companhia de Jesu na India nos annos de 600 e 601. Lisbon, 1603.
Inscriptions, ancient, Portuguese, and Dutch, at Cheol, etc., in the Colaba Agency. Selections from the Bombay Records, New Series, no. 7.
LINSCHOTEN, JAN HUYGEN VAN. Voyage. (Hakluyt Society.) 1885.
MONSERRATE. "Mongolicae legationis commentarius." Ed. by the Rev. H. Hosten, S.J. (Memoirs of the Asiatic Society of Bengal, no. 9. Calcutta, 1914.)
—— The commentary of Father Monserrate. Translated by J. S. Hoyland and annotated by S. N. Banerjee. Oxford, 1922.
NUNES, ANTONIO. O livro dos pesos, medidas, e moedas. (Ap. Felner, Subsidios para a historia da India Portugueza, q.v.)
OSORIUS. Histoire de Portugal comprinse en vingt livres dont les douze premiers sont traduit du latin de Jerosme Osorius, eveque de Sylves en Algarve. 1581.

Pieris, P. E., and Fitzler, M. A. H. Ceylon and Portugal. Part I, Kings and Christians 1539–52. Leipzig, 1927.
Pinto, Fernão Mendez. Peregrinação. Lisbon, 1614. Reprinted 1829, etc.
Puente, Martinez de la. Compendio de los descubrimientos, conquistas, y guerras de la India Oriental. Madrid, 1681.
Queroz, Fernão de. Conquista temporal e espiritual de Ceylão. Colombo, 1916.
Ramusio, Giovanni Battista. Navigationi e viaggi. Venice. 1550, etc.
Ribeiro, João. Fatalidade historica da ilha de Ceilão. (Academia Real das Sciencias.) Lisbon, 1836.
—— Translated by P. E. Pieris. Colombo, 1909.
Schurhammer, G. and Voretzsch, E. A. Ceylon zur Zeit des Königs Bhuvaneka Bahu und Franz Xavers. 2 vols. Leipzig, 1928.
Teive, Diogo de. Commentarius de rebus a Lusitanis in India apud Dium gestis anno 1546.
Teneiro, Antonio. Itinerario. Coimbra, 1565.
Varthema, Ludovico di. The travels of —— a.d. 1503–1508. (Hakluyt Society.) 1863.

(2) *ARABIC SOURCES*

An Arabic history of Gujarat. Zafar ul-Walih bi Muzaffar wa ālih, by 'Abdullah Muhammad bin 'Omar al-Makki, Al-Asafi, Ulughkhani. Ed. by E. Denison Ross. (Indian texts Series.) 3 vols. London, 1910–1928. This important work was completed after the *Mir'āt-i-Sikandarī*, which appeared in 1611.
Tohfut-ul-Mujahideen (by Sheikh Zeen-ud-Deen)....Translated into English by M. J. Rowlandson. (Oriental Translation Fund.) London, 1833.
Historia dos Portugueses no Malabar por Zinadim....Publicado e traduzido por David Lopes. (Sociedade de Geographia de Lisboa.) Lisbon, 1898.

(3) *PERSIAN SOURCES*

Mir'āt-i-Sikandarī. *Text.*
    Translations: The history of India as told by its own historians. The local Muhammadan dynasties. Gujarat. By...Sir E. C. Bayley. Partially based on a translation by...J. Dowson (of the Mir'āt-i-Sikandarī). London, 1886.
    Mirati Sikandari or the Mirror of Sikandar....Translated by Fazlullah Lutfullah Faridi. Bombay, 1899.
Mir'āt-i-Ahmadī. *Text.* Ed by Syed Nawab Ali. (Gaewad's Oriental Series.) Baroda, 1927. *In progress.*
    Translations: The political and statistical history of Gujarat, translated from the Persian of Ali Mohammed Khan...by J. Bird. (Oriental Translation Fund.) London, 1835.
    The supplement to the Mirat-i-Ahmedi, translated...by Syed Nawab Ali... and C. N. Seddon. Baroda, 1924.
Akbar-Namah. *Text.* Ed. for the Asiatic Society of Bengal. (Bibliotheca Indica.) 3 vols. Calcutta, 1877–87.
    Translation: The Akbarnāma of Abu-l-Fazl, translated...by H. Beveridge. (Bibliotheca Indica.) Calcutta, 1897– . *In progress.*
Abu Turāb Vali. A history of Gujarat....Edited...by E. Denison Ross. (Bibliotheca Indica.) Calcutta, 1909.
Firishtah. *Text.* Tarikh-i-Ferishta, or history of the rise of Mahomedan power in India, till the year a.d. 1612....Edited...by J. Briggs...assisted by...Mir Kheirat Ali Khan Mushtak. 2 vols. Bombay, 1831.
    Translation: History of the rise of the Mohomedan power in India...translated ...by J. Briggs. 4 vols. London, 1829.
Elliot, Sir H. and Dowson, John. The history of India as told by its own historians. 8 vols. 1867–75.

(4) TURKISH SOURCES

Sidi 'Alī, Ra'is. "Miroir des pays, ou Relation des Voyages de Sidi-Aly." Traduite sur la version allemande de M. de Diez, par M. Morris. (*Journal Asiatique*, Tome IX, Paris, 1826.)

(5) PALI SOURCES

The Mahāvamsa, or the Great Chronicle of Ceylon. Translated into English by W. Geiger....Assisted by M. H. Bode. (Pali Text Society.) London, 1912.

B. SECONDARY WORKS

Accursio das Neves, J. Considerações sobre os descobrimentos e possessões dos Portuguezes na Africa e na Asia. Lisbon, 1830.
ALMEIDA, FORTUNATO DE. Historia de Portugal. 4 vols. Coimbra, 1922–6.
ARAGÃO, A. TEIXEIRA D'. Vasco da Gama. Lisbon, 1898. 3rd ed.
ARGENSOLA. Histoire de la conquête des isles Moluques par les Espagnols, les Portugais, et les Hollandois. Translated by J. des Bordes. Amsterdam, 1707.
BALDAQUE DA SILVA, A. A. Noticia sobre a náo S. Gabriel em que Vasco da Gama foi pela primeira vez a India. Lisbon, 1892.
BALSEMÃO, ÉDOUARDO AUGOSTO DE SA NOGUEIRA PINTO. Os Portuguezes no Oriente. Goa, 1881.
BARCELLOS, C. J. DE SENNA. "Construcções de naus em Lisboa para a carreira da India no começo do secolo XVII." (*Bol. da Soc. de Geo. de Lisboa*, 1899.)
BEAZLEY, C. R. The dawn of modern geography. 3 vols. 1897–1906.
CALDWELL, R. A...history of the district of Tinnevelly. Madras, 1881.
CAMPOS, J. DE. "Numismatica indo-portugueza." (*Bol. da Soc. de Geo. de Lisboa*, 1901.)
CAMPOS, J. J. A. The Portuguese in Bengal. Calcutta, 1919.
COMMISSARIAT, M. S. "A brief history of the Gujarat Saltanat." (*Journal, Bombay branch, Royal Asiatic Society*, 1920.)
CORVO, J. DE ANDRADE. Estudos sobre as provincias ultramarinas. Lisbon, 1883–87. 4 vols.
—— Chaul and Bassein. Bombay, 1876.
DALGADO, SEBASTIÃO RODOLFO. Glossario Luso-Asiatico. 2 vols. Coimbra, 1919–21.
DAMES, M. LONGWORTH. "The Portuguese and the Turks in the Indian Ocean in the sixteenth century." (*Journal Royal Asiatic Society*, 1921, part I.)
DANVERS, F. C. History of the Portuguese in India. 2 vols. 1894.
FARIA Y SOUSA, MANOEL. Asia Portugueza. Lisbon, 1666–75.
FONSECA, JOSE NICOLAU DE. Goa. 1878.
Gazetteer of the Bombay Presidency. Bombay, 1877.
HEYD, W. Histoire du commerce du Levant. Translated by F. Raynaud. 2 vols. Reprinted Leipzig, 1923.
HUMMERICH, F. Vasco da Gama und die Entdeckung des Seewegs nach Ostindien. Munich, 1898.
INNES, C. A. Madras District Gazetteers—Malabar and Anjengo. Madras, 1903.
JAYNE, K. G. Vasco da Gama and his successors. 1910.
KLOGUEN, C. DE. Sketch of Goa. Madras, 1831.
LANNOY, C. DE, and LINDEN, H. VAN DER. L'expansion coloniale des peuples européens—Portugal et Espagne. Paris, 1907.
MAFFEII, J. P. Historiae Indicae. Bergomi, 1747.
MAJOR, R. H. Prince Henry the Navigator. 1868.
—— The discoveries of Prince Henry the Navigator, 1877.
MENDES, A. LOPES. A India Portugueza. Lisbon, 1886.
MOCQUET, JEAN. Voyages. Paris, 1830.
PIERIS, P. E. Ceylon: the Portuguese era. 2 vols. Colombo, 1913–14.

Ross, Sir E. D. "The Portuguese in India and Arabia between 1507 and 1517." (*Journal Royal Asiatic Society*, 1921, part II.)
Smith, V. A. Akbar the Great Mogul. Oxford, 1917.
Sousa Pinto, Manoel de. Dom João de Castro. Lisbon, 1912.
Ustariz. Teorica e pratica de comercio y marina. 3rd ed. Madrid, 1757.
Whiteway, R. S. The rise of the Portuguese power in India, 1497–1550. 1899.

CHAPTER II

THE DUTCH IN INDIA

A. ORIGINAL MATERIALS

Manuscript

The archives of the Dutch East India Company are now preserved at the Rijksarchief at the Hague. Among the papers sent over annually from Batavia were copies of the correspondence carried on by the Governor-General and Council with the various establishments in India. Further documents concerning these establishments preserved at Batavia were also transferred to the Hague in the third quarter of the nineteenth century. The Rijksarchief further possesses certain collections of private papers formed by servants of the Company. A work of great importance for the administrative and commercial history of the Company was composed at the request of the Seventeen by Pieter van Dam between 1689 and 1701; it fills eight large manuscript volumes, preserved in the Rijksarchief; its publication has been undertaken by the Rijks Geschiedkundige Publicatie Commissie.

At the India Office are seventy volumes of "Hague Transcripts" with thirty-six volumes of translations (see *List of General Records*); and a collection of volumes concerning relations with the Dutch down to 1824 (see Sir William Foster, *Guide to the India Office Records*, pp. 96–7). Numerous Dutch papers occur among the Mackenzie MSS (see C. O. Blagden, *Cat. of the Mackenzie Collections*, Part I).

At the Madras Record Office is preserved a large collection of records relating principally to Cochin, though it includes a number of transcripts of memoirs, obtained from Batavia, relating to Negapatam. See the *Catalogue of Madras Records*, and the *Press List of Ancient Dutch Records from 1657 to 1825* (Madras, n.d.).

At the Colombo Record Office are still preserved a great body of documents relating to the Dutch administration of that island, including some 3000 volumes of "General Records" and 700 volumes of the proceedings of the Council. See R. G. Anthonisz, *Report on the Dutch Records in the Government Archives at Colombo* (Colombo, 1907).

Published Documents

Chijs, J. A. van der. Nederlandsch-Indisch plakaatboek 1602–1811. 17 vols. Batavia, 1885–91.
Dagregister gehouden in't Casteel van Batavia. Batavia, 1887, etc. (Covers the period 1624–1693, and is to be continued.)
Heeres, J. E. Corpus Diplomaticum Neerlandico-Indicum. The Hague, 1907. (Only the first volume, down to 1650, has appeared.)
Lopes, D. "Cartas de Raja Singa rei de Candia aos Hollandezes." (*Bol. da Soc. de Geo. de Lisboa*, 1907.)
Mijer, P. Verzameling van instructiën, ordonnanziën, en reglementen voor de regeering van Nederlandsch Indie. Batavia, 1848.
Moreland, W. H. and P. Geyl. Jahangir's India: the Remonstrantie of Fr. Pelsaert, translated from the Dutch. Cambridge, 1925.
Rea, A. "Monumental remains of the Dutch E.I. Coy. in the Presidency of Madras." (*Arch. Sur. of India*, New Imp. Ser. vol. xxv. Madras, 1897.)

Selections from the Records of the Madras Govt. Dutch Records. Ed. by the Rev. Fathers A. J. van der Burg, P. Groot, and J. Fruictier, and A. Galletti, I.C.S. 15 vols. Sm. fol. Madras, 1908–11:

Gedenkschrift van J. V. S. van Gollenesse (1743). 1908.
Gedenkschrift geschreven in 1781 door Adriaan Moens. 1908.
Memorie van den afgaanden commandeur Fredrik Cunes (1756). 1908.
Memorie van J. G. van Angelbeek (1793). 1908.
Verhaal van den Nabab Aider Alij Chan van 1763. 1908.
Catalogus van hollandsche handschriften, brieven en officieele stukken (n.d.). 1909.
Copia memoria van den Commandeur C. Breekpot (1769). 1909.
Dagboek der gebeurtenissen gedurende den oorlog met den Zammorijn (1716–17). 1910.
Uittreksels uit de algemeene transports van de jaren 1743, 1761, en 1780. 1909.
Dagregister gehouden door...den E. Capitain J. Hackert gedurende den train tegen den Koning van Trevancoor (1739–40). 1909.
Memorie nagelaten door den commandeur C. de Jong (1761). 1910.
Memorie van den commandeur G. Weijerman (1765). 1910.
The Dutch in Malabar, being a translation of selections nos. 1 and 2. 1911.
Gedenkschrift geschreven in 1677 door H. A. van Rheede. 1911.
Verklaringen van brieven gezonden van Negapatnam (1748–58). 1911.

Memoirs of the Dutch Governors, etc. of Ceylon. 10 vols. Colombo, 1908–15.

Instructions from the Governor-General and Council of India, 1656–65. 1908.
Memoir left by Ryclof van Goens, 1679. 1910.
Memoir of H. Zwaar de Croon, 1697. 1911.
Memoir by Anthony Mooyaart 1766. 1910.
Memoir left by J. C. Pielat. 1734. n.d.
Memoir left by G. W. van Imhoff. 1740. 1911.
Memoir of C. J. Simons, 1707. 1914.
Memoir of H. Becker, 1716. 1914.
Diary of G. de Heere, 1697. 1914.
Memoir of T. van Rhee, 1697. 1915.

TRAVELS

BALDAEUS, PHILIPPUS. Nauwkeurige beschrijvinge van Malabar en Choromandel, ...en het machtige Eyland Ceylon. Amsterdam, 1672. English translation in Churchill's *Voyages*, vol. III, 1745.
HAVART, D. Op- en Ondergang van Coromandel. Amsterdam, 1693.
VALENTYN, Fr. Oud en Nieuw Oost Indiën. Dordrecht-Amsterdam, 1724–6.

B. SECONDARY WORKS

AALBERS, J. Rijcklof van Goens, Commissaris en Veldoverste der Oost-Indische Compagnie, en zijn arbeidsveld, 1653–54 en 1657–58. 1916.
BERCKEL, G. J. A. VAN. Bijdrage tot de geschiedenis van het Europeesch opperbestuur over Nederlandsch-Indië, 1780–1806. Leiden, 1880.
BRAKEL, S. VAN. De Hollandsche Handelscompagnieën der zeventiende Eeuw. 1908.
CHIJS, J. A. VAN DER. Geschiedenis der stichting van de vereenigde Oost-Indische Compagnie. 2nd ed. 1887.
COLENBRANDER, H. T. Koloniale Geschiedenis. 1925.
DUBOIS, J. P. L. Vies des gouverneurs-généraux de la Compagnie des Indes avec l'abrégé de l'histoire des établissements hollandais aux Indes orientales. The Hague, 1768.
GEER, W. VAN. De opkomst van het Nederlandsch gezag over Ceilon; eerste gedeelte. 1895 (no more published).

HODENPYL, A. K. A. GYSBERTI. "De Gouverneurs van Koromandel, Chr. van Teylingen (1761–65) en Pieter Haksteen (1765–71)." (*Bijdragen voor Vaderlandsche Geschiedenis*, v, x, 1923.)

IMHOFF, VAN. Considérations sur l'état présent de la Compagnie hollandaise des Indes Orientales. The Hague, 1741.

JONGE, J. K. J. DE. De opkomst van het Nederlandsch gezag in Oost Indië. 1862, etc.

KAMPEN, N. G. VAN. Geschiedenis der Nederlanders buiten Europa. 1831–3.

LANNOY, C. DE, and LINDEN, H. VAN DER. L'expansion coloniale des peuples européens: Néerlande et Danemark. Brussels, 1911.

MACLEOD, N. De Oost-indische Compagnie als zeemogendheid in Azië. 1602–50. 2 vols. and atlas. Rijswijk, 1927.

MEES, M. W. C. Het muntwezen in Nederlandsch-Indië. Amsterdam, 1851.

MORELAND, W. H. From Akbar to Aurangzeb. 1923.

NYPELS, GEORGE. Hoe Nederland Ceilon verloor. 1908.

"Papieren van D. BAVY wegens het voorgevallene te Bengalen, 1763." (*Bijdragen en Mededeelingen van het Historisch Genootschap*, 1879.)

PIERIS, P. E. The kingdom of Jaffnapatam, 1645. Colombo, 1920.

—— Ceylon, the Portuguese Period, 1505–1658. 1914.

—— Ceylon and the Hollanders, 1658–1796. 1918.

REUS, G. C. KLERK DE. "Geschichtlicher Ueberblick der administrativen, rechtlichen und finanziellen Entwicklung der Niederlandisch-Ostindischen Compagnie." (*Verhandelingen van het Bataviaasch Genootschap van kunsten en Wetenschappen*, dl. XLVII, 1894.)

—— "De expeditie naar Bengale in 1759." (*De Indische Gids*, 1889 and 1890.)

—— "De vermeestering van Chinsoera in 1781 en 1795." (*Verhandelingen van het Bataviaasch Genootschap van kunsten en Wetenschappen*, dl. XXXVIII.)

SOURATTE, RADICALE. "Beschrijving, anno 1758, door den beambte der Oost-Indische Compagnie D. van Rheeden." (*Bijdragen en Mededeelingen van het Historisch Genootschap*, 1883.)

STELLWAGEN. "Gustaaf Willem baron van Imhoff." (*De Indische Gids*, 1889.)

TERPSTRA, H. De vestiging van de Nederlanders aan de kust van Koromandel. 1911.

—— "De Nederlanders in Voor-Indië, bij de stichting van het fort Geldria te Paliacatta." (*De Indische Gids*, 1915.)

—— De opkomst der Wester-kwartieren van de Oost-Indische Compagnie. 1918.

TJASSENS, J. Zeepolitie der Vereenigte Nederlanden. 2nd ed. The Hague, 1670.

VETH, P. "Hendrik Adriaan van Reede tot Drakestein." (*De Indische Gids*, 1887, vols. III and IV.)

CHAPTER III

THE FRENCH FACTORIES IN INDIA

A. ORIGINAL MATERIALS

MANUSCRIPT

Les Archives anciennes du Ministère des Colonies (conservées, en ce qui concerne l'Inde, au Ministère même des Colonies et non pas aux Archives Nationales) contiennent la plupart des documents importants relatifs à l'histoire des débuts de l'Inde française dans les volumes de la *Correspondance générale* relatifs à l'Inde française pour les années 1666–1740 (C^2 62 à 80) et de son *Supplément* (C^2, 2e série, t. 1 à 5, 1666–1740). On trouvera également des pièces se rattachant à l'histoire de l'Inde soit dans les volumes de la *Correspondance générale* relatifs à l'Extrême-Orient et au Siam (C^1 22–25), soit dans le premier carton de la même *Correspondance générale* pour Madagascar (C^5 1, 1642–1674). A signaler encore dans la collection Moreau de Saint-Méry les copies de pièces contenues dans le registre F^3 238.

Il n'existe pas de répertoire de la Correspondance générale pour l'Inde, non plus que pour la Collection Moreau de Saint-Méry; mais la *Bibliographie de Madagascar* d'Alfred et de Guillaume Grandidier (Paris, Comité de Madagascar, 1906, 2 vols.) donne la liste des pièces contenues dans le carton 1 de la série 5 (t. xi, pp. 676–678), et Alfred Tantet, *Inventaire sommaire de la Correspondance générale de la Cochinchine*, 1686–1863 (Paris; Challamel, 1905, in-8) les documents se rattachant aux rapports de l'Inde et de l'Indochine au cours de la période dont traite le présent chapitre. Voir aussi Weber, *La Compagnie des Indes*, pp. xxvii–xxxii. Aux Archives Nationales se trouve le manuscrit des Mémoires de François Martin, un document considérable et dont on ne saurait exagérer l'importance pour l'histoire des tout premiers débuts de l'établissement des Français dans l'Inde. Ce manuscrit, qu'ont utilisé plusieurs historiens et que différents érudits ont projeté d'éditer, attend toujours sa publication intégrale. Il est intitulé "Mémoires sur l'établissement des Colonies françaises aux Indes Orientales, dressés par Messire François Martin, Gouverneur de la Ville et Fort-Louis de Pondichéry. Ces mémoires contiennent l'histoire de trente ans, depuis 1664 jusqu'en 1696" (in folio de 631 feuillets). La *Collection des Ouvrages anciens relatifs à Madagascar*, publiée par Alfred et Guillaume Grandidier et Henri Froidevaux (t. ix, pp. 429–633) contient le seul fragment un peu étendu des Mémoires de Martin qui ait jusqu'à présent vu le jour.

Comme on vient de le voir, ces mémoires ne vont pas plus loin que l'année 1696; ils ne dépassent même pas, en réalité, et quoi qu'en dise le titre, le mois de février 1694. Des lettres de François Martin conservées dans le carton K 1374 (Négociations, missions étrangères) et datées des années 1699–1702, permettent de les prolonger jusqu'au début du xviiie siècle, surtout si on les rapproche des fragments de son journal quotidien envoyés par lui à la Compagnie pour les périodes du 21 janvier 1703 (Arch. anc. Mre. Colonies, C^2 66, fol. 15–49 et 154–171).

Aux Archives Nationales sont déposées les Archives anciennes du Ministère de la Marine, dont les séries B^2 (*Dépêches et Ordres du Roi*) et B^4 (*Campagnes*) contiennent, l'une dans ses volumes 11–312 (1670–1740), l'autre dans ses volumes 3 à 44 (1666–1740) nombre de documents utiles (cf. l'*État sommaire des Archives de la Marine antérieures à la Révolution*; Paris, L. Baudoin, 1898, in-8). Il existe au Cabinet des Manuscrits de la Bibliothèque Nationale dans les *Mélanges Colbert* (vol. 119 et suivants), dans le *fonds Ariel* (MSS. Fa., nouv. acquis., nos. 8.925–8.930) et dans la *Collection Margry* (nos. 9.348–9.351) différents documents de réelle valeur sur l'histoire de l'Inde française au cours de la période. A remarquer parmi eux une copie des mémoires de François Martin (*Collection Margry*, nouv. acq. fr., 9.348–9.351).

Nous signalons encore l'existence de différentes pièces intéressantes dans plusieurs volumes des mémoires et documents du *fonds Asie* des Archives du Ministère des Affaires étrangères (tomes 2 à 6).

Dans l'Inde même, il existe à Pondichéry un dépôt d'archives dont, pour la Société de l'Histoire de l'Inde française, l'inventaire a été dressé par M. Alfred Martineau (*Inventaire des anciennes archives de l'Inde française*, Pondichéry, 1914, in-8 de 38 pages), et des manuscrits desquels M. Edmond Gaudart a commencé de publier le catalogue (*Catalogue des Manuscrits des anciennes Archives de l'Inde Française*, t. i, Pondichéry, 1690–1789. Paris-Pondichéry, 1922, in-8 de xxii–810–xvi pages).

PUBLISHED DOCUMENTS

CLÉMENT, PIERRE. Lettres, instructions et mémoires de Colbert. 7 vols. 4to. Paris, 1862–82.

DERNIS. Recueil et collection des titres concernant la Compagnie des Indes Orientales établie au mois d'août 1664. 4 vols. 4to. Paris, 1755–6.

FROIDEVAUX, HENRI. "Mémoires de Bellanger de Lespinay sur son voyage aux Indes Orientales." (*Bull. de la Société Arch. du Vendômois*, 1891–5.)

LA FARELLE. Mémoires du chevalier de La Farelle sur la prise de Mahé. Ed. by Lennel de la Farelle. 1889.

—— Mémoires et correspondance du chevalier et du général de la Farelle. Ed. by Lennel de la Farelle. 1896.

Publications of the Société de l'histoire de l'Inde française:

Délibérations du Conseil Supérieur de Pondichéry, 1701–39. 3 vols. Ed. by E. Gaudart and A. Martineau. 1911–14.

Lettres et conventions des gouverneurs de Pondichéry avec différents princes hindous. 1666-1793. Ed. by A. Martineau. 1914.

Correspondance du Conseil Supérieur de Pondichéry avec la Compagnie 1726–1738. Ed. by A. Martineau. 2 vols. 1920, 1921.

Correspondance du Conseil Supérieur de Pondichéry avec le Conseil de Chandernagor. Ed. by A. Martineau, 1728–57. 3 vols. 1915–18.

Actes de l'État Civil. Vol. 1, 1676–1735. 1917.

Catalogue des Manuscrits des anciennes archives. Ed. by E. Gaudart. Vol. 1, 1690–1789. 1922.

TRAVELS AND OTHER CONTEMPORARY PUBLICATIONS

BEAULIEU, AUGUSTIN DE. Expedition to the East Indies. (Ap. Harris, *Voyages*, vol. 1.)

BERNIER, FRANÇOIS. Travels in the Mogul Empire. Ed. Oxford.

CARRÉ. Voyages des Indes Orientales. 2 vols. 12mo. Paris, 1699.

CHALLES, DE. Journal d'un voyage fait aux Indes Orientales depuis le 24 fév. 1690 jusqu'au 20 août 1691. 3 vols. 12mo. Rouen, 1691. (Reprinted ap. Sottas, *q.v. infra*.)

DELLON, Dr. Relation d'un voyage des Indes Orientales, 1667–77. 2 vols. 12mo. Paris, 1685.

DU FRESNE DE FRANCHEVILLE. Histoire de la Compagnie des Indes. 4to. Paris, 1746.

Journal du voyage des Grandes Indes. 2 vols. 12mo. Paris, 1698.

LABOULLAYE LE GOUZ. Voyages et observations où sont décrites les religions, gouvernements, etc. de...Perse, Arabie, Grand Mogul, etc. 4to. Paris, 1657.

LE BLANC, VINCENT. Les voyages des Indes. Paris, 1648.

LEGUAT, FRANÇOIS. Voyage 1690–8. Ed. by Oliver. (Hakluyt Society.) 2 vols. 1890.

L'ESTRA, DE. Relation ou journal d'un voyage fait aux Indes Orientales 1671–8. 12mo. Paris, 1677.

LUILLIER. Voyage aux Grandes Indes. 12mo. Paris, 1705.

PYRARD DE LAVAL, FRANÇOIS. Voyage. Ed. by Gray and Bell. (Hakluyt Society.) 3 vols. 1887–9.

SOUCHU DE RENNEFORT. Histoire des Indes Orientales. 4to. Paris, 1688.

TAVERNIER, JEAN-BAPTISTE. Travels in India. Ed. by W. Crooke. 2 vols. Oxford, 1925.

THÉVENOT, JEAN DE. Voyages de M. de Thévenot. 1664–84.

B. SECONDARY WORKS

BENOÎT DU REY, E. Recherches sur la politique de Colbert. Paris, 1902.

CASTONNET DES FOSSES, H. L'Inde française avant Dupleix. Paris, 1887.

CLÉMENT, P. Histoire de Colbert et de son administration. Paris, 1874.

DELORT, THEODORE. "La première escadre de la France dans les Indes." Paris, 1876. (*Revue Maritime et Coloniale*, 1875.)

DU FRESNE DE FRANCHEVILLE. Histoire de la Compagnie des Indes Orientales. Paris, 1746, in-4.

GUET, I. "Origines de l'Inde Française." (*Revue Maritime*, août, 1892.)

KAEPPELIN, PAUL. Les origines de l'Inde Française; La Compagnie des Indes Orientales et François Martin. Paris, 1908.

LANIER, LUCIEN. "Relations de la France et du Royaume de Siam de 1662 à 1703." (*Mémoires de la Société des Sciences morales...de Seine-et-Oise*, t. XIII, 1883.)

MARTINEAU, A. Les origines de Mahé de Malabar. Paris, 1916.

MARTINEAU, A. "Quatre ans de l'histoire de l'Inde, 1726–1730." (*Revue de l'Histoire des colonies françaises*, t. VIII, 1919.)

—— "Benoist Dumas; notes biographiques." (*Revue de l'Histoire des colonies françaises*, t. IX, 1920.)

NEYMARCK, A. Colbert et son temps. 2 vols. 1877.

PAULIAT, L. Louis XIV et la Compagnie des Indes Orientales. Paris, 1886.

Revue de l'Histoire des Colonies françaises. Paris, 1913, etc.

SAINT YVES ET CHAVANON. "Documents inédits sur la Compagnie des Indes Orientales." (*Rev. des quest. historiques*, octobre, 1903.)

SOTTAS, JULES. Histoire de la Compagnie royale des Indes Orientales. Paris, 1905.

WEBER, HENRY. La Compagnie française des Indes. Paris, 1904.

CHAPTER IV

THE EAST INDIA COMPANY, 1600–1740

A. ORIGINAL MATERIALS

MANUSCRIPT

India Office. The Court Minutes of the East India Company. The Original Correspondence series of letters from the East. The Letter Books, containing copies of letters despatched thither. The early ships' journals in the Marine Records. The Factory Records. The Consultations received from the various Presidencies. For particulars see the *Guide to the India Office Records*, 1600–1858 (London, 1919).

Public Record Office. The series known as C.O. 77; also the Domestic State Papers.

British Museum. A number of miscellaneous MSS. Cf. S. A. Khan, *Sources for the history of British India in the XVIIth century* (Oxford, 1926).

PUBLISHED DOCUMENTS

Calendars of State Papers, East Indies, 1513–1634. By W. N. Sainsbury. 5 vols. London, 1862–92. These give abstracts of documents in the Public Record Office, India Office (Court Minutes and Original Correspondence only), and (to 1616) British Museum, relating to all parts of the East.

Court Minutes, etc., of the East India Company, 1635–79. By Miss E. B. Sainsbury, with introductions and notes by W. Foster. 8 vols. Oxford, 1907–29. (In progress.)

The English factories in India, 1618–69. By W. Foster. 13 vols. Oxford, 1906–27. Down to 1654 this series calendars the documents to be found in the India Office, Public Record Office, Indian Record Offices, and British Museum; from that date it is in narrative form, based on similar materials. A supplementary volume covering the period 1600–40 has been published (London, 1928).

The dawn of British trade to the East Indies. Ed. by Sir George Birdwood. London, 1886. This contains the text of the first volume of the Court Minutes.

The first Letter Book of the East India Company. Ed. by Sir George Birdwood and W. Foster. London, 1893. A printed version of the Miscellaneous Court Book, 1600–19.

Letters received by the East India Company from its servants in the East. Ed. by F. C. Danvers (vol. I) and W. Foster (vols. II–VI). This series gives the text of the first portion of the Original Correspondence.

Selections from the…State Papers preserved in the Bombay Secretariat. Maratha Series (1 vol.). Home Series (2 vols.). Ed. by G. W. Forrest. Bombay, 1885, 1887. Bombay, n.d.

Press lists of ancient documents preserved in the Bombay Record Office, 1646–1760. 4 vols.

Press lists of ancient documents in Fort St George, 1670–1800. 35 vols. Madras.

Calendar of Madras records, 1740–44. By H. H. Dodwell. Madras, 1917.

Diary and consultation books, Fort St George, 1681–85. Ed. by A. T. Pringle. 5 vols. Madras, 1893–5.

Notes on and extracts from the Government records, Fort St George, 1670–77. Madras, 1871.

Publications of the Madras Record Office. Ed. by H. H. Dodwell and K. Krishnaswami Ayyanger: Consultations, 1672–1702; Despatches from England, 1670–1706; Despatches to England, 1694–1711; Letters to other places, 1679–1702; Letters from other places, 1681–1700; Sundry Books, 1677–86. Madras, 1910–25. These are printed verbatim. There are gaps in all the series, due to the loss of volumes.

Papers relating to...the Company of Scotland. Ed. by G. P. Irish. Edinburgh, 1924.

TRAVELS AND OTHER CONTEMPORARY PUBLICATIONS

BERNIER, F. Travels of —— , 1656–68. Tr. and ed. by Archibald Constable, 1891. 2nd ed. (by V. A. Smith). Oxford, 1914.

BRUTON, W. Newes from the East Indies. 1638.

CHILD, Sir JOSIA. New discourse of trade. 1665.

COVERTE, R. A true and almost incredible report.... 1612.

DE LAET, J. De imperio magni Mogolis. Leiden, 1631.

DELLA VALLE, PIETRO. Travels of —— . Ed by E. Grey. 2 vols. (Hakluyt Society.) 1891.

DOWNING, C. History of the Indian Wars. Ed. by W. Foster. 1924.

Early annals of the English in Bengal. Ed. by C. R. Wilson. 3 vols. Calcutta, 1895–1917.

Early travels in India, 1583–1619. Ed. by W. Foster. 1921.

FRYER, J. New account of the East Indies and Persia. Ed. by W. Crooke. 3 vols. (Hakluyt Society.) 1909–15.

HAMILTON, A. New account of the East Indies. 2 vols. Edinburgh, 1727.

Hawkins' voyages, The. Ed. by C. R. Markham. (Hakluyt Society.) 1878.

HEDGES, WILLIAM. Diary of —— . Ed. by Col. H. Yule. 3 vols. (Hakluyt Society.) 1877–89.

HERBERT, THOMAS. Some yeares travale. 1634. Reprinted, ed. by Sir W. Foster, 1929.

JOURDAIN, JOHN. Journal of —— , 1608–17. Ed. by W. Foster. (Hakluyt Society.) 1905.

LANCASTER, Sir JAMES. Voyages of —— . Ed by C. R. Markham. (Hakluyt Society.) 1877.

LOCKYER, C. Account of the trade in India. 1711.

MANDELSLO, J. A. VON. Travels of —— . Tr. by J. Davies. 1662.

MANUCCI, NICCOLAO. Storia do Mogor. Translated and ed. by W. Irvine. 4 vols. 1907–8.

MASTER, STREYNSHAM. Diaries of —— . Ed. by Sir Richard Temple. 2 vols. 1911.

MIDDLETON, Sir HENRY. Voyage of —— . Ed. by Bolton Corney. (Hakluyt Society.) 1857.

MUNDY, PETER. Travels of —— . Ed. by Sir Richard Temple. 4 vols. (Hakluyt Society.) 1907–25. (In progress.)

OVINGTON, Rev. F. Voyage to Surat in 1689. 1696.

Purchas His Pilgrimes. 4 vols. 1625.

ROE, Sir THOMAS. Embassy of —— , 1615–19. Ed. by W. Foster. 2 vols. (Hakluyt Society.) 1899. 2nd ed. 1926.

TAVERNIER, J. B. Travels of —— . Translated and ed. by V. Ball. 2 vols. 1889.

TERRY, Rev. E. Voyage to East-India. 1655.

B. SECONDARY WORKS

ANDERSON, Rev. P. The English in Western India. Bombay, 1854.

BAL KRISHNA. Commercial relations between India and England, 1601–1757. 1924.

BRUCE, JOHN. Annals of the East India Company. 3 vols. 1810.

DALTON, Sir C. N. Life of Thomas Pitt. Cambridge, 1915.
DUFF, J. GRANT. History of the Mahrattas. Ed. by S. M. Edwardes. 2 vols. 1921.
EDWARDES, S. M. The rise of Bombay. Bombay, 1902.
—— Gazetteer of the City and Island of Bombay. 3 vols. Bombay, 1909–10.
ELPHINSTONE, MOUNTSTUART. The history of India. Ed by E. B. Cowell. 1905.
FENGER, J. F. History of the Tranquebar Mission. Tranquebar, 1863.
HALL, D. G. E. Early English intercourse with Burma. 1928.
HERTZ, G. B. "England and the Ostend Company." (*E.H.R.* April, 1907.)
HUISMAN, M. La Belgique commerciale sous l'Empereur Charles VI. Brussels, 1902.
HUNTER, Sir WILLIAM. History of British India. 2 vols. 1899, 1900.
LARSEN, KAY. De Dansk-Ostindiske Koloniers Historie. I. Trankebar. II. De Bengalske Loger Nikobarerne. Copenhagen, 1907, 1908.
LANNOY, C. DE, and LINDEN, H. VAN DER. Histoire de l'expansion coloniale des peuples européens. II. Néerlande et Danemark. III. Suède. Brussels, 1911, 1921.
LOVE, Col. H. D. Vestiges of Old Madras. 4 vols. 1913.
LYALL, Sir ALFRED. The British dominion in India. 1906.
MACPHERSON, D. History of the European commerce with India. 1812.
MALABARI, B. M. Bombay in the making. 1910.
MILBURN, W. Oriental commerce. 2 vols. 1813.
MILL, JAMES. History of British India. Ed. by H. H. Wilson. 10 vols. 1858.
MORELAND, W. H. India at the death of Akbar. 1920.
—— From Akbar to Aurangzeb. 1923.
RAWLINSON, H. G. British beginnings in Western India. Oxford, 1920.
RAYNAL, G. T. Histoire...des établissemens et du commerce des Européens dans les deux Indes. 10 vols. Geneva, 1782.
SCHLEGEL, J. H. Sammlung zur Dänischen Geschichte. 2 vols. Copenhagen, 1771–76.
SCOTT, W. R. Joint stock companies to 1720. 3 vols. Cambridge, 1910–12.
SHAFAAT AHMAD KHAN. The East India trade in the seventeenth century. 1923.
—— Anglo-Portuguese negotiations relating to Bombay, 1660–77. [1922.]
STRACHEY, R. and O. Keigwin's rebellion. Oxford, 1916.
THOMAS, P. J. Mercantilism and the East India trade. 1926.
WHEELER, J. T. Madras in the olden time. 3 vols. Madras, 1861–62.
—— Early records of British India. Calcutta, 1878.
WILSON, C. R. Old Fort William in Bengal. 2 vols. 1906.
WRIGHT, ARNOLD. Annesley of Surat. 1918.

CHAPTERS V, VI, and VIII

THE STRUGGLE WITH THE FRENCH

A. ORIGINAL MATERIALS

MANUSCRIPT

Among French records for the period of Dupleix, the following are the most important:

Archives du Ministère des Colonies. C^2 8^2 à E^2 90, année 1747 à 1756, lettres et actes divers.

Bibliothèque Nationale. Nouvelles acquisitions; 9192 à 9170: Lettres de Dupleix aux officiers de l'armée du Carnatic et du Deccan; lettres de Bussy et de divers officiers à Dupleix; correspondance de Dupleix avec divers; lettres de Moracin; comptes de Dupleix.

9356: Correspondance de Dupleix avec la Compagnie et avec Bussy.

9358: Journal de l'armée conduite par Bussy dans le Deccan (1751–1755).

9360 et 9361: Correspondance de Bussy et de Duval de Leyrit.

Archives de Seine-et-Oise. E 3746 à 3756 *bis*: Lettres de Dupleix à l'armée du Sud (3746); à l'armée de Trichinapoly (3747); à Bussy (3748); à Law et à Brenier (3750); aux officiers de Coblon, Chingleput et Valdaour (3751); au gouverneur de Madras (3752); aux syndics et directeurs de la Compagnie (3753); à l'armée de Golconde (3754); aux commandants de Karikal et Masulipatam (3755 et 3756); livre de compte pour 1754 (3756 *bis*).

For the period of Lally:

The d'Argenson papers at the Bibliothèque de l'Arsenal; documents relating to the trial of Lally in the Archives Nationales; the Collection Ariel in the Bibliothèque Nationale; the archives of the Ministère de la Marine.

The Pondicherry records contain little or nothing relating to this vexed period. The important papers were probably taken to Europe in connection with the suits of Dupleix and the trial of Lally, and must have suffered further dispersion by the capture and destruction of Pondicherry.

The Madras records (preserved at the Madras Record Office and the India Office for the most part in duplicate): especially the Madras Public Consultations for the whole period. Fort St David, 1747–52 (while it was the Presidency headquarters); the proceedings of the Madras Select Committee (usually known as the Military Consultations). At the India Office is also a collection "The French in India", see Foster, *Guide*, p. 96. Consult also Dodwell, *Handbook to the Madras Records*.

Important papers relating to the conduct of the squadron and of the king's forces in India will be found in the Public Record Office, especially Admiralty papers, I, 160–161, and War Office papers.

The Orme Collection (at the India Office) is particularly important. It was formed by Orme for the purpose of his history and has been admirably catalogued by the late Mr S. C. Hill. There is also a large collection of Clive MSS (in the possession of Lord Powis) which was calendared by Mr Rushbrook Williams, though his calendar still awaits publication.

PRINTED DOCUMENTS

D'ACHE, Despatches of. Ap. Moufle d'Angerville, *La vie privée de Louis XV*, Paris, 1781.

ANANDA RANGA PILLAI. Private diary. Ed. by Price and Dodwell. 12 vols. Madras, 1904–28.

DODWELL, H. H. Calendar of the Madras records, 1740–44. Madras, 1917.

—— Calendar of the Madras despatches, 1744–1755. Madras, 1920.

HILL, S. C. Catalogue of the Orme MSS. 1916.

Lettres édifiantes et curieuses. Ed. by Aimé-Martin. Vol. II. 1839.

LOVE, Col. HENRY DAVISON. Vestiges of old Madras. 3 vols. 1913.

NAZELLE, Marquis DE. Dupleix et la défense de Pondichéry. 1908.

Records of Fort St George (sm. fol. Madras):
French Correspondence 1750, 1751, 1752. 1914–16.
Journal of the siege of Madras. 1915.
Madras military consultations, 1752–1756. 1910–13.
Country correspondence, 1740–58. 1908–15.

Société de l'histoire de l'Inde française. Correspondance du conseil supérieur de Pondichéry et de la Compagnie. Vol. III, 1739–1742. 1922. Vol. IV, 1744–1749. 1924. Vol. V, 1755–1759. 1928.

—— Correspondance du conseil supérieur de Pondichéry avec le conseil de Chandernagor. Vol. II, 1738–1747. 1916. Vol. III, 1747–1757. 1918–19.

—— Pondichéry en 1746. 1911.

—— Actes de l'état civil. Vol. II, 1736–1761.

VINSON, JULIEN. Les Français dans l'Inde. 1894.

FRENCH CONTROVERSY AND MEMOIRS

Mémoire pour La Bourdonnais (and supplement). 4to. Paris, 1750–51.
Mémoire pour La Gatinais. 4to. Paris, 1750.

Mémoire pour la famille de Dupleix. 4to. Paris, 1751.

Histoire de la dernière révolution des Indes Orientales, par M. L. L. M. 12mo. Paris, 1757.

Relation du siège de Pondichéry. (Ap. Collection historique...pour servir à l'histoire de la guerre terminée (en 1748).) 12mo. London, 1758.

Lettre de Godeheu à Dupleix. 4to. Paris, 1760.

Mémoire pour Dupleix contre la Compagnie des Indes. 4to. Paris, 1763.

Mémoire pour la Compagnie des Indes contre Dupleix. 4to. Paris, 1763.

Plainte du Chevalier Law. 4to. Paris, 1763.

Réponse de Dupleix à la lettre de Godeheu. 4to. Paris, 1763.

Réfutation des faits imputés à Godeheu. 4to. Paris, 1764.

Mémoire pour Bussy expositif de ses créances sur la Compagnie des Indes. 4to. Paris, 1764.

Mémoire pour Bussy au sujet du mémoire que Lally vient de répandre dans le public. 4to. Paris, 1766.

Mémoire pour Lally contre le Procureur-général. 3 parts. 4to. Paris, 1766.

Lettres de d'Aché à Lally. 4to. Paris, 1766.

Lettres de Leyrit à Lally. 4to. Paris, 1766.

Mémoire pour d'Aché. 4to. Paris, 1766.

Mémoire pour Bussy contre la Compagnie. 4to. Paris, 1767.

Plaidoyer du Comte de Lally-Tollendal, curateur à la mémoire du feu Comte de Lally, son père. Rouen, 1780.

GENTIL. Mémoires sur l'Indoustan. 1822.

CONTEMPORARY ENGLISH TRACTS AND TRAVELS

[MONSON, WILLIAM.] A letter to a Proprietor of the East India Company. 8vo. 123 pp., n.d.

Narrative of the transactions of the British squadrons in the East Indies...by an officer who served in those squadrons. 8vo. 1751.

Journal...of the Boscawen's voyage to Bombay...by Philalethes. 8vo. 1750.

IVES, E. Voyage to India. 1773.

B. SECONDARY WORKS

BIDDULPH, Col. JOHN. Stringer Lawrence. 1901.

CAMBRIDGE, RICHARD OWEN. Account of the war in India. 1761.

CORBETT, J. England in the Seven Years' war. 2 vols. 1907.

CRÉPIN, PIERRE. Mahé de la Bourdonnais. Paris, 1922.

CULTRU, PROSPER. Dupleix: ses plans politiques: sa disgrâce. Paris, 1901.

DALTON, C. Memoir of Captain Dalton. 1886.

DODWELL, H. H. Dupleix and Clive: the beginning of empire. 1920.

DU TEIL, J., Baron. Une famille militaire au 18e siècle. Paris, 1896.

FORDE, Col. LIONEL. Lord Clive's right-hand man. 1910.

FORREST, Sir G. W. Life of Lord Clive. 2 vols. 1918.

GRANT, C. History of Mauritius. 4to. 1801.

GRANT, J. Sketch of the history of the East India Company. 1813.

GUET, I. Jan Begum. Paris, 1892.

HAMONT, TIBULLE. Dupleix d'après sa correspondance inédite. Paris, 1881.

—— Lally-Tollendal. Paris, 1887.

LACOUR-GAYET, G. La marine militaire sous le règne de Louis XV. Paris, 1910.

LA FLOTTE. Essais historiques sur l'Inde. Paris, 1769.

MALCOLM, Sir JOHN. Life of Robert Lord Clive. 3 vols. 1836.

MARTINEAU, ALFRED. Dupleix et l'Inde française. 4 vols. Paris, 1920-8.

ORME, ROBERT. History of the military transactions of the British nation in Indostan. 3 vols. 4to. 4th ed. 1803.

RICHMOND, H. W. The navy in the war of 1739-48. 3 vols. Cambridge, 1920.

WADDINGTON, R. La guerre des sept ans. 4 vols. Paris, 1899-1907.

WILKS, M. Historical sketches of the south of India. 3 vols. 1810-17.

WILSON, Col. W. J. History of the Madras army. 5 vols. Madras.

CHAPTERS VII and IX

THE CONQUEST OF BENGAL

A. ORIGINAL MATERIALS

MANUSCRIPT

The principal authority for the period consists of the Proceedings of the Bengal Council and Select Committee, preserved in duplicate at the Imperial Record Office, Calcutta, and at the India Office Library. See Foster, *Guide*, pp. 40–42.

Important matter is also contained in the Clive MSS and the Orme MSS, for which cf. p. 621 *supra*.

A number of papers relating to the period will also be found in the earlier portion of the Hastings MSS at the British Museum, for which cf. p. 625 *infra*.

PRINTED DOCUMENTS

AITCHISON, Sir C. Collection of treaties, engagements and sunnuds relating to India. 10 vols. Calcutta, 1892.

Bengal Government Records. Proceedings of the Select Committee, 1758.

Calendar of Persian Correspondence, 1759–1772. 3 vols. Calcutta, 1911–19.

[FORREST, G. W.] Bengal and Madras Papers, 1746–1785. 2 vols. Fo. Calcutta.

HILL, S. C. Abstract of the early records of the Foreign Department, 1756–62. Fo. Calcutta, 1901.

—— Bengal in 1756–57. 3 vols. 1905.

—— Catalogue of the Orme MSS. Oxford, 1916.

LAW, JEAN. Mémoire sur quelques affaires de l'empire mogul. Ed. Martineau. Paris, 1913.

LONG, Rev. J. Selections from the unpublished records of the Government of Bengal, 1748–1767. Calcutta, 1869.

Reports of the Select Committee of the House of Commons, 1772–73.

Reports of the Committee of Secrecy appointed by the House of Commons, 1772–73.

[VANSITTART, HENRY.] Original papers relative to the disturbances in Bengal, 1759–1764. 8vo. 1765.

—— Narratives of the transactions in Bengal from...1760 to...1764. 3 vols. 1766.

CONTEMPORARY TRACTS, ETC.

A comparative view of the Dutch, French and English East India Companies. 1770.

Address from...Holwell...to...Scrafton in reply to his...Observations on Mr. Vansittart's narrative. 1767.

A defence of the United merchants of England...against the complaints of the Dutch East India Company. 4to. 1762.

An authentic account of the proceedings of...Holland and West Friesland on the complaints laid before them by Sir Joseph Yorke. 4to. 1762.

BOLTS, WILLIAM. Considerations on Indian affairs. 3 vols. 4to. 1772–5.

[CAILLAUD, JOHN.] Narrative of what happened in Bengal in the year 1760. n.d.

CARACCIOLI, C. Life of Robert, Lord Clive. 4 vols. [1777.]

Debates in the Asiatic Assembly. 1767.

HOLWELL, J. Z. India Tracts. 2nd ed. 4to. 1764.

IVES, E. Voyage to India. 1773.

Letter from certain gentlemen of Council at Bengal...containing reasons against the revolution in favour of Meir Cossim Aly Chan. Sm. 4to. 1764.

Proceedings of the court-martial on Sir Robert Fletcher. n.d.

SCRAFTON, LUKE. Reflections on the government of Indostan. 1763.
—— History of the administration of the leader in the Indian direction. Sm. 4to. [1764.]
STRACHEY, H. Narrative of the Mutiny of the officers in Bengal. 1773.
VERELST, HARRY. Rise, progress and present state of the English Government in Bengal. 4to. 1772.
[WATTS, WILLIAM.] Memoirs of the revolution in Bengal in the year 1757. 1760.

B. SECONDARY WORKS

GENERAL

AUBER, PETER. Rise and Progress of the British power in India. 2 vols. 1837.
Bengal Past and Present. Calcutta, 1907– .
BEVERIDGE, HENRY. A comprehensive history of India civil, military, and social. 3 vols. 1867.
BURGESS, Dr JAMES. The chronology of modern India. 1913.
CURZON OF KEDLESTON, The Marquis. British Government in India. 2 vols. 1925.
ILBERT, Sir COURTENAY. The Government of India. 1915.
Imperial Gazetteer of India. Vol. I. Descriptive. Oxford, 1907. Vol. II. Historical. 1908. Vol. III. Economic. 1908. Vol. IV. Administrative. 1907. Atlas.
LYALL, Sir ALFRED. Rise and expansion of the British dominion in India. 1910.
MARSHMAN, JOHN CLARK. History of India from the earliest period to the close of Lord Dalhousie's administration. 3 vols. 1867.
MILL, JAMES. History of British India. 5th ed. With notes and continuation by H. H. Wilson. 10 vols. 1858.
MUIR, RAMSAY. Making of British India. Manchester, 1915.
MUKHERJI, P. Indian constitutional documents. 2 vols. 2nd ed. Calcutta, 1918.
ROBERTS, P. E. India. 2 vols. Oxford, 1916–20.
STRACHEY, Sir JOHN. India. 1888.
THORNTON, EDWARD. History of the British Empire in India. 6 vols. 1841.

SPECIAL

BROOME, A. Rise and progress of the Bengal army. Calcutta, 1850.
DODWELL, H. H. Dupleix and Clive. 1920.
FORREST, Sir G. W. Life of Lord Clive. 2 vols. 1918.
GENTIL. Mémoires sur l'Indoustan. 1822.
GHOSE, N. N. Memoirs of...Nubkissen. 1901.
HALLWARD, N. L. William Bolts. 1920.
HILL, S. C. Major-General Claud Martin. 1901.
—— Three Frenchmen in Bengal. 1903.
—— Major Randfurlie Knox Dilawar Jang Bahadur. 1917.
HYDE, H. B. The Parish of Bengal. 1899.
—— The parochial annals of Bengal. 1901.
KLERK DE REUS, G. C. "De expeditie naar Bengale." (De Indische Gids, 1889.)
MALCOLM, Sir JOHN. Life of Robert Lord Clive. 3 vols. 1836.
MALLESON, Col. G. B. Lord Clive. 1907.
ORME, ROBERT. Military transactions of the British nation in Indostan. 3 vols.

, Sir HENRY. Letters of Warren Hastings to Sir John Macpherson. historians. Vol. VIII. , and DOWSON, JOHN. The history of India as told b
Hansard's Parliamentary History. Vol. VIII and following. 1812.
History of the Trial of Warren Hastings, Esq. 1796.
FORREST, G. W. (Sir). Selections from the Letters, Despatches, and oth
    Papers preserved in the Foreign Department of the Government o
    1772–85. 3 vols. Fol. Calcutta, 1890.
—— Selections from the State Papers of the Governors-General of India.
    Hastings. 2 vols. Oxford, 1910.
GRIER, SYDNEY C. The letters of Warren Hastings to his wife. Edinburgh
Journals of the House of Commons.
Journals of the House of Lords.
Minutes of the evidence taken at the trial of Warren Hastings. 11 vols. 1
NANDAKUMAR. The trial of Maha Raja Nundocomar, Bahader, for forger
    4to. 1776.

CHAPTERS X–XIII and XVI–XVII

WARREN HASTINGS AND BENGAL, 1772–85

A. ORIGINAL SOURCES

MANUSCRIPT

In the India Office is a great mass of records dealing with the Hastings period. Foster's *Guide* (especially pp. 42–7) should be consulted. In the Home Miscellaneous Series, vols. 212–221 deal with Hastings' administration, and vols. 228–234 with the Impeachment. The following volumes in this series also deal with the period: 115, 118, 119, 123, 139, 140, 162, 172–4, 227, 372, 555, 683. Among other records for the period 1772–1785 are the Court Minutes (i.e. of the Court of Directors), 15 vols.; the General Court Minutes (i.e. of the Court of Proprietors), 4 vols.; Letters Received from Bengal, 13 vols.; Despatches to Bengal, 8 vols.; Bengal Public Consultations, 77 vols.; Bengal Secret and Military Consultations, 76 vols.; Bengal Revenue Consultations, 93 vols.; Bengal Foreign Consultations, 6 vols.; Calcutta Committee of Revenue Proceedings, 61 vols.

Duplicates of almost all the consultation volumes, similarly authenticated, are to be found in the Imperial Record Office, Calcutta.

At the Public Record Office are preserved the original correspondence of the Secretary of State (C.O. 77–24, 25, and 82, 83), but a great mass of further correspondence of the Secretary of State occurs in the Home Miscellaneous Series at the India Office (145–189). A great quantity of Lord North's East India Correspondence will be found in the Treasury Papers (T 49–1 to 9). Besides these there also occur in the Additional MSS three volumes of Robinson's correspondence with George III (37833–5); a volume of Clavering-Francis letters (34287); and the Impey papers (16259–74). The Hastings MSS form Additional MSS 28973–29236.

The private papers of Francis are lodged at the India Office. A volume of Clavering-Francis correspondence forms Add. MS 34287.

PRINTED DOCUMENTS

AITCHISON, Sir C. See p. 623 *supra*.
BOND, E. A. Speeches of the Managers and Counsel in the Trial of Warren Hastings. 4 vols. 1859–61.
Calendar of Persian Correspondence, 1772–5. Calcutta, 1925.
Debates of the House of Lords on the evidence delivered in the trial of Warren Hastings Esquire; Proceedings of the East India Company in consequence of his acquittal and testimonials of th... 1797.
DODWELL, H. ...
ELLIOT ...

NANDAKUMAR. The trial of Joseph Fowke, Francis Fowke, Maha Rajah Nundocomar and Roy Rada Churn, for a conspiracy against Warren Hastings Esq. 1776.

Reports (I-IX) of the Select Committee on the Administration of Justice in Bengal, Behar and Orissa. 1782-3.

SAIYID GHULAM HUSAIN KHAN. Siyar-al-mutakhkherin. Translated by Mustafa. 4 vols. Calcutta [1902].

TRACTS AND OTHER CONTEMPORARY WRITINGS

Answer of Philip Francis, Esq., to the charges exhibited against him, General Clavering, and Colonel Monson by Sir Elijah Impey, Kt. n.d.

Appeal from the hasty to the deliberative judgment of the people of England. 8vo. 1787.

BROOME, RALPH. A comparative review of the administration of Mr Hastings and Mr Dundas. n.d.

—— An elucidation of the articles of impeachment...against Warren Hastings. 1790.

CLIVE, Lord ROBERT. Lord Clive's Speech in the House of Commons, 30th March, 1772, on the motion made for leave to bring in a bill, for the better regulation of the affairs of the East India Company, and of their Servants in India, and for the due Administration of Justice in Bengal. London. n.d.

Examination of public measures proposed in 1782 both in the House of Commons and at the India House, as far as they concern W. Hastings, Esq. 1782.

Five letters from a free merchant in Bengal to Warren Hastings. 1783.

FOWKE, FRANCIS. Extracts from records at the East India House of proceedings relative to ——. 1782.

HAMILTON, C. An historical relation of the origin, progress, and final dissolution of the government of the Rohilla Afghans. 1787.

HASTINGS, WARREN. A narrative of the insurrection which happened in the Zemeendary of Banaris in the month of August 1781, and of the transactions of the Governor-General in that district; with an appendix of authentic papers and affidavits. [1782.]

—— Memoirs relative to the state of India. 1786.

—— Review of the state of Bengal. 1786.

HICKEY, WILLIAM. Memoirs, edited by Alfred Spencer. 4 vols. 1913-25.

HODGES, WILLIAM. Travels in India, during the years 1780, 1781, 1782, and 1783. London, 1793.

Letters of Albanicus to the people of England on the partiality and injustice of the charges brought against Warren Hastings. 1786.

Letters of Detector on the reports of the Select Committees. 1782.

containing a humble description of the trial

SHERIDAN, R. B. A narrative statement of the 2 bills for the better government of the British possessions in India brought into Parliament by Mr. Fox and Mr. Pitt, with explanatory observations. 1788.

Short account of the resignation of Warren Hastings, Governor-General of Bengal, in the year 1775. 1781.

THOMPSON, HENRY FREDERICK. Intrigues of a Nabob. 1780.

TIERNEY, G. The real situation of the East India Company. 1787.

B. SECONDARY WORKS

For general works see the list at p. 624 *supra*.

BEVERIDGE, H. The trial of Nanda Kumar. 1886.

BUSTEED, H. E. Echoes of old Calcutta. Calcutta, 1908.

GLEIG, G. R. Memoirs of Warren Hastings. 3 vols. 1841.

HASTINGS, G. W. Vindication of Warren Hastings. 8vo. Oxford, 1909.

IMPEY, ELIJAH BARWELL. Memoirs of Sir Elijah Impey. 1847.

LAWSON, Sir CHARLES. Private life of Warren Hastings. 1911.

LYALL, Sir ALFRED. Life of Hastings. 1908.

MACPHERSON, W. C. Soldiering in India, 1764–87. 1928.

MANNERS, Lady VICTORIA, and WILLIAMSON, Dr G. C. Life and work of John Zoffany. 4to. 1920.

MARKHAM, CLEMENTS R. Major James Rennell. 1895.

[MINTO, Lord.] Life and letters of Sir Gilbert Elliott, 1751–1806. 3 vols. 1874.

MONCKTON-JONES, M. E. Hastings in Bengal, 1772–1774. 8vo. Oxford, 1918.

PARKES, JOSEPH, and MERIVALE, HERMAN. Memoirs of Sir Philip Francis. 2 vols. 1867.

ROBERTS, P. E. "Warren Hastings and his accusers." (*Journal of Indian History*, vol. III, part 1, March, 1924.)

STANHOPE, Lord. Life and correspondence of William Pitt. 4 vols. 8vo. 1861.

STEPHEN, Sir JAMES FITZJAMES. Nuncomar and Impey. 2 vols. 1885.

STRACHEY, Sir JOHN. Hastings and the Rohilla War. 1892.

CHAPTER XIV

THE FIRST CONFLICT OF THE COMPANY WITH THE MARATHAS, 1761–82

A. ORIGINAL SOURCES

MANUSCRIPT

The English records consist principally of the Bombay Public and Secret, and Political Consultations (see Foster, *Guide*, pp. 84–5, and A. F. Kindersley, *Handbook of the Bombay Government Records*, pp. 20–21 and 41–42). But the student should also consult the Bengal records of the period and the Hastings MSS (see p. 625 *supra*).

The surviving Maratha papers consist of the Poona *Daftar*, of which no index or catalogue has yet been prepared; and the family papers of the principal chiefs, which still await examination.

Much regarding the first Maratha War occurs in the *Officios dos Governadores*, in the *Archivo Ultramarino* at Lisbon; and the correspondence of the Goa Government with its English and Maratha neighbours has been incorporated in the series *Livros dos Reis visinhos* in the Goa archives.

PRINTED DOCUMENTS

BRIGGS, J. "Early life of Nana Farnevis." (*Proc. Royal Asiatic Soc.* 1829.)

FORREST, Sir G. W. Selections from the letters, despatches and state papers preserved in the Bombay Secretariat. Home Series. Bombay, 1887. Maratha Series. Bombay, 1885.

PARASNIS, D. B. Itihas Sangraha. 7 vols. Bombay.
PARASNIS, D. B. and MAWJEE, P. V. Treaties, agreements and sanads.
RAJWADE, V. K. Marthyanchya Itihasanchi Sadhanen. 22 vols.

TRACTS AND OTHER CONTEMPORARY WRITINGS

FORBES, James. Oriental Memoirs, a narrative of 17 years' residence in India. 2nd ed. revised by his daughter, the Countess de Montalembert. 2 vols. 1834.
Historical account of the settlement and possession of Bombay by the English E.I.C. and of the rise and progress of the war with the Mahratta nation. 1781.
MOODIE, JOHN. History of the military operations in Hindustan from...1744 to the conclusion of peace...in 1784. 2 vols. 1788.

B. SECONDARY WORKS

For general works see the list at p. 624 *supra*.

BAINES, J. A. History of Gujarat—Maratha period (1760–1819). (Ap. Gazetteer of the Bombay Presidency, vol. I, part I, Bombay, 1896.)
Bombay Gazetteer, Materials.
DOUGLAS, JAMES. Bombay and Western India. 2 vols. 1893.
EDWARDES, S. M. The rise of Bombay.
—— Gazetteer of Bombay city and island. Vol. II. Bombay, 1909.
DUFF, JAMES GRANT. History of the Mahrattas. 3 vols. 1826.
KHARE, V. V. Adhikar Yoga.
KINCAID, C. A. and PARASNIS, D. B. History of the Maratha people. 3 vols. 1918–25.
WARING, E. S. A history of the Mahrattas. 1810.

CHAPTER XV

THE CARNATIC, 1761–84

A. ORIGINAL SOURCES

MANUSCRIPT

The principal source is the series of records of the governor and council of Madras, preserved for the most part in duplicate at the India Office and at the Madras Record Office. These consist mainly of two series of consultations, Public and Military. (See Foster, *Guide*, pp. 75–76, and Dodwell, *Report on the Madras Records*, pp. 20 *sqq.*)

The Madras Record Office contains a special group of volumes (Military Sundries, nos. 60–62) containing the reports, etc., of the commissioners who concluded the Treaty of Mangalore.

Papers relating to the conduct of the naval commander at Madras will be found divided between the Public Record Office and the India Office. The chief items at the former are C.O. 77.82 and T 49.1, 2, and 25; and at the latter Home Miscellaneous 99–114.

Among the Additional MSS at the British Museum is a large part of the Macartney papers, especially his private correspondence (22454–62). The Bodleian Library contains a number of MSS supplementing this last item (Bodley MSS, English History C 66–114). Macartney's correspondence with the Chairs forms Home Miscellaneous 246–7 at the India Office.

A considerable quantity of the Persian papers of the Nawab of the Carnatic is at the Madras Record Office.

Printed Documents

Forrest, Sir G. W. See p. 625 *supra*.
Ghulam Muhammad. Lives of Haidar 'Ali and Tipu Sultan. 1855.
Husain 'Ali Khan Kirmani. History of Hyder Naik. Translated by Miles. 1842.
Love, Col. H. D. Vestiges of old Madras. 3 vols. and index. 1913.
—— The Palk MSS. (Royal Hist. MSS Com.) 1922.
Reports (I–VI) of the committee of secrecy on the causes of the war in the Carnatic. 1781–2.

Tracts and other Contemporary Writings

Answer to the charges exhibited against Sir Thomas Rumbold...by himself. [1781.]
Benfield, Paul. Report of the Committee of Correspondence. 1780.
—— Heads of objections. 1780.
—— The case of Mr. Paul Benfield. 1781.
—— Opinion of W. Grant...relative to Mr. Benfield's claims. 1781.
—— Trial for an action for £37,000. 1782.
—— Letter to the creditors of Boyd, Benfield and Co. 1800.
—— Case of Paul Benfield Esq. 1803.
Boyd, Hugh. Miscellaneous works. Ed. by Lawrence Campbell. 2 vols. 1800.
Bristow, James. Ten years' captivity with Hyder and Tippoo. 1793.
Burke, Edmund. Speech on the Nabob of Arcot's debts, with an appendix containing several documents. 1788.
Campbell, Donald. Journey overland to India. 4to. 1796.
Campbell, Col. John. Account of the gallant defence made at Mangalore. 1786.
Curtis, Charles. Account of the diseases of India as they appeared in the English fleet at Madras, 1782–83. Edinburgh, 1807.
Defence of Lord Pigot. 1776.
Defences of George Stratton, Esq., and the majority of Council at Madras in answer to the accusations brought against them for the supposed murder of Lord Pigot. 1778.
Enquiry into the policy of making conquests for the Mahometans in India by British arms. London, 1779.
Essay towards illustrating the late conduct of...Sir Hector Munro. 1782.
Fullarton, William. A view of the English interests in India; and an account of the military operations in the southern parts of the peninsula, during the campaigns of 1782, 1783, and 1784. 1787.
King of Tanjore's memorial to the Court of Directors. 1776.
Le Couteur, Capt. John (100th Foot). Letters from India containing an account of the military transactions on the coast of Malabar. 1790.
[Maistre de la Tour.] Histoire d'Ayder-ali Khan. 1783.
Mangalore, Treaty of. Dallas-Huddlestone controversy. See *Asiatic Journal*, vols. V–VII.
Memoir of the public character and services of William Collins Jackson, late senior merchant on the Madras establishment. 1812.
Memoirs of the war in Asia. 1st ed. 2 vols. 1788; 2nd ed. 1 vol. 1789.
Mr. Floyer's case in the late disputes at Madras. 4to. 1778.
Narrative of the late revolution of the government of Madras. 1776 and 1778.
Oakes, Henry. Narrative of the treatment of the English prisoners at Bednur. 1785.
Observations on the proceedings in Council at Madras. 4to. [1778.]
Original letters from Warren Hastings, Esq., Sir Eyre Coote, K.B., and Richard Barwell, Esq., to Sir Thomas Rumbold, Bart., and Lord Macartney, K.B. 1787.
Original papers...and proceedings before the coroner's inquest upon the death of Lord Pigot. 1778.
Original papers relative to Tanjore. 4to. 1777.
Remarks on the most important military operations of the English forces on the western side of the peninsula of Hindoostan in 1783 and 1784...by a British officer. 1788.

Restoration of the King of Tanjore considered. [1776.]

Robson, F. The life of Hyder Ali. 1786.

Rous, G. The restoration of the King of Tanjore considered. 3 parts. 1777.

Scurry, James. Ten years' captivity by Hyder and Tippoo. 1824.

[Stanhope, Philip Dormer.] Genuine memoirs of Asiaticus. 1785.

State of the facts relating to Tanjore. [1776.]

Stuart, Andrew. Letter to the directors of the East India Company from —— respecting the conduct of Brigadier-General James Stuart at Madras. 4to. 1778.

—— Letters to the Rt. Hon. Lord Mansfield. Dublin, 1775.

[Stuart, Major-General James.] Correspondence during the indisposition of the commander-in-chief. 4to. n.d.

[Sulivan, R. J.] Analysis of the political history of India. 4to. 1779.

B. SECONDARY WORKS

For general works see the list at p. 624 *supra.*

Barrow, J. Some account of the public life and a selection from the unpublished writings of the Earl of Macnartney. 2 vols. 1807.

Biddulph, Col. John. The XIX and their times. 1899.

Bilgrami, S. H. and Wilmot, G. Historical and descriptive sketch of the Nizam's dominions. 2 vols. 1883–4.

Bowring, Lewin B. Haidar Ali and Tipu Sultan. Oxford, 1899.

Dodwell, H. H. "Warren Hastings and the assignment of the Carnatic." (*E.H.R.* lx, 375 *sqq.*)

Génin, E. Talents militaires d'Aider-aly, sa lutte contre les Anglais, 1780–82.

Hill, S. C. Yusuf Khan. 1914.

Lacour-Gayet, G. La marine militaire sous le règne de Louis XVI. 1905.

Lindsay, Lord. Lives of the Lindsays. 3 vols. 1849. (Vol. iii contains narratives of R., James, and John Lindsay.)

Mahan, A. T. The influence of sea-power upon history, 1660–1788. 1889.

Oakeley, Herbert. Some account of Sir Charles Oakeley. 1829.

Page, J. Schwartz of Tanjore. 1921.

Pearson, Hugh. Life...of Christian Frederick Swartz. 2 vols. 1834.

Richmond, Vice-Admiral Sir H. W. "The Hughes-Suffren Campaigns." (*Mariner's Mirror*, xiii, 219 *sqq.* 1927.)

Robins, Helen H. Our first ambassador to China. 1908.

Roux, J. S. Le Bailli de Suffren dans l'Inde. 1862.

Rumbold, E. A. Vindication of Sir Thomas Rumbold. 1868.

Staunton, Sir G. L. Memoirs of the life and family of the late ——. Havant, 1823.

Wilks, Mark. Historical Sketches of the South of India. 3 vols. 1810–17.

Wilson, Col. W. J. History of the Madras army. 5 vols. Madras.

Wright, Arnold, and Sclater, W. L. Sterne's Eliza. 1922.

Wylly, Col. H. C. Life of Coote. 1922.

CHAPTER XVIII

LEGISLATION AND GOVERNMENTS, 1786–1818

A. ORIGINAL MATERIALS

Manuscript

The principal surviving record series of the Board of Control at the India Office are summarised in Foster, *Guide*, pp. 33–6.

Castlereagh's correspondence when President of the Board forms vols. 502 *sqq.* of the Home Miscellaneous Series. The Dundas papers, which would have been invaluable for this subject, have been dispersed; but some letters occur in the Home Miscellaneous Series 731 *a.*

An interesting reference to the relations between the Board and the Company will be found in Additional MS 33108 at the British Museum, where the Wellesley and Liverpool papers may also be consulted.

Printed Documents

Debates at the India House on the Company's new charter. 1793.
Parliamentary Papers. Papers relating to the renewal of the Company's charter in 1813 occur in vols. VI and VII, session 1812, and VIII–X, session 1812–13. The evidence given before the Select Committee in 1831–2 also relates to the earlier period (vols. VIII–XII, session 1831–2). Correspondence relating to the constitution of the Indian Governments (session 1833, vol. XXV, 115, 185).
Ross, Charles. Correspondence of Charles, first Marquis Cornwallis. 3 vols. 1859.
Wellesley, Marquess. Despatches. 5 vols. 1836.

Tracts and other Contemporary Publications

Anderson, George. ...Variations...in the affairs of the East India Company since...1784. 1792.
[Bruce, J.] Historical view of plans for the government of India. 1793.
Considerations of an attempt of the East India Company to become manufacturers in Great Britain. 1796.
Considerations on the danger...of laying open the trade with India and China. 1813.
Elphinstone, Mountstuart. Opinions of...upon some of the leading questions connected with the government of British India examined and compared with those of the late Sir T. Munro and Sir J. Malcolm. 1831.
Grant, Robert. The Expediency maintained of continuing the system by which the trade and government of India are now regulated. 1813.
Hasty sketch of a debate at the East India House on the subject of the private trade. 1801.
Lauderdale, Earl of. An inquiry into the practical merits of the system of the government of India. Edinburgh, 1809.
Malcolm, Sir John. The government of India. 1833.
Memorandum of the relative importance of the West and East Indies to Great Britain. 1823.
Rickards, R. India or facts submitted to illustrate the character and condition of the native inhabitants. n.d.
Russell, F. A short history of the East India Company. 1793.
[Scott-Waring, Major T.] Observations on the present state of the East India Company. 1807.
Tucker, H. St G. Review of the financial situation of the East India Company. 1822.

B. SECONDARY WORKS

For general works see the list at p. 624 *supra*.

Auber, Peter. Analysis of the constitution of the East India Company. 1826.
Foster, Sir W. "The India Board." (*Trans. of the Royal Hist. Soc.* 1916.)
Kaye, J. W. Life and correspondence of Henry St George Tucker. 1854.
Macpherson, David. Annals of commerce. 4 vols. 1805.
—— European commerce with India. 1812.
Morris, Henry. Life of Charles Grant. 1904.
Seton, Sir Malcolm. The India Office. 1926.

CHAPTER XIX

THE EXCLUSION OF THE FRENCH, 1784–1815

A. ORIGINAL MATERIALS

MANUSCRIPT

The chief English records are the Bengal Political, Foreign, Military and Secret Consultations for the period (Foster, *Guide*, pp. 50 *sqq.*). But besides these a good deal of matter ready collected occurs in the series *The French in India* (*idem*, p. 96) and in the later part of the Factory Records: Persia and the Persian Gulf (*idem*, p. 99).

At the Public Record Office the series F.O. 60 contains the papers relating to the early Persian missions.

At Paris the archives of the Ministries of the Colonies and of Marine are especially important.

PRINTED DOCUMENTS

AITCHISON. Treaties. See p. 623 *supra*.
FORTESCUE MSS. (Hist. MSS Com.) 1894– .
GARDANE, Comte ALFRED DE. Mission du Général Gardane en Perse sous le premier empire. 1865.
GAUDART, E. Catalogue des manuscrits des anciennes archives de l'Inde française. 2 vols. Pondichéry, 1922–4.
LAW, JEAN. État politique de l'Inde en 1777. Pondichéry, 1913.
NAPOLÉON I. Correspondance. (Especially vol. xv.)

TRACTS, TRAVELS, AND OTHER CONTEMPORARY WRITINGS

BALDWIN, GEORGE. Political recollections relative to Egypt. 1801.
BRITTANICUS. Letter to Samuel Whitbread.... 1810.
CAPPER, J. Observations on the passage to India through Egypt, by Baghdad, etc. 1785.
COSSIGNY, CHARPENTIER. Voyage au Bengale. 1789.
FORSTER, GEORGE. Journey from Bengal to England through the northern parts of India.... 2 vols. 1808.
FRANCKLIN, Col. W. Observations made on a tour from Bengal to Persia, 1786–87. 1790.
GRANDPRÉ, L. DE. Voyage dans l'Inde et au Bengale, 1789–90. 2 vols. 1801.
HANWAY, JONAS. Historical account of the British trade over the Caspian Sea. 2 vols. 4to. 1754.
[HOPKINS, D.] The dangers to British India from the French and missionary establishments. 1808.
MORELLET, Abbé ANDRÉ. Mémoire sur la situation actuelle de la Compagnie des Indes. 1769.
PLAISTED, BARTHOLOMEW. A journey from Calcutta in Bengal by sea to Busserah: from thence across the great desert to Aleppo.... 1757.
SONNERAT. Voyage to the East Indies, 1774–81. Translated. Calcutta, 1788.
TAYLOR, Major J. Travels from England to India, with instructions for travellers and an account of the expenses of travelling. Maps. 2 vols. 1799.

B. SECONDARY WORKS

For general works see the list at p. 624 *supra*.

BARBÉ, ÉMILE. Le nabab René Madec. 1894.
BOIGNE, Comte DE. Mémoire sur la carrière militaire et politique de M. le Général Comte de Boigne. Chambéry, 1830.

BRETTE. La colonie de l'Isle de France en 1790. n.d.

BRYDGES, Sir HARFORD JONES. Account of the transactions of H.M.'s mission to the Court of Persia in the years 1807–11. 2 vols. 1834.

CHARLES-ROUX, FRANÇOIS. Autour d'une route: L'Angleterre, l'isthme de Suez, et l'Égypte au 18e siècle. 1922.

—— Les origines de l'expédition d'Égypte. 1910.

—— L'Angleterre et l'expédition française en Égypte. Cairo, 2 vols. 1925.

—— "Un projet français de commerce avec l'Inde par Suez sous le règne de Louis XVI." (Rev. de l'hist. des cols. fr. 1925, pp. 411 and 551.)

—— Les échelles de Syrie et de Palestine au XVIIIe siècle. [1927.]

CHEVALIER, E. Histoire de la marine française sous le consulat et l'empire. 1886.

DAUBIGNY, E. T. Choiseul et la France outremer. 1892.

DOURDON, Chevalier DE. "Voyage dans l'Inde par les deserts (1787)." (Rev. Hist. de l'Inde Française, i, 171.)

DRIAULT, ÉDOUARD. La politique orientale de Napoléon: 1806–1809. Sebastiani et Gardane. 1904.

GALLOIS, NAPOLÉON. Les corsaires français sous la république et l'empire. Le Mans. 2 vols. 1847.

HOSKINS, H. L. British routes to India. New York, 1928.

KAYE, J. W. The life of Sir John Malcolm. 2 vols. 1856.

LA GRAVIÈRE, JURIEN DE. Guerres maritimes sous la république et l'empire. 2 vols. 1860.

LARCHEY, L. Correspondance intime de l'armée d'Égypte interceptée par la croisière anglaise. Introduction et notes par L. Larchey. 12mo. 1866.

MAILLARD, L. Notes sur l'isle de la Réunion. 1862.

MASSON, PAUL. Histoire du commerce français dans le Levant au XVIIIe siècle. 1896.

MINTO, Lady. Lord Minto in India. 1880.

NOË, Comte DE. Mémoires relatifs à l'expédition partie de Bengale pour aller combattre en Égypte l'armée d'Orient. 1826.

PEARCE, ROBERT ROUILLERE. Memoirs and correspondence of...Richard Marquess Wellesley. 3 vols. 1846.

PINGAUD, L. Choiseul-Gouffier, la France en Orient au XVIIIe siècle. 1887.

PRENTOUT, H. L'île de France sous Decaen. 1901.

ROSE, J. HOLLAND. Life of Pitt. 1911.

—— Life of Napoleon. 1901.

SURCOUF, ROBERT. Un corsaire malouin, Robert Surcouf. n.d.

SYKES, Sir P. M. History of Persia. 2 vols. 1922.

TORRENS, W. M. The Marquess Wellesley. 1850.

CHAPTER XX

TIPU SULTAN, 1785–1802

A. ORIGINAL MATERIALS

MANUSCRIPT

Documents relating to Tipu's administration seem almost entirely to have disappeared (but see *infra s.v. Printed Documents*). Our main authorities consist therefore in the Proceedings of the Bengal and Madras Councils for the period (Foster, *Guide*, p. 50, and Dodwell, *Report on the Madras Records*, pp. xii–xiii and 33).

Essential private collections are the Cornwallis MSS at the Public Record Office and the Wellesley MSS at the British Museum.

PRINTED DOCUMENTS

AITCHISON. Treaties. See p. 623 *supra.*

GURWOOD, Lt.-Col. J. Dispatches of the...Duke of Wellington. 13 vols. 1834–9.

KIRKPATRICK, Col. W. Select letters of Tippoo Sultan. London, 1811.

Mysore State Papers. Mysore, 1922.

Ross, Charles. Correspondence of Charles 1st Marquis Cornwallis. 3 vols. 1859.

Société de l'histoire de l'Inde Française. Catalogue des manuscrits des anciennes archives. Vol. i. Pondichéry, 1690–1789. 1922. Vol. ii. Pondichéry, 1789–1815. 1924.

Stewart, Charles. Tippoo's oriental library, and memoirs of Hyder and Tippoo. 1809.

Wellesley, Marquess. Despatches, minutes and correspondence. Ed. by Montgomery Martin. 5 vols. 1836.

—— The Wellesley Papers. 2 vols. 1914.

Contemporary Writings and other Publications

Allan, Capt. A. Views in the Mysore country. (20 large aquatint views.) Oblong fol. 1794.

—— Account of the Campaign in Mysore, 1799. Ed. by Nares Chandra Sinha. Calcutta, [1913].

Beatson, Alexander. View of the war with Tippoo Sultan. 4to. 1800.

Campbell, Sir Archibald. Letters from the late Sir A. C. to the Rajah of Travancore, 5th, 17th and 30th April, and 12th August, 1788. 1792.

—— Letter to Major Bannerman, 12th August, 1788. 1792.

Dirom, Major. Narrative of the campaign in India which terminated the war with Tippoo Sultan in 1792. 1794.

Elers, George. Memoirs. Ed. by Ld. Monson and G. L. Gower. 1903.

Historical and political view of the Deccan. 1791.

Hollingberry, W. History of Nizam Alee Khaun. Calcutta. 1805.

Mackenzie, Lt. Roderick. Sketch of the war with Tippoo Sultan (1789–1792). 2 vols. 4to. Calcutta, 1794.

Michaud, Joseph François. Histoire des progrès et de la chute de l'empire de Mysore, sous les règnes d'Hyder-Aly et Tippoo-Saib. 2 vols. 1801.

Moleville, Bertrand de. Mémoires (for M. Leger, Tipu's envoy in 1791).

Moor, Edward. Narrative of the operations of Captain Little's detachment. 4to. 1794.

[Munro, Innes.] Narrative of the military operations...against the combined forces of the French, Dutch and Hyder Ally (1780–84). 4to. 1789.

Narrative of the operations of the British army in India April–July 1791. 4to. 1792.

Narrative sketches of the conquest of Mysore effected by the British troops and their allies. 1800.

Rennell, Major James. Marches of the British armies...during the campaigns of 1790 and 1791. 1792.

Salmond, James. Review of the origin, progress and result of the decisive war with Tippoo. 1800.

Tipu Sultan. Negotiations with the French. 1799.

Welsh, Col. James. Military reminiscences. 2nd ed. 2 vols. 1830.

Wood, Mark. A review of the origin, progress and result of the late decisive war in Mysore, in a letter from an officer in India. London, 1800.

B. SECONDARY WORKS

For general works see the list at p. 624 supra.

Biddulph, Col. John. The XIX and their times. 1899.

[Hook, Theodore.] Life of Sir David Baird. 2 vols. 1832.

Lushington, S. R. Life and service of General Lord Harris in America, the West Indies, and India. 1840.

Tantet, V. L'Ambassade de Tippou Saheb à Paris en 1788. 1899.

Teignmouth, Lord. Memoirs of the life and correspondence of John Lord Teignmouth. 2 vols. 1843.

Wilkin, Capt. W. H. Life of Sir David Baird. 1912.

Wilks, Mark. Historical sketches of the south of India. 3 vols. 1810–17.

Wilson, Col. W. J. History of the Madras army. 5 vols. Madras.

CHAPTER XXI

THE CARNATIC, 1785–1801

A. ORIGINAL MATERIALS

MANUSCRIPT

The principal source of information is the series of Madras Military and Secret Consultations for the period, but especially for the years 1795 and 1801, at the India Office and the Madras Record Office. In the Home Miscellaneous Series at the India Office vols. 271–84 are especially concerned with Tanjore and 285–328 with the Nawab of Arcot.

The Cornwallis MSS at the Public Record Office and the Wellesley MSS at the British Museum should also be consulted.

The Persian records of the Nawabs of Arcot are preserved at the Madras Record Office.

PRINTED DOCUMENTS

AITCHISON. Treaties. See p. 623 *supra*.
Parliamentary Papers. 1801–2, vol. v; 1802–3, vol. IX; 1806, vol. II; 1806–7, vol. VIII.
Ross. Cornwallis Correspondence. See p. 634 *supra*.
Wellesley Despatches. See p. 634 *supra*.

B. SECONDARY WORKS

For general works see the list at p. 624 *supra*.

PEARCE. Life of Wellesley. See p. 633 *supra*.
SAUNDERS, BAILEY. Life and letters of James Macpherson. 1894.
TEIGNMOUTH. Life of Shore. See p. 634 *supra*.
WILKS. Historical sketches of Southern India. See p. 634 *supra*.
WRAXALL, NATHANIEL. Memoirs. 4 vols. 1836.

OUDH, 1785–1801

A. ORIGINAL MATERIALS

MANUSCRIPT

The principal source of information is the Political and Secret Proceedings of the Bengal Council for the period (at the India Office and the Imperial Record Office, Calcutta).

In the Home Miscellaneous Series at the India Office vols. 577–83 are specially concerned with Oudh. Vols. 447–8 of the same series contains Shore's correspondence with the resident at Lucknow.

PRINTED DOCUMENTS

ABU TALIB. History of Asafu'Daulah. Translated by W. Hoey. Allahabad, 1885.
AITCHISON. Treaties. See p. 623 *supra*.
Parliamentary Papers. 1806, vols. XV–XVII.
Ross. Cornwallis Correspondence. See p. 634 *supra*.
Wellesley Despatches. See p. 634 *supra*.

B. SECONDARY WORKS

For general works see the list at p. 624 *supra*.
See also the list under this head for "The Final Struggle with the Marathas",
p. 637 *infra*.

CHAPTER XXII

THE FINAL STRUGGLE WITH THE MARATHAS, 1784–1818

A. ORIGINAL MATERIALS

MANUSCRIPT

The principal materials comprise the Proceedings of the Bengal and Bombay
Councils for the period at the India Office, the Imperial Record Office, Calcutta,
and the Secretariat, Bombay. See Foster, *Guide*; Kindersley, *Handbook of the Bombay
Government records*, and *Handbook to the records of the Government of India*.

The Home Miscellaneous Series at the India Office contains, among other items
of importance, letters from Duncan to Wellesley (vols. 470–8), correspondence
relating to the Marathas (vols. 616–27), and Nepal (vols. 643–56).

See also the Cornwallis MSS at the Public Record Office and the Wellesley MSS
at the British Museum.

For the Maratha records see p. 627 *supra*.

PRINTED DOCUMENTS

AITCHISON. Treaties. See p. 623 *supra*.
FORREST, Sir G. W. Selections from the minutes...of Mountstuart Elphinstone.
    1884.
—— Selections from the letters, despatches, and other papers preserved in the
    Bombay Secretariat. Maratha Series, Bombay. 1885.
GUPTE, B. A. Historical records of Baroda. Calcutta.
GURWOOD, Lt.-Col. J. The dispatches of...the Duke of Wellington. 13 vols.
    1834–9.
HASTINGS, Marquess of. Private diary. 2 vols. 1858.
JENKINS, RICHARD. Report on the territories of Nagpore. Calcutta, 1827.
KHARE, V. V. Aitihasik Lekha Sangraha. 12 vols. Poona. (Marathi.)
Papers relating to the Nepaul War (printed by the East India Company). [See
    also Parliamentary Papers, 1817, vol. XI.]
PARASNIS, D. B. Itihas Sangraha. 7 vols. Bombay. (Marathi.)
PARASNIS, D. B. and MAWJEE, P. V. Treaties, agreements and sanads. Bombay.
    (Marathi.)
Parliamentary Papers. 1803–4, vol. XII; 1805, vol. X; 1806, vol. XVI; 1818,
    vol. XI; 1819, vol. XVIII.
ROSS, C. Correspondence of...Marquis Cornwallis. 3 vols. 1859.
SETON-KARR, W. S. Selections from the Calcutta Gazettes 1784–1823. 5 vols.
    1864–9.
WELLESLEY, Marquess. Despatches. Ed. by Montgomery Martin. 5 vols. 1836.
—— The Wellesley Papers. 2 vols. 1914.

CONTEMPORARY PUBLICATIONS

Asiatic Annual Register. 1800–11.
Asiatic Journal. 28 vols. 1816–29.
Selections from the Asiatic Journal. 2 vols. Madras, 1875.
BLACKER, V. Memoir of the operations of the British army in India during the
    Mahratta War of 1817, 1818, and 1819. 2 vols. 4to. 1821.

Brief remarks on the Mahratta War and on the rise and progress of the French establishments in Hindoostan under Generals du Boigne and Perron. 1804.

BROUGHTON, THOMAS DUER. Letters written in a Mahratta camp during the year 1809. 1892.

BUSAWUN LAL. Memoirs of Ameer Khan. Tr. H. T. Prinsep. Calcutta, 1832.

CAMPBELL, L. D. Letter...on the articles of charge against Marquis Wellesley which have been laid before the House of Commons. 8vo. 1808.

DIROM, Major. Campaign in India in 1792. 1793.

DUFF, J. GRANT. History of the Mahrattas. 1826.

East India Military Calendar. Vol. III. 1826.

FORBES, J. Oriental memoirs. 2nd ed. 1834.

FRANCKLIN, W. History of the reign of Shah Aulum. 4to. 1798.

—— Military Memoirs of Mr George Thomas. 1805.

HEBER, REGINALD. Narrative of a journey through the upper provinces of India. 2nd ed. 3 vols. 1828.

MALCOLM, Sir JOHN. The political history of India from 1784 to 1823. 1826.

—— Memoir of Central India. 2 vols. 3rd ed. 1832.

Notes relative to the late transactions in the Mahratta empire. Calcutta, 1803.

Origin of the Pindarries preceded by historical notices on the rise of the different Mahratta states by an officer in the service of the Hon. East India Company. Calcutta, 1819.

PRINSEP, HENRY T. History of the political and military transactions in India during the administration of the Marquess of Hastings, 1813–1823. 2 vols. 1825.

—— Memoirs of...Ameer Khan. See Busawun Lal.

SCOTT-WARING, T. History of the Mahrattas. 1810.

SMITH, L. F. Sketch of the rise, progress and termination of the regular corps formed...by Europeans in the service of native princes of India. Calcutta, 1805.

THORN, Major WILLIAM. Memoir of the War in India. 1818.

VALENTIA, Viscount. Voyages and travels to India. 3 vols. 1809.

B. SECONDARY WORKS

For general works see the list at p. 624 *supra.*

BLAKISTON, Lieut. JOHN. Twelve years' military service in three quarters of the Globe. 2 vols. 1829.

Bombay Presidency Gazetteers. Bombay, 1877–94.

COLEBROOKE, Sir H. T. Life of Elphinstone. 2 vols. 1884.

COMPTON, HERBERT. European military adventurers of Hindustan, 1784–1803. 1892.

FORTESCUE, Sir JOHN W. History of the British Army. Vol. XI. 1923.

FRASER, JAMES. Military memoir of Colonel James Skinner. 1851.

GLEIG, G. R. Life of Sir Thomas Munro. 3 vols. 1830.

HOPE, J. The house of Scindea. 1863.

HUTTON, W. H. The Marquess Wellesley. 1897.

KAYE, Sir JOHN. Lives of Indian officers. 2 vols. 1889.

KAYE, J. W. Life of Sir John Malcolm. 2 vols. 1856.

—— Life and correspondence of Charles Lord Metcalfe. 2 vols. Rev. ed. 1858.

—— Selections from the papers of Lord Metcalfe. 1855.

KEENE, H. G. Hindustan under free lances. 1770–1820. 1907.

KELKAR, N. C. Maratha ani Ingraj. (Marathi.)

KHARE, V. V. Nana Phadnavis. (Marathi.)

LUARD, Lt.-Col. C. E. Central India State Gazetteer. Calcutta and Lucknow, 1907–8.

Mahratta and Pindari War. Compiled for the General Staff, India. Simla, 1910.

NATU. Mahadaji Sindhia. (Marathi.)

PARASNIS, D. B. Satara.

PARASNIS, D. B. Sangli State.
PEARCE, ROBERT ROUILLERE. Memoirs and correspondence of...Richard Marquess Wellesley. 3 vols. 1846.
PEARSE, Col. HUGH. The Hearseys, 1768–1893. 8vo. 1905.
—— Life and military services of Viscount Lake. 1907.
[PESTER, JOHN.] War and sport in India, 1802–6. n.d.
[PRICE, Major.] Memoirs of the early life and service of a field officer on the retired list of the Indian army. 1839.
TEIGNMOUTH, Lord. Memoirs of the life and correspondence of John Lord Teignmouth. 2 vols. 1843.
[WALLACE, R. G.] Fifteen years in India or sketches of a soldier's life...from the journal of an officer in H.M.S. 1822.

CHAPTER XXIII

MARATHA ADMINISTRATION

A. ORIGINAL MATERIALS

MANUSCRIPT

For the Maratha records see p. 627 *supra*.

PRINTED DOCUMENTS

ELPHINSTONE, M. Report on the territories lately conquered from the Paishwa. Calcutta, 1822.
JENKINS, R. Report on the territories of the Raja of Nagpur. Calcutta, 1827.
MAWJEE, P. V. and PARASNIS, D. B. Sanadpatra Nivadapatra.
Revenue and Judicial Papers. Published by the East India Company. Vols. III and IV. 1826.

B. SECONDARY WORKS

ATRE. Ganv Gada. (Marathi.)
Iniquities of the Inam Commission in the Presidency of Bombay compiled from the published selections from Government Records and other sources exposed for the information of Enamdars. 1859.
RANADE, M. G. Introduction to the Peshwas' Diaries.
SEN, S. N. Administrative System of the Marathas. 2nd ed. Calcutta, 1925.
SYKES, Lt.-Col. Statistics of the four Collectorates of Dukhan under the British Government. 1838.
—— "On the Land Tenures of the Dekkan." (*J.R.A.S.* 1835, pp. 205–33.)
—— "Land Tenures of Dukhun." (*J.R.A.S.* 1836, pp. 350–76.)
TONE, W. H. Illustrations of some institutions of the Mahratta people. Calcutta, 1818.

CHAPTER XXIV

THE CONQUEST OF CEYLON, 1795–1815

A. ORIGINAL MATERIALS

MANUSCRIPT

At the India Office is a group of 57 volumes covering the period of the Company's administration (see Foster, *Guide*, pp. 92–3).

The Public Record Office has an extensive series of records C.O. 54–9, beginning with 1794.

At the Record Office, Colombo, exists a great quantity of administrative papers.

At the Record Office, Madras, are volumes relating to the embassies of Pybus and Andrews (see Dodwell, *Report*, pp. 22 and 34).

The Wellesley MSS (especially Add. MSS, 13864–7) at the British Museum.

PRINTED DOCUMENTS

BOYD, HUGH. Miscellaneous Works. Vol. II. 1800.

Cleghorn Papers. Ed. by the Rev. W. Neil. 1927.

PYBUS, JOHN. Mission to the King of Kandy in 1762. 1862.

The Uva Rebellion 1817–18. (Reprinted from the Ceylon Government Gazette.) Colombo, 1889.

CONTEMPORARY PUBLICATIONS

CORDINER, JAMES. A description of Ceylon, containing an account of the country, inhabitants, and natural productions; with narratives of a tour round the island in 1800, the campaign in Candy in 1803, and a journey to Ramisseram in 1804. 2 vols. 1807.

DAVY, JOHN. An account of the interior of Ceylon, and of its inhabitants; with travels in that island. 1821.

D'OYLY, Sir JOHN. "A sketch of the constitution of the Kandyan kingdom." (*Trans. Royal Asiatic Soc.* vol. III, 1832.)

Narrative of events that have recently occurred in the island of Ceylon. 1815.

PERCIVAL, Captain ROBERT. An account of the island of Ceylon, containing its history, geography, natural history, with the manners and customs of its various inhabitants; to which is added, the Journal of an embassy to the Court of Candy. London, 1805.

PHILALETHES. A history of Ceylon...to the year 1815. 4to. 1817.

TURNOUR, GEORGE. An epitome of the history of Ceylon. 1836.

B. SECONDARY WORKS

BENNETT, JOHN WHITCHURCH. Ceylon, and its capabilities. 1843.

CAMPBELL, Lieut.-Col. JAMES. Excursions, adventures, and field-sports in Ceylon; its commercial and military importance, and numerous advantages to the British emigrant. 2 vols. 1843.

Ceylon: a general description of the island: historical, physical, statistical, by an officer, late of the Ceylon Rifles. 2 vols.

KNIGHTON, W. History of Ceylon. 1845.

MARSHALL, HENRY. Ceylon: a general sketch. 1846.

PRIDHAM, CHARLES. An historical, political and statistical account of Ceylon and its dependencies. 2 vols. 1849.

TENNENT, Sir JAMES EMERSON. Ceylon. 3rd ed. 2 vols. 1859.

CHAPTER XXV

THE REVENUE ADMINISTRATION OF BENGAL, 1765–86

A. ORIGINAL MATERIALS

MANUSCRIPT

The principal series are: Proceedings of the Committee of Circuit; Proceeding of the Committee of Revenue, 1772–1774; Proceedings of the Committee of Revenue, 1774–1781 (Governor-General's Proceedings); Public Proceedings, 1772–1779 (Home Department); Proceedings of the Committee of Revenue, 1781–1786; Report of Messrs Anderson, Croftes and Bogle, dated March 1781 (Government of Bengal Records, Revenue Department), and Reports of Mr John David Patterson on the Office of Kanungo dated 23 April 1781, and 18 May 1787, respectively (Government of Bengal Records, Revenue Department). The text used is that of the Imperial, and the Government of Bengal, records. See the *Hand-book to the records of the Government of India*, and the *Catalogue of the English records of the Government of Bengal*. For the series at the India Office see Foster, *Guide*, pp. 50–3.

PRINTED DOCUMENTS

Bengal Dt. Records. Chittagong. Vol. I. 1760–1773. 1923.
—— Midnapur. 3 vols. 1911–25.
—— Rangpur. Vol. I. 1770–1779. Vol. II. 1779–1782 Received. Vol. III. 1783–1785 Received. Vol. IV. 1779–1785 Sent.
—— Sylhet. 4 vols.
Bengal Government Records. Press List, Series I. Vol. II. Committee of Circuit, 1772–1773. Vol. IV. Revenue Proceedings, 1775. Vol. V. Revenue Proceedings, 1776. Supplement, 1771–1775.
—— Press List, Series II. Vol. I. Intermediate Rev. Authorities, 1765–1773. Vol. II. Intermediate Rev. Authorities, 1769–1774.
—— Press List, Series III. Vol. I. Controlling Correspondence of Commerce, 1771–1773. Vol. II. Board of Trade, 1774–1776.
—— I. Resident's Letter Bks, 1769–70. II. Controlling Council, 1770. III–VIII. Controlling Council, 1771. VII A. Controlling Council, 1771. IX. Controlling Council, 1772. X, XI, XII. Controlling Council, 1772–1774.
—— Copy-Book of the Supervisor of Rajshahi at Nator. Letters issued 30 Dec. 1769–15 Sept. 1772. 1925.
COLEBROOKE, Sir J. E. Digest of the laws and regulations. 1807.
FRANCIS, P. Original minutes of the Governor-General and Council of Fort William on the settlement and collection of the revenues of Bengal. 1782.
HALHED, NATHANIEL BRASSEY. A code of Gentoo laws. 1781.
HARRINGTON. Analysis of the Bengal Regulations. 3 vols. 1805.
LONG, J. Selections from the unpublished records of Government, 1748–67. Calcutta, 1869.
Proceedings of the Governor and Council of Fort William respecting the administration of justice amongst the natives in Bengal. 4to. 1774.
SMYTH, D. C. Original Bengalese Zumindaree Accounts. Calcutta, 1823.

CONTEMPORARY PUBLICATIONS

AMIR HAIDAR BILGRAMI. Dissertation concerning the revenues. Persian text, and trans. by F. Gladwin. 1796.
BOLTS, WILLIAM. Considerations on Indian affairs. 3 vols. 1772–5.
Plan for the Government of the Provinces of Bengal, addressed to the Directors of the E.I.C. 1772.
SCRAFTON, L. Observations on Mr. Vansittart's Narrative. n.d.
VANSITTART, H. Narrative of the transactions in Bengal. 3 vols. London, 1766.
VERELST, H. View of the rise... of the English Government in Bengal. 1772.

B. SECONDARY WORKS

For general works see the list at p. 624 *supra*.

ASCOLI, F. D. Early revenue history of Bengal and the fifth report. 1917.
BADEN-POWELL, B. H. Land-systems of British India. 3 vols. 1892.
COTTON, HENRY. Memorandum on the revenue history of Chittagong. 1880.
FIRMINGER, Rev. W. K. Introduction to his edition of the fifth report from the Select Committee of the House of Commons. 3 vols. Calcutta, 1917.
GLEIG, G. R. Memoirs of Warren Hastings. 3 vols. 1841.

RAMSBOTHAM, R. B. Studies in the Land Revenue History of Bengal 1769–1787. 1926.
RAY, S. C. Land revenue administration in India.
THOMPSON, W. H. Final settlement of Tippera and Noakhali. Calcutta, 1922.
WILSON, H. H. Glossary of judicial and revenue terms. 1855.
Zemindary Settlement of Bengal. 2 vols. Calcutta, 1879.

CHAPTER XXVI

THE BENGAL ADMINISTRATIVE SYSTEM, 1786–1818

A. ORIGINAL MATERIALS

MANUSCRIPT

India Office Records. Despatches to Bengal, vols. 15–94. (Index: vols. 3–10.) Letters received from Bengal, vols. 25–91. Home Miscellaneous Series, especially volumes 359, 372, 380–4. Bengal, Revenue Consultations, *passim*. Bengal, Judicial Consultations, *passim*.
Public Record Office. Cornwallis Correspondence, bundles 8–59. Chatham Papers, bundles 125, 362.

PRINTED DOCUMENTS

Bengal, Fort St George and Bombay Regulations 1813 to 1824.
Bengal Dt. Records. Dinajpur. Vol I, 1787–1789. 1914. Vol. II, 1786–1788. 1924.
COLEBROOKE, Sir J. E. Digest of the Regulations...of...Bengal. 3 vols. Calcutta, 1807.
Fifth Report...1812. Parl. Papers 1812. VII, 1. (Ed. by W. K. Firminger. 3 vols. Calcutta, 1917.)
HARRINGTON, J. H. Analysis of the Bengal Regulations. 3 vols. 1805.
Minutes of evidence taken before the Select Committee on the Affairs of the East India Company. Vol. III, Revenue. Parl. Papers 1831–2. XI, 1. Vol. IV, Judicial. Parl. Papers 1831–2. XII, 1.
Papers relating to the administration of justice in Bengal. Parl. Papers 1819. XIII, 479.
Regulations for Bengal, Behar and Orissa, 1793–1794. 1795.
ROSS, C. Correspondence of...Marquess Cornwallis. 3 vols. London, 1859.
Second Report from the Select Committee on the Affairs of the East India Company. 1810. Parl. Papers 1810. V, 13.
Selection of Papers from the records at the East India House. 4 vols. London, 1820–6.
Wellesley Despatches. 5 vols. 1836.

CONTEMPORARY PUBLICATIONS

[GALLOWAY, Sir ARCHIBALD.] Observations on the law and constitution of India, on the nature of landed tenures, and on the system of revenue and finance, as established by the Moohummadan law and Moghul government, with an enquiry into the revenue and judicial administration and regulations of police at present existing in Bengal. 1825.
[GREVILLE, J.] British India analyzed. 3 vols. 1795.
History of the Adawlat System in Bengal. 1820.
ROUSE-BOUGHTON, C. W. Dissertation concerning the landed property of Bengal. 1791.

41

B. SECONDARY WORKS

Ascoli, F. D. Early revenue history of Bengal and the fifth report. 1917.

Aspinall, A. The administrative and judicial reforms of Lord Cornwallis in Bengal. (An unpublished thesis.)

Baden-Powell, B. H. Land systems of British India. 3 vols. 1892.

Bradley-Birt, F. B. Sylhet Thackeray. 1911.

Hunter, Sir William Wilson. Bengal MS Records...letters in the Board of Revenue, Calcutta, 1782–1807. 4 vols. 1894.

—— Annals of rural Bengal. 1897.

Kaye, Sir J. W. Administration of the East India Company. 1853.

Minto, Lady. Lord Minto in India. 1880.

Morris, Henry. Life of Charles Grant. 1904.

Prinsep, H. T. Political and military transactions in India during the administration of the Marquess of Hastings. 2 vols. 1825.

Ray, S. C. Land revenue administration in India.

Teignmouth, Lord. Memoirs of Lord Teignmouth. 2 vols. 1843.

—— Memoirs of the life, writings and correspondence of Sir William Jones. 2 vols. 1835.

Twining, Thomas. Travels in India a hundred years ago. 1893.

Walpole, Sir S. History of England. Vol. VI. 1898.

Wilson, H. H. Glossary of judicial and revenue terms. 1855.

Zemindary Settlement of Bengal. 2 vols. Calcutta, 1879.

CHAPTER XXVII

THE MADRAS DISTRICT SYSTEM AND LAND REVENUE TO 1818

A. ORIGINAL MATERIALS

Manuscript

The main sources of information are the Revenue Consultations of the Madras Council from 1774; the records of the Board of Assigned Revenue 1781–85; and the records of the Board of Revenue from 1786. See Foster, *Guide*, pp. 76–7, and the *Madras Catalogue of records in the Revenue Department*. Copies of the judicial and revenue minutes of Sir Thomas Munro are at the British Museum (Add. MSS, 22077–9). For the records of the Nawab of the Carnatic see p. 635 *supra*.

Printed Documents

Arbuthnot, Sir A. J. Sir Thomas Munro: selections from his minutes. 2nd ed. Madras, 1886.

Baramahal Records. 7 vols. Fo. Madras, 1907–20.

Fifth Report...1812. Parl. Papers, 1812, vol. VII. (Ed. by W. K. Firminger. 3 vols. Calcutta, 1917.)

General Reports of the Madras Board of Revenue. (Printed for official use but not published.)

Huddlestone. Papers on mirassi tenures.

Irwin, Eyles. A collection of letters chiefly between the Madras Government and Eyles Irwin, 1781–85. Madras, 1888.

Minutes of evidence taken before the Select Committee on the affairs of the East India Company. Parl. Papers, 1831–2, XI–XII (especially the evidence of A. D. Campbell and Hodgson).

Mysorean Revenue Regulations. 1792.

Papers relating to the village panchayat and other judicial systems of administration. Fo. Madras, 1916.

Poligar Peshkash. Parl. Papers, 1808, XIII.

RAMASAWMY NAIDOO, B. Memoir on the internal revenue system of the Madras Presidency. (Selection from the records of the South Arcot district.) Cuddalore, 1870.

Regulations of the Presidency of Fort St George.

Reports of the Committee of Circuit (printed for official use but not published).

Second Report from the Select Committee on the affairs of the East India Company. 1810. Parl. Papers, 1810, v.

Selection of papers from the records at the India House. 4 vols. 1820–6.

CONTEMPORARY PUBLICATIONS

BUCHANAN, F. Journey through Mysore and southern India. 3 vols. 1807.

DU BOIS, Abbé. Hindu manners and customs. 1816. (Reprinted 1897, etc.)

FULLARTON, Col. View of the British interests in southern India. 1787.

HEYNE, BENJAMIN. Tracts, historical and statistical, on India; with journals of several tours through various parts of the peninsula. 1814.

SULIVAN, JOHN. Observations respecting the Circar of Masulipatam. Sm. 4to. 1780.

B. SECONDARY WORKS

For general works see the list at p. 624 *supra*.

BADEN-POWELL, B. H. Land systems of British India. 3 vols. 1892.

BRADSHAW, JOHN. Sir Thomas Munro. Oxford, 1906.

BRIGGS, Gen. JOHN. Land-tax in India. 1830.

District Gazetteers of the Madras Presidency. 25 vols. Madras.

GLEIG, G. R. Life and correspondence of Sir Thomas Munro. 3 vols. 1830.

PEARSON, HUGH. Memoirs of the life and correspondence of Christian Frederick Swartz. 2 vols. 1834.

RAY, S. C. Land revenue administration in India.

SRINIVASA RAGHAVA AIYANGAR. Forty years' progress of the Presidency of Madras. Madras, 1892.

SUNDARARAJA AIYANGAR, S. Land tenures in the Madras Presidency. Madras, 1916.

WILKS, MARK. Historical sketches of the south of India. 3 vols. 1810–17.

WILSON, H. H. Glossary of judicial and revenue terms. 1855.

CHAPTER XXVIII

AFGHANISTAN, RUSSIA AND PERSIA

A. ORIGINAL MATERIALS

MANUSCRIPT

The chief authorities are the Political Proceedings of the Government of India, at the India Office and the Imperial Record Office, and the Foreign Office series *Russia* and *Persia*, at the Public Record Office. Of these the Government of India papers are not, while the Foreign Office papers are, generally, accessible to the student. Besides these there are three private collections of great importance:

(1) The Ellenborough Papers at the Record Office. This vast mass of documents has now been arranged as follows: Files 1–36 miscellaneous loose letters and papers; files 37–69, letters to Lord Ellenborough from April, 1841, to July, 1844, from various men of note such as the Prince Consort, the Duke of Wellington, Sir

Robert Peel, and the various higher officials in India, *e.g.* Sir C. Napier, Major-General Pollock, Major-General Nott, the Commander-in-Chief, and Major Sleeman; files 70–73, miscellaneous papers, civil, European, military, political; files 74–106, letters from Lord Ellenborough to various important Indian officials and to the Secret Committee and Court of Directors; files 107–110, miscellaneous letters, civil, European, military and political. Some of these letters have been printed, others have not.

(2) The Broughton Papers at the British Museum. This collection of the correspondence and papers of John Cam Hobhouse, first Baron Broughton, fills 29 volumes, and was bequeathed to the British Museum at his death in 1869 with the condition that it was to be sealed up till the year 1900. It forms Add. MSS 36455–83. The important volumes are 36467–72, his general correspondence relating to the time when he was at the Board of Control; 36473–4, April, 1835–May, 1841, correspondence with Lord Heytesbury and then mainly with Lord Auckland. There are enclosures relating to Central Asia, Afghanistan.

(3) The Auckland Papers at the British Museum. This collection of thirty volumes of letters, books, and minute books forms Add. MSS 37689–718. Of these numbers 37689–707 consist of confidential letters to various eminent men; they run from 13 March, 1836 to 16 February, 1842. At folio 174 in 37707 is a letter (a little out of its right date) from Lord Auckland to Lord Ellenborough giving an account of recent events in Afghanistan. 37708 contains copies of a few letters from Lord Auckland to Sir Charles Metcalfe and others running from 24 September, 1836, to 3 April, 1837. 37709–13. Five volumes of minutes and memoranda by Lord Auckland, from 11 April, 1836, to 30 December, 1840.

PRINTED DOCUMENTS

Afghan War. Parl. Papers, 1839, XL, 29, 139, 159, 207, 217, 241, 269, 317; L, 89; 1840, XXXVII, 137; 1842, XLV, 125; 1843, XXXVII, 1, 3, 13, 17; 1859 (Session 2), XXV, 7 (Burnes's correspondence).
COLCHESTER, Lord. Indian administration of Lord Ellenborough. 1874.
LAW, Sir ALGERNON. India under Lord Ellenborough. 1926.

CONTEMPORARY PUBLICATIONS

ABBOT, Capt. J. Journey from Heraut to Khiva, Moscow and St. Petersburg. 2 vols. 1843. 3rd ed. 1884.
ATKINSON, JAMES. Expedition into Afghanistan 1839–40. 1842.
—— Sketches in Afghanistan. Fol. 1842.
BARR, Lieut. WILLIAM. Journal of a march from Delhi to...Cabul with the mission of Sir C. M. Wade. 1844.
Bengal Civilian. Lord Auckland and Lord Ellenborough. 1845.
Bengal Officer. Recollections of the first campaign west of the Indus. 1845.
BRYDGES, Sir HARFORD JONES. Account of H.M.'s mission to the Court of Persia in the years 1807–11. 1834.
BUIST, GEORGE. Outline of the operations of the British troops in Scinde and Afghanistan 1838–41. Bombay, 1843.
BURNES, ALEXANDER. Travels into Bokhara, etc. 3 vols. 1834.
—— Cabool: being a personal narrative. 1842.
CONOLLY, ARTHUR. Journey to the north of India overland from England. 2 vols. 1834.
CUMMING, Lieutenant JAMES SLATOR. (H.M.'s 9th.) Six years' diary. 1847.
Defence of Jellalabad...Drawn on stone by W. L. Walton. Fol. 1846.
DENNIE, WILLIAM H. Personal narrative of the campaigns in Afghanistan. Dublin, 1843.
ELPHINSTONE, MOUNTSTUART. Account of the kingdom of Caboul. 4to. 1815.
Étude diplomatique sur la guerre de Crimée. 1878.
EVANS, Lt.-Col. DE LACY. The designs of Russia. 1828.
—— On the practicability of an invasion of British India. 1829.

EYRE, Sir VINCENT. Military operations at Cabul, in January 1842. 1843. Ed. by G. B. M(alleson). 1879, under title "The Kabul Insurrection".
—— A retrospect of the Affghan War. 1869.
FANE, Col. H. E. Five years in India. 2 vols. 1842.
FERRIER, J. P. Caravan journeys...in Persia, Afghanistan, Turkistan, and Beloochistan. Translated by Captain W. Jesse. 1856.
FORSTER, GEORGE. Journey from Bengal to England through the northern part of India, Kashmire, Afghanistan, and Persia. 2 vols. 1798.
GLEIG, G. R. Operations of Sale's brigade. 1846.
GREENWOOD, J. Narrative of the late victorious campaign in Afghanistan under General Pollock. 1844.
GRIFFITH, W. Journals of travels. 1847.
GROVER, Captain. The Bokhara victims. 1845.
HALL, J. H. W. Scenes in a soldier's life (1839–43). 1848.
HARLAN, J. A memoir of India and Avghanistaun, with observations on the present exciting and critical state and future prospects of those countries. Philadelphia, 1842.
HAVELOCK, Capt. HENRY. Narrative of the war in Affghanistan in 1838–39. 2 vols. 1840.
[HOLDSWORTH, T. W. E.] The campaign of the Indus. 1840.
HOLME, F. Anglo-Indian policy during and since the Afghan War. Edinburgh, 1845.
HOUGH, Major W. Narrative of the march and operations of the Army of the Indus...1838–9. 1841.
India, Great Britain and Russia. 1838.
KENNEDY, R. H. Narrative of the campaign of the army of the Indus. 2 vols. 1840.
LAWRENCE, Sir GEORGE. Forty-three years in India. 1874.
Letters on recent events in India. 1842.
LOGIN, Dr J. S. Facts relating to Herat.
MACGREGOR, C. Report on the causes of the Caubul outbreak.
MALCOLM, Sir JOHN. Sketches of Persia. 1845.
MASSON, CHARLES. Narrative of a journey to Kalat. 1843.
—— Narrative of various journeys in Balochistan, Afghanistan and the Punjab. 3 vols. 1842.
MEYENDORFF, Baron G. DE. Voyage d'Orembourg à Boukhara, 1820. 1826.
Military service and adventure in the far East. 1847.
MOHAN LAL. Travels in the Panjab, Afghanistan, etc. 1846.
—— Life of Dost Mahomed. 2 vols. 1846.
MOSLEY, J. Russia in the right. 1853.
Narrative of the recent war in Affghanistan. By an officer in the H.E.I.C.'s service. 1842.
NASH, C. History of the war in Afghanistan. 1843.
NEILL, J. M. B. Recollections of four years' service in the East. 1845.
OUTRAM, Capt. JAMES. Rough notes of the campaign in Sinde and Afghanistan 1838–39. 1840.
PRICE, WILLIAM. Journal of the British embassy to Persia. 2 vols. Sm. oblong Fol. 1825.
Report of the East India Committee of the Colonial Society on the causes and consequences of the Affghan War. 1842.
Royal Engineer Papers. Vols. IV and VI.
SALE, Lady. Journal of the disasters in Afghanistan. 1843.
SHAHAMAT 'ALI. Picturesque sketches in India, with notices of the adjacent countries of Sindh, Multan, and the West of India. n.d.
STACY, L. R. Narrative...whilst in the Brahoe campaign. Serampore, 1844.
—— Narrative of services...in the years 1840, 1841, and 1842. 1848.
STOCQUELER, J. H. Memorials of Affghanistan. 1842.
URQUHART, DAVID. Exposition of transactions in Central Asia through which the independence of states and the affections of people, barriers to the British possessions in India, have been sacrificed to Russia by...Palmerston.... 1840.

VIGNE, G. T. A personal Narrative of a visit to Ghuzni, Kabul, and Afghanistan, and of a residence at the Court of Dost Mohamad. 1840.

WOLFF, REV. JOSEPH. Narrative of a mission to Bokhara. 2 vols. 1845.

Note. Much information is contained in contemporary periodicals, *e.g.* the *Quarterly Review* (especially vols. 64, 78), the *Edinburgh Review, Blackwood's Magazine,* the *Revue des deux Mondes* (1840–3), the *Asiatic Journal,* the *Calcutta Review,* and the *Calcutta Monthly Journal.*

B. SECONDARY WORKS

For general works see the list at p. 624 *supra.*

BELLEW, H. W. Afghanistan and the Afghans. 1879.

—— The races of Afghanistan. 1880.

BROADFOOT, Major W. Career of Major George Broadfoot in Afghanistan and the Panjab. 1888.

BROUGHTON, Lord. Recollections of a long life. 6 vols. 1909–11.

BURNES, JAMES. Notes on his name and family (including a memoir of Sir Alexander Burnes). Edinburgh, 1851.

COLVIN, Sir AUCKLAND. John Russell Colvin. 1895.

CURZON, Lord. Russia in Central Asia in 1889. 1889.

DAVIS, H. W. C. The Great Game in Asia—1800–1844. [1927.]

DURAND, Sir H. MARION. The first Afghan War and its causes. 2 vols. 1879.

DURAND, H. M. Life of Major-Gen. Sir Henry Marion Durand. 2 vols. 1883.

EDWARDES, Sir H. B. and MERIVALE, HERMAN. Life of Sir Henry Lawrence. 2 vols. 1872.

FERRIER, J. P. History of the Afghans. Trans. by Captain W. Jesse. 1858.

FORREST, G. W. Life of Sir Neville Chamberlain. 1909.

GARDNER, ALEXANDER. Memoirs. Ed. by Col. Hugh Pearse. 1898.

GOLDSMID, Sir F. J. James Outram 1802–63. 2 vols. 1881.

GRIFFIN, Sir LEPEL. Ranjit Singh. 1911.

HELLWALD, F. VON. The Russians in Central Asia. Tr. by Wirgman. 1874.

HUME, J. Selections from the writings...of the late H. W. Torrens. 2 vols. Calcutta, 1853.

JOHNSON, Capt. "Diary." (*Blackwood's Magazine*, March, 1906.)

KAYE, JOHN WILLIAM. Memorials of Indian government. 1853.

—— Life and correspondence of Henry St. George Tucker. 1854.

—— Life and correspondence of Sir John Malcolm. 2 vols. 1856.

—— Lives of Indian officers. 2 vols. 1889.

—— History of the war in Afghanistan. 3 vols. 1878.

LAYARD, Sir HENRY. Autobiography and letters. 2 vols. 1903.

LOW, C. R. Life of Sir George Pollock. 1873.

—— The Afghan War 1838–42. From the journal and correspondence of Major-Gen. A. Abbott. 1879.

McNEILL, Sir JOHN. Memoir of —— and of his second wife Elizabeth Wilson by their grand-daughter. 1910.

MALLESON, G. B. History of Afghanistan. 1878.

MARSHMAN, J. C. Memoirs of...Sir Henry Havelock. 3rd ed. 1867.

MILLER, HUGH. Conclusion of the war in Affghanistan. Edinburgh, 1870.

MORIARTY, G. P. Cambridge History of Foreign Policy. Vol. II, pp. 199–214. 1923.

RAIT, ROBERT S. Life of Lord Gough. 2 vols. 1903.

RAVERTY, Major H. G. Notes on Afghanistan and part of Beluchistan. Fol. 1883.

RAWLINSON, Sir HENRY. England and Russia in the East. 1875.

RAWLINSON, H. G. Indian historical studies. 1913.

SKRINE, F. H. The expansion of Russia. Cambridge, 1915.

SMITH, Sir HARRY. Autobiography. 2 vols. 1902.

SMITH, R. B. Life of Lord Lawrence. 2 vols. 1883.

STOCQUELER, J. H. Life of Sir William Nott. 2 vols. 8vo. 1854.

SYKES, Sir PERCY. History of Persia. 2nd ed. 2 vols. 1921.

TEER, EDWARD. Siege of Jellalabad. 1904.

THORBURN, S. S. Asiatic neighbours. 1894.

CHAPTER XXIX

THE CONQUEST OF SIND

A. ORIGINAL MATERIALS.

MANUSCRIPT

The principal source of information consists of the Political Proceedings of the Government of Bengal to 1834, and thereafter of the Government of India. These are not fully accessible to the student; but this disadvantage is partially made good by the Ellenborough MSS at the Public Record Office (see note at p. 643 *supra*).

PRINTED DOCUMENTS

COLCHESTER, Lord. Indian administration of Lord Ellenborough. 1874.
JACOB, Gen. JOHN. Record-book of the Scinde Irregular Horse. 1853–56.
Jagirs in Sind. Bombay Records, new series, no. 66. 1862.
LAW, Sir ALGERNON. India under Lord Ellenborough. 1926.
Memoirs on Shikarpur, etc. Bombay Records, new series, no. 17. 1855.
Parl. Papers, 1839, XL, 139; 1840, XXXVII, 129; 1843, XXXIX, 1, 9, 45; 1844, XXXVI, 511; 1846, XXXI, 375; 1847, XLI, 395, 421; 1852, XXXVI, 255.

CONTEMPORARY PUBLICATIONS

Affairs of Scinde. 1844.
BRYDGES, Sir HARFORD JONES. The Ameers of Scinde. 1843.
BUIST, GEORGE. Correction of a few of the errors contained in Sir W. Napier's Life of... Sir Charles Napier. 1857.
BURNES, JAMES. Narrative of a visit to the Court of Sinde at Hyderabad on the Indus, illustrated with plates and a map (pp. xviii, 168). 3rd ed. with A sketch of the history of Cutch (pp. xviii and 74). Edinburgh and London, 1839.
BURTON, R. Sindh the Unhappy Valley. 2 vols. 1851.
[EASTWICK, Capt. EDWARD.] Dry leaves from young Egypt. 1851.
EDWARDS, Lt. WILLIAM. Sketches in Scinde. Fol. 1846.
NAPIER, RICHARD. Remarks on Lt.-Col. Outram's work entitled "Our conquest of Sinde, a commentary". 1847.
NAPIER, Sir WILLIAM. The conquest of Scinde. 1845.
—— Sir Charles Napier's administration of Scinde. 1851.
—— Life of Sir Charles Napier. 4 vols. 1857.
OUTRAM, Sir JAMES. Conquest of Scinde, a commentary. Edinburgh, 1846.
—— Memoir of the public services rendered by Lt.-Col. Outram, C.B. 1853.
POSTANS, T. Personal observations on Sindh. 1843.
POTTINGER, Sir HENRY. Travels in Beloochistan and Scinde. 4to. 1816.
Scinde policy: a few comments on Major-Gen. W. F. P. Napier's defence of Lord Ellenborough's Government. 2nd ed. 1845.
SULLIVAN, J. and EASTWICK, Captain W. Speeches at the special court held at the East India House on the case of the Amirs of Sinde. 1844.
WILTON, J. H. Scenes in a soldier's life... in Scinde etc. 1839–43. 8vo. Montreal, 1848.

B. SECONDARY WORKS

For general works see the list at p. 624 *supra*.

BUTLER, Sir W. F. Sir C. J. Napier. 1894.
GOLDSMID, Sir F. J. James Outram. 2 vols. 1881.
HOLMES, T. RICE. Sir Charles Napier. 1925.
HUGHES, A. W. A Gazetteer of the Province of Sind. 2nd ed. 1876.
MACDOUGALL, Col. Sir Charles James Napier. 1860.
MORIARTY, G. P. See p. 646 *supra*.
YOUNG, Col. KEITH. Scinde in the forties. 1912.

CHAPTER XXIX

THE CONQUEST OF THE PANJAB

A. ORIGINAL MATERIALS

MANUSCRIPT

The principal source of information consists of the Political Proceedings of the Government of India, not fully accessible to the student. The Broughton MSS at the British Museum include Add. MSS 36475, correspondence with Lord Hardinge May, 1846–February, 1848, covering the first Sikh War; 36476–7, correspondence with Lord Dalhousie, January, 1848–March, 1852, covering the second Sikh War and including much of interest; 36478, correspondence with Indian officials, *e.g.* Sir Charles Napier, from 1846–1852; 36479–80, correspondence with the India House 1846–52.

PRINTED DOCUMENTS

BAIRD, J. G. Private letters of the Marquess of Dalhousie. 1910.
HARDINGE, Viscount HENRY, G.C.B. The war in India. Despatches of the Right Honourable Lt.-Gen. Viscount Hardinge, G.C.B., Governor-General of India; the Right Honourable General Lord Gough, G.C.B., Commander-in-Chief; Major-Gen. Sir Harry Smith, Bart., G.C.B., and other documents: comprising the engagements of Moodkee, Ferozeshah, Aliwal, and Sobraon. With a map of the country, and seven plans of the positions of the army. London, 1846.
Panjab Government Records. I. Delhi Residency and Agency 1807–1857. II. Ludhiana Agency 1808–1815. III. Lahore Pol. Diaries 1847–48. IV. Lahore Pol. Diaries 1846–49. V. Lahore Pol. Diaries 1847–49. VI. Lahore Pol. Diaries 1847–49. VII. Mutiny Correspondence. 2 parts. VIII. Mutiny Reports. 2 parts. IX. Birch's Note-book 1818–21.
Parl. Papers, 1839, XL, 29; 1846, XXXI, 161, 215; 1847, XLI, 173, 177; 1849, XLI, 1, 683.
SITA RAM KOHLI. Catalogue of the Khalsa Durbar Records. Vol. I (Sikh Army). 1919.

CONTEMPORARY PUBLICATIONS, ETC.

ARNOLD, EDWIN. The Marquis of Dalhousie's administration. 2 vols. 1862.
BUIST, GEORGE. Annals of India for the year 1848. Bombay, 1849.
COLEY, JAMES. Journal of the Sutlej campaign 1845–46. 1856.
COURT, Major H. History of the Sikhs. Lahore, 1888.
CUNNINGHAM, JOSEPH DAVEY. History of the Sikhs. Ed. by H. L. O. Garrett. Oxford, 1918.
DUNLOP, Dr J. Mooltan during and after the siege. 21 large tinted lithographs with descriptive text. 4to. 1849.
Economist. The annexation of the Punjab. (Repr. Lahore, 1897.)
EDWARDES, Sir H. B. A year on the Punjab frontier. 1851.
History of the campaign on the Sutlej and the war in the Punjaub. 1846.
History of the Punjab. 2 vols. 1846.
HUGEL, Baron CHARLES. Travels in Kashmir and the Panjab. 1845.
JACQUEMONT, VICTOR. Letters from India. 2 vols. 1834.
Journal of a subaltern. 1850.
LAWRENCE, Sir HENRY. Adventures of an officer in the service of Runjeet Singh. 2 vols. 1845.
—— Essays military and political. 1859.
Leaves from the journal of a subaltern during the campaign in the Punjab. Edinburgh, 1851.
McGREGOR, W. L. History of the Sikhs. 2 vols. 1846.

MALCOLM, Lieut.-Col. JOHN. Sketch of the Sikhs: a singular nation who inhabit the provinces of the Punjab, situated between the Rivers Jumna and Indus. London, 1812.

MOHAN LAL, MUNSHI. Travels in the Panjab, Afghanistan, and Turkistan, to Balk, Bokhara, and Herat; and a visit to Great Britain and Germany. 1846.

MOORCROFT, W. Travels in the Himalayan provinces of Hindostan and the Punjab. 2 vols. 1841.

ORLICH, LEOPOLD VON. Travels in India, including Sinde and the Punjab. Translated from the German by H. Evans Lloyd. 2 vols.

OSBORNE, the Hon. WILLIAM GODOLPHIN. The Court and Camp of Runjeet Sing. 1840.

PRINSEP, H. T. Origin of the Sikh power. 1834. 2nd ed. 2 vols. ?1842.

SHAHAMAT ALI. Hist. Account of the Sikhs and Afghans in connexion with India and Persia. [1847.]

STEINBACH, Lieut.-Colonel. The Punjaub, being a brief account of the country of the Sikhs; its extent, history, commerce, productions, Government, manufactures, laws, religion, etc. 1846.

THACKWELL, E. Narrative of the 2nd Sikh War. 2nd ed. 1851.

VIGNE, GODFREY T. Travels in Kashmir, Ladak, Iskardo, the countries adjoining the Mountain Course of the Indus, and the Himalaya, North of the Panjab. 2 vols. 1842.

B. SECONDARY WORKS
For general works see the list at p. 624 *supra*.

ARCHER, J. H. LAWRENCE. Commentaries on the Punjab campaign, 1848–49. 1878.

BROADFOOT, Major W. Career of Major George Broadfoot in Afghanistan and the Panjab. 1888.

BURTON, R. G. The first and second Sikh Wars. Simla, 1911.

COTTON, J. J. Life of General Avitabile. Calcutta, 1906.

EDWARDES, Sir H. B., and MERIVALE, HERMAN. Life of Sir Henry Lawrence. 2 vols. 1872.

EDWARDES, Lady. Memorials of the life of Sir H. B. Edwardes. 1886.

FIELD, D. The religion of the Sikhs. 1914.

GARDNER, ALEXANDER. Memoirs. Ed. Pearse. 1898.

GIBBON, FREDRICK P. The Lawrences in the Punjab. 1908.

GOUGH, Gen. Sir CHARLES and INNES, ARTHUR D. The Sikhs and the Sikh Wars: the rise, conquest and annexation of the Punjab State. 1897.

GRIFFIN, LEPEL H. The Rajas of the Punjab, being the history of the principal States in the Punjab, and their political relations with the British Government. 1873.

GRIFFIN, LEPEL H. and MASSEY, F. C. Chiefs and families of note in the Punjab. 3 vols. Lahore, 1909.

—— —— Ranjit Singh. Oxford, 1911.

HARDINGE, Viscount. Viscount Hardinge. Oxford, 1891.

INNES, J. J. McL. Sir Henry Lawrence. Oxford, 1898.

LATIF, SAYYID MUHAMMAD. History of the Panjab, from the remotest antiquity to the present time. Calcutta, 1891.

LEE-WARNER, Sir WILLIAM. Life of the Marquis of Dalhousie. 2 vols. 1904.

MACAULIFFE, M. The Sikh religion. 1909.

RAIT, R. S. Life of...Sir Frederick Haines. 1911.

SITA RAM KOHLI. "The army of Ranjit Singh." (*Journ. Indian Hist.* Feb. and Sept. 1922.)

SMITH, R. BOSWORTH. Life of Lord Lawrence. 6th ed. 2 vols. 1885.

SMYTH, Major G. CARMICHAEL. A history of the reigning family of Lahore, with some account of the Jummoo Rajahs, the Seik soldiers and their Sirdars: with notes on Malcolm, Prinsep, Lawrence, Steinbach, McGregor and the Calcutta Review. Calcutta, 1847.

THORBURN, S. S. The Punjab in peace and war. 1904.

WYLLY, Col. H. C. Military memoirs of Lt.-Gen. Sir Joseph Thackwell. 1908.

CHAPTER XXX

BURMA, 1782–1852

A. ORIGINAL MATERIALS

MANUSCRIPT

Bengal Secret and Political Consultations, years 1812, 1813, 1823, India Office copies.

Government of India, Foreign Dept., Secret and Political Consultations of 1829–52, including correspondence on the Ava residency, proposed retrocession of Tenasserim, journeys to the jade mines, Assam frontier, journals of Major Burney and other officers in charge of the residency, events leading up to the 1852 war, etc.

ARAKAN. Some one hundred and ninety volumes of correspondence, 1823–52, in the office of the Commissioner of Arakan, Akyab. The only reprint is *Précis of the Old Records (1823–4) of Historical Interest in the Office of the Commissioner of Arakan*, publ. Superintendent, Government printing, Rangoon, 1922.

TENASSERIM. Some ninety volumes of correspondence, 1825–52, in the office of the Commissioner of Tenasserim, Moulmein. The only reprints are by Mr J. S. Furnivall, I.C.S., *Correspondence for the years 1825–26 to 1842–43 in the office of the Commissioner, Tenasserim Division*, publ. Superintendent, Government printing, Rangoon, 1915, and *Selected Correspondence of Letters issued from and received in the office of the Commissioner, Tenasserim Division, for the years 1825–26 to 1842–43*, publ. *ibid.* 1916.

Eighty autograph letters of Lord Dalhousie to Sir Arthur Phayre 1852–6, in possession of the University of Rangoon.

Letters of Thomas Spears, Government Correspondent at the Court of Ava, to Captain Arthur Phayre, Commissioner of Pegu, 1854–60, in the Imperial Record Dept., Calcutta.

Journal of Sir Arthur Phayre 1852–9, two vols., in possession of the University of Rangoon.

RICHARDSON, DAVID. Journals, Burma. 1829–35. British Museum, Add. MS, 30354.

PRINTED DOCUMENTS

BAIRD, J. G. A. Private letters of the Marquess of Dalhousie. 1910.

CRAWFURD, J. Journal of an embassy from the Governor General of India to the Court of Ava (1826). 2 vols. 1834.

KONBAUNGSET YAZAWIN. Mandalay. 1905. (The standard vernacular Burmese chronicle from 1752.)

McLEOD, W. C. Journal of a mission from Moulmein to the Frontiers of China, 1836–37. 1869.

Papers relating to the first Burma War 1812–24. Parl. Papers, Session 1825, XXIV, 91.

Papers relating to the second Burma War. Parl. Papers, Session 1852, XXXVI, 139; 1852–3, LXIX, 351.

Papers relating to the route of Captain W. C. McLeod from Moulmein to the frontier of China and to the route of Dr Richardson on his fourth mission to the Shan provinces of Burma, or extracts from the same. Parl. Papers, Session 1868–9, XLVI, 281 *sqq.*

PEMBERTON, R. B. Report on the Eastern Frontier of British India...with a supplement by Dr Bayfield on the British Political Relations with Ava. Calcutta, 1835.

Report on the Progress of Arakan under British rule from 1826 to 1869. Rangoon, 1874.

SYMES, M. Account of an embassy to the kingdom of Ava. 4to. 1800.

WILSON, H. H. Documents illustrative of the Burmese War. 1827.

YULE, HENRY. Mission to the Court of Ava in 1855. 1858.

CONTEMPORARY PUBLICATIONS

ALEXANDER, Major-General Sir J. E. Travels from India to England comprising a visit to the Burman Empire. 4to. 1827.

BUCHANAN, FRANCIS. Religion and literature of the Burmas. Ap. Asiatic Researches, 1835.

[BUTLER, Major JOHN.] Sketch of the services of the Madras European Regt. during the Burmese War by an officer of the corps. 1839.

BUTLER, J. Travels and adventures in the Province of Assam during a residence of fourteen years. 1855.

Cox, H. Journal of a residence in the Burman Empire. 1821.

DOVETON, F. B. Reminiscences of the Burmese War in 1824-5-6. 1852.

GOUGER, H. Personal narrative of two years' imprisonment in Burmah. 1860.

GRIERSON, T. Select views of the seat of war. Oblong fol. Calcutta, 1825.

HAVELOCK, H. Memoir of the three campaigns of Major-General Sir Archibald Campbell's army in Ava. Serampore, 1828.

JUDSON, Mrs. An account of the American Baptist Mission to the Burman Empire. 1823.

LAURIE, Col. W. F. B. The second Burmese War. 1853.

—— Pegu, being a narrative of events during the second Burmese War. 1854.

—— Our Burmese wars and relations with Burma. 1885.

MARRYAT, Captain F. Olla Podrida. 1840.

MARSHALL, J. Narrative of the naval operations in Ava, during the Burmese War, in the years 1824, 1825, and 1826. 1830.

Maulmain Chronicle, The. Jan. 1849 to April 1850 (and other volumes).

MOORE, Lt. JOSEPH. Eighteen coloured views taken at or near Rangoon. Fol. 1825-6.

ROBERTSON, T. C. Political Incidents of the first Burmese War. 1853.

SNODGRASS, Major JOHN JAMES. The Burmese War. 1827.

[TRANT, Capt. THOMAS A.] Two years in Ava 1824-26. 8vo. 1827.

WHITE, Capt. W. A political history of the extraordinary events which led to the Burmese War. 1827.

B. SECONDARY WORKS

British Burma Gazetteer. 2 vols. Rangoon, 1879-80.

GAIT, E. A. A History of Assam. Calcutta, 1906. New ed. 1927.

HALL, D. G. E. Early English Intercourse with Burma. 1928.

LEE-WARNER, Sir WILLIAM. The Life of the Marquis of Dalhousie. 2 vols. 1904.

STEBBING, E. P. The Forests of India. 3 vols. 1922.

WAYLAND, F. A Memoir of the Life and Labours of the Rev. Adoniram Judson, D.D. 2 vols. Boston and London, 1853.

CHAPTER XXXI

THE INDIAN STATES, 1818-57

A. ORIGINAL MATERIALS

MANUSCRIPT

The principal source of information—the proceedings of the Government of India—is not generally accessible. In some degree this is made good by the large number of Parliamentary Papers, see *Printed Documents, infra*; and a good deal of matter occurs in the Home Miscellaneous series, see Hill's *India Office Records, Home Miscellaneous Series, passim*.

The chief private collections in which information may be sought are those described at p. 643 *supra*.

PRINTED DOCUMENTS

AITCHISON. Treaties. See p. 623 *supra.*

BAIRD, J. G. A. Private letters of the Marquess of Dalhousie. 1910.

COLCHESTER, Lord. Indian administration of Lord Ellenborough. 1874.

HASTINGS, Marquess of. Private journal. 2 vols. 1858.

JENKINS, RICHARD. Report 27th July 1826 on the territories of the Raja of Nagpore. 4to. Calcutta, 1827.

LAW, Sir ALGERNON. India under Lord Ellenborough. 1926.

LOGAN, W. Collection of treaties...relating to British affairs in Malabar. Sm. fol. Calicut, 1879.

Mysore Commissioner. Selections from the records. Bangalore, 1864.

Papers respecting a reform in the administration of the Nawab Wazir 1808–15. 1824. (Printed by the East India Company.)

Parliamentary Papers. Native States. General. 1831–2, XIV; 1844, XXXVI, 143, 165, 167; 1849, XXXIX, 135; 1850, XLI, 395.

    Annexations. 1856, XLV, 101; 1857–8, XLII, 151; 1859 (Session 2), XXV, 1.

    Baroda. Memorial of Crishna Rao Withul, 1847–8, XLVIII, 137. Correspondence, 1850, XLI, 41. Outram's removal, 1852, XXXVII, parts I and II. Corrupt practices, 1852–3, LXX–LXXIII. Guarantee to subjects of the Guicowar, 1852–3, LXIX, 255. Letters regarding succession, 1856, XLV, 161.

    Hyderabad. Cession of territory, 1854, XLVII, 263.

    Jhansi. Annexation, 1854–5, XL, 45.

    Nagpur. Annexation, 1854, XLVIII, 317. Correspondence, 1856, XLV, 37.

    Oudh. Bankers' claims, 1834, XLIV, 53, 101. Succession, 1837–8, XLI, 381, 411; 1839, XXXIX, 191. Loans from the king, and papers of 1855–6, XLV, 341, 659. Annexation, 1857 (Session 1), XI, 109.

    Satara. Commission of enquiry, etc., 1836, 1843, XXXVIII, 1, 109; Correspondence, 1839–44, 1844, XXXVI, 345. Correspondence, 1845, XXXIV, 433. Proceedings, 1846, XXXI, 347, 351, 373. Correspondence, 1838–47, 1847, XLI, 291, 315, 327. 339. Correspondence, 1846–48, 1847–8, XLVIII, 321, 379, 423. Correspondence, 1849, XXXIX, 137. Correspondence, 1850, XLI, 189, 203. Correspondence, 1851, XLI, 735, 741. Proceedings, 1852–3, LXIX, 535.

    Sindhia. Correspondence, 1805–20, 1844, XXXVI, 455. Correspondence, 1843–4, XXXVI, 165.

Pecuniary transactions of Messrs Palmer and Co. with the Nizam. Printed by the East India Company. 1824.

PLOWDEN, TREVOR CHICHELE. Précis of correspondence relating to the affairs of Mysore 1799–1878. Calcutta, 1878.

WILKS, M. Administration of Mysore. Calcutta, 1805.

CONTEMPORARY PUBLICATIONS

ARNOLD, Sir EDWIN. The Marquis of Dalhousie's administration of British India. 2 vols. 8vo. 1862.

BOILEAU, Lt. A. H. E. Personal narrative of a tour through the western states of Rajwara in 1835. 4to. Calcutta, 1837.

BRIGGS, H. G. The Nizam. 2 vols. 1861.

FRASER, HASTINGS. Our faithful ally the Nizam. 1865.

Historical sketch of the princes of India...by an officer in the service of the H.E.I.C. Edinburgh, 1833.

HOUGH, Major WILLIAM. History of the Bhopal principality. Calcutta, 1845.

JACKSON, Sir CHARLES. A vindication of the Marquis of Dalhousie's Indian administration. 1865.

JONES, B. S. Papers relating to the progress of the British power in India and the system of subsidiary alliances. n.d.

KNIGHTON, WILLIAM. Private life of an eastern king. Ed. Smith. 1921.

MIR HASAN 'ALI, Mrs. The Mussalmanns of India. Reprinted 1917.

PATTON, ROBERT. The principles of Asiatic monarchies. 1801.

SLEEMAN, Sir WILLIAM H. Journey through the kingdom of Oude in the years 1849–50. 2 vols. 1858.

SUTHERLAND, JOHN. Sketches of the relations subsisting between the British Government in India and the different native states. 1837.

B. SECONDARY WORKS

BILGRAMI, S. H. and WILLMOT, C. Historical and descriptive sketch of the Nizam's dominions. 2 vols. 1883–4.

COLEBROOKE, Sir H. T. Life of Elphinstone. 2 vols. 1884.

DALY, Major H. Memoirs of General Sir Henry Dermot Daly. 1905.

FRASER, Col. HASTINGS. Memoir and correspondence of General James Stuart Fraser. 1885.

HARDINGE, Viscount. Viscount Hardinge. Oxford, 1900.

HOPE, J. The house of Scindea. 1863.

KAYE, J. W. Life...of Charles, Lord Metcalfe. 2 vols. 1858.

LEE-WARNER, Sir WILLIAM. Life of the Marquis of Dalhousie. 2 vols. 1904.

—— The Native States of India. 1910.

LUARD, Capt. C. E. Central India. (Imp. Gaz. Prov. Ser. 1908.)

MALCOLM, Sir JOHN. Memoir of Central India. 3rd ed. 1832.

MALLESON, G. B. An Historical Sketch of the Native States of India in Subsidiary Alliance with the British Government. 1875.

MEHTA, M. S. Lord Hastings and the Indian States. (Unpublished thesis.)

MIRZA MEHDY KHAN. Hyderabad State. (Imp. Gaz. Prov. Ser. Calcutta, 1909.)

PRINSEP, H. T. Political and military transactions in India under the administration of the Marquess of Hastings. 2 vols. 1825.

RICE, B. L. Mysore and Coorg. (Imp. Gaz. Prov. Ser. 1908.)

SHAHAMET ALI. History of Bahawalpur. 1848.

TAYLOR, MEADOWS. Story of my life. Ed. Bruce. 1920.

TUPPER, CHARLES LEWIS. Our Indian Protectorate. 1893.

CHAPTER XXXII

THE DEVELOPMENT OF SOVEREIGNTY IN BRITISH INDIA

In general the reader should consult the previous bibliographies.

Home Miscellaneous Series 336 contains a collection of papers relative to the Moghul Emperor 1781–1812.

Parliamentary Papers, 1805, x, 757, contains papers relating to Wellesley's settlement; and 1859, session I, xviii, III, and session II, xxv, 331, contain papers relating to the trial of the King of Delhi.

The *Punjab Government Records*, vol. 1 (Lahore, 1911) contains very valuable selections from the records of the Delhi Residency 1807–57.

CHRONOLOGICAL TABLE

1497–8	Vasco da Gama's first voyage.
1500	Cabral's voyage; factory established at Cochin.
1502	Bull of Alexander VI.
1503	War between the Zamorin and Raja of Cochin. Albuquerque's first voyage.
1504	Duarte Pacheco's defence of Cochin.
1505	Francisco d'Almeida viceroy. Cochin the Portuguese headquarters.
1506	Albuquerque's second voyage: first siege of Ormuz.
1508	Lourenço d'Almeida defeated by the Egyptian squadron off Chaul.
1509	Francisco d'Almeida defeats the Egyptian squadron off Diu.

1509	Albuquerque governor of India.
1510	Goa occupied.
1511	Malacca taken by Albuquerque.
1513	Albuquerque's attempt on Aden.
1515	Albuquerque establishes Portuguese suzerainty over Ormuz.
	Death of Albuquerque.
1516	Soares' attempt on Aden.
1518	Expedition to Ceylon.
1520	Diogo Lopes' expedition to the Red Sea.
1521	De Brito besieged in Colombo.
1524	Vasco da Gama dies at Cochin.
1529	Nuno da Cunha governor of India.
1530	Goa becomes the Portuguese headquarters.
1534	Bassein ceded to the Portuguese.
	The Portuguese permitted to build a fort at Diu.
1537	Bahadur Shah's quarrel with the Portuguese and death.
	See of Goa established.
1538	The Turkish squadron attacks Diu.
	Garcia de Noronha viceroy.
1540	Portuguese treaty with the Zamorin.
1541	Portuguese expedition to Suakin.
	Francis Xavier arrives in India.
1545	João de Castro viceroy.
1546	Second siege of Diu.
1548	Death of João de Castro.
1550	Affonso de Noronha viceroy.
1552	Francis Xavier dies.
1554	Pedro de Mascarenhas viceroy.
1555	Portuguese war in Ceylon.
1557	Goa made a metropolitan see.
1559	Daman occupied by the Portuguese.
1560	Goa made an archbishopric.
1562	Siege of Daman.
1564	Portuguese war in Malabar.
1569	Luiz d'Atayde reduces Honawar.
	Camoens returns from Goa to Lisbon.
1570	Defence of Chaul.
1571	Dom Antonio de Noronha viceroy.
1578	King Sebastian killed in Morocco.
1579	Linschoten reaches Goa.
1586	Portuguese war with Raja Sinha.
1590	Capture of the *Madre de Dios*.
1595	Houtman's voyage.
1600	Charter to the London East India Company.
1602	Formation of the United Dutch East India Company.
	Spilbergen in Ceylon.
1603	Mildenhall at Agra.
1605	Death of Akbar and accession of Jahangir.
1606	Dutch blockade of Goa.
1609	Hawkins at Agra.
	Dutch factory at Pulicat.
1611	Middleton at Surat.
1612	Best at Surat.
	Danish East India Company founded.
1615	Roe at the Moghul Court.
1616	The Danes at Tranquebar.
1619	Anglo-Dutch treaty.
1622	The Portuguese expelled from Ormuz.
1623	The massacre of Amboyna.

1625	Dutch factory at Chinsura.
1629	Death of Jahangir and accession of Shah Jahan.
1634	Farman permitting English trade in Bengal.
1635	Courteen's Association formed.
1638	Dutch attack Portuguese in Ceylon.
1639	Fort St George founded.
1644	Temporary peace between the Dutch and Portuguese in the East.
1651	English factory at Hugli founded.
1654	Treaty of Westminster.
1657–8	Moghul war of succession; Aurangzib emperor.
1660	Portuguese completely driven from Ceylon.
1661	Charles II's charter to the East India Company.
	Cession of Bombay to the English.
1663	Publication of peace between the Dutch and Portuguese.
1664	Sivaji plunders Surat.
	Colbert founds the Compagnie des Indes.
1665	Humphrey Cooke obtains possession of Bombay.
1667	Treaty of Breda.
1670	Sivaji again plunders Surat.
1671	La Haye's expedition.
1673	The French besieged in St Thomé.
1674	François Martin founds Pondichery.
1680	Dedication of St Mary's Church in Fort St George.
1683	Keigwin's mutiny at Bombay.
1686	English war with the Moghuls.
1688	Heath's expedition to Bengal.
1690	Calcutta founded.
1693	Death of Job Charnock.
	The Dutch capture Pondichery.
1698	Formation of the English East India Company.
1702	Amalgamation of the English and London East India Companies.
1707	Death of Aurangzib; accession of Bahadur Shah.
1712	Accession of Jahandar Shah.
1713	Accession of Farrukhsiyar.
1715	Surman's embassy to Farrukhsiyar.
1719	Murder of Farrukhsiyar.
	Accession of Muhammad Shah.
	Law's Company formed.
1720	Baji Rao I Peshwa.
1722	Ostend East India Company set up.
1726	Lenoir governor of Pondichery.
	Charter establishing courts of law at the English presidencies.
1731	Dupleix *directeur* of Chandernagore.
	The Swedish East India Company founded.
1735	Dumas governor of Pondichery.
1737	The Marathas occupy Salsette.
1739	Nadir Shah's invasion of India.
1740	The Marathas raid the Carnatic; Nawab Dost 'Ali killed.
1741	Chanda Sahib captured by the Marathas.
1742	Dupleix governor of Pondichery.
	Murder of Safdar 'Ali, Nawab of the Carnatic.
1743	Nizam-ul-mulk's expedition to the Carnatic.
1744	War of the Austrian Succession.
	Anwar-ud-din Nawab of the Carnatic.
1746	La Bourdonnais takes Madras.
1748	Boscawen besieges Pondichery.
	Death of Nizam-ul-mulk.
	Ahmad Khan Durani invades the Panjab.
	Accession of Ahmad Shah.

1749	Chanda Sahib with French aid defeats and kills Anwar-ud-din at Ambur. Madras restored to the English.
1750	Defeat and death of Nasir Jang.
1751	Bussy establishes Salabat Jang as subahdar of the Deccan. Clive's seizure and defence of Arcot.
1752	Chanda Sahib killed by the Tanjoreans and Law surrenders to the English.
1753	Cession of the Northern Sarkars to Bussy.
1754	Conference of Sadras. Recall of Dupleix. Accession of 'Alamgir II. Truce between the French and the English.
1755	Clive returns to India.
1756	Capture of Gheria. Bussy's defence of the Chahar Mahal. Siraj-ud-daula captures Calcutta. The Seven Years' War.
1757	Clive recovers Calcutta and takes Chandernagore. The battle of Plassey. Mir Ja'far Nawab of Bengal.
1758	Lally's expedition. Capture of Fort St David. Bussy recalled from the Deccan. Lally besieges Madras.
1759	Forde captures Masulipatam. 'Ali Gauhar invades Bihar. The Dutch expedition against the English in Bengal. 'Alamgir II murdered by Ghazi-ud-din.
1760	Battle of Wandiwash. Clive returns to England. 'Ali Gauhar again in Bihar, and proclaims himself Shah 'Alam II. The Marathas capture Delhi. Mir Kasim made Nawab of Bengal.
1761	Battle of Panipat. Capitulation of Pondichery. Hyder 'Ali usurps Mysore. Nizam 'Ali imprisons his brother Salabat Jang.
1763	War with Mir Kasim; re-establishment of Mir Ja'far. Treaty of Paris.
1765	Clive returns to India and obtains a grant of the diwanni of Bengal.
1766	The Bengal officers' mutiny. Nizam 'Ali grants the Northern Sarkars to the English.
1767–9	The first Mysore War.
1769	Appointment of Scrafton, Forde, and Vansittart as supervisors.
1770	Lindsay at Madras.
1771	Shah 'Alam leaves Allahabad for Delhi.
1772	Warren Hastings governor of Fort William. Trial of Muhammad Reza Khan. Madhava Rao Peshwa dies.
1773	The Regulating Act passed. Taimur Shah succeeds to Ahmad Shah Durani. Narayana Rao murdered.
1774	The Rohilla War. Bogle's mission to Tibet. The Regulating Act comes into force.
1775	The treaty of Surat. The trial of Nandakumar.
1776	The treaty of Purandhar. Lord Pigot arrested by a majority of the Madras Council.

1776	Death of Colonel Monson.
1777	General Clavering dies.
1778	Sir Thomas Rumbold governor of Madras.
	Renewed war with the Marathas.
	Capture of Pondichery.
1779	Convention of Wadgaon.
	Capture of Mahé.
	Goddard's expedition.
1780	Popham's capture of Gwalior.
	Duel between Hastings and Francis.
	Second Mysore War.
1781	Battle of Porto Novo.
	Lord Macartney governor of Madras.
	Chait Singh deposed.
	Treaty of Chunar with Asaf-ud-daula.
1782	The French fleet under Suffren arrives on the Coromandel Coast.
	The Treaty of Salbai.
	Death of Hyder 'Ali.
1783	Arrival of Bussy's expedition at Cuddalore.
	Death of Sir Eyre Coote.
	News of peace with the French.
	Fox's India Bills.
1784	Treaty of Mangalore.
	Pitt's India Act.
1785	Warren Hastings resigns.
1786	Lord Cornwallis governor-general.
1788	Hastings' trial begins.
	Ghulam Kadir seizes and blinds Shah 'Alam.
1789	Tipu attacks Travancore.
1790	Third Mysore War.
1793	The Company's Charter renewed.
	The Permanent Settlement of Bengal.
	Capture of Pondichery.
	Sir John Shore governor-general.
1794	Mahadaji Sindhia dies.
1795	The battle of Kharda.
	Expedition against the Dutch in Ceylon.
	Death of Muhammad 'Ali Walajah.
1796	Baji Rao II Peshwa.
1797	Zaman Shah at Lahore.
	Death of Asaf-ud-daula.
1798	Wazir 'Ali deposed and succeeded by Sa'adat 'Ali.
	Tipu's mission to Mauritius.
	Lord Mornington governor-general.
	Subsidiary treaty with Nizam 'Ali.
1799	Fourth Mysore War.
	Marshman at Serampore.
	Malcolm's mission to Persia.
1800	Death of Nana Phadnavis.
	The College of Fort William established.
1801	Baird's expedition to the Red Sea.
	The assumption of the Carnatic.
	Treaty with Sa'adat 'Ali.
1802	Symes's mission to Ava.
	Treaty of Bassein.
1803	War with Sindhia.
	Treaties of Deogaon and Surji Arjungaon.
1804	War with Holkar.
1805	Siege of Bhartpur.

1805	Lord Cornwallis supersedes Lord Wellesley and dies.
1807	Lord Minto governor-general.
1808	Missions to Persia, Lahore, Peshawur and Sind.
1810	Bourbon and Mauritius captured by the English.
1811	Java occupied by the English.
1813	The Company's charter renewed, but its monopoly of the trade to India abolished.
	Lord Moira (Hastings) governor-general.
1814	The Nepal War.
1817	The last Maratha War.
1818	Baji Rao II deposed.
1823	Lord Amherst governor-general.
1824	The first Burmese War.
	Dutch settlements in India transferred to the English.
1825	The voyage of the *Enterprise*.
	The second siege of Bhartpur.
1827	Daulat Rao Sindhia dies.
1828	Lord William Bentinck governor-general.
1829	Measures against thagi.
	Prohibition of sati.
1830	Mysore rebellion.
1832	Treaty for the free navigation of the Indus.
1833	The Company's charter renewed but its trade abolished.
1834	The annexation of Coorg.
	Macaulay appointed Law member of council.
	Province of Agra formed.
1836	Lord Auckland governor-general.
1837	Burnes's mission to Kabul.
	Siege of Herat.
1838	The Tripartite Treaty.
1839	Shah Shuja enthroned at Kandahar.
	Death of Ranjit Singh.
1840	Dost Muhammad surrenders.
1841	The revolt at Kabul; murders of Burnes and later of Macnaghten.
1842	Massacre of the Kabul brigade.
	Lord Ellenborough governor-general.
	Withdrawal from Afghanistan.
1843	Conquest of Sind.
	Battle of Maharajpur.
1844	Lord Ellenborough recalled; Sir Henry Hardinge governor-general.
1845	Danish settlements transferred to the English.
	First Sikh War.
1846	Battle of Sobraon and peace with the Sikhs.
1848	Lord Dalhousie governor-general.
	Annexation of Satara.
	Second Sikh War.
1849	Battle of Gujrat and annexation of the Panjab.
1852	Second Burmese War.
1853	Railway opened from Bombay to Thana.
	Cession of Berar.
	Annexation of Nagpur.
	The Company's charter renewed.
1854	The Ganges Canal opened.
1855	Treaty with Dost Muhammad.
1856	Annexation of Oudh.
	Lord Canning governor-general.
	War with Persia.
1857	The Sepoy Mutiny.
1858	Assumption of government of India by the crown.

INDEX

Aba Selukar, 368
Abbas Mirza, 484, 489, 490
Abbasid Empire, 603, 608
Abbott, Captain, 503
Abdali, tribe, 483
Abdul Ghiyas Khan, 543
Abdul Karim Khan, *see* Sidis, the
Abdul Rahim, *see* Sidis, the
Abercromby, Sir John, 332
Abercromby, Sir Ralph, 328, 336
Abreu, —, 566
Abul Fazl, 23
Abwabs, 409
Accountant-general, the, 416
Aché, Comte d', 159, 160, 163
Achin, 41, 62, 92; threatens Malacca, 19, 85; trade, 32, 33, 39, 49; English at, 77
Adam's Bridge, 48
Adams, Major Thomas, 173, 174
Adas, battle of, 258
Aden, 2, 9, 11, 12, 13, 40; English at, 77
Adigar, 404, 405, 407
Adil Khan, *see* Bijapur
Adlercron, Colonel, 144, 145, 157
Admiralty Courts, 102
Adoni, 334
Adoption, 581–3; sanads, 586
Adrianople, 15; Treaty of, 489
Adyar river, action on, 122
Afghans, invade India, 146, 249, 350; relations with the English, 483 *sqq.*, 543–6; relations with Sind, 522, 524, 528; in the second Sikh War, 555, 556
Afrasiab Khan, 602
Africa, 17, 74
Afzal Khan, 505
Agnew, Patrick Alexander Vans, 554
Agra, 40, 66, 77, 84, 324, 364, 366, 579, 580; English factory at, 78, 79, 81, 91, 92, 100; taken by Lake, 374
Ahalya Bai, 252, 368, 369, 376; her opinion of Raghoba, 258
Ahmad II of Gujarat, 19
Ahmadabad, 22, 40, 84, 92, 267, 270; English factory, 81; district, 368, 376, 379, 382
Ahmad Mirza, 515
Ahmadnagar, kingdom, 3, 20, 21; city of, 135, 262, 370, 374
Ahmad Shah Abdali, 214, 249, 483, 484
Aislabie, W., 102 n.
Aix-la-Chapelle, Treaty of, 124, 591
Aiyaz Khan, 286
Ajit Singh Sindhianwala, 546, 547
Ajmir, 80, 381
Akalkot, raja of, 382
Akbar, 77, 383, 409, 412; reduces Gujarat, 22, 23; relations with the Portuguese, 23

Akbar II, 605, 606, 608
Akbar Khan Barakzai, *see* Muhammad Akbar
Akram Khan, 487
Akshah, 484
Akunwun, 566
Akyab, 562–5
Alagada Islands, 18
'Alamgir II, 169
'Alampur, 252
Alaungpaya, 558
Albuquerque, Affonso d', 15; commentaries, 3; voyages, 7, 9, 10; government, 10 *sqq.*, 17, 18
Albuquerque, Francisco d', 7
Alcantara, 24
Aldworth, Thomas, 79
Aleppo, 65, 70
Alexander the Great, route to India, 327, 331
Alexander I, 331, 489
Alexander VI, Pope, 2, 76
Alexandria, 1, 2, 9, 327, 328
'Ali II, Sultan of Bijapur, 20
'Ali Bahadur, 365
'Ali Gauhar, *see* Shah 'Alam II
'Ali Husain, 361, 362
'Ali Masjid, 512, 513, 520
'Ali Muhammad, 217, 220
'Ali Murad, 533–5, 537
Aliwal, 551
'Ali Wardi Khan, 112, 141, 142, 147, 423
Allahabad, city of, 176, 180, 215, 216, 218, 251, 253, 309, 354, 528, 596, 597; district of, 380, 597; Treaty of, 176, 273, 274, 592, 596
Allard, General, 542, 544
Almas 'Ali Khan, *see* Ilmas 'Ali Khan
Almeida, Francisco d', 8–10, 24
Almeida, Lourenço d', 8–10, 25
Almora, 546
Altamgha, 409
Alveiras, Conde d', 44
Alves, Captain, 559
Alwar, state of, 374, 577
Amar Singh Thapa, 378
Ambala, 540, 541, 549
Amboina, Massacre of, 84, 86, 326
Ambur, 336; battle of, 126, 127
America, 324
American Baptist Mission, 566
Amherst, 565–9
Amherst, Lord, and the Indian states, 577; and the emperor, 606
Amiens, Treaty of, 115, 329, 403, 596
Amins, 425
Amin-ul-lah Khan, 519
Amir Husain, *alias* Mir Hashim, 9, 10

42-2

Amir Khan, 376, 380, 381, 383, 573
Amir Mirjan, 13
Amir Singh, 360, 361
Amir-ul-umara, 361
Amrit Rao, 264, 372
Amritsar, 539
Amsterdam, 28, 58; chamber of, 31; Fort, see Caradiva
Amyatt, Peter, 173
An, 562
An Pass, the, 564
Anand, 258
Ananda Razu, 162
Anandi Bai, 250, 251, 254, 255, 257
Anand Rao, 375, 376, 382, 575
Anderson, Lieutenant, 554
Anderson, David, 269–71, 425, 427, 430, 431
Anderson, Sir George W., 508
Anderson's Horse, 510
Andrews, Robert, 403
Ange, Jean, 61
Angelbeck, van, 401, 402
Angria, 113, 114, 369. See also Babu Rao, Manaji, Raghuji
Anjadiva, 6, 8, 9, 10
Anjengo, 103
Antwerp, 28
Anwar-ud-din Khan, 119, 121, 124, 126
Appa Khande Rao, 366
Appa Sahib, 379–81, 574
Arabia, 9, 40, 62, 65
Arakan, 34, 558–60, 562, 565, 568; administration, 563; local battalion, 562, 564
Araxes, the, 489
Arcot, Nawab of, 117–9, 122. See also Carnatic; Prince of, 586; town of, 127, 284, 591; siege of, 129, 130
Argaon, battle of, 374
Arghandab, 502
Armagon, 88
Armenia, 486
Armenians, the, 143
Arras, see Adas
Arthasastra, the, 384, 387, 393, 394
Arthur, Sir George, 530
Aryankuppam, 130
Asaf Khan, 14
Asaf Khan (Itikad Khan), 40
Asaf-ud-daula, 222, 299 sqq., 309, 347 sqq.; Treaty of Faizabad with, 233
Ascension, the, 78
Ashta Pradhan, the, 384
Ashti, 381, 382
Asirgarh, 380, 381
Assada Association, the, 91
Assam, 558, 559, 578
Assaye, battle of, 374
Astruc, —, 131
Atar Singh Sindhianwala, 546, 547
Atayde, Dom Luiz d', 20, 21
Atta Muhammad, 488
Attock, 488, 541, 548, 555

Auckland, Lord, character, 490; and Russia, 483, 489; and Afghanistan, 490–508, 511, 512, 520; and Sind, 523, 524, 526–8, 538, 544; and the Sikhs, 545, 549; and the Indian states, 578, 583; recalled, 513
Aumont, —, 325
Aungier, Gerald, 100, 101
Aurangabad, 134–7
Aurangzib, 36, 66, 71, 93, 99–101, 105, 107, 411; conquers Golconda, 37, 104, 590
Aurore, l', 325
Austen, Sir Francis William, 561
Austen, Jane, 561
Austrian Succession, War of, 59, 117–24, 590
Auteuil, Louis Combault d', 126, 127, 129, 130
Ava, 558–62, 567, 568
Avitabile, General, 512, 542, 546
Ayyab Khan, 488
'Azim-ud-daula, 361, 362
Azizpur, 532
Azores, the, 24

Baber, Edward, 410, 412, 413
Babti, 395
Bab-ul-mandab, Straits of, 78
Babur, 14
Babu Rao Angria, 369
Badami, 334, 365
Baghdad, Khalif of, 608
Bagyidaw, 559, 560
Bahadur Shah II, 606, 607
Bahadur Sultan of Gujarat, 14, 15, 22
Bahawalpur, 483, 484, 499, 531–4, 536, 586
Bahur, 126
Baillie, Colonel William, 283, 284, 348
Baird, Sir David, 328, 341, 346
Baiza Bai, 578
Baj-baj, 145
Baji Rao I, 118, 253
Baji Rao II, 253, 257, 364, 370, 371, 386, 388, 390, 393, 396; and Tipu, 371; and the English, 377, 379 sqq., 574, 583; his pension, 586, 606
Baksar (Buxar), 296, 299; battle of, 174, 251, 254, 280
Bala Hissar, the, see Kabul
Balaji Baji Rao, 118, 135, 137, 138, 157, 249, 253, 384
Balaji Janardhan, see Nana Phadnavis
Balaji Vishvanath, 250, 384
Balasore, 41, 107, 115; English factory, 88, 106
Baldaeus, Philippus, 53
Baldeo Singh Raja, 577
Baldwin, George, 327
Balkh, 484
Balochis, the, 500, 513, 527, 536, 537
Balochistan, 484, 488, 530
Balu Mian, see Sidis, the
Bamyan, 504, 505, 507

Banda Islands, 83, 86, 326
Bandar Abbas, *see* Gombroon
Bandarmalanka, 139
Bandula, 559
Bangalore, 118, 275, 276, 336, 578
Bangkok, 568
Bankibazar, 115
Bankot, *alias* Fort Victoria, 114
Bannu, 495
Bantam, 29, 31–5, 39, 40, 49, 62, 67, 68, 71, 88; English factory, 77, 83, 84, 89, 93, 111
Bapu Gokhale, 381
Bara alute, the, 386
Bara balute, the, 386
Barakzai tribe and monarchy, 484–8, 490, 501, 502, 515, 519, 541
Baramahal district, 337, 467–71, 473, 474, 476
Barbosa, Duarte, 5
Bardas, 18
Barker, Sir Robert, 216–8, 223, 232
Barlow, Sir George H., 320, 343, 375, 378, 455, 570, 577
Barnett, Commodore Curtis, 120, 121
Baroda, 257, 267, 368, 376. *See also* Gaekwad, the
Baron, François, 70, 71
Barrackpore, 115
Barré, Colonel Isaac, 184, 186
Barreto, Antonio Moniz, 21, 23
Barreto, Francisco, 19
Barros, João de, 61
Barwell, Richard, 189, 225, 228, 231, 262, 420–4; character, 226–7; retires, 229; prosecutes Nandakumar, 235
Basalat Jang, 140, 281, 282, 600
Basian, 550
Basra, 66; English factory, 87, 90
Bassein, 14, 19, 23, 114, 249, 256, 257, 259, 260, 264, 268–70; Treaty of, 372–5, 379, 574
Bassein (Burma), 562
Bat chhapai, 396
Batavia, 35, 37, 38, 40–2, 44–7, 50, 56–60, 83, 84, 91, 101, 154, 402; founded, 32; taken by the English, 328
Batta, 178–9
Batticoloa, 32, 41–3, 407
Bayanor Raja, 74–5
Bayley, William Butterworth, 503
Bazi jama, 409
Beaulieu, Augustin de, 62
Béber, —, 66
Becher, Richard, 207
Becker, Hendrik, 54
Beckford, Alderman William, 184
Bednur, 286
Begar, 386
Belier, le, 329
Belle Poule, la, 329
Belli, John, 238
Benaru hills, 507
Benares, 270, 351, 360, 516, 553, 598, 602,

Benares (*continued*)
604; ceded to the Company, 233; reforms in, 305–6; Treaty of, 215–6, 218, 219. *See also* Chait Singh
Benasterim, 11, 21
Benfield, Paul, 273, 280, 287, 290, 292, 293, 355–7
Bengal, province of, 32; Dutch factories in, 40, 41, 57; French factories in, 62, 72, 73; Danish factory, 114, 115; Ostend factory, 115; Prussian trade in, 116; English factories in, 80, 88, 89, 91, 92, 103, 105–8, 112, 153; Clive in, 1756–60, 141 *sqq.*; French designs on, 135, 139, 147, 323; financial help from, 165; diwanni of, *see* Diwanni; English position, 1772, 206; governor's allowances, 234; sovereignty in, 591 *sqq.*
Bengal, Government of—position of nawab, 210; constitution under Regulating Act, 189 *sqq.*; and under the India Act, 200, 316, 317; working under Regulating Act, 225 *sqq.*; relations with other presidencies, 190, 200, 259, 277, 281, 282, 316, 317; relations with Supreme Court, 241 *sqq.*; policy in first Maratha War, 257–60, 263; policy in Second Mysore War, 284, 285; relations with Muhammad 'Ali, 291, 292; the secretariat, 446
Benson, Colonel, 560
Bentinck, Lord William Cavendish, 321, 476, 490, 491; and the Russian danger, 489, 542; and the Indian states, 577–9
Berar, kingdom of, 3; Maratha state of, 136, 250, 252, 254, 270, 367, 368, 376, 380, 598; annexation of, 581, 582; Nizam's province, 586
Berchem, Wemmer van, 34
Bernagore, 41
Bertie, Admiral Sir Albemarle, 332
Best, Thomas, 79
Bet, island of, 382
Beveridge, H., quoted, 236, 423, 424
Bezwada, 137
Bhag Singh, 540
Bhai Bir Singh, 547
Bhanpura, 376
Bharatpur, 374, 375, 542, 577
Bhatkal, 90
Bhawani, Charan Mitra, 422
Bhils, the, 391, 392
Bhonsle family, the, 249, 254, 260, 608. *See also* Appa Sahib, Chimnaji, Janoji, Khanduji, Mudaji, Parsaji, Raghuji, Sabaji
Bhopal, 266, 380, 573
Bhor Ghat, the, 269, 270
Bhung Bara, 532, 533, 536
Biana, 92
Bias, the, 552
Bidar, kingdom of, 3
Bihar, 92, 103, 106, 142, 151–3, 166, 169, 174, 183, 219, 377, 423, 449

Bijaigarh, 299
Bijapur, kingdom of, 3, 9–12, 70, 333; and the Portuguese, 18, 20
Bimlipatam, 37
Binot, —, 329
Birbhum, 416
Bisdom, Adriaan, 154
Bithur, 381
Black Hole of Calcutta, 113, 144, 156
Blackman, President, 94
Blundell, E. A., 565, 568
Board of Control, the, set up, 200; powers, 201, 313; paid, 314; President, 314; relations with the Company, 314–6
Bodawpaya, 558, 559
Bogambara, 408
Bogle, Sir Archibald, 562, 563, 565
Bogle, C., 425
Boigne, Comte Benoît de, 363, 366
Bokhara, 489, 503, 504
Bolan Pass, 499, 500, 515, 530
Bolts, William, 116, 590
Bombay, 56, 68, 84, 99, 105, 107, 108, 113, 157, 261, 491, 508, 530, 594; cession of, 86, 87; presidency of, 96, 100, 101, 102; courts at, 102, 114; besieged, 103; mint, 112; fortifications, 113; the Marine, 114; the Marine Yard, 275; docks at, 114; under the Regulating Act, 256, 259, 260, 277; form of government, 321; sovereignty at, 589; relations with the Marathas, 113, 114, 249 sqq., 256 sqq., 263 sqq.; relations with Mysore, 253, 275, 277, 279, 285, 286; Lindsay at, 279
Bonaparte, Île, see Bourbon, Isle of
Boone, C., 102, 113
Boscawen, Admiral Edward, 123, 124, 126
Boschhouwer, —, 42
Both, Pieter, 31, 32
Bourbon, Isle of, alias Île Bonaparte, 74, 163, 332
Bourchier, Richard, 280
Bourquin, Louis, 374
Bouvet, Lozier de, 123, 158
Bowyear, —, 558
Boyd, Hugh, 401
Boyd, J. P., 368
Braganza, Dom Constantine de, 19, 26
Brazil, 5, 46, 47, 49, 85
Brenier, —, 130, 131
Brereton, Major Cholmondley, 162
Brest, 329
Bristow, John, 301, 305, 306
Brito, Lopo de, 25
Brittany, 323
Broach, 22, 23, 40, 374; English factory, 81, 103; cession of revenues, 257, 260, 265, 270, 271
Broadfoot, Major George, 510, 512, 548–50, 565, 567, 568
Broadfoot, Lieutenant William, 506
Broughton, Lord, see Hobhouse, Sir John Cam
Browne, Major James, 601, 602

Brownrigg, Sir R., 408
Brydon, Dr, 510, 511
Buchanan, Francis, 345
Bukkur, 499, 500, 527, 529, 530, 532
Bundelkhand, 263, 265–7, 363, 374, 398, 583
Bundi, 380, 385
Burdwan, 422, 423, 444; ceded to the English, 168, 206, 593
Burgoyne, General John, 184–7
Burgoyne, General Sir John, 293
Burhanpur, 39, 40, 256, 266; Treaty of, 580
Burke, Edmund, 203; on the Company, 182, 186–8, 191, 192, 194; on Fox's bills, 196, 197, 199; on the Company's servants, 198; on the India Act, 202; on the governor-general's powers, 203; on Nandakumar's trial, 235; on the Arcot debt, 273, 355; on presents, 303; on Tanjore, 279; on Indian correspondence, 319; on Shore, 350; attacks Hastings, 205, 216, 233, 247, 307 sqq.
Burke, William, 279
Burma, 76, 324, 558 sqq.; first war, 542, 559, 560, 577; second war, 561, 562; administration of, 562 sqq.
Burnell, A. C., quoted, 53
Burnes, Sir Alexander, 491–3, 496, 497, 499, 500, 502, 505, 506, 508, 509, 523, 526, 527
Burnes, Charles, 506
Burnes, James, 523
Burney, Fanny, 307, 560
Burney, Major Henry, 560, 568
Burr, Colonel, 380
Bussy, Charles Castelnau de, takes Jinji, 127; in the Deccan, 128, 132, 134 sqq., 145, 147, 151, 152, 158, 162, 274; English plans against, 157; his recall, 162, 165; expedition of 1782, 287, 324, 325

Cabral, Antonio, 23
Cabral, Jorge, 18, 19
Cabral, Pedro Alvarez, 5, 6
Cachar, 559, 578
Caillaud, Colonel John, 166–9, 274
Cairo, 1, 2, 11, 328
Calcutta and Fort William, 105, 107, 112, 149, 153, 157, 158, 171, 172, 174, 175, 177, 179, 210, 230, 415, 453, 511, 514, 559, 560, 562, 564, 566, 593; foundation of, 108; early history, 113; courts at, 113; taken by Siraj-ud-daula, 139, 141, 142, 144, 148, 153; defences, 142, 143; recovered, 145–7, 205, 590, 592; customs house, 208; zamindary lands, 416
Calcutta Review, the, 538
Calicut, trade, 1; kingdom of, 3; Portuguese at, 5–10, 18, 20, 21, 25; Dutch at, 33, 49, 51; hostile to Cochin, 50; French at, 74; town of, 3, 51, 68, 286
Call, Sir John, 160
Camac, Major Jacob, 270

Camara, Jose da, 264
Cambay, 10, 19, 22, 23, 40, 257, 376; Gulf of, 78
Cambaya, kingdom of, see Gujarat
Cambridge Modern History, quoted, 538
Camoens, Luiz de, 18
Campbell, Sir Archibald, 320, 356
Campbell, Sir Archibald, 559, 560, 565
Campbell, Colonel John, 288
Canary Islands, 330
Canning, Captain, 559
Canning, Charles John, Lord, 583, 585; and the Moghul, 607
Canning, George, 320, 321
Canton, 494
Cantoo Babu, see Krishna Kantu Nandi
Cape Comorin, 68, 72, 383
Cape of Good Hope, 2, 28, 31, 62, 63, 74, 76, 77, 163, 326, 329
Cape Verde, 2
Capuchins, the, 62
Caradiva, 48
Carnac, General John, in Bengal, 169, 170, 174, 176; in Bombay, 264, 265
Carnarvon, Lord, 310
Carnatic, 34, 35, 41, 69, 117 *sqq.*, 273 *sqq.*, 355 *sqq.*; assignment of revenues, 290–2; revenue system, 462 *sqq.*; dependence on the empire, 591; title of nawab of — extinguished, 586, 591, 606
Caroline, the, privateer, 330
Caron, François, 45, 66–71
Cartier, John, 180, 413
Casearius, Johannes, 53
Caspian Sea, 489
Castlereagh, Lord, 315, 320
Castries, Marquis de, 324, 325, 327
Castro, Dom João de, 16, 17
Cawnpore, 374, 575
Ceded Districts, the, 471, 475, 478
Cedeme, 20
Central Asia, 331
Central India, 570, 571, 574, 576, 577, 581
Central Provinces, 574
Ceylon, 17, 56, 57, 62, 120; Portuguese in, 8, 24 *sqq.*; Dutch in, 32, 37, 38, 41 *sqq.*, 51, 57, 85, 87; rebellions against the Dutch, 54; Treaty of 1766, 55; French attack, 61, 66–8; Portuguese and Dutch influence, 402; English in, 285, 326, 329, 400 *sqq.*
Chahar Mahal, the, 138, 145, 152
Chait Singh, 230, 295 *sqq.*, 301, 302, 309; Impey's affidavits, 246, 301; vote on, 307, 308, 310
Chale, 21
Chalias, the, 51, 54
Chambal river, 380, 579, 580
Chambers, Sir Robert, 236
Champion, Colonel Alexander, 177, 219, 220, 222, 232, 304
Chanda district, 367
Chanda Sahib, 117, 118, 126, 130, 133, 159, 179

Chandernagore, 73, 137, 139, 142; taken by Clive, 146, 147, 157, 158; refortified, 278
Chand Kaur, 546, 547
Chandragupta Maurya, 394
Chandrakant, 558
Chandu Lal, 585
Changama, battle of, 276
Chaonga, 532
Charak, 550
Charikar, 507
Charles II, 50, 102, 104; his charters, 95
Charnock, Job, 107, 108
Charpentier, François, 63, 65
Charters, Samuel, 427, 430, 431
Chatham, Lord, 184, 187, 593
Chatter Singh, 554
Chattisgarh district, 367
Chaugula, the, 386
Chaul, 9, 261; siege of, 20, 21
Chauth, 118, 394, 395, 398
Cheduba island, 562
Chenab, the, 555, 556
Cherry, G. F., 351
Chetpattu, 158
Chet Singh, 545
Chevalier, —, 323, 324
Chhapa, 397
Chicacole, 136, 137
Chiengmai, 568
Chikka Rayalu, 118
Chilaw, 54, 55
Child, Sir John, 102, 103
Child, Sir Josia, 96, 97, 101, 102
Chilianwala, battle of, 555, 556
Chimnaji Appa, 256, 371
Chimnaji Bhonsle, 268, 269
China, 17, 31, 36, 41, 76, 90; Portuguese in, 13; English in, 111; Danes in, 115; Ostenders in, 115; Prussians in, 116; Swedes in, 115; Sikhs attack, 546; attacks Burma, 558
Chinapatam, see Madras
Chinese in Burma, 564, 568
Chingiz Khan, 20
Chingleput, 131, 161, 284; district, see Jagir, the
Chinsura, 41, 154, 155
Chitaldrug, 344
Chitnis, the, 388
Chitpavan sect, 385
Chittagong, town, 107, 108, 562, 564, 566; district, 168, 206, 558, 593
Chittur, 475
Chitu, 377, 380
Chitur Singh, 372
Chunar, 296
Churchill, 205
Cide Bofata, see Sayf-ul-muluk Miftah
Cis-Satlej Sikhs, see Sikhs
Clarendon, Lord, 494
Clarke, Sir Alured, 349
Clavering, General Sir John, 189, 191, 231, 236, 239, 298, 419, 420, 421, 425, 599;

Clavering, General Sir John (*continued*)
  character, 226, 414; claims the chair, 228; death, 228
Cleghorn, Hugh, 401, 402
Clerk, Sir George Russell, 508, 511, 518, 545, 547
Clive, Edward, Lord, 321, 339, 341, 343, 358, 359
Clive, Robert, Lord, 112, 117, 140, 234, 323, 589, 601; in the Carnatic, 129–31, 154; takes Gheria, 114; returns to India, 157; at Fort St David, 144; his first government, 141 *sqq.*, 158, 166, 168, 170, 171, 205, 215, 290; takes Chandernagore, 139; his jagir, 153, 175, 206; cooperates against Lally, 161; his second government, 174 *sqq.*, 409, 593, 596, 597, 599; his views in 1765, 251; his Military Fund, 180; attacked in parliament, 181, 184, 185, 187; on the Company, 183, 187, 190, 593
Close, Colonel Barry, 345, 346, 361
Coalition, the, 181
Cochin, 3, 68; Portuguese at, 5–8, 10, 11, 13, 14, 18, 19, 25, 26; taken by the Dutch, 49–51, 85; raja of, 335; as protected state, 574
Cockburn, Colonel William, 264, 265
Coen, Jan Pietersoon, 32, 39, 40, 60
Coimbatore, 288, 336, 337, 343; revenue system in, 471
Coinage, ceases to bear Moghul superscription, 606
Colbert, Jean-Baptiste, 63–8, 71, 74, 75
Colebrooke, Henry Thomas, 431
Coleroon river, 125, 129
Collectors, *see* Revenue
Colombo, 53, 54, 406, 407, 408; Portuguese in, 25–7, 43, 44, 46, 48; taken by the Dutch, 47, 52, 85; taken by the English, 401, 402
Columbus, Christopher, 1
Colvin, Sir Auckland, quoted, 490, 498
Colvin, John Russell, 490–4, 503, 504, 508, 511, 565
Combermere, Lord, 577
Conflans, Marquis de, 162
Conjeeveram, 130, 162, 283
Conolly, Captain Arthur, 504
Conolly, Edward, 505
Constantinople, 278, 340
Cooke, Humphrey, 156
Coorg, 337, 341, 578
Coote, Sir Eyre, 152, 163–5, 169, 170, 232; commands in Bengal, 229, 230; in second Mysore War, 269, 284–7, 290, 292, 293
Cope, Captain John, 125, 127
Coral companies, 63
Corbin, —, 568
Corbin, the, 61
Cornwallis, Lord, 177, 178, 181, 203, 212, 244, 320, 596; Dundas on, 195; appointment and early career, 434; separate powers, 317; patronage, 318, 319; re-

Cornwallis, Lord (*continued*)
  forms, 430, 433 *sqq.*, 456, 461; third Mysore War, 289, 326, 334 *sqq.*, 366; organises Baramahal, 467; and Benares, 299, 306; and Oudh, 306, 347; and the Carnatic, 356, 357, 359, 360; and the Sidi, 369; later appointment and government, 338, 375; policy towards the Indian states, 570, 577, 580, 603; character, 437
Coromandel Coast, 31–41, 49, 55, 57, 69, 71, 83, 87, 92, 93, 103, 113, 120
Coster, —, 42–4
Cotton, Sir Willoughby, 500, 502, 505, 506
Couper, Sir George, 584, 585, 587
Court, General, 542
Courteen, Sir William, 90, 91
Covelong, 131
Covenanted servants of the East India Company, 177, 178, 318; Burke on, 198; W. Hastings on, 198; provision for trial of, 202, 203; Hastings' reform of, 211, 212; salaries under Hastings, 213; ineligible as governor-general, 320; reforms of Cornwallis, 433 *sqq.*; at Madras, 467
Cox, Captain, 559
Craig, General Sir James, 349, 351
Cricklade, 230
Croftes, Charles, 416, 425, 427, 430, 431
Croissant, the, 61
Crommelin, Richard, 249
Cromwell, Oliver, treaty with Portuguese, 85; and the Dutch War, 86; his charter, 89, 91, 94, 95, 103, 106
Cuddalore and Fort St David, 123, 124, 127, 144; English factory, 104, 113, 130; Dupleix attacks, 122; English headquarters, 125; taken by Lally, 140, 159; occupied by Bussy, 287; battle of, 287
Cuddapah, 118, 128, 337
Cunha, Nino da, 13–5
Cunha, Tristão da, 8, 9, 11
Cunningham, J. D., quoted, 540, 543, 544, 549
Curia Muria Islands, 7
Currie, Sir Frederick, 554, 555, 583
Customs duties, Maratha, 397; internal, 208, 467, 481; board of, 213
Cutch, 523, 576
Cuttack, 268, 269, 367, 374

Daatzerom, Dutch at, 37
Dabo, battle of, 537
Dacca, 172, 226, 445, 453, 558; English factory at, 106, 148; customs house at, 208; provincial council of, 422
Dacoity, 456, 457, 563, 565, 568
Dacres, P. M., 414, 422–4
Dada Sahib, *see* Raghunath Rao; *see* Khasgi-wala
Dadula, 532
Dadur, 499, 515
Daftardar, the, 388

Daji, 535
Dakshina, 394
Dalhousie, Lord, 321; and the Sikhs, 554 *sqq.*; and Burma, 561, 562; and the Indian states, 574, 581–7, 591; and the Moghul emperor, 606, 607
Dalip Singh, 547, 553
Dallas, Robert, 309
Damaji Gaekwad, 257
Damalcheri Pass, 118
Daman, 19, 20, 23, 68, 79, 264
Dambudenia, 406
Danes, the, in India; the East India Company, 114; expedition to Ceylon, 42; breach with England, 330
Danubyu, 559
Darakhdars, the, 388
Darbar kharch, 388
Darien, 98
Darogas, the, 445, 452, 474, 480
Daulat Rao Sindhia, 367, 369, 371, 372, 578; and the English, 373 *sqq.*, 380 *sqq.*, 385, 539, 570, 580
Daulatabad, 140
Davie, Major, 405, 406
Davy, Dr, 407
Daylesford, 203, 312
Decaen, —, 329–32, 604
Deccan, the, 101; subahdar of, 117; Bussy in, 134 *sqq.*, 151. *See also* Nizam, the
Declaratory Act, the, 315
Dehra Ghazi Khan, 491, 495
Dehra Ismail Khan, 495
Delarche, Henri, 132
Delft, the, 33
Delhi, sultanat of, 3; city of, 23, 111, 113, 135, 153, 169, 180, 216, 306, 324, 380, 549, 571, 573, 577, 607; occupied by Marathas, 215, 253, 363, 364, 597; plundered by Rohillas, 365, 366; taken by the English, 374, 539, 604, 605; the palace, 607; the Diwan-i-khas, 606; the magazine, 607
della Valle, Pietro, 62
den Broecke, Pieter van, 39, 40
Dennie, Brigadier, 501, 505
Deogaon, Treaty of, 374
der Haghen, Admiral Steven van, 33, 49
der Meyden, Adriaan van, 47
Deslandes, —, 72, 73
Desmukh, the, 387, 388, 396
Despande, the, 387, 396
Devenampatnam, Dutch at, 33, 37, 42. *See also* Cuddalore
Devikottai, 125
Dewan, the, 388
Dewas, state of, 571
Dhaboi, 267
Dhar, fort, 257; state, 571
Dharapuram, 287, 343
Dharmapala, 26, 27
Dharna, 398
Dharwar, 336, 397
Dhian Singh, 545–7

Dhondu Pant, *alias* Nana Sahib, 586
Dias, Bartholomeu, 5
Dickinson, Captain, 562
Diemen, Antonie van, 32, 42
Dig, battle of, 375
Dindigul, taken by the English, 287; ceded, 337, 467; revenue settlement, 474, 475
Dinghi, 555
Diu, 10, 13, 14, 23, 25; first siege, 15; second siege, 16; French visit, 61
Divy Island, 126
Diwanni of Bengal, 176, 177, 183, 185, 188, 206, 409 *sqq.*, 448, 529, 593, 596; abolition of naib diwans, 209
Diwanni adalats, 415, 418, 421, 425, 440, 443, 453
Doddington, the, 157
Dominicans, the, at Goa, 21
Dorin, J. A., 584
Dost 'Ali Khan, 117, 118
Dost Muhammad Khan, 486, 488–93, 495, 496, 498, 499, 501, 503–5, 507, 508, 520, 543–6, 555, 557
Dow, Colonel Alexander, 423
Downton, Nicholas, 79
Drake, Sir Francis, 24, 76
Drake, Roger, 142, 156, 291
Drakensteyn, Adriaan van Rheede tot, 36–8, 53, 58
Draper, Daniel, 263
Draper, Lieutenant-colonel Sir William, 160, 162
Du Bausset, —, 132
Ducarel, G. G., 423, 424
Du Chemin, —, 285
Dudpatli, 559
Dudrenec, Chevalier, 366, 368
Duff, Grant, quoted, 257, 333
Duif, the, 34
Du Mans, Père Raphael, 62
Dumas, Benoist, 75, 126
Dumbara, 406
Duncan, Jonathan, 299, 435, 436, 499
Dundas, Henry, 192, 193, 325, 338, 347, 348, 356, 361, 434–7; his India bill, 194–6, 355; and W. Hastings, 202, 262, 307, 308; as President of the Board, 314; on foreign policy, 350; and Ceylon, 403; on revenue, 450, 451
Dundas, Robert, 458
Dundia Wagh, 346
Dupleix, Joseph, 323, 343, 558; and the Dutch, 59; his policy, 75, 117, 125, 154, 600; on Bengal, 142; desires neutrality, 119, 120; quarrels with La Bourdonnais, 121; relations with Anwar-ud-din, 122, 591; attacks Fort St David, 122, 123; defends Pondichery, 123, 124; the struggle in the Carnatic, 126 *sqq.*, 145, 150, 176
Durand, Sir Henry, 501, 565–7
Durani tribe, the, 483–5, 489, 501, 505, 515. *See also* Afghans
Durjan Sal, 577

Du Saussay, —, 131
Dutch in India, the; early voyages, 28 *sqq.*;
 company founded, 30; wars with the
 Portuguese, 31, 82, 83; organisation in
 India, 31; on the Coromandel Coast,
 33 *sqq.*; early relations with the English,
 82–4, 86, 91; the Company's servants,
 37; in Gujarat, 39, 40; in Bengal, 40, 41;
 in Ceylon, 41 *sqq.*; the Ten-year Truce,
 44–6; renewal of war, 47; peace with the
 Portuguese, 50, 85; organisation in
 Malabar, 51; in Ceylon, 52 *sqq.*; religious policy, 53; relations with Kandi,
 54, 55; sea-power, 56; third Anglo-
 Dutch War, 56; finance, 57, 60; defects
 of organisation, 57 *sqq.*; oppose the
 French, 59, 61, 67, 72, 104, 153; oppose
 Clive, 60, 153, 154, 162, 166; in the War
 of the American Revolution, 285, 289,
 401; projected French alliance, 325; in
 the Revolutionary and Napoleonic Wars,
 326, 329, 401 *sqq.*; convention of 1814,
 596; in Burma, 558
Du Tremblay, Père Joseph, 62

East India Company (English), early
 voyages, 76–8; founded, 30, 77; relations
 with the Portuguese, 76–8, 80–6, 113;
 relations with the Dutch, 56, 59, 60,
 82–6, 91, 104; early relations with the
 French, 72, 104; relations with the Danes,
 115; Malayan factories, 77; Hawkins's
 mission, 77; Middleton's voyages, 78;
 Roe's mission, 80; in Persia, 81, 82; development of trade, 87 *sqq.*, 91–4, 96,
 108 *sqq.*; on the Coast, 88, 89; early
 finance, 89; Courteen's association, 90;
 Assada association, 91; Cromwell's
 charter, 94, 95; Charles II's charters, 95,
 96; during the Revolution, 97, 98; the
 new company, 98, 99, 104, 105; union of
 the companies, 99, 100; Child's policy,
 101, 102; the Moghul War, 102, 103,
 107, 108; organisation in India, 102;
 troubles from pirates, 103; Surman's
 embassy, 111, 112; influence of Clive's
 victories, 175; relations with the state,
 181 *sqq.*, 278, 592; constitution under
 Regulating Act, 189, 190; Maratha
 policy, 261, 262; legislation regarding,
 1786–1818, 313 *sqq.*, 455; loses trade
 monopoly, 313; relations with the Board,
 314–6; Afghan policy, 498, 499, 505. *See
 also* Justice, Military forces, Covenanted
 servants, Secret Committees and the
 Indian presidencies under their several
 names
East India Mutiny Act, 180
Ecclesiastical authorities, 313
Eck, Governor van, 55
Eden, William, first Baron Auckland, 596.
 See also Auckland, Lord
Education, grant under act of 1813, 313;
 Munro's enquiry, 481; in Burma, 565, 566

Edwardes, Sir Herbert, 554, 555
Egerton, Colonel, 263–5
Egypt, 1, 9, 15; attacks the Portuguese, 9,
 13; Napoleon in, 327, 328, 331, 339;
 English projects in, 327
Eheylapola, 407, 408
Elizabeth, Queen, 24, 76, 77
Elizabethpol, 489
Ellenborough, Lord, 513, 578; and the
 Afghan War, 513 *sqq.*, 529; and Sind,
 522, 528 *sqq.*; and the Sikhs, 544, 546,
 547, 549, 579; and Gwalior, 579; and
 the directors, 579; and the Moghul
 emperor, 606
Elliot, Alexander, 598
Elliot, Sir Gilbert, *see* Minto, Lord
Ellis, Sir Henry, 490
Ellis, William, 172, 173
Ellore, 136
Elphinstone, Mountstuart, quoted, 222,
 388, 390, 397, 582; mission to Peshawar,
 487; resident at Poona, 379; in the
 Deccan, 571; governor of Bombay, 321;
 on the Afghan question, 498
Elphinstone, General W. G. K., 505–7,
 510, 511, 515
England, Brigadier, 515, 516, 519, 530
Enkhuizen, 29
Entertainment allowance, 234
Erivan, 489
Erskine, Sir James, 202, 309
Etheraja, 34
Ethiopia, Portuguese missionaries in, 5
Eurasians, 143
Evans, Sir De Lacy, 489
Evelyn, John, 96
Excise revenue, 564, 568
Eyloff, Pieter Ysaac, 33, 34
Eyre, Sir Charles, 108

Fairfax, Lord, 91
Faizabad, 301; Treaty of, 232, 233
Faizulla Khan, 220, 303 *sqq.*
Fakr-ud-din, 607
Falck, Iman Willem, 55
Famine policy, 481, 482
Fane, Sir Henry, 497, 499
Faridkot, 540, 541
Farmer, W., 261, 264, 265, 267
Farrer, —, 235, 236, 238, 239
Farrukhabad, 375
Farrukhsiyar, 104, 111
Fatehabad, 511
Fatehgarh, 347
Fatehpur Sikri, 365
Fateh Singh, 118
Fateh Singh Gaekwad I, 257, 258, 267,
 268, 270, 271
Fateh Singh Gaekwad II, 368, 381, 382,
 575
Fath 'Ali Khan Talpura, 484, 522
Fath 'Ali Shah Kajar, 486, 489, 490
Fath Jang, 519
Fath Khan Barakzai, 485–8, 541

Faujdari adalats, 415
Ferreira, Miguel, 12
Ferrier, J. P., 483
Fez, 24
Finkenstein, Treaty of, 331
Firozpur, 499, 512, 520, 534, 542, 544, 548–51, 555
Firozshah, 550, 551
Firoz-ud-din Sadozai, 488
Fitch, Ralph, 76
Fitzwilliam, Lord, 199
Fleetwood, Edward, 558
Fletcher, Sir Henry, 199
Fletcher, Sir Robert, 174, 179, 180, 280
Flint, Lieutenant William, 284
Floyer, Charles, 125, 128
Foote's Nabob, 283
Forde, Colonel Lionel, 155, 162, 207
Forests, Maratha revenue from, 397; Burmese, 566, 567
Fort Dauphin, 62, 66
Fort Gustavus, see Chinsura
Fort Macdowall, 406
Fort St David, 72. See also Cuddalore
Fort St George, see Madras
Fort Louis, see Pondichery
Fort Victoria, see Bankot
Fort William, see Calcutta
Fouquet, Nicolas, 62
Fowke, Joseph, 235, 420
Fox, H.M.S., 561
Fox, Charles James, 181, 186, 191, 223, 247, 309, 318; his India bills, 194 sqq., 201, 314, 355; his coalition with North, 198–200, 434; on the India Act, 202
Foxcroft, George, 104
France, Île de, see Mauritius
Francis, Philip, 189, 203, 212, 213, 224, 227, 228, 231, 236, 245, 307, 426, 435, 437, 599, 600, 601; his character, 225, 226, 414, 419; compact with Hastings, 229; leaves India, 230; and Nanda-kumar, 239, 240; and Chait Singh, 295; views on revenue, 423–5, 430
Franciscans, the, 18, 21
French in India, the; early voyages, 61, 62; relations with the Dutch, 56, 59, 61, 67 sqq., 72, 104; relations with the Portu-guese, 61; projected companies, 61, 62; in Madagascar, 62, 65–7; Colbert's com-pany, 63–5; early factories, 66; La Haye's expedition, 56, 67–70, 400; at Pondi-chery, 70, 71; in Burma, 558; early rela-tions with the English, 72, 104; Martin's policy, 73; Law's company, 74; in Bengal, 599; struggle with the English, see Dupleix; war of the American Revo-lution, 281; intrigues with Marathas, 261, 266; assist Hyder 'Ali, 268, 285 sqq.; adventurers in India, 323, 371; projected Dutch alliance, 325; influence of the Revolution, 326; designs on Portuguese settlements, 329; in the Napoleonic War,

French in India (continued)
see Napoleon; relations with the Sikhs, 544. See also Pondichery, Chanderna-gore, Mahé
Fryer, Dr John, 101
Fulaili river, 536, 537
Fullarton, Colonel William, 287, 288
Fulta, 144, 147

Gaekwad, the, 249, 250, 252, 254, 257, 368, 372, 373, 375, 379, 382; treaty with Fateh Singh, 267; as protected state, 574, 575, 578. See also Anand Rao, Damaji, Fateh Singh Govind Rao, Kanhoji, Sayaji
Galle, 25, 41, 44–6, 51, 52
Galloway, General Sir A., 607
Gama, Christovão da, 16
Gama, Estavão da, 6, 16
Gama, Vasco da, 1, 2, 16; first voyage, 3; at Calicut, 4; second voyage, 6, 7; viceroy, 13
Gambier, Robert, 256
Gaming farms, 568
Gandammak, 487, 506, 511, 519
Ganga Bai, 255, 256
Gangadhar Sastri, 379
Ganga Govind Singh, 427
Ganges, the, 92, 107, 146, 218, 219, 296, 324, 373, 381, 558
Ganjkottai, 337
Gardane, General, his mission, 331
Garhwal, 378
Garo, 546
Gaunggyok, 560, 566
Gawilgarh, 374
Gaya, 169
Gayer, Sir John, 102, 105
Gazzalhatti Pass, 336
Geldria Fort, see Pulicat
Genoa, 1
George III, 181, 307, 308, 598; and the India bills, 199, 200; "sovereign of the seas," 594
Georgia, 331, 486, 487, 489
Germain, Lord George, 186
Ghafur Khan, 573
Ghazipur, zamindar of, 233
Ghazi-ud-din Khan, 135, 136
Ghazni, 484, 488, 501, 502, 512–5, 517–9
Gheria, 114; captured, 157
Ghilzai tribe, 485, 488, 504–6, 511, 519
Ghorian, 493
Ghulam 'Ali, 522
Ghulam Kadir, 365, 366, 603
Ghulam Shah, 526
Gilgit, 547
Gillespie, Sir R. R., 378
Gilpin, Major, 301, 307
Gingens, Captain Rodolf de, 128, 129
Giriskh, 517
Gleig, Rev. G. R., quoted, 290, 306, 308, 343, 421
Globe, the, 83

Goa, 3, 13, 15–17, 19, 23, 26, 29, 31, 34, 43–9, 68, 79, 80, 91, 113, 264, 346, 382; taken by the Portuguese, 10, 11; their headquarters, 14; see of, 15; Jesuits at, 18; siege of, 20, 21; blockaded by the Dutch, 32, 42, 44, 83, 85; Dutch hanged at, 33, 39; Convention of, 85, 87, 89, 90
Goalpara, 558
Godavari river, 251
Goddard, General William, 229, 266–70
Godeheu, Charles Robert, 132, 133, 137, 138, 157
Godolphin, Lord, 99, 100
Godwin, Sir Henry Thomas, 561
Goens, Rijcklof van, 48–50, 56, 58, 60, 69, 70
Goeree, Adriaan, 39
Gogala, 15
Gohad, 267, 268, 270, 375
Golconda, 35, 36, 88, 589; Dutch relations with, 33–5, 38; Dutch factory at, 37; conquered by Moghuls, 38, 104, 590; attacks French at St Thomé, 56, 69–71; English relations with, 83
Goldsborough, Sir John, 102
Gombroon, alias Bandar Abbas, French at, 66; English at, 81, 82, 87, 90, 93, 94
Gondhalis, the, 397
Gondhs, the, 608
Gooty, 138, 344
Gopika Bai, 250, 251, 254
Gorakhpur, 378, 380
Goring, C., 421
Gotki, 532
Gough, Hugh, Lord, 549–51, 554–6, 579
Goupil, Louis Jérôme, 136
Governor-general, powers of, 189, 190, 194, 203, 206, 280, 316; appointment of, 203; separate powers, 317
Govinda Chand Mitra, 237
Govindpur, 108
Govind Rao Gaekwad, 257, 267, 268, 368, 375
Grafton, Duke of, 278
Graham, J., 414
Grand Alliance, the, 73
Grand Anglais, the, see Marie de Bon Secours
Grant, Ensign, 406
Grant, Charles, 232, 360, 435, 436, 441, 442, 450
Grant, Charles, Lord Glenelg, 320
Grant, James, 209, 398, 431, 432, 435–7, 447 sqq.
Grant, Sir John Peter, 584
Grasias, the, 572
Greenhill, Henry, 89
Gregory, R., 199
Grenville, William Wyndham, 198, 309
Greville, Charles C. F., 509, 520
Grey, Charles, second Earl, 297, 309
Grey, George, 282
Griffin, Sir Lepel, quoted, 542, 545
Griffin, Admiral Thomas, 123
Grose, J. H., 114
Guardafui, Cape, 10, 17

Gujarat, kingdom and province, 3, 9, 12, 14, 16, 19, 24, 32, 80, 261, 268, 374, 387; conquered by Moghuls, 22; Dutch factories in, 39–41; French factories in, 66; English factories in, 78, 87, 92; Maratha state, see Gaekwad, the
Gujrat, battle of, 556
Gulab Singh, 546, 548, 549, 552, 553
Gulbadan Begam, 23
Gulistan, Treaty of, 489
Guntoor, 281, 282, 284, 334, 366, 370
Gurdas, 210
Gurkhas, the, 377, 575; war with the Sikhs 541; regiments, 507
Gurramkonda, 344
Gwalior, 365, 497, 579, 580; taken by Popham, 268–70, 296; restored to Sindhia, 363, 375; Treaty of, 380, 381; state of, see Sindhia

Hafiz Rahmat Khan, 217, 219–22
Hague, the, 30, 44, 45, 50, 83
Haidarabad, see Hyderabad
Haidar 'Ali, see Hyder 'Ali
Haidar Beg Khan, 305, 347, 348
Haidar Jang, 140
Haidar Khan Barakzai, 501
Haidaru, 541
Haidar-ud-din Ghazi, 575, 578
Hakulzai, 515
Hala, 536
Hamid 'Ali Khan, 348
Hamilton, Charles, 221
Hamilton, William, 111
Handia, 380
Hanguraketa, 52
Hannay, Colonel, 222, 301, 302
Hanwella, 54
Hardinge, Henry, Lord, 513, 520; and the Sikhs, 549 sqq.; and the Indian states, 580, 583
Hariharpur, 88, 106
Harington, J. H., 415, 431
Hari Pant Phadke, 254, 257, 270, 271, 334, 365
Hari Singh, 543
Harkaras, the, 394
Harland, Sir Robert, 279
Harris, General George, 340, 341, 346
Hartley, Colonel James, 267
Hasham daftardar, 389
Hashamnavis, 389
Hashamphadnis, 389
Hastings, Marquess of (Lord Moira), 375; and the Gurkhas, 378; his Maratha policy, 379, 385 sqq., 486, 582; and the Indian states, 570 sqq., 578, 581, 587; his administrative reforms, 458, 459 sqq.; relations with the Moghul emperor, 605, 606
Hastings, Warren, 316, 323, 356, 364, 436, 437, 438, 439, 461, 589, 591; early service, 147, 167, 172, 173, 175, 180, 205 sqq.; on Lord Shelburne, 187; on the Regulating Act, 182, 190; on the Com-

Hastings, Warren (*continued*)
  pany, 183; appointed governor-general,
  189, 191; continued in office, 192; recall
  demanded, 193, 194; and Fox's bills,
  195, 196; on the India Act, 203; on the
  Company's servants, 198; his patronage,
  319; financial policy, 295; administration, 1772–74, 205 *sqq.*, 598; his foreign
  policy, 1772–74, 215 *sqq.*, 597, 598, 607;
  relations with the majority, 225 *sqq.*, 280,
  599, 600; resignation, 228; Maratha
  policy, 254, 257, 259, 261–3, 265–71;
  relations with Rumbold, 281; relations
  with Macartney, 287–90, 292, 317; policy
  towards Mysore, 284, 285, 333, 363; relations with Chait Singh, 295 *sqq.*; presents, 298, 302, 303; treatment of the
  begams, 300; treatment of Faizulla Khan,
  303; conduct in Oudh, 1784, 305; rela-
  tions with the shahzada, 306, 601; en-
  courages Suez route, 327; revenue ad-
  ministration, 413 *sqq.*; impeachment,
  181, 307 *sqq.*
Havaldar, the, 389
Havart, Daniel, 36–8
Havelock, Captain Henry, 512, 551, 560
Hawkins, William, 77, 78
Hay, William, 173
Hayat Muhammad Khan, 266
Hazara, 552, 554
Hazirinavis, 389
Heath, Captain William, 108
Heber, Mrs, 406
Hector, the, 77
Hedges, William, 106
Helmund, the, 501
Henrique, Dom, 24, 26
Henry IV, 61
Herat, 483–8, 490–8, 501–5
Herbert, Thomas, 62
Heytesbury, Lord, 490
Higginson, Nathaniel, 102
Hijili, island of, 107
Hindu Kush, the, 502, 503, 519
Hira Singh, 547, 548
Hislop, Sir Thomas, 376, 380, 381
Hobart, Lord, 317, 321, 357–60, 468
Hobhouse, Sir John Cam (Lord Brough-
  ton), 493, 497–9, 501, 503–5, 527, 606
Hodgson, John, 476, 477
Hodson, Major William, 554
Holkar, family of, 249, 250, 256, 257, 259,
  260, 262, 368, 381, 539, 570; after 1818,
  571, 573, 577. *See also* Jasvant Rao,
  Malharji, Malhar Rao, Kashi Rao,
  Khande Rao, Tukoji, Vithuji
Hollond, John, 281, 282, 317, 335
Holmes, Thomas, 265
Holwell, John Zephaniah, 141, 143, 156,
  166–9
Honawar, 286
Honfleur, 61
Hope, the, 79
Hornby, William, 193, 262, 264–6

Houtman, Cornelis de, 28–30, 76
Howe, Lord, 186
Hughes, Sir Edward, 285, 287, 401
Hugli district, 416; faujdar of, 590
Hugli river, 41, 55, 60, 107, 115, 120, 145,
  154, 158
Hugli town, 145, 146, 148; English factory
  at, 88, 91, 100, 103, 106, 107; customs
  house at, 208
Hulft, Gerard, 47
Humayun, 14, 22
Humayun Mirza Durani, 484
Humberstone, Colonel, 286
Hundikaris, 397
Hunter, —, 562, 563
Huriki, 549
Hurst, G., 423
Husain 'Ali, 522, 534
Hutchinson, John Hely, 328
Huzur Daftar, 385, 388
Huzur zilla land, 416
Hyde, Mr Justice, 235, 243
Hyderabad (Deccan), city, 136, 138, 274,
  281, 326, 327, 576; Bussy's defence of, 138,
  158; province of, 112, 134; contingent,
  341, 586. *See also* Nizam, the
Hyderabad (Sind), 500, 522–4, 526, 527,
  529–37
Hyder 'Ali, 51, 333, 346; rise to power,
  275; assists Lally, 163, 164; relations with
  the Marathas, 251–5, 259, 260, 276, 277;
  first Mysore War, 252, 275 *sqq.*; execution of treaty, 279; relations with Nizam
  'Ali, 277; relations with Bombay, 275,
  277, 279; allies against the English, 267,
  269; his Malabar conquests, 282; second
  Mysore War, 268, 270, 271, 282 *sqq.*;
  revenue administration, 462, 463; death,
  286; character, 321

Ibrahim Husayn, 22
Idalcão, *see* Yusuf Adil Khan
Ilbert, Sir Courtenay, quoted, 184, 202,
  247, 589
Île Dauphine, *see* Madagascar
Ilmas 'Ali Khan, 347, 351
Imad-ul-mulk, *alias* Madre Maluco, 19, 20
Imam Garh, 534, 535
Imhoff, Baron van, 53, 54, 59
Impey, Captain, 569
Impey, Sir Elijah, 226, 232, 235–8, 240,
  241, 243–5, 301, 302, 426; impeached, 246
Inams, 386, 387
India Act, Pitt's, 181, 194, 200 *sqq.*, 280,
  313, 355, 356, 358, 430, 595
Indian states, relations of the Company
  with, 570 *sqq.*
Indo-China, 559
Indore, 252, 256, 369; state of, *see* Holkar
Indus, the, 327, 483, 485, 488, 491, 495,
  497, 499, 500, 508, 513, 516, 523, 524,
  525, 527, 528, 529, 530, 531, 532, 533,
  534, 535, 538, 542, 543, 545, 552
Ingeram, English factory at, 136, 139

Inquisition, the, 18
Interlopers, 95–7, 102, 109
Internal trade of Bengal, 169–72, 177, 178, 208
Irrawaddy, the, 558
Irrigation, in South India, 463, 482
Ismail Beg, 365–7
Ismail Safavi, 12
Ispahan, 62
Istalif, 519
Itimad Khan, 19, 22

Jabbar Khan, 488, 501, 504
Jacatra, 31, 32
Jacob, General John, 538
Ja'far 'Ali, 136
Ja'far Khan, 112
Jaffnapatam, alias Jaffna, 48, 51, 52, 85, 401
Jagdallak, 511, 519
Jagir, Clive's, 153, 206; the Company's, 274, 467, 468, 471, 473, 474, 476, 482
Jahangir, 39, 77–9; Hawkins' mission to, 77 sqq.; Roe's mission to, 80 sqq.
Jahangir Sadozai, 488
Jaikottai, 335
Jaintia, 559, 578
Jaipur, 365, 374, 375, 380, 574, 578
Jaitak, 378
Jakat, 397
Jalandhar doab, the, 552
Jallalabad, 488, 495, 501, 502, 506, 507, 509–18, 520, 546
Jalla Pandit, 548
Jambi, 39
Jamenis, the, 388
James I, 77, 80, 97
James II, 96
James, Commodore, 114
Jammu, rajas of, 545–8. See also Suchet Singh
Jamrud, 489, 491, 512, 543
Janjira, the Sidis of, 101, 369
Jankoji Rao Sindhia, 578, 579
Janoji Bhonsle, 250–2
Jaora, 573
Japan, 31, 36, 61, 90
Jask, 81
Jastipatti, 396
Jasuds, the, 394
Jasvant Rao Holkar, 372, 373, 376; and the English, 374, 375
Jasvant Rao Lad, 381
Jats, the, 252, 253, 323, 374
Java, 29–32, 40–2, 55, 67, 76, 77, 332
Jawahir Singh, 547, 548
Jayaji Rao Sindhia, 579
Jedda, 1, 2, 9, 12, 13
Jeffreys, Chief-justice, 96
Jenkinson, Charles (Lord Liverpool), 199
Jessore, 416
Jesuits, the, 3, 18
Jhansi, 581–3
Jhelum, the, 555, 556
Jhusi (Joosee), 299
Jind, 540

Jindan Rani, 547, 548, 553
Jinji, 117, 130, 131, 163, 384; Dutch relations with, 33; French relations with, 72; English relations with, 104; taken by Bussy, 127; taken by the English, 164; river, 127
Jiwan Bakht, 607
João, Dom, 41, 42
Jodhpur (Marwar), 366, 380
Johar, see Sidis, the
Johnstone, Captain, 407
Johnstone, Governor George, 185, 192
Johore, 32
Jones, Sir Harford, 331, 487
Jones, Sir William, 436, 437, 445, 455, 461
Jumna, the, 92, 270, 354, 374, 380, 539, 541, 549
Junius, 160
Justice, Maratha administration of, 389 sqq.; early courts at Bombay, 100, 114; at Madras, 104, 589; at Calcutta, 590; Admiralty courts, 102; charter of 1726, 113; Supreme Court of Calcutta, 189; Company's courts in Bengal, 415, 426, 440; proposed amalgamation, 242 sqq., 426; Cornwallis's reforms, 433, 434, 436, 440, 443–5, 450, 452–4; Shore's amendments, 456, 457; Wellesley's amendments, 457; Minto's amendments, 457; Lord Hastings' amendments, 459, 460; in Southern India, 464, 472; Bengal system introduced, 474, 476–9; modified, 480; in Burma, 563, 564, 566; use of Persian in, 563; police in Bengal, 391, 451, 458, 459, 464; in Madras, 474, 479, 480

Kabaw valley, 560
Kabul, 483–5, 488, 491–6, 502, 504–12, 514, 515, 517–9, 546; the Bala Hissar, 491, 506, 507, 509, 510, 515, 519; the Great Bazaar, 519
Kachhi, 500, 502
Kafaristan, 483
Kalanga, 378
Kalat, 484, 500, 502–4
Kalora, tribe, 484, 522, 538, 543
Kalpi, 262, 268
Kalutara, 54
Kalyan, 268, 270
Kamal-ud-din, 235
Kamaran, 12
Kamavisdar, the, 387, 389, 396
Kamran Mirza Sadozai, 485, 486, 488, 490, 492, 493, 497, 501, 514
Kanara, 51, 343, 470, 471, 478
Kandahar, 87, 91, 483, 484, 486–8, 490–4, 497, 499, 500–5, 509, 512–7, 519, 530, 543, 544
Kandi, 34, 41–4, 46, 51, 54, 55, 69, 85, 400, 401, 403–8
Kangra district, 541
Kanhoji Gaekwad, 368, 375
Kannanur, 3, 341; Portuguese at, 5–10, 12; taken by the Dutch, 50, 85; taken by Macleod, 288

Kantu Babu, *see* Krishna Kantu Nandi
Kanund Mohendargarh, 366
Kanungos, the, 411, 412, 428–30, 432, 460
Karachi, 527, 529–32
Karam 'Ali, 522
Karauli, 583
Karens, the, 567
Karikal, 75, 126, 160, 163
Karim Khan, 377
Karja patti, 396
Karnal, 497, 549
Karnatak, 387
Karnul, 128, 578
Karrak, island of, 487, 494
Karvir, 377
Karwar, 90, 103
Kasauli, 549
Kashi Rao Holkar, 376
Kashmir, 484, 485, 487, 488, 495, 541, 542, 547, 552, 553
Kashmira Singh, 547
Kasijora case, 243, 246, 247, 426
Kasimbazar, English factory at, 88, 106, 142, 144, 148; French factory at, 145
Kasur, 549
Kathiawad, 368, 379
Kathmandu, 378, 379
Kautiliya, 384, 387, 393
Kavalgar, the, 464, 472
Kavari, the, 129, 341
Kavaripak, action at, 130
Kaway river, 337
Kaye, Sir John, quoted, 190, 491, 496, 503, 506
Kays, islet of, 48
Kaysar Mirza Sadozai, 486
Keane, John, Lord, 497, 499–502, 527
Keating, Colonel Thomas, 257–60
Kedda, 62
Keigwin, Richard, 102
Kelly, Colonel Robert, 336
Ken, 544
Kenghung, 568
Kerjean, Jacques Desnos de, 130
Khadki, battle of, 380
Khaibar Pass, 491, 502, 512–4, 516, 520
Khairpur, 522, 523, 526, 527, 530, 532–7, 543, 544
Khalsa, the, 210, 415, 416, 427, 447
Khande Rao, 275
Khande Rao Holkar, 376
Khandesh, 387
Khanduji Bhonsle, 368
Khaneri, island of, 101
Khankhanan, 39
Kharak Singh, 545, 546
Kharda, battle of, 328, 370, 371
Khasgi-wala, Dada, 579
Khem Savant, of Wadi, 369, 377
Khilat-i-ghilzai, 513, 515–8
Khiva, 489, 502–4
Khojak Pass, 515
Khorassan, 483–4, 488, 489
Khosas, the, 523

Khudawand Khan, *see* Khwaja Safar Salmani
Khudawand Khan Rajab, 20
Khudkasht ryot, 424
Khulum, 504, 505
Khurd Kabul Pass, 510, 519
Khurram, Prince, *see* Shah Jahan
Khwaja Petrus, 148
Khwaja Safar Salmani, *alias* Khudawand Khan, 15–17, 20
Killpatrick, Major James, 144, 145, 150
Kilwa, 8
Kineer, Major, 130
King's Bench, court of, 280, 315
Kirkee, *see* Khadki
Kirman, 483
Kirti Sri, 400
Kishm, island of, 81, 82
Kittur, 334, 365
Kizilbashis, the, 485, 488
Kohandil, 484, 488, 492
Koh-i-nur, the, 487, 541
Kohistan, 503, 505–7, 519
Kokand, 504
Kolaba, 369
Kolhapur, 369–72, 377, 382
Kolis, the, 397
Kondur, 162
Konimedu, 104
Konkan, the, 371, 372, 379
Kopargaon, 261, 364
Kora, 215, 216, 218, 251, 309, 597
Koregaon, 381
Kosseir, 328
Kotah, 366, 374, 380
Kotte, 26
Kotwal, 393
Kranganur, 49, 50, 68, 335
Krishna, the, 128, 337, 364, 365
Krishna Kantu Nandi, 421, 422
Krishna Rao Kadam, Mama Sahib, 579
Krishnaraja Udaiyar, 345, 578
Kubilai Khan, 23
Kulkarni, the, 386
Kulu, 484
Kumaon, 378, 379
Kuran, the, 397
Kutb, the, 607
Kutiari, 69
Kyaukpyu, the, 562, 564
Kyunok, the, 563

La Bourdonnais, Bertrand-François Mahé de, 119–22, 124, 160, 343
La Condamine, — de, 569
Lahar, 268
La Haye, Jacob Blanquet de, 56, 67–70
Lahna Singh Sindhianwala, 547
Lahore, 350, 485, 487, 492, 495, 496, 504, 524, 544–6, 548, 549, 552, 555; first Treaty of, 539; second Treaty, 552; revised, 553
Lahribandar, English factory at, 87
Lake, Edward John, 554

Lake, Gerald, Lord, 374, 375, 539, 540, 604, 605
Lakheri, 366
Lally, Comte de, 140, 158 sqq., 323
Lal Singh, 548–50, 553
Lambert, Commodore, 561
Lancaster, James, 76, 77
Lang, Colonel Ross, 293
Langhorne, Sir William, 104
La Rochelle, 67
Laswari, battle of, 374
La Touche, Prévôt de, 128
La Tour, Chevalier de, 122
Laval, François Pyrard de, 61, 63
Lavaur, Père, 132, 159
Laverolle, — de, 400
Law, Hindu and Muslim, 436, 444, 445, 455, 461, 464; in Burma, 568. See also Legislation
Law, Edward, first Lord Ellenborough, 309
Law, Edward, second Lord, see Ellenborough
Law, Jacques, 129, 131, 138, 139
Law, Jean, 74, 145–7, 152, 169, 601
Lawrell, J., 414
Lawrence, Sir George, 554
Lawrence, Sir Henry, 511, 549, 551, 553, 554, 556, 557
Lawrence, John, Lord, 320, 551, 553, 556, 557
Lawrence, General Stringer, 125, 130, 131, 149, 150, 160, 162
Leech, Lieutenant, 492, 515
Legislation, the Cornwallis code, 452, 454, 455; modified, 459, 461; applied in Madras, 474, 477, 479
Le Gouz, La Boullaye, 62, 66, 67
Lemaistre, Mr Justice, 235
Lenoir, Pierre Christophe, 75
Leslie, Alexander, 558
Leslie, Colonel Matthew, 262, 263, 265, 266
Lespinay, Bellanger de, 70, 71
Lestineau, —, 365
Levant, the, 1, 62, 77
Levant Company, the, 94
Lewis, —, 561
Lewis, William, 263
Lewisham, Lord, 199
Leyden, university of, 53
Leyden, see Ouratura
Leyrit, Duval de, 138, 158, 159
Lindsay, Sir John, 253, 277, 278, 279, 594
Linois, Admiral, 330
Linschoten, Jan Huyghen van, 28, 29, 31
Lisbon, 1, 3, 24, 25, 28, 76, 83
Littler, General, 550
Loknath Nandi, 422
London, city of, opposes the Regulating bill, 188
Lord, Dr, 505
Lorraine, regiment of, 158
Loughborough, Lord, 234, 310, 311

Louis XIII, 62
Louis XIV, 56, 61, 63, 65, 67, 68, 73, 75
Low, Sir John, 582, 584
Lucknow, 232, 300, 305, 306, 348, 349, 351, 352, 354, 585; English factory at, 100; the Imambarah at, 349; the Martinière, 349
Ludhiana, 378, 487, 491, 496, 497, 540, 541, 542, 543, 549, 550, 551
Lumsden, Sir Harry Burnett, 554
Lushington, Henry, 149
Lusiads, the, 18
Lyall, Sir Alfred, quoted, 221, 224, 230, 231, 236, 298

Macao, 85, 87
Macartney, Lord, 232, 287–93, 320, 356
Macassar, 114
Macaulay, Lord, quoted, 221, 225, 236, 240, 241, 245
McCaskill, Sir John, 519
Macdowall, General, 404
Macgregor, Captain Charles, 506, 510, 512
Mackeson, Frederick, 496
Maclaren, Brigadier, 515
McLeane, Colonel Laughlin, 228
Macleod, Lord, 283; his regiment, 283
Macleod, Brigadier, 288, 289
Macleod, Lieutenant, 501
Macleod, Major, 566, 568
Macleod, William, 471
Macnaghten, Sir William, 492, 494–7, 500–9, 520, 528, 545
McNeill, Sir John, 489, 490, 493, 494
Macpherson, James, 279
Macpherson, Sir John, 231, 278, 279, 287, 292, 296; appointed to council, 230; Maratha policy, 334, 364; Oudh in the time of, 347, 351; revenue administration under, 430 sqq., 443
Madagascar, alias Ile Dauphine, discovered, 5; French in, 62, 63, 65, 67; English in, 65, 90, 91; coffrees from, 120
Madapollam, 139
Madec, René, 323, 324
Madge, Captain, 406
Madhu Rao Peshwa, 218, 249–54, 279, 386, 388, 396
Madhu Rao Narayan Peshwa, 253, 263, 364, 367, 370
Madras, 35, 38, 83, 94, 105, 106, 108, 111, 117, 119, 123, 128, 130, 131, 143, 147, 157, 158, 164, 166, 168, 169, 178, 179, 284, 285, 287, 293; foundation of, 87, 88; presidency of, 89, 96, 100, 101, 103, 104, 106, 112, 113; courts at, 102, 113; municipality of, 103; trade with Burma, 558; taken by La Bourdonnais, 120–2, 590; rendition of, 124, 591; headquarters, 125; expedition against Siraj-ud-daula, 144, 145; besieged by Lally, 140, 157, 159–61; Hastings at, 205; relations with Hyder, 253, 275 sqq.; Maratha policy, 254; Lindsay and Harland at, 279; re-

Madras (*continued*)
lations with Bengal, 277, 281, 282; select committee at, 283, 284, 290, 291; form of government after 1786, 321; sovereignty over, 589, 590
Madre Maluco, *see* Imad-ul-mulk
Madrid, Treaty of, 84
Madura, nayak of, 48, 52; occupied by Muhammadans, 117; Yusuf Khan at, 279; poligars of, 357
Maetsuycker, Joan, 46, 52
Magellan, Straits of, 31, 77
Mahad, 372
Mahadaji Rao Sindhia, 254, 261–3, 265–8, 270–2, 288, 298, 324, 326, 333, 363 *sqq.*, 368, 369, 602–4; his widows, 371, 372
Mahal, the, 387, 389
Mahanadi, the, 88
Maharajpur, battle of, 579
Mahars, the, 391, 392, 396
Mahé, French factory, 74, 75, 164, 282, 324
Mahfuz Khan, 276
Mahi, river, 258, 267
Mahidpur, battle of, 376, 381, 573
Mahmud of Ghazni, his tomb, 518
Mahmud II, sultan of Turkey, 540
Mahmud III, sultan of Gujarat, 16, 18
Mahmud Shah Sadozai, 484–8
Mai Chand Kaur, *see* Chand Kaur
Mailapur, *see* St Thomé
Maine, Sir Henry, 483
Maingy, A. D., 565, 568, 569
Mainville, Chevalier de, 131, 132
Mairta, 366
Maissin, —, 131, 132
Makwanpur, 377, 378
Mal, 409; adalats, 444, 453, 460
Malabar Coast, 33, 43, 48, 55, 57, 61, 83; Dutch on, 49 *sqq.*, 58, 85; French on, 66–8, 71; English on, 87, 90, 94, 103; Danes on, 115; pirates on, 100, 101, 113, 114; Hyder's conquests on, 275, 282, 285, 286, 471; Tipu's cessions on, 337. *See also* Calicut, Cochin, etc.
Malabar district, transferred to Madras, 471
Malabar Hill, 261
Malacca, 16–9, 21, 26, 29, 31; taken by the Portuguese, 11, 12; taken by the Dutch, 32, 42–4, 85; taken by the English, 326
Malader, 532
Malaon, 378
Malartic, —, 328, 339
Malaya and the Malay archipelago, 29, 31, 36, 41, 53, 57, 61, 62, 66, 77, 92, 114
Malcolm, Sir John, quoted, 182, 194, 196, 211, 348, 353, 356, 369, 575; his missions to Persia, 331, 486, 487; in Central India, 381, 571, 572, 573; governor of Bombay, 392
Malda, English factory at, 106, 436, 441
Maldive Islands, 8, 25
Malet, Sir Charles, 257, 334, 335, 337, 365
Malharji Holkar, 252, 368

Malhar Rao Holkar, 376, 578
Malik Ayaz, 13
Mallavelly, 341
Malwa (Central India), 14, 266, 368, 372, 373, 380, 571, 573
Malwa (Cis-Satlej), 540
Malwan, 369, 370
Mama Sahib, *see* Krishna Rao Kadam
Mamlatdar, the, 387–91, 393, 396
Manaji Angria, 369
Manaji Gaekwad, 257, 368
Manar, 48
Mandal, the, 410
Mandasor, battle of, 14; Treaty of, 381, 573
Mangalore, 276, 286, 328, 339; siege of, 288; Treaty of, 288, 289, 333–5, 341, 363
Mangni, 534
Mangs, the, 391
Manikani family, the, 522
Manilla, 87
Manipur, 558–60
Mansell, Charles E., 556
Mansfield, Lord, 311
Manu, 389
Marathas, the, wars with the Moghuls, 101; in South India, 104, 118, 119; raids on Bengal, 112, 142; relations with Bombay, 113, 114; attack the Portuguese, 114; attack Salabat Jang and Bussy, 135, 136; northern ambitions, 180, 215, 252, 253, 597; attack the Rohillas, 217; Lindsay's relations with, 279; revolution of 1773, 218; first and second Maratha Wars, 229, 249 *sqq.*, 287; relations with Nizam 'Ali, 249–51, 255, 277, 333, 338, 370; relations with Hyder and Tipu, 252, 253, 255, 275–7, 325–7, 330, 333, 334, 338, 364, 370; French intrigues with, *see* St Lubin; relations with Macpherson, 334, 363; relations with Cornwallis, 335 *sqq.*, 366; position of the confederacy in 1794, 367; third Maratha War, 341–4, 373 *sqq.*, 539; pirates, 369, 382; fourth Maratha War, 379 *sqq.*, 486, 570, 576, 577; their administrative system, 384 *sqq.*; nobles, 385; the Huzur Daftar, 385. *See also* Military forces
Mariage, —, 66
Maria Theresa, 115, 116
Marie de Bon Secours, alias the *Grand Anglais*, 61
Marine, the Bombay, 114
Markham, —, 307
Marley, Major-general, 378
Marryat, Captain, 559
Marseilles, 63, 327
Martaban, 562, 568
Martin, General Claude, 349
Martin, François, 70–4
Marwar, *see* Jodhpur
Mascarenhas, Dom Francisco, 24
Mascarenhas, João, 16
Mascarenhas, Pero de, 18

Maskat, 17, 87
Masson, Charles, 490
Massowah, 16
Master, Sir Streynsham, 104
Mastung, 500, 502
Masulipatam, 136, 153; Dutch at, 33–5, 37, 38, 40, 59; French at, 62, 67, 70, 72, 74; English at, 83, 88, 89, 94, 103, 105, 113; their trade to Burma, 558; Danes at, 114; granted to the French, 126, 138; taken by Forde, 155, 162
Matara, 54
Mathews, Brigadier Richard, 286
Matturai, 45
Maulmain Chronicle, the, 566
Mauritius, 119, 158, 160, 165, 324, 328, 339, 561; Dutch in, 65; occupied by the French, 74; under La Bourdonnais, 120; d'Aché at, 163; privateers, 326, 328; taken by the English, 332
Maxwell, Colonel Hamilton, 336
Mazarin, Cardinal, 63
Mazaris, the, 543, 544
Mazumdar, the, 388, 389
Mecca, 11, 12, 15, 23
Medows, General, 336
Medway, H.M.S., 120
Meerut, 549, 551
Mekong delta, 74
Melbourne, Lord, 320, 490
Melville, Lord, see Dundas, Henry
Menezes, Dom Diego de, 23
Menezes, Duarte de, 13
Menezes, Henrique de, 13
Menou, —, 328
Meredith, George, 556
Mergui, 565, 568
Meshed, 490
Metcalfe, Charles, Lord, 320, 487, 494, 540, 571, 576, 577, 578, 582
Methwold, William, 85
Meuron, Comte de, 401; regiment of, 401, 402
Mewar, see Udaipur
Miani, battle of, 528, 536, 537
Middleton, Sir Henry, 78
Middleton, Nathaniel, 222, 232, 233, 300–4, 307
Middleton, S., 414, 422, 423
Midnapur, 410, 413, 416, 429; ceded to the English, 168, 206, 593
Mihrab Khan, 502
Military forces; the Maratha army, 393 *sqq.*; Company's army, revolt at Bombay, 102; batta, 178, 179; officers' mutiny, 179–80, 280; Clive's fund, 180; command of the Madras Army, 292, 293; local battalions, 562, 567; military boards, 321
Mill, James, quoted, 193, 201, 216, 221, 302, 341, 352, 358, 424
Minto, Lord (Sir Gilbert Elliot), 186, 199, 233, 246, 309; President of Board, 314; foreign policy, 331, 378; revenue ad-

Minto, Lord (*continued*)
ministration, 456–8; relations with Indian states, 570
Mints, Indian, 92; Maratha, 397; at Madras, 590; at Calcutta, 590, 592
Miran, 151, 153–5, 166, 167
Miranpur Katra, 219
Mirasdars, the, 395, 396, 468, 469, 476
Mir Hasham, see Amir Husayn
Mir Ja'far, 60, 147–52, 154–5, 166–72, 174, 180, 210, 592
Mir Jumla, 88
Mir Kasim, 167–74, 179, 377, 593
Mirpur, 522, 528, 532, 537
Mirtha, see Mairta
Mirza Bakr Gurgian, 526
Mirza Jiwan Bakht, 602
Mirzapur, 377
Misls, 542
Missionaries, admission of, 313; in Burma, 566
Mississippi, the, 133
Moghul Empire, Child's war against, 102; survival of, 571, 574, 575, 591, 592, 603 *sqq.*; French and English policy towards, 600, 601. *See also* Norris, Sir William; Roe, Sir Thomas; Jahangir; Shah Jahan; Aurangzib; Farrukhsiyar; Shah 'Alam II
Mohan Lal, 147
Mohan Prasad, 235
Mohaturfa, 397
Moira, Lord, see Hastings, Marquess of
Mokasa, 395
Mokha, 39, 40, 75, 81, 84; Middleton seized at, 78; English factory at, 93, 111
Molucca Islands, 29, 31, 32, 35, 39, 42, 61, 77, 82
Monckton, General Robert, 191
Mongir, 172, 173, 179
Mong Nai, 568
Monson, Colonel George, 164, 189, 231, 236, 239, 419; character, 226; death, 228, 422, 424
Monson, Colonel William, 374, 375
Montague, F., 199
Montigny, —, 324, 325
Montmorin, —, 596
Moore, Commodore John, 258
Moraba Phadnavis, 262
Moracin, Léon, 138, 162
Morari Rao Ghorpade, 129–32, 138
Morbihan, Company of, 63
Moriarty, G., quoted, 492
Mornington, Lord, see Wellesley, Marquess
Mostyn, Thomas, 252, 261
Motijhil, 168
Moucheron, Balthazar de, 41
Moulmein, 561, 565–8
Mountney, Nathaniel, 90
Mozambique, 17, 31
Mudaji Bhonsle, 266, 268–70, 334, 364, 365, 367
Mudki, battle of, 550
Muhammad, Mir, 522, 525, 527

Muhammad Akbar Khan, 489, 501, 507–13, 519, 543
Muhammad 'Ali Walajah, 88, 126–9, 132, 133, 135, 168, 179, 276, 591; relations with Macpherson, 230, 278; debts, 273, 280; retains administration, 274; nazim, 274; Maratha policy, 277; Lindsay's mission to, 278, 279, 594; and Tanjore, 279, 280, 355; leases Guntoor, 281; assigns revenues, 290–2; missions to Calcutta, 291, 292, 591; relations with Macartney, 293; later years, 355 *sqq.*; revenue administration under, 462
Muhammad Azim Barakzai, 488
Muhammad Beg, 364, 365
Muhammad Husam, 533
Muhammad Mirza (later Shah), 489, 490, 493
Muhammad Reza Khan, 206, 209, 211, 409, 414, 416, 431, 445, 599
Muir, Colonel Grainger, 270
Mukhya deshadhikari, 387
Mukund Dara Pass, 374
Mukur, 519
Mulgrave, Lord, 309
Mulraj, Diwan, 548, 554
Multan, 23, 484, 495, 541, 542, 544, 548, 554–6
Munir-ul-mulk, 576
Munni Begam, 210, 233, 234
Munro, Sir Hector, 174, 280, 281, 283, 284, 286
Munro, Sir Thomas, 321, 333, 342, 343, 346, 470–2, 475–82, 571, 582
Munsifs, 459, 480
Murad 'Ali, Mir, 522, 523
Murray, Colonel, 374
Murshidabad, 141, 142, 147–50, 152, 168, 174, 205, 208, 210, 211, 234, 413, 415, 445, 453, 558, 590; customs house at, 422
Murshidabad division, 422
Murshid Kuli Khan, 409, 410, 412
Murtaza 'Ali Khan, 119
Murtaza Nizam Shah, 20, 21
Mustafanagar, 136
Mustafa Rumi Khan, 14
Mutiny, the Sepoy, 607, 608
Mutuswamy, 404, 405
Muzaffar Jang, 126–8, 133, 134
Muzaffar Sultan, 22, 24
Myothugyi, 563
Mysore, Hindu rajas of, 163, 608; assist Muhammad 'Ali, 129, 135; help the French, 130–2; attacked by Salabat Jang, 138; under Hyder 'Ali, 251, 275; first Mysore War, 275, 276; second war, 282 *sqq.*; third war, 334 *sqq.*; fourth war, 339 *sqq.*, 475; re-establishment of Hindu family, 344–6, 382; as protected state, 574, 578

Nabha, chief of, 540, 548
Nadgaunda, 395
Nadia, distict of, 422

Nadir Shah, 483, 484, 486, 492
Nagaraka, the, 393
Nagelwanze, 37, 38
Nagpur, 367, 368, 372, 379–81, 574, 608. See also Bhonsle family, the
Nagur, 159
Nairs, the, 49, 50
Najib-ud-daula, 222
Najm-ud-daula, 174, 177
Nana Phadnavis, 250, 254, 255, 261–9, 271, 272, 333, 334, 363 *sqq.*, 372, 398
Nana Sahib, 381, 586
Nandakumar, 146, 169, 174, 209, 210; accuses Hastings, 232–4; trial, 235–9, 246
Nandi Raja, 131, 132
Nao Nihal Singh, 503, 543, 545, 546
Napier, Sir Charles, 530–9, 552, 556
Napier, Sir Robert, Lord, 551
Napier, Sir William, quoted, 537
Napoleon, his eastern projects, 327, 328, 331, 339, 540
Nara river, 534
Narayan Rao Peshwa, 253–4, 257
Narbada, the, 215, 266, 364, 373, 379, 381
Nargund, 333, 334, 365
Nasik, 379
Nasir Jang, 118, 134; in the Carnatic, 127, 128, 142, 150
Nasir Khan, 504
Nasir Khan, Mir, 522, 525, 527, 531
Nasir-ul-mulk, 604
Natyegan, 564
Nawshahra, 488
Nazarana, 581
Negapatam, Portuguese at, 33; Dutch at, 36–8, 48, 49, 85, 117, 154, 155; taken by the English, 60, 285
Negombo, 43–7
Negrais Island, 558
Nepal, the war with, 377 *sqq.*, 575, 577, 580
Nesselrode, Count, 494
Netherlands, the, 24, 596. See also Dutch in India, the
Neutrality projects, in the Carnatic, 119; in Bengal, 145, 146
Newspapers, 566
Newton's *Principia*, 349
Nga Chin Pyan, 558
Nicholson, John, 554
Nicobar Islands, 61, 76, 115
Nicolls, Sir Jasper, 504, 511
Nieuw Oranje, 50
Nimula, 487
Nimweguen, Peace of, 71
Nizam, the, as protected prince, 574–7; relations with Barlow, 375; relations with the Moghul emperor, 575, 602; the Berar question, 586. See also Nizam 'Ali, Nizam-ul-mulk
Nizam 'Ali, 140, 274, 398; relations with the Marathas, 249–52, 254, 255, 259, 260, 277, 328, 333, 334, 364, 370, 371; relations with Hyder, 275–7; relations with Madras, 252, 267–9, 271, 274–6, 281,

Nizam 'Ali (continued)
    282, 289; relations with Cornwallis, 334,
    335, 337, 366; relations with Shore, 338;
    relations with Wellesley, 328, 341, 344,
    353, 373, 471
Nizamat adalat, 440, 443, 445
Nizampatam, sarkar of, 128. See also
    Petapoli
Nizam-ul-mulk, 117-9, 126, 127, 135
Noronha, Antonio de, 21
Noronha, Dom Affonso de, 18, 19
Noronha, Garcia de, 15, 16
Norris, Sir William, 99, 104, 105
North, Colonel, 199
North, Frederick, 403, 404, 406
North, Lord, 181, 186, 191, 192, 228, 233,
    242, 289, 598, 600; coalition with Fox,
    198-200, 434; on Hastings, 205
North-east Passage, 29, 76
Northern Sarkars, the, granted to the
    French, 136; French administration,
    139; attacked by Forde, 162; ceded to
    the English, 274, 275, 281; revenue ad-
    ministration, 281, 467, 468, 474; pro-
    posed rendition, 289; raided by Pindaris,
    377; zamindars in, 463, 473, 474, 476
North-west Passage, 76
North-west Provinces, 511
Nott, General Sir William, 505, 507, 515-
    20, 529, 530
Nur Muhammad Khan, Mir, 522, 525-7
Nyayadhish, the, 390, 391

Oakeley, Sir Charles, 337
Ochterlony, Sir David, 375, 378, 540, 571,
    577
Ohio, the, 133
Okhamandal, 382
Oldenbarnevelt, Johan van, 30
Oman, Sea of, 483
Omichand, 141, 147-9, 151, 180
Ongole, 117
Opium revenue, 439, 440, 460, 564, 568
Orangist party, 325, 326
Orenburg, 502
Orissa, 88, 106, 183, 374
Orleans, Duke of, 62
Orleans, Iles d', 74
Orme, Robert, 144, 150, 151
Ormuz, 11, 12, 84; taken by the Portu-
    guese, 9, 10; their rule, 13, 17, 18; taken
    by the English and Persians, 81, 82
Orves, — d', 285
Ostend East India Company, 109, 114-6,
    142
Oudh, 153, 172-6, 179, 254, 360, 497;
    early relations of the English with, 152,
    597; the begams of, 230, 300 sqq., 309,
    310; condition of, 302; reforms of 1784,
    305; history 1785-1801, 347 sqq.; as pro-
    tected state, 574, 575, 577, 578, 580, 581,
    583; king of, 575, 606. See also Asaf-ud-
    daula, Shuja-ud-daula
Ouratura, 48

Outram, Sir James, 522, 528-33, 535, 536,
    538, 539, 583, 585
Oxenden, Sir George, 100
Oxus, the, 483

Pacheco, Duarte, 7, 8
Pagan, 560
Palakollu, 37
Palayams, 474, 475
Palghaut, 288
Palk, Sir Robert, 132, 273
Palliar, the, 131
Palmer and Company, 576
Palmerston, Lord, 494, 499
Panchayat, the, 389, 390, 464, 479, 480
Pandit Rao, the, 394
Panipat, third battle of, 180, 215, 249, 253,
    255
Panjab, the, relations with the Afghans,
    381, 483, 485; relations with the English,
    497, 503, 504, 520, 539 sqq., 576, 580.
    See also Ranjit Singh; Sikhs, the
Panniar, battle of, 579
Pant Pratinidhi, the, 377, 382
Pant Sachiv, the, 382
Paradis, Louis, 122
Pargana, 387, 412
Paris, Treaty of (1763), 278, 594, 595;
    (1814), 596
Parliament, and the East India Company,
    97, 98, 181 sqq.; select committee of 1772,
    181, 185, 186; secret committee of 1772,
    181, 186; select committee of 1781, 181,
    192, 247, 303, 433; secret committee of
    1781, 181, 192; impeachment of Hastings,
    307 sqq.; legislation 1786-1818, 313 sqq.,
    458, 595; select committee of 1808, 458,
    478
Parsaji Bhonsle, 379
Parvarti Bai, 255
Parwandurrah, 505
Paskievich, General, 489
Patan, 366
Patel, the, 386, 387, 389-93, 396
Patiala, 540
Patna, 152, 169, 170, 179, 208, 209, 378,
    413, 423-5, 453; Dutch factory at, 41;
    English factory at, 88, 92, 106; attacked
    by 'Ali Gauhar, 153, 166; Ellis at, 172,
    173; massacre of, 173; customs house at,
    208; the — case, 243, 246, 247
Paton, —, 562, 563
Patronage, in the time of Hastings, 212;
    under Fox's bill, 195; under the India
    Act, 318, 437
Pattakila, 386
Patterson, J., 412, 428
Patullo, H., 423
Patvardhans, the, 382, 385
Patwari, the, 460
Payandah Khan, 484, 485
Pearse, Colonel Thomas, 269
Peat, Captain, 501
Peel, Sir Robert, 516

Pegu, 17, 52, 115, 562, 566, 567; French in, 62

Pelham, Thomas, 309

Pembroke Dockyard, 566

Penang, 76

Pennar river, 337

Pensée, the, 61

Perron, Pierre Cuillier, *dit*, 326, 366, 374

Persia, 1, 62, 88, 91, 483, 560; relations with the Portuguese, 12, 81, 82; relations with the French, 65; relations with the Dutch, 84; relations with the English, 81, 82, 84, 93; Gardane's mission to, 331, 485, 486; English missions to, 486, 487, 489, 492–4; relations with Russia, 486, 489; relations with the Afghans, 487–90, 492–4, 496, 497, 514, 543; relations with Sind, 525–7

Persian Gulf, Portuguese trade in, 6, 81; French in, 66; English trade in, 92; disputes with the Turks in, 278; English influence in, 486, 494

Pertab Singh, 547

Peshawar, 484, 485, 487–90, 492–3, 495, 497, 504, 508, 511, 512, 515, 518, 520, 541–3, 546, 549, 555, 556

Peshawara Singh, 547, 548

Peshwa, the, origin and position of, 384, 574, 608. See also Marathas, the

Petapoli, Dutch at, 33, 34, 37; English defeated off, 56, 104

Peyton, Captain Edward, 120

Phadnavis, the, 250, 388, 389

Phayre, Sir Arthur, 562, 565

Philip II, 24, 26–8, 77

Philippine Islands, 31

Pigot, George, Lord, 144, 156, 158, 160, 161, 279, 280, 286, 293, 355, 360

Pilamé Talawé, 404–7

Pimienta, 18

Pindaris, the, 375–7, 379, 380, 383, 571

Pippli, 41

Pirates, 103, 105. *See also* Marathas, the

Pir Dil Khan, 488

Pitt, John, 105

Pitt, Thomas, 102, 104, 105, 111

Pitt, William, Lord Chatham, *see* Chatham, Lord

Pitt, William, 181, 213, 314, 320, 350, 358, 434, 437, 450, 451; on Fox's India bills, 195, 198, 199, 403; his India Act, 194, 200 *sqq.*, 355; and Hastings, 203, 307–9; and Impey, 247

Place, Lionel, 468, 471, 472, 482

Plancius, Petrus, 28

Plassey, battle of, 60, 149, 150, 152, 155, 169, 170, 321, 593

Plumer, Thomas, 309, 311

Plymouth, 24

Pocock, Sir George, 154, 158–60, 163

Poëte, Chevalier de, 160

Police, *see* Justice

Polier de Bottens, Major Paul, 159

Poligars, 357, 463, 464, 471–3, 475, 480

Polilur, first battle of, 283; second battle of, 284, 286

Pollock, Sir George, 511–20, 546

Pompadour, Madame de, 121

Pondichery, 117, 119–23, 126–8, 130–4, 137, 142, 143, 146, 158–61, 163, 261, 329; early history, 70–4; taken by the Dutch, 72; besieged by Boscawen, 123, 124; taken by Coote, 157, 163–5; taken in 1778, 281; taken in 1793, 326; proposed transfer of headquarters from, 324, 325

Pontchartrain, Jérôme, 73

Ponwars, the, 376

Poona, 118, 218, 249–52, 254–7, 259–64, 266, 324, 325, 367, 370–3, 379, 380, 608; police of, 393; collectorate of, 392; Treaty of, 575

Poonamallee, 127, 130

Popham, Captain, 268

Porakad, 50

Porter, Endymion, 90

Port Louis, 120

Porto Novo, 70; Dutch factory at, 37; English at, 104; battle of, 284

Portuguese in India, early voyages, 2 *sqq.*; chronicles, 3; oriental sources, 3; relations with Muslim powers, 6, 9, 10–13; atrocities, 6, 19; organisation, 8, 17; at Goa, 10; at Diu, 14; war with Turks, 15, 16, with Gujarat, 16, 18; their decline, 17; religious policy, 18, 53; war with Zamorin, 18; at Daman, 19, 20; relations with Akbar, 23; union with Spain, 24, 44; relations with the English, 24, 76 *sqq.*, 82 *sqq.*; in Ceylon, 24 *sqq.*; relations with the Dutch, 29, 31 *sqq.*, 44, 47, 50, 85; their influence, 53, 402; relations with the French, 61; cession of Bombay, 86, 87; relations with the Marathas, 114, 256, 264, 269, 334; French projects on their settlements, 329

Potdar, the, 388

Potnis, the, 388

Pottinger, Eldred, 493, 501, 507, 509, 510, 515

Pottinger, Colonel Henry, 497, 500, 523–8

Pozzo di Borgo, Count, 494

Prant, the, 387

Pratab Singh, raja of Tanjore, 125, 129

Pratinidhi, the, 384

Prentout, M., quoted, 330

Presents, after Plassey, 151; after revolution of 1760, 169; forbidden by the Company, 177; illegal, 303, 309, 310

Previous communications, 315, 316

Prinsep, H. T., quoted, 382

Privateers, French, 326, 328, 330, 332. *See also* Whitehill, John

Private trade, under the Dutch, 58; under the English, 94, 438, 442; prohibited, 419, 433, 443, 444

Prome, 562

Prussian companies, 116

Psyche, the, 330
Pudukottai, 132
Pulicat, 32, 34–8, 42, 44, 83, 88, 120
Pulo Kondor, 74
Pulo Run, 86, 91
Pulteney, —, 186
Purandhar, 255, 262; Treaty of, 260–3, 266, 270, 271
Purnaiya (Purniya), 344
Purnia, district of, 141, 142, 423, 428
Puttalam, 54, 55
Pybus, John, 400, 401

Quetta, 499, 500, 504, 515, 516, 519
Quilon, 47, 49, 50

Raghoba, *see* Raghunath Rao
Raghuji Angria, 369
Raghuji Bhonsle I, 118, 136
Raghuji Bhonsle II, 367, 368, 371, 379, 381; and the English, 373
Raghunath Rao, *alias* Raghoba, and Dada Sahib, 249 *sqq.*, 364
Rahmat Khan, *see* Hafiz Rahmat Khan
Rai Durlabh, 146, 147, 150–4, 169, 416
Rainier, Commodore Peter, 326, 328
Rai-raian, the, 209, 416, 418, 420, 427
Rais Salman, 13
Rajahmundry, 136, 162
Rajapur, 90, 103
Raja Rama, 384
Raja Sinha I, 26
Raja Sinha II, 42–8, 51, 52
Rajballabh, 416
Rajmahal, 141; English factory at, 106
Rajpurghat, Treaty of, 375
Rajputana, 375, 376, 381, 483, 557, 571, 573, 574, 576, 578, 583
Rajputs, the, 252, 253, 365, 366, 375, 376, 380, 398, 571, 577
Rajshahi, zamindari of, 422
Rakshasbhavan, 251
Ramazan Rumi Khan, 17
Ramdas Pandit, 135, 138
Ramghat, 218
Rammanakoil, 48
Ramnad, poligar of, 279, 475
Ramnagar, 555
Ramnarayan, 151–3, 169, 170
Ramosis, the, 391, 392
Rampur, 220, 222, 303, 304
Ramree, 562–5
Rangoon, 558–62, 566, 567, 607
Rangpur, 428, 429
Ranjit Singh, 304, 485, 487, 488, 490–7, 499, 503, 518, 523–5, 539 *sqq.*, 547, 548, 552, 557
Rasad, 388
Rasul, 556
Ratlam, 571
Ratnagiri, 250
Ravesteyn, Gilles van, 39
Ravi, the, 555
Rawlinson, Major Henry, 514

Raygamwatte, 47, 48
Raymond, François de, 326, 370
Raza Sahib, 126
Razilly, Isaac de, 61
Read, Colonel Alexander, 467–72, 477, 480
Red Sea, 1, 2, 10, 11, 13, 16, 25, 74, 105; Portuguese and trade through, 6–9; English in, 78, 79, 81, 84, 92, 111; route to India, 327, 328
Reede tot Drakenstein, — van, *see* Drakenstein
Regulating Act, 181, 188 *sqq.*, 277, 303, 419, 594, 599
Renault, *see* St Germain, Renault de
Revenant, the, 330
Revenue, Bengal, controlling boards, 208, 210; committee of, 213, 410; Hastings' administration, 309, 409 *sqq.*; permanent settlement recommended, 419, 423; Supreme Court and, 421; Macpherson's reforms, 431 *sqq.*, 443; Cornwallis's reforms, 433, 439, 440, 443, 444, 447 *sqq.*, 456; revenue courts, 444, 453; criticism of zamindari settlement, 458; sair revenue, 409, 439, 449, 467. *See also* Salt
Revenue, Burma, 562, 563, 567, 568
Revenue, Madras, 462 *sqq.*; in the Northern Sarkars, 281, 283, 473; assignment of the Carnatic, 290–2, 356; Board of Revenue, 319, 321, 467, 471–3, 476; permanent settlement, 473, 475, 476, 478; village settlements, 476–8; ryotwari established, 479, 480
Revenue, Maratha, division of, 385, 395; accounts etc., 387, 395 *sqq.*
Rezimont, Gilles de, 62
Richardson, Dr, 568
Richelieu, Cardinal, 61–3
Richmond, Colonel, 547, 548
Rigault, —, 62
Ripon, first Lord, 579
Rivett-Carnac, Sir James, 581
Roberts, Brigadier, 505
Robertson, Thomas Campbell, 511
Rochester, Bishop of, 311
Roe, Sir Thomas, 80 *sqq.*; and the Dutch, 39
Rogerius, Abraham, 53
Rohilkhand, 174, 217–22, 232
Rohillas, the, 252, 253, 348, 485
Rohilla War, 217 *sqq.*, 232, 303; vote on, 307, 308
Rohri, 530, 532–4
Rojhan, 543, 544
Rooke, William, 428
Rose, Professor Holland, quoted, 199, 307
Rotation government, at Calcutta, 105, 153
Rouen, merchants of, 61
Rous, Boughton, 421
Roussel, Colonel Jean-Baptiste, 162
Royal Society, the, 96
Roz kird, 386
Rumbold, Sir Thomas, 193, 280–3
Rupar, 542

Russell, Sir Henry, 576
Russia, 331, 483; relations with Persia, 486, 487, 489, 490, 494, 542, 544; relations with the Afghans, 492, 493, 496, 498, 503, 525; relations with the Turks, 489; relations with the Sikhs, 489; expedition against Khiva, 502–4
Rustam Khan (of Broach), 22
Rustam Khan, Mir, 522, 523, 526, 527, 533–5, 538
Ryotwari, see Revenue—Madras, Burma
Ryswick, Treaty of, 72

Sa'adat 'Ali, 349 sqq., 575
Sa, Garcia de, 17, 18
Sabaio, see Yusuf Adil Khan
Sabaji Bhonsle, 258
Sabathu, 549
Sabhasad, the, 388
Sabzalkot, 531–3, 536
Sachin state, 369
Sacre, the, 61
Sadar amins, 459
Sadar warid patti, 388
Sadashiv Rao Bhao, 255
Sadozai clan, 483, 485, 488, 493
Sadraspatam, alias Sadras, Dutch at, 37; conference at, 132
Sadr diwanni adalat, 242, 244–6
Sadullapur, 556
Safdar 'Ali Khan, 117–9
Safdar Jang, 519
Saffragam, 45
Sagar and Narbada Territories, 381, 574
Sagauli, Treaty of, 378
Saharanpur, 378
Sahotra, 395
St Anne's Church, Calcutta, 113
St Augustine's Bay, 65, 90
St George, Battle of, 219
St Germain, Renault de, 145
St Helena, 99
St Lubin, —, 261–3, 266, 324
St Malo, merchants of, 61, 73; Company of, 63
St Mary's Church, Fort St George, 104
St Petersburg, 490, 494
St Thomas Mount, 130, 161, 280, 284
St Thomé, alias Mailapur, Portuguese at, 33–5, 88; French at, 56, 69–71, 104; taken by Golconda, 103; occupied by Boscawen, 126, 127
Sair, revenue, see Revenue, Bengal
Saiyid Ahmad Shah Ghazi, 542
Saiyid Lashkar Khan, 135, 136, 138
Sakharam Bapu, 250, 254, 255, 260–3
Salabat Jang, 134, 135, 137–40, 144, 151, 162, 274, 594, 600
Salbai, Treaty of, 254, 270–2, 288, 289, 334, 363, 364
Sale, Florentia, Lady, 510
Sale, Sir Robert, 501, 505–7, 510, 512–4, 516, 520
Salsette, 18, 250, 256–61, 267, 271

Salt, 213; revenue, 439, 440, 467, 481
Sambhaji, 384
Sampaya, Lopo Vaz de, 13
Samru, Begam, 323
Sandoway, 562, 564
San Fiorenzo, the, 330
Sanivar Wada, the, 370
Saranjams, 385, 386, 394
Sarboji, 360, 361
Sardar Khan Singh, 554
Sardesmukhi, 394, 395
Saristadar, chief, 431, 432, 435, 447, 448
Sarji Rao Ghatke, 371
Sarkar, the, 387
Sarkhej, 92
Sarsubhedar, the, 387, 390, 391
Sartine, Gabriel de, 262
Sasvad, 392
Satara, 118, 249, 254, 262, 367, 372, 380, 382; position of the raja of, 384, 608; state, 574, 578, 581, 583
Sati, forbidden at Goa, 18; Ganga Bai proposes, 255; in the protected states, 580
Satlej, the, 378, 383, 483, 495, 497, 508, 511, 539–42, 549–52, 555, 579
Saugor, see Sagar
Saunders, Thomas, 128, 132, 133, 136, 154, 157
Savanur, 128, 138, 334
Sayaji Gaekwad, 257, 368
Sayf-ul-muluk Miftah, alias Cide Bofata, 19
Scheldt, the, 28
Schonamille, François de, 115, 142
Schreuder, Jan, 54
Scott, Major John, 193, 202, 213, 301, 307
Scott, Colonel W., 352, 353
Scottish East India Company, 97
Scrafton, Luke, 148, 150, 172, 207
Sebastian, Dom, 24
Secret Committee of the East India Company, the, 200, 201, 315, 337, 441
Sedasere, battle of, 341
Seignelay, Marquis de, 71, 72
Selim III, 340
Sena Khas Khel, the, 257, 368
Sena Sahib Suba, 368
Sepoy Troops, mutiny 1764, 174
Sequeira, Diogo Lopes de, 13
Serampore, 114, 330
Seringapatam, 336, 337, 340–3, 345, 346, 361, 470, 475; first Treaty of, 337, 338, 366; second Treaty of, 345, 346
Seths, the, 147, 148, 173
Seton, Alexander, 487
Seven Korles, 408
Seven Years' War, 59, 139, 145, 147, 157 sqq., 275, 280, 600
Seville, 28
Shadiwal, 556
Shah Abbas, 81
Shah 'Alam I, 111
Shah 'Alam II, 153, 166, 167, 169, 170, 173–5, 180, 323, 324, 602; Treaty of Allahabad with, 176, 251, 274, 409, 596;

Shah 'Alam II (*continued*)
    joins the Marathas, 215, 253; his tribute
    from Bengal, 215, 216, 264, 596, 597;
    relations with Sindhia, 333, 364, 367,
    602, 603; blinded, 365, 603; relations
    with the English, 374, 601 *sqq.*
Shahdad, 522
Shahdadpur family, the, 522
Shah Jahan (Prince Khurram), 39, 40, 80,
    606
Shahji, 125
Shah Nawaz Khan, 136, 138–40
Shah Nawaz Khan (of Kalat), 502
Shahpuri Island, 559
Shah Shuja, 106
Shah Shuja, *see* Shuja-ul-mulk Sadozai
Shahu, 384
Shah Wali Khan, 484
Shaikh Imam-ud-din, 553
Shaista Khan, 107
Shakespeare, Sir Richmond, 503, 519
Shal, 500, 502
Shan states, 558, 561, 568, 569
Shapur Mirza, 519, 520
Shaukat Jang, 142, 147
Shelburne, Lord, 187, 278, 434
Shelton, Brigadier, 506, 507, 509, 511
Sheppard, —, 561
Sheridan, R. B., 309, 310
Sher Khan Lodi, 70, 71
Shete mahajan, 389
Shikarpur, 495, 499, 523, 525, 530, 531,
    542–4
Shingshingoti, 397
Shir Muhammad, 522, 537, 538
Shir Singh, 545–7, 550, 554, 555
Shitab Rai, 206, 209
Shivpuri, *see* Sipri
Sholinghur, battle of, 285
Shore, Sir John, Lord Teignmouth, 307,
    317, 319, 320, 347, 350, 415, 420, 421;
    and Hastings' reforms, 211, 212, 427–31;
    his foreign policy, 338, 339, 370, 371;
    his Oudh policy, 348 *sqq.*; his Carnatic
    policy, 358; his Tanjore policy, 360; and
    Cornwallis's reforms, 435–7, 439, 443
    sqq.; appointed governor-general, 451;
    revenue policy, 456; accepts a khil'at, 604
Shuja-ud-daula, 172–4, 180, 300, 598; and
    Treaty of Allahabad, 176, 251; and the
    Rohillas, 217 *sqq.*; death, 233
Shuja-ud-daula Sadozai, 515
Shuja-ul-mulk Sadozai, Shah Shuja, 484,
    485, 487–90, 493–502, 504–6, 508, 512,
    513, 515, 517, 519, 524–6, 541–5, 549
Sialkot, 547
Siam, French in, 72, 73; frontier raids, 568
Sidis, the, Abdul Rahim, 369; Abdul
    Karim, *alias* Balu Mian, 369; Johar, 369.
    See also Janjira
Sihbandi, 387, 393
Sikhs, the, 365, 366, 386, 602; Metcalfe's
    mission to, 487, 540; war with the
    Gurkhas, 541; relations with the Afghans,

Sikhs (*continued*)
    491, 495, 496, 498, 502, 503, 512, 513,
    520, 541–5, 555, 556; designs on Sind,
    523, 524, 542, 543; and the French, 544;
    attack Chinese Tibet, 546; relations with
    the English, 513, 516, 518, 539 *sqq.*
Sikkim, 378
Silveira, Antonio da, 15
Simla, 496, 519, 549
Simonich, Count, 490, 493
Sind, 483, 515, 552; Portuguese in, 19;
    English factories in, 80, 87, 92; French
    designs on, 323, 522, 523; the Afghans in,
    484, 486, 488, 495, 522, 524, 528, 543;
    English relations with, 487, 491, 493,
    497, 499, 500, 513; Sikh designs on, 495,
    496, 523, 524, 542; Persian relations with,
    500, 525–7; conquest of, 522 *sqq.*, 580
Sindhia, family of, 249, 252, 256, 257, 259,
    260; their state, 571, 573, 578, 579. *See
    also* Daulat Rao, Jankoji Rao, Jayaji
    Rao, Mahadaji Rao
Sindhianwala family, 546, 547. *See also*
    Ajit Singh, Atar Singh, Lahna Singh
Sinfray, —, 149
Sipra river, 376
Sipri (Shivpuri), battle of, 270
Siraj-ud-daula, 139, 141–3, 145–52, 154,
    167, 205, 592
Sirhind, division, 529, 540
Sirpur, action of, 166
Sistan, 490, 493
Sitabaldi, 381
Sitke, 566
Sivaganga, poligar of, 279, 475
Sivaji, 71, 100–3, 253, 258, 372, 384, 385,
    387, 393–5, 398, 574, 608
Siva Rao, 360
Skardu, 546
Skinner's Horse, 510
Slavery, 481, 568; debtor, 568
Sleeman, Sir William H., 568, 583, 585
Smith, Sir Harry, 551
Smith, General Joseph, 276, 284
Smith, Colonel Lionel, 382
Soares, Lopo, 7, 12, 13, 25
Sobraon, battle of, 551, 557
Socotra, 9, 10
Sodre, Vincente, 6, 7
Sohrabani, family of, 522
Soldanha, —, 7
Somnath, Gates of, 518–20
Son river, action on the, 169
Sonars, 397
Sondhwada, 577
Souillac, Vicomte de, 324
Soupire, Chevalier de, 158
Sousa, Martin Affonso de, 16
Southampton, Lord, 347
South Arcot, 471
Sovereignty, question of British, in Bengal,
    241, 242, 314; in India, 589 *sqq.*
Spanish Armada, the, 76
Spanish Succession, War of the, 73

Spice Islands, *see* Moluccas, the
Spilbergh, Joris van, 41
Sraddha, 391
Srirangam, island of, 129–31
Stables, John, 230, 231
Stamps, 481
Stephen, Sir James, quoted, 225, 226, 233, 234, 235, 236, 237, 238, 239, 240, 241, 243, 244, 245, 302
Stewart, Captain, 267
Stewart, Major-General James, 341
Stoddart, Colonel, 494, 503, 504
Strachey, Sir John, quoted, 217, 220, 221, 222, 223, 224
Stuart, Charles, 436, 438, 442, 449
Stuart, Major-General James, 280, 286, 287, 292, 293
Stuart, Colonel James, 401
Subha, the, 387
Subhedar, the, 387
Subudar Khan, 522, 525, 526, 532, 534
Suchet Singh, 547, 548
Suez, 2, 9, 10, 13, 14, 16, 18, 327, 494
Suffren, the Bailli de, 164, 285, 287
Sukkur, 516, 517, 529–33
Sulaiman Mirza, 484
Sulaiman Pasha, 15
Sulaiman Sultan, 15
Sulivan, Laurence, 175, 184, 185, 231, 266, 268, 289, 290, 318
Sultan 'Ali Sadozai, 488
Sultan Muhammad, 488, 492, 493
Sumatra, 29, 32, 39, 61; English factories in, 77, 79
Sumer Singh, 255
Sunda, Straits of, 29, 84
Supervisors, sent out 1769, 207, 278, 411; proposed 1772, 187
Supervisors of revenue, 206, 208, 226, 411
Supreme Court of Calcutta, established, 189, 191, 225; decides between Hastings and Clavering, 228; its power of reprieve, 237; conduct of the court, 240 *sqq.*, 421, 426, 599; its powers limited, 192, 247
Surat, 20, 22–4, 31, 33, 56, 92, 105, 258, 260, 261, 266, 267, 369, 372; Dutch factory at, 39, 40, 57, 58, 84; French factory at, 66, 67, 71, 73; English factory at, 77–81, 90, 93, 96, 100–3, 107, 111, 112; nawab of, 603; Treaty of, 257, 260–2; revenues ceded, 257
Surcouf, Nicolas, 330
Surcouf, Robert, 330
Surji Arjungaon, Treaty of, 374, 380
Surman, John, 104, 111, 112
Sutanuti, 107, 108
Suvarndrug, 114
Swally Hole, 66, 68, 78, 79, 84
Swartz, Christian Frederick, 282, 360
Swedish East India Company, 116
Sydney, Lord, 314
Symes, Captain M., 559
Syriam, 558

Table Bay, 65
Tabriz, 12, 489
Tafazzul Hussain Khan, 349
Tagai, 396
Tahsildars, 449, 460, 563
Taimur, house of, *see* Moghul
Taimur Mirza, 501, 502, 516, 517, 519
Taimur Shan, 483, 484, 488
Takaza, 397
Talaings, the, 558–60, 562, 566–8; corps of, 567, 569
Talegaon, 264
Talpura, tribe, 484, 500, 522, 538
Tanjore, kingdom of, 59, 117, 118, 125, 130, 132; attacked by Chanda Sahib, 127, 159; attacked by Lally, 159, 160; relations with Muhammad 'Ali, 273, 279, 280, 355; relations with Madras, 290; French intrigue in, 330; Wellesley's settlement with, 352, 353, 360, 361; land values in, 465; village system of, 476; revenue system, 471; title extinguished 586, 606
Tankhwa, 571, 572
Tantia Jogh, 577
Tapasnavis, the, 393
Tapti, the, 77, 78, 252, 267
Tara Bai, 384
Tarai, the, 378, 379
Tarf, the, 387, 389
Tatta, 527, 531, 532, 535; plundered by the Portuguese, 19; English factory at, 87, 522
Tavernier, Jean-Baptiste, 62
Tavoy, 565, 568
Taylor, William, 259, 260
Teheran, 331, 486, 487, 489, 492; Treaty of, 489
Teignmouth, Lord, *see* Shore, Sir John
Tej Singh, 548–50
Tellicherri, 103
Temple, Lord, 200
Tenasserim, 558–60; administration of, 565 *sqq.*
Texel, the, 28, 29
Teylingen, Christiaan van, 59
Tezin, 519
Thackwell, General Joseph, 555
Thalbarit, 397
Thalmod, 397
Thanadars, the, 474, 480
Thana Fort, 256
Tharrawaddy, 560, 566
Thathameda, 563
Thebes, 328
Thijssen, —, 44, 46
Thomassen, Adolf, 34
Thomson, Captain, 501
Thugs, 568
Thugyi, 563, 566
Thurlow, Lord, 192, 202, 203, 207, 211, 310, 311, 598
Tibet, 219, 493; Chinese, 546
Tiku, 62

Tilsit, Treaty of, 331, 486
Tinnevelly, district of, 289, 358; poligars of, 357, 475
Tipu Sultan, 51, 271, 272, 286, 317, 318, 324, 327, 346, 356, 360, 366, 371, 467; succeeds his father, 286; peace with the English, 287, 288, 363; treatment of prisoners, 289; relations with the French, 324sqq., 339; war with the Marathas, 364; government and fall, 333 sqq., 574, 602; revenue administration, 463, 469; character, 341, 342
Tirupapuliyur, 33, 37, 49
Tiruvalur, 159
Tiruvannamalai, battle of, 276
Tiruvendipuram, 127
Tiruviti, 127, 130, 131
Tod, Lieutenant-Colonel James, 571, 573, 578
Todd, Major, 501, 503–5
Tomar, 24
Tone, Colonel, 398
Tonk, 380, 573
Tonkin, 71
Tordesillas, Treaty of, 2, 76
Torrens, Henry Whitelock, 494, 504
Trade, with Europe by the Levant, 1, 2; in the 17th century, 91, 92; in the 18th century, 438; Coromandel, 35; Company's monopoly abolished, 458; boards of trade, 321, 436, 438, 439, 441, 442, 447, 454, 458
Tranquebar, 114, 115, 330
Travancore, raja of, 317, 326; French intrigues in, 330; Tipu attacks, 335, 366; as protected state, 574
Trevor, Captain, 509
Trichinopoly, 179; Hindu state, 117; taken by Marathas, 118; retaken by Nizam, 119; Muhammad 'Ali at, 126, 127; attacked by the French, 128, 129, 131, 132, 135, 137–40, 150, 158, 160, 161
Trieste Company, 116
Trimbakji Danglia, 379
Trimbak Rao, Mama, 253, 255
Trinkomali, 42–4, 56, 60, 68, 69, 285, 324, 325, 328, 400, 401, 405–7
Tripartite Treaty, the, 495, 505, 525, 528, 543–5
Truce of Antwerp, 83
Tukoji Holkar, 252, 254, 262, 263, 266, 267, 270, 271, 334, 365–9, 371, 372
Tulsi Bai, 376
Tungabhadra river, 337
Tupai, 556
Turkestan, 507
Turkomanchai, Treaty of, 489
Turks, the, attack the Portuguese, 15, 18, 27; relations with Persia, 81; dislike Europeans in Egypt, 327; relations with the English, 540
Tutikorin, 48
Twenty-four Parganas, the, 153, 206, 593

Udaipur (Mewar), 380
Ujjain, 270
Umaji Naik, 392
Umarkot, 537
'Umdat-ul-Umara, 357, 359, 361, 362
Underi, island of, 101
Upri, 395, 396
Upton, Colonel John, 259–61
Utrecht, 37, 53; Treaty of, 115
Uva, 407
Uzbegs, the, 503

Valentia, Lord, 398
Valentyn, François, 53, 400
Valikondapuram, 70, 130; action at, 129
Valudavur, 127
Vandalur, 130
Vansittart, George, 235, 423
Vansittart, Henry, 132, 168–73, 175, 178, 207, 208, 601
Vellore, 33, 34, 118, 119, 126, 336, 341, 408; mutiny at, 330
Vengurla, 49, 51, 369
Venice, 1, 9, 11
Ventura, General, 542
Vepery, 113
Verelst, Harry, 180, 208, 234, 411, 412, 415
Vernet, —, 154
Versailles, Treaty of, 288, 324, 339, 595
Versluys, Pieter, 54, 58
Victoria, Queen, 514
Vijayadrug, 114
Vijayanagar, 3, 11, 88, 117
Vikkur, 500
Vikrama Raja Sinha, 404
Vikravandi, action at, 130
Village-systems, under the Marathas, 386; in Bengal, 410; in south India, 463–5, 468, 469, 471, 476, 477
Villiyanallur, 126, 164
Villupuram, 127, 130
Vincens, Marie, alias Chonchon, 134
Visaji Kishan, 252, 253
Vithuji Holkar, 372
Vitkevich, Captain, 490
Vitré, François Martin de, 61, 63
Vizagapatam, 104, 112, 113, 128, 136, 139, 145, 162
Vizianagram, 162
Vuyst, Pieter, 54, 58, 59
Vypin, 50

Wade, Colonel C., 496, 497, 501, 518, 525, 542, 545
Wadgaon (Wargaum), Convention of, 264, 265, 267
Wadi, 369, 377
Wadni, 550
Waite, Sir Nicholas, 102, 105
Wakil-i-mutlak, 364, 367, 604
Walajah, see Muhammad 'Ali Walajah
Walcot, 599
Wallace, Brigadier, 534, 536

Wallich, Dr Nathaniel, 567
Walpole, Horace, 186
Wandiwash, battle of, 140, 163; defence of, 284; chief of, 589
Wards, Court of, 429
Wargaum, see Wadgaon
Wasil Muhammad, 377
Watans, 387
Watson, Admiral Charles, 114, 139, 144–6, 149, 156–8
Watts, William, 141, 146, 148, 149, 152, 156
Wazir 'Ali, 350, 351
Weavers, 481
Webbe, Josiah, 361
Weddell, John, 90
Weert, Sebald de, 41
Wellesley, Arthur, Duke of Wellington, 339–41, 345, 346, 354, 358, 359, 361, 362, 373, 374, 498, 509, 517, 518, 520, 521, 535, 539, 544, 554
Wellesley, Henry, Lord Cowley, 353, 354
Wellesley, Richard, Lord Mornington, Marquis, 315, 317, 319, 320, 323; opposes the French, 327 sqq., 600; overthrows Tipu, 338 sqq.; relations with Persia, 486; with Oudh, 350 sqq., 583; with the Carnatic, 358 sqq.; with the Marathas, 371 sqq., 576; with the Indian states, 570, 587; revenue administration under, 456, 472; treatment of the Moghul emperor, 604, 605; his honours, 345; recalled, 375
Wellington, Duke of, see Wellesley, Arthur
Wesick, — van, 34
Western Ghats, the, 100
Westerwolt, —, 42, 43
West Indies, 321
Westminster, Treaty of, 86
Wheeler, General, 551
Wheler, Edward, 212, 228, 229, 231, 296, 301, 302, 426; character, 230
Whitehill, John, 193, 283, 284
Wilberforce, William, 199, 308, 313

Wild, Brigadier, 511, 512
Wilks, Colonel Mark, quoted, 335, 36, 337, 342, 344
William III, 97, 98, 108
William IV (of Orange), 59
Willock, Sir Henry, 498
Willshire, General, 502
Windham, William, 309
Winter, Sir Edward, 104
Wood, Major-General, 378
Wood, Benjamin, 76
Wood, Colonel John, 276
Wraxall, Nathaniel, 196, 307
Wynad, 343
Wynch, Alexander, 280

Xavier, St Francis, 8, 16, 18, 26

Yajnavalkya, 389
Yanam, 74
Yandabo, Treaty of, 559, 560, 567
Yar Lutf Khan, 148
Yar Muhammad Khan Barakzai, 541
Yar Muhammad Wazir, 490, 493, 501, 505
Yuagaung, 563
Yusaf Khan, 279
Yusuf Adil Khan, alias Idalcao and Sabaio, 10

Zabita Khan, 365
Zaman Shah, 350, 351, 484–6, 515
Zamindari daftar, 429
Zamindars, in Bengal, 409, 410, 448, 449, 452, 456, 457, 473; in the Northern Sarkars, 463, 473, 474, 480
Zamindar's Court, 590
Zamorin of Calicut, see Calicut
Zeeland, 38
Zeyla, 13
Zillah courts, 453, 454, 457, 458, 460, 474, 479
Zorawar Singh, 546
Zulfikar Khan, 104

CAMBRIDGE: PRINTED BY WALTER LEWIS, M.A., AT THE UNIVERSITY PRESS